Welfare Benef
Tax Credits Handbook

7th edition

Child Poverty Action Group

CPAG is the leading charity campaigning for the abolition of poverty among children and young people in the UK and for the improvement of the lives of low-income families. CPAG aims to: raise awareness of the extent, nature and impact of poverty; bring about positive income policy changes for families with children in poverty; and enable those eligible for benefits and tax credits to have access to their full entitlement. If you are not already supporting us, please consider making a donation or ask for details of our membership schemes and publications.

Published by Child Poverty Action Group

94 White Lion Street, London N1 9PF

020 7837 7979

Registered Company No. 1993854
Charity No. 294841

A CIP record f[illegible] Library

ISBN 1 901698 75 0

Design by Devious Designs 0114 275 5634
Printed in Great Britain by William Clowes Limited, Beccles, Suffolk

The authors

Consultant editor: Simon Osborne

Pamela Fitzpatrick is a welfare rights worker at CPAG.

Carolyn George is a part-time welfare rights worker at CPAG and a freelance writer on welfare rights.

Jacqui McDowell is a freelance writer and trainer based in Scotland. She is also the author of CPAG's *Child Support Handbook*.

Susan Mitchell is a freelance writer on welfare rights.

Simon Osborne is a welfare rights worker at CPAG, based at CPAG in Scotland.

Judith Paterson is a welfare rights worker at CPAG in Scotland.

David Simmons is a part-time welfare rights worker at CPAG. He is also a freelance welfare rights trainer and author.

Peter Turville is a welfare rights worker based at Oxfordshire Welfare Rights.

Paula Twigg is CPAG's welfare rights manager.

Barbara Williamson is an independent welfare rights trainer.

Stewart Wright is CPAG's legal officer.

Acknowledgements

The authors would like to thank Jon Blackwell, Jo Bontoft, Sarah Clarke, Barbara Gray, Arnie James, Beth Lakhani and Celia Minoughan for their invaluable comments.

We would also like to acknowledge the efforts of the many authors of previous editions of the *National Welfare Benefits Handbook*, the *Rights Guide to Non-Means-Tested Benefits* and the *Jobseeker's Allowance Handbook*, on which this book is based.

Thanks are due to James Marsh, Pauline Phillips, Stella Wood and Nicola Johnston for editing and managing the production of the book so efficiently, and to Paula McDiarmid and Helen Cartwright for proofreading the text. Particular thanks are due to Katherine Dawson for producing the index.

We would also like to thank, once again, staff at the Department for Work and Pensions, Child Support Agency, the Revenue, Department for Education and Skills and the Tax Credit Office for their help and co-operation.

We would also like to say thank you to the staff at KonnectSoft, David Lewis XML Associates and Clowes for keeping up with our schedules.

Finally, thanks go to all the families of the authors who endured many lost weekends during the writing of this book.

The law covered in this book was correct on 1 March 2005 and includes regulations laid up to this date.

Contents

How to use this *Handbook*

This *Handbook* covers the rules for all welfare benefits and tax credits.

The basic structure of the benefit and tax credit systems is summarised in Chapter 1. This chapter explains the differences between the various types of benefits and tax credits and includes a quick guide to the benefits and tax credits you can claim depending on your circumstances. You can use this guide to get an idea of which benefits and tax credits you might be able to get before turning to the chapters about each benefit and tax credit for more detail.

This *Handbook* also aims to give practical help in the areas where disputes are likely to arise between claimants and local authorities, the Department for Work and Pensions (DWP), the Revenue or other government departments. If you are challenging a decision related to your claim it is sometimes helpful to refer to the relevant law and official guidance, as well as caselaw – references are given in the notes found at the end of each chapter.

In this *Handbook* the chapters are organised into six parts to help you find your way around the information. Part 1 outlines the benefit and tax credit systems, Parts 2–5 are about benefits (including pension credit) and Part 6 is about tax credits. Broadly, all the information about individual benefits – in alphabetical order – is in Part 2, and all the benefit rules that apply to special groups, or are common to all of the benefits, are in Parts 3–5. Part 6 describes the two different tax credits as well as the rules common to both.

The notes to each chapter are at the end of each chapter and are numbered in the order they appear in the text. The notes are in abbreviated form, in order to save space, and the relevant abbreviations are all listed in Appendix 11.

For example, 'Reg 52(2) JSA Regs' is regulation 52(2) of the Jobseeker's Allowance Regulations 1996. The references are usually to Acts or Regulations, but sometimes they are to caselaw (social security commissioners' or court decisions) and guidance issued by the DWP. Appendix 2 and Appendix 3 suggest where to look for copies of the law and caselaw.

In the text, abbreviations are also used for most of the benefits in order to save space. There is a list of abbreviations used in the text at the front of this book. However, an abbreviated term is always given in full the first time it is used in a chapter or section.

The index contains entries in bold type which direct you to the general information on the subject or where the subject is covered more fully. Sub-entries under the bold headings are listed alphabetically and direct you to specific aspects of the subject.

The cross references in the text refer you to other information about the relevant topic.

The main subjects in each chapter are summarised in the contents pages at the front of this book. The main subject headings and page numbers are repeated at the beginning of each chapter.

Contents of this Handbook

Part 1 contains just one chapter introducing the main structure of the benefit and tax credit systems.

Part 2 covers the rules for all the non-means-tested and means-tested benefits.

Part 3 describes the special rules that apply to certain groups of claimants.

Part 4 gives the general rules that apply to all, or most of, the benefits.

Part 5 describes the administration of benefits and how to challenge decisions made about benefits or complain if you have been treated unfairly.

Part 6 covers the rules for tax credits, describes how they are administered and explains how to challenge tax credit decisions.

The benefit and tax credit rates listed in the following sections and throughout this *Handbook* are those applying from April 2005.

Abbreviations

AA	attendance allowance
BL	budgeting loan
CA	carer's allowance
CAB	Citizens Advice Bureau
CCG	community care grant
CL	crisis loan
CSA	Child Support Agency
CTB	council tax benefit
CTC	child tax credit
DEA	disability employment adviser
DfES	Department for Education and Skills
DHP	discretionary housing payments
DLA care	disability living allowance – care component
DLA mobility	disability living allowance – mobility component
DPTC	disabled person's tax credit
DWP	Department for Work and Pensions
EC	European Community
ECtHR	European Court of Human Rights
ECJ	European Court of Justice
EEA	European Economic Area
EO	employment officer
EU	European Union
EWC	expected week of childbirth
GP	general practitioner
HB	housing benefit
IB	incapacity benefit
ICA	invalid care allowance
IIDB	industrial injuries disablement benefit
IRS	Independent Review Service
IS	income support
JSA	jobseeker's allowance
LEA	local education authority
MA	maternity allowance
MP	Member of Parliament
MS	medical service
NI	national insurance
NICO	National Insurance Contributions Office
PAYE	Pay As You Earn
PC	pension credit
REA	reduced earnings allowance
SAAS	Student Awards Agency for Scotland
SAP	statutory adoption pay
SDA	severe disablement allowance
SF	social fund
SFI	social fund inspector
SFO	social fund officer
SHP	severe hardship payment
SLC	Student Loan Company
SMP	statutory maternity pay
SPP	statutory paternity pay
SSP	statutory sick pay
TAS	The Appeals Service
TCO	Tax Credit Office
WFTC	working families' tax credit
WTC	working tax credit

Means-tested benefit rates

Income support/income-based jobseeker's allowance

Personal allowances

		£pw
Single	16–17*	33.85
	18–24 (including some 16/17-year-olds)	44.50
	25 or over	56.20
Lone parent	Under 18*	33.85
	Under 18* (in certain cases)	44.50
	18 or over	56.20
Couple	Both under 18*	max. 67.15
	Both 18 or over	88.15

* For eligibility and amounts for under-18s, see p879

Premiums

Bereavement		25.85
Carer		25.80
Disability	Single	23.95
	Couple	34.20
Enhanced disability	Single	11.70
	Couple	16.90
Severe disability	One qualifies	45.50
	Two qualify	91.00
Pensioner	Single (JSA only)	53.25
	Couple	78.90

Children (Pre-6 April 2004 claims with no child tax credit)

Child under 19 personal allowance	43.88
Family premium	16.10
Disabled child premium	43.89
Enhanced disability premium (child)	17.71

Capital limits

	Lower	Upper
Under age 60	3,000	8,000
Aged 60 or over	6,000	12,000
Care homes	10,000	16,000

Tariff income £1 per £250 between lower and upper limit

Pension credit

Standard minimum guarantee	Single	109.45
	Couple	167.05
Severe disability addition	One qualifies	45.50
	Two qualify	91.00
Carer addition		25.80

Savings credit

Threshold	Single	82.05
	Couple	131.20
Maximum	Single	16.44
	Couple	21.51

Capital disregard

Standard	6,000
Care homes	10,000

No upper limit

Deemed income £1 per £500 above disregard

Housing benefit and council tax benefit

Personal allowances

Single	16–24	44.50
	25 or over	56.20
Lone parent	Under 18	44.50
	18 or over	56.20
Couple	Both under 18	67.15
	One or both 18 or over	88.15
Children	Under 19	43.88

Pensioner 60 or over

(not on IS or income-based JSA)	Single under 65	109.45
	Single 65 or over	125.90
	Couple both under 65	167.05
	Couple one or both 65 or over	188.60

Premiums

Bereavement		25.85
Carer		25.80
Disability	Single	23.95
	Couple	34.20
Disabled child		43.89

		£pw
Severe disability	One qualifies	45.50
	Two qualify	91.00
Enhanced disability	Single	11.70
	Couple	16.90
	Child	17.71
Family	Ordinary rate	16.10
	Some lone parents	22.20
	Baby addition	10.50
Pensioner (on IS or income-based JSA)	Single	53.25
	Couple	78.90

Capital limits

	Lower	Upper
Under age 60	3,000	16,000
Aged 60 or over	6,000	16,000
Care home (housing benefit only)	10,000	16,000
Pension credit guarantee credit		no limit

Tariff income £1 per £250 between lower and upper limit
£1 per £500 for those aged 60 or over not on IS/income-based JSA
No tariff income for those on PC guarantee credit

Social fund payments

Maternity grant		500.00
Cold weather payment		8.50
Winter fuel payment	60–69	200.00
	70–79	250.00
	80 or over	300.00
	Care home – 60–69	100.00
	Care home – 70–79	125.00
	Care home – 80 or over	150.00

Non-means-tested benefit rates

	Claimant £pw	Adult dependant £pw
Attendance allowance		
Higher rate	60.60	
Lower rate	40.55	
Bereavement benefits		
Bereavement payment (lump sum)	2,000.00	
Bereavement allowance (standard)	82.05	
Widowed parent's allowance	82.05	
Widowed mother's allowance	82.05	
Widow's pension (standard)	82.05	
Carer's allowance	45.70	27.30
Child benefit		
Only/eldest child	17.00	
Other child(ren)	11.40	
Only/eldest child (some lone parents)	17.55	
Child dependants' increase		
(For some existing claimants on carer's allowance, long-term incapacity benefit, retirement pension, severe disablement allowance, widowed mother's allowance and widowed parent's allowance)		
Only/eldest child	9.40	
Other child(ren)	11.35	
Disability living allowance		
Care component		
Higher	60.60	
Middle	40.55	
Lower	16.05	
Mobility component		
Higher	42.30	
Lower	16.05	

	Claimant £pw	Adult dependant £pw
Guardian's allowance	12.20	
Short-term incapacity benefit		
Lower rate	57.65	35.65
Higher rate	68.20	35.65
Lower rate (over pension age)	73.35	43.95
Higher rate (over pension age)	76.45	43.95
Long-term incapacity benefit	76.45	45.70
Age additions		
Under 35	16.05	
35–44	8.05	
Industrial disablement benefit		
18 or over	20%: £24.76 to 100%: £123.80	
Under 18	20%: £15.17 to 100%: £75.85	
Contribution-based jobseeker's allowance		
Under 18	33.85	
Under 25	44.50	
25 or over	56.20	
Maternity allowance		
Standard rate	106.00	35.65
Retirement pension		
Category A	82.05	49.15
Category B for a widow/widower	82.05	
Category B for a married woman	49.15	
Category D	49.15	
Severe disablement allowance	46.20	27.50
Age additions		
Under 40	16.05	
40–49	10.30	
50–59	5.15	
Statutory maternity, paternity and adoption pay		
Standard rate	106.00	
Statutory sick pay	68.20	

	£pw
National insurance contributions	
Lower earnings limit	82.00
Primary threshold	94.00
Employee's class 1 rate	11% of £94.01 to £630.00 1% above £630.00
Class 2 rate	2.10

Tax credit rates

Child tax credit		Daily rate	£ per year
Family element	Basic	1.50	545
	Baby element	1.50	545
Child element		4.64	1,690
Disability element		6.27	2,285
Severe disability element		2.53	920
Working tax credit			
Basic element		4.44	1,620
Couple element		4.37	1,595
Lone parent element		4.37	1,595
30-hour element		1.81	660
Disability element		5.94	2,165
Severe disability element		2.53	920
50-plus element	Working 16–29 hours	3.05	1,110
	Working 30 hours or more	4.55	1,660
Childcare element	70% eligible childcare costs to a weekly maximum of:		
	One child	25.00	175
	Two or more children	42.86	300
Thresholds			
First income threshold	WTC alone or with CTC		5,220
	CTC only		13,910
First taper			37%
Second income threshold			min. 50,000
Second taper			6.67%

Part 1

Introduction

Chapter 1

Introduction

This chapter covers:

1. The benefit and tax credit system

The government department responsible for overall administration and policy work concerning social security benefits (other than housing benefit – HB – and council tax benefit – CTB) is the **Department for Work and Pensions (DWP)**. Tax credits, child benefit and guardian's allowance are dealt with by **the Revenue**. **Note:** At the time of writing, the Inland Revenue was expected to merge with Customs and Excise to form a new department called Her Majesty's Revenue and Customs. This merger was expected to take place during April 2005. Therefore, references to 'the Revenue' should be taken to mean references to both the Inland Revenue and Her Majesty's Revenue and Customs.

HB and CTB are dealt with by the **local authority**. For the sake of simplicity, in this book we usually call the people dealing with your benefit claim the DWP. Where we are referring only to tax credits, we call the people dealing with your claim the Tax Credit Office, where we are referring to child benefit and guardian's allowance we call the people dealing with your claim the Revenue, and when we are referring only to HB or CTB we call the people dealing with your claim the local authority.

Since April 2002, an executive agency of the DWP, called **Jobcentre Plus**, administers most benefit claims for people under state retirement age. In some areas this service is still being delivered through two separate offices – a Jobcentre and a local social security office. It is expected that Jobcentre Plus will cover the entire country by 2006. Another executive agency of the DWP, the **Pension Service**, deals with the administration of state retirement pensions and pension credit (PC) which replaced income support (IS) for those aged 60 or over (see Chapter 18 for more details on PC). Another part of the DWP, the **Disability and Carer Service**, administers claims for **attendance allowance** and disability living allowance through regional Disability Benefit Centres and a Disability Benefits Unit in Blackpool, and carer's allowance through the Carer's Allowance Unit in Preston. Other executive agencies include the **Appeals Service** (administering appeals) and the **Child Support Agency** (administering the child support system).

The main types of benefit and tax credit

Some benefits are paid only if you have limited income and capital. These benefits are known as **means-tested benefits** (see p6) because there is an investigation into your means before you can be paid them. Examples of means-tested benefits are IS and HB.

Tax credits (see p7) are also means-tested. There are two types of tax credit dealt with in this book – child tax credit and working tax credit (see Chapters 49 and 50).

Some other benefits (known as 'passported' benefits) are payable if you qualify for particular means-tested benefits or tax credits (see p10). Some benefits are 'discretionary' even if you satisfy a means test (see p9).

Non-means-tested benefits (see p5) do not involve a detailed investigation of your means. You qualify if you satisfy certain basic conditions such as being available for work, disabled or widowed. It may still be relevant to ask whether you have any earnings or an occupational pension, because many of the benefits are designed to compensate for your loss of earnings, but normally your income or capital does not affect your entitlement. Examples of non-means-tested benefits are incapacity benefit and retirement pension (which replace earnings) and child benefit and disability living allowance (which are to meet specific needs).

One benefit is both a means-tested and a non-means-tested benefit. This is jobseeker's allowance (JSA) (see Chapter 15). There are two main types of JSA: *income-based* JSA (which is means-tested) and *contribution-based* JSA (which is non-means-tested). A third type, called joint-claim JSA, is a kind of income-based JSA, but has some special rules about claiming for certain couples.

This *Handbook* also covers the rules for **statutory sick pay, statutory maternity pay, statutory paternity pay** and **statutory adoption pay** which are paid, without any means test, by your employer, rather than by the DWP.

You may be entitled to a combination of non-means-tested and means-tested benefits. For example, you might receive incapacity benefit topped up by IS. In addition, you might also qualify for help with your rent (HB) and your council tax (CTB).

2. Non-means-tested benefits

The most important distinction for the non-means-tested benefits is between those which are contributory and those which are not.

One of the conditions of entitlement to **contributory benefits** is that you should, in the past, have paid sufficient contributions. These are known as 'contribution conditions'. To find out more about the contribution conditions for the benefit you want to claim, see Chapter 33.

You do not have to satisfy contribution conditions to qualify for **non-contributory benefits**.

Contributory benefits	*Non-contributory benefits*
Bereavement allowance	Attendance allowance
Bereavement payment	Carer's allowance
Incapacity benefit	Child benefit
Contribution-based jobseeker's allowance	Disability living allowance
Category A and B retirement pension	Guardian's allowance
Graduated retirement benefit	Industrial injuries benefits
Widowed mother's allowance (replaced by widowed parent's allowance for new claims from 9 April 2001)	Category D retirement pension
Widowed parent's allowance	Severe disablement allowance (abolished for new claims from 6 April 2001)
Widow's payment (replaced by bereavement payment for new claims from 9 April 2001)	
Widow's pension (replaced by bereavement allowance for new claims from 9 April 2001)	

If you qualify for contribution-based jobseeker's allowance (JSA) you might also qualify for income-based JSA (for some couples this may need to be joint-claim JSA) if:

- you qualify for any of the premiums that can be added to your basic personal allowance (see p878); *or*
- you need help with your mortgage interest or other types of housing costs (see Chapter 36).

Earnings replacement and other non-means-tested benefits

Some benefits are available to compensate you for your inability to work through unemployment, sickness, pregnancy or old age. These are known as 'earnings replacement' benefits. Other benefits exist to meet particular needs – eg, because you are disabled or have children, irrespective of your ability to work.

Earnings replacement benefits

- Carer's allowance
- Incapacity benefit
- Contribution-based jobseeker's allowance
- Maternity allowance
- Retirement pensions
- Severe disablement allowance (abolished for new claims from 6 April 2001)

Other benefits

- Attendance allowance
- Child benefit
- Disability living allowance
- Guardian's allowance
- Industrial injuries benefits

You may usually only receive one 'earnings replacement benefit' at a time (see p1102 for details of the overlapping benefit rules). However, you may receive any number of the other benefits listed above whether or not you also receive an 'earnings replacement benefit'.

Most 'earnings replacement benefits' have 'earnings rules' which limit the amount of earnings you may receive while remaining entitled to the benefit. Retirement pensions are an exception: your earnings do not affect the amount of retirement pension you get.

Bereavement benefits (ie, widows' benefits, widowed parent's allowance and bereavement allowance) have not been included in the list above. They exist to replace the earnings of your late spouse if you are a widow or widower and therefore your own earnings are ignored. Bereavement and widowed parent's allowance are not paid in addition to any other earnings replacement benefit which you may be entitled to in your own right.

3. Means-tested benefits

To be entitled to means-tested benefits you do not have to satisfy any contribution conditions (see p5). Instead, your income and capital must be sufficiently low for you to qualify. This involves detailed investigation of your means. The way means tests work is outlined on p8.

The main means-tested benefits

Income support

Income-based jobseeker's allowance

Pension credit

Housing benefit

Council tax benefit

Health benefits (other than free milk and vitamins)

It is not always necessary to consider all the benefits listed above separately because, if you qualify for income support, income-based jobseeker's allowance or pension credit that includes the guarantee credit, you automatically satisfy the means test for the other benefits.

4. Tax credits

To be entitled to tax credits you do not have to satisfy any contribution conditions (see p843). However, for child tax credit you must have responsibility for a child and for working tax credit you must be in full-time paid work (see p1342). For both tax credits you must satisfy a means test. The way means tests work is outlined on p9.

Tax credits

Child tax credit

Working tax credit

5. Working and means-tested benefits

Some means-tested benefits are restricted to those who are *not* in full-time paid work (see p757). Pension credit, housing benefit and council tax benefit are for people both in and out of full-time paid work. You might qualify for some of the means-tested benefits even if you are getting tax credits (see above).

Benefits only for people not in full-time work	*Benefits for people both in and out of work*
Free school meals	Council tax benefit
Income support	Health benefits
Income-based jobseeker's allowance	Housing benefit
Social fund budgeting loans, cold weather payments and community care grants (but you can still get these if in full-time work and getting pension credit)	Pension credit
	Social fund crisis loans, funeral payments and maternity payments, winter fuel payments

6. The way means tests work

Benefits

Means-tested benefits have similar ways of taking account of your needs. For benefits other than pension credit (PC), these involve adding up a personal allowance for you and your partner if you have one (or, in the case of housing benefit (HB) and council tax benefit (CTB), for each member of the family) and then adding on additional amounts, known as premiums, to take account of extra expenses you may have because of your or your partner's circumstances (and for HB and CTB, your children's circumstances) (see Chapter 35) and any eligible housing costs if you are a home owner. This figure is called your 'applicable amount' and is then compared with your total resources – your income and capital.

If you have too much capital, you are not entitled to any benefit at all. If you have a lesser amount of capital, it may reduce the amount of benefit to which you are entitled because it is treated as producing an income (see p977 for information about 'tariff income').

Once your needs and your income have been calculated, your benefit entitlement can be worked out. In the case of income support (IS), income-based jobseeker's allowance (JSA) and health benefits, this is done simply by deducting your income from your needs. In the cases of HB and CTB, there are more complicated formulae which take into account the amount of your rent or council tax as well as your other needs and your income. The higher your income, the less benefit you receive, but those with incomes substantially above IS or income-based JSA level may still receive some help. The formulae are set out on p303 (IS), p379 (income-based JSA), p193 (HB) and p109 (CTB).

Radical changes to the structure of IS and income-based JSA came into effect from 6 April 2004 as a result of the introduction of the new tax credits. From this date all amounts for children will be removed from IS and income-based JSA, leaving just the amounts for adults and any housing costs within an applicable amount. Families with a child(ren) will have to claim IS, JSA or working tax credit for themselves and child tax credit (CTC) for their child(ren). Those on IS or income-based JSA on 6 April 2004, who have not claimed CTC before this date, will have their IS or income-based JSA child amounts transferred to CTC at some point in 2005 (see p1310).

The guarantee credit of PC is calculated in a similar way to IS in that additional amounts may be added to your 'standard minimum guarantee' where you have any additional needs, for example due to a disability or caring responsibilities and any eligible housing costs if you are a home owner. The maximum amount of guarantee credit you can get is known as your 'appropriate minimum guarantee'. Your income is then deducted from your 'appropriate minimum guarantee'. The income rules are, on the whole, more generous for PC than they are for IS. There is no capital limit for PC but any capital that counts will be deemed to produce an income. For more information on PC see Chapter 18.

Tax credits

These work in a similar way to benefits in that amounts are aggregated according to your circumstances, such as whether you have a family, a disability, childcare costs, or you work over 30 hours a week. Your total income (including actual income from capital – although there is no capital limit) is taken into account by comparing this total to a set figure. For further details see Chapter 53.

Discretionary benefits

Where a benefit is discretionary, your means and other individual circumstances are obviously crucial in deciding whether or not to award the benefit. Social fund crisis loans (CLs), budgeting loans (BLs) and community care grants (CCGs) are paid on a discretionary basis, although certain rules also have to be followed (see Chapter 21).

To get a BL or CCG, you must be entitled to IS, income-based JSA or PC. You do not need to be on benefit to get a CL. Each local area has a limited budget for social fund payments, so your needs are assessed alongside those of other claimants.

Where local authorities have the power to make payments for things like school uniforms, they can do it on a purely discretionary basis. They often have local means tests similar to the IS means test. They also have the power to make discretionary housing payments to people entitled to HB and/or CTB who require further help in order to meet their housing costs.

Passported benefits

Some benefits and tax credits act as a 'passport' to other benefits. These are:

Passported benefit	*Passports*
Free school meals	Income support Income-based jobseeker's allowance Some recipients of child tax credit
Health benefits	Income support Income-based jobseeker's allowance Some recipients of child tax credit Some recipients of working tax credit Guarantee credit of pension credit
Sure Start maternity grants	Income support Income-based jobseeker's allowance Pension credit (either or both credits) Some recipients of child tax credit (see p549) Some recipients of working tax credit (see p549)
Social fund funeral expenses payments	Income support Income-based jobseeker's allowance Pension credit (either or both credits) Some recipients of child tax credit (see p551) Some recipients of working tax credit (see p551) Housing benefit Council tax benefit
Social fund cold weather payments, community care grants and budgeting loans	Income support Income-based jobseeker's allowance Pension credit (either or both credits)

In the case of community care grants and budgeting loans from the social fund, it is a further condition of entitlement that your capital is not above a certain level (see Chapter 21).

Receipt of certain other benefits should result in automatic social fund winter fuel payments so long as you satisfy other conditions of entitlement (see p559), otherwise a claim will be required. If you are on a low income, you might qualify for health benefits even if you do not get one of the 'passports'. Details of the low income scheme are in Chapter 9.

7. Bonuses

If you or your partner start working full time or increase your earnings, and as a result stop claiming income support or income-based jobseeker's allowance, you might be entitled to certain bonuses aimed at easing your transition into work after a period of time on benefit (see Chapter 3).You may be entitled to one or more of the following bonuses, depending on your circumstances: child maintenance bonus (but these are gradually being phased out) (see p54); job grant (see p66); mortgage interest run-on (see p62); extended payments of housing benefit and council tax benefit (you might also qualify for these if you are moving into work after a period on incapacity benefit or severe disablement allowance) (see p63); and an annual Christmas bonus if you are entitled to certain benefits (see p68).

Back-to-work bonus and lone parent run-on were abolished from 25 October 2004 but you might still be entitled to a back-to-work bonus if you had accrued one by this date (see p49). There are other government schemes that provide financial incentives to help you move from certain benefits into full-time work. For details of these ask at your local Jobcentre.

8. Which benefits or tax credits should you claim?

You may be able to claim a combination of non-means-tested benefits, means-tested benefits and tax credits. You should check to see:

- if you are entitled to any 'earnings replacement' benefits (see p6); *then*
- if you can get any benefits because of your circumstances – eg, because you are disabled or are looking after children; *and finally*
- whether you qualify for any means-tested benefits or tax credits to top up your benefit and other income.

Qualifying for some of the non-means-tested benefits means you qualify for some of the means-tested benefits at a higher rate. It is worth getting help to ensure you are claiming all the benefits to which you are entitled. See Appendix 2 for information about where you can go for advice and assistance. See pp12–13 for ideas of benefits you might claim in certain circumstances.

Remember:

- when you claim, ask for your claim to be backdated if relevant (see p1085);
- if getting one of the non-means-tested benefits you are claiming qualifies you for another benefit, claim the other benefit at the same time (see p1090).

The following table is an overview of the possible benefits and tax credits that you may be entitled to depending on your circumstances. You may find that more than one of the circumstances applies to you – for example, you may have a child, a disability, a mortgage and work part time; please refer to each separate circumstance that applies.

Summaries of the rules for each benefit/tax credit are provided in the text following this table; please refer to the relevant chapters for full details.

Whatever category below you are in, you might get the following benefits/tax credits if you do not have enough money to live on. These can be paid in addition to other benefits or on their own:

– income support or income-based jobseeker's allowance, if not in full-time paid work;
– working tax credit, if in full-time paid work;
– pension credit, if in or out of full-time paid work.

Your circumstance	*Benefits/tax credits you may be entitled to*
Bereaved	Bereavement payment
	Widowed parent's allowance
	Bereavement allowance
	Funeral expenses payment
Carer	Carer's allowance
Responsible for a child	Child tax credit
	Child benefit
	Guardian's allowance
	Statutory paternity pay
	Statutory adoption pay
	Working tax credit
	Health benefits
	Cold weather payment
Disabled	Disability living allowance
	Attendance allowance
	Industrial injuries benefits
	War disablement pension
	Cold weather payment
Incapable of work	Incapacity benefit
	Non-contributory incapacity benefit
	Statutory sick pay
	Severe disablement allowance
	Cold weather payment
Have a mortgage	Income support
	Income-based jobseeker's allowance
	Pension credit
	Council tax benefit

Not enough money to meet certain needs	Community care grant Budgeting loan Crisis loan
Pensioner	State retirement pension Pension credit Winter fuel payment Cold weather payment
Pregnant	Statutory maternity pay Maternity allowance Sure start maternity grant Health benefits
Student	Income support Jobseeker's allowance Pension credit
Tenant	Housing benefit Council tax benefit
Unemployed and seeking work	Contribution-based jobseeker's allowance Income-based jobseeker's allowance

Attendance allowance

- Attendance allowance (AA) is not means-tested and is for those who are 65 or over when they claim who need help with personal care (see Chapter 7).
- If you receive this benefit you may also be entitled to disability-related premiums if you claim housing benefit (HB) and/or council tax benefit (CTB) or an additional amount if you claim pension credit (PC) (see Chapter 35), or your partner claims income support (IS) or income-based jobseeker's allowance.
- If you get AA at any rate your carer may qualify for carer's allowance (CA) (but your carer should check whether this will affect any income support/income-based JSA/housing benefit/council tax benefit or pension credit you may be getting – see p14).

Bereavement allowance

- Bereavement allowance is paid for up to 52 weeks for widows or widowers who were 45 or over but under pension age when their spouse died.
- You cannot get bereavement allowance and widowed parent's allowance at the same time (see Chapter 2).

Bereavement payment

- Bereavement payment is a one-off lump sum payment for widows and widowers under pension age when their spouse died or whose late spouse was not entitled to state retirement pension (see Chapter 2).

Budgeting loan

- You may get an interest-free loan to help you with particular expenses – you have to be in receipt of a qualifying benefit when you claim and throughout the previous 26 weeks (see Chapter 21).

Carer's allowance

- Carer's allowance (CA) is paid if you are providing 35 hours or more care per week for a person who is entitled to disability living allowance (DLA) care component at the middle or higher rate, or AA (see Chapter 4).
- If you get CA you will qualify for a carer's premium if you claim IS, income-based JSA, HB and/or CTB, or a carer's additional amount if you claim PC, but the CA will count as income for these benefits. However, before you claim CA check whether this will affect the person for whom you are caring – if s/he gets a benefit that includes a severe disability premium or additional amount, then this could be stopped if you claim CA (see Chapter 35).

Child benefit

- Child benefit is not means-tested and is paid regardless of whether or not you are working (see Chapter 5).

Child tax credit

- Child tax credit (CTC) is paid whether you are in or out of work – the amount you may get will depend on a means test (see Chapter 49).

Cold weather payment

- Social fund cold weather payments are paid automatically if you are getting IS or income-based JSA that includes a qualifying premium or you have a child under five, or you are getting pension credit (see Chapter 22).

Community care grant

- You may get a grant specifically to help you live independently in the community – you have to be in receipt of a qualifying benefit when you claim (see Chapter 21).

Contribution-based jobseeker's allowance

- Contribution-based jobseeker's allowance (JSA) is paid for 26 weeks and where you satisfy the national insurance (NI) contribution conditions – it is not means-tested but earnings can affect the amount of benefit you receive (see Chapter 15).

Council tax benefit

- If you have a council tax liability and are on a low income you may get council tax benefit (CTB). It is paid whether you are in or out of work (see Chapter 6).

- If you are the only person liable for council tax on your home and you have an adult on a low income living with you, you might be able to get 'second adult rebate' instead of council tax benefit.For second adult rebate it does not matter how much income or capital you have and it is paid whether you are in or out of work (see Chapter 6).

Crisis loan

- A crisis loan may be payable if you have suffered an emergency or disaster and you do not have enough money to meet immediate short-term needs. You do not have to be in receipt of a benefit to get this loan but have to be likely to be able to repay it (see Chapter 21).

Disability living allowance

- Disability living allowance (DLA) is not means-tested and is paid where you need help with your mobility and/or your personal care. You must be under 65 when you first claim (see Chapter 7).
- If you receive this benefit you may also be entitled to disability-related premiums if you claim IS, income-based JSA, HB and/or CTB, or an additional amount if you claim PC (see Chapter 35).
- If you get DLA care at the middle or higher rate your carer may qualify for CA (but your carer should check whether this will affect any income support/ income-based JSA/housing benefit/council tax benefit or pension credit you are getting – see p14).

Funeral expenses payment

- To get help with the cost of a funeral through the social fund you have to receive a qualifying benefit (see Chapter 22).

Guardian's allowance

- Guardian's allowance is paid to you if you are looking after a child who is effectively an orphan (see Chapter 8).

Health benefits

- Health benefits include free prescriptions, dental treatment, milk and vitamins. If you get a qualifying benefit you will have a 'passported' entitlement to health benefits. Alternatively you may qualify on low-income grounds (see Chapter 9).

Housing benefit

- If you have rent to pay as a tenant and are on a low income you may get housing benefit (HB). It is paid whether you are in or out of work (see Chapter 10).

Incapacity benefit

- You have to satisfy the NI contribution conditions to be paid incapacity benefit (IB), unless you became incapable of work in youth (see Chapter 12).

Income-based jobseeker's allowance

- Income-based jobseeker's allowance (JSA) is means tested and non-contributory. It is paid for as long as you satisfy the conditions of entitlement. It can be paid in addition to contribution-based JSA where you have any additional needs – eg, a disability or eligible housing costs (see Chapter 15).
- If you work less than 16 hours a week you may be required to take up a full-time job (see Chapter 15).
- Some mortgage payments can be met by this benefit and if you are eligible you may have to serve a waiting period before you get this assistance (see Chapter 36).

Income support

- To qualify you have to fit into one of the categories of eligible claimants (eg, lone parents or disabled people) (see Chapter 13).
- Income support (IS) can be paid in addition to other benefits to top up your income to a certain level.
- Some mortgage payments can be met by this benefit and if you are eligible you may have to serve a waiting period before you get this assistance (see Chapter 36).

Industrial injuries benefits

- Industrial injuries benefits are paid if you are disabled as a result of being injured or contracting a disease at work (see Chapter 14).
- If you receive this benefit you may also be entitled to disability-related premiums if you claim IS, income-based JSA, HB and/or CTB (see Chapter 35).

Maternity allowance

- If you are pregnant or have recently had a baby and you are not entitled to SMP you may be eligible for maternity allowance (MA) – eg, if you are self-employed (see Chapter 17).

Non-contributory incapacity benefit

- If you do not qualify for incapacity benefit (IB) on the basis of your NI contribution record, you may qualify if you became incapacitated in youth (see Chapter 12).

Pension credit

- The guarantee credit of pension credit (PC) is paid to both men and women aged 60 or over and acts to top up a low income; it is means tested. The savings credit of PC is paid to men and women aged 65 or over (or whose partner is 65 or over) and acts as a reward for making provisions above the basic state pension (see Chapter 18).

- Some mortgage payments can be met by this benefit (see Chapter 36).

Severe disablement allowance

- Severe disablement allowance (SDA) was abolished for new claimants on 6 April 2001 but some claimants with entitlement before that date remain eligible to receive SDA (see Chapter 20).

State retirement pension

- State retirement pension is paid to women from the age of 60 and to men from the age of 65. It is based on the amount of your NI contributions (see Chapter 19).

Statutory adoption pay

- Statutory adoption pay is paid if you are, or have been, an employee who satisfies the continuous employment and earnings conditions, it is paid for 26 weeks where a child is placed or is expected to be placed with you for adoption (see Chapter 23).

Statutory maternity pay

- Statutory maternity pay (SMP) is paid if you are an employee who satisfies the continuous employment and earnings conditions – the earliest it can be paid is the 11th week before your expected week of childbirth and it is paid for up to 26 weeks (see Chapter 23).
- If you are not entitled to SMP you may be eligible for MA – eg, if you are self-employed (see Chapter 23).

Statutory paternity pay

- Statutory paternity pay is paid if you are, or have been, an employee who satisfies the continuous employment and earnings conditions, it is paid for two weeks where your partner has just given birth or you have adopted a child (see Chapter 23).

Statutory sick pay

- Statutory sick pay (SSP) is paid to employees for the first 28 weeks of incapacity (see Chapter 24).

Sure Start maternity grant

- To get a Sure Start maternity grant you have to receive a qualifying benefit (see Chapter 22).

War disablement pension

- If you receive this benefit you may also be entitled to disability-related premiums if you claim IS, income-based JSA, HB and/or CTB (see Chapter 35).

Widowed parent's allowance

- Widowed parent's allowance is for widows and widowers with children and for pregnant widows.
- You cannot get both widowed parent's allowance and bereavement allowance at the same time (see Chapter 2).

Winter fuel payment

- Social fund winter fuel payments are for people aged 60 or over, regardless of their means (see Chapter 22).

Working tax credit

- Working tax credit (WTC) is paid if you work 16 hours or more a week (or in some cases 30 hours or more a week) and have a low income (see Chapter 50).

9. Other financial help

This *Handbook* is mainly concerned with information about social security benefits and tax credits. However, there is a lot of other financial help to which you may be entitled, especially if you are on a low income, have children, have an illness or disability or other special needs, or are an older person.

More detail on such help can be found in CPAG's *Paying for Care Handbook* and in the *Disability Rights Handbook*, published by Disability Alliance. For details of financial support through welfare to work programmes see the *Welfare to Work Handbook* by Inclusion.

Education benefits

Free school meals

Children are entitled to free school meals if their families receive:

- income support (see Chapter 13), or income-based jobseeker's allowance (see Chapter 15); or pension credit (guarantee credit);
- child tax credit (but not working tax credit) and whose annual taxable income is £13,910 or less.

Also entitled are:

- 16–18-year-olds receiving the above benefits or tax credit in their own right;
- asylum seekers.

Clothing grants

Local education authorities (LEAs) can give grants for school uniforms and other school clothes. Each authority determines its own eligibility rules.

School transport

Education authorities must provide free transport to school for pupils under 16 where it is considered necessary to enable that pupil to get to the 'nearest suitable school'.

Education grants and loans

To find out what help is available to finance your studies, contact your LEA or college, also see CPAG's *Student Support and Benefits Handbook for England and Wales* and CPAG's *Benefits for Students in Scotland Handbook*. Education maintenance allowances (EMAs) are available to 16–19-year-olds who stay on in full-time education – for further details visit the Department for Education and Skills EMA website at www.ema.dfes.gov.uk or call the EMA student/parent helpline on 0808 1016219.

Health benefits

You may be entitled to help with NHS charges for prescriptions, dental treatment, sight tests, glasses, wigs and fabric supports, fares to hospital, milk, vitamins and health care equipment. For more detail, see Chapter 9.

Housing grants

Local authority grants

Your local authority may be able to provide you with a grant to help with the cost of improving your home. The main types of grant available are:

- renovation grants;
- disabled facilities grants;
- home repair assistance.

For more details, see CPAG's *Paying for Care Handbook*.

Home energy efficiency scheme

This scheme provides grants for insulating and draught-proofing your home.

For more details, see CPAG's *Paying for Care Handbook*, or contact the Energy Action Grants Agency, Freepost NEA 12054, Newcastle upon Tyne, NE2 1BR (freephone 0800 072 0150).

Help from social services

Local authority social services departments have statutory duties to provide a range of practical and financial help to families, children, young people, older people, people with disabilities and asylum seekers.

If you are an asylum seeker, see Chapter 26.

For more details, see CPAG's *Paying for Care Handbook*.

Special funds for sick or disabled people

A variety of help is available for people with an illness or disability to assist with things like paying for care services in their own home, equipment, holidays, furniture and transport needs, and for people with haemophilia or HIV contracted via haemophilia treatment.

For more information, see CPAG's *Paying for Care Handbook* and the *Disability Rights Handbook*, published by Disability Alliance.

Charities

There are hundreds of charities that provide a variety of help to people in need. Your local authority social services department or local advice centre may know of appropriate charities that could assist you, or you can consult publications, such as the *Guide to Grants for Individuals in Need* and the *Charities Digest*, in your local library.

Part 2

Benefits

Chapter 2

Bereavement benefits

This chapter contains the rules about bereavement benefits. It covers:

If your spouse has died, you may qualify for bereavement benefits. The three main benefits, collectively known as bereavement benefits, are:

- a **bereavement payment** – a lump-sum payment of £2,000;
- **widowed parent's allowance** – a weekly benefit paid to widows who are pregnant and to widows and widowers who have children; *and*
- **bereavement allowance** – a weekly benefit paid for up to 52 weeks to widows and widowers who are at least 45 years of age when their spouse dies.

Bereavement benefits were introduced on 9 April 2001. They can be claimed by men and women whose spouse died on or after 9 April 2001. Widowed parent's allowance (but not bereavement payment or bereavement allowance) can also be paid to men whose wives died before 9 April 2001 (but see p36). Bereavement benefits replaced the old system of widows' benefits, which were only payable to women. If you are a woman whose husband died before 9 April 2001 you may still qualify for widows' benefits (see p35).

You can only qualify for bereavement benefits if your late spouse either satisfied the national insurance contribution conditions or died as the result of an industrial accident or disease. Your entitlement to bereavement benefits is not affected by any work that you do, nor by any income or savings that you have.

To qualify for bereavement benefits you must be a widow or widower. For who counts as a widow or widower, see p31. If you do not know whether your spouse is dead, see p34.

There are some groups of claimants to whom special rules apply (see p35).

Certain people claiming widowed parent's allowance and bereavement allowance may be required to attend a work-focused interview (see p1092).

Provisions in the Civil Partnership Act 2004 will affect the bereavement and widow's benefit rules. At the time of writing, the Civil Partnership Act was not in force but it is expected to come into force on 5 December 2005. Once it is in force, you will effectively be treated as a widow or widower if your civil partner dies (see p811 for the meaning of civil partner) and will be able to qualify for bereavement benefits, as long as s/he met the national insurance contribution conditions, or died as a result of an industrial accident or disease, and you satisfy the other normal qualifying conditions for these benefits. Similarly, just as remarriage ends entitlement to widowed parent's allowance, bereavement allowance, widowed mother's allowance or widows pension, entering into a civil partnership will end your entitlement to these benefits too. In addition, your entitlement to any of these benefits will be suspended if you live with someone of the same sex as if you were civil partners, and you will not qualify for a bereavement payment if, at the time of your spouse's or civil partner's death, you were living with someone of the same sex as if you were civil partners. See CPAG's *Welfare Rights Bulletin* for updates.

1. Bereavement payment

A bereavement payment is a one-off, lump-sum payment which you can be paid in addition to widowed parent's allowance or bereavement allowance.

Who can claim a bereavement payment

You qualify for a bereavement payment if:[1]

- you are a widow or widower and your spouse died on or after 9 April 2001 (see p31 for the meaning of widow and widower); *and*
- you claim within 12 months of your spouse's death unless your spouse died before 1 April 2003 when you must have claimed within three months of her/his death[2] (but see p42 if you were not aware that your spouse had died, and see p25 if you and your spouse were not in Great Britain (GB) when s/he died); *and either*
- your late spouse satisfied the national insurance (NI) contribution conditions (see p845); *or*
- your late spouse died as the result of an industrial injury or disease (see p35); *and either*
- you were under pension age when your spouse died (ie, under 60 if you are a woman or under 65 if you are a man); *or*
- if you were over pension age, your spouse was not entitled to a Category A retirement pension when s/he died.

Disqualification

Your entitlement to a bereavement payment is not affected if you remarry after the death of your late spouse. However, you are not entitled to a bereavement payment if, at the time of your spouse's death, you were cohabiting with someone else (ie, living together with someone of the opposite sex as husband and wife – see p34).[3]

If your spouse was not in GB at the time s/he died you cannot qualify for a bereavement payment unless:[4]

- you were in GB on the date of your spouse's death; *or*
- you returned to GB within four weeks of her/his death. In this circumstance it may be possible to argue that you can qualify for a bereavement payment if you claim it within 12 months of your return to GB if your spouse died on or after 1 April 2003, or within three months of your return if s/he died before that date; *or*
- your spouse's NI contribution record is sufficient for you to satisfy the contribution conditions for widowed parent's allowance and bereavement allowance (see p846).

The rules about your age

There is no lower age limit for entitlement to a bereavement payment. However, as you will only qualify for a bereavement payment if you are a widow or widower, you must be at least old enough to marry legally.

For details of the upper age limit for qualifying for a bereavement payment see p24.

Claiming for others

A bereavement payment is a lump-sum payment and there are no additions made to it for any of your dependants.

The amount of bereavement payment

A bereavement payment is a lump sum of **£2,000**.[5] If you are receiving a means-tested benefit, child tax credit paid at a rate that exceeds the family element or working tax credit which includes the disability or severe disability element, you may be entitled to a funeral expenses payment as well (see p551).

See p38 for details of how to claim a bereavement payment.

2. Widowed parent's allowance

Widowed parent's allowance is a weekly benefit paid to widows who are pregnant or to widows and widowers who have qualifying children. You cannot receive widowed parent's allowance and bereavement allowance at the same time but you may become entitled to bereavement allowance after your entitlement to widowed parent's allowance ends (see p29).

In addition to your widowed parent's allowance you may also qualify for a bereavement payment (see p24).

Who can claim widowed parent's allowance

You qualify for widowed parent's allowance if:[6]

- you are a widow or widower (see p31) whose spouse died on or after 9 April 2001 and you are under pension age (ie, 60 for a woman, 65 for a man); *or*
- you are a man whose wife died before 9 April 2001, you were under 65 on 9 April 2001 and you are still under pension age, and you have not remarried; *and either*
- your late spouse satisfied the national insurance (NI) contribution conditions (see p845); *or*
- your late spouse died as the result of an industrial injury or disease (see p35); *and either*
- you are entitled to child benefit (or treated as entitled to child benefit if the child has been absent from Great Britain[7]) in respect of at least one qualifying child (see below); *or*
- you are a widow and either:
  - you are pregnant by your late husband; *or*
  - you were residing with your late husband immediately before his death and you are pregnant as a result of artificial insemination by a donor or *in vitro* fertilisation which was carried out before his death.

A 'child'

For who counts as a child see p86. The definition of a child for widowed parent's allowance is the same as the definition for child benefit purposes.

Qualifying children

A child only counts as a qualifying child if *either*:[8]

- s/he is living with you (see p90); *or*
- you are contributing to the cost of supporting the child. The payments you make must be at least equal to the amount of any child benefit payable for that child (see p95) plus £12.20; *and either*
- the child is a child of yours and your late spouse; *or*
- you were residing with your late spouse immediately before s/he died and you were entitled to child benefit for the child at that time; *or*
- immediately before s/he died, your late spouse was entitled to child benefit for the child.

If you and your spouse were living apart at the time of her/his death, you can still be considered to have been residing with her/him if your separation was only intended to be temporary.[9] See p800 for the meaning of 'residing with'. If you were not residing with your spouse at the time of her/his death, unless the child is a child of yours and your late spouse, you will only qualify for widowed parent's allowance for the child if your late spouse was getting child benefit for her/him.

Disqualification and suspension

Widowed parent's allowance is paid for as long as you satisfy the qualifying conditions. It ceases if you remarry, and you are not able to re-qualify for it even if you subsequently get divorced. It is suspended during any period in which you are cohabiting (see p34) but is reinstated if you stop cohabiting.[10]

The rules about your age

There is no lower age limit for widowed parent's allowance. However, in order to qualify for it you must be at least old enough to have been legally married. Widowed parent's allowance cannot be paid once you reach pension age (ie, 60 if you are a woman, 65 if you are a man) but you may then qualify for a Category A or B retirement pension (see p487).

Claiming for others

Increases for your dependent children that could be claimed with widowed parent's allowance were abolished on 6 April 2003 and replaced with child tax credit, which is means tested (see Chapter 49). You were only entitled to an increase in your widowed parent's allowance in respect of a child dependant if:

- you were entitled to basic widowed parent's allowance (if you were only entitled to the additional earnings-related payment of widowed parent's allowance (see p28) you could not qualify for an increase for a child); *and*
- the child was a qualifying child (see p26); *and*
- you were entitled, or treated as entitled (see p799), to child benefit for the child (see p799 for the circumstances when, even if you receive child benefit for a child, you are treated as if you are not); *and*
- you made a claim for the increase.

If you were entitled to an increase for a dependent child on 5 April 2003 you may be able to continue to receive it after that date if you continue to satisfy the above conditions (see p798). Claims for certain other benefits – such as child benefit – may be treated as a claim for an increase in your widowed parent's allowance for your child dependant. If such a claim was made no more than three months after 5 April 2003, this may help you to qualify for an increase in your widowed parent's allowance now.

You cannot claim an increase in widowed parent's allowance for an adult dependant. (See pp31 and 34 for the effect of remarriage and co-habitation on your entitlement to bereavement benefits.)

The amount of widowed parent's allowance

Widowed parent's allowance is made up of:

- a basic widowed parent's allowance;
- an additional earnings-related payment based on your late spouse's earnings under the additional state pension scheme (see p499) if her/his NI contribution record qualifies you for this.

If you are entitled to widowed parent's allowance you will also be entitled to a Christmas bonus (see p68). If, before 6 April 2003, you were entitled to an increase in your widowed parent's allowance for a child dependant you may still be able to receive this although such increases have been abolished from that date (see p27).

	£pw
Basic widowed parent's allowance	82.05
Increase for child dependant	
– Eldest eligible child (for whom child benefit is paid)	9.40
– Other eligible children (each)	11.35

The amount of your basic widowed parent's allowance may be reduced if your late spouse's national insurance record was incomplete (see below).

Your widowed parent's allowance may also be reduced if, without good cause, you fail to attend a work-focused interview when you are required to do so (see p1097).

You may qualify for the additional earnings-related payment even if your late spouse's contribution record is not sufficient for you to qualify for basic widowed parent's allowance.[11]

See p38 for details of how to claim widowed parent's allowance.

Reduction in the basic widowed parent's allowance

You may receive a reduced rate of the basic widowed parent's allowance if your spouse's contribution record was incomplete (see p847).[12] In this case, you may be able to increase your entitlement by paying Class 3 contributions on your spouse's behalf (which you may do even though s/he has died – see p834 for further details and p837 for the time limits for making such payments). Write to your local NI contributions office quoting your own national insurance number and your late spouse's and ask whether you could benefit from this rule. You can obtain the address of your local office by telephoning any local office of the Revenue – the details are in the telephone directory.

3. Bereavement allowance

Bereavement allowance is a weekly benefit paid for up to 52 weeks to widows or widowers who were 45 or over when their spouse died. You cannot receive both widowed parent's allowance and bereavement allowance at the same time, but you may qualify for bereavement allowance when you stop being entitled to widowed parent's allowance.

In addition to qualifying for bereavement allowance you may also be entitled to a bereavement payment (see p24).

Who can claim bereavement allowance

You qualify for bereavement allowance if:[13]

- you are a widow or widower and your spouse died on or after 9 April 2001 (see p31 for the meaning of widow and widower); *and*
- you were aged 45 or over but under pension age (ie, under 60 if you are a woman, 65 if you are a man) when your spouse died (see below); *and*
- you are still under pension age; *and*
- not more than 52 weeks have passed since your spouse died; *and either*
- your late spouse satisfied the national insurance (NI) contribution conditions (see p846); *or*
- your spouse died as the result of an industrial injury or disease.

Disqualification and suspension

Bereavement allowance ceases if you remarry and you cannot re-qualify for it even if you subsequently get divorced. It is suspended while you are cohabiting but will be reinstated if you stop cohabiting (see p34).[14]

The rules about your age

You must be 45 or over at the time your spouse died to qualify for bereavement allowance.

You cannot receive bereavement allowance if you are over pension age (ie, 60 or over if you are a woman or 65 or over if you are a man). However, you may qualify for retirement pension based on your own or your late spouse's NI contributions (see Chapter 19).

Claiming for others

You cannot get an increase in your bereavement allowance for any dependants that you have.

The amount of bereavement allowance

The full rate of bereavement allowance is **£82.05** a week.[15]

However, the amount of bereavement allowance you receive may be reduced if:

- your late spouse's NI contribution record was incomplete; *or*
- you were under 55 when s/he died.

See below for details of the way your benefit is reduced.

If you are required to attend a work-focused interview and without good cause you fail to do so, your bereavement allowance may also be reduced (see p1097).

Your late spouse's contribution record

If your late spouse's NI contribution record was not complete, the amount of basic bereavement allowance you receive is reduced proportionately (see p847). Just as for widowed parent's allowance, you may be able to increase your entitlement by paying Class 3 contributions on your spouse's behalf (see p28).

Your age

Your bereavement allowance is reduced if you were under 55 when your spouse died.[16]

For each year, or part of a year, by which you were under 55 when your spouse died your bereavement allowance is reduced by 7 per cent. This percentage reduction remains the same for as long as you receive bereavement allowance.

The full rate of bereavement allowance is **£82.05**. So, if your spouse had a complete NI contribution record the amount you would receive is as follows:

Age when widowed	*Rate of bereavement allowance* *£pw*
54	76.31
53	70.56
52	64.82
51	59.08
50	53.33
49	47.59
48	41.85
47	36.10
46	30.36
45	24.62

4. Definition of terms

Who counts as a widow or widower

In order to qualify for bereavement benefits you must be a widow or widower. The question of who counts as a widow or widower is not always straightforward. You are a widow or widower if you were married to your spouse at the date of her/his death and the marriage was considered valid under UK law.

However, the Court of Appeal decided that a woman who was not actually married to her partner could be presumed to be validly married following a Sikh ceremony of marriage (held in England) and a long period of cohabitation. Although the temple in which the couple held their marriage ceremony was not registered for marriages, she believed herself to be married. The Court decided that she still counted as the man's widow.[17] This contrasts with an earlier commissioner's decision in which it was decided that a couple were not validly married, although they had believed themselves to be so, because their marriage was conducted in a bogus registry office.[18]

In Scotland (but not the rest of Great Britain) you are also a widow or widower if you were married 'by cohabitation with habit and repute' even if you did not go through a formal wedding ceremony.[19] This is more than simply living together, as there must have been something about the relationship which meant that it could be inferred that you and your partner consented to marriage and nothing existed which would have prevented a valid marriage taking place (eg, either party already being married to someone else).[20] In addition, your relationship must have been such that other people generally believed that you were married.[21]

If you have been widowed more than once, your entitlement to bereavement benefits depends on the contribution record of your most recent spouse.

See p33 for details about invalid marriages.

Separation, divorce and remarriage

If you were divorced when your ex-spouse died, you are not a widow or widower. But a divorce becomes effective only when the decree absolute is pronounced. So, if you were in the process of obtaining a divorce, you are still entitled to bereavement benefits if your spouse died before the decree was made absolute.

If you were living apart from your spouse when s/he died but without being divorced from her/him you are a widow or widower. This applies even if you were judicially separated as long as you were not actually divorced.

If you remarry, you are no longer a widow or widower and lose all entitlement to widowed parent's allowance and bereavement allowance based on your previous spouse's contribution record.[22]

The DWP may claim that you are not entitled to bereavement benefits as your marriage was bigamous (and therefore invalid because it is 'void' – see p34), or was polygamous (see p32), because it disputes the validity of a divorce given by a foreign court. For example, a commissioner decided a Muslim talaq divorce was not effective because it was proclaimed in this country and under English law such proceedings are only valid if instituted in a court of law.[23]

A commissioner held that when entitlement to bereavement benefits is dependent on the validity of a foreign divorce, the validity of that divorce should be judged according to the law of the country in which a couple was domiciled at the time of their subsequent marriage. If this was also abroad, then it will be a matter of foreign law. The interpretation of foreign law is a question of fact to be proved by evidence. So, while commissioners' decisions on such matters may be helpful as evidence, they are not binding on decision makers.[24]

If you are living with someone of the opposite sex as husband and wife but have not remarried see p34.

Polygamous marriages

If your marriage was polygamous you are not normally entitled to bereavement benefit following the death of your spouse. This is because, as a general rule, the law in England, Wales and Scotland does not treat a man and a woman as legally married unless their marriage is a monogamous one.[25]

A marriage is only considered polygamous if the law of the country where the marriage takes place permits either party to have another wife or husband.[26] Usually it is the husband who is allowed to have more than one wife but the rules apply in the same way if it is the wife who is permitted two or more husbands.[27] However, there are occasions when a polygamous marriage can give rise to an entitlement to bereavement benefits:

- if it is only potentially polygamous (ie, if neither the husband nor the wife has ever had more than one spouse); *or*
- when it is formerly polygamous (ie, if the husband or wife have had other spouses in the past but all such spouses have now died or been divorced),

but not on any day when it is actually polygamous (ie, the husband has more than one wife or the wife more than one husband).

This means that you are treated as a widow or widower if, on the day s/he died, neither you nor your spouse had any other husband or wife.

If you are refused bereavement benefits because your marriage was or is polygamous, you should take advice. The law on the recognition of polygamous marriages is complex and it is quite possible that even if you think your marriage is polygamous, the law will not agree with you.

This depends on whether you were your spouse's first wife or husband and on where you and your spouse were 'domiciled' at the time of your marriage and any subsequent marriage. **'Domicile'** is a difficult legal concept but in very general terms it means the country in which you have chosen to make your permanent home.[28] Domicile is not the same as 'presence' (see p697), 'residence' (see p698), 'ordinary residence' (see p698) or nationality.

In particular, no one who is domiciled in England and Wales is allowed to contract a polygamous marriage anywhere in the world even if the local law would allow it.[29]

Decision makers refer any questions about whether a marriage is to be treated as monogamous or polygamous to a special section of the DWP, called the Validity of Marriage Unit.

See p31 if the DWP considers that you were polygamously married because it disputes the validity of an earlier divorce.

Example

At the time of their wedding, Shaznaz and her husband were domiciled in Pakistan and were married under Islamic law. After the wedding they came to live in England and made their permanent home here and had no intention of returning to live in Pakistan at any time. Later her husband returned temporarily to Pakistan and married a second wife. As her husband was domiciled in England rather than Pakistan at the time of the second marriage, English law does not recognise the second marriage and therefore regards Shaznaz as her late husband's only wife. Provided she meets the other conditions of entitlement, she is entitled to bereavement benefits.[30] Conversely, if her husband had re-acquired domicile in Pakistan at the time of his second marriage, and his second wife is still alive, both marriages are polygamous, and neither wife can claim bereavement benefits.[31]

Following the incorporation of the European Convention on Human Rights into domestic law in October 2000, there is a possible argument that bereavement benefits should be extended to widows of polygamous marriages (see p1290).

Invalid marriages

Sometimes the law treats a monogamous marriage as invalid even though you have been through a formal wedding ceremony. An invalid marriage can be either 'voidable' or 'void' (see below and p34).

As with polygamous marriages (see p32), questions about the validity of marriage can be deceptively difficult. The DWP has a Validity of Marriage Unit that decides questions in this area. If it claims that your marriage was invalid, you should seek advice (see Appendix 2).

'Voidable' marriages

A 'voidable' marriage (eg, one that has not been consummated) still exists until annulled by a court, and is treated as a valid marriage until a decree absolute of annulment is pronounced.[32] So, if your spouse dies before the marriage is finally annulled, you may claim bereavement benefits. If you are widowed and then enter a 'voidable' marriage, that marriage ends your entitlement to bereavement benefits based on the contributions of your first spouse, even after it is annulled.

'Void' marriages

A 'void' marriage (eg, a bigamous one) does not exist at all and, from a legal point of view, has no consequences and can simply be ignored (although for most practical purposes, it is necessary to confirm the position by getting a court order).

For social security purposes, this means that if your marriage is 'void' it does not give rise to entitlement to benefits such as bereavement benefits that are based on marital status even if your marriage has not been annulled.[33] For the same reason, if you have been married or widowed more than once and your most recent marriage is held to be 'void', you may still be entitled to bereavement benefits based on the contributions of your previous spouse.

See p31 if the DWP disputes the validity of a divorce.

Proving that your spouse is dead

It is up to you to prove to the DWP decision maker that your spouse is dead and that you were married to her/him when s/he died.

Normally this is not a problem. When you register the death you get an extra death certificate for social security purposes, called a Certificate of Registration of Death, and if you complete the form on the back and forward it to the DWP, you are sent the claim form for bereavement benefits. See p38 for further information about claiming bereavement benefits.

If your spouse's whereabouts are unknown

It may be difficult to establish your entitlement to bereavement benefits if your spouse goes missing and you think that s/he has died. In this situation you can request that a decision maker at the DWP determines whether your spouse has died or can be presumed to have died. In Scotland, a Decree of Presumption of Death must be accepted as sufficient proof of death for benefit purposes. In England and Wales, if a court has presumed death this is normally accepted by a decision maker unless the decision maker has evidence to the contrary which the court did not consider. Even without a decision from a court, the decision maker may presume that your spouse has died if s/he has been missing for seven years and during that time there has been no evidence to suggest that s/he is alive and the people that would be expected to have heard from her/him have not done so.[34] The decision maker makes enquiries to try to find out whether your spouse has been seen by or been in contact with anyone. If your spouse has been missing for less than seven years a decision maker may still decide that s/he can be presumed to be dead if there is strong evidence to suggest that s/he died at an earlier date. See p42 for details of backdating bereavement benefits if you were unaware of your spouse's death.

Cohabitation

You are not entitled to a bereavement payment if you are living with someone of the opposite sex as husband and wife (cohabiting) at the time of your spouse's death. Your widowed parent's allowance or bereavement allowance is suspended if you are cohabiting, but becomes payable again if the cohabitation ends.[35]

Deciding whether or not you are living together as husband and wife may not be straightforward. For information about whether you count as living together as husband and wife, see p813.

If the DWP decides that you are cohabiting and you do not agree you can challenge its decision (see Chapters 43 and 44 for how to request a revision or supersession, or appeal against a decision of the DWP).

Industrial accident or disease

The meaning of 'industrial accident or disease' is discussed on p321. To qualify for bereavement benefits the industrial accident or disease must have been a cause of death, but it need not have been a direct cause or the only cause.[36]

5. Special rules for special groups

There are some groups of claimants to whom special rules apply. These are covered below and in Chapters 25, 26 and 28. Special rules apply to:

- widows whose husbands died before 9 April 2001 (see below);
- widowers whose wives died before 9 April 2001 (see p36);
- people who have obtained a gender recognition certificate (see p37);
- people who are in hospital (see p715);
- people who are abroad (see p686);
- people who are in prison or detention (see p731).

Widows whose husbands died before 9 April 2001

If your husband died before 9 April 2001 you are not entitled to bereavement benefits but instead may claim widows' benefits. Widows' benefits consist of:

- widow's payment;
- widowed mother's allowance; *and*
- widow's pension.

For an explanation of the qualifying conditions for widows' benefits see the 2nd edition of this *Handbook* and see the table at the beginning of this edition for the current rates of widows' benefits.

You could only qualify for a **widow's payment** if you made a claim within three months of your husband's death (or within a longer period if you were not aware that he had died – see p128 of CPAG's *Welfare Benefits Handbook* 2000/2001). If you satisfy the qualifying conditions for **widowed mother's allowance**, you can continue to receive this for as long as you have a qualifying child, as there is no upper age limit for receipt of widowed mother's allowance.

If your entitlement to widowed mother's allowance ends, or if you are not entitled to widowed mother's allowance, you may qualify for a **widow's pension**. This can be paid until you reach 65, if you satisfy the qualifying conditions.

If you were entitled to widows' benefits and invalidity benefit prior to 12 April 1995, you may benefit from transitional rules – see p132 of CPAG's *Welfare Benefits Handbook* 2000/2001 for details.

Widows' benefits and retirement pension

If your husband died before 9 April 2001 and you are 60 or over you may be entitled to both retirement pension and either widow's pension or widowed mother's allowance. Because of the overlapping benefit rules you cannot receive both benefits in full at the same time but see p132 of CPAG's *Welfare Benefits Handbook* 2000/2001 if you are in this position.

If you qualify for a Category B retirement pension on the basis of your late husband's national insurance (NI) contribution record, this can continue to be paid even if you remarry after reaching the age of 60. This is in contrast to the position of widows whose husbands died on or after 9 April 2001 who are not entitled to Category B retirement pension if they remarry.

Widowers whose wives died before 9 April 2001

If you are a man and your wife died before 9 April 2001 you may be in a less favourable position than a woman whose husband died before 9 April 2001. This is because a woman whose husband died before 9 April 2001 may qualify for widows' benefits but you cannot. For example, while you may claim widowed parent's allowance this can only be paid until you reach 65. In contrast, a woman in the same position could claim widowed mother's allowance which is payable after pension age if the other qualifying conditions are met.

Prior to the introduction of bereavement benefits, the fact that there were no widowers' benefits equivalent to the widows' benefits available to women was challenged on the basis that it breached the non-discrimination principle contained in the European Convention on Human Rights (ECHR). The Government settled two cases being taken to the European Court of Human Rights (ECtHR), paying money to the two men involved which was equivalent to the widow's payment and widowed mother's allowance they would have received had they been women.[37]

Another case which did reach the ECtHR involved a man whose wife died before 9 April 2001 and who, had he been a woman, would have qualified for widow's payment, widowed mother's allowance and, from 2006, widow's pension.[38] The Court decided that:

- widow's payment and widowed mother's allowance counted as possessions for the purpose of the ECHR, even though entitlement was based on NI contributions paid by the claimant's late wife;[39] *and*

- the refusal to award him the equivalent of widow's payment and widowed mother's allowance was discrimination which could not be objectively justified.

However, the Court did not give a ruling on the issue of widow's pension entitlement as it said that the case on this point was premature. The argument on widow's pension, particularly on whether the Government can objectively justify the discrimination between men and women in entitlement to pensions, is to be considered by the Court in two other cases (see CPAG's *Welfare Rights Bulletin* for updates on the progress of these).[40] However, the legal position of widowers whose wives died before 9 April 2001 is extremely complicated, particularly as a recent decision in the Court of Appeal raises questions about which courts – the ECtHR or the domestic courts – should be used to resolve these issues.[41] Seek expert advice.

If you are a man and you are over pension age you may qualify for a Category B retirement pension based on your late wife's national insurance contribution record (see p488) or if you are incapable of work you may qualify for incapacity benefit under the special rules for widowers (see p278).

People who have obtained a gender recognition certificate

If you have been living in the opposite gender or have changed gender and you have obtained a full gender recognition certificate your entitlement to bereavement and widow's benefits may be affected. (An interim gender recognition certificate does not affect your benefit entitlement.) The following is a summary of the rules. If you are likely to be affected by them, seek advice.[42]

- If you are married when you apply for gender recognition, you will only be given an interim certificate as any existing marriage must be dissolved or annulled before a full certificate is issued. Following the annulment you will not be entitled to any bereavement benefit on the basis of the death of your ex-spouse. However, if you marry *after* obtaining the full certificate, you may qualify for bereavement benefits if your spouse subsequently dies.
- If your spouse died before your full gender recognition certificate was issued and you were married at the time of her/his death, you may still qualify for bereavement benefits after the issue of the full certificate on the basis of your late spouse's contributions (or on the basis that her/his death was a result of an industrial accident or disease). However, any entitlement to widow's pension will end after the issue of a full certificate, and if you were entitled to widowed mother's allowance (or would have been had you made a claim for it) before the full certificate was issued, you will instead qualify for widowed parent's allowance after you get the full certificate.

6. Claims and backdating

To be entitled to bereavement benefits you must make a claim.[43] The rules on claiming are outlined briefly below. This section should be read in conjunction with the more detailed information about claims and claiming contained in Chapter 40. It may be possible to claim in advance (see p41) or to get your claim backdated (see p41 and Chapter 40). If you wish, you may amend or withdraw your claim before it is assessed by writing to the DWP.

If you are under 60 you may be expected to take part in a work-focused interview in order to qualify for widowed parent's allowance or bereavement allowance (see p1092 for details). Once benefit is in payment you may also be required to attend further work-focused interviews.

Making a claim

A claim for bereavement benefits must be in writing and must usually be made on the correct application form (a BB1 form which you can get from any DWP, JobCentre or Jobcentre Plus office or from the DWP website – see Appendix 1). This form serves as a claim for a bereavement payment, widowed parent's allowance and bereavement allowance. In certain circumstances, the decision maker may accept a written application which is not on the correct form (see p1079).[44] However, the procedure you should follow in order to make your claim depends on whether you live in the catchment area of a Jobcentre Plus office – you can check your local telephone directory or the Jobcentre Plus website (www.jobcentreplus.gov.uk) to see if you live in a Jobcentre Plus area. If you live in a Jobcentre Plus area see below. If not, your claim should be taken or sent to the DWP office which covers your local area. If you are 60 or over you may also be able to make your claim by taking or sending it to a designated 'alternative office' (see p1078 for details). Whichever procedure you follow to claim it is advisable to keep a copy of your claim form in case queries arise.

For more details about making a claim see p1076.

Jobcentre Plus areas

If you live in a Jobcentre Plus area, then you will usually be required to start your claim by telephoning a **'contact centre'**. (Your local Jobcentre Plus office will have this number, and it may also be displayed in local advice centres, libraries, etc.) The contact centre will take basic details, and then issue you with a claim form. The contact centre may also arrange an appointment for an initial work-focused interview (see p1092). However, if you send in a claim form before telephoning the contact centre then usually your claim will be processed and the interview arranged (where necessary) without you having to telephone the contact centre.

If you cannot or do not want to use the telephone to start your claim, then Jobcentre Plus say that they can still deal with your claim in other ways. You might for example be invited for a 'face-to-face' interview to gather the relevant details, or in some cases they may accept a BB1 claim form. Seek advice if you are unable to use a telephone and the Jobcentre Plus office will not let you start your claim in any other way.

If you live in a Jobcentre Plus area and there is some delay in you making a claim for bereavement benefit it may be advisable for you to obtain and immediately submit a BB1 form rather than waiting for the form to be sent to you by the contact centre. This is because the date of your claim is the date your completed claim form is received by the DWP or Jobcentre Plus office and not the date on which you telephone the contact centre. As widowed parent's allowance and bereavement allowance can only be backdated for up to three months (and you will normally only be entitled to bereavement payment if you claim within 12 months of your spouse's death), you should do this if it is likely that your claim form will otherwise reach the Jobcentre Plus office more than three months after your entitlement to bereavement benefits would have begun (or more than 12 months after your spouse's death in the case of bereavement payment), to avoid losing money.

Information to support your claim

When you claim bereavement benefits, you must satisfy what is known as the 'national insurance (NI) number requirement'. In most cases this means you must provide your NI number.[45] See p1083 for further details.

You can also be asked to supply 'certificates, documents, information and evidence' considered relevant to your claim.[46] You will therefore normally be expected to supply your spouse's death certificate or the Certificate of Registration of Death (see p34 if you do not have proof of whether your spouse has died), and your marriage certificate if you have one. Evidence or documents relating to your claim can be taken or sent to your local DWP or Jobcentre Plus office. If you are 60 or over, your local housing benefit or council tax benefit office may also be able to accept evidence and documents from you in connection with your claim, as long as it is a designated 'alternative office' (see p1078).

If you are asked to provide evidence or documents which you do not have, ask what other evidence would be acceptable. Ask the DWP to explain what is required and why and complain if you feel any requests for information are unreasonable.

See p1082 for further details of evidence which may be required to support your claim.

Who should claim

You must normally claim bereavement benefits on your own behalf. However, bereavement benefits can be claimed by another adult on your behalf if you are not able to act for yourself. This person is known as your 'appointee' (see p1075 for further details).

The date of your claim

The date of your claim is important as it determines whether you will qualify for a bereavement payment. It also determines the date from which you will be paid widowed parent's allowance or bereavement allowance (see p42). The date of your claim is normally the date it is received at the DWP or Jobcentre Plus office or, if you are 60 or over and submit your claim to a designated 'alternative office' (see p1078), the date it is received by that office.[47] A claim can be counted as having been received even on a day when the office is closed if that is the day it would have normally been delivered.[48]

If the claim you submit is incomplete or not on the correct form you may be asked to provide further information or to complete the correct form. As long as this additional information or form is submitted within a month of it being sent back to you (or longer if the decision maker thinks that the delay is reasonable), your claim is treated as being made on the date that the initial claim was received.[49] But see p1092 if you are required to take part in a work-focused interview.

In some circumstances you can claim before you qualify for bereavement benefits (see p40) or the date of your claim can be backdated (see p41).

See p42 if you claim late because you did not know that your spouse had died.

If you claim the wrong benefit

The decision maker may treat a claim for retirement pension as a claim for bereavement benefits.[50] A claim for retirement pension may therefore help you to qualify for a bereavement payment if the pension claim is made (or is treated as made) within 12 months of your spouse's death (but if your spouse died before 1 April 2003 the claim must have been made (or treated as made) within three months of her/his death). See p25 if you and your spouse were not in Great Britain (GB) when s/he died. A claim for retirement pension may also allow you to get your widowed parent's allowance or bereavement allowance backdated for more than the normal three months (see p41). If your retirement pension claim is accepted as a claim for widowed parent's allowance or bereavement allowance, your claim can be backdated for up to three months from the date of your retirement pension claim, if you satisfy the qualifying conditions over that period. **Note:** if you make late payments of Class 3 national insurance contributions for any of the tax years from 1996/97 to 2001/02 in the circumstances described on p836 your retirement pension claim can be treated as if it was made on a date which is earlier than the date it is received by the DWP.[51]

See p1084 for details of interchanging claims in this way.

Claiming in advance

You can claim bereavement benefits up to three months before you expect to qualify. In most circumstances you will not know of your need to claim benefit in advance, but this may be relevant if, for example, you know that you will no longer be cohabiting.[52] It is helpful to claim in advance if you can as the DWP can then gather the information it may need and decide your claim in good time.

How your claim is dealt with

Your claim is dealt with by the DWP office that covers your local area, although it may refer certain questions relating to your claim to other offices. Queries about your claim should be made to the office covering your area.

You may be able to claim an interim payment while waiting for a decision on your claim (see p1108) or to claim means-tested benefits or tax credits if your income is low (see p44). You may also be able to apply for a crisis loan if you need money to tide you over (see Chapter 21).

See p1091 for more information on the processing of claims.

Backdating your claim

A claim for a **bereavement payment** must be made within 12 months of your spouse's death, unless your spouse died before 1 April 2003 when it must be made within three months of her/his death (but see p25 if you and your spouse were not in GB when s/he died). If you do not claim within this time you will not be entitled to a bereavement payment, unless you were not aware that your spouse had died (see p42).

There is no time limit for claiming **widowed parent's allowance** or **bereavement allowance** and payment of these benefits can be backdated for up to three months before the date that you make your claim, if you satisfy the qualifying conditions over that period. You do not need to show reasons why your claim was late (see p1085). If you were not aware of your husband's death you may be able to get your claim backdated further – see p42. However, it is important to remember that bereavement allowance is only payable for the 52-week period running from the date your spouse died. As long as you claim widowed parent's allowance or bereavement allowance within three months of your spouse's death you will not lose any money.

If you might have qualified for benefit earlier but did not claim because you were given the wrong information or were misled by the DWP you could:

- ask for an ex gratia payment (see p1304); *or*
- complain to the Ombudsman via your MP (see p1302).

See p40 if you claimed retirement pension instead of bereavement benefits. See p1086 for more details about backdating claims.

If you were unaware of your spouse's death

The time limit for claiming a bereavement payment and the three-month time limit on backdating of widowed parent's allowance and bereavement allowance can be waived if:[53]

- it is more than 12 months since your spouse died or since the date that s/he is presumed to have died;

and either:

- your spouse's body has not been found or identified (or if it has you were not aware of this when you asked the decision maker at the DWP to decide whether s/he had died); *and*
- the decision maker has decided that your spouse has died or that it can be presumed s/he is dead; *and*
- you claim bereavement benefits within 12 months of the decision maker's decision;

or:

- your spouse's body has been found or identified and you learn of this within 12 months of the discovery or identification; *and*
- you claim bereavement benefits within 12 months of finding out about your spouse's death.

Bereavement benefits can be backdated to the date that the decision maker has determined was the date of your spouse's death in the former situation. In the latter circumstances bereavement benefits can only be backdated for a maximum of two years. This is because you must claim within 12 months of finding out about your spouse's death and, in turn, you must have learnt about your spouse's death within 12 months of her/his body being identified.[54]

7. Getting paid

A **bereavement payment** is a lump-sum one-off payment.

Widowed parent's allowance and **bereavement allowance** are weekly benefits and so cannot be paid for periods of less than a week. Payment of widowed parent's allowance or bereavement allowance is normally made by direct credit transfer into your bank (or similar account).[55] If you are unable to open or manage an account payment can be made by cheque. Such cheques can be paid into an account or cashed at the post office (see p1099 for details).

Payments are normally made either four-weekly in arrears or weekly in advance on a Tuesday, although the DWP may choose another day as your normal payday.[56] If you qualify for widowed parent's allowance or bereavement allowance payments will normally run from the first payday after the date of your claim (see p40), unless the date of your claim is on your payday, when they will run from that day.[57]

If the amount of benefit to which you are entitled is less than £5 a week a decision maker at the DWP can decide how often you are paid, although you must be paid at least once a year.[58]

Payment of bereavement benefits may be made to someone else on your behalf if you are unable to act for yourself (called your 'appointee' – see p1075).

If your entitlement to widowed parent's allowance or bereavement allowance ends, payment of benefit will continue up to, but not including, the following payday unless your entitlement ends on a payday when your benefit will be paid up to, but not including, that day.

If your benefit cheque is lost or stolen, see p1104. If payment of your widowed parent's allowance or bereavement allowance is suspended, see p1105. If your widowed parent's allowance or bereavement allowance has been reduced because you failed to attend a work-focused interview, see p1097.

You may not be paid widowed parent's allowance or bereavement allowance if you have been sanctioned for benefit offences (see p1169).

Delays and complaints

If payments of your bereavement benefits are delayed, you might be able to get an interim payment. See p1108 for further details.

If you experience delays, or wish to complain about how your claim has been dealt with, see pp1300 and 1305. You might be able to claim compensation (see p1304).

Change of circumstances

It is your duty to report any change in your circumstances which might affect your entitlement to, the amount of, or the payment of your benefit.[59] You should do this promptly in writing or by telephone to the office handling your claim (although in individual cases notification might be accepted in a form other than in writing or by telephone). In some cases, however, the decision maker might say you must report changes in writing. In any case, you might want to report the change in writing and keep a copy in case of a dispute in the future. If you do not promptly report any such change, any resulting overpayment may be recoverable from you (see Chapter 40). If you are considered deliberately to have acted falsely or dishonestly, you may also be guilty of an offence (see Chapter 42).

Widowed parent's allowance and bereavement allowance are normally awarded for an indefinite period, unless your circumstances are likely to change shortly after the award.[60] In order for payment of benefit to be stopped or adjusted, the decision on your entitlement must first be revised or superseded (see Chapter 43). If, following a change in your circumstances, the decision on your claim is superseded and your entitlement to benefit is affected, the date from which the new decision takes effect depends on whether or not it is advantageous to you and whether you reported the change in time (see p1204 for further details).

Overpayments and fraud

If you are overpaid bereavement benefits, you might have to repay them. The rules on overpayments are covered in Chapter 41.

If you have been accused of fraud, see Chapter 42.

8. Challenging bereavement benefits decisions

You can apply for a revision or supersession of a bereavement benefit decision, or appeal against it (see Chapters 43 and 44). The advice given there applies equally to bereavement benefits.

Certain decisions are not open to appeal, although you can request that such decisions be revised or superseded (see p1221).[61]

9. Tax, tax credits and other benefits

The lump-sum bereavement payment is not taxable. Widowed parent's allowance and bereavement allowance are taxable apart from any increase to widowed parent's allowance in respect of children.[62]

Tax credits

If your income is low and you work for sufficient hours each week (see Chapter 51) you may qualify for working tax credit (WTC – see Chapter 50) as well as bereavement benefits. If you have at least one dependent child you may also qualify for child tax credit (CTC – see Chapter 49). Bereavement payment is ignored when calculating your entitlement to WTC and CTC, widowed parent's allowance counts in full as pension income (see p1384) and bereavement allowance counts in full as benefit income (see p1378). If you are at least 50 and are entitled to WTC, receipt of widowed parent's allowance or bereavement allowance may help you to qualify for a 50-plus element within your WTC (see p1358).[63]

Means-tested benefits

If you have a low income you may be entitled to means-tested benefits, which can be paid in addition to bereavement benefits. A bereavement payment is counted as capital for the purposes of all means-tested benefits (see p968). Widowed parent's allowance and bereavement allowance (less any tax payable on them) are counted as income. However, £10 of your weekly widowed parent's allowance is ignored when calculating your entitlement to income-based jobseeker's allowance[64] (JSA – see Chapter 15), income support[65] (IS – see Chapter 13) and pension credit (PC – see Chapter 18).[66]

£15 of your weekly widowed parent's allowance or widowed mother's allowance (see p35) is ignored when calculating your entitlement to housing benefit[67] (HB – see Chapter 10) and council tax benefit[68] (CTB – see Chapter 6). However, if you are getting both widowed parent's allowance and only the savings credit of PC, the income used to calculate your HB and CTB is that used by the DWP to calculate your entitlement to PC (which includes only a £10 disregard from your widowed parent's allowance).

Bereavement allowance is counted in full as income when calculating your entitlement to income-based JSA, IS, HB, CTB and PC.

Certain widows and widowers can qualify for an additional amount of income-based JSA, IS, HB and CTB when their bereavement allowance stops – known as a bereavement premium (see p897). See p897 for the time limits for claiming this.

In certain circumstances you can qualify for IS on the basis of being a widow or a widower (see p295).

Non-means-tested benefits

Your entitlement to non-means-tested benefits is not affected by your entitlement to a bereavement payment.

Widowed parent's allowance and bereavement allowance are affected by the overlapping benefit rules and so you may not qualify for these benefits if another earnings replacement benefit is being paid to you (see p1102).

Although increases in non-means-tested benefits for children were abolished on 6 April 2003, some people will continue to be entitled to them with their widowed parent's allowance (see p27). You cannot receive both guardian's allowance for a child and an increase in your widowed parent's allowance for the same child.[69]

If you are receiving an increase in your widowed parent's allowance for a child, the amount of that increase is adjusted if you receive child benefit for that child paid at the rate for the eldest eligible child (see p1104). You cannot receive the lone parent rate of child benefit for a child for whom you receive an increase in your widowed parent's allowance. Instead you will get the standard rate of child benefit.

Once you reach pension age you may qualify for a Category A or B retirement pension on the basis of your late spouse's national insurance contribution record (see p487).

When your bereavement benefit stops (unless it stops because you have remarried or are cohabiting), you are credited with national insurance contributions for each year that bereavement benefit was paid to you, up to and including the year in which it stops, for the purpose of allowing you to satisfy the second contribution condition for incapacity benefit and JSA (see p840).[70]

Passports and other sources of help

If you are on a low income, you might be entitled to certain health service benefits, such as free prescriptions (see Chapter 9). You may also qualify for other sources of help (see Chapter 1) or a social fund payment (see Chapters 21 and 22). If you are getting IS, income-based JSA or, in some circumstances, CTC and have children attending school your children will qualify for free school meals (see p18).

For general practical advice about preparing funerals and registering deaths, obtain DWP leaflet D49, *What to Do After a Death in England and Wales* or *What to Do After a Death in Scotland* published by the Scottish Executive Justice Department.

Help with the costs of a funeral

If you receive income-based JSA, IS, HB, CTB, PC, the disability or severe disability element of WTC, or CTC paid at a higher rate than the family element, you may be entitled to a grant for funeral expenses from the social fund (see p551).

Notes

1. **Bereavement payment**
   1 ss36 and 60(2) and (3) SSCBA 1992
   2 Reg 19(3A) SS(C&P) Regs; reg 4 Social Security (Claims and Payments and Miscellaneous Amendments)(No.3) Regs 2002, SI 2002 No.2660
   3 s36(2) SSCBA 1992
   4 Reg 4(2B) SSB(PA) Regs
   5 Sch 4 Part II SSCBA 1992

2. **Widowed parent's allowance**
   6 ss39A and 60(2) and (3) SSCBA 1992
   7 Reg 16ZA SS(WB&RP) Regs
   8 ss39A(3) and 77(5) SSCBA 1992
   9 Reg 2(4) SSB(PRT) Regs
   10 s39A(4) and (5)(b) SSCBA 1992
   11 Reg 6(2) SS(WB&RP) Regs
   12 Reg 6 SS(WB&RP) Regs

3. **Bereavement allowance**
   13 ss39B and 60(2) and (3) SSCBA 1992
   14 s39B(4) and (5) SSCBA 1992
   15 ss39C and 44 SSCBA 1992
   16 s39C(5) SSCBA 1992

4. **Definition of terms**
   17 *CAO v Bath, The Times*, 28 October 1999 (CA)
   18 R(G) 2/70
   19 R(G) 5/83
   20 R(G) 1/71
   21 CSG/7/1995; CSG/681/2003

22 ss39A(4) and 39B(4) SSCBA 1992
23 R(G) 1/94; see also R(P) 1/98 where a panchayat (Hindu) in India was valid
24 R(G) 2/00; but see also CG/2581/2001
25 *Hyde v Hyde* [1866]; reg 2 SSFA(PM) Regs
26 Reg 1(2) SSFA(PM) Regs
27 Reg 1(4) SSFA(PM) Regs; s6 IA 1978
28 R(S) 2/92
29 s11(3) MCA 1973
30 R(G) 1/95
31 R(G) 1/93
32 R(G) 1/73
33 R(G) 2/63
34 *Chard v Chard* [1956] P.259
35 ss39A(5) and 39B(5) SSCBA 1992
36 CI/142/1949; R(I) 14/51

5. **Special rules for special groups**
37 *Cornwall v UK* [2000] No.36578/97; *Leary v UK* [2000] No.38890/97
38 *Willis v UK* [2002] No.36042/97
39 Art 1 Protocol 1 Human Rights Act 1998
40 *White and Runkee v United Kingdom* (ECtHR)
41 *R (Hooper and others) v Secretary of State for Work and Pensions* [2003] EWCA Civ 813, 3 All ER 673 (CA) (an appeal against this decision was heard by the House of Lords in February 2005. At the time of writing, judgment was awaited – see *Welfare Rights Bulletins* for updates); see also *Welfare Rights Bulletins* 175 and 176 for write up of case and discussion of its implications
42 ss4 and 5 and Sch 5 paras 3-5 Gender Recognition Act 2004

6. **Claims and backdating**
43 s1 SSAA 1992
44 Reg 4(1) SS(C&P) Regs
45 s1(1A) and (1B) SSAA 1992
46 Reg 7(1) SS(C&P) Regs
47 Reg 6(1) SS(C&P) Regs
48 R(SB) 8/89
49 Regs 4(7) and 6(1) SS(C&P) Regs
50 Reg 9(1) and Sch 1 Part I SS(C&P) Regs
51 Reg 6(31) SS(C&P) Regs
52 Reg 13 SS(C&P) Regs
53 s3 SSAA 1992
54 CG/7235/1995

7. **Getting paid**
55 Reg 21 SS(C&P) Regs
56 Reg 22(1) and (3) and Sch 6 para 6 SS(C&P) Regs
57 Reg 16(1) SS(C&P) Regs
58 Reg 22(2) SS(C&P) Regs
59 Reg 32(1B) SS(C&P) Regs;
60 Reg 17 SS(C&P) Regs

8. **Challenging bereavement benefits decisions**
61 s12(1) and Sch 2 SSA 1998; regs 3(8) and 6(2)(d) SS&CS(DA) Regs

9. **Tax, tax credits and other benefits**
62 ss577-579, 661 and 676 Income Tax (Earnings and Pensions) Act 2003;
63 Reg 18(9) WTC(EMR) Regs
64 Reg 103 and Sch 7 para 17(e) JSA Regs
65 Reg 40 and Sch 9 para 16(h) IS Regs
66 Sch IV para 7 SPC Regs
67 Reg 33 and Sch 4 para 14A(b) HB Regs
68 Reg 24 and Sch 4 para 14A(b) CTB Regs
69 Reg 7(4) SS(OB) Regs
70 Reg 8C SS(Cr) Regs

Chapter 3

Bonuses

This chapter covers:

If you take up full-time paid work (see p750) you no longer qualify for income support (IS) or jobseeker's allowance (JSA). Likewise, if your weekly pay increases, you may no longer qualify for IS or JSA on income grounds. In both of these situations, there are a number of bonuses you might be able to get. These can give you some financial help in the first weeks after your IS or JSA ceases – eg, before you get your first pay from full-time paid work. You might be entitled to a **child maintenance bonus** and to **mortgage interest run-on** and **extended payments of housing benefit (HB) and council tax benefit (CTB)**. You might also be entitled to a **job grant**.

You may also qualify for extended payments of HB and CTB if you move into work after receiving incapacity benefit or severe disablement allowance.

If you are taking up full-time paid work, you should also check to see if you might be entitled to working tax credit. See Chapter 50 for further information.

Two types of bonus were abolished on 25 October 2004 – **back-to-work bonus** and **lone parent run-on**. However, if you had accrued a back-to-work bonus by 25 October 2004 you might still be entitled to one. See p49 for further information.

If you are in receipt of certain benefits, you are automatically entitled to a **Christmas bonus** (see p68).

Other incentives to help you go into work

The Government provides a number of other financial incentives to help you make a transition from benefits to work. These depend on where you live and whether you are in a pilot scheme area. Examples include the return to work credit (available in 'Pathways to

Work' pilot scheme areas) and worksearch and job preparation premiums. Ask at your local JobCentre to see what is available.

1. Back-to-work bonus

Back-to-work bonus was abolished on 25 October 2004. However, if you or your partner worked part time while receiving jobseeker's allowance (JSA) or (if you were under 60) income support (IS) and earnings were taken into account before 25 October 2004, you still might be entitled to a back-to-work bonus of up to £1,000. This is the case if you returned to work or increased your hours or your pay, or turned 60 or pension age by 28 January 2005, and as a result were no longer entitled to IS or JSA.

An outline of the back-to-work bonus rules and information about claiming are given below. For full details, see CPAG's *Welfare Benefits and Tax Credits Handbook* 2003/2004.

There is a strict time limit for claiming a back-to-work bonus. See p51 for further information.

Who can claim a back-to-work bonus

You qualify for a back-to-work bonus if:[1]

- you or your partner were entitled, or treated as entitled, to IS or JSA for at least 91 days. This is called the 'waiting period'. Two or more periods of entitlement could link and count as one if they were separated by not more than 12 weeks or one of a number of types of connecting period;
- you or your partner satisfied the 'work condition' (see p50) prior to 28 January 2005 and prior to the day before:[2]
  - your 60th birthday if you were coming off IS; *or*
  - you reached pension age (60 for women and 65 for men) if you were coming off JSA.

  Special rules apply if you did not satisfy the work condition before those ages;
- you or your partner had earnings from part-time work which reduced your weekly rate of IS or JSA during what was known as the 'bonus period'.[3] Your **'bonus period'** is the period starting with the first day after the end of your waiting period and ending on the earlier of:[4]
  - the date that you stopped being entitled to IS or JSA (ie, because you met the work condition or reached age 60 or pension age); *or*
  - 24 October 2004;
- you claim within the time limit (see p51). In some cases your time limit for claiming can be extended.

There are special rules for couples who started sharing a household or separated while claiming IS or JSA and for partners of people who died while claiming IS or JSA.

What happens after 25 October 2004?

You must have served your waiting period by 24 October 2004 when back-to-work bonus was abolished. You cannot accrue any more bonus after that date. However, in some circumstances, you can claim and be paid the bonus you have already accrued, even if this is after 24 October 2004. You must have satisfied the work condition, or have reached age 60 or pension age by 28 January 2005.

You can be paid a back-to-work bonus if you satisfied all the rules for getting a bonus (see p49) by 28 January 2005 and you:[5]

- make a claim within the time limit if this is required – see p52); *or*
- if you are claiming outside of the time limit, your late claim can be backdated because you have 'good cause' (see p52).

The work condition

The work condition is satisfied if you or your partner:[6]

- took up a new job or the waged option of the New Deal or returned to work (but not if you returned to work for the same employer at the same place of work following a trade dispute[7]); *or*
- increased your weekly hours of work and so counted as in full-time paid work (see p750); *or*
- had an increase in earnings. This includes where the combined earnings of you and your partner increased to a level at which you were no longer entitled to IS or income-based JSA.

If entitlement to IS or JSA stopped for another reason, you still qualify for a bonus if, by 28 January 2005:

- you satisfied the work condition, this was within 14 days of IS or JSA ceasing,[8] and you claimed a bonus within 12 weeks of this; *or*
- you stopped getting IS or JSA (or a connecting period ended) and within 12 weeks you went on a training course for which you received a training allowance and you claimed within 12 weeks of the training course ending. Within 14 days of finishing the training course you must have:[9]
  - begun working 16 hours or more a week; *or*
  - had earnings from work that were equal to or more than the training allowance you received in the last week of the course.

If there was another change in your or your partner's circumstances which caused entitlement to IS or JSA to end at the same time that you or your partner satisfied the work condition, you still qualify for the bonus.[10]

If you have separated from your partner but you satisfied the work condition within 14 days of this, you can qualify for a bonus if:[11]

- you or your partner were entitled to IS or JSA at the time of the separation; *and*
- the separation took place before you reached the age of 60.

Note: mortgage interest run-on (see p62) does not count as IS for the purpose of the work condition.

The amount of back-to-work bonus

The amount of bonus you receive depends on the amount of earnings you or your partner received which were taken into account in calculating your JSA and IS during your bonus period.[12] Disregarded earnings (see pp963 and 948) and earnings paid during your waiting period are not counted.

The **maximum bonus** is £1,000.[13] If you and your partner were both entitled to IS or JSA as single people within the 12 weeks before you became a couple and were both within a bonus period (see p49) your bonuses are added together up to a maximum of £2,000.[14] However, they are not added together where both of you were entitled to contribution-based JSA.[15]

If your back-to-work bonus would be less than £5 you are not paid at all.

The bonus is calculated by:[16]

- adding up all the earnings which have been taken into account for IS or JSA during the bonus period. This includes your partner's earnings if you were getting IS or income-based JSA; *and*
- dividing by two.

Example

James is single and has been claiming JSA for six months. He begins to work for one day a week as a waiter for which he earns £25 a week. After 12 weeks James is taken on full time. His JSA stops.

While James was working part time, £5 of his earnings were disregarded. The remaining £20 a week were taken into account in calculating his JSA.

Back-to-work bonus is calculated as follows:

£20 a week x 12 weeks = £240

£240 ÷ 2 = £120 back-to-work bonus

Claims

A claim for a back-to-work bonus must be in writing and on the appropriate form.[17] The rules are the same as for child maintenance bonus (see p59).

Who should claim

If you have served, or are treated as having served, a waiting period, are one of a couple and the qualifying benefit is IS or income-based JSA, the person who was claiming the benefit must make the claim for the back-to-work bonus.[18] In all other cases, you claim the back-to-work bonus if you are the person who accrued it.

When to claim

You must claim within the time limits as follows:[19]

- within the 12 weeks after you or your partner stop getting IS or JSA; *or*
- where you are claiming following attendance on a training course (see p50), within 12 weeks of finishing the course; *or*
- where you are claiming following separation from your partner, within 12 weeks of the separation; *or*
- where you are claiming because you stopped getting IS or JSA in the 12 weeks before you reached age 60/pension age (see below), no later than 12 weeks after you reach that age.

The time limit could be **less than this** if you become entitled to IS or JSA again within 12 weeks of your previous entitlement ceasing or after any of the connecting periods that link two claims.[20]

Your claim is usually treated as made on the date it is received by the DWP office.[21]

Your claim can be **backdated**, but only if you can show that, throughout the period between the date by which you should have claimed and the date you actually claimed, you had 'good cause' for failing to claim.[22] However, your claim can never be backdated more than 12 months. See p221 for information about what counts as 'good cause' for a late claim.

Different rules apply if you are an appointee claiming the back-to-work bonus of someone who has died (see p53).

Special rules if you reach age 60 or pension age

You can get a back-to-work bonus **without having to make a claim**, even if you did not satisfy the work condition (see p50) if, by 28 January 2005, you:[23]

- turned 60 and on the day before you were entitled to IS and in a bonus period; *or*
- reached pension age (60 for women and 65 for men) and on the day before you were entitled to JSA and in a bonus period; *or*
- stopped getting JSA after your 60th birthday but before you reached pension age and you became entitled to pension credit (PC) within 12 weeks or after a connecting period.

You do not have to complete a claim form. Any bonus should be paid automatically.

You can get a back-to-work bonus even if you did not satisfy the work condition (see p50) but **you have to make a claim** if you stopped being entitled to IS 12 weeks before you reached age 60, or you stopped being entitled to JSA 12 weeks before you reached pension age.[24] You must claim within 12 weeks of attaining that age.

Death of the person entitled to a back-to-work bonus

If someone who had been accumulating a back-to-work bonus dies, the bonus s/he had accumulated can be paid to an appointee (see below). In addition, the bonus could help her/his partner get a bonus.[25]

Payment to an appointee

If a person satisfied all of the conditions of entitlement to a back-to-work bonus described on p49 but did not claim and s/he died within 12 weeks of her/his entitlement to IS or JSA ceasing, a decision maker can appoint someone to claim in her/his place.[26] You must apply to be an appointee within six months of the date of death. You must then claim the bonus within six months of being appointed. The time limits for applying for permission to claim, or for claiming, can be extended in exceptional circumstances up to a maximum of 12 months from the date of death. However, if the time limit for one is extended, the other is shortened by the same amount of time. Any time between the date you apply to be an appointee and the date you are appointed is ignored.

If the person for whom you want to claim satisfied all the conditions of entitlement to a bonus other than making a claim on or before 28 January 2005 (if this was required), and it is now after that date, apply to be appointed and make the claim as soon as possible. Argue that the person had good cause for her/his late claim (see p52) and so comes within the special rules.

Challenging a back-to-work bonus decision

You can apply for a revision or supersession of a back-to-work bonus decision or appeal against it (see Chapters 43 and 44).

Tax, tax credits and other benefits

The bonus is not taxable.

Back-to-work bonus is treated as capital for IS, JSA, housing benefit (HB) and council tax benefit (CTB). [27] However, if you are under 60 or you or your partner are on IS or income-based JSA, it is disregarded for 52 weeks for HB and CTB purposes (or until 28 January 2006 if this is earlier).[28] It is disregarded as income for working tax credit and child tax credit.[29] It does not count as income or capital for PC or for HB and CTB if you are 60 or over and neither you or your partner are on IS or income-based JSA.

You should check to see if you qualify for any of the other bonuses in this chapter.

2. Child maintenance bonus

If you have been getting, or were meant to be paid, child maintenance while on income support (IS) or income-based jobseeker's allowance (JSA), you can be paid a child maintenance bonus of up to £1,000. This is the case if you or your partner return to work or increase your hours or your pay and, as a result, you are no longer entitled to IS or income-based JSA. See p58 to find out how much you can get. See p811 to see who counts as your partner.

Child maintenance for these purposes is:[30]

- child support maintenance (see p854);
- maintenance paid to you for your child(ren) by agreement or under a court order;
- maintenance being deducted from the benefit of a non-resident parent (see p862) who is liable to maintain your child(ren).

Abolition of child maintenance bonus

Child maintenance bonus is gradually being phased out. Currently, you cannot accrue child maintenance bonus once you instead qualify for a child maintenance premium (see p972). However, special rules allow you to claim the bonus you have already accrued. There is a very strict time limit for doing so. See below for further information.

Who can claim a child maintenance bonus

You qualify for a child maintenance bonus if:[31]

- you were paid (or were meant to be paid) child maintenance (see above) during a period when you or your partner were on IS or income-based JSA (what is known as your 'bonus period' – see p56); *and*
- you or your partner satisfy the 'work condition' within the time limit (see p57). Special rules apply once you qualify for a child maintenance premium (see p57). You must satisfy the work condition prior to the day before:
  - your 60th birthday if you are coming off IS; *or*
  - you reach pension age (60 for women and 65 for men) if you are coming off income-based JSA.

  Special rules apply if you do not satisfy the work condition before those ages (see p60); *and*
- you claim within the time limit (see p59).

There are special rules where the person with the care of a child dies (see p61).

If you qualify for a child maintenance premium

You cannot accrue a child maintenance bonus once you instead qualify for a child maintenance premium. This happens when you:[32]

- come under the child support scheme 'new rules' (see p855). The Government says that existing child support cases will only come under the 'new rules' when the scheme is working well. See CPAG's *Welfare Rights Bulletin* for updates;
- are first paid child maintenance by agreement or under a court order, if this is on or after 3 March 2003.

If you have already accrued a bonus, you will still be able to claim it in some circumstances:

- If you qualify for a child maintenance bonus before the date you qualify for a child maintenance premium (eg, you satisfy the 'work condition' but a decision is outstanding or you have not yet claimed) – see below.
- If you do not qualify for a child maintenance bonus because you have not yet satisfied the 'work condition' when you qualify for a child maintenance premium, there is a strict time limit for satisfying that condition (see p57).

Note: you may also qualify for a child maintenance premium if you are first paid voluntary maintenance (that is not paid by agreement or under a court order) on or after 16 February 2004. This type of maintenance cannot help you accrue a child maintenance bonus.

If you qualify for a bonus before the date you qualify for child maintenance premium

If you qualify for a child maintenance premium (see p54), you can no longer accrue a child maintenance bonus. Your bonus period ends on the date you qualify if it has not ended already (see p56). You can be paid a bonus you have already accrued if, prior to the date you qualify for a child maintenance premium:[33]

- you satisfy the 'work condition' and claim the bonus but no decision is made before that date. This includes where a late claim is accepted; *or*
- you are someone to whom the special rules for those who reach age 60 or pension age apply (see p60); *and*
  - if you are someone who can get a bonus without having to make a claim, the DWP has not yet determined your entitlement; *or*
  - if you are someone who can get a bonus but has to make a claim, you claim the bonus prior to the date you qualify for a child maintenance premium but no decision is made before that date. This includes where a late claim is accepted; *or*
- you qualify for a bonus, but do not claim the bonus until on or after that date. You must claim within the time limit. You can make a late claim in some circumstances (see p60).

If you do not yet satisfy the 'work condition' when you qualify for a child maintenance premium, see p57. If you satisfy the 'work condition' within a strict time limit, you can still claim your child maintenance bonus.

The bonus period

You accumulate a child maintenance bonus during a bonus period – that is, days when:[34]

- you or your partner were entitled, or treated as entitled, to IS or income-based JSA whether or not it was paid. Days when you are getting an urgent cases payment of IS or income-based JSA do not count unless you get the payment because you are a 'person subject to immigration control' (see p654); *and*
- you are getting, or are meant to be paid, child maintenance (see p54) for a child who lives with you but whose other parent does not. Your child still counts as living with you if s/he is away temporarily, but not for more than 12 weeks. You count as getting child maintenance if:[35]
  - it is being collected by the DWP on your behalf, (including where this is done by the Child Support Agency) (see p854), even if it retains the payments; *or*
  - it is being taken into account as income in working out how much IS or income-based JSA you can get (see p865).

The earliest your bonus period could start was 7 April 1997.

When a bonus period ends

When your bonus period ends, in order to qualify for a child maintenance bonus you must satisfy the 'work condition' within a strict time limit (see p57). A bonus period ends:[36]

- when the rules above no longer apply (eg, you satisfy the 'work condition' and your IS or income-based JSA ceases or your child's other parent no longer has to pay maintenance to you[37]); *or*
- when the person with the care of the child dies. See p61 for further information; *or*
- if your bonus period has not already ended for one of the above reasons, once you qualify for a child maintenance premium – see p54.[38]

If your bonus period ends but you cannot claim a child maintenance bonus (eg, because you do not satisfy the work condition – see p57) you do not necessarily lose out. Two bonus periods can be linked to count as one if they are separated by not more than 12 weeks *or* one of the following 'connecting periods':[39]

- while you are getting maternity allowance (see p456); *or*
- not more than two years throughout which you were getting incapacity benefit, carer's allowance (called invalid care allowance prior to April 2003) or severe disablement allowance (see Chapters 12, 4 and 20).

Example

Beth stopped getting IS when her ex-partner began to pay her additional maintenance but could not claim a child maintenance bonus as she was not working (see below). Eight weeks later she started getting IS again. When Beth takes up full-time work the DWP should look at the child maintenance she was paid during both bonus periods when it calculates her child maintenance bonus.

Although bonus periods can link, it is best to claim your child maintenance bonus as soon as your bonus period ends and you satisfy the work condition (see below) – eg, if you are uncertain how long a temporary job will last. Remember: you must satisfy the work condition within a strict time limit after your bonus period ends. See p59 for information about how and when you must claim.

The work condition

You qualify for a bonus if your or your partner's entitlement to IS or income-based JSA ceases because one of you satisfies the work condition, that is:[40]

- takes up a new job or the waged option of the New Deal or returns to work (but not if you return to work for the same employer at the same place of work following a trade dispute[41]); *or*
- increases your weekly hours of work and so counts as in full-time paid work (see p750); *or*
- has an increase in earnings. This includes where the combined earnings of you and your partner have increased to a level at which you are no longer entitled to IS or income-based JSA.

Unless your bonus period ends because you qualify for a child maintenance premium (see below), you must satisfy the work condition:

- within the 14 days after your bonus period ends (see p56); *or*
- within 12 weeks of the earliest of the dates an absent parent dies or stops being habitually resident in the UK or is found not to be your child(ren)'s parent; *or*
- where you get maintenance for one child and s/he dies, within 12 months of her/his date of death.

If you qualify for a child maintenance premium

The time limits within which you must satisfy the work condition are different if, before the date you qualified for a child maintenance premium (see p54):[42]

- you claimed a bonus, but did not satisfy the work condition before that date; *or*
- you did not claim a bonus, did not satisfy the work condition before that date and on the day before that date:
  - you or your partner were entitled to (or treated as entitled to) IS or income-based JSA; *and*

– you were getting child maintenance or were meant to be paid child maintenance (see p54) for a child who lives with you but whose other parent does not.

In either of these cases, you must satisfy the work condition:[43]

- within one month after your bonus period ends. Your bonus period ends on the date you qualify for a child maintenance premium if it has not already ended (see p56); *or*
- within 12 weeks of the earliest of the dates an absent parent dies or stops being habitually resident in the UK or is found not to be your child(ren)'s parent, if this happened before you qualified for a child maintenance premium; *or*
- where you get maintenance for one child and s/he dies before the date you qualify for a child maintenance premium, within 12 months of her/his death.

The amount of child maintenance bonus

To calculate your child maintenance bonus, the DWP looks at how much child maintenance (see p54) you were paid, or were meant to be paid, during your bonus period (see p56). Your child maintenance bonus is the lower of the following amounts:[44]

- £5 for every week when you were meant to be paid at least £5 child maintenance *plus* for each week you were meant to be paid less than £5, the amount due; *or*
- the actual amount of child maintenance you were paid. If it is not clear how much maintenance is being paid for your child(ren) because you are also getting it for yourself, £5 is taken into account as child maintenance (or all of what you are paid if this is less than £5).[45] Any child maintenance you get above what has been taken into account as income in working out your IS or income-based JSA (see p865), or what has been collected on your behalf by the DWP (see p854) is not included; *or*
- £1,000.

Examples

Avni's ex-husband, Sanjay, agreed to pay £20 child maintenance a week. He did so during her bonus period of 250 weeks.

£5 x 250 = £1,250 *or*

£20 x 250 = £5,000

Avni gets a child maintenance bonus of £1,000.

Sarah's ex-husband, Phil, was meant to pay £20 child maintenance a week during her bonus period of 100 weeks. During that time Phil actually paid her £4 a week.

£5 x 100 weeks = £500 *or*

£4 x 100 weeks = £400

Sarah gets a child maintenance bonus of £400.

Lynn's former partner, Robert, was meant to pay £12 child maintenance a week during her bonus period of 50 weeks. He actually paid £6 a week.

£5 x 50 = £250 *or*

£6 x 50 = £300

Lynn gets a child maintenance bonus of £250.

If your child maintenance bonus would be less than £5, you are not paid at all.[46]

While you are on IS or income-based JSA, the DWP can send estimates of how much child maintenance bonus you might be paid were you to take up work.[47] If the DWP knows you are getting child maintenance (see p54) you should get a statement every six months. However, you can ask for a statement at any time – eg, if you are considering taking a job and want to know how much child maintenance bonus you have accumulated.

Claims

A claim for child maintenance bonus must be in writing and on the appropriate form.[48] You can get the form from DWP offices or from its website (see Appendix 1). You should return the form to a DWP office.

If you do not complete the form properly (the decision maker refers to this as a 'defective claim'), you are asked to do so, usually within one month.[49] You can be given longer than this if the decision maker thinks it is reasonable. It is important that you reply in time. If you do not complete the form properly, you might not get a child maintenance bonus unless you can show that you have 'good cause' for claiming late (see p60). However, your claim should *not* count as defective simply because your employer fails to complete her/his declaration on your form.[50] If you disagree with a decision that your claim is defective, you can seek a revision or appeal. See p1189 and Chapter 44 for further information.

You can be asked to provide information or evidence to support your claim.[51] You are given one month to do so (longer if the decision maker thinks this is reasonable). If you fail to provide the information or evidence required, your claim is decided without it.[52]

You can ask for your claim to be amended or withdrawn.[53] You must do this in writing before a decision is made about your claim.

Who should claim

If you are one of a couple, you should claim the child maintenance bonus if you are the one caring for a child for whom child maintenance (see p54) is paid.[54] If both you and your partner care for different children for whom child maintenance is paid, you can both qualify for a child maintenance bonus. In this case, each of you must claim. If you separate, you count as entitled to IS or income-based JSA on days when your former partner was claiming for you.[55] If you are not one of a couple, you claim the child maintenance bonus if you are the person who accrued it.

When to claim

You can claim in the week before the week in which your or your partner's entitlement to IS or income-based JSA ceases. This is useful, for example, where you know you or your partner are returning to work. Otherwise, you must claim within the time limits as follows:[56]

- no later than 28 days after you or your partner stop getting IS or income-based JSA; *or*
- where you are claiming because you stopped getting IS/income-based JSA in the 12 weeks before you reached age 60/pension age (see below), no later than 28 days after you reach that age.

Different rules apply if you are an appointee claiming the child maintenance bonus of someone who has died (see p61).

The date of your claim

Your claim is usually treated as having been made on the date it is received by the DWP office.[57] Your claim can be backdated, but only if you can show that throughout the period between the date by which you should have claimed and the date you actually claimed you had 'good cause' for failing to claim.[58] However, your claim can never be backdated more than six months. See p221 for what counts as 'good cause' for a late claim.

Special rules if you reach age 60 or pension age

You can get a child maintenance bonus **without having to make a claim** even if you do not satisfy the work condition (see p57) if you:[59]

- turn 60 and on the day before your claim you or your partner were entitled to IS; *or*
- reach pension age (60 for women and 65 for men) and on the day before your claim you or your partner were entitled to income-based JSA; *or*
- stop getting income-based JSA after your 60th birthday but before you reach pension age and you become entitled to pension credit (PC) within 12 weeks or during any of the periods listed on p56 that link bonus periods.

You can get a child maintenance bonus even if you do not satisfy the work condition (see p57), but **you have to make a claim** (see p59) if your or your partner's entitlement to IS ceases in the 12 weeks before your 60th birthday or to income-based JSA ceases in the 12 weeks before you reach pension age.[60]

Your bonus period ends when you are paid a child maintenance bonus. You cannot get another one.[61]

Death of the person with care of the child

If someone dies, the child maintenance bonus s/he has already accumulated can be paid to an appointee or can help the person who takes over the care of her/his child(ren) get a higher child maintenance bonus.

Payment to an appointee

If a person satisfies all of the conditions of entitlement to a child maintenance bonus described on p54 but does not claim and s/he dies within 28 days of her/his entitlement to IS or income-based JSA ceasing, a decision maker can appoint someone to claim in her/his place.[62] You must apply to be an appointee within six months of the date of death and claim the child maintenance bonus, in writing, within six months of the date you are appointed. An application for appointment or a claim for the bonus can be accepted up to 12 months after the date of death in exceptional circumstances. However, if the time limit for one is extended, the other is shortened by the same amount of time. Any time between the date you apply to be an appointee and the date you are appointed is ignored.

Payment to a new carer

If you take over the care of someone's child(ren) when s/he dies, you might be able to claim any child maintenance bonus accumulated at the date of her/his death or within 12 weeks of that date. Unless you have already accumulated a bonus for the same weeks, weeks in her/his bonus period (see p56) must be treated as part of yours if:[63]

- on the date the person died, s/he or her/his partner was entitled to IS or income-based JSA or had been within the 12 weeks before the death;
- you are her/his close relative (see p906); *and*
- you or your partner were entitled to IS or income-based JSA on the date of her/his death or within 12 weeks of when s/he was last entitled to those benefits.

Challenging a child maintenance bonus decision

You can apply for a revision or supersession of a child maintenance bonus decision or appeal against it (see Chapters 42 and 43).

Tax, tax credits and other benefits

The bonus is not taxable.

A child maintenance bonus is treated as capital for IS, JSA, housing benefit (HB) and council tax benefit (CTB) purposes.[64] However, if you are under 60 or you or your partner are on IS or income-based JSA, it is disregarded for 52 weeks for HB and CTB purposes.[65] It is disregarded as income for the purposes of working tax credit and child tax credit.[66] It does not count as income or capital for the purposes of PC or for HB or CTB if you are 60 or over and neither you nor your partner are on IS or income-based JSA.

You should check to see if you qualify for any of the other bonuses in this chapter.

3. Mortgage interest run-on

When you return to work or increase your hours and so count as in full-time paid work, you no longer qualify for income support (IS) or income-based jobseeker's allowance (JSA). However, you might qualify for what is known as mortgage interest run-on. If you do, you are paid your IS or income-based JSA housing costs for the first four weeks after you go into full-time paid work.

Who can claim mortgage interest run-on

You qualify for mortgage interest run-on if:[67]

- you or your partner take up a new job or increase your weekly hours of work and so count as in full-time paid work (see p750). You must expect the work to last for at least five weeks;
- throughout the 26 weeks before the day you count as in full-time paid work, you or your partner were getting IS or income-based JSA. Periods when you were getting mortgage interest run-on do not count towards the 26 weeks;[68] *and*
- on the day before you or your partner commenced the work, your IS or income-based JSA applicable amount included the following housing costs:
  - mortgages and other home purchase loans (see p910); *or*
  - loans for repairs and improvements (see p916); *and*
- you or your partner are still liable to pay the housing costs.

If you qualify, you are paid IS for the housing costs for the first four weeks of full-time paid work.[69] Mortgage interest run-on is paid to you, *not* direct to your lender.[70]

The amount of mortgage interest run-on

You are paid the lowest of:[71]

- the weekly amount of IS or income-based JSA housing costs that you were getting immediately before you or your partner took up full-time paid work (see p750). See Chapter 36 for information about how these costs are calculated; *or*
- your or your partner's IS or income-based JSA entitlement in the week before you took up full-time paid work (or the amount to which you would have been entitled had you not been getting a training allowance). See pp303 and 379 for information about how your IS or income-based JSA is calculated.

Your mortgage interest run-on can be adjusted if there are changes in:[72]

- the IS applicable amount (see p303);
- the amount of housing costs you can get because:
  - the standard rate of interest used to calculate housing costs (see p915) or your non-dependant deductions (see p924) have changed; *or*
  - you have been entitled to IS for 26 weeks.

Your earnings from the full-time paid work and any other income you get are disregarded.[73] All of your capital is also disregarded.[74]

Claims

Although you do not have to make a claim to qualify for mortgage interest run-on,[75] you must let your local DWP office know you are starting full-time paid work. Mortgage interest run-on should then be paid automatically.

Challenging a mortgage interest run-on decision

You can apply for a revision or supersession of a mortgage interest run-on decision or appeal against it (see Chapters 42 and 43).

Tax, tax credits and other benefits

Mortgage interest run-on is not taxable.

Mortgage interest run-on is a payment of IS. You might, therefore, get health benefits (see Chapter 9) and education benefits (see p18). You might also qualify for social fund payments (see Chapters 21 and 22).

You should check to see if you qualify for any of the other bonuses in this chapter.

4. Extended payments of housing benefit and council tax benefit

If you are on income support (IS), income-based jobseeker's allowance (JSA), incapacity benefit (IB) or severe disablement allowance (SDA) and your entitlement ends because you start work, or increase your hours or pay, you may be entitled to continue to receive the same amount of housing benefit (HB) and council tax benefit (CTB) as you did before your entitlement ended. This is paid for up to four weeks. We refer to these as extended payments of HB and CTB in this *Handbook*. If you get extended payments because your entitlement to IB or SDA ends, the local authority may call these 'extended payments (severe disablement allowance and incapacity benefit)'.

Who can claim extended payments

You qualify for extended payments of HB or CTB if:

- the DWP has certified that you or your partner:[76]
  - were entitled to and in receipt of IS or income-based JSA and your entitlement ended because you or your partner started work (including self-employed work) or increased your earnings from, or hours of, work. Mortgage interest run-on ceasing (see p62) does not count for these purposes; *and*
  - had been continuously entitled to, and in receipt of, either IS or JSA or a combination of these for 26 weeks. This includes periods of less than five weeks when you counted as in full-time paid work (see p750) because you were on an employment zone programme; *or*
- unless you are getting pension credit, you or your partner:[77]
  - were *not* entitled to or in receipt of IS; *and*
  - were entitled to and in receipt of IB or SDA and your entitlement ended because you or your partner started work (including self-employed work) or increased your earnings from, or hours of, work; *and*
  - had been continuously entitled to, and in receipt of, either SDA or IB or a combination of these for 26 weeks.

If you move home, you can still qualify for extended payments of HB and CTB, so long as the day you moved was in the same week, or the week before, you or your partner started work or increased your earnings from or hours of work.[78]

You only qualify for extended payments of HB or CTB if, in addition, you (or your partner) notify the local authority or DWP that:[79]

- you (or your partner) have started, or are about to start, full-time paid work (see p750) or increase your hours or earnings; *and*
- you expect the work (or increase in hours or pay) to last for five weeks or more.

You must notify the local authority or DWP within four weeks of starting work or of the increase in your hours or pay. The time limit is very strict. If you miss it, try to claim HB and CTB on the basis of your income and ask for your claim to be backdated (see p221).

Your entitlement to HB and CTB also ends in the circumstances described above (see p225). If you do not notify within the four-week time limit, you could be overpaid HB or CTB and you might have to repay it. See pp1144 and 1156 for further information.

Amount of the extended payment of housing benefit

The weekly amount of your extended payment is the actual HB payable in your last full week of your IS, income-based JSA, IB or SDA claim (ignoring rent-free weeks).[80] This amount is paid for four weeks unless:[81]

- any of the weeks count as rent-free periods (see p211); *or*

- you move to local authority accommodation (but see below); *or*
- your liability to pay rent ceases altogether within the four weeks.

If you were being paid discretionary housing payments (see p235), ask for these to continue for the extended payment period.

If you move house (unless you move into local authority accommodation – see below), you continue to get the weekly amount of HB payable on your old home.[82] No account is taken of changes in circumstances over the extended payment period – eg, non-dependants (see p211), rent increases, increases in income, rent-free weeks.

If you move into local authority accommodation, the amount of the extended payment is the eligible rent (see p207) at your new address minus any non-dependant deductions (see p211) which applied at the old address.[83] However, if you are getting extended payments because you stopped getting IB or SDA, you are paid the amount of weekly HB payable in your last week of entitlement if this is lower.[84]

Even if you get an extended payment, you may still qualify for HB on two homes (see p203).[85]

If you claim HB on the basis of your income from work, and your new entitlement is higher than your extended payment, you can be paid up to the level of your new entitlement (see p66).

Amount of the extended payment of council tax benefit

The weekly amount of your extended payment of CTB is the amount of CTB you got in the last week before your entitlement to IS, income-based JSA, IB or SDA ceased.[86] The rules on how long the payment lasts are the same as for extended payments of HB (see p64). However, you *are* paid extended payments of CTB during rent-free periods. If you move, you get the maximum CTB (see p114) applicable to your new address minus any non-dependant deductions (see p115) which applied at your old address.[87] However, if you are getting extended payments because you stopped getting IB or SDA, you are paid the amount of weekly CTB payable in your last week of entitlement if this is lower.[88]

If you were being paid discretionary housing payments (see p235), ask for these to continue for the extended payment period.

If you claim CTB on the basis of your income from work, and your new entitlement is higher than your extended payment, you can be paid up to the level of your new entitlement (see p66).

Claims

Although you do not have to make a claim for extended payments of HB and CTB,[89] you must let your local authority and DWP office know you are starting work or increasing your hours or earnings. You must do this within a strict four-week time limit (see p64). Your extended payments of HB and CTB should then be made automatically.

Challenging a decision

You can apply for a revision or supersession of an extended payments decision or appeal against it (see Chapters 43 and 44). However, if you disagree with what the DWP has certified (eg, whether or not you were entitled to and in receipt of IS or income-based JSA continuously), you need to take this up with the DWP.[90]

In-work claims for housing benefit and council tax benefit

You are treated as entitled to and getting HB (or CTB):[91]

- during the four weeks for which you are paid extended payments; *or*
- until your liability to pay rent (or council tax) ends, if this is sooner.

If you claim HB or CTB again within the period above that applies to you, or within the four weeks after, your HB or CTB entitlement will be continuous. This means, for example, that if you are exempt from the local reference rent rules (see p249), you should continue to be exempt unless you move home.

In some cases, your new entitlement to HB or CTB on the basis of your income from work might be more than the amount of your extended payment. This could happen where, for example, your rent increases or a non-dependant with a high income moves out. In this case HB and CTB can be paid up to the level of your new HB and CTB entitlement.[92]

Your new HB and CTB claims are given priority if you claim within 14 days of the day after the day your IS or income-based JSA ceased.[93] You only get priority if you notified the local authority or DWP (see p64) within 14 days of this happening.

Tax, tax credits and other benefits

Extended payments are not taxable. They are not taken into account as income or capital in working out your entitlement to means-tested benefits or tax credits.

You should check to see if you qualify for any of the other bonuses in this chapter.

5. Job grant

If you take up full-time paid work, you may be entitled to a job grant.[94]

Who can claim a job grant

You can qualify for a job grant if:

- you have received one of, or a combination of, the following benefits or allowances continuously for the previous 26 weeks, including where this is while you are in Northern Ireland:
  - IS;
  - JSA;
  - IB;
  - severe disablement allowance (SDA);
  - a New Deal scheme or Jobcentre Plus allowance based on IS, JSA, IB or SDA; *or*
  - employment zone payments based on JSA, so long as you are still getting some income-based JSA.

  Days when you are on jury service count towards the 26 weeks if you would otherwise have been entitled to benefit. Days when you were getting hardship payments also count towards the 26 weeks. In both cases, you must have been getting benefit immediately before and after this; *and*
- you have not already received a job grant relating to the same 26 week period; *and*
- you go into full-time paid work of 16 hours or more each week (or your partner goes into full-time paid work of 24 hours per week). This includes waged options of the New Deal and where you count as employed on Work Based Learning for Adults and Training for Work. You can add the hours from more than one job or scheme together; *and*
- you and your partner both stop getting benefit (this includes contribution-based JSA). You must move straight from benefit into work – eg, you cannot leave benefit for some other reason, then start work later; *and*
- you expect the work to last five weeks or more.

Even if you satisfy the rules above, you *cannot* qualify for a job grant if:
- you are under 25 and the benefit you have been getting is JSA, unless you are a lone parent; *or*
- you were claiming JSA or IB, did not receive benefit, but did receive national insurance credits (see p838); *or*
- your partner is the one starting full-time paid work and *you* are still signing on for national insurance credits; *or*
- your entitlement to benefit has ceased because of proven fraud – ie, you were working while claiming benefit.

The amount of job grant

The amount of job grant you get is:
- £100 if you are single or a member of a couple and you do not have any children; *or*
- £250 if you are a lone parent or a member of a couple with children.

Claims

You do not have to make a claim for a job grant. A job grant is paid automatically if you notify the DWP of the details of your job within 21 days of full-time paid work commencing.

Challenging a job grant decision

You do not have a right of appeal against a job grant decision. However, if you disagree with a decision you can ask a different decision maker to reconsider the case.

Tax, tax credits and other benefits

A job grant is not taxable. It should be treated as capital in assessing your entitlement to other benefits and tax credits.

6. Christmas bonus

You qualify for a Christmas bonus of £10 if you receive one or more of the 'qualifying benefits' (see below) in respect of at least part of what is known as the relevant week (even if the benefit is paid later).[95] You must be present or ordinarily resident in the UK, the Channel Islands, the Isle of Man, Gibraltar or any other European Economic Area state at some time during the 'relevant week'. The **'relevant week'** is usually the week beginning with the first Monday in December.[96]

The **'qualifying benefits'** are:[97]

- long-term incapacity benefit (see p263);
- severe disablement allowance (see Chapter 20);
- carer's allowance (see Chapter 4);
- widowed mother's or widowed parent's allowance (see pp25 and 35);
- widow's pension (see p35);
- retirement pension (see Chapter 19);
- disability living allowance (see pp127 and 136);
- attendance allowance (see p147);
- mobility supplement;
- disablement benefit (but only if unemployability supplement or constant attendance allowance is payable) (see p333);
- industrial death benefit for widows or widowers;
- war disablement pension (but only if you are at least 65 before the end of the relevant week);[98]
- war widow's pension;
- pension credit (PC – see Chapter 18).

You are treated as entitled to a benefit (other than PC) if you are not receiving it because some other payment is being made to you or your partner from public funds. You are treated as entitled to PC if you are normally entitled to it but your or your partner's income was too high in the relevant week for you to qualify.[99]

Couples

You may also claim an extra bonus for your partner (a further £10) if s/he has not received a bonus in her/his own right, and:[100]

- you are both at least pension age (currently 60 for women and 65 for men) and you are entitled, or may be treated as entitled, to an increase of one of the qualifying benefits in respect of her/him (see Chapter 31); *or*
- you are both at least 60 and the only qualifying benefit you get is PC.

You are treated as entitled to an increase in respect of your partner if the reason for it not being paid is either that some other payment is being made from public funds or that s/he earns too much.[101]

Claims

In most cases it is not necessary to make a claim for a Christmas bonus. It is paid automatically. However, you should contact the DWP if you have not obtained your bonus within a year. Otherwise, your right is lost.[102]

Challenging a Christmas bonus decision

You do not have a right of appeal against a Christmas bonus decision, but you *can* seek a revision or a supersession of, or appeal against, the decision about whether you are entitled to a qualifying benefit. See Chapters 43 and 44 for further information about revisions, supersessions and appeals.

Tax, tax credits and other benefits

The bonus is not taxable and has no effect on other benefits. It is disregarded as income for the purposes of working tax credit and child tax credit.[103]

Notes

1. **Back-to-work bonus**
1 Reg 7 SS(BTWB) Regs
2 Reg 7(2)(d) and (4)(e) SS(BTWB) Regs
3 Reg 7(2)(a) SS(BTWB) Regs
4 Regs 1(2), definition of 'bonus period' and 17(3) SS(BTWB) Regs; reg 10(2)(a) and (3) SS(BTWB&LPRO)(Amdt) Regs
5 Reg 10(1) SS(BTWB&LPRO)(Amdt) Regs
6 Reg 7(2)(b) SS(BTWB) Regs
7 Reg 19(8) SS(BTWB) Regs
8 Reg 7(3) SS(BTWB) Regs
9 Reg 7(4) SS(BTWB) Regs
10 Reg 7(6) SS(BTWB) Regs
11 Reg 7(5)(a) SS(BTWB) Regs
12 Reg 1(2) SS(BTWB) Regs, definition of 'earnings; CIS/2397/1996
13 Reg 8(6) SS(BTWB) Regs
14 Reg 13(1) and (2) SS(BTWB) Regs
15 Reg 13(5) SS(BTWB) Regs
16 Reg 8 SS(BTWB) Regs
17 Regs 22 and 23 SS(BTWB) Regs; CIS/2397/1996; CIS/2838/2001
18 Reg 22(6) SS(BTWB) Regs
19 Reg 22(1)(b) SS(BTWB) Regs
20 Reg 23(5) SS(BTWB) Regs
21 Reg 23(3) SS(BTWB) Regs
22 Reg 23(6) SS(BTWB) Regs
23 Reg 17(1)(a)(2) and (4) SS(BTWB) Regs
24 Reg 17(5) SS(BTWB) Regs
25 Reg 18 SS(BTWB) Regs
26 Reg 26 SS(BTWB) Regs
27 Reg 21 SS(BTWB) Regs
28 Sch 5 para 49 HB Regs; Sch 5 para 49 CTB Regs; reg 9 SS(BTWB&LPRO)(Amdt) Regs
29 Reg 7 Table 3 para 2 TC(DCI) Regs

2. **Child maintenance bonus**
30 Reg 1(2) SS(CMB) Regs
31 Reg 3 SS(CMB) Regs
32 Regs 1 and 4 SS(CMPMA) Regs
33 Reg 4(2) SS(CMPMA) Regs
34 Reg 4 SS(CMB) Regs
35 Reg 2(1) SS(CMB) Regs
36 Reg 4(7) SS(CMB) Regs
37 CIS/3544/2002
38 Reg 4(7) SS(CMB) Regs, as modified by reg 4(6) SS(CMPMA) Regs
39 Reg 4(2)-(5) SS(CMB) Regs
40 Reg 3(1) SS(CMB) Regs
41 Reg 3(2) and (3) SS(CMB) Regs
42 Reg 4(3) and (4) SS(CMPMA) Regs
43 Reg 3(3)(1)(f) SS(CMB) Regs, as modified by reg 4(5) SS(CMPMA) Regs
44 Reg 5 SS(CMB) Regs
45 Reg 1(5) SS(CMB) Regs
46 Reg 5(5) SS(CMB) Regs
47 Regs 2(2) and 6 SS(CMB) Regs
48 **CMB** Reg 10(1) SS(CMB) Regs
BTWB Reg 22(1) SS(BTWB) Regs
49 **CMB** Reg 10(3)-(4) SS(CMB) Regs
BTWB Reg 22(3) and (4) SS(BTWB) Regs
50 CJSA/2838/2001
51 **CMB** Reg 10(5) SS(CMB) Regs
BTWB Reg 22(5) SS(BTWB) Regs
52 CJSA/2838/2001
53 **CMB** Reg 11(1) and (2) SS(CMB) Regs
BTWB Reg 23(1) SS(BTWB) Regs
54 Reg 9 SS(CMB) Regs
55 Reg 9(4) and (5) SS(CMB) Regs
56 Reg 10 SS(CMB) Regs
57 Reg 11(3) SS(CMB) Regs
58 Reg 11(4) SS(CMB) Regs
59 Reg 8(1) and (2) SS(CMB) Regs
60 Reg 8(4) and (5) SS(CMB) Regs
61 Reg 8(3) SS(CMB) Regs
62 Reg 13 SS(CMB) Regs
63 Reg 7 SS(CMB) Regs
64 Reg 14 SS(CMB) Regs
65 Sch 5 para 52 HB Regs; Sch 5 para 52 CTB Regs
66 Reg 7 Table 3 paras 13,16 and 17 TC(DCI) Regs

3. **Mortgage interest run-on**
67 Reg 6(5) and (8) IS Regs
68 Reg 6(7) IS Regs
69 Reg 6(6) IS Regs
70 Sch 9A para 3(9) SS(C&P) Regs
71 Sch 7 para 19A(1) IS Regs
72 Sch 7 para 19A(2) and (3) IS Regs
73 Schs 8 para 15C and 9 para 74 IS Regs
74 Sch 10 para 62 IS Regs
75 Reg 3(h) SS(C&P) Regs

4. Extended payments of housing benefit and council tax benefit

76 **HB** Reg 62A(1)-(3), (5) and (7) and Sch 5A para 2 HB Regs
CTB Reg 53A(1)-(3), (5) and (7) and Sch 5A para 2 CTB Regs
77 **HB** Reg 62ZB(1)-(3) and (5) HB Regs
CTB Reg 53ZB(1)-(3) and (5) CTB Regs
78 **HB** Regs 62A(1)(b) and 62ZB(1)(b) HB Regs
CTB Regs 53A(1)(b) and 53ZB(1)(b) CTB Regs
All CH/1762/2004
79 **HB** Schs 5A para 3 and 5B para 1 HB Regs
CTB Schs 5A para 3 and 5B para 1 CTB Regs
80 Schs 5A para 4 and 5B para 2 HB Regs
81 Regs 62A(6)and 62ZB(6) and Schs 5A para 4(5) and 5B para 2(5) HB Regs
82 Schs 5A paras 6, 7 and 8 and 5B paras 4, 5 and 6 HB Regs
83 Sch 5A para 8(b) and Sch 5B para 6(b) HB Regs
84 Sch 5B para 6(b)(ii) HB Regs
85 Schs 5A para 10 and 5B para 8 HB Regs
86 Schs 5A para 4and 5B para 2 CTB Regs
87 Schs 5A paras 5 and 6 and 5B paras 3-5 CTB Regs
88 Sch 5B para 4(b) CTB Regs
89 **HB** Regs 62A(2) and 62ZB(2) HB Regs
CTB Regs 53A(2) and 53ZB(2) CTB Regs
90 CH/5553/2002
91 **HB** Regs 62A(6) and 62ZB(6) HB Regs
CTB Regs 53A(6) and 53ZA(6) CTB Regs
Both Reg 28 HB&CTB(ABP) Amdt Regs
92 **HB** Schs 5A para 11 and 5B para 9 HB Regs
CTB Schs 5A para 7 and 5B para 6 CTB Regs
93 **HB** Reg 76(4) HB Regs
CTB Reg 66(4) CTB Regs

5. Job grant

94 Job grants are paid under arrangements made under s2(2) ETA 1973

6. Christmas bonus

95 ss148(1)and 149(1) SSCBA 1992
96 s150(4) SSCBA 1992
97 s150(1) SSCBA 1992
98 s149(4) SSCBA 1992
99 s149(2) SSCBA 1992
100 ss148(2) and (5) and 150(2) SSCBA 1992, definition of 'the qualifying age for state pension credit'
101 s149(3) SSCBA 1992
102 Reg 38 SS(C&P) Regs
103 Reg 7 Table 3 para 5 TC(DCI) Regs

4

Chapter 4

Carer's allowance

This chapter covers:

Carer's allowance (CA) is a benefit that may be paid to you if you care for someone who is severely disabled. You do not have to have paid national insurance contributions to qualify for CA and, although your entitlement will depend on the level of any earnings that you have, it is not affected by the level of your savings. Until 1 April 2003 CA was called invalid care allowance.[1]

1. Who can claim carer's allowance

You qualify for carer's allowance (CA) if:[2]

- you satisfy the residence conditions (see p699);
- you are not subject to immigration control[3] (see p654);
- you are caring for a person receiving either the higher or middle rate of disability living allowance (DLA) care component (see p136), attendance allowance (AA) (see p147) or constant attendance allowance in respect of industrial or war disablement (see p333);
- the care you give is regular and substantial (see p73);
- you are not gainfully employed or in full-time education (see p73);
- you are aged 16 or over.

There are some groups of claimants to whom special rules apply (see p75).

Regularly and substantially caring

To qualify for CA you must be engaged in caring for the disabled person 'regularly and substantially'. You satisfy this requirement during any week in which you are (or are likely to be) engaged and regularly engaged in caring for her/him for 35 hours or more.[4] Caring might include supervision as well as assistance and if some of the time you spend on caring in the week is time spent preparing for the disabled person to come to stay with you, or clearing up after their visit, this can also count towards the 35 hours.[5] However, it is not possible to meet the rules of caring for 35 hours a week by showing that you care for more than 35 hours in some weeks and less in others. The rules require that you care for 35 hours a week in the week in question.[6]

You also do not qualify if you are caring for two or more disabled people for a total of 35 hours a week. You have to show that you are caring for one of the disabled people for at least 35 hours a week (for CA, a week runs from Sunday to Saturday).[7]

See p80 if the person you care for dies.

Breaks from caring

Once you have been caring for a disabled person for a while, temporary breaks in your care do not lead to the loss of your benefit. If you have been providing care for at least 35 hours a week in 22 of the last 26 weeks (or for at least 14 of the last 26 weeks, if the reason you did not provide care for 22 weeks was that either you or the disabled person were in hospital or in a similar institution – see p715), you can still get CA. Weeks before you claimed CA can be counted. Effectively, you can have four weeks' break from caring in any period of six months, or 12 weeks' break if one of you was in hospital for at least eight weeks.[8]

However, CA stops if the AA, constant attendance allowance or DLA of the disabled person for whom you are caring stops because s/he is in hospital or certain other special sorts of accommodation (see Chapter 28).[9]

Gainfully employed

You cannot qualify for CA if you are 'gainfully employed'. You are considered to be gainfully employed if your earnings in the previous week (from employment and/or self-employment) were more than the lower earnings limit for national insurance contributions which was in force at the end of that week. This means that for the tax year 2005/06 you will not qualify for CA if your earnings are more than £82 a week (for the way earnings are calculated, see p941 and for the lower earnings limits for other years, see p827).[10] Your earnings are ignored if you are working during a period when you are not actually caring for the disabled person – eg, because s/he is in hospital or you are on your four weeks' break from caring (see above).[11]

Full-time education

If you are in 'full-time education' you cannot get CA. The rules about what counts as full-time education for CA are different than for other benefits (see p634).[12]

2. The rules about your age

You can claim carer's allowance (CA) if you are aged 16 or over.[13]

Before 28 October 2002, you could only get invalid care allowance (ICA – now called carer's allowance) after reaching the age of 65 if you were entitled to it immediately before you became 65 (or if you would have been entitled to it but for the overlapping benefit rules – see p1102). You could then continue to be entitled to ICA after 65, even if you were no longer caring for the disabled person or if you had started gainful employment (see p73), as long as you satisfied all the other conditions of entitlement. If you were entitled to ICA and aged 65 or over immediately before 28 October 2002, you can continue to receive CA on this basis.[14]

From 28 October 2002, there is no upper age limit for claiming CA, and so you can claim it even if you are 65 or over. However, in order to qualify you must satisfy all the normal qualifying conditions, including caring for a disabled person and not being in 'gainful employment'.

Before 28 October 1994 there were different upper age limits for claiming ICA for men and women (60 for women, 65 for men). This discrimination was found to be unlawful and the upper age limit for claiming was changed to 65 for both men and women from 28 October 1994. Women who were 65 before 28 October 1994 and who would have qualified for ICA but for the discriminatory age rules may still be able to claim now, whether or not they claimed before, even if they no longer care for a disabled person or are gainfully employed.[15] If you are in this situation, seek advice.

Remember that if you qualify for retirement pension as well as CA you will not be paid both benefits in full because of the overlapping benefit rules (see p1102).

3. Claiming for others

If you are the person providing care you can claim the basic rate of carer's allowance (CA) for yourself. You can also claim an increase for your spouse or for someone who cares for your child (see Chapter 31). Your entitlement to the increase may be affected by your spouse's, or your adult dependant's, earnings or by any occupational or personal pension payments or overlapping benefits s/he receives (see pp797 and 1102). If you have been entitled to an increase in your CA for your partner for at least six months and you are both 18 or over but under 60, then your partner may be required to take part in a work-focused interview and your benefit can be reduced if s/he fails to do so without good cause (see p1094).

Increases for your dependent children, which could also be claimed with CA, were abolished on 6 April 2003 and replaced with child tax credit, which is means tested (see Chapter 49). However, if you were entitled to an increase in your CA for a dependent child on 5 April 2003 you may be able to continue to receive it after that date (see p798).

You may choose not to claim increases to which you may be entitled if, for example, this would take you over the income limit for income support or income-based jobseeker's allowance (but see p81).

4. The amount of benefit

The amount of carer's allowance (CA) you get depends on whether you are claiming for any dependants (see p74).[16]

Note: Increases for child dependants have been abolished from 6 April 2003 (but see p798 for details of who can continue to receive them).

	£pw
Claimant	45.70
Adult dependant	27.30
Child dependant (first child)	9.40
Child dependant (each subsequent child)	11.35

While receiving CA, you are credited with Class 1 national insurance contributions (see p839).

If two or more people each spend 35 hours a week caring for the same disabled person, only one of them can receive CA. If they cannot agree on who this should be then the decision maker at the Department for Work and Pensions will decide. If someone cares for two or more disabled people for more than 35 hours a week each that carer can still only qualify for one award of CA.[17]

The amount of your benefit may be reduced, or not paid at all, if you are required to take part in a work-focused interview and fail to do so (see p1092). See p1094 if your partner is required to take part in a work-focused interview because you get an increase in your CA for her/him.

If you are on CA, you are entitled to a Christmas bonus (see p68).

5. Special rules for special groups

Special rules may apply to you if:

- you have come from or are going abroad (see Chapter 26);
- you, or the person you are caring for, are in hospital (see p715);
- the person you are caring for goes into residential accommodation (see p725);
- you are in prison or detention (see p731).

6. Claims and backdating

The main rules on claiming and backdating are contained in Chapter 40. The following section explains the specific rules that relate to carer's allowance (CA). If you are claiming a means-tested benefit see p81 before you decide whether to also claim CA, as the effect of CA on other benefits means that it is not always advisable for you to claim it.

If you decide to claim CA you should not delay your claim or you may lose benefit. If you are caring for a disabled person who is in the process of claiming disability living allowance (DLA) or attendance allowance (AA) you should not wait until her/his claim is decided before you claim CA. You might lose benefit if you do. Instead, you should claim CA at the same time as the disabled person claims DLA or AA or as soon as possible after this (but see p1090 if your claim is refused because, when your claim is decided, the person you care for has not been awarded DLA or AA).

If you are under 60, you may be required to take part in a work-focused interview in order to qualify for CA (see p1092).

Once benefit is in being paid you may also be required to attend further work-focused interviews.

Making a claim

A claim for CA must be made in writing and must be on an appropriate form – form DS700. In certain circumstances, the Secretary of State may accept a written application which is not on the correct form (see p1079).[18] Form DS700 can be obtained from your local Department for Work and Pensions (DWP), JobCentre or Jobcentre Plus office or can be printed out from the DWP's website (see Appendix 1). Alternatively you can ring the Carer's Allowance Unit on 01253 856123 (textphone 01772 899489) to obtain a claim form. You should send your completed claim form to the Carer's Allowance Unit, Palatine House, Lancaster Road, Preston, PR1 1NS. If you are 60 or over you may also be able to make your claim by taking or sending it to a designated 'alternative office' – see p1078 for details.

If you have access to the internet, you may also claim CA by completing an online application form and submitting it to the DWP via its website (see Appendix 1) as long as the DWP accepts this form of communication from you (see p78).

Whichever procedure you follow in order to claim, it is advisable to keep a copy of your claim form in case queries arise.

See p1076 for the detailed rules on making a claim.

Information to support your claim

When you claim CA, you must satisfy what is known as the 'national insurance (NI) number requirement'. In most cases this means you must provide your NI number, as well as the NI number of any adult dependant for whom you are claiming (see p1083).

Who should claim

You must normally claim CA on your own behalf. However, CA can be claimed by another adult on your behalf if you are unable to act for yourself. This person is called your 'appointee' (see p1075 for further details).

Before deciding whether to claim you should be aware of how CA affects your entitlement to means-tested benefits (see p81).

The date of your claim

The date of your claim is normally the date on which your completed claim form is received by the DWP or, if you are 60 or over and submit your claim to a designated 'alternative office' (see p1078), the date it is received by that office.[19] If you make a claim for CA in writing, but not on the correct form (form DS700), or if the claim form you submit is incomplete, you may be asked to provide further information or to complete the correct form. As long as this additional information or form is returned within a month of it being sent back to you (or longer if the decision maker thinks that the delay is reasonable – see p1082), the decision maker can treat your claim as made on the date that your initial written application or form was received by the DWP.[20] If you submit your claim online via the DWP website (see p78), then the date of your claim will normally be the date it is received by the DWP, although a decision maker has the discretion to treat it as having been received on an earlier or later date than this.

The date of your claim may be backdated (see p78). See p1092 if you are required to take part in a work-focused interview.

If you claim the wrong benefit

If you have made a claim for income support (IS) instead of CA then this may be treated as a claim for CA (see p1084).[21] This rule may enable you to get round the strict time limits on backdating (see p78). Decision makers are not obliged to treat an IS claim as a claim for CA, and there is no right of appeal against a decision not to do so. The only legal challenge is by way of judicial review.[22] A decision maker can treat an IS claim as a CA claim if s/he is satisfied that a reasonably alert official, asking the proper questions, would have recognised that you were entitled to CA.

Claiming in advance

If you are not currently entitled to CA, but will become entitled in the future (eg, you are currently earning more than £82 a week but you plan to stop work), you can make a claim up to three months in advance.[23] The decision maker can award benefit from a future date if s/he believes that you will satisfy all the CA qualifying conditions on that date.

How your claim is dealt with

A decision on your claim will be made by a decision maker at the Carer's Allowance Unit. The DWP aims to deal with new claims for CA within three weeks.

Using the internet

As well as sending claims and information by post, in certain circumstances you may use the internet to:

- make a claim for CA;
- notify the DWP of a change in your circumstances.

You can do this by logging on to the DWP's website (www.dwp.gov.uk), looking up CA under 'benefits and services A–Z', following the links for the CA e-service and completing the claim form or relevant change of circumstances form online. After submitting the relevant form you will be given a transaction number. You should keep a record of this number in case problems arise, as it can be used to trace your claim or notification. Although in many circumstances the decision maker has the power not to accept the information or a claim from you when it is sent via the internet, as long as you submit the information or claim through the DWP's website (rather than by email), using the forms on the site when appropriate, and follow the procedure given on the website for submitting the information or claim, this would be unusual.

At the time of publication it was not possible to send any documents or papers to support your claim over the internet. You would have to forward these separately to the DWP by post.

Backdating your claim

A claim for CA can be backdated for up to three months if you satisfy the qualifying conditions over that period. You do not have to show any reasons why your claim was late. The rules on backdating are covered on p1085.

If your CA claim is refused because the person that you care for is not receiving the middle or higher rate DLA care component, AA or constant attendance allowance, but one of those benefits is subsequently awarded to her/him you may be able to get your CA backdated beyond the normal limit.[24]

Similarly, if:

- your CA is stopped because the person you care for has had her/his DLA, AA or constant attendance allowance reduced or stopped; *and*
- s/he subsequently gets her/his benefit reinstated; *and*
- you make a further claim for CA within three months of the DWP's decision to reinstate DLA, AA or constant attendance allowance,

your benefit can be backdated to the date that your earlier claim ended or the date from which middle/higher rate DLA care component, AA or constant attendance allowance was re-awarded, whichever is later.[25]

If you might have qualified for benefit earlier but did not claim because you were given the wrong information by the DWP or because you were misled by the DWP you could:

- ask for an ex gratia payment (see p1304); *or*
- complain to the Ombudsman (see p1302).

7. Getting paid

Payment of carer's allowance (CA) is normally made by direct credit transfer into your bank (or similar) account.[26] If you are unable to open or manage an account, payment can be made by cheque. Such cheques can be paid into an account or cashed at the post office (see p1099 for details).

CA is paid either weekly in advance or at four-weekly intervals.[27] You will normally be paid CA on Mondays. However, if the person for whom you are caring receives constant attendance allowance with their industrial injuries disablement benefit or war pension, you will be paid on Wednesdays.[28] If you are entitled to CA, payments will normally run from the first payday (ie, Monday or Wednesday) after the date of your claim, unless the date of your claim is on your payday, when they will run from that day.

CA awards can be made for a fixed period or indefinitely.[29]

If you are unable to act for yourself, CA can be paid to someone else on your behalf, called your appointee (see p1075). Direct deductions to repay debts cannot be made from CA.

If your benefit cheque is lost or stolen, see p1104. If payment of your CA is suspended, see p1105. If your CA has been reduced because you, or your partner, failed to take part in a work-focused interview, see p1097.

You may not be paid CA if you have been sanctioned for benefit offences (see p1169).

Delays and complaints

If payment of your CA is delayed, you might be able to get an interim payment. See p1108 for further details.

If you suffer delays, see p1305. If you wish to complain about how your claim has been dealt with, see p1300. You might be able to claim compensation (see p1304).

Change of circumstances

It is your duty to report any change in your circumstances which might affect your entitlement to, or the payment of, your benefit. You should do this promptly by writing to the Carer's Allowance Unit of the Department for Work and Pensions (DWP). You can also send notification of your change of circumstances to the DWP over the internet via the DWP's website (see p78), as long as the DWP accepts this form of communication from you. While in certain circumstances you may be able to report changes of circumstances by telephone, or by some other means, it is advisable to write, or to confirm a telephone conversation in writing so that there is a clear record of the information you have given and to keep a copy of the letter you send in case problems arise. If you do not promptly report any such change, any resulting overpayment may be recoverable from you (see Chapter 41). If you are considered deliberately to have acted falsely or dishonestly, you may also be guilty of an offence (see Chapter 42).

If, following a change in your circumstances, the decision on your claim is superseded and your entitlement to benefit is affected, the date from which the new decision takes effect depends on whether or not it is advantageous to you and whether you reported the change in time (see p1204 for further details).

If the person receiving care dies

If the person you care for dies you continue to be entitled to CA for a further eight weeks, even though you are no longer providing care, as long as you satisfy the other qualifying conditions. The eight-week period runs from the Sunday following the death unless the death occurred on a Sunday, when it will run from that day.[30]

Overpayments and fraud

If you are overpaid CA, you might have to repay it. The rules on overpayments are covered in Chapter 41. If you have been accused of fraud, see Chapter 42.

8. Challenging a carer's allowance decision

You can apply for a revision or supersession of a carer's allowance (CA) decision, or appeal against it – see Chapters 43 and 44. The advice given in those chapters applies equally to CA.

9. Tax, tax credits and other benefits

Carer's allowance (CA) is taxable except for any increases for children.[31]

Tax credits

If your income is low you may qualify for child tax credit (CTC) (if you have at least one dependent child – see Chapter 49) and working tax credit (WTC) (if you or your partner, if you have one, are in qualifying remunerative work – see Chapters 50 and 51). But remember, you cannot get CA if you are in gainful employment (see p73). CA is counted in full as income for both these tax credits. If you are receiving CA and you are 50 or over you may qualify for the 50-plus element of WTC.

Means-tested benefits

If you are under 60, have a low income and you (and your partner if you have one) are not in full-time paid work (see p750) you may be entitled to income support (IS) in addition to your CA. This is because, if you receive CA, you come within one of the groups of people who can claim IS (see p294).[32] If you are not receiving CA, but you are regularly and substantially caring for a person who receives or has claimed attendance allowance (AA) or the higher or middle rate of the care component of disability living allowance (DLA), you can likewise claim IS (see p297). In this context you are not necessarily required to provide care for 35 hours a week to be regularly and substantially caring for someone.[33] If your partner is claiming income-based jobseeker's allowance (JSA) and you are a member of a 'joint claim couple' for JSA (see p394) you will not be required to be available for work, to actively seek work or to enter into a jobseeker's agreement to make a joint claim if you are a carer who is entitled to claim IS (see p297). However, in these circumstances you should consider claiming IS instead of income-based JSA.

If your income is low you may also qualify for housing benefit (HB) and council tax benefit (CTB).

Before you claim CA, you should consider how your claim might affect your entitlement to these means-tested benefits. In particular you should be aware of the following points:

- If you receive CA (or are entitled to it but do not receive it because of the effect of the overlapping benefit rules – see p1102) you get a carer's premium of £25.80 a week included in the calculation of your IS, income-based JSA, HB or CTB (see p896).[34]
- However, CA is counted in full as income (less any tax payable on it) when calculating your entitlement to IS, income-based JSA, HB and CTB.[35] This means that if you are getting IS or income-based JSA, claiming CA normally

reduces your entitlement to those benefits and only increases your overall income by the amount of the carer's premium.

- If you also work, the situation may be slightly different. This is because if you get CA, and so receive a carer's premium, £20 of your earnings can be disregarded (rather than the standard £5 or £10 – see p963) when working out your entitlement to IS, income-based JSA, HB and CTB. (**Note:** The rule for calculating your earnings for entitlement to CA is different.)
- Claiming CA may mean that your income is too high for you to qualify for benefits such as IS and income-based JSA, even if the carer's premium is awarded to you. In this situation, losing entitlement to IS or income-based JSA can mean your entitlement to HB and CTB is reduced and that you no longer qualify for benefits like free school meals for your children and social fund payments. You will need to calculate whether the increase in your weekly income compensates you for the loss of these benefits. If in doubt, seek advice.
- If the person you care for gets one of these means-tested benefits and the middle or higher rate care component of DLA or AA, s/he may be receiving a severe disability premium within her/his IS, income-based JSA (if the person qualifies for this despite her/his disability), HB or CTB (see p891). If you get CA, s/he will lose entitlement to that premium. You will therefore need to discuss whether or not a claim for CA is a good idea. It is important to bear in mind that the severe disability premium is worth more than the carer's premium.
- For means-tested benefits you can be treated as if you receive income that you deliberately do not claim in order to gain benefit for yourself or your family (see p984). So if you choose not to claim CA, the Department for Work and Pensions (DWP) might treat you as if you receive it and reduce your benefit accordingly. But for this 'notional income' rule to apply there has to be no doubt that you would qualify for CA and this may be difficult for the DWP to establish if you have not claimed or been awarded CA already.
- If the person you care for is not a member of your family, you cannot be treated as having notional income if you do not claim CA or stop claiming it so that s/he can qualify for a severe disability premium.

If you are 60 or over you may qualify for pension credit (PC – see Chapter 18) in addition to your CA.

CA is treated as income (less any tax payable on it) when calculating your entitlement to PC. However, if you receive CA (or are entitled to it but do not receive it because of the overlapping benefit rules) you should qualify for the additional amount for carers in the guarantee credit of PC. The situation is more complicated for the savings credit. As CA counts as qualifying income, claiming CA may also affect your entitlement to the savings credit. How your entitlement is affected will depend on the amount of other qualifying income you have. Just as for the other means-tested benefits mentioned above and on p81, if you get CA and you work, £20 of your earnings can be disregarded when calculating your entitlement to PC. If the person you care for gets PC and her/his benefit includes an additional amount for severe disability, this additional amount will not be payable if you start getting CA for caring for her/him. For further information, see p896.

Non-means-tested benefits

CA is subject to the overlapping benefit rules, which mean that you may not qualify for CA in full if another earnings replacement benefit is paid to you (see p1102).

For each week that you receive CA you will receive a credited Class 1 national insurance (NI) contribution (but your contribution record may be protected anyway through home responsibilities protection – see p842). Even if you are receiving another earnings replacement benefit it may still be worth claiming CA if this would qualify you for a carer's premium within your means-tested benefit (see pp 81–82) or for credited NI contributions.

Passports and other sources of help

If you are on a low income, you might be entitled to certain health service benefits such as free prescriptions (see Chapter 9). You may also qualify for a social fund payment (see Chapters 21 and 22). If you are getting income support, income-based JSA or, in some circumstances, CTC, any children that you have will qualify for free school meals (see p18).

Notes

1 Art 2 RR(CA)O

1. Who can claim carer's allowance

2 s70 SSCBA 1992; regs 3 and 9(1) SS(ICA) Regs
3 s115 IAA 1999
4 Reg 4(1) SS(ICA) Regs
5 CG/6/1990
6 R(G) 3/91
7 Reg 4(1A) SS(ICA) Regs
8 Reg 4(2) SS(ICA) Regs
9 *Secretary of State for Work and Pensions v Pridding* [2002] EWCA Civ 306, *The Times*, 3 April 2002
10 Reg 8(1) SS(ICA) Regs
11 Reg 8(2) SS(ICA) Regs
12 Reg 5 SS(ICA) Regs

2. The rules about your age

13 s70(3) SSCBA 1992
14 Art 4 RR(CA)O
15 *Secretary of State v Thomas* [1993] QB 747; R(G) 2/94; CG/5425/95; DMG vol 10 para 60063

4. The amount of benefit

16 Sch 4 SSCBA 1992
17 s70(7) SSCBA 1992

6. **Claims and backdating**
18 Reg 4(1) SS(C&P) Regs
19 Reg 6(1)(a) SS(C&P) Regs
20 Reg 6(1)(b) SS(C&P) Regs
21 Reg 9(1) and Sch 1 SS(C&P) Regs
22 R(A) 3/81
23 Reg 13 SS(C&P) Regs
24 Reg 6(16)-(18) SS(C&P) Regs
25 Reg 6(19)-(22) SS(C&P) Regs

7. **Getting paid**
26 Reg 21 SS(C&P) Regs
27 Reg 22(1) SS(C&P) Regs
28 Reg 22(3) and Sch 6 SS(C&P) Regs
29 Reg 17 SS(C&P) Regs
30 s70(1A) SSCBA 1992

9. **Tax, tax credits and other benefits**
31 ss660, 661 and 676 IT(EP)A 2003
32 Reg 4ZA and Sch 1B para 4(b) IS Regs
33 Reg 4ZA and Sch 1B para 4(a) IS Regs; R(IS) 8/02
34 Sch 2 para 14ZA IS Regs and HB Regs; Sch 1 para 16 CTB Regs; Sch 1 para 17 JSA Regs
35 Reg 40 IS Regs; reg 33 HB Regs; reg 24 CTB Regs; reg 103 JSA Regs

Chapter 5

Child benefit

This chapter contains the rules about child benefit. It covers:

Child benefit is a benefit paid to people who are responsible for a child. If you qualify for it, child benefit is paid for each child for whom you are responsible, with a higher amount paid for your eldest eligible child. You do not have to be a parent of a child to qualify for child benefit for her/him and the child does not necessarily have to live with you. It is not necessary to have paid national insurance contributions to qualify for child benefit and your entitlement to child benefit is not affected by any income or savings that you have.

Although it has now been abolished, some lone parents are still entitled to a higher lone parent rate of child benefit (see p95).

The Revenue is responsible for the administration of child benefit.

Disability living allowance, child tax credit and guardian's allowance are also available for children (see Chapters 7 and 8).

Changes in 2006

The Government is proposing to change the rules on entitlement to child benefit for young people aged 16 or over from 10 April 2006.[1] At the time of writing it was proposed that child benefit for a young person will be paid until the 31 August after her/his 16th birthday, unless s/he is in either:

– full-time non-advanced education at a school or college, when entitlement will continue until s/he finishes that education or until s/he reaches the age of 20, if that happens earlier (but you will only qualify for child benefit for a young person between 19 and 20 if s/he began the course before reaching 19); *or*

– approved training which has not been provided through an employer, when entitlement will continue until the training ends or until s/he reaches 20, if that happens earlier (as long as that training was started before s/he was 19).

These new rules will not apply to young people who are 19 before 10 April 2006. See CPAG's *Welfare Rights Bulletin* for updates.

1. Who can claim child benefit

You qualify for child benefit for a child if:[2]

- s/he counts as a child for child benefit purposes. This means that s/he must be:[3]
  - under 16; *or*
  - 16 or over but under 19 and receiving full-time non-advanced education (see below and p87); *or*
  - aged 16 or over but under 18 and have ceased full-time education but still be within the 'extension period' (see p88); *and*
- you are responsible for the child *either* because:
  - the child lives with you (see p90); *or*
  - you contribute to the cost of supporting the child (see p91) at a rate of at least the amount of child benefit for that child; *and*
- you have priority over other potential claimants (see p92); *and*
- you and the child satisfy the residence conditions (see p699); *and*
- you are not subject to immigration control (see p654).

Child benefit may not immediately stop once a child reaches 16 or leaves full-time non-advanced education. See p88 for when child benefit stops. See p94 for details of when child benefit will not be paid.

There are some groups of claimants and children to whom special rules apply (see p97). If your child has died, see p104.

16–19 and in full-time non-advanced education

If your child is under 16 the kind of education s/he receives is not relevant to your entitlement to child benefit for her/him.

If your child is 16 or over but under 19 you can qualify for child benefit for her/him if s/he is:

- attending a full-time course of non-advanced education (see p87) at a recognised educational establishment; *or*
- attending a full-time course of non-advanced education elsewhere (but see p87), if a decision maker recognises the education.

Recognised educational establishment

A 'recognised educational establishment' is a school, college or university or somewhere comparable.

A course at a recognised educational establishment counts as full time if it is for more than 12 hours a week during term time, including instruction, tuition, supervised study, exams, practical work and experiments or projects provided for in the curriculum, but excluding meal breaks and unsupervised study.[4] If your child has finished a course but is enrolled on and starts another, s/he can still be considered to be in full-time education during any normal holiday between the two courses.

'Supervised' study requires the close proximity of a teacher or tutor to enforce discipline and provide encouragement and help.[5]

Education elsewhere

The above definition of full-time education only applies to a course at a recognised educational establishment. The meaning of full time is not defined if the education is provided elsewhere. In these circumstances 'full time' should be given its natural and ordinary meaning and it may be possible to argue that unsupervised, as well as supervised, study should be counted when assessing whether such a course is full time.

If a child of 16 or over could reasonably be expected to attend a recognised educational establishment, but is being educated elsewhere (such as at home), the decision maker may only recognise the education if s/he is satisfied that the education was being provided in the same way immediately before the child reached 16.[6]

Non-advanced education

Once your child reaches 16 you can still receive child benefit for her/him if s/he is undertaking a full-time course of education which is non-advanced. The main examples of advanced and non-advanced courses[7] are set out below and on p88. There may be others.

Non-advanced courses	*Advanced courses*
GCSEs	a university degree
A-levels	NVQ level 4
NVQ level 3 and below	Higher National Diploma (HND)
SVQ level 3 and below	Diploma of Higher Education
Ordinary National Diploma (OND)	a teaching qualification
Scottish National Qualifications (higher or advanced higher level)	Scottish Vocational Education Council Higher National Diploma
National Certifcate of Edexcel	Business & Technician Education Council Higher National Diploma

Scottish Vocational Education Council
National Certificate
Business & Technician Education Council
Diploma

Interruption of education

If your child's education is interrupted, her/his absence from her/his studies can be ignored for up to six months if it is found to be 'reasonable' in the circumstances. In practical terms this means that your child can still be considered to be in full-time education. An interruption to your child's education may be ignored indefinitely if it is caused by your child having a physical or mental illness or disability and the length of the absence is found to be reasonable given the circumstances.[8]

However, if your child starts, or is likely to start, a training course for which a training allowance is paid, or a course of education connected to her/his employment after the interruption in her/his education, the interruption cannot be ignored.[9] In these circumstances your child would no longer be considered to be in full-time education.

If your child leaves full-time non-advanced education but returns to it after a period of work or unemployment, child benefit becomes payable again until your child is 19 years old or until s/he leaves full-time education again.

The extension period

If a child is 16 or over but under 18 child benefit can continue to be paid during an **'extension period'** if s/he:[10]

- is registered as available for work or training with the Careers Service or Connexions Service; *and*
- is not working for 24 hours a week or more (unless the work is not done for payment or in expectation of payment); *and*
- is not in full-time education; *and*
- is not on a training scheme for young people for which s/he receives a training allowance.

Child benefit can only be paid during the extension period if it was payable immediately before the extension period started and you apply in writing.[11] See p90 for details of when the extension period ends and see p94 for circumstances when child benefit will not be paid.

When child benefit stops

Payment of child benefit may not stop immediately your child reaches 16 or leaves full-time non-advanced education. As long as you continue to meet the normal qualifying conditions for child benefit and you do not stop being entitled to child benefit for one of the reasons described on p94, child benefit will continue to be paid until the date the young person stops counting as a child. This depends on when s/he reaches 19, when s/he leaves full-time non-advanced education, or when her/his child benefit extension period ends.

Reaching 19

If your child is still in full-time non-advanced education when s/he reaches 19, your child benefit will stop from the first child benefit payday on or after s/he reaches 19.[12]

Leaving full-time non-advanced education

If your child leaves full-time non-advanced education before reaching 19, unless the rules allowing payment during an extension period apply (see p88), the general rule is that you will stop receiving child benefit for her/him:[13]

- if s/he left school before reaching the end of compulsory school age (the date that s/he is legally allowed to finish her/his education – see below), on the first 'terminal date' (see below) which falls after the date her/his compulsory school age ends; *or*
- if s/he left full-time non-advanced education after the end of compulsory school age, on the first 'terminal date' which falls after the date s/he left.

However, if your child has not reached 16 on the relevant terminal date then child benefit will stop from the first child benefit payday on or after s/he reaches 16.

The first **'terminal date'** is the Sunday after the:

- first Monday in January; *or*
- first Monday after Easter Monday; *or*
- first Monday in September.

A child who will return to sit an external examination is treated as still being at the school or college until the date of the last exam.[14] See the table on p90 for forthcoming terminal dates that may apply to your child.

In England and Wales, **compulsory school age** ends on the last Friday in June in the school year in which the child reaches 16.

In Scotland, if the child reaches the age of 16 between:

- 1 March 2005 and 30 September 2005, compulsory school age ends on 31 May 2005;
- 1 October 2005 and 28 February 2006, it ends on the first day of the Christmas holiday if the child is attending school, otherwise 21 December 2005;
- 1 March 2006 and 30 September 2006, it ends on 31 May 2006.

End of the extension period

If you are entitled to child benefit under the rules allowing payment during an extension period (see p88) child benefit will stop either on the date the extension period ends,[15] or, if your child reaches 18 during the extension period, from the first child benefit payday on or after s/he reaches 18.[16]

If your child reaches the end of compulsory school age or leaves school between (see p88):	*child benefit is paid until the terminal date (but see p89):*	*the extension period is:*
06.09.04 – 02.01.05	09.01.05	10.01.05 – 03.04.05
03.01.05 – 03.04.05	10.04.05	11.04.05 – 03.07.05
04.04.05 – 04.09.05	11.09.05	12.09.05 – 01.01.06
05.09.05 – 01.01.06	08.01.06	09.01.06 – 02.04.06
02.01.06 – 23.04.06	30.04.06	01.05.06 – 23.07.06
24.04.06 – 03.09.06	10.09.06	11.09.06 – 31.12.06

Responsible for a child

You are only entitled to child benefit for a child if you are responsible for her/him. You count as responsible for a child in any week in which:[17]

- you have the child living with you (see below) *or*
- you contribute to the cost of providing for the child (see p91).

A child 'living with' you

To be living with you, the child 'must live in the same house or other residence as [you] and also be carrying on there with [you] a settled course of daily living'.[18] This does not mean the same as 'residing together' or 'presence under the same roof'.[19] A child may be 'living with' you even while away. There are special rules if your child is in care or being looked after by a local authority (see p97).

Absence from home

If the child is absent from home, s/he is still treated as living with you as long as s/he has not been away for more than 56 days in the last 16 weeks.[20] In calculating whether a child has been absent from home for 56 days, certain days of absence are ignored. These are days when the child is away only for the purpose of:

- receiving full-time education at a recognised educational establishment, such as a boarding school;[21] *or*
- staying in certain forms of residential accommodation, if this is only necessary because of a disability which the child has or because her/his health would be 'significantly impaired or further impaired' if s/he was not staying in the accommodation (but see p91);[22] *or*
- receiving inpatient treatment at a hospital or similar institution (but see p91).

In the latter two situations a maximum of 12 weeks' absence can be ignored, unless you are regularly incurring expenditure in respect of the child, when the period of absence can be ignored indefinitely.[23] (As long as you are making visits, or giving the child pocket money, this condition is likely to be satisfied.) Two or more periods in hospital or residential accommodation separated by 28 days or less are treated as one in calculating the 12-week period.

If the child's absence is not solely for one of the three reasons listed on p90 her/his days of absence cannot be ignored and s/he will no longer be considered to be living with you if s/he has been away for more than 56 days in the last 16 weeks.

However, even if a child is not living with you, you may still qualify for child benefit for her/him if you are contributing to the child's maintenance.

See p699 if your child is abroad.

Example

Amy's son was in hospital for 18 weeks, but she visited him regularly, taking him the food, drinks and comics that he liked. On being discharged he went to stay with his grandmother for a further nine weeks to convalesce before returning home. Amy is entitled to child benefit for her son for the whole time that he was in hospital. Although he was there for over 12 weeks Amy regularly incurred expenditure for him and so he is still treated as living with her for the time he was an inpatient. Amy continues to be entitled to child benefit for the first eight weeks of her son's stay with his grandmother. This is because he can be treated as still living with Amy when he has been absent for 56 days or less in the last 16 weeks. The period he was in hospital is ignored when calculating the 56-day period. Amy will be entitled to child benefit again on her son's return home.

Contributing to the cost of supporting a child

If a child is not living with you, you can still qualify for child benefit if you contribute to the cost of providing for her/him. To satisfy this condition you must contribute at least the amount of child benefit payable for the child (see p95).[24]

Contributions must be regular, although the odd hiccup may be ignored.[25] Payments in kind rather than cash may be accepted.[26] If a husband and wife are residing together, any contribution made by one may be treated as a contribution by the other.[27] Similarly, if you and another person (or persons) each contribute less than the amount of child benefit payable for the child, but your total contributions are at least equal to the amount of child benefit payable, one of you is treated as contributing the whole sum. If you do not agree on which one of you it is to be, the Revenue decides.[28] If you qualify for child benefit on this basis, once benefit has been awarded you alone must actually contribute at least the amount of child benefit paid for the child in order to continue to be entitled.

See p800 for the way the amount of contribution is calculated in difficult cases.

Priority between claimants

Potentially, it is often possible for more than one person to be entitled to child benefit for the same child – eg, when a child is living with one parent and maintained by the other. However, only one person can be awarded child benefit for a particular child. There is an order of priority which governs who receives child benefit when two or more people would otherwise be entitled.[29]

No one is entitled to child benefit without making a claim (see p99) and the priority rules do not apply unless at least two people have claimed child benefit for the same child and both of them would qualify for it.[30]

Then, claimants take priority in the following order:[31]

- a person with whom the child lives;
- a wife, where a husband and wife are residing together (see p93);
- a parent (this includes a step-parent and adoptive parent);[32]
- the mother, where the parents are unmarried and are residing together (see p93);
- in any other case, a person agreed by those entitled;
- if there is no agreement, a person selected by a decision maker at the Revenue (in which case there is no appeal against the decision[33] – but see p1221).

Even if the new claim carries priority over an existing claim, child benefit continues to be paid on the existing claim for the three weeks following the week in which the new claim is made, unless the existing claimant withdraws her/his claim prior to this.[34] In addition, even if your claim has priority you normally cannot receive child benefit for a period for which it has already been paid to someone else for the same child – see p103 for details.[35]

If you have claimed child benefit but you want someone who has equal priority to you, or who has lower priority than you, to receive child benefit for a child instead of you, you should write to the Child Benefit Office.[36]

The Revenue has a secure computer messaging service which allows you to make such requests over the internet (see p101).

It may be important to concede priority to a person looking after a child so that s/he can claim home responsibilities protection (see p842). Where the child's mother and father live together, for example, and the mother goes out to work while the father stays at home to look after the children, the father can protect his entitlement to retirement pension (see Chapter 19) by claiming child benefit. To enable him to do so the mother would have to write to the Child Benefit Office conceding her prior claim.

It may also be important to concede priority if the claimant with priority frequently travels abroad (see p98).

Separation and the priority rules

Problems can arise when there are competing child benefit claims for a child from a mother and father who have just separated. When the mother was receiving child benefit before the separation and the child continues to live with her, she continues to be entitled to child benefit. But if the mother was receiving child benefit before the separation and the child goes to live with the father, as long as he has made a valid claim for child benefit, his claim should have priority when any one of the following applies:[37]

- the mother either withdraws her child benefit claim or elects that he receive it instead of her; *or*
- the father and mother are no longer considered to be residing together. If their separation is permanent this should normally be from the date that they separate (see below); *or*
- the child is no longer treated as living with her/his mother (normally after the child has been away from her for 56 days, see p90).

However, in this situation, even if the father's claim has priority, the mother will continue to be entitled to child benefit instead of him for the three weeks following the week in which the father makes his claim, unless she either withdraws her claim before this, or she stops qualifying for child benefit for another reason. Also the father cannot receive child benefit for a period for which it has already been paid to the mother unless she pays it back or it has been formally claimed back from her by the Revenue and this decision is final or the time limit for appealing it has expired.[38]

Parents 'residing together'

It may be important to know whether a couple who are responsible for a child are 'residing together' (or 'residing with' each other)[39] because if they are and they are married, the wife's claim has priority over the husband's, and if they are not married the mother's claim has priority over the father's. Also, the question of whether you are residing with your partner may determine your entitlement to the higher rate of child benefit for lone parents if you come within one of the groups of people that are still able to receive this (see p95). The rules on whether a couple are residing together are not the same for child benefit as for other benefits.

Even if you are apart, if you are married, you and your spouse are treated as residing together if:

- the absence from each other is not likely to be permanent;[40] *or*
- the reason for the absence is only because one or both of you is receiving treatment as an inpatient at a hospital or a similar institution, whether this is likely to be temporary or permanent.[41]

Even if a married couple have not lived together, they can be treated as residing together if their absence from each other is not likely to be permanent.[42]

It is possible to be absent from your spouse while you are living under the same roof if you are maintaining separate households.[43]

If you and your child's other parent are not married but are apart, you are still considered to be residing together if your absence from each other is not likely to be permanent.[44]

When child benefit is not paid

You are not entitled to child benefit for a child if:

- s/he is married[45] or living with someone as husband and wife[46] (see p813) (unless the child is not living with her/his spouse or her/his spouse or partner is in full-time education. But a spouse or partner can never be the claimant even in these circumstances[47]); *or*
- s/he is 16 or over and working for 24 hours a week or more (if the work is done for payment or in expectation of payment);[48] *or*
- s/he is 16 or over but under 19 and in full-time education and s/he receives incapacity benefit (if this is paid on the basis of her/his incapacity for work in youth – see p267), severe disablement allowance (see Chapter 20), income support (see Chapter 13), income-based jobseeker's allowance (see Chapter 15), working tax credit (see Chapter 50) or child tax credit (see Chapter 49) in her/his own right;[49] *or*
- s/he has spent more than eight consecutive weeks in prison or other custody (but see p97);[50] *or*
- s/he has spent more than eight consecutive weeks in the care of the local authority (but see p97);[51] *or*
- s/he is 16 or over but under 19 and in full-time education and s/he is an employed trainee. A child in full-time education which is received because of her/his employment counts as an employed trainee unless it is likely that s/he will not receive any payment or financial support from her/his employer for a continuous period of at least six months (apart from money to cover the cost of books, equipment, tuition, exam fees and travelling expenses).[52]

2. The rules about your age

There is no upper or lower age limit for entitlement to child benefit.

3. Claiming for others

Child benefit can be claimed for each child for whom you are responsible. No increase in child benefit is paid for any other dependants that you have.

4. The amount of benefit

Child benefit is payable at the following weekly rates:[53]

	£pw
Eldest eligible child:	
Lone parent rate	17.55 (but see below)
Standard rate	17.00
Other children (each)	11.40

Entitlement to child benefit does not qualify you for national insurance (NI) credits. However, if you receive child benefit for a child aged under 16 throughout a tax year (or, in some circumstances, for at least nine months in a tax year) you will qualify for home responsibilities protection for that tax year. This protects your NI contribution record for pension purposes (see p842).

Lone parent rate of child benefit

The lone parent rate of child benefit, which replaced the former one parent benefit in April 1997, was abolished from 6 July 1998. However, you may still be able to receive the lone parent rate of child benefit if you satisfy the conditions for it (see p96) and:[54]

- you have been getting the lone parent rate of child benefit continuously since at least 5 July 1998; *or*
- although you did not actually receive the lone parent rate on 5 July 1998, you were later paid the lone parent rate for the week including 5 July 1998 in one of the circumstances described on p78 of the 2002/2003 edition of this *Handbook; or*
- you were not receiving the lone parent rate of child benefit on 5 July 1998 because on that date you were receiving *either*:[55]
  - a child's special allowance (a benefit now only paid to women who were entitled to it before 6 April 1987); *or*
  - an increase in widowed mother's allowance, invalid care allowance (now called carer's allowance), disablement pension or Category A, B or C retirement pension for a dependent child (see p798); *or*
  - a child's allowance under the industrial death benefits scheme; *or*
  - an allowance under the war pension scheme for a child because of the death of a person due to service or war injury; *and*

  you apply for the lone parent rate of child benefit within one month of payment of any of the above benefits stopping; *or*
- you were receiving child benefit on 5 July 1998 (but not the lone parent rate of child benefit); *and*

- you stopped receiving income support (IS) or income-based jobseeker's allowance (JSA) because you started paid work; *and*
- on the date that you last received IS or income-based JSA your benefit included *either:*
  - the higher rate of the family premium paid to lone parents (see p885); *or*
  - a pensioner premium, an enhanced pensioner premium, higher pensioner premium (see p890) or a disability premium (see p886), but only if you were a lone parent on 5 April 1998 and your benefit included one of those premiums or the higher rate of the family premium paid to lone parents on 5 April 1998; *and*
- you apply for the lone parent rate of child benefit within a month of your IS or income-based JSA stopping; *and*
- it is the first time you have applied for a review of your child benefit since 5 July 1998.

Note: The last of the above routes for qualifying for the lone parent rate of child benefit has been limited by the introduction of pension credit (PC – see Chapter 18) and child tax credit (CTC – see Chapter 49). It is now not possible for a lone parent to receive any of the pensioner premiums within her/his IS (as people aged 60 or over cannot qualify for IS) and only men aged 60–64 can qualify for a pensioner (or higher pensioner) premium within their income-based JSA (as women aged 60 or over cannot qualify for JSA). Also, lone parents receiving the higher rate of the family premium within their IS or income-based JSA will, at some time after 6 April 2004, be automatically awarded CTC, at which point all payments for children within their IS or income-based JSA (including the higher rate of the family premium) will stop.

If you do qualify for the lone parent rate of child benefit you will continue to receive it until you no longer satisfy the qualifying conditions for it or until, as a result of the Government's uprating of child benefit, the standard rate of child benefit for the oldest eligible child equals the lone parent rate.

The lone parent rate of child benefit can only be paid for the eldest eligible child if the child is living with you (see p90) *and if either:*[56]

- you are not married; *or*
- you are married but do not 'reside with' (see p93) your spouse; *and in either case*
- you are not 'living with' (see p813) someone as if you were married.

If you do not qualify for the lone parent rate of child benefit, you will get the standard rate of child benefit for your eldest eligible child (ie, £17 a week).

Although increases in non-means-tested benefits for children have been abolished from 6 April 2003, some people will continue to receive them (see p798). If you are receiving an increase in your retirement pension, widowed parent's allowance, widowed mother's allowance or carer's allowance for a child, you will not qualify for the lone parent rate of child benefit for the same child.

Instead you will receive the standard rate of child benefit for the child (see p95).[57] See p1104 if you receive an increase in another benefit for a child for whom you receive the lone parent rate of child benefit.

5. Special rules for special groups

There are some groups of claimants to whom special rules apply. These are covered below and in Chapters 25, 26 and 28. Special rules apply to:

- children being looked after by a local authority or in prison or detention (see below);
- children in hospital (see p715);
- people who go abroad frequently (see p98);
- children who go or come from abroad (see pp688 and 699);
- people subject to immigration control (see p653);
- people in prison (see p732).

Prison, detention or looked after by the local authority

If a child is away from home and, for at least one day a week in the last eight consecutive weeks, is *either*:[58]

- in the care of a local authority and is being provided with accommodation under the Children Act 1989 or the Children (Scotland) Act 1995 and at least part of the cost of either the accommodation or the child's maintenance is being paid out of local authority or public funds (but see below); *or*
- subject to a supervision requirement and residing in residential accommodation under the Social Work (Scotland) Act 1968; *or*
- in prison or another form of detention such as a detention centre, borstal, or young offenders' institution,

child benefit is not usually payable for her/him after the eight-week period.[59]

This rule does not apply if the child is placed in accommodation by the local authority because of a disability which s/he has, or on the grounds that her/his health would be significantly impaired or further impaired were s/he not in the accommodation. In these circumstances see p90.

There are also some other exceptions to this rule.

- As child benefit only stops after the child has been in the care of the local authority or in prison for at least one day a week in the last eight consecutive weeks, if the child comes out of care or prison for at least a week (ie, from Monday to Sunday), the eight-week period should start again if s/he is subsequently placed in care or detained once more.
- You can continue to get child benefit after the first eight weeks as long as the child 'ordinarily' lives with you for at least one whole day each week (which,

in practice means at least two nights – see below) even if s/he is not actually at home in that particular week.[60]

- After the first eight weeks' absence, even if the child remains in detention or in the care of the local authority and does not 'ordinarily' live with you for at least one day a week, you will still qualify for child benefit when the child comes to stay with you if s/he comes to stay for a week or more.[61]
- If the child is detained in a hospital or a similar institution because of mental health problems you continue to be entitled to child benefit for her/him in the circumstances described on p718 unless s/he was taken there from prison or another place of detention and is still within the term of her/his sentence.[62]
- If the child has been detained in custody but at the conclusion of criminal proceedings is not sentenced to a term of imprisonment or detention, you are entitled to child benefit for her/him for the period of her/his earlier detention.[63]

A **'week'** means seven days beginning with a Monday.[64] A **'day'** means from midnight to midnight.[65] Because the child must live with you 'throughout' the day,[66] this means that in practice s/he has to stay with you for two nights to be regarded as living with you for one day.

The requirement that a child 'actually' be living with you is regarded very strictly, and even one night's absence by a child can result in a loss of benefit. On the other hand, a brief absence by you for two nights or so may be regarded less severely.[67] This is not a problem if the child 'ordinarily' lives with you at least one day a week because then it does not matter if the child is away during any particular week.

Fostering and adoption

Even if you qualify for child benefit under the rules on pp97–98, you cannot receive it if, for any day in a week, the local authority has arranged for the child to be boarded out with you under placement, looking after or fostering arrangements and the local authority is paying you an allowance towards the cost of the child's accommodation or maintenance.[68] Also, child benefit is not paid to anyone for a child who has been placed for adoption in the house of her/his prospective adopters if the adopters are receiving payments from the local authority for the child's accommodation or maintenance, unless the child has been placed with you for adoption and you were entitled to child benefit before 6 April 1987.[69]

Your entitlement to child benefit is not affected if you are looking after a child under private fostering arrangements.

People who go abroad frequently

One of the residence conditions for child benefit is that you must normally be physically present in Great Britain to qualify for child benefit[70] (although temporary absences of up to eight weeks – or in some circumstances 12 weeks – are ignored – see p688). If you have a partner and you spend a lot of time out of the country but your partner does not, it may be advisable for your partner to claim child benefit even if s/he would not normally have priority (see p92). For more on the residence conditions and what happens if you or your child goes abroad, see p699.

6. Claims and backdating

To be entitled to child benefit you must make a claim for it.[71] The rules for claiming are explained in brief below. The more detailed rules are explained in Chapter 39. It may be possible to claim child benefit in advance (see p101) or to get your claim backdated (see p102).

Making a claim

A claim for child benefit must be made in writing on the correct form – a CH2 form, which can be obtained from the Child Benefit Office, any Revenue enquiry centre, the Revenue website (see Appendix 1) or from Jobcentre Plus offices. A decision maker at the Revenue has the discretion to accept a written claim which is not on the correct form if it is sufficient in the circumstances (see p1079).[72] Your claim should be sent to the Child Benefit Office (Washington), PO Box 1, Newcastle upon Tyne, NE88 1AA. Claims can also be taken or sent to a Revenue enquiry centre or a Jobcentre Plus office. Keep a copy of your claim in case queries arise.

You can also complete a child benefit claim form online and submit it to the Revenue via its website at www.ir.gov.uk[73] as long as the Revenue accepts this form of communication from you (see p101). The Revenue will usually still need to see an original copy of your child's birth certificate (see below).

If you wish, you may amend or withdraw your claim before it is assessed by writing to the Child Benefit Office.

For more details about making a claim see p1076.

Information to support your claim

When you claim child benefit you must satisfy what is known as the 'national insurance (NI) number requirement' (see p1083). This means that, in most cases, you must provide your NI number when making a claim for child benefit. You can also be asked to supply 'certificates, documents, information and evidence' considered relevant to your claim[74] such as the child's birth or adoption certificate.

The Revenue has a secure computer messaging service which allows you to submit some kinds of information (but not birth certificates) over the internet (see p101).

The Revenue will usually still need to see an original copy of your child's birth certificate, so you will either have to send this to the Child Benefit Office by post or take it to your local Revenue enquiry centre or Jobcentre Plus office.[75] If you have claimed child benefit over the internet (see p101) you will have been given a transaction number to identify your claim. You should include the transaction number when you submit your child's birth certificate.

If you are asked to provide evidence or documents which you do not have, ask what other evidence would be acceptable. Ask the Revenue to explain what is required and why and complain if you feel any requests for information are unreasonable.

Who should claim

You must normally make a claim for child benefit on your own behalf. However, child benefit can be claimed by another adult on your behalf if you are unable to act for yourself. This person is known as your 'appointee' (see p1075).

If someone else makes a claim for child benefit for the same child on their own behalf you will only be entitled to child benefit for that child if you have priority over the other claimant. See p92 for details of priority between claimants.

The date of your claim

The date of your claim is important as it determines the date from which you will be paid child benefit (see p102). The date of your claim is normally the date it is received at either the Child Benefit Office, a Revenue enquiry centre or a Jobcentre Plus office.[76] If you submit your claim online via the Revenue website (see p101), then the date of your claim will normally be the date it is received by the Revenue, although a decision maker has the discretion to treat it as having been received on an earlier or later day than this. If the claim you submit is incomplete or not on the correct form you may be asked to provide further information or to complete the correct form. As long as this additional information or form is submitted within a month of it being sent back to you (or longer if the decision maker thinks that the delay is reasonable), your claim is treated as being made on the date that the initial claim was received at one of the above offices.[77]

In some circumstances you can claim before you qualify for child benefit (see p101), or the date of your claim can be backdated (see p102).

If you claim the wrong benefit

The decision maker has the discretion to treat a claim for guardian's allowance (see Chapter 8) as a claim for child benefit for the same child.[78] If, before 7 April 2003, you claimed maternity allowance (as long as this was claimed after your baby was born) or an increase in incapacity benefit (IB), widowed mother's allowance, widowed parent's allowance, retirement pension, severe disablement allowance (SDA), or carer's allowance (CA) for a child dependant the decision maker may also treat this as a claim for child benefit for the same child. Although increases in non-means-tested benefits for children have been abolished from 6

April 2003, some people will continue to receive them (see p798). If your claim for one of the benefits on p100 is accepted as a claim for child benefit, your claim can be backdated for up to three months before the date you claimed that benefit, if you satisfy the qualifying conditions for child benefit over that period. This may allow you to get your claim for child benefit backdated for more than the normal three months.

See p1084 for further details of interchanging claims in this way.

Claiming in advance

You cannot claim child benefit before a child is born because you will not know the precise date of birth. In other situations you can claim up to three months before you expect to be entitled to benefit – eg, when a child is returning from care.[79]

How your claim is dealt with

Your claim is dealt with by the Child Benefit Office and queries about your claim should be made to that office.

You may be able to claim an interim payment while waiting for a decision on your claim (see p1108) or claim means-tested benefits or tax credits if your income is low (see p105).

See p1091 for more information about the processing of claims.

Using the internet

As well as sending claims and information by post, in certain circumstances you may use the internet to:

- make a claim for child benefit;
- inform the Revenue of a change in your circumstances;
- send or receive messages from the Child Benefit Office using their secure computer messaging service.

In many circumstances the decision maker has the power not to accept the information or a claim from you when it is sent via the internet, but as long as you submit the information or claim via the Revenue's website (rather than by email), using the forms on the site when appropriate, and follow the procedure given on the website for submitting the information or claim, this would be unusual.

The intention of the Revenue's secure computer messaging service is to allow you to send any written communication about your child benefit claim (or guardian's allowance claim, if you receive it – see Chapter 8) to the Revenue over the internet and to receive correspondence from it over the internet, if you agree to this. To start using the secure messaging service, you will first need to register on the 'Government Gateway' website (www.gateway.gov.uk) in order to obtain a user ID number and an activation PIN number. These numbers will be sent to you by post. You must use the activation PIN number the first time you use the secure messaging service on the Revenue's website (www.ir.gov.uk and follow the links for child benefit), and after that you will only need to quote your user ID number and a password that you have chosen, each time you wish to use the service.

Certain information will not be accepted via the internet, such as birth certificates (see p99).

Backdating your claim

You should make a claim for child benefit within three months of becoming entitled to it. If you claim late, you can only receive up to three months' arrears of benefit (although there are special rules if you were getting child benefit and move between Great Britain and Northern Ireland or if you have been recognised as a refugee – see p669).[80] You do not have to show any reason why your claim was late. However, if someone else who is also entitled to child benefit for the same child has already been receiving it, you will not be entitled to arrears. Instead, if your claim takes priority (see p92), you will be paid child benefit from the fourth week after the week in which you claim, unless the other person withdraws her/his claim prior to this.[81]

If you might have qualified for child benefit earlier but did not claim because you were given the wrong information or misled by the Department for Work and Pensions or the Revenue you could:

- ask for an ex gratia payment (see p1304); *or*
- complain to the Ombudsman via your MP (see p1302).

If you have claimed guardian's allowance, or before 7 April 2003 you claimed maternity allowance (if this was claimed after your baby was born), or you claimed an increase in IB, widowed mother's allowance, widowed parent's allowance, retirement pension, SDA, or CA (previously invalid care allowance) for a child dependant instead of child benefit for the same child, your claim for one of these benefits may be treated as a claim for child benefit – see p100.

See p1086 for more details about the backdating of claims.

7. Getting paid

Child benefit is a weekly benefit, which means that it cannot be paid for periods of less than a week. If you qualify for child benefit, your benefit will be paid from the Monday after the date of your claim (see p100).[82] However, if the date of your claim is a Monday it is arguable that payment should actually begin from that day. As your date of claim can be backdated for up to three months, if you claim within three months of your child's birth and you satisfy the qualifying conditions, child benefit will normally be paid from the Monday after your child was born.[83]

If you are making a claim for child benefit and someone else who is also entitled to child benefit for the same child is already receiving it, you will only receive child benefit if your claim has priority over that of the existing claimant's (see p92). In these circumstances, your benefit starts from the beginning of the fourth week after the week in which you claim, unless the existing claimant withdraws her/his claim prior to this. However, even if your claim has priority you cannot receive child benefit for a period for which it has already been paid to someone else for the same child, unless that person pays it back to the Revenue, or the Revenue has formally claimed it back from her/him and this decision is final or the time limit for appealing it has run out.[84]

Child benefit is normally paid by direct credit transfer into your bank account (or similar account). If you are unable to open or manage an account, payment can be made by cheque. Such cheques are sent to your home address and can be paid into an account or cashed at the post office (see p1099 for details).[85]

Although the decision maker has discretion to choose any day of the week as your normal payday, child benefit is generally paid every four weeks on a Monday (unless the decision maker has arranged for you to be paid on a Tuesday) for three weeks in arrears and one week in advance.[86] Weekly payments of child benefit can be made only if:

- you were receiving child benefit before 15 March 1982 and have been receiving it continuously since then and you applied in writing before, or within the 26 weeks after, your first four-weekly payment[87] (or if you were absent from Great Britain on 15 March 1982 because you or your partner were a serving member of the Forces, you applied in writing within 26 weeks of the first week in which child benefit was payable following your return[88]); *or*
- you are a lone parent;[89] *or*
- you or your spouse (or the person with whom you are living as husband and wife) are entitled to income-based jobseeker's allowance or income support (see Chapters 15 and 13);[90] *or*
- the decision maker is satisfied that four-weekly payment 'is causing hardship'.[91]

If you are in one of these categories, you need to inform the Revenue in writing that you want to receive the benefit weekly.

Payment can also be made to someone else on your behalf – called your 'appointee' (see p1075) if you are unable to act for yourself.

Alternatively, if you reside with your partner the Child Benefit Office can arrange for your child benefit to be made payable either to you or to your partner on your behalf.[92] However, if you are also receiving guardian's allowance and have asked the Revenue not to make your guardian's allowance payable to your partner, your child benefit will not be payable to your partner either.[93]

If your entitlement to child benefit ends, payment of benefit will continue up to, but not including, the following payday.[94] However, if your entitlement ends on your normal payday your benefit will be paid up to, but not including, that day. If a benefit cheque is lost or stolen, see p1104. If payment of your child benefit is suspended, see p1105.

Delays and complaints

If payment of your child benefit is delayed, you might be able to get an interim payment. See p1108 for further details.

If you experience delays, or wish to complain about how your claim has been dealt with, see Chapter 47. You might be able to claim compensation (see p1304).

Change of circumstances

It is your duty to report any change in your circumstances which might affect your right to, the payment of or the amount of your benefit, such as when your child leaves school or college.[95] You should do this promptly either by writing to, or speaking to someone in, the Child Benefit Office, a Revenue enquiry centre or your local Jobcentre Plus office. If you do not promptly report any such change, any resulting overpayment may be recoverable from you (see Chapter 41). If you are considered deliberately to have acted falsely or dishonestly, you may also be guilty of an offence (see Chapter 42). If you report a change of circumstances verbally you should make a note of the time and date of your conversation, and the name of the person you informed. It is also advisable to confirm your conversation in writing, keeping a copy of your letter in case problems arise.

You can also inform the Revenue of changes in your circumstances via its website (see Appendix 1), as long as the Revenue accept this form of communication from you (see p101).[96]

Child benefit is normally awarded for an indefinite period (unless your circumstances are likely to change shortly after the award).[97] In order for payment of child benefit to be stopped or adjusted the decision on your entitlement must first be revised or superseded (see Chapter 43).[98] If, following a change in your circumstances the decision on your claim is superseded and your entitlement to benefit is affected, the date from which the new decision takes effect depends on whether or not it is advantageous to you and whether you reported the change in time (see p1204 for further details).

If your child dies

If your child dies and you were entitled to child benefit for her/him in the week in which s/he died (or you would have been had s/he not died in the same week that s/he was born), child benefit will continue to be paid for a period of eight weeks, unless s/he would have reached 19 in that period, when it will be paid until the Monday after s/he would have reached 19. If it was your spouse or partner who was getting child benefit for the child and s/he also dies, you will be entitled to child benefit for the eight-week period. This only applies if you were living with your spouse or partner at the time s/he died. In this context partner means someone that you were living with as husband and wife.[99]

Overpayments and fraud

If you are overpaid child benefit, you might have to repay it. The rules on overpayments are covered in Chapter 41.

If you have been accused of fraud, see Chapter 42.

8. Challenging a child benefit decision

You can apply for a revision or supersession of a child benefit decision, or appeal against it (see Chapters 43 and 44). The advice given there applies equally to child benefit. Certain decisions – such as who should receive child benefit when two people, whose claims have equal priority, cannot agree (see p92) – cannot be appealed. However, you may ask for such decisions to be revised or superseded (see p1221).[100]

9. Tax, tax credits and other benefits

Child benefit is not taxable.[101]

Tax credits

If your income is low you may qualify for working tax credit (if you or your partner, if you have one, are in full-time paid work – see p1342) and child tax credit (CTC – see Chapter 48). Child benefit is ignored when calculating your entitlement to tax credits.[102]

Means-tested benefits

If you have a low income you may be entitled to means-tested benefits which can be paid in addition to child benefit. From 6 April 2004, if you make a new claim for income support (IS) or income-based jobseeker's allowance (JSA), or if you have been awarded CTC, any child benefit you receive will be ignored when calculating your entitlement to IS and income-based JSA.[103] If you have been getting IS or income-based JSA since before 6 April 2004 with an amount for a child included in your claim, and have not yet been awarded CTC, your child benefit will be taken into account in full as income when calculating your entitlement to IS or income-based JSA. However, if you get child benefit for a child under one year old and still get IS or income-based JSA for the child rather than CTC, £10.50 of your child benefit is ignored when calculating your entitlement to IS or income-based JSA (even if you have more than one child).[104]

Child benefit is ignored when calculating entitlement to pension credit.[105]

If you or your partner are getting IS, income-based JSA or the guarantee credit of pension credit (PC) you will be passported on to the maximum rate of housing benefit (HB – see Chapter 10) and council tax benefit (CTB – see Chapter 6), and so your child benefit will not directly affect your entitlement to HB and CTB (see p206). If you or your partner are getting the savings credit of PC, child benefit is ignored when calculating your HB and CTB entitlement. If you or your partner are not getting IS or income-based JSA, your child benefit will be counted in full as income when calculating your entitlement to HB[106] and CTB[107] unless either of you are 60 or over, when it will be ignored.

Non-means-tested benefits

If you are entitled to another non-means-tested benefit, you may be receiving an increase in that benefit in respect of a child. Such increases for children were abolished on 6 April 2003, but some people will continue to be entitled to them (see p798). However, the increase is reduced if you also receive child benefit for that child paid at the rate for the eldest eligible child (ie, £17) – see p1104.

If you receive an increase in your incapacity benefit (IB) or severe disablement allowance (SDA) for a child and are entitled to the lone parent rate of child benefit for the same child (ie, £17.55), the increase in your IB or SDA will be reduced (see p1104).

If you receive an increase in your retirement pension, widowed parent's allowance, widowed mother's allowance or carer's allowance for a child you cannot receive the lone parent rate of child benefit for that child but instead will receive the standard rate of child benefit (see p95).

Your entitlement to any other non-means-tested benefit is not affected by your entitlement to child benefit.

Passports and other sources of help

If you are on a low income, you might be entitled to certain health service benefits, such as free prescriptions (see Chapter 9). You may also qualify for a social fund payment (see Chapters 21 and 22). If you are getting IS, income-based JSA or, in some circumstances, CTC, your child(ren) will qualify for free school meals (see p18).

Young people between the ages of 16 and 19 who are in non-advanced education may qualify for an educational maintenance allowance (EMA) or other financial help with their studies. Details of the EMA scheme in England are available in the leaflet 'Financial Help for Students' (DfES/0169/2004) available from the Department for Education and Skills (DfES) or from the DfES website (www.dfes.gov.uk/financialhelp). Details of the scheme in Wales are available from www.emawales.gov.uk and in Scotland are available from www.emascotland.com.

From 2005, the Government is introducing a child trust fund scheme.[108] Details of the scheme are published on the Revenue's website (www.ir.gov.uk).

Notes

1 Child Benefit Bill 2004; Draft Child Benefit (Definition of Qualifying Young Person) Regulations 2004

1. Who can claim child benefit

2 ss141, 143, 144, 146 and 146A SSCBA 1992
3 s142(1) and (2) SSCBA 1992
4 Reg 5 CB Regs
5 R(F) 1/93
6 s142(2) SSCBA 1992
7 Reg 1(2) CB Regs
8 Reg 6(1) CB Regs
9 Reg 6(2) CB Regs
10 Regs 8(1) and 9 CB Regs
11 Reg 8(1)(d) and (e) CB Regs
12 Reg 7(1) CB Regs
13 Reg 7 CB Regs
14 Reg 7(1) CB Regs
15 Reg 8(2) CB Regs
16 Reg 14 CB&GA(Admin) Regs
17 s143 SSCBA 1992
18 R(F) 2/81
19 R(F) 2/79
20 s143(2) SSCBA 1992
21 s143(3)(a) SSCBA 1992
22 s143(3)(c) SSCBA 1992; reg 2 CB Regs
23 s143(3)(b) and (c) and (4) SSCBA 1992; reg 3 CB Regs
24 s143(1)(b) SSCBA 1992
25 R(U) 14/62
26 R(U) 3/66
27 Reg 4(4) CB Regs
28 Reg 4 CB Regs
29 s144(3) and Sch 10 SSCBA 1992
30 s13(1) SSAA 1992
31 Sch 10 SSCBA 1992
32 s147(3) SSCBA 1992
33 Sch 2 para 4 SSA 1998
34 Sch 10 para 1(2) SSCBA 1992
35 s 13(2) SSAA 1992; reg 38 CB Regs
36 Regs 14 and 15 CB Regs
37 CF/1771/2003
38 Sch 10, para 1 SSCBA 1992; s13(2) SSAA 1992; reg 38 CB Regs
39 *Grove v Insurance Officer*, reported as an appendix to R(F) 4/85
40 Reg 34(a) CB Regs
41 Reg 34(b) CB Regs
42 R(F) 4/85
43 R(F) 3/81
44 Reg 34(a) CB Regs
45 Sch 9 para 3 SSCBA 1992
46 Reg 12 CB Regs
47 Regs 12(2)(a) and 13(a) CB Regs
48 Regs 1(2), 7(2) and 8(1)(b) CB Regs
49 Sch 9 para 5 SSCBA 1992; reg 10 CB Regs
50 Sch 9 para 1(a) SSCBA 1992; reg 16 CB Regs
51 Sch 9 para 1 SSCBA 1992; reg 16 CB Regs
52 Sch 9 para 2 SSCBA 1992; reg 11 CB Regs

4. The amount of benefit

53 Reg 2(1) CB&SS(FAR) Regs
54 Reg 4 CB&SS(FAR) Amdt Regs
55 Reg 3 CB&SS(FAR) Amdt Regs
56 Reg 2(2) CB&SS(FAR) Regs
57 Reg 2(4)(a) and (5) CB&SS(FAR) Regs

5. Special rules for special groups

58 Sch 9 para 1 SSCBA 1992; regs 16-18 CB Regs
59 Reg 16(1)(a) CB Regs
60 Reg 16(1)(b)(iv) CB Regs
61 Reg 16(1)(b)(i)-(iii) CB Regs
62 Reg 17(2)-(5) CB Regs
63 Regs 1(2) and 17(1) CB Regs

64 s147(1) SSCBA 1992
65 R(F) 3/85
66 Reg 16(2) CB Regs
67 R(F) 1/81
68 Reg 16(3) CB Regs
69 Reg 16(4) and (5) CB Regs; reg 8 CB(Amdt) Regs
70 s146(2) SSCBA 1992

6. **Claims and backdating**

71 s13 SSAA 1992
72 Reg 5 CB&GA(Admin) Regs
73 Reg 2 and Sch 2 CB&GA(Admin) Regs
74 Reg 7 CB&GA(Admin) Regs
75 Regs 3(2) and 5(5) CB&GA(AA) Regs
76 Reg 5(3) CB&GA(Admin) Regs
77 Reg 10 CB&GA(Admin) Regs
78 Reg 11 CB&GA(Admin) Regs
79 Reg 12 CB&GA(Admin) Regs
80 Reg 6 CB&GA(Admin) Regs
81 Sch 10 para 1(2) SSCBA 1992

7. **Getting paid**

82 Reg 13 CB&GA(Admin) Regs
83 s147 SSCBA 1992
84 sch 10, para 1 SSCBA 1992; s13(2) SSAA 1992; reg 38 CB Regs
85 Reg 17 CB&GA(Admin) Regs
86 Reg 18(2) CB&GA(Admin) Regs
87 Reg 20(1) and (2)(a) CB&GA(Admin) Regs
88 Reg 20(1) and (2)(b) CB&GA(Admin) Regs
89 Reg 19 CB&GA(Admin) Regs
90 Reg 19 CB&GA(Admin) Regs
91 Reg 18(3) CB&GA(Admin) Regs
92 Reg 34(1) CB&GA(Admin) Regs
93 Reg 34(2) CB&GA(Admin) Regs
94 Reg 14 CB&GA(Admin) Regs
95 Reg 23(4) CB&GA(Admin) Regs
96 Reg 2 and Sch 2 CB&GA(Admin) Regs
97 Reg 15 CB&GA(Admin) Regs
98 Reg 15 CB&GA(Admin) Regs
99 s145A SSCBA 1992; reg 20 CB Regs

8. **Challenging a child benefit decision**

100 s12(1) and Sch 2 SSA 1998; regs 9 and 13(2) CB&GA(DA) Regs

9. **Tax, tax credits and other benefits**

101 s677 Income Tax (Earnings and Pensions) Act 2003
102 Reg 7 TC(DCI) Regs
103 Sch 9 para 5B IS Regs; Sch 7 para 6B JSA Regs
104 Reg 40 IS Regs; reg 103 JSA Regs; regs 1, 7 and 8 SS(WTCCTC)(CA) Regs
105 Regs 9 and 15(1)(j) SPC Regs
106 Reg 33 HB Regs; regs 23 and 25 HB Regs as modified by regs 2 and 8 HB&CTB(SPC) Regs
107 Reg 24 CTB Regs; regs 15 and 17 CTB Regs as modified by regs 12 and 17 HB&CTB(SPC) Regs
108 Child Trust Funds Act 2004; Child Trust Funds Regulations 2004 No.1450

Chapter 6

Council tax benefit

This chapter covers:

Council tax benefit (CTB) is paid to people with a low income who pay council tax. It is paid whether or not the claimant is available for or in full-time paid work and may be paid in addition to other benefits and tax credits. CTB is paid by local authorities, although it is a national scheme and the rules are mainly determined by DWP regulations.

There are two types of CTB: **main CTB** and alternative maximum CTB, which is known as **second adult rebate**. If you are eligible for both, you are paid whichever is the higher.

You do not have to have paid national insurance contributions to qualify for CTB.

If you are entitled to income support (IS), income-based jobseeker's allowance (JSA) or the guarantee credit of pension credit, you automatically qualify for maximum CTB (see p114). Otherwise, your CTB is calculated using a special formula.

The rules for CTB are often the same as for housing benefit (HB – see Chapter 10). In this chapter, where the rules are the same or similar, reference is made to the chapter on HB. Footnotes in that chapter contain references to both the HB and CTB legislation where applicable.

See CPAG's *Council Tax Handbook* for further explanation of the rules relating to council tax liability, valuations, reductions, discounts and benefits.

If you are 60 or over

The CTB rules for people who are 60 or over who are not (and whose partners are not) getting IS or income-based JSA are different (and more generous) than those for other claimants. Where these are the same as for HB, see Chapter 10 for details.

If you turn 60, you should check to see if you qualify for CTB even if you did not do so before that age. The different rules for income, capital and applicable amounts are covered in other chapters, but a summary of the income and capital rules is given on p194.

1. Who can claim council tax benefit

Main council tax benefit

You qualify for main council tax benefit (CTB) if:[1]

- you are liable for council tax in respect of the home where you are 'resident' (see p112); *and*
- your income is low enough (see Chapter 38); *and*
- unless you or your partner are getting the guarantee credit of pension credit (PC), your savings and other capital are worth £16,000 or less (see Chapter 39). There is no capital limit if you or your partner are getting the guarantee credit of PC;[2] *and*
- you are not a full-time student (although there are certain limited exceptions – see p630). This rule does not apply if you are 60 or over and neither you nor your partner are getting IS or income-based JSA;[3] *and*
- you satisfy the habitual residence test (see p702); *and*
- you are not a 'person subject to immigration control' (see p654).

There are some groups of claimants to whom special rules apply (see p120).

Second adult rebate

Second adult rebate is designed to help you if you have certain other residents (referred to as second adults) in your home who do not share liability for council tax with you and who do not pay rent to you.

You qualify for a second adult rebate if:[4]

- you are liable for council tax in respect of the home where you are 'resident' (see p112); *and*
- you are the only person liable for the council tax on the home (with certain exceptions – see p111); *and*
- no one living in your home pays you rent (with certain exceptions – see p111); *and*
- you have one or more 'second adults' (see p111) living with you who are on a low income; *and*

- you satisfy the habitual residence test (see p702); *and*
- you are not a 'person subject to immigration control' (see p654).

Note: the whole of your income and capital is ignored when you claim second adult rebate. So you can get it even if *you* have a high income and/or capital worth more than £16,000.[5] For second adult rebate it does not matter if you are a student.

Second adult rebate is an alternative type of CTB that can be paid instead of, but not as well as, main CTB. Whenever you claim CTB the local authority must assess you for both types and award whichever is the greater.[6]

Who counts as a second adult

A **'second adult'** is someone who is resident with you. In practice, residents classified as second adults are mainly the same people as those treated as non-dependants for main CTB purposes (see p115). You must have one or more second adults residing with you to qualify for second adult rebate. Someone residing with you does *not* count as a second adult if:[7]

- s/he is aged under 18;[8] *or*
- s/he has what is known as a status discount – ie, s/he is ignored for council tax purposes.[9] For example, full-time students and people who are severely mentally impaired have status discounts; *or*
- s/he is your partner with whom you are jointly liable for council tax;[10] *or*
- s/he is jointly liable to pay the council tax on the dwelling with you – eg, because s/he is a joint owner or tenant with you. Although you cannot get second adult rebate for her/him, s/he can claim main CTB for her/his own share of the bill – see p115);[11] *or*
- s/he is residing with you and:[12]
  - you are living with at least one other person and all of you are jointly liable for council tax (eg, as joint owners or tenants); *and*
  - at least two of those of you who are jointly liable do *not* have status discounts.

If you are a member of a couple or polygamous marriage, no one who resides with you counts as a second adult, unless both you and your partner (or in the case of a polygamous marriage, at least two of the members) have status discounts.[13]

Residents liable to pay rent

You cannot qualify for second adult rebate if a second adult who resides with you is liable to pay rent to you in respect of her/his occupation of your home. Any people paying you rent who do not count as second adults are ignored for these purposes.[14] Some local authorities think you are not entitled to second adult rebate if *any* resident is liable to pay you rent. You should argue that if a person paying you rent does not come within the description of second adult, s/he does not prevent you receiving second adult rebate.

Liability to pay council tax

There is not sufficient space in this *Handbook* to describe the rules relating to the council tax itself. See CPAG's *Council Tax Handbook* for further information. If you are jointly liable to pay council tax this may affect the amount of main CTB or second adult rebate you receive (see pp115 and 120).

Where you are resident

For CTB purposes, you are a resident in the home where you have your 'sole or main residence'.[15] This is the same criterion as for liability for council tax, so any decision on your sole or main residence should be the same for CTB purposes. Your main residence is the property that a reasonable onlooker with knowledge of the facts would regard as your home.[16] A property can count as your sole or main residence even if you spend substantial periods of time away from it, if you consider it to be the main place where you live.[17] You can get CTB for your sole or main residence if you are on bail and have to live away from your home and no bail hostel place is available to you.

There are rules about temporary absence from your home which are similar to those for HB (see p202).

2. The rules about your age

You must be aged 18 or over to qualify for council tax benefit (CTB). If you are under 18 you cannot be liable for council tax, so you do not need to claim CTB.

If you are 60 or over and neither you nor your partner are getting income support or income-based jobseeker's allowance, different (more generous) CTB rules apply.

3. Claiming for others

You claim council tax benefit for your family. See Chapter 32 for who counts as your family.

4. The amount of benefit

Calculating main council tax benefit

The amount of main council tax benefit (CTB) you get depends on:

- your 'applicable amount' (see Chapter 35). This is made up of personal allowances and premiums for any special needs;
- your 'maximum CTB' (see p114); *and*
- how much income and capital you have (see Chapters 38 and 39).

If you do not qualify for CTB currently, you may qualify when:

- the benefit rates go up. Personal allowances and premiums are increased every April; *or*
- you or your partner turn 60. Your applicable amount is then higher. In addition, if neither you nor your partner are on income support (IS) or income-based jobseeker's allowance (JSA), the income and capital rules are more generous; *or*
- you or your partner turn 65. Your personal allowance is increased by the equivalent of the amount of the maximum savings credit, whether or not you receive this, so long as neither you nor your partner are on IS or income-based JSA.

In addition, if your income is too high for you to qualify for CTB currently, you might qualify once you or a member of your family becomes entitled to another benefit (a 'qualifying benefit'). See p121 for further information.

If you need extra financial assistance to meet your council tax, you might be entitled to discretionary housing payments (see p235).

Remember that if you:

- come off IS, income-based JSA, incapacity benefit or severe disablement allowance because of starting work or increasing your income from work, you may be entitled to an extended payment of CTB (see p63);
- come off IS or income-based JSA because you are moving onto pension credit (PC), you may be able to continue to receive CTB at the same rate for four weeks (see p123);
- have been incapable of work but move into work or training, you might count as a 'welfare to work' beneficiary (see p769). This means you retain entitlement to the disability or higher pensioner premium (see pp886 and 890) if you become incapable of work again within 52 weeks.

If you are on IS, income-based JSA or the guarantee credit of PC

Entitlement to IS, income-based JSA or the guarantee credit of PC acts as an automatic passport to maximum CTB (once you have made a claim for CTB) – see p114. You therefore do not need to work out applicable amounts, income or capital. CTB = maximum CTB.

For these purposes, you are treated as entitled to income-based JSA:[19]

- when you satisfy the conditions of entitlement but are not being paid it because of a sanction (see Chapter 16);
- on your waiting days (see p377); *and*

- when it is not paid because of the 'loss of benefit' rules (see p1169).

You continue to be passported to full CTB entitlement if your entitlement to IS or income-based JSA ceases because your help with housing costs no longer includes charges for support services (see p919).[20] This only applies if you were entitled to IS or income-based JSA on 31 March 2003 (or someone who was your partner on that date was entitled to one of those benefits) and entitlement ceased on or before 5 April 2003.

If you are not on IS, income-based JSA or the guarantee credit of PC

- Step one: Check that your capital is not too high (see Chapter 38).
- Step two: Work out your maximum CTB (see below).
- Step three: Work out your applicable amount (see Chapter 35).
- Step four: Work out your income (see Chapter 38 but also p630 if you are a student and p468 if you are getting the savings credit of PC).
- Step five: Calculate CTB:
  - If your income is **less than or equal to** your applicable amount, CTB = 'maximum CTB'.
  - If your income is **greater than** your applicable amount, work out the difference. CTB = 'maximum CTB' minus 20 per cent of the difference between your income and your applicable amount.

Maximum council tax benefit

Maximum CTB is your net weekly liability for council tax after any of the following reductions and discounts have been applied:[21]

- a disability reduction;
- a discount;
- transitional reduction;
- any non-dependant deductions (see p117).

Net weekly liability for council tax

Net weekly liability is assessed by dividing your annual council tax liability by the number of days in the financial year (365 or 366) and then multiplying this by seven.[22]

Example

Cara's net council tax liability is £490

Divide this by 365 = £1.342466

Multiply this by 7. Cara's net weekly liability = £9.397262

DWP guidance recommends that the figures should not be rounded until the final annual amount of CTB is worked out, and that calculations should usually be done to six decimal places.[23] When notifying you of your CTB a rounded figure can be specified.[24]

If you are jointly liable for council tax, see below.

Joint liability

If you are a member of a couple and are jointly liable for council tax, one of you must claim CTB for both of you.[25] If you are also jointly liable with one or more other residents, you can claim on a two-person share of the bill. See p811 for who counts as a couple.

If you are (or count as) a single person and are jointly liable for council tax, the local authority calculates your maximum CTB by dividing the total net liability for council tax by the number of liable people. Any liable person who is a student not entitled to CTB is ignored.[26]

Example

Ravi, Maxine and Bill share a flat. They are jointly liable for a net annual council tax bill of £600. £600 divided by 3 = £200. They can each make a separate claim for CTB on £200 liability. Ravi and Maxine become a couple. Either of them can make a claim for CTB on £400 liability (a two-person share), with Bill making a separate claim on £200 liability (a one-person share).

Bill becomes a full-time student and is therefore excluded from entitlement to CTB. Ravi and Maxine can now claim CTB on the full £600 liability.

Under the council tax rules, a person who is jointly and severally liable for council tax can be held responsible for the full amount of council tax due on the property while receiving CTB only on her/his share. Note, however, that students who share with non-students are not jointly and severally liable for council tax with the non-students.[27]

Deductions for non-dependants

If other people normally live with you in your home who are not part of your family for benefit purposes (see p809) and are not liable for council tax – they are called **'non-dependants'** – a set deduction is usually made from your CTB.[28] This is because it is assumed the non-dependant makes a contribution towards your outgoings, whether or not s/he does so. Examples of non-dependants are adult sons or daughters, or elderly relatives who share your home. You may therefore need to ask your non-dependant(s) for a contribution.

The rules for whether a person is a non-dependant are the same as for HB (see p211). However, the categories of people who are not non-dependants are slightly different.

People who are not non-dependants

The following people do *not* count as non-dependants, even if they normally live with you:[29]

- a member of your family for benefit purposes (see p809);
- if you are in a polygamous marriage, a partner of yours and any child or young person in your household (see p820) for which you or a partner is responsible;
- a child or young person living with you who is not a member of your household (see p813);
- someone who is employed by a charitable or voluntary organisation as a resident carer for you or your partner and who you pay for the service. This can also apply if a public body pays on your behalf;
- someone who is jointly liable to pay council tax in respect of your home;
- someone who is liable to pay rent on a commercial basis (see p199) to you or your partner. However, although no non-dependant deduction can be made for her/him, the rent s/he pays can count as your income (see p976).

If the person comes within the last two categories above, s/he can still be treated as your non-dependant if s/he falls within any of the following categories:[30]

- you or your partner are her/his landlord, s/he resides with you and *either* s/he is:
  - a close relative of you or your partner; *or*
  - the agreement to pay rent or council tax is not a commercial one. The meaning of these terms is the same as for HB (see p199);
- you or your partner are her/his landlord and the agreement to pay rent or council tax has been created to take advantage of the CTB scheme. This does not apply if s/he had a legitimate liability to pay you or your partner within the eight weeks prior to entering into the agreement.
  For the meaning of 'taking advantage' see p200, but remember that just because someone is taking advantage of the HB scheme does not mean that s/he is taking advantage of the CTB scheme. You should argue that the local authority should consider the two schemes separately;
- s/he is jointly liable with you for council tax on the home and within the last eight weeks was a non-dependant of one or more residents there, who were liable for the tax. This does not apply if you can persuade the local authority that the liability to pay council tax was not made to take advantage of the CTB scheme.

When no non-dependant deduction is made

The rules on when no non-dependant deduction is made are the same as for HB (see p213) except that:[31]

- all non-dependants on IS or income-based JSA are ignored and not just those under 25; *and*

- no deduction is made for the following people with what are known as status discounts:
  - people under 19 if child benefit is payable;
  - recent school and college-leavers under 20;
  - student nurses;
  - foreign language assistants;
  - apprentices;
  - people who are 'severely mentally impaired'(see below);
  - certain carers;
  - members of visiting armed forces, members of international headquarters and defence organisations and their dependants; *and*
  - foreign spouses or dependants of students;
- no non-dependant deduction is ever made for a full-time student – even if s/he works during the summer vacation.

A person counts as **'severely mentally impaired'** if a doctor has certified that s/he has a severe impairment of intelligence and social functioning which appears to be permanent.[32] S/he must also be entitled to a qualifying benefit.[33] See CPAG's *Council Tax Handbook* for further information.

The amount of deductions

Once it is established that you have one or more non-dependants, deductions are usually made for each non-dependant in your household. As for HB, the amount of the deduction depends on the gross weekly income of your non-dependant. For situations when no deduction is made, see above.

A deduction is made for every non-dependant living in your household except in the case of a non-dependant couple (see p118). The amounts are shown below.[34]

Circumstances of the non-dependant	*Deduction*
18 or over and in full-time paid work with a weekly gross income of:	
£322 or more	£6.95
£258–£321.99	£5.80
£150–£257.99	£4.60
Up to £150	£2.30
Others aged 18 or over (for whom a deduction is made)	£2.30

The income bands only apply to non-dependants in full-time paid work. See p213 for further information about income and Chapter 29 for what counts as full-time paid work. Remember:

- A non-dependant who is not in (or treated as in) full-time paid work does not attract the higher levels of deduction even if her/his income exceeds £150.

- If someone is getting IS or income-based JSA for more than three days in a benefit week, s/he does not count as in full-time paid work in that week. This means no deduction is made.[35]

As with HB, your CTB can be assessed using the income and capital of a non-dependant, instead of your own, if you are trying to take advantage of the CTB scheme (see p215).[36]

Only one deduction is made for a non-dependant couple (or the members of a polygamous marriage). The deduction made is the highest that would have been made if they were treated as individuals.[37] For the purpose of deciding which income band applies (see below), their joint income counts even if only one of them is in full-time paid work.[38]

If you share liability for the council tax with others, the amount of the non-dependant deduction is divided equally between you, even if the others are not claiming CTB.[39] However, if the local authority thinks that the non-dependant deduction only belongs to one of you, the whole deduction is made from that person's CTB. If you are a member of couple and share liability with someone, your CTB is reduced by two-thirds of the non-dependant deduction.

Discretionary housing payments

If you need extra financial assistance to meet your housing costs (including your council tax), you might be able to claim discretionary housing payments to top up your CTB. See p235 for further information.

Extra benefit for war pensioners

As for HB, the local authority has the power to pay extra CTB to people getting war disablement pension, war widow's or war widower's pension.[40] See p215 for further information.

Calculating second adult rebate

The amount of second adult rebate you get is a percentage of your gross council tax liability minus any reductions for disability. The percentages are:[41]

Income of second adult(s)	*Second adult rebate*
Second adult (or all second adults) on:	
IS/income-based JSA/PC	25 per cent
Second adult(s) total gross weekly income:	
up to £150	15 per cent
£150–£193.99	7.5 per cent
£194 or more	Nil

The maximum second adult rebate you can get is always 25 per cent of your council tax liability, even where you would have received a 50 per cent discount, or would have been exempt altogether, were it not for the presence of two or more second adults in your home.

Example

Liam is a student who lives alone in a home he owns, so he is exempt from paying council tax. His friend Brian who is on IS comes to lodge with him, so Liam is now liable for council tax. Liam claims second adult rebate. This is 25 per cent of his council tax liability.

Council tax liability used for a second adult rebate

Second adult rebate is based on your gross council tax liability, after any disability and transitional reductions have been applied.[42] Note that this is not the same figure as used for main CTB. However, the procedure for converting annual to weekly amounts is the same (see p114). Where you have received a discount it must be added back on to the net amount of council tax payable to arrive at the figure used in the second adult rebate calculation. This is only done for the purposes of the CTB calculation – you still receive your discount in practice.

Assessment of second adult income

To obtain a second adult rebate, you must give the local authority details of the gross income of any second adults living with you. Where there is more than one second adult, their combined gross income is used.[43]

Gross income includes the second adult's:

- earnings;
- non-earned income, including social security benefits;
- actual income from capital (as opposed to, for example, 'tariff income'). The capital itself is ignored.

Gross income does *not* include:

- any income of a second adult on IS, income-based JSA or PC;[44]
- any attendance allowance or disability living allowance;[45]
- certain payments from the MacFarlane Trusts, the Eileen Trust, the Skipton Fund, the Fund and the Independent Living Funds (see p973);[46]
- the income of any person with a status discount (see p111), except where that person has a partner who is not ignored for discount purposes (in which case the gross income of both partners, less disregarded income, is taken into account).[47]

A basic problem with second adult rebate is that it involves looking at the income of someone who may not always wish to give you that information. If you have difficulty establishing the income of your second adults you may find that the local authority automatically assumes the highest income and that you are not entitled to CTB. If you cannot persuade your second adults to give details of their income to you, they may be prepared to tell the local authority directly. Failing this, you could try finding out the going rate for the type of work they do, or social security benefits they receive, and ask the local authority to make a reasonable estimate based on that.

Second adult rebates and jointly liable claimants

In contrast to main CTB, where there is more than one resident liable for the council tax in your dwelling, any second adult rebate is always calculated on the (pre-discounted) liability for your dwelling as a whole. Unless you are jointly liable with your partner, every jointly liable person must make her/his own separate claim in order to get a share of the second adult rebate. Any second adult rebate is then split equally between all the jointly liable residents.[48] If you are jointly liable with your partner, one of you claims on behalf of both and receives the entire second adult rebate (or if you are sharing with other liable residents, a couple's share).[49]

Discretionary housing payments

You cannot claim discretionary housing payments to top up your second adult rebate unless you would have been entitled to CTB if you had not received a second adult rebate.[50] See p235 for further information.

5. Special rules for special groups

There are some groups of claimants to whom special rules apply. These are covered in Chapters 25, 26 and 28. Special rules apply to:

- people subject to immigration control (see p654);
- people in hospital (see p715);
- students (see p630);
- prisoners (see p731);
- people in care homes (see p725).

6. Claims and backdating

The rules for claiming council tax benefit (CTB) are the same as for housing benefit (HB). See p216 for full details, substituting CTB where it says HB. Note, however, that the Government says that to encourage people to claim CTB, it intends to send out claim forms automatically if you contact the DWP to claim pension credit. The different rules for CTB are covered below. Remember that:

- you can claim CTB even if you have already paid your council tax bill in advance;
- if you are in arrears with your council tax bill this does not affect your right to claim CTB. You may even be able to get your claim backdated for up to 52 weeks (see below and p221);
- if you want to claim discretionary housing payments, you must claim separately. See p236 for further information.

Claiming in advance

The rules about advance claims for CTB are generally the same as for HB (see p220). There is a further situation when an advance claim for CTB can be made. You can claim CTB up to eight weeks before you become liable for council tax and you are treated as having claimed on the day your liability begins.[51]

Council tax benefit after an award of a 'qualifying benefit'

You might not be entitled to CTB currently, but would be once you or a member of your family become entitled to another 'qualifying benefit' – eg, disability living allowance or carer's allowance (see Chapters 7 and 4). Alternatively, you might be entitled to a higher rate of benefit once the qualifying benefit is awarded. If you are already entitled to CTB when the qualifying benefit is awarded, see pp1194 and 1201. If you only qualify for CTB when the qualifying benefit is awarded, see p220.

Backdating your claim

The rules about late claims and backdated CTB are the same as for HB (see p221).[52] In addition, if you did not claim CTB because your name was not put on the council tax bill, you should argue that you have good cause for a late claim because you did not realise you were liable for council tax as the local authority had failed (via the council tax bill) to inform you of this.

There is a special rule if your local authority has not set its council tax rate by the beginning of the financial year.[53] As long as you claim within four weeks of the council tax being set or imposed, your claim is backdated to 1 April, or the date you first became entitled to CTB, if that is later.

Notice of a decision

You receive separate decision notices for HB and CTB. However, the information which must be included is the same (see p223) except that those items specifically relating to rent are excluded in a CTB decision notice and, instead, it must show your weekly council tax liability rounded to the nearest penny.[54] It should also include the following, where relevant:

- if you have been assessed for, and are entitled to, both main CTB and second adult rebate, the amount of benefit entitlement in each case and the fact that you can only be paid the higher amount;[55]
- if you have been assessed for a second adult rebate, the gross income of any second adult(s) used to determine the rate of CTB, including where any second adult is on income support or income-based jobseeker's allowance;[56]
- details of how any of the figures supplied on the decision notice have been rounded (ie, to the nearest penny).[57]

7. Getting paid

There is no minimum entitlement to council tax benefit (CTB). This means that you are paid CTB however low your entitlement is.

If you are 60 or over and your claim has been automatically backdated for up to 12 months (see p221) **your entitlement to CTB** starts:[58]

- if you became liable for council tax in the first of the weeks in respect of which you are claiming, from the Monday of that week; *or*
- in all other cases, from the benefit week following the first date in respect of which you are claiming.

Otherwise your entitlement to CTB starts:[59]

- if you have only just become liable for council tax and you claim in the same week in which your liability begins, from the Monday of that week; *or*
- in all other cases, in the benefit week following your date of claim.

The rules for when your **entitlement to CTB ends** are the same as for HB (see p225). Remember: you must let the local authority know about certain changes in your circumstances and the local authority can review your claim regularly.

Payment of CTB is normally made by means of a reduction to your annual council tax bill. Your weekly benefit is converted to a daily figure by dividing by seven and then multiplying the answer by the number of days between your first day of entitlement and the following 31 March.

If you are jointly liable for council tax with one or more other residents, apart from your partner, remember that any CTB they receive is also credited to the same bill as your own. You need to take this into account when agreeing with them how any remaining balance of council tax liability should be shared between you.

Where your CTB cannot be used to reduce your bill (eg, where you have already paid your bill in full), payment can be made direct to you.[60] Usually you must ask for the money. If you do not, your CTB is likely to be credited against your next year's council tax bill.[61] However, if you are no longer liable for council tax in an authority's area, it must send you any outstanding CTB within 14 days if possible.[62] Payment is normally made to you as the claimant or to your appointee if you have one (see p1075).[63]

Continuing payments where pension credit is claimed

To avoid problems caused by delays in reassessing your CTB when you move from income support (IS) or income-based jobseeker's allowance (JSA) onto pension credit (PC), so long as you otherwise continue to qualify for CTB, you continue to receive it for:[64]

- a period of four weeks from the day after your IS or income-based JSA ceases; *or*
- if the four-week period ends before the last day of a benefit week, until the end of the benefit week in which the end of the four-week period falls.

It is paid at the same rate as before this happens (but see below). The DWP calls these 'continuing payments'.

You qualify for continuing payments if you are entitled to CTB,[65] *and:*

- your partner has claimed PC and the DWP has certified this; *or*
- your IS ceased because you turned 60 or if you were getting income-based JSA beyond that age, this ceased because you turned 65 and the DWP has certified this and also that you are required to claim, or have claimed, PC (or are treated as having done so).

Your maximum CTB (see p114) is re-calculated if your liability for council tax increases or there is a change in the non-dependant deductions (see p115) that should be made.[66]

Suspending benefit

Local authorities have powers to suspend and terminate benefit. See p1105 for details.

Delays and complaints

The rules are the same as for HB (see p229).

Payments on death

If a claimant dies, any outstanding CTB can be paid to her/his personal representative or, if there is none, to the next of kin aged 16 or over.[67] A written application for this must be sent to the local authority within 12 months of the death.

Change of circumstances

It is your duty to report any change in circumstances which might affect your right to, or the amount of, your CTB or payment of your benefit.[68] You should do this promptly in writing to the office handling your claim (although in individual cases notification might be accepted in a form other than in writing). If you do not report any such change promptly in writing, any resulting overpayment may be recoverable from you (see Chapter 41). If you are considered deliberately to have acted falsely or dishonestly, you may also be guilty of an offence (see Chapter 42).

The rules are the same as for HB (see p230) except that:

- you do not need to notify any changes in rent for council tax purposes; nor do you have to tell the local authority the amount of council tax you pay. It has this information already.[69]
- if you are getting second adult rebate, you must write and tell the local authority of any changes in the number of adults living in your home and any changes to their gross income.[70]

There are additional changes you have to report if you are getting PC. The rules are the same as for HB (see p231).

When changes in circumstances take effect

The rules about when changes in circumstance take effect are generally the same as those for HB (see p232), but there are some differences. As with HB, normally, a change affects your CTB from the Monday after it occurs.[71] However, the following changes affect your benefit from the date they occur:[72]

- a change in the amount of your council tax;
- changes to the CTB regulations;
- the fact that you have become part of a couple;
- the death of, or separation from, your partner.

If two or more changes occur in the same week and each takes effect from a different date under the above rules, they are all taken into account from the date of the first change.[73]

Overpayments and fraud

If you are overpaid CTB, you might have to repay it. The rules on overpayments are covered in Chapter 41.

If you have been accused of fraud, see Chapter 42. You might get a reduced amount of CTB if you have been sanctioned for benefit offences (see p1169).

8. Challenging a council tax benefit decision

You can apply for a revision or supersession of a council tax benefit decision or appeal against it (see Chapters 43 and 44).

9. Tax, tax credits and other benefits

Council tax benefit (CTB) is not taxable.

Means-tested benefits

If you stop getting income support (IS), income-based jobseeker's allowance (JSA), incapacity benefit or severe disablement allowance because you start work or increase your hours or earnings, you may be entitled to an extended payment of housing benefit (HB) or CTB. This means you can usually continue to get the same amount of benefit for four weeks (see p63).

If you were previously incapable of work and getting IS, HB or CTB, then start work or training and count as a 'welfare to work' beneficiary (see p769), you retain the disability or higher pensioner premium if you become incapable of work again within 52 weeks.

Passports and other sources of help

If you are on a low income, you might qualify for certain health benefits, such as free prescriptions (see Chapter 9). You may also qualify for other sources of help (see Chapter 1) or a social fund payment or maternity grant or funeral expenses payment (see Chapters 21 and 22).

Notes

1. **Who can claim council tax benefit**

1 s131(1)(a) and (3)-(5) SSCBA 1992
2 Reg 14 CTB Regs, as substituted by reg 17 HB&CTB(SPC) Regs
3 Reg 40 CTB Regs; reg 18(a) HB&CTB(SPC) Regs
4 s131(1)(b), (3) and (6) SSCBA 1992
5 Reg 54 and Sch 5 para 45(1) CTB Regs
6 s131(9) SSCBA 1992
7 s131(7) SSCBA 1992
8 s6(5) LGFA 1992
9 Sch 1 LGFA 1992
10 Reg 55(a) CTB Regs
11 Reg 55(c) CTB Regs
12 Reg 55(d) CTB Regs
13 Reg 55(b) CTB Regs
14 s131(6)(a) and (7) SSCBA 1992
15 s131(11) SSCBA 1992; s6(5) LGFA 1992
16 *Williams v Horsham District Council* [2004] unreported, EWCA Civ 39, 21 January 2004
17 *Ward v Kingston-upon-Hull MBC* [1993] RA 71 (QBD)
18 Regs 4B and 4C CTB Regs; CH/2111/2003 decided that reg 4C(3) CTB Regs was of no effect.

4. **The amount of benefit**

19 Reg 2(3A) CTB Regs
20 Sch 4 para 4B CTB Regs; HB/CTB Circular A7/2003
21 Reg 51(1) and (2) CTB Regs
22 Reg 51(1) CTB Regs
23 para B3/3.300 GM
24 Sch 6 paras 9-10 CTB Regs
25 Reg 51(4) CTB Regs

26 Reg 51(3) CTB Regs
27 **England and Wales** ss6(4) and 9(2) LGFA 1992
Scotland ss75 and 77 LGFA 1992
All Sch 1 para 4(2) LGFA 1992
Note that the definition of student is different for these purposes than for CTB
28 Regs 3(1) and 51(1) CTB Regs
29 Reg 3(2) CTB Regs
30 Reg 3(3) CTB Regs
31 Reg 52(6)-(8) CTB Regs
32 Sch 1(2) LGFA 1992
33 Reg 3 CT(DD)O
34 Reg 52(1), (2) and (9) CTB Regs
35 Reg 4(5) CTB Regs
36 Reg 12 CTB Regs
37 Reg 52(3) CTB Regs
38 Reg 52(4) CTB Regs
39 Reg 52(5) CTB Regs
40 s139(6) SSAA 1992; reg 24(2A) CTB Regs
41 Reg 54 and Sch 2 para 1 CTB Regs
42 Reg 54 and Sch 2 para 1(2) CTB Regs
43 Reg 54 and Sch 2 para 1 Table CTB Regs
44 Sch 2 para 1(2) CTB Regs
45 Sch 2 para 2(a) CTB Regs
46 Sch 2 para 2(b) and (c) CTB Regs
47 Reg 54 and Sch 2 para 3 CTB Regs
48 Reg 54(2) CTB Regs
49 Reg 54(3) CTB Regs
50 Reg 3(e) DFA Regs

6. **Claims and backdating**

51 Reg 62(10) CTB Regs
52 Reg 62(16) CTB Regs
53 Reg 62(11) CTB Regs
54 Sch 6 paras 9(1)(a) and 10(a) CTB Regs
55 Sch 6 paras 12(b), 14(b) and 15 CTB Regs
56 Sch 6 para 13(c) and (f) CTB Regs
57 Sch 6 paras 9, 10, 13 and 15 CTB Regs

7. **Getting paid**

58 Reg 56(3) and (4) CTB Regs
59 Reg 56(1) and (2) CTB Regs
60 Reg 77(1)(b) and (3) CTB Regs
61 Reg 77(3)(a)(ii) CTB Regs
62 Reg 77(3)(b) CTB Regs
63 Reg 78 CTB Regs
64 Reg 53B(3)-(4) CTB Regs, as inserted by reg 20 HB&CTB(SPC) Regs
65 Reg 53B(1) and (2) CTB Regs, as inserted by reg 20 HB&CTB(SPC) Regs
66 Reg 53B(5) CTB Regs as inserted by reg 20 HB&CTB(SPC) Regs
67 Reg 81 CTB Regs
68 Reg 65(1) CTB Regs; reg 4 SS(NCC) Regs
69 Reg 65(2) CTB Regs
70 Reg 65(4) CTB Regs
71 Reg 59(1) CTB Regs
72 Reg 59(2)-(6) CTB Regs
73 Reg 59(7) CTB Regs

Chapter 7

Disability living allowance and attendance allowance

This chapter covers:

Disability living allowance (DLA) is a benefit for those who are under 65 when they claim. It has both mobility and care components. Although there are separate components, DLA is a single benefit for which you only have to make one claim. Throughout we refer to these components as 'DLA mobility' and 'DLA care'. Each component can be paid at different rates. Attendance allowance (AA) is a benefit for those who are aged 65 or over when they claim.

You do not have to have paid national insurance contributions to qualify for DLA or AA.

There are some groups of claimants to whom special rules apply (see p148).

1. Disability living allowance mobility component

Disability living allowance mobility component (DLA mobility) is for people who have difficulties with walking. There are two rates: higher rate and lower rate.

Who can claim

You qualify for DLA mobility if:[1]

- you satisfy the residence conditions (see p699);

- you are not subject to immigration control (see p660);
- you satisfy the age rules (see p145), that is:
  - for the *higher rate* of DLA mobility you must be aged 3 or over, but under 65;
  - for the *lower rate* of DLA mobility you must be aged 5 or over, but under 65;
- you are not in hospital (although sometimes DLA mobility is paid in hospital) (see p716);
- you are likely to be able, from time to time, to benefit from enhanced facilities for locomotion (see below);
- you satisfy the **'disability'** conditions, that is:
  - for the *higher rate* of DLA mobility: *either*
    - you have a physical disability that means you are unable, or virtually unable, to walk (see below); *or*
    - you are both deaf and blind (see p131); *or*
    - you were born without feet, are a double amputee or otherwise without both legs (see p131); *or*
    - you are 'severely mentally impaired', and have severe behavioural problems, and qualify for the highest rate of DLA care component (DLA care) (see p131);
  - for the *lower rate* of DLA mobility you must show that, although you are able to walk you are so severely disabled, physically or mentally, that, ignoring any ability to use familiar routes, you are unable to take advantage of your walking abilities outdoors without guidance or supervision from another person most of the time.[2] There is also an extra test if you are claiming on behalf of a child under 16 (see p135);
  - for *both rates* you must satisfy one of the disability conditions for at least three months before the start of your award and be likely to satisfy it for the next six months (unless you are terminally ill – see p134).

To 'benefit from enhanced facilities for locomotion'

To qualify for either rate of DLA mobility you must be able to 'benefit from enhanced facilities for locomotion'. This means you must be able to take advantage of outdoor journeys. It is not essential that you are interested in or enjoy going out provided it would be beneficial for you to do so.[3] For example, you can get DLA mobility even if you have to be carried out to a car for a ride.

The disability conditions for higher rate mobility

'Unable or virtually unable to walk'

You are eligible for higher mobility if 'your physical condition as a whole is such that, without having regard to circumstances peculiar to [you] as to the place of residence or as to the place of, or nature of, employment:

- you are unable to walk; *or*

- your ability to walk out of doors is so limited, as regards:
  - the distance over which; *or*
  - the speed at which; *or*
  - the length of time for which; *or*
  - the manner in which

  you can make progress on foot without severe discomfort, that you are virtually unable to walk; *or*
- the exertion required to walk would constitute a danger to your life or would be likely to lead to a serious deterioration in your health'.[4]

Your personal circumstances should not be taken into account. It is not, for instance, relevant that you may live a long way from your nearest bus stop,[5] or that you may no longer be able to use public transport.

Physical disability

To qualify for higher mobility the cause of your inability or virtual inability to walk must be connected to your physical condition. For example, you would not qualify for the higher rate mobility component solely because you have agoraphobia (a fear of going out). However, you may well qualify for the lower rate (see p133). On the other hand, if you have a psychological disorder that causes paralysis then you can argue that you should qualify.[6] If you have myalgic encephalomyelitis (ME) or chronic fatigue syndrome, this should be accepted as having a physical origin unless there is evidence that your mobility restrictions have only a psychological cause.[7]

If the reason for your pain, where this limits your walking, is undiagnosed or is psychological, you may have difficulty qualifying. Pain is a physical symptom but could be a symptom of a psychological or physical condition.[8] In some cases, real pain has been accepted as a physical disability regardless of what causes it.[9] In particular, chronic regional pain syndrome should be accepted as a physical disability.[10] In other cases, pain arising solely from depression or other psychological conditions has not been accepted as a physical disability.[11] However, it can be argued that it should be accepted where the depression was itself caused by a physical condition.[12]

Unable to walk

You are unable to walk if you cannot move your body along by alternate, weightbearing steps of the feet.[13]

Prostheses, aids and medication

Your ability to walk is considered after taking into account any prosthesis or artificial aid you habitually wear or use, or that would be suitable for you.[14] You may not qualify if you are able to walk with a stick or crutches. However, someone with one leg and no artificial limb suitable for them to use is regarded as 'unable to walk', even if they can get around on crutches.[15] If you have no feet you qualify automatically (see p131).[16]

Your walking is assessed taking account of any medication you normally use and reasonably use (eg, it may not be practical to carry a bulky nebuliser).[17] But you should not be expected to undergo surgery, and if you do not take the prescribed medicines or treatment, your walking should be assessed as you are now, not how you might be if you accepted the treatment.[18]

Out of doors

The test is whether you can walk out of doors, not indoors. If you have problems with your balance on uneven pavements and roads, or you have a lung or other condition which is made worse by wind or rain, these are relevant factors in deciding your claim.[19]

Distance

The law does not lay down a specific distance to be used to determine whether you are virtually unable to walk. In one case, a commissioner refused to accept that a person who had walked less than 50 yards was virtually unable to walk.[20] But, in other cases, people who have been able to walk much greater distances have been judged to be 'virtually unable to walk'.[21] One relevant consideration may be how long it takes you to recover after walking a certain distance – eg, 50 metres. If you can walk another 50 metres after only a minute's rest, your walking ability is obviously greater than that of a person who has to lie down for an hour after walking such a distance. You should remember that distance is just one factor among others which should be taken into account when assessing your overall walking ability.[22] As well as distance, decision makers should also take into account your walking speed, the length of time you can walk for, and your manner of walking.

Without severe discomfort

Any walking you can achieve only with severe discomfort should be ignored when considering whether you are virtually unable to walk.[23] If, when you walk, you feel severe discomfort – eg, pain or breathlessness brought on by walking[24] – you should make this clear. In practice, you may be able to walk a distance without severe discomfort, followed by a further distance which does cause you severe discomfort, and then have to stop altogether. In this case it would be incorrect to decide that discomfort became severe only when it was so great as to prevent you walking.[25] The correct test is 'how far the person can walk before severe discomfort is occasioned by going any further'. But further walking (ie, without severe discomfort) after a brief rest stop could be taken into account.[26] If you are already in severe discomfort before you start to walk, even if the pain gets no worse, you should count as virtually unable to walk so long as your disability affects the physical act of walking. For example, someone with an injured foot qualified in this way.[27] You do not, however, count as virtually unable to walk if something unconnected with walking causes the discomfort. For example, someone whose skin blistered in sunlight was held not to be virtually unable to walk even though he was in severe discomfort outdoors.[28]

The exertion required to walk

You can qualify for higher mobility if walking is dangerous to your health. The 'exertion required to walk' must lead to a danger to life or a serious deterioration in health. It is not necessary for the possible serious deterioration in your health to be permanent or long-lasting.[29] On the other hand, in one case a person with ME, who needed a few days' rest after walking, did not satisfy the test. You need to show that you would never recover, or recovery would take a significant period of time (eg,12 months) or would require some form of medical intervention.[30]

Blind and deaf

You are treated as being unable to walk if:

- the degree of disablement resulting from your loss of vision is 100 per cent; *and*
- the degree of disablement resulting from your loss of hearing is 80 per cent on a scale where 100 per cent represents absolute deafness;[31] *and*
- the combined effects of the blindness and deafness mean that you are unable to walk to any intended or required destination while out of doors, without the help of another person.[32]

100 per cent disablement through 'loss of vision' means 'loss of sight to such an extent as to render the claimant unable to perform any work for which eyesight is essential'.[33] This is the same definition as that used when someone is registered as blind (and the same as that used in the industrial injuries scheme).[34] In practice, therefore, if you are registered as blind then you should be treated as 100 per cent disabled. You do not need to be totally blind to be registered as blind.

Disablement through **hearing loss** is assessed in the same way as occupational deafness.[35] You may be required to undertake a hearing test. If your average level of hearing loss due to all causes at 1, 2 and 3 kHz is at least 87dB in both ears, you will satisfy the 80 per cent disablement test.[36] The assessment of your hearing ability takes into account any hearing aid you use or could reasonably be expected to use.[37]

People without feet

If you do not have legs or feet (missing from the ankle or above) you are automatically treated as being unable to walk.[38] This is so even if you can walk with prostheses.

Severe mental impairment and behavioural problems

There is another route to *higher rate* DLA mobility for those with severe behavioural difficulties.

You qualify if:

- you are **'severely mentally impaired'** – ie, you suffer from arrested or incomplete development of the brain, which results in severe impairment of intelligence and social functioning; *and*
- you display severe behavioural problems – ie:
  - you exhibit disruptive behaviour which is extreme; *and*
  - you regularly require someone else to intervene and physically restrain you in order to prevent you causing injury to yourself or others or damage to property; *and*
  - you are so unpredictable that another person has to be present and watching over you whenever you are awake; *and*
- you qualify for the highest rate of DLA care.[39]

If you do not meet all of the above elements of the severe mental impairment test – eg, you may not be sufficiently unsettled at night to get the highest rate DLA care, there is nothing to stop you trying to qualify for higher mobility on the basis that you are virtually unable to walk (see p128). You could argue that your disability prevents you from walking effectively, causing so many refusals to walk that you can be said to be virtually unable to walk.[40]

Arrested or incomplete development

You can only be regarded as suffering from 'arrested or incomplete development of the brain' if this is something that occurs before the brain reaches its final development, which medical opinion suggests is at or before the age of 30. Someone with Alzheimer's disease, a degenerative condition which occurs after the brain has fully developed, would not qualify under this route.[41] In the case of an illness such as schizophrenia you may qualify via the 'severe mental impairment' route but the age at which your illness began is very significant and you also need to have a severe impairment of intelligence *and* of social functioning (see below).[42]

Severe impairment of intelligence

If your IQ is 55 or less that is generally accepted as a 'severe impairment of intelligence'. However, some people may have a higher IQ but an inability to apply it practically.[43] The test requires you to have a severe impairment of intelligence *and* social functioning. Decision makers should recognise that 'in some cases at least an impairment of social function will shade into an impairment of intelligence'. Your 'degree of judgement in relation to everyday living' should also be taken into account.[44] For example, an autistic child with no awareness of danger may have severely impaired intelligence even if their IQ is over 55.[45]

Physical restraint

Physical restraint may involve as little as a hand on the arm. You do not need to show that any force is used.[46] If the presence of those who watch over you is enough to prevent you from being disruptive altogether or a specially adapted environment allows you to be safely left alone, you may not pass the test.[47]

The disability condition for lower rate mobility

You qualify for *lower rate* DLA mobility if you are 'so severely disabled physically or mentally' that you cannot walk outdoors 'without guidance or supervision from another person most of the time'.[48]

Any walking that you can accomplish in familiar routes is ignored for the purposes of this test – but inability to walk, whether on familiar or unfamiliar routes, should be considered.[49] If you experience pain or discomfort as a result of walking, but you do not satisfy the 'virtually unable to walk' test for *higher rate* DLA mobility (see p128), you do not necessarily qualify for *lower rate* DLA mobility. Qualification for lower rate DLA mobility is based on an assessment of your need for supervision or guidance rather than your physical ability to walk.[50]

'Guidance' and 'supervision' clearly overlap and some forms of assistance could be treated as either guidance or supervision (see below).

Physical and mental disablement

You can qualify for the lower rate on the basis of mental as well as physical disablement. If you have an anxiety disorder and you are mentally disabled to the extent that you need an escort to overcome your fear of going outside, you may satisfy the 'guidance or supervision' requirement.[51] However, if no amount of reassurance can persuade you to go outside, you may not be able to qualify.[52]

If it is fear or anxiety that stops you going out on your own, it must be a symptom of a mental disability or a mental disability itself in order to count, and it must be severe enough to prevent you going out without someone to guide or supervise you.[53] If your physical disability causes you so much fear or anxiety that you can be said to be mentally disabled, and because of that you cannot go outside without a companion, you may qualify.

Although the law says that you must be 'severely disabled physically or mentally' there is no separate test of the severity of your disability. If your disability gives rise to a need for guidance or supervision to enable you to walk outdoors, ignoring any ability you have on familiar routes, you satisfy the test.[54]

Guidance

'Guidance' can take a number of different forms. It can mean physically leading or directing you, giving oral suggestion or persuasion, helping you avoid obstacles or places which upset you, or leading or persuading you when you become disorientated or have a panic attack.

If you are visually impaired and use a guide dog or a long cane you may still need guidance to follow directions, avoid obstacles or to help you cross roads. A profoundly deaf person, whose primary method of communication is sign language, may require guidance in unfamiliar places if s/he is unable to ask for or follow directions.[55] Even though the deaf person's companion may only intervene occasionally, s/he will still be guiding or supervising 'most of the time', because otherwise the deaf person would not know when to change direction. However, deaf people may not qualify if they are 'capable of studying maps, reading street signs or communicating with passers by, either in writing or by speaking or lip reading'.[56]

Supervision

'Supervision' can also take different forms. It can take a precautionary form of accompanying and watching over you, in order to monitor your physical, mental or emotional state in case you need more positive action to encourage you to continue walking. Similarly, it can mean monitoring the route ahead for obstacles, dangers, places or situations which might upset you. Alternatively, supervision can take more active forms, such as encouraging, persuading or cajoling you, or distracting you from possibly alarming situations through conversation.[57]

Unlike the 'continual supervision' condition for DLA care, it is not a condition of lower rate DLA mobility that supervision must be required to prevent 'substantial danger'.[58] However, if you qualify for DLA care because you require continual supervision you may also qualify for lower rate DLA mobility.[59] This does not mean you will be automatically passported onto lower rate mobility. Your eligibility must be assessed on the mobility criteria alone.[60]

The supervision does not need to actually improve your walking ability, but should enable you to 'take advantage of the faculty of walking'. If you need supervision because, for example, you are at risk of fits or seizures, even though you do not have problems with orientation, you can qualify for lower rate mobility.[61]

Terminal illness

Terminal illness is defined in the same way for the mobility component as for DLA care (see p149). However, if you are terminally ill you do not automatically qualify for DLA mobility. The only special treatment given is that, where a claim is made specifically on the basis that you are terminally ill, you do not have to satisfy the three-month backward qualifying condition.[62] The forward qualifying condition is modified to last for the remainder of your life, rather than the usual six months.

The rules about your age

DLA mobility has lower and upper age limits described below.

Age limits for children

Children can get higher rate DLA mobility from the age of three onwards and lower rate DLA mobility from the age of five.[63] The three months before the child reaches the age at which s/he can get DLA mobility can form the backward qualifying period (see p136), enabling payment from her/his birthday.

Children under 16 who are applying for lower rate mobility must also satisfy an extra test.

The extra test for children

A child under 16 will only qualify for lower rate mobility if, in addition to the normal guidance or supervision condition (see p133), you can also show that *either*:

- the child requires substantially more guidance or supervision (see p133) than children of her/his age in normal physical and mental health would; *or*
- children of the same age in normal physical and mental health would not require such guidance or supervision.[64]

This extra test for children does not apply to higher rate mobility.

The fact that no young children are allowed to travel unsupervised on unfamiliar outdoor routes should not, in itself, prevent disabled children from satisfying this extra test. What matters is the nature and extent of the guidance and supervision required by a disabled child, on familiar or unfamiliar routes, compared with that required by a non-disabled child of the same age.[65]

Your child may require substantially more outdoor guidance or supervision either because of the extra time you spend providing such assistance or by virtue of the quality or degree of that assistance.[66] Whereas able-bodied children may only require adults to accompany them, children with, for example, visual impairments or learning disabilities may need adults physically to hold or guide them, or to watch over them much more attentively (see p157 for tips on answering the mobility questions on the children's claim form). Similarly, a young deaf child may need someone to stay within touching distance or maintain eye contact, whereas a hearing child would not.[67]

It would be wrong to compare the outdoor supervision needed by a child with behavioural problems to that required by a badly behaved child who requires more supervision than the average. The correct comparison is with an 'average child' – ie, a child of average intelligence, whose behaviour is neither particularly good nor bad.[68]

Aged over 65

The upper age limit for claiming either rate of DLA mobility is 65. You must make your claim and be sufficiently disabled to qualify before the date of your 65th birthday but you need not have completed the three-month backward qualifying period by then.

Although you must be under 65 to qualify, once DLA mobility is awarded it can be paid beyond the age of 65. However, you cannot change rates, up or down, if your condition worsens or improves. If your condition improves so you no longer satisfy the disability conditions for the higher rate, your DLA mobility entitlement stops altogether even if you would meet the lower rate conditions. You can renew a DLA mobility award after age 65 but you must reclaim within a year of the previous award ending.[69]

If you have an award of DLA care that was made before your 65th birthday, you can ask for a revision or supersession of that award to include DLA mobility after age 65, providing you can show that you have satisfied the disability conditions for the mobility component since before age 65.[70] Similarly, if you have an award of lower rate DLA mobility that was made before your 65th birthday, you can ask for it to be revised or superseded to give you the higher rate if you can show that you met the disability conditions for the higher rate since before age 65.

Claiming for others

You can only claim DLA mobility for yourself. If your spouse or partner also has mobility problems s/he should make a separate claim in her/his own right. A child under 16, however, cannot make a claim in her/his own right. A claim must be made on a child's behalf by an appointee, who is usually a parent or guardian (see p160).[71]

The amount of benefit

For how much DLA mobility you can get, see p148.

2. Disability living allowance care component

Disability living allowance care component (DLA care) is for people with care or supervision needs.

Who can claim

You qualify for DLA care if:[72]

- you satisfy the residence conditions (see p699);
- you are not subject to immigration control (see p660);
- you are under the age of 65 when you first claim (see p145);
- you are not resident in certain types of accommodation (see p721);
- you satisfy the 'disability' conditions, for either:
  - the lower rate of the care component (see p137); *or*
  - the middle rate of the care component (see p137); *or*
  - the higher rate of the care component (see p137); *or*
  - you are terminally ill (see p149);
- you have satisfied the disability condition throughout the period of three months immediately before your award begins (see p152 if you are reclaiming

within two years) and you are likely to continue to satisfy the disability conditions for the next six months *or* you are terminally ill.

Children under 16 also have to satisfy an extra disability test (see p146).

Disability conditions for lower rate care component

You qualify for the lower rate of DLA care if:[73]

- you are 16 or over and you are so severely disabled physically or mentally that you cannot prepare a cooked main meal for yourself if you have the ingredients (the 'cooking test' – see p138); *or*
- you are so severely disabled physically or mentally that you require, in connection with your bodily functions, attention from another person for a significant portion of the day, whether during a single period or a number of periods (see p143).

Disability conditions for middle rate care component

To qualify for the middle rate of DLA care you must show that you are so severely disabled physically or mentally that you require (see p139):[74]

- frequent attention from another person throughout the day in connection with your bodily functions (see p140); *or*
- continual supervision throughout the day in order to avoid substantial danger to yourself or others (see p144); *or*
- prolonged or repeated attention at night (see p144) in connection with your bodily functions (see p140); *or*
- another person to be awake at night for a prolonged period or at frequent intervals to watch over you (see p145) in order to avoid substantial danger to yourself or others.

This means you must have either daytime or night-time attention or supervision needs.

Disability conditions for higher rate care component

To qualify for the higher rate of DLA care you must be so severely disabled physically or mentally that:

- you require frequent attention throughout the day in connection with your bodily functions, *or* continual supervision throughout the day to avoid substantial danger to yourself or others; *and*
- you require prolonged or repeated attention at night in connection with your bodily functions, *or* in order to avoid substantial danger to yourself or others you require another person to be awake at night for a prolonged period or at frequent intervals to watch over you;[75] *or*
- you are terminally ill (see p149).[76]

This means you must have both daytime and night-time requirements, *or* you must be terminally ill.

'So severely disabled physically or mentally'

To qualify, you must be 'so severely disabled physically or mentally' that you need attention or supervision. You must have a disability caused by a medically recognised physical or mental condition,[77] even if doctors cannot agree on an exact diagnosis.[78] Problems sometimes arise where, for example, a child has behavioural problems that have not been attributed to a disability. In one case, a child was eligible for DLA despite not having a specific diagnosis for the behavioural problems; it was accepted that they did stem from a disability.[79]

There is no extra test of severity; your disability is regarded as severe if you satisfy one of the disability tests.[80]

Care needs resulting from any disability caused or made worse by alcohol dependency should be taken into account whether or not you can control your drinking. On the other hand, care needs resulting from intoxication alone are not taken into account.[81]

The cooking test

You qualify for lower rate DLA care if you can show that you are so severely disabled, physically or mentally, that you cannot prepare a cooked main meal for yourself if you have the ingredients. This test does not apply to children under the age of 16.[82] The meal in question is a labour intensive main meal for one person, freshly cooked on a traditional cooker.[83] It is a hypothetical test about what you can reasonably do – it does not matter what you actually do or do not do.[84]

It is not enough to argue that you simply do not know how to cook. The test assumes that those who do not know how are at least willing to learn.[85]

The test is a broad view of your ability – it does not necessarily matter if there are some days when your ability is more or less than it is the rest of the time.[86]

You need to show that your disability makes you unable to perform the tasks that are needed to cook such a main meal. You need to explain about your ability to plan a meal and to prepare and cook it – eg, to:

- peel and chop vegetables;
- use taps;
- use cooking utensils;
- use a cooker;
- lift hot or heavy pans;
- drain vegetables;
- tell if food is cooked properly.

In order to cook a main meal you need to be able to manage both physical tasks (eg, lifting, carrying, bending, and manipulating kitchen equipment) and mental tasks such as concentrating and planning.

- If you are at risk of seizures or blackouts (eg, you have epilepsy) you may be able to satisfy this test. Although you might physically and mentally be able to cook, in practice you may not cook because it is potentially too dangerous an activity for you.
- If you have a visual impairment you should qualify if you are unable to read labels or cooking instructions, check whether vegetables have been adequately prepared and washed or see whether food is properly cooked.
- If, as a consequence of a mental illness, such as severe depression, you lack the motivation or concentration to cook, you should satisfy the test.[87]
- You may qualify if you can perform some of the individual cooking tasks (eg, chopping meat or vegetables) but overall you do not have the stamina to prepare an entire meal. For example, if you have chronic back pain and cannot stand for long periods, it may not be reasonable to expect you to prepare a meal and wait for it to cook while sitting down.[88]
- You may qualify if breathing difficulties stop you cooking in a hot, steamy kitchen.[89]

Kitchen aids and adaptations

There is some confusion about whether the availability of cooking aids and adaptations is a relevant consideration for the cooking test. Since this is simply a hypothetical test of what you can or cannot reasonably do, you could argue that it is not appropriate, or reasonable, to consider whether your kitchen is, or could be, specially adapted.[90] It would certainly be incorrect to expect you to use a microwave to heat up convenience food.[91] However, cooking aids and adaptations may be taken into account if it is 'reasonable' to do so – eg, if they are readily obtainable by you.[92] If it is suggested you use a slotted spoon instead of draining vegetables from the pan, explain any difficulties you might still have lifting pans of water on and off the cooker.

Reasonableness

Only those who could 'reasonably' be expected to prepare a cooked main meal should be regarded as being able to do so. What is reasonable depends on the circumstances of your case. In one case, a person suffering from haemophilia was judged to be at some risk and to experience some anxiety when cooking, but not to the extent that it was unreasonable for him to prepare a cooked main meal.[93]

Attention and supervision

'Requires'

In order to satisfy the attention or supervision conditions (see p136) you have to show that you 'require' this assistance from another person. This means that the assistance must be 'reasonably required' rather than 'medically required'.[94] For example, if you are incontinent and need help changing your bedding, that help should count as 'reasonably required' even if not actually required to help protect your skin.

The correct test is 'whether the attention is reasonably required to enable the severely disabled person as far as reasonably possible to live a normal life'.[95] Having a social life, taking part in recreation and cultural activities can be part of normal life, and it is reasonable to want to be involved in them.[96] It is, therefore, reasonable for a blind person to have someone read newspapers, describe television pictures, or guide her/him during social outings. Similarly, it is reasonable for a person with learning disabilities to have assistance in order to travel to, or take part in, social and recreational pursuits. What is reasonable in each case depends on the age and interests of the disabled person.[97]

Reasonably requires supervision

What is reasonable also applies to a person's requirement for supervision. You are not expected to avoid doing anything which might cause a risk of harm in order not to need any supervision. People who are at risk of falls as a result of their condition might be able to avoid the risk of danger in this way. You can avoid most risks by staying in a chair all day but that may be totally unreasonable.[98] It is not reasonable to expect you to avoid all situations in which you might fall.[99]

In considering your need for continual supervision (see p144), the fact that such supervision is actually provided should be regarded as strong evidence that it is required. As one chief commissioner said: 'Mothers would be unlikely to exhaust themselves by providing it unnecessarily for years.'[100]

If such supervision is not provided, because you live alone, then you may be told that your choice is 'a strong indication that ... [continual] ... supervision is not required'.[101] But this always depends on the facts of your particular case. You may reasonably require supervision even if you do not receive it. You should be very clear about the difficulties you have when your needs are not met, and about what help you think you need.[102]

Refusing medical treatment

Refusing medical treatment may affect the assessment. If you would be able to cope with less help were you to accept treatment you have been offered by your doctor, the help you need may not be regarded as reasonably required. You should argue that it is reasonable for you not to take the treatment – eg, because of the side effects. Refusing invasive surgery should be accepted. It should also be accepted as reasonable if your psychiatric condition causes you to refuse treatment.[103]

Attention

The attention you require must be in connection with **'bodily functions'**, which have been defined as including:

> breathing, hearing, seeing, eating, drinking, walking, sitting, sleeping, getting in or out of bed, dressing, undressing, eliminating waste products and the like, all of which an ordinary person who is not suffering from any disability does for himself. But they do not include cooking, shopping, or any of the other things which ... generally ... one of the household does for the rest of the family.[104]

The attention is in connection with the bodily function if it provides a substitute method of providing what the bodily function would provide if it were not totally or partially impaired.[105] For example, guiding a blind person so that s/he is able to walk outside should be treated as attention with the bodily function of 'seeing', rather than of 'walking'. A guide assists with 'seeing' by acting 'as the eyes' of a blind person.

'Attention' is 'a service of a close and intimate nature ... involving personal contact carried out in the presence of the disabled person'. The attention must need to be given in the physical presence of the disabled person.[106] Although attention must usually involve personal contact, this does not need to take the form of *physical* contact. Contact established by the spoken word may count if, for example, you are blind.[107] Thus, reading, describing or giving verbal instructions can be attention. Similarly, if you would neglect yourself unless cajoled or stimulated to do routine tasks you may require attention in the form of active stimulation.[108] Spoken reassurance counts as long as the carer is required to be physically in the same place as the disabled person. Reassurance provided over the telephone and other types of support not required to be given in the physical presence of the disabled person cannot qualify as attention.[109]

Attention or supervision

'Attention' involves a service of an 'active nature'[110] whereas **'supervision'** is passive and 'may be precautionary or anticipatory, yet never result in intervention'.[111] However, where supervision does lead to intervention, this constitutes attention, so you should not regard the two categories as completely separate. For example, if you need to be supervised because you are likely to fall and injure yourself, you receive attention every time your carer gives you a steadying hand or warns you of an obstacle you are about to trip over.[112] If that attention is frequent you qualify for middle rate DLA care, even if the supervision is not 'continual' throughout the day. Sometimes an act can be both supervision and attention. It is, therefore, important to emphasise the full extent of your needs without trying to fit them neatly into either 'attention' or 'supervision' categories at the expense of leaving things out.

Communicating

Hearing and speaking are both bodily functions so you can qualify if you are profoundly deaf (eg, a sign language user who cannot speak or easily understand spoken English) and you require an interpreter to enable you to communicate.[113] But although communication with other people via an interpreter is a clear attention need, it does not necessarily follow that if you communicate easily with members of your family by sign language you are receiving attention from them in the course of such communication.[114] If, on the other hand, extra effort is required to initiate a two-way conversation, or if someone takes time away from their ordinary duties to communicate with you, this could constitute attention.[115]

Help in explaining written information to a deaf person with poor literacy skills can count as attention.[116] Similarly, others whose disability means they need help with written information may qualify.[117]

Domestic duties

Attention must normally be carried out in the presence of the disabled person.[118] A period of attention can also include incidental activities which could take place outside the presence of the claimant. For example, where a carer strips a soiled bed at night, the additional tasks of wringing out the sheets, putting sheets to soak or hanging them up to dry could count as attention if done on the spot, as would cleaning a soiled carpet or furniture after an episode of incontinence.[119] Taking the washing away or doing the cleaning at a different time would not qualify as attention.

Other kinds of domestic tasks can usually be performed by a carer outside your presence and, therefore, do not normally count as attention. But it is different if you do your own domestic tasks with the help of a carer. If you are blind and someone helps you to cook for yourself by reading cooking instructions to you, this is assistance with the bodily function of 'seeing' and can count as attention.[120] Similarly, if you have a learning disability and go shopping, you may need help to communicate your requirements. There are, however, conflicting commissioners' decisions on whether assistance of this kind, which enables someone to perform her/his own domestic tasks, is attention reasonably required.[121] You should argue that if a disabled person, given help, is able to shop or cook for her/himself, this is part of what constitutes a 'normal life' (see definition of 'requires' on p139).[122]

Childcare

The assistance given to disabled parents to enable them to look after their children can also count as attention.[123] For example, lifting or holding babies so that their mother can feed them is a sufficiently intimate service.[124] Similarly, assisting a disabled mother to take part in outdoor activities with her children can allow her to lead a normal social life.[125] When assessing the *parent's* care needs a distinction must be made between help provided to the parent, which counts as attention, and that given directly to the child, which does not count.[126]

Special diets

Attention only counts if it needs to be given in the physical presence of the disabled person. So it will often be difficult to have help with food preparation included. Arguably though, this type of help may, nonetheless, count as attention if it forms part of a broader sequence of care tasks. For example, the various parts of the process of regulating the blood sugar levels of a diabetic child, some of which require personal contact and some of which do not, should nonetheless *all* be treated as attention because they are integral elements of an overall regime.[127]

'Attention... for a significant portion of the day'

If you can show that you need attention for a 'significant portion of the day' you qualify for lower rate DLA care.[128] A significant portion of the day can be either during a single period or a number of periods.

You may qualify for lower rate DLA care if you only need help for *part* of the day, rather than *throughout* the day (see p144) – eg, you need help with activities connected to 'getting up', such as dressing and washing, at the beginning of the day and with activities connected to 'going to bed', such as undressing and washing, at the end of the day, but are otherwise able to care for yourself without help. Help at night does not count for the lower rate.[129]

The term **'a significant portion of the day'** is often taken to mean an hour or thereabouts.[130] But if your carer spends less time than that in total but has to give help for a brief period on a number of small occasions then that might qualify.[131] Or if your carer does not have much time available or the help they give is in spells of particularly concentrated activity, less than an hour's help may be enough. Factors like the amount, importance or effect of the attention could count towards its significance.[132]

Night and day

An adult who needs help going to the toilet at 3am, a time when most people are asleep, clearly needs that help at night. Problems do sometimes arise when children or adults need supervision or attention in the late evening or early morning.

'Night' has been defined as 'that period of inactivity, or that principal period of inactivity, through which each household goes in the dark hours' beginning when 'the household, as it were, closes down for the night'.[133] This may be somewhere between 11pm and 7am, but the pattern of activities of the particular household needs to be taken into account. If a carer stays up into the small hours to help you but would otherwise go to bed earlier, that should count as night care.[134] Similarly if a carer gets up early in the morning to help you but would otherwise get up later with the rest of the household, that should count as night care.[135] If you live alone and go to bed unusually late or get up unusually early, your 'night' may be assumed to begin at a more average time of 11pm or to end at 7am.[136]

The definition of 'night' for a child is the same as for an adult, so that attention given to a child in the evening before the adults have gone to bed counts only towards satisfaction of the day condition.[137]

Frequent attention throughout the day

To satisfy the day attention condition you need to show that attention is required **frequently throughout the day**. A frequent need might include help with toileting (whether that be to reach the toilet, use a commode, or deal with zips and buttons), or needing help to walk within your own home. These are both examples of activities which most people would reasonably engage in with some frequency during the course of a normal day. Most people who satisfy the 'frequency' condition do so by virtue of a range of different types of care needs which, when added together, occur frequently and throughout the day. For this test, it is the pattern of the needs across the day which is crucial. If you only need help at the beginning and end of the day you are unlikely to satisfy the test. The help you need must be both **'frequent'**, meaning 'several times – not once or twice'[138] and required 'at intervals spread over the day'.[139] However, even if the spread is uneven and there are lengthy periods when you do not need help, this should not necessarily disqualify you.[140]

Prolonged or repeated attention at night

The help that needs to be given in the night has to be either prolonged or repeated. The Department for Work and Pensions usually regards 20 minutes of attention as **'prolonged'**.[141] **'Repeated'** simply means twice or more.[142]

Because sleeping is a 'bodily function', soothing a child back to sleep counts as giving attention in connection with a bodily function.[143]

Continual supervision

You satisfy the **daytime supervision** condition if you require another person to provide 'continual supervision' throughout the day to prevent the risk of substantial danger, either to yourself or to others.[144] This supervision test consists of four parts:[145]

- **There must be a substantial danger to yourself or someone else as a result of your medical condition.** What constitutes a 'substantial danger' must be decided on the facts of each case. For example, if an elderly person falls, this is more likely to constitute a 'substantial danger' than if a younger person falls but only sustains minor bruises.
- **The substantial danger must be one against which it is reasonable to guard.** This involves weighing the remoteness of the risk and the seriousness of the consequences should it arise. While the risk of a house catching fire may be remote (but not fanciful), the consequences of leaving a disabled person who is unable to move alone in a house which did catch fire would be catastrophic. Similarly, the consequences of allowing a child to run out onto the road could

be dire even though such an incident may be isolated.[146] Thus, it can be argued that you reasonably require continual supervision.[147] In assessing the likelihood of danger, the decision maker must look not only at what has happened in the past but at what may happen in the future.[148]

- **There must be a need for the supervision.** What should count as supervision is the level of supervision you 'reasonably require' (see p139). Although you may not receive much supervision (perhaps because you live alone), you may still qualify if you can show you ought to be receiving it.
- **The supervision must be continual.** This is something less than 'continuous', but supervision which is required only occasionally or spasmodically is insufficient. The 'characteristic nature of supervision is overseeing or watching over considered with reference to its frequency or regularity of occurrence'.[149] Supervision can be precautionary and anticipatory. It does not necessarily involve direct intervention.
  If you are liable to epileptic fits without warning you may need continual supervision, although attention for the period between the fits is not required.[150] Even if you have warning of the fits so that you can prevent yourself from falling, you may require continual supervision if you suffer from prolonged periods of confusion afterwards.[151] If you are a parent with a young child you may need supervision so that there is someone to look after your child when you have a fit.

If you have mental health problems you may need supervision to help prevent you harming yourself. It is wrong to assume, without fully investigating your case, that if you really were at risk of harming yourself you would be a hospital in-patient.[152] Further, if you are at risk of committing suicide, it would also be wrong to suggest that no amount of supervision would prevent a determined suicide attempt and supervision is therefore not required. The correct approach is to decide whether supervision would result in 'a real reduction in the risk of harm to the claimant'.[153]

Watching over

You satisfy the night-time supervision condition if you need someone to be awake to watch over you at night to prevent the risk of substantial danger to yourself or others.[154] The person watching over you has to be awake for a 'prolonged period' or 'at frequent intervals'. A 'prolonged period' may mean 20 minutes or more.[155] The term 'at frequent intervals' means more than twice.

The rules about your age

Children

There is no lower age limit for claiming DLA care. However, as with other claimants, a baby has to meet the qualifying conditions for three months before the allowance becomes payable, unless s/he is terminally ill.

Children under the age of 16 cannot qualify for lower rate DLA care via the cooking test (see p138). A child can only qualify for lower rate DLA care if s/he requires attention for a 'significant portion of the day' (see p143).

For all rates of DLA care, there is also an extra test for children.

The extra test for children

Children under 16 can only qualify for the care component if they satisfy an extra test in addition to the normal care or supervision conditions. You must show that, *either*:

- the child has attention or supervision requirements 'substantially in excess of the normal requirements' of a child of the same age; *or*
- the child has substantial attention or supervision requirements which younger children in normal physical and mental health may also have, but which children of the same age and in normal physical and mental health would not have.[156]

The extra test does not apply if you claim the care component for a child who is terminally ill.[157]

As all young children require assistance throughout the day, it can be difficult to explain how you are providing attention or supervision which is 'substantially in excess' of what is normally required (see p156 for tips on filling out the children's claim form). It may be either because of the extra time you devote to these tasks, or 'by virtue of the quality or degree of attention or supervision which is required'.[158] For example, non-disabled children may need their food cut up, whereas disabled children may also need their food spooned into their mouths.

The comparison should be with an 'average child' – ie, a child of average intelligence whose behaviour is neither particularly good nor bad.[159] So the help given to a child with behavioural problems should be compared to an average child, not to a non-disabled but badly behaved child who requires more supervision than normal.

Aged over 65

The upper age limit for claiming DLA care is 65. You cannot claim DLA care for the first time once you have reached the age of 65 (unless you already get DLA mobility – see p147).[160] If you are above this age limit you have to claim attendance allowance (AA) instead.

There is no upper age limit for receipt of DLA care once you qualify and you can continue to receive it after you are 65. If your condition improves you can drop from higher to middle rate or lose DLA care entitlement altogether but you cannot drop to lower rate DLA care.[161] If your condition worsens, you can move up to middle or higher rate DLA care. You have to show that you have met the qualifying conditions for the middle or higher rate for six months before it can be awarded, not three months. This is because the rules about qualifying periods for those in receipt of DLA care above the age of 65 are the same as those for AA.[162] If it has been over a year since your previous award ended, you must claim AA instead of DLA care.

If you have an award of DLA mobility that was made before your 65th birthday, you can ask for a revision or supersession of that award to include DLA care after age 65, but to get the lower rate you must show that you have satisfied the disability conditions for the lower rate since before age 65.[163] To get the middle or higher rate DLA care, you must meet the disability conditions for a qualifying period of six months.[164]

Claiming for others

You can only claim DLA care in respect of your own care or supervision needs. If your spouse or partner also has care or supervision needs s/he should make a separate claim in her/his own right. A child under 16, however, cannot make a claim in her/his own right. A claim must be made on a child's behalf by an appointee, who is usually a parent or guardian (see p160).[165]

The amount of benefit

For how much DLA care you can get, see p148.

3. Attendance allowance

Attendance allowance (AA) is a benefit for people aged 65 and over with attention or supervision needs. There is a higher rate and a lower rate, the rules of which are similar to those for the higher and middle rates of the disability living allowance care component (DLA care) respectively (see p137). AA, unlike disability living allowance (DLA), does not have a mobility component.

Who can claim

You qualify for AA if:[166]

- you satisfy the residence conditions (see p699);
- you are not subject to immigration control (see p660);
- you are 65 or over when you first claim (see p148);
- you are not resident in certain types of accommodation (see p721);
- you satisfy the 'disability' conditions – ie:
  - you meet one or more of the day or night conditions (see p137); *and*
  - you meet the condition(s) throughout a period of six months in the two years before your award begins (see p152 if you are reclaiming within two years); *or*
  - you are terminally ill (see p149).

The disability conditions

The disability conditions for AA are the same as those for the middle or higher rates of DLA care. There is no equivalent in AA of the lower rate of DLA care. You get lower rate AA if you satisfy the disability conditions for middle rate DLA care (see p137). You get higher rate AA if you satisfy the disability conditions for higher rate DLA care (see p137).

The rules about your age

You can claim AA if you are aged 65 or over.

If you already get disability living allowance mobility component when you reach 65, you can claim DLA care instead of AA after age 65. However, you cannot get lower rate DLA care unless you satisfied the disability test for the lower rate before age 65. If you are approaching your 65th birthday it is usually better to claim DLA since DLA has a mobility component and the extra lower rate care component.

4. The amount of benefit[167]

Disability living allowance mobility component (DLA mobility) is paid at two weekly rates:

- the *lower rate* of DLA mobility (see p127) is £16.05;
- the *higher rate* of DLA mobility (see p127) is £42.30.

Disability living allowance care component (DLA care) is paid at three weekly rates:

- the *lower rate* of DLA care (see p137) is £16.05;
- the *middle rate* of DLA care (see p137) is £40.55;
- the *higher rate* of DLA care (see p137) is £60.60.

Attendance allowance (AA) is paid at two weekly rates:

- the *lower rate* of AA is £40.55;
- the *higher rate* of AA is £60.60.

In addition, you are entitled to a Christmas bonus (see p68). You are not credited with national insurance contributions by virtue of receiving disability living allowance or AA.

5. Special rules for special groups

There are some groups of claimants to whom special rules apply. These are covered on p149 and in Chapters 25, 26 and 28. Special rules apply to:

- people on renal dialysis (see below);
- people who are terminally ill (see below);
- people subject to immigration control (see Chapter 26);
- people who have gone abroad (see Chapter 26);
- people in care homes (see p725);
- people in hospital (see p715);
- people in hospices (see p716);
- people in prison (see p731).

People on renal dialysis

Special rules apply if you are undergoing renal dialysis on a kidney machine.[168] You receive middle rate disability living allowance care component (DLA care) or lower rate attendance allowance (AA).

To qualify, you need to have such treatment regularly for two or more sessions a week. You also need to show that either the dialysis is of a type which requires the attendance or supervision of another person or that you in fact require attention or supervision from another person while you are dialysing.

These rules also apply if you dialyse in hospital as an outpatient and have no help from any member of the staff. Others who dialyse in hospital do not qualify by this special route but you can count these spells of hospital dialysis towards the qualifying periods. This helps those who alternate between dialysis in hospital and at home to get AA or DLA care more quickly for the times they dialyse at home. There is nothing to prevent those who undergo renal dialysis in a manner that does not qualify them under this route from qualifying for DLA care (see p136) or AA (see p147) under the ordinary conditions.

People who are terminally ill

You are regarded as **'terminally ill'** if you are suffering from a progressive disease and can reasonably be expected to die within six months as a result of that disease.[169] This does not mean that it must be more likely than not that you will die within this period. It simply means that death within six months would not be unexpected.

A terminally ill claimant is automatically treated as satisfying the conditions for higher rate DLA care and there is no requirement to satisfy the three-month qualifying period.[170] Similarly, higher rate AA is paid straight away without you having to serve the six-month qualifying period.[171] If you are terminally ill, you do not automatically get disability living allowance mobility component (DLA mobility). You must satisfy the usual disability conditions for DLA mobility but the award can start as soon as you do, without serving the usual three-month qualifying period.

The Department for Work and Pensions (DWP) aims to deal with these claims within eight working days. They are referred to as 'claims under the special rules'.

The special rules apply only if your claim is made on that basis, or if an application for revision or supersession on an existing claim is made on that basis. Any notification to the DWP that someone is terminally ill should be treated as an application for a claim, revision or supersession, provided that the notification refers to DLA or AA.[172]

Someone else is allowed to make a claim, or apply for a revision or supersession, on behalf of a terminally ill person without her/his knowledge or authority.[173]

The DWP can supersede your award if your condition or prognosis improves so that you are no longer regarded as 'terminally ill'.

6. Claims and backdating

The success of a disability living allowance (DLA) or attendance allowance (AA) claim can often depend on how well you have completed the claim form. Therefore, you should read the following section carefully before you make a claim.

Making a claim

A claim for AA or DLA should be made on the relevant Department for Work and Pensions (DWP) claim form – an AA1 for AA or a DLA1 for DLA. You can obtain the claim pack by contacting your local disability benefits centre, or by ringing the DWP freephone Benefit Enquiry Line for people with disabilities on 0800 882 200 (textphone 0800 243 355). Alternatively, you can request a claim form by sending in the tear-off coupon from leaflet DS702 for AA, or DS704 for DLA. You will then be sent a claim form by post (it may be wise to keep a record of the date you asked for it). The claim form is date-stamped and you have six weeks, from the date of your request, to return the completed form to the DWP.[174]

The claim packs are also available from citizens advice bureaux and other advice agencies, and can be found on the DWP website (see Appendix 1). These packs are not date-stamped so you must send in the completed form as soon as possible to secure your date of claim. The date of claim is the date on which your form is received by the DWP (see p151). Keep a copy of your claim in case queries arise. The law allows you to return your claim to any DWP office but, in practice, you should send the completed claim pack to the disability benefits centre that covers your area.

Claims under the special rules for terminally ill people are made in a different way (see p151).

In certain circumstances the Secretary of State may accept a written application which is not on the correct form (see p1079).[175]

Information to support your claim

When you claim DLA or AA, you must satisfy the national insurance (NI) number requirement. In most cases this means you must provide your NI number. These requirements do not apply if you are claiming DLA on behalf of a child under 16.[176] See p1083 for further details.

Who should claim

A claim for DLA or AA is normally made by the disabled person her/himself. A claim for a child under 16 or a person unable to manage her/his own affairs is made by the disabled person's appointee (see p1075).

Claiming for terminally ill people

If a claim is being made on the basis that a person is terminally ill (see p149), it may be made without that person's knowledge or authority. This applies equally to claims for AA, disability living allowance care component (DLA care) or disability living allowance mobility component (DLA mobility) (although in this latter case, as explained on p134, terminal illness only exempts the claimant from the rules about qualifying periods).[177]

These claims are known as 'claims under the special rules'. People claiming under these rules need to provide Form DS1500, completed by their GP or consultant, detailing their medical condition. They do not need to fill in the parts of the claim form relating to their need for personal care. If they wish to claim for DLA mobility, then they do need to answer the relevant questions.

It is possible for someone acting on behalf of a terminally ill person to request a revision or supersession of an unfavourable decision, and even to appeal to a tribunal, without that person's knowledge or authority.

The date of your claim

The date of your claim is the date your request for a claim pack is received by the DWP, providing you return the properly completed form within six weeks of the date of your request.[178] There is discretion to extend the six-week deadline, so if you return the form late explain why it is late.

If you are using a claim form issued by an advice agency or downloaded from the internet, your date of claim is the date your completed form is received by the DWP. As the DLA claim form comes in different sections, you can establish your date of claim by sending in section 1 first (see p153).

If you claim the wrong benefit

A claim for DLA can be treated as a claim for AA and vice versa (see p1084).[179] A claim for an increase of industrial injuries disablement benefit where constant attendance is needed can be treated as a claim for DLA or AA and vice versa (see p1084).[180]

Claiming in advance

A claim for DLA or AA can be made before you have satisfied the three-month qualifying period for DLA[181] (see pp127 and 136), or the six-month qualifying period for AA[182] (see p147). As long as you claim no more than three months before you would qualify for DLA, or six months before you would qualify for AA, and you satisfy the other qualifying conditions, you can be awarded DLA or AA in advance of your date of entitlement.

Renewal claims

DLA and AA can be awarded for fixed periods (see p159). Renewal claims are usually invited up to six months before your old award expires. It is important that you send back your completed renewal claim form before your old award expires as no backdating is possible.

Decision makers will normally treat your renewal claim as a new claim beginning the day after your old award runs out.[183] However, they may use the information you give in the renewal claim to revise or supersede your existing award, in which case your entitlement may be changed earlier.[184] Therefore, if you feel you have a strong case for an increased award, you should send your renewal form back early and ask for a revision or supersession. If this is not the case, it is advisable to send the form back nearer the date your current award runs out.

Reclaiming within two years

If your award has ended and you reclaim within two years, perhaps because your condition has worsened again, you can be paid from the date of claim. You do not have to serve the standard three-month qualifying period again, provided that you meet all the other qualifying conditions for the rate you were getting before.[185] This is because the qualifying period is taken to be the last three months of your previous award.[186] If you reclaim a different rate, you do have to serve the standard qualifying period.

Reclaiming over age 65

If your DLA award ended after you reached 65 and you reclaim the same rate within one year, you can be paid immediately without having to serve the standard three- or six-month retrospective qualifying period again. To reclaim another rate (see p146), you do have to serve the qualifying period again. If it has been over a year since your previous award ended, you must claim AA instead of DLA care, and you will not be able to reclaim DLA mobility.[187]

If your AA award has ended, you can reclaim the same rate within two years without having to serve the standard six-month qualifying period again.[188]

Completing the claim form

Make sure you get the correct form. There are two DLA claim packs – one for those under the age of 16 (DLA1 Child) and one for those aged 16 and over (DLA1) – and one AA claim pack (AA1). See p154 for tips on filling in your claim form.

If you find it difficult to complete the form, the DWP can help you complete it by telephone, or in some circumstances can send a visiting officer to do so. Most advice agencies can also help you.

Attendance allowance claims

The AA claim form has just one section to complete. The decision maker may phone you to get more details about your care needs. Try not to underestimate the help you need. Although the forms are different, the information given below regarding the longer claim forms for DLA, other than the sections on DLA mobility, is just as elevant for AA claims.

Disability living allowance claims

Unless you are part of the new claim form trial in the Glasgow area in which a shorter claim pack is being used, the DLA pack comes in two parts:

- **Section 1** asks for various factual details about the person claiming the allowance.
- **Section 2** asks about the sort of help the disabled person needs with personal care and getting around.

Note: a shorter claim form, consisting of just one section, may be introduced during 2005. With such forms, the decision maker may phone you to get more details about your care needs and/or your problems with getting around. However, the information below about the longer claim forms will remain relevant

Section 1 of the pack is, technically, the benefit claim and should be returned without delay, even if you will take longer to complete Section 2. In each section there is space for another person to sign your form. The same person, or two different people, can sign these statements. It can be someone who knows you well in either a professional or personal capacity – eg, a carer, social worker, friend, relative or doctor. If your doctor signs the form s/he will not charge you. If you are unable to get other people to complete the form you should send it in anyway, as the DWP can arrange for this.

DLA claim packs cover mobility and care needs, but you do not need to answer all the questions (although care and mobility questions may overlap – see p155). You can answer only the questions that relate to mobility needs if you only want to claim for DLA mobility. When you complete Section 2 you should look carefully at the descriptions of the qualifying conditions for the various rates of the allowances given earlier in this chapter.

The claim pack for adults

The DLA form asks you questions about your mobility problems, your supervision and attention needs, and your ability to cook a main meal. Do not worry if a lot of the questions do not apply to you. You can, for example, qualify for the lower rate of DLA care because of the problems you have cooking a main meal (see p138), which only takes up one page of the claim pack.

You should give as much detail as you can. Do not feel bound by the size of the boxes. If you need extra space to explain your situation in full, use a separate piece of paper.

Unmet care needs

It can be difficult, if you do not receive any help from another person, to describe your attention or supervision needs. Many disabled people struggle to perform daily tasks on their own. If you do not have a carer you should still describe your problems. You should ask yourself whether certain activities cause you pain, or make you dizzy, tired or breathless. If you take a long time to perform particular tasks you should explain this. You should also say if you are not able to perform a particular activity adequately. For example, if you cannot bend down you may not be able to reach your feet when washing.

Aids and adaptations

If a decision maker thinks that you can use a particular aid or adaptation s/he may decide that you do not need attention or supervision. For example, if you have a commode the decision maker may conclude you do not need someone to help you get to the toilet at night. You should, therefore, try to explain how useful any equipment actually is and whether you still need help from another person in spite of the equipment. If, for instance, you have had a bath rail fitted, but find it very difficult to climb in or out of a bath, you should explain this.

Frequency, variability and duration

You are asked throughout the form to estimate how long you need help for, how many times a day, and how many days a week.

- The questions about 'how long' you need help for are important if you need attention for a 'significant portion of the day' (see p143) or you need 'prolonged' attention at night (see p144).
- The questions about 'how many times a day' you need help are important if you need 'frequent attention throughout the day' (see p144) or 'watching over' at frequent intervals during the night (see p145).
- The questions about 'how many days a week' you need help are designed to assess your overall needs, particularly if you have a variable or fluctuating condition. If your condition does not vary but you only receive help on certain days you should still say that you need help seven days a week. It is the help you need, not the help you actually get, that counts. If you need attention or

supervision or have difficulties walking most days of the week, your needs are taken into account. However, if you only have problems a few days a week, you will not necessarily be refused DLA.[189] In this case, explain fully the help you need on your 'bad' days but include the help you need on your 'good' days as well so that you are giving an overall picture.

As you have some weeks before you need to return Section 2 of the claim pack, it may well be a good idea to keep a diary over a period of a week or more, so that you can answer the questions about the pattern of your needs more accurately.

Walking outdoors

The section on 'walking outdoors' is for the higher rate of DLA mobility. If walking causes you 'severe discomfort' you may be regarded as being virtually unable to walk (see p128).

- You are asked to say how far you can walk before you feel discomfort and how long on average it takes you to walk this distance. If you are not sure how to answer this you should get someone to walk outdoors with you to measure the distance you can walk without severe discomfort and the time it takes you to walk this far.
- You should explain what sort of discomfort you experience, such as pain or breathlessness.
- You should also describe your manner of walking. For example, you may have problems with balance, or you may walk with a limp, drag your feet, or shuffle.
- If you need to stop to rest you should try to explain how far you can walk before you need to stop, and for how long you need to rest.

Guidance or supervision

If you are able to walk but need guidance or supervision outdoors, at least in unfamiliar places, you may qualify for the lower rate of DLA mobility (see p133). The section on 'having someone with you when you are outdoors' relates directly to this qualifying condition. Explain clearly what your companion does or might need to do to help you – eg, does s/he physically lead you, or give directions or help you avoid obstacles, or does s/he monitor your condition or monitor the route ahead or encourage or calm you. Say why you need your companion to do these things. If you need supervision because you are at risk of danger, the questions on 'falls or stumbles', 'someone keeping an eye on you', and 'dizzy spells, fits, seizures or something like this', which relate primarily to the 'continual supervision' test for the care component (see p144), may also help you qualify for the lower rate of the mobility component.

Mental disabilities

There is a section on 'the way you feel about your mental health'. This relates to both supervision and attention needs. There is also a section on 'communicating with other people', as well as questions throughout the claim pack which ask if someone has to 'tell you or encourage you' to perform a particular activity. These questions are also designed for people with mental disabilities who may need reminding or persuading to attend to their bodily functions. The section on 'the help you need when you go out during the day or in the evening' may also be appropriate for people with mental disabilities who need assistance to undertake social, leisure and recreational activities.

Sensory impairments

The section on 'communicating with other people' applies to deaf claimants who need an interpreter, or blind people who need to have newspapers or correspondence read to them (see p140). Blind people who need someone to tell them if they have stains on their clothes or if their hands are clean should explain these problems in the 'dressing' and 'washing' sections. It is especially important that people with sensory impairments complete the section on 'the help you need when you go out during the day or in the evening' to explain about the help needed to perform social and recreational activities .

The claim pack for children

When claiming on behalf of a child you must show that a disabled child's attention or supervision needs are 'substantially in excess' of what is required by a non-disabled child (see pp135 and 146). All very young children require attention and supervision and it can be difficult to identify what help is given 'in excess' of a child's normal care or supervision needs. The questions on 'development' in the DLA child pack help to address this problem.

If your child needs supervision to prevent them doing something that would be dangerous, you should explain why you cannot rely on the child to take the necessary precautions themselves. Decision makers tend to take a mechanical view of child development and assume that children adapt to particular disabilities by set ages. This leads to fixed-period awards that expire when a child reaches a certain age. However, it is wrong to assume that all disabled children respond to the problems they face in the same way. In one case a child with photosensitive epilepsy was known to watch television even though he was not supposed to. It could not be said that he was 'old enough to know better', as there was evidence that he persisted in doing things that were known to be bad for him.[190]

Some issues, such as how to answer the questions on frequency, variability and duration of needs, are similar to those faced by people filling in the adult pack (see p154). You should, therefore, read the section on the adult claim pack, as well as this section, if you are completing a child pack. You should consider the following issues, which are specific to claiming for children.

When the child is in bed at night

It is explained in the claim form that 'night' means 'when the household has closed down at the end of the day'. This is usually some time after a child has gone to bed. Any attention you provide after a child has gone to bed, but before you have, should count towards the daytime attention conditions, not the night-time needs (see p144).

Mobility

The form reminds you that children can only qualify for DLA mobility from the age of three, but points out that problems with getting around may indicate care or supervision needs. It can be difficult to explain how a disabled child requires 'substantially more' guidance or supervision (see p135) outdoors in order to qualify for the lower rate of DLA mobility (see p133). This is because most young children do not go out, at least in unfamiliar places, on their own. A child with a sensory impairment or learning disability may require much more direct or close supervision than a non-disabled child.[191] Whereas a non-disabled child may be allowed to walk in the presence of an adult, a disabled child may require an adult physically to hold or guide her/him. Also, a 'familiar route' to a non-disabled child may be a hazardous obstacle course to a child whose sight is impaired.

Extra attention or supervision

When explaining about your child's 'extra' requirements you should bear in mind that the extra 'attention or supervision' can be 'substantially in excess' of that required by a non-disabled child, either in terms of additional time, or 'by virtue of the quality or degree' of the assistance (DLA mobility, see p135; DLA care, see p146).[192]

For example, you may let a non-disabled child play outdoors in the street and instruct her/him not to cross roads. You may be able to supervise the child indirectly without having to watch her/him all the time. However, you may have to supervise directly a child with sensory impairments or behavioural problems or confine her/him indoors. Or perhaps a child with attention deficit disorder would need to be accompanied to school or to local shops, whereas a non-disabled child would be allowed to go on her/his own.[193]

About the child's development

The questions on development are extremely important when trying to show that disabled children need extra care or supervision.

Disabled children may need extra help in order to develop daily living skills, language, social skills and so on. For example, babies with sensory impairments may require much more physical stimulation in order to aid parental bonding and develop communication skills. Children learn spontaneously through play, but a disabled child may need help to use toys, or may need to be coaxed to explore her/his environment. Children with learning or sensory disabilities require extra help to develop daily living or language skills. They may also develop these skills later than non-disabled children.

If you have no experience of bringing up children you may not know exactly when a child should be crawling, walking, speaking, feeding her/himself and so on. If you are not sure you should ask your health visitor or paediatrician. For example, most children pick up and eat food by 8 to 12 months. Therefore, if you are still feeding a child after 12 months you are providing attention that a non-disabled child of the same age would not need.

School-age children

Disabled children, particularly those with sensory impairments or learning disabilities, usually require extra help with their school work. Extra help in the classroom or with homework can count towards a child's attention needs.[194] A statement of special educational needs may provide useful supporting evidence of the extra help needed with her/his studies.

Communicating

Pre-lingual deaf children, whose first language is British Sign Language, may need help to understand or communicate in written or spoken English. Blind children will not only need help to understand written information, but may also need help to learn Braille. Children with behavioural problems may need help to express themselves or understand other people.

How your claim is dealt with

Claims are initially dealt with at regional disability benefit centres. A decision maker can award DLA or AA on the basis of your claim form alone but may choose to contact someone you have named on the form for more information, perhaps your doctor. S/he may also arrange for you to be given a medical examination by a doctor acting on behalf of the DWP.

The Secretary of State has the power to refer you to a doctor for an examination to get further information in connection with the claim (see p161).[195] All initial decisions on claims are made by a decision maker (see p1180).[196]

If you refuse to attend a medical examination 'without good cause' then the decision maker has to decide your claim against you.[197]

The DWP aims to deal with new claims for DLA within 39 working days and new claims for AA within 24 working days. Claims made under the 'special rules' for terminal illness (see p149) should be decided within eight working days.

Backdating your claim

It is very important to claim in time. A claim for DLA or AA cannot be backdated.[198]

If you might have qualified for benefit earlier but did not claim because you were given the wrong information or misled by the DWP you could:

- ask for an ex gratia payment (see p1304); *or*
- complain to the Ombudsman via your MP (see p1302).

7. Getting paid

Payment of disability living allowance (DLA) or attendance allowance (AA) is normally made by credit transfer ('direct payment') into a bank account (or similar account). You will still have the option of opening an account that allows you to collect your benefit at the post office (see p1099).[199] If you are unable to open or manage an account, it may be possible to be paid by cheque. For more information about these payment methods, see p1099.

AA and DLA are normally paid every four weeks.[200] In practice, they are normally paid in arrears. AA can be paid weekly in advance. If you are claiming DLA under the special rules for terminal illness, it can be paid weekly.

If you are expected to return to hospital or a care home within 28 days, DLA and AA can be paid at a daily rate for days at home (see Chapter 28).[201]

DLA and AA are normally paid on Wednesdays, but the Secretary of State can vary the payday.[202]

Higher rate disability living allowance mobility component (DLA mobility) can be paid directly to Motability if you are purchasing a car through the scheme (see p164).

Payment can also be made to someone else on your behalf, called your 'appointee' (see p1075), if you are unable to act. Direct deductions cannot be made from DLA or AA to repay debts (see Chapter 40). If payment of your DLA or AA is suspended, see p1105.

Length of awards

Awards of DLA or AA can be made for either fixed or indefinite periods.[203] The length of an award depends on how long a decision maker estimates your current needs may last for. If you have an indefinite award (previously called a life award), you will not have to make a renewal claim at any stage but it is always open to the Department for Work and Pensions (DWP) to reduce or stop your award if they have grounds to revise or supersede it.[204]

In practice, awards are usually made for at least six months because of the DLA requirement that you must be likely to satisfy the disability conditions for the next six months. However, there is no legal minimum length for an award.[205] If you think benefit should be awarded for longer, perhaps because your condition is such that your care or mobility needs will not decrease, or because you need a longer period award of DLA mobility to take advantage of the Motability scheme (see p164), you should consider asking for a revision (see p1189). You should, however, bear in mind that, if you challenge the length of your award, the rate of your award may also be reconsidered. If your award is for a limited period you will be invited to make a renewal claim six months before the award runs out (see p152).

Although DLA has two components there can only be a single DLA award, consisting of one or both components. You can have an indefinite award of one component combined with a limited period award of the other. However, you cannot be awarded both components for two different fixed periods – both award periods must be aligned to end on the same day.[206]

Payment to children

DLA for a child under the age of 16 is usually paid to an adult with whom the child is living, whom the Secretary of State appoints to act on her/his behalf (often called an 'appointee'). This is normally the child's mother or father.[207] Children cannot make valid claims on their own behalf.[208]

The allowance can continue to be paid to the appointee in some circumstances when the child and appointee are not living together, including during a temporary separation of up to 12 weeks, or when the child is absent at a boarding school or in hospital (although other rules may mean that payment stops – see p715). DLA ceases to be paid to the appointee immediately when the child is being looked after by a local authority or any similar arrangement, unless the arrangement is not intended to last for more than 12 weeks.[209]

Delays and complaints

If payment of your DLA or AA is delayed, you might be able to get an interim payment. See p1108 for further details.

If you suffer delays or wish to complain about how your claim has been dealt with, see Chapter 47. You might be able to claim compensation (see p1304).

Change of circumstances

It is your duty to report any change in your circumstances which might affect your right to, the amount of, or payment of your benefit.[210] You should do this promptly by writing to or telephoning the Disability Benefits Unit (although in individual cases notification might be accepted in a form other than in writing or by telephone). In some cases, however, the decision maker might say you must report changes in writing. In any case, you might want to report the change in writing and keep a copy in case of a dispute in the future. If you do not promptly report any such change, any resulting overpayment may be recoverable from you (see Chapter 41). If you are considered deliberately to have acted falsely or dishonestly, you may also be guilty of an offence (see Chapter 42).

If your condition deteriorates so that you become eligible for a higher rate or another component, benefit can be backdated to the end of the three-month (for DLA) or six-month (for AA) qualifying period, as long as you tell the DWP no later than a month after completing the qualifying period. If payment (but not entitlement) of DLA or AA has stopped – eg, while you are in hospital or a care home – the decision to resume payment will take effect from the day you left if you tell the DWP within a month. If you do not report a change of circumstances within the month, benefit can still be backdated if you do so within 13 months and there were 'special circumstances' that meant it was not practical to report the change earlier.[211]

If your condition improves so that you should drop down a rate, lose a component or lose benefit altogether, the new decision normally takes effect from the date you tell the DWP of the improvement, or from the date of the decision if the DWP changed it without you asking. It would only take effect from an earlier date (and cause an overpayment) if you should have realised earlier that the change should have been reported. The DWP recognises that it is difficult for claimants to realise when a gradual improvement begins to affect benefit entitlement.[212]

Overpayments and fraud

If you have been overpaid DLA or AA, you might have to repay it. The rules on overpayments are covered in Chapter 41.

If you have been accused of fraud, see Chapter 42.

Periodic enquiries

Since June 1999 the DWP has been checking existing DLA awards as part of a 'periodic enquiry process'. AA recipients are not currently having their awards checked.

The enquiry process applies to people on all rates of DLA, including those originally awarded DLA 'for life' or indefinitely. Each year only a relatively small proportion of awards are checked. There is a higher chance of selection from among those groups that the DWP considers more prone to change – those getting just one DLA component – but within groups selection is random. Overall, in nine out of 10 cases, checked awards either remain unchanged or are increased.

Certain groups of people are exempt from periodic enquiries. You should not be contacted if:[213]

- you have a fixed-period award which ends within three years;
- you receive higher rate DLA mobility *and either* middle *or* higher rate disability living allowance care component (DLA care); *and*
  - you are paraplegic, tetraplegic or quadriplegic, both deaf and blind (see p131), severely mentally impaired (see p131), a double amputee (see p131), aged 65 or over, or your award was made before April 1992;
- you receive higher rate DLA care because you are terminally ill and qualify under the 'special rules' (see p149);
- you receive higher rate DLA mobility *and* higher rate DLA care; *and*

- your main disabling condition has been recorded as cystic fibrosis, motor neurone disease, dementia, multiple allergy syndrome, multiple sclerosis, hyper kinetic syndrome, neurological disease (including muscular dystrophy), Parkinson's disease, learning difficulties, haemodialysis or total parenteral nutrition.

Awards to children under 16 are currently not being checked. The periodic enquiry process is still under review so the exemption list may change.

The DWP contacts you by sending a postal questionnaire (DLA300). You have a duty to supply any information requested by the DWP that may affect benefit entitlement.[214] If you do not respond to the enquiry, the DWP may notify you that your benefit may be suspended within a month.[215] This one-month limit can be extended if necessary to arrange for someone to help you complete the questionnaire.[216] If, after your benefit has been suspended for a month, you still have not complied with the enquiry, your award can be terminated.[217]

As part of the initial investigation into an existing award the DWP can require that you undergo a medical examination.[218] If you fail, without good cause, to submit to a medical examination on two consecutive occasions, your benefit can be suspended.[219] If, after your benefit has been suspended for one month, you still have not submitted to a medical examination, your benefit can be terminated.[220]

8. Challenging a decision

If you disagree with a disability living allowance or attendance allowance decision you can challenge it by a revision (see p1189), supersession (see p1199), or appeal (see p1218).

9. Tax, tax credits and other benefits

Tax

Attendance allowance (AA) is not taxable, nor is any part of disability living allowance (DLA).[221]

Tax credits

DLA and AA are ignored as income when calculating child tax credit (CTC) and working tax credit (WTC). An award of AA or DLA at any rate counts as a qualifying benefit for the disability element of WTC which you may get if you are working. A disability element is included in CTC for each child who gets DLA (any rate). If s/he gets higher rate DLA care, you may get a severe disability element in CTC. If you or your partner get higher rate DLA care or higher rate AA, a severe disability element is included in WTC. See Chapter 52 for more information.

Means-tested benefits

Neither AA nor any rate of DLA is taken into account as income when calculating income support (IS), income-based jobseeker's allowance (JSA), housing benefit (HB), council tax benefit (CTB) or the guarantee credit or savings credit of pension credit (PC). DLA and AA are paid on top of these benefits; indeed, you may be entitled to extra benefit.

If you or your partner are entitled to AA or DLA, then IS, income-based JSA, HB and CTB will include the disability premium, or higher pensioner premium if either of you are aged over 60 (see p882). If you or your partner are entitled to higher rate DLA care and aged under 60, you also get an enhanced disability premium (see p888). A severe disability premium is included in IS, income-based JSA, HB or CTB, or an addition for severe disability is included in the guarantee credit of PC if you receive AA or higher or middle rate DLA care and meet the other conditions for that premium. For further information, see p891.

If your child is entitled to DLA, HB/CTB will include a disabled child premium. If s/he gets higher rate DLA care, HB/CTB will include an enhanced disability premium. These premiums are also included in IS and income-based JSA if you do not yet get CTC.

If you or your partner are entitled to AA or DLA care then 'non-dependant deductions' (see p924) are not made from any benefits for housing costs you claim (ie, HB, CTB and mortgage interest payments included in IS, income-based JSA and the guarantee credit of PC).

Non-means-tested benefits

DLA and AA may be paid in addition to any other non-means-tested benefits described in this *Handbook* except that:

- AA and disability living allowance care component (DLA care) overlap with constant attendance allowance under the industrial injuries scheme (see p333) or war pensions scheme;[222] *and*
- Disability living allowance mobility component (DLA mobility) overlaps with the war pensioners' mobility supplement payable under the war pensions scheme.[223]

If you are receiving higher or middle rate DLA care or AA and someone regularly looks after you, that person may be entitled to carer's allowance (see Chapter 4).

If you get higher rate DLA care you are automatically treated as being incapable of work under the personal capability assessment (see p772), and the long-term rate of incapacity benefit is payable after 28 weeks instead of 52 weeks.

Passports and other sources of help

If you are on a low income, you might be entitled to certain health service benefits such as free prescriptions (see Chapter 9). You may also qualify for other sources of help (see Chapter 1) or a social fund payment (see Chapters 21 and 22) or free school meals (see p18).

If you get higher rate DLA mobility, you or your carer can be exempt from paying vehicle excise duty (**road tax**) on a car used solely by you or for your purposes. Contact the Disability Benefits Unit (see Appendix 1) for an application form.

If you get higher rate DLA mobility you should qualify for the **Blue Badge scheme** of parking concessions which operates throughout Great Britain and in the European Economic Area (with certain local variations). You should contact your local authority for further information.

If any member of your household receives AA or DLA at any rate you can get a grant from the **Warm Front** scheme (**Warm Deal** in Scotland; **Warm Homes** in Northern Ireland) (formerly the Home Energy Efficiency Scheme) for home insulation and other heating improvements (see p19). To obtain further information you should contact the freephone numbers below:

- England: 0800 316 6011 (textphone 0800 072 0156);
- Scotland: 0800 072 0150 (textphone 0800 072 0156);
- Wales: 0800 316 2815 (textphone 0800 072 0156);
- Northern Ireland: 0800 181 667 (textphone 019 1233 1054).

If you are aged over 16 and under 66 and you are getting higher rate DLA care you may be eligible for money from the **Independent Living Funds** to finance care provision (see p20).

Motability

Motability is a charity incorporated by Royal Charter. It runs a scheme to help you lease or buy a car if you receive higher rate DLA mobility (see p127).

DLA mobility is paid direct to Motability.[224] You may also have to make a down payment. If you drive more than 12,000 miles a year you may have to make further annual payments. For further information, write to Motability, Goodman House, Station Approach, Harlow, Essex CM20 2ET, or telephone 0845 456 4566. Motability produces leaflets on its schemes for car leasing and hire purchase of new cars, used cars and electric wheelchairs.

Notes

1. **Disability living allowance mobility component**
   1 s73 SSCBA 1992
   2 s73(1)(d) SSCBA 1992
   3 CM/5/1986
   4 Reg 12(1)(a) SS(DLA) Regs
   5 R(M) 3/78
   6 CDLA/3323/2003. However, CDLA/3612/2003 says that the cause of the problem must be physical. See *Welfare Rights Bulletin* 181, p8 for more detail.
   7 CDLA/2822/1999; CDLA/4329/1999
   8 CDLA/15106/1996
   9 CDLA/948/2000; CDLA/265/1997
   10 CDLA/1898/2003
   11 CDLA/15106/1996
   12 CSDLA/894/2001 and CDLA/3612/2003
   13 R(M) 2/89; CDLA/97/2001
   14 Reg 12(4) SS(DLA) Regs
   15 R(M) 2/89
   16 Reg 12(1)(b) SS(DLA) Regs
   17 CDLA/3188/2002
   18 R(M) 1/95; CSDLA/171/1998
   19 CM/208/1989; CSDLA/0044/2002
   20 CM/47/1986 and CSDLA/252/1994, but see also R(M) 5/86
   21 CDLA/608/1994. This was not disapproved of in R(DLA) 5/04; see *Adviser* 71 for an analysis of this issue.
   22 CDLA/1389/1997
   23 R(M) 1/81
   24 R(M) 1/83
   25 CM/627/1993
   26 CDLA/608/1994; R(DLA) 4/03
   27 R(DLA) 4/04
   28 *Hewitt and Diment v CAO* 29 June 1998 (CA), reported as R(DLA) 6/99
   29 CM/23/1985
   30 R(M) 1/98
   31 Reg 12(2) SS(DLA) Regs
   32 Reg 12(3) SS(DLA) Regs
   33 Sch 2 SS(GB) Regs
   34 s64 NAA 1948
   35 R(DLA) 3/95
   36 Sch 3 Part II SS(IIPD) Regs
   37 Reg 12(2) SS(DLA) Regs
   38 Reg 12(1)(b) SS(DLA) Regs
   39 s73(3) SSCBA 1992; reg 12(5) and (6) SS(DLA) Regs
   40 R(M) 3/86
   41 R(DLA) 2/96
   42 R(DLA) 3/98
   43 *M (a child) v CAO* 29 October 1999 (CA), reported as R(DLA) 1/00
   44 CDLA/95/1995
   45 CDLA/3215/2001
   46 CDLA/2054/1998
   47 R(DLA) 7/02; R(DLA) 9/02; CDLA/3244/2001
   48 s73(1)(d) SSCBA 1992
   49 R(DLA) 6/03
   50 CDLA/42/1994
   51 CDLA/42/1994; R(DLA) 3/04
   52 There are conflicting decisions on whether a person who needs guidance or supervision, but cannot take advantage of the faculty of walking, can qualify. See CDLA/2364/1995 and CDLA/42/1994.
   53 Reg 12(7) and (8) SS(DLA) Regs; R(DLA) 3/04
   54 CDLA/153/1994
   55 The tribunal of commissioners' decision in R(DLA) 4/01 means that CSDLA/223/1998, CSDLA/867/1997 and CSDLA/840/1997 should no longer be followed
   56 R(DLA) 4/01
   57 CDLA/42/1994
   58 CDLA/42/1994
   59 CDLA/52/1994; CDLA/3360/1995; CSDLA/591/1997; CDLA/2643/1998
   60 R(DLA) 4/01
   61 The tribunal of commissioners' decision in R(DLA) 4/01 means that CDLA/757/1995 should not be followed
   62 s73(12) SSCBA 1992
   63 s73(1A) SSCBA 1992
   64 s73(4) SSCBA 1992
   65 CSDLA/76/1998; CDLA/4806/2002. See CPAG's *Welfare Rights Bulletin* 147 for an analysis of the extra test for children.
   66 CA/92/1992; CSDLA/91/2003
   67 CDLA/2268/1999
   68 CA/92/1992
   69 Sch 1 paras 1, 5 and 6 SS(DLA) Regs
   70 Sch 1 para 1 SS(DLA) Regs; see also CSDLA/388/2000
   71 Reg 43 SS(C&P) Regs

2. **Disability living allowance care component**

72 s72 SSCBA 1992
73 s72(1)(a) SSCBA 1992
74 s72(1)(b) and (c) SSCBA 1992
75 s72(4)(a) SSCBA 1992
76 s72(5) SSCBA 1992
77 CDLA/944/2001; CDLA/4400/2001; R (DLA) 10/02
78 CSDLA/552/2001; CDLA/944/2001; CDLA/3908/2000
79 CDLA/15467/1996 (heard with CDLA/1659/1997) held that a child with behavioural problems could qualify without a medical diagnosis or label (see also CDLA/948/2000). A number of later decisions have disagreed, suggesting that some medical diagnosis is normally needed. See CDLA/944/2001.
80 R(DLA) 10/02
81 CDLA/2408/2002; CDLA/394/2004
82 s72(6)(a) SSCBA 1992
83 R(DLA) 2/95
84 R(DLA) 7/03
85 *R v Secretary of State for Social Security ex parte Armstrong* [1996] (CA)
86 *Moyna v Secretary of State for Work and Pensions* [2003] (HL) reported as R(DLA) 7/03
87 CSDLA/80/1996
88 CDLA/7374/1995; R(DLA) 8/02
89 CDLA/20/1994; CDLA/4214/2002
90 R(DLA) 2/95 which nonetheless allows for the use of 'certain devices to assist' which may form part of 'normal reasonable facilities' for cooking. See also R(DLA) 7/03 which held that the cooking test is a notional test and a thought experiment.
91 CDLA/20/1994. R(DLA) 2/95 insists on a traditional cooker but note CDLA/770/2000, which allows fresh food to be prepared in a microwave. See also CDLA/3778/2002.
92 CDLA/17329/1996 and CDLA/770/2000, both of which would appear to accord more weight to the use of special cooking aids than R(DLA) 2/95; see CPAG's *Welfare Rights Bulletin* 163
93 R(DLA) 1/97
94 R(A) 3/86 and *Mallinson v Secretary of State for Social Security* 21 April 1994 (HL), reported as R(A) 3/94
95 *Secretary of State for Social Security v Fairey* (aka *Halliday*) 21 May 1997 (HL), reported as R(A) 2/98
96 *Secretary of State for Social Security v Fairey* (aka *Halliday*) 21 May 1997 (HL), reported as R(A) 2/98
97 *Secretary of State for Social Security v Fairey* (aka *Halliday*) 21 May 1997 (HL), reported as R(A) 2/98
98 R(A) 3/89
99 R(A) 5/90
100 R(A) 1/73
101 CDLA/899/1994
102 See for example, R(A) 3/86 and *R v Secretary of State for Social Services ex parte Connolly* [1986] 1 WLR 421 (CA)
103 R(DLA) 10/02
104 *R v National Insurance Commissioner ex parte Secretary of State for Social Services* [1981] 1 WLR 1017 (CA), also reported as R(A) 2/80
105 *Mallinson v Secretary of State for Social Security* 21 April 1994 (HL), reported as R(A) 3/94
106 *R v National Insurance Commissioner ex parte Secretary of State for Social Services* [1981] 1 WLR 1017 (CA), also reported as R(A) 2/80; reg 10C SS (DLA) Regs
107 *Mallinson v Secretary of State for Social Security* 21 April 1994 (HL), reported as R(A) 3/94
108 CA/177/1988; CDLA/14696/1996
109 Reg 10C SS(DLA) Regs; reg 8BA SS(AA) Regs
110 R(A) 3/74
111 R(A) 2/75
112 CA/86/1987
113 *R v Social Security Commissioner ex parte Butler* February 1984, unreported and *Secretary of State for Social Security v Fairey* (aka *Halliday*) 21 May 1997 (HL), reported as R(A) 2/98
114 CDLA/240/1994
115 R(DLA) 1/02, R(DLA) 2/02 and R(DLA) 3/02 review the issue in the light of *Fairey* 15 June 1995 (CA)
116 R(DLA) 2/02
117 CDLA/3607/2001
118 *R v National Insurance Commissioner ex parte Secretary of State for Social Services* [1981] 1 WLR 1017 (CA), also reported as R(A) 2/80
119 *Cockburn v CAO and Another* 21 May 1997 (HL), reported as R(A) 2/98; *Ramsden v Secretary of State for Work and Pensions* 31 January 2003 (CA), reported as R(DLA) 2/03
120 CDLA/267/1994

121 CDLA/267/1994, CDLA/11652/1995, CDLA/3711/1995, CDLA/12381/1996, CDLA/16996/1996,CDLA/16129/1996 and CDLA/4352/1999 are useful, but conflict with CSDLA/281/1996 and CSDLA/314/1997. See CPAG's *Welfare Rights Bulletin* 145 for an analysis of this issue.
122 *Secretary of State for Social Security v Fairey* (aka *Halliday*) 21 May 1997 (HL), reported as R(A) 2/98
123 CDLA/16129/1996, CDLA/16996/1996 and CDLA/4352/1999 are helpful, but conflict with CSDLA/314/1997
124 CDLA/4352/1999 and CDLA/5216/1998, the latter being more restrictive
125 CDLA/4352/1999
126 CDLA/5216/1998
127 R(DLA) 1/98
128 s72(1)(a)(i) SSCBA 1992
129 R(DLA) 8/02
130 CDLA/58/1993
131 CSDLA/29/1994
132 Ramsden v Secretary of State for Work and Pensions 31 January 2003 (CA), reported as R(DLA) 2/03
133 *R v National Insurance Commissioner ex parte Secretary of State for Social Services* [1974] 1 WLR 1290 (DC), also reported as R(A) 4/74
134 CDLA/2852/2002
135 CDLA/997/2003
136 R(A) 1/04
137 R(A) 1/78
138 *R v National Insurance Commissioner ex parte Secretary of State for Social Services* [1981] 1 WLR 1017 (CA), also reported as R(A) 2/80. See also CDLA/5465/2002 and CDLA/492/2004 which prefer the phrase 'frequent ... throughout' the day to be looked at as a whole and given its ordinary, everyday meaning, taking account of all relevant factors.
139 CA/281/1989
140 CA/140/1985
141 CDLA/5465/2002 and CDLA/492/2004
142 *R v National Insurance Commissioner ex parte Secretary of State for Social Services* [1981] 1 WLR 1017 (CA), also reported as R(A) 2/80
143 R(A) 3/78
144 ss64(2)(b) and 72(1)(b)(ii) SSCBA 1992
145 R(A) 1/83
146 CA/15/1979, approved in R(A) 1/83
147 R(A) 2/89
148 CA/33/1984
149 R(A) 2/75
150 *Moran v Secretary of State for Social Services, The Times,* 14 March 1987 (CA), reported as R(A) 1/88
151 R(A) 5/81
152 R(A) 2/91
153 R(A) 3/92
154 ss64(3)(b) and 72(1)(c)(ii) SSCBA 1992
155 para 61165 DMG
156 s72(6) SSCBA 1992
157 R(DLA) 1/99
158 CA/92/1992; see also *Welfare Rights Bulletin* 147 for a useful analysis of the extra test for children
159 CA/92/1992
160 s75 SSCBA 1992
161 Sch 1 para 3 SS(DLA) Regs
162 Sch 1 para 3(2)(b) SS(DLA) Regs
163 Sch 1 para 1 SS(DLA) Regs; see also CSDLA/388/2000
164 Sch 1 para 7 SS(DLA) Regs
165 Reg 43 SS(C&P) Regs

3. **Attendance allowance**
166 s64 SSCBA 1992; reg 3 SS(AA) Regs

4. **The amount of benefit**
167 Sch 4 SSCBA 1992; reg 4 SS(DLA) Regs

5. **Special rules for special groups**
168 Reg 5 SS(AA) Regs; reg 7 SS(DLA) Regs
169 s66(1) and (2) SSCBA 1992
170 s72(5) SSCBA 1992
171 s66(1) SSCBA 1992
172 Regs 3(9)(b) and 6(6)(c) SSD&A Regs
173 ss66(2)(b) and 76(3) SSCBA 1992

6. **Claims and backdating**
174 Reg 6(8), (8A) and (9) SS(C&P) Regs
175 Reg 4(1) SS(C&P) Regs
176 Reg 1A SS(DLA) Regs
177 s66(2)(b) and s76(3) SSCBA 1992; s1(3) SSAA 1992
178 Reg 6(8), (8A) and (9) SS(C&P) Regs
179 Reg 9(1) and Sch 1 SS(C&P) Regs
180 Reg 9(1) and Sch 1 SS(C&P) Regs
181 Reg 13A(1) SS(C&P) Regs
182 s65(6) SSCBA 1992
183 Reg 13C SS(C&P) Regs
184 CDLA/14895/1996
185 Regs 6 and 11 SS(DLA) Regs
186 Regs 6 and 11 SS(DLA) Regs
187 Regs 6 and 11 and Sch 1 paras 3 and 5 SS(DLA) Regs
188 Reg 3 SS(AA) Regs
189 R(A) 2/74; see also Moyna v Secretary of State for Work and Pensions 31 July 2003 (HL) reported as R(DLA) 7/03
190 CDLA/339/1994

191 CDLA/2268/1999
192 CA/92/1992; CSDLA/91/2003
193 CDLA/4806/2002
194 CDLA/3737/2002, which concerned a visually impaired child. It is not disapproved by the CA in *Secretary of State for Work and Pensions v Hughes (a Minor)*, reported as R(DLA) 1/04, although the Court says its decision is not a precedent.
195 s19(1) SSA 1998
196 s8(1)(a) SSA 1998
197 s19(3) SSA 1998
198 ss65(4) and 76(1) SSCBA 1992

7. **Getting paid**
199 Reg 21 SS(C&P) Regs
200 Reg 22 SS(C&P) Regs
201 Reg 25 SS(C&P) Regs
202 Reg 22(3)and Sch 6 SS(C&P) Regs
203 ss65(1)(a) and 71(3) SSCBA 1992
204 s67(1) WRPA 1999
205 R(DLA) 11/02
206 s71(3) SSCBA 1992
207 Reg 43 SS(C&P) Regs
208 CDLA/1326/1995
209 Reg 43 SS(C&P) Regs
210 Reg 32(1B) SS(C&P) Regs
211 Reg 7(9) SS&CS(DA) Regs
212 Reg 7(2)(c) SS&CS(DA) Regs
213 House of Commons, *Hansard*, 10 March 1999, col 251
214 Reg 32(1) SS(C&P) Regs
215 Reg 17 SS&CS(DA) Regs
216 Reg 17(4)(a)(ii) SS&CS(DA) Regs; see also House of Commons, *Hansard*, 2 February 1998, cols 496-97
217 Reg 18 SS&CS(DA) Regs
218 Reg 19(1) SS&CS(DA) Regs
219 Reg 19(2) SS&CS(DA) Regs
220 Reg 19(3) and (4) SS&CS(DA) Regs

9. **Tax, tax credits and other benefits**
221 s677 IT(EP)A 2003
222 Sch 1 para 5 SS(OB) Regs
223 Reg 42(1)(b)(ii) SS(C&P) Regs
224 Regs 44, 45 and 46 SS(C&P) Regs

Chapter 8

Guardian's allowance

This chapter covers:

Guardian's allowance is a benefit paid to people looking after children who are effectively orphans. It is not necessary for you to be a child's legal guardian to qualify for guardian's allowance. It is also not necessary for both of the child's parents to have died. Guardian's allowance may be paid if one parent has died and the whereabouts of the other is unknown or the surviving parent is in prison. It is not necessary for you to have paid national insurance contributions to qualify for guardian's allowance. Your entitlement is not affected by whether or not you work or by any savings or income that you have. The Revenue is responsible for the administration of guardian's allowance.

Disability living allowance, child tax credit and child benefit are also available for children (see Chapters 7, 49 and 5).

1. Who can claim guardian's allowance

You qualify for a guardian's allowance if:[1]

- you are entitled to, or treated as entitled to, child benefit for the child (see p170); *and*
- the child is a 'qualifying child' (see p170); *and either*
  - the child is living with you (see p90); *or*
  - you, or if you are residing with your spouse, you and/or your spouse make contributions to the cost of providing for the child at the rate of at least

£12.20 a week in addition to any payment you are making to qualify you for child benefit for the child (see below and p91); *and*

- the residence conditions are satisfied (see p700).

Even if you are not making contributions to the cost of providing for the child, you can be treated as if you are if you give a written undertaking to make the contributions once benefit is paid to you. Any decision to pay you guardian's allowance on this basis may be revised if you do not actually make contributions once benefit is paid to you.[2]

If a child for whom you get guardian's allowance dies, see p176.

There are some groups of claimants for whom special rules apply (see p173).

Treated as entitled to child benefit

In order to qualify for guardian's allowance you must either be entitled to child benefit (see Chapter 5) or you must be treated as entitled to child benefit for the child. You are treated as being entitled to child benefit:[3]

- if you are residing with your husband or wife and s/he is entitled to child benefit for the child;[4] *or*
- for a week in which you are living in Great Britain and would have been entitled to child benefit for the child had you (or your spouse, if you reside with your spouse) not been getting a family benefit from another country; *or*
- for a week in which you (or your spouse, if you reside with your spouse) would have been entitled to child benefit had the child been born at the end of the week before her/his actual birth; *or*
- for the week before the first week that guardian's allowance is paid to you, if you would have been entitled to guardian's allowance for that week had child benefit been paid.

As both child benefit and guardian's allowance are normally paid from the Monday after you become entitled to them, the latter two provisions ensure that you do not have to wait a further week to qualify for guardian's allowance.

A 'child'

For who counts as a 'child' see p86. The rules on who counts as a child and on when a young person no longer counts as a child for the purposes of guardian's allowance are the same as those for child benefit.

'Qualifying' children

A child is a **'qualifying child'** if:[5]

- both the child's parents have died (see below if the child is adopted or has a step-parent); *or*

- one of the child's parents has died and the whereabouts of the other parent is unknown and was unknown at the time of the death (see below); *or*
- one of the child's parents is dead and the other is sentenced to a term of imprisonment of two years or more or is detained in hospital by order of a court (see p172).

Parents, adoptive parents and step-parents

The general rule is that a parent of a child may not claim guardian's allowance for that child.[6]

If a child is adopted, her/his adoptive parents are the ones who count as parents.[7] Guardian's allowance is payable if both of the adoptive parents have died or if one has died and the other is in prison or her/his whereabouts are unknown. If only one person adopts a child, a claim can be made for guardian's allowance if that person dies. If a child's adoptive parents have died, the child's natural parents may claim guardian's allowance.[8] However, adoptive parents may continue to receive guardian's allowance if they were entitled to it immediately before the adoption.[9]

If, when a child was born, her/his parents were unmarried, guardian's allowance is payable after the death of the mother, provided that paternity has not been clearly established.[10]

Guardian's allowance is also payable if a child's natural or adoptive parents were divorced and one parent has died, and at the time of her/his death the other parent did not have custody of the child (and there is no court order granting her/him custody) and was not maintaining the child (and was not liable for maintenance for the child under a court order or under a child support maintenance assessment or calculation). However, you cannot qualify for guardian's allowance if you are the surviving parent of the child.[11]

A step-parent does not count as a parent for guardian's allowance and so may be entitled to guardian's allowance for a stepchild.

Missing parents

Guardian's allowance can be paid if one of the child's parents is dead and, from the date of the death until a decision maker at the Revenue makes a decision on the guardian's allowance claim, the whereabouts of the other parent is unknown.[12] You will be expected to show that you have taken reasonable steps to find the missing parent, including asking known relatives and friends and checking old addresses. If contact has been made with a surviving parent since the death of the other parent (but prior to the decision maker's decision on the claim), guardian's allowance cannot be paid, as the whereabouts of the surviving parent has been known.[13] This applies even if the contact was only fleeting, such as at the funeral. If such contact has not been made, the position is less clear. If you are able to communicate with the surviving parent in some way this is likely to be sufficient to show that the whereabouts of that parent are known.[14] 'Whereabouts' is not the same as an address, so merely showing that you do not know where the surviving parent actually lives may not be sufficient if you know the locality in which s/he is based. However, the locality must be sufficiently defined – if all that is known is that the surviving parent is in a large urban area then you could argue that her/his whereabouts are unknown.

If the surviving parent's whereabouts have been established after the death, but before the decision maker's decision on your claim, you cannot qualify for guardian's allowance even if the surviving parent subsequently disappears.

If you qualify for guardian's allowance on this basis, you will continue to be entitled, even if the whereabouts of the surviving parent later becomes known, as long as her/his whereabouts only became apparent after the decision maker decided you were entitled to benefit.

Prison sentences

If one of the child's parents is dead and the other is in prison, you are only entitled to guardian's allowance if the surviving parent is serving a sentence of at least two years' imprisonment, or is detained in hospital by order of a court.[15] This includes custodial sentences (such as detention, including detention in a young offenders' institution) as well as prison sentences, but it does not include any period of imprisonment for contempt of court. There are detailed rules for calculating whether the length of a sentence amounts to two years, so if you are affected by these rules seek advice.

2. The rules about your age

There is no upper or lower age limit for entitlement to guardian's allowance.

3. Claiming for others

Guardian's allowance is payable for each qualifying child. No additional guardian's allowance is paid for any other dependants that you have.

4. The amount of benefit

Guardian's allowance is payable at the rate of £12.20 a week for each qualifying child.[16]

Entitlement to guardian's allowance does not qualify you for national insurance (NI) credits. However, if you also receive child benefit for a child under 16 throughout a tax year (or, in some circumstances, for at least nine months in a tax year), you will qualify for home responsibilities protection for that tax year. This protects your NI contribution record for retirement pension purposes (see p842).

5. Special rules for special groups

There are some groups of claimants to whom special rules apply. These are covered in Chapters 25, 26 and 28. Special rules apply to:

- people going abroad (see p686);
- people coming from abroad (see p700);
- qualifying children who are in legal custody (see p732);
- qualifying children whose parents were born outside the UK (see p700).

6. Claims and backdating

In order to be entitled to guardian's allowance you must make a claim for it.[17] The rules for claiming are described briefly below. The rules are explained in more detail in Chapter 39. You may claim guardian's allowance before you become entitled to it or your claim can be backdated (see p175).

Making a claim

Claims for guardian's allowance should be made in writing on the correct claim form – a BG1 form. You can obtain a claim form from the Child Benefit Office (telephone: 0845 302 1464, textphone: 0845 302 1474), your local Revenue enquiry centre, the Revenue's website (see Appendix 1), or from Jobcentre Plus offices. The Revenue decision maker has the discretion to accept a written claim which is not on the correct form if it is sufficient in the circumstances (see p1082).[18] You can submit your claim to the Guardian's Allowance Unit, Child Benefit Office (Washington), PO Box 1, Newcastle upon Tyne, NE88 1AA, a Revenue enquiry office or to a Jobcentre Plus office.

Keep a copy of your claim in case queries arise.

You may amend or withdraw your claim before it is assessed by writing to the Guardian's Allowance Unit. See p1076 for more details about making a claim.

Information to support your claim

When you claim guardian's allowance you must satisfy what is known as the 'national insurance (NI) number requirement' (see p1083). This means that, in most cases, you must provide your NI number when making a claim for guardian's allowance. You can also be asked to supply 'certificates, documents, information and evidence' considered relevant to your claim.[19] For example, you may be asked to supply the birth certificate(s) of the child or children for whom you are claiming.

If you are asked to provide evidence or documents which you do not have, ask what other evidence would be acceptable. Ask the Revenue to explain what is required and why and complain if you believe any requests for information are unreasonable.

Who should claim

You must normally claim guardian's allowance on your own behalf. However, if you are unable to manage your own affairs, another person can claim guardian's allowance for you by becoming your 'appointee' (see p1075).

If you are a married woman and you reside with your husband it is you, rather than your husband, who will be entitled to guardian's allowance. However, the guardian's allowance will be made payable to either you or your husband unless you inform the Revenue that you do not want payment to be made to your husband. You should inform the Revenue of this in writing by completing a form which you can obtain from the Revenue, although the decision maker may accept a written request which is not on such a form if it is sufficient in the circumstances. You may make such a request over the internet using the Revenue's secure messaging service (see p101 for further details).[20]

The date of your claim

The date of your claim is important, as it determines the date from which you will be paid guardian's allowance (see p175). The date of your claim is normally the date your claim is received at either the Child Benefit Office, a Revenue enquiry centre or a Jobcentre Plus office.

If the claim you submit is incomplete or not on the correct form you may be asked to provide further information or to complete the correct form. As long as this additional information or form is submitted within a month of it being sent back to you (or longer, if the decision maker thinks that the delay is reasonable), your claim is treated as having been made on the date that the initial claim was received at one of the above offices.[21]

In some circumstances you can claim before you qualify for guardian's allowance or the date of your claim can be backdated (see p175).

If you claim the wrong benefit

The decision maker can treat a claim for child benefit for a child as a claim for guardian's allowance for the same child.[22] This may allow you to get your claim for guardian's allowance backdated for more than the normal three months. If your child benefit claim is accepted as a claim for guardian's allowance, your claim can be backdated for up to three months from the date you claimed child benefit, if you satisfy the qualifying conditions over that period.

See p1084 for details of interchanging claims in this way.

Claiming in advance

You can claim guardian's allowance up to three months before you expect to qualify for it – eg, if you know you will be taking responsibility for a child.[23] It is helpful to claim in advance if you can, as the Revenue can then gather the information it needs and decide your claim in good time.

How your claim is dealt with

Your claim is dealt with by the Guardian's Allowance Unit of the Child Benefit Office and queries about your claim should be made to that office.

You may be able to claim an interim payment while waiting for a decision on your claim (see p1108) or to claim means-tested benefits if your income is low (see p177). See p1091 for more information about the processing of claims.

Backdating claims

Your claim for guardian's allowance can be backdated for up to three months from the date that you make your claim if you satisfy the qualifying conditions over that period.[24] You do not have to show any reasons why your claim was late. The rules on backdating are covered on p1086. (There are special rules if you were getting guardian's allowance and move between Great Britain and Northern Ireland or if you have been recognised as a refugee – see p669.[25])

If you might have qualified for benefit for an even earlier period but did not claim because you were given the wrong information or were misled by the Department for Work and Pensions or the Revenue, you could:

- ask for an ex gratia payment (see p1304); *or*
- complain to the Ombudsman via your MP (see p1302).

If you claimed child benefit instead of guardian's allowance, see p174.

7. Getting paid

Guardian's allowance is a weekly benefit and so cannot be paid for a period of less than a week. The decision maker at the Revenue can decide how your guardian's allowance is paid. Payment of guardian's allowance is normally made by direct credit transfer into your bank account or similar account. If you are unable to open or manage an account, payment can be made by cheque. Such cheques are sent to your home address and can be paid into an account or cashed at the post office (see p1099 for details). If you also receive child benefit, guardian's allowance will be paid at the same time and in the same way as your child benefit (see p102).[26]

Payment of guardian's allowance starts from the first Monday after the date of your claim (see p174), unless your date of claim is a Monday, when it starts on that day.[27] For details of when your date of claim can be backdated, see above.

If your entitlement to guardian's allowance ends, payment of benefit will continue up to, but not including, the following payday (which will normally be either Monday or Tuesday) unless your entitlement ends on a payday, when your benefit will be paid up to, but not including, that day.[28] If your benefit cheque is lost or stolen, see p1104. If payment of your guardian's allowance is suspended, see p1105.

Delays and complaints

If payment of your guardian's allowance is delayed, you might be able to get an interim payment. See p1108 for further details. If you suffer delays, or wish to complain about how your claim has been dealt with, see Chapter 47. You might be able to claim compensation (see p1304).

Change of circumstances

It is your duty to report any change in your circumstances which might affect your right to, the amount of, or the payment of your benefit.[29] You should do this promptly either by writing to, or speaking to someone in, the Guardian's Allowance Unit of the Child Benefit Office, a Revenue enquiry centre or a Jobcentre Plus office. If you do not report any such change promptly, any resulting overpayment may be recoverable from you (see Chapter 41). If you are considered deliberately to have acted falsely or dishonestly, you may also be guilty of an offence (see Chapter 42). If you report a change of circumstances verbally you should make a note of the time and date of your conversation and the name of the person you informed. It is also advisable to confirm your conversation in writing, keeping a copy of your letter in case problems arise. The rules about when your benefit will be adjusted following a change in your circumstances are the same as those for child benefit (see p104).

If a child dies

If a child for whom you are receiving child benefit dies, you can qualify for guardian's allowance for the eight-week period that child benefit remains in payment for that child (see p104), as long as you meet the normal qualifying conditions for guardian's allowance over that time (other than the condition that the child either must be living with you, or you must be contributing to her/his maintenance).[30]

Overpayments and fraud

If you are overpaid guardian's allowance, you might have to repay it. The rules on overpayments are covered in Chapter 41.

If you have been accused of fraud, see Chapter 42.

8. Challenging a guardian's allowance decision

You can apply for a revision or supersession of a guardian's allowance decision, or appeal against it – see Chapters 43 and 44.

9. Tax, tax credits and other benefits

Guardian's allowance is not taxable.[31]

Means-tested benefits and tax credits

If you have a low income you may be entitled to means-tested benefits, which can be paid in addition to guardian's allowance. Guardian's allowance is ignored when calculating your entitlement to income-based jobseeker's allowance (JSA)[32] (see Chapter 15), income support (IS)[33] (see Chapter 13), pension credit[34] (see Chapter 18), housing benefit[35] (see Chapter 10), council tax benefit[36] (see Chapter 6), working tax credit (see Chapter 50) and child tax credit (CTC)[37] (see Chapter 49).

Non-means-tested benefits

Although increases in non-means-tested benefits for children were abolished on 6 April 2003, some people will continue to be entitled to them (see p798). You cannot get guardian's allowance and an increase in non-means-tested benefit for the same child (see Chapter 31).[38] Other than this, guardian's allowance can be paid in addition to any other non-means-tested benefit.

Passports and other sources of help

If you are looking after a child but you are not the child's parent, and you do not qualify for guardian's allowance, you might consider approaching the local authority social services department for a fostering allowance.

If you are on a low income, you might be entitled to certain health service benefits, such as free prescriptions (see Chapter 9). You may also qualify for other sources of help (see Chapter 1) or a social fund payment (see Chapters

21 and 22). If you are getting IS or income-based JSA or, in some circumstances, CTC, your child(ren) will qualify for free school meals (see p18).

Notes

1. Who can claim guardian's allowance

1 s77 SSCBA 1992
2 Reg 5 SSB(Dep) Regs
3 Reg 4A SSB(Dep) Regs
4 s122(4) SSCBA 1992
5 s77(2) SSCBA 1992; reg 7 GA(Gen) Regs
6 s77(10) SSCBA 1992
7 Reg 4 GA(Gen) Regs
8 s77(10) SSCBA 1992; R(G) 4/83 (appendix)
9 s77(10) and (11) SSCBA 1992
10 Reg 5 GA(Gen) Regs
11 s77(10) SSCBA 1992; reg 6 GA(Gen) Regs
12 s77(2)(b) SSCBA 1992
13 CG/60/1992; R(G) 2/83; CSG/8/1992
14 CG/60/1992; CF/2735/2003
15 Reg 7 GA(Gen) Regs

4. The amount of benefit

16 Sch 4 Part III SSCBA 1992

6. Claims and backdating

17 s1 SSAA 1992
18 Reg 5 CB&GA(Admin) Regs
19 Reg 7 CB&GA(Admin) Regs
20 s77(9) SSCBA 1992; reg 10(4) GA(Gen) Regs; Sch 2 CB&GA(Admin) Regs
21 Reg 10 CB&GA(Admin) Regs
22 Reg 11 CB&GA(Admin) Regs
23 Reg 12 CB&GA(Admin) Regs
24 Reg 6(1) CB&GA(Admin) Regs
25 Reg 6(2) CB&GA(Admin) Regs

7. Getting paid

26 Regs 16(2), 17(5) and 18(4) CB&GA(Admin) Regs
27 Reg 13 CB&GA(Admin) Regs
28 Reg 14 CB&GA(Admin) Regs
29 Reg 23(4) CB&GA(Admin) Regs
30 s145A(4) SSCBA 1992

9. Tax, tax credits and other benefits

31 s677 Income Tax (Earnings and Pensions) Act 2003
32 Sch 7 para 6A(1) JSA Regs
33 Sch 9 para 5A(1) IS Regs
34 Reg 15(1)(g) SPC Regs
35 Regs 23 and 25 HB Regs as substituted by regs 2 and 8 HB&CTB(SPC) Regs; Sch 4 para 50 HB Regs
36 Regs 15 and 17 CTB Regs as substituted by regs 12 and 17 HB&CTB(SPC) Regs; Sch 4 para 49 CTB Regs
37 Reg 7 TC(DCI) Regs
38 Reg 7(4) SS(OB) Regs

Chapter 9

Health benefits

This chapter covers:

1. Charges and exemptions

Although the NHS generally provides free health care, there are fixed charges for some items and services such as prescriptions, dental treatment, sight tests, glasses, wigs and fabric supports.

You are exempt from these charges, however, if:[1]

- you, or a member of your family (see p809), are receiving income support (IS), income-based jobseeker's allowance (JSA) or the guarantee credit of pension credit (PC);
- you or your partner are receiving:
  - child tax credit (CTC – see Chapter 49); *or*
  - CTC and working tax credit (WTC – see Chapter 50); *or*
  - WTC including a disability or severe disability element (see p1357); *and*

  your gross annual income, as calculated by the Revenue for tax credit purposes at the time of your tax credit award, does not exceed £15,050. Members of your family for tax credit purposes (see p1316) are also exempt from charges if you satisfy these conditions.

  If this applies to you, the Revenue will inform the Prescription Pricing Authority of the Health Benefits Divison (see Appendix 1) which should then send you an exemption card which is normally valid until the end of the tax year. You can also use your tax credit award notice as proof of entitlement;

- you are a permanent resident in a care home and your place is being partly or wholly funded by a local authority (see p721). If your place is *not* being funded by a local authority, you may qualify for help with health charges under the low income scheme (see p186), or on other grounds;
- you are a hospital in-patient, in which case all medication and NHS treatment is provided free of charge (including glasses and contact lenses if prescribed through the Hospital Eye Service). If you are an out-patient, medication taken and treatment given while you are in the hospital is also provided without charge (but you may be charged for dentures and bridges);
- you are an asylum seeker, or a dependant of an asylum seeker, who is receiving support from the National Asylum Support Service (NASS) or a local authority (see p667);
- you are a war disablement pensioner and need the relevant item or service because of your war disability;
- you are aged 16 or 17 and are being financially maintained by a local authority in England or Wales after being in local authority care on or after 1 October 2001 (see p713);
- you are receiving support from a local authority in Scotland under section 29(1) of the Children (Scotland) Act 1995, after leaving care;
- you are in prison, or a young offender's institution.

You may also be exempt from some charges because of your age or health condition. See the following sections for details.

If you are not exempt on any of the above grounds, you may be entitled to full or partial remission of charges on the grounds of low income. The low income scheme is covered on p186.

2. Prescriptions

Free prescriptions

You qualify for free prescriptions if:[2]

- you are in one of the exempt groups listed above; *or*
- your income is low enough (see p189); *or*
- you are aged 60 or over; *or*
- you are aged under 16 (under 25 in Wales only), or under 19 and are in full-time education; *or*
- you are pregnant, or have given birth in the last 12 months; *or*
- you suffer from one or more of the following conditions:
  - a continuing physical disability which prevents you leaving your home except with the help of another person;
  - epilepsy requiring continuous anti-convulsive therapy;

- a permanent fistula, including a caecostomy, ileostomy, laryngostomy or colostomy, needing continuous surgical dressing or an appliance;
- diabetes mellitus (except where treatment is by diet alone);
- diabetes insipidus and other forms of hypopituitarism;
- myxoedema;
- hypoparathyroidism;
- forms of hypoadrenalism (including Addison's disease), for which specific substitution therapy is essential;
- myasthenia gravis.

Reduced-cost prescriptions

You cannot get reduced-cost prescriptions under the low income scheme.

If you need a lot of prescriptions, however, but are not exempt from charges, you can reduce the cost by buying a pre-payment certificate for four months or a year.[3] This will save you money if you need more than five prescription items in four months or 14 items in a year. You apply for a certificate on Form FP95 in England, EC95 in Scotland or FP95W in Wales, which you can get at a DWP office or chemist. A refund can be claimed in certain circumstances if you buy a pre-payment certificate and then qualify for free prescriptions or die (contact your health authority for details and time limits).

3. Dental treatment and dentures

Free treatment

You qualify for free NHS dental treatment (including check-ups) and appliances (including dentures) if, when your treatment is arranged or charges are made:[4]

- you are in one of the exempt groups listed on p179; *or*
- your income is low enough (see p188); *or*
- you are under 18, or under 19 and in full-time education; *or*
- in Wales only and for an examination only, you are under 25 or are 60 or over; *or*
- you are pregnant or have given birth within the last 12 months; *or*
- you are a patient of the Community Dental Service (this service is available for people who have difficulty getting treatment because of a disability or other reasons – contact your health authority for details) or an NHS Hospital Dental Service. Note, however, that there may be a charge for dentures and bridges.

Reduced-cost treatment

If you do not qualify for free treatment, you may qualify for reduced-cost treatment and appliances on the ground of low income. See p186 for details.

4. Sight tests and glasses

Free sight tests

You qualify for a free NHS sight test if:[5]

- you are in one of the exempt groups listed on p179; *or*
- your income is low enough (see p189); *or*
- you are aged 60 or over; *or*
- you are under 16, or under 19 and in full-time education; *or*
- you are registered blind or partially sighted; *or*
- you have been prescribed complex or powerful lenses (ie, one lens which has a power in any one meridian of at least plus or minus ten dioptres, or which is a prism-controlled bifocal lens); *or*
- you have been diagnosed as having diabetes or glaucoma or are at risk of getting glaucoma; *or*
- you are aged 40 or over and are the parent, brother, sister or child of someone suffering from glaucoma; *or*
- you are a patient of the Hospital Eye Service.

Reduced-cost sight tests

If you do not qualify for a free sight test, you may be entitled to a reduced-cost sight test on low income grounds.[6] See p186 for details. There is no set charge for a sight test, so it is worth shopping around if you are not entitled to a free test.

Vouchers for glasses and contact lenses

If you are given a prescription for glasses following an eye test, you are entitled to a voucher which you can use to buy (or repair) glasses or contact lenses if:[7]

- you are in one of the exempt groups listed on p179; *or*
- your income is low enough (see p189); *or*
- you are under 16, or under 19 and in full-time education; *or*
- you are a Hospital Eye Service patient needing frequent changes of glasses or contact lenses; *or*
- you have been prescribed complex or powerful lenses (see above).

You are entitled to a voucher if:[8]

- you require glasses or contact lenses for the first time; *or*
- your new prescription differs from your old one; *or*
- your old glasses have worn out through fair wear and tear; *or*
- you are under 16; *or*
- because of illness (or disability in Scotland) you have lost or damaged your glasses or contact lenses and the cost of repair or replacement is not covered by insurance or warranty; *and*

- you, or a member of your family, are exempt from charges because you are receiving income support, income-based jobseeker's allowance, the guarantee credit of pension credit, or tax credits (see p179); *or*
- your income is low enough (see p189); *or*
- you have been prescribed complex lenses (see p182).

Vouchers are issued by opticians or a hospital (if it has prescribed you with complex lenses or you need to change your lenses frequently). Each voucher has a coded value depending on the type of lenses (or repair) you need.[9] You can redeem the voucher at any supplier when you buy glasses (or have them repaired) or contact lenses. Vouchers are, however, only valid for six months[10] and they may not cover the full cost of the glasses or lenses you choose to buy. Prices vary and you may need to shop around if you do not want to pay the extra cost.

Reduced-value vouchers

You may be entitled to a reduced-value voucher on the grounds of low income. See p186 for details.

5. Fares to hospital

Full help

You qualify for full help with your fares to attend a hospital or any other establishment for NHS treatment or services if:[11]

- you are in one of the exempt groups listed on p179; *or*
- your income is low enough (see p189); *or*
- you are a patient at a genito-urinary medicine clinic more than 15 miles from your home (more than five miles if you need to attend on a weekly basis); *or*
- you live in the Isles of Scilly or the Scottish Islands or Highlands and have to travel more than a specified distance for hospital treatment.

The law allows help with the cost of travelling by the cheapest means of transport available and where necessary, the cost of overnight accommodation.[12] This usually means standard-class public transport. If you have to go by car or taxi, you should be paid your petrol costs or taxi fares. The travel expenses of an escort can also be met if you need to be accompanied for a medical reason. Special rules (including maximum costs) apply if you live in the Isles of Scilly or the Scottish Islands or Highlands.[13]

You should claim at the hospital (ask for the office which deals with claims). You may be able to request payment in advance of travelling, where this is necessary or, alternatively, you could apply for a social fund crisis loan from the DWP (see p538).

If you are travelling abroad to receive NHS treatment, you are entitled to payment for the cost of travel to and from the airport, ferry port or international train station if you are in one of the above groups. You are also entitled to payment or repayment of onward travelling expenses to the treatment centre, whether or not you fall within one of the above groups. The amount and mode of transport and payment is determined by the health authority or board prior to travel.

If you are receiving income support, income-based jobseeker's allowance or pension credit and are visiting a close relative or partner, you may be eligible for a social fund community care grant to help with your fares (see p528).

Partial help

You may qualify for partial help with your hospital fares on the grounds of low income. See p186 for details.

6. Free milk and vitamins

Note: The Government proposes to replace the current system of free milk and vitamins with a new scheme called 'Healthy Start'. The new scheme will be piloted in Devon and Cornwall from the summer of 2005 and will then be introduced in the rest of the UK in 2006. It will include the replacement of milk tokens by fixed value weekly vouchers which can be exchanged for milk, infant formula, fruit and vegetables. Further details of the proposals can be found in CPAG's *Welfare Rights Bulletin* 179 and on the Department of Health website (www.dh.gov.uk). Proposed changes to the current scheme prior to national roll out of 'Healthy Start' are noted below.

Milk tokens

The following people qualify for milk tokens which can be exchanged for free milk (liquid or dried):[14]

- expectant mothers who are entitled to income support (IS), income-based jobseeker's allowance (JSA) or the guarantee credit of pension credit (PC – see Chapter 18) or who are members of the family of someone who is entitled (see p809);
- children under five who are members of the family of someone who is entitled to IS, income-based JSA, the guarantee credit of PC, or child tax credit (CTC) provided, in the latter case, that the person's gross income (as calculated by the Revenue for tax credit purposes) at the time of the CTC award does not exceed £13,910 and s/he is not entitled to working tax credit (WTC);
- disabled children aged 5 to 16 who do not attend a school because of their disability.

Note:

- If you are an asylum seeker being supported by the National Asylum Support Service (NASS) (see p666) you should receive an additional payment for milk or infant formula if you are pregnant or have a child under three.
- The Government are proposing that from the commencement of the piloting of the new 'Healthy Start' scheme (see p184), the guarantee credit of PC will no longer be a qualifying benefit for milk tokens and that disabled children aged 5-16 who do not attend school because of their disability will no longer qualify (but may receive a one-off compensation payment).

Each qualifying person is entitled to one milk token a week.[15] Tokens can be used within four weeks of issue to obtain 7 x 568 millilitres or 8 x 500 millilitres of liquid milk at any participating retailer (includes most shops and milk deliverers) or 900 grammes of dried milk for a child under one from a child or maternity clinic.[16]

If you are more than 10 weeks pregnant, you should complete the form at the back of the leaflet 'Free Milk for Pregnant Women' (available from maternity clinics and the Department of Health website – see p184) to obtain your milk tokens. The form must be countersigned by a health professional to certify that you are pregnant and have received health advice. Once your child is born, you should inform the Revenue by calling 0845 300 3900 to continue to get milk tokens. A claim should be made for a disabled child not attending school on Form FW20. You should receive your tokens by post if your benefit is paid directly into your account. If you cash your benefit at a post office, you should be given your tokens at the same time. If you do not receive tokens to which you think you are entitled, or have any other problems with your tokens, you should contact your local DWP or tax credits office.

Free milk for children in daycare

Children under five are entitled to 189-200 millilitres of free milk on each day they are looked after for two hours or more:

- by a registered childminder or daycare provider; *or*
- in a school, playcentre or workplace nursery which is exempt from registration; *or*
- in local authority daycare.[17]

Children under one are allowed fresh or dried milk. Providers must apply for approval to the Secretary of State.

Reduced-cost dried milk

You are entitled to buy 900 grammes of dried milk a week at a reduced rate from a child or maternity clinic for each child under the age of one for whom you are responsible if:[18]

- you are entitled to CTC and WTC and your gross income for tax credit purposes as assessed by the Revenue at the time of your award does not exceed £15,050; *or*
- you are entitled to CTC, but not WTC, and your gross income for tax credit purposes at the time of your CTC award is between £13,910 and £15,050; *and*
- you are not getting milk tokens for that child.

You should automatically receive a certificate of entitlement from the Revenue which you can use to make a claim at the clinic. You can buy the dried milk within four weeks of the claim.

Note: The Government are proposing to remove the provision of reduced-cost dried milk from the commencement of the piloting of the new 'Healthy Start scheme' (see p184).

Free vitamins

The following people qualify for free vitamins:[19]

- expectant mothers, or those breastfeeding a child under age one, who are receiving IS or income-based JSA, the guarantee credit of PC, or CTC (or who are members of the family of someone who is entitled to one of these benefits), provided in the case of CTC, that the claimant's gross income for tax credit purposes, as assessed by the Revenue at the time of the award, does not exceed £13,910 and s/he is not entitled to WTC;
- children under five who are members of the family of someone who is entitled to IS, income-based JSA, the guarantee credit of PC, or CTC, provided in the case of CTC, that the person's gross income, as described above, does not exceed £13,910.

Children and expectant mothers are entitled to 20 millilitres of vitamin drops every 13 weeks. Breastfeeding mothers can have the same or 90 tablets. Vitamins can be obtained from child and maternity clinics.

7. The low income scheme

You or a member of your family may be entitled to full or partial remission of NHS charges on the grounds of low income if you are not exempt on other grounds. The low income scheme is administered by the Health Benefits Division (see Appendix 1).

To qualify for help under the scheme, you must have less than £8,000 capital, or £12,000 (£12,250 in Scotland) if you or your partner are aged 60 or over, or £20,500 (£20,000 in Scotland) if you live permanently in a care home (see p1024). Your capital is calculated as for other means-tested benefits (see Chapter 38). Tariff income from capital is calculated as for IS, unless you are a permanent resident in a care home (see below).

To determine whether you qualify for help under the low income scheme, your 'requirements' (see below) are compared with your 'income' (see below). If your income does not exceed your requirements by more than £3.25 (50 per cent of the current cost of a prescription), you are exempt from charges.[20] If your income exceeds your requirements by more than £3.25, you will be entitled to partial remission of charges as follows:[21]

- Dental charges and charges for wigs and fabric supports which are higher than three times the amount by which your income exceeds your requirements (your 'excess income') are remitted.
- The cost of a sight test is reduced to the amount of your excess income, if lower, plus the amount by which the cost exceeds the NHS sight test fee.
- The value of a voucher for glasses or lenses is reduced by twice your excess income.
- The amount you can claim for hospital fares is reduced by the amount of your excess income.

You cannot get partial help with the cost of prescriptions under the low income scheme (but see p181 for pre-payment certificates).

Calculating your requirements

Your 'requirements' are similar to the income support (IS) 'applicable amount' (see Chapter 35). The most significant elements and differences are set out below. **Note:** there are no exclusions or reductions for people who are subject to immigration control or not habitually resident in the UK, or for students, people engaged in a trade dispute or people without accommodation.

Your **'requirements'** are made up of the following elements:[22]

- **Personal allowance(s):**

Single person aged under 25	£44.50
Single person aged 25-59 and lone parent aged under 60	£56.20
Single person and lone parent, aged 60 or over	£109.45
Couples, both partners aged under 60	£88.15
Couples, one or both partners aged 60 or over	£167.05

- **Premiums:** the disability, enhanced disability, severe disability, bereavement and carer's premiums are added to your requirements if you would qualify for them under IS rules (see p882).
- **Amounts for children:** if you are receiving child tax credit (CTC – see Chapter 49) but are not exempt from charges, your requirements do not include any amounts for children. If you are not receiving CTC, your requirements include £43.88 for each dependent child or young person for whom you are responsible (see p818). Also included are a family premium of £16.10 and a disabled child

premium and enhanced disability premium for each child who would qualify for them under IS rules (see p882).[23]

- **Weekly council tax *less* any council tax benefit** (see Chapter 6).
- **Weekly rent *less* any housing benefit** (HB) (see Chapter 10) and any non-dependant deductions applicable under the rules relating to IS housing costs (see p924). Deductions for fuel and ineligible service charges are made in accordance with HB rules.
- **Weekly mortgage interest and capital payments on loans** secured on a home, or to buy a home, or to adapt a home for the special needs of a disabled person, **and payments on an endowment policy** relating to the purchase of a home. Deductions are made in respect of non-dependants in accordance with IS rules (see p924).
- **If you live permanently in a care home** (see Chapter 28), your 'requirements' are:
  - your weekly accommodation charge, including meals and services; *plus*
  - a personal expenses allowance of £18.80 in England or Scotland (£18.40 in Wales).

Calculating your income

Your income is calculated as for IS (see p952), with the following modifications:[24]

- The IS rules on attribution of income (see p990) do not apply. Your income will normally be taken into account in the week in which it is paid. If you are affected by a trade dispute, your normal earnings are taken into account.
- You are entitled to an earnings disregard of £20 if you would qualfy for a disability premium (see p886), or you or your partner are aged 60 or over.
- Regular liable relative payments count as weekly income. Irregular payments are averaged over the 13 weeks prior to your claim. Lump-sum payments are treated as capital. Child maintenance and child benefit only count if amounts for children are included in your requirements (see p187).
- Student loans are divided by 52, unless you are in your final year or are doing a one-year course, in which case the loan is divided by the number of weeks you are studying. The £10 disregard from student loans only applies if you are eligible for a premium (see p886) or you receive an allowance because of deafness or you are not a student but your partner is.
- Insurance policy payments for housing costs not met by IS count as income, but payments for unsecured loans for repairs and improvements (including premiums) are ignored.
- The capital limit for tariff income is £12,500 if you are permanently in residential or nursing care.
- The savings credit of pension credit is ignored as income.

8. Claims and refunds

Claiming full help with health costs

- If you are exempt from charges on the grounds of your **age**, **receipt of a qualifying benefit** or because you are a **full-time student under 19**, you should complete the back of the prescription form, or complete the appropriate form at your dentist, optician or hospital.
- If you are exempt from charges because you are **pregnant** or have **given birth** in the last 12 months, you should obtain an exemption certificate by completing Form FW8, which you can get from your doctor, midwife or health visitor.
- If you are entitled to free prescriptions because you have a **prescribed condition**, you should apply for an exemption certificate on Form FP92A (EC92A in Scotland), which you can get from your doctor, hospital or pharmacist.
- If you are exempt from charges because you are an **asylum seeker** you should apply to the Health Benefits Division (see Appendix 1) for an HC2 exemption certificate by completing an HC1 application form, which you can get from a DWP office or by ringing 08701 555 455.
- If you are exempt because you live in a **care home** or you are a **16/17-year-old care leaver** you will also need an HC2 certificate (see above), but you can apply for one on a special short form HC1(SC).
- If you are exempt because you are a **war disablement pensioner**, you should contact the Veterans Agency Treatment Group (Norcross, Blackpool FY5 3WP; telephone 0800 169 2277).
- To claim full or partial help with health costs under the low income scheme, see below.

Claiming under the low income scheme

To apply for remission of charges on the grounds of low income, you need to complete Form HC1 (obtainable from DWP offices or post offices) and send it to the Health Benefits Division of the Prescription Pricing Authority (see Appendix 1), or your local social security office in Northern Ireland.

If your income is low enough to qualify for free services you will be sent a certificate HC2. If you qualify for partial remission of charges, you will be sent a certificate HC3. Another person can apply on your behalf if you are unable to act. Certificates are normally valid for six months, or 12 months if you are aged 60 or over, entitled to a disability premium, or living in residential or nursing care. If you are self-employed, certificates normally last for 13 months. If you are a full-time student, your certificate will normally last until the end of your course or the start of the next academic year. You should make a repeat claim on Form HC1 shortly before the expiry date. Changes of circumstances (eg, starting work) do not affect the validity of a certificate but if the change could result in increased help, you can re-apply for a fresh assessment before the certificate expires.[25]

Proof of entitlement

You will normally be asked for proof that you are entitled to full or partial help with charges, although you should not be denied an item or service if you are unable to provide the required evidence. If you have an HC2 or HC3 certificate (see p189) you should show this to the dentist, optician, hospital or pharmacist (you may also have to enter details on the appropriate form). In other cases, you may need to show evidence of your date of birth, student status, FP92 exemption certificate, tax credit exemption certificate (see p179) or benefit order book or award letter.

If you receive help to which you were not entitled, you can be issued with a penalty notice requiring you to pay the charge you should have paid plus a penalty of five times that charge (up to a maximum of £100), unless you can show that you did not act 'wrongfully' or with 'any lack of care'. The penalty can be increased by up to £50 if you do not pay it within 28 days, and court proceedings can be taken to recover the debt. Anyone wrongly claiming help with charges on your behalf can themselves be liable to pay a penalty charge. You can also be prosecuted if you wrongly obtain help on the basis of a false statement or representation.[26]

Delays and problems

There is no right of appeal against a decision on whether you are entitled to full or partial help with health costs, but you can always write to the Health Benefits Division (see Appendix 1) or relevant service provider asking for a re-consideration of the decision.

If there are delays in obtaining a certificate, you can complain to the customer services manager. If necessary, you could pay for the treatment or items you need then try and obtain a refund (see below).

Refunds

If you pay for an item or service which you could have got free, or at reduced cost, you can apply for a refund. You should do this within three months of paying the charge, although the time limit can be extended if you can show good cause for applying late (eg, you were ill).[27]

You should apply for a refund of a prescription charge on Form FP57 (EC57 in Scotland). For other items and services, you should apply for a refund on Form HC5. You can get the forms from a DWP office or post office. You will need to submit a receipt or other documents to show that you have paid the charge. If you need an HC2 or HC3 certificate and have not applied for one, you should also send a Form HC1 with your application for refund.

9. Health care equipment

Health care equipment, such as special footwear, leg appliances, wigs, surgical supports, wheelchairs, commodes, incontinence pads, hearing aids and low vision aids can be provided by health authorities, hospitals and GPs, either free of charge or on prescription (see p180). Equipment for daily living can also be provided by social services but may be subject to a reasonable charge.

Notes

1. **Charges and exemptions**
 1 Regs 4-6 NHS(TERC) Regs 2003; regs 3-6 NHS(TERC) Regs; regs 3-5 NHS(TERC)(S) Regs

2. **Prescriptions**
 2 Regs 4-6 NHS(TERC) Regs 2003; regs 3-6 NHS(TERC) Regs; regs 3-5 NHS(TERC)(S) Regs; reg 7 NHS(CDA) Regs; reg 7 NHS(CDA)(S) Regs; reg 8 NHS(CDA)(W) Regs
 3 Reg 9 NHS(CDA) Regs; reg 8 NHS(CDA)(S) Regs; reg 10 NHS(CDA)(W) Regs

3. **Dental treatment and dentures**
 4 Regs 4-6 NHS(TERC) Regs 2003; regs 3-6 NHS(TERC) Regs; regs 3-5 NHS(TERC)(S) Regs; Sch 2 NHS(DC) Regs and NHS(DC)(S) Regs; Sch 12 NHSA 1977

4. **Sight tests and glasses**
 5 Reg 13 NHS(GOS) Regs; reg 3 NHS(OCP) Regs and NHS(OCP)(S) Regs
 6 Reg 3 NHS(OCP) Regs and NHS(OCP)(S) Regs
 7 Regs 8 and 15 NHS(OCP) Regs and NHS(OCP)(S) Regs
 8 Regs 9 and 15 NHS(OCP) Regs and NHS(OCP)(S) Regs
 9 Schs 1-3 NHS(OCP) Regs and NHS(OCP)(S) Regs
 10 Reg 12(1) NHS(OCP) Regs and NHS(OCP)(S) Regs

5. **Fares to hospital**
 11 Regs 3, 5 and 6 NHS(TERC) Regs 2003; regs 3-6 NHS(TERC) Regs; regs 3-5 NHS(TERC)(S) Regs
 12 Regs 5 and 6 NHS(TERC) Regs 2003; reg 3 NHS(TERC) Regs; regs 3-5 NHS(TERC)(S) Regs
 13 Reg 5B NHS(TERC) Regs 2003; reg 7 NHS(TERC)(S) Regs

6. **Free milk and vitamins**
 14 Regs 3-4 WF Regs
 15 Reg 10 WF Regs
 16 Regs 4, 11 and 14 WF Regs
 17 Reg 18 WF Regs
 18 Reg 7 WF Regs
 19 Reg 5 WF Regs

7. **The low income scheme**
 20 Reg 5(2)(e) NHS(TERC) Regs 2003; reg 4(2)(j) NHS(TERC) Regs; reg 4(2)(c) NHS(TERC)(S) Regs
 21 Reg 6 NHS(TERC) Regs 2003; reg 5 NHS(TERC) Regs; reg 5 NHS(TERC)(S) Regs; regs 1, 3, 7, 14 and 19 NHS(OCP) Regs and NHS(OCP)(S) Regs
 22 Reg 17 and Sch 1 Part II NHS(TERC) Regs 2003; reg 6 and Sch 1 Part II NHS(TERC) Regs; reg 8 and Sch 1 Part II NHS(TERC)(S) Regs

23 The inclusion of allowances and premiums for children, confirmed by Prescription Pricing Authority internal staff instructions, appears to be on an extra-statutory basis
24 Reg 16 and Sch 1 Part I NHS(TERC) Regs 2003; reg 6 and Sch 1 Part I NHS(TERC) Regs; reg 8 and Sch 1 Part 1 NHS(TERC)(S) Regs

8. Claims and refunds

25 Reg 8 NHS(TERC) Regs 2003; reg 7 NHS(TERC) Regs; reg 10 NHS(TERC)(S) Regs
26 ss122A, 122B and 122C NHSA 1977; ss99ZA and 99ZB NHS(S)A 1978
27 Reg 11 (NHS)(TERC) Regs 2003; reg 8 NHS(TERC) Regs; reg 11 NHS(TERC)(S) Regs; reg 10 (NHS)(CDA) Regs; reg 9 (NHS)(CDA)(S) Regs; reg 11 NHS(CDA)(W) Regs; regs 6 and 20 NHS(OCP) Regs and NHS(OCP)(S) Regs

Chapter 10

Housing benefit and discretionary housing payments

This chapter covers:

Housing benefit (HB) is paid to people with a low income who pay rent. It is paid whether or not the claimant is available for or in full-time paid work and may be paid in addition to other benefits or tax credits. HB is paid by local authorities, although it is a national scheme and the rules are mainly determined by DWP regulations.

You do not have to have paid national insurance contributions to qualify for HB.

If you are entitled to income support, income-based jobseeker's allowance or the guarantee credit of pension credit, you automatically qualify for maximum HB (see p206). Otherwise, your HB is calculated using a special formula (see p206).

1. Who can claim housing benefit

You qualify for housing benefit (HB) if:[1]

- your income is low enough (see p205);

- unless you or your partner are getting the guarantee credit of pension credit (PC), your savings and other capital are worth £16,000 or less (see Chapter 39). There is no capital limit if you or your partner are getting the guarantee credit of PC;[2]
- the payments you make can be met by HB (see below);
- you or your partner count as liable to pay rent (see p196);
- the payments you make are for the home in which you normally live (see p201), or you are only temporarily absent from it;
- you satisfy the habitual residence test (see p702); *and*
- you are not a person subject to immigration control (see p654).

There are some groups of claimants to whom special rules apply (see p215). If you are 16 or 17 and have been looked after by a local authority in England or Wales on or after 1 October 2001, you cannot usually claim HB. Instead, your local authority should support and accommodate you. See p714 for exceptions to the rules. Similar rules apply in Scotland if you cease to be looked after by a local authority on or after 1 April 2004 (see p713).

If you are 60 or over

The HB rules for people who are 60 or over who are not (and whose partners are not) getting income support (IS) or income-based jobseeker's allowance (JSA) are different (and more generous) than those for other HB claimants. If you turn 60, you should check to see if you qualify for HB even if you did not do so before that age. The different rules for income, capital and applicable amounts are covered in other chapters, but a summary of the income and capital rules is given below.

For further details see Chapters 38 (income and means-tested benefits), 39 (capital) and 35 (applicable amounts).

Income and capital

If you are **on the guarantee credit of PC**, for HB purposes all of your income and capital is ignored.[3] This means there is no capital limit if you get the guarantee credit of PC and you automatically qualify for maximum HB.

If you are **on the savings credit of PC but not the guarantee credit**:[4]

- the local authority uses the assessment of your income and capital that the DWP used for working out your PC entitlement (known as the 'assessed income figure') as the basis for working out your income and capital for HB. The local authority may modify this figure to take certain income into account – eg, the amount of savings credit you receive is taken into account as income for HB;
- if your capital rises above £16,000 while you are on HB and there is an assessed income period in force (see p480), the local authority then calculates your capital according to the HB rules for those who are 60 or over and not on IS or income-based JSA – these are broadly the same as those for PC. If the calculation

confirms that you have capital over £16,000 then you are no longer entitled to HB.

You cannot appeal against the local authority's use of the 'assessed income figure'.[5] If you disagree with the DWP assessment of your income and capital, you need to lodge your appeal with the DWP, not the local authority. However, if the local authority modifies your 'assessed income figure', you do have a right of appeal against the modification. You may, therefore, need to appeal against both decisions in some circumstances. If you lodge an appeal with the local authority and the situation is ambiguous, the local authority should advise you to also lodge an appeal with the DWP.[6]

If you are **not on either the guarantee credit or the savings credit of PC**, the local authority works out your capital and income using the HB rules for those who are 60 or over and not on IS or income-based JSA.

Payments which can be met by housing benefit

HB can meet rent that you pay to your landlord. It can also meet other types of payment, such as payments as a licensee and payments for bed and breakfast and hostel accommodation. In this *Handbook*, we refer to any payments you make as 'rent'. Some types of payment cannot be met by HB (see p196).

The following payments can be met by HB:[7]

- rent paid in respect of a tenancy. This can include ground rent payable in respect of a lease of 21 years or less.[8] If your lease is for longer than 21 years, the ground rent might be met by IS, income-based JSA or PC – see p918;
- payments in respect of a licence or other permission to occupy premises;
- 'mesne profits' (in Scotland, 'violent profits') which include payments made if you remain in occupation when a tenancy has been ended;
- other payments for the use and occupation of premises (including boat licence and mooring permit fees if you live in a houseboat[9]);
- payments of eligible service charges (see p209);
- rent, including mooring charges, for a houseboat;
- site rent for a caravan or mobile home (but not a tent, although that might be met through IS, income-based JSA or PC – see p918);
- rent paid on a garage or land (unless used for business purposes). Either you must be making a reasonable effort to end your liability for it, or you must have been unable to rent your home without it;[10]
- contributions made by a resident of a charity's almshouse;
- payments made under a rental purchase agreement under which the purchase price is paid in more than one instalment and you do not finally own your home until all, or an agreed part of, the purchase price has been paid;
- in Scotland, payments in respect of croft land.

The payment must be in return for your occupation of the home. This usually means that the payments must be made to the person who has the right to let you occupy it or somebody acting on her/his behalf. Payments to someone else might not qualify for HB.[11] If you think you may be in this situation, seek advice.

Even if you make payments that can be met by HB, you might not qualify if:

- you are required to live in an approved bail or probation hostel (see p201); *or*
- you are treated as not liable to pay rent (see p199).

Payments which cannot be met by housing benefit

HB cannot meet payments if:

- you live in a care home owned or managed by a local authority and the charge includes meals.[12] Even if meals are not provided you cannot get HB for your accommodation costs if you were in the home on 31 March 1993 and excluded from HB at that time;[13]
- you own your accommodation or have a lease of more than 21 years – unless you have a shared ownership tenancy with a housing association or housing authority (ie, buying part of your house or flat and renting the rest), in which case you can get HB on the part you rent.[14] You are treated as the owner of the property if you have the right to sell it – even though you may not be able to do this without the consent of other joint owners.[15] The payments might be met by IS, income-based JSA or PC instead (see Chapter 36);
- you are getting IS or income-based JSA for these.[16] If you are now getting your housing costs met through IS or income-based JSA but were previously getting HB for the same accommodation, your HB continues for your first four weeks on IS or income-based JSA, but this is deducted from your IS or income-based JSA. Remember that if you buy a home and immediately before that you were renting accommodation and getting HB, you might not get your full housing costs met (see p914);[17]
- you are a Crown tenant. The payments might be met by IS, income-based JSA or PC instead (see p918). Some landlords of Crown tenants have rent rebate schemes that are similar to HB;[18]
- you make payments under a co-ownership scheme under which you will receive a payment related to the value of the accommodation when you leave. The payments might be met by IS, income-based JSA or PC instead (see p918);[19]
- you make payments under a hire purchase (eg, for the purchase of a mobile home), credit sale or a conditional sale agreement except to the extent that it is in respect of land. The payments might be met by IS, income-based JSA or PC instead (see p910).[20]

Liability to pay rent

You count as liable to pay rent (see p197) if:[21]

- you or your partner are liable; *or*

- you are treated as liable. You are treated as liable if:
  - your former partner is liable to make the payments on your home but is not doing so and you have to pay rent in order to remain living there. It does not matter whether or not the landlord is prepared to transfer the tenancy to you or wants to evict you. If you are a local authority tenant and the local authority refuses to accept your HB claim in this situation, point out that the eligibility rules for HB and for transferring local authority tenancies are quite separate; *or*
  - you have taken over paying the rent but are not the former partner of the liable person and you have to pay rent in order to remain living there. The local authority can treat you as liable if it considers that it is reasonable to do so.[22] If it refuses to exercise this discretion in your favour, request a revision or appeal (see Chapters 43 and 44); *or*
  - your landlord allows you a rent-free period as compensation for undertaking repairs or re-decoration which s/he would otherwise have had to carry out. This only applies for a maximum of eight benefit weeks in respect of any one rent-free period. You must have actually carried out the work. If you expect the work to last for more than eight weeks, you should arrange with your landlord to schedule the work in periods of eight weeks or less, separated by at least one complete benefit week where you resume paying rent; *or*
  - you are the partner of a full-time student (see p621) who is treated as not liable to pay rent (see p199). This means that you can qualify for HB even if your partner cannot do so.

Even if you fall into one of these categories, you can still be treated as not being liable to pay rent and so not entitled to HB in certain circumstances (see p199).

If you pay your rent in advance, you are still treated as liable to pay it, even where you paid it before claiming HB.[23]

What 'liable' means

In order for you to be 'liable' to pay rent, your agreement must be legally enforceable.[24] It is not enough if you only have a moral obligation, such as a promise to pay something whenever you can afford to do so. You can count as liable to pay rent even if someone else has been paying it on your behalf (eg, the social services department is paying it because of its duty to safeguard and promote the interests of children in need in its area).[25] You can be liable to pay rent by yourself or you can be jointly liable to do so (see p198).

It is always better to have your agreement with your landlord **in writing**. If you have a written agreement, the local authority uses this to decide if you are liable to pay rent and whether the liability is a genuine part of the agreement between you and your landlord. Even if the local authority accepts this, it might still treat you as not liable to pay rent (see p199).[26]

Your agreement can be enforceable even if it is **not in writing**. If you have made a firm promise to pay money to your landlord in return for your occupation of the property, that should be treated as sufficient to allow you to claim HB. If the local authority refuses to accept that you have a legal liability unless you produce a written agreement, a rent book or some other evidence in writing of the agreement, argue that this is wrong and seek a revision or appeal (see Chapters 43 and 44).[27]

16- and 17-year-olds

People under 18 can be liable to pay rent and, therefore, entitled to HB. This applies where there is an intention to create legal relations, regardless of the precise wording of the agreement.

If you are aged under 16, an adult or social services department is generally responsible for the rent. However, HB departments should not make decisions on HB entitlement based on what services they think the social services department ought to provide.

Joint liability

If you are a member of a couple and are jointly liable for the rent, only one of you can claim HB (see p218).[28] See p811 for who counts as a couple.

The way a group of single people living together and paying rent to their landlord is treated depends on whether you are all liable under the agreement, some of you are liable or only one of you is liable. If all, or some of you, have joint liability for the rent, you can each make a separate claim and be paid HB on your share (unless the local authority thinks the joint tenancy has been created to take advantage of the HB scheme – see p200). The local authority apportions the eligible rent between you by considering:[29]

- the number of jointly liable people in the property (including any students who are treated as not liable to pay rent – see p199);[30] *and*
- the proportion of the rent actually paid by each liable person; *and*
- any other relevant circumstances, such as:[31]
  - the number of rooms occupied by each jointly liable person;
  - whether any formal or informal agreement exists between you regarding the use and occupation of the home; *and*
  - if one of the jointly liable people has gone, the demands being made by the landlord on those who remain or the possibility of getting other accommodation.

In some circumstances, it could be appropriate to apportion the whole of the rent to you even if you are jointly liable.[32]

Where the rent includes any ineligible service charges, etc. these are apportioned between you on the same basis as the rent.[33] If only one of you is liable for the rent, s/he is treated as the tenant and the other(s) as a non-dependant(s) (see p211).

People treated as not liable to pay rent

Even if you or your partner are liable to pay rent, or you are treated as liable, you cannot qualify for HB if you are treated as though you are not liable to do so. You are treated as not liable to pay rent if:

- you are a full-time **student**[34] and you do not come into one of the categories of those who can get HB (see p631);
- you are a person **subject to immigration control** (see p654) or you **do not satisfy the habitual residence test** (see p702);[35]
- you are a member of, and are fully maintained by, a **religious order**;[36]
- you are living in a **care home**[37] (but see p725);
- you **pay rent to someone you live with and that person is a close relative** of you or your partner.[38] You are regarded as living with your landlord if you share some accommodation with her/him, other than a bathroom, toilet or a hall or passageway.[39] It does not matter if you use the accommodation at different times or if you pay to use it.[40] A **'close relative'** is a parent, parent-in-law, son, son-in-law, daughter, daughter-in-law, brother, sister, step-parent, step-son or step-daughter or the partner of any of these.*[41] It also includes half-brothers and sisters.[42] Relations with in-laws or step-relatives are severed by divorce but arguably not by death;[43]
- your **agreement to pay rent is not on a commercial basis.**[44] In deciding whether or not your agreement is commercial, the local authority must look at the whole agreement, taking into account all the circumstances. It must consider, among other things:
  - whether your agreement includes terms which are not legally enforceable.[45] DWP guidance suggests that this might arise, for example, where a tenant does household chores (although if you do chores in exchange for a lower rent, it could be considered commercial);[46]
  - your agreement to pay rent. The rent need not necessarily be a market rent.[47] Your agreement can count as commercial even if your landlord is not collecting the full contractual rent from you – eg, where it is not being met by HB because of the rent restriction rules (see Chapter 11);[48]
  - your relationship to your landlord. Just because you are a relative of, or have a close friendship with, the person to whom you pay rent, or your landlord provides you with care and support, does not mean that your agreement is non-commercial;[49]
- you are **renting from:**[50]
  - your ex-partner and the home is your former joint home; *or*
  - your partner's ex-partner and the home is your partner's former joint home with her/his ex-partner;

* From 5 December 2005, 'step' and 'in-law' relations of a civil partner can also count as close relatives.

- you or your partner are **responsible for a child of your landlord**.[51] Being responsible for a child means more than caring for her/him. It only applies in situations where the child is included in your HB claim (see p818).[52]
  This rule was challenged under the Human Rights Act 1998,[53] but the Court decided that the Regulation did not conflict with the Act;
- you, your partner, your ex-partner, your partner's ex-partner or a close relative of you or your partner who lives with you is *either*:[54]
  – a **director or employee of a company which is your landlord**; *or*
  – a **trustee or beneficiary of a trust which is your landlord.**
  However, you should be treated as liable if you can show the arrangement was not intended to take advantage of the HB scheme (see below);
- you are renting accommodation from a trustee of a trust, of which your child or your partner's child is a **beneficiary**;[55]
- you were **previously the non-dependant** of someone who lived, and continues to live, in the accommodation.[56] This should not apply to you if you can show that the agreement was not created to take advantage of the HB scheme (see below);[57]
- you or your current partner **previously owned the accommodation** and less than five years have passed since you last owned it.[58] Whether you were legally or practically compelled to give up ownership is relevant, but your motivation for doing so is not.[59]
  This rule does not apply if you can show that you could not have continued to remain in the accommodation without giving up ownership. It also does not apply if you lived elsewhere before returning to live in the accommodation;[60]
- you or your partner are employed by your landlord and are **occupying your accommodation as a condition of employment**. This should not apply if you continue to live in the accommodation after ceasing employment;[61]
- where none of the above apply, but the local authority considers that your **liability to pay rent has been created to take advantage of the HB scheme.**[62]

Agreements taking advantage of the housing benefit scheme

In order for your agreement to count as 'taking advantage of the housing benefit scheme', it must be shown that it amounts to an abuse of the scheme, and that the main reason for you entering the agreement was to obtain HB.[63] All the circumstances should be taken into account in deciding if this is the case, including what your landlord has to say.[64]

Your agreement does not take advantage of the HB scheme just because your landlord is your parent[65] or because you hope to be able to claim HB to help you with your rent. In the latter case, your main purpose is to get accommodation for yourself, not to obtain HB.[66] In particular, you should not be seen as taking advantage of the HB scheme just because you seek to find out the eligible rent (see p207) from the rent officer before moving in.

It is not necessary for you and your landlord to have plotted to take advantage of the HB scheme.[67] Tenants of a landlord who deliberately charges high rents to try and get them paid by HB may fall foul of this provision, even if they had no such intention themselves.[68] However, the fact that a rent is above the market average does not mean that the liability takes advantage of the HB scheme,[69] unless perhaps the rent is extremely high. If your landlord is going to evict you if you cannot get HB, that suggests that the agreement does not take advantage of the HB scheme.[70]

If the local authority refuses you HB on the basis that you are taking advantage of the HB scheme, you should always request a revision or appeal (see Chapters 43 and 44).

Occupying accommodation as your home

HB is paid for the home in which you normally live.[71] You cannot usually be paid for any other home. There are special rules if you:

- have just moved into your home (see below);
- are temporarily away from home (see p202);
- are liable to pay rent on more than one home (see p203);
- are in certain other situations (see p204) – ie, you:
  - left home in fear of violence; *or*
  - are a single claimant (including a lone parent), and you are either a student who is not excluded from HB entitlement or on a training course; *or*
  - had to move into temporary accommodation due to essential repairs being carried out on your main home.

If you have to live in a bail hostel or approved probation hostel, you are not treated as occupying that accommodation as your home.[72] This means that you cannot qualify for HB towards the rent you pay to the hostel.

Moving home

If you have just moved into your home but were liable to pay rent before moving in, you can get HB on your new home for a period of up to four weeks before you moved in.[73] If you have given up your previous home and have no other home, you can try to argue that the date you move in is the date you move your furniture and belongings in.[74] You qualify if your delay in moving was reasonable, you claimed HB before moving in, *and*:

- you were waiting for a social fund payment for a need connected with the move – eg, removal expenses or to help you set up home. This only applies if:
  - you have a child of five or under living with you; *or*
  - you are 60 or over and neither you nor your partner are getting IS or income-based JSA;[75] *or*
  - you qualify for one of the pensioner premiums or a disability, severe disability or disabled child premium (see pp886–891); *or*

- you were waiting for adaptations to be finished to meet needs you or a member of your family have because of a disability; *or*
- you became liable to make payments on your new home while you were a hospital patient or in residential accommodation.

Your HB is not actually paid until you move in. If an earlier claim for HB you made before you moved in was turned down, you must claim again within four weeks of moving to qualify.

Also, if you are not liable to pay rent in your new accommodation (this includes, for example, prison), you can get HB for up to four weeks for your former home if you:[76]

- were liable for rent on it immediately before moving into your new accommodation and continue to be liable; *and*
- could not reasonably have avoided liability for rent on your former home.

If you are obliged to pay rent for your old home as well as your new accommodation, you can only get HB for one of these unless you are covered by the rules described on p203 (eg, you were waiting for adaptations to be finished to meet needs because of a disability).[77]

Temporary absence from home

If you are temporarily away from your normal home, have not rented it out and intend to return, your HB can continue to be paid for a period. You can try to argue that you count as temporarily absent from home even if you have not yet stayed there – eg, you move your furniture and belongings in but then have to go into hospital.[78]

You can get HB for **13 weeks** for your normal home while you are away, whatever the reason. You must be unlikely to be away for longer than this.[79]

You can get HB for **52 weeks** for your normal home if you are unlikely to be away for longer than this (or in exceptional circumstances, unlikely to be away for substantially longer than this) and:[80]

- you are a remand prisoner held in custody pending trial or sentence;
- you are required to live in a bail hostel or an address away from your normal home as a condition of bail;
- you are a hospital inpatient;
- you or a dependant are undergoing medical treatment or medically-approved convalescence in the UK or abroad;
- you are providing, or receiving, 'medically approved' care (ie, certified by a medical practitioner) in the UK or abroad;
- you are caring for a child whose parent or guardian is away from home receiving medically approved care or medical treatment;

- you are undertaking a training course in the UK or abroad which is provided by, or on behalf of, or approved by a government department, the Secretary of State, Scottish Enterprise or Highlands and Islands Enterprise;
- you are a student who is not excluded from HB (see p631) and you neither fall into the first category under 'Other situations' on p204 nor are entitled to HB on two homes (see below);
- you are in a care home for short-term respite care. However, if you are in the home for a trial period to see if you wish to move there permanently, you can only get HB for up to 13 weeks.[81] You must intend to return home if the accommodation is not suitable; once you decide to become a permanent resident, this rule no longer applies (but see p202).[82] If the home does not suit your needs, you can have further trial periods in other homes so long as you are not away from home for more than 52 weeks;
- you are away from home through fear of violence. You need not have suffered actual violence, but you must be in fear of violence in your home or from a former family member. The former category includes violence by neighbours and racial attacks on your home. See below if you need to claim for two homes and p204 if you do not intend to return to your former home.

Whether or not you are unlikely to be away for longer than 13/52 weeks should be considered initially based on the circumstances on the date you leave your home.[83] If at any time after that date it becomes likely that you will be away from home for more than the 13/52 weeks, your entitlement can be reconsidered.

A new period of absence starts if you return home for even a short stay. A stay of at least 24 hours may be enough.[84] This does not apply, however, if you are a prisoner on temporary leave.[85]

Housing benefit for more than one home

You can usually only get HB for one home. However, if you have to pay rent for two homes, you can get HB for both:

- for up to **four weeks** if:
  - you have moved into a new home and you could not reasonably avoid having to pay rent on your old home.[86] The local authority must consider the reasons why you had to move quickly. For example, if you were forced to move quickly to take advantage of better accommodation you may not have been able to avoid leaving without giving notice;[87] *or*
  - you qualify for HB on a new home because a move was delayed while you were adapting your new home for the disability needs of a member of your family (see p201).[88] You can get HB on both homes for the four weeks prior to the date you move;
- for up to **52 weeks**, if you have left your home due to fear of violence (see above for what counts as violence). You must intend to return to your former home, and it must be reasonable for you to receive HB for both homes;[89]

- **indefinitely**, if:
  - you are a couple and you or your partner are a student who is not excluded from HB (see p631) or a trainee on a government course, and it is necessary for you to live apart, and it is reasonable for you to receive HB for both homes;[90]
  - your family is large and the local authority has housed you in more than one home.[91]

Other situations

If you have left your home due to a fear of violence (see p203 for what counts as violence) and cannot be paid HB for two homes (see p203) or while temporarily absent from home (see p202) – eg, you do not intend to return to your former home – you can get HB for four weeks for your former home.[92] This only applies if your liability to pay rent was unavoidable (eg, you must give your landlord notice that you are leaving but had to leave in a hurry because of the violence).

If you have **two homes**, and you make payments for only one of them (including mortgage payments), you are treated as occupying the home for which you pay and therefore get HB for that home. This applies if:

- you are a single claimant (including a lone parent), and you are either a student who is not excluded from HB entitlement (see p631) or on a training course (see p203), and you live in one home during periods of study or training and another home for vacations;[93] *or*
- you had to move into temporary accommodation due to essential repairs being carried out on your main home.[94] '**Essential repairs**' means basic works rather than luxuries, but they need not be crucial to make the house habitable.[95]

2. The rules about your age

There are no lower or upper age limits for claiming housing benefit (HB). However, if you are:

- under 16, there may be a question about whether you have a legally enforceable liability for rent (see p198);
- 16 or 17 and have been looked after by a local authority in England or Wales on or after 1 October 2001, you usually cannot claim HB. Instead, your local authority should support and accommodate you. See p714 for exceptions to the rules. Similar rules apply in Scotland if you cease to be looked after by a local authority on or after 1 April 2004 (see p713);
- 60 or over and neither you nor your partner are getting income support or income-based jobseeker's allowance, different (more generous) HB rules apply.

3. Claiming for others

You claim housing benefit for your family. See Chapter 32 for who counts as your family.

4. The amount of benefit

The amount of housing benefit (HB) you get depends on:

- your 'applicable amount' (see Chapter 35). This is made up of personal allowances and premiums for any special needs;
- your 'maximum HB'. This is your 'eligible rent' (see p207) minus any deductions which are made for your non-dependants (see p211);[96]
- how much income and capital you have (see Chapters 38 and 39); *and*
- whether your 'eligible rent' is restricted (see Chapter 11). **Note:** if you live in a Pathfinder area, the amount of your HB is based on a local housing allowance. See p254 for further information.

If you do not qualify for HB currently, you may qualify when:

- the benefit rates go up. Personal allowances and premiums are increased every April; *or*
- you or your partner turn 60. Your applicable amount is then higher. In addition, if neither you nor your partner are on income support (IS) or income-based jobseeker's allowance (JSA), the income and capital rules are more generous; *or*
- you or your partner turn 65. Your personal allowance is increased by the equivalent of the amount of the maximum savings credit, whether or not you receive this, so long as neither you nor your partner are on IS or income-based JSA.

If your income is too high for you to qualify for HB currently, you might qualify once you, or a member of your family, become entitled to another benefit (a 'qualifying benefit'). See p220 for further information.

If you need extra financial assistance to meet your housing costs, you might be entitled to discretionary housing payments (see p235).

Remember that if you:

- come off IS, income-based JSA, incapacity benefit or severe disablement allowance because of starting work or increasing your income from work, you may be entitled to extended payments of HB (see p63);
- come off IS or income-based JSA because you are moving onto pension credit (PC), you may be able to continue to receive HB at the same rate for four weeks (see p225);

- have been incapable of work but move into work or training, you might count as a 'welfare to work' beneficiary (see p769). This means you retain entitlement to the disability or higher pensioner premium (see pp886 and 890) if you become incapable of work again within 52 weeks.

If you are on IS, income-based JSA or the guarantee credit of PC

Entitlement to IS, income-based JSA or the guarantee credit of PC acts as an automatic passport to maximum HB (once you have made a claim for HB). You therefore do not need to work out your applicable amount, income or capital.[97] In these circumstances HB = 'maximum HB'.

For these purposes, you are treated as entitled to income-based JSA:[98]

- when you satisfy the conditions of entitlement but are not being paid it because of a sanction (see Chapter 16);
- on your waiting days (see p377); *and*
- when it is not paid because of the 'loss of benefit' rules (see p1169).

Example

Mr and Mrs Feinstein and their adult son live together in a flat. Mr Feinstein is the sole tenant and pays rent of £65 a week, which includes all their fuel. Mr Feinstein receives income-based JSA for himself and his wife while they are looking for work. Their son earns £110 a week gross. Mr Feinstein claims HB.

His eligible rent is £51.10 a week (ie, £65 – £13.90 deducted because of the fuel charges – see p208).

His son counts as a non-dependant and the appropriate deduction for him is £17 a week (see p211).

Therefore, Mr Feinstein's maximum HB is £34.10 a week (£51.10 – £17).

Because he receives income-based JSA, his HB is £34.10 a week. The amount is lower than his actual rent because his fuel charge is not covered by HB and because his son is expected to make a contribution to the rent.

If you are not on IS, income-based JSA or the guarantee credit of PC

- Step one: Check that your capital is not too high (see Chapter 39).
- Step two: Work out your 'maximum HB' (see p205).
- Step three: Work out your applicable amount (see Chapter 35).
- Step four: Work out your income (see Chapter 38 but also p633 if you are a student and p482 if you are getting the savings credit of PC).
- Step five: Calculate HB:
  - If your **income is less than or equal to your applicable amount**, HB = 'maximum HB'.
  - If your income is greater than your applicable amount, work out the difference. HB = 'maximum HB' minus 65 per cent of the difference between your income and your applicable amount.

Examples

Mr Jopling is aged 45. He is unemployed. Mrs Jopling is aged 46. She works 21 hours per week. She is paid £165 a week after deductions of tax and national insurance contributions. The couple are joint tenants who pay £67 rent a week. Mrs Jopling claims HB. Her eligible rent is £67 a week.

Mr and Mrs Jopling have no non-dependants. Therefore, her maximum HB is £67 a week.

Mrs Jopling's applicable amount is £88.15 (the standard rate for a couple – see p879).

Her income to be taken into account is £155 a week (because £10 of her earnings are disregarded – see p965).

The difference between her income and her applicable amount is therefore £66.85 a week.

65% of £66.85 a week is £43.45 a week.

Mrs Jopling's HB is therefore £67 – £43.45 = £23.55 a week.

Mr Haralambous is 67 years old. He receives the savings credit of PC, totalling £14.22 a week. His weekly income from his private and state pensions is £115 – this is too high to qualify for the guarantee credit of PC. His total weekly income is therefore £129.22 (£115 + £14.22). He is a sole tenant and has no non-dependants. His eligible rent is £65 a week.

His applicable amount is £125.90 (adult personal allowance for a single person aged 65 or over).

The difference between his income and applicable amount is £3.32 a week.

65% of £3.32 a week is £2.16 a week.

Mr Haralambous's HB is therefore £65 – £2.16 = £62.84 a week.

Eligible rent

Your 'eligible rent' is the amount of your rent which is taken into account for the purpose of calculating your HB. It may be less than the actual amount that you pay.

Your eligible rent is your contractual rent, minus:

- any ineligible charges (see below). If you are in supported accommodation, see p210; *and*
- any amount above the level to which your rent is restricted under the rent restriction rules (known as your 'maximum rent' – see Chapter 11).

The local authority also has general powers to decrease your eligible rent to an amount it considers appropriate (see p252). It should have evidence which justifies it doing so and must exercise its discretion properly. If it decreases your eligible rent in this way, you can seek a revision or appeal (see Chapters 43 and 44).

Ineligible charges

You may find that your HB is less than your contractual rent because ineligible charges are deducted. Ineligible charges include:

- most fuel charges (see p208);

- some service charges (see p209);
- charges for meals (see p210);
- water charges;[99]
- payments for any part of your accommodation which is used exclusively for business purposes;[100]
- rent supplements charged to clear your rent arrears;[101]
- any amount above the level to which your rent is restricted under the rent restriction rules (see Chapter 11).[102]

Fuel charges

Fuel charges cannot be met by HB unless they are for communal areas (see p209).[103] If your fuel charge is:

- specified on your rent book or is **readily identifiable** from your agreement with your landlord the full amount of the charge is deducted from the rent you pay to arrive at your eligible rent.[104] Where your fuel charge is specified but the local authority considers it to be unrealistically low in relation to the fuel provided, the charge is treated as unspecified and a flat-rate deduction made instead (see below).

  This is also the case where your total fuel charge is specified but contains an unknown amount for communal areas. If you are a council tenant, the regulations assume your fuel charges are always specified or readily identifiable, since the local authority is also your landlord.[105]
- **not readily identifiable**, a flat-rate deduction is made from the rent you pay to arrive at your eligible rent. The flat-rate fuel deductions are:[106]

Where you and your family occupy more than one room:	
For heating (other than hot water)	£10.55
For hot water	£1.25
For lighting	£0.85
For cooking	£1.25
Where you and your family occupy one room only:	
For heating alone, or heating combined with either hot water or lighting or both	£6.33
For cooking	£1.25

These amounts are added together where fuel is supplied for more than one purpose. If you are a joint tenant, all the deductions are apportioned according to your share of the rent.[107]

If flat-rate fuel deductions have been made in calculating your HB, the local authority must notify you about this and explain that if you can produce evidence from which the actual or approximate amount of your fuel charge can be estimated, the flat-rate deductions may be varied accordingly.[108]

The DWP says that the lower deduction for one room should apply where you occupy one room exclusively – even if you share other rooms (such as a bathroom or kitchen, or communal lounge in a hotel).[109] You should also argue that the lower level of deductions should be made where you are forced to live in one room because the other room(s) in your accommodation are, in practice, unfit to live in – eg, because of severe mould/dampness etc.

Fuel for communal areas

If you pay a service charge for the use of fuel in communal areas, and that charge is separately identified from any other charge for fuel used within your accommodation, it may be included as part of your eligible rent.[110] Communal areas include access areas like halls and passageways, but not rooms in common use except those in sheltered accommodation – eg, a shared TV lounge or dining room etc.[111] If you pay a charge for the provision of a heating system (eg, regular boiler maintenance) this is also eligible where the amount is separately identified from any other fuel charge you pay.[112]

Service charges

Many service charges are covered by HB, but only if payment is a condition of occupying the accommodation rather than an optional extra.[113] Eligible and ineligible service charges are listed below. If the local authority regards any of the eligible charges as excessive it estimates a reasonable amount given the cost of comparable services.[114] If you are in supported accommodation, see p210.

The following services are **eligible** for HB:

- services for the provision of adequate accommodation including general management costs, gardens, children's play areas, lifts, entry phones, communal telephone costs, portering and rubbish removal. TV and radio relay is covered, but only relay for ordinary UK channels and not satellite dishes or decoders. Cable TV is excluded unless it is the only practicable way of providing you with ordinary domestic channels;[115]
- laundry facilities (eg, a laundry room in an apartment block), but not charges for the provision of personal laundry;[116]
- furniture and household equipment, but not if there is an agreement that the furniture will eventually become yours;[117]
- cleaning of rooms and windows in communal areas and the outside of windows where neither you nor any member of your household is able to clean them yourself, unless payment for these is made by your local authority or the National Assembly for Wales.[118]

The following services are **not eligible** for HB:[119]

- food, including prepared meals (see p210);
- sports facilities;
- TV rental and licence fees (but see above);

- transport;
- personal laundry service;
- provision of an emergency alarm system;
- medical expenses;
- nursing and personal care;
- counselling and other support services;
- any other charge not connected with the provision of adequate accommodation and not specifically included in the list of eligible charges above.

If you are in supported accommodation, your support services are funded by your local authority's 'supporting people team' not by HB. See below for further information.

Any ineligible service charge must be deducted in full from your rent to arrive at your eligible rent. Where the ineligible charge is specified, this amount is deducted. Local authorities have the power to substitute their own estimate where they consider the amount to be unreasonably low.[120] Where the amount is not specified in your rent agreement, the local authority estimates how much is fairly attributable to the service, given the cost of comparable services.[121]

Charges for meals

Where your housing costs include an amount for meals, the local authority makes set deductions.[122] These always apply, regardless of the actual cost of your meals.

Where at least three meals a day are provided:

For the claimant and each additional member of the family aged 16 (see below) or over	£20.05
For each additional member of the family aged under 16	£10.15
Where breakfast only is provided:	
For the claimant and each additional member of the family, regardless of age	£2.45
In all other cases (part-board):	
For the claimant and each additional member of the family aged 16 or over	£13.35
For each additional member of the family aged under 16	£6.70

For these purposes, a person is treated as having reached the age of 16 on the first Monday in September following her/his 16th birthday.

The standard deductions are made for everyone who has meals paid for by you – including meals for someone who is not part of your family, such as a non-dependant.[123]

Service charges in supported accommodation

If you live in supported accommodation, you can claim HB to help you pay your rent. However, HB is not available for the support services provided with your accommodation. Instead, the local authority's 'supporting people team' funds your landlord (eg, a registered social landlord or voluntary organisation) to provide these.

In some cases, the local authority can charge you for the support services you get. Your local authority uses its means test to determine how much you have to pay. See CPAG's *Paying for Care Handbook* 4th edn, pp82–84 for further information.

Calculating a weekly amount of housing benefit

HB is always paid for a specific benefit week – a period of seven consecutive days beginning with a Monday and ending on a Sunday.[124] If you pay rent at different intervals (eg, monthly) the amount has to be converted to a weekly figure before HB can be calculated.[125]

If the rent period is not a whole number of weeks, the figure is divided by the number of days in the period. This daily rent is then multiplied by seven to give the equivalent weekly figure to be used in the HB calculation.[126]

Rent-free periods

If you have a regular rent-free period (eg, you pay rent on a 48-week rent year) you get no HB during your rent-free period. Your applicable amount, weekly income, non-dependant deductions, the set deductions for meals and fuel charges and the minimum amount payable (but not your eligible rent) are adjusted.[127] The rules for doing this are:

- Where your rent is paid weekly or in a whole multiple of weeks, you should multiply the figures to be converted by 52 (or 53 as appropriate) to give the annual amounts. Then divide by the number of weeks in the year in which you actually pay rent. So, for a 48-week rent year, all the figures would need to be multiplied by 52 and the result divided by 48.[128]
- Where your rent is paid on some other basis, you should multiply all the figures to be converted by 365 (or 366 as appropriate) and divide the result by the number of days in the rent year for which rent is actually payable. So, if you pay rent every calendar month except December (31 days), all the figures would need to be multiplied by 365 and the result divided by 334 (365 – 31).[129]

Note: if you pay your rent in instalments, but it is an annual rent covering the whole year, this rule does not apply.[130] In addition, it does not apply if your landlord has temporarily waived the rent in return for you doing repairs (see p197).

Deductions for non-dependants

If other people normally live with you in your home who are not part of your family for benefit purposes (see p809) – they are called **'non-dependants'** – a set deduction is usually made from your HB.[131] This is because it is assumed the non-dependant makes a contribution towards your outgoings, whether or not s/he does so. Examples of non-dependants are adult sons or daughters, or elderly relatives who share your home. You may, therefore, need to ask your non-dependant(s) for a contribution.

A person can only be treated as **living with you** if s/he shares some accommodation with you.[132] A person who is separately liable to pay rent to your landlord does not count as living with you, nor does a person who only shares a bathroom, lavatory, or a communal area such as a hall, passageway or a room in common use in sheltered accommodation. For example, where part of your home has been converted to include a self-contained 'granny-flat', the person occupying it would not be a non-dependant even though s/he may share your bathroom and toilet. However, if any other areas of the house are shared, such as the kitchen, the other person is treated as living with you. This is the case even if you only use it at different times and you maintain different households (see p812 for the meaning of 'household').[133]

A person does not **normally live with** you if s/he has not been there long enough to regard your home as her/his normal home.[134] If you think the local authority has wrongly assumed that a person is normally living with you, ask for a revision or appeal – see Chapters 43 and 44. A number of factors have to be taken into account to decide whether a person is normally living with you:[135]

- the relationship between you;
- how much time the person spends at your address;
- where the person has her/his post sent;
- where the person keeps most of her/his clothes and personal belongings;
- whether the person's stay or absence from your address is temporary or permanent;
- whether the person has another place that could be regarded as home or whether s/he just travels around.

People who are not non-dependants

The following people cannot count as non-dependants even if they normally live with you:[136]

- a member of your family for benefit purposes (see p809);
- if you are in a polygamous marriage , a partner of yours and any child or young person in your household (see p818) for which you or a partner are responsible;
- a child or young person living with you who is not a member of your household (see p821);
- someone who is employed by a charitable or voluntary organisation as a resident carer for you or your partner and who you pay for the service. This can also apply if a public body pays on your behalf;
- any person, or a member of their household, to whom you or your partner are liable to pay rent on a commercial basis;
- someone who jointly occupies your home and is either a co-owner or jointly liable with you or your partner to make payments in respect of occupying it.

You do not jointly occupy the home with someone unless you made a joint agreement with your landlord to occupy the home. The fact that you live in the same home does not make you joint occupiers;[137]

- someone who is liable to pay rent on a commercial basis (see p199) to you or your partner. However, although no non-dependant deduction can be made for her/him, the rent s/he pays can count as your income (see p976).

If the person comes within the last three categories above, s/he *does* count as a non-dependant if s/he is treated as not liable for rent under the rules explained on p199 (unless s/he is a student or has failed the habitual residence test or is a person subject to immigration control).[138]

When no non-dependant deduction is made

No non-dependant deductions are made if either you or your partner:[139]

- are registered blind or have regained your eyesight within the last 28 weeks; *or*
- receive attendance allowance (AA), constant attendance allowance, or the care component of disability living allowance (DLA).

No deduction is made in respect of any non-dependant who is:[140]

- currently staying in your household but whose normal home is elsewhere;
- receiving a Work-Based Learning for Young People allowance;
- a full-time student during her/his period of study. Unless you or your partner are 65 or over and neither of you are on IS or income-based JSA, this only applies during the summer vacation if the student is not in full-time work;
- in hospital for more than 52 weeks;
- in prison;
- under 18 years old;[141]
- aged under 25 and receiving IS/income-based JSA;[142]
- on pension credit.[143]

The amount of deductions

Once it is established that you have one or more non-dependants, deductions are usually made for each non-dependant in your household. The amount of the deduction depends on the gross weekly income of your non-dependant. For situations when no deduction is made, see above.

You should try to provide information to show which deduction applies. If you cannot, ask the local authority to consider your circumstances – eg, if your non-dependant is doing a job which is normally very low paid. The DWP says that local authorities are not expected to investigate the income of non-dependants in every case.[144] A deduction is made from your eligible rent for every non-dependant living in your household except in the case of a non-dependant couple (see p214). The amounts are as shown below.[145]

Circumstances of the non-dependant	*Deduction*
Aged 18 or over and in full-time paid work with a weekly gross income of:	
£322 or more	£47.75
£258–£321.99	£43.50
£194–£257.99	£38.20
£150–£193.99	£23.35
£101–£149.99	£17.00
All others (for whom a deduction is made)	£7.40

Gross income includes wages before tax and national insurance are deducted, plus any other income the non-dependant has (apart from AA, constant attendance allowance, DLA and payments from any of the Macfarlane Trusts, the Eileen Trust, the Skipton Fund, the Fund and the Independent Living Funds[146]).

The income bands only apply to non-dependants in full-time paid work. The rules on full-time paid work are covered in Chapter 28. Remember:

- A non-dependant who is not in (or is treated as not in) full-time paid work does not attract the higher levels of deduction even if her/his weekly gross income is £101 or more.
- If someone is getting IS or income-based JSA for more than three days in a benefit week, s/he does not count as in full-time paid work in that week.[147] This means the lower deduction (£7.40) is made (or no deduction is made, if the non-dependant is under 25 and getting IS or income-based JSA).

If you are 65 or over

If you or your partner are 65 or over and a non-dependant moves in with you so a deduction should be made, or a there has been a change of circumstances in respect of a non-dependant, the effect of this can be delayed for 26 weeks (see p233).

Non-dependant couples

Only one deduction is made for a married or unmarried couple (see p811) (or the members of a polygamous marriage) who are non-dependants. The deduction made is the highest that would have been made if they were treated as individuals.[148] For the purpose of deciding which income band applies (see above), their joint income counts, even if only one of them is in full-time work.[149]

Non-dependants of joint occupiers

Where you share a non-dependant with any other joint occupiers, the deduction is divided between you, taking into account the proportion of housing costs paid by each of you. But no apportionment should be made between the members of a couple.[150] Where the person is a non-dependant of only one of you, the full deduction is made from that person's benefit only.

Income and capital of a non-dependant is greater than yours

Normally, the income and capital of any non-dependant is only relevant in deciding which non-dependant deduction applies. However, your HB entitlement is assessed on the basis of your non-dependant's income and capital rather than your own if:[151]

- you are not on IS/income-based JSA; *and*
- the income and capital of your non-dependant are both greater than yours; *and*
- the local authority is satisfied you have made an arrangement with your non-dependant to take advantage of the HB scheme (see p200).

Any income and capital normally treated as belonging to you is completely ignored, but the rest of the calculation proceeds as normal. If you think this has been applied to you wrongly, seek a revision or appeal (see Chapters 43 and 44).

Discretionary housing payments

If you need extra financial assistance to meet your housing costs (including your council tax) you might be able to claim discretionary housing payments to top up your HB. See p235 for further information.

Extra benefit for war pensioners

The local authority has the power to pay extra HB to people getting either a war disablement pension, a war widow's pension or war widower's pension, including similar pensions paid by non-UK governments, by disregarding some or all of them as income, rather than just disregarding £10.[152] If the authority uses this power it must apply the income disregard to all people in receipt of these pensions. See p971 for further information.

5. Special rules for special groups

There are some groups of claimants to whom special rules apply. These are covered in Chapters 25, 26 and 28. Special rules apply to:

- students (see p630);
- people subject to immigration control (see p654);
- people in hospital (see p715);
- prisoners (see p730);
- people in care homes (see p725).

6. Claims and backdating

You should claim housing benefit (HB) as soon as you think you might be entitled or you may lose benefit. The rules about backdating are explained on p221. If you are claiming because your entitlement ended when you or your partner started work (or increased your hours or your pay) and stopped getting income support (IS), income-based jobseeker's allowance (JSA), incapacity benefit (IB) or severe disablement allowance, see pp225 and 66.

If you want to claim discretionary housing payments, you must claim separately. See p236 for further information.

Making a claim

All claims must be made in writing on a properly completed claim form.[153] You must provide any information and evidence required on the claim form. You can claim in some other written form (eg, by letter) so long as the written information and evidence you provide is sufficient. Claim forms are available from your local authority. In addition, if you are claiming:

- IS or income-based JSA (see Chapters 13 and 15) there is an HB and council tax benefit (CTB) claim form (HCTB1) in your IS/JSA claim pack.[154] This is also available from the DWP website (see Appendix 1);
- pension credit (PC), HB and CTB forms are not given with the PC claim form. Instead, a claim form (HCTB1(PC)) is sent separately to you if you are not already getting HB or CTB and you indicate that you wish to claim HB and/or CTB at the time you claim PC. You may be asked to provide further information if, for example, you have children or are working or have non-dependants living with you. If you are 60 or over and you are already getting HB, the DWP passes your details on to the local authority who treats this as your claim for HB.

The local authority might ask you to complete its own form. You should do this as soon as possible.

If you are claiming HB or CTB within 12 weeks of a previous entitlement ending, you might be able to make a 'rapid reclaim' (see p217).

You cannot claim by telephone. However, if you telephone to ask for a claim form, state on the form that you would like your claim to be backdated to the date of your phone call (or earlier, if appropriate) because you have good cause for a late claim (see p221).

Send your claim in as soon as you can so you do not lose benefit. Keep a copy of your claim in case queries arise. Remember: the local authority might ask you for other information and evidence (see pp217 and 218).

You may amend or withdraw your claim in writing at any time before it has been assessed. Amendments must be made in writing and are treated as though they were part of your original claim.[155] A notice to withdraw your claim takes effect from the day it is received.[156]

Making sure your claim is valid

It is very important that you provide any information or evidence required on the claim form. Until you do, you may not count as having made a valid claim (eg, if you do not complete your claim form properly or you claim by letter and you do not provide sufficient information and evidence) the local authority calls this a 'defective claim'. However, if you have:

- not completed the claim form properly, the local authority can return it to you or ask you for further information or evidence;[157] *or*
- claimed by letter, the local authority can send you a claim form to complete properly or ask you for further information or evidence.[158]

If you return the form properly completed or provide the information or evidence within four weeks, your claim is treated as though it was received on the date of your original claim.[159] The local authority can allow you longer than four weeks if it thinks this reasonable.

Rapid reclaim

You might be able to complete a shortened HB and CTB claim form (HBRR1) – known as 'rapid reclaim' – if you are claiming within 12 weeks of a previous entitlement to HB or CTB ending.[160] This only applies if:

- you are also making a 'rapid reclaim' for IS or JSA (see pp306 and 392); *and*
- you are entitled to IS or income-based JSA. Local authorities may also allow a 'rapid reclaim' if you are re-awarded contribution-based JSA; *and*
- your circumstances have not changed since the last time you were claiming HB or CTB, unless the only change is that you, or someone you are claiming for, are now pregnant.

You are given the shortened form by the DWP with your claim form for IS or JSA. You must send your HB and CTB claim to the local authority, *not* to the DWP. If you fill in the form properly, the local authority should be able to make a decision on your HB or CTB claim without asking you for further information. However, if you do not do so, or any of your details have changed since the last time you claimed HB or CTB, the local authority may send you a full HB or CTB form to complete or ask you for further information.

Where to make your claim

You must usually send or give your HB claim to the local authority's designated office for the receipt of HB and CTB claims.[161] The address is usually on the claim form or a notice accompanying it. You can also send or give your claim to:[162]

- your DWP office *or* to the local authority's designated office for HB/CTB claims, if you or your partner are claiming IS, IB or JSA. The HCTB1 form tells you to send the form to the local authority. However, if you send your HB/CTB claim to the DWP, unless your HB/CTB claim is on the same form as your IS, IB or JSA claim, the DWP must forward it to the local authority within two working days of the date your HB/CTB claim was received or as soon as reasonably practicable after that.[163]

It may be wise to send your HB/CTB form directly to the local authority. If you do this, the local authority verifies your entitlement to IS, IB or income-based JSA before assessing your HB. This may speed up your HB/CTB claim; *or*

- if you are at least the qualifying age for PC (currently 60), any office nominated by the DWP and authorised by the local authority to receive your claim; *or*
- a ONE office, if you are 16 or over but under 60 and live in a ONE scheme area.

Keep a copy of your claim form wherever possible. Ask for confirmation that you have delivered it to the relevant office.

Information to support your claim

Where possible, your claim for HB should be accompanied by all the information and evidence needed to assess it,[164] but you should not delay your claim just because you do not have all the evidence ready to send. Even if you provide all the information required by the claim form, the local authority might ask you for further evidence or information. You must then supply this within four weeks – or longer if the local authority thinks you need more time.[165] Contact the local authority as soon as possible with the information requested and ask it to extend the four-week period if you need more time.

Unless you are living in a hostel, you and your partner must satisfy the national insurance (NI) number requirement (see p1083). If you have claimed HB in association with a claim for PC, IS, JSA or IB and the DWP has accepted that you satisfy the NI number requirement, the local authority can accept that it is also satisfied for HB purposes.[166] If your claim is for contribution-based JSA or IB, the local authority may still need to verify your partner's NI number and identity.

The local authority might ask you to provide information after you are awarded HB. If you fail to do so, your HB could be suspended or even terminated.

Who should claim

If you are a single person or a lone parent, you make a claim for HB on your own behalf. If you are one of a couple, or a partner in a polygamous marriage, you can decide between you who should claim. See p811 for who counts as a couple. The choice of claimant may affect the level of HB you receive – eg, if one of you is a full-time student and not entitled to HB (see p631). In particular, if you are exempt from the local reference rent rules (see p249) and are considering changing the claim into your partner's name, you should check whether doing so could result in you losing your exemption and becoming subject to harsher rent restriction rules (see p244). If you cannot agree who should be the claimant, the local authority can decide for you.[167]

If a person is either temporarily or permanently unable to manage her/his own affairs, the local authority must accept a claim made by someone formally appointed to act legally on her/his behalf – eg, someone appointed with power of attorney, a receiver appointed by the Court of Protection or, in Scotland, a judicial factor or any guardian appointed under the Adults with Incapacity (Scotland) Act 2000 administering the person's estate.[168]

If no one has been formally appointed to look after a claimant's affairs, the local authority can decide to make someone aged over 18 an appointee who can act on her/his behalf.[169] For the purpose of the claim, an appointee has the responsibility of exercising all rights and duties as though s/he were the claimant.[170]

You can write to ask to be an appointee, and can resign after giving four weeks' notice. The local authority may terminate any appointment at any time.[171] If someone is given a formal legal appointment, that person automatically takes over from the person appointed by the local authority.[172]

The date of your claim

Your date of claim is important because it affects the date from which your HB begins (see p224). Usually, your claim is treated as being made on the day your properly completed claim form (see p216) is received by the designated office (see p217), not the date on which you post it.[173]

The only exceptions are if:

- you or your partner have successfully claimed IS, income-based JSA or the guarantee credit of PC and your HB claim reached the DWP within four weeks of your IS, income-based JSA or PC claim being received by the DWP. Your HB claim is treated as having been made on the first day of entitlement to IS, income-based JSA or PC (including the three waiting days for JSA);[174]
- you or your partner have unsuccessfully claimed IS, income-based JSA or the guarantee credit of PC. Your HB claim is treated as having been made on the day it reached either the DWP or the local authority's designated office, whichever was earlier;[175]
- you or your partner claimed HB on the same form as a claim for IB or contribution-based JSA. Your HB claim is treated as made on the date it was received at the DWP office;[176]
- you are at least the qualifying age for PC (currently 60) and sent or gave your claim to an office nominated by the DWP and authorised by the local authority to receive it. Your HB claim is treated as made on the date it was received at that office;[177]
- you claimed PC and you were not entitled or were only entitled to the savings credit. Your HB claim is treated as made on the date on which your HB claim

was received at the DWP office or the designated office, whichever was earlier;[178]

- you have made an advance claim (see below);
- you make your claim at a ONE office (see below);
- you or your partner are on IS, income-based JSA or the guarantee credit of PC and have just become liable to pay rent. If your HB claim form reaches the local authority's designated office or DWP office within four weeks of you becoming liable, it is treated as being made on the date that you first became liable.[179]

See p224 for information about when your entitlement starts.

Claiming from a ONE office

At the time of writing this *Handbook*, only a small number of ONE offices still exist. Special rules apply if you claim HB or CTB from a ONE office. See CPAG's *Welfare Benefits Handbook 2002/2003*, p212 for further information.

Claiming in advance

You can claim HB in advance if:

- you become liable for rent for the first time but cannot move into your accommodation until after your liability begins. You must claim HB as soon as you are liable. Then, once you have moved in, you may be able to receive HB for up to four weeks prior to moving in. See p201 for further information;
- you are not entitled to HB now, but will become entitled within 13 weeks of claiming (17 weeks, if you or your partner will be 60 or over within 17 weeks). The local authority can treat your claim as having been made in the benefit week immediately before you are first entitled.[180] If this happens, you do not need to make a further claim later on.

Housing benefit after an award of a 'qualifying benefit'

You might not be entitled to HB currently, but would be once you or a member of your family become entitled to another 'qualifying benefit' – eg, disability living allowance or carer's allowance (see Chapters 7 and 4). Alternatively, you might be entitled to a higher rate of benefit once the 'qualifying benefit' is awarded. If you are already entitled to HB when the qualifying benefit is awarded, see pp1194 and 1201.

If you only qualify for HB (or CTB) when the qualifying benefit is awarded, the rules operate in an unfair way. You should, therefore, claim HB (or CTB) while waiting to hear about the claim for a qualifying benefit. Then:

- ask the local authority to check whether you are entitled to HB (or CTB) on the basis of your circumstances, regardless of whether you are entitled to a qualifying benefit. If you are, it should award HB (or CTB). If you later get a qualifying benefit your award should be revised or superseded (see pp1194 and 1201);

- if you do not qualify for HB (or CTB) until awarded a qualifying benefit, ask the local authority to wait to make a decision on your claim until the award of qualifying benefit is made. This is what is known as 'stockpiling' your claim.

If the local authority refuses to stockpile your claim, you can try to argue that its failure to delay making a decision on your claim was an 'error of law' and therefore that there are grounds for an 'any time' revision (see p1193).[181] If you are refused HB (or CTB) but have since been awarded a qualifying benefit, claim again and ask for your claim to be backdated. You should argue that you have good cause for your late claim (see below). If you lose benefit because of the way the rules operate, ask your local authority for an extra statutory payment to cover the period before your fresh HB (or CTB) claim.

Backdating your claim

It is very important to claim in time. A claim for HB can be backdated:

- if you are 60 or over and neither you nor your partner are on IS or income-based JSA, for up to 12 months. You only need to show that you qualified for HB during that period;[182] *or*
- in all other cases, for up to 52 weeks. However, you must show that you qualified for HB during that period and prove you have continuous 'good cause' for your failure to claim throughout the whole time for which you want to claim.[183]

Any backdated HB is calculated based on your circumstances and the HB rules as they were over the backdating period.

You must ask for your HB to be backdated for this to be considered. You should claim backdated HB as soon as possible. HB can only be backdated from the date of your request for backdating, not from the date of your original claim for HB.

If you would have been entitled to HB for an earlier period, you could:

- ask for an 'any time' revision if there are grounds (see p1193);
- ask for an extra-statutory payment from the local authority if you were given wrong information or misled by it (see p1304);
- complain to the Ombudsman (see p1303).

If you only qualify for HB when a 'qualifying benefit' is awarded, see above.

Good cause for claiming late

You count as having 'good cause' for your late claim if you can show there is something that would probably have caused a reasonable person of your age and experience to act (or fail to act) as you did, having regard to all the circumstances (including your state of health and the information which you received and which you might have obtained).[184] It is your mental age, not your chronological age that is relevant.[185] If you have a mental health problem that makes you act unreasonably, then that must be borne in mind.[186]

The following are examples of situations where you might have good cause for making a late claim:

- You sought advice about your rights but were misled by someone on whom you were entitled to rely. You are entitled to rely on officers from the local authority or the DWP,[187] or independent advisers such as solicitors,[188] citizens advice bureaux,[189] trade union officials[190] or accountants.[191] Relying on the advice of work colleagues, friends,[192] or even a doctor,[193] is not enough. The inquiries that you made need not have been specific, provided the situation is such that you ought to have been told about your possible entitlement.
- You did not seek advice about your rights because either you mistakenly thought that you understood them,[194] or you mistakenly thought that you had no entitlement and there was nothing for you to enquire about.[195] Generally, you are expected to find out about your rights but if it was reasonable for you to form one of these views, you can still have good cause.
- The delay was due to some factor beyond your control, such as the failure of the post,[196] or the failure of someone you asked to help with your claim, provided you have checked whether the claim has arrived in good time.[197]
- You are unable to claim due to physical or mental ill-health.[198] However, you might reasonably be expected to seek the assistance of friends or relatives if available.
- You have difficulty communicating in English, or understanding documents, or have little knowledge of the benefits system. These matters should be taken into account[199] but are not usually good cause in themselves.[200]
- You only qualify for HB or CTB when a 'qualifying benefit' is awarded (see p220).

Notice of the decision

If you are a person affected by an HB decision you must be notified of it by the local authority within 14 days or as soon as 'reasonably practical'.[201] This is sometimes called a 'decision notice'. You can request reasons for a decision. Your request must be in writing and it must be signed by you.[202]

You are a person affected by a decision if you are:[203]

- a claimant;
- someone acting for a claimant who is unable to act for her/himself – eg, an appointee, a receiver, a guardian (in Scotland) or a person with power of attorney;
- someone from whom the local authority decides to recover an overpayment (including a landlord); *or*
- a landlord or agent, where the decision concerns whether or not to make a direct payment of HB to you.

Information a decision notice should contain

The local authority must include a minimum amount of information in its decision notice.[204] In addition, it may also include other relevant information.[205]

If the decision is one against which you have a right of appeal (see p1219) you must be informed of:[206]

- your right to appeal against the decision; *and*
- your right to a written statement of reasons for the decision (if this is not already included – see p1184).

Other information that must be provided varies with the particular circumstances of your case. All the following should be included in any local authority decision where relevant:[207]

- the normal weekly amount of HB to which you are entitled;
- your weekly eligible rent (see p207);
- the amount of any notional fuel deductions, why they have been made, and that they can be varied if you can provide evidence of the actual amount involved;
- the amount and category of any non-dependant deductions (see p211);
- if you are a private tenant, the day your HB will be paid and whether payment will be made weekly, monthly, etc;
- the date on which your entitlement starts;
- if you are not receiving IS or income-based JSA or you are on PC but are only entitled to the savings credit, how your applicable amount is calculated;
- if you are not receiving IS or income-based JSA, how your income has been assessed;
- if you are on PC but are only entitled to the savings credit:
  - the amount of the savings credit and any child tax credit or child benefit taken into account;
  - the amount of income and capital notified to the local authority by the DWP which has been taken into account. The local authority must also tell you about any modifications it makes to your income or capital;
  - the amount of capital the local authority has taken into account, if the DWP notified the local authority that your capital was less than £16,000 but it has increased to more than that figure while an assessed income period was in force (see p480);
- if your level of HB is less than the minimum amount payable, that this is the reason why you have no entitlement;
- if your claim was successful, your duty to notify the local authority of any change in circumstances which might affect your entitlement and what kinds of changes should be reported;
- if your claim was unsuccessful, a statement explaining exactly why you are not entitled;

- if it has been decided to pay your rent allowance direct to your landlord, information saying how much is to be paid to your landlord and when payments will start, and also that where recovery of an overpayment is made from a landlord (see p1152) and recovery is made from a tenant other than the one who was overpaid, that tenant is treated as if the full payment of HB had been made;[208]
- if the income and capital of a non-dependant has been used instead of yours to calculate your HB (see p215), additional information saying that this has happened and why.

7. Getting paid

No housing benefit (HB) is payable if the amount would be less than 50 pence a week.[209] A local authority may round any figure used in working out your entitlement to the nearest penny (a half-penny is rounded upwards).

When your entitlement starts

If you are 60 or over and your claim has been automatically backdated for up to 12 months (see p221), your entitlement to HB starts:[210]

- if you became liable for rent for your home in the first of the weeks in respect of which you are claiming, from the Monday of that week; *or*
- in all other cases, from the benefit week following the first date in respect of which you are claiming.

Otherwise your entitlement to HB starts:[211]

- if you have only just become liable for rent on your home and you claim in the same week in which your liability begins, from the Monday of that week.
- in all other cases, in the benefit week following your date of claim.

A benefit week is a period of seven days running from Monday to Sunday.[212]

This means that if you claim HB in the same week in which your liability for rent began or you became liable for rent in the first of the weeks in respect of which you are claiming:

- if your rent is due weekly or at intervals of a multiple of a week, your HB starts at the beginning of the week in which liability starts – ie, you receive a full week's benefit for that first week, even if your tenancy did not start until part-way through that week;[213]
- if your rent is due at other intervals, your HB starts on the same day your liability actually begins.[214]

When your entitlement ends

Your entitlement to HB ends if your circumstances change in a way that means you no longer satisfy the rules described in this chapter. In addition, your entitlement to HB ends, even if you would otherwise continue to qualify, if:[215]

- you or your partner:
  - were entitled to and in receipt of IS or income-based JSA (including joint-claim JSA) and your entitlement ended because either of you started work (including self-employed work) or increased your earnings from or hours of work; *and*
  - had been continuously entitled to and in receipt of either IS or JSA or a combination of these for at least 26 weeks.This includes periods of less than five weeks when you counted as in full-time paid work (see p750) because you were on an employment zone programme; *and*
  - expect the work (or increase in hours or pay) to last for five weeks or more; *or*
- unless you are getting pension credit (PC), you or your partner:
  - were entitled to and in receipt of incapacity benefit (IB) or severe disablement allowance (SDA) and that entitlement ended because you or your partner started work (including self-employed work) or increased your earnings from, or hours of, work; *and*
  - were not entitled to or in receipt of IS; *and*
  - had been continuously entitled to and in receipt of either IB or SDA or a combination of these for 26 weeks; *and*
  - expect the work (or increase in hours or pay) to last for five weeks or more.

This applies even if you would be entitled to HB on the basis of your income from work. Your entitlement ends at the end of the benefit week in which entitlement to IS, income-based JSA, IB or SDA ceases. You *must* make a fresh claim for HB to continue to qualify. In order to ensure your claim is continuous, you must claim within a strict time limit (see p66).

In all of these situations, you might qualify for extended payments of HB and council tax benefit (CTB) – see p63.

Note: The Government is considering amending these rules. See CPAG's *Welfare Rights Bulletin* for updates.

Continuing payments where pension credit is claimed

To avoid problems caused by delays in reassessing your HB when you move from IS or income-based JSA onto PC, so long as you otherwise continue to qualify for HB, you continue to receive it for:[216]

- a period of four weeks from the day after your IS or income-based JSA ceases; *or*
- if the four-week period ends before the last day of a benefit week, until the end of the benefit week in which the end of the four-week period falls.

HB is paid at the same rate as before this happened (but see below). The DWP calls these 'continuing payments'. You qualify for continuing payments if you are entitled to HB[217] *and:*

- your partner has claimed PC and the DWP has certified this; *or*
- your IS ceased because you turned 60, or if you were getting income-based JSA beyond that age, this ceased because you turned 65 and the DWP has certified this and also that you are required to claim or have claimed PC (or are treated as having done so).

Your maximum HB (see p205) is recalculated if your rent increases or there is a change in the non-dependant deductions (see p211) that should be made.[218]

How your benefit is paid

If your landlord is the housing authority responsible for the payment of HB, you receive HB in the form of a reduction in your rent. This is called a rent rebate.[219]

If you are a private tenant (or a housing association tenant), you receive HB in the form of a rent allowance which is usually paid to you although, in some cases, it may be paid direct to your landlord (see p227) or to someone acting on your behalf (see below).[220]

Although rent allowances are normally paid in the form of a cheque, the local authority has the discretion to pay you by whatever method it chooses but, in doing so, it must have regard to your 'reasonable needs and convenience'.[221] It should not insist on payment into a bank account if you do not have one, nor make you collect it if it involves a difficult journey.[222] If it does, you can complain to your local councillor. If that has no effect, ask your MP to take the matter up with the local authority (see p1302), and also complain to the Ombudsman (see p1303).

If the local authority refuses to replace a payment which has never arrived, you should threaten to sue in the county court. The process is the same as for payments from the DWP (see p1105). If payment of your HB is suspended see p1105.

Payment to someone acting on your behalf

Where an appointee or some other person legally empowered to act for a claimant has claimed HB on her/his behalf, that person can also receive the payments.[223]

If you are able to claim HB for yourself, you can still nominate an agent to receive or collect it for you. To do this you must make a written request to the local authority. Anyone you nominate must be aged 18 or over.[224] The DWP says that this can only be done where you are unable to collect the payment yourself, but the regulations do not make such a restriction.[225]

If a claimant dies, any unpaid HB may be paid to her/his personal representative or, where there is none, to her/his next of kin aged 16 or over.[226] For payment to be made, a written application must be received by the local authority within 12 months of the claimant's death. However, the time limit can be extended at the local authority's discretion. Where HB was being paid to the landlord prior to the claimant's death, the local authority can pay any outstanding HB to clear remaining rent due.

Payment direct to a landlord

Your HB can be paid directly to your landlord (or the person to whom you pay rent) in specific circumstances (see below). Your landlord could contact the local authority about this.[227] If the local authority is suspicious of your landlord, see p228.

If you are granted refugee status and receive a retrospective award of HB, part of, or the whole of, the award can be paid direct to your landlord (see p671).[228]

If you have just claimed HB, and the local authority thinks you have not already paid your rent and that it would be in the interests of the 'efficient administration' of HB, it may make the first cheque payable to your landlord although it will be sent to you.[229]

Both you and your landlord should be notified if HB is to be paid to your landlord. If it is *not* in your interests to have HB paid directly to your landlord it is worth trying to persuade the local authority to withhold it rather than paying it to your landlord where there are more than eight weeks' arrears. However, you should always consider seeking housing advice before you do so.

When payment must be made

The local authority *must* pay your HB, including payments on account,[230] directly to your landlord (or the person to whom you pay rent) if:

- you or your partner are on IS, income-based JSA or PC and the DWP has decided to pay part of your benefit to your landlord for arrears (see p1112);[231] *or*
- you have rent arrears equivalent to eight weeks' rent or more, unless the local authority considers it to be in your overriding interest not to make direct payments.[232] Once your arrears have been reduced to less than eight weeks' rent, compulsory direct payments stop. The local authority might then choose to continue direct payments on a discretionary basis (see below).

The rules above also apply if you live in a Pathfinder area and the 'local housing allowance' rules apply to you (see p253). However, the maximum the local authority can pay to your landlord is the amount of rent and arrears of rent you are liable to pay.[233] This is the case even if the amount of HB to which you are entitled is higher than your rent liability.

When payment may be made

The local authority *may* pay your HB directly to your landlord (or the person to whom you pay rent):[234]

- if you have requested or agreed to direct payments; *or*

- without your agreement, if it decides that direct payments are in the best interests of yourself and your family.

These rules do *not* apply if you live in a Pathfinder area and the 'local housing allowance' rules apply to you (see p253), but see below.

Whether or not you live in a Pathfinder area, the local authority may also pay your HB directly to your landlord (or the person to whom you pay rent) without your agreement if you have left the address for which you were getting HB and there are rent arrears. In this case, direct payments of any unpaid HB due in respect of that accommodation can be made, up to the total of the outstanding arrears.[235]

If the 'local housing allowance' rules apply to you

In addition to the rules described above, if you live in a Pathfinder area and the 'local housing allowance' rules apply to you (see p253), the local authority may pay your HB directly to your landlord if:[236]

– your HB was calculated based on a standard local housing allowance that was set within the last six months and this allowance has not since changed; *and*

– you have been continuously entitled to HB for the same home since that date.

However, direct payment can only be made if the local authority:

– thinks you are likely to have difficulty managing your own affairs; *or*

– thinks it is improbable that you will pay your rent; *or*

– has already made direct payments during your current award of HB in any of the situations when payments must be made (see p227).

The maximum the local authority can pay to your landlord is the amount of rent and arrears of rent you are liable to pay.[237] This applies even if the amount of HB to which you are entitled is higher than your rent liability.

When the local authority is suspicious about a landlord

If HB is being paid to a landlord, or a request is made for payment to a landlord, and the local authority suspects impropriety on the part of the landlord, it may require a landlord or her/his agent to provide information to the local authority.[238] The information must be supplied in written or printed form (or in handwritten or electronic form if the local authority agrees) within four weeks. A further four weeks can be allowed if a written request for an extension of time is made within four weeks of the request for information.[239] The local authority may also refuse to make direct payments where it 'is not satisfied that the landlord is a fit and proper person'.[240]

However, direct payments may be made if:[241]

- the requirements for discretionary direct payments are met; *and*
- the local authority is satisfied that it is in the best interests of you and your family that direct payments are made.

If the local authority decides not to make payments to your landlord, it can make payments to you (including by sending you a cheque payable to the landlord) or to a trusted third party such as a social worker or solicitor.[242]

Time of payment

HB is normally paid in arrears. Payments are made at intervals of a week, two weeks, four weeks or a month, depending on when your rent is normally due. It can also be paid at longer intervals if you agree.[243]

If your rent allowance is less than £1 a week, the local authority can choose to pay your benefit up to six months in arrears.[244]

You can insist on two-weekly payments if your rent allowance is more than £2 a week unless HB is paid direct to your landlord (see p227).[245] The local authority can pay your rent allowance weekly either to avoid an overpayment or where you are liable to pay rent weekly and it is in your interests for HB to be paid weekly.[246]

Before 7 October 1996, HB was usually paid two weeks before the end of the period in respect of which it was paid. Payments for two weeks were made in advance and payments for four weeks or a month midway through the period.[247] To see if this still applies to you, see CPAG's *Welfare Benefits and Tax Credits Handbook 2004/2005*, pp232–33.

Direct payments to your landlord

Payments made direct to your landlord are made four-weekly or monthly in arrears. If HB is also paid to your landlord for other tenants, the first payment for you can be made at a shorter interval so that your payments are brought into line with the cycle of payments for the other tenants.[248]

Suspending benefit

Local authorities have powers to suspend and terminate benefit. See p1105 for details.

Delays and complaints

The local authority must make a decision on your claim, tell you in writing what the decision is, and pay you any HB to which you are entitled within 14 days, or, if that is not reasonably practicable, as soon as possible after that.[249] In practice, many local authorities take considerably longer than 14 days to deal with claims. If you consider a delay is unreasonable, write to the HB manager and threaten a formal complaint of maladministration to the Ombudsman (see p1303). In serious cases you may want to seek advice on whether you have grounds for judicial review (see p1253).

If you are a private (or housing association) tenant and have not received your rent allowance within 14 days of your claim, you can get a payment on account – known as an 'interim payment'.

Interim payments

If you are a private (or housing association) tenant and the local authority has not been able to assess your HB within the required period, you should receive a payment on account – known as an interim payment – while your claim is being sorted out.[250] The local authority should automatically do this. You do not have to request an interim payment.[251]

Some local authorities treat interim payments as though they are discretionary. However, the local authority *must* pay you an amount which it considers reasonable, given what it knows about your circumstances.[252]

Interim payments can only be refused if it is clear that you will not be entitled to HB or the reason for the delay is that you have been asked for information or evidence in support of your claim and you have failed, without good cause, to provide it (see p218).[253] If the delay has been caused by a third party (eg, the rent officer, your bank or employer) this does not affect your right to an interim payment. If your local authority has not made a payment on account, you should complain. You could also argue that it is guilty of maladministration and complain to the Ombudsman (see p1303).

If the local authority makes a payment on account, it should notify you of the amount and that it can recover any overpayment which occurs if your actual HB entitlement is different from the interim amount.[254]

If your interim payment is less than your true entitlement, your future HB can be adjusted to take account of the underpayment.[255]

Change of circumstances

It is your duty to report any change in your circumstances which might affect your right to, the amount of, or payment of, your HB.[256] You should do this promptly in writing to the office handling your claim (although in individual cases notification might be accepted in a form other than in writing). In any case, you might want to report the change in writing and keep a copy in case of a dispute in the future. If you do not report any such change promptly in writing, any resulting overpayment may be recoverable from you (see Chapter 41). If you are considered deliberately to have acted falsely or dishonestly, you may also be guilty of an offence (see Chapter 42). Remember:

- the local authority must tell you in writing about the changes you have to report;[257]
- it is important that you report any changes to the right department. Your duty to notify changes is to the HB department, not to the local authority as a whole;[258]
- if your benefit is paid to someone else on your behalf, the duty to report any relevant changes extends to her/him as well.[259]

If you are in a ONE scheme area (see p220), you can report a change of circumstances for HB in writing to a ONE office.[260] If you made your claim at a

ONE office, you can report a change of circumstances to that or any other ONE office you are told about on or with your claim form.[261]

Remember, if in doubt, always report changes in circumstances. If you think that the local authority might have forgotten to look at your HB entitlement after you report a change, you should check with it.

If you do not get pension credit

If you do not get PC, you must always report the following changes:[262]

- any change to your rent, unless you are a local authority tenant;
- entitlement to IS or income-based JSA ending . You should not assume that the DWP does this on your behalf. Make sure that you make a fresh claim for HB if you are still on a low income after coming off IS, income-based JSA, incapacity benefit or severe disablement allowance because of increased hours of work or earnings. You should also check to see if you qualify for extended payments of HB and CTB (see p63);
- a member of your family is no longer a child for benefit purposes (see p818);
- the number of, or circumstances of, any non-dependants that may affect the level of deductions made to your benefit (see p211).

Examples of other changes you must also report are:

- if you are not getting IS or income-based JSA, family income or capital;
- the number of boarders or sub-tenants or in the payments made by them;
- your status (eg, marriage, cohabitation, separation or divorce).

If you get pension credit

If you get either the guarantee or the savings credit of PC you must report the following changes:[263]

- any change to your tenancy, apart from changes in your rent if you are a local authority tenant;
- any changes affecting a non-dependant normally living with you or with whom you normally live;
- any absence from your home which is, or is likely to be, for more than 13 weeks.

If you are only getting the savings credit of PC, you must also report the following changes:[264]

- changes affecting a child who lives with you which could affect how much HB you get. You need not report changes in the child's age;
- changes affecting child tax credit or child benefit;
- any changes to your capital which do or could take it above £16,000;
- any change in the income or capital of a non-dependant of yours, if your HB has been assessed on the basis of this instead of your own (see p215), and whether s/he has stopped or resumed living with you;

- any change in the income or capital of your partner that has not been taken into account since the determination of your PC award, and whether your partner has stopped or resumed living with you.

If you are on PC, these are the only changes you have to report to the local authority.[265] Other relevant changes in your circumstances should be passed on to the local authority by the DWP.

Other changes

There may be other changes which the local authority requires you to report, depending on the particular circumstances of your case. The need to report these additional changes must be drawn to your attention at the time you claim and also if you are asked for further information.[266] This is important because you only have a duty to report changes which you 'might reasonably be expected to know' could affect your HB.[267]

You do not have to report:[268]

- any changes in your rent if you are a local authority tenant;
- changes in the ages of members of your family, or of non-dependants, unless the change results in a young person ceasing to count as a member of your family (because s/he turns 16, or 19 if in relevant education).[269]

When changes in circumstances take effect

If you claim HB and then report a change of circumstances before the local authority has assessed your claim, your application is assessed on the basis of the revised information you have provided.

If a change of circumstances takes place once benefit has been awarded, the local authority must establish the date on which that change actually occurred.[270] Where you have ceased to be entitled to some other social security benefit, the date the change occurred must always be taken as the day after your last day of entitlement to that benefit.[271]

In most cases, a change takes effect from the start of the benefit week after the one in which the change actually occurred.[272] This applies whether or not a decision is advantageous to you. This means that, on whatever day of the week the change actually occurs, the change is implemented as from the following Monday.

Exceptions to the rule

There are exceptions to the general rule described above. These include:

- If the change is one you are required to notify to the local authority (other than one relating to you having to take part in a work-focused interview – see p1092 – or if you are on PC, one of the exceptions to the rules described on p233) and it is advantageous to you, you must notify the change within one month of it taking place.[273] The one-month period can be extended in certain circumstances (see p1206). If you notify the change outside the one-month period (or any longer period allowed by the local authority) the date of notification is treated as if that is the date the change occurred.

- Where a child or young person reaches the age of 11 or 16, the personal allowance in respect of her/him (see p881) increases from the first Monday in September following the 11th or 16th birthday.[274]
- A change in your rent is taken into account from the first day of the benefit week in which it actually occurs. If you pay your rent weekly, or in a multiple of weeks, the change is taken into account on the Monday of the week in which it occurs. If you pay rent monthly, the change is taken into account on the day it actually occurs.[275] However, if the change in your rent happens on a day that is not the first day of a benefit week and this ends your entitlement to HB, the change is taken into account from the first day of the benefit week following the date the change occurred.[276]
- A payment of income (or arrears of income) for a past period is taken into account from the date it would have been taken into account had it been paid to you on time.[277] If as a result you receive too much HB, the overpayment may be recoverable (see p1144). Remember that arrears of some benefits, as well as working tax credit, child tax credit and discretionary housing payments, count as capital not income and can be disregarded for a period after they are paid (see p1035).
- If you or your partner are at least 65 and either a non-dependant comes to live with you, or there is a change in respect of a non-dependant, so that a higher non-dependant deduction should be made, the change takes effect 26 weeks after the date on which the change occurred (or where more than one of this type of change occurs, 26 weeks after the date of the first of these), if this is the first day of a benefit week.[278] Otherwise, it takes effect on the first day of the next benefit week to commence after that date.

If two or more changes occurring in the same benefit week would, according to the above rules, normally take effect in different benefit weeks, they are treated as taking effect in the same benefit week in which they occur. They take effect from the beginning of that benefit week (unless one of the changes relates to monthly rent, in which case all the changes take effect on the same day as the rent changes).[279] However, if the changes happen on a day that is not the first day of a benefit week and these end your entitlement to HB, they are taken into account from the first day of the benefit week following the date the changes occurred.[280]

Additional exceptions if you get pension credit

There are additional exceptions to the rules described above if you are on PC and the amount of this changes because of a change in your circumstances or the correction of an official error (see p1193), and this means there is a change in the amount of HB you can be paid. This includes where you are only getting the savings credit of PC and the change is as a result of a change in the DWP assessment of your income or savings. The change to your HB takes effect from:[281]

- the first day of the benefit week in which the rate of your PC changes, where:
  - your PC increases or decreases and as a result your HB increases; *or*
  - you failed to notify the DWP of a change in your circumstances in time, your PC decreases and as a result your HB decreases;
- where you or your partner are awarded PC or your PC increases or decreases and as a result your HB decreases, from the first day of the benefit week after the later of:
  - the date the local authority receives notification from the DWP of the increase in your PC; *or*
  - your PC increases;
- the first day of the benefit week in which the guarantee credit of PC is payable where as a result of the award of guarantee credit your HB increases.

If you are getting 'continuing payments' of HB (see p225) and one of the changes above occurs within the four-week period, the change instead takes effect on the first day of the benefit week starting after the four-week period ends.

Overpayments and fraud

If you are overpaid HB, you might have to repay it. The rules on overpayments are covered in Chapter 41.

If you have been accused of fraud, see Chapter 42. You might get a reduced amount of HB if you have been sanctioned for benefit offences.

8. Challenging a housing benefit decision

You can apply for a revision or a supersession of a housing benefit decision, or appeal against it (see Chapters 43 and 44).

9. Tax, tax credits and other benefits

Housing benefit (HB) is not taxable.

Mean-tested benefits

If you stop getting income support (IS), income-based jobseeker's allowance, incapacity benefit or severe disablement allowance because you start work or increase your hours of work, you may be entitled to extended payments of HB or council tax benefit (CTB) – see p63.

If you were previously incapable of work and getting IS, HB or CTB, then start work or training and count as a 'welfare to work' beneficiary (see p769), you retain the disability or higher pensioner premium if you become incapable of work again within 52 weeks.

Passports and other sources of help

If you are on a low income, you might qualify for certain health benefits such as free prescriptions (see Chapter 9). You may also qualify for other sources of help (see Chapter 1) or a social fund payment, maternity grant or funeral expenses payment (see Chapters 21 and 22).

10. **Discretionary housing payments**

Discretionary housing payments are extra payments that can be paid to you by your local authority to help meet your rent or council tax liability. They do not count as housing benefit (HB) or council tax benefit (CTB) and have different rules.

You do not have a 'right' to discretionary housing payments. They are paid from a cash-limited budget allocated to your local authority by the Government. There are some restrictions on when payments can be made (see below).

Who can claim discretionary housing payments

A local authority can pay you discretionary housing payments if:[282]

- you are entitled to HB or CTB; *and*
- you appear to require some financial assistance in addition to your HB or CTB to meet your housing costs (this includes council tax).

Local authorities have discretion whether to pay you, what amount to pay you (with certain limits) and over what period to pay you.[283] You cannot be paid for rent or council tax for which you were liable before 2 July 2001.[284]

Payments not met by discretionary housing payments

Discretionary housing payments cannot be made to you if your need for financial assistance arises as a consequence of:[285]

- ineligible service charges under the HB scheme (see p209);
- water and sewage charges;
- council tax liability if you are entitled to HB but not CTB;
- liabilities that can be met by HB if you are entitled to CTB but not HB;
- council tax liability if you are only entitled to the second adult rebate and are not or would not have been entitled to CTB if you had not received the rebate;

- your rent payments being increased to cover arrears of rent, service charges or other unpaid charge;
- a reduced benefit direction benefit penalty because you failed to co-operate with the Child Support Agency (see p859);
- your benefit being reduced because you refused to attend a work-focused interview (see p1092);
- your jobseeker's allowance (JSA) being stopped or reduced because you left your work voluntarily (see p419) or you lost your job because of misconduct (see p416);
- your benefit being suspended (see p1105);
- your benefit being restricted:
  - because a court has decided that you failed to comply with a community order without a reasonable excuse (see p1117); *or*
  - under the 'loss of benefit for benefit offences' rules (see p1169).

The amount of discretionary housing payments

Discretionary housing payments are normally paid in weekly amounts. It is up to the local authority to decide for how long you can be paid and how far your payments can be backdated.[286] You cannot be paid more than:[287]

- in the case of an amount to assist you to meet your council tax liabilities, your weekly council tax liability;
- in the case of an amount to meet payments in respect of your home, other than council tax, an amount to meet your rent and other amounts listed on p195 (payments which can be met by HB) less any amounts paid for ineligible service charges and rent-free periods.

Claims

A claim for discretionary housing payments is separate from your claim for HB or CTB. You claim from your local authority and you should ask it how to make a claim. The local authority may accept a claim from you, or from someone acting on your behalf, as long as you are entitled to HB or CTB.[288] Your local authority does not have to insist your claim is made in writing but it decides what 'form or manner' your claim should take.[289]

You must provide grounds for your claim and provide any other information that the local authority specifies.[290] If you want your claim to be backdated, tell the local authority.

Getting paid

You must be given written notice of the local authority's decision on your claim and the reasons for its decision as soon as is 'reasonably practical'.[291] It can pay you or, if reasonable, someone else where appropriate.[292]

Change of circumstances

It is your duty to report any change in your circumstances which might affect your right to, the amount of, or payment of your benefit. You should do this promptly in writing to the office handling your claim (although in individual cases notification might be accepted in a form other than in writing). In any case, you might want to report the change in writing and keep a copy in case of a dispute in the future. If you do not report any such change promptly in writing, any resulting overpayment may be recoverable from you (see Chapter 41). If you are considered to have acted dishonestly, you may also be guilty of an offence (see Chapter 42).

Challenging a discretionary housing payment decision

You do not have the right of appeal to an independent appeal tribunal against a discretionary housing payment decision. However, you do have the right to ask the local authority for a review of its decision.[293] Local authorities must have a review procedure. You are entitled to written notice and reasons for the review decision as soon as is 'reasonably practicable'.[294] You might be able to challenge a review decision by judicial review (see p1253).

Tax, tax credits and other benefits

Discretionary housing payments are not taxable.

Discretionary hardship payments are disregarded as income and capital for income support, JSA, HB and CTB, working tax credit and child tax credit purposes.[295]

Notes

1. Who can claim housing benefit

1 s130 SSCBA 1992
2 Reg 22 HB Regs, as substituted by reg 8 HB&CTB(SPC) Regs
3 Reg 22 HB Regs, as substituted by reg 8 HB&CTB(SPC) Regs; reg 14 CTB Regs, as substituted by reg 17 HB&CTB(SPC) Regs
4 Reg 23 HB Regs, as substituted by reg 8 HB&CTB(SPC) Regs; reg 15 CTB Regs, as substituted by reg 17 HB&CTB(SPC) Regs
5 Sch para 6 HB&CTB(DA) Regs
6 Housing Benefit and Council Tax Benefit Pension Credit Handbook para 1103
7 Regs 8(1) and 10(1) HB Regs
8 CH/3110/2003
9 CH/844/2002
10 Reg 2(4)(a) HB Regs
11 *R v Cambridge CC ex parte Thomas,* 10 February 1995 (QBD)
12 Reg 8(2)(b) HB Regs
13 Reg 8(2ZA) HB Regs
14 Reg 10(2)(a) and (c) HB Regs

15 Reg 2(1) HB Regs, definition of 'owner'; *Burton v New Forest District Council* [2004] EWCA Civ 1510, 12 November 2004, to be reported as R(H) 7/05
16 Reg 8(2)(a) HB Regs
17 Reg 8(3) HB Regs
18 Reg 10(2)(e) HB Regs; Part A8 GM
19 Reg 10(2)(b) HB Regs
20 Reg 10(2)(d) HB Regs
21 Reg 6(1) HB Regs
22 Reg 6(1)(c)(ii) HB Regs
23 Reg 6(2) HB Regs
24 *R v Rugby BC HBRB ex parte Harrison* [1994] 28 HLR 36 (QBD)
25 CH/3579/2003
26 R(H) 3/03
27 *R v Poole BC ex parte Ross* [1995] 28 HLR 351 (QBD); *R v Warrington BC ex parte Williams* [1997] 29 HLR 872 (QBD)
28 s134(2) SSCBA 1992; reg 71(1) HB Regs
29 Reg 10(5) HB Regs
30 *R (Naghshbandi) v Camden LBC* [2002] EWCA Civ 1038 *The Times, 5 August* 2002, unreported (CA)
31 CH/3376/2002
32 CH/3376/2002
33 Reg 10(3) HB Regs
34 Reg 48A(1) HB Regs
35 s115 IAA 1999; reg 7A HB Regs
36 Reg 7(1)(j) HB Regs
37 Reg 7(1)(k) HB Regs
38 Reg 7(1)(b) HB Regs
39 Reg 3(4) HB Regs
40 *Thamesdown BC v Goonery* [1995] 1 CLY 2600 (CA)
41 Reg 2(1) HB Regs
42 R(SB) 27/87; paras A3/3.33-3.34 GM
43 paras A3/3.36-3.37 GM
44 Reg 7(1)(a) HB Regs; R(H) 1/03; CH/1171/2002
45 Reg 7(1A) HB Regs
46 para A3/3.46 GM
47 para A3/3.47 GM
48 CH/1076/2002
49 *R v Poole BC ex parte Ross* [1995] 28 HLR 351 (QBD); CH/1076/2002; CH/296/2004; CH/1097/2004
50 Reg 7(1)(c) HB Regs
51 Reg 7(1)(d) HB Regs
52 para AA3/3.54 GM
53 R (Tucker) v Secretary of State [2001] EWCA Div 1646, unreported (EWCA)
54 Reg 7(1)(e) HB Regs
55 Reg 7(1)(f) HB Regs
56 Reg 7(1)(g) HB Regs
57 Reg 7(1B) HB Regs
58 Regs 2(1), definition of 'owner' and 7(1)(h) HB Regs; CH/1278/2002; CH/0296/2003
59 CH/3853/2001; CH/396/2002
60 CH/716/2002
61 Reg 7(1)(i) HB Regs; HB/CTB Circular A1/99
62 Reg 7(1)(l) HB Regs
63 *R v Solihull MBC ex parte Simpson* [1995] 1 FLR 140 (CA)
64 *R (Mackay) v Barking and Dagenham HBRB* [2001] EWHC Admin 234 (HC)
65 *R (Mackay) v Barking and Dagenham HBRB* [2001] EWHC Admin 234 (HC)
66 *R v Sutton LBC HBRB ex parte Keegan* [1992] 27 HLR 92 (QBD)
67 para A3/3.87 GM
68 *R v Manchester CC ex parte Baragrove Properties Ltd* [1991] 23 HLR 337 (QBD)
69 *R v Gloucestershire CC ex parte Dadds* [1997] 29 HLR 700 (QBD)
70 *R v Poole BC ex parte Ross* [1995] 28 HLR 351 (QBD)
71 s130(1) SSCBA 1992; reg 5(1) and (2) HB Regs
72 Reg 5(4A) HB Regs
73 Reg 5(6) HB Regs
74 CH/2957/2004
75 Reg 5(6)(c)(ii) HB Regs, modified by reg 4 HB&CTB(SPC) Regs
76 Reg 5(5A) HB Regs
77 CH/2201/2002
78 CH/2957/2004
79 Reg 5(8) HB Regs
80 Reg 5(8B) HB Regs
81 Reg 5(7B) and (7C) HB Regs
82 CH/1854/2004
83 CH/1237/2004
84 *R v Penwith DC ex parte Burt* [1988] 22 HLR 292 (QBD); para A3/3.141 GM
85 Reg 5(8A) HB Regs
86 Reg 5(5)(d) HB Regs
87 paras A3/3.201-3.206 GM
88 Reg 5(5)(e) HB Regs
89 Reg 5(5)(a) HB Regs
90 Reg 5(5)(b) HB Regs
91 Reg 5(5)(c) HB Regs
92 Reg 5(7A) HB Regs
93 Reg 5(3) HB Regs
94 Reg 5(4) HB Regs
95 R(SB) 10/81

4. **The amount of benefit**

96 Reg 61 HB Regs
97 s130(3) SSCBA 1992; Schs 4 para 4 and 5 para 5 HB Regs; Schs 4 para 4 and 5 para 5 CTB Regs; reg 22 HB Regs, as substituted by reg 8 HB&CTB(SPC) Regs; reg 14 CTB Regs, as substituted by reg 17 HB&CTB(SPC) Regs; *R v Penwith DC ex parte Menear* [1991] 24 HLR 120 (QBD); *R v South Ribble DC HBRB ex parte Hamilton* [2000] 33 HLR 104 (CA)
98 Reg 2(3A) HB Regs; reg 2(3A) CTB Regs
99 Reg 10(3)(b)(i) and (6) HB Regs; *R v Bristol City Council ex parte Jacobs* [1999] 32 HLR 82 (QBD)
100 Reg 10(4) HB Regs
101 Reg 8(2A) HB Regs
102 Reg 10(3)(a) HB Regs
103 Reg 3(b)(ii) and Sch 1 para 4 HB Regs
104 Sch 1 para 5(1) HB Regs
105 Sch 1 para 5(1)(a) HB Regs
106 Sch 1 para 5(2) and (2A) HB Regs
107 Reg 10(3)(b) HB Regs
108 Schs 1 para 5(3) and 6 para 9(c) HB Regs
109 para A4/4.233 GM
110 Sch 1 paras 4 and 5(1)(b) HB Regs
111 Sch 1 para 7 HB Regs, definition of 'communal area'
112 Sch 1 para 7 HB Regs, definition of 'fuel'
113 Reg 10(1)(e) HB Regs
114 Sch 1 para 3 HB Regs
115 Sch 1 para 1(a)(iii) HB Regs
116 Sch 1 para 1(a)(ii) HB Regs
117 Sch 1 para 1(b) HB Regs
118 Sch 1 para 1(a)(iv) HB Regs
119 Reg 10(3)(b)(ii) and Sch 1 para 1 HB Regs
120 Reg 10(3)(b)(iii) and Sch 1 para 2(1A) HB Regs
121 Sch 1 para 2 HB Regs
122 Sch 1 para 1(a)(i) and 1A(1) HB Regs
123 Sch 1 para 1A(5) and (6) HB Regs
124 Reg 2 HB Regs, definition of 'benefit week'
125 Reg 69 HB Regs
126 Reg 69(2)(b) HB Regs
127 Reg 70(3) and Sch 1 para 6(2) HB Regs; paras A5/5.133 GM
128 Reg 70(3)(a) and Sch 1 para 6(2)(a) HB Regs
129 Reg 70(3)(b) and Sch 1 para 6(2)(b) HB Regs
130 CH/4714/2003. It is understood that the Government intends to amend the rules to reverse the effect of this decision (HB/CTB U11/2004)
131 Regs 3(1) and 61 HB Regs; regs 3(1) and 51(1) CTB Regs
132 Reg 3(4) and Sch 1 para 7 HB Regs
133 *Thamesdown BC v Goonery* [1995] ICLY 2600 (CA)
134 CIS/14850/1996
135 Para A5/5.165 GM
136 Reg 3(2) HB Regs; reg 3(2) CTB Regs
137 *R v Chesterfield BC ex parte Fullwood* [1993] 26 HLR 126 (CA)
138 Reg 3(3) HB Regs
139 Reg 63(6) HB Regs; reg 52(6) CTB Regs
140 Reg 63(7) HB Regs; reg 52(7) CTB Regs
141 Reg 63(1) HB Regs; reg 52(1) CTB Regs
142 Reg 63(8) HB Regs
143 Reg 63(10) HB Regs
144 para A5/5.175 GM
145 Reg 63(1) and (2) HB Regs
146 Reg 63(9) HB Regs; reg 52(9) CTB Regs
147 Reg 4(5) HB Regs; reg 4(5) CTB Regs
148 Reg 63(3) HB Regs; reg 52(3) CTB Regs
149 Reg 63(4) HB Regs; reg 52(4) CTB Regs
150 Reg 63(5) HB Regs
151 Reg 20 HB Regs; reg 12 CTB Regs
152 ss134(8) and 139(6) SSAA 1992; reg 33(2A) HB Regs

6. **Claims and backdating**

153 Reg 72(1) and (9) HB Regs; reg 62(1) and (9) CTB Regs
154 Reg 72(2) HB Regs; reg 62(2) CTB Regs
155 Reg 74(1) HB Regs; reg 64(1) CTB Regs
156 Reg 74(2) HB Regs; reg 64(2) CTB Regs
157 Reg 72(7)(a) HB Regs; reg 62(7)(a) CTB Regs
158 Reg 72(7)(b) and (8) HB Regs; reg 62(7)(b) and (8) CTB Regs
159 Reg 72(8) HB Regs; reg 62(8) CTB Regs
160 paras A2/2.98-2.102 GM
161 Reg 72(4) HB Regs; reg 62(4)(b) CTB Regs
162 Reg 72(4)(a) and (d)-(f) HB Regs; reg 62(4)(a) and (d)-(f) CTB Regs
163 Reg 72(4)(c) HB Regs; reg 62(4)(c) CTB Regs
164 Reg 72(1) and (9) HB Regs; reg 62(1) and (9) CTB Regs
165 Reg 73(1) HB Regs; reg 63(1) CTB Regs
166 HB/CTB Circular A28/03
167 Reg 71(1) HB Regs; reg 61(1) CTB Regs
168 Reg 71(2) HB Regs; reg 61(2) CTB Regs
169 Reg 71(3) and (5) HB Regs; reg 61(3) and (5) CTB Regs
170 Reg 71(6) HB Regs; reg 61(6) CTB Regs
171 Reg 71(4) HB Regs; reg 61(4) CTB Regs
172 Reg 71(4)(c) HB Regs; reg 61(4)(c) CTB Regs
173 Regs 72(5)(d) and 72B(1) HB Regs; regs 62(5)(e) and 62B(1) CTB Regs

174 Reg 72(5)(a) HB Regs; reg 62(5)(a) CTB Regs
175 Reg 72(5)(aaa) and (b) HB Regs; reg 62(5)(aaa) and (b) CTB Regs
176 Reg 72(5)(aa) HB Regs; reg 62(5)(aa) CTB Regs
177 Reg 72(5)(c) HB Regs; reg 62(5)(d) CTB Regs
178 Reg 72(5)(aaa) HB Regs; reg 62(5)(aaa) CTB Regs
179 Reg 72(5)(bb) HB Regs; reg 62(5)(c) CTB Regs
180 Reg 72(11) and (11A) HB Regs; reg 62(12) and (12A) CTB Regs
181 CG/1479/1999; CIS/217/1999
182 Reg 72BA HB Regs; reg 62BA CTB Regs
183 Reg 72(15) HB Regs; A2/2.274-2.78 and Annex A GM; reg 62(16) CTB Regs
184 R(S) 2/63 (T); CH/2659/2002; CH/474/2002; CH/393/2003; A2/Annex A GM
185 CH/393/2003
186 CH/474/2002
187 R(SB) 6/83
188 CS/50/1950
189 R(U) 9/74
190 CI/146/1991; CI/142/1993
191 *R v Canterbury CC ex parte Goodman*, 11 July 1995, unreported (QBD); CFC/39/1993
192 R(U) 5/56
193 R(S) 5/56
194 R(SB) 6/83
195 CI/37/1995
196 R(S) 25/52
197 R(P) 2/85
198 R(S) 10/59; R(SB) 17/83
199 CSB/813/1987
200 R(G) 1/75
201 Reg 77 HB Regs; reg 10 HB&CTB(DA) Regs
202 Reg 77(4) HB Regs; reg 10 HB&CTB(DA) Regs
203 Reg 3 HB&CTB(DA) Regs
204 Reg 77 and Sch 6 HB Regs; reg 67 and Sch 6 CTB Regs
205 Sch 6 para 6 HB Regs; Sch 6 para 6 CTB Regs
206 Reg 10(1) HB&CTB(DA) Regs
207 Sch 6 paras 9-13 HB Regs; Sch 6 paras 9-13 CTB Regs
208 Sch 6 paras 11 and 11A HB Regs

7. **Getting paid**

209 Reg 64(2) HB Regs
210 Reg 65(4) and (5) HB Regs; reg 56(3) and (4) CTB Regs
211 Reg 65(1) and (2) HB Regs; Reg 56(1) and (2) CTB Regs
212 Reg 2(1) HB Regs; reg 2(1) CTB Regs
213 Reg 69(4)(a) HB Regs
214 reg 69(2)(b), (5)(a) and (6) HB Regs
215 Regs 65A and 65B HB Regs; regs 56A and 56B CTB Regs
216 Reg 62B(3)-(4) HB Regs, as inserted by reg 10 HB&CTB(SPC) Regs
217 Reg 62B(1) and (2) HB Regs, as inserted by reg 10 HB&CTB(SPC) Regs
218 Reg 62B(5) HB Regs, as inserted by reg 10 HB&CTB(SPC) Regs
219 s134(1A) SSAA 1992
220 s134(1B) SSAA 1992; reg 92(1) HB Regs
221 Reg 88(1)(b) HB Regs; reg 77(1) and (3) CTB Regs
222 para A6/6.120 GM
223 Reg 92(2) HB Regs; reg 78(2) CTB Regs
224 Reg 92(3) HB Regs
225 para A6/6.148 GM
226 Reg 96 HB Regs; reg 81 CTB Regs
227 *R v Haringey LBC ex parte Azad Ayub* [1992] 25 HLR 566 (QBD)
228 Sch A1 para 8(4) HB Regs; Sch A1 para 7(4) CTB Regs
229 Reg 94(1A) HB Regs
230 *R v Haringey LBC ex parte Azad Ayub* [1992] 25 HLR 566 (QBD)
231 Reg 93(1)(a) HB Regs; Sch 9 SS(C&P) Regs
232 Regs 93(1)(b) HB Regs
233 Reg 93(2A) HB Regs
234 Reg 94(1)(a) and (b) HB Regs
235 Regs 93(2A) and 94(1)(c) HB Regs
236 Reg 94(1C)(b) HB Regs
237 Reg 93(2A) HB Regs
238 s126A SSAA 1992; regs 3 and 4 HB(ILA) Regs
239 Reg 5 HB(ILA) Regs
240 Regs 93(3) and 94(1B) HB Regs
241 Reg 94(1B) HB Regs
242 HB/CTB Circular A48/97
243 Reg 90(1) and (4) HB Regs
244 Reg 88(2) HB Regs
245 Reg 90(3) HB Regs
246 Reg 90(4) HB Regs
247 Reg 90(2) HB Regs (pre-October 1996); reg 11 HB(Amdt) Regs 1996
248 Reg 90(2A) and (2B) HB Regs
249 Regs 76(2), 77(1)(a) and 88(3) HB Regs; regs 66(2), 67(1)(a) and 77(3)(b) and (c) CTB Regs
250 Reg 91(1) HB Regs
251 *R v Haringey LBC ex parte Azad Ayub* [1992] 25 HLR 566 (QBD)
252 paras A6/6.137-6.141 GM
253 Reg 91(1) HB Regs; *R v Haringey LBC ex parte Azad Ayub* [1992] 25 HLR 566 (QBD)

254 Reg 91(2) HB Regs
255 Reg 91(3) HB Regs
256 Reg 75(1) HB Regs; reg 4 SS(NCC) Regs
257 Sch 6 paras 9(1)(i) and 10(a) HB Regs; Sch 6 paras 9(1)(f) and 10(a) CTB Regs
258 Regs 2(1), 73(2) and 75(1) HB Regs; regs 2, 63(2) and 65(1) CTB Regs
259 Reg 75(1) HB Regs; reg 65(1) CTB Regs
260 Reg 75(4) HB Regs; reg 65(5) CTB Regs
261 Reg 75(1A) HB Regs; reg 65(1A) CTB Regs
262 Reg 75(1), (2)(a) and (e) and (3) HB Regs; reg 65(1), (2)(d), (3) and (4) CTB Regs
263 Reg 75(5) HB Regs; reg 65(6) CTB Regs
264 Reg 75(6) HB Regs; reg 65(7) CTB Regs
265 Reg 75(7) HB Regs; reg 65(8) CTB Regs
266 Regs 73(2) and 77 and Sch 6 HB Regs; regs 63(2) and 67 and Sch 6 CTB Regs
267 Reg 75(1) HB Regs; reg 65(1) CTB Regs
268 Reg 75(2) HB Regs; reg 65(2) CTB Regs
269 Reg 75(3) HB Regs; reg 65(3) CTB Regs
270 Reg 68 HB Regs; reg 59 CTB Regs; reg 8 HB&CTB(DA) Regs
271 Reg 68(1) HB Regs; reg 59(1) CTB Regs
272 Reg 68(1) HB Regs; reg 59(1) CTB Regs; reg 8(2) HB&CTB(DA) Regs
273 Reg 8(3) HB&CTB(DA) Regs
274 Schs 2 para 2 and 2A para 2 HB Regs; Schs 1 para 2 and 1A para 2 CTB Regs
275 Reg 68(2) HB Regs
276 Reg 68(13) and (14) HB Regs
277 Reg 68(6) and (7) HB Regs; reg 59(8) and (9) CTB Regs
278 Reg 68(9)-(12) HB Regs; reg 59(10)-(13) CTB Regs
279 Reg 68(4) HB Regs
280 Reg 68(13) and (14) HB Regs
281 Reg 68B HB Regs; reg 59B CTB Regs

10. **Discretionary housing payments**
282 s69 CSPSSA 2000; reg 2(1) DFA Regs
283 Reg 2(2) DFA Regs
284 Reg 2(3) DFA Regs
285 Reg 3 DFA Regs
286 Reg 5 DFA Regs
287 Reg 4 DFA Regs
288 Reg 6 DFA Regs
289 Reg 6(1)(a) DFA Regs
290 Reg 7 DFA Regs
291 Reg 6(3) DFA Regs
292 Reg 6(2) DFA Regs
293 Reg 8 DFA Regs
294 Reg 6(3) DFA Regs
295 Schs 9 para 71 and 10 para 7(1)(d) IS Regs; Schs 7 para 71 and 8 para 12(1)(d) JSA Regs; Schs 4 para 74 and 5 para 8(1)(e) HB Regs; Schs 4 para 73 and 5 para 8(1)(f) CTB Regs; reg 7 Table 3 para 9 TC(DCI) Regs

Chapter 11

Housing benefit rent restrictions

This chapter covers:

The amount of your eligible rent for housing benefit (HB) purposes (see p207) may be restricted if you are a private tenant or housing association tenant. **The rules described in this chapter do not apply if you are a local authority tenant or are liable to pay the local authority for your accommodation.**

There are three sets of rules:

- the 'local reference rent rules';
- if you live in a Pathfinder area (see p254), the 'local housing allowance' rules; *and*
- the pre-January 1996 rules.

If your eligible rent is restricted, your HB is calculated using this figure, *not* the rent that you are supposed to pay, and there could be a shortfall. If you do not pay the shortfall you could fall into arrears and risk losing your home. Remember that:

- you might be able to negotiate a reduced rent with your landlord;
- if you have to make payments towards the shortfall:
  - you might be able to get discretionary housing payments (see p235);
  - you might be able to increase your income by taking in lodgers (see p976 for how this affects your means-tested benefits);
  - payments made directly to your landlord by relatives, friends or a charity towards the amount of your rent not being met by HB can be ignored in calculating your means-tested benefits (see p985).

Seek advice *before* taking in lodgers or having payments made directly to your landlord to find out exactly how this might affect your benefit claims.

1. The local authority procedure

Unless you are in a Pathfinder area and are covered by the 'local housing allowance' rules, the local authority must follow the steps below:

Step 1: The local authority decides whether your tenancy should be referred to the rent officer (see below).

Step 2: The rent officer makes determinations as to the level of rent and size of your accommodation (see p245).

Step 3: The local authority decides whether you are exempt from the 'local reference rent rules' (see p249).

Step 4: If you are not exempt, the 'local reference rent rules' apply. The local authority calculates your maximum rent on the basis of the rent officer's determinations (see p250).

Step 5: The local authority checks to see whether there should be a delay before any restriction is imposed (see p251).

Step 6: If you are exempt from the 'local reference rent rules', the local authority decides whether to restrict your rent using the rules in force before January 1996 (see p255). The local authority checks to see whether there should be a delay before any restriction is imposed (see p258).

Step 1: Should your tenancy be referred to the rent officer

Unless your tenancy is an 'excluded tenancy' (see p244), the local authority must make a reference to the rent officer if:[1]

- you make a new claim for housing benefit (HB), unless a rent officer determination has been made for the same tenancy (or a tenancy in the same dwelling) on substantially the same terms, within the last 52 weeks.[2] This means that a determination made for a previous tenant may be valid for your HB claim. A new referral *is* needed if you are a young individual and no single room rent determination has yet been made (see p247);[3]
- you live in a hostel and make a new claim for HB, unless a rent officer determination has been made for similar accommodation within the hostel, sleeping the same number of people as yours, within the last 12 months and there has been no change of circumstances in respect of that accommodation;[4]
- you move to another private rented or housing association home while entitled to HB;

- a previous reference to the rent officer was made in respect of your claim more than 52 weeks ago; *or*
- there has been one of the following changes of circumstances:[5]
  - the number of occupiers has changed (except in a hostel);
  - there has been a substantial change in the condition of the dwelling or the terms of the tenancy (other than a rent increase);
  - there has been an increase in rent and the previous determination was not a significantly high rent, a size-related rent or an exceptionally high rent determination (see p245);
  - a size-related rent determination (see p245) was made and there has since been a change in the composition of the household, or a child living with you has reached the age of 10 or 16.

The following are **'excluded tenancies'** and are *never* referred to the rent officer:[6]

- a regulated or protected tenancy (ie, a tenancy entered into before 15 January 1989 or, in Scotland, 2 January 1989);
- a tenancy in a Home Office bail hostel or probation hostel. Remember, however, that in any case, if you are required to live in a bail hostel or approved probation hostel, you cannot claim HB towards the rent you pay to the hostel (see p201);
- a housing action trust tenancy;
- a former local authority or new town letting which has been transferred to a new owner, unless there has been a rent increase since the transfer: *and*
  - the local authority considers your rent to be unreasonably high; *or*
  - if the transfer took place before 7 October 2002 only, the local authority considers your accommodation to be unreasonably large;
- a registered housing association letting, unless the local authority considers your accommodation to be unreasonably large or your rent unreasonably high.

If your tenancy is excluded, the local authority can still use its general power to decrease your eligible rent (see p252) to an amount it considers 'appropriate'. It should have evidence which justifies doing so and must exercise its discretion properly. If it decreases your eligible rent in this way, you can seek a revision or appeal (see Chapters 43 and 44).

2. The 'local reference rent' rules

If your tenancy is not excluded (see above), the local authority refers it to the rent officer and asks her/him to make determinations. The rent officer can ask for further information if this is needed.[7]

Step 2: Rent officer determinations

The rent officer makes determinations about the rent for your home, comparing it with the rent for other private sector tenancies in the neighbourhood or vicinity. The determinations are:

- significantly high rent (see below);
- size-related rent (see below); *and*
- exceptionally high rent (see p246).

The lowest of these is what is known as the 'claim-related rent' (see p247).

S/he also makes determinations which indicate the average rents for specific types of accommodation in the locality:

- the local reference rent (see p247);
- a single room rent (see p247).

For these purposes, a **'locality'** is two or more neighbourhoods, including the one where your home is. Each must adjoin at least one of the others. In addition, it must be an area where:[8]

- you could reasonably be expected to live, taking into account the facilities and services there are for health, education, recreation, banking and shopping in (or accessible to) the neighbourhood where you live. The rent officer must take the distance you have to travel by public and private transport into account; *and*
- there are a variety of kinds of residential accommodation and types of tenancy.

A **'neighbourhood'** is:[9]

- *if you live in a town or city,* the part of the town or city where your home is located which is a distinct area of residential accommodation; *or*
- *if you do not live in a town or city,* the area surrounding your home which is a distinct area of residential accommodation which includes homes of the same size as yours (or of a size you are allowed under the size criteria – see p246).

Significantly high rent determination

If your rent is significantly higher than that paid for similar tenancies and dwellings in the vicinity, the rent officer determines an amount your landlord might reasonably be paid for your tenancy.[10] For these purposes, a **'vicinity'** is the immediate area around your home.

Size-related rent determination

If your accommodation is larger than you are allowed under the size criteria, the rent officer determines an amount your landlord might reasonably be paid for a similar tenancy in the vicinity of an appropriate size for you.[11] For these purposes, **'vicinity'** means the immediate area around your home, or where there is no dwelling in that area of a size you are allowed under the size criteria, the nearest area where there is one.[12]

Remember that if you are a single person under 25, the rent officer must identify a single room rent. See p247 for further information.

The size criteria

To work out what size of dwelling you are allowed under the size criteria, the rent officer, ignoring for example your kitchen, bathroom and toilet, allows one bedroom, or room 'suitable for living in', for each of the following occupiers (each occupier coming only into the first category for which s/he is eligible):[13]

- a married or unmarried couple (see p811);
- a person who is not a child (ie, someone aged 16 or over);
- two children of the same sex;
- two children under 10;
- a child.

In addition, you are allowed the following number of rooms 'suitable for living in':

Number of occupiers	*Number of rooms*
Less than 4	1
4 to 6	2
7 or more	3

A person counts as an 'occupier' if the local authority includes her/him on the form used to refer your tenancy to the rent officer.[14] This can include people who are not part of your family for benefit purposes (eg, your non-dependants). However, if you share the care of a child, the child is considered to be occupying the home of only one parent – the parent with whom the child normally lives.[15]

If any of the rooms in your home are not suitable for living in (eg, because of their size or lack of ventilation), you should argue that they should be ignored.

Example

Alice and Len have three children. Their two sons are 12 and 14 and their daughter is 17. Applying the size criteria, Alice and Len are allowed one room for themselves, one for their two sons and one for their daughter – three bedrooms (or rooms 'suitable for living in'). They are also allowed two other rooms 'suitable for living in'. They are therefore allowed five rooms, as well as a kitchen, bathroom and toilet.

Exceptionally high rent determination

If the rent officer considers the 'rent payable' for your home to be exceptionally high, s/he determines the highest amount that your landlord might reasonably be paid for an assured tenancy in the neighbourhood (see p245) which is the same size as your home (or the size you are allowed under the size criteria).[16]

'Rent payable' means:

- the size-related rent determination; *or*
- if there is no such determination, the significantly high rent determination; *or*
- in any other case, the rent you are supposed to pay.

Claim-related rent

The rent officer also identifies what is known as the claim-related rent. This is the lowest of the above determinations or, if no such determination was made, the rent you are supposed to pay.[17]

Local reference rent

The local reference rent is the midpoint of 'reasonable market rents' for assured tenancies in the locality (see p245) appropriate to the size of property that you are living in (or the size you are allowed under the size criteria – see p246).[18] It is only provided if your rent, or the lowest of the rent officer determinations (excluding the single room rent), exceeds it.

Single room rent

If you are a **single claimant** under the age of 25 – known as a 'young individual' – in most cases, the rent officer identifies a single room rent.[19] Your maximum rent (see p250) is based on this figure unless you:[20]

- qualify for a severe disability premium as part of your applicable amount (see p891); *or*
- have a non-dependant living with you (see p211).

You do *not* count as a young individual and the single room rent rules do *not* apply if you are:[21]

- a housing association tenant;
- under the age of 22 and:
  - were in the care of or under the supervision of a local authority under specific legal provisions after you turned 16; *or*
  - were provided with accommodation by the local authority under s20 of the Children Act 1989.

  Remember, however, that if you are 16 or 17 and have been looked after by a local authority in England or Wales on or after 1 October 2001, you usually cannot claim HB. Instead the local authority should support and accommodate you. See p714 for exceptions to the rules. Similar rules apply in Scotland if you cease to be looked after by a local authority on or after 1 April 2004 (see p713).

However, even if your maximum HB is not based on the single room rent or you do not count as a young individual, the other 'local reference rent' rules described in this chapter can still apply.

The single room rent is the midpoint of 'reasonable market rents' for accommodation in the locality (see p245), in which the tenant has exclusive use of one bedroom only and other than that only shares a living room, kitchen, a toilet and bathroom and makes no payment for board or attendance.[22]

Notification to the local authority

The rent officer notifies the local authority of the claim-related rent and, if lower, the local reference rent or single room rent.[23] This must be done within five working days of the local authority's request for determinations (25 days if the rent officer intends to visit the property) or as soon as is practicable after that.[24] If the rent officer needs further information, the five (or 25) days run from the date this is received. The local authority uses these to determine your 'maximum rent' for HB purposes (see p250).

Example 1

Tina, aged 35, lives in a one-bedroom flat. It has a separate living room. Her rent is £60 a week. The rent officer decides that, although the accommodation is an appropriate size, the rent is too high for the tenancy. He makes a significantly high rent determination (£55) and identifies this as the claim-related rent. He notifies the local authority of the following:

Claim-related rent	£55
Local reference rent	£50

Example 2

Ross, aged 23, has a one-bedroom flat. It has a separate living room. He pays £60 a week rent. The rent officer decides that the rent is too high for the tenancy. He makes a significantly high rent determination (£55). Ross counts as a young individual so the local authority is notified of the following:

Claim-related rent	£55
Single room rent	£40

Example 3

Paul and Sarah have a two-bedroom flat which has a living room and a dining room. They pay £75 a week rent. The rent officer decides that the accommodation is too big and the rent too high for the property. He makes significantly high and size-related rent determinations. The lowest of these, the size-related rent determination (£60), is the claim-related rent. The local authority is notified of the following:

Claim-related rent	£60
Local reference rent	£50

Example 4

Carl, aged 55, has a two-bedroom flat with two living rooms. He pays £90 a week rent. The rent officer decides that not only is the flat too big but the rent is too high. She also thinks that the rent is exceptionally high. She makes significantly high, size-related and exceptionally high rent determinations. The lowest of these, the exceptionally high rent determination (£70), is the claim-related rent. The local authority is notified of the following:

Claim-related rent	£70
Local reference rent	£50

Service charges in rent officer determinations

The local authority notifies the rent officer of the amount of rent you are supposed to pay, whether this includes service charges and the amount of the charges that can and cannot be met by HB (see p207).[25] The claim-related rent determined by the rent officer does not include ineligible charges. The only exception is where you live in one-room accommodation and the landlord provides substantial board and attendance. In these cases the claim-related rent and local reference rent (though not the single room rent) include charges for meals.[26]

Step 3: Exemption from the local reference rent rules

The local authority must decide whether you are exempt from the 'local reference rent rules'. You are exempt if you are either an 'exempt claimant' or live in exempt accommodation.[27]

You are an **'exempt claimant'** if:

- you have been continuously entitled to and in receipt of HB since 1 January 1996. Breaks in your claim of up to four weeks (52 weeks if you or your partner are a 'welfare to work' beneficiary – see p769) are ignored;[28] *and*
- you continue to occupy the same property as your home (except where you are forced to move because fire, flood or natural catastrophe makes it uninhabitable).

If you are thinking of making any changes to your claim, you should check whether you would lose your exemption by doing so. This happens, for example, if you move (including moving rooms within the same house) or if your partner takes over the claim (but see below).

An exemption can be transferred to you if:[29]

- you claim HB because an exempt claimant dies and you are a member of the former claimant's family, or any relative (see p251) occupying the same accommodation without a separate right to do so. You must continue to occupy the same property and make your claim within four weeks of the death;
- you claim HB because your partner (who was exempt) has been detained in custody and is not entitled to HB under the temporary absence rules (see p202). You must continue to occupy the same property and must make your claim within four weeks of the imprisonment;

- you claim HB because your former partner (who was exempt) has left the dwelling and you are no longer living together as husband and wife. You must continue to occupy the same property and claim within four weeks of the date s/he left.

In all three cases, if you can get your claim backdated (see p221) to within the four weeks, you can try to argue that the exemption should be transferred to you.

The exemption can only be transferred if either the exempt claimant was in receipt of HB at the time s/he died or left the dwelling as the case may be, or had become a 'welfare to work' beneficiary (see p769) within the previous 52 weeks.[30]

You live in **'exempt accommodation'** if:[31]

- you live in hostel accommodation for people without a fixed way of life which is funded by the Resettlement Agency;
- you live in accommodation provided by a housing association, non-metropolitan county council, registered charity or voluntary organisation where that body, or a person acting on its behalf, also provides the claimant with care, support or supervision.

If you are exempt, the local authority might still decide to restrict your rent using the pre-January 1996 rules (see p255).

Step 4: The local authority determines the maximum rent

If you are not exempt, the local reference rent rules apply and the local authority calculates your 'maximum rent' on the basis of the rent officer's determinations. This figure is then used to calculate your HB (see p205) even if the rent you pay is higher than this.

Your '**maximum rent'** is restricted to:[32]

- the lowest of the claim-related rent, the local reference rent or, if you are a single person under 25 and it is relevant, the single room rent; *or*
- if you have transitional protection, the lowest of the local reference rent (plus half the difference between the local reference rent and the claim-related rent) or, if you are a single person under 25 and it is relevant, the single room rent. You have transitional protection if you have been continuously entitled to, and in receipt of, HB for the same property since 5 October 1997.[33] If you or your partner are a 'welfare to work' beneficiary (see p769) breaks in your claim of up to 52 weeks are ignored.[34]

In certain circumstances, the rent restriction cannot be applied for a period (see p251).

Example

Jo and Louis live by themselves in a three-bedroom private flat with a living room and separate dining room. They are joint tenants who pay rent of £80 per week. Louis is unemployed and gets contribution-based jobseeker's allowance of £56.20 per week. Jo works part-time and takes home £100 after deduction of tax and National Insurance contributions. Jo claims HB. The rent officer decides that the accommodation is too big and that the rent is too high. He notifies the local authority of a claim related rent of £70 and a local reference rent of £60. Maximum rent (and therefore maximum HB) is £60 per week.

Her applicable amount is £88.15 (the standard rate for a couple).

Income to be taken into account is £146.20 a week (because £10 of her earnings are disregarded – see p965).

The difference between her income and her applicable amount is therefore £58.05 a week.

65% of £58.05 a week is £37.73 a week.

Jo's HB is therefore £60 – £37.73 = £22.27 a week.

The rent Jo and Louis pay is £80. Taking the HB into account, they are left with a shortfall to find of £57.73 per week (£80 – £22.27).

Renegotiating your rent

Once the maximum rent figure has been set, your HB is paid on the basis of this until the next time the local authority makes a reference to the rent officer about your claim. However, if you negotiate with your landlord and s/he agrees a new rent which is lower than the maximum rent, your HB is re-calculated using your new rent.[35] The same applies if you renegotiate your rent following a pre-tenancy determination (see p252).[36]

Step 5: Delay in applying rent restrictions

A rent restriction can be delayed in some circumstances:

- If a member of your family (or a relative who lives in the same accommodation as you without a separate right to do so) dies:[37]
  - no restriction applies for 12 months from the date of death if no maximum rent applied at the time of the death; *or*
  - any maximum rent which applied at the time of death continues to do so for the 12 months from the date of death.
- If you, or a member of your family (or a relative who lives in the same dwelling as you without a separate right to do so) could meet the costs of the dwelling when you took them on (this could include other bills as well as the rent), no restriction can be made for 13 weeks provided you did not receive HB in the 52 weeks before your current award of HB (see p224).[38]

For these purposes, **'relative'** means a close relative (see p199) or a grandparent, grandchild, uncle, aunt, nephew or niece.[39]

Discretionary housing payments

If the way the rent restriction rules operate means that you need some financial assistance to meet your rent, you might be able to get discretionary housing payments. For information about how to claim, see p235.

Discretion to decrease entitlement

If the local reference rent rules have been applied but the local authority does not think it reasonable for the full amount of your eligible rent (see p207) to be met by HB, it has discretion to decrease your weekly entitlement further.[40] It may only reduce your HB to a reasonable level. All the circumstances should be taken into account, including your health and financial circumstances,[41] the special housing-related needs of anyone occupying your home and whether alternative accommodation is available to HB claimants.[42] Since the whole point of having rent officer determinations is to determine reasonable rent levels, local authorities should rarely use their powers to decrease your HB in this way. If your HB is reduced under this rule you should ask for a revision or appeal (see Chapters 43 and 44).

Pre-tenancy determinations

If you are thinking of renting accommodation privately and are likely to claim HB, you can apply to the local authority for a pre-tenancy determination.[43] This tells you the rent figure that will be used to calculate your HB if you take the accommodation. You can also apply if you are already receiving HB and your tenancy is due for renewal. Your current tenancy agreement must have started at least 11 months before your request.[44]

You must apply in writing on the appropriate form available from your local authority. You must complete the form properly and both you and your prospective landlord must sign it. Return it to the local authority, who must forward it to the rent officer within two days of receipt.[45] The rent officer must send you, the prospective landlord and the local authority the rent figures which s/he has decided within five working days (unless s/he needs more information from the local authority) or as soon as is practicable after that.[46] If the rent officer needs further information, the five days runs from the date this is received.

A pre-tenancy determination is valid for a year unless there is a change in your tenancy agreement or family circumstances.[47] This means that if someone else applied for a pre-tenancy determination for your accommodation in the previous 12 months, her/his pre-tenancy determination applies to you.

You cannot appeal against a pre-tenancy determination. However, if you accept the tenancy and claim HB, you can ask the rent officer to consider the determination again (see below).

If you subsequently negotiate a lower rent with your landlord, see p251.

Challenging rent officer determinations

You cannot appeal against the rent officer's determinations. However, the local authority *can* ask for them to be redetermined on your behalf.[48] You must apply to the local authority in writing no later than six weeks after the date you are notified of its decision on your HB claim. The local authority must then apply to the rent officer for a redetermination and pass any representations you make or evidence you supply to her/him within seven days.[49] In practice, if you seek a revision or appeal against a HB decision and this relates in whole or in part to the rent officer's determinations, the local authority should apply for a redetermination.[50]

While it is not easy to challenge rent officers, it may be possible in some circumstances. If, for example, the rent officer has said your rent is significantly high, you may be able to get her/him to reconsider by providing evidence of similar tenancies where tenants who are not on HB are paying the same rent as you. The rent officer must get the advice of one or two other rent officers and notify the local authority of her/his decision within 20 working days.[51]

The local authority has the power to ask for a rent officer redetermination, even if you have not done so.[52] In this case, you can ask for a further redetermination. Otherwise, you are limited to one request for each fresh rent officer determination.[53] If the local authority discovers an error in the referral to the rent officer (eg, if it made a mistake as to the number of occupiers) or if the rent officer discovers an error (other than in the application of professional judgement), the local authority must apply for a substitute determination.[54] You can seek a redetermination in this situation.

The rent officer's redetermination might reduce your maximum rent so you need to consider your position carefully before requesting a redetermination (or asking for a revision or an appeal). You could end up with less HB as a result. However, if the redetermination reduces your maximum rent (see p250), it only applies from the date of the new decision so you cannot have been overpaid.[55] If it increases your maximum rent, it applies from the date of the original decision and you should be paid any HB arrears.

3. The 'local housing allowance' rules

The 'local housing allowance' rules are being piloted in a number of Pathfinder areas. They replace the rent restriction rules for tenants in the deregulated private sector. If the pilots are successful, the rules will be introduced nationwide, the Government says, by March 2008. This section gives an outline of the rules.

For further details and information about the 'local housing allowance' rules in practice, see CPAG's *Welfare Rights Bulletin* 179, pp5-7. The DWP guidance to local authorities, the *Housing Benefit Local Housing Allowance Guidance Manual*, is available at www.dwp.gov.uk/housingbenefit/lha/guidance-manual-inc-amt-1.pdf.

The Pathfinder areas

The 'local housing allowance' rules apply to you if you live in a current Pathfinder area. Additional Pathfinder areas will begin to pilot the 'local housing allowance' rules between April and August 2005.

Current Pathfinder areas

Blackpool; Brighton and Hove; Conwy; Coventry; Edinburgh; Leeds; London Borough of Lewisham; Northeast Lincolnshire; Teignbridge

Additional Pathfinder areas

Argyll and Bute; East Riding of Yorkshire; Guildford; Norwich; Pembrokeshire; Salford; South Norfolk; St. Helens; Wandsworth

An outline of the scheme

The scheme applies if you are a tenant in the deregulated private sector. It does not apply where your landlord is a registered social landlord or you live in the types of exempt accommodation on p250 or you pay rent for a hostel, a houseboat, a caravan or a mobile home or for board and attendance.[56]

If you were already claiming housing benefit (HB) when the 'local housing allowance' scheme began in your area, you should not be worse off. Some claimants have what is known as 'transitional protection'.[57]

The rules in brief

The rules include the following:

- Your HB is based on a flat rate 'local housing allowance' depending on the area where you live and the size of your household. The 'local housing allowance' is set by the rent officer and is based on a mid-range local market rent for a property of the appropriate size in the area in which you live.[58] It must be made public.[59] The size criteria are broadly the same as those for the 'local reference rent' rules.[60] Local housing allowances are changed by the rent officer from time to time, if s/he considers it appropriate having regard to the rules.[61]
- Your HB is based on the local housing allowance that is appropriate when your claim is assessed, and this lasts for a year even if the allowance changes.[62] The local authority reassesses your claim annually, using the allowance that is then appropriate for your property. However, your claim can be reassessed earlier if your circumstances change and this means a different allowance is appropriate

(eg, your child comes to live with you, a rent increase is built into your tenancy agreement or you are a single claimant who turns 25).[63]

- If the appropriate local housing allowance for you should be reduced, because of the death of a member of your family or a relative who lives with you, the decrease can be delayed for 12 months.[64]
- A rent restriction can be delayed for 13 weeks if you or a member of your family or a relative could meet the costs of the dwelling when you took them on.[65]
- If your rent is lower than the local housing allowance, you can keep the difference.[66] This even applies if you move to cheaper accommodation in the area and if you renegotiate your rent with your landlord. The extra HB does not affect your other benefits (eg, income support or income-based jobseeker's allowance).
- In most cases, HB is paid to you, not to your landlord. However, direct payments to landlords are still possible in some situations (see p227).

4. The pre-January 1996 rules

If you are exempt from the local reference rent rules (see p249) and are not covered by the 'local housing allowance' rules (see p253), the local authority can use the pre-January 1996 rules to decide whether to restrict your eligible rent (see p207). If it does, this figure is then used to calculate your housing benefit (HB – see p205) even though the rent you pay is higher than this.

If the local authority decides to impose a rent restriction in your case, you should insist on a full explanation. If you believe that the local authority has failed to apply all the proper tests or has been influenced by irrelevant facts, you should ask for a revision or appeal (see Chapters 43 and 44).

The procedure

The local authority must:

- consider whether your accommodation is unreasonably large or your rent unreasonably high (see below);
- if it thinks your accommodation is unreasonably large or your rent is unreasonably high, consider whether you are in a 'protected group' (see p257);
- decide whether to restrict your HB to an appropriate level (see p258). If you are in a protected group, the local authority cannot restrict your rent unless there is suitable alternative accommodation available to you and it is reasonable to expect you to move (see p258);
- if your rent is to be restricted, consider whether there should be a delay before the restriction applies.

Is your accommodation unreasonably large?

The local authority can consider your accommodation unreasonably large if it is larger than is reasonably needed for you and anyone who also occupies the accommodation (including non-dependants and sub-tenants), taking account of suitable alternative accommodation occupied by other households of the same size.[67] The important question is the size of home that you need, rather than the size of home that you want.[68]

The needs of everyone living in your accommodation, whether or not they are part of your family, must be considered. For example, you might need additional space because someone has a disability, or lives elsewhere but regularly comes to visit you. If you are elderly and have lived in a house for a long time, you should argue that because you are used to living there and are settled, you need to stay in your existing accommodation.

Is your rent unreasonably high?

The local authority can consider your rent too high if it is unreasonably high compared with that for suitable alternative accommodation elsewhere.[69] 'Rent' includes, among other things, any service charges or licence fees you have to pay.[70]

When deciding whether your rent is unreasonably high, the local authority may ask a rent officer to assess a reasonable rent for your property, but the figures are not binding on the local authority. *It* (not the rent officer) must decide whether your rent is unreasonably high – a different criterion from that used by the rent officer.[71]

It is not enough for the local authority to argue that your rent is merely higher than that for suitable alternative accommodation. It must be unreasonably higher.[72] In making this comparison, the local authority must consider the full spectrum of rents which could be paid for such accommodation and not just the cheapest.[73] If your rent is within the range[74] or just above it,[75] the local authority may find it difficult to justify a finding that your rent is unreasonably high.

What is suitable alternative accommodation?

The local authority should only make comparisons with suitable alternative accommodation which forms part of an active housing market. This means that the accommodation must currently be available for rent, although not necessarily to you.[76] The local authority might produce a list of comparable properties to justify its assertions that there is suitable alternative accommodation. Local authorities should not make comparisons with other parts of the country where accommodation costs differ widely from those which apply locally,[77] but it may compare your property with one in a less expensive area within a city.[78]

It is not sufficient for the local authority to show that cheaper or smaller alternative accommodation exists. It must also be 'suitable' for the age and health of all the people that the local authority must take into account, having regard to the nature of the accommodation and the facilities available.[79] The local authority must consider these factors, even if you do raise your housing needs yourself.[80] The people that the local authority must consider are:[81]

- you;
- members of your family;
- if you are in a polygamous marriage, any of your partners or children for whom you or they are responsible;
- any relative (see p251) who lives in the same dwelling as you without a separate right to do so.[82]

The local authority must compare your home with properties that have reasonably equivalent facilities. It is not sufficient, for example, just to compare flats with the same number of bedrooms. Some effort must be made to establish what other facilities are available.[83]

If you currently have security of tenure, then the local authority must compare your home with other properties offering the same security of tenure.[84] For example, if you have an assured tenancy, the local authority may not rely on comparison with accommodation which is only let on an assured shorthold tenancy,[85] or with council or housing association properties.[86] If you are not sure what type of tenure you have, seek housing advice.

The local authority is not required to exclude properties that you cannot take because the landlord wants a deposit which you cannot afford.[87]

Are you in a protected group?

If the local authority decides that your rent, or the size of your accommodation, is unreasonable, it must then consider whether you are in a 'protected group'.[88] If you are, the local authority must consider whether cheaper suitable alternative accommodation is available and whether it is reasonable to expect you to move.

You are in a protected group if any of the people that the local authority must consider (see above):

- is aged 60 or over; *or*
- satisfies any of the tests of being incapable of work for social security purposes (see p764); *or*
- has a child or young person living with her/him for whom s/he is responsible (see p820).

Is there cheaper suitable alternative accommodation available?

The local authority must prove that suitable alternative accommodation does not merely exist, but is actually available to you. However, if a local authority considers that suitable alternative accommodation is available, it does not need to refer to specific properties, but must have sufficient evidence to demonstrate the existence of an active housing market comprising accommodation of a suitable type, rent and location for you.[89] See p256 for information about 'suitable alternative accommodation'.

In considering whether accommodation is 'available', the local authority must have regard to personal factors, such as whether you can afford to pay a deposit.[90] You should insist on being told exactly what accommodation is being referred to, why it is considered suitable for you and those who live with you, and on what evidence it is considered to actually be available to you. Even if the local authority produces a list of properties which are available to you, you can try to show that they are not available due to your personal circumstances.[91]

Is it reasonable to expect you to move?

The local authority must show that it is reasonable to expect you to move. It must consider the adverse effects of a move on the following:[92]

- your ability to retain your job; *and*
- the education of any child or young person living with you. In considering this, the local authority must justify any decision that it is reasonable to make the child travel to or move school.[93]

The local authority may say that it does not need to consider any other factors, such as your health.[94] You can argue that this is wrong, since the Regulations only say that the local authority *must* take into account the two factors above.[95]

The rent restriction

The local authority *must* reduce your eligible rent if it finds that:

- your accommodation is too large or too expensive; *and*
- if you are in a protected group only, that:
  - cheaper suitable alternative accommodation is available to you; *and*
  - it is reasonable to expect you to move.

Although the local authority cannot decide not to reduce your rent, it has discretion as to how much it reduces it by. It must take into account the cost of suitable alternative accommodation and other circumstances that are reasonably relevant to the decision (eg, pregnancy, the difficulty of finding suitable alternative accommodation and whether the local authority would have to rehouse you if you had to move).[96] Although the local authority should not be unduly influenced by the amount of subsidy it is paid by the government, it can take this into account when deciding on a reasonable level of rent. It cannot be reduced below that payable for suitable alternative accommodation.[97]

Delay before a restriction is applied

No restriction can be made within 12 months of the death of a member of your family (or a relative – see p251) who lives in the same dwelling as you without a separate right to do so.[98] If you or a member of your family (or a relative who lives in the same dwelling as you without a separate right to do so) could meet the costs of the dwelling when you took them on (this could include other bills as well as the rent), no restriction can be made for 13 weeks provided you did not receive HB in the 52 weeks before your current award of HB.[99]

Rent increases

If the pre-January 1996 rules apply to you, and your landlord increases your rent, the local authority cannot increase your HB by the full amount if it decides that:[100]

- the increase is unreasonably high compared with those in suitable alternative accommodation. The amount of the increase is not the only factor that the local authority must consider. It should also look at such things as the quality of the accommodation, your age and state of health, whether you would have to move if the increase is not met and how a move would affect you;[101] *or*
- the increase is unreasonable because a previous increase has occurred within the preceding 12 months.

If the local authority considers a rent increase to have been unreasonable, it may either refuse to meet all of that increase or only so much of it as it considers appropriate. If your rent has been increased for the second time in under 12 months but it is still below the market level for suitable alternative accommodation, or the increase reflects improvements made to your accommodation, you should press for the full amount to be allowed. If the local authority refuses, you should ask for a revision or appeal (see Chapters 43 and 44).

Notes

1. **The local authority procedure**
 1 Reg 12A(1) and (8) HB Regs
 2 Sch 1A para 2(1) and (2) HB Regs
 3 Sch 1A para 2(3)(f) HB Regs
 4 Reg 12A(2)(a) and (7) HB Regs
 5 Sch 1A para 2(3)(a)-(e) HB Regs
 6 Reg 12A(2)(b) and Sch 1A paras 3-12 HB Regs

2. **The 'local reference rent' rules**
 7 Art 5 RO(HBF)O; Art 5 RO(HBF)(S)O
 8 Sch 1 para 4(6) RO(HBF)O; Sch 1 para 4(6) RO(HBF)(S)O
 9 Sch 1 para 3(5) RO(HBF)O; Sch 1 para 3(5) RO(HBF)(S)O
 10 Sch 1 para 1 RO(HBF)O; Sch 1 para 1 RO(HBF)(S)O
 11 Sch 1 para 2 RO(HBF)O; Sch 1 para 2 RO(HBF)(S)O 1997
 12 Sch 1 para 1(4) RO(HBF)O; Sch 1 para 1(4) RO(HBF)(S)O
 13 Sch 2 RO(HBF)O; Sch 2 RO(HBF)(S)O
 14 Art 2(1) RO(HBF)O; Art 2(1) RO(HBF)(S)O
 15 *R v Swale Borough Council HBRB ex parte Marchant* [1999] 1 FLR 1087 (QBD); [2000] 1 FLR 246 (CA)
 16 Sch 1 para 3 RO(HBF)O; Sch 1 para 3 RO(HBF)(S)O

17 Sch 1 para 6 RO(HBF)O; Sch 1 para 6 RO(HBF)(S)O
18 Sch 1 para 4 RO(HBF)O; Sch 1 para 4 RO(HBF)(S)O
19 Reg 11(3A) HB Regs
20 Reg 11(3B) HB Regs
21 Reg 2(1) HB Regs, definition of 'young individual'
22 Sch 1 para 5 RO(HBF)O; Sch 1 para 5 RO(HBF)(S)O
23 Sch 1 para 9 RO(HBF)O; Sch 1 para 9 RO(HBF)(S)O
24 Art 2(1) RO(HBF)O; Art 2(1) RO(HBF)(S)O
25 Reg 12A(1A) HB Regs
26 Sch 1 paras 7(1)(a)(ii) and 5(2)(c) RO(HBF)O; Sch 1 paras 7(1)(a)(ii) and 5(2)(c) RO(HBF)(S)O
27 Reg 10 HB(Amdt) Regs
28 Reg 10(1)(a), (2) and (2A) HB(Amdt) Regs
29 Reg 10(3), (4), (5) and (5B) HB(Amdt) Regs
30 Reg 10(6) HB(Amdt) Regs, definition of 'previous beneficiary'
31 Reg 10(1)(b) and (6), definition of 'exempt accommodation' HB(Amdt) Regs
32 Reg 11(3A) and (4) HB Regs
33 Reg 4(2A) HB&CTB(Amdt) Regs
34 Reg 4(2AB) and (2AC) HB&CTB(Amdt) Regs
35 Reg 11(6) HB Regs
36 Reg 11(6A) and (6B) HB Regs
37 Reg 11(7), (11) and (12) HB Regs
38 Reg 11(9)-(12) HB Regs
39 Reg 2(1) HB Regs, definition of 'relative'
40 Reg 10(6B) HB Regs
41 *R on the application of Laali v Westminster CC* [2002] HLR 179 (HC)
42 *R v Macclesfield BC HBRB ex parte Temsemani* 1999, unreported (QBD); A10 Annex C GM
43 Reg 12A(1)(c) HB Regs
44 Reg 12A(8) HB Regs, definition of 'prospective occupier'
45 Reg 12A(3) HB Regs
46 Art 2(1) RO(HBF)O
47 Reg 12A(2A)(b) and Sch 1A para 2(2)(b) HB Regs
48 Reg 12CA HB Regs
49 Reg 12CA(2) HB Regs
50 Reg 12CA(1)(b) HB Regs
51 Arts 2(1), definition of 'relevant period' and 4 and Sch 3 RO(HBF)O; Arts 2(1), definition of 'relevant period' and 4 and Sch 3 RO(HBF)(S)O
52 Reg 12B HB Regs
53 Reg 12CA(3) and (4) HB Regs
54 Reg 12C HB Regs
55 Reg 12CA(5) HB Regs

3. **The 'local housing allowance' rules**

56 Reg 11A(2) HB Regs
57 Reg 10(3B), (3C) and (3I)(a)-(c) HB Regs
58 Reg 11A(3) HB Regs; Sch 3A RO(HBF)O; Sch 3A RO(HBF)(S)O
59 Reg 11B HB Regs
60 Reg 11A(9) HB Regs, definition of 'size criteria'
61 Art 4B RO(HBF)O; Art 4B RO(HBF)(S)O
62 Reg 10(3A) HB Regs
63 Regs 10(3A)(b)(ii) and 11A(1)(iv) HB Regs
64 Reg 10(3D), (3E), (3H) and (3I)(d) HB Regs
65 Reg 10(3F)-(3H) and (3I)(e) HB Regs
66 Reg 11A(8) HB Regs

4. **The pre-January 1996 rules**

67 Reg 11(2)(a) HB Regs (pre-January 1996)
68 *R v Kensington and Chelsea RBC HBRB ex parte Pirie*, 26 March 1997, unreported (QBD)
69 Reg 11(2)(c) HB Regs (pre-January 1996)
70 *R v Beverley District Council HBRB ex parte Hare* [1995] 27 HLR 637 (QBD)
71 *R v Kensington and Chelsea RBC HBRB ex parte Sheikh*, 14 January 1997, unreported (QBD)
72 *R v Kensington and Chelsea RBC ex parte Abou-Jaoude*, 10 May 1996, unreported (QBD)
73 *Macleod v Banff and Buchan District HBRB* [1988] SLT 753 (CS); *Malcolm v Tweedale District HBRB* [1994] SLT 1212 (CS); CH/4970/2002
74 *R v Kensington and Chelsea RBC ex parte Abou-Jaoude*, 10 May 1996, ureported (QBD)
75 *R v Coventry CC ex parte Waite*, 7 July 1995, unreported (QBD)
76 *R v East Devon DC HBRB ex parte Gibson* [1993] 25 HLR 487 (QBD)
77 *R v Waltham Forest LBC ex parte Holder* [1996] 29 HLR 71 (QBD)
78 *R v Kensington and Chelsea RBC HBRB ex parte Sheikh*, 14 January 1997, unreported (QBD)
79 Reg 11(6)(a) HB Regs (pre-January 1996)
80 CH/4306/2003
81 Reg 11(7) HB Regs (pre-January 1996)
82 Reg 11(8) HB Regs (pre-January 1996)

83 *R v Lambeth LBC HBRB ex parte Harrington*, 22 November 1996, unreported (QBD)
84 Reg 11(6)(a) HB Regs (pre-January 1996)
85 *R v Kensington and Chelsea RBC ex parte Pirie*, 26 March 1997, unreported (QBD)
86 *R v Coventry CC ex parte Waite*, 7 July 1995, unreported (QBD)
87 *R v Waltham Forest LBC ex parte Holder* [1996] 29 HLR 71 (QBD); *R v Slough BC ex parte Green*, 15 November 1996, unreported (QBD)
88 Reg 11(3) HB Regs (pre-January 1996)
89 *R v East Devon DC HBRB ex parte Gibson* [1993] 25 HLR 487 (QBD); CH/4306/2003
90 *R v Waltham Forest LBC ex parte Holder* [1996] 29 HLR 71 (QBD)
91 *R v Oadby and Wigston DC ex parte Dickman* [1995] 28 HLR 806 (QBD)
92 Reg 11(6)(b) HB Regs (pre-January 1996)
93 *R v Kensington and Chelsea RBC HBRB ex parte Sheikh*, 14 January 1997, unreported (QBD)
94 *R v Kensington and Chelsea RBC HBRB ex parte Carney* [1997] Crown Office Digest 124 (QBD)
95 Reg 11(3) HB Regs (pre-January 1996)
96 *R v City of Westminster HBRB ex parte Mehanne* [1992] 2 All ER 317 (CA)
97 *R v Brent LBC HBRB ex parte Connery* [1989] 22 HLR 40 (QBD)
98 Reg 11(3A) HB Regs (pre-January 1996)
99 Reg 11(4) and (5) HB Regs (pre-January 1996)
100 Reg 12 HB Regs (pre-October 1997)
101 CH/2214/2003

Chapter 12

Incapacity benefit

This chapter covers:

Incapacity benefit (IB) is a benefit paid to people who are incapable of work and who have either paid or been credited with sufficient national insurance contributions or who became incapable of work in youth. There are special rules which also allow some widows and widowers to qualify for IB. Your entitlement to IB does not depend on whether or not you are employed (although you must be incapable of work) and is not affected by any savings that you have. Although your entitlement to IB may be affected by any personal, occupational or public service pension that you receive, it is not affected by any other income that you have.

If you are employed but are off work because of sickness you normally receive statutory sick pay (SSP) from your employer for the first 28 weeks of your incapacity for work (see Chapter 24). After that, if you satisfy the qualifying conditions, you can claim IB from the Department for Work and Pensions. If you are not entitled to SSP you may qualify for IB from the start of your incapacity for work.

IB is payable at three rates: a lower short-term rate, a higher short-term rate and a long-term rate, according to the length of time the incapacity has lasted (see p274 for details).

Certain people claiming IB and their partners may be required to attend a work-focused interview (see pp1092 and 1094).

Certain IB claimants living in pilot areas may be required to take part in a more intensive work-focused interview procedure under the Pathways to Work or Working Neighbourhoods pilot schemes (see p1095).

See Chapter 30 for details of how your incapacity for work is assessed.

1. Who can claim incapacity benefit

You qualify for incapacity benefit (IB) if:[1]

- you are assessed as, or treated as, incapable of work (see pp263 and 764); *and*
- you are within a 'period of incapacity for work' (see p265); *and*
- for short-term IB you are not more than five years above pension age and for long-term IB you are not over pension age (see p272). For the meaning of short-term IB and long-term IB see p274; *and*
- you are not entitled to statutory sick pay (SSP – see Chapter 24);[2] *and either*
- you have paid (or been credited with) sufficient national insurance (NI) contributions (see p844); *or*
- you qualify as someone who became incapable of work in youth (see p267); *or*
- you are no more than five years over pension age (60 for a woman, 65 for a man), your period of incapacity for work began before you reached pension age, and you would qualify for a Category B retirement pension as a widow or widower, or a Category A retirement pension had you not deferred claiming it or 'de-retired' (see Chapter 19). (**Note:** This provision only allows you to qualify for short-term IB); *or*
- your spouse died before 9 April 2001 and you qualify as a widow or widower (see p278).

For the effect of the Civil Partnerships Act 2004, see p273.

There are some groups of claimants to whom special rules apply (see p278).

Incapable of work

In order to qualify for IB you must be incapable of work or treated as incapable of work. Whether you are incapable of work is determined by the **own occupation test** or the **personal capability assessment** described in Chapter 30. See below for the details of when you can be treated as incapable of work. In some circumstances even if you are incapable of work you are treated as if you are not and so will not qualify for IB (see p264).

If you satisfy the other qualifying conditions you are entitled to IB for days on which you are incapable of work which fall within a 'period of incapacity for work' (see p265).

Treated as incapable of work

You are treated as incapable of work on days on which:

- you are deemed to be incapable of work without having to satisfy the own occupation test or the personal capability assessment (see p768); *or*
- you are exempt from the personal capability assessment (see p773); *or*
- having failed the personal capability assessment, you are in 'exceptional circumstances' (see p778); *or*
- you are entitled to maternity allowance (MA), and have not been disqualified from receiving it (see p458).[3] (**Note:** You cannot be paid both MA and IB in full because of the overlapping benefit rules – see p1102 – but days on MA count towards the periods required to qualify for the higher short-term rate and long-term rate of IB – see p274); *or*
- you work at night in the circumstances described below.

See p267 if you were getting SSP and you are claiming IB on the basis that you became incapable of work in youth.

If you work at night

If you work night shifts you may end one shift and start another on the same day (a day runs from midnight to midnight). If you are incapable of working on only one of those shifts it would normally be difficult to show that the day is a day of incapacity for work. This is because you are normally treated as capable of work on a day on which you do some work. For this reason, there are special rules to help people who work a shift that spans midnight.

- If you worked a different number of hours before and after midnight, you are treated as incapable of work on the day that you work the least hours if you are incapable of work for the rest of that day.[4]
- If you worked the same number of hours before and after midnight, you are treated as incapable of work on the first day of that shift if the shift falls at the end of a period of incapacity for work (see p265), or on the second day of that shift if the shift falls at the beginning of a period of incapacity for work.[5]

Treated as not incapable of work

Even if it has been decided that you are incapable of work, you will be treated as capable of work (and so will not be entitled to IB) in any weeks in which you actually do work, unless that work can be ignored. See p765 for details.

Also, even if you are incapable of work you are treated as capable of work on certain other days including those on which:[6]

- you have been disqualified from receiving IB during a period of absence from Great Britain (GB) or a period when you are imprisoned or detained in legal custody, if that disqualification is for more than six weeks; *or*
- you are on a training course for which you get a training allowance, unless either you finished (or stopped attending) the course before your claim for IB,

or the allowance you receive is only to cover your meal or travel expenses. (However, days when you are on a training course count as days of incapacity for work for the purpose of qualifying for IB while temporarily absent from GB – see p687); *or*

- you are receiving statutory maternity pay (SMP) or statutory adoption pay (SAP – see Chapter 23) (but days on SMP or SAP sometimes count towards the periods required to qualify for the higher rate of short-term IB, or long-term IB – see pp274 and 290);[7] *or*
- you do not satisfy the 'NI number requirement' when making your claim (see p1083).[8]

Period of incapacity for work

You are only entitled to IB for any day on which you are incapable of work which forms part of a 'period of incapacity for work'.

A **'period of incapacity for work'** is either:

- a period of four or more consecutive days when you are incapable of work;[9] *or*
- if you are having plasmapheresis, chemotherapy or radiotherapy, or regular weekly kidney dialysis or total parenteral nutrition, a period of two days when you are incapable of work. These days do not have to be consecutive as long as they are within a period of seven consecutive days.[10] In these circumstances, you are treated as incapable of work on the days that you have this treatment.[11]

Two or more periods of incapacity for work can sometimes be linked together to form a single period – see below.

The linking rules

Two or more periods of incapacity for work separated by eight weeks or less are linked together to form a single period.[12] If you are a 'welfare to work' beneficiary (see p769) two periods of incapacity for work can be linked in this way if they are separated by 52 weeks or less.

You will not be entitled to IB for the periods between the linked periods of incapacity for work,[13] but if periods are linked in this way it means that:

- the question of whether or not you satisfy the contribution conditions is decided at the beginning of the first period of incapacity for work and is not reconsidered if you have periods when you get better but then become ill again;
- you do not have to serve a further three waiting days before being entitled to payment of IB (see p271);
- for the purpose of calculating the date from which you become entitled to the higher rate of short-term or long-term IB, previous periods when you were entitled to IB in a linked period of incapacity for work can be counted;
- you can continue to qualify for IB on the grounds that you were incapable of work in youth, if this is the basis on which you qualified before, and if you still

have not paid or been credited with sufficient NI contributions to qualify otherwise.

Tax credits and the linking rules

In certain circumstances, if you stop claiming IB your period of incapacity for work does not end as long as you claim IB again within two years. This applies if:[14]

- you were in full-time paid work (defined on p750) and you claim IB after stopping this work; *and*
- you were incapable of work on the day after you stopped work; *and*
- you were previously entitled to the higher rate of short-term IB or long-term IB at some time in the two-year period ending with the day after you finish work; *and either*
  - you were entitled to the disability element of working tax credit (WTC – see p1355) on the day before you stopped work, or you would have been had your (and your partner's, if you have one) income not been too high; *and*
  - you were paid WTC or the child, disabled child or severely disabled child element of child tax credit (CTC) for the day before you stopped work; *or*
  - you claim IB on or before 6 April 2005 and the day before you stopped work fell before 7 April 2003 and was in a week in which you were entitled to disabled person's tax credit (DPTC).

In these circumstances, any day during that two-year period will be treated as a day of incapacity for work if it is a day:

- which falls within a week in which you were entitled to DPTC; *or*
- on which you were both:
  - entitled to the disability element of WTC (or you would have been had your income not been too high); *and*
  - for which you were paid WTC, or the child, disabled child or severely disabled child element of CTC.

Training for work and the linking rules

Your period of incapacity for work also does not end if:[15]

- you were on a training for work course (see below); *and*
- you were entitled to the higher rate of short-term or long-term IB at some time in the eight weeks before you started your training; *and*
- you are incapable of work on the day after your training stops; *and*
- this day falls within two years of the last day on which you were entitled to IB.

In these circumstances any day on which you were doing such training counts as a day of incapacity for work.

'Training for work' means training provided under the Employment and Training Act 1973 or, in Scotland, the Enterprise and New Towns (Scotland) Act

1990, or one which you attend for 16 hours or more a week if the primary purpose of the training is teaching occupational or vocational skills.[16]

Incapable of work in youth

If you do not qualify for IB on the basis of your NI contribution record you may still qualify if you became incapable of work in youth.

You will qualify for IB on the basis of incapacity in youth if:[17]

- you are aged 16 or over; *and*
- you have been incapable of work for at least 196 consecutive days (see p267); *and*
- you were under 20 (or, in some circumstances, under 25 – see p268) when your period of incapacity for work started and you claim in time (see below); *and*
- you satisfy the residence and presence conditions (see p696); *and*
- you are not subject to immigration control (see p653); *and*
- if you are under 19, you are not in full-time education (see p270).

If you previously qualified for IB on the basis of your incapacity for work in youth but your entitlement ended, you may be able to requalify for IB on the same basis if you become incapable of work again even if you are over 20 (or 25) (see p270).

If you were under 20 on 6 April 2001 and were getting severe disablement allowance (SDA), your SDA would have stopped on 5 April 2002. You would then have automatically qualified for long-term IB on the basis of your incapacity for work in youth.

The 196-day qualifying period

In order to qualify for IB as someone who became incapable of work in youth, you must have been incapable of work, or treated as incapable of work, for at least the 196 days immediately before the first day on which your entitlement can begin. See Chapter 30 for details of when you are considered incapable of work and p264 for details of when you can be treated as incapable of work. Days on which you were entitled to SSP can also count towards the 196-day qualifying period.[18]

The 196 days must be consecutive and for this purpose Sundays count, so that 196 days is 28 weeks. The linking rules described on p265 do not apply here. As the 196 days must be consecutive, any break in your incapacity for work within the qualifying period means that the 196 days must begin again. Entitlement to the lower rate of short-term IB only begins once you have served the 196-day qualifying period.

If you have not been incapable of work for 196 consecutive days when you make your claim, but you will have been at some point during the three months after you claim, as long as you meet the other qualifying conditions you can be paid IB from the 197th day of your incapacity for work. This is because you can claim IB up to three months in advance (see p284).

If you have already been incapable of work for 196 days before you claim, you should include a backdated medical certificate covering the full qualifying period.

Although you must be at least 16 to qualify for IB on the basis of your incapacity for work in youth, days when you are incapable of work that fall before your 16th birthday can still be counted when calculating the 196-day period as long as you are at least 16 on the day after the 196-day period.

If you have a break in your claim, you do not have to serve the 196-day qualifying period again before being paid IB on a new claim if your new period of incapacity for work is linked to your earlier period of incapacity for work (see p265).[19]

Age

You must have been under 20 when your period of incapacity for work started (or under 25 in the circumstances given below). It is not necessary for you to be under 20 (or 25) on the date of your claim for IB. According to the Department for Work and Pensions (DWP), however, if you are over 20 (or 25) and you fail to claim within three months of the end of your 196-day qualifying period (which must begin before your 20th (or 25th) birthday), you will not be able to qualify for IB on the basis of incapacity in youth.[20]

Once you qualify for IB on the grounds of your incapacity for work in youth you can continue to receive it even after you reach 20 (or 25) as long as your period of incapacity for work continues. If there is a break in your period of incapacity for work, as long as the linking rules described on p265 allow your present period of incapacity for work to be linked to one in which you qualified for IB on the grounds of your incapacity for work in youth, you can requalify for IB on this basis.

You can also requalify for IB after your 20th (or 25th) birthday in the circumstances detailed on p270.

Under-25-year-olds

The age condition is relaxed to include some people over the age of 20 who have been studying or training, and who have not paid or been credited with sufficient NI contributions to qualify for IB otherwise.

If you are under 25 when your period of incapacity for work starts, you can still qualify for IB on the basis of your incapacity for work in youth if, in addition to the main conditions described on p267:[21]

- you registered on a course of full-time advanced or secondary education, or on a course of vocational or work-based training (see below for definitions), at least three months before you became 20; *and*
- within an academic term of registering, you attended that course of education or training; *and*
- you started the course at least three months before you reached 20; *and*

- you finished the course some time after the start of the last two complete tax years which fall before the benefit year in which you claim IB (see p844).

Type of education or training

For the meaning of 'advanced education', see p621. **'Secondary education'** is a course of education below advanced level which you attend at a recognised educational establishment, such as a school or college, or which you attend elsewhere if the Secretary of State is satisfied that the education you receive is equivalent to that given at a recognised educational establishment.[22]

'Full-time' education is not defined and so it can be argued that it should be given its ordinary and natural meaning, and could include periods of unsupervised as well as supervised study.

However, if you are on a part-time course because you have a disability which means that you cannot attend full time, then you are treated as if you are attending a full-time course.[23]

'Vocational training' includes training described as 'training for work' on p266, and also includes any training which is provided by someone recognised by the Secretary of State and is for people with a mental or physical disability, if the main purpose of the training is to teach occupational or vocational skills.

'Work-based training' is vocational training which you do on an employer's premises.

You are still treated as attending a course of education or training if your attendance is interrupted because of illness or a domestic emergency.[24]

Attending more than one course

The rules on course attendance are not entirely clear if you have attended more than one course, each with different finishing dates. If you satisfy the above conditions for under-25-year-olds for more than one course, it is the end date of the last of those that is relevant. However, if you started one course at least three months before you reached 20 and started another course less than three months before your 20th birthday, and so you meet the above conditions in relation to the first but not the second course, the position is less clear. If there is a gap between the two courses (other than just a normal end-of-term holiday) it is the date on which the first course ends which governs your entitlement.

If there is no gap between the courses (other than an end-of-term holiday) the DWP states that the intention is that the above time limits apply to the end of the second course. The regulations may not achieve this, however, and arguably the time limits for claiming relate to the end of the course which you started at least three months before you reached 20, rather than to the end of any subsequent course. In these circumstances, you may be entitled to IB once your first course of education or training ends, even if you are still attending a subsequent course, as long as you meet the other qualifying conditions. If you are refused IB in these circumstances, seek advice. Note, however, that you cannot qualify for IB if you are on a training course for which you get a training allowance unless the allowance you receive only covers your meal or travel expenses (see p264).

Under 19 and in full-time education

If you are under 19 you will only qualify for IB on the basis of being incapable of work in youth if you are not on a full-time course of education (but see below if the course you attend is designed for people with disabilities). For this purpose you will be considered to be in full-time education if you attend a course for 21 hours or more a week.[25] Temporary interruptions in your education are disregarded. If you are 19 or over and studying either full or part time, or if you are under 19 and studying for under 21 hours a week, you can qualify for IB as long as you meet the other conditions of entitlement.

Courses for people with disabilities

When calculating whether you are studying for 21 hours a week or more, only the instruction or tuition you receive which would be suitable for someone of the same age or sex as you who did not have a physical or mental disability is counted.[26] Both the course content and the method of teaching must be considered in deciding whether the education is suitable for someone without a disability.[27] If part of your course is suitable for people without disabilities but part is not (eg, because some of it makes use of information in Braille), only the part of the course that is suitable for students who do not have a disability is counted.

Requalifying on the basis of your incapacity for work in youth

If you previously qualified for IB on the basis of your incapacity for work in youth, there are rules that allow you to requalify for IB on this basis even if you are over 20 (or 25).

If your present period of incapacity for work is linked to an earlier period when you received IB on the grounds of your incapacity for work in youth, you can requalify on this basis (see p265 for when periods can be linked). If your periods of incapacity for work are linked in this way your previous period on IB is counted when assessing whether you qualify for the higher rate of short-term IB or long-term IB.

If your present period of incapacity for work cannot be linked with an earlier one, you can still qualify for IB on the basis of your incapacity for work in youth in the circumstances detailed below. In these circumstances you will return to the lower rate of short-term IB even if you were previously receiving the higher rate of short-term IB or long-term IB. You can qualify for IB in this way if:[28]

- you were previously entitled to IB on the basis of your incapacity for work in youth; *and*

- your last claim for IB did not end because you were either found to be capable of work or because it was decided that you could be treated as capable of work (see p264); *and*
- you are 20 or over (or 25 or over, if you would otherwise qualify under the rules for people between 20 and 25 – see p268); *and either*
- your last claim for IB ended only because you were planning to take up employment or training in the circumstances detailed below (whether or not you actually did so); *or*
- your last claim for IB ended only because you were absent from GB in the circumstances detailed below.

Taking up employment or training

You can requalify if you meet the above conditions and:

- any earnings that you received over the period from when your last IB claim ended until your current period of incapacity for work began were so low that you do not meet the first NI contribution condition for IB (see p844); *and either*
- you meet the second NI contribution condition for IB and within the last tax year relevant to that condition you received at least one credited contribution on the basis that you were receiving DPTC. **Note:** DPTC was abolished from April 2003 (see p841); *or*
- you reclaim IB not more than 56 days after the day you stopped work.

Absence from Great Britain

If your last claim for IB only ended because you went abroad you can requalify if you meet the above conditions and:

- you have been incapable of work for at least 196 consecutive days since you returned to GB; *and*
- you reclaim IB within three months of the end of that 196-day period.

Waiting days

Except in the circumstances detailed below, you are not entitled to IB for the first three days in your period of incapacity for work. These three days are called 'waiting days'.[29]

You do not have to serve these three waiting days, and so can qualify for IB from the first day of your period of incapacity for work, if:

- your period of incapacity for work can be linked to a previous one (see p265); *or*
- you were previously receiving SSP and your period of incapacity for work falls within the 57 days after your entitlement to SSP ended;[30] *or*
- you are receiving IB on the grounds of your incapacity for work in youth (see p267);

- you were discharged from the forces after 3 May 2003 and you have had at least four consecutive days of recorded sickness absence from duty, the last of which falls no more than eight weeks before the start of your entitlement to IB.

Disqualification from benefit

You can be disqualified from receiving IB for up to six weeks for one of the reasons below[31] (you can appeal against the fact of disqualification, or the period, or both).

- You are incapable of work because of your own misconduct. This means conduct which is blameworthy or wrong, and does not include playing dangerous sports or having an accident. Involuntary alcoholism is not 'misconduct', but drunkenness is.[32] You cannot be disqualified for misconduct if you become pregnant or contract a sexually transmitted disease.
- You refuse suitable treatment without good cause (see below). You are not required to subject yourself to 'invasive' treatment – eg, inoculation, vaccination or surgery (unless it is very minor). The DWP recognises that many people fear or mistrust such treatment and that it has risks.
- You fail to refrain from behaviour calculated to slow down your recovery, without good cause.
- You are away from home without leaving word as to where you may be found without good cause. This is so that you can be called to a medical examination or be seen by a visiting officer from the DWP if necessary. If you are going away (eg, to stay at a friend's or relative's house) write to the DWP giving details of the period you will be away, and where you are going (but see p687 if you are going abroad).

'**Good cause**' in this context is not defined by the legislation. The decision maker should consider all the circumstances when deciding whether you have good cause. Good cause may, for example, include a refusal to take medical treatment on religious grounds.

2. The rules about your age

Lower age limit

In order to qualify for incapacity benefit (IB) on the grounds that you have been incapable of work in youth (see p267) you must be 16 or over.

If you qualify for IB on the basis of your national insurance (NI) contribution record there is no lower age limit but in order to satisfy the second NI contribution condition for IB (see p845), you must have paid or been credited with NI contributions over a period of at least two years. You do not have to start paying NI contributions on earnings until you are 16 years of age (see p828).

Upper age limit

You are not entitled to long-term IB after you reach pension age.[33] Pension age is 60 for a woman and 65 for a man.

If you are not more than five years over pension age you are entitled to short-term IB if:

- you would have been entitled to a Category A or, on the basis of your late spouse's NI contributions, a Category B retirement pension had you not deferred claiming it or de-retired (see p490); *and*
- your period of incapacity for work began before you reached pension age; *and*
- the period of 364 days during which IB is paid at the short-term rate has not yet run out.[34]

Note: When the Civil Partnership Act 2004 comes into force, you will also be able to qualify for short-term IB if:

- you would have qualified for a Category B retirement pension on the basis of your late civil partner's NI contribution record had you not deferred claiming it or de-retired; *and*
- you are over pension age but not more than 5 years over; *and*
- your period of incapacity for work began before you reached pension age.[35]

The Civil Partnership Act 2004 is expected to come into force on 5 December 2005 (see CPAG's *Welfare Rights Bulletin* for updates).

See p275 for details of the amount of IB paid after you reach pension age and p290 for details of whether you may be better off claiming your retirement pension or remaining on IB after reaching pension age.

3. Claiming for others

If you are getting incapacity benefit (IB) (either the short-term or long-term rates) you may be entitled to an increase for your spouse or someone who looks after your children (see p793).[36] Your entitlement to such an increase may be affected by the level of any earnings or pension s/he receives (see p797). The earnings rule is more generous for long-term IB than for short-term IB. This means that if your spouse or adult dependant is earning too much to entitle you to an increase when you are receiving short-term IB, you may become entitled once you begin to be paid at the long-term rate. If so, you must make a separate claim for this increase within three months of becoming entitled to the long-term rate. If you do not, only three months' arrears are paid.[37] If you have been entitled to an increase in your IB for your partner for at least six months and you are both 18 or over but under 60, then your partner may be required to take part in a work-focused interview and your benefit can be reduced if s/he fails to do so without good cause (see p1094).[38]

Increases for your dependent children, which could be claimed with the higher rate of short-term IB or long-term IB (or, if you were over pension age, with the lower rate of short-term IB as well) were abolished on 6 April 2003 and replaced with child tax credit, which is means tested (see Chapter 49). However, if you were entitled to an increase for a dependent child on 5 April 2003 you may be able to continue to receive it after that date (see p798). If your partner works or receives an occupational or personal pension, your entitlement to an increase for a child may be affected by the level of her/his earnings or pension (see p798).

4. The amount of benefit

Rates of incapacity benefit

Incapacity benefit (IB) is paid at three rates. The rate you receive depends on the length of time that you have either been entitled to IB, or treated as entitled to IB (see below):

- The lower rate of short-term IB is paid for the first 28 weeks of entitlement.
- The higher rate of short-term IB is paid after 28 weeks of entitlement (ie, from the 197th day of entitlement).
- Long-term IB is paid after 52 weeks of entitlement (ie, from the 365th day of entitlement).
- If you are terminally ill or receiving the higher rate of disability living allowance (DLA) care component (see Chapter 7), you are paid an amount equivalent to the long-term rate after 28 weeks of entitlement. The definition of 'terminally ill' is the same as for DLA (see p149).[39]

Treated as entitled to incapacity benefit

The rate of IB you receive is determined by the number of days on which you have either been entitled to IB or 'treated as entitled' to IB. Days on which you are disqualified from receiving IB (see p272) do not count.[40]

You are treated as entitled to IB on the following days:[41]

- the first three days of your 'period of incapacity for work' (you cannot always receive IB for these days, which are called 'waiting days' – see p271);
- days on which you are entitled to maternity allowance (see p456);
- days on which you are entitled to statutory maternity pay (SMP) or statutory adoption pay (SAP) but only if:
  - you are incapable of work, and on the day before your SMP or SAP started you were within a period of incapacity for work (see p265) or were receiving statutory sick pay (SSP); *and*

  - the days are not days on which you are treated as capable of work for IB purposes (see p264); *and*
  - you satisfy the contribution conditions for IB on the first day in your period of incapacity for work or on a day on which you were receiving SSP;[42]
- days on which you satisfied the contribution conditions for IB and were entitled to SSP, as long as your period of entitlement to SSP ended not more than 57 days before your current period of incapacity for work began (see p289);[43]
- certain days of sickness absence from duty if you were a member of the forces and were discharged after 3 May 2003.

Amount paid

The full weekly rates of IB are as follows, but your IB may be reduced if you receive a personal, occupational or public service pension (see p277).

	Claimant under pension age £pw	*Claimant of pension age or over £pw*
Long-term IB		
Claimant	76.45	N/A
Adult dependant	45.70	N/A
Child dependant:		
Eldest eligible child	9.40	N/A
Each other child	11.35	N/A
Short-term IB (higher rate)		
Claimant	68.20	76.45
Adult dependant	35.65	43.95
Child dependant:		
Eldest eligible child	9.40	9.40
Each other child	11.35	11.35
Short-term IB (lower rate)		
Claimant	57.65	73.35
Adult dependant	35.65	43.95
Child dependant:		
Eldest eligible child	N/A	9.40
Each other child	N/A	11.35

If you are entitled to long-term IB, you may also be entitled to an age-related addition (see below). If IB is payable for a period of less than a week it is paid at a daily rate of one-seventh of the weekly amount.

Long-term IB is not payable after you reach pension age (60 for a woman and 65 for a man). Short-term IB is reduced after you reach pension age if your retirement pension, had you claimed it, would have been reduced because your national insurance (NI) contribution record was incomplete (see p847).[44] However, as for people under pension age, you can receive the equivalent of the long-term rate of IB after the first 196 days of incapacity for work if you are terminally ill or if you are getting the higher rate of DLA care if this would be more favourable to you than receiving the higher rate of short-term IB.[45]

Benefit is also paid at a reduced rate if you are a local councillor and your net councillor's allowances exceed £78 a week (see p938).[46]

If you are on long-term IB, you are entitled to a Christmas bonus (see p68).

See p273 and Chapter 31 for details of the qualifying conditions for payment of an increase in your IB for dependants.

The amount of your benefit may be reduced, or not paid at all, if you are required to take part in a work-focused interview and fail to do so (see p1094). See p273 if your partner is required to take part in a work-focused interview because you get an increase in your IB for her/him.

For each week that you receive IB you are entitled to be credited with a Class 1 NI contribution (see p838). This is because you receive a credit for each week during which you are incapable of work.

Age-related additions

Once you are entitled to long-term IB you are paid an age-related addition to your benefit if you were under 45 *either*:[47]

- on the first day of your period of incapacity for work (see p265); *or*
- on the first day of any previous periods of incapacity for work linked to your current one (see p265); *or*
- on the first day of your period of entitlement to SSP (see p596), if you were previously on SSP and your current period of incapacity for work started not more than 57 days after your SSP stopped.

Special rules apply to certain widows or if you are a serving member of the forces.[48]

This age-related addition is paid at two rates depending on your age on the relevant day, as follows:

Age	*£pw*
Under 35	16.05
Under 45	8.05

If you receive a guaranteed minimum pension from your late spouse's contracted-out occupational pension scheme the amount of your age addition will be reduced by the amount of your guaranteed minimum pension.[49]

Reduction in incapacity benefit for pension payments

If your entitlement to IB started on or after 6 April 2001 your benefit may be reduced if you receive certain kinds of pension payments (but see below if you receive the highest rate of DLA care).

If the total amount of the gross pension you receive amounts to more than £85 a week your IB will be reduced by half of the amount of pension that is paid above £85 a week.[50]

Example

Ebadur is entitled to IB from 30 April 2003. He is receiving two pensions, a personal pension of £52 a week gross and a public service pension of £43 a week gross. The pensions total £95 a week. As these amount to £10 more than £85, his IB is reduced by £5 a week (50 per cent of £10).

Your benefit is reduced proportionately if you get IB for a period of less than a week. If the total gross pension you receive amounts to £85 or less each week then your IB is unaffected.

Pensions that are taken into account

Pensions that are taken into account are periodic payments made under:[51]

- any personal pension scheme; *and*
- any occupational scheme; *and*
- any public service pension scheme; *and*
- any permanant health insurance policy arranged by your employer which provides payments in connection with ill-health or disability after your employment ends. However, if you contributed more than 50 per cent of the pension premiums the amount you receive from this kind of pension will be ignored.

Other types of pension payments (including one-off lump sum payments) are ignored for the purpose of calculating your entitlement to IB. The following types of payment are also ignored and so will not affect your IB:

- any part of your pension paid direct to an ex-wife or ex-husband by the pension scheme trustees under an earmarking order of the court;[52] *and*
- any payments you receive as a result of the death of the pension holder[53] (but see p276 if you get an age addition with your IB and a guaranteed minimum pension from your late spouse's contracted-out occupational pension scheme).

If you are entitled to the highest rate of DLA care (see Chapter 7) all pension payments you receive are ignored and so do not affect your entitlement to IB.[54]

If you were entitled to incapacity benefit before 6 April 2001

If you were entitled to IB before 6 April 2001 and you have continued to be entitled to IB since that time, any pension payments you receive will not affect your IB entitlement.[55] However, see p276 if you get an age addition with your IB and a guaranteed minimum pension from your late spouse's contracted-out occupational pension scheme.

If you break your claim for IB but later requalify for IB, pension payments you receive can still be ignored if your period(s) of incapacity for work can be linked (see p265).

5. Special rules for special groups

There are some groups of claimants to whom special rules apply. These are covered below and in Chapters 25, 26 and 28. Special rules apply to:

- widows and widowers (see below);
- people who have been incapable of work since 12 April 1995 (see p279);
- people going abroad (see p687);
- people in hospital (see p715);
- people in prison or detention (see p731).

Widows and widowers

If you are a widow or widower and your spouse died before 9 April 2001, you may qualify for incapacity benefit (IB) even if you do not satisfy the national insurance (NI) contribution conditions. If so, you can be paid long-term IB even if you have not received short-term IB first.

If you are a widow you are entitled under these rules if:[56]

- your husband died before 9 April 2001; *and*
- you were not entitled to widowed mother's allowance after your husband died or you are no longer entitled to widowed mother's allowance; *and*
- the date when your husband died *or* your widowed mother's allowance stopped was after 5 April 1979; *and*
- you are incapable of work and your current period of incapacity for work (see p265) began either before your husband died or before your widowed mother's allowance stopped, and has lasted for at least 364 days (or 196 days if you are terminally ill, see p149); *and*
- you would have been entitled to widow's pension if you had been over 45 when your husband died or when your widowed mother's allowance stopped, or you receive a reduced widow's pension because of your age at the relevant time (see p35); *and*
- you would not otherwise be entitled to any rate of IB – eg, because you have not paid or been credited with sufficient contributions.

In these circumstances, you receive the long-term rate of IB or, if you are receiving a reduced rate of widow's pension, you receive that and the difference between the rate of widow's pension you receive and the long-term rate of IB.[57]

If you are a widower you are entitled if:[58]

- your wife died after 5 April 1979 but before 9 April 2001; *and*
- you were incapable of work when she died or you became incapable of work within 13 weeks of the day after her death; *and*
- your period of incapacity for work has lasted for at least 364 days (or 196 days if you are terminally ill – see p149); *and*
- you would not otherwise be entitled to any rate of IB – eg, because you have not paid or been credited with sufficient contributions.

In these circumstances you receive the long-term rate of IB. If you are a widower who has a qualifying child you may also qualify for widowed parent's allowance (see p25). However, the overlapping benefit rules mean that you cannot receive both widowed parent's allowance and IB in full (see p1102).

Days in receipt of statutory sick pay (see Chapter 24) count towards the 364-day (or 196-day) period of incapacity for work for both widows and widowers.

You cannot qualify for long-term IB under these provisions if you are over pension age, but you may qualify for a Category A pension under these rules instead.[59]

If you have obtained a full gender recognition certificate and you were entitled to long-term IB on the basis of being a widow or widower before the certificate was issued, your entitlement will end following the issue of the certificate. To obtain a gender recognition certificate you must have been living in the opposite gender or have changed gender. An interim gender recognition certificate does not affect your benefit entitlement.[60]

People incapable of work since 12 April 1995

IB was introduced on 13 April 1995 and replaced sickness benefit and invalidity benefit (IVB). (For details of sickness benefit and IVB see the 17th edition of CPAG's *Rights Guide to Non-Means-Tested Benefits*.) Some people are still protected by transitional rules if they were getting IVB before IB was introduced, including some who qualified on the basis of an industrial injury (see p280).

People who were receiving invalidity benefit

If you were receiving IVB immediately before the introduction of IB, you automatically received a transitional award of long-term IB.[61] Transitional long-term IB can continue to be paid until you reach pension age (60 for a woman, 65 for a man), or until you are no longer incapable of work, whichever is earlier.

People who qualified following an industrial accident or disease

Even if you did not satisfy the NI contribution conditions it was possible to qualify for sickness benefit and IVB if your incapacity for work was a result of an industrial accident or disease. If you were receiving sickness benefit on 12 April 1995 on this basis, you became entitled to transitional short-term IB and, after a year, ordinary long-term IB.[62]

If you were receiving IVB on 12 April 1995 as a result of an industrial accident or disease, you are entitled to a transitional award of long-term IB until you reach pension age (60 for a woman, 65 for a man) or until you are no longer incapable of work as a result of your industrial accident or disease.

Transitional long-term incapacity benefit

If you receive transitional long-term IB, in effect you continue to receive the old IVB (including the old, more generous, age-related invalidity allowance) under a different name. For further details you should refer to the 17th edition of CPAG's *Rights Guide to Non-Means-Tested Benefits*.

Note that:

- if you were receiving an additional pension under the additional state pension scheme (see p499) with your IVB, it is frozen at its 1994/95 level (the rest of your transitional IB is uprated in the normal way);
- increases for adult dependants continue to be paid under the old rules that applied to IVB;[63]
- your transitional long-term IB is tax free and will be ignored when calculating your entitlement to working tax credit and child tax credit;
- if you break your claim you can requalify for transitional long-term IB, including any increase for an adult dependant, if your current period of incapacity for work can be linked to an earlier one when you were entitled to transitional long-term IB – see p769.[64]

6. Claims and backdating

To be entitled to incapacity benefit (IB) you must make a claim for it.[65] The main rules for claiming are described in Chapter 40. The following section explains the specific rules that relate to IB.

You may be required to attend a work-focused interview in order to qualify for IB (see p1092). Certain IB claimants living in pilot areas may be required to take part in a more intensive work-focused interview procedure under the Pathways to Work or Working Neighbourhoods pilot schemes (see p1095).[66]

It may be possible to claim in advance (see p284) or to get your claim backdated (see p284).

If you wish, you may amend or withdraw your claim in writing before it is assessed.

Making a claim

A claim for IB must be made in writing on the appropriate application form. The decision maker at the Department for Work and Pensions (DWP) may accept a written application that is not on the correct form if this is sufficient in the circumstances (see p1079).[67] You must also make a written claim for an increase for a dependant (see Chapter 31). The IB claim forms contain a separate section for making such claims.

The procedure you should follow in order to make your claim depends on whether you live in the catchment area of a Jobcentre Plus office – you can check your local telephone directory or use the Jobcentre Plus website (www.jobcentreplus.gov.uk) to see if you live in a Jobcentre Plus area. If you live in a Jobcentre Plus area see below. If not, you should claim IB by completing an SC1 form or, if you are claiming on the grounds of being incapable of work in youth, an IB(Y)1 form. You can obtain these claim forms from any DWP or Jobcentre Plus office. They are also available on the Jobcentre Plus website. You should send or take your completed claim form to the DWP office that covers your local area (you should be able to find the address in the telephone directory). If you are 60 or over you may also be able to make your claim by taking or sending it to a designated 'alternative office' (see p1078 for details).

Whichever procedure you follow to claim, it is advisable to keep a copy of your claim in case queries arise.

See p1076 for the detailed rules on making a claim.

If you are employed, see p282.

Jobcentre Plus areas

If you live in a Jobcentre Plus area, then in practice you will usually be required to start your claim by telephoning a 'contact centre'. (Your local Jobcentre Plus office will have this number, and it may also be displayed in local advice centres, libraries, etc.) The contact centre will take basic details, then call you back to go through the details of your claim. Also, the date of an initial work-focused interview (see p1092) will be set, unless it is agreed that you do not need to attend one. You will then be sent a statement recording those details, which you will be asked to sign. The signed statement of details will form your official claim, instead of an SC1 or IB(Y)1 claim form.

It is best for you to start your claim in this way if you can. However, if you cannot or do not want to use the telephone to start your claim, then Jobcentre Plus say that they can still deal with your claim in other ways. You might, for example, be invited for a 'face-to-face' interview to gather the relevant details, or in some cases they may accept an SC1 or IB(Y)1 claim form. Seek advice if you are unable to use a telephone and the Jobcentre Plus office will not let you start your claim in any other way.

If you satisfy the qualifying conditions IB can be backdated for up to three months, so the delay between the date of your phone call to the contact centre and the date you return your signed statement will normally not result in any loss of benefit. However, if you claim late and it is likely that your signed statement will reach the Jobcentre Plus office more than three months after your entitlement to IB would have begun, it is advisable to make a written application immediately on an SC1 (or IB(Y)1, if you are claiming on the basis of being incapable of work in youth), without waiting to receive the statement, to ensure that you do not lose money.

If you are employed

You should normally be paid statutory sick pay (SSP – see Chapter 24) for the first 28 weeks of your incapacity for work. If your employer thinks that you are not entitled to SSP or if your entitlement to SSP has run out, they should complete and give you an SSP1 form and you should claim IB from your local DWP or Jobcentre Plus office as described above. You will normally have to include the SSP1 form and a medical certificate with your claim. If you disagree with your employer's decision to refuse to pay you SSP or to stop paying you SSP, you can refer the matter to the Revenue (see p608), but do not delay claiming IB while you do so. If you have asked the Revenue to decide whether you should qualify for SSP you should explain this on your IB claim form. See p283 if you are claiming IB after your employer has refused your claim for SSP.

Information to support your claim

When you claim IB, you and any adult dependant for whom you are claiming must satisfy the national insurance number requirement (see p1083).

When you make a claim for IB you can be asked to supply 'certificates, documents, information and evidence' considered relevant to your claim.[68] For example, you will normally be expected to provide medical evidence of your incapacity for work. Evidence or documents relating to your claim may be taken or sent to your local DWP or Jobcentre Plus office. If you are 60 or over, your local housing benefit or council tax benefit office may also be able to accept evidence and documents from you in connection with your claim, as long as it is a designated 'alternative office' (see p1078).

If you are asked to provide evidence or documents which you do not have, ask what other evidence would be acceptable. Always ask the DWP to explain what is required and why and complain if you feel any requests for information are unreasonable.

Medical evidence

For the first seven days of your incapacity for work the DWP should accept a self-certificate. After seven days you need to provide proof of your incapacity for work in the form of a medical certificate from your doctor. If it is unreasonable to expect you to provide a medical certificate (MED 3) from a doctor, the DWP should accept other evidence if this is sufficient to show that you should not work because of some specific disease or bodily or mental disablement.[69] If you have been (or are likely to be) unfit for work for more than seven days you should send the medical certificate with the claim form.

When making a decision on your claim the decision maker may refer your case to a medical practitioner (normally a Medical Service doctor – see p764) for a report and a medical examination. If you fail to attend a medical examination without good cause your claim can be refused.[70]

Who should claim

You must normally claim IB on your own behalf. However, IB can be claimed by another adult on your behalf if you are not able to act for yourself. This person is your 'appointee' (see p1075 for further details).

The date of your claim

The date of your claim is important as it determines the date from which you will be paid IB (see p285). The date of your claim is normally the date your claim form (or signed statement – see p281) is received at a DWP or Jobcentre Plus office or, if you are 60 or over and submit your claim to a designated 'alternative office' (see p1078), the date it is received by that office.[71] A claim can be counted as having been received at the office even on a day when the office is closed if that is the day it would have normally been delivered.[72]

If the claim you submit is incomplete or not on the correct form you may be asked to provide further information or to complete the correct form. As long as this additional information or form is returned within a month of it being sent back to you (or longer if the Secretary of State thinks that the delay is reasonable), your claim is treated as made on the date the initial claim was received (see p1082).[73] But see p1092 if you are required to take part in a work-focused interview in order to qualify for IB.

In some circumstances you can claim before you qualify for IB or the date of your claim can be backdated (see p284).

If you claim the wrong benefit

If you are employed and have claimed SSP but your employer decides that you are not entitled to SSP, and you claim IB within three months of being notified of your employer's decision in writing, your claim for IB is treated as having been made on the date of your claim for SSP.[74]

A claim for maternity allowance (MA) may be treated as a claim for IB.[75] This may allow you to get your claim for IB backdated for more than the normal three months. If your MA claim is accepted as a claim for IB, your IB can be backdated for up to three months before the date you claimed MA if you satisfy the qualifying conditions over that period. See p1084 for details of interchanging claims in this way.

Claiming in advance

You can claim IB up to three months before you expect to qualify for it.[76] It is helpful to claim in advance if you can, as it can allow the DWP time to gather the information it may need to decide your claim in good time.

How your claim is dealt with

Your claim is dealt with by the DWP office that covers your local area and queries about your claim should be made to that office.

You may be able to claim an interim payment while waiting for a decision on your claim (see p1108) or to claim means-tested benefits if your income is low (see p288), or apply for a crisis loan to tide you over until benefit is paid (see p538).

See p1091 for more information about the processing of claims.

Backdating your claim

A claim for IB can be backdated for up to three months as long as you satisfy the qualifying conditions over that period. You do not have to show reasons why your claim was late.[77]

If you were previously entitled to IB but your benefit was stopped because you were not thought to be incapable of work and:

- when your IB stopped you had made a claim for disability living allowance (DLA), or constant attendance allowance (AA), and the claim had not been decided; *and*
- your claim for that benefit was successful and you were awarded the higher rate of the DLA care component, or constant AA paid at a rate which is higher than the 'lower weekly rate' (which means that you are exempt from the personal capability assessment); *and*
- you make a further claim for IB within three months of the decision to award you the other benefit,

your later claim for IB can be backdated either to the date that your previous claim for IB stopped, or to the date from which you were awarded the other benefit, whichever is later.[78]

If you might have qualified for benefit earlier but did not claim because you were given the wrong information or were misled by the DWP you could:

- ask for an ex gratia payment (see p1304); *or*
- complain to the Ombudsman via your MP (see p1302).

If you have claimed SSP or MA instead of IB, see p283.

See p1086 for more details about the backdating of claims.

At the end of your claim

If you start work within a week of your entitlement to IB stopping, you may be able to benefit from the rules for 'welfare to work' beneficiaries (see p769). To qualify as a 'welfare to work' beneficiary, within the month after the date that your benefit stopped you need to notify the DWP that you have started work (unless you have successfully appealed against a decision that you were capable of work – see p770). If you are a 'welfare to work' beneficiary you can return to the same level of IB that you were previously receiving if you become incapable of work again within your 52-week linking period (see p770).

When you recover and return to work, or sign on for jobseeker's allowance (see Chapter 15), or claim income support (see Chapter 13) you are given a form by the DWP. You should keep it (if you are not employed), or give it to your employer. If you fall sick again within eight weeks of the end of your previous period of incapacity for work (see pp265 and 265), you can then claim IB and not SSP (but see above if you are a 'welfare to work' beneficiary). This may be beneficial because IB paid at the higher short-term rate or the long-term rate is more than SSP, and can include additions for dependants. If you do go off work again within eight weeks your employer should give you Form SSP1(E). This, along with any medical certificates, should be sent to your local DWP office or Jobcentre Plus office.

Certain IB claimants in pilot areas may be entitled to a 52-week return to work credit if they come off IB to start work for 16 hours or more a week and they earn £15,000 a year or less. To qualify you must have been getting IB for at least three months or have been getting SSP for at least 13 weeks before your IB started.[79]

You may be able to claim an extended payment of housing benefit and council tax benefit if your entitlement to IB stops because you either start work, your hours of work increase or your earnings go up (see p64). Certain IB claimants may also qualify for a job grant on starting work (see p66).

7. Getting paid

Incapacity benefit (IB) is a daily benefit, which means that it can be paid for periods of less than a week. The daily rate is one-seventh of the weekly amount.

IB is normally paid by direct credit transfer into your bank (or similar) account. If you are unable to open or manage an account payment can be made by cheque. Such cheques are sent to your home address and can be paid into an account or cashed at the post office (see p1099 for details).[80]

If you satisfy the qualifying conditions, you are paid IB from the date of your claim, although you normally receive payment of IB fortnightly in arrears unless:

- immediately before you claimed IB you were claiming income support (IS – see Chapter 13) because you were too ill or disabled to work and IS was being paid to you weekly, in which case IB is paid weekly in arrears;[81] *or*
- you have been continuously entitled to IB since 13 April 1995 and were entitled to sickness benefit or invalidity benefit (which were replaced by IB) on 12 April 1995, in which case IB is paid weekly in arrears;[82] *or*
- the amount you are due is less than £1 a week, in which case it may be paid four-weekly in arrears, but see below if your IB is reduced because of pension payments you receive;[83] *or*
- your IB is reduced to less than £5 a week because of pension payments that you receive (see p277), in which case the Department for Work and Pensions (DWP) decision maker can decide how often you are paid, although you must be paid at least once a year.[84]

Payment may be made to someone else on your behalf if you are unable to act for yourself (called your 'appointee' – see p1075). If you just want someone else to be able to get your benefit for you, but you do not need someone to act for you as you are able to deal with your own benefit claim, you can request that the decision maker authorises that person to receive benefit on your behalf, by writing to the DWP.[85]

If your IB has been reduced because you (or your partner) failed to take part in a work-focused interview, see p1097.

Your IB may be suspended and eventually stopped if you are asked by the DWP to provide a medical certificate and you do not do so.[86] If payment of your IB is suspended, see p1105.

If your benefit cheque is lost or stolen, see p1104.

Delays and complaints

If payment of your IB is delayed, you might be able to get an interim payment. See p1108 for further details.

If you suffer delays (see p1305), or wish to complain about how your claim has been dealt with, see p1300. You might be able to claim compensation (see p1304).

Change of circumstances

It is your duty to report any change in your circumstances that might affect your entitlement to, or the payment of, your benefit.[87] You should do this promptly in writing or by telephone to the office handling your claim (although in individual cases notification might be accepted in a form other than in writing or by telephone). In some cases, however, the decision maker might say you must report changes in writing. In any case, you might want to report the change in writing and keep a copy, in case of a dispute in the future. If you do not promptly report any such change, any resulting overpayment may be recoverable from you (see Chapter 41). If you are considered deliberately to have acted falsely or dishonestly, you may also be guilty of an offence (see Chapter 42).

IB is normally awarded for an indefinite period, unless your circumstances are likely to change shortly after the award.[88] In order for payment of IB to be stopped or adjusted, the decision on your entitlement must first be revised or superseded. The rules about when a decision on your IB claim can be revised or superseded, and about the date from which a new decision takes effect, are described in Chapter 43. See that chapter for details, specifically:

- if a Medical Service doctor has provided a new medical report on you to the DWP see p1201;
- if a decision on your entitlement to IB has been superseded because it has been decided that you can be treated as incapable of work as you are exempt from the personal capability assessment[89] see p1208;
- if you have had a personal capability assessment while still subject to the own occupation test see p1205;
- if you have become entitled to the highest rate of disability living allowance care component and as a result you are entitled to the long-term rate of IB[90] see p1208;
- if your IB stops because of a change in your incapacity for work[91] see p1206;
- if your IB stops because you have started work (or for another reason not related to the personal capability assessment) see p1206;
- if you are entitled to more benefit as a result of a change in your circumstances see p1205.

Overpayments and fraud

If you are overpaid IB, you might have to repay it. The rules on overpayments are covered in Chapter 41.

If you have been accused of fraud, see Chapter 42. You may not be paid IB if you have been sanctioned for benefit offences (see p1169).

8. Challenging an incapacity benefit decision

You can apply for a revision or supersession of an incapacity benefit (IB) decision, or appeal against it (see Chapters 43 and 44).

If you are appealing a question that relates to whether you are incapable of work under the personal capability assessment, your appeal will be heard by an appeal tribunal, which must include at least one medically qualified and one legally qualified person.[92] The chair of the tribunal may refer you for a medical examination if this is necessary to help the tribunal decide whether you are incapable of work.[93] See p787 for advice on appeals about your incapacity for work. If you make a fresh claim for IB while waiting for your appeal to be decided, the decision on that claim can be revised on the basis of the appeal tribunal's eventual decision.[94]

Certain decisions are not open to appeal although you can request that they be revised or superseded (see p1221).

9. Tax, tax credits and other benefits

Apart from the lower rate of short-term incapacity benefit (IB), which is tax free, IB is taxable.[95] Your benefit is not taxable if you were receiving invalidity benefit on 12 April 1995 and you are in receipt of transitional long-term IB (see p279). You also do not have to pay tax on an increase in your IB paid for a child dependant.

Tax credits

In addition to IB you may qualify for child tax credit (CTC – see Chapter 49) if you have at least one dependent child. If your partner works, or if you are receiving the lower rate of short-term IB and were in full-time paid work (see Chapter 51) immediately before your IB began, you may qualify for working tax credit (WTC – see Chapter 50). However, the higher rate of short-term IB and long-term IB count in full as income for CTC and WTC (unless it is transitional long-term IB, see p280, which is ignored). The lower rate of short-term IB is also ignored when calculating your entitlement to CTC and WTC.[96]

If your partner works and you pay for childcare, your entitlement to the higher rate of short-term or long-term IB can help you qualify for a childcare element with WTC (see p1360).

Your past entitlement to IB may help you to qualify for WTC if you now work for at least 16 hours a week and may qualify you for the disability element and, if you or your partner are at least 50, the 50-plus element of WTC (see pp1355 and 1358 for details).[97]

You normally cannot qualify for CTC for a young person who is receiving IB in her/his own right (see p1320). Therefore, if a backdated payment of IB is made to a young person for a period when CTC was being paid for her/him, an overpayment of CTC may arise.

Means-tested benefits

If you have a low income, in addition to IB you may be entitled to income support if you are under 60 (IS – see Chapter 13), or pension credit if you are 60 or over (PC – see Chapter 18). You may also be entitled to housing benefit (HB – see Chapter 10) and council tax benefit (CTB – see Chapter 6). If you live with a partner s/he may be entitled to income-based jobseeker's allowance (JSA – see Chapter 15). If you are a member of a 'joint-claim couple' for JSA (see p394) you will not be required to be available for work, to actively seek work or to enter into a jobseeker's agreement if you are incapable of work, or treated as incapable of work. IB counts in full as income for all these benefits (less any tax payable on it) although it is not treated as qualifying income for the savings credit of PC.

If you are receiving IB at the long-term rate (or if your IB is paid at a rate equivalent to the long-term rate because you are terminally ill) and are under 60 you qualify for a disability premium for IS, income-based JSA, HB and CTB (see p886). Your entitlement to long-term IB (or to IB which is paid at a rate equivalent to the long-term rate because you are terminally ill) can also qualify your partner for a higher pensioner premium within her/his income-based JSA (if either of you is 60 or over) or IS (if you are 60 or over but s/he is not). In some circumstances, if you are entitled to IB, certain childcare costs may be deducted from your partner's earnings and/or from your own earnings, if you have any, when calculating your entitlement to HB and CTB (see p965). In some cases your earnings and any WTC and CTC you or your partner receive can be added together before applying this deduction.

Certain IB claimants in pilot areas may be entitled to a 52-week return to work credit if they stop claiming IB and start working for 16 hours or more a week (see p285). You may be able to claim an extended payment of HB and CTB if your entitlement to IB stops because you either start work, your hours of work increase or your earnings go up (see p63).

Non-means-tested benefits

IB is affected by the overlapping benefit rules, which means that you may not qualify for IB in full if another earnings replacement benefit is paid to you (see p1102).

Statutory sick pay

You cannot receive IB if you are receiving statutory sick pay (SSP).[98] But, as long as:

- your period of entitlement to SSP ended not more than 57 days before your current period of incapacity for work; *and*
- you would have satisfied the contribution conditions for IB (see p844),

any week during which you received a whole week's SSP counts as seven days of short-term IB for the purpose of satisfying the qualifying periods for long-term, and the higher rate of short-term, IB if you claim IB after your SSP ends.[99]

Odd days of entitlement to SSP are also taken into account.[100]

Days on which you receive SSP can also count towards the 196 days for which you must be incapable of work in order to qualify for IB on the grounds of your incapacity for work in youth (see p267) .

Statutory adoption pay and statutory maternity pay

Days within the maternity pay period (see p574) and the adoption pay period can count towards the qualifying period for long-term, or the higher rate of short-term, IB (see p274).

If you are entitled to statutory maternity pay (SMP) or statutory adoption pay (SAP) and either the higher short-term rate of IB or long-term IB, your IB will be reduced by the gross amount of SMP or SAP to which you are entitled. If you are only entitled to the lower short-term rate of IB you will not qualify for IB while you are entitled to SMP or SAP.[101]

Jobseeker's allowance

You cannot normally qualify for JSA and IB at the same time. This is because you must be capable of work to qualify for JSA (although short periods of sickness can be ignored – see p352) and incapable of work to qualify for IB.[102]

A period of incapacity for work can sometimes link two or more 'jobseeking periods' – ie, periods during which you are entitled to JSA (see p348). This can be advantageous – eg, if you are getting JSA then become too ill to work but claim JSA again as soon as you get better, you do not have to serve another three waiting days (see p377) before you are paid JSA. On the other hand, it can be disadvantageous. For example, the linking rules can prevent a fresh period of six months' entitlement to contribution-based JSA from arising. For detailed advice, see Chapter 15.

If a decision maker decides that you are no longer entitled to IB, perhaps because s/he considers you are capable of work, you will often not receive notification of this until after the date your entitlement ends. So that you do not lose out in these circumstances, you may be able to get your JSA backdated for up to a month (see p1088).

Retirement pension

You cannot receive IB if you are receiving Category A retirement pension or Category B retirement pension as a widow or widower.

Short-term IB is paid at a higher rate after you reach pension age. However, if your retirement pension, had you claimed it, would have been reduced because your national insurance contribution record is incomplete, your short-term IB is reduced by the same proportion.

If you are terminally ill or you are getting the highest rate of disability living allowance (DLA) care component (see p137) you receive the equivalent of the long-term rate of IB after the first 196 days of incapacity for work, if this is more than the amount you would receive otherwise.[103]

If you received the age-related addition to long-term IB at any point during the eight weeks before you reach pension age, an equivalent amount is added to your retirement pension.[104]

The circumstances in which it may be advisable to remain on short-term IB rather than claim your retirement pension are:

- if you have sufficient income from other sources to pay income tax during the first six months of your entitlement to short-term IB when, unlike retirement pensions, IB is not taxable; *or*
- if you are not entitled to a full-rate retirement pension and you are terminally ill or getting the highest rate of DLA care component, if the amount of IB paid after 196 days would be higher than the rate of retirement pension to which you are entitled.

Passports and other sources of help

If you are on a low income, you might be entitled to certain health service benefits, such as free prescriptions (see Chapter 9). You may also qualify for other sources of help (see Chapter 1) or a social fund payment (see Chapters 21 and 22). If you are getting IS or your partner gets income-based JSA or, in some circumstances, CTC, your children will qualify for free school meals (see p18).

Certain IB claimants may also qualify for a job grant on starting work (see p66).

Notes

1. **Who can claim incapacity benefit**

1 s30A SSCBA 1992
2 Sch 12 para 1 SSCBA 1992
3 s30C(2) SSCBA 1992
4 Reg 5(1) SS(IB) Regs
5 Reg 5(2) SS(IB) Regs
6 Reg 4 SS(IB) Regs
7 s171ZP(1) and Sch 13 para 1 SSCBA 1992; regs 7A and 7B SS(IB) Regs
8 Reg 4(1)(a)(iv) SS(IB) Regs
9 s30C(1)(b) SSCBA 1992
10 Reg 6 SS(IB) Regs
11 Reg 13 SS(IFW) Regs
12 s30C(1)(c) SSCBA 1992
13 *CAO v Astle* [1999] 6 Journal of Social Security Law, Issue 4
14 s30C(5), (5A) and (5B) SSCBA 1992
15 s30C(6) SSCBA 1992
16 s30C(6) SSCBA 1992; reg 3 SS(IB) Regs
17 s30A(1)(b)and (2A) SSCBA 1992
18 Reg 4A SS(IB) Regs
19 s30A(2A)(c) SSCBA 1992
20 Letter from DSS 15 February 2001. The rules themselves are not clear.
21 Reg 15 SS(IB) Regs
22 Reg 15(5) SS(IB) Regs
23 Reg 15(5) SS(IB) Regs
24 Reg 15(4) SS(IB) Regs
25 Reg 17(2) SS(IB) Regs
26 Reg 17(3) SS(IB) Regs
27 R(S) 2/87
28 Reg 18 SS(IB) Regs
29 s30A(3) SSCBA 1992; reg 2 SSCBA 1992 (Modifications for Her Majesty's Forces and Incapacity Benefit) Regulations 2003, SI 2003 No.737; reg 7C SS(IB) Regs
30 Sch 12 para 4 SSCBA 1992
31 s171E SSCBA 1992; reg 18 SS(IFW) Regs
32 R(S) 2/53

2. **The rules about your age**

33 s30A(5) SSCBA 1992
34 s30A(2)(b) SSCBA 1992
35 Sch 24 para 14 CPA 2004

3. **Claiming for others**
36 s86A SSCBA 1992; reg 9 SS(IB-ID) Regs
37 Reg 19(2) and (3) SS(C&P) Regs
38 Regs 2 and 3 Social Security (Jobcentre Plus Interviews for Partners) Regulations 2003, SI 2003 No.1886

4. **The amount of benefit**
39 s30B(4) SSCBA 1992
40 s30D(4) SSCBA 1992
41 s30D SSCBA 1992; reg 3 SSCBA 1992 (Modifications for Her Majesty's Forces and Incapacity Benefit) Regulations 2003, SI 2003 No.737; reg 7C SS(IB) Regs
42 Regs 7A and 7B SS(IB) Regs
43 s30D(3) SSCBA 1992; reg 7 SS(IB) Regs
44 s30B(3) SSCBA 1992
45 s30B(4) SSCBA 1992
46 s30E SSCBA 1992; regs 8 and 9 SS(IB) Regs
47 s30B(7) SSCBA 1992; regs 10 and 11 SS(IB) Regs
48 Regs 12 and 13 SS(IB) Regs
49 s46(3) Pension Schemes Act 1993
50 s30DD SSCBA 1992; CIB/65/2004
51 s30DD(5) SSCBA 1992; regs 20 and 21 SS(IB) Regs
52 CIB/638/2003
53 Reg 21 SS(IB) Regs
54 Reg 26 SS(IB) Regs
55 Reg 6 SS(IB)MA Regs

5. **Special rules for special groups**
56 s40 SSCBA 1992
57 s40(5) SSCBA 1992
58 s41 SSCBA 1992
59 ss40(6) and 41(5) SSCBA 1992
60 Sch 5 para 6 GRA 2004
61 Reg 17(1) SS(IB)(T) Regs
62 Regs 11 and 14 SS(IB)(T) Regs
63 Reg 25 SS(IB)(T) Regs
64 Regs 17B, 21 and 24 SS(IB)(T) Regs

6. **Claims and backdating**
65 s1 SSAA 1992
66 Social Security (Incapacity Benefit Work-focused Interviews) Regulations 2003 No.2439; Social Security (Working Neighbourhoods) Regulations 2004 No.959. See CPAG's *Welfare Rights Bulletin* 177, p7 and 180, p5 for details
67 Reg 4(1) SS(C&P) Regs
68 Reg 7(1) SS(C&P) Regs
69 Regs 2 and 5 SS(ME) Regs
70 s19 SSA 1998
71 Reg 6(1) SS(C&P) Regs
72 R(SB) 8/89; CIB/2805/2003
73 Regs 4(7) and 6(1) SS(C&P) Regs
74 Reg 10(1) and (2) SS(C&P) Regs
75 Reg 9 and Sch 1 Part I SS(C&P) Regs
76 Reg 13 SS(C&P) Regs
77 Reg 19(1)and sch 4 SS(C&P) Regs; CIB/2805/2003
78 Reg 6(23) and (24) SS(C&P) Regs
79 See *Welfare Rights Bulletin* 175 p7 for details

7. **Getting paid**
80 Reg 21 SS(C&P) Regs
81 Reg 24(2)(b) SS(C&P) Regs
82 Reg 24(2)(a) SS(C&P) Regs
83 Reg 24(3) SS(C&P) Regs
84 Reg 24(3A) SS(C&P) Regs
85 Reg 20A(2) SS(C&P) Regs
86 Reg 17 SS&CS(DA) Regs
87 Reg 32(1B) SS(C&P) Regs
88 Reg 17 SS(C&P) Regs
89 Reg 7(11) SS&CS(DA) Regs
90 Reg 7(10) SS&CS(DA) Regs
91 s10(5) SSA 1998; reg 7(2)(c)(ii) SS&CS(DA) Regs

8. **Challenging an incapacity benefit decision**
92 Reg 36 SS&CS(DA) Regs
93 s20 SSA 1998; reg 41 SS&CS(DA) Regs
94 Reg 3(5A) SS&CS(DA) Regs

9. **Tax, tax credits and other benefits**
95 ss660-664 and 676 Income Tax (Earnings and Pensions) Act 2003
96 Reg 7 TC(DCI) Regs
97 Regs 9 and 18 WTC(EMR) Regs
98 Sch 12 para 1 SSCBA 1992
99 s30D(3) SSCBA 1992; reg 7 SS(IB) Regs
100 Reg 7(2)(b) SS(IB) Regs
101 s171ZP(1) and Sch 13 para 1 SSCBA 1992; regs 7A and 7B SS(IB) Regs
102 Reg 55 JSA Regs
103 s30B(3) and (4) SSCBA 1992
104 s47(1) SSCBA 1992

Chapter 13
Income support

This chapter covers:

Income support (IS) is a benefit for people with a low income. It is not paid to unemployed people who have to be available for and actively seeking work. They may be able to claim jobseeker's allowance instead (see Chapter 15). IS is not paid to people in full-time paid work (see p750), who may be able to claim working tax credit (see Chapter 50).

Whether or not you are in full-time paid work, you may be able to claim child tax credit (see Chapter 49).

You do not have to have paid national insurance contributions to qualify for IS.

In some situations, while you are on IS you are credited with Class 1 national insurance contributions. See p837 for further details. You might instead be entitled to 'home responsibilities protection' (see p842).

1. Who can claim income support

You qualify for income support (IS) if:[1]

- you fit into one of the groups of people who can claim IS (see p294);
- neither you nor your partner count as in full-time paid work (see p298 and Chapter 29). You can claim if you are temporarily away from full-time work – eg, you are sick or on unpaid 'parental leave' or paternity leave (see p296). If you have just started full-time paid work, you might be able to get 'mortgage interest run-on' (see p62);

- you are not studying full time. There are exceptions to this rule (see p624). See p619 if you are at school or college. See p627 if you are studying part time;
- you are not getting contribution-based jobseeker's allowance (JSA) and neither you nor your partner are getting income-based JSA (either individually or as a 'joint-claim couple' see p394). See Chapter 15 for further information about JSA;
- your partner is not getting pension credit (PC – see Chapter 18);
- you are at least 16 and are under 60. If you are 60 or over, you can claim PC instead;
- your income is less than your applicable amount (see p303);
- your savings and other capital are worth £8,000 or less (£12,000 if your partner is 60 or over; £16,000 if you live in a care home – see p1024). Some capital (in particular, your home) is ignored (see Chapter 39); *and*
- you satisfy the 'habitual residence test' and are present in Great Britain. To find out if you are exempt from the habitual residence test, see p702. To see if you can claim IS during a temporary absence abroad, see p688.

There are some groups of claimants to whom special rules apply (see p305). In addition, if you do not satisfy the normal rules for IS, you may be able to get an urgent cases payment of IS (see p299).

If you are 16 or 17 and have been looked after by a local authority in England or Wales on or after 1 October 2001, you usually cannot claim IS. Instead, your local authority should support and accommodate you. See p713 for further information and for exceptions to this rule. Similar rules apply in Scotland if you cease to be looked after by a local authority on or after 1 April 2004 (see p714).

In some cases, you (or your partner if you have one) might be required to attend a work-focused interview. See pp299 and 1092 for further information.

Groups of people who can claim income support

You can claim IS if you satisfy the other rules for getting IS described above and fit into one of the groups described below.[2] If you fit into one of the groups on any day in a benefit week, you count as doing so for the whole week.

Age[3]

- On 6 October 1996, or at any time in the previous eight weeks you were getting IS; *and*
  - you were aged at least 50; *and*
  - you had not been in full-time paid work (see p750) for 10 years and were not required to sign on as available for and actively seeking work during that period (or would not have been required to sign on had you claimed IS); *and*
  - you had no prospect of getting full-time paid work.

If you stop claiming IS for up to eight weeks you can still qualify under this rule when you claim again, so long as you do not do full-time paid work (see p750) during this period.

Bereaved people[4]

- On 9 April 2001, you were aged at least 55 but under 60; *and*
  - you are claiming IS as a single person; *and*
  - your late spouse died on or after 9 April 2001.

Sick and disabled people[5]

- You are incapable of work because of illness or disability and you:
  - are entitled to statutory sick pay (see Chapter 24); *or*
  - satisfy the 'own occupation test' (see p771) or the 'personal capability assessment' for incapacity benefit (IB – see p772); *or*
  - are treated as incapable of work by a decision maker, for example because you suffer from a severe condition or have an infectious disease or are blind (see p765); *or*
  - are treated as capable of work because you are disqualified from receiving IB due to misconduct or failure to accept treatment (see p272).

  If you have been claiming JSA (see Chapter 15) and are only likely to be sick for a short time, you do not necessarily have to claim IS. When you are sick for less than two weeks, you can sometimes continue to claim JSA even though you are incapable of work (see p352).
- You are appealing a decision that you are not entitled to a benefit (eg, IS or IB) because you are not treated as incapable of work under:
  - the own occupation test – see p771 (if you continue to send in medical certificates during the period of your appeal); *or*
  - the personal capability assessment – see p772 (but you might be paid at a reduced rate – see below).

  You *must appeal* to fit into this group of people who can get IS.[6] You must appeal against the decision refusing you benefit or national insurance credits, not the determination that says you are fit for work. You can get IS until your appeal has been finally determined.[7]

  You do *not* come within this group of people who can claim IS if:
  - you simply ask for a revision (see p1189); *or*
  - you are appealing any other type of decision about your incapacity for work – eg, where you are treated as capable of work because you failed to attend a medical without good cause (see p784).

  If you are in these situations, you cannot get IS unless you come within any of the other groups of people who can claim described in this chapter.
- You are mentally or physically disabled and because of this your earnings or the number of hours you work are reduced to 75 per cent or less of that for a person without your disability in the same or a comparable job.

- You are registered blind (certified blind in Scotland). If you regain your sight you continue to be treated as blind for 28 weeks after you have been taken off the register.
- You work while living in a care home (see p758).

Reduced rate IS if you are appealing about the personal capability assessment

If you are claiming IS while appealing about the personal capability assessment and you do not come within any of the other groups of people who can claim IS described in this chapter, you are given a 'benefit penalty'.[8] Your IS is reduced by 20 per cent of the personal allowance for a single claimant of your age (see p879).

If you are given a benefit penalty, you may be better off signing on and claiming JSA (see p790 for more information about claiming JSA in this situation). Your claim for JSA should not influence the decision on your appeal about your incapacity for work.

If your appeal is successful, any reduction in the amount of your benefit, for example because you lost the disability premium (see p886), must be repaid to you.

People with childcare responsibilities and carers[9]

- You are a lone parent who is responsible for a child under 16 (see p301) who lives in your household (see p301).[10] Once your only or youngest child turns 16, you cannot claim IS unless you fit into one of the other groups of people who can claim.
- You are entitled to and on leave from work to look after your child(ren) – called 'parental leave';[11] *and*
  - during the period for which you are claiming IS, you are not entitled to a payment of any kind from your employer; *and*
  - you and your child(ren) live in the same household (see p301); *and*
  - you were entitled to working tax credit (WTC), child tax credit (CTC) payable at a higher rate than the family element, housing benefit (HB) or council tax benefit (CTB) on the day before your parental leave began.
- You are entitled to and on paternity leave;[12] *and*
  - you are not entitled to statutory paternity pay (see p565) or to a payment of any kind from your employer during the period for which you are claiming IS; *or*
  - you were entitled to WTC, CTC payable at a higher rate than the family element, HB or CTB on the day before your paternity leave began.
- You are fostering a child under 16 through a local authority or voluntary organisation and are not a member of a couple (see p811).
- You are looking after a child under 16 because the parent or the person who usually looks after her/him is temporarily away or ill.[13]
- You are responsible for a child under 16 (see p301) who lives in your household (see p301) and your partner is temporarily out of the UK.

- You are pregnant; *and*
  - incapable of work because of your pregnancy. You only have to show that you are incapable of work, not that there is a serious risk to your health or that of your baby;[14] *or*
  - there are 11 weeks or less before the week your baby is due.
- You had a baby not more than 15 weeks ago.
- You are looking after your partner, or a child under 19 for whom you are responsible (see p301) and who lives in your household (see p301), who is temporarily ill.
- You are a carer; *and*:
  - receive carer's allowance (CA) (see Chapter 4), or would receive it had it not been restricted under the 'loss of benefit for benefit offences' rules (see p1169); *or*
  - the person for whom you care receives attendance allowance (AA) or the highest or middle rate care component of disability living allowance (DLA) (see Chapter 7); *or*
  - the person for whom you care has been awarded AA or the highest or middle rate care component of DLA on an advance claim but it has not yet gone into payment; *or*
  - the person for whom you care has claimed AA or DLA. You are entitled to IS for up to 26 weeks from the date of the claim for AA/DLA or until the claim is decided, whichever comes first.

  You must be 'regularly and substantially engaged' in providing care. For CA, this means for at least 35 hours a week. However, to qualify for IS if you do not receive CA, the decision maker must look at the quality and quantity of care you provide. This could be less than 35 hours a week.[15]

  If you cease meeting these conditions or stop being a carer, you can continue to claim IS for a further eight weeks. After that, you cannot get IS unless you fit into one of the other groups of people who can claim described in this chapter.

Pupils, students and people on training courses[16]

- You are a person in 'relevant education' who can qualify for IS (see p618).
- You are a student who can claim IS (see p624).
- You are aged 16 to 24 and on a training course being provided by the Learning and Skills Council for England, the National Council for Education and Training for Wales, or in Scotland, by a Local Enterprise Company.

  You receive a training allowance while on a course. In many cases this means that your income is too high for you to qualify for IS. However, you are likely to qualify for IS if you:
  - are a 16-year-old on a lower rate of training allowance;
  - qualify for a disability premium (see p886);
  - have to live away from home (see p880); *or*
  - are aged 18 or over.

Some participants in training schemes have the legal status of employees (and are normally given contracts of employment). If you are an employee, you do not qualify for IS if you are in full-time paid work (see p750). You might qualify for WTC instead (see Chapter 50).

Others[17]

- You have to go to court as a JP, juror, witness or party to the proceedings.
- You have been remanded in custody, or committed in custody but only until your trial or until you have been sentenced (see p729). You can only get IS for your housing costs (see Chapter 36). If you pay rent, you may qualify for HB (see p193) and if you pay council tax, you may qualify for CTB (see p112).
- You have been accepted by the Home Office as a refugee (but only from the date of your claim for asylum to the date the decision was made on this — see p669).
- You are a refugee who is learning English in order to obtain employment. You must be on a course for more than 15 hours a week and, at the time the course started, you must have been in Britain for a year or less. You can get IS for up to nine months.
- You are subject to immigration control but you are entitled to the urgent cases rate of IS (see p664).
- You are not treated as in full-time work because you qualify for mortgage interest run-on (see pp62 and 758).
- You are involved in a trade dispute or have been back to work for 15 days or less following a trade dispute (see p735).

Full-time paid work

You cannot usually get IS if you or your partner are in full-time paid work. If you are the one claiming IS, this means working 16 hours or more each week. For your partner it means 24 hours or more each week. If you both work less than this, you can get IS. In some situations you are treated as *not* in full-time work even if you work more than 16/24 hours (see p757). See p752 for details of how your hours are calculated and p752 for what counts as paid work.

If you or your partner normally work 16/24 hours or more but are off sick or on maternity, paternity or adoption leave you do not count as in full-time paid work.[18] You may therefore be able to claim IS if you fit into one of the groups of people who can claim. You might also qualify for WTC (see Chapter 50).

If you work less than 16 hours and your partner works at least 16 hours but less than 24 hours each week, you or your partner might be able to claim WTC. In some cases, you might be able to claim both WTC and IS. See p759 for further information. You should seek advice to see how you would be better off financially.

If your partner is 60 or over and either of you are working 16/24 hours or more each week, your partner might be able to claim pension credit (PC – see Chapter

18) or WTC (or both if your income is low enough). There is no full-time paid work rule for PC but earnings are taken into account when working out how much PC you can get.

If you have just started full-time paid work, you might be able to claim bonuses. See Chapter 3 for further information.

Remember, if you are claiming IS because you are incapable of work (see p295), you should consult the DWP *before* you do any work, even if this is for less than 16/24 hours or the work is unpaid. If you work, you might be treated as capable of work. If this happens, you cannot claim IS unless you fit into one of the other groups of people who can claim described in this chapter. See p765 for further information about work you may do while you are incapable of work.

Work-focused interviews

In some situations when you claim IS, you (or your partner) might be asked to attend a work-focused interview. **You** might be required to attend a work-focused interview if:

- you are a lone parent or live in a ONE or Jobcentre Plus scheme area. If you fail to do so without good cause:
  - when you first claim IS, you might not count as making a valid claim (see p1097);
  - when you are already getting IS, you might be paid IS at a reduced rate (see p1097);
- you live in a 'Pathways to Work' pilot scheme area, are aged at least 18 and are claiming IS because you are incapable of work or because you are appealing a decision about whether you satisfy the 'own occupation test' or the 'personal capability assessment' (see p295). If you fail to do so without good cause, your IS might be paid at a reduced rate (see p1095).

If you have a partner, and you and your partner are both 18 or over but under 60, **your partner** might be required to attend a work-focused interview. If s/he fails to do so without good cause, your IS might be paid at a reduced rate (see p1094).

Urgent cases payments

'Urgent cases payments' are payments of IS at a reduced rate (see p664). You may be able to get these if:[19]

- you are a person subject to immigration control and meet certain conditions; *or*
- you are treated as possessing income which was due to be paid to you but which has not been paid (see p985). The income you are treated as possessing must not be readily available to you and the decision maker must be satisfied that if you do not get an urgent cases payment, you, your partner or any child(ren) for whom you are responsible (see p301) and who live in your

household (see p301) will suffer hardship.[20] If you were due to receive a *benefit* but it has not been paid you are *not* treated as possessing it.

Urgent cases payments are calculated in a special way (see p664). An urgent cases payment is a payment of IS, so you are automatically eligible for other benefits (see p315). Even if your partner is entitled to ordinary IS you can claim urgent cases payments instead if the amount you receive would be higher. You do not have to make a separate claim for urgent cases payments.[21]

2. The rules about your age

You must be at least 16 to qualify for income support (IS). Some special rules apply if you are aged 16 or 17 (see p305). If you are 16 or 17 and do not qualify for IS, check if you qualify for jobseeker's allowance (JSA) instead (see p382). Even if you cannot get IS or JSA you may qualify for housing benefit and council tax benefit (see Chapters 10 and 6).

You cannot claim IS if you are 60 or over. Instead, you can claim pension credit (PC). See Chapter 18 for further information.

3. Claiming for others

You claim income support (IS) for yourself and your partner, if you have one. See p811 for who counts as a couple. If you do not fit into one of the groups of people who can claim IS (see p294) but your partner does, s/he could be the claimant. Whichever one of you claims IS, the other should seek advice about how to protect her/his national insurance record. See Chapter 33 for more details about national insurance credits. If you and your partner are both 18 or over but under 60, even if you are not the claimant you might be required to attend a work-focused interview (see p1094).

Children

New rules from 6 April 2004

From 6 April 2004, if you make a new claim for IS you do not claim for your children. Instead you claim child tax credit (CTC). If you were already claiming IS on 6 April 2004, but have not yet claimed CTC, you continue to get allowances and premiums for your children until you are transferred onto CTC. See p818 for further information about the transitional rules.

There are some situations when you must show that you are 'responsible' for a child who is living in your household – eg, you may need to show that you are a lone parent in order to fit into one of the groups of people who can claim IS.

To count as responsible for a child, you do not have to be the child's parent.[22] You can count as responsible for any child under 16. You can also count as responsible for any young person under 19 if s/he is still in full-time 'relevant' education (see p618 for what this means). We refer to these young people as 'children' in this *Handbook*.

Note: certain 16/17-year-olds who have left local authority care do not count as your children (see p713).

Responsibility for a child

You are treated as 'responsible' for a child if you get child benefit for the child (see Chapter 5).[23] Where no one gets child benefit you count as 'responsible' if you are the only one who has applied for it. Otherwise, you count as 'responsible' if you are the person with whom the child 'usually lives'. Where a child for whom you are 'responsible' gets child benefit for another child, you also count as 'responsible' for that child.[24]

It is essential to look first at who gets or has applied for child benefit, and only where this is not decisive is it relevant to look at where the child usually lives. This means that in some situations one parent may count as responsible for a child for IS purposes while the other parent can claim HB or CTB for the same child at the same time. See p818 for the different rules for HB and CTB.

The rules say that for

IS purposes, a child can only be the responsibility of one person in any week.[25] However, if you share actual responsibility for the child (eg, you share responsibility with your ex-partner) and are a 'substantial minority carer' (ie, you have the child with you for at least 104 nights a year), then following a recent court decision it may be arguable that you should be regarded as responsible for the child even if you do not get child benefit.[26] Seek advice and see CPAG's *Welfare Rights Bulletin* for updates.

See p302 for when a child stops counting as a child.

Living in the same household

If you count as responsible for a child, then that child is usually treated as a member of your household despite any temporary absence (see below). For the meaning of household, see p812.

However, a child does *not* count as a member of your household, even if s/he is staying with you, if s/he:[27]

- is being fostered by you under a specific statutory provision. However, a child counts as a member of your household if you are fostering privately or where the social services department has made a less formal arrangement for the child to live with you;

- is living with you in order to attend school, but you do not count as responsible for her/him;
- is living with you prior to adoption, and has been placed with you by social services or an adoption agency.

In addition, a child does not count as a member of your household, even if s/he normally does, if s/he:[28]

- is boarded out or has been placed with someone else prior to adoption;
- is in the care of, or being looked after by, the local authority and not living with you. The child should count as a member of your household on the days when s/he comes home – eg, for the weekend or a holiday;[29]
- has been in hospital or a local authority home for more than 12 weeks, and you or other members of your household have not been in regular contact with her/him. The 12 weeks run from the date s/he went into the hospital or home, or from the date you claim IS, if later.[30] However, if you were entitled to income-based jobseeker's allowance (JSA) immediately before your claim for IS, the 12 weeks run from the date s/he went into the hospital or home;[31]
- is in custody on remand or serving a sentence. The child should count as a member of your household on the days when s/he comes home – eg, for the weekend or on leave;[32]
- has been abroad for more than four weeks, or for more than eight weeks if the absence abroad is to get medical treatment for the child.[33] The four- or eight-week periods run from the day s/he went abroad or from the day you claim IS, if later. However, if you were entitled to income-based JSA immediately before your claim for IS, the four- or eight-week periods are calculated from the day after the child went abroad.[34]

Temporary absence from home

Your child continues to count as a member of your household while s/he is temporarily away from home, unless s/he:[35]

- has no intention of resuming living with you; *or*
- is likely to be away for more than 52 weeks (or s/he is unlikely to be away for substantially more than 52 weeks and there are exceptional circumstances).

Remember that in some situations a child *cannot* count as a member of your household while s/he is away from home, even if the absence is temporary (see above).

When someone stops counting as a child

Someone continues to count as a child until s/he is 16 (or 19 if s/he is in 'relevant education' – see p618). Children who have left school count as in relevant education until the 'terminal date' (see p89). **Note:** this does not apply in any

week where the child does full-time paid work.[36] **'Full-time'** paid work for these purposes means at least 24 hours a week.

A 16/17-year-old who has left school or college may continue to count as a child for a few months after the terminal date – what is known as the 'child benefit extension period' (see p88 for details and dates).

Some 16/17-year-olds can get IS or income-based JSA in their own right (see p305) and they cannot count as your child.[37]

4. The amount of benefit

Income support (IS) tops up your income to a level set by the government that changes every April. The amount you get depends on your needs – this is called your 'applicable amount' – and on how much income and capital you have.[38] For the rules on income see Chapter 38, and on capital, Chapter 39. There are three steps involved in working out your IS (see below).

You might get a reduced amount of IS if:

- you are unwilling to apply for child support maintenance or to provide information to the Child Support Agency that is needed to make a maintenance assessment (see p854). If you come under the 'new rules' this includes refusing to submit to a DNA test; *or*
- you are claiming IS while appealing a decision of the DWP which says that you are capable of work under the personal capability assessment (see p296). This does not apply if you fit into one of the other groups of people who can claim IS (see p294); *or*
- you are getting an urgent cases payment of IS (see p299); *or*
- you are someone who was required to attend a work-focused interview and failed to do so without good cause (see p1092); *or*
- you have a partner, you are both 18 or over but under 60 and your partner has failed to attend a work-focused interview without good cause (see p1094); *or*
- a court has decided that you failed to comply with a community order without a reasonable excuse (see p1117); *or*
- your IS has been restricted under the 'loss of benefit for benefit offences' rules (see p1169).

Step one: calculate your applicable amount

Your applicable amount consists of:

- **a personal allowance** (see p878); *plus*
- **premiums** (see p882) for any special needs; *plus*
- **housing costs**, principally for mortgage interest payments (see Chapter 36).

Personal allowances and premiums are increased every April. If you do not qualify for IS currently, you might qualify when the rates go up.

If you have children

It is important to remember that if you claim IS from 6 April 2004 it does not include allowances and premiums for your children. Instead you should claim child tax credit (CTC – see Chapter 49). CTC does not count as income for IS, nor does child benefit.

If you were getting IS on 5 April 2004 and this included allowances and premiums for your children but you were not yet entitled to CTC, you will be transferred onto CTC. The DWP says this will happen sometime in 2005. See p819 for further information.

Step two: calculate your income

This is the amount you have coming in each week from other benefits, part-time earnings, tax credits, maintenance, etc (see Chapter 38). If you have capital over £3,000 (£6,000 if your partner is 60 or over; £10,000 if you live in a care home) it also includes your tariff income (see p977).

Step three: deduct income from applicable amount

Example

Mr and Mrs Hughes, aged 27 and 29, have a daughter aged 8. Mr Hughes has been incapable of work for two years. He gets long-term incapacity benefit (IB) of £76.45. Mrs Hughes gets child benefit and CTC. The couple have no housing costs to be covered by IS.

Their applicable amount is:

£88.15	Personal allowance
£23.95	Disability premium
£112.10	Total

Their income to be taken into account is £76.45 (IB). Child benefit and CTC are ignored.

Their IS is £112.10 (applicable amount) minus £76.45 (income) = £35.65.

If your income is too high for you to qualify for IS currently, you might qualify once you or a member of your family become entitled to another benefit (a 'qualifying benefit'). You should make your claim for IS at the same time as your claim for the qualifying benefit (see p1090).

Different rules for calculating your benefit apply if you are:

- in hospital (p715);
- a prisoner (p729);
- a person without accommodation (p734);
- aged 16 or 17 (p879);
- affected by a trade dispute (p735).

People who are members of, and fully maintained by, a religious order do not get any IS at all.

5. Special rules for special groups

There are some groups of claimants to whom special rules apply. These are covered below and in Chapters 25, 26 and 28. Special rules apply to:

- 16/17-year-olds (see below);
- people subject to immigration control (see p653);
- people without accommodation (see p734);
- people involved in a trade dispute (see p735);
- people in hospital (see p715); *and*
- prisoners (see p729).

16/17-year-olds

If you are 16 or 17 you are entitled to income support (IS) in your own right if you satisfy the normal rules of entitlement described in this chapter.[39] You must fit within one of the groups of people who can claim IS listed on pp294– 298.[40] You should not have your claim refused or be turned away by the DWP simply because of your age.

However, you should remember the following:

- If you have been looked after by a local authority in England or Wales on or after 1 October 2001, you usually cannot claim IS. Instead, your local authority should support and accommodate you. See p714 for exceptions to the rules. Similar rules apply in Scotland if you cease to be looked after by a local authority on or after 1 April 2004 (see p713).
- If you count as in 'relevant education', you are only entitled to IS in specified circumstances (see p619).[41] If you are in or have recently left non-advanced education and so count as a child and are living with someone who counts as responsible for you, s/he might be able to claim child tax credit (CTC) for you (see Chapter 49). If you count as someone's child for IS or income-based jobseeker's allowance (JSA) purposes and s/he is claiming, you cannot claim IS yourself.[42]
- Your IS personal allowance depends on your (and your partner's) age and circumstances (see p879).
- In certain circumstances, you may satisfy the rules for both IS and income-based JSA,[43] but you cannot claim both.[44] It is usually better to claim IS to avoid the requirement to be available for and actively seeking work and training and the attendant risk of benefit sanctions (see Chapter 16). You can still look for work if you want to. If you claim IS rather than JSA, however, you might not receive national insurance credits (see Chapter 33 for information about credits).
- You should check to see if you are entitled to any of the other benefits in this *Handbook*. If you are, you could qualify for a higher amount of IS. See p11 for some ideas about what you might be able to claim.

If you are not entitled to IS, you may be entitled to income-based JSA if you satisfy the special rules which apply to 16/17-year-olds (see p381) . If you are not entitled to IS or JSA, you can claim discretionary payments of JSA if you would otherwise suffer severe hardship (see p384) .

6. Claims and backdating

You should claim income support (IS) as soon as you think you might be entitled, or you might lose benefit. The rules about claiming and backdating are in Chapter 39. This section tells you about the specific rules that apply to IS.

You might be required to attend a work-focused interview as a condition of getting IS if:

- you are a lone parent (see p1096); *or*
- you are at least 18 and are claiming IS because you are incapable of work or are appealing a decision about your incapacity (see p295) and you live in a 'Pathways to Work' pilot scheme area (see p1095); *or*
- you live in a ONE scheme or Jobcentre Plus area (see p307).

If you have a partner and you are both 18 or over but under 60, your partner might be required to attend a work-focused interview. If s/he fails to do so without good cause, your IS might be paid at a reduced rate (see p1094).

If you do not live with your child(ren)'s other parent, you might be required to apply for child support maintenance and provide information to the Child Support Agency that is needed to make a maintenance assessment (see p854).

Making a claim

To be entitled to IS, you must normally make a claim.[45] This must be in writing and on the appropriate form which is free of charge.[46] If you are a self-employed contractor this is Form B16. In all other cases, this is Form A1. Unless you live in a JobCentre Plus area, the DWP sends you a claim form if you telephone your local office, write a letter, have someone contact it on your behalf, or send in the wrong form. If you live in a JobCentre Plus area, see below.

Forms are available from your local DWP office as well as the DWP website (see Appendix 1). They are often also available at your local CAB, welfare rights service or advice centre. If you download a claim form or get one from, for example, an advice centre, it is still important to telephone your local DWP office to let them know you want to claim IS. If you do not, you might lose benefit. Be ready to give the DWP your national insurance number. However you get your form, you should complete it and return it to your local office within one month of your initial contact. See p309 for further information about your date of claim.

Keep a copy of your completed claim form in case queries arise. If you want to withdraw or amend your claim, notify the DWP office before it makes its decision.[47]

If you are claiming IS within 12 weeks of a previous claim, you might be given a shortened claim form. This is known as 'rapid re-claim'.

If you qualify for mortgage interest run-on (see p62) you do not have to make a claim.

You have to make a separate claim to your local authority for **housing benefit (HB)** and for **council tax benefit (CTB)**. You are given a claim form with your IS claim form (or it is available on the DWP website – see Appendix 1). If you are claiming IS in a JobCentre Plus area, your claim for HB and CTB is made via what the DWP calls an 'input document'. If you are making a 'rapid re-claim' for IS, you may also be able to make a 'rapid re-claim' for HB and CTB. See pp216 and 120 for further information about claiming HB and CTB.

If you or your partner are required to attend a **work-focused interview**, an appointment is arranged to see a personal adviser at the local JobCentre (or ONE scheme/Jobcentre Plus office). See p1097 for further information. If you fail to attend your interview without good cause, you might not count as making a valid IS claim. If your partner fails to attend an interview without good cause, your IS might be paid at a reduced rate.

JobCentre Plus areas

If you live in a Jobcentre Plus area, then in practice you are usually required to start your claim by telephoning a 'contact centre'. Your local Jobcentre Plus office has this number, and it may also be displayed in local advice centres, libraries, etc. The contact centre takes basic details, then calls you back to go through the details of your claim. Also, the date of an initial work-focused interview (see p1092) is set, unless it is agreed that you do not need to attend one. You are then sent a statement recording those details, which you are asked to sign, and details of the evidence and information you should bring with you to the interview. The signed statement of details forms your official claim, instead of the old-style claim form.

It is best for you to start your claim in this way if you can. However, if you cannot or do not want to use the telephone to start your claim, then Jobcentre Plus say that they can still deal with your claim in other ways. You might, for example, be invited for a 'face-to-face' interview to gather the relevant details, or in some cases they may accept an old-style claim form. Seek advice if you are unable to use a telephone and the Jobcentre Plus office will not let you start your claim in any other way.

Information to support your claim

When you claim IS, you must satisfy the national insurance (NI) number requirement. In most cases this means you must provide your NI number as well as your partner's. See p1083 for further details. You may also be asked to provide proof of your identity (see p1083) and information to support your claim (see below). If you are asked to provide information which you do not have, ask what other evidence would be accepted. Press the DWP to be clear about what is required and why, and complain if you feel that any requests for information are unreasonable (see p1300).

You must usually claim on the first day you want your benefit to start. See p309 for more information about your date of claim and p1085 for when your claim can be backdated.

Providing information with your claim

It is very important that you provide any information or evidence required on the claim form – known as the 'evidence requirement'. Until you do, you may not count as having made a valid claim and you could lose benefit.[48] See p1080 for further information about the evidence requirement and to see if you are exempt from this requirement.

On the IS claim form you are currently asked for:

- payslips;
- proof of your income. You should provide proof of any money you have coming in that is not being paid to you by the DWP, for example, child tax credit, statutory sick pay, statutory maternity pay, a work pension, war widow's pension, maintenance payments, student grants or loans and training allowances;
- proof of savings over £2,500;
- proof of any payments from a credit insurance policy;
- proof of any pension you have told the DWP about;
- proof of any war widows pension;
- details of any payments you received on ceasing work – eg, redundancy payments, lump-sum payments or holiday pay;
- proof of the service charges and ground rent you pay;
- if you or your partner are an asylum seeker, proof of any application made.

If you are claiming IS because you are incapable of work and do not have an employer or are not already getting incapacity benefit or severe disablement allowance, you are usually asked to complete an SC1 form (an IB(Y)1 form if you became incapable of work in youth – see p267). Return this with your IS claim. The DWP might try to say your claim is not valid if you fail to do so. If this happens, you should seek advice.

If you have a mortgage, you are given Form MI12 to give to your lender, who will provide details about your mortgage and return the form to the DWP.

If it is not possible to assess your housing costs (see Chapter 36) accurately or your entitlement to the severe disability premium (see p891) the decision maker can exclude these from your IS until they can be calculated.[49]

Information and evidence you must supply after you claim

Even if you have provided all that is required (see above), a decision maker might need additional evidence or information to enable her/him to make a decision about your claim. You can be asked to supply any certificates, documents, information or evidence considered relevant to your claim or to an issue arising from your claim.[50] If your partner is 60 or over, this includes details of any personal pension scheme or retirement annuity contract which you or your partner have taken out.[51]

You must provide the information or evidence within one month of the request. A decision maker can allow you longer than this if s/he thinks it is reasonable. The one-month time limit runs from the date of the decision maker's request for the additional information, *not* the date you made your IS claim. In some cases, if you fail to provide information when required to do so, your IS could be suspended or even terminated (see p1106).

Who should claim

If you are a single person or a lone parent you claim on your own behalf. If you are one of a couple you must choose which one of you claims for you both. See p811 for who counts as a couple. If you are a member of a couple claiming backdated IS after one of you is awarded refugee status (see p669), the claim must be made by the refugee.[52] Where you have a choice about who can claim and you cannot agree, a decision maker decides.[53]

You can change which partner claims, provided the partner previously claiming is agreeable.[54] It can be worth swapping who claims, for example, if:

- it would entitle you to a disability premium (see p886);
- one of you is about to go abroad or otherwise lose entitlement – eg, become a student;
- one of you fits into one of the groups of people who can claim IS but not the other (see p294). However, you should both seek advice about how to protect your NI record;
- one of you is working less than 16 hours a week and the other is working between 16 and 24 hours a week (see p750 for what counts as full-time paid work). In this case, you and your partner might also be able to claim working tax credit (WTC – see p759). However, you should seek advice to see how you would be better off financially.

If you cannot make your claim yourself – eg, you are mentally ill or suffering from dementia, an 'appointee' (see p1075) can claim on your behalf.

The date of your claim

You are usually not entitled to IS for any day before your 'date of claim'.[55] However, in some cases you can claim in advance before you qualify (see p310) and sometimes your date of claim can be backdated (see p311). If you want this to be done you should make this clear when you claim or the DWP might not consider it.

Your **'date of claim'** is usually the earliest of:[56]

- the date you first contact a benefit office (eg, you ask to claim IS by telephone or letter) or someone does this on your behalf so long as a fully completed form and all the information and evidence required (see p307) are provided within one month; *or*
- the date your fully completed claim form and all the information and evidence required (see p307) are received in the benefit office.

Something counts as being received in the benefit office even if it arrives on a day on which the office is closed.[57] If you send something by post it should be accepted as having been delivered unless it is proved not to have been. However, you have to persuade the DWP that you did post it.[58] If your local DWP office has a 'bulk surcharge account' with the Post Office but the Post Office retains your claim because you sent it with insufficient postage, it counts as being received by the benefit office on the day it would have been delivered.[59]

If you claim the wrong benefit

If you claim WTC (see Chapter 50) when you should have claimed IS, the day you claimed WTC counts as your date of claim for IS. However, you must:[60]

- have been refused WTC because neither you nor your partner are in full-time paid work for WTC purposes (see Chapter 51); *and*
- claim IS within 14 days of the decision refusing your claim.

You can ask for your IS claim to start on a later date, for example, where you have just finished work and have earnings that will be taken into account for a certain period of time (see p942).

If you claim IS when you should have claimed carer's allowance (CA – see Chapter 4), a decision maker can treat your IS claim as a claim for CA.[61] This could help you qualify for backdated carer's premium (see p896).

Claiming in advance

You can claim IS up to three months before you qualify,[62] thus giving the DWP time to ensure you receive benefit as soon as you are entitled. This can be useful if you know you are going to qualify – eg, you are due to come out of hospital or a care home. In this case, your date of claim (see p310) is the date from which you are claiming.[63]

You should let the DWP know you want to claim in advance when you claim. You might have to persuade the DWP that it can accept a claim in advance.

You might not be entitled to IS currently, but would be once you or a member of your family become entitled to another 'qualifying benefit', for example, disability living allowance or CA (see Chapters 7 and 4). In this case, you should also make a claim in advance. You should make your claim for IS at the same time as the claim for the qualifying benefit. If you are refused IS:

- claim again when you get a decision about the qualifying benefit; *and*
- ask for your IS to be backdated to the date of your first IS claim or to the date from which the qualifying benefit is paid, if that is later. See p1090 for further information.

Note: if you are entitled to IS even before the qualifying benefit is awarded, you might be entitled to a higher rate once the outcome of the claim for the qualifying benefit is known. In this case, your award can be revised or superseded. See p1209 for further information.

How your claim is dealt with

Claims are dealt with by your local DWP or Jobcentre Plus office (in some cases, this is your local JobCentre). London claimants may have their claims dealt with by benefit centres set up to deal with work which does not require face-to-face contact with claimants. The benefit centres decide your claim. You should still use your branch office if you want to hand your claim in personally or speak to someone face-to-face.

It is very unlikely that you will get an immediate decision on your claim because the facts need to be checked and your benefit calculated. If you think it is taking too long to deal with your claim, see p313.

Backdating your claim

It is very important to claim in time. A claim for IS can be backdated for a maximum of three months but only in exceptional circumstances. See p1085 for the general rules on backdating. There are exceptions to the rule. Your claim can be backdated more than three months if:

- you are claiming backdated IS after being awarded a qualifying benefit and an earlier IS claim had been refused because you did not at that time get a qualifying benefit (see p1090);[64]
- you are claiming backdated IS after you are awarded refugee status (see p669);
- you claimed WTC when you should have claimed IS (see p310).

If you might have qualified for benefit earlier but did not claim because you were given the wrong information by the DWP or because you were misled by it you could:

- ask for an ex gratia payment (see p1304); *or*
- complain to the Ombudsman (see p1303).

7. Getting paid

You can be paid income support (IS) by direct payment into your bank (or similar) account (see p1099).[65] In some cases, you may instead be paid by cheque.[66] It may be possible to be paid in cash in some circumstances.[67] Payment can also be made to someone else on your behalf, called your 'appointee' (see p1075). In some circumstances part of your IS can be deducted and paid to other people and organisations on your behalf (see p1109). You can indicate which method of payment you prefer when you claim IS, although a decision maker decides how IS is paid.

IS is a weekly benefit. However, if you are only entitled to IS for part of a week, you are only paid for the part week.[68]

If you are entitled to less than 10 pence a week you are not paid IS at all, unless you are receiving another social security benefit which can be paid with IS.[69] If you are entitled to less than £1 a week a decision maker can decide to pay you quarterly in arrears.[70] If your IS includes a fraction of a penny it is rounded up to a full penny if it is half a penny or more. Otherwise the fraction is ignored.[71]

You are paid in advance if you are:[72]

- receiving widows' or bereavement benefits (but only if you are not providing or required to provide medical evidence of incapacity for work); *or*
- returning to work after a trade dispute .

If you are paid in advance, your entitlement to IS usually begins on the first payday of any widows' or bereavement benefit to which you are entitled (or would be entitled if you had sufficient national insurance contributions) following the date of your claim for IS. For example, widowed parent's allowance is paid on a Tuesday. If you claim IS on a Wednesday you are entitled to IS in advance from the following Tuesday. But if you claim on a Tuesday, you get it from that day.

You are paid in arrears if you are not in one of the above groups, although your entitlement to IS usually starts from the date of your claim (see p310).[73] You might be able to get a crisis loan to tide you over while you are waiting to be paid your IS (see p538).

Once your entitlement has been worked out, a decision maker decides how often and on what day you are paid unless you are entitled to incapacity benefit (IB), severe disablement allowance, or widows' or bereavement benefits.[74] If you are entitled to one of these (or would be if you satisfied the contribution conditions), you are paid IS on the same day of the week as that other benefit and at the same intervals.[75] If you are incapable of work and not getting IB you are paid fortnightly in arrears.[76]

If your cheque is lost or stolen or you have forgotten your PIN, see p1104. If payment of your IS is suspended, see p1105.

Delays and complaints

If payment of your IS is delayed, you might be able to get an interim payment (see p1108 for further details). You may be able to get a crisis loan from the social fund to tide you over until your benefit is paid (see p538).

If you suffer delays, or wish to complain about how your claim has been dealt with, see p1300. You might be able to claim compensation (see p1304).

Change of circumstances

It is your duty to report any change in your circumstances which might affect your right to or the amount of your IS or payment of your benefit. You should do this promptly in writing or by telephone to the office handling your claim (although in individual cases notification might be accepted in a form other than in writing or by telephone). In some cases, however, the decision maker might say you must report changes in writing. In any case, you might want to report the change in writing and keep a copy in case of a dispute in the future.

If you do not report any such change promptly, any resulting overpayment may be recoverable from you (see Chapter 41). If you are considered deliberately to have acted falsely or dishonestly, you may also be guilty of an offence (see Chapter 42). A change of circumstances could mean that you qualify for more IS or less IS or even that you are no longer entitled.

The DWP can ask your mortgage lender about any changes to the amount you owe or the interest payable during your claim. If you have this information (eg, from an annual statement you receive from your lender) you must also advise the DWP just in case your lender fails to do so. Make sure the DWP takes this information into account so you are not overpaid IS (see p1141).

When there has been a relevant change of circumstances (see p1200), a decision maker looks at your claim again and makes a new decision, called a 'supersession' (see p1199). Your IS is then adjusted from the date this new decision takes effect. When this is depends on whether the new decision is to your advantage, and whether you reported the change in time. See p1204 for further information about when a supersession takes effect.

When your income support is adjusted

As a general rule, your IS is adjusted as follows:[77]

- If you are paid IS in arrears, your IS is adjusted from the beginning of the week in which the change of circumstances takes effect (see p1204).
- If you are paid IS in advance, your IS is adjusted from the date the change of circumstances takes effect if this is the day you are paid benefit. If it is not, your IS is adjusted from the next week.

There are exceptions to the rules above.

- If a decision is to your advantage, but you failed to notify the DWP of a change within the time limit (see p1204), your IS is adjusted:[78]
  - if you are paid in arrears, from the beginning of the week in which you notified the change; *or*
  - if you are paid in advance, from the day on which you notified the change, if this is the day you are paid benefit. If it is not, your IS is adjusted from the next week.
- Your IS is adjusted from the date of the change of circumstances (or the day on which this is expected to take place) if:[79]
  - you are paid IS in arrears and the change of circumstances means you no longer qualify for IS. However, the ordinary rule (see above) applies if the reason you no longer qualify is that your income is too high;
  - a child or young person (see p300) only stays with you for part of the week and the rest of the week is in care or in custody;
  - your IS has been reduced because you, your partner or a child for whom you are responsible (see p300) have been in hospital for a period (see p715) and the change of circumstances is that the person who has been in hospital is coming home for less than a week;
  - you are going into or coming out of prison (see p729);
  - the change is that you or your partner are no longer treated as being involved in a trade dispute because you are incapable of work or in your maternity period (see p736);
  - you claim IB or bereavement benefits and, as a result, the day of the week you are paid benefit changes (see p312).
- Where you have income that is counted as paid on a particular day (see p991) and this changes (or such a change is expected), your IS is adjusted from the day the income counts as being paid.[80]
- Where a decision has been made that you failed to take part in a work-focused interview without 'good cause' (see p1097), your IS is adjusted from the week after that decision.[81]

If a change of circumstances means the amount of your IS should go down but the decision maker certifies that it is not practical to adjust your IS on the days outlined above, your IS is adjusted from the beginning of the week following the week in which the new decision is made (or in which the change is expected to occur if this has not yet happened).[82] This does not apply where the change is that you have claimed IB or bereavement benefits or where there is a change in income which counts as paid on a particular day.

Overpayments and fraud

If you are overpaid IS, you might have to repay it. The rules on overpayments are covered in Chapter 41.

If you have been accused of fraud, see Chapter 42. You might get a reduced amount of IS if you have been sanctioned for benefit offences (see p1170).

8. Challenging an income support decision

You can apply for a revision or supersession of an income support decision, or appeal against it (see Chapters 42 and 43).

9. Tax, tax credits and other benefits

Income support (IS) is not taxable except where you are involved in a trade dispute and you are claiming it in respect of your partner.

Tax credits

If you work less than 16 hours a week and your partner works at least 16 hours but less than 24 hours a week, you and your partner might be able to claim working tax credit. See p759 for further information. However, before deciding which to claim you should seek advice to see how you would be better off financially.

Whether or not you are in work, you might be able to claim child tax credit (CTC). CTC is not taken into account as income in working out your IS.

Means-tested benefits

If you pay rent or council tax you may be entitled to housing benefit (HB – see Chapter 10) and council tax benefit (CTB – see Chapter 6), as well as IS.

You might be able to choose whether to claim IS or income-based jobseeker's allowance. If you have a partner and s/he is 60 or over, s/he might be able to claim pension credit for you instead of you claiming IS. See p410 for further information.

Non-means-tested benefits

The non-means-tested benefits (see p5) in this *Handbook* (other than attendance allowance (AA), disability living allowance (DLA), guardian's allowance and, if you are getting CTC, child benefit) are taken into account as income when working out the amount of IS you get (see p303). However, it can still be worth claiming these benefits. If you or your partner qualify for certain non-means-tested benefits (including AA and DLA) you also qualify for certain premiums (see p882) and therefore a higher rate of IS. To find out which benefits help you qualify for:

- disability premium, see p886;
- enhanced disability premium, see p888;

- higher pensioner premium, see p890;
- severe disability premium, see p891;
- carer's premium, see p896.

If you think you might qualify you should seek advice to see if you would be better off .

Note: if your IS still includes allowances and premiums for your child(ren), you may also be entitled to a disabled child or enhanced disability premium if your child qualifies for DLA.

Example

Gloria is a lone parent aged 36. She has one child, aged 13. She gets child benefit and CTC. She spends a lot of her time caring for her disabled Aunt Lydia who lives with her. Aunt Lydia is claiming AA.

Claiming as a lone parent, Gloria's IS applicable amount (see Chapter 34) is:

£56.20	Personal allowance
£56.20	Total

She has no income to be taken into account. Child benefit and CTC are ignored.

Her IS is £56.20.

If Gloria qualifies for carer's allowance because she cares for Aunt Lydia (see Chapter 4), her IS applicable amount is:

£56.20	Personal allowance
£25.85	Carer premium
£82.05	Total

Her income to be taken into account is £45.70 carer's allowance. Child benefit and CTC are ignored.

Her IS is £82.05 (applicable amount) minus £45.70 (income) = £36.35. However, the combination of IS and carer's allowance is £82.05.

You might only qualify for IS once you or a member of your family are awarded another benefit, known as a 'qualifying benefit'. To make sure you do not lose out while awaiting the outcome of a claim for a qualifying benefit, claim IS at the same time. If your IS claim is refused, once the qualifying benefit is awarded claim IS again and ask for it to be backdated to the date of your first claim. See p1090 for details.

Passports and other sources of help

If you are entitled to IS you also qualify for:

- health benefits such as free prescriptions (see Chapter 9); *and*
- education benefits such as free school meals (see p18).

You may also qualify for social fund payments (see Chapters 21 and 22).

Bonuses

If you stop getting IS because you or your partner start work or your earnings or hours in your existing job increase, you might be able to get:

- child maintenance bonus;
- mortgage interest run-on, if you have a home loan;
- extended payments of HB or CTB, if you pay rent or council tax;
- job grant.

See Chapter 3 for further information about the bonuses you can claim. **Note:** if you accrued one by 25 October 2004, you may also be able to claim a back-to-work bonus.

Notes

1. **Who can claim income support**
 1 s124 SSCBA 1992
 2 Reg 4ZA and Sch 1B IS Regs
 3 Sch 1B para 16 IS Regs
 4 Sch 1B para 16A IS Regs
 5 Sch 1B paras 7-9, 13 and 24-27 IS Regs
 6 CIS/1614/2004
 7 CIS/2654/1999
 8 Reg 22A IS Regs
 9 Sch 1B paras 1-6, 14, 14A, 14B and 23 IS Regs
 10 CIS/2260/2002
 11 The rules on parental leave are in Part III Maternity and Parental Leave etc. Regulations 1999, SI 1999 No.3312
 12 The rules on paternity leave are in Part 2 Paternity and Adoption Regulations 2002, SI 2002 No.2788
 13 CIS/866/2004
 14 CIS/0542/2001
 15 R(IS) 8/02
 16 Sch 1B paras 10-12, 15 and 28 IS Regs
 17 Sch 1B paras 9A, 18-22 IS Regs
 18 Reg 5(3A) IS Regs
 19 Reg 70(2) IS Regs
 20 Reg 70(4) IS Regs
 21 para 31350 DMG

3. **Claiming for others**
 22 s137(1) SSCBA 1992; reg 14 IS Regs
 23 Reg 15(1) IS Regs
 24 Reg 15(1A) IS Regs
 25 s134(2) SSCBA 1992; reg 15(4) IS Regs
 26 *Hockenjos v Secretary of State for Social Security* [2004] EWCA Civ 1749, 21 December 2004, unreported. This applies only to JSA; however, it may support arguments concerning IS based on the Human Rights Act.
 27 Reg 16(4) and (7) IS Regs
 28 Reg 16(5) IS Regs
 29 Regs 15(3) and 16(6) IS Regs
 30 Reg 16(5)(b) IS Regs
 31 Reg 16(5A) IS Regs
 32 Regs 15(3) and 16(6) IS Regs
 33 Reg 16(5)(a) and (aa) IS Regs
 34 Reg 16(5A) IS Regs
 35 Reg 16(1) and (2) IS Regs
 36 Regs 1(2), definition of 'remunerative work' and 7(2) CB Regs
 37 s134(2) SSCBA 1992

4. **The amount of benefit**
 38 s124(4) SSCBA 1992

5. **Special rules for special groups**
 39 s124(1)(a) SSCBA 1992
 40 s124(1)(e) SSCBA 1992; Sch 1B IS Regs
 41 s124(1)(d) SSCBA 1992; reg 13 IS Regs
 42 s134(2) SSCBA 1992

43 Reg 61(1)(c) JSA Regs
44 s124(1)(f) SSCBA 1992; s3(1)(b) JSA 1995

6. Claims and backdating

45 s1 SSAA 1992
46 Reg 4(1A) and (5) SS(C&P) Regs
47 Reg 5(2) SS(C&P) Regs
48 Regs 4(1A) and (9) and 6(1A) SS(C&P) Regs
49 Reg 13 SS&CS(DA) Regs
50 Reg 7 SS(C&P) Regs
51 Reg 7(4) and (5) SS(C&P) Regs
52 Reg 4(3C) SS(C&P) Regs
53 Reg 4(3) SS(C&P) Regs
54 Reg 4(4) SS(C&P) Regs
55 Reg 19(1) and Sch 4 para 6 SS(C&P) Regs
56 Reg 6(1A) SS(C&P) Regs
57 R(SB) 8/89
58 CIS/759/1992
59 CIS/4901/2002
60 Reg 6(28) SS(C&P) Regs
61 Reg 9(1) and Sch 1 SS(C&P) Regs
62 Reg 13(1) SS(C&P) Regs
63 Reg 6(1A) SS(C&P) Regs
64 Reg 6(16)-(18) SS(C&P) Regs

7. Getting paid

65 Reg 21 SS(C&P) Regs
66 Reg 20 SS(C&P) Regs
67 para 5039 IS Guide (payments volume)
68 s124(5) and (6) SSCBA 1992; reg 73 IS Regs
69 Reg 26(4) SS(C&P) Regs
70 Sch 7 para 5 SS(C&P) Regs
71 Reg 28 SS(C&P) Regs
72 Reg 26(1) and Sch 7 paras 2, 3 and 6(2) SS(C&P) Regs
73 Sch 7 paras 1, 3 and 6(1) SS(C&P) Regs
74 Sch 7 para 3(2) SS(C&P) Regs
75 Sch 7 para 3(1) SS(C&P) Regs
76 Sch 7 para 3(1A) SS(C&P) Regs
77 Reg 7and Sch 3A para 1 SS&CS(DA) Regs
78 Reg 7(2)(b) SS&CS(DA) Regs
79 Sch 3A paras 2 and 3 SS&CS(DA) Regs
80 Sch 3A para 4 SS&CS(DA) Regs
81 Reg 7(25) SS&CS(DA) Regs
82 Sch 3A para 5 SS&CS(DA) Regs

Chapter 14

Industrial injuries benefits

This chapter covers:

Industrial injuries benefits are paid if you were disabled as a result of an accident at work or a disease caused by your job. The main benefit is **disablement benefit** (see p331). You may also qualify for **reduced earnings allowance** (see p334) or **retirement allowance** (see p338).

You do not have to have paid national insurance contributions to get industrial injuries benefits.

1. Who can get industrial injuries benefits

For all industrial injuries benefits (except industrial death benefit) you must satisfy the **'industrial injury condition'**, that is:[1]

- you have suffered a 'personal injury' in an 'industrial accident' (see p321) or you are suffering from a 'prescribed industrial disease' (see p325); *and*
- at the time of the injury you are an employed earner (see p320); *and*
- as a result of that accident or disease you have suffered a 'loss of faculty' (see p327); *and*
- as a result of that 'loss of faculty' you are 'disabled'.

You are not covered by the scheme if your disability is caused by an industrial accident which happened before, or by a disease the onset of which was before, 5 July 1948. However, you may still be able to claim allowances under either the Workman's Compensation (Supplementation) Scheme 1982 or the Pneumoconiosis, Byssinosis and Miscellaneous Diseases Scheme 1983. See leaflets WS1 and PN1, available from the Department for Work and Pensions (DWP).

You can only qualify for reduced earnings allowance (REA – see p334) and retirement allowance (see p338) if your accident or disease occurred before October 1990.

For information about industrial death benefit, which would only be relevant if your spouse died before April 1988, see the 17th edition of CPAG's *Rights Guide to Non-Means-Tested Benefits*.

If you have been injured by your work, you may also have the right to sue your employer. Legal help (formerly legal aid) may be available and you may be able to get a free consultation with a solicitor under the ALAS scheme. Your right to compensation from your employer is separate from your rights to benefit under the industrial injuries scheme (although your compensation may be reduced if you have received benefits from the DWP – see p1119).

Employed earners

You can claim industrial injuries benefits only if you were an 'employed earner' whose accident or disease was caused by your employed earner's employment.[2] You are an employed earner if you are gainfully employed under a contract of service. This means that there is some obligation by an employer to pay you remuneration as an employee for tasks that you are bound to perform for the employer under the contract of employment.[3] Therefore, if you are self-employed you are excluded from the scheme, as are most trainees on government training schemes.

Entitlement to industrial injuries benefits is not dependent on you having paid national insurance contributions. However, payment of contributions is a way of deciding whether or not you are an employed earner.

If you pay, or ought to pay, Class 1 contributions (see p831) as an employed earner you can qualify for industrial injuries benefits. This includes those paying Class 1 (and, in the case of volunteer development workers, Class 2 – see p833) contributions while abroad.[4] You can qualify if your earnings are too low to pay contributions; mostly this is because of part-time work but can also apply to those who are too young to pay contributions. Finally, you are also treated as being an employed earner if you are an apprentice, mine inspector or rescue worker, special constable, taxi driver, office cleaner, agency worker, minister of religion, lecturer, member of an aircrew, mariner, or in some situations an offshore oil or gas worker.[5]

You are treated as *not* being an employed earner if:[6]

- you are employed by your spouse and either your employment is not for the purpose of her/his employment or your earnings are normally below the lower earnings limit (see p827). So a man employed by his wife to help run her shop, and earning less than £82 a week (the current lower earnings limit), is not an employed earner; *or*

- you are employed by a close relative (parent, step-parent, grandparent, son, daughter, step-child, grandchild, brother, sister, half-brother or half-sister) in a private house where you both live, and your employment is not for your relative's trade or business carried out there; *or*
- you are a member of visiting armed forces, or a civilian employed by them, unless you are normally resident in the UK.

Personal injury

Personal injury includes the obvious, such as broken legs or arms,[7] but also covers the less obvious, such as strains and psychological injury.[8] So an assault at work causing slight physical injury might give a far greater injury to the mind by causing agoraphobia or a breakdown. In difficult cases, the question is whether or not you have suffered a physiological or psychological change for the worse. It is not enough just to suffer pain if the pain is merely a symptom of an existing condition and does not make that condition substantially worse.[9] The damage must be to you or part of you. Dislocation of an artificial hip joint counts as a personal injury,[10] but damage to a pair of spectacles[11] or an artificial leg[12] does not.

Accident

The term **'accident'** has been defined as an 'unlooked-for occurrence' or 'mishap'.[13] However, an accident need only be unexpected from the worker's point of view. It does not matter that it could have been anticipated by an expert.[14] If you do a heavy or dangerous job where accidents are common, a resulting injury is just as much an accident as if your job is sedentary and comparatively safe. If your heavy lifting causes a heart attack, it is the heart attack which is the accident, not the heavy lifting.[15] Deliberate acts by third parties can be accidents – eg, assaults on security workers or on staff in shops and hospitals.[16] However, if you start a fight at work and injure your hand punching somebody, that is not an industrial accident.

An accident will be 'industrial' if you can show a connection with your work. For accidents this connection factor is established if the accident arose 'out of and in the course of your employment'.[17] It is important to realise that despite the name, it is not only industrial workers who can suffer from 'industrial accidents' all employees can suffer 'industrial accidents'. For example, if you are an office worker and a badly loaded filing cabinet tilts and falls on you, that would count as an 'industrial accident'. The term 'industrial accident' conjures up images of a very dramatic event, but any accident sustained while you are doing your job can qualify – eg, spilling a hot drink and scalding yourself can be an industrial accident. In one decision a commissioner found that an illness brought on by conversation can count as being caused by an industrial accident.[18]

Accident or process

One of the most difficult problems is to distinguish between an 'accident', for which benefit is payable, and a 'process', for which it is not (unless it causes a 'prescribed disease' – see p325). Clearly, to fall from a ladder and break your leg is an 'accident'. Equally clearly, to work for many years as a heavy manual worker and have a sore back is a cumulative 'process'.[19] However, sometimes a series of events, over a period of time, can be viewed as an 'accident' for the purposes of the benefit.[20] The cumulative effect of a series of incidents can also result in an accident.[21] Furthermore, you should not be excluded from entitlement to benefit simply because you cannot identify which of the incidents caused the injury.[22]

Example

Cyril's job is trimming excess rubber from hot water bottles with a pair of scissors. A particularly hard batch of rubber comes through and each cut requires greater strength. Over two or three days he suffers a strain injury in his hand. The series of cuts constitutes a series of 'accidents' that meets the definition.

It is easier to establish the series of events as an accident if the period of time is fairly short,[23] or is noticed at an identifiable moment.[24] An accident is proved if you can establish that an identifiable occurrence must have happened, even if it is impossible to prove when.[25]

In the course of employment

The accident (see p321) must arise 'in the course of employment'. It has been said that:

> an accident befalls a man in the course of his employment if it occurs while he is doing what a man so employed may reasonably do within a time during which he is employed, and at a place where he may reasonably be during that time to do that thing.[26]

Difficulties arise when work rules are broken, or when you do something not directly connected with work.

Generally speaking, when you arrive at your employer's factory or shop, and are on her/his private property, you are 'in the course of your employment'. You do not have to have clocked in or have reported to your actual workplace. If you arrive early to get ready for work, or to have a meal in the works canteen,[27] you are covered, though if you arrive early to fit in a game of billiards you are not.[28] You are probably covered during breaks from working if you remain on the employer's property,[29] but probably not if you go elsewhere. So if, during a tea break, you go to a local shop to buy a snack, you are outside the course of your employment.[30] If you are allowed to have a snack either at home or at work while still on duty (such as may happen with a police officer) you are covered.[31]

While at work most activities are considered to be 'in the course of employment'.[32] Smoking,[33] chatting,[34] or passing sweets[35] are all 'reasonably incidental' to the employment, provided they are not done in breach of instructions.[36] Even if you were doing something in breach of instructions you are still covered if what you were doing was done for the purposes of, or in connection with, your employment.[37]

Example 1

Clara works as a labourer in a paper factory where there is an absolute ban on riding on the load of a forklift truck. She is seen riding on the load, falls off and is injured. Usually she would not be covered, but she saw the load was slipping and rode on the truck in order to hold it on. This was done for the purposes of her employment and so, this time, she is covered.

Example 2

Maureen is a supervisor in an office where central heating has been removed, but not replaced or the holes patched. It is cold and her staff are threatening not to work in the draught. The employer does not respond to her pleas for help. She goes onto the roof to patch the holes with papers and falls through it. She is 'in the course of employment' even though the employer would have disapproved of her activities.

Even if you are at home you may, depending on the requirements of your contract, be covered. This may even include a person on sick leave.[38]

In putting forward your claim (see p339) or arguing your case at an appeal (see Chapter 43), you should consider all aspects of your employment, including the wording of your contract and the degree of flexibility in the arrangements between you and your employer.[39]

Accidents while travelling

As more people are injured on journeys to and from work than are injured at work itself, accidents while travelling have been a source of much dispute. You are not in the course of your employment (see p322) during ordinary journeys to and from work, unless you are travelling on transport operated by or on behalf of your employer or by arrangement with your employer and not in the ordinary course of public transport service.[40]

Many employees have no set place of work – eg, lorry drivers, local authority home helps, gas and electricity company employees. Obviously a lorry driver is at work when driving her/his lorry, but gas company workers, travelling directly from home to their first job of the day are not always in the course of employment (see p322), even if driving a company van. It depends on the circumstances, including the rules for the use of the van.[41] A home help has been found to be in the course of her employment travelling between jobs, but not going to the first job or from the last. This is because she became engaged in her employment once she started at the first job and remained engaged until the end of the day.[42]

Some employees with no fixed hours of work may be regarded as covered from the moment of leaving home.[43] Recent cases have eased the rules on travelling – eg, to conferences or meetings. You must look at all the factors in a common sense way when deciding whether or not you were in the course of your employment. So a police officer who had to travel about 40 miles from home to a training course was in the course of his employment while travelling.[44] Provided you go reasonably directly, with no marked deviation from a proper route, and do not embark on activities unrelated to the journey, you may be covered.

One important factor in deciding whether you are in the course of your employment is whether you receive wages for travelling.[45] However, if you receive a flat-rate travelling allowance as compensation for having to work at a workplace other than your normal base, this may not be enough to make your journey to your alternative workplace part of your work.[46]

Out of employment

As well as arising in the course of your employment (see p322), the accident (see p321) must arise 'out of' your employment, so that it can be said that in some way the employment contributed to it. The fact that you suffered a displaced retina at work is not sufficient to show it arose 'out of' the employment, but medical evidence which shows that it was caused by sudden head movements while inspecting a production line enables you to establish that an industrial accident (see p321) took place. An unexplained fracture while walking at work is not an industrial accident,[47] but it is if you slip and the fracture occurs while you are falling onto the ground. You are covered even if you are more susceptible to injury because, for example, your bones are brittle[48] or your eyes are weak.

Example

Joe, a farm worker, suffers sudden pain in the groin while doing his normal job of digging. It is found that a previous hernia, which had been surgically repaired, has given way again. The decision maker says that this could have happened at any time and so did not arise 'out of' the employment. Joe's doctor says it could have happened at any time but probably did so at that time because of the heavy digging. A tribunal awards him benefit.

An accident also arises out of your employment if it arises in the course of employment (see p322), *and* it is caused by:[49]

- another's misconduct, skylarking or negligence; *or*
- the behaviour or presence of an animal (including a bird, fish or insect); *or*
- your being struck by any object or by lightning; *and*

- you did not directly or indirectly induce or contribute to the accident happening by your conduct outside the employment or by any act not incidental to the employment.

An accident is deemed to arise out of and in the course of your employment if you are helping people in an emergency, or trying to save property at or near where you are employed.[50] A milkman was covered when he was helping to put out a fire at a customer's home.[51]

Prescribed industrial disease

It is necessary for the disease to be a **'prescribed industrial disease'**. This means it is on a list, produced by the DWP, of diseases which are known to have a link to a particular occupation, called a 'prescribed occupation' (see below).[52] Each prescribed disease has a statutory definition and you must fit within that definition. It is not sufficient simply to have a medical diagnosis that you suffer from a particular condition.[53] From time to time new diseases are added to the list. However, you cannot claim for a disease for any period prior to it being added to the list.[54] Each prescribed industrial disease has a letter and number to identify it – eg, prescribed disease A12 is carpal tunnel syndrome and prescribed disease D1 is pneumoconiosis. The complete list is in Appendix 8. Whether or not you suffer from a prescribed industrial disease is known as the 'diagnosis question'.[55]

If the DWP accepts that you are suffering from a prescribed industrial disease, other diseases which result from it (eg, amnesia resulting from methyl bromide poisoning prescribed disease C12) are included when assessing your 'loss of faculty' and disablement.[56] See p327 for further information on how your disablement is assessed.

Prescribed occupations

Different diseases are 'prescribed' for different types of jobs because different jobs have different health risks. To qualify for benefit on grounds of a prescribed industrial disease it is not enough to be suffering from a disease which happens to be on the list. You must also prove:

- that you have worked in one or more of the jobs for which that disease is prescribed ('prescribed occupations'); *and*
- that your job caused the disease.

If the DWP refuses to accept that you have worked in a prescribed occupation you should take advice, preferably from your trade union if you have one, or from an advice agency. An expert's report may help to prove your case.

Time limits

For most prescribed diseases you do not have to have worked in a prescribed occupation for any minimum length of time. You can also claim at any time, even if it is many years since you worked in that occupation. However, there are exceptions to these general rules. If you are suffering from occupational deafness (prescribed disease A10) you have to have worked in a prescribed occupation for ten years and to claim within five years of having done so.[57] If you have occupational asthma (prescribed disease D7) you have to claim within ten years of working in a prescribed occupation.[58] If you have coal miners' chronic bronchitis or emphysema (prescribed disease D12) you have to have been working in a prescribed occupation for 20 years.[59] If you have cataracts (prescribed disease A2) you must have worked in a prescribed occupation for five years or more in aggregate.[60] Commissioners have ruled in two cases that in calculating periods of exposure, account may be made of self-employment.[61] However, from 10 July 2000 regulations specify that only periods of employment rather than self-employment can be used to calculate the relevant periods. These regulations do not apply to claims made prior to 10 October 2000.[62]

Causation

You must prove that the prescribed disease is due to your occupation, but it is normally assumed that if you suffer the disease within one month of last working in the prescribed occupation (see p325), the occupation caused the disease.[63] With carpal tunnel syndrome (prescribed disease A12) and dermatitis (prescribed disease D5) there is no such presumption. The presumption operates with slightly different time conditions for occupational deafness (prescribed disease A10), tuberculosis (prescribed disease B5), pneumoconiosis (prescribed disease D1), byssinosis (prescribed disease D2) and chronic bronchitis and emphysema (prescribed disease D12). The connection for carpal tunnel syndrome and dermatitis therefore has to be proved. The DWP investigates the connection issue, and you may need to ask your GP or consultant to help with a report linking the disease to your occupation. DWP guidance on the diagnosis of diseases is available (see Appendix 8). However, it is not necessary to prove the link beyond any reasonable doubt and to rule out all other possibilities. It is necessary only to establish the link 'on a balance of probabilities'; in other words, it is more likely than not that there is a connection.

Example

Connie, a hospital cleaner, uses a new cleaning material. A rash develops on her hands and she has to give up the job. The medical evidence shows that the cleaning material could have caused the problem but so could several things with which Connie had been in contact outside work. There is a strong argument that the cleaning material caused the rash because the rash developed so soon after using it.

Onset and recrudescence

The **'onset'** (date of starting) of a prescribed disease is taken as the date of the first day you suffered a relevant 'loss of faculty' (see below). In deafness cases it is the later of either the date you first suffered the loss of faculty or the date you successfully claimed benefit.[64]

In diseases other than deafness, asthma and respiratory conditions, you can improve and then worsen again. It is important to know whether it is a **'recrudescence'** (fresh outbreak of the existing disease) or a completely new attack. The first enables an immediate supersession;[65] with the second, you have to wait for 15 weeks before disablement benefit can be claimed. If a further attack commences during a current period of assessment, it is assumed to be a recrudescence unless the contrary is proved.

Loss of faculty and disablement

In addition to showing the link between your injury or disease and your occupation, you also need to establish that you have suffered a 'loss of faculty' and are 'disabled'.

'Loss of faculty' is the damage or impairment of part of the body or mind caused by the industrial accident or disease. **'Disability'** is the inability to do something that is caused by that damage or impairment. **'Disablement'** is the total of all of your disabilities which, taken together, amount to a disablement. This disablement is expressed as a percentage.

In assessing your disablement, there are three disablement questions:[66]

- Has the relevant industrial accident (see p321) or prescribed disease (see p325) resulted in a loss of faculty (see below)?
- What is the extent of disablement resulting from a loss of faculty (this is expressed as a percentage – see p328)?
- What period is to be taken into account by the assessment (see p331)?

These questions are decided by decision makers (see Chapter 44).

Has the relevant accident or disease resulted in a loss of faculty?

A **'loss of faculty'** is an 'impairment of the proper functioning of part of the body or mind'[67] caused by an accident or disease. A 'loss of faculty' is not the same as disablement. It includes disfigurement even if the disfigurement is not accompanied by a loss of physical faculty.[68] A decision that there has been a personal injury resulting from an industrial accident (see p321) does not itself prevent a decision maker or tribunal from finding that there is no loss of faculty, but this is rare.[69]

What is the extent of disablement?

In order to qualify for disablement benefit (see p331), generally you must reach a threshold of at least 14 per cent disablement. However, a finding of at least 1 per cent may permit a claim for reduced earnings allowance (REA – see p334).

The extent of your disablement is assessed on a percentage basis. Any assessment between 14 and 19 per cent is treated as being 20 per cent (except for those entitled to disablement gratuities).[70] If the total disablement from all industrial accidents and diseases is more than 20 per cent, it is rounded to the nearest multiple of 10 per cent with multiples of 5 per cent being rounded upwards.[71]

Some assessments of disablement are set out in regulations.[72] These are known as 'prescribed degrees of disablement' and include various amputations (eg, loss of a hand or a leg) and degrees of hearing loss (see Appendix 7). However, even in these cases the decision makers must take into account the real disablement resulting from an injury, and increase or decrease the figure to arrive at a reasonable assessment[73] – eg, the loss of a right hand is more disabling for a right-handed person than for a left-handed person. However, impaired function of the pleura, pericardium or peritoneum caused by diffuse mesothelioma automatically has an assessment of 100 per cent disablement.[74]

Apart from age, sex and physical and mental condition, the personal circumstances of a claimant must be ignored, so that particular problems you may have, like the location of your office, or the distance to the nearest bus stop, are not taken into account.

Your disablement should be assessed by comparing you to a person of the same age and sex whose physical and mental condition is normal.[75]

When there is no prescribed degree of disablement (see above), and these form the vast majority of cases, the authorities assess you on the basis of their experience but may refer to the prescribed percentages to help them decide.[76] Although you may suggest that your assessment should be a particular percentage, by analogy with the percentage figures in the regulations, those assessing your claim come to their own medical judgement.[77] One point in favour of claimants is that 100 per cent is given to people who are far from totally disabled (eg, those with no disabilities other than total deafness) and presumably other assessments should reflect this.

It is important that you are very straightforward with the examining doctor. The authorities have checks to establish that your symptoms are consistent with the injury, and that your movements are consistent with the disablement you claim you have. Therefore, how you walk into the room and how you undress are looked at as carefully as how you respond to the examination. Do make sure, though, that those who are examining you are aware of all the things that you now cannot do (your disabilities – see p327) as a result of your injury or disease.

Offsets if your disability has more than one cause

If a disability has more than one cause, the rules for assessment are complex. If a disability is congenital or arose before an industrial one, it is deducted from the total disability.[78] The reduction is often called the **'offset'**. The procedure on offsets is complex and frequently leads to disputes. Mistakes are sometimes made because the decision maker incorrectly offsets for medical conditions which were not causing any disability.

Example 1

Sam loses a hand, which would normally be 60 per cent, but he had previously lost the index finger. So 14 per cent is deducted, leaving 46 per cent (rounded up to 50 per cent).

Example 2

Sian has a back injury as a result of an industrial accident. A decision maker has reduced her assessment by 5 per cent on the grounds of a pre-existing disability of which she knew nothing. Many people have spines that are slightly curved due to lifting things. The decision maker may have looked at an X-ray, correctly considered that her curved spine was not due to the relevant accident and then incorrectly reduced her assessment.

In Example 2, what the decision maker should have done was consider whether the pre-existing loss of faculty (see p327), the curved spine, really has (or would have) led to disablement which would have occurred even if the industrial accident (see p321) had not happened. S/he should have considered, among other things, whether the loss of faculty led to disablement before the industrial accident occurred. There is no physical disablement if you do not suffer any pain or restriction of movement and it is, therefore, wrong to reduce your assessment unless there is a good reason for deciding that disablement would have arisen during the period of assessment even if the industrial accident had not occurred.

In Example 2, depending on the medical opinion:

- there might be no offset (see above); *or*
- it might be proper to make a life award (see p331) with some uniform offset over the whole period in respect of the future back problems Sian would have been likely to have; *or*
- it might be proper to make a stepped assessment, making no offset initially but bringing one in at some future date, or applying different levels of offset for different parts of the period covered by the award.[79]

No reduction is made if 100 per cent is a reasonable assessment for the industrial accident.[80]

The decision maker should also bear in mind that even if you did have a pre-existing problem which caused a disability, the accident may worsen the effects of it, as well as causing a new problem. In such a case, the assessment should reflect the increase in the original problem as well as the new disability.[81]

If another disability arose after an industrial accident then the decision maker first has to assess the disablement arising from the purely industrial injury. If it is less than 11 per cent any disability from the other cause is ignored; if it is more than 11 per cent any extra disablement caused by the effect of the industrial injury on the other disability is added.[82]

Example 3

Ali loses a little finger in an industrial accident and is assessed as 7 per cent disabled as a result. He then loses the other fingers of that hand in a non-industrial accident. He continues to be assessed as 7 per cent disabled due to the industrial accident.

Example 4

Paul loses the middle, ring and little fingers of one hand in an industrial accident and is assessed as 30 per cent disabled as a result. He then loses the index finger of that hand in a non-industrial accident. His total disablement is now 50 per cent. But loss of the index finger only would have been 14 per cent. The disablement resulting from his industrial accident may therefore be reassessed at 36 per cent (50 per cent *minus* 14 per cent) which is rounded up to 40 per cent.

Two or more industrial accidents or diseases

If you have more than one industrial accident, the percentages of disablement (see p327 and Appendix 7) can be added together and may entitle you to benefit, even if neither accident would do so on its own. If you have two or more industrial accidents you may end up in a situation where the second or later accident is made worse by the interaction with the effect of the previous accident(s). The assessment process can allow for this.[83] Your most recent assessment should include an increase for any such interaction.[84] The same would apply where an industrial disease (see p325) interacts with the effects of an industrial accident.

Example 5

Steve has a fall at work and seriously injures his left leg. He receives a life assessment of 10 per cent. Years later, he has a further fall and seriously injures the other leg. He is assessed as 10 per cent disabled for that accident, with a further 5 per cent for the extra disability he suffers as a result of the interaction between the two injuries. The total of 25 per cent is rounded up, resulting in payment of a 30 per cent pension.

There are special rules if you have pneumoconiosis. The rules allow for certain conditions to be taken into account in order to increase the assessment even though these conditions did not arise from the pneumoconiosis. Any effect of tuberculosis is assessed with the effects of the pneumoconiosis.[85] If your disability is assessed at 50 per cent due to the pneumoconiosis, any added disability due to chronic bronchitis or emphysema is added.[86] If you have made such a claim for pneumoconiosis you cannot then make an effective separate claim for chronic bronchitis or emphysema.[87]

What period is to be taken into account by the assessment?

The decision maker or appeal tribunal makes an assessment (see p328) for a period 'during which the claimant has suffered and may be expected to continue to suffer from the relevant loss of faculty'. Percentage assessments are usually made for six months or for one or two years, or are given for life,[88] but definite dates must be given.

An assessment is either final or provisional.[89] You get a provisional assessment when there is doubt as to what will happen in the future, and you are automatically called for another assessment at the end of the period.[90] Life assessments are final.

If you are given a final assessment for a fixed period this means that the authorities believe that you will no longer be affected by your accident or disease by the end of that period. If you think that the effects of the accident or disease will last for longer than that, you should consider an immediate appeal against that assessment (see p1222).

If your condition deteriorates during a period of assessment, or if you still have a disability at the end of a period for which you have been given a final assessment, you should apply for a supersession (see p1199).

An assessment of disablement for occupational deafness is for life.[91]

2. Industrial injuries disablement benefit

The main industrial injuries benefit is industrial injuries disablement benefit (IIDB). There are also a number of benefits which are paid as increases to IIDB. The most important are:

- constant attendance allowance (see p333); *and*
- exceptionally severe disablement allowance (see p333).

Who can claim industrial injuries disablement benefit

You qualify for IIDB if:[92]

- you satisfy the industrial injury condition (see p319) as a result of one or more industrial accidents (see p321) or prescribed diseases (see p325);
- your resulting disablement is assessed as being at least 14 per cent (1 per cent in the case of pneumoconiosis, byssinosis and diffuse mesothelioma) (see p328 and Appendix 7);

- 90 days (excluding Sundays) have elapsed since the date of the accident or onset of the prescribed disease or injury (those suffering from the prescribed disease of mesothelioma can be paid without serving this waiting period).

There are some groups of claimants for whom special rules apply (see p339).

Disqualification

You may be disqualified for misconduct on similar grounds as for incapacity benefit (see p272).[93]

The rules about your age

You must be old enough to be an employed earner. If you are aged under 18 you receive a lower rate of benefit.

Claiming for others

There are no dependant increases unless you are getting unemployability supplement (a benefit that was abolished for new claims after 5 April 1987).

The amount of benefit

The amount of benefit you get depends on the extent of your disablement (see p328 for how this is assessed).[94]

Extent of disablement	*Benefit per week (£) Claimant aged under 18 not entitled to an increase in respect of dependant*	*Benefit per week (£) Any other claimant*
100%	75.85	123.80
90%	68.27	111.42
80%	60.68	99.04
70%	53.10	86.66
60%	45.51	74.28
50%	37.93	61.90
40%	30.34	49.52
30%	22.76	37.14
11%–20%	15.17	24.76

Since 1 October 1986, IIDB has been paid only if the assessment of your disablement is at least 14 per cent,[95] except in the cases of pneumoconiosis, byssinosis and diffuse mesothelioma, when benefit is paid if the assessment is at least 1 per cent.[96]

Until 1 October 1986, IIDB was paid in respect of any assessment of disablement of at least 1 per cent. The old rules are still in force for assessments following claims made before that date.[97] If you are getting a payment as a result of such a small percentage assessment, see p176 of the 17th edition of CPAG's *Rights Guide to Non-Means-Tested Benefits*.

You might be able to get an increase of benefit (see below). In addition, if you are getting unemployability supplement (a benefit that was abolished for new claims after 5 April 1987) or constant attendance allowance (see p333) you are entitled to a Christmas bonus (see p68).

Increases of industrial injuries disablement benefit

You get increased IIDB if you qualify for constant attendance allowance or exceptionally severe disablement allowance.

Constant attendance allowance

You qualify for constant attendance allowance if:[98]

- you are entitled to a basic industrial injuries disablement pension based on a degree of disablement assessed at 100 per cent; *and*
- you require constant attendance as a result of the relevant loss of faculty (see p327).

Disablement as a result of pre-1948 industrial accidents and diseases, war injuries and injuries suffered while on police or fire duty, may be taken into account in considering the degree of your disablement.[99]

There are two rates:

- The **higher weekly rate** of £99.20 is paid if you are 'so exceptionally severely disabled as to be entirely, or almost entirely, dependent on (constant) attendance for the necessities of life, and [are] likely to remain so dependent for a prolonged period and the attendance so required is whole-time'.[100]
- The **lower weekly rate** of £49.60 is paid if you are 'to a substantial extent dependent on (constant) attendance for the necessities of life and [are] likely to remain so dependent for a prolonged period'. This may be increased up to £74.40 a week if 'the extent of such attendance is greater by reason of the beneficiary's exceptionally severe disablement'. If attendance is part-time only, the amount payable is 'such sum as may be reasonable in the circumstances' (usually £24.80 a week).[101] Some claimants may be better off claiming the care component of disability living allowance (see p136) or the ordinary attendance allowance instead (see p147).

Exceptionally severe disablement allowance

This is paid at the weekly rate of £49.60 if:

- you are entitled to constant attendance allowance (or would be if you were not in hospital) at a rate in excess of £49.60 a week; *and*
- you are likely to remain so permanently.[102]

3. Reduced earnings allowance

Reduced earnings allowance (REA) is available only if you had an accident or started to suffer from a disease before 1 October 1990. A successful first claim can still be made now if you had such an accident or disease before that date.

The amount of REA you get depends on whether your current earnings, or earnings in a job which it is considered you could do, are less than the current earnings in your previous 'regular occupation' (see p336).

Who can get reduced earnings allowance

You qualify for REA if:[103]

- you satisfy the industrial injury condition (see p319) due to an industrial accident (see p321) before 1 October 1990 or an industrial disease (see p325), the onset of which was before that date (see p327); *and*
- your resulting disablement is assessed as being at least 1 per cent (see p327 and Appendix 7 for how this is done); *and*
- as a result of a relevant loss of faculty *either*:
  - you are incapable and likely to remain permanently incapable of following your regular occupation (see p335) and are incapable of following employment of an equivalent standard (see p336) which is suitable in your case (the 'permanent condition' – see below); *or*
  - you are, and have been at all times since the end of the 90-day qualifying period for disablement benefit, incapable of following your regular occupation or employment of an equivalent standard (see p336) which is suitable in your case ('the continuing condition' – see p335); *and either*
- you are under pension age (but see below); *or*
- you have not given up regular employment (see p336); *and*
- you have not been in receipt of REA since 1 October 1990 and subsequently ceased to be entitled to it for at least one day (see p336).

Some claimants have been successful in claiming REA after pension age and retaining that REA rather than moving onto the lower rate of benefit in retirement allowance (see p338). This is on the basis that there is a loophole in the law that allows a person who is over pension age and claiming REA for the first time to be paid REA rather than retirement allowance.[104]

In addition to those rules of entitlement, if you were entitled to REA on either 10 April 1988 or 9 April 1989 and on that date you were over pension age and were retired, or were treated as retired, you remain entitled to the allowance for life. For the meaning of 'retired or treated as retired' in that context, see p69 of the 12th edition of CPAG's *Rights Guide to Non-Means-Tested Benefits*.

There are some groups of claimants for whom special rules apply (see p339).

Reduced earnings

Although REA compensates for loss of earnings, the fact that you are losing money as a result of an industrial accident or disease is not, in itself, enough. You must meet either the permanent, or continuing, conditions outlined below.

The permanent condition

Only incapacity at the time of your claim and in the future are relevant. The phrase 'likely to remain permanently incapable' relates only to your 'regular occupation' (see p335) and not to 'employment of an equivalent standard' (see p336). So you do not need to prove at a tribunal that you are likely to remain incapable of employment of an equivalent standard; just that you are not likely to be able to perform your normal job.

If you suffer from pneumoconiosis, and you are advised not to work by a decision maker, then you are deemed not to be able to work unless the decision maker proves otherwise.[105]

If your condition could be improved by an operation, and you refuse to have it, the decision maker may disqualify you, but only if the operation is a very minor one.[106] You have the right to refuse a more serious operation.

The continuing condition

Only incapacity at the time of your claim and in the past are relevant, so there is less scope for argument than when assessing the future. However, if you returned to work but were 'sheltered' by your workmates, you can still argue that you were 'incapable' of following your regular occupation (see below). Specific provision is made so that, if you have worked since the end of the 90-day period, but this work was approved by the Secretary of State or done on the advice of a doctor for rehabilitation, testing or training, it can be disregarded. So, also, is employment before obtaining surgical treatment, and six months of employment thereafter.[107] If you have given up work due to pneumoconiosis on the advice of a decision maker you are deemed to have been continuously incapable of following that regular occupation.[108]

Regular occupation

Deciding what your 'regular occupation' is involves looking at your work history (part time[109] as well as full time) and the content of the job, as opposed to its title. For example, a docker still employed to work as a docker but unable to earn as much because he is unable to do the full range of his duties, was found incapable of his regular occupation.[110]

If an accident happens when you have just started a new job, that job may well be treated as your regular occupation. Your intentions and prospects need to be considered.[111] But a stop-gap occupation, taken on during ill-health, would not be treated as your regular occupation.[112] If you are a full-time student, any part-time work counts as your regular occupation.[113] If your earnings are derived from several jobs you may face problems. Any employment which is subsidiary to your usual or main job does not count. If you would have been fairly sure to have been promoted by the time of your claim, but for the accident, then the promoted position may count as the regular occupation. It is possible to make a number of separate claims for REA. If you suffer a number of industrial accidents and have to downgrade your employment each time, you can be compensated for each accident. The crucial point is whether each accident has led to a change in your regular occupation.[114]

If you suffer from a prescribed disease (see p325) and, because of this, gave up a job before you applied for benefit, it may count as your regular occupation.[115]

Employment of an equivalent standard which is suitable

Employment is of an equivalent standard if the normal earnings are the same as the normal earnings in your regular occupation (see above).[116] If these earnings include a great deal of overtime, so that you have to do a lot more hours to earn the same, those overtime earnings are disregarded. It is the total earnings 'package' that matters, not how it is made up. Suitability is judged by looking at your education, experience, training, work history and general health.[117] Only employed earner's employment can be treated as suitable, so self-employed work is not considered.[118]

If your regular occupation (see above) was part time, full-time work is not of an equivalent standard even if you are medically fit to do it. Like must be compared with like. However, if there are no jobs of the same number of hours, different work for a similar number of hours may be regarded as equivalent.[119]

Regular employment

If you are over pension age, you are only entitled to REA if you are in 'regular employment'. During any period when you are not entitled to REA because you have given up 'regular employment', you receive retirement allowance instead (see p338). This is paid to you at a much lower rate.

The definition of 'regular employment' was changed with effect from 24 March 1996. **'Regular employment'** since then means working for an average of 10 hours or more a week within a period of five or more weeks of such employment.[120] This definition was imposed from 24 March 1996 with no transitional protection. This means it immediately affected those who were over pension age but not working.[121] The practical effect was as follows:

- If you were already over pension age on 24 March 1996 but not treated as being in regular employment, you were transferred to retirement allowance (see p338).
- If you reached pension age after 24 March 1996 but were not then treated as being in regular employment, you will be transferred to retirement allowance (see p338).

- If you are in regular employment now and are over pension age, or you reach pension age while you are still in regular employment, you retain REA but will be transferred to retirement allowance (see p338) as soon as you give up regular employment.

This does not apply to you if you were entitled to the allowance on 10 April 1988 or 9 April 1989 and were then already over pension age and retired. Instead, you receive REA at a 'frozen' rate (see p338).

The effects of European law

In practice, most people losing REA now do so because they reach retirement age. This is 60 for a woman, 65 for a man. Although this discriminates against women, the European Court of Justice has held it to be lawful.[122]

The rules about your age

You need to be old enough to be an employed earner. REA is paid until you reach pension age and it is then replaced with retirement allowance (see p336). If you are now over pension age but have never claimed REA even though you meet the conditions for entitlement, you do not appear to be excluded under the regulations from claiming REA. The DWP currently is making awards of REA on such claims. If you are considering making a claim for REA and you are about to reach pension age you should seek advice before delaying a claim for REA.

Claiming for others

There are no dependant increases.

The amount of benefit

The amount of REA you get is the amount by which your current earnings, or earnings in a job which it is considered you could do, are less than the current earnings in your previous regular occupation (see p335).[123] Earnings include overtime.

For most claimants this is a fairly routine calculation. However, if you are unemployed:

- the DWP's doctors are asked for your limitations;
- the DWP disability employment advisers are asked to say what job they think you could do; *and*
- the JobCentre (or ONE/Jobcentre Plus office) is asked to quote a wage which such a job would command in your area.

You should look carefully at all the elements of the calculation and assess whether the jobs quoted are realistic for you to do, whether the wages seem correct and if a proper allowance has been given for you as an individual.

Example

Alice was employed as a 'silver service' waitress, but injured her knee and cannot walk very easily. She is unemployed and there are few jobs of any description in the area for someone of her age (mid-50s) and physical restriction. She would have been earning £125 a week including tips. The disability employment adviser suggests that she could become a receptionist and quotes £90 to £110 as a range of wages. The decision maker usually takes an average and so allows her £125 – £100 = £25 a week. She argues that, given her disabilities and lack of experience, an employer would pay at the very bottom of the range. She finds adverts for jobs offering less than £90. At worst, she should be able to argue for £125 – £90 = £35 a week for at least a year or two.

Once the first assessment has been made, the amount is usually increased in line with earnings in that industry or workplace, unless that regular occupation (see p335) has ceased to exist.[124] In that case, it is calculated as rising in line with the nearest 'occupational group' as defined by the DWP. You can ask for a fresh assessment to take into account your normal prospects of advancement, though here you have to show that promotion would have happened, say at the end of a period of employment or training, not just that it may have happened if you had been particularly diligent.[125]

The maximum amount of reduced earnings allowance

The maximum amount you may receive for any one award is £49.52 a week.[126] The total you can receive by way of industrial injuries disablement benefit (IIDB) and REA (whether for one or more awards) is 140 per cent of the standard rate of IIDB – ie, £173.32 a week.[127] If you were over pension age and retired before 6 April 1987 your allowance will be reduced if it would otherwise mean that you would be receiving more than 100 per cent disablement benefit.[128]

If you qualified for REA and were retired or treated as retired on either 10 April 1988 or 9 April 1989, you continue to receive the allowance at the same 'frozen' rate. Its value, therefore, erodes over time.[129]

4. Retirement allowance

Retirement allowance is really a reduced rate of reduced earnings allowance (REA – see p334) for people over pension age.

Who can claim retirement allowance[130]

You qualify for retirement allowance if:

- you are over pension age – currently 60 for women and 65 for men;
- you have given up regular employment (see p336);

- you were entitled to REA at a rate of at least £2 a week (in total, if you had more than one award) immediately before you gave up regular employment (see p336);
- you are not entitled to REA.

There are some groups of claimants for whom special rules apply (see p339).

The rules about your age

You must be over pension age to qualify.

Claiming for others

There are no dependant increases.

The amount of benefit[131]

The amount of retirement allowance you get is £12.38 a week or 25 per cent of the amount of REA you were receiving, whichever is the lower.

5. Special rules for special groups

There are some groups of claimants to whom special rules apply. These are covered in Chapters 25, 26 and 28. Special rules apply to prisoners. Industrial injuries disablement benefit is paid for up to one year of any sentence in addition to any period on remand.[132]

6. Claims and backdating

Making a claim

A claim for benefit should usually be made on the appropriate form and returned to your local Department for Work and Pensions (DWP) office. There are a number of different claim forms depending on the benefit claimed and on the type of accident or disease. In certain circumstances, the Secretary of State may accept a written application which is not on the correct form (see p1079).[133]

You can apply for a declaration that you have had an industrial accident, even if you do not wish to claim any benefit. You do this on Form BI95, obtainable from your local DWP office. This may be wise if you have had an accident but are not sure whether you wish to proceed with a claim to benefit.[134]

Keep a copy of your claim in case queries arise.

Information to support your claim

When you claim industrial injuries benefits, you must satisfy the national insurance number requirement. In most cases this means you must provide your national insurance number as well as your partner's. See p1083 for further details.

Who should claim

You claim for yourself unless you are unable to act on your own. In such cases it may be appropriate for an appointee to make the claim (see p1075).

The date of your claim

The date of your claim is the date it is received at the appropriate DWP office.

If you claim the wrong benefit

In some circumstances, it is possible for a claim for one benefit to be treated as a claim for a different benefit (see p1084). However, for industrial injuries benefits it is only possible to 'interchange' constant attendance allowance with disability living allowance and attendance allowance. There is no right of appeal against such a refusal.

Claiming in advance

It is not possible to claim industrial injuries benefits in advance.

Renewal claims

Assessments can be provisional or final, and for a limited period or for life. A provisional assessment means that the decision maker considers that your medical condition has not yet settled down, and might get worse or better. At the end of a provisional assessment you will be invited to be re-examined. A final assessment means that the medical authorities consider that your condition has settled down and your case is dealt with once and for all. At the end of a period of award you therefore need to apply for a renewal of benefit.

If you are awarded disablement benefit for a particular disease, you may recover at some point but subsequently suffer a further attack. If there is a continuation or recrudescence of the old disease you do not have to wait 15 weeks before gaining entitlement to disablement benefit.

How your claim is dealt with

The DWP states that claims for industrial injuries benefit resulting from an accident will be processed within 70 days, and claims as a result of a prescribed diseases within 100 days.

Backdating claims

It is very important to claim in time. Your claim can be backdated for up to three months if you satisfy the qualifying conditions over that period. You do not have to show any reasons why your claim was late. The rules on backdating are covered on p1085.

If you might have qualified for benefit earlier but did not claim because you were given the wrong information or were misled by the DWP you could:

- ask for an ex gratia payment (see p1304); *or*
- complain to the Ombudsman via your MP (see p1302).

7. Getting paid

Industrial injuries benefits are weekly benefits paid in advance by credit transfer into a bank or similar account, order book or giro on a Wednesday.

Payment can also be made to someone else on your behalf – called your appointee (see p1075).

If your order book is lost or stolen, see p1104. If payment of your industrial injuries benefit is suspended, see p1105.

Delays and complaints

If payment of your industrial injuries benefit is delayed, you might be able to get an interim payment. See p1108 for further details.

If you experience delays or wish to complain about how your claim has been dealt with, see p1299. You might be able to claim compensation (see p1304).

Change of circumstances

It is your duty to report any change in your circumstances which might affect your right to, the amount of, or payment of, your benefit. You should do this promptly in writing or by telephone to the office handling your claim (although in individual cases notification might be accepted in a form other than in writing or by telephone). In some cases, however, the decision maker might say you must report changes in writing. In any case, you might want to report the change in writing and keep a copy in case of a dispute in the future. If you do not promptly report any such change in writing, any resulting overpayment may be recoverable from you (see Chapter 41). If you are considered deliberately to have acted falsely or dishonestly, you may also be guilty of an offence (see Chapter 42).

Overpayments and fraud

If you are overpaid industrial injuries benefits, you might have to repay them. The rules on overpayments are covered in Chapter 41.

If you have been accused of fraud, see Chapter 42.

8. Challenging an industrial injuries benefit decision

You can apply for a revision or a supersession of an industrial injuries benefit decision, or appeal against it (see Chapters 43 and 44).

9. Tax, tax credits and other benefits

Industrial injuries benefits are not taxable.[135]

Tax credits

Industrial injuries benefits are ignored as income for tax credits.

Means-tested benefits

Industrial injuries disablement benefit, reduced earnings allowance and retirement allowance are taken into account in full for income support (IS), income-based jobseeker's allowance (JSA), housing benefit, council tax benefit and pension credit (PC).

Non-means-tested benefits

In general, the overlapping benefits rule does not apply to industrial injuries benefits and it is possible for them to overlap – eg, to receive full disablement benefit as well as full incapacity benefit (IB).

Carer's allowance (see Chapter 4) may be paid to someone who is 'regularly and substantially caring' for you while you are receiving constant attendance allowance (see p333).

If you were receiving sickness benefit or IB because of an industrial accident or disease on 12 April 1995 you can continue to qualify for IB, even though you do not satisfy the contribution conditions, provided that you remain incapable of work because of the accident or disease.[136]

Passports and other sources of help

If you have, or are, a dependant of someone who has died and who had, pneumoconiosis (including asbestosis, silicosis and kaolinosis), byssinosis, diffuse mesothelioma, diffuse pleural thickening, or primary carcinoma of the lung if accompanied by asbestosis or diffuse pleural thickening, and you cannot get compensation from your employer (eg, because s/he has ceased trading), or you do not have a realistic chance of obtaining damages from that employer, you may be able to get a one-off lump-sum payment in addition to any industrial injuries benefit.

If you are on a low income, you might be entitled to certain health benefits, such as free prescriptions (see Chapter 9). You may also qualify for a social fund payment (see Chapters 21 and 22). If you are getting IS, the guarantee cedit of PC or income-based JSA, your child(ren) qualify for free school meals (see p18). You may also be entitled to health benefits and free school meals if you are getting tax credits (see Chapter 48).

If your spouse died as a result of an industrial accident or disease you may qualify for a bereavement benefit even though the national insurance contribution conditions are not satisfied (see p29).[137]

Notes

1. **Who can get industrial injuries benefits**

1 s94(1) SSCBA 1992
2 ss94(1) and 108(1) SSCBA 1992
3 s2(1) SSCBA 1992; *Vandyk v Minister of Pensions and National Insurance* [1954] QB 29
4 Reg 10(6)(c) SSB(PA) Regs as amended
5 Regs 2, 4 and 6 SS(EEEIIP) Regs
6 Reg 3 SS(EEEIIP) Regs
7 CI/257/1949; CI/159/1950
8 R(I) 22/59
9 R(I) 1/76
10 R(I) 8/81
11 R(I) 1/82
12 R(I) 7/56
13 *Fenton v Thorley* [1903] AC 443 (HL)
14 CI/123/1949
15 *Jones v Secretary of State for Social Services* [1972] AC 944 (HL), also reported as an appendix to R(I) 3/69
16 *Trim Joint District School Board of Management v Kelly* [1914] AC 667 (HL)
17 s94(1) SSCBA 1992
18 CI/105/1998
19 *Roberts v Dorothea Slate Quarries Co. Ltd* [1948] 2 All ER 201 (HL)
20 R(I) 24/54; R(I) 43/55
21 CI/3370/1999 (*14/01)
22 *Mullen v Social Security Commissioner* 17 January 2002, unreported (CS)
23 R(I) 43/61; R(I) 4/62
24 R(I) 18/54
25 CI/159/1950
26 *Moore v Manchester Liners Ltd* [1910] AC 498 at p500 (HL)
27 *R v National Insurance Commissioner ex parte East* [1976] ICR 206 (DC), also reported as an appendix to R(I) 16/75
28 R(I) 1/59
29 *R v Industrial Injuries Commissioner ex parte AEU* [1966] 2 QB 31 (CA), also reported as an appendix to R(I) 4/66
30 R(I) 10/81
31 *R v National Insurance Commissioner ex parte Reed* (DC), reported as an appendix to R(I) 7/80
32 s94(3) SSCBA 1992
33 *R v Industrial Injuries Commissioner ex parte AEU* [1966] 2 QB 31 (CA), also reported as an appendix to R(I) 4/66
34 R(I) 46/53
35 R(I) 17/63
36 *R v Industrial Injuries Commissioner ex parte AEU* [1966] 2 QB 31 (CA), also reported as an appendix to R(I) 4/66
37 s98 SSCBA 1992
38 In CI/14111/1996 which referred to R(I) 67/52, a Benefits Agency officer, assaulted by a claimant while at home on sick leave, was found to have been injured 'in the course of her employment'. Although this case was subsequently overturned by the Court of Appeal, the Court ruled that a person might be in the course of his employment if at the relevant time he

was carrying out some duty he was contracted to do; *CAO v Rhodes*, *The Times*, 25 August 1998.
39 *Nancollas v Insurance Officer* [1985] 1 All ER 833 (CA), also reported as an appendix to R(I) 7/85
40 s99 SSCBA 1992
41 R(I) 1/88
42 R(I) 12/75
43 R(I) 4/70
44 *Nancollas v Insurance Officer* [1985] 1 All ER 833 (CA), also reported as an appendix to R(I) 7/85
45 *Smith v Stages* [1989] 2 WLR 529 (HL)
46 R(I) 1/91
47 R(I) 6/82
48 R(I) 12/52
49 s101 SSCBA 1992
50 s100 SSCBA 1992
51 R(I) 6/63
52 ss108(1) and 109(1) SSCBA 1992; reg 2 SS(IIPD) Regs
53 CI/1819/01; CI/2314/01; CI/2885/01; CI/51310/01
54 CI/6027/99; R(I) 4/96
55 Reg 12 SS&CS(DA) Regs
56 Reg 3 SS(IIPD) Regs
57 Regs 2(c) and 25 SS(IIPD) Regs. Although at one time it was held that the time limit in respect of occupational deafness had been imposed unlawfully, it was made valid retrospectively by Sch 6 para 4(3) SSA 1990.
58 Reg 36 SS(IIPD) Regs
59 Sch 1 SS(IIPD) Regs
60 Reg 2(3) SS(IIPD) Regs
61 CI/286/1995; CSI/89/1996
62 Reg 25(2)(a) SS(IIPD) Regs
63 Reg 4 SS(IIPD) Regs
64 Reg 6(2)(c) SS(IIPD) Regs
65 Reg 7 SS(IIPD) Regs
66 s45(1)(a) and (b) SSAA 1992
67 *Jones v Secretary of State for Social Services* [1972] AC 944 at p1009 (HL), also reported as an appendix to R(I) 3/69
68 CI/499/2000 (*24/01)
69 s30 SSA 1998
70 s103(3) SSCBA 1992
71 s103(2) and (3) SSCBA 1992; regs 15A and 15B SS(IIPD) Regs, as amended
72 Sch 2 SS(GB) Regs; Sch 3 SS(IIPD) Regs
73 Reg 11(6) SS(GB) Regs
74 Reg 20A SS(IIPD) Regs
75 Sch 6 para 1 SSCBA 1992
76 Reg 11(8) SS(GB) Regs
77 CI/636/1993; although the commissioner said that, where there are specific submissions backed with expert medical evidence on the percentage assessment, it would be an error of law to arrive at a different figure without giving reasons for this
78 Reg 11(3) SS(GB) Regs
79 CI/34/1993
80 Reg 11(7) SS(GB) Regs
81 R(I) 3/91, which contains a definitive survey of the situations where reg 11 SS(GB) Regs comes into play
82 Reg 11(4) SS(GB) Regs
83 Reg 11(5) SS(GB) Regs
84 R(I) 1/91
85 Reg 21 SS(IIPD) Regs
86 Reg 22 SS(IIPD) Regs
87 Reg 2(d) SS(IIPD) Regs
88 Sch 6 para 6 SSCBA 1992
89 Sch 6 para 7 SSCBA 1992
90 s45(3) SSAA 1992
91 Reg 29(a) SS(IIPD) Regs

2. **Industrial injuries disablement benefit**
92 ss103 and 108 SSCBA 1992
93 Reg 40 SS(GB) Regs
94 Sch 4 SSCBA 1992
95 s103(1) and Sch 7 para 9(1) SSCBA 1992
96 Reg 20(1) SS(IIPD) Regs
97 Sch 7 para 9(1)(a) SSCBA 1992; regs 12 and 14 SS(II&D)MP Regs
98 s104 SSCBA 1992
99 Reg 20 SS(GB) Regs
100 Sch 4 SSCBA 1992; reg 19(b) SS(GB) Regs
101 Sch 4 SSCBA 1992; reg 19(a) SS(GB) Regs
102 s105 SSCBA 1992

3. **Reduced earnings allowance**
103 Sch 7 paras 11 and 12(1), (2) and (7) SSCBA 1992
104 Sch 7 para 13(1) SSCBA 1992
105 Reg 23(a) SS(IIPD) Regs; Sch 8 para 9 SSAO No.8
106 Reg 40 SS(GB) Regs; R(I) 2/86
107 Reg 17 SS(GB) Regs
108 Reg 23(b) SS(IIPD) Regs; Sch 8 para 9 SSAO No.8
109 *R v National Insurance Commissioner ex parte Mellors* [1971] 2 QB 401 (CA), also reported as an appendix to R(I) 7/69
110 R(I) 28/51
111 R(I) 65/54
112 CI/80/1949
113 Reg 2 SS(II&D)MP Regs

114 *Hagan v Secretary of State for Social Security* [2001] EWCA Civ 1452
115 Reg 17 SS(IIPD) Regs
116 *R v Deputy Industrial Injuries Commissioner ex parte Humphreys* [1966] 2 QB 1 (CA), also reported as an appendix to R(I) 2/66
117 R(I) 22/61
118 Sch 7 Part IV para 11(4)-(7) SSCBA 1992
119 R(I) 3/83
120 Reg 2 SS(IIRE) Regs; R(I) 3/93
121 Reg 3 SS(IIRE) Regs, as amended
122 *Hepple and Others* EC Case C-196/98 [2000] (ECJ)
123 Sch 7 para 11(10) SSCBA 1992
124 Sch 7 para 11(14) SSCBA 1992
125 R(I) 8/67
126 Sch 7 para 11(10) SSCBA 1992
127 Sch 7 para 11(10) SSCBA 1992
128 Sch 7 para 11(11) SSCBA 1992
129 Sch 7 para 12(6) SSCBA 1992

4. **Retirement allowance**
130 Sch 7 para 13 SSCBA 1992
131 Sch 7 para 13(4) SSCBA 1992

5. **Special rules for special groups**
132 Reg 2(6) and (7) SS(GB) Regs

6. **Claims and backdating**
133 Reg 4(1) SS(C&P) Regs
134 s29 SSA 1998

9. **Tax, tax credits and other benefits**
135 s617 ICTA 1988
136 Regs 14, 17 and 21 SS(IB)(T) Regs
137 s60(2) and (3) SSCBA 1992

Chapter 15

Jobseeker's allowance: main rules

This chapter covers:

Jobseeker's allowance (JSA) is a benefit for people who are unemployed or who work for less than 16 hours a week and who are looking for full-time work. You must normally satisfy what are known as the 'labour market conditions' (see below). JSA is not paid to people in full-time paid work (see p750) who may be able to claim working tax credit instead (see Chapter 50). Whether or not you are in full-time paid work, you may be able to claim child tax credit (see Chapter 49).

There are two main types of JSA. **Contribution-based JSA** is paid if you satisfy the national insurance (NI) contributions conditions. **Income-based JSA** is paid if you pass the means test.

A third type of JSA, **joint-claim JSA**, is very similar to income-based JSA. It is paid if you are a member of a 'joint-claim couple'. Both of you must usually satisfy all the conditions for getting JSA (see p350 for exceptions). Most of the rules are the same as for income-based JSA, although there are important differences for claims. See p394 for further details. Unless otherwise stated, references in this *Handbook* to income-based JSA are also references to joint-claim JSA. We only refer to joint-claim JSA where the rules are significantly different.

You do not have to have paid NI contributions to qualify for income-based JSA.

It is possible to receive contribution-based JSA with an income-based JSA (including joint-claim JSA) top-up. Both types of JSA can be claimed at the same time. There are some situations where you might want to claim income support or pension credit instead of JSA (see p410).

Even if you are entitled to JSA, you may find you are not paid if you are 'sanctioned' – eg, if you lose your job through misconduct or fail to take up a job or training scheme opportunity. If this happens, you might qualify for hardship payments. You might also qualify for hardship payments if there is a doubt whether you satisfy the labour market conditions. See Chapter 16 for further information.

1. Who can claim jobseeker's allowance

You qualify for jobseeker's allowance (JSA) if you:[1]

- do not count as being in full-time paid work (see pp352 and 750) and if you are claiming income-based JSA, nor does your partner; *and*
- are capable of work. However, in certain circumstances, people who are sick can get JSA (see p352); *and*
- are not in 'relevant education' (see p618). If you are a full-time student you usually cannot get JSA. See p353 for further information; *and*
- satisfy what are known as the 'labour market conditions'. This means that you must:
  - be 'available for work' (see p354); *and*
  - be 'actively seeking work' (see p365); *and*
  - have a current 'jobseeker's agreement' with the Department for Work and Pensions (DWP) (see p369).

  You are required to attend the JobCentre to sign on (unless you are allowed to do this by post – see p400), to assess whether you are still meeting these criteria and to decide if you need extra help to find work. If you are part of a 'joint-claim couple' (see p394) both you and your partner must usually fulfil all these criteria in order to receive benefit. For exceptions to the rules, see p350; *and*
- are below pensionable age (currently 60 for women and 65 for men); *and*
- are not getting income support (IS); *and*
- are in Great Britain (GB). JSA can continue to be paid in limited circumstances while you are temporarily away (see p690) and contribution-based JSA can be 'exported' if you are unemployed and looking for work in a European Economic Area country (see p677).

In addition, you must satisfy extra rules. For contribution-based JSA see p349. For income-based JSA (or joint-claim JSA) see p349.

You are usually not entitled to JSA for the first three days of your 'jobseeking period' (see below). These are known as 'waiting days' (see p377).

There are some groups of claimants to whom special rules apply (see p380). If you do not satisfy the normal rules for getting JSA, you may be able to get an urgent cases payment of JSA (see p373).

Jobseeking periods

A **'jobseeking period'** is the period during which you either meet the basic conditions of entitlement for JSA (see p347), or do not satisfy the labour market conditions but receive hardship payments (see p443).[2]

It is not necessary to satisfy the extra rules on pp349 and 349 for a jobseeking period to exist.

Linked jobseeking periods

In some cases, a jobseeking period may be 'linked' with an earlier one. This means the earlier jobseeking period is treated as continuing, so that:[3]

- the question of whether you satisfy the national insurance (NI) contribution conditions for contribution-based JSA (see p844) is decided by looking at your situation at the beginning of the first jobseeking period and not at the beginning of your current claim;[4]
- you do not have to serve another three 'waiting days' (see p377) before you get JSA;
- if the jobseeking periods together are longer than 182 days, you cannot get any more contribution-based JSA (see p378);
- if the jobseeking periods together are at least two years, you might be able to get JSA while attending a 'qualifying course' (see p353).

Two jobseeking periods are treated as linked if they are separated by one or any combination of the following:[5]

- any period of no more than 12 weeks; *or*
- a period during which you are doing jury service; *or*
- a 'linked period' (see below); *or*
- any period of no more than 12 weeks which comes between two linked periods or between a jobseeking period and a linked period.

'Linked periods' are any periods during which you are:[6]

- entitled to carer's allowance (CA – see Chapter 4) but only if this allows you to get contribution-based JSA when you would not otherwise satisfy the contribution conditions; *or*
- incapable of work or treated as incapable of work (see p764); *or*
- getting maternity allowance (see p456); *or*
- undergoing training, including on the New Deal, and receiving a training allowance; *or*
- not entitled to JSA because you count as being in full-time paid work (see p750) or your earnings or income are too high and you are on:

  - a New Deal option – ie, the self-employed employment, environment task force or voluntary sector option of the New Deal for young people, or the 'intensive activity period' of the New Deal for people aged 25 to 50 or for people aged 50 plus; *or*
  - an employment zone programme.

Although you could only claim JSA from 7 October 1996, your jobseeking period might have begun earlier than this if you were unemployed before that date.[7]

What is not counted as part of the jobseeking period

The following do not count as part of a jobseeking period:[8]

- days for which you do not claim (or are not treated as claiming) JSA;
- days for which you lost your entitlement to JSA because you failed, without good cause, to attend the JobCentre when required or to sign on (see p403);
- a period for which you claimed backdated benefit, but which has been refused (see p399);
- any week (Sunday to Saturday) for which you are not entitled to JSA because you were involved in a trade dispute for all or part of that week (see p735);
- days on which you are not entitled to JSA because you have not provided your or your partner's NI number (see p393).

Extra rules for contribution-based jobseeker's allowance

To get contribution-based JSA, in addition to satisfying the basic rules of entitlement (see p347), you must:[9]

- satisfy the contribution conditions (see p844). This depends on your record of NI contributions and credits (see Chapter 33) in the two tax years immediately before the benefit year in which your jobseeking period begins; *and*
- not have earnings above a specified amount – known as the 'prescribed amount' (see p948). If you have earnings below this amount, your JSA is reduced to take account of them.

Extra rules for income-based jobseeker's allowance

If you do not qualify for contribution-based JSA, or if you do but need additional benefit (for your partner or housing costs), you can qualify for income-based JSA if:[10]

- your income is less than your applicable amount (see p379); *and*
- your savings and other capital are worth £8,000 or less (£12,000 if you or your partner are 60 or over; £16,000 if you live in a care home, see p1024). Some capital (in particular your home) is ignored (see Chapter 39); *and*
- you are not receiving pension credit (PC), nor is your partner if you have one; *and*
  - if you are *not* a 'joint-claim couple' (see p394), your partner is not receiving either IS or income-based JSA; *or*

  - if you *are* a 'joint-claim couple' (see p394), neither you nor your partner are receiving IS.

  If you or your partner can qualify for IS or PC check if this would make you better off than if you were to claim income-based JSA; *and*
- no one else is claiming IS or income-based JSA for you as part of their family (see p374); *and*
- you (or if you are a 'joint-claim couple' – see p394 – at least one of you) are aged 18 or over but if you are a 16/17-year-old you might get income-based JSA if you satisfy special rules (see p382); *and*
- you satisfy the 'habitual residence test'. To find out if you are exempt from the test, see p702.

Exemptions for 'joint-claim couples'

If you are a member of a 'joint-claim couple' (see p394) and do not satisfy all the rules for claiming JSA although your partner does, the two of you can still qualify for joint-claim JSA if you fit into one of the exempt groups below.[11] If you fit into an exempt group, you do not have to satisfy the labour market conditions or be in GB. However, you must be below pensionable age and must not count as being in full-time paid work (see p750). Even if you are in an exempt group, if you claim a specified benefit you can be required to attend a work-focused interview (see p1092).[12]

Exempt groups

You fit into an exempt group if, for at least one day in a week, you are:[13]
- studying full time. You count as studying full time for these purposes if you are:
  - at least 16 but under 19 years old and in full-time non-advanced education (see p86) or are a full-time student (see p621); *and*
    - you were when you and your partner claimed JSA; *or*
    - when you and your partner claimed JSA you had been allocated a place on a full-time course of study from the next academic year or term or had applied for such a place and had not yet received a decision; *or*
    - you applied to commence a full-time course of study within one month of the last day of a previous course or within one month of the day you received examination results from one. This does not apply to applications for courses of study beyond the level of a first degree course; *or*
    - someone who can claim IS while in 'relevant education', other than a refugee learning English (see p619).

  You can only fit into this exempt group for one JSA claim made jointly with your partner, unless another joint claim is made because the first ceased when one of you started full-time paid work or was summoned to do jury service or was within any of the linked periods on p348;[14] *or*

- a carer who can claim IS (see p296). If you cease meeting this condition or stop being a carer, you continue to fit into an exempt group for a further eight weeks; *or*
- incapable of work because of illness or disability; that is, you:
  - are entitled to statutory sick pay (SSP – see Chapter 24); *or*
  - satisfy the own occupation test or the personal capability assessment for incapacity benefit (IB – see pp771 and 772); *or*
  - are treated as incapable of work by a decision maker – eg, you have a severe condition or have an infectious disease or are blind (see p765); *or*
  - are treated as capable of work because you are disqualified from receiving IB due to misconduct or failure to accept treatment (see p272); *or*
- treated as not being in full-time work because you are living in a care home (see p758); *or*
- mentally or physically disabled and because of this, your earnings or the number of hours you work are reduced to 75 per cent or less of that for a person without your disability in the same or a comparable job; *or*
- a disabled student (see p624); *or*
- registered blind (certified blind in Scotland). If you regain your sight, you continue to be exempt for 28 weeks after being taken off the register; *or*
- incapable of work because of pregnancy. You only have to show that you are incapable of work, not that there is a serious risk to your health or that of your baby;[15] *or*
- aged 60 or over. In practice, this only applies if you are a man aged 60 or over but under 65. In this situation you might be better off if you claim PC rather than JSA; *or*
- a refugee learning English in order to obtain employment. The course must be for more than 15 hours a week and at the time the course started, you must have been in GB for a year or less. You can only be exempt for nine months on this ground; *or*
- required to go to court as a justice of the peace (JP), juror, witness or party to the proceedings; *or*
- aged 16–24 years and on a training course provided by the Learning and Skills Council for England, the National Council for Education and Training in Wales or in Scotland by a local enterprise company (sometimes called 'Work-based Learning for Young People'); *or*
- involved in a trade dispute (see p740).

You might be able to choose whether to claim IS or JSA (or if you are 60 or over, PC). If you fit into one of the exempt groups above (other than the first one, studying full time), you should also qualify for IS. To find out if you can claim IS while studying full time, see pp618 and 624. See p410 for further information before deciding what to do.

Full-time paid work

You cannot get JSA if you are in full-time paid work. You cannot get income-based JSA if either you or your partner are in full-time paid work. If you are the JSA claimant, this means 16 hours or more each week.[16] For your partner, this means 24 hours or more each week.

If you are a member of a 'joint-claim couple' you cannot get joint-claim JSA if either of you is in full-time paid work. If one of you is working less than 16 hours a week, the other can then work up to 24 hours a week. The person working 16 to 24 hours does not have to claim joint-claim JSA.

In some situations you are treated as *not* being in full-time work even if you work more than 16/24 hours (see p757). See p752 for details of how your hours are calculated and p752 for what counts as paid work.

If you work less than 16 hours and your partner works at least 16 hours but less than 24 hours each week, you and your partner might be able to claim working tax credit (WTC – see Chapter 50). In some cases, you might be able to claim both WTC and JSA. See p759 for further information. You should seek advice to see how you would be better off financially.

If you or your partner are 60 or over and either of you are working 16/24 hours or more each week, you might be able to claim PC or WTC (or both if your income is low enough). There is no full-time paid work rule for PC, but earnings are taken into account in working out how much you can get.

If you have just started full-time paid work, you might be able to claim mortgage interest run-on (see p62).

Capable of work

To qualify for JSA, you must be capable of work.[17] There are two tests for deciding whether you are capable or incapable of work. See Chapter 30 for further details. If a decision maker has decided for the purpose of some other benefit that you are capable (or incapable) under the tests, you are automatically treated as being capable (or incapable) of work for JSA.[18] You still have to show that you are available for work if you suffer from ill-health or disability, but there are some special rules to help you do this (see p361).

Periods of sickness when you can claim JSA

Even if you are incapable of work, you do not have to stop claiming JSA in some situations.

Two-week periods of sickness

You are treated as being capable of work and as available for and actively seeking work (see p354 and p365) for up to two weeks if the only reason why you would not otherwise qualify for JSA is that you are unable to work because you are sick.[19] You have to make a written declaration that you have been incapable of work from a specific date or for a specific period, on a special form available at the JobCentre.[20] However, the rules do not apply if you have stated in writing that you are going to claim or have claimed IB, severe disablement allowance (SDA – see Chapter 20) or IS.[21]

You are allowed up to two two-week periods of sickness in a 'jobseeking period' (see p348) or if your jobseeking period has lasted more than 12 months, in any successive 12-month periods.[22] If you are sick more often than this, or for a longer period, you must claim IB and/or IS (PC if you are 60 or over) instead of JSA for the time you are unable to work.

The rules on two-week periods of sickness do not apply to you if you were getting one of the following benefits in the eight weeks before you were sick:[23]

- IB (see Chapter 12);
- SDA (see Chapter 20);
- SSP (see Chapter 24);
- IS, paid because you were sick and including a disability premium (see Chapter 13 and p886).

Instead, you can claim benefit as being incapable of work without having to serve any 'waiting days' (see p271 and 600).

NHS hospital treatment abroad

From 4 October 2004, you can be treated as being capable of work and as available for and actively seeking work (see p354 and p365) if the only reason why you would not otherwise qualify for JSA is that you are incapable of work and temporarily absent from GB for the purpose of getting NHS hospital treatment under certain provisions.[24] You have to make a written declaration that you will be incapable of work from a specific date or for a specific period, on a special form available at the JobCentre.[25] However, the rules do not apply if you have stated in writing before the period of temporary absence abroad begins that you have claimed IB, SDA or IS immediately before the beginning of the period.[26]

Note: the provisions under which arrangements for undergoing NHS hospital treatment abroad are made currently only apply in England and Wales, not in Scotland.

Full-time training and study

You cannot usually get JSA if you are studying full time (see p621). To find out if you can claim JSA while studying full time, see p624. You might be able to get JSA while studying part time (see p627).

In some situations, you *can* take a full-time 'qualifying course' and continue to get JSA. While you are on the course, you are treated as available for and actively seeking work (see pp354 and 365). You can get JSA while attending a 'qualifying course' if you:[27]

- are aged 25 or over; *and*

- had been 'receiving benefit' (see below) during a jobseeking period (see p348) for at least two years at the time the course starts. In working out whether you have been 'receiving benefit' for two years, the rules for linking jobseeking periods apply (see p348); *and*
- have been given approval to attend the course by an employment officer (EO); *and*
- satisfy the conditions for being treated as available for and actively seeking work (see pp358 and 368).

For these purposes, **'receiving benefit'** means getting:[28]
- JSA, IS or unemployment benefit as an unemployed person; *or*
- NI credits for unemployment or because you are 60 or over; *or*
- IS as an asylum seeker, but only if you have been accepted as having refugee status or have been granted 'exceptional leave to remain' in the UK, and you were getting IS as an asylum seeker, or were subsequently paid backdated IS, at some time in the 12 weeks before the start of the 'jobseeking period' (see p348), which includes the date that your course starts.

A course can be a **'qualifying course'** if it:[29]
- is employment-related; *and*
- lasts no more than 12 consecutive months; *and*
- is a course of further or higher education. A higher level course can also be a qualifying course if your EO agrees.

Once you have started the course, the course becomes compulsory. This means that if you abandon your course without 'good cause' or are dismissed from it because of misconduct, you could be sanctioned (see p430).

Available for work

To qualify for JSA you must be available for work in each 'benefit week' you claim JSA. To be available for work you must be 'willing and able' to take up work 'immediately'.[30]

In some circumstances you can be treated as being available for work even if you are not actually available (see p357). Special rules allow you to count as available for work for the first 13 weeks of a period when you are laid off or on short-time working (see p380). If you are not available, or treated as available, for work you cannot get JSA but you may be able to get hardship payments (see p443). You should also check to see if you qualify for any of the other benefits in this *Handbook*.

The DWP can decide that you are not available for work without having to show that you have turned down a job.[31] However, the fact that you turn down a job does not necessarily mean that you are not available.

In some situations you can place restrictions on the jobs you are prepared to accept (see p361). However, you must:

- be prepared to work at least 40 hours a week, but also be willing to work for less than 40 hours a week if required to do so. Carers, people with disabilities and short-time workers can restrict the number of hours they are prepared to work to less than 40 hours a week (see p362);
- if you are placing restrictions on your availability, have a 'reasonable prospect' of getting work (see p365). Note that if the restrictions are reasonable in view of your physical or mental condition you do not have to have a reasonable prospect of getting work (see p361).

Willing and able to take up work immediately

Being **willing** to work is essentially a test of your attitude. The DWP looks at your desire and willingness to return to work. What you do in practice to display this willingness is usually dealt with under the rules for actively seeking work (see p365).

You must be prepared to take up work as an employed person – being only available for self-employment is not sufficient.[32] However, this means that you do not count as being unavailable for work if you refuse to work as a self-employed person.

In order to be **able** to work it must be lawful for you to work in GB.[33] Your immigration status may affect this – eg, if a condition of your entry is that you do not work. In addition there must be nothing to prevent you from receiving job offers (eg, because you are away from home for more than a short time) and nothing to prevent you acting on them straight away (eg, because you are involved in other commitments you cannot abandon easily).

Being able to take up work **immediately** means that you must usually be able to start work without any delay, with little more than the time needed to get washed and dressed and have breakfast.[34] You can be allowed more time than this in the following situations. You only need to be available for work:

- on **one week's notice** if you are doing voluntary work.[35] You must be willing and able to attend an interview in connection with opportunities for work on 48 hours' notice. Voluntary work is work which is done for a charity or other not-for-profit organisation or for anyone other than a member of your family (see p374) for which you receive no payment other than reimbursement of your reasonable expenses;
- on **48 hours' notice** if you have caring responsibilities because you are looking after a member of your household (see p812 on the meaning of household) or a close relative (see below) who is a child under 16, someone over pension age or someone who needs care because of her/his medical condition;[36]
- on **24 hours' notice** if you are providing a service, whether paid or not, but do not qualify as a carer or a volunteer.[37] This includes services you provide for family or friends on an entirely non-commercial basis, such as giving someone

a regular lift to work in your car.[38] It also includes activities that are of service to the community in general. For example, it could cover:[39]
- jurors (see below);
- witnesses in criminal proceedings;
- JPs;
- tribunal members (eg, appeal tribunals and employment tribunals);
- people doing community orders (see below);
- people who are working;
- **after your notice period** has passed if you are working part time. This applies if you have a duty to give your employer notice that you are leaving work under employment law.[40] If you must give longer notice than this under the terms of your contract of employment, argue that a longer notice period should apply.

Note: if you have said that you are only available to work at certain times (see p363) you are *not* required to be able to take up employment at times that you are not available.[41] However, you must be willing and able to take up the offer as soon as you reach the next period in your pattern of availability (see p363).

You can take advantage of the cumulative effect of the above rules. For example, if you have caring responsibilities and so only need to be available on 48 hours' notice, and have also agreed a pattern of availability under which you are not available on Saturday or Sunday, you can count as available on a Thursday or Friday if you are ready to start work the following Monday.[42]

'Close relative' means partner, parent, step-parent, parent-in-law, grandparent, son, step-son, son-in-law, daughter, step-daughter, daughter-in-law, brother, sister, grandchild or partners of any of these.

If you are selected as a **juror** you must attend court when asked to do so. You are therefore not available for work while you are on jury service and cannot qualify for JSA. You should not presume that if you lose JSA this will be made up by the Court. The information provided by the Court says that you should show the certificate of loss of earnings it sends you to the DWP and that the DWP will tell you how being on jury service affects your claim. Rather than complete the certificate for you to return to the Court, the DWP may instead say you should claim IS (see p298).[43] You might count as being available for work if you only have to attend the court for one day because you only have to be available for work on 24 hours' notice. This could also apply on your last day of jury service. However, you should always make enquiries or seek advice about what you should claim *before* you go on jury service.

If you are an **offender** you may be required, as part of your punishment, to do unpaid work in the community – under a community order. You count as being available for work if arrangements are made so that you can be notified of a vacancy or interview and you can leave the unpaid work in order to take up a job within 24 hours.[44] If you are required to attend a probation course you have to be available for work immediately because this does not count as providing a service. To be considered available for work you should make sure that you can be contacted at short notice and are allowed to leave the course to attend an interview if required to do so. An offender who is released early from prison under the Home Detention Curfew Scheme can be available for work during daytime hours.

Treated as being available for work

Even if you are not actually available for work, you can be treated as if you are in limited circumstances, for short periods during your claim. When you can be treated as being available for work and the length of the period depends on the circumstances. You must still satisfy the other conditions of entitlement to JSA – eg, you must be actively seeking work or treated as if you are (see p365). Remember that special rules allow you to count as available for work for the first 13 weeks of being laid off or on short-time working (see p380).

General rules

You are treated as available for work:[45]

- at the **beginning of your claim**, from your date of claim until the day of the week on which your signing day falls if, in respect of all the days concerned, you are available in line with any agreed restrictions on your availability (see p361); *and*:[46]
  - you have an agreed pattern of availability or are allowed to restrict your availability because of a physical or mental condition, caring responsibilities or because you are on short-time working; *or*
  - you do not have an agreed pattern of availability and are available for work of eight hours each day;
- during the **last week of your claim**, until the day your entitlement to JSA ends (except where your claim ends on the day of the week you would sign on if it were a signing-on week);
- if you are **sick** for a two-week period (see p352) or are temporarily absent from GB for the purpose of getting NHS hospital treatment (see p353);
- if you were **recently found capable of work**. This only applies if your time limit for claiming JSA is extended because your entitlement to IS or IB ended but you were not told this before it happened so could not claim JSA in time. You are treated as being available for work for the period of the extension.

Studying and training

In some cases, you can study or take part in training courses while on JSA so long as you satisfy the rules of entitlement. See p618 for further information about studying and claiming JSA. Some people getting training allowances do not have to satisfy the labour market conditions (see p389).

In some situations, you would not normally count as being available for work while studying. However, you count as doing so:[47]

- for one period of up to two weeks in any 12 months, when:
  - you are a full-time student (see p621) **on an employment-related course** which has been approved in advance by your EO. See below for more generous rules if you are on a 'qualifying course'; *or*
  - when you are **attending a residential work camp** in GB, organised by a charity, local authority or voluntary organisation for the benefit of the community or the environment;[48]
- if you are attending a compulsory residential course as part of an **Open University course** (for up to one week for each course);
- if you are attending a residential training programme run by **the Venture Trust** (for one programme only for a maximum of four weeks in any 12-month period).

Special rules apply if you are attending a **'qualifying course'** with the approval of an EO (see p353). You are treated as being available for work in any week:[49]

- which falls entirely or partly in term time, so long as you provide written evidence, within five days of it being requested, confirming that you are attending and making satisfactory progress on the course. This must be signed by you and by the college or educational establishment;
- in which you are taking examinations relating to the course; *or*
- which falls entirely in a vacation, if you are willing and able to take up any 'casual employment' immediately. **'Casual employment'** means employment that you can leave without giving notice or if you must give notice, that you can leave before the end of the vacation.

Temporary absence from Great Britain

You are treated as available for work when you are temporarily absent from GB and you are:[50]

- taking a child or young person, who is a member of your household (see p375) and for whom you are responsible (see p375), abroad temporarily for medical treatment (for a maximum of eight weeks). The treatment must be under the supervision of a person qualified in medical, physiotherapeutic or similar practices; *or*
- attending a job interview, provided you have told your EO in advance and confirmed it in writing if required to do so (for a maximum of seven days); *or*
- a member of a couple and the pensioner, enhanced pensioner, higher pensioner, disability or severe disability premium is being paid for your partner (see Chapter 35) and you are both away from GB (for a maximum of four weeks); *or*

- temporarily absent from GB for the purpose of getting NHS hospital treatment (see p353); *or*
- on the date of the JSA claim, you are a member of a 'joint-claim couple' (see p394) and on the day the other member of the couple makes the claim for JSA, you are:
  - in Northern Ireland (for a maximum of four weeks) but only if you are unlikely to be away for more than 52 weeks; *or*
  - attending a job interview (for a maximum of seven days).

If you are looking after a child because your partner is temporarily absent from the UK, see below.

Other

You are treated as available for work:[51]

- if you are **looking after a child**. This only applies (for a maximum of eight weeks) if you are:
  - a member of a couple and looking after a child who is a member of your household (see p375) and for whom you are responsible (see p375) while your partner is temporarily absent from the UK; *or*
  - looking after a child on a full-time basis because the person who normally looks after the child is ill or temporarily away from home or looking after a member of the family who is ill;
- if you have been **discharged from detention** in prison, a remand centre or a youth custody institution (for one week from the date of discharge). This does not apply if you were detained in a police cell;[52]
- if you are engaged in crewing or launching a lifeboat, are carrying out duties as a part-time firefighter or are engaged during an emergency as a member of an organised group which is helping to save lives, prevent injury or a serious threat to the health of others, or protect property;
- if you are dealing with circumstances arising from:
  - a domestic emergency affecting you or a close friend or 'close relative' (see p356); *or*
  - the death, serious illness or funeral of a close friend or 'close relative' (see p356); *or*
  - the death of someone for whom you were caring.

  You can only be treated as being available in these circumstances for up to a week at a time and for no more than four occasions in any 12-month period.

The period you are treated as available for work

If you are treated as being available for work at the beginning or end of your claim, you are treated as being available for the whole of any part-week. If you are treated as being available because of a domestic emergency, death, serious illness or funeral, you are only treated as being available during the time it takes to deal with the matter. If any of the other circumstances listed above apply to you for less than a full week, you are treated as being available for work:[53]

- if you have not agreed a 'pattern of availability' (see p363), for eight hours on each of the days when the circumstances apply; *or*
- if you have agreed a 'pattern of availability', for the number of hours (if any) you would normally be available in accordance with the pattern of availability on each of the days when the above circumstances apply.

Treated as being unavailable for work

Even if you are available for employment or you can be treated as if you are available (see p357), you are nevertheless treated as unavailable for work if:[54]

- you are a full-time student, *unless* you are:
  - on a 'qualifying course' (see p358); *or*
  - a member of a couple who are both students, it is the summer vacation and one of you is responsible for a child or young person (see p375); *or*
  - treated as being available for work (see p357) because you are on an employment-related course or on a residential training programme run by the Venture Trust;
- you are on temporary release from prison;
- you are receiving maternity allowance (see p456) or statutory maternity pay (see p566);
- you are on paternity leave or ordinary adoption leave;
- it is the beginning of your claim, from the date of claim until the day of the week on which your signing day falls, unless you come under the rule for being treated as being available for that period (see p357).

Unavailability for part of a week

A situation may arise which makes you unavailable for work for a short period during a benefit week. This might be, for example, because:

- you were away from home for a few hours;
- you were arrested and held by the police for a short time but then released on bail.

If this happens to you and you have put restrictions on the times that you are available (see p363):[55]

- your JSA is not affected, if the period you are not available comes entirely outside your 'pattern of availability' (see p363); *or*
- you lose JSA for the whole of that benefit week, if all or part of the period you are not available comes within your 'pattern of availability'.

If this happens to you and you have *not* put any restrictions on the hours that you are available, you may find that you lose benefit for that week because you are not available to take up work immediately.[56] For this reason it is best to avoid signing a jobseeker's agreement with totally unrestricted hours.

Restrictions on availability for work

If you have a physical or mental condition, you can restrict your availability in any way if the restrictions are reasonable (see below). Otherwise, if you can prove that you still have a reasonable prospect of securing employment (see p365), you can make some restrictions on the work you are available to do. These are:[57]

- the **type of work** you are prepared to do (see below);
- the **hours** you are prepared to work (see p362);
- the **times** you are prepared to work (see p363);
- the **terms and conditions** of employment you are prepared to accept, including the rate of pay (see p364);
- the **location** of the job (see p364).

Physical or mental condition

You can restrict your availability for work in any way if the restrictions are reasonable in view of your physical or mental condition.[58] If the restrictions you impose are reasonable ones for you, you do not have to show that you have reasonable prospects of securing employment (see p365).

You are normally expected to provide medical evidence and you might be referred to an adviser at the JobCentre (see p402). But if you have no prospects of work at all, you should consider whether you really are capable of work. If not, it may be in your interest to claim IB, IS or PC instead of JSA (see Chapters 12, 13 and 18). If you have been found fit for work following a personal capability assessment and are appealing against the decision, see p790 for information about claiming JSA during this period.

If you also place restrictions on your availability for work that are *not* connected with your physical or mental condition, you must show that you have a reasonable prospect of securing employment with all your restrictions.[59] You should therefore think carefully before placing additional restrictions on your availability.

Restrictions on the type of work you are prepared to do

The general rule is that you have to be available for any type of employment, but you are allowed to place restrictions on the sort of job you are prepared to do so long as you have a reasonable prospect of securing employment (see p365). In addition, special rules allow you to make restrictions:

- during your 'permitted period' if you have one (see p362);
- if you have been laid off or are working part time (see p380);
- because of your physical or mental condition (see above);
- because of a sincerely held religious belief or conscientious objection (see p362).

Permitted periods

A **'permitted period'** is a period of between one and 13 weeks from the date you claim JSA during which you are allowed to be available only for vacancies in your normal line of work (your 'usual occupation') and to refuse to take or look for jobs that are not what you would normally do or which pay less than you would normally receive.[60] Any other restrictions you place on your availability during your permitted period must be consistent with the conditions of work that are normal in your usual occupation.

The term 'usual occupation' is not defined in the rules and the DWP has to decide if you have one. If you had only recently started a new occupation before claiming JSA, it may still be treated as being your usual occupation if you intend to follow that type of employment in future.[61]

Not everyone is allowed a permitted period. Your jobseeker's agreement (see p369) says whether or not you have been allowed one and, if so, when it starts and finishes.[62]

In deciding whether you can have a permitted period and how long it can last, the DWP must consider the following factors:[63]

- your 'usual occupation'; *and*
- any relevant skills or qualifications you may have; *and*
- the length of time you have spent training for or have worked in the occupation or since you have worked in the occupation; *and*
- the availability and location of jobs in that area of work.

A permitted period can be, and often is, less than 13 weeks. The minimum permitted period is one week.

Religious or conscientious objection

You do not have to be available for work that offends a sincere religious belief or a sincere conscientious objection – eg, a job in a company associated with live animal exports if you have a conscientious objection to these.[64] You must still have reasonable prospects of securing employment despite those restrictions (see p365).[65] You can only rely on a religious or conscientious belief to restrict the type of employment you are prepared to do, not to restrict the total number of hours or level of pay you are prepared to accept.

Restrictions on the hours you are prepared to work

The general rule is that in order to qualify as being available for work:[66]

- you must be prepared to take a job which would involve working for *at least* 40 hours a week; *and*
- you must also be prepared to work for less than 40 hours a week if required to do so. In practice, this means that you must be prepared to work part time.

You are allowed to restrict the number of hours you are prepared to work if:

- this is reasonable in view of your physical or mental condition (see p361); *or*
- you are a short-time worker (see p380); *or*
- you have caring responsibilities (see p363).

You must be prepared to work for the maximum number of hours for which you are available or for a lower number.

You are allowed to refuse a job formally notified to you which would be for less than 24 hours a week.[67] If it has been agreed that you need only be available for less than 24 hours a week – eg, because you have responsibilities as a carer (see below) you can refuse a job which would be for less than 16 hours a week. This is because you can show 'good cause' for refusing to apply and cannot be sanctioned (see p428). If the DWP issues you with a jobseeker's direction requiring you to apply for a job for less than 24 hours a week, you should argue that because of the 'good cause' rules, such a direction would be unreasonable.

Caring responsibilities

You may restrict the total hours for which you are available to less than 40 hours a week if:[68]

- you are caring for a child, a person over pensionable age or someone who needs care because of a physical or mental condition. S/he must be in the same household as you or a close relative (see p356). 'Household' is not defined, but see p812; *and*
- you are available for employment for as many hours as your responsibilities as a carer permit and for at least 16 hours a week; *and*
- you have a reasonable chance of securing employment (see p365) despite the restricted hours you are prepared to work.

When deciding whether you qualify under this rule, the DWP must consider relevant factors. These include the particular hours and days you spend caring, whether your caring responsibilities are shared with someone else and the age and physical and mental condition of the person being cared for.[69]

If you are a carer and you cannot make yourself available for work at least 16 hours a week, consider claiming CA (see Chapter 4) and IS (see Chapter 13) or, if you are 60 or over, PC (see Chapter 18) rather than JSA.

The times you are prepared to work

To count as being available for work, the general rule is that you must be prepared to work at any time of the day or on any day of the week. However, you are allowed to put restrictions on the times you are prepared to work if:[70]

- the total hours during which you are prepared to work are at least 40 a week (unless you are someone who is allowed to restrict your hours);
- you have agreed with the DWP a 'pattern of availability' (ie, the particular days and hours that you are available for work) and this has been recorded in your jobseeker's agreement (see p369);

- you still have reasonable prospects of securing employment despite the restrictions (see p365); *and*
- the restrictions do not *considerably* reduce your prospects of securing employment.

If you are doing voluntary work and you have placed restrictions on the total number of hours you are available to work, any voluntary work you do within your 'pattern of availability' must be ignored for the purpose of deciding if you are available, so long as you are willing and able to rearrange the voluntary work within:[71]

- one week's notice, in order to take up any job whose hours fall within your pattern of availability;
- 48 hours' notice, to attend an interview in connection with an opportunity for work at a time that falls within your pattern of availability.

There is a similar rule if you are a part-time student (see p629).

The terms and conditions of employment you will accept

You can make restrictions on the terms and conditions of employment you are prepared to accept (including the rate of pay – but see below) so long as you can show you still have reasonable prospects of securing employment despite those restrictions (see p365).[72]

The rate of pay you are prepared to accept

You can only restrict the rate of pay you are willing to accept in three situations:

- If you have a 'permitted period' (see p362) you can restrict your rate of pay to the rate you are accustomed to receive in your usual occupation during your permitted period.[73]
- You can restrict the rate of pay that you are willing to accept for six months from the date you claimed JSA, so long as you still have reasonable prospects of securing employment (see p365).[74]
- You can place restrictions on the rate of pay that you are prepared to accept indefinitely if this is reasonable in view of your physical or mental condition (see p361).[75]

Remember that you should not be expected to work for a rate of pay below the national minimum wage (see p451).

The location of the job

You can make restrictions on the localities within which you are available for work so long as you can show you still have reasonable prospects of securing employment despite those restrictions (see below).[76]

A 'reasonable prospect' of securing employment

You must show that you have a reasonable prospect of securing employment despite any restrictions you are allowed to place on your availability.[77] If you impose more than one type of restriction, it is the cumulative effect on your job prospects that is considered. In deciding whether you still have a reasonable chance of securing employment, the DWP must consider all the evidence and in particular:[78]

- your skills, qualifications and experience; *and*
- the type and number of job vacancies within daily travelling distance of your home; *and*
- the length of time you have been unemployed; *and*
- the job applications which you have made and their outcome; *and*
- whether you are willing to move home to take up a job, but only where you are placing restrictions on the type of job you are prepared to do.

Your job prospects may be poor. However, if you do not put any restrictions on the work you will take, you are accepted as being available no matter how poor your prospects of finding work may be. You should therefore think carefully if it is sensible to apply restrictions if this applies to you.

Actively seeking work

In order to qualify for JSA you must be actively seeking work, or be treated as if you are (see p367).[79] Special rules apply if you have been allowed a 'permitted period' (see p362).

To be actively seeking work you must take, in each benefit week, such 'steps' as you can reasonably be expected to have to take in order to have the best prospects of securing employment.[80] You are expected to take more than two steps during a week unless taking one or two steps is all that it is reasonable for you to do.[81] On rare occasions, if your jobseeker's agreement (see p369) says you do not have to take any steps to seek work during a week, you can try to argue that it is reasonable for you not to take any steps, for example if you are doing a part-time job that is the most work that you can be expected to do in view of your state of health.[82]

The normal actively seeking work rule is adapted to cover any part-week at the beginning of your claim. You satisfy the test so long as you take such steps as are reasonable in the part-week to ensure you have the best chance of getting a job.[83]

In order to check that you are actively seeking work, the DWP asks you to give details of the 'steps' you have taken when you sign on every fortnight (see p399). It is therefore extremely important that you keep records of your attempts to get a job.

What counts as a 'step'

Anything you do that might lead to your being offered employment should count as a **'step'**. 'Steps' include:[84]

- applying for jobs in writing, personally or by phone;
- seeking information from advertisements, advertisers, agencies or employers;
- registering with an agency;
- appointing someone else to help you find work – eg, appointing an agent if you are looking for work in the entertainment field;
- preparing a CV;
- asking a previous employer for a reference;
- preparing a list of or looking for information about employers who may be able to offer you a job;
- looking for information about an occupation with a view to finding a job in that occupation;
- getting specialist advice on how to improve your chances of finding a job – eg, from a disability employment adviser.

When the DWP decides whether you have been actively seeking work in a week, it must disregard a step if (unless there are reasons beyond your control) you:[85]
- act in a violent or abusive manner; *or*
- spoil an application if the step is completing a job application; *or*
- undermine your prospects of getting a job by your behaviour or appearance.

In these circumstances, the DWP might issue a jobseeker's direction (see p423) and sanction you if you fail to comply with it.

Deciding what steps are reasonable

You might not count as actively seeking work if it is considered that you should be taking more steps or ones that give you a better chance of finding work. You may be asked at an advisory interview to change the steps you must take (see p402). In this case, the EO may propose a variation in your jobseeker's agreement (see p372).

When the DWP decides what steps are reasonable, all the circumstances in your individual case must be considered, including:[86]
- your skills, qualifications and abilities;
- any physical or mental limitations you may have;
- how long you have been unemployed, and your work experience;
- the steps you have taken in previous weeks and how those steps have improved your chances of finding a job;
- the availability and location of job vacancies;
- any time you have spent:
  - launching or crewing a lifeboat or acting as a part-time firefighter, undertaking duties as a member of the Territorial Army or reserve force, attending an outward bound course or taking part in an organised group helping in an emergency;

  - undertaking voluntary work and the extent to which it may have improved your chances of finding a paid job;
  - improving your chances of finding a job by training to use aids to overcome any physical or mental disabilities you may have or, if you are blind, training to use a guide dog;
  - as a part-time student on an employment-related course or time you have spent on an employment or training programme for which no training allowance is paid, if this is for less than three days a week;
- any circumstances which have resulted in you being treated as being available for work (see p357);
- whether you have applied for, taken part in or accepted a place on a course funded by the Government or European Community, which is designed to help you select, train for, obtain or retain employment or self-employment;
- if you are homeless, the fact that you have no accommodation and the steps which you need to take and did take to find a home. It should be accepted that being homeless may limit the steps you can take to look for work and that you need time to look for somewhere to live.

If your chances of getting work are poor, there may only be a limited number of steps you can take each week but it may be reasonable for the DWP to expect you to pursue all of them every week. If your chances of getting work are good, there may be many steps you could take each week but it would not be reasonable for the DWP to expect you to take all of them.[87]

Actively seeking work during your 'permitted period'

If you have been allowed a 'permitted period' (see p362) you count as actively seeking work during that period even if you are only looking for jobs in your normal line of work or at your normal level of pay, or both.[88] If you have been self-employed in your usual occupation at any time within the 12 months before you claim JSA you count as actively seeking work if you are seeking self-employment in that occupation.

Treated as actively seeking work

Even if you are not actively seeking work you can be treated as if you are in some circumstances:

- You can count as actively seeking work while you are laid off or working short time (see p380).[89]
- You are allowed two weeks (longer in some circumstances) during which you are seen as actively seeking work while away from home (see p368).
- Other situations where you can be treated as actively seeking work generally mirror those where you are treated as 'available for work' and have the same maximum lengths (see p357).[90] However, in most cases you are only considered

to be actively seeking work if the situation affects you for at least three days in the benefit week. There are differences:

- You are treated as actively seeking work in any week which is part of a period in which you are taking active steps to become self-employed under a scheme to assist people to do so.[91] This only applies during a single period lasting no more than eight weeks in any period of entitlement to JSA, starting with the week in which you are accepted on a place under the scheme. The scheme must be provided or funded by:
  - in Wales, the Secretary of State; *or*
  - in England, the Secretary of State, the Urban Regeneration Agency, an urban development corporation or a housing action trust; *or*
  - in Scotland, the Secretary of State or Scottish Enterprise or Highlands and Islands Enterprise.
- You are treated as actively seeking work for any week in which you spend at least three days on an employment or training programme for which you are not paid a training allowance.[92]

If you are attending a 'qualifying course' with the approval of an EO (see p353) and are treated as being available for work (see p354), you are also treated as actively seeking work.[93] If this is in any week which falls entirely in a vacation, you must take such steps as can reasonably be expected in order to have the best prospects of securing 'casual employment' (see p358).

Absence from home

While you are on JSA, you can be treated as actively seeking work while away from home – eg, on holiday.[94] You must inform the DWP before you go away. You still have to be available for work, so you are expected to give an assurance that you are willing and able to cut your absence short if notified of a job. In any 12-month period, you can be away from home for up to:[95]

- three weeks, if during each week you spend at least three days on an outward bound course; *or*
- if you are blind, two weeks, plus up to four other weeks spent attending training in the use of guide dogs for at least three days a week; *or*
- two weeks, in any other case.

If you are away for longer than this and so cannot be treated as actively seeking work, you must show that you are looking for work while you are away from home.

If you are considering going away from home, remember:

- You must inform the DWP before you go away, normally on a 'holiday form'.
- You must be available for work (see p354), and able to receive information about job offers. You must therefore provide details of how you can be contacted or how you plan to contact the DWP while you are away. You are

unlikely to qualify for JSA if the nature of the work you are looking for involves being personally present when job offers are made (eg, casual labouring on building sites).[96]

- You must usually be in GB to qualify for JSA. To see if you can get JSA while temporarily away, see p690. If you are unemployed and want to look for work in a European Economic Area country, see p677 to see if you can export your contribution-based JSA. See p353 if you are going to be temporarily absent from GB for the purpose of getting NHS hospital treatment.
- When you return home you must sign on (see p399) the very next day your JobCentre is open even if that is not your usual signing on day. If you do not, you may lose benefit for the whole of the period you were away unless you can show that you had 'good cause' for failing to do so (see p404).

The jobseeker's agreement

To qualify for JSA you must enter into (ie, agree and sign) a 'jobseeker's agreement'. It enables the DWP to monitor and direct your search for a job. It also gives you a chance to put any restrictions in your availability for work that are agreed on record. The jobseeker's agreement is discussed with you during your interview (see p393).

Until you have agreed the contents of the jobseeker's agreement with your EO, your claim for JSA is not passed to a decision maker to decide whether you have paid sufficient NI contributions (see p349) or whether you pass the means test (see p349). However, see p370 for situations when you can be treated as having signed an agreement.

The agreement is not valid until it has been signed by you and the EO.[97] You are given a copy and you should take it with you every time you sign on.[98] To find out when your agreement can be backdated, see p371. For what happens if you cannot agree, see p371.

If a decision on your claim is delayed or JSA is refused because you have not entered into a jobseeker's agreement you may be able to get hardship payments.

What is in the jobseeker's agreement

A jobseeker's agreement must contain the following information:[99]

- your name;
- unless you say that you are prepared to work at any time, the total number of hours that you are available for work each week, with a breakdown of what hours you are available on each day. This is what is known as your **'pattern of availability'**. For information on restricting the number of hours and the times for which you are available, see pp362 and 363;
- other restrictions you are placing on the work you are prepared to do (eg, the type of work, the level of pay or the distance you are prepared to travel) (see p361);
- the type of job you are looking for;

- the steps you are to take to seek work or to improve your chances of finding work (see p365);
- if you have been allowed a 'permitted period' (see p362), the dates on which it starts and ends;
- a statement of your rights if you and the EO cannot agree on what should be in the agreement;
- the date of the agreement.

The agreement also confirms that you must be capable of, available for and actively seeking work. It advises you to keep a record of what you do to find work and that if you do not do enough, your JSA might be affected.

Your jobseeker's agreement is not binding on you or the DWP. There is no penalty if you fail to keep it. However, whether or not you keep to your jobseeker's agreement, the DWP might still decide that you are not available for or actively seeking work. However, if you have done everything in your jobseeker's agreement, you can try to argue that you should not be accused of not actively seeking work.[100]

Treated as signing a jobseeker's agreement

You can be treated as if you have signed a jobseeker's agreement even if you have not done so. This enables JSA to be paid before you have your interview (see p393).

You are treated as signing an agreement:[101]

- for the period from your date of claim until the date of your interview with a visiting EO, where you are allowed to make a claim for JSA by post (see p391);
- if you stop claiming JSA before your new jobseeker's interview;
- for as long as you are treated as being available for work (see p357) because of circumstances which arose between the date of your claim and your new jobseeker's interview;
- if there are circumstances affecting the normal procedures for claiming, awarding or paying JSA (eg, a computer failure at the DWP, a strike by staff or severe weather) which make it impracticable or difficult for you to comply with them;[102]
- where you sign on at the JobCentre after a period claiming JSA while getting a training allowance (and so not having to be available for work), from the date your training course ends until your interview;
- for the period of your temporary absence from GB, if you are a member of a 'joint-claim couple' (see p394) and on the date that the other member of the couple makes a claim for JSA, you are:
  - in Northern Ireland (for a maximum of four weeks) but only if you are unlikely to be away for more than 52 weeks; *or*
  - attending a job interview (for a maximum of seven days).

Disputes about a jobseeker's agreement

Your EO is not allowed to sign your jobseeker's agreement unless s/he is satisfied that you would qualify as being available for and actively seeking work (see pp354 and 365) if you complied with its terms.[103] If s/he thinks you are placing unreasonable restrictions on your availability for work or that the steps you are proposing to take to actively seek work are not sufficient, s/he will not sign the agreement.

If this situation arises the EO may refer the proposed jobseeker's agreement to a decision maker. If you ask your EO to do so, s/he must refer the proposed agreement to a decision maker immediately.[104]

The decision maker decides:[105]

- whether it is reasonable to expect you to have to comply with it; *and*
- whether you would qualify as being available for and actively seeking work if you were to comply with its terms.

The decision maker may also direct the EO to enter into a jobseeker's agreement on whatever terms s/he considers appropriate and may also order that if the agreement is entered into, it should be backdated.[106]

The decision maker must make a decision within 14 days of the agreement being referred unless to do so would be impracticable.[107] You are notified of the decision.[108] If you are happy with the decision, you have to make another appointment to see your EO and sign the agreement. If you are unhappy with it, you can ask for the decision to be revised or superseded, or appeal to an appeal tribunal (see pp1189, 1199 and Chapter 44).

If your proposed jobseeker's agreement is referred to a decision maker, you should immediately apply for hardship payments (see p443). See Chapter 47 for information about dealing with delays and making complaints.

If the decision maker decides in your favour, your jobseeker's agreement is normally backdated and you are paid arrears of JSA from the date of your claim. However, if the decision maker decides against you, you are unlikely to get any backdating. You, therefore, risk losing benefit if you refuse to sign the jobseeker's agreement and insist on its referral to a decision maker.

Rather than refuse to sign the jobseeker's agreement, you might do better to sign it and then write to the DWP saying that you would like to change it (see p372). You should not lose JSA so long as you comply with the original jobseeker's agreement while the variation is being considered. It is important you make it clear that you intend to do so. If there is a doubt whether you are available for or actively seeking work (see pp354 and 365), your JSA could be suspended (see p1105).

Backdating the jobseeker's agreement

A jobseeker's agreement is automatically backdated to the first day on which you claimed JSA so long as you and your EO can agree about what it should contain and it is not referred to a decision maker.[109] This includes any date to which your claim has been backdated (see p1087).

If the agreement is referred to a decision maker it is only backdated if the decision maker makes a direction ordering this.[110] When deciding whether to make a direction, the decision maker must consider all the relevant circumstances including the following factors:[111]

- whether it was reasonable for you to refuse to accept the agreement proposed by the EO; *and*
- whether the terms of any alternative agreement which you may have proposed are reasonable; *and*
- whether you have subsequently said that you would be prepared to accept the agreement proposed by the EO; *and*
- the date on which you were first prepared to enter into an agreement which the decision maker considers to be reasonable; *and*
- the fact that the first opportunity you had to sign a jobseeker's agreement was later than the date of your claim for JSA (unless, exceptionally, your new jobseeker's interview – see p393 – was on the same day as your claim).

Changing your jobseeker's agreement

The terms of your jobseeker's agreement can be changed by agreement between you and your EO. Any variation must be in writing and signed by you and the EO.[112]

Both you and the EO can propose changes at any time. It is best to put your proposals in writing. Your letter should contain full details of the changes you want to make and the reasons why you want to make them. An EO cannot agree to a variation unless s/he considers that the terms mean that you satisfy the labour market conditions.[113]

If you propose a change to your agreement, you are usually called in for an interview. If the EO is prepared to accept the changes you want to make, you can both sign a new jobseeker's agreement there and then and you are given a copy.[114]

If either you or the EO do not agree to a proposed change it can be referred to a decision maker.[115] It *must* be referred to a decision maker if you request this. If the decision maker believes that both your and the EO's proposals are reasonable and you would qualify as being available for and actively seeking work (see pp354 and 365), s/he must give preference to your proposals.[116]

When a proposed variation to an agreement is referred to a decision maker, the existing agreement remains in force until the decision maker's decision is made. Your JSA may be suspended if you do not stick to the terms of your existing agreement until the decision maker's decision, if this causes a doubt about whether you are available for or actively seeking work.

The decision maker can direct a variation of the jobseeker's agreement and the terms on which you and the EO must agree to vary it.[117] If you fail to sign the new agreement within 21 days, the decision maker can bring your jobseeker's agreement to an end.[118] If this happens, you no longer get JSA, including during any revision or appeal period, unless you qualify for hardship payments (see p443).

If you are unhappy with the decision maker's decision you can request a revision or appeal to an appeal tribunal (see p1189 and Chapter 43). If your appeal is eventually allowed, the original jobseeker's agreement revives and you are owed arrears even if the tribunal or commissioner directs another variation in the agreement.[119]

Urgent cases payments

'Urgent cases payments' are payments of JSA at a reduced rate (see p664). You may be able to get these if you are:[120]

- a person subject to immigration control and meet certain conditions; *or*
- treated as possessing income which was due to be paid to you but which has not been paid (see p985). The income you are treated as possessing must not be readily available to you and the decision maker must be satisfied that if you do not get an urgent cases payment, you, your partner or any children for whom you are responsible (see p375) and who live in your household (see p375) will suffer hardship.[121] If you were due to receive a *benefit* but it has not been paid you are *not* treated as possessing it.

Urgent cases payments are calculated in a special way (see p664). An urgent cases payment is a payment of income-based JSA so you are automatically eligible for passported benefits (see p411). Even if you or your partner are entitled to ordinary income-based JSA you can claim urgent cases payments instead if the amount you receive would be higher. You do not have to make a separate claim for urgent cases payments.[122]

There may be situations when you come under the rules for an urgent cases payment and hardship payments (see p443) for the same period. If so, your JSA is assessed at a particularly low rate.

2. **The rules about your age**

There is no minimum age for entitlement to **contribution-based jobseeker's allowance (JSA)** but in practice, because you can only qualify if you have paid or been credited with sufficient national insurance (NI) contributions in the two tax years before the benefit year in which you claim (see p844), you are unlikely to qualify before the age of 18.

You cannot usually qualify for **income-based JSA** until you are 18. There are special rules that can help you qualify if you are 16 or 17 (see p381). If you do not qualify, see if you might qualify for income support (IS) instead (see Chapter 13).

Even if you cannot get JSA or IS you may qualify for housing benefit (see Chapter 10).

You cannot usually qualify for **joint-claim JSA** unless you and your partner are both 18. If only one of you is 18 or over, the other must qualify for income-based JSA in her/his own right as a 16- or 17-year-old (see p381).[123]

You cannot claim JSA if you are pension age or over (currently 60 for a woman and 65 for a man). In practice there is usually no point in remaining on income-based JSA if you are a man aged 60 or over, as from that time you qualify for pension credit (PC) on the grounds of age without having to sign on as unemployed (see Chapter 18). You also receive automatic NI credits (see p841).

You (and your partner) should be no worse off on PC than on income-based JSA. See p410 for further information.

3. Claiming for others

If you claim **contribution-based jobseeker's allowance** (JSA) you can only claim for yourself. You cannot claim any additions for your partner or your children.

You and your partner must usually both claim **joint-claim JSA** if you are what is known as a 'joint-claim couple' (see p394).

If you claim **income-based JSA** (but not joint-claim JSA), you claim for yourself and your partner, if you have one. If you are a member of a couple who does not have to claim joint-claim JSA, you or your partner may claim income-based JSA for you both. See p811 for who counts as a couple. Whichever one of you claims, the other can make a claim for credits in order to protect her/his national insurance record (see p838). If you are both 18 or over but under 60, the non-claimant might be required to attend a work-focused interview (see p1094). If s/he fails to do so without good cause, income-based JSA might be paid at a reduced rate.

In some cases, you need to know who counts as a 'member of your family' for JSA purposes. **'Member of the family'** means your partner and any child or young person who is a member of your household and for whom you count as 'responsible' (see below).[124]

Children

New rules from 6 April 2004

From 6 April 2004, if you make a new claim for income-based JSA you do not claim this for your children. Instead you claim child tax credit (CTC). If you are already claiming JSA on 6 April 2004, but have not yet claimed CTC, you continue to get allowances and premiums for your children until you are transferred onto CTC. See p818 for further information about the transitional rules.

There are some situations where you need to show that you are 'responsible' for a child who is living in your household. You do not have to be the child's parent.[125] This includes a child under 16, or a young person under 19 if s/he is still in full-time 'relevant' education (see p618 for what this means).[126] We refer to these young people as 'children' in this *Handbook*. **Note:** Certain 16/17-year-olds who left local authority care on or after 1 October 2001 do not count as your children (see p713). To see when someone stops counting as a child, see p376.

Responsibility for a child

You are treated as 'responsible' for a child if you get child benefit for the child. Where no one gets child benefit you count as 'responsible' if you are the only one who has applied for it. Otherwise, you count as responsible if the child 'usually lives' with you.[127] Where a child for whom you are 'responsible' gets child benefit for another child, you count as responsible for that child.

If your child lives with more than one person (eg, you and her/his other parent from whom you are separated), your child counts as usually living with you if s/he spends more time with you than with anyone else.[128] This is not decided by looking at the position on a week-by-week basis, but by looking at what is usual over a longer period.[129]

The rules say that for JSA purposes, a child can only be the responsibility of one person in any week.[130] However, if you share actual responsibility for the child (eg, you share responsibility with your ex-partner), then a recent court decision means that even if you do not get child benefit for the child, you should be regarded as responsible for the child if you are a **'substantial minority carer'** – ie, you have the child with you for at least 104 nights a year.[131] However, the DWP is contesting this decision and may not treat you as responsible if you do not get child benefit.[132] Seek advice (see Appendix 2) and see CPAG's *Welfare Rights Bulletin* for updates.

See p376 for when a child stops counting as a child.

Note: There are different rules about children for the purpose of deciding whether you must claim joint-claim JSA. See p395 for further information.

Living in the same household

If you count as responsible for a child, then that child is usually treated as a member of your household even during any temporary absence (see below). For the meaning of household, see p812.

A child does *not* count as a member of your household, even if s/he is staying with you, if s/he:[133]

- is being fostered by you under a specific statutory provision. However, a child counts as a member of your household if you are fostering privately or where social services has made a less formal arrangement for the child to live with you;

- is living with you in order to attend school but you do not count as responsible for her/him;
- is living with you prior to adoption, and has been placed with you by social services or an adoption agency.

In addition, a child does *not* count as a member of your household, even if s/he normally does, if s/he:[134]

- is boarded out or has been placed with someone else prior to adoption;
- is in the care of, or being looked after by, the local authority and not living with you. The child should count as a member of your household on the days when s/he comes home – eg, for the weekend or a holiday;[135]
- has been in hospital or a local authority home for more than 12 weeks, and you or other members of your household have not been in regular contact with her/him. The 12 weeks run from the date s/he went into the hospital or home, or from the date you claim income-based JSA, if later.[136] However, if you were entitled to income support (IS) immediately before your claim for income-based JSA, the 12 weeks runs from the date s/he went into the hospital or home;[137]
- is in custody on remand or serving a sentence. The child should count as a member of your household on the days when s/he comes home – eg, for the weekend or on leave;[138]
- has been abroad for more than four weeks, or for more than eight weeks if the absence abroad is to get medical treatment for the child.[139] The four- or eight-week periods run from the day s/he went abroad or from the day you claim income-based JSA, if later. However, if you were entitled to IS immediately before your claim for income-based JSA, the four- or eight-week periods are calculated from the day after the child went abroad.[140]

Temporary absence from home

Your child continues to count as a member of your household while s/he is temporarily away from home, unless s/he:[141]

- has no intention of resuming living with you; *or*
- is likely to be away for more than 52 weeks (or s/he is unlikely to be away for 'substantially' more than 52 weeks and there are exceptional circumstances).

Remember that in some situations, a child *cannot* count as a member of your household while s/he is away from home, even if the absence is temporary (see above).

When someone stops counting as a child

Someone continues to count as a child until s/he is 16 – or 19 if s/he is in 'relevant education' (see p618).[142] Children who have left school still count as in relevant education until the 'terminal date' (see p89), or until they get full-time paid work if that is earlier. 'Full-time' work for these purposes means at least 24 hours a week.[143]

A 16/17-year-old who has left school or college may continue to count as a child for a few months after the terminal date – known as the child benefit extension period (see pp88 and 90 for details and dates).

Some 16/17-year-olds can get IS or income-based JSA in their own right (see p381) and they cannot count as your child.[144]

4. The amount of benefit

The amount of jobseeker's allowance (JSA) you get depends on whether you are claiming contribution-based JSA or income-based JSA. While you are on JSA you are entitled to be awarded a credit for national insurance (NI) contributions purposes. See p837 for further details.

Waiting days

You are not entitled to either income-based or contribution-based JSA for the first three days ('waiting days') of any jobseeking period (see p348) unless:[145]

- your claim is linked to a previous claim for JSA (see p348). For 'joint-claim couples' this includes a previous claim made by either of you separately; *or*
- you (or for 'joint-claim couples' only – see p394 – either of you) have been entitled to income support (IS), incapacity benefit or carer's allowance within the 12 weeks before you become entitled to JSA; *or*
- you are the member of a 'joint-claim couple' nominated to be paid JSA (see p406) and are in receipt of a training allowance; *or*
- you are 16 or 17 and getting JSA under the severe hardship rules (see p384).

In addition, if you and your partner swap which of you claims IS or JSA for both of you, and the new claim is for JSA, you do not have to serve any waiting days.[146]

If you receive income-based JSA you are entitled to maximum housing benefit and/or council tax benefit during any waiting days (see pp112 and 206).

Amount of contribution-based jobseeker's allowance

Contribution-based JSA is paid at the following weekly rates:[147]

Age of claimant	*£pw*
Under 18	33.85
18–24	44.50
25+	56.20

You are not paid an allowance for your partner or children.

These amounts are reduced penny for penny if you receive an occupational or personal pension of more than £50 in any week (see p948).[148] Contribution-based JSA may also be reduced penny for penny by any earnings you have from working part time. For more on how earnings are calculated and for when certain earnings are ignored, see p947. Other types of income and any capital including any earnings and capital of your partner do not affect your contribution-based JSA.[149]

Contribution-based JSA is only paid for a limited period. You can claim income-based JSA (including joint-claim JSA) to top up your contribution-based JSA if you satisfy the means test.

Duration of contribution-based jobseeker's allowance

You cannot receive more than 182 days of contribution-based JSA in any jobseeking period (see p348) or in two or more jobseeking periods where entitlement is based on NI contributions in the same two contribution years.[150] However, you can have another 182 days of contribution-based JSA for a later claim if:[151]

- you satisfy the contribution conditions; *and*
- at least one of the two contribution years used to decide whether you satisfy the contribution conditions is later than the second contribution year used to decide your previous entitlement.

Each day for which you are entitled to contribution-based JSA, even if you are not paid, counts towards the 182-day total. Because JSA is a weekly benefit, you are entitled on Saturdays and Sundays.

Days when you are entitled to contribution-based JSA but are not paid include days you:

- satisfy the contribution conditions to contribution-based JSA but:[152]
  - you have been sanctioned (see Chapter 16); *or*
  - your JSA is not payable because a court has decided that you failed to comply with a 'community order' without a reasonable excuse (see p1117); *or*
  - JSA is not paid because of the 'loss of benefit for benefit offences' rules (see p1169); *or*
- meet conditions of entitlement but a pension, or a combination of a pension and earnings, means that the amount paid is reduced to nil (see p948); *or*
- are refused contribution-based JSA because you do not meet the labour market conditions *and* you are receiving a hardship payment (see p444).[153]

Days when you are not entitled to JSA, and which do *not* count towards the 182-day total include:

- waiting days (see p377);
- days in any benefit week where you are not entitled to JSA because you earn more than the prescribed amount (see p948);

- days when you are refused contribution-based JSA because you do not meet the labour market conditions and you are *not* getting a hardship payment.

Amount of income-based jobseeker's allowance

Income-based JSA tops up your income to a level set by the government that changes every April. The amount you get depends on your needs – the Department for Work and Pensions calls this your 'applicable amount' – and on how much income and capital you have.[154] For the rules on income see Chapter 38 and on capital, Chapter 39.

Your 'applicable amount' consists of:

- a **personal allowance** (see p878); *and*
- **premiums** (see p882) for any special needs; *and*
- **housing costs**, principally for mortgage interest payments (see Chapter 36).

The way income-based JSA is calculated is the same as for IS. See pp303–304 for details of how IS is calculated.

If you have children

It is important to remember that from April 2004, income-based JSA does not include allowances and premiums for your children. Instead you claim child tax credit (CTC – see Chapter 49). CTC does not count as income for income-based JSA.

If you were getting income-based JSA on 5 April 2004 and this included allowances and premiums for your children, but you were not yet entitled to CTC, you will be transferred onto CTC some time after 6 April 2004. See p819 for further information.

You might get a reduced amount of JSA if:

- you are unwilling to apply for child support maintenance or to provide information to the Child Support Agency that is needed to make a maintenance assessment (see Chapter 34). If you come under the 'new rules' this includes refusing to submit to a DNA test; *or*
- you are getting an urgent cases payment of JSA (see p373); *or*
- you are required to make a joint claim for JSA but your partner has not fulfilled all the eligibility conditions (see p396) or has been sanctioned (see Chapter 16); *or*
- you have a partner, you both are 18 or over but under 60 and your partner has failed to attend a work-focused interview without good cause (see p1094); *or*
- you are receiving a hardship payment of income-based JSA (see Chapter 16); *or*
- a court has decided that you failed to comply with a 'community order' without a reasonable excuse (see p1117); *or*
- your JSA has been restricted under the 'loss of benefit for benefit offences' rules (see p1169).

Different rules for calculating your JSA can sometimes apply if you are in one of the groups to whom special rules apply.

5. Special rules for special groups

There are some groups of claimants to whom special rules apply. These are:

- workers who are laid off or working short time (see below);
- 16/17-year-olds (see p381);
- people in receipt of a training allowance (see p389);
- people coming from abroad (see Chapter 26);
- people without accommodation (see Chapter 28);
- people involved in a trade dispute (see Chapter 28);
- people in hospital (see Chapter 28);
- people who are studying full time or part time (see Chapter 25).

Laid-off and short-time workers

If, because of 'temporary adverse industrial conditions' you have a job but:[155]

- your work and wages have been suspended, you count as being **laid off**. For example, you count as being laid off if you are a farm worker whose work is suspended because of a scare about food safety;
- your hours of work have been reduced, you count as being on **short-time working**. For example, you count as short-time working if you are a secretary in a solicitor's office whose hours are reduced because the property market is flat and there is no conveyancing to be done.

Special rules allow you to be seen as being available for and actively seeking work (see pp354 and 365) for up to 13 weeks if you have been laid off or put on short-time working even though you are still subject to your normal employment contract and so have a duty to return to work or to working full time as soon as your employer calls on you to do so.

The days you claim jobseeker's allowance (JSA) under these rules count towards your 182 days of contribution-based JSA entitlement. So, if you think that you are likely to become fully unemployed in the foreseeable future, and you are not claiming income-based JSA, you might gain more JSA overall by not claiming it until you become fully unemployed. However, if your earnings drop below the lower earnings limit (see p827) you do not have any national insurance (NI) contributions deducted. You may then wish to sign on for JSA which entitles you to NI credits (see p838).

Availability for work

You count as being available for work (see p354) for the first 13 weeks of a period of being laid off or of short-time working so long as:[156]

- you are willing and able to return immediately to:
  - the job from which you were laid off; *or*
  - full-time working in the job in which you are being kept on short time; *and*
- you are willing and able to take up immediately (subject to the rules on p355) any casual work which is within daily travelling distance of your home. If you are a short-time worker, this only has to be during the hours when you are not working in your normal job; *and*
- in the case of short-time working only, the weekly total of the number of hours during which you are working and the number of hours during which you are available for casual employment is at least 40 hours (unless you are restricting your hours of availability to less than 40 because of a physical or mental condition or because of caring responsibilities – see pp361 and 363).

A **'week'** for this purpose means any period of seven consecutive days.[157] **'Casual employment'** is work which the employer is prepared for you to leave without giving any notice.[158]

You are not entitled to a 'permitted period' (see p362) if you are claiming JSA under these rules.[159] If you are receiving JSA while laid off or kept on short time and then lose your job completely, you are then allowed a permitted period but it must end by a date no more than 13 weeks after the start of your JSA claim.

Actively seeking work

You are treated as actively seeking work (see p365) during any benefit week in which you are subject to the special rules on availability described above, for at least three days. You must take all the steps which you can reasonably be expected to take which give you the best prospects of finding casual work.[160]

16/17-year-olds

You can qualify for JSA if you are aged 16 or 17 in some circumstances. You can qualify for:

- **contribution-based** JSA (see p349) if you satisfy the contribution conditions;
- **income-based** JSA if you satisfy the basic rules of entitlement and you are entitled under the rules described below. This includes severe hardship payments (see p384);
- **joint-claim** JSA, if you satisfy the basic rules of entitlement, only one of you is 18 or over and the other would be entitled to income-based JSA under the rules described below. This includes severe hardship payments (see p384).

If you are claiming any type of JSA, you can apply for ordinary hardship payments if you are sanctioned or there is a doubt about you meeting the labour market conditions (see p443).

If you have already had a job or training place and are looking for another one, you can claim a payment called a 'bridging allowance' (see p388). This is not part of the JSA scheme.

When you cannot qualify for income-based jobseeker's allowance

You cannot qualify for JSA if you:

- are a member of the family (see p374) of someone who is claiming income support (IS) or income-based JSA;[161] *or*
- leave local authority care in England and Wales, having been in care on or after 1 October 2001.[162] Instead, your local authority should support and accommodate you. See p713 for further information and exceptions to the rules. Similar rules apply in Scotland if you cease to be looked after by a local authority on or after 1 April 2004 (see p714).

In addition, remember that in most cases, you cannot claim JSA if you are in 'relevant education'.

Entitlement to income-based jobseeker's allowance

You can qualify for income-based JSA while you are 16 or 17 if you are a person who can claim:

- at any time before age 18 (see below); *or*
- during the child benefit extension period (see p383); *or*
- during other limited periods (see p383); *or*
- on a discretionary basis. This applies if you do not qualify for income-based JSA under the rules listed above but would otherwise suffer severe hardship (see p384). In this case you are paid severe hardship payments.

You must satisfy all the other rules of entitlement to income-based JSA (see pp347 and 349). You must register for work and training and must usually show that you are actively seeking both of these. There are special rules for calculating your JSA 'applicable amount' (see p879).

Qualifying at any time before age 18

You can qualify for income-based JSA at any time before you are 18 if you satisfy the normal conditions of entitlement (see p347), *and*:[163]

- you come within one of the groups of people who can claim IS (see p294). In this case, you can choose whether to claim JSA or IS; *or*
- you are one of a couple and you are responsible for a child in your household (see p374); *or*
- you have never been sanctioned (unless the sanction was for failing to carry out a jobseeker's direction) and have accepted an offer to enlist in the armed forces within eight weeks of the offer being made and were not in employment or training when the offer was made. See Chapter 16 for further information about sanctions.

Qualifying during the child benefit extension period

You may be able to claim income-based JSA during the child benefit extension period (see p88) – a short period after leaving school or college. You qualify for income-based JSA during the child benefit extension period if:[164]

- you are a member of a married couple and your partner is:
  - 18 or over; *or*
  - under 18, does not qualify for contribution-based JSA and is:
    - registered for work and training; *or*
    - treated as being responsible for a child who is a member of her/his household (see p374); *or*
    - laid off or on short-time working and is available for work under the special rules described on p380; *or*
    - temporarily absent from Great Britain and is taking a child or young person, for whom you are responsible and who is a member of your household (see p374), abroad for treatment (for the first eight weeks of the absence); *or*
    - incapable of work and training because of a physical or mental condition and a doctor confirms s/he is likely to remain incapable for a period of at least 12 months; *or*
  - under 18, does not qualify for contribution-based JSA and fits into certain of the groups of people who can claim IS. These are:
    - people with childcare responsibilities and carers (other than those on parental or paternity leave – see p296);
    - pupils, students and people on training courses (see p297);
    - people who are blind, or who are refugees learning English, or who are subject to immigration control but entitled to the urgent cases rate of IS (see p298).

  Satisfying these rules helps you to qualify for the highest rate of personal allowance for a couple. In many of these cases your partner can claim either JSA or IS, but this allows you to be the claimant instead; *or*
- you are a person who qualifies for the higher rate personal allowance for any of the reasons listed on p880 (other than the first or last reason).

Qualifying during other limited periods

Even if you are not someone who can claim income-based JSA at any time before you are 18 (see p382), you may be able to claim it for a limited period:

- You can claim after the end of the child benefit extension period (see p88) if one of the following applies:[165]
  - You are discharged from custody or detention after the child benefit extension period ends, and you are in one of the groups of people who can claim income-based JSA during the child benefit extension period (see above). You can claim income-based JSA for up to eight weeks from the day after you were discharged.

  - You have to live away from your parents and anyone acting as your parent following a stay in accommodation provided by a local authority. You can claim income-based JSA for up to eight weeks from the date of leaving the accommodation. That date can be either before or after the end of the child benefit extension period. If you leave the accommodation less than eight weeks before the end of the child benefit extension period, you are first entitled to income-based JSA under the rules on p383, and then your benefit can continue under this rule until the end of the eight-week period. Remember that some people cannot claim JSA when they leave local authority care (see p713).
- You can claim during any period that you are laid off or are on short-time working and are available for work under the special rules described on p380.[166]

Qualifying for severe hardship payments

If you do not qualify for income-based JSA under any of the rules for 16- or 17-year-olds above or for IS (see Chapter 13), you can still be paid income-based JSA on a discretionary basis if you would otherwise suffer severe hardship (see below).[167] We refer to this type of JSA as 'severe hardship payments' in this *Handbook*.

If it is decided that you are in severe hardship or will suffer severe hardship, a 'severe hardship direction' is issued. You must have a 'severe hardship direction' to get severe hardship payments. If you are one of a couple and you are only getting income-based JSA at one of the lower rates (see p879), you may be eligible for the couple rate if a 'severe hardship direction' is made in respect of your partner.

Remember that:

- severe hardship payments are payments of JSA so you are automatically eligible for other benefits (see p409);
- there are special rules about sanctions that only apply to severe hardship payments (see p440).

All your circumstances should be considered when deciding whether you are suffering or likely to suffer severe hardship, but the following factors should be taken into account:[168]

- your financial circumstances, including income, capital and debts;
- whether you are homeless or at risk of homelessness if severe hardship payments are not paid;
- whether you have any health problems or are pregnant or are vulnerable and at risk for any reason;
- whether you are making reasonable efforts to get work or a training place;
- whether anybody can support you.

A 'severe hardship direction' normally lasts for eight weeks but it can be longer or shorter than this depending on your circumstances.[169] For example, you can try to argue that a short-term direction should be made if you are starting work or training soon, or have not yet signed on or registered for training because it is difficult to get to the different offices, or evidence to support your application is not easily available.

When your 'severe hardship direction' ends, you can apply for it to be renewed. You can then continue to get severe hardship payments. Before awarding a new severe hardship direction the Department for Work and Pensions (DWP) should review your circumstances. However, if your 'severe hardship direction' is revoked, you can no longer get severe hardship payments. A direction can (but does not have to) be revoked if:[170]

- your circumstances have changed and you would no longer suffer severe hardship if you did not receive severe hardship payments; *or*
- the direction was given in ignorance of, or because of a mistake about, a material fact. This could give rise to a recoverable overpayment (see Chapter 41);[171] *or*
- you failed to follow up an opportunity of a place on a training scheme or rejected an offer of a place and cannot show good cause for having done so. 'Good cause' is not defined in the rules. If your 'severe hardship direction' is revoked on this ground, you can apply for another one straight away but if one is made, your severe hardship payments are reduced for a two-week period. See p440 for further information about severe hardship payment sanctions.

Labour market conditions

If you are 16 or 17, in general you are subject to the same labour market conditions as people aged 18 or over.[172] For information about the rules on availability for and actively seeking work see pp354 and 355. However, there are some important differences to these rules.

Availability for work

Usually you can restrict your availability to jobs where the employer provides 'suitable training' (but see below for exceptions).[173] You do not have to show that you have a reasonable prospect of securing employment (see p365) despite this restriction.

You *cannot* restrict your availability for work to jobs offering 'suitable training' if:

- you have been sanctioned either under the normal rules (see p388) or under the special rules for severe hardship payments (see p440), unless the sanction was for failing to carry out a 'jobseeker's direction';
- you are claiming JSA under the special rules for people laid off or on short-time working (see p380);
- you are claiming under the special rules for people waiting to enlist in the armed forces (see p382).

Deciding whether training is **'suitable training'**[174] involves considering factors such as your personal abilities and skills, your preference and the preference of your training provider, the level of qualification you are aiming for, the length of the training, how easily you can travel to the training and how soon the training will begin.

If you have only worked for a short time but you received training for that type of work or obtained relevant qualifications, you could argue that you have a usual occupation and so should be given a 'permitted period' (see p362).

Actively seeking work

If you are 16 or 17:[175]

- you are expected to take more than one step during a week unless taking one step is all that it is reasonable for you to do;
- you must usually take at least one step to find work and one to find training every week;
- you are required to actively seek both work *and* training;
- in addition to the normal list of activities that count as a step (see p365), the activities of seeking training and seeking full-time education also count.

For this purpose training means 'suitable training' (see above).

These exceptions do not apply if you are claiming under the special rules for people laid off or on short-time working or for people waiting to enlist in the armed forces (see pp380 and 382). The first three exceptions do not apply if you have been sanctioned either under the normal JSA rules (see p415) or under the additional rules for severe hardship payments (see p440), unless the sanction was for failing to carry out a 'jobseeker's direction'.

Jobseeker's agreement

If you are 16 or 17, in general, your jobseeker's agreement is the same as those for people aged 18 or over, although it places emphasis on training. However, unless you are claiming JSA because you are laid off or on short-time working (see p380) or you have accepted an offer to enlist in the armed forces, your jobseeker's agreement must explain the rules about sanctions for claimants under 18 (see p438).[176] It should also include details of what you agreed with the Careers Service or the Connexions service about your training or employment options.

Claiming jobseeker's allowance if you are 16 or 17

To claim JSA including severe hardship payments you must first register for both work and training with the Careers Service or Connexions.[177] Either service gives you a referral form to take to the JobCentre where you are interviewed.

You do not have to register with the Careers Service or Connexions if:

- you are claiming under the special rules for people laid off or on short-time working (see p380) or if you have accepted an offer to enlist in the armed forces (see p382);[178] *or*

- there is an emergency at the Careers Services or Connexions or you would suffer hardship because of the extra time it would take to register there.[179] If this applies, you can register with the DWP at the JobCentre on a temporary basis.

If you are claiming severe hardship payments, remember to state this when you claim JSA. Always insist on your right to make a claim under the severe hardship rules and refuse to be turned away. Try to take as much evidence as you can to your interview to show that you would suffer severe hardship without payments. Be ready to explain fully why your parents are not supporting you or why they should not be expected to continue to do so and, if relevant, why it could be damaging if they were to be contacted.

If you are claiming JSA (other than severe hardship payments) the normal rules about claims and payments apply (see p390).

How your claim for severe hardship payments is dealt with

To qualify for severe hardship payments, a decision must first be made on whether to issue a 'severe hardship direction'.

Decisions about 'severe hardship directions' are made by designated DWP staff at the JobCentre or by the Under Eighteens Support Team (UEST – see Appendix 1). DWP staff in the JobCentre can grant, but not refuse, severe hardship directions.[180] Your application should be referred to the UEST for a decision if your case is considered to be sensitive or borderline. It should make a decision within 24 hours. Your case should be referred if:[181]

- your application is likely to be refused; *or*
- you are subject to a care order; *or*
- you have a partner; *or*
- you do not have good cause for refusing to give permission to contact your parents or a third party; *or*
- no one at the JobCentre is authorised to issue a severe hardship direction.

You should not be refused a severe hardship direction just because you are living at home. If you are living away from home the DWP seeks confirmation that you cannot return home. If you say your parents cannot or will not support you , the DWP may want to verify this by contacting them. It cannot do this without your permission. If you refuse permission without good reason, however, your case is referred directly to the UEST.

If you have written evidence from, or are accompanied by, a 'responsible third party', such as a relative, social worker or recognised voluntary worker, further enquiries from, or contact with, your parents may not be necessary.[182] If there is difficulty in obtaining evidence from your parents or a third party, the interviewing officer should consider a short-term direction. You can then receive severe hardship payments while further enquiries are made.

Once a severe hardship direction is issued, the normal rules and procedures for claiming income-based JSA apply. Severe hardship payments are paid in arrears, but if payment is due immediately, a 'counter payment' can be made. If you need money urgently you could apply for a social fund crisis loan (see Chapter 21).

Challenging a jobseeker's allowance decision

You can challenge a decision about whether you satisfy the rules for entitlement to JSA in the usual way. See p409 and Chapters 43 and 44 for further information.

For severe hardship payments only, you *cannot* appeal against the decision whether:[183]

- you would suffer severe hardship;
- to issue or revoke a 'severe hardship direction' or how long a direction should last.

However, you have a right to ask for a revision or seek a supersession of a decision against which you do not have a right of appeal (see pp1189 and 1199). You do not have to show specific grounds in this situation. Any reasons you give for disagreeing with the decision should be considered.

You can also complain to your MP. You might be able to apply for a judicial review (see p1253). If, for example, you obtain more evidence of your hardship, you could also make a new claim.

Sanctions

The normal rules on sanctions apply if you are claiming contribution-based JSA. If you are aged 16 or 17 and receiving income-based JSA (including severe hardship payments – see p384), you can be sanctioned in the same way as other claimants if you have:

- left a job voluntarily without just cause (see p419); *or*
- lost a job because of misconduct (see p416).

See Chapter 16 for further information about the normal rules on sanctions. Where the sanctions are for other reasons, special rules apply if you are 16 or 17 years old (see p438) or are getting severe hardship payments (see p440).

Bridging allowances

Bridging allowances can be paid by the DWP while you are between jobs or training places.[184] They are not social security benefit payments.

To be eligible for a bridging allowance, you must:[185]

- be under 18;
- have left a job or training place;
- be registered for work and training;
- not have a parent or guardian who is claiming child benefit for you.

Bridging allowances are normally only paid if you are *not* entitled to income-based JSA (see above). However, you can get a bridging allowance while getting income-based JSA if:[186]

- you are registered disabled; *or*
- it is after the child benefit extension period (see p383); *and*
  - you have been discharged from custody. This only applies if your parents were entitled to child benefit on your 'terminal date' (see p89); *or*
  - you lost your job or training place during the child benefit extension period; *or*
  - because you were sick, you were unable to take up a job or a training course but you have since recovered; *or*
  - you are a trainee who is affected by (but not involved in) a trade dispute.

A bridging allowance can be paid for up to eight weeks (40 days) in a 52-week period (indefinitely if you are registered disabled). If you are liable to pay rent and have no other income you get maximum housing benefit while receiving a bridging allowance. A bridging allowance counts as income for income-based JSA.

If you refuse a suitable training place, the DWP can refuse to pay you a bridging allowance on the grounds that you are voluntarily unemployed.

You claim a bridging allowance at the Careers Office (or JobCentre) where you register for training. The allowance is paid fortnightly. You have to sign on fortnightly and register for training.

People in receipt of a training allowance

If you are receiving training and getting a training allowance you can get income-based JSA without having to satisfy the labour market conditions.[187] This also applies if you would have been getting a training allowance if a court had not decided that you failed to comply with a 'community order' without a reasonable excuse (see p1117). For these purposes, 'training' does not include training for people aged 16–24 provided by the Learning and Skills Council for England, the National Council for Education and Training for Wales or by Scottish Enterprise or Highlands and Islands Enterprise (sometimes called 'Work-based Learning for Young People'). However, if this is the type of training you are doing, you might qualify for IS (see p297).

Training allowance

'Training allowance' means an allowance payable to you for your maintenance or in respect of a member of your family (see p374) out of public funds by a government department or by or on behalf of the Secretary of State for Education and Employment, Scottish Highlands and Islands Enterprise, the Learning and Skills Council for England or the National Assembly for Wales.[188] It must be payable for the period or part of a period of a course of training or instruction provided by or under arrangements made with that department, or approved by it.

6. Claims and backdating

You should claim jobseeker's allowance (JSA) as soon as you think you may be entitled, or you might lose benefit. The rules about claims and backdating are in Chapter 40. This section tells you about the specific rules that apply to JSA.

While you are getting JSA, you must show that you are available for and actively seeking work (see pp354 and 365). For this reason, as well as completing claim forms (see below), you are expected to attend:

- an interview when you claim (see p393); *and*
- an interview when you sign on fortnightly (see p399); *and*
- further interviews as required (see p402).

If you fail to sign on or attend an interview, your entitlement to JSA could end (see p403).

If you are claiming income-based JSA and you do not live with your child(ren)'s other parent, you might be required to apply for child support maintenance and to provide information to the Child Support Agency which is needed to make a maintenance assessment (see p854).

If you have a partner, and you both are 18 or over but under 60, your partner might be required to attend a work-focused interview (see p1094). If s/he fails to do so without good cause, your income-based JSA might be paid at a reduced rate.

JSA is administered by the Department for Work and Pensions (DWP). Two types of officer deal with JSA claims – decision makers and employment officers (EOs) (see p1180).

Making a claim

A claim for JSA must be made in writing and on the appropriate form.[189] You are also required to attend an interview (see below). JSA claim forms are only available from JobCentres. If you live in a Jobcentre Plus area, see below.

To claim JSA, you should normally go to the JobCentre which is nearest your home address but you may go to another one if you have a good reason to do so (eg, it is more accessible by public transport, has easier access for disabled people or is in the area where you are looking for work). It is possible to make contact with the JobCentre by telephone or letter. The date of your first contact is important because it usually determines the date on which your claim is treated as made (see p396).

When your forms are issued (or if you live in a Jobcentre Plus area, when you first contact the office), you are usually given an appointment at the JobCentre for an interview (see p393). You should take your completed forms to this interview. If you want to withdraw or amend your claim, notify the JobCentre before it makes its decision.[190]

If you are 16 or 17 years old, you normally have to register for work and training at the Careers Service or Connexions (see p386).

Jobcentre Plus areas

If you live in a Jobcentre Plus area, then in practice you are usually required to start your claim by telephoning a 'contact centre'. Your local Jobcentre Plus office has this number, and it may also be displayed in local advice centres, libraries, etc. The centre takes basic details, then calls you back to go through the details of your claim. Also, the date of an interview (see p393) is set. You are then sent a statement recording those details, which you are asked to sign, and details of the evidence and information you should bring with you to the interview. The signed statement of details forms your official claim, instead of the old-style claim form.

It is best for you to start your claim in this way if you can. However, if you cannot or do not want to use the telephone to start your claim, then Jobcentre Plus say that they can still deal with your claim in other ways. You might for example be invited for a 'face-to-face' interview to gather the relevant details, or in some cases they may accept an old-style claim form. Seek advice if you are unable to use a telephone and the Jobcentre Plus office will not let you start your claim in any other way.

Postal claims

You are normally required to attend the JobCentre (or ONE or Jobcentre Plus office if you live in a scheme area) for an interview (see p393), but this requirement can be waived if attending the JobCentre would mean that you would have to be away from home for more than eight hours. In this case you are allowed to send in your forms by post and your jobseeker's agreement is treated as existing until your interview is carried out by a 'visiting employment officer'.

If you make your first visit to the JobCentre in person, but it is clear that you qualify to claim by post, the DWP may arrange to carry out your interview while you are still there.

Even if you are not exempt from attending the JobCentre for your interview, you may still be allowed to sign on by post (see p400).

Claiming national insurance credits

If you are claiming national insurance (NI) credits but not JSA (see p838), the normal procedures for getting JSA apply to you. You must make your application in writing. You therefore have to arrange an appointment for an interview (see p393) and complete the 'Helping You Back to Work' form (see p392) if this is required.

Forms

Unless you are claiming in a Jobcentre Plus area, the JSA claim pack contains two main forms:

- a JSA claim form for claiming both contribution-based and income-based JSA. You must answer all the questions in the section of the form about contribution-based JSA, even if you think you only qualify for income-based JSA. You do not have to apply for income-based JSA, but if you are not sure whether you are entitled you should always claim it just in case; *and*
- a form called 'Helping You Back to Work'. This is important as it forms the basis of your jobseeker's agreement. For tips on completing it, see below.

You are also given a form telling you what information and evidence to bring to your interview (see p393). If you are claiming in a Jobcentre Plus area, see above.

If you are claiming JSA within 12 weeks of a previous claim, you may be given a shortened claim form known as 'rapid re-claim' and your interview is arranged more quickly.

You have to make a separate claim to your local authority for housing benefit (HB) and council tax benefit (CTB). You are given a claim form with your JSA claim form. If you are claiming JSA in a Jobcentre Plus area, your claim for HB and CTB is made via what the DWP calls an 'input document'. If you are making a 'rapid re-claim' for JSA, you may also be able to make a 'rapid re-claim' for HB and CTB. See pp120 and 216 for further information about claiming HB and CTB.

The 'Helping You Back to Work' form

Completing the 'Helping You Back to Work' form is not compulsory as the information needed to agree your jobseeker's agreement can be given during your new jobseeker's interview (see p393). However, if you are asked to complete one, a refusal may create a negative impression about your willingness to find work. As everyone's circumstances are different, there are no 'right' answers, but there are a number of general rules to bear in mind:

- Remember that you are stating the steps that you will take to find work. If you do not keep to these, the decision maker might say you are not actively seeking work.
- You are allowed to place restrictions on the sort of work you are prepared to do and where and when you will do it as long as you still have reasonable prospects of securing employment despite those restrictions (see p365):
  - You can restrict your availability for work in any way if the restrictions are reasonable in view of your mental or physical condition (see p361);
  - You should mention any good reasons why you cannot take certain types of job or jobs in certain areas;
  - If you have not agreed in advance that there are certain types of work which you cannot, or are unwilling, to do, it may prove very difficult to justify turning down such a job if it is offered to you later.

- If English is not your first language or if you have difficulties with reading and writing, ask someone (preferably not an employee of the DWP) to help you.
- Keep a copy of your answers.
- It is *vital* that the wage or salary you say you are willing to accept should not be higher than the going rate for the jobs you have said you are looking for. Bear in mind any entitlement you may have under the national minimum wage (see p451).

The interview

You and, if you are claiming joint-claim JSA, your partner, must usually attend the JobCentre for an interview to discuss what work you are looking for and what you intend to do to find it. You are interviewed by an EO. The aims of the interview are:

- to help you back into work as quickly as possible;
- to make sure that you are eligible to claim JSA;
- to draw up a jobseeker's agreement (see p369).

If you have been sent a claim form to complete, you should do this before your interview. If you do not provide all the evidence and information required (either by the instructions on the form or in the information you get from Jobcentre Plus), your interview might not go ahead unless you come within one of the categories on p1081. If you need help completing a form, you should contact the JobCentre before your interview or arrive a few minutes early if only some parts of the form are incomplete.

The interview forms the basis of the jobseeker's agreement which both you and the EO must sign. The EO may refer you to a job vacancy immediately but a jobseeker's agreement should still be completed to establish entitlement in case you do not get a job.

The interview also covers what you were doing before you became unemployed and, in particular, why you left your previous job. If the EO thinks that you may have left voluntarily or been dismissed for misconduct (and therefore might be liable to be sanctioned – see p415) you are asked to complete a form explaining your side of the story.

Remember that if you have a partner, and you both are under 60, your partner might be required to attend a work-focused interview (see p1094). If s/he fails to do so without good cause, your income-based JSA might be paid at a reduced rate.

Information to support your claim

When you claim JSA you must satisfy the NI number requirement. In most cases this means that you must provide your NI number as well as your partner's (see p1083). You may also be asked to provide proof of your identity (see p1083) and information to support your claim (see p394).

If you are asked to provide information which you do not have, ask what other evidence would be accepted. Press the DWP to be clear about what is required and why, and complain if you feel that any requests for information are unreasonable (see p1300).

Providing information with your claim

It is very important that you provide any information or evidence required on the claim form – known as the 'evidence requirement'. Until you do, you might not count as having made a valid claim and you could lose benefit. See p1080 for further information about the evidence requirement and to see if you are exempt from it.

If you have a mortgage you are given an additional form to give to your lender, who will provide details about your mortgage and return the form to the DWP.

Information and evidence you must supply after you claim

Even if you have provided all that is required, a decision maker might need additional evidence or information to enable her/him to make a decision about your claim. You can be asked to supply any certificates, documents, information or evidence considered relevant to your claim or to an issue arising from your claim.[191] You must do this within seven days of the request. A decision maker can allow you longer than this if s/he thinks it is reasonable. The seven-day time limit runs from the date of the decision maker's request for the additional information, *not* the date you made your JSA claim. If you do not provide the information, the decision maker is likely to decide your claim in the way most adverse to you. In some cases, if you fail to provide information when required to do so, your JSA could be suspended or even terminated (see p1106).

Who should claim

You can only claim **contribution-based JSA** for yourself.

For **income-based JSA**, if you are a single person or a lone parent you claim on your own behalf. Unless you must make a joint claim for JSA (see below), if you are a member of a couple you must choose which one of you claims for you both. See p811 for who counts as a couple. If you cannot agree who should claim, a decision maker decides.[192] If you are not the person claiming JSA, you may wish to make a claim for NI credits to protect your NI record (see p838) or to gain help from back-to-work schemes.

Joint claims for jobseeker's allowance

You must make a joint claim for JSA if you are a member of a couple (see p811) and:[193]

- at least one of you:
  - was born after 28 October 1957; *and*
  - is 18 or over; *and*

- neither of you are responsible for children in the circumstances listed below.

You are known as a **'joint-claim couple'**. You can only be a member of one 'joint-claim couple'. Where you are potentially a member of more than one 'joint-claim couple' you can choose from which to claim. If you do not choose, a decision maker decides.[194]

If you are a 'joint-claim couple' both of you must usually:

- claim JSA; *and*
- satisfy all the rules for getting income-based JSA (see pp347 and 349).

For exceptions to these rules, see pp350 and 396.

Responsible for children

You do not have to claim joint-claim JSA if you or your partner count as being responsible for a child or young person. For these purposes, you count as being responsible for a child or young person if:[195]

- you are entitled to child benefit for her/him; *or*
- no one is receiving child benefit for her/him but:
  - you count as responsible because s/he usually lives with you; *or*
  - you are the only person who has claimed child benefit for her/him; *or*
- someone else is responsible for her/him but s/he is staying with you so that s/he can attend school; *or*
- you are looking after her/him for the local authority or a voluntary organisation under specific provisions; *or*
- you are looking after her/him with a view to adoption.

Even if you do not get child benefit for your child and none of the other rules above apply, if you share actual responsibility for the child (eg, you share responsibility with your ex-partner) and are a 'substantial minority carer' (ie, you have the child with you for at least 104 nights a year), then following a recent court decision it may be arguable that you should still be regarded as responsible for the child.[196] However, the DWP is contesting this decision and may not treat you as responsible if you do not get child benefit.[197] Seek advice and see CPAG's *Welfare Rights Bulletin* for updates.

If you and your partner **become responsible** for a child or young person while you are claiming joint-claim JSA you must provide the DWP with evidence of this if required.[198] You and your partner must notify the DWP which of you is to continue claiming income-based JSA for you both. Your claim for JSA then continues without interruption.

If you and your partner **stop being responsible** for any children or young people while you are claiming income-based JSA, or they have all died or have reached the age of 16 and are no longer in full-time education, you and your partner must then claim joint-claim JSA.[199] Your claim for JSA can continue without interruption if the DWP has sufficient information to award you joint-claim JSA and you or your partner have told the DWP which of you has been nominated to receive payment for you both.

If your partner does not claim jobseeker's allowance

If you are a member of a 'joint-claim couple' and you satisfy all the rules for getting income-based JSA (see pp347 and 349), in certain circumstances you can qualify for JSA even if your partner has not made a joint claim with you. This is the case if your partner:[200]

- failed to attend the interview (see p393); *or*
- failed to meet the labour market conditions; *or*
- is temporarily absent from Great Britain (GB); *or*
- is subject to immigration control (see p654); *or*
- has failed to satisfy the habitual residence test (see p702); *or*
- is over pension age (60 for women and 65 for men). In this situation, you both might be better off if your partner were to claim pension credit for you rather than JSA; *or*
- works 16 or more but under 24 hours a week; *or*
- has claimed maternity allowance or statutory maternity pay; *or*
- is pregnant and there are 11 weeks or less before the week the baby is due; *or*
- had a baby not more than 15 weeks ago; *or*
- is receiving an unemployment benefit from another country under a reciprocal agreement (see p691); *or*
- is receiving statutory sick pay and was working 16 hours or more a week immediately before s/he became incapable of work.

In the first four cases (interview attendance, labour market conditions, temporary absence and immigration control), your JSA entitlement is calculated as if you were a single claimant.[201] However, in all other respects you are treated as a couple and, therefore, any income or capital of your partner is taken into account. In the remaining cases, JSA entitlement is calculated for both of you in the normal manner.

The date of your claim

You are usually not entitled to JSA for any day before your 'date of claim'.[202] However, in some cases you can claim in advance before you qualify (see p398) and sometimes your claim can be backdated (see p399). If you want this to be done, you should make this clear when you claim or the DWP might not consider it.

Your **'date of claim'** is usually:

- if you (and your partner if you are a 'joint-claim couple') attend your interview (see p393) at the time specified by the DWP and provide a properly completed claim form with all the information and evidence required (see p393), the date you first contact the JobCentre (eg, by telephone or letter);[203] *or*

- if you are allowed a postal claim (see p391), the earliest of:[204]
  - the date you first contact the JobCentre, so long as a properly completed claim form with all the information and evidence required (see p394) is provided within one month of your first contact; *or*
  - the date on which a properly completed claim form with all the information and evidence required (see p394) is received at the JobCentre;
- if you are a 'joint-claim couple' and only one of you is required to attend an interview, the earliest of:[205]
  - the date on which a properly completed claim form with all the information and evidence required (see p393) is received at the JobCentre, so long as the person who is required to attend an interview does so; *or*
  - the date you and your partner first contact the JobCentre, so long as a properly completed claim form with all the information and evidence required (see p394) is provided within one month of your first contact.

If you (or you or your partner if you are a 'joint-claim couple') **fail to attend an interview** at the time specified by the DWP and cannot show good cause for this, the rules above do not apply. If, without good cause, you fail to attend an interview or attend at the wrong time, so long as a properly completed claim form with all the information and evidence required is provided (see p394), your date of claim is:

- for 'joint-claim couples' only:
  - if you are both required to attend an interview, the date one of you eventually goes to the JobCentre. However, in this situation, you can only get the single person's rate of JSA (see p396); *or*
  - if only one of you is required to attend an interview, the date the person who is required to attend eventually goes to the JobCentre; *or*
- if you are not a 'joint-claim couple', the date you eventually go to the JobCentre.

'Good cause' is not defined. All relevant circumstances must be considered. These may relate to your abilities or to external factors. The general test is whether there is some factor that would probably cause a reasonable person of your age and experience to act, or fail to act, as you did.[206]

The DWP can extend the time you have to provide a properly completed claim form by up to one month from the date you first contacted the JobCentre to claim JSA.[207] This is discretionary, so you should provide your claim form within the time limit wherever possible.

If you are a member of a couple and one of you claims contribution-based JSA but is not entitled to it and a subsequent income-based JSA claim is made by your partner (or you and your partner if you are a joint-claim couple), the date of claim for income-based JSA is the date of the earlier claim for contribution-based JSA.[208] If your partner has been claiming contribution-based JSA, this expires and you claim income-based JSA, the date of claim for your income-based JSA is the day after your partner's entitlement expires.[209]

If you claim the wrong benefit

If you claim working tax credit (WTC – see Chapter 50) when you should have claimed JSA, the day you claimed WTC counts as your date of claim for JSA. However, you must:[210]

- have been refused WTC because neither you nor your partner are in full-time paid work for WTC purposes (see Chapter 51); *and*
- claim JSA within 14 days of the decision refusing your claim.

You can ask for your JSA claim to start on a later date instead – eg, where you have just finished work and have earnings that will be taken into account for a certain period of time (see p942).

Claiming in advance

You can claim JSA up to three months before you qualify,[211] thus giving the DWP time to ensure you receive benefit as soon as you are entitled. In this case, your date of claim (see p396) is the date from which you are claiming.[212] You should let the DWP know you want to claim in advance when you claim and at your interview. You might have to persuade the DWP that it can accept a claim in advance.

You might not be entitled to JSA currently, but would be once you or a member of your family (see p374) become entitled to another 'qualifying benefit' – eg, disability living allowance or carer's allowance (see Chapters 7 and 4). You should make your claim for JSA at the same time as the claim for the qualifying benefit. If you are:

- refused JSA, claim again when you get a decision about the qualifying benefit and ask for your JSA to be backdated to the date of your first JSA claim or to the date from which the qualifying benefit is paid, if that is later. See p1090 for further information;
- awarded JSA, you might be entitled to a higher rate once the outcome of the claim for the qualifying benefit is known. Seek a revision or a supersession if you think this applies to you. See p1209 for further information.

How your claim is dealt with

The decision on your claim is made by a decision maker (see p1180) and there may be some unavoidable delay in making the decision. For contribution-based JSA your NI contribution record needs to be checked. For income-based JSA your benefit needs to be calculated. If the delay is caused by doubt as to whether you meet the labour market conditions you may be able to receive hardship payments (see p443). But if any delay seems unreasonable, you should make a complaint (see Chapter 47).

Backdating your claim

It is very important to claim in time. A claim for JSA can be backdated for a maximum of three months, but only in exceptional circumstances. The rules on backdating are covered on p1085. Note that for JSA your claim cannot be backdated on the grounds that it was delayed due to your illness or disability. There are special backdating rules if you are making a new claim for JSA after you failed to sign on or attend an interview (see p405).

There are exceptions to the rule. Your claim can be backdated more than three months if:

- you are claiming JSA after being awarded a qualifying benefit and an earlier JSA claim had been refused because you did not at that time get a qualifying benefit (see p1090);
- you claimed WTC when you should have claimed JSA (see p398).

If you might have qualified for benefit earlier but did not claim because you were given the wrong information or misled by the DWP you could:

- ask for an extra statutory payment (see p1304); *or*
- complain to the Ombudsman, via your MP (see p1302).

If you want to get your jobseeker's agreement backdated, see p371.

After your claim has been accepted

Once your claim for JSA has been accepted, in order to continue to receive JSA you have to:

- sign on regularly at the JobCentre (or by post if you live some distance from the JobCentre) and attend regular interviews; *and*
- attend further interviews as required (see p402).

Signing on and regular interviews

Unless you are allowed to sign on by post (see p400), while you are getting JSA you (and if you are a joint-claim couple, both of you) must normally attend the JobCentre in order to sign a declaration that:[213]

- you have been available for and actively seeking work or could be treated as if you were (see pp354 and 365); *and*
- there has been no change in your circumstances which might affect the amount of or your right to JSA (other than those you may have already notified to the DWP).

Generally, you must sign on every fortnight. This is the case even if you are paid weekly. You can be notified of the time and place you should attend by phone, post or electronic means.[214] To find out if you must sign on more frequently, see below. If you are told you are not entitled to JSA, you can argue that you no longer have to sign on – eg, while you are appealing against the decision.[215] However, if your appeal is successful, in order to be paid arrears you need to show that you have satisfied the labour market conditions since the last time that you signed on, which can often be difficult. So it is always best to continue to sign on to protect your position.

Each time you sign on, you are interviewed. The aims of the interview are to:

- keep a regular check on what you are doing to find work and make sure that your jobseeker's agreement remains up-to-date and relevant. You should take your records of your attempts to find work with you (see p401);
- discuss any difficulties you are experiencing and identify any help and support which the DWP can give you;
- check whether there have been any relevant changes in your circumstances;
- refer you to job, training or employment scheme vacancies (see p401).

Any record of the interview should be made while you are present. You may be referred to an EO for a more in-depth interview if what you say raises a doubt as to whether you remain entitled to JSA.

More frequent signing on

You may be required to sign on weekly for six weeks after your first 'restart interview' (see p402). You may be required to sign on and attend interviews more frequently than once every two weeks if you are suspected of fraud or you are of no fixed abode.

Because decisions about how often you have to sign on and attend interviews are made by EOs, you do not have a right of appeal. However, you can ask for the frequency to be altered – eg, if your circumstances change or the cost of travel causes hardship. If you are told that you are suspected of fraud, see Chapter 42.

Signing on by post

The DWP allows you to sign on by post if:[216]

- the journey time by public transport from your home to the nearest JobCentre is more than an hour door-to-door; *or*
- attending the JobCentre would result in your being away from home for more than four hours; *or*
- you have a mental or physical disability which restricts your mobility.

If no public transport is available, the DWP looks at whether or not you can reasonably be expected to walk from home to the JobCentre in one hour.[217] You should not be asked to walk more than three miles.

Even if you do not normally have to attend the JobCentre in person, you must attend for your interview (see p393) and further interviews as required (see p402) unless to do so would result in your being away from home for more than eight hours. In this case, an interview is arranged with a visiting EO nearer your home.

Even if you are allowed to sign on by post, you still have to show that you are available for and actively seeking work (see pp354 and 365). Every time you send in the declaration, you are expected to provide evidence of what you have been doing to look for work (see below). Tell the DWP if you have literacy problems. The JobCentre should be prepared to telephone you each time you send in declarations. Alternatively, a friend or relative could provide written evidence on your behalf. If you have not provided evidence of the steps you have taken to find work and you cannot be contacted by telephone, JSA is usually withheld and you are asked to attend the JobCentre, if this is appropriate.[218]

If your declaration is not received within five working days of your postal signing date, your entitlement to JSA ends unless you can show 'good cause' for the delay (see p404). If you cannot show good cause, you must make a fresh claim for JSA and attend a new jobseeker's interview (see p393).

Proving that you are actively seeking work

It is very important to keep careful records of the steps you take to get a job. You should:

- make a note every time you make a phone call or visit a JobCentre, potential employer or agency or do anything else which might count as a 'step' towards actively seeking work (see p365). Include the dates and times, who you spoke to and what was said;
- keep copies of any letters you send and of any advertisements to which you reply;
- tell the EO if you have difficulty reading or writing, or with the English language. You can get a friend or relative to help you compile your record (and to help you look for jobs). The DWP may be prepared to accept an oral report. You could keep a written record in your first language and take an interpreter or ask for an interpreter to be provided if you cannot take anyone with you.

Referral to job, training or employment programme vacancies

While you are claiming JSA, the DWP may refer you to a job vacancy. If there are a number of possible vacancies you should always be offered the vacancies with the highest rates of pay before those paying lower rates. Bear in mind that the law now gives some workers minimum rights regarding hours, rest breaks and holidays (see p451) and you should not be expected to accept jobs that do not meet those standards.

If you are not considered ready for a job you are likely to be referred to a place on a training scheme or employment or New Deal programme. Some of these are compulsory. If you are on a 'compulsory' New Deal programme you can be sanctioned or have your claim terminated for failing to attend options, or for leaving options early (see p430). A scheme or programme that is not compulsory may become so if you are issued with a jobseeker's direction – see p423.

You risk being sanctioned if, without good cause, you refuse to apply for a notified job vacancy (see p424). Alternatively, you could be issued with a jobseeker's direction and risk being sanctioned if you refuse or fail to carry it out (see p423). A refusal to apply for a job or vacancy on a scheme or programme may also raise doubts about whether you are available for work (see p354).

Referral to a disability employment adviser

If you have a disability which impedes your search for work you may be eligible for specialist help from the DWP, including referral to a disability employment adviser (DEA). Every JobCentre has a disability adviser who is responsible for good practice relating to disabled people.

You may want to ask to be referred to a DEA if, for example:

- you feel that the normal service from the JobCentre is not meeting your needs; *or*
- you have a new disability or health problem and need specialist help; *or*
- your health problem or disability has worsened significantly; *or*
- you need new skills in order to do a job; *or*
- you need practical help with looking for a job (eg, help in getting interviews or identifying specialist equipment); *or*
- you are not clear about the effect your disability has on the job options that are open to you.

Further interviews as required

If you remain unemployed for a period of time you must attend a number of other interviews – restart and advisory interviews.

Restart interviews

You are normally asked to attend an interview after you have been claiming JSA for 13 weeks (or at the end of your permitted period – see p362), 6 months, 12 months and 24 months. These are called 'restart interviews'. The timing of the interviews is linked to the length of time you have to be unemployed to qualify for various schemes to help you get back into work. You might be required to sign on weekly for six weeks after your first restart interview.

At the interview, an EO reviews your situation, the type of work you are looking for and the steps you are taking to find it. You may be asked to agree to a variation of your jobseeker's agreement (see p372) to record any change in the type of work for which you are looking or steps you will take to find it.

Advisory interviews

You can be called in for an 'advisory interview' at any time. You are likely to be given an advisory interview if the DWP thinks that you need more help with your search for work or there is a question about whether you fulfil the 'labour market conditions' (see p347).

Travel expenses

Your travel expenses to and from the JobCentre to **sign on** are *not* reimbursed. If this causes you hardship, you should ask to sign on by post. The DWP has a discretion to allow you this even if you are not in one of the circumstances listed on p400.

You *can* have your travel costs reimbursed if you are given an appointment for an **interview** on a day other than the day you normally attend to sign on, or if you have to attend a different office on your normal signing on day and you incur additional costs.[219] If you are signing on by post but are required to visit the JobCentre for an interview you are also entitled to a refund of your travel costs.

Payment of expenses covers the cost of the cheapest public transport route or, if you are justified in using your own car, a set amount per mile by the most direct route. Only in exceptional cases is the cost of a taxi reimbursed (eg, if you have a disability and cannot use private or public transport).

Failure to sign on or attend an interview

Your entitlement to JSA can end if you fail to sign on, whether by going to the JobCentre or by post, or you fail to attend an interview when required to do so. Your benefit can be suspended while a decision maker is considering the matter (see p1106).

Unless you can show 'good cause' for your failure within five working days (see below) your entitlement to JSA ends if you fail to:[220]

- attend at a place specified by an EO in a notification (eg, the JobCentre):
  - at the right time, but you do attend sometime on the right day and it is not the first time that you have been late. The DWP must have sent you a written notice warning you that your JSA could cease if you fail to attend your next appointment; *or*
  - on the right day. The rules do not make any explicit provision for you to be given a warning in the way that they do for the situation where you attend late but on the right day.

  Notification can be in writing, by telephone or by electronic means (eg, email). If you can show you did not receive the notification, this means that you have not failed to attend and your entitlement to JSA should therefore not be ended. However, the law normally assumes that when a letter has been sent correctly addressed and with the full postage paid, it will be received. So you need to put forward a good case to show why this assumption should not be made – eg, you have always responded properly to other notifications when these were received from the JobCentre or there are problems with your postal address.[221]

If the requirement to attend is for a training scheme or employment programme, your entitlement does not end. However, you can be sanctioned instead (see p430); *or*

- sign a declaration, whether this is at the JobCentre or by post.[222]

'Good cause'

You may be able to avoid your entitlement to JSA ending if, within five working days of your failure to attend or sign on, you provide an explanation which shows that you had 'good cause' for the failure.[223] The decision maker decides whether you have good cause and you have the right to appeal against her/his decision. You have **automatic good cause** for a failure to attend when required to do so if:[224]

- you have caring responsibilities or are engaged in voluntary work and you were given less than 48 hours' notice or you are providing a service and you were given less than 24 hours' notice (see p355); *or*
- on the day you failed to attend you were someone who was treated as being available for employment in the circumstances listed on pp357–359, other than:
  - at the beginning or end of your claim for JSA; *or*
  - because you were discharged from a prison, remand centre or youth custody; *or*
  - for 'joint-claim couples' only, when you and your partner are both temporarily absent from GB and the pensioner, higher pensioner, disability or severe disability premium is being paid for your partner; *or*
  - for 'joint-claim couples' only, when you are temporarily absent from GB on the date of claim; *or*
  - you were recently found capable of work; *or*
- the day you failed to attend was in a week during which you were treated as actively seeking work because of an absence from home (see p368).

If you do not have automatic good cause (see above), you may still have **good cause for other reasons**. When deciding good cause, the decision maker must take into account *all* the circumstances of your case, including whether you misunderstood what you had to do because of language, learning or literacy difficulties or because you were misled by an EO. In addition, the decision maker must take into account:

- if you failed to attend:[225]
  - whether you (or someone for whom you are caring) were attending a medical or dental appointment which it would have been unreasonable to expect you to rearrange;
  - any transport difficulties;
  - any religious reasons why you could not attend;

  - whether you were attending a job interview;
- if you failed to sign on, adverse postal conditions (for postal claimants only).[226]

When your entitlement to jobseeker's allowance ends

If you fail to attend an interview or to sign on, you lose JSA for the period between the date on which your entitlement ends and the date on which you are treated as having claimed again.

The date on which your entitlement to JSA ends is the *earliest* of the following days:[227]

- the day after the last day for which you have provided information which shows you continue to be entitled to JSA (eg, at your regular fortnightly interview). In many cases this means the day after the last day on which you signed on;
- if you failed to attend or attend at the wrong time, the day on which you should have attended;
- if you failed to sign on, the day on which you should have done so.

The date on which you are treated as having claimed JSA again is normally the first day on which you contact the JobCentre again. But if this was the same day as the failure to attend (ie, you came on the right day but were late for the appointment) you are treated as having made your fresh claim on the *following* day.[228] See below to see if your new claim can be backdated.

The effect of this is that, if you fail to sign on, you may lose JSA for the full two weeks for which you would have been paid if you had signed on at the right time. In addition, you lose JSA for the days between the day you missed signing on and the day you next contact the JobCentre. If you have missed signing, it is possible to provide the necessary information at a later date.[229] So as soon as you contact the JobCentre again, ask it to accept the information you would have provided on the signing day. If this is accepted, the decision maker should revise the decision that stopped your benefit so that you are paid up to the date you failed to sign on.

Backdating your new claim

Where your entitlement to JSA has ceased because you failed to attend an interview or to sign on and you have to make a new claim, it may be possible to get your new claim backdated and so avoid some, or all, of the loss of JSA. Your claim can be backdated:

- under any of the normal rules (see p1085); *or*
- under the special rules described below.

Your claim can be backdated to the day after your entitlement to JSA ended if:[230]

- you failed to attend because of one of the circumstances listed on pp357–359 which allow you to be treated as being available for employment and you make a new claim for JSA no later than the day after those circumstances cease

to apply. However, this rule does not apply where you are treated as being available for employment:
- at the beginning or end of your claim for JSA; *or*
- because you were discharged from a prison, remand centre or youth custody; *or*
- because you were recently found capable of work; *or*
- for 'joint-claim couples' only, when you and your partner are both temporarily absent from GB and the pensioner, enhanced pensioner, higher pensioner, disability or severe disability premium is being paid for your partner; *or*
- for 'joint-claim couples' only, when you are temporarily absent from GB on the date of claim; *or*

- you failed to attend because you were away from home while eligible to be treated as actively seeking work because of an absence from home (see p368), and you make a new claim for JSA no later than the day after you returned home; *or*
- you are normally allowed to sign on by post, you did not receive the instruction to attend the JobCentre and you make a new claim for JSA immediately you were informed that you had failed to attend the appointment.

7. Getting paid

You can be paid jobseeker's allowance (JSA) by direct payment into your bank (or similar) account (see p1099). In some cases, you may instead be paid by cheque. In limited circumstances you can also collect your JSA from the JobCentre – known as 'personal issue' (see p407). You can indicate which method of payment you prefer when you claim JSA, although a decision maker decides how JSA is paid.

Where you and your partner are a 'joint-claim couple' you must nominate which one of you receives payment for you both. Where you cannot agree, a decision maker decides.[231] Even if you are not the person nominated to receive the JSA, if you separate from your partner and s/he cannot be traced, you can be paid any arrears of JSA that are due.[232]

In some circumstances, your JSA can be paid to other people and organisations on your behalf – these are called 'direct payments' (see p1109).

JSA is a weekly benefit.[233] Most questions about entitlement are decided in relation to a particular **'benefit week'** – ie, the period of seven days ending on the day of the week on which you sign on.[234]

JSA is normally paid fortnightly in arrears, although the DWP can decide to make other arrangements in particular cases.[235] You are usually paid for the last two benefit weeks up to and including the day you (and your partner if you are a 'joint-claim couple') sign on. If you do not sign on, you are not paid.

If you are entitled to less than 10p a week you are not paid JSA at all,[236] but you are still eligible for national insurance credits (see p838). If you are entitled to less than £1 a week, a decision maker can decide to pay you quarterly in arrears.[237]

If your cheque is lost or stolen or you have forgotten your PIN, see p1104. If payment of your JSA is suspended, see p1105.

Personal issue

In limited circumstances you may be allowed or required to collect your JSA from the JobCentre, normally on the day that you are required to sign on. People who receive their JSA in this way are described by the Department for Work and Pensions (DWP) as being on 'personal issue'. Payment by personal issue may be appropriate if:

- you live at an address that is unsafe for postal deliveries and you cannot provide an alternative address;
- you are suffering hardship due to late postal deliveries;
- you are suspected of falsely reporting that you have not received giros;
- you have no accommodation and you cannot provide an address for correspondence.

Before putting you on personal issue, the DWP is likely to ask you whether you wish to receive payment directly into a bank (or similar) account instead.

Delays and complaints

If payment of your JSA is delayed, you might be able to get an interim payment. See p1108 for further details. You may also be eligible for a crisis loan (see p538).

If you suffer delays, or wish to complain about how your claim has been dealt with, see Chapter 47. You might be able to claim compensation (see p1304).

Change of circumstances

It is your duty to report any change in your circumstances which might affect the amount of, your right to, or payment of, JSA.[238] You should do so promptly and in writing to the office handling your claim (although in individual cases notification might be accepted in a form other than writing). In any case, you might want to report the change in writing and keep a copy, in case of a dispute in the future. You must also report any change in your circumstances that you know is likely to occur.[239] If you do not notify any such change promptly and in writing, any resulting overpayment may be recoverable from you (see Chapter 41). If you are considered deliberately to have acted falsely or dishonestly, you may also be guilty of an offence (see Chapter 42).

A change in your circumstances may mean that the decision about your current benefit entitlement is superseded.

If you have a mortgage, the DWP can ask your lender about any changes in the amount you owe or the interest payable during your JSA claim. If you have this information – eg, from an annual statement you receive from your lender, you must also advise the DWP just in case your lender fails to do so. Make sure the DWP takes this information into account so you are not overpaid JSA (see p1141).

When your jobseeker's allowance is adjusted

As a general rule, your JSA is adjusted from the first day of the benefit week in which the change occurs or is expected to do so.[240] See p1204 for further information about the general rule.

There are exceptions to the rule:

- If a decision is to your advantage, but you failed to notify the DWP of a change within the time limit (see p1204), your JSA is adjusted:[241]
  - if you are paid in arrears, from the first day of the benefit week in which you notified the change; *or*
  - if you are paid in advance, from the day on which you notified the change, if this is the day you are paid benefit. If it is not, your JSA is adjusted from the next week.
- Your JSA is adjusted from the date of the change of circumstances (or the day on which this is expected to take place) if:[242]
  - the change of circumstances means you no longer qualify for JSA. However, the ordinary rule (see above) applies if the reason that you no longer qualify is that your income is too high;
  - a child or young person (see p374) only stays with you for part of the week and the rest of the week is in care or in custody;
  - if you are a 'joint-claim couple', you cease to be a couple;
  - your partner, child, or a young person for whom you are responsible (see p374) comes home from hospital for a stay of less than a week.

  This also applies if your circumstances change back again.
- Where you have income that is counted as being paid on a particular day (see p991) and this changes (or such a change is expected), your JSA is adjusted from the day the income counts as being paid.[243] But this does not apply to an adjustment to your contribution-based JSA due to a change in your occupational pension.

If a change of circumstances means the amount of your JSA should go down (or is expected to go down) but a decision maker accepts it would not be practicable to adjust your JSA on the days outlined above, your JSA is adjusted from the first day of the benefit week following the one in which the change occurred.[244]

Overpayments and fraud

If you are overpaid JSA, you might have to repay it. The rules on overpayments are covered in Chapter 41.

If you have been accused of fraud, see Chapter 42. You might get a reduced amount of JSA if you have been sanctioned for benefit offences (see p1169).

8. Challenging a jobseeker's allowance decision

You can apply for a revision or a supersession of a jobseeker's allowance (JSA) decision, or appeal against it (see Chapters 43 and 44). Remember that if you are told you are not entitled to JSA, you can argue that you no longer have to sign on – eg, while you are appealing against the decision.[245] However, it is always best to continue to sign on to protect your position.

You cannot seek a revision or a supersession of an employment officer's (EO's) decision or appeal against it. If you disagree with an EO's decision, see p1186. There is a special procedure used in cases where you disagree about the content of your jobseeker's agreement (see p371).

9. Tax, tax credits and other benefits

Jobseeker's allowance (JSA) is taxable.[246] The maximum amount of JSA that is taxable is:

- if you are claiming for yourself, an amount equal to the appropriate personal allowance for a person of your age (see p878); *or*
- if you are a member of a couple, an amount equal to the income-based JSA personal allowance for an adult couple (half this amount if your partner is unable to claim JSA because s/he is involved in a trade dispute).

The tax is not deducted while JSA is being paid but reduces the refund you would otherwise receive through Pay As You Earn (PAYE) when you return to work. Any tax refunds of PAYE payments are paid to you at the end of the tax year to which they relate. Any other tax refund is paid only when you stop getting JSA.

Tax credits

If you work less than 16 hours each week and your partner works at least 16 hours but less than 24 hours each week, you and your partner might be able to claim working tax credit. See p759 for further information. However, before deciding whether to claim you should seek advice to see how you would be better off financially.

Whether or not you are in work, you might be able to claim child tax credit (CTC). CTC does not count as income for income-based JSA purposes.

Means-tested benefits

If you pay rent or council tax you may be entitled to housing benefit (HB) and council tax benefit (CTB) as well as JSA. If you are getting contribution-based JSA, you may also be entitled to income-based JSA to top this up. Your contribution-based JSA counts as income for the purposes of those benefits.

If you are a man aged 60 or over, but less than 65 you might be able to claim pension credit (PC) instead of income-based JSA. You could be better off doing so if you have savings or other capital (see below).

Claiming income support or pension credit instead of jobseeker's allowance

You cannot claim both JSA and income support (IS) at the same time. You cannot claim income-based JSA and PC at the same time. If you have a partner, your partner can claim IS or PC and you can claim contribution-based JSA (but not income-based JSA).

You therefore need to choose whether to claim income-based JSA or IS (or PC) in some situations. You should consider the following when deciding what to do:

- The rates of IS, the guarantee credit of PC and income-based JSA are usually the same but you do not have to sign on, or look for work or risk being sanctioned if you are claiming IS or PC (nor does your partner). For more information about who can claim IS see Chapter 13 and PC, see Chapter 18.
- You may want to claim JSA instead of IS in order to receive national insurance (NI) contribution credits (see p838). You might not be entitled to NI credits if you claim IS.
- You may have to claim IS or PC (instead of income-based JSA) if your circumstances change – eg, if you are ill for more than two weeks.
- If you are sanctioned, you or your partner should claim IS or PC if eligible. You cannot get hardship payments (see p443) if you or your partner come within one of the groups of people who can claim IS, even if you do not claim it.
- If you claim PC:
  - there is no capital limit and the tariff income rules are more generous;
  - you can qualify for the savings credit of PC if you or your partner are 65 or over;
  - there is no rule that prevents you or your partner doing full-time paid work (known as 'remunerative work'), although any earnings from work are taken into account in working out how much PC you can get;
  - the HB and CTB rules are more generous if you or your partner are 60 or over and neither of you is getting IS or income-based JSA. See Chapters 6 and 10 for further information.

Non-means-tested benefits

The non-means-tested benefits in this *Handbook* (other than attendance allowance (AA), disability living allowance (DLA), guardian's allowance and if you are getting CTC, child benefit) are taken into account when working out the amount of income-based JSA you can get (see p379). However, it can be worth claiming these benefits. If you or your partner qualify for certain non-means-tested benefits (including AA and DLA) you also qualify for certain premiums (see p882) and therefore a higher rate of income-based JSA.

You might only qualify for income-based JSA once you or a member of your family are awarded another benefit known as a 'qualifying benefit'. To make sure you do not lose out while awaiting the outcome of a claim for a qualifying benefit, claim JSA at the same time. If your claim for income-based JSA is refused, once the qualifying benefit is awarded claim JSA again and ask for it to be backdated to the date of your first claim. See p1090 for further details.

Contribution-based JSA is affected by the overlapping benefit rules (see p1102).

If you qualify for DLA or industrial injuries disablement benefit, this may indicate that you should be regarded as incapable of work and entitled to incapacity benefit if you satisfy the other qualifying conditions. You should seek advice to see how you would be better off.

Passports and other sources of help

If you are entitled to income-based JSA you also qualify for:

- health benefits, such as free prescriptions (see Chapter 9); *and*
- education benefits, such as free school meals (see p18).

You may also qualify for social fund payments (see Chapters 21 and 22).

Bonuses

If you stop getting JSA because you or your partner start work or your earnings or your hours in your existing job increase, you might be able to get:

- a child maintenance bonus;
- mortgage interest run-on, if you have a home loan;
- extended payments of HB or CTB, if you pay rent or council tax;
- job grant.

See Chapter 3 for further information about the bonuses you can claim.

Notes

1. Who can claim jobseeker's allowance

1 ss1-3 and 3A JSA 1995
2 Reg 47(1) and (2) JSA Regs
3 Sch 1 para 3 JSA 1995
4 s2(1) and (4) JSA 1995
5 Reg 48 JSA Regs
6 Reg 48(2) and (3) JSA Regs
7 Regs 47A and 48(2)(e) JSA Regs
8 Reg 47(3) JSA Regs
9 s2 JSA 1995
10 ss3, 3A and 13 JSA 1995
11 Reg 3D JSA Regs; Sch 1 para 8A JSA 1995
12 Reg 8 SS(JPI) Regs
13 Sch A1 JSA Regs
14 Reg 3D(3) and (4) JSA Regs
15 CIS/0542/2001
16 Reg 51 JSA Regs
17 s1(2)(f) JSA 1995
18 Sch 1 para 2 JSA 1995; reg 10 SS&CS(DA) Regs; reg 6(3) SS(IFW) Regs
19 Reg 55(1) JSA Regs
20 Reg 55(2) JSA Regs
21 Reg 55(1) JSA Regs
22 Reg 55(3) JSA Regs
23 Reg 55(4) JSA Regs
24 Reg 55A(1) JSA Regs
25 Reg 55A(2) JSA Regs
26 Reg 55A(1) JSA Regs
27 Reg 17A(2), (3) and (5) JSA Regs
28 Reg 17A(7), (7A) and (7B) JSA Regs
29 Reg 17A(7) and (8) JSA Regs
30 s6(1) JSA 1995; regs 6 and 10 JSA Regs
31 R(U) 44/53
32 s6(1) JSA 1995
33 *Shaukat Ali v CAO*, appendix to R(U) 1/85
34 *Secretary of State for Social Security v David*, 15 December 2000 (CA), reported as R(JSA) 3/01
35 Regs 4 and 5(1)(b) and (6) JSA Regs
36 Regs 4 and 5(1)(a) JSA Regs
37 Reg 5(2) JSA Regs
38 C(U) 96/1994
39 para 21277 DMG
40 Reg 5(3) JSA Regs; para 21299 DMG
41 Reg 5(4) JSA Regs
42 CJSA/924/2003
43 CIS/1010/2003; the Court Service booklet, *You and your Jury Service*, available at www.courtservice.gov.uk/forms_and_guidance/forms/you_your.pdf
44 paras 21287-21293 DMG
45 Reg 14(1)(i), (j), (l), (ll) and (o) JSA Regs
46 Reg 14(2A) JSA Regs
47 Reg 14(1)(a), (b), (f) and (k) JSA Regs
48 Reg 4 JSA Regs, definition of 'work camp'
49 Reg 17A(3) and (7) JSA Regs
50 Reg 14(1)(c), (ll), (m), (n), (nn), (p) and (q) JSA Regs
51 Reg 14(1)(d), (e), (g), (h) and (2) JSA Regs
52 CJSA/5944/1999
53 Reg 14(3) JSA Regs
54 Reg 15 JSA Regs
55 Reg 7(3) JSA Regs
56 *Secretary of State for Social Security v David* (CA), 15 December 2000, reported as R(JSA) 3/01
57 s6(3) JSA 1995; regs 6,7 and 8 JSA Regs
58 Reg 13(3) JSA Regs
59 Reg 8 JSA Regs
60 s6(5)(7) and (8) JSA 1995; reg 16 JSA Regs
61 para 21404 DMG
62 Reg 31(f) JSA Regs
63 Reg 16(2) JSA Regs
64 para 21451 DMG
65 Reg 13(2) JSA Regs
66 Reg 6 JSA Regs
67 Reg 72(5A)(b) JSA Regs
68 Regs 4 and 13(4) JSA Regs
69 Reg 13(5) JSA Regs
70 Reg 7(1) and (2) JSA Regs
71 Reg 12 JSA Regs
72 Reg 8 JSA Regs
73 Reg 16(1) JSA Regs
74 Regs 8 and 9 JSA Regs
75 Reg 13(3) JSA Regs
76 Reg 8 JSA Regs
77 Reg 10 JSA Regs
78 Reg 10(1) JSA Regs
79 ss1(2)(c) and 7 JSA 1995
80 s7(1) JSA 1995
81 Reg 18(1) JSA Regs
82 CJSA/2162/2001

83 Reg 18A JSA Regs
84 Reg 18(2) JSA Regs
85 Reg 18(4) JSA Regs
86 Reg 18(3) JSA Regs
87 paras 21616-20 DMG
88 Reg 20 JSA Regs
89 Reg 21 JSA Regs
90 Reg 19 JSA Regs
91 Reg 19(1)(r) JSA Regs
92 Reg 19(1)(q) JSA Regs
93 Reg 21A JSA Regs
94 Reg 19(1)(p) JSA Regs
95 Reg 19(2) JSA Regs
96 R(U) 4/66
97 s9(3) JSA 1995
98 s9(4) JSA 1995
99 s9(1) JSA 1995; reg 31 JSA Regs
100 CJSA/2162/2001
101 Reg 34 JSA Regs
102 CJSA/935/1999
103 s9(5) JSA 1995
104 s9(6) JSA 1995
105 s9(6)(a) and (b) JSA 1995
106 s9(7)(b) and (c) JSA 1995
107 s9(7)(a) JSA 1995
108 s9(8)(b) JSA 1995; reg 33 JSA Regs
109 Reg 35 JSA Regs
110 s9(7)(c) JSA 1995
111 s9(8)(a) JSA 1995; reg 32 JSA Regs
112 s10(1) and (2) JSA 1995
113 s10(4) JSA 1995
114 s10(3) JSA 1995
115 s10(5) JSA 1995
116 s10(7)(a) JSA 1995; reg 39 JSA Regs; para 21951 DMG
117 s10(6)(b) JSA 1995
118 s10(6)(c) JSA 1995; reg 38 JSA Regs
119 CJSA/4435/1998
120 Reg 147 JSA Regs
121 Reg 147(6) JSA Regs
122 para 31350 DMG

2. **The rules about your age**
123 s3A(1)(e)(ii) JSA 1995; reg 58 JSA Regs

3. **Claiming for others**
124 s35(1) JSA 1995
125 s35 JSA 1995; reg 77 JSA Regs
126 Regs 1(3), definition of 'young person', and 76 JSA Regs
127 Reg 77(1)-(3) JSA Regs
128 CFC/1537/1995
129 CJSA/4890/1998
130 Reg 77(5) JSA Regs
131 Reg 77 JSA Regs, as applied in *Hockenjos v Secretary of State for Social Security* [2004] EWCA Civ 1749, 21 December 2004
132 DMG Letter 01/05 (January 2005). This implies that the DWP intends to apply the JSA rule without applying either *Hockenjos v Secretary of State for Work and Pensions*, or the earlier decision in CJSA/4890/1998.
133 Reg 78(4) and (8) JSA Regs
134 Reg 78(5) JSA Regs
135 Regs 77(4) and 78(7) JSA Regs
136 Reg 78(5)(c) JSA Regs
137 Reg 78(6) JSA Regs
138 Regs 77(4) and 78(5)(i) and (7) JSA Regs
139 Reg 78(5)(a) and (b) JSA Regs
140 Reg 78(6) JSA Regs
141 Reg 78(1) and (2) JSA Regs
142 Reg 76 JSA Regs; s142 SSCBA 1992; regs 5-8 CB Regs
143 Regs 1(2), definition of 'remunerative work', and 7 CB Regs
144 Reg 76(2)(b) and (c) JSA Regs

4. **The amount of benefit**
145 Sch 1 para 4 JSA 1995; reg 46 JSA Regs
146 Reg 14A SS&CS(DA) Regs
147 s4(1) and (2) JSA 1995; reg 79 JSA Regs
148 ss4(1)and 35(1) JSA 1995; reg 81(1) JSA Regs
149 Reg 80(2) JSA Regs
150 s5(1) JSA 1995
151 s5(2) JSA 1995
152 Reg 47(4)(b)(ii) JSA Regs
153 Reg 47(2) and (4)(c) JSA Regs
154 ss4(3) and (3A) and 13 JSA 1995

5. **Special rules for special groups**
155 Reg 4 JSA Regs
156 Reg 17(1)-(3) JSA Regs
157 Reg 17(5) JSA Regs
158 Reg 4 JSA Regs
159 Reg 17(4) JSA Regs
160 Reg 21 JSA Regs
161 ss3(1)(c) and (d) and 3A(1)(b) and (c) JSA 1995
162 s6 C(LC)A 2000; reg 2(2) C(LC)SSB Regs
163 ss3(1)(f)(iii) and 3A(1)(e)(ii) JSA 1995; reg 61(1)(b), (c) and (f) and (2)(a) and (b) JSA Regs
164 ss3(1)(f)(iii) and 3A(1)(e)(ii) JSA 1995; regs 57(2)-(4) and 59 JSA Regs
165 ss3(1)(f)(iii) and 3A(1)(e)(ii) JSA 1995; reg 60 JSA Regs
166 Reg 61(1)(a) JSA Regs
167 ss3(1)(f)(ii), 3A(1)(e)(i) and 16 JSA 1995
168 Ch 9 ESG 16/17 vol (internal DWP guidance)
169 s16(2) and (4) JSA 1995
170 s16(3) JSA 1995

Notes

171 s71A SSAA 1992
172 Regs 64-66 JSA Regs
173 Reg 64(2) and (3) JSA Regs
174 Reg 57(1) JSA Regs, meaning of 'suitable training'
175 Regs 65 and 65A JSA Regs
176 Reg 66 JSA Regs
177 Reg 62 JSA Regs
178 Reg 62(1) JSA Regs
179 Reg 62(2) and (3) JSA Regs
180 para 5 Ch 7 ESG 16/17 vol (internal DWP guidance)
181 para 42 Ch 8 ESG 16/17 vol (internal DWP guidance)
182 para 17 Ch 8 ESG 16/17 vol (internal DWP guidance)
183 Sch 2 para 1(a) SSA 1998
184 para 30920 DMG
185 *Youth Training Bridging Allowances*, Allowance Payments Guide
186 para 30921 DMG
187 Reg 170 JSA Regs
188 Reg 1(3) JSA Regs, definition of 'training allowance'

6. **Claims and backdating**
189 Regs 4(1A) and (6) SS(C&P) Regs
190 Reg 5 SS(C&P) Regs
191 Reg 24 JSA Regs
192 Reg 4(3B)(a) SS(C&P) Regs
193 s1(2B) and (4) JSA 1995; reg 3A(1) JSA Regs
194 s1(2D) JSA 1995; reg 3A(2) JSA Regs
195 s1(4) JSA 1995; reg 3A(1) JSA Regs
196 *Hockenjos v Secretary of State for Social Security* [2004] EWCA Civ 1749, 21 December 2004
197 DMG letter 01/05 (January 2005)
198 Sch 1 para 9A JSA 1995; reg 3B JSA Regs
199 Sch 1 paras 9B and 9C JSA 1995; reg 3C JSA Regs
200 s1(2C) JSA 1995; reg 3E JSA Regs
201 Sch 5 paras 10(2)(b), 13A and 17A JSA Regs
202 Reg 19(1) and Sch 4 para 1 SS(C&P) Regs
203 Reg 6(4ZB)(a) and (4A)(a)(i) SS(C&P) Regs
204 Reg 6(4A)(b) SS(C&P) Regs
205 Reg 6(4ZC)(a) and (b) SS(C&P) Regs
206 CS/371/1949
207 Reg 6(4AB) SS(C&P) Regs
208 Reg 4(3B)(b) SS(C&P) Regs
209 Reg 4(3B)(c) SS(C&P) Regs
210 Reg 6(28) SS(C&P) Regs
211 Reg 13(1) SS(C&P) Regs
212 Reg 6(4ZB) and (4A) SS(C&P) Regs
213 s8 JSA 1995; reg 24(6) JSA Regs
214 Regs 23 and 23A JSA Regs
215 CJSA/1080/2002
216 para 2 Postal Jobseekers ESG I vol (internal DWP guidance)
217 para 4 Postal Jobseekers ESG I vol (internal DWP guidance)
218 para 31 Postal Jobseekers ESG I vol (internal DWP guidance)
219 paras 30-35 Ch 13 ESG I vol (internal DWP guidance)
220 s8(2) JSA 1995; regs 25 and 27 JSA Regs
221 Regs 23 and 23A JSA Regs; s7 Interpretation Act 1978; R(JSA) 1/04
222 *Secretary of State for Work and Pensions v Michael Ferguson* [2003] EWCA Civ 536, reported as R(JSA) 6/03
223 Reg 27 JSA Regs
224 Reg 30 JSA Regs
225 Reg 28 JSA Regs
226 Reg 29 JSA Regs
227 Reg 26 JSA Regs; *Secretary of State for Work and Pensions v Michael Ferguson* [2003] EWCA Civ 536, reported as R(JSA) 6/03; R(JSA) 2/04
228 Reg 6(4C) SS(C&P) Regs
229 R(JSA) 2/04
230 Reg 6(4B) SS(C&P) Regs

7. **Getting paid**
231 s3B JSA 1995
232 Reg 30A SS(C&P) Regs
233 s1(3) JSA 1995
234 Reg 1(3) JSA Regs, definition of 'benefit week'
235 Reg 26A SS(C&P) Regs
236 Reg 87A JSA Regs
237 Reg 26A(3) SS(C&P) Regs
238 Reg 24(7)(a) JSA Regs; reg 3 SS(NCC) Regs
239 Reg 24(7)(b) JSA Regs
240 Reg 7 and Sch 3A para 7 SS&CS(DA) Regs
241 Reg 7(2)(b) SS&CS(DA) Regs
242 Sch 3A paras 8 and 9 SS&CS(DA) Regs
243 Sch 3A para 10 SS&CS(DA) Regs
244 Sch 3A para 11 SS&CS(DA) Regs

8. **Challenging a jobseeker's allowance decision**
245 CJSA/1080/2002

9. **Tax, tax credits and other benefits**
246 ss671-675 IT(EP)A 2003

Chapter 16

Jobseeker's allowance: sanctions and hardship payments

This chapter covers:

1. When sanctions can apply

Even if you are entitled to jobseeker's allowance (JSA) you may find that you are not paid for a period if a decision maker decides you should be sanctioned. This can only be done if you are in one of the situations when a sanction can be applied (see p p416 and 430). The Department for Work and Pensions sometimes refers to an action which results in a sanction as an 'offence'.

The length of time for which you are sanctioned (known as a 'sanction period') can be fixed or variable (see p434).

See p437 for further information about the amount of JSA payable during the sanction period. If your JSA is not paid or is paid at a reduced rate, you might be able to get hardship payments (see p443). Remember that while your claim is referred to a decision maker to decide whether you should be sanctioned, JSA can be paid, so long as you satisfy the other conditions for getting it.

Special rules apply if you are 16 or 17 (see p438).

Additional rules apply if:

- a court has decided you failed to comply with a community order without reasonable excuse (see p1117);
- you have been sanctioned because of benefit offences (see p1169).

If you disagree that you should be sanctioned, or with the period for which you have been sanctioned, you can challenge the decision. See p442 for further information.

During a sanction period, you are treated as entitled to JSA. Therefore, days in the period count towards your 182 days of entitlement to contribution-based JSA (see p378) even if you are not actually paid any benefit. You remain entitled to maximum housing benefit and council tax benefit (see p450) if you are treated as entitled to income-based JSA.

If you are sanctioned, you should check whether you can claim income support (IS – see Chapter 13) or pension credit (PC – see Chapter 18) instead. If you are not a member of a 'joint-claim couple' and you have a partner s/he may qualify for JSA, IS or PC instead of you. If you are a member of a joint-claim couple, check to see if either of you might qualify for IS or PC instead of JSA. If you (or if you are a 'joint-claim couple', you and your partner) must continue to claim JSA, check to see if you qualify for hardship payments (see p443).

2. Employment-related sanctions

You can be sanctioned if you:[1]

- lose a job because of 'misconduct' (see below); *or*
- leave a job voluntarily (see p419); *or*
- refuse or fail to carry out a jobseeker's direction (see p423); *or*
- fail to apply for or accept a job (see p424); *or*
- 'neglect to avail' yourself of a job (see p425).

Employment for these purposes does not include self-employment or self-employment on an employment programme or the 'intensive activity period' (see p430).[2] However, employment on the Employed Option of the New Deal for Young People *is* included. In considering whether you should be sanctioned the decision maker should only look at your last employment preceding your claim and your subsequent actions.[3]

For information about challenging a sanction decision, see p442.

Losing a job because of misconduct

You can be sanctioned if you lose your job through misconduct (see p417).[4] This includes where you are suspended from work for misconduct[5] or if you resigned rather than be dismissed.[6] You cannot be sanctioned for misconduct in self-employment.

The sanction period is variable (see p436).

Deciding if you should be sanctioned

You are asked to give your reasons for claiming jobseeker's allowance (JSA) when you claim. If you indicate that you left or were dismissed from a job you are asked to explain why. Your claim could then be referred to a decision maker.

If it appears that there may have been misconduct, your former employer is usually asked to complete a statement. You should then be given an adequate chance to comment on what your former employer said.[7] Your remarks may, in turn, be passed to your former employer for further comments.

Make sure you give full details of your case and why you disagree with the allegation of misconduct. If you are going to an employment tribunal to make a claim of unfair dismissal, you should say so. In this case you may want to discuss your reply with whoever is advising you on this, as you may be asked questions at the employment tribunal hearing by your former employer about what you have said.

What is misconduct?

'Misconduct' is not defined in the rules. Not every breach of your employer's rules or instructions amounts to misconduct – everyone makes mistakes or is inefficient from time to time. So, for example, if you are a naturally slow worker who, despite making every effort, cannot produce the output required by your employer, you are not guilty of misconduct even if the poor performance may justify your dismissal.[8]

Even if you were sacked or forced to resign because of inadequate work, you are guilty of misconduct only if your actions or omissions are 'blameworthy'. This does not mean that it has to be established that you did anything dishonest or that you deliberately did something wrong. Serious carelessness or negligence may be enough.[9]

The misconduct has to have some connection with your employment, either directly or indirectly, so as to give a reason for your employer to dismiss you. It does not have to take place during working hours to count as misconduct. A sanction cannot be imposed if the acts or omissions took place before your employment began.[10] The Department for Work and Pensions (DWP) is likely to say that this applies to things you said or failed to say when applying for the job from which you were eventually dismissed.[11]

Although evidence from your employer is taken into account, the fact that s/he did not describe your actions as 'misconduct' does not guarantee that you can escape a sanction.[12] However, you should argue that the fact that your employer did not view your action as misconduct must go heavily in your favour.

Some behaviour is clearly misconduct. This includes:

- a conviction for any offence of **dishonesty** whether or not connected with your work. This may amount to misconduct if it causes your employer to dismiss you because s/he no longer trusts you;[13]
- **arson** and other forms of deliberate damage;
- **assaults** on your employer, fellow employees or customers;
- **drunkenness** at work or working under the influence of **illegal drugs**.

Some behaviour is not necessarily misconduct, for example:

- **bad time-keeping** and failing to report in time that you are sick. To amount to misconduct, it has to be shown that you were persistently late or that you failed to report that you were sick on a number of occasions. Absence from work that was unavoidable, or justified, is not in itself misconduct.[14] However, you are expected to have complied with your employer's rules about notification of absence;
- **instructions not obeyed**. A refusal to carry out a *reasonable* instruction by an employer is usually misconduct, but not if you had a good reason for refusing or your failure was due to a genuine misunderstanding or you reasonably, but mistakenly, believed you were entitled to refuse;[15]
- if your job has rules covering **personal conduct**, breaking such a rule may be misconduct, depending on the seriousness of the breach.[16] A breach of a trivial rule may not be misconduct;[17]
- **a refusal to work overtime** is misconduct if you were under a duty to work overtime when required and the request to do it was reasonable. Even if there is nothing in writing about such a duty, the law may say that it is part of the custom and practice of your workplace.

Whether misconduct caused the loss of employment

Your misconduct need not be the only cause of the loss of your employment, but it must be an immediate and substantial reason for you losing your job.[18] If this is the case, it is not relevant that your dismissal was unreasonable or an over-reaction on your employer's part. However, you should seek advice to see if you might have a case for unfair dismissal at an employment tribunal. **Note:** you may have to follow your employer's internal procedure for resolving disputes before you can complain to an employment tribunal. If your misconduct was not the real reason for your dismissal – eg, your employer used this as an excuse to dismiss you but really only wanted to reduce numbers of staff – you should not be sanctioned.

If there was misconduct, the exact way in which you lost your employment is not important. You may be summarily dismissed, be dismissed with notice or resign as an alternative to probable or possible dismissal.[19]

Leaving your job voluntarily

You can be sanctioned if you leave your job 'voluntarily' without 'just cause' (see p420).[20]

A sanction for leaving a job voluntarily can only be imposed if:

- you were in employment (not self-employment); *and*
- you were not in a 'trial period' (see p426).

The decision maker has to show that you left your employment voluntarily, but once this is shown, you must then show that you had 'just cause' for leaving if you want to avoid a sanction.

The **sanction period** is variable (see p436).

Deciding if you should be sanctioned

You are asked to give your reasons for claiming JSA when you claim. If you indicate that you left a job you are asked to explain why. Your claim could then be referred to a decision maker.

If it appears that you may have left your job voluntarily without just cause, your former employer is usually asked to complete a form. You should then be given an adequate chance to comment on what your former employer wrote.[21] Your remarks may, in turn, be passed to your former employer for further comments.

Make sure you give full details of your case and say why you feel you had 'just cause' (see p420) for leaving your job.

Whether you left voluntarily

'Voluntarily' is not defined in the rules, but the DWP says it means that you have brought your employment to an end by your own acts and of your own free will.[22] You have not left your employment voluntarily if you had no choice in the matter or there is convincing evidence (eg, medical evidence from your GP) that you were not responsible for your actions.

If you resign because you genuinely believe that your employer is about to end your employment or because you were given the 'choice' of resignation or dismissal you have not left your job voluntarily. However, the DWP may then consider whether you lost your job through misconduct (see p416).

You are likely to be treated as leaving your job voluntarily if you resign giving notice. However, when deciding the length of the sanction period, the decision maker should take into account whether you:[23]

- were willing to work your notice (but your employer would not allow you to do so) and you might have had a better chance of finding other work while you were still in the job;
- tried to withdraw your notice, even if this was not accepted.

Your employer may have given you notice to end your employment but then cancelled or suspended the notice, allowing you to continue in the same employment. If you decide not to continue in the employment and it is clear that you have a genuine choice to remain, you are likely to be treated as leaving voluntarily.[24] However, the circumstances may be such as to amount to 'just cause' (see p420) or to justify a reduction in the sanction period (see p436).

Volunteering for redundancy

You do not count as leaving your job voluntarily if you volunteer for redundancy or accept your employer's proposal for redundancy.[25] This only applies where there is a 'redundancy situation' at your workplace.[26] For example, a redundancy situation can exist where a whole factory or department is closing down, and also where there is a cut in the number of people needed to carry out certain tasks.

You cannot be said to have left employment voluntarily if your job was abolished, even if you were offered or you could have applied for alternative jobs with the same employer. However, if you could have taken other work but refused it, you might be sanctioned for another reason – eg, if the decision maker says you have refused employment or 'neglected to avail' yourself of an opportunity of employment (see pp424 and 425).

There is no special rule to help you if you take early retirement (see p422).

Change in terms and conditions of employment

The DWP says that if your employer ends your contract of employment you have *not* left a job voluntarily.[27] A change in your terms or conditions by your employer may mean that your employer has ended your existing contract of employment. This is more likely to be the case if a change is imposed without your agreement and the new terms are a lot less favourable than before. If you refuse to accept the new contract and you leave your employment as a result, you can try to argue that you have not left your job voluntarily but have been dismissed. Even if this is not accepted, you may be able to show that you had 'just cause' for leaving.

'Just cause' for leaving your job

If the decision maker says that you left your job voluntarily, it is up to you to show that you had 'just cause' for doing so. 'Just cause' is not defined in the rules. It is not the same as 'good cause', which applies to other sanctions.

Showing you had 'just cause' for leaving your job involves balancing your interests against those of the general public. You must show not only that you acted reasonably in leaving, but also that the circumstances of your case make it proper that the community should support you.[28] This means that you are expected if at all possible to take steps through the proper channels to sort out any problems – eg, by raising the problem with your employer or using the grievance procedure (if there is one), rather than leave immediately.[29] You are also expected to look for another job seriously before giving one up. Even if it is decided that you do not have 'just cause' for leaving your job, these factors may work in your favour in reducing the sanction period (see p436).

If the circumstances in which you left employment 'fall just short' of providing 'just cause', the DWP says that your chances of getting other employment, including self-employment, should be taken into account. If your chances of getting employment were good you *may* have acted reasonably in leaving your job and have 'just cause'.[30]

You may have 'just cause' for leaving a job in the following situations.

Your job is unsatisfactory

You cannot argue you had 'just cause' simply because the conditions of your employment were poor, but see p451 if there was a breach in the law on minimum working conditions. However, you may have 'just cause' if, for example:

- you genuinely did not know or were mistaken about the conditions of the job and you gave it a fair trial before leaving. For example, if the job was of a different kind to what you normally do, but you tried it because there were no jobs in your type of work you should argue that you had 'just cause'.[31] The issue is whether it was reasonable for you to have left at the time you did;
- the job was beyond your physical and mental capacity or it was harmful to your health.

Personal or domestic reasons

If you leave your job for personal or domestic reasons you may have 'just cause' if, for example, you give up work to:

- look after a sick relative;[32] *or*
- move with your partner who has taken a job elsewhere. Married women who have left jobs to live with their husbands who have been posted elsewhere by their employers have not usually been sanctioned.[33] Men who leave jobs to live with their wives should also receive the same treatment.[34]

The DWP is likely to say that the circumstances must usually have become very pressing or urgent to justify leaving your job before looking for alternative employment. It could be helpful if you can show that you tried to negotiate an arrangement with your employer that would resolve the problem – eg, a reduction in your hours or time off work.

Change in your terms and conditions

If your employer makes a change in the terms and conditions of your employment which does not amount to an ending of your contract of employment, you may have 'just cause' for leaving. You are expected to use any grievance procedure first.

The rules for JSA do not allow the decision maker to take 'any matter relating to the level of remuneration' in your job into account when deciding whether or not you have 'just cause' for leaving it (but see p451 if your employer is paying below the national minimum wage).[35] This appears to mean that if you leave your job because your employer cuts your wages unilaterally you are not able to show 'just cause'. However, a cut in pay can mean that your existing contract of employment has ended and therefore you have been dismissed rather than having left your job. Matters relating to the level of pay can be taken into account when it comes to deciding the length of the sanction period.

If you give notice hastily when your terms of work are changed and then try to revoke it but are not allowed to by your employer, you should argue that the sanction period should be reduced.[36]

Firm offers of other employment

You may have left your job because of a firm offer of alternative employment, but then have to claim JSA because the offer fell through. You should be treated as having 'just cause' for leaving unless:[37]

- the offer was cancelled before you left your previous employment and either you could have stayed in the existing employment or you did not ask your employer whether you could stay; *or*
- you changed your mind and did not take the new job but you could have stayed or asked to stay in your existing employment.

Taking retirement

Some employers lay down a general retirement age but allow you to apply for permission to leave before that age (known as 'early retirement') or to carry on beyond that age. If you do take early retirement or do not take advantage of an opportunity to continue working after retirement age, you might be regarded as having left your job voluntarily.[38] However, you might be able to show 'just cause' if, for example, you can show that the work was getting too much for you because of your age or you would have been employed on worse terms and conditions than before.

Employers sometimes institute special early retirement schemes which run for a limited period. This is often in order to deal with a 'redundancy situation'. In that case, you come under the special rules about redundancy (see p420). Employers often try to avoid using the word redundancy and you may have to prove to the decision maker that a redundancy situation existed.

Where you take early retirement under some other special scheme, you cannot show 'just cause' merely because your action was in your employer's interest.[39] But this should be taken into account when deciding the length of the sanction period. It might be a particularly strong argument if you worked in the public sector and could say that your action was in the public interest.[40]

Refusing or failing to carry out a jobseeker's direction

You can be sanctioned if you refuse or fail to carry out a reasonable jobseeker's direction (see below), without 'good cause' (see p427).[41]

The **sanction period** is fixed at two or four weeks (see p435).

A jobseeker's direction

A **'jobseeker's direction'** is a written notice from your employment officer (EO) telling you to take specific action to help you find a job or increase your chances of being employed.[42] The written notice must make it clear that you are being given a jobseeker's direction. For example, you might be directed to apply for a specific job vacancy, to send your CV and a covering letter to a particular employer, to attend a voluntary training scheme or re-motivation course or to improve your appearance or behaviour so as to present yourself better to potential employers. Remember that a jobseeker's direction can be given:

- **at any time.** If you are given one it states the time within which you are expected to comply with it and you are given a further interview shortly afterwards to check that you have done so;
- **more than** once telling you to take the same action. Each refusal to carry out a direction could result in you being sanctioned. However, every jobseeker's direction must be reasonable.

Before you are given a jobseeker's direction the DWP says you should first be warned that a direction might be issued if you continue to refuse or fail to take action on a voluntary basis.

Is a jobseeker's direction 'reasonable'?

A jobseeker's direction must be reasonable. A jobseeker's direction would not be reasonable if it:

- would not help you find a job or increase your chances of being employed; *or*
- was at odds with your sincere conscientious or religious beliefs; *or*
- where it might unlawfully discriminate on grounds such as gender, religion or nationality.

Any jobseeker's direction must be relevant to *your* needs and to the circumstances of the local labour market.

A jobseeker's direction might require you to apply for a job that is for less than 24 hours a week if it improves your prospects of finding further work.[43] However, you can try to argue that you have good cause for refusing or failing to carry it out or that the direction is unreasonable, as there is a rule that says you should not be sanctioned for refusing to apply for, or to accept, a notified job vacancy which is for less than 24 hours a week (see p428).

Deciding if you should be sanctioned

If you refuse or fail to carry out a jobseeker's direction you should be asked by the DWP for your reasons. If the EO accepts that a jobseeker's direction was unreasonable, or could not be carried out in the time required, s/he cancels the direction. If the direction is not cancelled, your case is referred to a decision maker to decide whether you should be sanctioned.

Failing to apply for or accept a job

You can be sanctioned if you are notified by the DWP of a job vacancy, and without 'good cause' (see p427):[44]

- you do not apply for it; *or*
- you refuse to accept it if it is offered to you.

If you repeatedly fail to take jobs that are offered to you, a decision maker might also decide that you are not really available for or actively seeking work (see pp354 and 365) and refuse you JSA altogether.

The **sanction period** is variable (see p436).

Deciding if you should be sanctioned

A decision maker decides whether you refused to apply for or accept a job, although what the employer says might be taken into account. The DWP might treat you as having refused to apply for or accept a job if:[45]

- you fail to complete the job application form properly or give inappropriate answers to questions on the form. However, if you submit your application to the DWP and it does not pass this on to a potential employer (eg, because you did not provide a photograph to go with it), you can argue that you did not fail to apply for the job. The issue may be whether an employer's request for a photograph or other details is reasonable;[46] *or*
- you fail to attend a job interview;[47] *or*
- it believes that you behaved in such a way that you lost the chance of getting the job. However, this should only apply to things you actually said or did (or refused to do) and should not apply just because a prospective employer disliked your appearance or manner; *or*
- you impose unreasonable conditions so that an employer withdraws a job offer; *or*
- you accept a job but then fail to start it.

You can be expected to apply for and accept temporary work. You cannot escape a sanction on the grounds that a job is temporary, but the decision maker should take the date the job would have ended into account when deciding the period of any sanction (see p436).

Changing your mind

If you refused or failed to apply for a vacancy but then change your mind, you are not sanctioned if you apply for it or accept it before the vacancy has been filled.[48] If a sanction has already been imposed, you should ask for the decision to be revised (see p1189).

Notification of a job vacancy

To be sanctioned, you must have been notified of a job vacancy by the DWP. You are normally notified of vacancies orally or in writing when you attend to sign on, or during an advisory interview (see p402), although you could be notified by telephone or post. You should argue that no sanction should be imposed at all if you did not receive the notification.

You must be given sufficient information to enable you to pursue the vacancy or to make an informed decision as to whether to pursue it.[49] A job advert that is simply displayed in a JobCentre or Jobcentre Plus office so that it can be read does not by itself amount to a notification by the DWP. However, if you identify a vacancy yourself from the display and then discuss it with a DWP adviser, the vacancy might be considered as being 'notified' to you, providing the adviser made sufficient enquiries to be satisfied of your suitability for the job.[50] You risk being sanctioned if you do not apply for the job, do not attend for interview or refuse the job if it is offered to you.

If you are notified of a vacancy and are unsure about what your financial situation would be, check the amount of 'in-work benefits' for which you would qualify if you took the job. This includes any entitlement to working tax credit (see Chapter 50), council tax benefit (see Chapter 6) and housing benefit (see Chapter 10). If you need help with the calculations, seek advice from one of the agencies listed in Appendix 2. Remember that you might not be able to show 'good cause' for refusing a job because of your income or the rate of pay (see p429).

'Neglecting to avail' yourself of a job

You can be sanctioned if you fail to take up – known as 'neglecting to avail' yourself of – a reasonable opportunity of employment without 'good cause' (see p427).[51] You do not have to be notified of a vacancy by the DWP for this sanction to apply.

You count as 'neglecting to avail' yourself of an opportunity if you have the chance to return to a job with a former employer but you fail to take it up. However, this rule does not apply if the 'opportunity' is for further work with an employer you have been working for during a 'trial period' (see p426).

The **sanction period** is variable (see p436).

Deciding if you should be sanctioned

In practice, this sanction usually applies in situations where you do not return to work with your former employer after what was originally intended to be a temporary break – eg, if you decide not to resume work after maternity leave. A sanction should only be imposed if the job vacancy was in a 'qualifying former employment' (see below). This is because you automatically have good cause for 'neglecting to avail' yourself of the job if it is *not* a qualifying former employment (see p428).[52]

The DWP is likely to apply a sanction if:[53]

- you knew, or had the means to find out, how to get the job; *and*
- you had a reasonable chance of getting the job; *and*
- you did not take the steps necessary to make use of the opportunity to get the job; *and*
- you were not in a trial period (see below); *and*
- the job was not vacant due to a stoppage of work caused by a trade dispute.

Qualifying former employment

A job counts as a 'qualifying former employment' if:[54]

- it is employment with an employer you previously worked for or with an employer who took over the business from your former employer; *and*
- it is not more than a year between the date you last worked for the employer and the date the question of a sanction arises; *and*
- the terms and conditions are not less favourable than those of the job you had when you last worked for the employer.

The date on which you last worked for the employer is the date you last attended work, not the last date for which you were paid.

Trial periods

In certain circumstances you may take a job for a 'trial period' and leave the job without the risk of being sanctioned for leaving voluntarily or for 'neglecting to avail' yourself of a reasonable opportunity of employment (see pp419 and 425).[55]

You *must* leave the employment within the trial period to avoid being sanctioned. You do not have to have agreed with the DWP that you were taking up the employment on a trial basis.

If you are dismissed or you leave the job as an alternative to being dismissed, you might still be sanctioned if this was because of misconduct (see p416).

The trial period rule applies if, for at least 13 weeks before the day you begin employment, you have not:[56]

- worked (including as a self-employed person); *or*
- been a full-time student (see p621) or in 'relevant education' (see p618). You do not count as a full-time student if you were in receipt of a training allowance.[57]

A **'trial period'** is the period of eight weeks starting with the beginning of your fifth week and ending at the end of your twelfth week in the job. However, for this purpose, weeks in which you work for fewer than 16 hours are ignored.[58] The DWP includes periods when you are not actually working but you are required by contract to be in a certain place in order to carry out a job.[59] Periods when you are off work sick or on holiday, even if you are paid, do not count when calculating the number of hours.

To be sure you are covered by this rule, you must work at least some of the fifth week and leave before you have worked all of the twelfth. In calculating the fifth and the twelfth weeks, the 'week' starts on the day you begin work and ends at midnight seven days later.[60]

Remember that if you do not claim JSA for more than 12 consecutive weeks (ie, until after the trial period), a new 'jobseeking period' (see p348) begins when you next claim. This means:

- you have to serve a further three waiting days (see p377) before getting JSA; *and*
- you may not qualify for contribution-based JSA if you no longer satisfy the contribution conditions (see p844).

Employment-related sanctions and 'good cause'

Certain sanctions cannot be imposed if you have 'good cause' for acting as you did. These are:

- refusing or failing to carry out a reasonable 'jobseeker's direction' (see p423);
- failing to apply for, or refusing to accept, a job after you were notified of the vacancy by the DWP (see p424);
- 'neglecting to avail' yourself of a job opportunity (see p425).

The factors which may mean you have 'good cause' depend on the sanction. In deciding whether you have 'good cause' the decision maker must take all the circumstances into account and must also consider whether there are circumstances which:

- give you automatic 'good cause' (see p428);
- must be taken into account when deciding whether you have 'good cause' (see p428);
- cannot give you 'good cause' (see p429).

A different 'good cause' rule applies when a sanction is connected with a training scheme or employment programme (see p432). Remember that you can be sanctioned for leaving a job voluntarily without 'just cause' rather than 'good cause' (see p419).

Automatic good cause

You automatically have 'good cause' if:

- you refuse to apply for, or do not accept, a job involving less than 24 hours work a week (16 hours if you have been allowed to restrict your availability for work to less than 24 hours a week – see p362).[61] This ground does not apply if you refuse or fail to carry out a jobseeker's direction. However, you may be able to challenge the jobseeker's direction on the grounds that it is unreasonable (see p423) ;
- you do not accept a job which is vacant because of a trade dispute – ie, you are not required to be a strike-breaker;[62]
- you are within your 'permitted period' (see p362) and you do not take up the offer of a job (unless this is one in your usual occupation and for at least your usual rate of pay);[63]
- you have trained for a particular type of work for at least two calendar months. You do not have to accept work in any other kind of employment for four weeks after your training ends (a **'week'** for these purposes means any period of seven consecutive days).[64] 'Training' for these purposes is not defined and should be given its ordinary everyday meaning;
- you have 'neglected to avail' yourself of an opportunity of employment, unless it is a 'qualifying former employment' (see p426);[65]
- you are laid off or on short time and have been accepted as available only for casual work (see p380) and you refuse to take some other type of work;[66]
- you come under the rules that exempt you from having to be able to start work immediately (see p355), or you have said that you are only available to work at certain times and you are therefore not required to be able to take up employment at times when you are not available (see p356), and you refuse to take a job where you would have to do so;[67]
- you fail or refuse to apply for or accept a notified job vacancy or 'neglect to avail' yourself of an opportunity of employment with a qualifying former employer (see pp424 and 425) while on a 'qualifying course' (see p353);[68] *and*
  - this happens in the four weeks before the end of the course or your examinations; *or*
  - it is other than a casual job during your vacation, unless it is permanent full-time paid work (16 hours or more a week).

Circumstances which must be taken into account

If you do not have automatic good cause, the decision maker must take the following circumstances into account to decide whether you have 'good cause':[69]

- any discrepancy between the restrictions you have been allowed to place on your availability for work and the requirements of the job, although minor differences might not count;

- any condition or personal circumstance which suggests that a particular job or carrying out a jobseeker's direction would be likely to cause you excessive physical or mental stress or significant harm to health;
- any sincerely held religious or conscientious objection;
- any caring responsibilities (see p363) which make it unreasonable for you to do the job or carry out a jobseeker's direction;
- the travelling time involved between your home and the place of work and back again (but see below);
- any expenses which would be unavoidably incurred in doing the job or carrying out the jobseeker's direction plus your travelling costs, if they would amount to an unreasonably high proportion of the income you would receive. The DWP says that this does not include the cost of childcare.[70]

These are not the only circumstances that can be taken into account. The decision maker should also take account of any other factor that appears to be relevant. See, in particular, p451 for when the terms of the job on offer break the laws on minimum working conditions. It is easier to argue you have good cause for failing to take a job if any of these reasons are included in your jobseeker's agreement (see p369).

What cannot give you good cause

You cannot show good cause if you refuse or fail to apply for a job or to carry out a jobseeker's direction because of:[71]

- your **income or outgoings** or those of any member of your household (see p812), either as they are now or as they would become if you took the job or carried out the direction. For these purposes, 'outgoings' do not include any expenses taken into account that would be an unreasonably high proportion of your income (see above).

  This means that you cannot, for example, argue that you need a high wage because you have a large mortgage or an expensive lifestyle. You might be able to show good cause if:[72]
  - you have been allowed to place restrictions on the rate of pay you would accept in a job because of your physical or mental condition (see p361) or under the rules about a 'permitted period' (see p362); *or*
  - the job you have refused to accept would have been paid on a commission-only basis; *or*
- unless because of your health or your caring responsibilities (see p363) the time is unreasonable, the **travelling time** involved between your home and the place of work and back again if this is less than:[73]
  - one hour either way, during the first 13 weeks you are entitled to JSA; *or*
  - one and a half hours either way, in all other cases.

Remember that you cannot refuse to apply for a job simply because of the **rate of pay** offered.[74] However, see p451 if the rate of pay is below the minimum wage.

3. New Deal, training scheme and employment programme-related sanctions

You can be sanctioned if you:[75]

- lose your place on a compulsory training scheme or employment programme because of 'misconduct' (see p432); *or*
- give up or fail to attend a place on a compulsory training scheme or employment programme (see p432); *or*
- fail to apply for or accept a place on a compulsory training scheme or employment programme (see p432); *or*
- 'neglect to avail' yourself of a place on a compulsory training scheme or employment programme (see p432).

The **sanction period** is fixed (two or four weeks or 26 weeks for some New Deal sanctions). See p435 for further information.

For information about challenging a sanction decision, see p442.

Compulsory training schemes and employment programmes

Compulsory training schemes and employment programmes include many of the New Deal options. Training scheme, employment programme and New Deal providers are required by their contract with the Department for Work and Pensions (DWP) to tell the DWP if one of the grounds for imposing a sanction applies, unless the scheme is training for 16/17-year-olds or a Modern Apprenticeship.

At the time this *Handbook* was written, the following training schemes and employment programmes were 'compulsory' for the purposes of the rules about sanctions:[76]

Training scheme sanctions

Work-Based Learning for Young People

New Deal scheme sanctions

The full-time education and training option of the New Deal for Young People
The self-employed employment option of the New Deal for Young People
The voluntary sector option of the New Deal for Young People
The environment task force option of the New Deal for Young People
The 'intensive activity period' of the New Deal for people aged 25 or over but less than 50
The 'intensive activity period' 50 to 59 pilot (in pilot areas only)

In addition, if you are on a 'qualifying course', and are therefore treated as available for work (see p358), your course counts as compulsory and you can be sanctioned if you give up your place on or fail to attend the course without good cause, or you lose your place on it through misconduct.[77]

Schemes can be added to or removed from the list of compulsory training schemes and employment programmes. You should seek advice if you are in any doubt about whether a scheme or programme is compulsory.

Although other training schemes and initiatives to help you find work are not compulsory, your employment officer (EO) can compel you to attend one by issuing a jobseeker's direction (see p423).

New Deal schemes

Whether and when you can be required to attend any particular New Deal scheme depends on your age and the length of time you have been unemployed. In certain situations it is possible to join a New Deal scheme earlier than the compulsory date, but if you subsequently agree to embark on any options they become compulsory and you could be sanctioned for leaving them. During the 'gateway' period when you first enter the New Deal, if you fail, without good cause, to attend set interviews, your jobseeker's allowance (JSA) claim is terminated under the rules about failing to attend interviews (see p403). If you claim again, you go back on to the 'gateway' where you left off.

If you refuse to start an option on a compulsory New Deal programme once you have received your official referral letter or if you leave an option without good cause or are dismissed for misconduct, you can be sanctioned.

Remember:

- If you are self-employed while on a New Deal option or the 'intensive activity period' any sanction related to this self-employment is a New Deal sanction.[78]
- If you are on the Employed Option of the New Deal, employment-related sanctions apply, not New Deal sanctions.

Employment zone programmes

An employment zone programme is a programme designed to help JSA claimants obtain sustainable employment, which is established in an employment zone.[79] An employment zone is an area in Great Britain designated as such under s60 of the Welfare Reform and Pensions Act 1999. Further information is available at www.employmentzones.gov.uk.

Losing your place because of 'misconduct'

You can be sanctioned if you lose your place on a compulsory training scheme or employment programme through 'misconduct'.[80] The information in the section on losing a job through misconduct (see p416) also applies to training scheme and employment programme sanctions. References in that section to an employer should be read as references to your training or employment programme provider.

Giving up or failing to attend

You can be sanctioned if you give up or fail to attend a place on a compulsory training scheme or employment programme without 'good cause' (see p432).[81] You are treated as failing to attend a scheme or programme if you have been absent without authorisation, even if the absence is only for one day.[82]

The DWP usually gets a statement from your scheme or programme provider about why you left. Before imposing a sanction, the decision maker should give you an adequate chance to comment on any evidence that is to be used against you.[83]

Failing to apply for or accept a place

You can be sanctioned if you are notified of a place on a compulsory training scheme or employment programme and, without 'good cause' (see below):[84]

- you do not apply for it; *or*
- you refuse to accept it if it is offered to you.

The information in the section about failing to apply for or accept a job (see p424) also applies to training scheme and employment programme sanctions. References in that section to an employer should be read as references to your training or employment programme provider. As with job vacancies, you must be properly notified by the DWP (see p425).

'Neglecting to avail' yourself of a place

You can be sanctioned if you fail to take up ('neglect to avail' yourself of) a reasonable opportunity of a place on a compulsory training scheme or employment programme without 'good cause'.[85] You do not have to be notified by the DWP for this sanction to apply.

Training scheme and programme-related sanctions and 'good cause'

Certain sanctions cannot be imposed if you have 'good cause' for acting as you did. These are:

- giving up or failing to attend a compulsory training scheme or employment programme (see p432); *or*

- failing to apply for or accept a place on a compulsory training scheme or employment programme (see p432); *or*
- 'neglecting to avail' yourself of a place on a training scheme or employment programme (see p432).

A different 'good cause' rule applies for employment-related sanctions (see p427).

When deciding whether you have 'good cause', the decision maker must consider all the circumstances of your case, but certain circumstances count as automatic good cause. You may also have good cause in other situations. The decision maker should consider all the reasons you put forward.[86] The rules do not specify any particular factors to be taken into account.

Automatic good cause

You automatically have 'good cause' if:[87]

- you had a disease or physical or mental disability which meant that:
  - you were unable to attend the scheme or programme; *or*
  - your health, or that of others, would have or would likely have been at risk if you had done so;
- your failure to participate in the scheme or programme resulted from a sincerely held religious or conscientious objection;[88]
- your travelling time to and from the scheme or programme would have exceeded one hour in each direction. If there are no appropriate schemes within an hour's travelling distance, you may be expected to travel for over one hour. You may have good cause if travel is difficult – eg, due to disability or poor health or if the distance involved is very long;
- you are on a 'qualifying' full-time educational course (see p353) and you:[89]
  - fail to attend or abandon the course if this:
    - happens less than four weeks after the first day of your course; *or*
    - was because the course was 'unsuitable'. This is defined as meaning that it was unsuitable for you 'in vocationally relevant respects', including your ability, preference and the qualification you are aiming for; *or*
    - was due to your lack of ability; *or*
  - fail to apply for or attend an employment programme, if this was at a time which would have prevented you from attending the qualifying course;
- you had caring responsibilities (see p363) and no close relative (see p356) of the person cared for or member of that person's household was available to perform them for you and it was not practical to make other arrangements;
- you were on jury service or attending court as a witness or a party to the proceedings;
- you were arranging or attending the funeral of a close relative or a close friend;
- you had to deal with a domestic emergency. The decision maker considers the nature of the emergency, when it arose and whether you could have made alternative arrangements;

- you were crewing or launching a lifeboat, working as a part-time firefighter or doing work as part of an organised group for the benefit of others in an emergency;
- you gave up a place on a scheme or programme and your continued participation in the scheme or programme would have, or was likely to have, put your health and safety at risk.

For **New Deal scheme sanctions** only, if you fail to start or leave any of the options early you automatically have good cause if you were not given a written notification by the DWP referring to the employment programme or training scheme in question that warned you:[90]

- about the circumstances in which you can be sanctioned; *and*
- that your JSA could be paid at a reduced rate or cease to be paid altogether.

4. Sanction periods and amount of jobseeker's allowance payable

If it is decided that a sanction should be applied under any of the rules described above, a decision maker must then decide how long the sanction period should be. A sanction period may be for a **fixed period** (always two or four weeks, or in the case of some New Deal scheme sanctions, 26 weeks) or **variable** (between one week and 26 weeks). The length of a variable sanction period is at the discretion of the decision maker and depends on the circumstances of the case (see p436).

For information about the amount of jobseeker's allowance (JSA) payable if you are sanctioned, see p437. If your JSA is not paid or is paid at a reduced rate, you might be able to get hardship payments (see p443).

Special rules apply to some sanctions if you are 16 or 17 (see p440).

If you disagree that you should be sanctioned or with the length of the sanction period, you can challenge the decision (see p442).

Sanction	*Period*
Losing a job because of misconduct (see p416)	Variable: 1–26 weeks
Leaving a job voluntarily (see p419)	Variable: 1–26 weeks
Failing to apply for or accept a job (see p424)	Variable: 1–26 weeks
'Neglecting to avail' yourself of a job opportunity (see p425)	Variable: 1–26 weeks
Failing to carry out a jobseeker's direction (see p423)	Fixed: 2 or 4 weeks
New Deal sanctions (see p430)	Fixed: 2, 4 or 26 weeks
Gateway to Work sanctions (see p430)	Fixed: 2 weeks
Other training scheme/employment programme-related sanctions (see p430)	Fixed: 2 or 4 weeks

Once a sanction period has begun, it continues unbroken until the sanction period comes to an end.[91] This means that if you take a job or training for a short period but then claim again during the period of the sanction, you are still caught by the sanction.

Fixed sanction periods

A fixed-period sanction is either:[92]

- two weeks; *or*
- four weeks if you have already had a fixed-period sanction within the past 12 months; *or*
- 26 weeks for some New Deal sanctions (see below).

The sanction usually starts from the day following the end of the benefit week (see p406) in which the decision to sanction you was made.[93]

Sanctions other than for New Deal schemes

Unless it is a New Deal sanction (see below) a sanction is imposed for two weeks or four weeks if it is not a Gateway to Work sanction and you are sanctioned within 12 months of a previous fixed-period sanction.[94] The 12 months run from the first day of the previous sanction to the date of the decision imposing the current sanction.

If you are given a four-week sanction but later the first (two-week) sanction is removed (eg, by a tribunal), ask a decision maker to reduce the four-week sanction period to two weeks.[95] If s/he fails to do so, appeal. If you have already appealed against the second sanction, the tribunal should take the removal of the first sanction into account.[96]

New Deal scheme sanctions

A fixed-period New Deal scheme sanction (see p430) is imposed for two weeks.[97] However, other than for sanctions relating to a Gateway to Work programme, the period is:

- four weeks if you have already had a sanction imposed within the last 12 months and both sanctions relate to the 'intensive activity period' of the New Deal (this includes the intensive activity period for people aged 50 to 59 but only if you live in a pilot scheme area) or both sanctions relate to New Deal schemes (other than the 'intensive activity period' of the New Deal);[98] *or*
- 26 weeks if you are given a sanction on three or more occasions, each sanction has been within 12 months of the previous one and all of the sanctions relate to the 'intensive activity period' of the New Deal (this includes the intensive activity period for people aged 50 to 59 but only if you live in a pilot scheme area) or all of the sanctions relate to New Deal schemes (other than the 'intensive activity period' of the New Deal).[99]

If this is the first time a 26-week sanction period is applied to you, and the Department for Work and Pensions (DWP) notifies you that you no longer have to participate in the scheme (eg, because you have completed the option) you can get income-based JSA again even if your 26-week sanction period has not ended.[100] Your income-based JSA starts on the later of:
- the date from which you no longer have to participate in the New Deal scheme; *or*
- the date four weeks after your JSA ceased.

Any other sanctions given in the previous 12 months do not affect the period of a New Deal scheme sanction.

Variable sanction period

A variable sanction can be any length from one week to 26 weeks.[101] Sanction periods are usually complete weeks, but there is nothing in the rules to prevent them including part weeks. However, a sanction of at least one week must be imposed, even if the decision maker thinks that the appropriate sanction period is less than one week.

The sanction period starts from the date the decision maker decides it should begin.[102] If you have been given more than one sanction, see p437.

Deciding how long you should be sanctioned

In deciding the length of the sanction period, the decision maker can take into account anything that provides some excuse for your conduct. You should be given a chance to provide information and evidence.[103]

If the reason for the sanction is anything other than misconduct (see p416) and there is no evidence to explain your action or failure to act, the DWP says you are likely to get the maximum sanction.[104] It is therefore important that you give as much information as you can to explain and justify your action or failure.

You should argue that 26 weeks should only be imposed in the most serious cases. Much of the caselaw referred to by decision makers was decided when the minimum period of a sanction was one day and the maximum six weeks. Although the principles for deciding the length of a sanction period still apply, you should argue that the fact that the maximum sanction period is now 26 weeks should be taken into account and the principles applied less harshly.

The rationale behind sanctions is to protect public funds. You can try to argue that there should be a difference in the sanction imposed where you have simply failed to apply for a job vacancy, rather than for refusing to accept an offer of employment or losing your job through misconduct.[105] This is particularly so if you can show that it is not likely that you would have been offered the job had you applied for it, as in this case public funds would not have suffered a loss.

Decision makers must give particular consideration to the following:[106]

- how long the employment you left or failed to take up was likely to have lasted, if this was less than 26 weeks. The decision maker should not impose a sanction for a period longer than the job would have lasted;
- where you have stopped work because of misconduct but your employer is prepared to take you back, the date you are to resume work. The decision maker should end the sanction period on that date;
- where you have voluntarily left a job in which the hours were 16 or less a week, the rate of pay and hours of work in that job. If the job did not provide you with an adequate income this is a mitigating factor in deciding the length of the sanction period;
- where you have left a job voluntarily or 'neglected to avail' yourself of a reasonable opportunity of employment, any physical or mental stress connected with the job. In some cases such stress provides 'just cause' for leaving the job, but if it is not sufficient for that purpose, it can still be a mitigating factor in deciding the length of the sanction period.

The decision maker should also take account of any time that has passed during which you were not receiving JSA since the date you, for example, stopped work. Having calculated the length of the sanction period that is appropriate in your case, s/he subtracts days you were not receiving JSA.[107] No deduction is made for days on which you did not qualify for JSA because you received a compensation payment in respect of the termination of your employment from your last employer and were therefore treated as in full-time paid work (see p959). The result of this deduction may be that the sanction period is reduced to nothing. This means that unless a compensation payment is involved, you are not sanctioned if more than 26 weeks have passed between you leaving your last job and claiming JSA.

More than one sanction

A decision maker might decide that more than one sanction should be applied to you. S/he must consider each separately but only one sanction should be applied in respect of a particular loss or refusal of work. The DWP says that in this situation, sanctions cannot be kept back and applied consecutively. This means that if decisions to apply sanctions are made at different times or for different periods, the sanction periods may overlap.[108]

Amount of jobseeker's allowance payable

JSA is **not** paid during the sanction period if you are sanctioned and you are a single person or a member of a couple (other than a 'joint-claim couple'), or if you are member of a 'joint-claim couple' and both of you are sanctioned.[109]

JSA is **paid at a reduced rate** during the sanction period if you are member of a 'joint-claim couple' and only one of you is sanctioned.[110] In this situation, the JSA is paid to the person who has not been sanctioned. However, unless you are on Work-Based Learning for Young People, JSA is paid at the full rate that applies to you if you (or if you are a member of a joint claim couple, one of you) are getting a training allowance.[111]

If your JSA is not paid or is paid at a reduced rate, you might be able to get hardship payments (see p443). You should also check to see if you qualify for income support (IS) or pension credit (PC) instead of JSA. If you are a member of a couple (other than a 'joint-claim couple') your partner might be able to claim JSA, IS or PC instead of you. If you are a member of a joint-claim couple, check to see if either of you might qualify for IS or PC instead of JSA.

Reduced amounts of jobseeker's allowance for joint-claim couples

If you are a member of a 'joint-claim couple' and one of you is sanctioned, the other is paid at the rate of:[112]

- contribution-based JSA, if s/he satisfies the rules for claiming it (see pp347 and 349); *or*
- hardship payments, if you and your partner qualify (see p448); *or*
- in any other case, income-based JSA calculated as if s/he is a single person (see p379 and Chapter 35). However, any income or capital either of you have is taken into account in the calculation (see Chapters 38 and 39).

5. Special rules for 16/17-year-olds

If you are aged 16 or 17, you can be sanctioned in the same way as claimants aged 18 and over if you are receiving:

- contribution-based jobseeker's allowance (JSA);[113] *or*
- income-based JSA, including under the severe hardship rules (see p384); *and*
  - have left a job voluntarily without 'just cause' (see p419); *or*
  - have lost a job because of misconduct (see p416).

Where the sanctions are for other reasons, special rules apply to 16- or 17-year-olds for:

- good cause (see p439);
- sanction periods and the amount of JSA you can be paid (for sanctions other than severe hardship payment sanctions) (see p440);
- severe hardship payment sanctions (see p440).

If you are 16 or 17, you may apply for hardship payments (see p443) in the same way as people 18 and over.

Good cause

Certain sanctions do not apply if you can show 'good cause' for acting or failing to act as you did. When deciding whether you have 'good cause', the decision maker should consider the factors that apply to sanctions for people aged 18 and over (see pp427 and 432). You might also have good cause under additional rules applying to 'training-related' sanctions and to 'employment-related' sanctions for 16- and 17-year-olds.

Training-related sanctions

There are a number of situations in which you can be sanctioned in respect of compulsory training schemes and employment programmes (see p430). If you give up or fail to attend such a course or fail to accept or 'neglect to avail' yourself of a place on one, you cannot be sanctioned if you can show 'good cause'. In addition to any other ground on which you can argue 'good cause' (see p432), you have this automatically if:[114]

- it is the first time that you have acted or failed to act in a way which could lead to a sanction; *and*
- you were a 'new jobseeker' (see below):
  - when you first started the scheme or programme, if a sanction is being considered because you gave up a place; *or*
  - at the time of the act or omission, if the sanction is for another reason.

You are a **'new jobseeker'** for these purposes if, since you left full-time education, you have never:[115]

- worked for 16 hours or more a week; *or*
- done a complete training course; *or*
- failed to complete a training course without 'good cause'; *or*
- given up a place on a training scheme or employment programme without 'good cause'; *or*
- lost a place on a training scheme or employment programme because of misconduct.

Employment-related sanctions

If you have neglected to avail yourself of a reasonable opportunity of a job (see p425), or refused or failed to apply for a notified job vacancy (see p424), in addition to any other ground on which you can argue 'good cause' (see p427) you have automatic 'good cause' if your employer did not offer you suitable training (see p385).[116] This rule does not apply if:

- your JSA, including payment under the severe hardship rules, has been reduced in the past for the same reasons or because of a training-related sanction (see p430); *or*

- your JSA has been stopped in the past because you lost a job because of misconduct or left a job voluntarily without 'just cause' (see pp416 and 419); *or*
- you are claiming under the special rules for 16/17-year-olds who are on short-time working, have been laid off or who have accepted a firm offer to join the armed forces (see p382).

Sanction periods and amount of jobseeker's allowance payable

A fixed sanction period of two weeks applies where:[117]

- a fixed-period sanction (of whatever length) would be applied to you if you were 18 or over (see p435); *or*
- you fail to apply for, or to accept, a job (see p424) or 'neglect to avail' yourself of a job opportunity (see p425).

The two weeks starts at the beginning of the first benefit week after the decision maker makes her/his decision to apply a sanction.

During the sanction period you continue to be paid benefit but at a reduced rate. You do not have to claim hardship payments in this situation. If you stop claiming JSA before the two weeks is over and then claim again, you are paid JSA at the reduced rate for the remainder of the two-week period. If you reach the age of 18 before the end of your two-week sanction, the sanction ends and you are paid the full rate of JSA for an 18-year-old.

Your JSA is reduced by 40 per cent of the single person's (or lone parent's) allowance for a person in your circumstances, even if you are a member of a couple (see p878), or by 20 per cent if you or any member of your family (see p374) are pregnant or seriously ill. 'Seriously ill' is not defined.

If you are getting severe hardship payments, in some circumstances you cannot be sanctioned under the normal rules. Instead, different rules apply (see below).

If you are being sanctioned for any other reason, the ordinary sanction periods apply (see p434). In this situation, you can apply for hardship payments in the usual way (see p443).

Severe hardship payment sanctions

If you are getting severe hardship payments (see p384), different rules for training-related sanctions apply if you behave in such a way as to risk:[118]

- your severe hardship direction being revoked because, without 'good cause' you:
  - 'neglect to avail' yourself of a reasonable opportunity of a place on a training scheme (see p432); *or*
  - refuse or fail to apply for a notified place on a training scheme (see p432).

If your severe hardship direction is revoked, you can apply for severe hardship payments again immediately, but these are paid at a reduced rate for 14 days;

- having your JSA paid at a reduced rate because:
  - you give up a place on or fail to attend a training scheme without 'good cause'. If you can show good cause, you are given a 'certificate of good cause' by the Department for Work and Pensions. **Note:** if you are refused a certificate, you cannot appeal against the refusal;[119] *or*
  - you lose a place on a training scheme through misconduct.

'Good cause' is not defined in the rules.

Reduced rates of severe hardship payments

You are paid a reduced rate of severe hardship payments for two weeks if:[120]

- you stopped getting severe hardship payments because your severe hardship direction was revoked when you failed to pursue an opportunity of obtaining training or rejected an offer of training without good cause; *or*
- you failed to pursue an opportunity of obtaining training or rejected an offer of training without good cause or failed to complete a course of training and did not get a 'certificate of good cause'. In addition, your benefit must have been reduced or stopped at least once in the past as a result of a sanction either under these rules or because:
  - of a training scheme or employment programme sanction (see p430); *or*
  - you lost a job because of misconduct (see p416); *or*
  - you voluntarily left a job without just cause (see p419).

Your severe hardship payments are also paid at a reduced rate for two weeks if you fail to compete a training course, are not given a 'certificate of good cause' and:[121]

- on the day before you started the course, you were not a new jobseeker (see p439); *or*
- you lost your place on the course through misconduct; *or*
- on a previous occasion when you were a new jobseeker (see p439) you:
  - 'neglected to avail' yourself of a reasonable opportunity of a place on a training scheme, or refused or failed to apply for a notified training place without 'good cause' while you were getting severe hardship payments; *or*
  - without good cause or only with the special 'good cause' described on p439 have:
    - 'neglected to avail' yourself of a reasonable opportunity of a place on a training scheme or employment programme; *or*
    - refused or failed to apply for a notified scheme or programme vacancy; *or*
    - failed to attend a training scheme or employment programme; *or*
- on a previous occasion, you started a training scheme at a time when you were a new jobseeker (see p439) but you:

- failed to complete a training scheme while you were getting severe hardship payments and were not given a 'certificate of good cause'; *or*
- gave up a place on a training scheme either without 'good cause' or only with the special 'good cause' described on p439.

Your severe hardship payments are reduced by 40 per cent of the single person's (or lone parent's) allowance for a person in your circumstances, even if you are a member of a couple (see p811), or by 20 per cent if you or any member of your family (see p374) are pregnant or seriously ill.[122]

6. Challenging a sanction decision

If you disagree with a sanction decision, you can challenge it.[123] You can challenge:

- the decision to give you a sanction; *and*
- the length of the sanction period.

You can apply for a revision or supersession of a sanction decision, or appeal against it in the usual way. See Chapters 43 and 44 for further information.

If you are sanctioned for failing to comply with a jobseeker's direction (see p423) you can challenge this on the basis that the direction which led to the sanction was not reasonable or that you have 'good cause' for not complying with it (see p427).

Appeals

It is often worth appealing to a tribunal. Even if the tribunal agrees that a sanction should be applied, it can reduce the length of a variable sanction period. However, an appeal tribunal could decide to extend your sanction period or could decide that the circumstances justify a different sanction. You should seek advice if you are worried this might happen in your case.

An appeal gives you a chance to put your case to an appeal tribunal and, if relevant, to challenge your former employer's version of events. Employers can be invited to attend appeal hearings, but rarely do so. See p1254 for further information about the evidence tribunals can consider.

If you do not attend a hearing and fresh allegations are made against you, the Department for Work and Pensions (if represented at the hearing) should normally request an adjournment to allow you to attend or to answer the allegations in writing[124] and the tribunal should consider one.

Relationship with unfair dismissal and other proceedings

Sometimes the same facts have to be considered by other bodies – eg, employment tribunals and the criminal courts. The questions and legal tests which these other bodies use may not be the same as the ones which apply to jobseeker's allowance (JSA) entitlement.

The benefit decision-making authorities and employment tribunals are entirely independent of each other – decisions by one are not binding on the other. This means, for example, that a finding by an employment tribunal that a dismissal was fair does not prevent a decision maker or an appeal tribunal from concluding that you did not lose your job through misconduct. It is important to remember that decision makers and appeal tribunals are not bound to decide the facts in the same way as an employment tribunal.[125]

Similarly, although appeal tribunals normally accept a criminal conviction as proof that you have done what is alleged, it must still go on to consider whether this was connected with your employment, whether it amounts to misconduct and whether the misconduct was the reason you lost your employment.

A decision maker or appeal tribunal does not have to wait for the outcome of other proceedings before making a decision,[126] although they are more likely to do so if there is a conflict of evidence. Any evidence to support your claim for JSA must be considered properly.

7. Hardship payments

Hardship payments are reduced-rate payments of income-based jobseeker's allowance (JSA) that are made in limited circumstances. You can get hardship payments if you have been sanctioned, and also in other situations. In addition:

- you must be in a 'vulnerable group' (see p446); *or*
- if you are not in a vulnerable group, a decision maker must be satisfied that you or your partner would suffer hardship if you are not paid (see p447).

For information about the amount of hardship payments, see p448.

When you can get hardship payments

You can qualify for hardship payments:

- at the beginning of a claim if you are waiting for a decision about whether you satisfy the labour market conditions (see p444);
- if you do not qualify for JSA because you do not satisfy the labour market conditions (see p444);
- if your benefit is suspended because of a doubt about whether you continue to satisfy the labour market conditions (see p445);
- if you have been sanctioned (see p445).

You cannot qualify for hardship payments if you or your partner are entitled to income support (IS) or come within one of the groups of people who can claim IS (see Chapter 13).[127] In this case, you or your partner can claim IS instead of hardship payments. If you or your partner are 60 or over, you (or your partner) might be able to claim pension credit (PC) instead of hardship payments.

Whether or not you qualify for hardship payments, you may be able to claim an interim payment of JSA (see p1108).

If, after receiving hardship payments, you are awarded full income-based JSA, IS or PC for the same period, the income-based JSA, IS or PC is reduced by the amount of hardship payments you were paid.[128]

At the beginning of a claim

You qualify for hardship payments at the beginning of a claim for JSA if you are waiting for a decision about whether you (or if you are a member of a 'joint-claim couple', you or your partner) are available for work or actively seeking work, or about your jobseeker's agreement.[129] If there is any other reason for the delay in deciding your claim you are not eligible.

You get hardship payments until the decision maker makes a decision on your claim, so long as you continue to satisfy the other conditions for getting income-based JSA (see p349).

If you cannot qualify for hardship payments, you might be able to get a crisis loan. See p538 for further information.

If you are **in a vulnerable group** (see p446) you get hardship payments from the later of:
- the fourth day after your claim for JSA (ie, after the three waiting days) or the date of your claim if the waiting days rule does not apply (see p377); *or*
- the date from which a decision maker decides that you count as in a vulnerable group.

Normally you can only get hardship payments from the day that you make a 'hardship statement', but a payment can be made for a period before the date of the statement if the decision maker is satisfied that you have suffered hardship because of a lack of resources during that period.[130] You cannot, however, get hardship payments for any period before your claim for JSA is made, unless it is a period for which a backdated claim is accepted.

If you are **not in a vulnerable group** (see p446) you get hardship payments from the later of:[131]
- the 18th day after your claim for JSA or the 15th day after your claim if the waiting days rule does not apply (see p377); *or*
- the date you submitted your hardship statement (see p449).

The labour market conditions are not satisfied

If a decision maker decides that you (or if you are a member of a 'joint-claim couple', you or your partner) are not available for work, not actively seeking work or that you do not have a valid jobseeker's agreement (known as the 'labour market conditions'), you can qualify for hardship payments, but only if you are **in a vulnerable group** (see p446).[132] This does not apply if you are treated as unavailable for work for one of the reasons listed on p360.

You get hardship payments from the day the decision maker decides that you do not satisfy the labour market conditions. You must continue to satisfy the other conditions for getting JSA (see p347). You get hardship payments indefinitely.

Jobseeker's allowance is suspended

You can qualify for hardship payments if your JSA is suspended because there is doubt about whether you (or if you are a member of a 'joint-claim couple', you or your partner) are meeting the labour market conditions.[133]

You get hardship payments until the decision maker makes a decision, so long as you satisfy the other conditions for getting income-based JSA (see p349). If you are a member of a 'joint-claim couple', both of you must satisfy these conditions (or one of you if the other is in an exempt group – see p350). If the decision maker eventually decides that you do not satisfy the labour market conditions, you can only continue to get hardship payments if you are in a vulnerable group (see above).

If you are **in a vulnerable group** (see p446), you get hardship payments from the date that the suspension begins.

If you are **not in a vulnerable group**, you cannot get hardship payments until the 15th day of the suspension.[134] If you are subject to successive 14-day suspensions (eg, at each signing day the employment officer (EO) doubts that you took sufficient steps to find work) and so never reach the 15th day of any suspension period and receive payment, seek advice as this may be unlawful.

Jobseeker's allowance is not paid because of sanctions

If you are sanctioned, JSA is not paid to you during the sanction period unless you qualify for hardship payments.[135]

If you are **in a vulnerable group** (see p446) you get hardship payments from the first day of the sanction period. If you are **not in a vulnerable group** you cannot get hardship payments until the 15th day of the sanction. This means that if the sanction period is for two weeks or less you do not get benefit for the sanction period at all unless you are in a vulnerable group.

If during a sanction period another sanction is imposed for a different reason, you cannot get hardship payments for the first 14 days of the period of the new sanction.[136]

Hardship payments continue until the end of the sanction period so long as:

- if you are a single person or a member of a couple (but not a 'joint-claim couple'), you satisfy the other conditions for getting income-based JSA; *or*
- if you are a member of a 'joint-claim couple', you both satisfy the other conditions for getting income-based JSA, or one of you does and the other is

someone who does not have to. See p350 for further information about exemptions for 'joint-claim couples'.

New Deal sanctions

If you (or if you are a 'joint-claim couple', you or your partner) are sanctioned for failing to take up or attend or for leaving a compulsory New Deal scheme (see p430), without good cause, you cannot receive hardship payments unless you are in a vulnerable group, no matter how long the sanction period lasts.[137] If you cease to be required to participate in an option, you may qualify for a hardship payment if the sanction has already lasted 14 days. If a 26-week sanction period has been awarded but you subsequently complete an option without being sanctioned again, see p435.

Hardship and vulnerable groups

Even if you come within one of the situations when hardship payments can be made, you cannot get them unless the decision maker is satisfied that you are in a 'vulnerable group' (see p446) or that you or your partner would suffer hardship if payments were not made.[138] Hardship payments can be made sooner if you are in a 'vulnerable group'. In some situations, you can only get hardship payments if you are in a vulnerable group.

Vulnerable groups

You are in a 'vulnerable group' if:[139]

- you or your partner are **pregnant** and would suffer hardship if no payment is made;
- you are a member of a couple and one of you is **responsible for a child under 16 or a young person** who would suffer hardship if no payment is made. See p374 for when you count as responsible for a child or young person;
- you are not a member of a couple and are **responsible for a young person** who would suffer hardship if no payment is made. See p374 for when you count as responsible for a young person. If you are responsible for a child under 16 you can claim IS and cannot claim hardship payments;
- your income-based JSA includes a **disability premium** (see p886) or would include one if your claim were to succeed and the person for whom the premium is paid would suffer hardship if no payment is made;
- you or your partner have a **chronic medical condition** and as a result your (or your partner's) functional capacity is 'limited or restricted by physical impairment', and the decision maker is satisfied that:
  - it has lasted or is likely to last for at least 26 weeks; *and*
  - the health of the person with the condition would decline further than that of a 'normal healthy adult' within the next two weeks and that person would suffer hardship if no payment is made.

The decision maker first considers whether the medical condition makes you or your partner incapable of work (see p764) and therefore entitled to IS.[140] In this case, you cannot claim hardship payments and should claim IS instead;

- you and/or your partner:
  - are **caring for someone** who:
    - is getting attendance allowance (AA) or the higher or middle rate of the care component of disability living allowance (DLA) (see Chapter 7) or has claimed one of these benefits, but only for up to 26 weeks from the date of the claim or until the claim is decided, whichever is first; *or*
    - has been awarded AA or the higher or middle rate of DLA care component but it has not yet gone into payment; *and*
  - would not be able to continue caring if no hardship payment is made. You do not have to show that the person you are caring for would suffer hardship.

  The care must be provided for a considerable portion of each week. This rule does not apply if the person who is being cared for is in a care home;[141]
- you or your partner are **16/17-year-olds** who can claim income-based JSA (see p381) and would suffer hardship if no payment is made;
- you or your partner are claiming JSA on the basis of a **severe hardship direction** (see p384). You do not have to show that you would suffer hardship. However, you do not count as in a 'vulnerable group' if you do not satisfy the labour market conditions (see p385); *or*
- you (or if you are a 'joint-claim couple', at least one of you) are under 21 at the date of your hardship statement and within the last three years were **being looked after by the local authority** or were someone the local authority had a duty to keep in touch with under the Children Act 1989 or who qualified for advice and assistance. Remember that if you are 16 or 17 and have been looked after by a local authority in England or Wales on or after 1 October 2001, you usually cannot claim income-based JSA. Instead, your local authority should support and accommodate you. See p713 for further information and exceptions to the rule. Similar rules apply in Scotland if you cease to be looked after by a local authority on or after 1 April 2004 (see p713).

For information about what the decision maker must consider in deciding whether a person would suffer hardship, see below.

Deciding hardship

'Hardship' is not defined in the rules. The Department for Work and Pensions (DWP) says that it means 'severe suffering or privation' (meaning 'a lack of the necessities of life').[142] When deciding whether or not someone would suffer hardship, the decision maker must consider:[143]

- whether you, or a member of your family (see p374), are so ill or disabled that you qualify for a disability premium (see p886) or the disability element or severe disability element of child tax credit (CTC) (see p1354);

- the resources likely to be available to you or a member of your family (see p374) if no hardship payments are made, how far these fall short of the amount of hardship payments to which you would be entitled (see p448) and the length of time this is likely to be the case. These include any resources that may be available from someone in your household who is not a member of your family;
- whether there is a 'substantial risk' that you or a member of your family (see p374) would be without essential items (eg, food, clothes, heating and accommodation) or that they would be available at considerably reduced levels and, if so, for how long.

The decision maker should consider all of your circumstances and those of your partner and other members of your family (see p374).

If your claim is refused, you should always consider applying for a revision or appealing (see Chapters 43 and 44). The decision maker must record the reasons for rejecting any evidence you provided or if there is conflicting evidence, for deciding what evidence to accept.[144] It could be useful to obtain a copy.

Available resources

When deciding whether you have resources available to you, the decision maker normally takes into account income and capital that is disregarded when calculating income-based JSA – eg, DLA or savings below £3,000 (see Chapter 7 and p1023).

You should only be treated as having resources that are likely to be actually available to you. For example, you may have savings in a bank account but they are subject to a notice period for withdrawal; therefore you may suffer hardship until you get access to your capital.

The rules about your age

You cannot usually qualify for hardship payments until you are 18. However, if you are aged 16 or 17, you can claim if you come into any of the categories of 16/17-year-olds who qualify for income-based JSA (see p382). If you are 16 or 17, and have been sanctioned, in many situations you do not need to claim hardship payments because you continue to get income-based JSA but at a reduced rate (see p440).

The amount of hardship payments

The weekly amount of hardship payments you get depends on your needs. Your personal allowance, premiums and housing costs are calculated as for income-based JSA (see p379). The normal disregards for capital and income are applied when calculating your hardship payments. However, your applicable amount is normally reduced by 40 per cent of:[145]

- if you are not a member of a couple, the appropriate personal allowance for a single person of your age;
- if you are a member of a couple (other than a joint-claim couple), the appropriate personal allowance for a single person:
  - aged 16 or 17, if both of you are aged 16 or 17;
  - aged 18–24, if one of you is between 18 and 24 years old and the other is a 16/17-year-old who does not qualify for income-based JSA;
  - aged 25 or over, in all other cases, so long as one of you is 18 or over;
- if you are a 'joint-claim couple', the appropriate personal allowance for a single person:
  - aged 18–24, if one of you is between 18 and 24 years old and the other is a 16/17-year-old who can claim income-based JSA (other than severe hardship payments);
  - aged 25 or over, in all other cases, so long as one of you is 18 or over.

The reduction is only 20 per cent if you or a member of your family (see p374) are pregnant or seriously ill. The amount of the reduction is rounded to the nearest 5p (or rounded down if it is exactly 2.5p).

'Seriously ill' is not defined in the rules, but the DWP says it means an important, significant or severe illness (it does not have to be long term or permanent).[146]

Claiming hardship payments

Because hardship payments are not a separate benefit, you do not have to make a claim for them. But, in order to be satisfied that you are in hardship, the decision maker needs to know a great deal more about your circumstances than you are likely to have stated when you claimed income-based JSA. You cannot get hardship payments until you have made and signed a **'hardship statement'**.[147]

The DWP should arrange to interview you as soon as it is known that you need hardship payments. Your hardship statement is normally recorded at the interview. You are asked a number of questions about your personal circumstances and medical conditions, what savings you have, what other benefits you are getting, what other money you have coming in and how much you owe. You are asked to give permission for the DWP to contact your GP if further medical evidence is required.

Although you cannot receive hardship payments until you have made your hardship statement, there is no general rule to prevent you from receiving hardship payments for a period before the date on which you made the statement. A special rule applies where you qualify for hardship payments because you are waiting for a decision at the beginning of your JSA claim (see p444).

The likelihood of being able to convince the decision maker that you are suffering hardship increases over time. You should make a fresh hardship claim at any time that you are without the normal payment of JSA.

Getting paid

While you are receiving hardship payments, you normally have to make a 'hardship declaration' at the JobCentre/Jobcentre Plus office each time you sign on, to confirm that you are still in hardship.[148] If it seems that you are no longer in hardship, the decision maker can revise or supersede the decision to award you hardship payments.

Challenging a hardship payment decision

If you are refused hardship payments you have a right of appeal to an appeal tribunal (see Chapter 44) but this takes time and you may be able to get matters resolved more quickly if you ask first for the decision to be revised (see p1189). To help you do this, you can ask for a written statement of reasons for the decision if this has not already been provided (see p1184).

Remember to tell the DWP if your circumstances worsen while you are seeking a revision or appealing. Ask the DWP to consider whether hardship payments can now be paid based on your new circumstances. If you have a partner, check to see if s/he can claim IS, PC or JSA instead of you (see below).

Tax, tax credits and other benefits

Hardship payments are taxable in the same way as any other type of JSA (see p409).

Claiming other benefits or tax credits

As hardship payments are paid at a reduced rate, if you have a partner, you should consider whether s/he could claim JSA (or IS or PC) instead of you. If so, you should continue to claim hardship payments until her/his claim has been decided (to cover the period while the claim is being processed). However, you should let the DWP know that this is what you are doing so that there is no overpayment. If your partner's claim for benefit is accepted, your entitlement to hardship payments ends. You may wish to continue to sign on to protect your national insurance record (see p838).

If you have children, check to see if you qualify for CTC (see Chapter 49). If your partner counts as in full-time paid work for working tax credit (WTC) purposes (see Chapter 51), check to see if you might be better off claiming WTC.

Passported benefits

Hardship payments are a type of income-based JSA and you are still entitled to full housing benefit and council tax benefit, payments from the social fund[149] and other passported benefits in the usual way (see p411).

8. Laws about minimum working conditions

Employers are required to provide certain minimum working conditions. These rules are relevant to the jobseeker's allowance (JSA) rules about sanctions and being available for work. A brief summary of the rules follows.

The Working Time Regulations

These regulations are designed to protect the health and safety of workers. The main rules are:

- a limit on the working week to 48 hours (averaged over a period – usually 17 weeks);
- minimum annual holiday entitlement of four weeks;
- entitlement to breaks from work (both daily breaks and a longer break once a week) and to rest periods while at work;
- special protection for night workers.

This *Handbook* cannot cover the detailed rules nor the complicated system of exceptions to them. You should seek specialist advice if you think your employer is breaking these rules.

The National Minimum Wage Act

This Act provides that the minimum hourly rate of pay in any job should be:

- if you are aged 22 or over, £4.85;
- if you are aged 18–21, £4.10;
- if you are under age 18 and not of compulsory school age, £3.00.

If you are not paid on an hourly basis, there are rules by which you can calculate what hourly rate of pay you are receiving.

The effect on jobseeker's allowance

The rules about minimum working conditions can affect your claim for JSA if you leave a job and also if you are looking for work.

Leaving a job voluntarily

If you give up a job because you believe that your employer is not complying with the legal requirements described above, you cannot necessarily argue 'just cause' (see p420). This is because of the principle that leaving a job must always be seen as the last resort and you should first do everything else possible to resolve problems before giving up your job.

If all else fails or if you feel that the hours you are being expected to work or the amount of pay you are receiving is intolerable, you might decide to give up work. In that case the laws about minimum working conditions could help you to show 'just cause'. You should point out that the intention of the Working Time Regulations is to protect the health and safety of workers, so conditions that do not comply with them should be regarded as unacceptable.

In considering 'just cause', no account should be taken of the 'level of remuneration' of the job in question (see p421). However, the Department for Work and Pensions (DWP) says this does not apply if you left your job because you tried to get your employer to pay the national minimum wage and your employer is not doing so.[150]

Placing restrictions on your availability

It should be possible for you to place a restriction on your availability for work, that you will not accept a job the terms of which do not comply with the legal requirements (eg, where an employer is offering a job at less than the minimum wage). You can try to argue that the rule that says you must still have reasonable prospects of finding work despite the restriction (see p365) should not apply as the DWP ought to assume that all employers will obey the law.

Refusing to apply for a job

You should try to argue that you have 'good cause' (see p427) for not applying for any job where the terms do not comply with the legal requirements. You need to be careful to make sure that this is so, particularly where the Working Time Regulations are concerned, in view of the many exceptions and opt-outs that might apply. If the terms offered break the rules about the 48-hour limit on the average working week, it is possible that the DWP might suggest that you should agree to an 'individual opt-out'. You should argue that this would be unreasonable, as the working time rules are intended to protect the health and safety of workers. The DWP says you *do* have good cause for refusing a job if you do so because it does not pay at least the national minimum wage that applies to you.[151]

Notes

2. **Employment-related sanctions**

1 ss19(5)(a), (6) and 20A(2)(a) and (d)-(g) JSA 1995
2 Reg 75(4) JSA Regs
3 CJSA/3304/1999
4 ss19(6)(a) and 20A(2)(d) JSA 1995
5 R(U) 10/71
6 R(U) 2/76
7 paras 34077-34081 DMG
8 para 34106 DMG
9 R(U) 8/57, para 6
10 R(U) 26/56; R(U) 1/58
11 para 34194 DMG
12 para 34109 DMG
13 R(U) 10/53
14 para 34173 DMG
15 R(U) 14/56
16 R(U) 24/56

17 R(U) 24/56
18 para 34199 DMG; R(U) 1/57; R(U) 14/57; CU/34/1992
19 R(U) 2/76
20 ss19(6)(b) and 20A(2)(e) JSA 1995
21 paras 34228-34231 DMG
22 para 34241 DMG
23 R(U) 1/96; R(U) 27/59
24 para 34256 DMG
25 ss19(7) and 20A(9) JSA 1995; reg 71 JSA Regs; R(U) 3/91
26 Reg 71(2) JSA Regs
27 R(U) 25/52; para 34259 DMG
28 *Crewe v Social Security Commissioner* [1982] 1 WLR 1209 (CA), also reported as R(U) 3/81; R(U) 20/64(T); R(U) 4/87
29 R(U) 20/64(T)
30 paras 34379-34383 DMG; R(U) 4/73
31 para 34290 DMG; R(U) 3/73
32 R(U) 14/52
33 R(U) 19/52
34 R(U) 4/87, para 9
35 ss19(9) and 20A(9) JSA 1995
36 R(U) 27/59
37 paras 34384-34386 DMG
38 R(U) 26/51; R(U) 20/64; R(U) 4/70; R(U) 1/81
39 R(U) 3/81
40 R(U) 4/87
41 ss19(5)(a) and 20A(2)(a) JSA 1995
42 ss19(10)(b) and 20A(9) JSA 1995
43 para 34651 DMG
44 ss19(6)(c) and 20A(2)(f) JSA 1995
45 para 34400 DMG
46 CJSA/2082/2002
47 CJSA/2692/1999
48 para 34401-34402 DMG
49 R(U) 32/52
50 para 34399 DMG
51 ss19(6)(d) and 20A(2)(g) JSA 1995
52 Reg 72(8) JSA Regs
53 paras 34591-34592 DMG
54 Reg 72(9) JSA Regs
55 ss20(3) and 20B(3) JSA 1995
56 Reg 74 JSA Regs
57 Reg 1(3) JSA Regs, definition of 'full-time student'
58 Reg 74(4) JSA Regs
59 para 34237 DMG
60 Reg 75(2) JSA Regs
61 Reg 72(5A) JSA Regs
62 ss20(1) and 20B(1) JSA 1995
63 Reg 72(5)(a) JSA Regs
64 Reg 72(4) JSA Regs
65 ss19(6)(d) and 20A(2)(g) JSA 1995; reg 72(8) and (9) JSA Regs
66 Reg 72(5)(a) JSA Regs
67 Reg 72(5)(b) JSA Regs
68 Reg 72(3A) and (3B) JSA Regs
69 Reg 72(2) JSA Regs
70 paras 34506 and 34686 DMG
71 Reg 72(6) JSA Regs
72 Reg 72(7) JSA Regs
73 Reg 72(6)(b) JSA Regs
74 ss19(9) and 20A(9) JSA 1995

3. New Deal, training scheme and employment programme-related sanctions

75 ss19(5) and 20A(2)(b) and (c) JSA 1995
76 Regs 1(3), definition of 'the New Deal options' and 75(1) JSA Regs
77 Reg 75(1)(b)(iii) JSA Regs
78 Reg 75(4) JSA Regs
79 Reg 1(3) JSA Regs, definition of 'employment zone'; the Employment Zones Regulations 2003 No. 2438
80 ss19(5)(c) and 20A(2)(c) JSA 1995
81 ss19(5)(b)(iii) and (iv) and 20A(2)(b)(iii) and (iv) JSA 1995
82 para 34743 DMG
83 para 34738 DMG
84 ss19(5)(b)(ii) and 20A(2)(b)(ii) JSA 1995
85 ss19(5)(b)(i) and 20A(2)(b)(i) JSA 1995
86 para 34791 DMG
87 Reg 73(2) JSA Regs
88 R(JSA) 7/03 discusses the meaning of 'conscientious objection' in this context
89 Reg 73(2B) and (4) JSA Regs
90 Reg 73(2A) JSA Regs

4. Sanction periods and amount of jobseeker's allowance payable

91 R(U) 24/56
92 ss19(2) and 20A(3) JSA 1995; reg 69(1) JSA Regs
93 Reg 7(8)(a) SS&CS(DA) Regs; reg 69(2) JSA Regs
94 Reg 69(1)(a) and (b) JSA Regs
95 Reg 3(6) SS&CS(DA) Regs
96 CJSA/2375/2000
97 Reg 69(1)(a) JSA Regs
98 Reg 69(1)(b) JSA Regs
99 Reg 69(1)(c) and (d) JSA Regs
100 Reg 69(3) and (4) JSA Regs
101 ss19(3) and 20A(4) JSA 1995
102 Reg 7(8)(b) SS&CS(DA) Regs
103 R(U) 8/74(T)
104 para 34040 DMG
105 CJSA/3875/2002
106 Reg 70 JSA Regs
107 paras 34046 DMG
108 para 34007 DMG
109 ss19(1) and 20A(5)(a) JSA 1995
110 s20A(5)(b) and (7) JSA 1995

111 Reg 74A JSA Regs
112 s20A(6) JSA 1995; reg 74B JSA Regs

5. **Special rules for 16/17-year-olds**
113 Reg 57 JSA Regs, definition of 'young person'
114 Reg 67(1) JSA Regs
115 Reg 67(3) JSA Regs
116 Reg 67(2) JSA Regs
117 Reg 68 JSA Regs
118 ss16(3)(b), 17(3)(b) and (c) and 20(2)(b) JSA 1995; reg 63 JSA Regs
119 s17(4) JSA 1995; Sch 2 para 1(b) SSA 1998
120 Reg 63(1)(a) and (b) JSA Regs
121 Reg 63(1)(c)-(f) JSA Regs
122 Reg 63 JSA Regs

6. **Challenging a sanction decision**
123 Sch 3 para 3(d) SSA 1998
124 paras 34082, 34231 and 34739 DMG
125 R(U) 2/74
126 R(U) 10/54

7. **Hardship payments**
127 Regs 140(3) and 146A(3) JSA Regs
128 Regs 146 and 146H JSA Regs; reg 5 SS(PAOR) Regs
129 Regs 141(2), 142(2), 146C(2) and 146D(2) JSA Regs
130 Regs 141(3) and 146C(3) JSA Regs
131 Regs 142(2) and 146D(2) JSA Regs
132 Regs 141(4) and 146C(4) JSA Regs
133 Regs 141(5), 142(3), 146C(5) and 146D(3) JSA Regs
134 Regs 142(4) and 146D(4) JSA Regs
135 Regs 141(6), 142(5), 146C(6) and 146D(5) JSA Regs
136 para 35304 DMG
137 Regs 140(4A), 140A, 146A(5) and 146B JSA Regs
138 Regs 140(1) and (2) and 146A(1) and (2) JSA Regs
139 Regs 140(1) and 146A(1) JSA Regs
140 para 35073 DMG
141 Regs 140(4) and 146A(4) JSA Regs
142 para 35155 DMG
143 Regs 140(5) and 146A(6) JSA Regs
144 para 35162 DMG
145 Regs 145 and 146G JSA Regs
146 R(SB) 19/82; para 35314 DMG
147 Regs 143 and 146E JSA Regs
148 Regs 144 and 146F JSA Regs
149 SF Dirs 8 and 25

8. **Laws about minimum working conditions**
150 para 34284 DMG
151 para 34437 DMG

Chapter 17

Maternity allowance

This chapter covers:

If you are pregnant or have recently given birth, and you are not entitled to statutory maternity pay (SMP – see Chapter 23), you may qualify for **maternity allowance (MA)**. MA is paid by the Department for Work and Pensions for a maximum of 26 weeks.

You do not have to have paid national insurance contributions to qualify for MA. Although you must satisfy an employment and an earnings condition, your entitlement to MA is not affected by any other income or savings that you may have.

You cannot receive MA for any week in which you are entitled to SMP. So, for example, you may get MA rather than SMP if:

- you are self-employed; *or*
- you do not satisfy the earnings condition or continuous employment rule for SMP because you have a low income or you changed jobs during pregnancy; *or*
- you gave up work just before or during your pregnancy (but see p577 for details of when you may still qualify for SMP in these circumstances).

If you do not qualify for MA (or SMP), you may be entitled to statutory sick pay (unless you are within the periods mentioned on p603) or to incapacity benefit (see Chapter 12).

Definitions of some of the terms that are used in this chapter are given on p587.

1. Who can claim maternity allowance

You qualify for maternity allowance (MA) if:[1]

- you are pregnant or have recently given birth, and you are within your 'maternity allowance period' (see below);
- you satisfy the employment condition (see below);
- you satisfy the earnings condition (see below);
- you are not working;[2]
- you are not entitled to statutory maternity pay (SMP).

See p458 for details of when you can be disqualified from receiving MA.

Maternity allowance period

MA is payable for a period of up to 26 consecutive weeks (known as the 'maternity allowance period'). The earliest your 26-week MA period can start is from the beginning of the 11th week before the expected week of childbirth (EWC – see p464), unless your baby is born before this, and the latest is the Sunday after your baby is born. The rules for when your MA period starts are the same as those for SMP[3] (see p574) except that:

- if you are not working at the beginning of the 11th week before your EWC, your MA period will start from the Sunday of that week; *and*
- if you are not entitled to MA during the 11th week before your EWC, but you become entitled to it before your baby is born (perhaps because you then meet the earnings or employment condition), your MA period will start from the Sunday after you stop work.[4]

Employment condition

In order to qualify for MA you must have worked as an employee and/or been self-employed for at least 26 weeks in the 66 weeks immediately before your EWC (see p464). This 66-week period is known as the **'test period'**.[5] If you work for just part of a week, the whole of that week counts towards the 26-week requirement. The 26 weeks do not need to be consecutive and you do not need to have worked for the same employer for the whole period. You need only show that you have been employed and/or self-employed for any part of each of the 26 weeks.

Earnings condition

To qualify for MA your average weekly earnings (or, if you are self-employed, the average weekly earnings you are treated as having) must be at least equal to the MA threshold – currently £30 a week. It is the MA threshold that is in force in the tax year in which your 66-week test period begins (see p464) that is used to assess your entitlement.[6]

Earnings from employment

If **you are employed**, your gross earnings are used to calculate your average weekly earnings. What counts as earnings for MA purposes is the same as for SMP (see p570).[7]

Any backdated pay rises which are paid for the period over which your earnings are averaged (see below) are included.[8]

Earnings from self-employment

If you are self-employed you are treated as earning the following amount each week and this figure is used to calculate your average weekly earnings, irrespective of the amount you actually earn:[9]

- for each week that you hold a national insurance (NI) small earnings exception certificate (see p833), you are treated as having weekly earnings equal to the MA threshold in force at the end of that week (currently £30 a week); *and*
- for each week for which you have paid a Class 2 NI contribution you are treated as having weekly earnings of an amount 90 per cent of which is equal to the maximum amount of MA that can be paid for that week. From 11 April 2005, as the maximum amount of MA that can be paid is £106, you are treated as having earnings of £117.78 a week. (For weeks between 4 April 2004 and 10 April 2005 you would be treated as having weekly earnings of £114.23.) If you have paid a Class 2 contribution for at least 13 weeks in your 66-week test period you will qualify for MA of £106 a week.[10]

Calculating average earnings

Your average weekly earnings are calculated as follows:

- If you have paid Class 2 contributions as a self-employed person for at least 13 of the weeks in your 66-week test period, your earnings in the first 13 such weeks in your test period are added together and the total is divided by 13. In this situation you will qualify for MA of £106 a week.
- If you have not paid Class 2 contributions in at least 13 weeks in your 66-week test period, perhaps because you were not self-employed or because your earnings from self-employment were not high enough, your average weekly earnings are calculated by adding together your earnings in the 13 weeks in your 66-week test period (see p464) when your earnings are highest, and dividing the total by 13.[11]

In both cases the 13 weeks do not need to be consecutive and if you have more than one job, the earnings from all your jobs, including earnings you are treated as having from self-employment, are counted.[12] If you are not paid weekly you work out your weekly earnings by dividing the payments you receive by the nearest number of weeks in the period for which they are paid.[13]

More than one job

Even if, as a result of having more than one job, you satisfy the conditions for MA more than once, you can only receive one 26-week payment of MA at a time. If you are receiving SMP from one job, you will not be able also to receive MA for the same week from another job or from self-employment.

Disqualification from benefit

You can be disqualified from receiving MA if:[14]

- you work (whether you are employed or self-employed) during your MA period;
- without good cause, you fail to take 'due care of your health' or to answer 'reasonable enquiries' from the Department for Work and Pensions (DWP) about whether you are doing so. The enquiries should not relate to any medical exam, treatment or advice you have or have not been given;
- prior to the birth of your baby you fail to attend a medical examination without good cause. You must have been given written notice of the examination at least three days beforehand.

In any of these circumstances the DWP can disqualify you for as long as is reasonable given the circumstances. However, if you have worked, the disqualification must be for at least the same number of days as you worked. If you are disqualified for not having attended a medical examination, the disqualification cannot continue once you have given birth. The question of whether or not you have good cause for your behaviour will depend on your circumstances. If you disagree with the DWP's decision on whether you have good cause or on the length of the disqualification period you can challenge their decision (see p463).

2. The rules about your age

There are no upper or lower age limits for receiving maternity allowance.

3. Claiming for others

When you receive maternity allowance you may be entitled to an increase in your benefit for an adult dependant – ie, your spouse or for someone who cares for your child (see Chapter 31).

4. The amount of benefit[15]

	£ per week
Claimant	the lesser of 106 or 90% of earnings
Adult dependant	35.65
MA threshold	30.00

You will only qualify for maternity allowance (MA) if your average weekly earnings are at least equal to the MA threshold (see p464).[16] See p457 for how your average earnings are calculated. The amount of MA you receive is either 90 per cent of your average weekly earnings or £106 a week, whichever is less. MA is only payable during your 'maternity allowance period' (see p456).

5. Special rules for special groups

There are some groups of claimants to whom special rules apply. These are covered below and in Chapters 26 and 28. Special rules apply to you if:

- you are in prison or legal custody (see p731);
- you go abroad (see p688).

There are also special rules if you have returned from abroad where you worked in the 12 months immediately before the end of the 15th week before your expected week of childbirth and you are ordinarily resident in Great Britain.[17]

6. Claims and backdating

To be entitled to maternity allowance (MA) you must make a claim for it.[18] The rules for claiming are described on p460. More detailed rules are explained in Chapter 40. It may be possible to claim in advance (see p462) or to get your claim backdated (see p462).

If you are working, you may be entitled to statutory maternity pay (SMP) from your employer and you should make a claim for this (see p581). If you are not entitled to SMP, your employer must give you Form SMP1 which you should send to the Department for Work and Pensions (DWP) to support your claim for MA. If you disagree with your employer's decision you should also send a copy of the SMP1 form to the your local Revenue National Insurance Contribution Office (NICO – see p586).

If you are employed, and your employer does not give you form SMP1, or does not make a decision about your SMP entitlement in good time, you should contact your local NICO (see p586). You should also make a claim for MA while you are waiting for a decision about your SMP.

Making a claim

A claim for MA must be made in writing on the appropriate application form (an MA1 form). Your local antenatal clinic may have the form or you can get one from any DWP, JobCentre or Jobcentre Plus office or from the Jobcentre Plus website (www.jobcentreplus.gov.uk). The decision maker at the DWP may accept a written application that is not on the correct form if this is sufficient in the circumstances (see p1079).[19] Your claim will not be accepted unless it is received after the 15th week before your expected week of childbirth (EWC).[20]

If you want to receive an increase in your MA for an adult dependant (see Chapter 31), you must also make a claim for this. The DWP will send you a claim form regarding the increase if you tick the relevant box on the MA1 form.

However, the procedure you should follow in order to make your claim for MA depends on whether you live in the catchment area of a Jobcentre Plus office. You can check your local telephone directory or the Jobcentre Plus website (see above) to see if you live in a Jobcentre Plus area. If you live in a Jobcentre Plus area see below. If not, you should send your claim, together with the SMP1 form from your employer (if applicable, see p459), to your local DWP office. You can find the address in the telephone directory.

Whichever procedure you follow to claim it is advisable to keep a copy of your claim in case queries arise.

Jobcentre Plus areas

If you live in a Jobcentre Plus area, then in practice you will usually be required to start your claim by telephoning a 'contact centre'. (Your local Jobcentre Plus office will have this number, and it may also be displayed in local advice centres, libraries, etc.) The contact centre will take basic details, and then issue you with a claim form. However, if you send in a claim form before telephoning the contact centre then usually your claim will be processed without you having to telephone the contact centre.

If you cannot or do not want to use the telephone to start your claim, then Jobcentre Plus say that they can still deal with your claim in other ways. You might for example be invited for a 'face-to-face' interview to gather the relevant details, or in some cases they may accept an MA1 claim form. Seek advice if you are unable to use a telephone and the Jobcentre Plus office will not let you start your claim in any other way.

If you live in a Jobcentre Plus area and there is some delay in you making your claim for MA it may be advisable for you to obtain and immediately submit an MA1 form rather than waiting for a claim form to be sent to you by the contact centre. This is because the date of your claim is the date your completed claim form is received by the DWP or Jobcentre Plus office and not the date on which you telephone the contact centre. As MA can only be backdated for up to three months, you should do this if it is necessary to ensure that your claim form is received within three months of the date that your entitlement to MA would have started, otherwise you may lose money.

Information to support your claim

When you claim MA, you and any adult dependant for whom you are claiming must satisfy the national insurance number requirement. See p1083 for further details. You must also provide medical evidence, normally a certificate from your doctor or a registered midwife, giving the expected date of birth of your child (Form MAT B1).[21] This certificate will not be accepted if it is issued before the 20th week before your EWC. If you cannot obtain a MAT B1 form, the DWP can accept other medical evidence of the expected date of birth, if this is sufficient in the circumstances. If you are claiming MA after your baby is born you will also have to provide proof of the date of the baby's birth – eg, a birth certificate.

If you have been employed you will need to provide the DWP with pay slips or some other written proof of your earnings – eg, a letter from your employer and an SMP1 form from any employer that you worked for during the 15th week before your EWC.

Do not delay sending in your claim for MA because you are waiting for your MAT B1, SMP1, or evidence of your earnings. You can send these in later, as soon as you get them.

Who should claim

If you are unable to manage your own affairs, another person can claim MA for you by becoming your 'appointee' (see p1075).

The date of your claim

The date of your claim is normally the date it is received at a DWP office.[22]

If the claim you submit is incomplete or not on the correct form you may be asked to provide further information or to complete the correct form. As long as this additional information or form is returned within a month of it being sent back to you (or longer if the decision maker thinks that the delay is reasonable), your claim is treated as made on the date the initial claim was received at the DWP office (see p1082).[23] In some circumstances you can claim before you qualify for MA, or the date of your claim can be backdated (see p462).

If you claim the wrong benefit

A claim for incapacity benefit (IB – see Chapter 12) may be treated as a claim for MA and vice versa (see p1085).[24] This may allow you to get your claim for MA backdated for more than the normal three months. If you claim SMP from your employer but your claim is refused, and you claim MA within three months of being notified of your employer's decision in writing, your claim for MA is treated as having been made either on the date of your claim for SMP or at the beginning of the 14th week before your EWC, whichever is later.[25]

Claiming in advance

You cannot make a claim for MA until after the 15th week before your EWC (until week 26 of pregnancy) but you should make your claim as soon as possible after that.[26] However, it may be worth waiting a few weeks before claiming if that means that you will have higher average earnings. If you plan to stop work after the 11th week before the EWC and you claim while you are still working, the DWP will send you Form BM25A, notifying you of your entitlement and asking to be informed of the actual date that you stop work.

How your claim is dealt with

Your claim is dealt with by the DWP office that covers your local area, and queries about your claim should be made to that office.

You may be able to claim an interim payment if you are waiting for a decision on your claim (see p1108) or a crisis loan to tide you over until benefit is paid (see p538). You could also claim means-tested benefits if your income is low (see p465).

See p1091 for more information about the processing of claims.

Backdating your claim

A claim for MA can be backdated for up to three months if you satisfy the normal MA qualifying conditions. You do not have to show any reasons why your claim was late.[27]

If you might have qualified for benefit earlier but did not claim because you were given the wrong information or misled by the DWP you could:

- ask for an *ex gratia* payment (see p1304); *or*
- complain to the Ombudsman via your MP (see p1302).

If you have claimed IB or SMP instead of MA, see p461.

7. Getting paid

Maternity allowance (MA) is paid from the start of the MA period (see p456) for up to 26 weeks. It is a daily benefit which means that it can be paid for periods of less than a week. The daily rate is one-seventh of the weekly amount.[28]

MA is normally paid by direct credit transfer into your bank (or similar account). If you are unable to open or manage an account, payment can be made by cheque. Such cheques are sent to your home address and can be paid into an account or cashed at the post office (see p1099 for details).[29]

Payments are normally made each Friday for payment from the previous Sunday.[30] You are entitled to national insurance contribution credits for each week you receive MA.

If your benefit cheque is lost or stolen, see p1104. If payment of your MA is suspended, see p1105.

Delays and complaints

If payment of your MA is delayed, you might be able to get an interim payment (see p1108).

If you suffer delays, or wish to complain about how your claim has been dealt with, see pp1300 and 1305. You might be able to claim compensation (see p1304).

Change of circumstances

It is your duty to report any change in your circumstances which might affect your entitlement to, the amount of, or the payment of, your benefit, such as if you work during the MA period. You should do this promptly in writing or by telephone to the office handling your claim (although in individual cases notification might be accepted in a form other than in writing or by telephone). In some cases, however, the decision maker might say you must report changes in writing. In any case, you might want to report the change in writing and keep a copy, in case of a dispute in the future. If you do not promptly report any such change, any resulting overpayment may be recoverable from you (see Chapter 41). If you are considered deliberately to have acted falsely or dishonestly, you may also be guilty of an offence (see Chapter 42).

If the change affects your entitlement to MA, a decision maker will look at your claim again and make a new decision (see p1199). The date from which the new decision takes effect depends on whether or not it is advantageous to you and whether you reported the change in time (see p1204 for further details).

Overpayments and fraud

If you are overpaid MA, you might have to repay it. The rules on overpayments are covered in Chapter 41.

If you have been accused of fraud, see Chapter 42.

8. Challenging a maternity allowance decision

You can apply for a revision or supersession of a maternity allowance decision, or appeal against it – see Chapters 43 and 44. Certain decisions are not open to appeal, although you can request that they be revised or superseded (see p1221).

9. Definitions of terms

- The **'expected week of childbirth'** (sometimes called the 'expected week of confinement') is the week, starting on a Sunday, in which your baby is due to be born.
- The **'maternity allowance period'** is the period of up to 26 weeks during which maternity allowance (MA) is paid. See p456 for when it can start.
- The **'test period'** is the period of 66 weeks immediately before the week in which your baby is due which is used to calculate entitlement to MA.
- The **'maternity allowance threshold'** is the minimum level of average earnings you need to qualify for MA.

Example

Rita's baby is due on Saturday 23 July 2005. The following dates apply:

– The 'expected week of childbirth' begins on the Sunday before – ie, Sunday 17 July 2005.

– The first week before the 'expected week of childbirth' begins on Sunday 10 July 2005, the second on Sunday 3 July 2005 and so on.

– The 11th week before the 'expected week of childbirth' begins on Sunday 1 May 2005. This is important because it is normally the earliest date from which Rita can be paid MA (or statutory maternity pay).

– The 66-week 'test period' runs from Sunday 11 April 2004 to Saturday 16 July 2005.

Calculating the weeks can be confusing. To help you with this, Appendix 5 contains a table of dates for all the weeks in 2005/06.

10. Tax, tax credits and other benefits

Maternity allowance (MA) is not taxable.[31]

Tax credits

If you are receiving MA or you are on ordinary maternity leave, and your income is low, you may qualify for working tax credit (WTC – see Chapter 50), as long as you were in full-time paid work immediately before your MA began, or before your maternity leave started (see p1348).

If you did not count as being in full-time paid work immediately before your MA started or before going on maternity leave but you were working for at least 16 hours a week you may qualify for WTC from the date your baby is born.

If you are entitled to WTC, you may be able to get help with the cost of childcare for your new baby even before you return to work (see p1360).

If you have a dependent child you may also qualify for child tax credit (CTC – see Chapter 49).

MA is ignored when calculating your entitlement to tax credits.

Means-tested benefits

If you have a low income you may be able to get income support (IS – see Chapter 13) while you are on maternity leave. See p296 for details of whether you may qualify for IS while on leave. If your partner is 60 or over you may instead qualify for pension credit (PC – see Chapter 18).

If you have a low income you may also be entitled to housing benefit (HB – see Chapter 10) and council tax benefit (CTB – see Chapter 6). If you are getting MA you may be able to get an allowance for childcare costs deducted from your earnings when calculating your entitlement to HB and CTB – see p965.

You cannot claim jobseeker's allowance (JSA) if you are getting MA because you are treated as unavailable for work, but your partner may qualify.[32] If you are a member of a couple who would normally have to make a joint claim for JSA (see p394) then:

- if you are incapable of work because of your pregnancy but you are not getting MA (or statutory maternity pay – SMP), and it is earlier than the 11th week before your expected week of childbirth (EWC), you do not need to meet the labour market conditions – only your partner must;
- your partner can receive JSA for you both without you needing to make a joint claim if you are getting MA (or SMP), or from the 11th week before your EWC until 15 weeks after the baby is born.

The MA you get is taken into account in full when calculating your entitlement to IS, income-based JSA, HB and CTB.

For PC, any MA you receive counts as benefit income although it is ignored when calculating your qualifying income for the savings credit of PC (see Chapter 18).[33]

Non-means-tested benefits

MA is affected by the overlapping benefits rules (see p1102).

You cannot get contribution-based JSA (see Chapter 15) or statutory sick pay (SSP) if you are receiving MA. See p603 for how your SSP entitlement is affected if you are pregnant.

Incapacity benefit

While you are pregnant you can be treated as incapable of work for incapacity benefit (IB) purposes (and so you may qualify for IB) in the circumstances explained on p768, and for any period when you are entitled to MA.[34]

However, while you can qualify for both MA and IB at the same time, you cannot receive payment of both MA and IB in full because of the overlapping benefit rules. Remember that a claim for MA can be treated as a claim for IB and vice versa (see p1085).

Days on which you were entitled to MA count when calculating whether you are entitled to the higher rate of short-term IB or long-term IB.

Passports and other sources of help

If you are receiving IS, income-based JSA, PC, the disability or severe disability element of WTC, or CTC paid at a higher rate than the family element you may be entitled to a Sure Start maternity grant of £500 per child from the social fund. You might be able to get other help from the discretionary social fund (see Chapters 21 and 22).

If you or your partner receive IS, income-based JSA, or, in some circumstances, CTC, you qualify for free school meals for your children (see p18).

For information on your possible entitlement to free prescriptions, free NHS dental treatment and free milk and vitamins (or, from summer 2005 if you live in certain areas, 'Healthy Start' welfare food vouchers), see Chapter 9.

Notes

1. **Who can claim maternity allowance**
   1 s35 SSCBA 1992
   2 Reg 2(1)(a) SS(MatA) Regs
   3 s35(2) SSCBA 1992
   4 Reg 3(2A) SS(MatA) Regs
   5 s35(1)(b) SSCBA 1992
   6 ss35(1)(c) and 35A(4) SSCBA 1992
   7 s35A(4)(a) SSCBA 1992; reg 2 SS(MatA)(E) Regs
   8 Reg 6(2) SS(MatA)(E) Regs
   9 Reg 3 SS(MatA)(E) Regs
   10 s35A(5)(c), (5A) and (5B) SSCBA 1992; reg 5 SS(MatA)(E) Regs
   11 Reg 6(1) SS(MatA)(E) Regs
   12 Reg 4(1) SS(MatA)(E) Regs
   13 Reg 6(3) SS(MatA)(E) Regs
   14 Reg 2 SS(MatA) Regs

4. **The amount of benefit**
   15 ss35(1) and 35A SSCBA 1992
   16 s35(1)(c) SSCBA 1992

5. **Special rules for special groups**
   17 SS(MatA)(WA) Regs

6. **Claims and backdating**
   18 s1 SSAA 1992
   19 Reg 4(1) SS(C&P) Regs
   20 Reg 14(1) SS(C&P) Regs
   21 Reg 2(3) SS(ME) Regs
   22 Reg 6(1) SS(C&P) Regs
   23 Regs 4(7) and 6(1) SS(C&P) Regs
   24 Reg 9 and Sch 1 Part I SS(C&P) Regs
   25 Reg 10(3) and (4) SS(C&P) Regs
   26 Reg 14 SS(C&P) Regs
   27 Reg 19(2) SS(C&P) Regs

7. **Getting paid**
   28 s35(5) SSCBA 1992
   29 Reg 21 SS(C&P) Regs
   30 Reg 24(4) SS(C&P) Regs

10. **Tax, tax credits and other benefits**
   31 s677 IT (EP)A 2003
   32 Reg 15(c) JSA Regs
   33 Regs 9 and 15(1) SPC Regs
   34 s30C(2) SSCBA 1992; reg 14 SS(IFW) Regs

Chapter 18

Pension credit

Pension credit (PC) came into force on 6 October 2003 and replaces income support for those over the age of 60, also known as minimum income guarantee. The purpose of the new credit is to ensure that pensioners have a guaranteed level of income and are rewarded for having made provisions for retirement above the basic state pension.

PC consists of two elements:
- guarantee credit;
- savings credit.

You may be entitled to either or both of these elements. PC is administered by the Pension Service, an executive agency of the DWP.

1. Who can claim pension credit

Guarantee credit

You are entitled to a guarantee credit if:[1]
- you are 60 or over (see p468);[2]
- you are in Great Britain (GB) (with exceptions for periods of temporary absence) and satisfy the 'habitual residence test' (see p702);[3]
- you have no income or your income is below the appropriate minimum guarantee (see p469);[4]
- you are not a 'person subject to immigration control' (see p654).[5]

Savings credit

You are entitled to a savings credit if:[6]

- you or your partner are 65 or over (see below);[7]
- you are in GB (with exceptions for periods of temporary absence) and satisfy the 'habitual residence test' (see p702);[8]
- you are not a 'person subject to immigration control' (see p654);[9]
- you have 'qualifying income' that exceeds the 'savings credit threshold' but is not too high to produce a nil award (see p472).[10]

2. The rules about your age

Entitlement to pension credit is linked to the minimum qualifying age at which a woman can receive state pension, which is currently 60.[11] However, this age will rise steadily to 65 between 2010 and 2020, by virtue of the Pensions Act 1995.

Additionally, you or your partner must be 65 or over in order to qualify for the savings credit element.[12]

3. Claiming for others

You claim for yourself and your partner (if you have one) and for each additional spouse in a polygamous marriage. If you have a child for whom you are responsible, you should claim child tax credit (see Chapter 49) as there are no child amounts payable with pension credit. See Chapter 32 for who counts as your family.

4. The amount of the credit

How much pension credit (PC) you receive depends on whether you are single or a member of a couple, have any disabilities, any caring responsibilities or any eligible housing costs. The maximum amount of guarantee credit you could receive is reduced by your income (subject to any applicable disregards). For savings credit the rules are slightly more complicated (see p472). The income and capital provisions differ from those for income support (IS), although there are some similarities (for the details on income and capital see Chapters 38 and 39). However, for the details on qualifying income for the purposes of savings credit see p472.

Guarantee credit

Your maximum guarantee credit is known as the 'appropriate minimum guarantee'[13] and is made up of:

- standard minimum guarantee; *and*
- where applicable, additional amounts.

Standard minimum guarantee

If you do not have any additional needs you will receive an award of PC which will ensure that your weekly income is brought up to one of the following standard minimum guarantee levels.

Single person[14]	£109.45
Couple (married or unmarried)[15]	£167.05
Each additional spouse in a polygamous marriage[16]	£57.60

Additional amounts

If you have additional needs, such as a disability, caring responsibilities or housing costs, your award will bring your income to the level of the standard minimum guarantee plus additional amounts. These will broadly correspond to the premiums and housing costs payable within IS, with an additional transitional amount to ensure that those in receipt of IS or income-based jobseeker's allowance (JSA) at the time they first become entitled to PC are not worse off as a result of the change (see below).

The additional amounts are:

Severe disability[17] The qualifying rules for this amount are broadly the same as for the severe disability premium within IS (see p891).	£45.50 (single)	£91.00 (where both partners qualify)
Carer[18] The rules are the same as those for the carer's premium within IS (see p896).	£25.80	£25.80 (for each partner who qualifies)
Housing costs[19] These provisions are covered in Chapter 36 and broadly mirror those for IS, but with some exceptions.	See Chapter 36	
Transitional[20]	See below	

Transitional amount[21]

If you are in receipt of IS or income-based JSA when you first become entitled to PC, in order to ensure that you are not worse off by moving onto PC, your appropriate minimum guarantee may include a 'transitional amount'. You will be eligible for this extra amount if, on the day you first become entitled to PC, your IS or income-based JSA applicable amount (less any deductions below) exceeds your appropriate minimum guarantee.

The amounts to be deducted from the applicable amount are:[22]

- any personal allowance or premiums for dependent children;
- any residential allowance.

Where you have some existing transitional protection paid under Income Support (Transitional) Regulations 1987 the applicable amount will be increased by this amount.[23] See the 19th edition of CPAG's *National Welfare Benefits Handbook*, section 17.

The transitional amount will reduce over time by any increase in your appropriate minimum guarantee and will cease when:[24]

- any increase in your appropriate minimum guarantee equals or exceeds the transitional amount (ignoring any increase due solely to you no longer being a hospital inpatient); *or*
- you or your partner cease to be entitled to PC (disregarding any break in entitlement of less than eight weeks).

The guarantee credit calculation

Step one: calculate your appropriate minimum guarantee

This consists of:

- standard minimum guarantee for you and your partner, if you have one; *plus*
- additional amounts for any special needs and/or housing costs.

Step two: calculate your income[25]

This is the amount you have coming in each week from some state benefits, private pensions, earnings etc. Not all income counts (eg, disability living allowance (DLA), attendance allowance (AA), child tax credit and child benefit) and some income is subject to disregards (see Chapter 37, but also see p480 for the new assessed income periods). If you have capital over £6,000 (£10,000 if you live in a care home) you will be treated as having £1 for every £500 (or part of £500) capital that exceeds £6,000 (or £10,000 if you live in a care home).[26]

Step three: deduct income from appropriate minimum guarantee

The amount of your guarantee credit will be your appropriate minimum guarantee less any relevant income you have.[27] If your income is above the appropriate minimum guarantee you will not qualify for any guarantee credit but you might qualify for some savings credit. Additionally, you might qualify for guarantee credit if you or your partner become entitled to a qualifying benefit, like AA, which would increase the amount of your appropriate minimum guarantee.

Example 1

Mehmet is single and aged 67. He lives in rented accommodation.

His appropriate minimum guarantee is:

£109.45 standard minimum guarantee (single person rate).

His weekly income is basic state pension of £82.05.

He is therefore entitled to £27.40 guarantee credit to bring the income level up to £109.45.

He is not entitled to any savings credit guarantee as he has no qualifying income above the savings threshold (see p472).

He will also be entitled to maximum housing benefit (HB) and council tax benefit (CTB) and any other passports that might apply.

Example 2

Barbara is single and aged 68. She is in receipt of AA. She lives alone and no one gets carer's allowance for looking after her. She has no eligible housing costs as she has paid off her mortgage.

Her appropriate minimum guarantee is:

£109.45	standard minimum guarantee (single person rate)
£45.50	severe disability additional amount
£154.95	total

Her weekly income is basic state pension of £74.00. AA is ignored as income.

She is therefore entitled to £80.95 guarantee credit to bring her total income up to £154.95.

She is not entitled to any savings credit as she does not have any qualifying income above the savings credit threshold (see p472).

She will also be entitled to maximum CTB and any other passports that may apply.

Example 3

Maria and Geoff are a couple. Maria is 62 and Geoff is 67. Their 24-year-old daughter lives with them and she is in receipt of income-based JSA. They have eligible weekly housing costs of £49.00. Maria receives the middle rate care component of DLA and Geoff gets AA.

Their appropriate minimum guarantee is:

£167.05	standard minimum guarantee (couple rate)
£49.00	eligible housing costs
£216.05	total

Their joint weekly income for calculating PC is £218.20 made up of basic state pension of £131.20 (Maria £49.15, Geoff £82.05) and occupational pension of £84.00 and £3.00 deemed income from £7,500 savings. DLA and AA are ignored as income.

They are not entitled to any guarantee credit because their income exceeds their appropriate minimum guarantee of £216.05. Their appropriate minimum guarantee does not include a severe disability addition because their 24-year-old daughter lives with them.

However, they would be entitled to some savings credit as they have qualifying income above the savings credit threshold (see below).

Savings credit

In order to qualify for this element of PC you must have qualifying income above the **'savings credit threshold'** of:[28]

Single person	£82.05
Couple	£131.20

'Qualifying income' for the purposes of entitlement to savings credit is all income that counts for guarantee credit (see Chapters 38 and 39) except the following:[29]

- working tax credit;
- incapacity benefit;
- contribution-based jobseeker's allowance;
- severe disablement allowance;
- maternity allowance;
- maintenance payments for you, or your partner, from a spouse or former spouse.

The amount of savings credit to which you are entitled is subject to a maximum figure known as the **'maximum savings credit'**.[30] This is 60 per cent of the difference between the standard minimum guarantee and the savings credit threshold. Remember these differ for a single claimant and a couple. The maximum is therefore:

Single person	£16.44
Couple	£21.51

The savings credit calculation[31]

Calculating any savings credit to which you may be entitled is slightly more complicated than working out the guarantee credit. If you have already calculated whether you are entitled to the guarantee credit you will already have worked out the amounts in steps one and two. If you are entitled to the guarantee credit then you only need to follow steps one to four below.

Step one: calculate your total income figure

This is any income that counts for PC purposes and includes qualifying income.

Step two: calculate your appropriate minimum guarantee

This is the standard minimum guarantee plus any additional amounts.

Step three: calculate 60 per cent of any qualifying income you have which is above the savings credit threshold that applies to you (subject to the maximum savings credit payable)

This is 60 per cent of all your income that counts for the guarantee credit, other than non-qualifying income listed on p472, above the savings credit threshold of £82.05 (if you are single) or £131.20 (if you are a couple). The figure you calculate is the maximum savings credit you can receive, but it is subject to a cap: you cannot get more than £16.44 if you are single, or £21.51 if you are a couple.

Step four: compare your total income with your appropriate minimum guarantee

If your total income (Step one) is less than your appropriate minimum guarantee (Step two) **the amount at Step three will be your savings credit.** If your total income is more than your appropriate minimum guarantee, go to Step 5.

Step five: calculate 40 per cent of your total income that exceeds your appropriate minimum guarantee

This is 40 per cent of your total income, not just qualifying income, above your appropriate minimum guarantee.

Step six: deduct the amount at Step five from the amount at Step three

This is your savings credit.

If you cannot deduct it because it is more than the amount at Step three then you will not get any savings credit.

Example 1

Terry and Julie are a couple over 65. They have a total weekly income of £155.20 made up of £131.20 basic state pension and £24 personal pension – all of this is qualifying income.

Step one: their total income is £155.20.

Step two: their appropriate minimum guarantee is £167.05 (standard minimum guarantee with no additional amounts).

Step three: their total qualifying income of £155.20 exceeds the savings credit threshold of £131.20 by £24. Sixty per cent of £24 is **£14.40.**

Step four: their total income (Step one) is less than their appropriate minimum guarantee (Step two) so the amount in Step three (£14.40) is their savings credit.

They would also qualify for a guarantee credit of £11.85 to bring their income to the standard minimum guarantee (£167.05) for a couple. Their total income would then be £181.45 (£155.20 + £11.85 guarantee credit + £14.40 savings credit).

They may also be entitled to maximum HB and CTB and other passports (see p483).

Example 2

Angelina and Michael are a couple. Michael is 67 and Angelina is 58. They have a total weekly income of £214.50 made up of £82.05 state pension, £52 private pension, £76.45 incapacity benefit in respect of Angelina, and £4.00 deemed income from £8,000 savings. They have eligible housing costs of £15.00 a week.

Step one: their total income is £214.50.

Step two: their appropriate minimum guarantee is £182.05 (£167.05 standard minimum guarantee + housing costs of £15.00).

Step three: their total qualifying income of £138.05 (state pension, private pension, and deemed income from savings) exceeds the savings credit threshold of £131.20 by £6.85. 60 per cent of £6.85 is **£4.11**. The £76.45 incapacity benefit is not qualifying income.

Step four: their total income (Step one) is more than their appropriate minimum guarantee (Step two) so proceed to Step five.

Step five: their total income of £214.50 exceeds their appropriate minimum guarantee of £182.05 by £32.45. Forty per cent of £32.45 = £12.98.

Step six: the amount at Step five (£12.98) cannot be deducted from the amount of Step three (£4.11) so they have no entitlement to savings credit.

They also have no entitlement to a guarantee credit as their income is greater than their appropriate minimum guarantee.

5. Special rules for special groups

There are some groups of claimants to whom special rules apply which can affect the calculation of, and entitlement to, pension credit (PC). These are covered in Chapters 26 and 28. Special rules apply to:

- 'people subject to immigration control' (see Chapter 26);
- people in hospital (see p715);
- people in care homes (see p721);
- prisoners (see p729).

You will not be entitled to any PC if you are a member of, and are fully maintained by, a religious order.[32]

6. Claims and backdating

The rules about claiming and backdating are covered in Chapter 40. This section explains specific rules that apply to pension credit (PC) – it tells you how you (or your partner) can make a claim for PC, the details you need to provide, when to claim and the date your claim will start from.

Making a claim

A claim can be made in one of the following ways:[33]

- in writing on an approved form or other such manner accepted as sufficient by the Secretary of State; *or*
- over the telephone; *or*
- in person.

The claim must be made to an office of the DWP or local authority housing benefit or council tax benefit office or an alternative office. Claims made to a local authority or alternative office must be in writing.

Although the legislation states that a claim can be made in any of the above ways, in practice a claim can be made as follows:

- by telephone to the PC application line on 0800 99 1234 or text phone on 0800 169 0133 from 8am to 8pm, Monday to Friday and 9am to 1pm on Saturday. The form can be completed over the phone and will then be sent to you for you to sign and post back to the appropriate pension centre in order to make it a valid claim.[34] If you choose not to have help with the form over the phone, it will be sent to you to complete. If English is not your first language, someone can telephone the application line above, on your behalf, and say that you want to apply using another language and a member of staff and an interpreter will call you back at an agreed to time to help you apply;
- by post either by completing the tear-off slip at the back of leaflet PC1L, *Pension Credit. Pick it up – it's yours*, or by writing a letter stating that you want to apply for PC. The tear-off slip or letter should be sent to: Freepost NAT 3780, PO Box 457, Mexborough S64 9ZZ.
  The PC1L leaflet should be available at some post offices, on the PC website (see below) and from organisations such as Age Concern and Help the Aged. It is also being included in the Pension Service's mailing to all people over the age of 60. For details of what happens to the tear-off slip or letter, see p477;
- via the website (www.pensions.gov.uk/pensioncredit). At the time of writing, it was not possible for the form to be sent online. Instead, it can be completed online, printed out, signed and sent by post. You can also print it off and complete it by hand.

If you are under 65 and have been awarded the guarantee credit, when you turn 65 the DWP will contact you in order to assess whether you are entitled to any savings credit and whether to give you an assessed income period. This will be done via completion of a review form. The DWP will either telephone you and complete the form over the telephone and then send you the form for you to check and return or send you the form in the post for completion. You must provide the information requested as part of this review within one month of being asked to do so.[35]

Information and evidence to support your claim

When you claim you will need to satisfy the national insurance number requirement in order to be entitled to PC.[36] In most cases you and your partner must satisfy this condition (see p1083 for further details). You may also be required to provide any additional information and evidence relevant to your claim. For example, specific details of any personal pension scheme to which you belong.[37] Additionally, you may be required to provide, within one month of being notified of the requirement, information and evidence in respect of any likely future changes in circumstances that are needed to enable the decision maker to decide whether to apply an assessed income period and if so the length of that period.[38] If the claim was made in writing to the local authority, the local authority can accept and obtain information and evidence and give advice relating to the PC claim.

For claims made in the advance period (the four months before you reach the qualifying age) the one-month time limit starts to run from the day after the advance period ends.[39]

Who should claim

If you are a single person or one of a lesbian or gay couple you must claim on your own behalf. However, the rules for same-sex couples are due to change later in 2005 (see p811). If you are one of a heterosexual couple you must choose which one of you claims for both of you (see p811). Where you have a choice about who can claim but you cannot agree, a decision maker decides.[40]

You can swap who claims as long as the partner previously claiming agrees. It may be worthwhile doing so, for example, if one of you is about to go abroad.

An 'appointee' can claim on your behalf if you cannot claim for yourself – eg, if you have a mental health condition (see p1075).

The date of your claim

You are normally not entitled to PC on any day before your 'date of claim'. However, you can claim PC in advance before you qualify (see p477) and your date of claim can be backdated (see p477).

Your **'date of your claim'** (unless the backdating rules apply) is the earliest of:[41]

- the date your written or telephone claim, properly completed with all the required information and evidence, is received at the appropriate office (this is the DWP or local authority housing benefit or council tax benefit office); *or*
- the date you contact the appropriate office of your intention to claim, and you provide all the information and evidence to support the claim within one month of this date. This includes where you call the application line and when you send a tear-off slip or letter to the Mexborough address.

This will be the date of claim even if your PC claim is defective and you correct it within one month of being notified by the Secretary of State of the defect.[42] If you are making an advance claim for PC before you have reached the qualifying age and your claim is defective you may correct it at any time before the end of the advance period.[43]

Claiming in advance

You can make an advance claim for PC to give the DWP time to ensure that you receive your benefit as soon as you become entitled. PC can be claimed up to four months before you qualify, whether this is before you reach the qualifying age[44] and know you will be entitled when you reach that age, *or* after you reach the qualifying age when you know you will have a future entitlement – perhaps due to a drop in income. The date of claim is the date you qualify.[45]

For details about claiming PC prior to 6 October 2003 see CPAG's *Welfare Benefits and Tax Credits Handbook* 2003/2004, p484.

How your claim is dealt with

If you claim via the application line, your call goes to a call centre but you return your completed form to a pension centre that will deal with your claim. If you claim by post using the PC1L tear-off slip, to the Mexborough address, an application pack will be sent to you but if you send a letter this will be forwarded to a pension centre to be dealt with – if your letter requested a claim form, the pension centre will send one to you. Response to a tear-off slip will therefore be faster so claimants are encouraged to use the tear-offs if they can. As long as you send your properly completed form back within one month, your date of claim will be the date your letter or tear-off slip arrived at the Mexborough address.

The pension centre may request further information in relation to your claim and will aim to do this by telephone or post. In some cases, they may arrange a date for an interview or a home visit. The interview would normally be held at the premises of an organisation they work in partnership with (eg, Age Concern).

Backdating your claim

It is important that you claim in time because PC can only be backdated for up to 12 months. The rules for PC are more generous than those for income support. Your claim can be backdated if you satisfy the qualifying conditions over the period for which you require backdating – you do not have to show why your claim was late.[46] If you want your claim to be backdated it is important that you request this as claims are not automatically backdated – you can request this at Part 10 of the application form and if you are making a claim over the phone we understand that you should be asked about the date you want your claim to start from.

If you claim backdated PC after being awarded a qualifying benefit and an earlier PC claim had been refused because you did not at that time get a qualifying benefit, your PC can be backdated to the date of your earlier PC claim or the date when the qualifying benefit was first payable, whichever is later[47] (see p1090 for more information on qualifying benefits).

For general rules on backdating, see Chapter 40.

7. Getting paid

You can be paid pension credit (PC) by order book, giro, or direct credit transfer into a bank, building society or post office account.

PC is a weekly benefit. You can be paid for a part-week if you:

- were entitled to income support (IS) or income-based jobseeker's allowance (JSA) immediately before your first day of PC entitlement; *and*
- your PC entitlement is likely to continue throughout the first full benefit week that follows the part-week.

When calculating the amount of PC for a part-week your income and that of your partner is ignored; the guarantee credit is divided by seven and then multiplied by the number of days in the part-week, rounding up a fraction of a penny.[48]

Other than for direct credit transfer, PC is paid in advance on Mondays or on the same day as any retirement pension is paid.[49] If you were entitled to IS immediately before 6 October 2003 and your IS was paid in arrears then your PC will also be paid in arrears.[50] If you are paid via direct credit transfer your PC will be paid within seven days of your PC payment start date.[51]

If you are entitled to less than 10 pence a week you are not paid PC, unless you are receiving another social security benefit that can be paid with PC[52] – although you will still have an underlying entitlement. If your entitlement is less than £1 a week a decision maker can decide to pay you quarterly in arrears.

Unless you fit into the exceptions below or your PC award falls on the first day in your benefit week, your PC is payable in the benefit week following your claim.[53] The **'benefit week'** runs for seven days starting from Mondays or the day of the week any state retirement pension is paid.[54]

Therefore, if the first day of your benefit week is a Monday and you claim PC on a Tuesday, it will be paid the following Monday.

Exceptions:[55]

- If you were entitled to IS or income-based JSA immediately before reaching the qualifying age (see p468) and have been awarded PC from that date, your entitlement to guarantee credit will begin from the first day of the PC award.
- If you were entitled to income-based JSA after reaching the qualifying age and have been awarded PC from the day after your income-based JSA ended, your

guarantee credit will begin from the first day of the PC award (this will only apply to men because of the different qualifying ages for PC and JSA).

Delays and complaints

If you are dissatisfied with the way your claim has been handled, you may wish to complain (see Chapter 47). You might be able to claim compensation (see p1304).

If payment of your PC is delayed, you may be able to get an interim payment (see p1108) or a social fund crisis loan (see Chapter 21) to help you until your benefit is paid.

Change of circumstances

It is your duty to report any change in circumstance that may affect your right to, the amount of, or payment of your PC, but see p480 for circumstances that do not need to be reported during the assessed income period. You report a change promptly in writing or by telephone to the office handling your claim (although in individual cases notification might be accepted in a form other than in writing or by telephone). In some cases, however, the decision maker might say you must report changes in writing. In any case, you might want to report the change in writing and keep a copy in case of a dispute in the future. If you fail to report any changes promptly an overpayment may result which may be recoverable from you (see Chapter 41). If you are considered deliberately to have acted falsely or dishonestly, you may also be guilty of an offence (see Chapter 42). If your circumstances change you may be entitled to more or less PC or even none at all.

Where there are any changes to the amount of housing costs you owe or the interest payable, your lender is required to report these to the DWP. If you have this information you must also inform the DWP just in case your lender fails to do so. To avoid an overpayment, make sure that the DWP takes this information into account.

Where there has been a relevant change of circumstances, your claim is looked at again by a decision maker and a new decision is made – this is called a 'supersession' (see p1199). Your PC is then adjusted from the date the new decision takes effect. When this is depends on whether the new decision is advantageous to you and whether you reported the change in time. See p1204 for more details on when a supersession takes effect.

When your pension credit is adjusted

Generally, your PC is adjusted from the day the change occurs or is expected to occur, if this is the day you are paid benefit. If it is not, your PC is adjusted from the start of the next benefit week.[56]

Exceptions to the general rule above:

- from the start of the benefit week (see p478) in which that change occurs or from the first day of the next week, if that is more practicable, where your

income has changed (other than due to deemed income from capital or a payment of, or increase in, working tax credit);[57]
- from the date the change occurs, or is expected to occur, if:
  - you cease to be, or become, a prisoner; *or*
  - you are awarded another benefit and as a result your benefit week changes or is expected to change;[58]
- where you cease being a hospital inpatient and become a patient again in that same week, the change in respect of ceasing to be a patient takes effect from the start of that benefit week;[59]
- from the day after the previous assessed income period ended if that period ended due to one of the circumstances listed on p481 and the amount of PC payable is changed.[60]

Assessed income period[61]

An assessed income period is a set period during which you are not required to report any changes in certain types of your income, known as 'retirement provision'.

'Retirement provision' means income from:[62]
- retirement pension (other than one payable under the Social Security Contributions and Benefits Act 1992);
- an annuity (other than retirement pension income);
- capital.

The effect of this is that if you have an increase in, or subsequently start to receive, your 'retirement provision' during your assessed income period you will not have to report this to the DWP. All other income changes that affect your PC entitlement must be reported to the DWP as soon as they occur.

An assessed income period will only be specified if you or your partner are 65 or over. An assessed income period will not be made if:
- you are a member of a couple and one of you is under 60; *or*
- you have been awarded PC or your PC has been increased because an element of your 'retirement provision' that is due to be paid has temporarily stopped; *or*
- you have failed to provide sufficient information, as requested by the DWP at the end of the assessed income period, to enable the DWP to determine whether your 'retirement provision' will vary throughout the 12 months that follow the day the previous assessed income period ends.[63]

An assessed income period can be set for five years[64] (or seven years[65] if you or your partner were awarded PC from the 6 October 2003 and were 65 on or before that date – this is to avoid a build-up of reassessments ocurring in 2008). An assessed income period may be made for less than five years or not at all where the amount assessed as your 'retirement provision' seems unlikely to represent your typical 'retirement provision' throughout the following 12 months.[66]

Deemed increases in retirement provision

If the terms of your retirement provision do provide for periodic increases and the date and amount of such increases and the DWP is informed of these, then the increase will be in line with these terms.[67] Otherwise, the increase will be in line with the social security uprating for additional pensions.[68] There will be no deemed increase if your pension or annuity does not provide for periodic increases in the amount payable.[69] If your retirement provision includes income from capital it will be deemed not to change unless it is capital that counts as having a tariff income.[70] In that case, it may be deemed to increase or decrease in line with any changes made to the tariff income rules – presently £1 for every £500 (or part of £500) over £6,000 (£10,000 if you live in a care home).

If the adjustment to your 'retirement provision' results in a change in the amount of PC you are entitled to, the DWP will amend your PC payment automatically[71] to take effect from the start of the benefit week where the increase or uprating date also falls on that day, in all other cases, from the start of the next benefit week.[72] However, if the period for which the first increase in retirement provision is paid is not the same length as the period of the last regular payment the adjustment takes effect from the date of the second payment of the increased amount if that falls on the same day as the start of the benefit week; otherwise from the start of the next benefit week. For example, your occupational pension is paid at the end of each month. Your last payment was made on 31 March 2005. An annual increase of 1.8 per cent takes effect on 16 April 2005 and is first included in the payment on 30 April 2005. The period from 16 April to 30 April (15 days) is not the same length as the last regular payment (one month) so any resulting adjustment to the PC is not applied until the start of the benefit week following the second payment of the increased amount.

Decreases in retirement provision

If your 'retirement provision' decreases during an assessed income period you can report this and your PC will be adjusted. This will not end the period but instead will be treated as a supersession.[73] It is in your interests to report decreases in order to gain from any increased PC during a current assessed income period, otherwise you will have to wait until the reassessment at the end of the period where any PC adjustment would only apply from the start of your next assessed income period.

The ending of an assessed income period

Certain circumstances will bring your assessed income period to an end. These are where:

- you marry or cohabit and your initial claim was as a single person;[74]
- you cease to be a member of a couple;[75]

- you or your partner reach the age of 65;[76]
- you are no longer entitled to PC;[77]
- you are single and enter a care home on a permanent basis;[78]
- payments of retirement pension due to you stop temporarily or are less than the amount due and your PC award is superseded as a result.[79]

Overpayments and fraud

If you are overpaid PC, you might have to repay some or all of it. The rules on recovery are the same as those for IS and these are covered in Chapter 41. If you have been accused of fraud, see Chapter 42. Your PC might be reduced if you have been sanctioned for benefit offences (see p1170).

8. Challenging a pension credit decision

The same rules governing revisions, supersessions and appeals apply to pension credit as for other benefits (see Chapters 43 and 44).

9. Tax, tax credits and other benefits

Pension credit (PC) is not taxable.

Tax credits

PC acts as a passport to tax credits, although you need to make a separate claim for tax credits. If you have responsibility for a child you may be entitled to child tax credit (CTC). CTC does not count as income when calculating PC.[80]

If you are working 16 hours or more a week you might also be entitled to working tax credit (WTC) (see Chapter 49). Because PC has no 16-hour work rule, it may be possible to get WTC and PC if your income is low enough, but any WTC you receive will count as income when calculating your PC entitlement.[81]

Means-tested benefits

If you pay rent and/or council tax you may qualify for housing benefit (HB – see p193) and/or council tax benefit (CTB – see p109) as well. The rules on HB and CTB changed from 6 October 2003 for those who attain the qualifying age for PC and who are (or whose partner is) not in receipt of IS or income-based JSA to bring them in line with the PC provisions (see Chapters 10, 38 and 39).

If you receive the guarantee credit you automatically qualify for maximum HB and/or CTB but you still have to make a separate claim. If you are only entitled to the savings credit element your HB/CTB claim is subject to a standard calculation.

The Pension Service provides the local authority with the assessed income figure (this is the figure the DWP used for working out your PC entitlement). The local authority may modify this figure to take certain income into account – eg, savings credit.[82] Although savings credit counts as income for HB and CTB, the HB/CTB applicable amount for people 65 or over is increased by an amount equal to the maximum savings credit (see p472) to minimise any loss in HB/CTB as a result of having more qualifying income (see Chapter 35).

The £16,000 capital limit will not apply if you receive the guarantee credit (with or without the savings credit). In all other cases it will continue to apply, including if you receive just the savings credit.

If you are a man aged between 60 and 65 you will be able to choose between claiming income-based JSA or PC. This is because income-based JSA is paid to those who are below pensionable age and this is 65 for a man and 60 for a woman, whereas the qualifying age for PC is linked to the pensionable age for a woman. When deciding which benefit to claim you will need to be aware of the different rules governing these two benefits to ensure that you will be better off. For example, there is no capital limit or a 16-hour work rule for PC but there is for income-based JSA. Furthermore, to benefit from the new HB/CTB rules that came into effect on 6 October 2003 neither you nor your partner must be in receipt of IS or income-based JSA. You should, therefore, seek advice from your local advice centre. See Chapters 38 and 39 for more details of the treatment of income and capital.

Non-means-tested benefits

The non-means-tested benefits in this *Handbook* (other than attendance allowance, disability living allowance, bereavement payment, guardian's allowance, constant attendance allowance, exceptionally severe disablement allowance, statutory sick pay, statutory maternity pay, statutory paternity pay, statutory adoption pay and child benefit) are taken into account as income when calculating any entitlement to PC (see Chapter 38).

However, qualifying for certain non-means-tested benefits can help you qualify for more PC. For example, if you get carer's allowance you may be entitled to a carer's additional amount within your appropriate minimum guarantee.

Passports and other sources of help

If you are entitled to PC you may also be eligible for the following (but some are only accessible if you are getting the guarantee credit of PC):

- health benefits if you are getting the guarantee credit of PC (see Chapter 9);
- free school meals if you are also getting CTC (but not WTC) and have annual taxable income of £13,910 or below (see Chapter 1);
- social fund payments (both discretionary and regulated) if you receive either or both elements of PC (see Chapters 21 and 22);

- home insulation grants and discretionary grants from the local authority towards the cost of home improvements (see p19);
- free milk if you are an expectant mother and you are entitled to, or are a member of the family of a person who is entitled to, the guarantee credit (see Chapter 9);
- free vitamins if you are an expectant mother or breastfeeding a child under the age of 1 and you are entitled to, or are a member of the family of a person who is entitled to, the guarantee credit (see Chapter 9).

Notes

1. **Who can claim pension credit**
 1 s2 SPCA 2002
 2 s1(6) SPCA 2002
 3 s1(2)(a) SPCA 2002; regs 2-4 SPC Regs
 4 s2(2) SPCA 2002; reg 6 SPC Regs
 5 s4(2) SPCA 2002
 6 s3 SPCA 2002
 7 s3(1) SPCA 2002
 8 s1(2)(a) SPCA 2002; regs 2-4 SPC Regs
 9 s4(2) SPCA 2002
 10 s3(2) SPCA 2002

2. **The rules about your age**
 11 s1(6) SPCA 2002
 12 s3(1) SPCA 2002

4. **The amount of the credit**
 13 s2(3) SPCA 2002
 14 Reg 6(1)(b) SPC Regs
 15 Reg 6(1)(a) SPC Regs
 16 Reg 6 and Sch 3 para 1(5) SPC Regs
 17 Reg 6(4) and (5) SPC Regs
 18 Reg 6(6)(a) SPC Regs
 19 Reg 6(6)(c) SPC Regs
 20 Reg 6(6)(b) SPC Regs
 21 Reg 6(6)(b) and Sch 1 para 6 SPC Regs
 22 Sch 1 para 6(5) SPC Regs
 23 Sch 1 para 6(6) SPC Regs
 24 Sch 1 para 6(8)-(9) SPC Regs
 25 s15 SPCA 2002; regs 14-24 SPC Regs
 26 Reg 15(6) SPC Regs
 27 s2(2) SPCA 2002
 28 Reg 7(2) SPC Regs
 29 Reg 9 SPC Regs
 30 s3(7) SPCA 2002; reg 7(1)(a) SPC Regs
 31 s3(3) SPCA 2002; reg 7(1)(b)-(c) SPC Regs

5. **Special rules for special groups**
 32 ss2(9) and 3(8) SPCA 2002; regs 6(2)(b) and 7(3)(b) SPC Regs

6. **Claims and backdating**
 33 Reg 4D SS(C&P) Regs
 34 Reg 4D(6) SS(C&P) Regs
 35 Reg 7(1B) SS(C&P) Regs
 36 s1(1A) and (1B) SSAA 1992
 37 Reg 7(4) SS(C&P) Regs
 38 Reg 7(1A) and (1B) SS(C&P) Regs
 39 Reg 7(1C) SS(C&P) Regs
 40 Reg 4D(7) SS(C&P) Regs
 41 Reg 4F SS(C&P) Regs
 42 Reg 4D(10) and (11) SS(C&P) Regs
 43 Regs 4D(12) and 4E(3) SS(C&P) Regs
 44 Reg 4E SS(C&P) Regs
 45 Reg 13D SS(C&P) Regs
 46 Reg 19(1)and Sch 4 para 12 SS(C&P) Regs
 47 Reg 6(16) SS(C&P) Regs

7. **Getting paid**
 48 Reg 13A SPC Regs
 49 Reg 26B SS(C&P) Regs
 50 Reg 36(6) SPC(CTMP) Regs
 51 Reg 26B(3)(a) SS(C&P) Regs
 52 Reg 13 SPC Regs
 53 Reg 16A(1) SS(C&P) Regs
 54 Reg 16A(4) SS(C&P) Regs
 55 Reg 16A(2) SS(C&P) Regs

56 Reg 7 and Sch 3B para 1(b) SS&CS(DA) Regs
57 Reg 7 and Sch 3B para 2 SS&CS(DA) Regs
58 Reg 7 and Sch 3B para 4 SS&CS(DA) Regs
59 Reg 7 and Sch 3B para 5 SS&CS(DA) Regs
60 Reg 7 and Sch 3B para 1(a) SS&CS(DA) Regs
61 ss6-10 SPCA 2002; regs 10-12 SPC Regs
62 s7(6) SPCA 2002
63 Reg 10(1) SPC Regs
64 s9 SPCA 2002
65 Reg 37 SPC(CTMP) Regs
66 s9(2) SPCA 2002
67 Reg 10(4) SPC Regs
68 Reg 10(6) SPC Regs
69 Reg 10(2)(a) SPC Regs
70 Reg 10(2)(b) and (7) SPC Regs
71 s10 SPCA 2002
72 Reg 10(5)-(7) SPC Regs
73 s8 SPCA 2002
74 s9(4)(a) SPCA 2002
75 s9(4)(b) SPCA 2002
76 s9(4)(c) and (d) SPCA 2002
77 Reg 12(a) SPC Regs
78 Reg 12(c) SPC Regs
79 Reg 12(b) SPC Regs

9. **Tax, tax credits and other benefits**
80 s7(2) TCA 2002; reg 4(d) TC(ITDR) Regs
81 s15(1)(b) SPCA 2002
82 Reg 23 HB Regs and reg 15 CTB Regs, as substituted by regs 8 and 17 HB&CTB(SPC) Regs

Chapter 19

Retirement pensions

This chapter covers:

There are three main categories of retirement pension.

- Category A retirement pension is payable on your own national insurance (NI) contribution record.
- Category B retirement pension is payable by virtue of your spouse's NI record.
- Category D retirement pension is a non-contributory pension payable to those over 80.

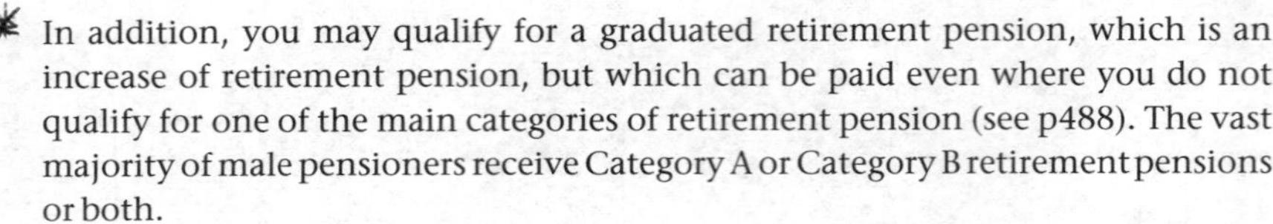

* In addition, you may qualify for a graduated retirement pension, which is an increase of retirement pension, but which can be paid even where you do not qualify for one of the main categories of retirement pension (see p488). The vast majority of male pensioners receive Category A or Category B retirement pensions or both.

1. Who can claim retirement pensions

You can get a retirement pension when you reach 'pensionable age'. **'Pensionable age'** is currently 65 for a man and 60 for a woman.[1] This rule discriminates on grounds of sex but is not contrary to European Community (EC) law (see p1285). However, pensionable age for women will be increased from 60 to 65 between 2010 and 2020 (see p491). You do not automatically become entitled to your retirement pension just by reaching pensionable age. You must claim. If you do

* From 5 December 2005, you will also be able to qualify for Category A and B retirement pensions on the basis of a civil partner's contribution record.

not claim you are treated as having deferred your retirement (see p489). If you are claiming a dependant's increase in your pension (see p793) you will need to claim separately on the appropriate form.[2]

You do not have to retire. You can choose whether or not to give up work. If you decide to go on working, your earnings do not reduce the pension you receive (although if your spouse is still working you may not be able to get an increase in your pension for her/him – see p794).

If you are getting transitional long-term incapacity benefit (see p279) you should take advice before claiming (see p507). Do not wait for more than three months after reaching pensionable age before making a decision or you may lose out (see p1085).

There are some groups of claimants to whom special rules apply (see p494).

Category A retirement pension

You qualify for a Category A pension if:[3]

- you satisfy the contribution conditions (see p846) on the basis of your own contribution record (unless you are a widow, a widower or divorced); *and*
- you are over pensionable age.

Category B retirement pension for a spouse

If you are married you qualify for a Category B pension if:[4]

- your spouse has satisfied the contribution conditions (see p846);
- you and your spouse are both over pensionable age; *and*
- your spouse has become entitled to a Category A retirement pension.

If your spouse was receiving an increase of Category A retirement pension in respect of you before you receive this pension, that increase is replaced by this pension, which is normally paid at the same rate.

Category B retirement pension for a widow

If you are a widow you qualify for a Category B pension if:[5]

- your late husband satisfied the contribution conditions (see p846); *or*
- your late husband died as a result of an industrial injury or disease (see p23); *and either*
- you were over 60 when he died; *or*
- you were a widow immediately before you reached pension age and you are entitled to a widow's pension (see Chapter 2) or would be but for one or more of the reasons given below.

If you are a widow who is approaching 60 and considering remarriage you should assess your position and, if necessary, take advice. There may be considerable financial benefits in postponing any wedding so that you are still a widow immediately before attaining pensionable age.[6]

If you are a widow whose widows'/bereavement benefits were suspended before you were 60 because you were cohabiting, you are entitled to have any Category B pension, to which you may be entitled, paid from your 60th birthday. But to get this you must claim the pension. If you do not, the Department for Work and Pensions (DWP) continues to treat you as entitled to widows'/bereavement benefits (and therefore continues to suspend payment during cohabitation) until your 65th birthday (see p498).

Category B retirement pension for a widower

If you are a widower, you are entitled to a Category B pension if:[7]

- your wife satisfied the contribution conditions (see p846); *and*
- your wife died on or after 6 April 1979; *and*
- your wife died when you were both over pensionable age.

The different conditions of entitlement for widows and widowers discriminate against men on the grounds of sex (because a man can never receive a Category B pension if his wife died before she reached pensionable age) but this is not contrary to the equal treatment provisions in EC law (see p1285). **Note:** if your wife died before she was 60 you may be able to use her contributions to help you get a Category A pension (see p495). The discriminatory rules for Category B pensions are to be abolished with effect from 6 April 2010.[8]

Period of payment

The pension is paid indefinitely and does not cease if you remarry or live with a woman as her husband.[9]

Category D retirement pension

You qualify for a Category D pension if:[10]

- you are aged 80 or over;
- you were ordinarily resident in Great Britain (GB – see p698) on the day you reached the age of 80;
- you have been resident in GB for a period of at least 10 years in any continuous period of 20 years immediately before you attained the age of 80; *and*
- you are entitled either to no other retirement pension or to an amount of retirement pension less than the current rate of a Category D retirement pension.

Graduated retirement benefit

'Graduated retirement benefit' is an increase in the weekly rate of retirement pension. However, although described as an increase in pension rate, graduated retirement benefit can be paid to a person over pension age who is not entitled to a retirement pension because s/he does not satisfy the national insurance (NI) contribution conditions. Between 1961 and 6 April 1975, those paying flat-rate Class 1 contributions also paid graduated contributions. For every £7.50 contributed by a man or £9.00 contributed by a woman, during that period, that person is now entitled to £5.16 a year.[11]

You are also entitled to an age addition of 25p a week if you are over 80 and receiving graduated retirement benefit but not (for some reason) receiving any other retirement pension.[12]

If you are a widow, you may add half of your husband's entitlement to your own. Similarly, a widower entitled to a Category B retirement pension (or who would be if he did not have a Category A retirement pension) may also add half his wife's entitlement to his own.[13]

Graduated retirement benefit may be paid even if you are not entitled to any retirement pension. But if you are entitled to only a very small amount, you receive a lump-sum payment instead of weekly payments. It is increased if you defer entitlement to a retirement pension (see below).[14]

The contribution conditions for graduated retirement benefit discriminate against women on the grounds of their sex, but are probably not contrary to EC law (see p1285).

Deferring your retirement pension

During the first five years after you reach pensionable age, you are allowed to defer entitlement to a Category A or Category B retirement pension. In return for doing so, you later become entitled to a higher rate of pension.*

For each week you defer entitlement, the pension you eventually receive is increased by one-seventh of 1 per cent.[15] The same applies to graduated retirement benefit (see p488).[16] This means that if you defer entitlement for the whole five-year period, you then receive slightly over 37 per cent extra retirement pension each week.

The benefits which are increased in this way include any additional pension under the additional state pension scheme (see p501), an incapacity increase and any increase resulting from your late spouse's deferment, but not increases for dependants or age additions.[17]

If you are a widow and your husband had deferred his entitlement to pension, you become entitled to the increase he would have gained through his deferment provided you do not remarry before you reach the age of 60. If you are a widower, you can similarly become entitled to an increase resulting from your wife's deferment, but only if you were over pensionable age when she died.[18]

It is important to realise that any day on which you receive any other contributory benefit, severe disablement allowance, carer's allowance or maternity allowance is not counted when your increased pension is calculated,[19]

*If you defer for 12 months or more, you may be able to get a lump sum payment instead of a higher rate of pension. The lump sum is based on the weekly rate of pension that you would have been entitled to during the period you deferred it.

nor is any day for which you would have been disqualified from receiving a Category A or B retirement pension because you were in prison.[20]

In particular, this rule applies to graduated retirement benefit (see p488).[21] As payments of graduated retirement benefit are usually very small, this can mean that an increment to a Category A or B retirement pension worth many pounds can be lost because of payments of graduated retirement benefit of as little as a few pence a week. This is a problem which particularly affects married women but everyone should think carefully, and if necessary take advice, before claiming graduated retirement benefit unless they are claiming their retirement pension at the same time (particularly since the graduated retirement benefit is itself increased if you defer claiming it).

If you are thinking of deferring your retirement, you should consider the following:

- You should think very carefully before deferring your pension now that the earnings rules for retirement pensions have been abolished. Even if you can afford to live without the money from your pension at present, you may be better off claiming it now and investing it. Apart from anything else, if you die within five years of reaching pensionable age, any money you have claimed and invested will go to your family, but if you die before you claim only your spouse, and not other members of your family, can benefit from the deferment of your pension, and even then only in certain circumstances (see p489).
- If you are receiving a means-tested benefit, deferring your retirement pension may lead to a problem under the notional income rules which sometimes entitle the DWP (or your local authority in the case of housing benefit and council tax benefit) to treat you as if you were claiming your pension, even though you are not, when your entitlement to benefit is calculated. For further details of the notional income rules, see p983.

De-retirement

You can usually defer your retirement pension (see p489) simply by not claiming it but, once you have become entitled, you may only defer by notifying the DWP of your intention on the proper form.[22] This is what is known as **'de-retiring'**. You may de-retire in this way at any time during the first five years after you reach pensionable age.[23] You can also cancel your deferment at any time, but you cannot then de-retire a second time.[24]

If you are a man who is entitled to a Category A retirement pension and you have a wife who is entitled to a Category B pension by virtue of your contributions, you cannot de-retire without your wife's consent unless that consent is unreasonably withheld.[25]

*If you start deferring your pension on or after 6 April 2005, you will not be entitled to an increase for any day on which your partner is getting an increase for you in their own non-means-tested benefit which would not have been paid if you had actually received your pension. See the 'overlapping benefit' rules described on p1102 for the benefits that are taken into account.

2. The rules about your age

Category A or B pension can be claimed when you reach pensionable age (currently 65 for a man, 60 for a woman). Category D pension can be claimed if you are over 80.

Pensionable age for women will be increased from 60 to 65 between 2010 and 2020.[26] These changes will affect women who were born after 5 April 1950. Women born after 5 April 1955 will reach pensionable age at 65 and those born between 6 April 1950 and 5 April 1955 will reach it at an age between 60 and 65. If you are in the latter category, the precise date on which you will reach pensionable age depends on your date of birth. Appendix 6 contains a table with further details.

If you are a married man who was born after 5 April 1945 or a widower whose late wife was born after 5 April 1950, the rules for Category B retirement pension will be the same as those which currently apply to women.[27] The discriminatory rules about increases to a Category A retirement pension for a dependent adult are also to be abolished with effect from 6 April 2010.[28]

From the same date, the five-year maximum time limit for the deferment of retirement pension (see p489) is to be abolished and each year of deferment will produce an increment of 10 per cent as opposed to 7.5 per cent at present.[29]

3. Claiming for others

You may qualify for an increase in your retirement pension if you have any dependants (see Chapter 31).

4. The amount of benefit

The amount of your retirement pension depends on which type of pension you get.

Category A retirement pension[30]

	£pw
Claimant	82.05
Adult dependant	49.15

Note: increases for children have largely been replaced by tax credits – see p798.

In addition, you may receive:

- an age addition of 25p a week if you are over 80;
- graduated retirement benefit based on earnings between 1961 and 1975 (see p488);
- an additional state pension if you reached pensionable age after 5 April 1979 (see p501);
- a higher pension if you deferred entitlement to pension (see p489);
- an amount equal to the age-related addition to long-term incapacity benefit if you were receiving this within eight weeks of reaching pensionable age (see p486).[31] If you have an additional state pension, this amount is set off against it;[32]
- a Christmas bonus (see p68).

You may receive less than the standard amount of pension if you only partially satisfy the contribution conditions (see p846). If so, it may be possible to improve your contribution record by paying Class 3 contributions (see p834). These can be paid even after you reach pensionable age but you should do so as soon as possible or you may lose the opportunity (see p835).

In addition, if you are a married woman and you are entitled to both a Category A pension at a reduced rate on the basis of your own contributions and a Category B pension on your husband's contributions (see below), there are special rules which allow your pension to be increased to the maximum of £49.15.[33]

Category B retirement pension for a spouse[34]

	£pw
Claimant	49.15

In addition, you may receive:

- an age addition of 25p a week if you are over 80;
- a higher pension from deferring entitlement to pension (see p489);
- a Christmas bonus (see p68).

You may receive less than the standard rate because your spouse only partially satisfies the contribution conditions (see p846, but see also p835). If so, it may be possible for your spouse to improve her/his contribution record (or for you to improve your own and become entitled to a Category A retirement pension in your own right) by paying Class 3 contributions (see p834). These can be paid even after you reach pensionable age, but you should do so as soon as possible or you may lose the opportunity (see p835).

Category B retirement pension for a widow or widower[35]

	£pw
Claimant	82.05

In addition, you may receive:
- an age addition of 25p a week if you are over 80;
- graduated retirement benefit based on your husband/wife's graduated contributions between 1961 and 1975 (see below);
- a higher pension if your husband/wife deferred entitlement to pension (see p489);
- an additional state pension based on your husband's earnings after 5 April 1979 (see p499). **Note:** special rules apply if your spouse died after October 2002 (see p505);
- a Christmas bonus (see p68).

You may receive less than the standard amount of pension because your spouse only partially satisfied the contribution conditions (see p847). If so, it may be possible to improve her/his contribution record by paying Class 3 contributions (see p834). These can be paid even after your spouse's death but you should do so as soon as possible or you may lose the opportunity (see p837).

If you are a widow and formerly received widow's pension (see p29) which was reduced because you were under the age of 55 when your husband died, or when you ceased to be entitled to widowed mother's allowance, your Category B retirement pension is reduced in the same way.[36] An identical reduction is made if you would have been receiving a bereavement pension but you were disqualified (eg, while you were living with a man as his wife).[37]

Category D retirement pension[38]

	£pw
Claimant	49.15

In addition, you receive:
- an age addition of 25p a week because you are over 80;
- a Christmas bonus (see p68).

Graduated retirement benefit

The amount of graduated retirement benefit you can receive depends upon the amount of special graduated contributions paid on earnings between 1961 and 1975 (see p488).

5. Special rules for special groups *

There are some groups of claimants to whom special rules apply. These are covered below and in Chapters 25, 26 and 28. Special rules apply to:

- divorced people (see below);
- widows and widowers (see p495);
- people coming from or going abroad (see Chapter 26).

Divorced people

There are special rules which may help you qualify for a Category A retirement pension if you are divorced and you cannot qualify on the basis of your own contributions. In practice, what these rules mean is that if your former spouse had a full contribution record, you can use it to replace your own, *either*:

- for all the years in your working life up to and including the one in which you were divorced; *or*
- for all the years during which you were married.

If your former spouse's contribution record was incomplete you are not necessarily treated as satisfying the second contribution condition for all of those years. But this may still be more than you would qualify for on the basis of your own contributions. These rules apply if:

- you have been divorced; *or*
- your marriage was not void (see p33) and has been annulled by a court; *and either*
- your decree absolute of divorce or nullity is dated after you reach pensionable age; *or*
- your decree absolute of divorce or nullity is dated before you reach pensionable age and you do not remarry before you reach that age.

If you are in one of these categories, you are treated as satisfying the first contribution condition (see p846) for a Category A retirement pension if your former spouse did so in any year of her/his working life (see p846) up to and including the year in which your marriage ended.[39]

In addition, you can use your former spouse's contribution record instead of your own in order to increase the number of years in which you satisfy the second contribution condition (see p846).[40]

To do this, you divide the number of years in which your former spouse met the second contribution condition by the number of years in her/his working life (in both cases up to but excluding the year in which your marriage ended). You can then *either*:

- multiply this figure by the number of years in your own working life (up to and including the year in which your marriage ended) and then round up to the

* The provisions described in this section apply in general to former civil partners and surviving civil partnersin the same way that they apply to divorced people, widows and widowers. Seek further advice if necessary.

next whole number and add the number of years after that year in which you satisfy the second contribution condition; *or*

- multiply this figure by the number of years for which you were married (including both the year in which you were married and the year in which your decree absolute was given) and then round up to the next whole number and add the number of years both before and after your marriage in which you personally satisfied the second contribution condition.

You are then taken as having satisfied the second contribution condition for whichever number of years is higher.[41]

These rules may mean that if your spouse is continuing to work and pay contributions, it is to your advantage not to get divorced when your marriage breaks up, unless and until one of you wants to remarry. If you are considering remarrying, have an incomplete contribution record and are approaching pensionable age, you should think carefully about the timing of your wedding as it may be to your financial advantage to postpone it until after you have reached pensionable age. Conversely, in some cases there may be a financial advantage in bringing the wedding forward. This depends both on whether you are male or female and on the contribution records of your former and your prospective spouses. You should take advice.

If you have been married more than once, only your most recent marriage counts for these purposes.[42]

Widows and widowers

The rules for divorced people (see p494) also apply to all women who are widows on the day they reach pensionable age.[43] They apply to men who are widowers in the following circumstances:

- Your late wife died before you reached pensionable age and you did not remarry before you reached that age;[44] *or*
- You are a man and were widowed after you reached pensionable age but before your late wife's 60th birthday[45] (a woman in the equivalent position would not need to use these rules because of her entitlement to Category B retirement pension at the widow's rate).

You cannot benefit from the rules if you had already reached pensionable age by 5 April 1979 unless your late wife did not die until after that date.[46]

In addition, if you are entitled to both a Category A pension at a reduced rate on your own contributions and a Category B pension on the contributions of your late spouse, there are special rules which allow you to increase your pension by up to £49.15.[47]

People coming from or going abroad

If you have lived elsewhere than the UK during your working life, your pension may be affected. For example, it may be paid at a reduced rate. However, there are reciprocal arrangements with many countries which may assist you. Equally, if you have worked in another European Economic Area (EEA) state you may benefit from European Community law (see p672). If you go abroad your pension will not be uprated unless you go to another EEA state or to a country with whom the UK has a reciprocal arrangement. A challenge to the lack of uprating of pensions was rejected by the Court of Appeal but is now being appealed to the House of Lords. The appeal is due to be heard in 2005.[48]

6. Claims and backdating

Making a claim

Normally the Department for Work and Pensions (DWP) sends you a claim form (BR19) about four months before you reach pensionable age. If you wish to claim an increase in your pension for a dependant you must complete the appropriate form for dependant increases. The DWP has a tele-claim service for pensions. It is available for people who are within four months of pension age to claim their retirement pension over the telephone. The service is available from 8am to 8pm Monday to Friday on 0845 300 1084. You can also at any time request a forecast of the amount of pension that you will receive, by phoning 0845 300 0168. From 2 May 2005 it is possible to both make a claim and amend a claim for retirement pension or graduated retirement pension by telephone.[49]

If you have not received a form three months before you want to receive the pension, ask for one from your local DWP office. Claim forms should be returned to your local DWP office.

If the DWP tells you that you have not paid enough contributions, you may still be able to get your pension if you make up the missing contributions now. The DWP does not always tell you this, so it is worth asking specifically whether or not this rule applies to you.

You can defer claiming your Category A or Category B retirement pension during the first five years after you reach pensionable age. In return for doing so, you later become entitled to a higher rate of pension. See p489 for further details. You can also de-retire after claiming (see p490).

Keep a copy of your claim in case queries arise.

If you live in a Jobcentre Plus area, then in practice you will usually be required to start your claim by telephoning a 'contact centre'. (Your local Jobcentre Plus office will have this number, and it may also be displayed in local advice centres, libraries, etc.) The contact centre will take your basic details and then issue you with a claim form. If you send in a claim form before telephoning the contact centre then usually your claim will be processed and the interview arranged (where necessary) without you having to telephone the contact centre.

If you cannot or do not want to use the telephone to start your claim, Jobcentre Plus says that it can still deal with your claim in other ways. You might, for example, be invited for a face-to-face interview to gather the relevant details, or in some cases an old-style claim form may be accepted. Seek advice if you are unable to use a telephone and the Jobcentre Plus office will not let you start your claim in any other way.

Information to support your claim

When you claim retirement pension, you must satisfy the national insurance (NI) number requirement. In most cases this means you must provide your NI number (as well as your partner's, if you are claiming a dependant's addition). See p1083 for further details.

Proving your age

It is up to you to prove that you have reached pensionable age. For most claimants it is sufficient to produce your birth certificate but problems can occur if you were born in a country which did not have a formal system of registering births. Other evidence which can prove your birth date includes:

- passport or identity card;
- school or health records;
- army records;
- statements from people who know you.

The date of your claim

The date of your claim is the date it is received by the appropriate DWP office.

If you claim the wrong benefit

In certain circumstances if you have claimed the wrong benefit, it is possible for your claim to be interchanged with another benefit. For retirement pensions this interchange is only possible with widows' benefits or bereavement benefits.

Claiming in advance

Claims for retirement pensions may be made up to, but no more than, four months in advance.[50] You should take advantage of this, as it can take a long time to sort out your contribution record.

Exceptions to the rule on claiming[51]

Provided you meet the other conditions of entitlement, you need not claim Category D retirement pension if you were 'ordinarily resident' in Great Britain (see p698) on your 80th birthday and you are already receiving another retirement pension.

If you are a widow, you need not claim your Category A or B retirement pension if *either*:

- you are over 65 when you stop getting widowed mother's allowance; *or*
- you are getting a widow's pension immediately before your 65th birthday.[52]

In either of these situations, your retirement pension should be paid to you automatically as soon as you stop getting widowed mother's allowance or reach 65. However, it may be advantageous to you to claim your retirement pension – eg, because you are cohabiting.

How your claim is dealt with

The DWP states that it aims to process most claims within 20 days and more complex cases within 55 days.

Backdating your claim

It is very important to claim in time. Your claim can be backdated for up to three months if you satisfy the qualifying conditions over that period.[53]* You do not have to show any reasons why your claim was late. The rules on backdating are covered on p1085.

If you might have qualified for benefit earlier but did not claim because you were given the wrong information by the DWP or because you were misled by it you could:

- ask for an *ex gratia* payment (see p1304); *or*
- complain to the Ombudsman via your MP (see p1302).

The rules about backdating of claims changed on 7 April 1997. If you claimed backdated retirement pension before that date, see CPAG's *Rights Guide to Non-Means-Tested Benefits 1996/1997*.

7. Getting paid

Pensions are usually paid by credit transfer into a bank or similar account, or by order book. You can choose to be paid by direct credit transfer either four-weekly or quarterly in arrears (see p1099 for details).

Payment can also be made to someone else on your behalf, called your appointee (see p1075).

***However, if you are claiming between 6.7.05 and 5.4.06 (inclusive), your claim can be backdated to 5.4.05, and if you claim on or after 6.4.06, your claim can be backdated for up to 12 months.**

If your order book is lost or stolen, see p1105. If payment of your retirement pension is suspended, see p1105.

Delays and complaints

If payment of your retirement pension is delayed, you might be able to get an interim payment. See p1108 for further details.

If you suffer delays, or wish to complain about how your claim has been dealt with, see p1305. You might be able to claim compensation (see p1304).

Change of circumstances

It is your duty to report any change in your circumstances which might affect your right to, the amount of, or payment of your benefit. You should do this promptly in writing or by telephone to the office handling your claim (although in individual cases notification might be accepted in a form other than in writing or telephone). In some cases, however, the decision maker might say you must report changes in writing. In any case, you might want to report the change in writing and keep a copy in case of a dispute in the future. If you do not promptly report any such change in writing, any resulting overpayment may be recoverable from you (see Chapter 41). If you are considered deliberately to have acted falsely or dishonestly, you may also be guilty of an offence (see Chapter 42).

Overpayments and fraud

If you are overpaid retirement pension, you might have to repay it. The rules on overpayments are covered in Chapter 41.

If you have been accused of fraud, see Chapter 42.

8. Challenging a retirement pension decision

You can apply for a revision or supersession of a retirement pension decision, or appeal against it (see Chapters 43 and 44). The advice given there applies equally to retirement pension.

9. The additional state pension scheme

Introduction

Most employees pay national insurance (NI) contributions which give entitlement to the basic state retirement pension. Those employees, but not the self-employed, can also earn additional pension. The additional state pension provides for earnings-related pensions to be paid to people receiving retirement and bereavement pensions who have paid (or whose late spouses have paid) Class 1 contributions in excess of the minimum required for entitlement to those benefits.

The rules for the additional state pension were subject to major changes from April 2002. Prior to this the additional state pension was calculated under the state earnings-related pension scheme (SERPS). The rules since April 2002 are based on the state second pension. The rules after that date are to all intents a simplified and more generous version of SERPS. In particular, under the new scheme certain low-paid employees will be deemed to have a minimum level of earnings. For 2005/06 this will be £12,100. This deeming provision will also apply to certain carers and people with a long-term disability.

You are not in the additional state pension scheme if you are either contracted out by your employer (see below) or a member of an appropriate personal pension scheme (see p501).

If you were receiving invalidity benefit immediately before it was abolished in April 1995 and were receiving an earnings-related addition to your basic invalidity pension (for which you would have had to pay Class 1 contributions at some point between April 1978 and April 1991), you will continue to receive the same amount as an addition to your incapacity benefit (IB). However, unlike the rest of your IB, this earnings-related component will not be uprated for inflation each year and its real value will therefore diminish over time.

Contracting out of the additional state pension scheme

You may be contracted out of the additional state pension scheme by your employer if your employment counts for the purpose of either a salary-related occupational pension (where the pension you eventually get is linked to your final salary) or if your employer makes certain minimum payments to a contracted-out money purchase scheme (where the pension you eventually get depends on what your pension fund can afford to buy in the open market when you come to retire). To enable you to be contracted out, either sort of scheme must be covered by a certificate from the Occupational Pensions Board.[54]

The effect of being contracted out is that you and your employer pay NI contributions at a lower rate than other employees and their employers (see p831).[55] This means that you do not build up any entitlement to pensions under the additional state pension scheme (although, until April 1991, you did as an addition to invalidity pension).[56] However, you will have to contribute to your employer's scheme and will receive a benefit from that.

An employer cannot compel you to be a member of any particular scheme, so you can opt out and join an appropriate pension scheme of your choice (see p501).[57]

Appropriate personal pension and stakeholder pension schemes

If a personal pension scheme satisfies certain conditions, the trustees or managers of the scheme may obtain an appropriate scheme certificate from the Revenue.[58]

If you then choose to become a member of an appropriate personal pension scheme, the Secretary of State pays to the scheme the difference between your contracted-in NI contributions and those you would have paid had you been contracted out.[59] The main difference is that it is your decision to join the scheme and not your employer's.

Since 6 April 2001 it has been possible to use a stakeholder pension scheme to contract out of the additional state pension scheme. The advantage of doing this is that strict rules about charges and penalties apply to stakeholder pensions.

If you are employed and earn above the lower earnings limit, your employer must offer you access to a stakeholder pension scheme even if it does not offer an occupational pension scheme. You will be then be able to make contributions by deductions from your pay. There are exceptions for employers who have fewer than five employees, who offer an occupational pension scheme to all employees within a year of their joining or who contribute at least 3 per cent of salary to certain types of approved personal pensions.

If you contract out of the additional state pension scheme by either method, you are then treated as not contributing to the additional state pension and must build up your personal pension or stakeholder pension instead.

Calculating the additional state pension

The way in which the additional state pension is calculated was subject to major changes from 6 April 2002. From that date the additional pension is calculated by adding together:

- the amount of additional pension accrued under the rules up to 6 April 2002 (under SERPS); *and*
- the amount of additional pension accrued under the new, more generous rules for the additional state pension (the state second pension).

For Category A retirement pension, the additional pension depends on your earnings factor (see p827) in each relevant year in which you have paid contributions. For bereavement benefit or Category B retirement pensions, the additional pension depends on your spouse's earnings factor in each relevant year for which s/he has paid contributions.[60] In certain circumstances, a widow or widower may be entitled to an additional pension based both on her/his own contributions and those of her/his spouse (see p495).

If you do not have all the necessary figures available to you, or if you wish to check the Contributions Office records, you can write to the Revenue Contributions Office asking for a pensions forecast. You should receive a reply stating how much additional pension it thinks you are entitled to at current values and an estimate of the additional pension which you will receive if you continue working.

To calculate the additional pension, you must first identify which years are relevant to your claim. These are:

- in the case of Category A retirement pension, contribution years from 1978/79 up to, but excluding, the year in which you reached pensionable age;
- in the case of bereavement benefits or Category B retirement pensions, contribution years from 1978/79 up to, but excluding, the year your spouse reached pensionable age or died under that age.

For each relevant year, you need to calculate the excess earnings (ie, earnings above the lower earnings limit – see p827). To obtain this figure you take the earnings factor and increase it by the appropriate percentage to take account of inflation. The appropriate percentages are those coming into force during the final relevant year. The final relevant year is the one *before* the one in which you reach pensionable age or die. Therefore, for anyone reaching pensionable age this financial year the relevant year is 2004/05 and the relevant order is the one in force from April 2004 which gives the following percentages:[61]

1978/79	545.9%	1991/92	75.6%
1979/80	470.1%	1992/93	64.9%
1980/81	376.3%	1993/94	57.0%
1981/82	298.9%	1994/95	52.3%
1982/83	262.3%	1995/96	45.9%
1983/84	236.4%	1996/97	41.9%
1984/85	211.5%	1997/98	35.1%
1985/86	192.2%	1998/99	29.2%
1986/87	168.3%	1999/2000	24.0%
1987/88	149.8%	2000/01	16.6%
1988/89	129.8%	2001/02	12.2%
1989/90	107.4%	2002/03	7.5%
1990/91	93.3%	2003/04	3.8%

You then deduct a figure equal to 52 times the lower earnings limit in force in the *last* relevant year (ie, £4,108 or 52 x £79 if the last relevant year was 2004/05).

What happens next depends on whether you reached pensionable age before 6 April 1999.[62]

Additional state pension accrued between 1978 and 2002

This section sets out the calculation for additional state pension accrued under the rules for SERPS between 1978 and 2002. The sum is then added to any additional pension accrued under the rules since April 2002.

The rules in this section apply to you if you are a man born on or after 6 April 1934 or a woman born on or after 6 April 1939. People who reach pensionable age after this date have a lower entitlement under the additional state pension scheme than would have been the case if the pre-1999 rules had continued to apply.

First of all, for people in this category any working families' tax credit (WFTC) or disabled person's tax credit (DPTC) you received in the year 1995/96 or any subsequent year can be used to increase your earnings factors for those years.[63] The rules on this are particularly favourable for people on those benefits with an earnings factor of less than the qualifying level of 52 times the lower earnings limit for the year, as the full amount of your WFTC or DPTC is used to calculate the additional pension, however low your other earnings are.[64] WFTC and DPTC were abolished in April 2003 – for details of these benefits see CPAG's *Welfare Benefits Handbook* 2002/2003.

The earnings factor for each relevant year is uprated for inflation in the way explained on p502 and the years are then divided into two groups – those from 1978/79 to 1987/88 (inclusive) and those from 1988/89 to the end of the contributor's working life.

- The uprated earnings factors for the first group of years (ie, 1978/79 to 1987/88) are added together, *and then*:
  - *multiplied* by 25 per cent; *and*
  - *divided* by the number of years between 1978/79 and the end of the last relevant year.
- The uprated earnings factor for the second group of years (ie, 1988/89 onwards) are added together, *and then:*
  - *multiplied* by a percentage of between 25 per cent and 20 per cent depending on when the contributor reached pensionable age, as follows:

Year in which pensionable age reached	%
1999/2000	25.0
2000/01	24.5
2001/02	24.0
2002/03	23.5
2003/04	23.0
2004/05	22.5
2005/06	22.0
2006/07	21.5
2007/08	21.0
2008/09	20.5
2009/10 or later	20.0

and
- *divided* by the number of years between 1978/79 and the end of the last relevant year.

The results of these two sets of calculations are then added together to calculate the annual additional state pension and divided by 52 to reach a weekly figure.

Once the calculation has been done for the first time, it is not repeated each year. Instead, the additional pension is simply increased in line with inflation.

Claimants who reached pensionable age before 6 April 1999

If you reached pensionable age before 6 April 1999 (ie, if you are a man who was born before 6 April 1934 or a woman who was born before 6 April 1939) the rules were generally more favourable. For an example of how this worked in practice, see the 21st edition of CPAG's *Rights Guide to Non-Means-Tested Benefits*, p244.

Accrual of additional pension from 6 April 2002

From 6 April 2002, entitlement to an additional pension accrues under the state second pension. At present, this scheme is earnings-related but at some point in the future it may be replaced by a flat-rate pension.

For years from (and including) 2002/03 earnings above the 'qualifying earnings factor' (which is 52 x the weekly lower earnings limit) are divided into three bands. For 2005/06, these are as follows:

Band	*Earnings (£pa)*	*Value of earnings in the band (£pa)*
1	4,264–12,100	7,836
2	12,101–27,800	15,700
3	27,801–32,760	4,959

The rate at which entitlement to an additional pension accrues depends on when you will reach pensionable age and into which band your earnings fall. If you reach pensionable age on or after 6 April 2009 (ie, if you are a man who was born on or after 6 April 1944 or a woman who was born on or after 6 April 1949) the rates are as follows:[65]

Band	*Rate*
1	40%
2	10%
3	20%

If you reach pensionable age after 5 April 2003 but before 6 April 2009, entitlement accrues at a higher rate as follows:[66]

Pensionable age reached	*Band 1*	*Rate Band 2*	*Band 3*
2003/04	46.00%	11.50%	23.00%
2004/05	45.00%	11.25%	22.50%
2005/06	44.00%	11.00%	22.00%
2006/07	43.00%	10.75%	21.50%
2007/08	42.00%	10.50%	21.00%
2008/09	41.00%	10.25%	20.50%

Different rules apply for any tax year during which you were a member of a contracted-out pension scheme (see p500) or an appropriate personal pension scheme (see p501) for part of the year.[67]

Under the new scheme, carers who have no earnings or earnings below the annual lower earnings limit will be treated for additional state pension purposes as though they had earnings at the low earnings threshold (£12,100 in 2005/06) for any complete tax year in which:

- they receive child benefit for a child under 6;
- they are entitled to carer's allowance; *or*
- they are given home responsibilities protection because they are caring for a sick or disabled person.

Those entitled to long-term incapacity benefit throughout a tax year will also be treated as if they had an earnings factor of £12,100 in that year. But in order to qualify under this rule you must have worked and paid Class 1 national insurance contributions for at least one-tenth of your working life since 1978 when the additional state pension was introduced.

Payment of additional state pension to widows and widowers

At present, a widow or widower who is eligible for a basic state retirement pension based on her/his husband's or wife's contributions can, in certain circumstances, also receive any additional state pension based on her/his spouse's contributions. The rules are complex and it is easier for a woman to claim or inherit her late husband's additional state pension than vice versa. The rules discriminate against men on the grounds of their sex but are almost certainly not contrary to European Community law (see p1285).

Under plans introduced in 1986 by the previous government, it was originally intended that people whose spouses died after 5 April 2000 would only inherit a maximum of 50 per cent of that spouse's additional state pension entitlement. However, because of a major failure by the (then) DSS to advise people about the change, the present Government decided not to implement the change to inherited additional state pensions from SERPS until 6 October 2002 and to phase the reduction over a period of 10 years rather than introduce an immediate 50 per cent cut. This phased reduction only applies to the additional pension inherited under the SERPS scheme. Any additional pension derived from the state second pension scheme will only be inheritable at 50 per cent. The percentage of the deceased person's additional state pension entitlement from SERPS which can be inherited by her/his surviving spouse will be reduced if the deceased person reached pensionable age from 5 October 2002 as follows:[68]

Date when deceased person reached pensionable age	*Maximum % of additional pension passing to surviving spouse*
6.10.02 to 5.10.04	90
6.10.04 to 5.10.06	80
6.10.06 to 5.10.08	70
6.10.08 to 5.10.10	60
6.10.10 onwards	50

Note: it is the date on which the deceased person reached pensionable age which is important for this purpose, not the date on which s/he died.

People who are able to prove that they were given incorrect or incomplete information about the reduction in inherited SERPS additional pension and who have suffered financial loss as a result may also be able to claim compensation for maladministration (see p1304).

The maximum amount of inherited additional pension from state second pension is 50 per cent.

10. Tax, tax credits and other benefits

Retirement pensions are taxable.[69]

Tax credits

Retirement pensions are partially taken into account for tax credits (see Chapter 53).

Means-tested benefits

It is possible to get a retirement pension and also pension credit (PC – see Chapter 18) and other means-tested benefits such as housing benefit and/or council tax benefit.

Retirement pensions are taken fully into account for the purposes of means-tested benefits, but pensioners receive a higher rate of some means-tested benefits.

Non-means-tested benefits

If you were entitled to invalidity benefit on 12 April 1995 you can continue to receive transitional long-term incapacity benefit (IB) if you were over pension age on that date. There may be advantages in doing this as IB is not taxable and award of this benefit can lead to payment of some other means-tested benefits at a higher rate.

Retirement pensions are affected by the overlapping benefit rules (see p1102).

Retirement benefit overlaps with jobseeker's allowance, IB, severe disablement allowance, carer's allowance, widowed parent's allowance and bereavement allowance.

There are special rules if you are entitled to both a Category A and Category B retirement pension (see p492).

Passports and other sources of help

People over 60 get free prescriptions and eye tests regardless of income. If you are on a low income, you may also qualify for other sources of help (see Chapter 1) or a social fund payment (see Chapters 21 and 22). If you are getting PC you may qualify for free dental treatment and school meals (see p18).

Notes

1. **Who can claim retirement pensions**
   1 s122(1) SSCBA 1992; Sch 4 PA 1995
   2 CP/216/2001
   3 s44(1) SSCBA 1992
   4 s48A and Sch 3 Part I para 5 SSCBA 1992
   5 s48B and Sch 3 Part I para 5 SSCBA 1992
   6 ss37, 38 and 48B SSCBA 1992
   7 s51 SSCBA 1992
   8 ss48A-48C SSCBA 1992; Sch 4 PA 1995
   9 s51(4) SSCBA 1992
   10 s78(3) SSCBA 1992; reg 10 SS(WB&RP) Regs
   11 s36 NIA 1965, as kept in force by Sch 1 SS(GRB) No.2 Regs; Art 7(1) SSBU(No.2)O 1991
   12 Reg 17(1)(h) and (3) SS(WB&RP) Regs
   13 s37 NIA 1965, as kept in force by Sch 1 SS(GRB) No.2 Regs
   14 s36(4) NIA 1965, as kept in force by Sch 1 SS(GRB) No.2 Regs
   15 Sch 5 paras 1 and 2 SSCBA 1992
   16 Sch 2 SS(GRB) No.2 Regs
   17 Sch 5 para 2(5) SSCBA 1992
   18 Sch 5 para 4 SSCBA 1992
   19 Reg 4(1)(b)(i) SS(WB&RP) Regs
   20 Reg 4(1)(a) SS(WB&RP) Regs
   21 Reg 4(1)(b)(ii) SS(WB&RP) Regs
   22 s54 SSCBA 1992; reg 2(3) SS(WB&RP) Regs
   23 Reg 2(1) SS(WB&RP) Regs
   24 Reg 2(2)(a) SS(WB&RP) Regs
   25 s54 SSCBA 1992; reg 2(2)(b) SS(WB&RP) Regs

2. **The rules about your age**
   26 s126 and Sch 4 PA 1995
   27 ss48A-48C SSCBA 1992, as inserted by Sch 4 para 3 PA 1995
   28 s83A SSCBA 1992, as inserted by Sch 4 para 2 PA 1995
   29 Sch 4 para 6 PA 1995

4. **The amount of benefit**

30 ss44(4) and 45 SSCBA 1992
31 ss34(3) and 47(1) SSCBA 1992
32 s47(2) SSCBA 1992
33 s51A SSCBA 1992
34 s48 and Sch 4 SSCBA 1992
35 s48B SSCBA 1992
36 ss38, 39(4) and 48B SSCBA 1992
37 Reg 7 SS(WB&RP) Regs
38 s78(6) and Sch 4 para 7 SSCBA 1992

5. **Special rules for special groups**

39 Reg 8(2) and (3) SS(WB&RP) Regs
40 Reg 8(2) and (4) SS(WB&RP) Regs
41 Sch 1 SS(WB&RP) Regs
42 s48(3) SSCBA 1992
43 Sch 7 SSA 1975, as preserved by Sch 1 para 20 Social Security Act 1979 and Sch 3 Social Security (Consequential Provisions) Act 1992
44 s48 SSCBA 1992; reg 8(1)(a) SS(WB&RP) Regs
45 s48 SSCBA 1992; reg 8(1)(c) SS(WB&RP) Regs
46 s48(2) SSCBA 1992
47 s52 SSCBA 1992
48 *Carson and Reynolds v Secretary of State for Work and Pensions* [2003] EWCA 797 (CA)

6. **Claims and backdating**

49 The Social Security (Claims and Payments and Payments on Account, Overpayments and Recovery) Amendment Regulations 2005 SI No.34
50 Reg 15 SS(C&P) Regs
51 Reg 3 SS(C&P) Regs
52 However, it may be worth claiming your Category A retirement pension as soon as you reach 60 if your contribution record, or the combined record of you and your late husband, is better than your late husband's record taken on its own
53 Reg 19 and Sch 4 SS(C&P) Regs

9. **The additional state pension scheme**

54 s7(3) and (4) PSA 1993
55 s41 PSA 1993
56 s46 PSA 1993
57 ss160 and 161 PSA 1993
58 s7 PSA 1993
59 ss43(1) and 45(1) PSA 1993
60 ss48A-48C SSCBA 1992
61 Art 2 Social Security Revaluation of Earnings Factor Order 2004 SI No.262
62 ss45 and 46 SSCBA 1992
63 s45A SSCBA 1992; Schs 1(2) and 4 TCA 1999; reg 2 SS(EoFCoEF) Regs
64 s45A(1)(b) SSCBA 1992; Schs 1(2) and 4 TCA 1999
65 Sch 4A para 2(4) SSCBA 1992
66 Sch 4A para 2(3) SSCBA 1992
67 Sch 4A Part III SSCBA 1992
68 Social Security (Inherited SERPS) Regulations 2001, SI No.1085

10. **Tax, tax credits and other benefits**

69 s617 ICTA 1988

Chapter 20

Severe disablement allowance

This chapter covers the transitional rules on severe disablement allowance (SDA). It contains:

Note: SDA was abolished for new claimants on 6 April 2001.[1] However, certain people entitled to SDA before that date can continue to receive it.

This chapter is mainly concerned with the transitional rules for deciding who remains entitled to SDA. For the usual rules that continue to apply if you are still entitled to SDA, see Chapter 4 of the 2000/2001 edition of the *Welfare Benefits Handbook*.

1. Who is still entitled to severe disablement allowance

To be entitled to severe disablement allowance (SDA):[2]

- your current period of incapacity for work (see p265) must have started before 6 April 2001; *and*
- you must have been entitled to SDA on any day of incapacity for work in that period of incapacity for work.

Since SDA was abolished on 6 April 2001, to qualify you need to have been entitled to SDA for at least one day before 6 April 2001 in your current period of incapacity for work. The only way it would have been possible to establish entitlement to SDA for the first time on or after that date is if you made a backdated claim and, on the basis of this, SDA was awarded for a day prior to 6 April 2001.

The people who remain entitled to SDA are:

- those who were aged 20 or over on 6 April 2001 and who were already getting SDA immediately before 6 April 2001, including those who backdated their claim to before that date (see below);
- those who can re-establish entitlement using the linking rules (see below).

See p511 if you were under 20 on 6 April 2001.

If you were already getting severe disablement allowance before 6 April 2001

If you were aged 20 or over on 6 April 2001, were receiving SDA immediately before 6 April 2001 and remain incapable of work from that date, you will continue to receive SDA. This will also apply if you were able to backdate your claim to that time. However, you still need to continue to satisfy the usual SDA rules – see Chapter 4 of the 2000/01 edition of this *Handbook* for those rules.

Note that although you could normally only backdate a claim for SDA for a maximum of three months, a claim for incapacity benefit (IB) or maternity allowance (MA) may be treated as a claim for SDA (see p1084). If your claim for IB or MA was made no later than three months after 5 April 2001 and is accepted as a claim for SDA, you may be able to establish your entitlement to SDA after 6 April 2001.

If you were under 20 on 6 April 2001 you would only have continued to be entitled to SDA for a maximum of a year and then, if you remained incapable of work, would have qualified for IB (see p511 for details).

Entitlement under the linking rules

Even if you were not actually receiving SDA immediately before 6 April 2001, or if your entitlement ceases for a time after that date, you may still be entitled to receive SDA again now if you were 20 or over on 6 April 2001 and if you can link a past period of incapacity for work in which you were entitled to SDA, to your present period of incapacity for work. The linking rules may help you to re-establish entitlement to SDA if you were once entitled to it and then were capable of work for a period of time. The linking rules are the same as those that apply to incapacity benefits – see p265.

---

2. Remaining entitled to severe disablement allowance

If you are still entitled to severe disablement allowance (SDA) under any of the rules on p509, you will only continue to receive it if you satisfy the usual SDA qualifying conditions – see Chapter 4 of the 2000/2001 edition of the *Welfare Benefits Handbook* for those rules.

Note, however, that the amounts for you and any adult or child dependants that you may have, and the earnings rules that apply to the amounts for dependants, may well change from year to year. You may need to check these in the current edition of the *Welfare Benefits and Tax Credits Handbook*. Increases for dependent children have been abolished from 6 April 2003, and replaced with child tax credit, which is means tested (see Chapter 49). Some people will continue to qualify for increases in their SDA for child dependants after that date (see p798 for details). Certain people claiming SDA, and in some circumstances their partners, may be required to attend a work-focused interview (see p p1092 and 1094).

When severe disablement allowance stops[3]

If you are still entitled to SDA, and you were aged 20 or over on 6 April 2001, then you will remain entitled to it indefinitely (as long as you continue to satisfy the usual SDA rules).

If you had a continuing entitlement to SDA, and you were aged under 20 on 6 April 2001, then you remained entitled to SDA for one year from that date (as long as you continued to satisfy the usual SDA rules over that period). You should then have been transferred on to long-term incapacity benefit (IB) on 6 April 2002. As this would be IB for people incapacitated in youth (see p267), you did not need to satisfy the national insurance contribution conditions to qualify for it.[4]

Notes

1 s65 WRPA 1999; WRPA(No.9)O

1. **Who is still entitled to severe disablement allowance**
   2 Art 4 WRPA(No.9)O

2. **Remaining entitled to severe disablement allowance**
   3 Art 4 WRPA(No.9)O; reg 19 SS(IFW) Regs
   4 Reg 19 SS(IB) Regs

21

Chapter 21

Social fund: discretionary payments

This chapter covers:

The social fund (SF) is a government fund that makes two types of payments to people in need:

- Sure Start maternity grants, funeral expenses, cold weather payments and winter fuel payments are available from the **regulated social fund**. You are legally entitled to a payment if you satisfy the conditions of entitlement which are laid down in regulations. The regulated SF is covered in Chapter 22.
- Community care grants, budgeting loans and crisis loans are available from the **discretionary social fund** to meet a variety of other needs. You are eligible for a payment if you satisfy the qualifying rules, but payments are discretionary and budget limited. The discretionary SF is covered in this chapter. SF reviews are covered in Chapter 45.

SF payments are not taxable and not counted as income when calculating entitlement to means-tested benefits and tax credits.

1. General matters

The discretionary social fund (SF) is different from most other social security provision because:

- it is strictly budget limited and there is no legal entitlement to a payment;
- most payments are in the form of loans, recoverable by deductions from weekly benefit; *and*
- there is no right of appeal to an independent tribunal, although there is an internal review system and the right to request a further review by a quasi-independent social fund inspector (see p1277).

The discretionary nature and restricted scope of this part of the SF scheme has been heavily criticised. It nevertheless remains an important source of help for many people.

Legal framework

Payments can be made from the discretionary SF in the form of:

- community care grants (CCGs) to meet needs relating to community care;
- budgeting loans (BLs) to meet intermittent expenses;
- crisis loans (CLs) to meet immediate, short-term needs.[1]

Decisions are made on behalf of the Secretary of State by 'appropriate officers', more commonly referred to as decision makers, based in local Department for Work and Pensions (DWP) offices.[2]

Legally binding 'directions' set out the eligibility conditions for each type of payment, the procedure for reviews, and the criteria for managing district budgets.[3]

The rules relating to the procedural aspects of applying for a grant, loan or review and to the acceptance and recovery of loans are set out in Regulations.[4]

Decisions of the higher courts create binding caselaw, although they are sometimes only relevant to the particular case in question. Social fund inspector (SFI) decisions (see p1278) do not create binding caselaw but can be useful guidance (see p1278).

Legislation relating to the SF, together with commentary, can be found in *The Social Fund: Law and Practice* (see Appendix 3). The SF directions can be found in the *Social Fund Guide* (see p514).

Budgetary control

The Government sets the total budget for the discretionary SF each year (which runs from April). Each DWP district is then allocated a fixed sum for grants and another for loans.[5]

An area decision maker (normally the district office manager) is responsible for planning and monitoring expenditure on a monthly basis and issuing guidance to decision makers on what needs the budget can afford to meet (see p514).[6] There is, however, no monthly limit on expenditure. The directions only prohibit expenditure in excess of the annual district budget.[7] It is possible for the Secretary of State to allocate additional funds to a district in the course of a year and this frequently happens.[8] There is also nothing to stop district managers asking for more funds if their budgets are under pressure, although they may be reluctant to do so in the current climate of constraints on social security expenditure. A local campaign, however, could be persuasive in highlighting the need for an increase in the district budget. There appears to be a national system for the reallocation of funds between districts to top up loan budgets which are running short of funds.

Decision makers must have regard to the budget when deciding whether to make a payment and how much to award.[9] The budget is only one factor they must take into account, however, and refusal of an application solely on budgetary grounds without consideration of the urgency and priority of the application would be unlawful, unless the district budget is exhausted. The High Court has ruled that when an application for a CCG is being considered, need and priority should be assessed before budgetary considerations are taken into account and this is now reflected in official guidance.[10]

The SF directions require the district budget to be managed so that as far as possible, high priority applications for CCGs and CLs can be met and the maximum amounts payable for budgeting loan applications can be maintained throughout the year.[11] The aim is to achieve consistent decision making. Critics, however, have described the SF as a lottery because whether you receive a payment can depend on when you apply and where you live – ie, the amount available in the district budget.

Guidance

The Secretary of State issues national guidance to decision makers on how to administer the SF, interpret the law and directions and prioritise applications, and when to make payments. The guidance, together with the SF directions, is published in the *Social Fund Guide* (see Appendix 3). You can access the *Guide* on the DWP's website at www.dwp.gov.uk. Decision makers must take account of the guidance when making decisions but it is not legally binding.[12]

Decision makers must also take account of local guidance (also not legally binding) issued by area decision makers in each district.[13] Local guidance must specify whether the district budget can afford to meet high, medium or low priority applications for CCGs and CLs. It must also identify the maximum BL payable in respect of an application of the lowest weighting (see p531).[14] The local guidance must be reviewed at least every month and may be revised depending on the state of the budget. Copies of the guidance should be available from your local DWP office.

Other useful sources of guidance (which are not, however, binding in any way on decision makers) include the following:

- **Decisions of the SFIs** (see p1277). These can act as useful guides to interpretation and decision making. The SF Independent Review Service (IRS – see Appendix 1) publishes a *Journal* three times a year which includes a digest of decisions. The complete digest (and copies of the *Journal)* is available on the IRS website at www.irs-review.org.uk.
- **Social Fund Commissioner's Advice.** The SF Commissioner is responsible for the IRS and issues guidance to SFIs on specific areas of the law, which they are expected to follow. The guidance is published on the IRS website and in the *Journal* (see above) and is referred to in the footnotes to this chapter, with the date it was issued.

Applications

Where and how to apply

An application for a payment from the discretionary SF should normally be made to your local Jobcentre Plus office. If you are moving out of care and claiming a CCG, you should apply to the office which covers the area you are moving to, unless you are only claiming removal expenses and/or fares. If you are applying for a CL, you can apply to the office nearest to where your need arises.

Applications for CCGs and BLs must be made in writing, either on an approved form (SF300 for CCGs and SF500 for BLs), or in some other written form which is accepted as sufficient by the Secretary of State.[15] An application for a CL can be made in writing on Form SF401, or in some other written or verbal way (eg, over the telephone) which is accepted as sufficient by the Secretary of State.[16] If a CL is awarded following a verbal application, you must provide satisfactory evidence of your identity and confirm the details of your application in writing before you are paid. If a CL is refused following a verbal application, you should still receive a written decision together with notification of your right to request a review. If you have difficulty making yourself understood on the telephone, you should be offered an immediate office interview instead.[17]

You can get the application forms from your local DWP office, or download them from the DWP website (see Appendix 1).

An application is no longer treated as an application to the SF as a whole. An application for a CL can be considered as an application for a CCG, however, and vice versa.[18] This should happen where, for example, information given in support of a CL application clearly suggests that a CCG should or could be awarded.[19] There is nothing to stop you asking for your application to be considered for both a CCG and a CL and requesting a review if you are offered a loan rather than a grant. An application for a BL cannot be treated as an application for a CCG or a CL, but if it contains information which suggests that a CCG or a CL may be appropriate, that information can be treated as an application for a CCG or a CL.[20] Alternatively, you could be invited to withdraw your BL application and re-apply for a CCG or CL on the appropriate form.[21]

You should always apply for a CCG rather than a loan, if you may be eligible. You can always apply for a loan if your application for a CCG is refused. If you accept a loan for an item for which you have also requested a CCG, the DWP may decide that you no longer have a need for the item in question. BLs, however, are not awarded for specific items, so the fact that you have applied for or been awarded a BL should not, in itself, affect a separate application for a CCG.

An application can be made on your behalf by another person, so long as you give your written consent (this is not necessary, however, if an appointee is acting for you).[22]

Your application is treated as made on the day it is received by the DWP.[23] If your application was incomplete and you comply with a request for additional information, your application is treated as made on the day it was originally received.[24] You are not normally required to produce corroborating evidence and should not be asked for evidence for which you have to pay.[25] It is sometimes helpful, however, to submit supporting evidence which confirms the existence and urgency of your need.

Repeat applications

If you have been awarded or refused a CCG or CL for an item or service, you cannot get a CCG or CL for the same item or service if you re-apply for it within 26 weeks of a previous application, unless there has been a relevant change of circumstances.[26] This rule does not apply to BLs. A relevant change in circumstances could be a change in your personal circumstances, or, for example, an increase in the amount available from the district budget.[27]

You should also note the following points relating to repeat applications:

- Applications by different partners are not caught by the above rule. The second application must be made by the same person who made the first application for the rule to apply.[28]
- The rule should not apply if your first application was incomplete, or you withdrew it before a decision was made, or you declined or did not respond to a CL offer.[29]
- Only payments for the 'same item or service' are excluded. An application for the same or a similar or related item should not be excluded if it is for a different need (eg, an application for a bed for one child is different to an application for a bed for another child, while an application for bedding may be different to an application for sheets, pillow cases and eiderdown). Applications for different items of clothing or for travel expenses for different periods should not be caught by the rule.[30]

Decisions

Although awards are discretionary, decision makers must act in accordance with the SF directions and take account of the national and local guidance (see p514).[31] They are also told to 'take particular care that their decisions are not in any way affected by bias or prejudice on such grounds as colour, ethnic or national origin, sexual orientation, sex or religion'.[32]

The consistency and standard of decision making has been heavily criticised. In part, this is a reflection of the contradictory nature of the SF's aim to meet need within a strictly limited budget.

You should receive a written decision on your application, with an explanation for a refusal or part refusal, together with a notification of your right to request a review (see p1272).

There are no legal time limits within which the DWP must make decisions, but the *Social Fund Guide* instructs decision makers to decide applications 'without delay' once they have all the necessary information and never to delay a decision until the need has passed.[33] Applications for a CL should, where possible, be dealt with on the day the need arises.[34] If there are unreasonable delays, you should complain to the district manager and, if necessary, consider asking your MP to take up your case with the manager or the Ombudsman (see p1302).

Payments and overpayments

Payment should normally be made to you, but the DWP can decide to pay a supplier directly,[35] and, where appropriate, pay you in the form of food vouchers, travel warrants, cash or instalments. You can request a review of a decision to pay a supplier directly.

If you misrepresent or fail to disclose any material fact, any payment you receive in consequence is recoverable from you.[36] For more details about overpayments and recovery, see Chapter 41. You must be notified in writing of any overpayment decision and you have the right to request a review (see Chapter 45).[37]

Tax

Social fund loans and grants are not taxable.

Other benefits and tax credits

Payments from the discretionary SF are disregarded as income and capital for the purposes of means-tested benefits and tax credits and do not affect entitlement to any non-means-tested benefits.

2. Community care grants

Community care grants (CCGs) are non-repayable grants to help people live independently in the community. There is no legal entitlement to a CCG, but you do have the right to request a review if you are not satisfied with a decision (see Chapter 45).

Eligibility

To be eligible for a CCG, you must satisfy all of the following conditions, which are laid down in legally binding directions.

- **You must be in receipt of income support (IS), income-based jobseeker's allowance (JSA) (including payments on account and hardship payments) or pension credit (PC) (guarantee or savings credit** – see Chapter 18) **when your application for a CCG is treated as made** (see p515).[38] The only exception to this rule is if you are due to leave institutional or residential care (see p523) within six weeks of the date your application for a CCG is made and you are likely to get IS, income-based JSA or PC when you leave.[39] If you receive a backdated award of IS, income-based JSA or PC which covers the date you applied for CCG, you are eligible for a CCG.[40] You are not eligible, however, if you apply for a CCG on one of the three 'waiting days' for JSA (see p377) unless you are moving out of institutional or residential care (see p523).[41] You are treated as being 'in receipt of' IS,income-based JSA or PC if it is being paid to you, or to an appointee on your behalf.[42] The High Court has held that you are not 'in receipt of IS/income-based JSA' if your partner or another member of your family is the claimant.[43] If you are a member of a 'joint-claim couple' (see p394), you are only eligible for a CCG if you are the partner being paid JSA.[44]

- **You must not have too much capital.** Any CCG awarded is reduced by the amount of capital you have in excess of £500 (£1,000 if you or your partner are 60 or over).[45] Capital is calculated as for IS, income-based JSA or PC, depending on which benefit you are receiving[46] (see Chapter 39). Payments made from the Family Fund to you, your partner or child are ignored.[47] Capital held by your children should be disregarded. Capital below £500 (or £1,000) should not be taken into account as a resource from which a need could be met (see p521).
- **You or your partner must not be involved in a trade dispute** unless your claim is for travel expenses to visit a sick person. See p528 for details.
- **The CCG must not be for an excluded item** (see p520).
- **You must be awarded a CCG of at least £30**, unless your award is for daily living expenses or travel expenses.[48]
- **You must need a CCG for one or more of the following purposes:**[49]
  - to help you, or a member of your family, or other person for whom you or a member of your family will be providing care, to establish yourself (or her/himself) in the community following a stay in institutional or residential accommodation in which you (or s/he) received care (see p523);
  - to help you, or a member of your family, or other person for whom you or a member of your family will be providing care, to remain in the community rather than enter institutional or residential accommodation in which you (or s/he) will receive care (see p523);
  - to help you to set up home in the community as part of a planned resettlement programme following a period during which you have been without a settled way of life (see p525);
  - to ease exceptional pressures on you and your family (see p526);
  - to allow you, or your partner, to care for a prisoner or young offender on temporary release (see p528);
  - to help you, or one or more members of your family, with travel expenses within the UK in certain circumstances (see p528).

Excluded items

The social fund (SF) directions exclude payment for the items listed below.[50]

Items excluded from community care grants and crisis loans

- A need which occurs outside the UK. This rule may constitute unlawful discrimination in the case of European Economic Area nationals (see p680).
- An educational or training need, including clothing and tools.
- 'Distinctive' school uniform, or any equipment or sports clothes for school use. You may, however, be eligible for a budgeting loan (BL) (see p529). You may also be eligible for a grant for school uniform from your local education authority.
- Travel expenses to and from school. You may, however, be eligible for a BL (see p529). You may also be eligible for help from your local education authority.
- Meals taken during school holidays by children who are entitled to free school meals.
- Expenses in connection with court proceedings (including a community service order) – eg, legal fees, court fees, fines, costs, damages and travel expenses. You can, however, get a crisis loan (CL) for emergency travel expenses (see p543).
- Removal charges where you are permanently re-housed following a compulsory purchase order, a redevelopment or closing order, or where there is a compulsory exchange of tenancies or you are permanently re-housed as homeless under the Housing Acts. In all these circumstances your local authority may help you. Alternatively you may be eligible for a BL (see p529).
- The cost of domestic assistance or respite care. This would include the cost of home care or short breaks in residential care.
- Repairs to property owned by public sector housing bodies including local authorities, most housing associations, housing co-operatives and housing trusts.
- Medical, surgical, optical, aural or dental items or services. A medical item does not include an everyday item needed because of a medical condition – eg, cotton sheets and non-allergic bedding when a person is allergic to synthetics, built-up shoes, special beds, incontinence pads. If an item is not in ordinary, everyday use, it should only be treated as a medical item if its sole purpose is to cure, alleviate, treat, diagnose or prevent a medical condition. Wheelchairs (or parts for them) and stairlifts should not be excluded under this test, but you can be refused a payment if help is available from the NHS, social services or elsewhere.[51]
- Work-related expenses. The *Social Fund Guide* says this includes fares when seeking work and the cost of work clothes.[52] You may be able to get help with fares to interviews from the Department for Work and Pensions (DWP). Alternatively you may be eligible for a BL (see p529).

- Debts to government departments. These could include national insurance arrears, income tax liabilities and customs charges.
- Investments.
- Council tax, council water charges, arrears of community charge, collective community charge contributions and community water charges.
- Housing costs (other than those listed below), including:
  - repairs and improvements to your home, including garage, garden and outbuildings (but see below for minor repairs and improvements);
  - deposits to secure accommodation;
  - mortgage payments, rent, service charges, water and sewerage charges and any other accommodation charges.

  Note: Repairs and improvements are only excluded if they relate to the structure or permanent fixtures of your home (eg, windows) as opposed to movable items (eg, stairlifts).[53]

Housing costs which are not excluded

You can be awarded:

- a CCG or CL for minor repairs and improvements ('minor' is not defined but relevant factors include the nature and extent of the work, the time needed to complete it and the cost of materials and labour[54]);
- a CCG for overnight accommodation as part of a travel expenses payment (see p528);
- a CL for rent in advance for fresh accommodation where the landlord is not a local authority;
- a CL for housing costs not met by housing benefit, IS or income-based JSA or not eligible for direct deductions from IS or income-based JSA (see p1109) – eg, emptying cesspits or septic tanks;
- a CL for board and lodging or hostel charges.

A BL is also payable for rent in advance, removal expenses, and the improvement, maintenance and security of the home (see p529).

Additional items excluded from community care grants[55]

- The cost of purchasing, renting or installing a telephone and of any call charges. You may, however, be eligible for help from your local authority social services department if you are chronically sick or disabled.
- Any expenses which the local authority has a statutory duty to meet (discretionary powers do not trigger the exclusion, nor should statutory duties not undertaken by the local authority).
- The cost of any fuel and standing charges.
- Any daily living expenses such as food and groceries except where incurred in caring for a prisoner on temporary release, or where the maximum amount for a CL has already been awarded (see p544).

- Any item worth less than £30, or several items which together are worth less than £30 (unless the award is for daily living expenses or travel expenses).[56]

Maternity and funeral expenses

The discretionary SF can only meet needs other than maternity and funeral expenses, which are provided for in the regulated part of the SF (see Chapter 22).[57] The *Social Fund Guide* concedes, however, that maternity and funeral expenses are not defined and that they may not include items such as clothing for a pregnant woman or a growing (as opposed to newborn) baby, funeral clothing and headstones.[58] The SF Commissioner's Advice states that only maternity expenses to meet the immediate needs of a recently born baby (and not the mother) are excluded from the discretionary SF.[59] A CCG could therefore be paid for items such as highchairs, stair gates, prams and even a cot or carrycot if the baby already has something to sleep in.

Decision making and priorities

When deciding an application for a CCG, the law requires decision makers to have regard to all the circumstances of each case and, in particular:[60]

- the nature, extent and urgency of the need;
- the existence of resources which could meet the need;
- whether any other person or body could wholly or partly meet the need;
- the district budget (see p513);
- the SF directions (see p514);
- national and local guidance (see p514).

The High Court has ruled that need and the priority of an application (see below) should be assessed before budgetary considerations are taken into account.[61] This is confirmed in the *Social Fund Guide,* which also stresses that the budget is not a factor in deciding the priority of an application.[62] Decision makers must have regard to the district grants budget, however, when they go on to decide whether to award a CCG and how much to pay.

The *Social Fund Guide* states that decision makers must take into account the circumstances of each individual case and exercise their discretion flexibly and sensitively.[63] They are also advised to avoid a rigid interpretation of the guidance and that the absence of guidance relating to a particular situation does not mean that a payment should be refused.[64] In spite of this, decision makers tend to use the *Social Fund Guide* as a rulebook, even though the guidance is not legally binding and the standard and consistency of decision making has been heavily criticised in many reports.

The *Social Fund Guide* suggests applications for CCGs are prioritised as follows:[65]

- High priority should normally be given if a CCG will have a substantial effect in the immediately foreseeable future in resolving or improving the circumstances of the applicant and meeting one of the purposes for which a CCG can be awarded (see p517).

- Medium priority should normally be given if a CCG will have a noticeable (but not substantial or immediate) effect in achieving the above aims.
- Low priority should normally be given if a CCG will only have a minor effect in meeting the above aims.

Examples given in the *Social Fund Guide* of circumstances which may affect priority include:[66]

- mental or physical disability and illness and general frailty;
- physical or social abuse or neglect;
- a long period of sleeping rough;
- unstable family circumstances;
- behavioural problems – eg, due to drug or alcohol misuse.

The *Social Fund Guide* suggests higher priority is given where an award of an item would significantly reduce the risk of you going into care, or would immediately alleviate exceptional pressure on your family in a substantial and noticeable way, or where the lack of an item would seriously undermine you becoming established in the community.[67]

Local guidance (see p514) specifies which level of priority can be met by the budget. Unfortunately, the pressure on district budgets means that, invariably, only high priority applications are specified, while the vagueness of the definition of a high priority application in the *Social Fund Guide* (see above) often results in restrictive and cautious decision making.

When deciding whether there are other resources which could meet your need, decision makers should not take into account any capital you have below £500 (£1,000 if you or your partner are 60 or over), or your IS, income-based JSA or PC. Any other income you have should only be taken into account if it is available to meet your need and is not required to meet other expenses. Attendance allowance and the care component of disability living allowance (DLA) should be treated as required to meet disability-related expenses, unless there is evidence to the contrary (the mobility component of DLA must always be disregarded).[68]

Amount and payment

The *Social Fund Guide* states that the amount you request should normally be allowed if it is within the broad range of prices for an item of serviceable quality, taking into account prices charged in national catalogue outlets and high street chain retailers.[69] It is not normally necessary to submit written estimates from a supplier, unless you are asking for removal expenses. An award should be sufficient to obtain new or reconditioned items from a reputable dealer.[70] You may be offered less than the appropriate amount if the budget is under exceptional pressure but the amount must still be sufficient to cover the cost of the item or service needed.[71] There is no legal maximum award but the minimum in most cases is £30 (see p518). If you are dissatisfied with the amount you have been awarded, you should consider requesting a review (see p1272).

An award should normally be paid to you but can also be paid directly to a supplier on your behalf. This should only happen in exceptional circumstances – eg, where there is firm evidence that the grant will not be used for its intended purpose.[72]

Tactics

- You should always apply for a CCG if you are eligible, rather than a loan, which has to be repaid from your benefit. Despite the restrictive nature of the SF, the eligibility conditions for a CCG are wide. You can apply for help with anything other than an excluded item (see p519), and the purposes for which a CCG can be awarded (see p518) can cover a wide range of circumstances. Bear in mind the rules about repeat applications (see p516).
- When completing the application form (SF300), you should give full details of each of the items you need. Try to be as specific as possible (eg, list each item of furniture or clothing you need, rather than just asking for 'furniture' or 'clothes') and include the actual cost or a reasonable estimate of the cost of each item. Further guidance on what you might claim for is given below in the sections on moving out of care (see below), staying out of care (see p524) and easing exceptional pressures on families (see p526).
- Your application must establish that you need a CCG for one of the purposes set out on p518. You should, therefore, explain how the payment you are requesting will help the relevant person to become established or remain in the community, or will help ease exceptional pressures on you and your family.
- You should also show why your application should be given high priority, bearing in mind the guidance on priorities and what constitutes a high priority application (see p521). You can obtain a copy of the local guidance from your local DWP office (see p514) and refer to it if appropriate. You could also submit supporting evidence – eg, from a doctor or social worker.
- If you are dissatisfied with a decision (eg, you have been refused a payment, or awarded less than you need), you should consider asking for a review (see p1272).

Moving out of institutional or residential accommodation

A CCG can be paid to help you, or a member of your family, or other person for whom you or a member of your family will be providing care, to establish yourself (or her/himself) in the community, following a stay in institutional or residential accommodation in which you (or s/he) received care.[73]

Interpretation

- None of the terms at the foot of p523 is defined in the SF directions. They are, therefore, open to interpretation according to your circumstances.
- See p527 for the meaning of 'family'.
- The *Social Fund Guide* says institutional or residential accommodation means accommodation where residents receive a significant and substantial amount of care, supervision or protection because they are unable to live independently in the community or might be a danger to others in the community.[74] Examples of accommodation given are hospitals, care homes, foster care , group homes, supported lodgings, sheltered housing, hostels, prisons and youth centres.[75] Decision makers are told to treat applications from discharged prisoners with particular urgency and sensitivity, bearing in mind the pressures they face and the risk of re-offending.[76] If you cannot establish that you lived in institutional or residential accommodation, you may still be eligible for a CCG to help you remain in the community, or for planned resettlement (see below and p525).
- You should be eligible if you are establishing yourself in the community for the first time because, for example, you have always lived in care, or you have recently arrived in the UK and have been in a refugee camp overseas or a refugee hostel in the UK (the High Court has ruled that 'the community' is restricted to the UK).[77] The High Court has said that you must be actually or imminently in the community to qualify.[78]
- The *Social Fund Guide* suggests that a 'stay in' institutional or residential accommodation normally means at least three months, or a pattern of frequent or regular admission.[79] The High Court has ruled, however, that undue importance should not be attached to the reference to three months[80] and the SF Commissioner advises that a stay of less than three months can satisfy the direction.[81]

What to claim for

You can claim for help with any expenses which are not excluded (see p519). Examples include:

- furniture, cookers, beds, bedding and household equipment, floor covering, curtains and connection charges, when setting up home;
- moving expenses including removal costs, fares, connection charges and storage charges;
- clothing and footwear;
- items needed because of a disability (including wheelchairs, stairlifts and special clothing and furniture).

Staying out of institutional or residential accommodation

A CCG can be paid to help you, or a member of your family, or other person for whom you or a member of your family will be providing care, to remain in the community, rather than enter institutional or residential accommodation in which you (or s/he) will receive care.[82]

Interpretation

- None of the above terms is defined in the SF directions. They are, therefore, open to interpretation according to your circumstances.
- See p524 for guidance on the meaning of 'institutional or residential accommodation'.
- See p527 for the meaning of 'family'.
- There is no requirement that a CCG must be able to 'prevent' you going into institutional or residential accommodation. The legal test is whether a CCG will 'help' you remain in the community. Decision makers should consider whether a CCG would improve your independent life in the community and therefore reduce the risk of your admission into care or delay such an admission.[83] Going into hospital, even for a short admission, should count as entering care in this context.[84] The risk of care does not have to be immediate, but should be more than a remote possibility (if it is immediate, the application should be given higher priority).[85] If your condition makes you liable to repeated stays in care, you could still get a CCG if it could reduce the frequency or length of such stays.
- Actual or potential risk to physical or mental health because of a lack of items such as basic furniture, cooking facilities, clothes, bedding and heaters can be used to argue that a CCG for such items will lessen the risk of entry into hospital or other types of institutional or residential accommodation.

What to claim for

You can claim for help with any expenses which are not excluded (see p519). Examples include:

- items which will improve your living conditions, such as minor repairs, redecoration and refurbishment, heaters, installation of a prepayment meter, bedding, washing machines;
- moving expenses, furniture and household equipment if a move to more suitable accommodation will help you to remain in the community, or if you are moving to help look after a vulnerable person;
- items needed because of a disability (including wheelchairs, stairlifts, special clothing, an orthopaedic mattress or an upright armchair);
- expenses of setting up home where, for example, you have been living rough or in temporary accommodation.

Planned resettlement

A CCG can be paid to help you set up home in the community as part of a planned resettlement programme.[86]

Interpretation

- None of the terms at the foot of p525 is defined in the SF directions. They are, therefore, open to interpretation according to your circumstances.
- A programme of resettlement involves help to set up home and help with matters such as budgeting skills, literacy skills, careers guidance and benefits advice. 'Setting up home' involves more than just moving into a new property and may still be in process (or even begin) some time after a move has occurred.[87]
- The *Social Fund Guide* says people without a settled way of life may have been in a night shelter, hostel, emergency shelter, temporary supported lodging scheme, or temporary accommodation provided by the Home Office to asylum seekers, or sleeping rough, but that this is not an exhaustive list.[88] It could also, for example, cover people moving between the houses of friends or relatives.[89]
- The *Social Fund Guide* also says planned resettlement programmes may be run by local authorities, voluntary organisations, housing associations and registered charities.[90] Again, this is not an exhaustive list and you can argue you are part of a programme planned by any other organisation or person (including yourself), even if they are unconnected to your accommodation.[91] Decision makers are told they may need to check that a resettlement programme exists at the accommodation you are moving from and that you are on such a programme.[92]
- If you cannot qualify for a CCG under this section, you may still be eligible for a CCG to help you move out of, or stay out of, institutional or residential accommodation (see pp523 and 524).

What to claim for

You can claim for help with any expenses which are not excluded (see p519). Examples include:

- furniture and household equipment;
- removal expenses, storage and connection charges on moving home;
- clothing and footwear.

Easing exceptional pressures on families

A CCG can be paid to ease exceptional pressures on you and your family.[93] The scope for applications on this basis is very wide.

When making your application, always fully explain all the pressures your family is experiencing and how a CCG will ease those pressures and help you to continue living independently in the community.

Exceptional pressures

The term 'exceptional pressures' is not defined in the SF directions (see p514) and should be given its normal, everyday meaning. The following points may be of relevance:

- Comparisons with 'normal' families are usually based on generalised assumptions. The level of pressure should be considered in terms of its effect on the individual family in question. Clearly though, 'exceptional' means something greater than the normal range of pressures experienced by most families.[94]
- The overall effect of the different pressures on a family should be assessed, including their cumulative impact.[95] You should always, therefore, list all the pressures affecting your family and explain their overall effect.
- Whether the pressures were foreseeable or are common is irrelevant, although the *Social Fund Guide* suggests higher priority should be given to a new, unforeseeable need.[96]
- The breakdown of a relationship, particularly involving domestic violence, is a common source of exceptional stress, as is disability.[97]
- Low income, lone parenthood and poor or overcrowded living conditions can be the source of exceptional pressures.
- Pressures that arise from a sudden event (eg, a disaster or fire) can be exceptional and traumatic. Pressures which have existed for a long time do not necessarily become easier to handle.
- There does not have to be any risk of a person going into care for exceptional pressures to exist.
- Mental stress, anxiety, depression, disability and illness are all sources and symptoms of exceptional pressures. The fact that an applicant does not appear stressed at an interview does not mean that exceptional pressures do not exist.
- Exceptional pressures experienced by children are entirely valid – eg, health risk or discomfort arising from lack of clothes or facilities in the home.
- The *Social Fund Guide* says refugees moving into the community from temporary accommodation provided by the Home Office may face exceptional family pressures.[98]
- Letters of support from professionals can help your case.

Family

The law refers to 'easing exceptional pressures on a person and his family'. This implies that people not living in a family are excluded. This interpretation was endorsed in a High Court case.[99]

The word 'family' is not defined in the SF directions. The *Social Fund Guide* says it can be given a flexible interpretation beyond the conventional 'nuclear' family (eg, two elderly sisters living together).[100] The SF Commissioner advises that a family could include:

- couples (with or without children, married or unmarried and with same or different sex partners);
- 'nuclear' and extended families;

- relationships of long-term interdependence, even where there are no blood or marriage ties;
- a woman who has been pregnant for 24 weeks or more.[101]

What to claim for

You can claim for any items that are not excluded (see p519). Examples include:

- items which will improve your family's living conditions or physical or mental health (including clothing, footwear or household items);
- maternity and funeral expenses that are arguably not covered by the regulated SF (see p549);
- moving and setting up home expenses if you move to more suitable accommodation or following the breakdown of a relationship;
- minor structural repairs;
- repairs or replacement of items damaged by behavioural problems;
- items needed because of a disability (including wheelchairs, stairlifts, special clothing and furniture).

Prisoners on temporary release

A CCG can be paid to allow you or your partner to care for a prisoner or young offender on temporary release under rule 6 of the Prison Rules 1964 (Part XIV of the Prisons and Young Offenders Institutions Rules 1994 in Scotland).[102]

Amount

The *Social Fund Guide* suggests it is normally reasonable to award one-seventh of your IS, income-based JSA or PC personal allowance for each day you are caring for a prisoner or young offender. If the prisoner is your partner, the suggested amount is one-seventh of the difference between your personal allowance and the couple rate.[103] The £30 minimum rule (see p518) does not apply.[104]

Travel expenses

A CCG can be paid to assist you and/or a member of your family with travel expenses in the UK (including overnight accommodation charges) to:[105]

- visit someone who is ill (in hospital or elsewhere); *or*
- attend a relative's funeral; *or*
- ease a domestic crisis (not defined); *or*
- visit a child who is with the other parent pending a court decision on which parent the child is to live with; *or*
- move to suitable accommodation.

Amount

The *Social Fund Guide* suggests that a CCG for travel expenses should be calculated as follows:[106]

- the cost of standard rate public transport (excluding air fares); *or*

- the cost of petrol, either up to the cost of public transport if available or in full if public transport is not available or you are unable to use it; *or*
- taxi fares, if public transport is unavailable or you or your partner cannot use public transport and have no access to private transport; *plus*
- the cost of an escort's fare if you cannot travel alone; *plus*
- the reasonable cost of necessary overnight accommodation.

The £30 minimum rule (see p518) does not apply to a CCG for travel expenses.[107]

Note: The *Social Fund Guide* suggests that any benefit or tax credits (other than premiums or the DLA mobility component) you are receiving for a hospital patient which exceeds £16.40 a week may be offset against the cost of hospital visiting. This should only apply, however, if the money is available to use for fares because you have fewer expenses due to the person being in hospital.[108] You can request a review of any decision to refuse or reduce a CCG on this basis (see Chapter 45).

3. Budgeting loans

Budgeting loans (BLs) are interest-free loans intended to help people with intermittent expenses which are difficult to budget for after a period on income support (IS), income-based jobseeker's allowance (JSA) or pension credit (PC). There is no legal entitlement to a BL, but unlike community care grants (CCGs) and crisis loans (CLs) (see pp517 and 538), decision making is based on legally binding factual criteria relating to your personal circumstances, rather than discretion. The criteria are applied nationally but the amount you receive is still dependent on the district budget (see p533).

Most BL refusals are on the grounds that the applicant cannot afford to repay the loan (see p534). Although you have the right to request a review (see p516) if you are refused a BL, or are given less than you asked for, a decision is only likely to be changed if it was based on incorrect information about your circumstances, or if the amount you are allowed to borrow has increased (see p1275).

Eligibility

To be eligible for a BL, you must satisfy all of the following conditions, which are laid down in legally binding directions.

- **You must be in receipt of IS, income-based JSA(including payments on account and hardship payments) or PC (guarantee or savings credit** – see Chapter 18) **when your BL application is determined.**[109] You are treated as being in receipt of IS, income-based JSA or PC if it is being paid to you, or to an appointee on your behalf.[110] You are eligible if you receive a backdated award of IS or income-based JSA covering the date your application is determined.[111] The High Court has held that you are not 'in receipt of' IS or income-based JSA if your partner or another member of your family is the claimant.[112] If you are a member of a 'joint-claim couple' (see p394), you are only eligible for a BL if you are the partner being paid JSA.[113]

- **You and/or your partner, between you, must have been receiving IS, income-based JSA (including payments on account and hardship payments) or PC throughout the 26 weeks before the date on which your application is determined, disregarding any number of breaks of 28 days or less.**[114] A period covered by a payment of arrears should count, as should any benefit received while in Northern Ireland.[115] The three waiting days at the start of a jobseeking period (see p377) do not count.[116] 'Partner' is not defined and is therefore not confined to its IS/JSA/PC meaning. More than one partner could help you satisfy the qualifying period.
- **You must not have too much capital.**[117] The rules are the same as for CCGs (see p518).
- **You, or your partner, must not be involved in a trade dispute** (see p735).[118]
- **The loan must be for one or more of the following categories of allowable expenses:**[119]
  - furniture and household equipment;
  - clothing and footwear;
  - rent in advance and/or removal expenses to secure fresh accommodation;
  - improvement, maintenance and security of the home;
  - travelling expenses;
  - expenses associated with seeking or re-entering work;
  - hire purchase (HP) and other debts for any of the above items.

  You are required to tick the category of expense for which you need the loan on the application form. You are not required to specify the particular items you need (eg, bed, winter coat). The exclusions which apply to CCGs and CLs (see p519) do not apply to BLs.
- **The loan must be a minimum of £30 and a maximum of £1,000 (less any outstanding social fund (SF) loans you and your partner have).**[120] You must state how much you are asking for on your application.
- **You must be likely to be able to repay the loan** (see p534).[121]

Decision making and priorities

When deciding a BL application, the law requires decision makers to have regard to:[122]

- prescribed factual criteria relating to the applicant's personal circumstances (see p645);
- the existence of resources which could meet the need;
- whether any other person or body could wholly or partly meet the need;
- the district budget (see p512);

- the SF directions;
- national and local guidance (see p514);
- the likelihood of repayment and the time it would take.

In practice, decisions are determined by two factors:

- **The 'weighting' of your application.** Each application is given a weighting (expressed in terms of a figure) based on prescribed criteria. This determines the relative priority of the application. See below for more details.
- **The district budget.** Local guidance (see p514) must specify the maximum amount payable for an application of the lowest weighting (this would apply to a single person who has been getting IS, income-based JSA or PC for 26 weeks only – see p532). The maximum payable for applications with a higher weighting is calculated by multiplying this base figure by the weighting of the application. If, for example, the base figure is £300, the maximum payable for an application with a weighting of three will be £900. The base figure may change over the course of the year depending on the demands on the district loans budget and will also vary from district to district.

The actual amount you can borrow also depends on the amount you can repay within 78 weeks and whether you already have any outstanding BLs (see p535 for details). Some examples of how the scheme works are given on p536.

Although decisions are legally made by decision makers, decision making is largely an automated process, with weightings and awards automatically calculated by computer.

Factual criteria and the weighting of applications

Initially, two factual criteria are used to determine the weighting of your application. If you cannot be offered a BL loan of at least £30 on the basis of the two initial criteria, a set of wider criteria is considered which may enhance the weighting of your application.

Initial criteria

The two initial criteria are as follows:[123]

- The length of time you, or your partner, have been receiving IS, income-based JSA (including payments on account and hardship payments) or PC (guarantee or savings credit) when your BL application is determined, subject to a minimum of 26 weeks and maximum of three years. Breaks (any number) of 28 days or less are disregarded. Backdated awards of benefit count for the period for which they are paid. The longer you have been on benefit, the higher will be the weighting of your application, as follows:
  - the minimum period of 26 weeks on benefit is given a weighting of one;
  - the maximum period of three years is given a weighting of one and a half;

- any point between the two will attract a *pro rata* weighting, depending on the number of full months on benefit (eg, the halfway point, which is 21 months, would be weighted at one and a quarter).

- The number of people (including yourself) who are members of your household for IS/income-based JSA purposes, including any children for whom you are responsible (see p809). The larger your family, the higher will be the weighting of your application, as follows:
  - you, as the BL applicant, are given a weighting of one;
  - your partner is given a weighting of one-third;
  - your first child is given a weighting of two-thirds;
  - additional children are given a total weighting of one-third.

The total weighting of your application is calculated by multiplying the weighting for the time you have spent on benefit by the weighting for your family size. An application from a single person who has been on IS or income-based JSA for 26 weeks would therefore attract the lowest weighting of one. Local guidance must specify the maximum amount of loan payable for such an application.

Example

Jack and Jill have been receiving IS for three years. They have one child, John.
Weighting for time on benefit = 1.5
Weighting for family size = 2 (one for Jack, one-third for Jill, two-thirds for John)
Total weighting = 1.5 x 2 = 3
If the district budget pays £300 for an application of the lowest weighting, Jack and Jill will be eligible for a maximum budgeting loan of 3 x £300 = £900.

Wider criteria

If you cannot be awarded a BL of at least £30 on the basis of the initial criteria, a set of wider criteria is considered.[124] If they apply, the weighting of your application will be enhanced. The wider criteria are used *in addition to* the initial criteria to determine the total weighting of your application. The purpose of the wider criteria is to incorporate greater flexibility into the scheme and avoid rigid cut-off points. You should note, however, that the wider criteria can only apply where you cannot be offered a loan of at least £30 on the basis of the initial criteria (if, for example, you apply for £800 and are offered £50, the wider criteria cannot then be considered).

The wider criteria and their effects on the weighting of an application are as follows:[125]

- The length of time you or your partner have been receiving working tax credit which includes a disability or severe disability element (see p1334), child tax credit at a rate higher than the family element (see p1321), working families tax credit, housing benefit or council tax benefit (CTB) ('secondary benefits')

can be added to the time you have been receiving IS, income-based JSA or PC, to enhance the weighting given for the length of time you have been receiving benefit (see p531). Note, however, that:
  - only time spent on *one* of the secondary benefits (the longest) counts;
  - only time spent on a secondary benefit in the three years prior to the date your BL application is determined counts;
  - only a period spent on a secondary benefit which ended 28 days or less before you became entitled to IS, income-based JSA or PC counts;
  - you must be in receipt of the secondary benefit continuously, apart from breaks (any number) of 28 days or less.
- Anyone who shares your private residence but is not a member of your household (see p812) and who is receiving IS, income-based JSA or PC (or is a member of the family of such a person), is given the same weighting as members of your family, to enhance the weighting given for family size.
- If you or your partner are pregnant, the child(ren) you are expecting count as members of your family, to enhance the weighting given for family size.

In addition, BLs taken out when you were with a former partner are disregarded if your current BL application relates directly to your separation. This can result in you being offered a higher loan under the wider criteria, where you have an outstanding BL debt (see below).

Amount

The actual amount of BL you will be offered depends on the following factors:[126]
- **The amount you request.** You will not be offered more than you ask for, but you may be offered less because of the factors below.
- **The legal minimum and maximum amounts and the capital rules.** You cannot be offered a loan of less than £30 or more than £1,000 (less any outstanding SF loans). The amount of your award will also be reduced if you have too much capital (see p518).
- **The weighting of your application** (see p531) and the maximum amount payable by the district budget for an application of that weighting (see p531).
- **The amount of any outstanding BL debt you or your partner have.**
  - If you have no outstanding BLs, you will be offered the maximum amount appropriate to the weighting of your application, or the amount you have requested, if this is lower.
  - If you do have an outstanding BL debt, the maximum amount you can borrow is reduced by double the amount of your outstanding BL debt. This means that where, for example, the appropriate maximum is £400, you will not be able to obtain a further BL until you have reduced your existing BL debt to below £200. This rule is designed to prevent you from continually topping up your debt to the maximum level, but it results in many applications being refused on the grounds of inability to repay the loan.

- **The amount you are likely to be able to repay.** The *Social Fund Guide* interprets this as the amount you can repay within 78 weeks (see below for details).[127]

Repayments

All loans must be repaid to the Department for Work and Pensions (DWP).[128]

There are three standard repayment rates:

- 15 per cent of your IS/income-based JSA applicable amount or PC appropriate minimum guarantee (see pp876 and 468) excluding housing costs, if you have no 'continuing commitments';
- 10 per cent of the above amount if you have 'continuing commitments' of up to £8.45 a week;
- 5 per cent of the above amount if you have higher 'continuing commitments'.

There is no definition of 'continuing commitments' but the BL application form asks for details of regular payments (other than normal living expenses such as fuel and food bills), including fines and catalogue, loan and HP repayments.

You can also agree to a higher repayment rate not exceeding 25 per cent of your applicable amount/appropriate minimum guarantee.

You are not allowed to borrow more than you are able to repay within 78 weeks and this may restrict the amount of loan you are offered.[129]

If you and your partner have no outstanding SF debts, you will be given up to two offers:

- an award repayable at the standard rate (5, 10 or 15 per cent of your applicable amount/appropriate minimum guarantee, excluding housing costs) subject to a maximum award of 78 times the standard repayment rate;
- an award repayable at a higher rate (up to 25 per cent of the above amount), subject to a maximum award of 78 times 25 per cent of your applicable amount/appropriate minimum guarantee.

The second option will offer you a larger loan at a higher repayment rate.

If you and your partner do have outstanding SF debts, you will be given up to three offers:

- an award repayable at the standard rate (5, 10 or 15 per cent of your applicable amount/appropriate minimum guarantee, excluding housing costs), subject to a maximum award of the standard repayment rate times the number of weeks remaining between the repayment of your existing budgeting loan debt and 78;
- an award repayable at a higher rate (up to 25 per cent of the above amount), subject to a maximum award of 25 per cent of your applicable amount/appropriate minimum guarantee multiplied by the number of weeks remaining as above;

- an award repayable at a rate equal to the total of your outstanding and proposed loans, divided by 78, subject to a maximum rate of 25 per cent of your applicable amount/appropriate minimum guarantee.

The first and second options involve repaying the new loan after the existing loan has been repaid. The second option will offer you a larger loan at a higher repayment rate. The third option will also offer you a larger loan if you agree to increase the repayment rate on your current loan.

See below for examples of repayment options.

You will receive a written decision on your application for a BL with details of any loan offers and repayment terms. You have 14 days from the date the decision was sent to return the declaration agreeing to one of the offers made to you (the time limit can be extended for 'special reasons').[130]

Methods of repayment

Both BLs and CLs are nearly always recovered by direct deductions from benefit, although you can make a payment at any time to pay off, partially or wholly, the debt. Deductions can only be made from the following benefits:[131]

- IS;
- PC;
- JSA (contributory or income-based);
- incapacity benefit;
- severe disablement allowance;
- carer's allowance;
- disablement benefit, reduced earnings allowance and industrial death benefit;
- bereavement benefits (excluding the lump-sum bereavement payment) and widows' benefits;
- retirement pensions (all types);
- maternity allowance.

Increases of benefit for age and dependants, and additional benefit under the additional state pension scheme, are also subject to deduction.

Deductions from benefit can be made even where an order for bankruptcy or sequestration has been made.[132]

A loan can be legally recovered from:

- you (the applicant) or the person who the loan was for;[133]
- your partner, if you are living together as a married or unmarried couple as defined for IS purposes (see p811);[134]
- a 'liable relative' (see p867) or a person who has given a sponsorship undertaking (see p662).[135]

Challenging repayment terms

You cannot request a review of a decision relating to repayment terms or recovery.[136] If you have accepted a loan, however, and the repayment terms are causing hardship (eg, because your financial situation has deteriorated), you can ask the DWP to reschedule the loan by lowering the weekly repayment rate.

Examples

The following examples are designed to illustrate how the scheme works.

All the people are single and live alone.

Example 1

Anna has been in receipt of IS and CTB for three years. She applies for a BL of £200. The maximum BL for an application of the lowest weighting in her district is £300. Her application attracts a weighting of 1.5 (see p531), which means the maximum she can borrow is £450 (£300 x 1.5). This figure is reduced by £430, however, because she already has an existing outstanding BL of £215 (see p530). This means that the maximum she can borrow is only £20, which is less than the legal minimum award of £30. None of the wider criteria applies (see p532) because although she has been receiving CTB for the past three years, this was not prior to her receipt of IS. She therefore receives a nil decision.

Example 2

Balbir, who is in receipt of income-based JSA and has no savings, applies for a BL of £800 for furniture and household equipment for his new home. The maximum BL for the weighting of his application is £650. He has no savings or SF debts but is paying £5 a week off a credit card debt. He receives two BL offers:

– £438.36 repayable at £5.62 a week. This is the amount repayable in 78 weeks at £5.62 a week (10 per cent of his applicable amount of £56.20);

– £650 repayable at £8.33 a week. This is the maximum award repayable in 78 weeks, at a rate equivalent to approximately 15 per cent of his applicable amount.

Example 3

Carmela receives IS and has no savings. She is pregnant and expecting twins. She applies for a BL of £500 for home improvements. The maximum BL for the weighting of her application under the initial criteria (see p531) is £500. She has no savings but has an outstanding BL of £250, which she is repaying at £8.43 a week (15 per cent of her applicable amount of £56.20). This reduces her maximum award by £500 to nil (see p531). The application of the wider criteria, however, doubles the weighting of her application because of her pregnancy (see p533). This increases her maximum award to £1,000. After the reduction of £500 because of her existing loan, she is able to borrow up to £500.

She receives three offers:

– £404.65 repayable at £8.43 a week (15 per cent of her applicable amount). This is the amount repayable in 48 weeks (her current outstanding loan of £250 will take approximately another 30 weeks to clear, leaving 48 weeks to repay the new loan within the maximum 78-week period);

– £500 repayable at £10.42 a week. This is the full amount of the loan applied for, repayable in 48 weeks at a rate equivalent to approximately 19 per cent of her applicable amount;
– £500 repayable at £9.61 a week (approximately 17 per cent of her applicable amount). This will repay both her new and existing loan (a total of £750) in 78 weeks.

Tactics

- You should always apply for a CCG, if you are eligible (see p517), rather than a BL, as the former is not repayable. Note that your application for a BL will *not* normally be considered for a CCG (see p515).
- When completing the BL application form SF500, it is important to give the information requested about your circumstances to ensure that your application will be properly weighted under the initial and wider criteria (see p531). You should also give details requested about your debts and commitments, as these will affect the standard repayment rate of any loan offer (see p533). You do not have to specify the precise items of expenditure for which you need the loan, but you must indicate that they fall within the broad categories for which a BL can be given (see p530).
- You must state how much you are applying for. Bear in mind the minimum and maximum amounts (see p530) and the capital rules (see p518). It is difficult (but possible) to work out how much loan you will be offered. The local guidance, which is obtainable from your local DWP office (see p514), should indicate the maximum BL applicable to applications with the lowest weighting (see p530). You can use this figure to work out roughly how much you are likely to be offered, depending on your circumstances (see p533). Remember that you will need to reduce any outstanding BL debt you have to below half of your maximum award before you can get a further BL (see p533).
- If you are refused a BL or awarded less than you asked for, you can request a review (see p1272). You should note, however, that a decision is only likely to be revised if it was based on an error relating to the factual criteria or if there has been an increase in the maximum amount of loan available from your district office (see p530). This could apply if your office has been allocated additional funds during the year (see p513).
- You can re-apply for a BL at any time. There is no rule preventing repeat applications for the same or different items of expenditure. If you are refused a BL and your circumstances relating to the factual criteria (see p531) change, you may be eligible if you re-apply. The longer you are on IS, income-based JSA or PC and the more of your current debt you have repaid, the more likely you are to be offered a loan. Also, if there has been an increase in the maximum amounts available from your district office, it may be worth re-applying.
- You should give careful consideration to the repayment terms before accepting a BL. Deductions of significant amounts from your weekly benefit may leave

you seriously short of money. Remember though, that BLs, unlike most commercial loans, are at least interest-free. You should return the declaration accepting a loan within 14 days or explain why it is late. If you have accepted a BL and are experiencing hardship because of the repayment terms, you should consider requesting a rescheduling of the loan (ie, asking for the repayment rate to be lowered).

4. Crisis loans

Crisis loans (CLs) are interest-free loans which are intended to help people with their immediate short-term needs in a crisis. Unlike budgeting loans (BLs), you do not have to be in receipt of benefit to qualify. There is no legal entitlement to a CL, but you do have the right to request a review if you are refused a payment or given less than you asked for (see p1272).

Eligibility

To be eligible for a CL, you must satisfy all of the following conditions, which are laid down in legally binding directions.

- **You must be aged 16 or over.**[137]
- **You must be without sufficient resources to meet the immediate short-term needs of yourself and/or your family** (see below for details).[138]
- **You must not be an excluded person** (see p539).[139]
- **The CL must not be for an excluded item** (see p541).[140]
- **The CL must be to help you meet:**[141]
  - expenses in an emergency, or as a consequence of a disaster, where a CL is the only means by which serious damage or serious risk to the health and safety of yourself or a member of your family may be prevented (see p541); *or*
  - rent in advance payable to a landlord who is not a local authority and where a community care grant (CCG) is being awarded following a stay in institutional or residential accommodation (see p543).
- **The loan cannot exceed £1,000** (less any outstanding social fund (SF) loans you and your partner have).[142] There are also more specific maximum amounts relating to items, services and living expenses (see p544 for details). There is no legal minimum amount of CL.
- **You must be likely to be able to repay the loan** (see p544).[143]

Resources

You must be without sufficient resources to meet the immediate short-term needs of yourself and/or your family. 'Resources' are not defined in the SF directions. The *Social Fund Guide* says all resources which are actually available to you, or could be obtained in time to meet the need, should be taken into account.[144] Resources available on credit should only be taken into account if you are not on income support (IS), income-based jobseeker's allowance (JSA) or pension credit (PC) and can afford the required repayments.[145]

The *Social Fund Guide* says the following resources should be disregarded:[146]

- other SF payments, housing benefit (HB) and the mobility component of disability living allowance;
- any run-on payments of HB, council tax benefit or mortgage interest (see Chapter 3);
- the value of your home, premises acquired for occupation within the next six months, and premises occupied by a relative or your ex-partner;
- the value of any reversionary interest – ie, an interest in property or capital which you will only be able to enjoy in the future, when a specified event occurs;
- your business assets;
- any sum paid to you because of damage to, or loss of, your home or personal possessions and intended for their repair or replacement;
- any sum acquired on the express condition that it is used for essential repairs or improvements to your home;
- any compensation award set aside for the replacement of lost livelihood;
- personal possessions, except those acquired for the purpose of qualifying for a CL;
- any payments from the Independent Living Funds, the Macfarlane Trust, the Variant Creutzfeldt Jakob Disease Trusts and the Skipton Fund;
- payments made under section 17 of the Children Act (section 22 of the Children (Scotland) Act), unless they are for the same need as the CL.

Decision makers are also advised to disregard other resources if it is reasonable to do so.[147] You could argue that money set aside to meet forthcoming bills (eg, council tax, fuel bills) is not available and should be disregarded. The SF Commissioner advises social fund inspectors (SFIs) to start from the premise that IS premiums, other benefits and capital are not available to meet the need, unless there is clear evidence to the contrary.[148]

Decision makers are told to not routinely refer applicants to employers, relatives or close friends unless there is reason to believe their help will be forthcoming.[149] They are also reminded that social services do not normally meet financial needs.[150] The possibility of getting a BL should not be used as a reason for refusing a CL.[151]

Excluded people

People excluded in all circumstances

The following people are excluded by the SF directions from getting a CL in all circumstances:[152]

- people in hospital and care homes (independent or local authority), *unless* their discharge is planned to take place within the next two weeks (**note:** people in a care home in Scotland are only excluded if they are receiving nursing or personal care[153]);
- prisoners and people lawfully detained, including those released on temporary licence (but not those released on parole or on bail pending a court hearing);[154]
- members of religious orders who are fully maintained by the order;
- people in 'relevant education' (see p618) who are not entitled to IS or income-based JSA.

People excluded in some circumstances

The following people are excluded by the directions from getting a CL except in very limited circumstances:

- full-time students not on IS, income-based JSA or PC (including payments on account) can only get a CL for expenses arising out of a disaster;[155]
- people who are 'subject to immigration control' (see p653) can only get a CL for expenses arising out of a disaster[156] (note that if you are an overstayer, subject to a deportation order, or an illegal entrant, you should not apply for a CL before getting advice about regularising your status);
- people involved in a trade dispute (see p735 for details);
- people subject to certain JSA disallowances or sanctions (see below for details).

People subject to jobseeker's allowance disallowances or sanctions

If you are subject to a JSA disallowance or sanction (see Chapter 16) in any of the circumstances specified below, you can only get a CL for expenses arising from a disaster (see p541), or for items needed for cooking or space heating (including fireguards), for the periods stated. This restriction does not apply, however, if you are a lone parent who is subject to the work-focused interviews for lone parents scheme (see p1096). It also does not apply if you are receiving hardship payments of JSA (see p443) but the amount of CL you can get for living expenses is restricted (see p544).[157] Your partner can claim a CL if you are subject to a disallowance or sanction but the amount payable for living expenses is also restricted (see p544).

- Your claim for JSA has been disallowed because you do not satisfy the labour market conditions (eg, you are not available for or actively seeking work – see p354). A CL can only be paid for the above expenses for 14 days, from the first day of the benefit week following the disallowance decision, or the day of the decision if it is made on the first day of a benefit week.[158]
- You are not getting JSA because you have been sanctioned for failing to take up or complete a New Deal employment or training option (see p430). A CL can only be paid for the above expenses during your sanction period, which is either two or four weeks.[159]
- You are not getting JSA because you have been sanctioned for another reason (eg, for leaving a job without just cause – see p419). A CL can only be paid for

the expenses on p540 for the 14 days following the end of the period during which you cannot get JSA (other than hardship payments).[160] If, for example, JSA is not payable for the first two weeks of a 26-week sanction period and hardship payments are awarded for the remaining 24 weeks, the CL restriction will apply during weeks three and four of the sanction. As JSA is paid in arrears, this will coincide with the period when you are without any JSA.
- You have failed, without good cause, to take part in a work-focused interview where this is required (see p1092).[161] A CL can only be paid for the expenses on p540 until you have taken part, or are no longer required to take part, in an interview. Note that this does not apply to some lone parents (see p540).

Notes
- After the periods specified have expired and during any period you are receiving JSA hardship payments (see p443), you are eligible for a CL without any restrictions.
- See p544 for details of the amount of CL payable for living expenses when you are subject to JSA disallowance or sanction.
- Your partner can apply for a CL if you are subject to a disallowance or sanction, but the amount payable for living expenses is restricted (see p531).

Excluded items

You cannot get a CL for any of the items listed on p519.

In addition, you cannot get a CL for the following items:[162]
- telephone purchase, installation, call and rental charges (see p19 if you are chronically sick or disabled and need a telephone);
- mobility needs (this does not include travel expenses);
- holidays;
- television or radio, TV licence, aerial, TV rental;
- garaging, parking, purchase and running costs of any motor vehicle except where payment is being considered for emergency travel expenses.

See p521 if you need help with maternity or funeral expenses.

Emergencies and disasters

Most CLs can only be awarded in an emergency or following a disaster. Neither of these terms is defined in the Directions. The SF Commissioner's advice defines an emergency as 'an unforeseen circumstance or pressing need, either of which requires immediate remedy or action' and a disaster as 'an event that causes great distress or destruction'.[163] Both the risk of an emergency, as well as an emergency or disaster that has already occurred could trigger a payment. You should always explain why a particular situation constitutes an emergency or disaster for you or your family. The consequences, rather than the causes, of the crisis should be the key issue.[164] Self-inflicted crises are not excluded and decision makers should not deny you a CL based on their judgements about your behaviour. Loss of money in the past should not prejudice the payment of a CL needed because of a further loss.

A CL has to be the only means of preventing serious damage or serious risk to health or safety. If a decision maker suggests there are 'other means', which you believe are impractical or unavailable, ask for a review. The burden of proof is on the decision maker (or SFI) to show that there are other means which are actually available to you.[165] 'Health' and 'safety' are not defined but health includes both physical and mental health, while safety relates to actual or potential danger.[166] Lack of adequate cooking, heating or sleeping facilities could seriously undermine your health, particularly if you already have health problems.[167]

Any supporting evidence you can get from your doctor, social worker, etc will help your case.

Survival for a period without money or a CL does not mean that a CL is not the only means of preventing serious damage or risk to your health or safety.

If you have been refused a BL, decision makers must consider whether the refusal has contributed to the emergency or disaster.[168]

Decision making and priorities

When deciding an application for a CL, the law requires decision makers to have regard to all the circumstances of each case and, in particular:[169]

- the nature, extent and urgency of the need;
- the existence of resources which could meet the need;
- whether any other person or body could wholly or partly meet the need;
- the district budget (see p513);
- the SF directions (see p514);
- national and local guidance (see p514);
- the likelihood of repayment and the time it would take.

The High Court has ruled that need and the priority of an application should be assessed before budgetary considerations are taken into account.[170] The *Social Fund Guide* states that an application for a CL to prevent serious damage or risk to health or safety will by its nature be high priority.[171]

Unlike BL decision making, decision makers must exercise individual discretion when deciding an application for a CL. The *Social Fund Guide* stresses that decision makers should take account of all the circumstances of each individual case and exercise their discretion flexibly. They are also advised to avoid a rigid interpretation of the guidance and that the absence of guidance relating to a particular situation does not mean that a payment should be refused.[172] In spite of this, decision makers tend to use the *Social Fund Guide* and local guidance (see p514) as a rulebook, even though they are not legally binding.

The standard and consistency of decision making have been heavily criticised and the discretionary SF likened to a lottery.

The *Social Fund Guide* gives examples of situations where a CL may be appropriate. These are set out below. They are not exhaustive, however, and you can apply for a loan in any situation so long as you satisfy the eligibility conditions (see p538).

Living expenses for a short period

The *Social Fund Guide* suggests a CL could be awarded to meet day-to-day living expenses in the following situations:

- you are waiting for your first benefit payment or wages;[173]
- you are suffering hardship because your employer has imposed a compulsory unpaid holiday;[174]
- you have lost money or you have lost a giro and replacement is delayed or not made (see p1104 on lost giros);[175]
- you cannot get IS or income-based JSA because your capital is over the prescribed limit (see p1023) but you cannot realise your assets immediately;[176]
- you are homeless and need living expenses (the *Social Fund Guide* stresses the risk to physical and mental health brought about by sleeping rough and prolonged homelessness);
- you have been discharged from prison and have insufficient money to meet your needs until your first payment of benefit (this can apply even if you have been paid a discharge grant).[177]

The *Social Fund Guide* suggests a CL should only cover living expenses for more than 14 days in exceptional circumstances – eg, a continuing crisis, loss of money which would normally cover you until your next income is due, or no money because of misfortune or mismanagement.[178]

Other needs

The *Social Fund Guide* suggests a CL could also be awarded to meet the following needs:

- emergency travel expenses if you are stranded away from home, or emergency fares to hospital;[179]
- fuel reconnection charges and fuel debts[180] (the *Social Fund Guide* says that if you need a CL to pay for a powercard or token, an amount to meet fuel arrears should be awarded separately from amounts for current consumption);[181]
- up to four weeks' rent (up to the level of your likely HB) payable in advance to a landlord other than a local authority, where a CCG is also awarded to help you return to the community;
- disasters – eg, fire or flood (see p541);[182]
- other urgent needs for which you cannot get a BL because you have not been receiving IS, income-based JSA or PC for 26 weeks.[183]

Amount

There is no legal minimum. There is a general legal maximum of £1,000 less any outstanding SF loan(s) you have.[184] You also cannot be awarded more than you can afford to repay,[185] usually calculated by multiplying your weekly repayment rate by 78 (see below). If you already have one or more loans you may find you are offered less than you asked for.

There are also more specific legal maximums for items, services and living expenses.

Items and services:[186] The maximum you can get is the reasonable cost of purchase (including delivery and installation) or the cost of repair, if cheaper. You should not normally be required to provide estimates and decision makers are not expected to check the amount requested against a price list.[187]

Living expenses:[188]

- The normal maximum you can get is 75 per cent of the appropriate IS or income-based JSA personal allowance for you *and* any partner (see pp811 and 879) plus £43.88 for each child.
- If you have been disallowed JSA because you have been sanctioned (see Chapter 16), or have failed to satisfy the labour market conditions, the maximum CL payable to your partner for living expenses is restricted to 75 per cent of her/his JSA personal allowance (see p879) plus £43.88 for each child.
- If you are getting a hardship payment of JSA (see p443), the maximum CL you can get for living expenses is the lesser of:
  - 75 per cent of the normal income-based JSA personal allowance for you and any partner (see pp811 and 879) plus £43.88 for each child;
  - the hardship rate of income-based JSA payable for you and any family.

Repayments

All CLs must be repaid to the Department for Work and Pensions (DWP). The rate of repayment, the repayment period and the method of recovery are not subject to review.[189] You can, however, request a change in your repayment terms (see p545).

The rate and period of repayment

There is no law specifying repayment rates or periods. The DWP normally seeks to recover CLs over a period of 78 weeks or, exceptionally, 104 weeks at the weekly rate of:

- 15 per cent of your IS/income-based JSA applicable amount or PC appropriate minimum guarantee (see p879), excluding housing costs (see p904) if you have no 'continuing commitments';
- 10 per cent of the above amount, if you have 'continuing commitments' of up to £8.45 a week;
- 5 per cent of the above amount, if you have higher 'continuing commitments'.

Recovery of a loan should be deferred until any existing loans are repaid. If you are receiving the hardship rate of JSA, you should argue that you should not be required to repay until your JSA is restored to the normal rate, or that recovery should be at the 5 per cent rate.

Methods of repayment

Crisis loans can be recovered by weekly deductions from most benefits. The rules are the same as for BLs (see p534).

Challenging repayment terms

You cannot request a review of a decision relating to the rate of repayment or the recovery of loans. You can request a change in your repayment terms, however, by writing to the DWP, either before accepting a loan, or at any time after accepting a loan (rescheduling), explaining why the repayment terms are unacceptable (eg, because they will cause you more hardship). You should give details of your financial commitments and any relevant changes in your financial circumstances.

Tactics

- You should always apply for a CCG (see p517) if you are eligible, rather than a CL, as the former is not repayable. Your application for a CL should be considered for a CCG if it contains information to indicate that a grant may be appropriate (see p517). You could also consider applying for a BL if you are eligible (see p529).
- You can apply for a CL on Form SF401, or verbally (eg, on the telephone – see p515). You should always insist that your application is formally determined by an SF decision maker and that you are given a written decision, together with a notification of your right to request a review. It is common for DWP counter staff to 'advise' potential applicants that they will not be given a loan.
- You are normally interviewed in connection with your application. You should ensure that the interviewing officer is aware of all your needs and circumstances and that full details are included in your written application. You will need to establish that you satisfy the eligibility rules (see p538), including the condition that a CL is the only way you can avoid a serious health risk (see p544). Bear in mind the rules relating to repeat applications on p516.
- You should insist on, and normally receive, a decision on the day your need arises. If there are unreasonable delays, you should complain to the district manager and, if necessary, ask your MP or an advice agency to intervene. Decisions should be based on your circumstances when you apply and a decision should never be delayed on the basis that the need will pass.
- If you are refused a CL, or given less than you asked for, you should consider requesting a review (see p1272). You should insist on the review being carried

out speedily. You can challenge the repayment terms of a loan if they are causing you hardship (see p545).

Notes

1. General matters

1 s138 SSCBA 1992
2 s139(1) SSCBA 1992; SF Dirs; SFG
3 ss138 and 140 SSCBA 1992; s66 SSAA 1992; SF Dirs
4 SF(App) Regs; SF(AR) Regs; SF(RDB) Regs; SF(Misc) Regs
5 s168 SSAA 1992
6 SF Dir 41; paras 7250-7265 SFG
7 SF Dir 42
8 s168(3)(c) and (d) SSAA 1992; paras 7042 and 7044 SFG
9 s140(1)(e) SSCBA 1992
10 *R v SFI ex parte Taylor* [1998] COD 152 (HC); para 3350 SFG; SF Commissioner's Advice on 'Approach to Budgets' 28/10/03
11 SF Dirs 40 and 41
12 s140(2) SSCBA 1992; s66(7) and (7A) SSAA 1992
13 s140(5) SSCBA 1992; ss64(3) and 66(a) SSAA 1992
14 SF Dir 41
15 Reg 2(1) SF(App) Regs
16 Reg 2A SF(App) Regs
17 para 4069 SFG
18 s140(4)(aa) SSCBA 1992; SF Dir 7
19 paras 5200-01 SFG
20 para 1072 SFG
21 para 3840 SFG
22 Reg 2(4) SF(App) Regs
23 Reg 3(a) SF(App) Regs
24 Reg 3(b) SF(App) Regs
25 paras 2071-72 and 4078-79 SFG
26 s140(4)(a) SSCBA 1992; SF Dir 7
27 paras 2152-53 and 4502-03 SFG
28 s140(4)(a) SSCBA 1992; SF Commissioner's Advice on 'Direction 7 (Repeat Applications)' 1/12/01
29 paras 2150 and 4500 SFG
30 SF Commissioner's Advice on 'Direction 7 (Same Item or Service)' 1/12/01
31 s140 SSCBA 1992
32 para 1026 SFG
33 paras 2028 and 6062 SFG
34 para 4063 SFG
35 s138(3) SSCBA 1992
36 s71ZA SSAA 1992; SF Dir 43
37 SF Dir 44

2. Community care grants

38 SF Dir 25
39 SF Dir 25(2)(b)
40 SF Dir 25(3)
41 SF Dir 25(4)
42 SF Dir (General)
43 *R v SFI ex parte Davey* 19 October 1998, unreported (HC)
44 SF Dir (General); para 2093 SFG
45 SF Dir 27
46 SF Dir 27(2)
47 SF Dir 27(2)
48 SF Dir 28(b)
49 SF Dir 4
50 SF Dirs 23and 29
51 CSB/1482/1985; *R v SFI ex parte Connick* 8 June 1993, unreported (HC); para 4570 SFG; SF Commissioner's Advice on 'Excluded Items' 18/6/01
52 para 4573 SFG
53 SF Commissioner's Advice on 'Housing Costs (General)' 1/3/03
54 paras 2301-2 and 4563-4 SFG
55 SF Dir 29
56 SF Dir 28(a)
57 s138(1)(b) SSCBA 1992; *R v SFI ex parte Harper* [1998] COD 221 (HC)
58 paras 2245-53 and 4583-91 SFG
59 SF Commissioner's Advice on 'Maternity Expenses' 2/1/02
60 s140 SSCBA 1992
61 *R v SFI ex parte Taylor* [1998] COD 152 (HC)
62 paras 3350 and 3360 SFG
63 para 2024 SFG
64 paras 2024 and 3321 SFG
65 paras 3323-27 SFG

66 para 3328 SFG
67 para 3329 SFG
68 SF Commissioner's Advice on 'Capital Resources' and 'Income Resources' 18/6/03 and 14/10/03
69 paras 3371-72 SFG
70 paras 3371 and 3375 SFG
71 paras 3377-79 SFG
72 paras 3120-21 and 3376 SFG
73 SF Dir 4(a)(i)
74 para 2401 SFG
75 paras 2408, 2460 and 2480 SFG
76 para 2481 SFG
77 *R v SFI ex parte Mohammed* [1993] COD 263 (HC)
78 *R v Secretary of State for Social Security ex parte Healey* [1991] COD 68 (HC)
79 para 2403 SFG
80 *R v SFI ex parte Sherwin* [1991] COD 68 (HC)
81 SF Commissioner's Advice on 'Direction 4(a)(i)' 1/5/01
82 SF Dir 4(a)(ii)
83 paras 2603-04 SFG; SF Commissioner's Advice on 'Direction 4(a)(ii)' 1/10/03
84 SF Commissioner's Advice on 'Direction 4(a)(ii)' 1/10/03
85 para 2601 SFG
86 SF Dir 24(a)(ii)
87 SF Commissioner's Advice on 'Direction 4(a)(v)' 1/5/03
88 para 3070 SFG
89 SF Commissioner's Advice to SFIs, *IRS Journal*, Winter 2001/02
90 para 3090 SFG
91 SF Commissioner's Advice on 'Direction 4(a)(v)' 1/5/03
92 para 3092 SFG
93 SF Dir 4(a)(iii)
94 para 2750 SFG
95 SF Commissioner's Advice on 'Direction 4(a)(iii)' 4/2/02
96 para 2755 SFG
97 para 2751 SFG
98 para 2753 SFG
99 *R v Secretary of State for Social Security ex parte Healey* [1991] COD 68 (HC)
100 para 2758 SFG
101 SF Commissioner's Advice on 'Direction 4(a)(iii)' 4/2/02
102 SF Dir 4(a)(iv)
103 para 3002 SFG
104 SF Dir 28(b)
105 SF Dir 4(b)
106 paras 3271-73 SFG
107 SF Dir 28(b)
108 paras 3152-58 SFG

3. **Budgeting loans**
109 SF Dir 8(1)(a)
110 SF Dir (General)
111 para 6151 SFG
112 *R v SFI ex parte Davey* 19 October 1998, unreported (HC); para 6180 SFG
113 para 6093 SFG
114 SF Dir 8(1)(c)
115 para 6151 SFG
116 SF Dir 8(3)
117 SF Dir 9
118 SF Dir 8(1)(b)
119 SF Dir 2
120 SF Dir 10
121 SF Dir 11
122 s140(1A) SSCBA 1992
123 SF Dirs 50 and 52
124 SF Dirs 51 and 52
125 SF Dirs 51 and 52
126 SF Dir 53
127 paras 6750-56 SFG
128 s78(1) SSAA 1992
129 para 6756 SFG
130 Reg 2 SF(Misc) Regs
131 Reg 3 SF(RDB) Regs
132 *Mulvey v Secretary of State for Social Security* [1997] SC 105 (HL); *R v Secretary of State for Social Security ex parte Taylor and Chapman, The Times*, 5 February 1996 (HC); s78(3A) and (3B) SSAA 1992
133 s78(3)(a) SSAA 1992
134 s78(3)(b) SSAA 1992
135 s78(3)(c) SSAA 1992
136 s38(13) SSA 1998

4. **Crisis loans**
137 SF Dir 14(a)
138 SF Dir 14(b)
139 SF Dirs 15-17
140 SF Dir 23
141 SF Dir 3
142 SF Dir 21
143 SF Dir 22
144 para 4101 SFG
145 para 4102 SFG
146 paras 4120-21, 4140-41 and 4160-65 SFG
147 paras 4120 and 4180-81 SFG
148 SF Commissioner's Advice on 'Crisis Loans and Resources' 18/6/01
149 para 4201 SFG
150 para 4220 SFG
151 SF Commissioner's Advice on 'Direction 3 – Only Means' 29/4/01
152 SF Dir 15
153 SF Dir 15(3)
154 para 4255 SFG

155 SF Dir 16(a)
156 SF Dir 16(b)
157 SF Dir 17(b)-(g)
158 SF Dir 17(b)
159 SF Dir 17(d)
160 SF Dir 17(c)
161 SF Dir 17(e)
162 SF Dir 23(2)
163 SF Commissioner's Advice on 'Direction 3 – Emergency/Disaster' 11/8/03
164 SF Commissioner's Advice on 'Direction 3 – Emergency/Disaster' 11/8/03
165 SF Commissioner's Advice on 'Direction 3 – Only Means' 29/4/02
166 SF Commissioner's Advice on 'Direction 3 – Serious Risk' 11/8/03
167 SF Commissioner's Advice on 'Direction 3 – Serious Risk' 11/8/03
168 SF Dir 3(2)
169 s140 SSCBA 1992
170 *R v SFI ex parte Taylor* [1998] COD 152 (HC)
171 para 4802 SFG
172 paras 4023 and 4800 SFG
173 paras 4713-15 SFG
174 para 4716 SFG
175 paras 4708-09 SFG
176 paras 4717-18 SFG
177 paras 4730-33 SFG
178 paras 4710-12 SFG
179 paras 4706-07 and 4719-20 SFG
180 para 4721 SFG
181 paras 4920-22 SFG
182 para 4702 SFG
183 paras 4734-36 SFG
184 SF Dirs 18, 20 and 21
185 SF Dir 22
186 SF Dir 21
187 para 5040 SFG
188 SF Dirs 18 and 20
189 s78(1) and (2) SSAA 1992

Chapter 22

Social fund: regulated payments

This chapter covers:

Unlike the discretionary social fund (see Chapter 21), the regulated social fund makes payments by right to people who satisfy conditions of entitlement which are laid down in regulations. As with most other benefits, decisions can be challenged by appealing to an appeal tribunal (see Chapter 44).

1. Sure Start maternity grants

You are entitled to a Sure Start maternity grant if you satisfy all of the following rules:

- You or your partner have been awarded a qualifying benefit in respect of the day you claim a maternity grant. The following are qualifying benefits:
  - income support (IS);
  - income-based jobseeker's allowance (including hardship payments);
  - child tax credit paid at a rate which exceeds the family element (see p1354);
  - working tax credit which includes the disability or severe disability element (see p1357);
  - pension credit (guarantee or savings credit – see Chapter 18).[1]

  You are eligible if you receive a backdated award of a qualifying benefit which covers the date you claim a maternity grant. If you are waiting for a decision on a claim for a qualifying benefit, the Department for Work and Pensions (DWP) may defer making a decision on a claim for a maternity grant until the qualifying benefit claim has been decided. If your claim for a maternity grant is refused while you are waiting for a decision on a claim for a qualifying benefit, you should re-claim a maternity grant within three months of being awarded the qualifying benefit (see p1090). Note, however, that if you do not claim a maternity grant within the time limits (see p551), a backdated award of a qualifying benefit will not qualify you for a grant. If you are not entitled to a qualifying benefit in your own right because you are under 16, or under 19 and in 'relevant education' (see p618), a member of your family can claim a maternity grant for you if s/he is getting a qualifying benefit in respect of you.

- One of the following applies:[2]
  - you or a member of your family are pregnant or have given birth in the last three months (including stillbirth after 24 weeks of pregnancy[3]);
  - you or your partner have adopted a child who is less than 12 months old when you claim a maternity expenses payment;
  - you and your spouse have been granted a parental order allowing you to have a child by a surrogate mother.

  In the last two cases, you are entitled to a payment even if one has already been made to the natural mother or a member of her family.[4]
- You or your partner are not involved in a trade dispute (see p735), unless specified circumstances apply (see p735).[5]
- You claim within the time limits (see p551).
- You have received health and welfare advice from a health professional (see below).

The terms 'partner' and 'family' in the above rules have almost identical meanings as they do for IS purposes (see p809).[6]

The rules about your age

There are no special rules relating to age.

Amount[7]

You are entitled to a grant of £500 for each child or expected child. The payment is not affected by any capital you have.

Claiming and getting paid

You should claim on Form SF100, which you can get from your local Jobcentre Plus office or from the DWP's website (see Appendix 1). There are strict time limits for claiming (see p551). The back of your claim form must be signed by a health professional (ie, midwife, health visitor or doctor), to confirm that you have received health and welfare advice relating to your baby or your maternal health.

Your date of claim is normally the date your form is received by the DWP.[8] If you make a written claim in some other way, you should be sent the appropriate form to complete. If you return it within one month, or such longer period as the Secretary of State considers reasonable, your date of claim is the date the DWP received your initial application.[9] See p549 for when your claim can be backdated if you are subsequently awarded a qualifying benefit.

If you claim before confinement, you need to submit a maternity certificate (Form MAT B1), a note from your doctor or midwife or an ante-natal clinic appointment card showing your expected date of confinement. If you claim after your child is born, you are usually asked for a maternity, birth or adoption certificate.[10]

The rules on getting paid and the recovery of overpayments are as for most other benefits (see pp1099 and 1142).

Time limits[11]

You can claim a maternity grant at any time from 11 weeks before the first day of your expected week of confinement until three months after your actual date of confinement. If you adopt a child or have a child by a surrogate mother, you can claim up to three months following the date of the adoption or parental order. There is no provision for claiming outside the time limits.

Challenging decisions

Decisions are made by decision makers on behalf of the Secretary of State and can be challenged by revision, supersession or appeal. The rules are the same as for most other benefits (see Chapters 43 and 44).

2. Funeral expenses payments

You qualify for a funeral expenses payment if you satisfy all of the following rules:

- You or your partner (see p554) have been awarded a qualifying benefit in respect of the day you claim a funeral payment.[12] The following are qualifying benefits:
  - income support (IS);
  - income-based jobseeker's allowance (including hardship payments);
  - housing benefit (HB);
  - council tax benefit (including second adult rebate where you are the 'second adult' – see p110);
  - child tax credit paid at a rate which exceeds the family element (see p1354);
  - working tax credit which includes the disability or severe disability element (see p1355);
  - pension credit (guarantee or savings credit – see Chapter 18).

  You are eligible if you receive a backdated award of a qualifying benefit which covers the date you claim a funeral payment. If you are waiting for a decision on a claim for a qualifying benefit, the Department for Work and Pensions (DWP) may defer making a decision on a claim for a funeral payment until the qualifying benefit claim has been decided.[13] If your claim for a funeral payment is refused while you are waiting for a decision on a claim for a qualifying benefit, you should re-claim a funeral payment within three months of being awarded the qualifying benefit (see p1090). Note that if you do not claim a funeral payment within the time limits (see p557), a backdated award of a qualifying benefit will not qualify you for a grant.

- You or your partner are in one of the categories of eligible people, listed below, who can be treated as responsible for the funeral expenses.
- You or your partner accept responsibility for funeral expenses (see p554).[14] If you are claiming as a close relative or close friend (see p554), it must also be reasonable for you to accept responsibility (see p554).
- The funeral (ie, burial or cremation)[15] takes place in the UK, unless you or your partner are covered by specified European Community (EC) legislation, in which case the funeral can take place in any European Economic Area (EEA) state or in Switzerland[16] (see p555).
- A social fund funeral payment has not already been made in respect of the deceased (but the amount of a previous award can be revised up to the maximum allowed under the rules).[17]
- The deceased was 'ordinarily resident' in the UK when s/he died.[18] See p696 for the meaning of ordinarily resident.
- You claim within the time limits (see p557).

Eligible people

You are only eligible for a funeral payment if you or your partner fall into one of the following categories of people who can be treated as responsible for the funeral costs. See p554 for definitions of the terms used.

- You were the 'partner' of the deceased when s/he died.[19]
- The deceased was a 'child' for whom you were responsible when s/he died and there is no 'absent parent', or there is an absent parent but s/he (or her/his partner) was getting a qualifying benefit (see p551) when the child died. If there is an absent parent who was not getting a qualifying benefit when the child died, you may qualify for a payment as a close relative of the deceased under the rules below. If the deceased was a 'stillborn child', you are eligible for a funeral payment if you were the parent or parent's partner and it does not matter whether there is an absent parent.[20]
- You were a parent, son or daughter of the deceased and it is reasonable for you to accept responsibility for the funeral expenses (see p554).[21]
- You were another 'close relative' or a 'close friend' of the deceased (see p554) and it is reasonable for you to accept responsibility for the funeral expenses (see p554). You cannot get a payment, however, if there is a parent, son or daughter of the deceased who could accept responsibilty for the funeral expenses and it is reasonable for her/him to do so.[22]

Exclusion of certain close relatives/friends

If you claim as a 'close relative' or 'close friend' of the deceased (see p554), you cannot get a payment if any of the following circumstances apply:

- The deceased had a partner (unless that partner died before the funeral without making a claim for a funeral payment).[23]
- The deceased was a child or stillborn child and a responsible person or parent is able to claim a funeral payment under the rules set out on p552.[24]
- There is a parent, son or daughter of the deceased, apart from the following:[25]
  - anyone under the age of 18;
  - anyone who (or whose partner) has been awarded a qualifying benefit (see p551);
  - anyone estranged from the deceased when s/he died (estranged is not defined but has connotations of emotional disharmony);[26]
  - students aged 18 doing a full-time course of advanced education (see p618), or aged 19 to pension age doing any full-time course (see Chapter 25);
  - members of a religious order which fully maintains them;
  - prisoners (including those in youth custody or a remand centre) who (or whose partners) were getting a qualifying benefit immediately before being detained;
  - inpatients receiving free treatment in a hospital or similar institution, who (or whose partners) were getting a qualifying benefit immediately before becoming a patient;
  - asylum seekers receiving asylum support from the National Asylum Support Service or a local authority (see p666);
  - anyone who is ordinarily resident (see p696) outside the UK.
- There is a close relative of the deceased who was in *closer contact* with the deceased than you were, taking into account the nature and extent of such contact.[27]
- There is a close relative of the deceased who was in *equally close contact* with the deceased as you were and who (or whose partner) is not getting a qualifying benefit (see p551).[28]

Note: The last two bullet points do not apply where:

- the close relative referred to was under the age of 18 when the deceased died, or was ordinarily resident outside the UK;[29] *or*
- the deceased was a child and there is no absent parent, or there is an absent parent who was getting a qualifying benefit when the child died.[30]

It is up to the DWP (and not you) to establish that there is another close relative who is not getting a qualifying benefit, if you are refused a payment on this ground.[31]

Example 1

Jane is not entitled to a funeral payment because, although she looked after her brother for many years before he died, he had a son who is not getting a qualifying benefit (see p551). Although the son rarely saw his father, they were not estranged.

Example 2

Yuri is entitled to a funeral payment when his close friend Robert dies because although Robert had two surviving close relatives, a son and a sister-in-law, the son is getting HB and Yuri was in closer contact with Robert than either of them were.

Definitions

- **Child** is defined as for IS purposes (see p818).[32] You are 'responsible' for a child if you get, or could get, child benefit for her/him (see p820).[33]
- **Stillborn child** means a child born dead after 24 weeks of pregnancy.[34]
- **Absent parent** means a parent of a deceased child, where the child:
  - was not living in that parent's household at the date of death; *and*
  - was living with another person who was responsible for her/him.[35]
- **Close relative** means parent, parent-in-law, son, son-in-law, daughter, daughter-in-law, step-parent, step-son, stepson-in-law, step-daughter, step-daughter-in-law, brother, brother-in-law, sister, sister-in-law.[36]
- **Close friend** is not defined in the law. It can include a relative who is not a close relative (eg, a grandparent or grandchild).[37]
- **Partner** has the same meaning as for IS (see p811).[38] You also count as a partner, however, if you were living in a care home (see p721) when the deceased died, *and*:
  - you and your spouse were living in the same home; *or*
  - you were a member of a couple before one or both of you moved into such a home.[39]

  This rule is designed to enable a surviving partner to claim a funeral payment where one or both partners were in a home at the date of death.

Accepting responsibility for funeral costs

To qualify for a funeral payment, you or your partner must 'accept responsibility' for funeral expenses.[40] The key factor is whether you are liable to pay the costs of a funeral, rather than whether you have made the arrangements for the funeral.[41]

If the funeral director's account or contract is in your name, you should normally be treated as having accepted responsibility. If the account or contract is in someone else's name (or, in the first case below, another person has paid the bill), you can still be 'responsible' if:

- s/he is acting as your agent – eg, because you are too distressed to act on your own behalf;[42] *or*

- s/he transfers liability to you, prior to full payment, with the consent of the funeral director (novation of the contract).[43]

If you are a close relative (see p554) or close friend of the deceased, it must also be 'reasonable' for you to accept responsibility for the funeral expenses, in the light of the nature and extent of your contact with the deceased.[44] In one case, it was held reasonable for a person to have accepted responsibility for his father's funeral even though he had not seen him for 24 years. This did not erase the contact they had had in the previous 30 years.[45]

EEA nationals

You can get a funeral payment for a funeral that takes place in any state of the EEA or in Switzerland (see p672) if you fall into one of the following categories:[46]

- You are a worker for the purposes of EC Regulations 1612/68 or 1251/70 (see p681).
- You are a member of the family of a worker for the purposes of EC Regulation 1612/68, or a member of the family of a worker who has died and who was covered by EC Regulation 1251/70 (see p681). The following count as family members:[47]
  - the worker's spouse;
  - the worker's or spouse's children, grandchildren and other descendants who are either under 21 or dependent;
  - dependent relatives of the worker or spouse in the ascending line (eg, parents, grandparents).
- You have the right to reside in the UK under EC Directive 68/360 or 73/148 (see p682).

For more details on the benefit rights of EEA nationals, see p672.

If you have ever been refused a payment for a funeral which took place in an EEA state and you satisfied the above rules, you should ask for a revision (see p1193). You could also try asking for lost interest or compensation for past non-payment.

The rules about your age

There are no special rules relating to age.

Amount of the payment

You are entitled to a payment sufficient to cover the following expenses:[48]

- The necessary costs of purchasing a new burial plot with the exclusive right of burial in it and necessary burial fees. The burial of ashes following cremation is not, however, covered.[49]
- Necessary cremation fees, including medical references and certificates and the fee for removing a pacemaker (restricted to £20 if not carried out by a doctor).[50]

- The costs of documentation necessary for the release of the deceased's assets.[51]
- The reasonable cost of transport for the portion of journeys in excess of 50 miles, undertaken to:
  - transport the body within the UK to a funeral director's premises or to a place of rest;[52]
  - transport the coffin and bearers in a hearse and the mourners in another vehicle from the funeral director's premises or place of rest to the funeral.[53] The cost of this plus burial in an existing plot cannot exceed the cost of such transport plus the purchase and burial costs of a new plot.[54]
- The necessary expenses of one return journey for the responsible person to arrange or attend the funeral. The maximum allowed is the cost of a return journey from home to the place where the burial or cremation costs are incurred.[55]
- Up to £700 for any other funeral expenses (eg, funeral director's fees, religious costs, flowers, other transport costs).[56]

Notes

- The cost of any items or services provided under a pre-paid funeral plan or equivalent arrangement cannot be met. Expenses not covered by the plan can be met if they fall into the above categories, but the maximum allowed under the last category is restricted to £120.[57]
- Costs relating to religious requirements cannot be included in the amount allowed for burial and transport.[58]
- If the amount awarded does not cover your funeral expenses, you could try making an application for a community care grant (eg, for the cost of a headstone), but see p521.

Deductions from awards

The amounts below are deducted from an award of a funeral payment:

- any of the deceased's assets available to you or a member of your family (defined as for IS purposes – see p1022) without probate or letters of administration.[59] Assets at the date of death count, even if you have spent or distributed them prior to your claim for a funeral payment.[60] Arrears of the deceased's attendance allowance (and probably other benefits) paid to you as next-of-kin also count;[61]
- any lump sum legally due to you or a member of your family from an insurance policy, occupational pension scheme, burial club or equivalent source on the death of the deceased;[62]
- any contribution towards funeral expenses made to you or a member of your family by a charity, or a relative of yours or of the deceased;[63]
- any funeral grant paid by the Government for a war disablement pensioner;[64]
- any amount paid or payable under a pre-paid funeral plan or equivalent arrangement (whether or not the plan was fully paid for).[65]

Any capital you have apart from the above has no effect on the amount of the funeral payment. Any payments from the Macfarlane Trust, the Macfarlane (Special Payments) Trusts, the Fund, the Eileen Trust, the CJD Trusts or the Skipton Fund (see p20) are not deducted from an award of a funeral payment.[66]

Claiming and getting paid

You should claim on Form SF200, which you can get from your local Jobcentre Plus office or from the DWP's website (see Appendix 1). There are strict time limits for claiming (see below). When completing the form, bear in mind the rules about accepting responsibility for the funeral expenses and your contact with the deceased (see p554).

Your date of claim is normally the date the form is received by the DWP.[67] If you do not complete the SF200 properly or apply in writing but not on the form, you should be sent the form to complete or correct. If you submit it within one month, or such longer period as the Secretary of State considers reasonable, your claim is treated as made on the date you originally applied.[68] See p551 for when your claim can be backdated if you are subsequently awarded a qualifying benefit.

Payment is normally made directly to the funeral director, unless you have already paid the bill.[69]

The rules relating to the recovery of overpayments are as for other benefits (see p1127) but see below for recovery from the deceased's estate.

Time limits

You can claim at any time from the date of death up to three months after the date of the funeral.[70] There is no provision for late claims. See above for details of the date your claim is treated as made.

Recovery from the deceased's estate

The Secretary of State is entitled to recover funeral expenses payments from the deceased's estate and normally seeks to do so.[71] Funeral expenses are a first charge on the estate, in priority to anything else (although there may be insufficient assets for full repayment).[72]

Challenging a decision

Decisions are made by decision makers on behalf of the Secretary of State and can be challenged by revision, supersession or appeal. The rules are the same as for most other benefits (see Chapters 43 and 44 for details).

3. Cold weather payments

You qualify for a cold weather payment if:

- a period of cold weather has been forecast or recorded for the area in which your normal home is situated (see below);[73] *and*
- you have been awarded pension credit (guarantee or savings credit) for at least one day during the period of cold weather; *or*
- you have been awarded income support (IS) or income-based jobseeker's allowance (JSA) for at least one day during the period of cold weather *and:*
  - your IS or income-based JSA includes one or more of the following premiums: disability; severe disability; disabled child; pensioner; or higher pensioner (see p882); *or*
  - you are responsible for a child under five; *or*
  - you are getting child tax credit which includes a disability or severe disability element (see p1354);[74] *and*
- you are not living in a care home (see Chapter 28).[75]

A period of cold weather

This is a period of seven consecutive days during which the average of the mean daily temperature forecast or recorded for that period is equal to or below 0 degrees celsius. The mean daily temperature is the average of the maximum and minimum temperatures recorded for that day.[76] The Regulations divide the country into local areas, each covered by a weather station at which temperatures are forecast or recorded.[77] The area your home is in is normally determined by your postcode.

The rules about your age

There are no special rules about your age.

Amount of the payment

The sum of £8.50 is paid for each week of cold weather.[78]

Claiming and getting paid

You do not need to make a claim for a cold weather payment. The Department for Work and Pensions (DWP) should automatically send you a giro if you qualify.[79] Your district DWP should publicise when there are periods of cold weather in your area by placing advertisements in local newspapers, by radio broadcasts, and by distributing posters and leaflets – eg, to doctors' surgeries and local advice centres.[80] If you do not receive a giro and you think you are entitled, contact your local Jobcentre Plus office. The rules relating to the recovery of overpayments are as for other benefits (see p1127).

Time limits

There are no time limits for claiming a cold weather payment, as there is no requirement to submit a claim. If you have missed out on a payment, you should contact your local DWP office and if necessary, submit a claim in writing.

Challenging decisions

If you do not receive a payment to which you think you are entitled, you should submit a written claim and ask for a written decision. If you are refused, you can request a revision or appeal (see Chapters 43 and 44).

4. Winter fuel payments

You qualify for a winter fuel payment if:[81]

- you are aged 60 or over in the week beginning on the third Monday in September (the qualifying week); *and*
- you are ordinarily resident in Great Britain (see p698);
  Note: You may be entitled to a payment if you are currently residing in another European Economic Area country or in Switzerland (see p673); *and*
- if a claim is required, you claim in time (see p560); *and*
- you are not excluded from a payment under the rules below.

Exclusions

You are excluded from entitlement to a payment if you fall into one of the following categories in the qualifying week (see p560):[82]

- You are serving a custodial sentence.
- You have been receiving free inpatient treatment for more than 52 weeks in a hospital or similar institution (see p715).
- You are receiving pension credit (PC) or income-based jobseeker's allowance (JSA) and you are living in residential care. You count as **'living in residential care'** if you are living in a care home (ie, an independent home which is registered or exempt from registration, or a local authority home which provides board) throughout the qualifying week and the 12 preceding weeks, disregarding temporary absences.[83]
- You are subject to immigration control (see p1457). If you become entitled to backdated income support (IS) in respect of the qualifying week when you are no longer subject to immigration control (eg, when you are granted refugee status – see p669), you are also entitled to a winter fuel payment.[84]

The rules about your age

You must be aged 60 or over in the qualifying week (see above).

Amount

Subject to the rules below, you are entitled to a winter fuel payment of:

- £200 if you are aged 60–69 (inclusive) in the qualifying week (see p559); *or*
- £250 if you are aged 70–79 (inclusive) in the qualifying week (see note below); *or*
- £300 if you are aged 80 or over in the qualifying week.[85]

If you are sharing accommodation as a mutual home with another person who is entitled to a winter fuel payment, only one payment is made per household (£200 if you are both or all aged 60–69; £250 if one of you is aged 70–79 – see note below); £300 if one of you is aged 80 or over). The payment will be split between you, unless you are getting PC, IS or income-based JSA as a couple (in which case either of you can be paid).[86]

If you are living in residential care (see p559) in the qualifying week and are not getting PC or income-based JSA, you are entitled to a payment of £100 if you are aged 60–69, £125 if you are aged 70–79 (see note below), or £150 if you are aged 80 or over.[87]

Note: The extra payments for people aged 70–79 were announced in the Government's Pre-Budget Report 2004 but at the time of writing had not yet been put into legislation. See CPAG's *Welfare Rights Bulletin* for updated information.

Claiming and getting paid

You should automatically receive a payment without having to make a claim if you received a payment the previous year, or you are getting a state retirement pension or any other social security benefit (apart from child benefit, housing benefit or council tax benefit) in the qualifying week.[88]

Otherwise, you must claim a winter fuel payment before 31 March following the qualifying week.[89] To ensure you receive your payment before Christmas, you should submit your claim before the qualifying week. A claim can be accepted in any written format but it is best to use the designated form, which you can get by ringing the winter fuel payment helpline on 08459 151515 (local rate) (textphone: 08456 015613), or from the DWP's website (see Appendix 1). There is a separate helpline for the additional age-related payments (02920 428106).

If you are a member of a couple and your partner is receiving IS, the payment can be made to either of you (even if your partner is under 60).[90]

The Government says it aims to make payments between mid-November and Christmas.

Claiming for previous winters

The Government introduced annual winter fuel payments in 1997/98, but for the first three winters payments were restricted to people aged 60 or over receiving IS or income-based JSA and people over pension age receiving other prescribed benefits. In December 1999, the European Court of Justice ruled that the exclusion of men aged 60–64 receiving benefits other than IS or income-based JSA was unlawful discrimination.[91] The Government responded by extending the scheme from 2000/01 to anyone over the age of 60 (see p559) and allowing anyone unlawfully excluded from entitlement in respect of the previous three winters to claim backdated payments.

You can still claim backdated payments for the winters of 1997/98, 1998/99 and 1999/2000 if:

- you did not receive a payment for the relevant year(s); *and*
- you were aged 60 or over in the relevant qualifying week (see below); *and*
- you did not fall within any of the excluded categories listed on p559 in the relevant qualifying week.

The qualifying weeks and the amounts you can claim in respect of each year are as follows:

Year	*Qualifying week*	*Amount*
1997/98	5–11 January 1998	£20*
1998/99	9–15 November 1998	£20*
1999/2000	20–26 September 1999	£100*

*You will only receive 50 per cent (ie, £10 or £50) if you were living with a partner who was entitled to a payment in their own right.

To make a claim for previous winters, you should complete a special claim form, which you can get by ringing the helpline (see p560).

Challenging decisions

Decisions can be challenged by revision, supersession or appeal in the same way as other benefits (see Chapters 43 and 44). To get a decision, you may have to submit a written claim and request a written decision. Backdated payments for previous winters are not covered by the regulations and it is unclear whether there is a right of appeal against refusal of a payment for previous years. If you feel you have been wrongly refused a backdated payment, you should request a written explanation and seek further advice if you are unhappy with the response.

Notes

1. Sure Start maternity grants

1 Reg 5(1)(a) SFM&FE Regs
2 Reg 5(1)(b) SFM&FE Regs
3 Reg 3(1) SFM&FE Regs
4 Reg 4(2) SFM&FE Regs
5 Reg 6 SFM&FE Regs
6 Reg 3(1) and (2) SFM&FE Regs
7 Reg 5(2) SFM&FE Regs
8 Reg 6(1)(a) SS(C&P) Regs
9 Regs 6(1)(b) and 4(7) SS(C&P) Regs
10 para 39012 DMG
11 Reg 19 and Sch 4 para 8 SS(C&P) Regs

2. Funeral expenses payments

12 Reg 7(1)(a) SFM&FE Regs
13 DMG Memo Vol JSA/IS 22
14 Reg 7(1)(e) SFM&FE Regs
15 Reg 3(1) SFM&FE Regs
16 Reg 7(1)(b) SFM&FE Regs
17 Reg 4(3) and (4) SFM&FE Regs
18 Reg 7(1)(c) SFM&FE Regs
19 Reg 7(1)(e)(i) SFM&FE Regs
20 Reg 7(1)(e)(ii) SFM&FE Regs
21 Reg 7(1)(e)(iii) SFM&FE Regs
22 Reg 7(1)(e)(iii) and (iv) SFM&FE Regs; R(IS) 7/04
23 Reg 7(1)(e)(iii) and (iv) and (2) SFM&FE Regs
24 Reg 7(1)(e) SFM&FE Regs; R(IS) 7/04
25 Reg 7(3) and (4) SFM&FE Regs
26 R(SB) 2/87
27 Reg 7(6)(a) SFM&FE Regs
28 Reg 7(6)(b) SFM&FE Regs
29 Reg 7(7) SFM&FE Regs
30 Reg 7(6) SFM&FE Regs
31 *Kerr v Department for Social Development (NI)* 6 May 2004 (HL)
32 Reg 3(1) SFM&FE Regs
33 Reg 7(1)(e)(ii)(aa) SFM&FE Regs
34 Reg 3(1) SFM&FE Regs
35 Reg 3(1) SFM&FE Regs
36 Reg 3(1) SFM&FE Regs
37 CIS/788/2003
38 Reg 3(1) SFM&FE Regs
39 Reg 3(1A) SFM&FE Regs
40 Reg 7(1)(e) SFM&FE Regs
41 CSB/488/1982
42 CIS/12344/1996; CIS/975/1997
43 CIS/85/1991
44 Reg 7(1)(e)(iii) and (iv) and (5) SFM&FE Regs
45 CIS/12783/1996
46 Reg 7(1A) SFM&FE Regs
47 Art 10 EC Reg 1612/68; Art 2 EC Reg 1251/70
48 Reg 7A(1) SFM&FE Regs
49 Reg 7A(2)(a) SFM&FE Regs; CIS/16192/1996
50 Reg 7A(2)(b) SFM&FE Regs
51 Reg 7A(2)(c) SFM&FE Regs
52 Reg 7A(2)(d) SFM&FE Regs
53 Reg 7A(2)(e) SFM&FE Regs
54 Reg 7A(4A) SFM&FE Regs
55 Reg 7A(2)(f) and (4B) SFM&FE Regs
56 Reg 7A(2)(g) SFM&FE Regs
57 Reg 7A(5) SFM&FE Regs
58 Reg 7A(4) SFM&FE Regs
59 Reg 8(1)(a) SFM&FE Regs
60 R(IS) 14/91
61 R(IS) 12/93
62 Reg 8(1)(b) SFM&FE Regs
63 Reg 8(1)(c) SFM&FE Regs
64 Reg 8(1)(d) SFM&FE Regs
65 Reg 8(1)(e) SFM&FE Regs
66 Reg 8(2) SFM&FE Regs
67 Reg 6(1)(a) SS(C&P) Regs
68 Regs 4(7) and 6(1)(b) SS(C&P) Regs
69 Reg 35(2) SS(C&P) Regs
70 Sch 4 para 9 SS(C&P) Regs
71 s78(4) SSAA 1992; CIS/616/1990
72 R(SB) 18/84

3. Cold weather payments

73 Reg 2(1) and (2) SFCWP Regs
74 Reg 1A(1) SFCWP Regs
75 Reg 1A(2) SFCWP Regs
76 Reg 1(2) SFCWP Regs
77 Schs 1 and 2 SFCWP Regs
78 Reg 3 SFCWP Regs
79 para 104 CWPH
80 paras 500-11 CWPH

4. Winter fuel payments

81 Reg 2 SFWFP Regs
82 Reg 3 SFWFP Regs
83 Reg 1(2), (3) and (3A) SFWFP Regs
84 Reg 4(2) SFWFP Regs
85 Reg 2 SFWFP Regs
86 Reg 2(1)(ii)(aa), (2) and (3) SFWFP Regs

87 Reg 2(2)(b) SFWFP Regs
88 Reg 4 SFWFP Regs
89 Reg 3(1)(b) and (2) SFWFP Regs
90 Reg 36(2) SS(C&P) Regs
91 *Taylor* ECJ Case C-382/98, 16 December 1999

* From 5 December 2005, you can also qualify for SPP if your civil partner has recently given birth or is adopting a child or is jointly adopting a child with you, and SAP if you are jointly adopting a child with your civil partner.

Chapter 23

Statutory maternity, paternity and adoption pay

This chapter covers:

Statutory maternity pay (SMP), statutory paternity pay (SPP) and statutory adoption pay (SAP) are benefits which are paid to employees by their employers.

If you are pregnant or have recently given birth you may be entitled to **statutory maternity pay (SMP).** (If you do not qualify for SMP you may qualify for maternity allowance instead – MA see Chapter 17). You may qualify for **statutory paternity pay (SPP)** if your spouse or partner has recently given birth or if s/he is adopting a child, or if you are jointly adopting a child with her/him. **Statutory adoption pay (SAP)** may be paid if you are adopting or jointly adopting a child. The table on p565 details which benefit you may qualify for, given your circumstances. *

SMP and SAP are paid for a maximum of 26 weeks. SPP is paid for up to two weeks. You do not have to have paid national insurance contributions to qualify for SMP, SPP, or SAP, although there is an employment and an earnings condition for each. Your entitlement to SMP, SPP and SAP is not affected by any other income or savings that you may have.

If you qualify for either SMP, SPP or SAP, each is the minimum amount of pay that the law requires employers to pay you during maternity, adoption or paternity leave. However, many groups of employees have negotiated the right to higher amounts of pay under their contracts. Details of your employer's own contractual maternity, paternity and/or adoption schemes may be available from your trade union representative, your employer's personnel department, or contained in your written particulars of employment.

Some terms used in this chapter apply to SMP, SPP and SAP. Definitions of these terms are covered on p587.

Overseas adoptions

You may qualify for SPP or SAP in respect of a child adopted from abroad if s/he entered Great Britain on or after 6 April 2003. However, in the case of an overseas adoption the normal rules of entitlement explained below are modified. See pp578-580 for details of the modifications.

1. Who can claim

The table below details which benefit you may qualify for, given your circumstances. If you are jointly adopting a child with your spouse or partner you will be able to choose whether to claim statutory paternity pay (SPP) or statutory adoption pay (SAP). Although the amount of SPP and SAP is the same, SAP is payable for up to 26 weeks, while SPP is only paid for up to two. In this situation, your spouse or partner may be able to qualify for SPP while you claim SAP or vice versa. However, you both cannot qualify for SAP for the same adoption and you cannot receive SPP for any week you are entitled to SAP.[1] While only women can qualify for statutory maternity pay (SMP), men or women can qualify for SAP or SPP. The qualifying conditions for SMP, SPP and SAP are described below.

If you **are pregnant or have recently given birth** and do not qualify for SMP or maternity allowance (MA) you may be entitled to statutory sick pay (SSP) (unless you are within the periods mentioned on p603) or to incapacity benefit (see Chapter 12).

There are some groups of claimants to whom special rules apply (see p576).

Event	*Circumstances*	*Benefit you may qualify for*
Adoption	If you are the sole adopter	SAP
	If you and your spouse or partner are jointly adopting a child	SAP or SPP (adoption)
	If your partner or spouse is the adopter	SPP (adoption)
Birth	If you are the mother of the baby	SMP or MA
	If you are the partner or spouse of the mother	SPP (birth)

Statutory maternity pay

You qualify for SMP if:[2]

- you are pregnant and within 11 weeks of your 'expected week of childbirth' (EWC – see p587), or you have recently given birth;[3] *and*
- you are employed for at least part of the 15th week before your EWC (see p587); *and*
- you satisfy the continuous employment rule (see p567);[4] *and*
- you satisfy the earnings condition (see p570);[5] *and*
- you have given your employer the appropriate notice and information (see p581); *and*
- you have ceased working for the employer paying you SMP (but see p572); *and*
- you do not work for other employers after the birth (but see p572 for an exception).

Statutory paternity pay

SPP can be paid for a child who is adopted – referred to in this chapter as SPP (adoption) – and for a child your spouse or partner has given birth to – referred to as SPP (birth). If a reference in the chapter is to SPP, the rules described relate to both SPP (adoption) and SPP (birth).

See p565 for details of the relationship between SPP and SAP. See p590 if you are entitled to SSP.

You qualify for SPP if:[6]

- you satisfy the continuous employment rule (see p567); *and*
- you satisfy the earnings condition (see p570); *and*
- you have given your employer the required notice and information (see p582); *and*
- you are not working for the employer paying you SPP (see p572); *and*
- you do not do any work for other employers (but see p572 for an exception).

In addition, the following must apply:

For SPP (adoption):

- your spouse or partner is adopting a child, or you and your spouse or partner are jointly adopting a child (see p567 for the meaning of partner); *and*
- the person adopting the child (the adopter) is doing so under UK law (but see p578 if the child is adopted from abroad); *and*
- you have, or you expect to have (along with the adopter or the other adopter) the main responsibility for the upbringing of the child; *and*
- while receiving SPP you intend to care for the child or to support the person adopting the child; *and*
- you have not elected to receive SAP.

For SPP (birth):

- while receiving SPP you intend to care for the child or to support the child's mother; *and either*
- you are the child's father and you will have responsibility for the upbringing of the child; *or*
- the child's mother is your spouse or partner and you will have, apart from the mother's responsibility, the main responsibility for the upbringing of the child (see below for the meaning of partner).

Who counts as a partner

For the purpose of SPP you count as the partner of the adopter or of the child's mother if you live with her/him and the child in an 'enduring family relationship'. Same-sex partners as well as partners of the opposite sex can claim SPP. However, a parent, grandparent, sister, brother, aunt, uncle, half-sister or half-brother cannot count as your partner, and if you are adopted neither can your adoptive parents, nor vice versa.[7]

Statutory adoption pay

See p565 for details of the relationship between SPP and SAP. See p590 if you are entitled to statutory sick pay.

You qualify for SAP if:[8]

- a child has been, or is expected to be, placed with you for adoption under UK law (but see p578 if the child is adopted from abroad); *and*
- you satisfy the continuous employment rule (see below); *and*
- you satisfy the earnings condition (see p570); *and*
- you have given your employer the required notice and information (see p584); *and*
- you have not elected to receive SPP; *and*
- if a child has been placed with both you and your spouse for adoption, your spouse is not claiming SAP; *and*
- you have ceased working for the employer paying you SAP (see p572); *and*
- you do not do any work for other employers (but see p572 for an exception).

Continuous employment rule

To be entitled to SMP, SPP or SAP you must be, or have been, an employee of an employer who pays secondary Class 1 national insurance (NI) contributions for you or who would pay them if your earnings were high enough (see p831).[9] The question of whether you are an employee is similar to the question of whether you are an 'employed earner' for industrial injuries benefits (see p320). To count as an employee you must be over 16.

It is not necessary for you to have a written contract of employment to count as an employee and your employer cannot restrict your right to SMP, SPP or SAP by its own rules or contract with you – it is a right established by law. Nor can your employer require you to contribute towards the cost of SMP, SPP or SAP.[10] Periods of employment for the same employer in another European Economic Area state may count towards your period of continuous employment.[11] However, even if you are an employee you may not be entitled to SMP, SPP or SAP if your employer is based outside Great Britain (see p577).[12]

Continuous employment for SMP and SPP (birth)

To qualify for **SMP** or **SPP** (birth):

- you must have been employed by your employer for a continuous period of at least 26 weeks ending with the 15th week before the EWC (see p587);[13]
- for SPP (birth) you must also have been continuously employed by that same employer from the end of the 15th week before the EWC to the day that the child is born.[14]

For both SMP and SPP (birth), if your baby is born in or before the 15th week before the EWC, you satisfy the continuous employment rule if you would have done so had the baby been born on the expected date.[15]

For SMP only, even if you are employed for only part of the 15th week the whole week still counts towards your period of continuous employment.[16]

Continuous employment for SAP and SPP (adoption)

To qualify for **SAP** or **SPP** (adoption):[17]

- you must have been employed by your employer for a continuous period of at least 26 weeks ending with the week in which you are notified that you have (or, for SPP, you or your partner or spouse has) been matched with a child for adoption (see p588);
- for SPP (adoption) only, you must also have been continuously employed by that same employer from the end of the week in which you were notified until the day the child is placed with you for adoption.

The date you are notified is the date you receive the adoption agency's notification rather than the date it is sent.[18] For SAP only, even if you are employed for only part of the week in which you receive the notification, the whole week still counts towards your period of continuous employment.[19]

Calculating 26 weeks' continuous employment

For **SMP**, **SPP** and **SAP**, if you return to work for the same employer following a break in your contract of employment, certain weeks when you were not employed can still count towards your 26 weeks of continuous employment. These include weeks in which, for all or part of the week, you were:[20]

- incapable of work due to sickness or injury, unless your incapacity lasted for more than 26 consecutive weeks;

- absent due to a temporary cessation of work because your employer had none to offer you (eg, you are an agency worker and the agency is unable to find you work in any particular week);
- absent from work in circumstances such that, by arrangement or custom, you are regarded as continuing in employment (eg, public holidays, annual shutdown, or certain teachers employed on term-by-term contracts);
- for SMP only, absent from work wholly or partly because of pregnancy or childbirth if there was not more than 26 weeks between your contracts with your employer, and you were employed by your employer both before and after you had your baby but not during the period of your absence;
- for SMP only, absent from work while on paternity, adoption or parental leave.

If it is your employer's practice to offer work for separate periods of six months or less, at least twice a year, to people who have worked for them before (eg, if you are a supply teacher or agency worker), then you do not have to have returned to work in order to benefit from the above rules as long as your absence was either:

- due to your incapacity for work arising from a specific disease or bodily or mental disablement; *or*
- if you are claiming SMP, due wholly or partly to your pregnancy or childbirth.

However, for SMP and SAP in these circumstances, if you had a contract of employment for only part of the 15th week before your EWC you can only count that part towards your 26 weeks' continuous employment and cannot count the whole week.[21]

The Revenue may say that even if you are still employed by your employer during periods when you are off work, you will only be considered to be in continuous employment for the period of your absence in the circumstances given above. This would mean, for example, that if you are off work sick but remain employed while you are absent, only a period of up to 26 weeks' absence would count towards your continuous employment. However, it is arguable that periods when you are off work, because of sickness or maternity leave, for example, can still count towards your continuous employment irrespective of the length of your absence as long as you continued to be employed by your employer over these periods.

If your employment is legally transferred from one employer to another your employment is unbroken.[22]

See p741 if your continuity of employment is affected by a strike and p577 if you have been dismissed by your employer. If you have been reinstated or re-engaged following an unfair dismissal claim, any period between your dismissal and reinstatement or re-engagement counts towards your 26 weeks' continuous employment. Similarly, if you are reinstated or re-engaged on or after 6 April 2005 as a result of a statutory dispute resolution procedure, then any period between your dismissal and reinstatement or re-engagement counts towards your period of continuous employment.[23]

The earnings condition

To qualify for SMP, SPP or SAP your average gross weekly earnings during the 'relevant period' (see p571) must be at least equal to the lower earnings limit for NI contributions.[24] For the tax year 2005/06 the lower earnings limit is £82 a week (see p827 for the amounts for other years).

- For **SMP** or **SPP** (birth), it is the lower earnings limit in force at the end of the 15th week before the EWC that is used (see p587), unless your baby is born prior to or during the 15th week before the EWC, in which case the lower earnings limit in force immediately before the week of the birth is used.[25]
- For **SAP** and **SPP** (adoption), it is the lower earnings limit in force at the end of the week in which the adopter (or you, if you are jointly adopting a child with your spouse or partner) is notified by the adoption agency of being matched with the child (see p588).

If your average weekly earnings during the relevant period fall below the lower earnings limit (eg, because you are sick and receiving just SSP) you will not qualify for SMP, SPP or SAP.

See p577 if you have been dismissed because of your pregnancy.

What counts as earnings

As well as your gross wages, bonuses and any overtime pay you receive during the relevant period, your earnings include:[26]

- SSP;
- SMP, SAP and SPP;
- arrears of pay following reinstatement or re-engagement in your job or a continuation of your contract of employment under the Employment Rights Act 1996; *and*
- payment of a protective award under the Trade Union and Labour Relations (Consolidation) Act 1992.

Pay rises

For SMP, if you are awarded a pay rise which affects your wages for any part of the period which runs from the first day of your relevant period (see p571) until the last day of your statutory maternity leave, then your employer should reassess your average earnings to take account of this increase. If you would have been awarded a pay rise but for being on maternity leave, then you are still treated as receiving it. For these purposes 'statutory maternity leave' includes both ordinary and additional maternity leave under the Employment Rights Act 1996. Your employer should recalculate your average weekly earnings as if your earnings in each of the weeks of your relevant period included the increase, and pay any arrears of SMP due to you.[27]

If you become entitled to SMP as a result of the pay rise, your employer should deduct any payments of maternity allowance that you have received for the same period from the SMP you are owed.[28]

This represents a change in the rules regarding treatment of pay rises for SMP following a ruling by the European Court of Justice (ECJ). Prior to 6 April 2005, the regulations stated that only backdated pay rises which were paid for the relevant period should be included in the calculation of your average earnings for SMP. However, the ECJ ruled that the inclusion of a pay rise in the assessment of average earnings should not just be limited to cases where the pay rise is backdated and covers the relevant period, but should include pay rises that are awarded at any time between the beginning of the relevant period and the end of the period of maternity leave.[29] You should therefore seek advice if at some time before the end of your maternity leave you have been awarded a pay rise, and this increase in your wages has not been included in the assessment of your average earnings when calculating your entitlement to SMP.

For SPP and SAP, any part of a backdated pay rise which is paid for the relevant period should be included in the calculation of your average earnings. Your employer should recalculate your average weekly earnings following the rise and pay any arrears of SPP or SAP due to you.[30]

Meaning of the 'relevant period'[31]

For **SMP** and **SPP** (birth) the **'relevant period'** is the period between:

- the last normal payday that falls either:
  - in or before the 15th week before the EWC (see p587); *or*
  - prior to the Sunday immediately before the baby was born (or, if s/he was born on a Sunday, prior to that day),

  whichever is earlier; *and*
- the day after the last normal payday falling at least eight weeks before that.

For **SAP** and **SPP** (adoption), the relevant period is the period between:

- the last normal payday that falls in or before the week in which you or the adopter are notified of being matched with a child for adoption (see p588). For this purpose a week runs from Sunday to Saturday; *and*
- the day after the last normal payday falling at least eight weeks before that.

In practice this normally means an average based on two months' earnings.

Your average weekly earnings are calculated by adding together your gross earnings during the relevant period, *and either*:[32]

- dividing by the number of weeks covered by the payments (if you are weekly paid); *or*

- dividing by the number of calendar months in the relevant period (to the nearest number of whole months), multiplying by 12 and dividing by 52 (if you are paid at intervals of one or more calendar months); *or*
- dividing by the number of days in the relevant period and multiplying by seven (if you are paid at irregular intervals).

Ceasing work

In order to qualify for SMP or SAP you must have ceased work. (But even for SPP – just as for SMP and SAP – your employer does not have to pay you benefit for any particular week in which you do any work for them – see below). Ceasing work does not necessarily mean ending your employment; it can mean having the right not to attend work for a period either by statute or agreement and so includes starting your period of maternity or adoption leave.[33]

It is not necessary for you to intend to return to work after your maternity, paternity or adoption leave to qualify for SMP, SPP or SAP.

See p577 if you give up your job or have been dismissed.

Working during your statutory maternity, paternity or adoption pay period

Working for the employer who is paying you benefit

If, during the maternity, paternity or adoption pay period (see p574), you work for the employer who is paying you SMP, SPP or SAP, you lose a week's benefit for every week in which you work, even if you only work for part of the week. This applies even if you are working for the employer under a different contract than the one you had before your maternity, paternity or adoption pay period began.[34] You lose SMP at the lower rate first – see p573.

For SMP, if you go back to work for your employer but you are subsequently off work sick during the maternity pay period you will be entitled to SMP rather than SSP for each week in which you are off work for a whole week. If, after your maternity pay period has ended, you are still off work for medical reasons you may qualify for incapacity benefit (IB – see Chapter 12) or possibly SSP (see Chapter 24).

Working for another employer

The general rule is that if you work for another employer (who is not liable to pay you SMP, SPP or SAP) while on maternity, paternity or adoption leave you lose your entitlement to SMP, SPP or SAP for the week in which you work and for any subsequent week.[35]

However, this rule is subject to two exceptions:

- For SMP, if the work is done while you are on maternity leave but before your baby is born your entitlement to SMP is unaffected.[36]

- For SMP, SPP and SAP, any work that you do for such an employer does not affect your entitlement to SMP, SPP or SAP if you were also working for that employer:
  - in the 15th week before the EWC, for SMP and SPP (birth); *or*
  - in the week in which you or your spouse or partner were notified that you had been matched with a child for adoption, for SPP (adoption) and SAP.[37]

You should notify the employer paying you SMP, SPP, or SAP of any work that you do for another employer within seven days of the first day in your maternity, paternity or adoption pay period on which you do such work. For SPP and SAP, your employer has the right to request this information in writing.[38]

2. The rules about your age

You must be 16 or over to get SMP, SPP or SAP.[39]

3. Claiming for others

You are not entitled to an increase in SMP, SPP or SAP for any dependants that you have.

4. The amount of benefit

	Period of payment	*Amount*
SMP	First six weeks	90% of average weekly earnings
	Remaining 20 weeks (but see below)	Lesser of £106 or 90% of average weekly earnings
SPP	Two weeks	Lesser of £106 or 90% of average weekly earnings
SAP	26 weeks	Lesser of £106 or 90% of average weekly earnings

Statutory maternity pay

Statutory maternity pay (SMP) lasts for up to 26 weeks. For the first six weeks it is paid at the 'earnings-related' rate of 90 per cent of your average weekly earnings in the relevant period (see p571), and for the remaining 20 weeks you receive either £106 a week or the earnings-related rate, whichever is lower.[40]

If you are on maternity leave, you should claim national insurance (NI) credits for any week in which your maternity pay falls below the lower earnings limit (see p840) by writing to your local Revenue National Insurance Contributions Office. It is very important to do this. If you do not, your future entitlement to contributory benefits such as retirement pension may be affected.

Statutory paternity pay and statutory adoption pay

Both statutory paternity pay (SPP) and statutory adoption pay (SAP) are paid at the same rate. The amount you receive is either 90 per cent of your average weekly earnings calculated over the relevant period (see p571) or £106 a week, whichever is less.[41]

Period of payment

Statutory maternity pay[42]

The period during which SMP is paid is called the 'maternity pay period'. The maternity pay period normally starts on the Sunday after you stop work and begin your maternity leave and lasts for up to 26 weeks. The earliest it can begin is at the start of the 11th week before the expected week of childbirth (EWC), unless your baby is born before this and the latest is the Sunday after your baby is actually born. Within these limits, when your SMP starts is normally up to you. However:

- if your baby is born before you planned to start your maternity pay period then your SMP will run from the day after you have your baby;
- if you are off work with a pregnancy-related absence in the four weeks immediately before your EWC, your SMP will start on the day after the first day of such absence in those four weeks. This does not apply if your absence is not pregnancy-related;[43]
- if you leave your job before your maternity pay period has started but in or after the 11th week before your EWC, your SMP will start on the Sunday after your job ends.[44]

Once your maternity pay period has begun, the actual date of your baby's birth will not affect your SMP. If the birth takes place earlier than expected, it does not entitle you to more than the 26 weeks' maximum period of SMP – the maternity pay period simply starts and ends sooner.

Statutory paternity pay

SPP can be paid for a maximum of two consecutive weeks – called the paternity pay period – although you can choose to receive it for just one week, if you prefer.[45] The earliest SPP can be paid is the from the child's date of birth, for SPP (birth), or the date of the child's placement for adoption, for SPP (adoption), and the latest is eight weeks after those dates. If the child is born before the EWC (see p587), the latest SPP (birth) can be paid is eight weeks after the first day of the EWC.[46]

As long as you request that your SPP be paid within this period and you give your employer sufficient notice of when you want it to be paid (see p582), you can choose when you want you SPP to begin. You may specify that you want it to begin either on:[47]

- a particular date; *or*
- the day of the baby's birth, or the day of the child's placement for adoption (without specifying an actual date); *or*
- a day falling a certain number of days after that (without specifying an actual date).

If you have chosen to start your paternity pay period either on the day that the baby is born or on the day that the child is placed for adoption but you are at work on that day, your paternity pay period will begin on the next day. See p572 if you work for the employer paying you SPP or for another employer during your paternity pay period. See p577 if you give up or lose your job.

Statutory adoption pay

You can receive SAP for a maximum of 26 weeks – called the adoption pay period. The earliest the adoption pay period can begin is 14 days before the day you expect the child to be placed with you (unless the child is actually placed with you earlier than expected when, even if you have not given the normal period of notice of your intention to claim SAP, your SAP will start from the date of placement). The latest date on which your SAP can normally start is on the date of placement. As long as you request that your SAP starts within that period and give your employer the required period of notice (see p584), you can choose for the 26-week adoption pay period to begin either:[48]

- on a particular date (as long as it is not a date falling after the expected date of placement or more than 14 days before it); *or*
- on the day of placement (without specifying an actual date). If it turns out that you are working on that day your adoption pay period will begin on the next day.

However, your adoption pay period may start on a different date than the one you have chosen in the following circumstances:

- If you have told your employer that you want your SAP to start on a particular date but the child is placed with you before that date, then the adoption pay period will begin on the date of placement, even if this means you have given less than 28 days' notice of the start date to your employer.[49]
- If you qualify for SAP but your job ends before your adoption pay period was due to start, it will start 14 days before the expected date of placement, or if your job ends after this, on the day after you finish work.[50] In this situation you do not need to give your employer 28 days' notice of the date on which your SAP will begin.

Your adoption pay period may end early if the child either:[51]

- is returned to the adoption agency after being placed with you; *or*
- dies, if this happens after being placed with you for adoption; *or*
- is not actually placed with you but your adoption pay period has already begun.

In these circumstances, your adoption pay period will end eight weeks after the end of the week the child is returned, or dies, or that you are notified that the placement is not to take place, if this is earlier than it would have otherwise ended. In this situation a week runs from Sunday to Saturday.

See p572 if you work for the employer paying you SAP or for another employer during your adoption pay period. See p577 if you give up or lose your job.

More than one job

If you satisfy the conditions of entitlement to SMP, SPP or SAP with more than one employer (or under two or more contracts with the same employer), you can get benefit from each job (although if your earnings from any of your jobs are aggregated for calculating your liability to pay NI contributions, those jobs are counted as one and the amount of SMP, SPP or SAP your employers have to pay is apportioned between them).[52] If your contracts are with different employers you do not have to take maternity, paternity or adoption leave from both jobs at the same time but if you give up one job and continue to work at the other you only get SMP, SPP or SAP for the one you have given up until you give up the other. If you get SMP, SPP or SAP for two or more contracts with the same employer you will only be paid if you do no work under any contract for that employer.

If you are self-employed in one of your jobs you will only get SMP, SPP or SAP for the job in which you are employed. If you receive SMP for one job you will not be entitled to maternity allowance for the same week for the job in which you are self-employed.[53]

5. Special rules for special groups

There are some groups of claimants to whom special rules apply. These are covered below and in Chapters 28 and 26. Special rules apply to you if:

- you are in prison or detention (see p732);[54]
- you are outside Great Britain (GB – see p577);
- you give up your job or have been dismissed (see p577);
- you have been involved in a trade dispute (see p741);
- your baby is stillborn, you have had a multiple birth or adopted more than one child (see p578);
- you have adopted a child from abroad (see p578).

People outside Great Britain

Your entitlement to statutory maternity pay (SMP), statutory paternity pay (SPP) or statutory adoption pay (SAP) is not affected by any absence from GB as long as you meet the qualifying conditions, including being an employee. Even while employed abroad you count as an employee if:[55]

- your employer is required to pay secondary Class 1 national insurance (NI) contributions for you; *or*
- you are employed in another European Economic Area country and, had you been employed in GB, you would have been considered an employee, and the UK is the competent state under European Community legislation (see Chapter 26); *or*
- you are a continental-shelf worker or, in certain circumstances, a mariner.

However, you do not count as an employee if your employer is not present or resident in GB, or does not run a business in GB, or is exempt from the social security legislation by international treaty.[56]

If you give up your job or are dismissed

Special rules may apply to you if you give up your job or are dismissed by your employer.

Your employer is liable to pay you SMP, SPP or SAP if any one of the following apply:[57]

- after your maternity pay period, paternity pay period or adoption pay period (see p574) has started, you give up your job, are dismissed or your job ends. Your employer will continue to be liable to pay you SMP, SPP or SAP until your maternity, paternity or adoption pay period finishes (but see p585 if your employer is insolvent);
- your employer dismisses you at any time if the dismissal was 'solely or mainly' to avoid paying SMP, SPP or SAP and you had been employed by that employer for at least eight continuous weeks. In these circumstances the amount of the earnings-related rate of SMP, SPP or SAP to which you may be entitled (see p573) is calculated using your average earnings for the eight-week period ending with the last day for which you were paid;[58]
- for SMP and SAP only, you satisfy qualifying conditions for SMP or SAP and your job ends for any reason at any time after:
  - the beginning of the 15th week before your expected week of childbirth (EWC), for SMP; *or*
  - the beginning of the week in which you were notified of being matched with a child for adoption, for SAP.

For SMP, if your job ends at any time after the start of the 15th week before your EWC, or for SAP, if it ends before the adoption pay period is due to start, you are not required to have given your employer notice of your intention to take maternity or adoption leave, although you will still need to give your employer information to support your claim as detailed on p581 – eg, evidence of the expected date of birth, for SMP.[59]

If you are dismissed while pregnant or on paternity or adoption leave, seek advice about your right to claim unfair dismissal.

If you start work for another employer after giving up your job or being dismissed, see p572.

Stillbirths and multiple births and adoptions

If your baby is stillborn after the 24th week of pregnancy, SMP or SPP (birth) is payable in the same way as for a live birth.[60] If the baby is stillborn earlier, this is treated as a miscarriage and SMP or SPP (birth) is not payable. SSP (see Chapter 24) or incapacity benefit (see Chapter 12) may be paid if you are incapable of work. If the baby is born alive but then dies (even after only a moment), then this is a live birth and you can get SMP or SPP (birth) even if it happens in or before the 24th week of pregnancy.

No additional SMP, SPP, or SAP is payable if you (or your wife or partner) give birth to more than one baby, or have more than one child placed with you for adoption, unless this happens as part of a different adoption arrangement.[61]

If you are adopting a child from abroad

You may qualify for SPP (adoption) if you have jointly adopted a child from abroad with your spouse or partner, or if your spouse or partner has adopted a child from abroad (an overseas adoption – see p588). Alternatively, you may be entitled to SAP for an overseas adoption if you have adopted or jointly adopted a child from abroad. Where such a placement is made under UK law the normal rules of entitlement to SPP and SAP apply.

In order to qualify for SPP or SAP for an overseas adoption you must satisfy the normal rules of entitlement described in this chapter with the modifications explained below. As you will not have been matched with a child for adoption by UK authorities under UK law, it is primarily the rules that refer to the date of placement and the date of notification of being matched for adoption (both of which do not apply to overseas adoptions) that are modified. In order to qualify for SPP or SAP for an overseas adoption the child must have entered GB on or after 6 April 2003.[62]

Continuous employment and overseas adoptions

To qualify for SPP (adoption) or SAP for an overseas adoption, you must have been employed by your employer for a continuous period of at least 26 weeks.[63] In addition, for SPP (adoption) you must have been continuously employed by the same employer from the end of a week in which you met the 26-week continuous employment rule, or from the end of the week in which official notification regarding the adoption was sent to you, if that is later, up to the date the child enters GB.

Earnings condition and overseas adoptions

To satisfy the earnings condition (see p570) the relevant period for calculating your average weekly earnings is the period between:

- your last normal payday in or before a week in which you met the 26-week continuous employment rule, or the week in which official notification regarding the adoption was sent to you or the adopter (see p588), if that is later; *and*
- the day after the last normal payday falling at least eight weeks before that.

Your average earnings over this period must have been at least equal to the NI lower earnings limit (see p827). The lower earnings limit that is used is either the one that was in force at the end of the week in which official notification regarding the adoption was sent to you or, if this is later, the one that was in force at the end of the week in which you met the 26-week continuous employment rule.[64]

Working for another employer and overseas adoptions

If, during your paternity or adoption pay period, you work for another employer who is not liable to pay you SPP or SAP, you will lose your entitlement to SPP or SAP for the week in which you work and any subsequent week unless you were working for that employer in the week in which you received official notification regarding the adoption (see p588).[65]

Period of payment for overseas adoptions

The earliest that SPP can be paid is from the date the child enters GB and the latest is eight weeks after that.

As long as payment falls within this period and you have given your employer the correct period of notice (see p582) you can either choose a particular date on which you want your SPP to start or you can ask that it starts on the day the child enters GB without giving an actual date.[66]

If you are claiming SAP, as long as you have given your employer the correct period of notice (see p584) you can ask your employer to start paying SAP from either:[67]

- a specific date (which is no later than 28 days after the date that the child enters GB); *or*
- the day the child enters GB (without giving an actual date).

If you give up your job or are dismissed

For SAP, if your job ends, for any reason, before your adoption pay period has begun your employer is still liable to pay you SAP as long as you satisfy the qualifying conditions. However, if your adoption pay period begins more than six months after your job ends the Revenue should pay your SAP instead, unless you subsequently become entitled to SAP from another employer within the adoption pay period, when that new employer will then take over responsibility for paying your SAP.[68]

Making a claim for SPP for an overseas adoption

In order to qualify for SPP you must give your employer the notice and information described on p582. However, instead of giving your employer notice of the date of placement or expected placement of the child and of the date of notification of being matched with the child for adoption, you must instead give your employer:[69]

- a declaration stating that you have received official notification (see p588) regarding the adoption; *and*
- notice of the date that you expect the child to enter GB, or the date s/he did enter GB if s/he has already done so.

Making a claim for SAP for an overseas adoption

In order to qualify for SAP you must give your employer the following notice and information at least 28 days before your adoption pay period is due to start, or if that is not practicable as soon as is reasonably practicable after that date:[70]

- a copy of the official notification regarding the adoption (see p588);
- a declaration that you wish to receive SAP, not SPP;
- the date that you expect the child to enter GB, or if s/he has already arrived the date s/he entered GB.

Additional information to be provided for an overseas adoption

In addition to the information outlined above, to qualify for SPP and SAP for an overseas adoption you must inform your employer of:[71]

- the date on which you (or your spouse or partner) received official notification regarding the adoption (see p588).You should notify your employer of this either within 28 days of:
  - receiving the official notification; *or*
  - being employed by your employer for 26 continuous weeks, if that is later; *and*
- the date of the child's arrival in GB, within 28 days of her/his arrival. For SAP, but not for SPP, you must also give evidence of the child's arrival to your employer (eg, airline tickets or the child's passport showing the date of entry).

If, after you have given the information on p580, your employer decides that you are not entitled to SPP or SAP s/he must provide you with details of the decision and the reasons for it within 28 days of the date you provided the information.[72]

6. Claims and backdating

You must claim statutory maternity pay (SMP), statutory paternity pay (SPP) and statutory adoption pay (SAP) from your employer rather than from the Revenue. The rules for claiming are described below. It may be possible to get your claim backdated (see p585).

Making a claim

To qualify for SMP, SPP or SAP you must give your employer certain notice and information. The rules differ according to which benefit you are claiming and are detailed below and on pp582 and 584.

Notification sent to your employer in a properly addressed and pre-paid letter is treated as having been given on the day it is put in the post.[73]

It is important to remember that there are different notice requirements for entitlement to statutory maternity, paternity and adoption leave. In addition, if your employer offers its own maternity, paternity or adoption pay scheme in addition to SMP, SPP or SAP, the notice requirements for this scheme may also be different. Check this with your employer.

If the Revenue requests information from you in connection with your claim, see p587.

Notice and information for statutory maternity pay

In order to qualify for SMP you must give your employer:

- notice (in writing if your employer requests this) of the date from which you expect your employer to pay you SMP. This notice must be given at least 28 days before you expect your employer to start paying you, or if that is not practicable, as soon as reasonably practicable after that.[74] See p574 for when it is possible for your benefit to start; *and*
- evidence of the expected date of birth. You must provide this evidence no more than three weeks after the start of your maternity pay period. This time limit can be extended to the end of the 13th week of the maternity pay period if you have good cause for the delay.[75]

The meaning of 'as soon as reasonably practicable' and 'good cause' is not defined in the regulations – you would have to show that your delay was reasonable given your circumstances.

The details of the expected date of birth are on Form MAT B1, which is issued by your doctor or a registered midwife. The earliest you can be issued with a MAT

B1 form is the start of the 20th week before your expected week of childbirth (EWC). Your employer needs to be given this form. If you do not have a MAT B1 your employer can accept other medical evidence, but it must be substantially like Form MAT B1.[76]

If you give your employer less notice than this or you do not provide the above evidence within the time limit your employer may not pay you SMP. If you think your employer's decision is wrong you can challenge it (see p586).

If your employment ends in or after the 15th week before your baby is due see p577.

If your baby is born prematurely

If your baby is born prematurely, before the date you planned to start your maternity pay period, you may not have been able to give your employer any notice, or sufficient notice, of the date you wanted your SMP to start. Even if you did give your employer the correct notice, your maternity pay period will normally begin on the day after you had your baby, rather than the day that you planned.

To qualify for SMP you must inform your employer (in writing if your employer requests this) of the date on which your baby was born if either:

- your baby is born during or before the 15th week before your EWC; *or*
- your baby is born before your maternity pay period was due to begin and, although you had informed your employer of the date from which you wanted your SMP to start, the baby was born before that date.

You must do this within four weeks of the birth or if that is not practicable as soon as reasonably practicable after that.[77]

In addition, if your baby is born before you intended to start your maternity pay period you must give your employer evidence of the week in which you had the baby (eg, a birth certificate) as well as evidence of the expected date of birth, within three weeks of the start of your maternity pay period. This time limit can be extended to the end of the 13th week of the maternity pay period if you have good cause for the delay.[78]

Notice and information for statutory paternity pay

In order to qualify for SPP you must tell your employer in writing:

- when you would like your SPP to start. See p574 for when it is possible for your benefit to start; *and*
- whether you want to get SPP for one week or two.

You must give your employer this information at least 28 days before your paternity pay period is due to start, or if that is not practicable, as soon as is reasonably practicable after that date (see p585).[79]

Within the same time limit you must also give your employer the following information, in writing:

For SPP (birth):

- the EWC (or the date of birth, if the child has already been born); *and*
- a declaration stating that:
  - you will care for the child or support the child's mother while getting SPP; *and either*
  - you are the child's father and will have responsibility for her/his upbringing; *or*
  - you are the spouse or partner of the child's mother and, apart from the mother's responsibility, you will have the main responsibility for the upbringing of the child.

For SPP (adoption):

- the date you expect the child to be placed for adoption (or the date s/he was placed, if the placement has already happened); *and*
- the date on which the adopter was notified that the child had been matched with her/him for adoption (see p588); *and*
- a declaration stating that:
  - you and your spouse or partner are jointly adopting a child, or your partner or spouse is adopting a child; *and*
  - you have, or expect to have, the main responsibility for the upbringing of the child (apart from the responsibility of the adopter or, if you are jointly adopting the child, of the other adopter); *and*
  - while getting SPP you intend to care for the child or support the child's adopter; *and*
  - you elect to be paid SPP rather than SAP.

You may use an SC3 form for SPP (birth), or an SC4 form for SPP (adoption), to provide the above information to your employer. These forms are produced by the Revenue and are available on the Revenue's website (see Appendix 1).

If you give your employer less notice than this or you do not provide the above information within the time limit your SPP can begin later, once the necessary time limit for providing the notice or information has passed, as long as payment would still fall within the eight-week period in which SPP can be paid (see p574).

In addition, if you notified your employer that you want to start your paternity pay period:

- on the day the child is born or is placed with you for adoption, or on a day falling a certain number of days after the birth or placement, then you need to tell your employer the date the child was born or the date on which the placement occurred, as soon as is reasonably practicable after that date;[80]

- on a specific date, but the child is not born or placed with you until after that date then you must give you employer notice of the new date on which you want your paternity pay period to start, as soon as is reasonably practicable.[81]

Notice and information for statutory adoption pay

In order to qualify for SAP you must give your employer the following notice and information at least 28 days before your adoption pay period is due to start, or if that is not practicable, as soon as is reasonably practicable after that date (see p585):[82]

- notice (in writing if your employer requests this) of:
  - when you want your SAP to start (see p575 for when it is possible for your benefit to start);
  - the date on which you expect the child to be placed with you for adoption;
- a written declaration that you want to receive SAP rather than SPP; *and*
- documents from the adoption agency giving:
  - its name and address and your name and address; *and*
  - the date on which the child is expected to be (or was) placed with you; *and*
  - the date on which it informed you that the child would be placed with you for adoption.

  The adoption agency should provide you with a 'matching certificate' which will give this information.

If you give your employer less notice than this or you do not provide the above information within the time limit your employer may not pay you SAP. In this situation it may be possible to argue that your SAP should start later, once the necessary time limit for providing the notice or information has passed, as long as payment would still fall within the adoption pay period (see p575). This may mean, however, that you might not be entitled to SAP for a full 26 weeks. If you are in this position, seek advice. If you think your employer's decision is wrong you can challenge it (see p586).

In addition to the above notice, if you choose to start your adoption pay period on the day the child is placed with you then you must give your employer further notice of the date on which the placement occurs, as soon as is reasonably practicable.[83]

If your employment ends before your adoption pay period begins, see p577.

Who should claim

If you are entitled to SMP, SPP or SAP but are not well enough to deal with your own affairs, the Revenue can appoint someone else to act for you.[84] This person is your 'appointee' (see p1075). An application for someone to be your appointee should be made to your local Revenue National Insurance Contributions Office.

If you claim the wrong benefit

If you are sick with a pregnancy-related illness in the four weeks before the week your baby is due and you make a claim to your employer for SSP, your employer can start your maternity leave (even if it is sooner than you had planned) and pay you SMP. It cannot do this if your illness is *not* pregnancy-related.

If you make a claim for SMP and it is turned down, your claim can be treated as a claim for maternity allowance (MA) in certain circumstances (see p461).

Backdating your claim

In order to qualify for **SMP**, **SPP** or **SAP** you must normally give your employer at least 28 days' notice of when you want your benefit to start. If you are not able to do so, your notice must be given as soon as is reasonably practicable after that date. If your employer accepts that you gave notice as soon as was practicable, then your SMP, SPP or SAP should be paid from the day you have chosen to start your maternity, paternity or adoption pay period (see p574). In order to qualify you will also have to give your employer the information and evidence detailed on pp581-584 within the time limits outlined on those pages.

What amounts to 'as soon as is reasonably practicable' is not defined in the regulations – you would have to show that your delay was reasonable given your circumstances. If you disagree with your employer's decision you can ask the Revenue to consider your entitlement (see p586).

7. Getting paid

Your employer usually pays SMP, SPP or SAP in the same way as your normal wage or salary.[85] If you are also entitled to contractual maternity, paternity or adoption pay from your employer, SMP, SPP or SAP will form part of your payments. Any payment of SMP, SPP or SAP goes towards discharging your employer's liability to make payments to you for the same period that are required by your contract.[86] Your employer cannot pay you SMP, SPP or SAP by making a payment in kind, or by providing board and lodging, a service or some other facility.[87]

See p574 for the period over which you can be paid SMP, SPP or SAP.

If your employer is liable to pay you SMP, SPP or SAP but is insolvent, the Revenue should pay you.[88] It is also the Revenue that will pay you if you are entitled to SAP after a period of imprisonment or detention (see p732) or for a period when you were in detention if you were subsequently released without charge, found not guilty or given a non-custodial sentence.[89]

Delays and complaints

See p586 for details of when you can ask the Revenue to make a decision on your entitlement to SMP, SPP or SAP if your employer cannot, or will not, pay you. If the Revenue (or tax appeal commissioners) decides that you are entitled to benefit, your employer may be required to pay you within a certain time. The rules about when your employer should pay are the same as for SSP (see p611).

See p1300 if the Revenue is deciding on your entitlement to SMP, SPP or SAP and you wish to complain about its delay in dealing with your application.

Change of circumstances

You have to keep your employer informed of any change of circumstances which may affect your entitlement, such as starting work for someone else during the maternity, paternity or adoption pay period (see p588).[90]

Overpayments

The rules about overpayments and recovery of overpaid benefit explained in Chapter 41 do not apply to SMP, SPP or SAP.

However, if your employer pays you SMP, SPP or SAP and later decides that you were not entitled to it, they may attempt to recover the sum considered overpaid by making a deduction from your wages. If this happens you should seek advice. You may be able to challenge your employer's decision to make deductions from your wages.

See below if you wish to challenge your employer's decision that you are not entitled to SMP, SPP or SAP.

If your employer decides that you have been paid SMP in error, you should consider claiming maternity allowance (MA) immediately. You may be able to get your MA backdated – see p461.

8. Challenging your employer's decision

If your employer decides you are not entitled to statutory maternity pay (SMP), statutory paternity pay (SPP) or statutory adoption pay (SAP) you must be provided with details of the decision and the reason for it. This information is normally given on an SMP1 form for SMP, a SPP1 form for SPP, or a SAP1 form for SAP.

For **SMP**, your employer must give you this information within seven days of the decision or, if earlier, within 28 days of you notifying your employer of your intention to take maternity leave (or of your baby being born). Your employer must also return your MAT B1 form to you.

If you consider that you are owed SMP by an employer or if you are paid an amount you consider to be wrong, you can also ask for a written statement showing:

- if SMP has been refused, the detailed reason why;

- if SMP is being paid but the amount seems wrong to you, how many weeks they consider it should have been paid for and the amount they consider should have been paid in those weeks.[91]

For **SPP** (birth) the information must be provided by your employer within 28 days of the day you gave them notice of your intended absence or the end of the 15th week before the EWC, if this is later.[92]

For **SAP** and **SPP** (adoption) this information must be given not more than 28 days after the end of the week in which you are notified of having been matched with a child for adoption (see p588). For this purpose, the end of the week falls seven days after the day you were notified.[93]

Your employer should also return any evidence you gave them in connection with your claim for SPP or SAP.

If you disagree with your employer's decision on your entitlement to **SMP**, **SPP** or **SAP**, or if they have failed to make a decision, you can ask the Revenue to make a formal decision on your entitlement. To do this, you should send your request, which should normally be made on an SMP14 form (for SMP), SPP14 form (for SPP) or SAP14 form (for SAP), along with the SMP1, SPP1 or SAP1 form, if you have one of these forms, to your local Revenue National Insurance (NI) Contributions Office within six months of the earliest day for which your SMP, SPP or SAP entitlement is in issue. The rules for challenging a decision are the same as for SSP (see p607). An SMP14, SPP14 or SAP14 can be obtained from your local NI Contributions Office. You can obtain the address of your local NI Contributions Office by telephoning any local office of the Revenue.

If the Revenue requests information from you

If the Revenue is making a decision about your claim for SMP, SPP or SAP, it may request that you supply information to it. You must provide this information within 30 days of receiving the Revenue's request. If you do not provide the information or documents which the Revenue reasonably needs to decide on your entitlement, you may be liable for a penalty of up to £300 and further penalties of up to £60 for each day you fail to produce the information after the initial penalty was imposed.[94] For SMP these penalties apply from 6 April 2005. Until 6 April 2005 the rule for SMP was that you must have provided information requested by the Revenue within 10 days or risk prosecution.

For SPP and SAP notification sent to the Revenue in a properly addressed and pre-paid letter is treated as having been given on the day it is put in the post.[95]

9. Definitions of terms

- The **'expected week of childbirth' (EWC)** (sometimes called the 'expected week of confinement') is the week, starting on a Sunday, in which your baby is due to be born.

- The **'relevant period'** is the period which is used to calculate your average earnings for statutory maternity pay (SMP), statutory paternity pay (SPP) and statutory adoption pay (SAP). See p571 for how the period is worked out.
- **'SPP (birth)'** means statutory paternity pay (SPP) which you qualify for on the basis either of your spouse or partner giving birth to a child, or you being the father of a child.
- **'SPP (adoption)'** is SPP that you qualify for on the basis that a child has been, or is to be, placed with your spouse or partner for adoption or with you and your spouse or partner for joint adoption.
- The **'maternity pay period'** is the period of up to 26 weeks during which SMP is payable. See p574 for when it may start.
- The **'adoption pay period'** is the period of up to 26 weeks when statutory adoption pay is payable. See p575 for when it can start.
- The **'paternity pay period'** is the period of one or two weeks when SPP is payable. See p574 for when it can start.
- You are **'matched for adoption'** when an adoption agency decides that you would be a suitable adoptive parent for a particular child. The adoption agency should be able to provide you with a **matching certificate** to verify that you have been matched with a child for adoption.
- **'Overseas adoption'** is one in which the child enters Great Britain for the purpose of the adoption and the adoption does not involve the placement of the child under UK law.
- **'Official notification regarding the adoption'** is a letter issued by or on behalf of the Welsh Assembly, Scottish Ministers or the Secretary of State informing you that they have issued, or are going to issue, a certificate to the overseas authority confirming that you are approved for adoption.

Example

Rita's baby is due on Saturday 23 July 2005. The following dates apply:
– The 'expected week of childbirth' begins on the Sunday before – ie, Sunday 17 July 2005.
– The first week before the 'expected week of childbirth' begins on Sunday 10 July 2005, the second on Sunday 3 July 2005 and so on.
– The 11th week before the 'expected week of childbirth' begins on Sunday 1 May 2005. This is important because it is normally the earliest date from which Rita can be paid SMP (or maternity allowance).
– The 15th week before the 'expected week of childbirth' runs from Sunday 3 April to Saturday 9 April 2005.

Calculating the weeks can be confusing. To help you with this, Appendix 5 contains a table of dates for all the weeks in 2005/06.

10. Tax, tax credits and other benefits

Statutory maternity pay (SMP), statutory paternity pay (SPP) and statutory adoption pay (SAP) are treated as earnings and you pay tax and national insurance contributions as appropriate.[96]

Tax credits

If your income is low and you are receiving SMP, SPP, or SAP, or you are on ordinary maternity, paternity or adoption leave you may also qualify for working tax credit (WTC – see Chapter 50) as long as you were in full-time paid work immediately before your SMP, SPP, or SAP began, or before your maternity, paternity or adoption leave started (see p1348).

If you did not count as being in full-time paid work immediately before your SMP, SPP, or SAP started or before going on maternity, paternity or adoption leave but you were working for at least 16 hours a week you may qualify for WTC from the date of birth or adoption of your child.

If you are entitled to WTC, you may be able to get help with the cost of childcare for your new baby or the child placed with you for adoption even before you return to work (see p1360).

If you have a dependent child you may also qualify for child tax credit (CTC – see Chapter 49).

The first £100 of your weekly SMP, SPP or SAP is ignored when calculating your entitlement to WTC and CTC, and any SMP, SPP or SAP you receive over £100 is counted as employment income.

Means-tested benefits

If you have a low income and are under 60, you may be able to get income support (IS – see Chapter 13) while you are on maternity, paternity or adoption leave. See p296 for details of whether you may qualify for IS while on leave. If you are 60 or over you may instead qualify for pension credit (PC – see Chapter 18). If you have a low income you may also be entitled to housing benefit (HB – see Chapter 10) and council tax benefit (CTB – see Chapter 6). If you are getting SMP, SPP, or SAP you may be able to get an allowance for childcare costs deducted from your earnings when calculating your entitlement to HB and CTB – see p965.

You cannot claim jobseeker's allowance (JSA) if you are getting SMP, or if you are on paternity or ordinary adoption leave, because you are treated as unavailable for work, but your partner may qualify.[97] If you are a member of a couple who would normally have to make a joint claim for JSA (see p394) then:

- if you are incapable of work because of your pregnancy but you are not getting SMP (or maternity allowance – MA), and it is earlier than the 11th week before your expected week of childbirth (EWC), you do not need to meet the labour market conditions – only your partner must;

- your partner can receive JSA for you both without you needing to make a joint claim if you are getting SMP (or MA), or from the 11th week before your EWC until 15 weeks after the baby is born.

Your net SMP, SPP or SAP (after deductions for Class 1 national insurance (NI), tax and half of any occupational or personal pension payments), is taken into account in full for IS and income-based JSA. SMP, SPP and SAP are treated as earnings for HB and CTB, and so you may be entitled to an earnings disregard.

For PC, your net payments of SMP, SPP or SAP (after any deductions for tax, NI and half of any occupational or personal pension payments) will be taken into account as earnings.[98]

Non-means-tested benefits

You cannot get contribution-based JSA if you are receiving SMP (see Chapter 15), or if you are on paternity or ordinary adoption leave. You cannot get statutory sick pay (SSP) when you are receiving SMP. See p603 for how your SSP entitlement is affected if you are pregnant. You cannot receive SPP or SAP for any week in which you are entitled to SSP.[99]

Incapacity benefit

While you are pregnant you can be treated as incapable of work for incapacity benefit (IB) purposes (and so you may qualify for IB) in the circumstances explained on p768.[100]

You can qualify for SMP or SAP and for the higher rate of short-term or long-term IB at the same time, but your IB (including any increase for a dependant) will be reduced by the gross amount of SMP or SAP you receive. If you are only entitled to the lower rate of short-term IB you will not qualify for IB while you are entitled to SMP or SAP.[101]

Days on which you were entitled to SMP or SAP in the circumstances described on p274 count when calculating whether you were entitled to the higher rate of short-term IB or long-term IB.

Passports and other sources of help

If you are receiving IS, income-based JSA, PC, the disability or severe disability element of WTC, or CTC paid at a higher rate than the family element you may be entitled to a Sure Start maternity grant of £500 per child from the social fund. You might be able to get other help from the discretionary social fund (see Chapters 21 and 22).

If you or your partner receive IS, income-based JSA, or, in some circumstances, CTC, you qualify for free school meals for your children (see p18).

For information on your possible entitlement to free prescriptions, free NHS dental treatment and free milk and vitamins (or from summer 2005 if you live in certain areas: **'Healthy Start'** welfare food vouchers), see Chapter 9.

Notes

1. Who can claim

1 ss171ZB(4) and 171ZL(4) SSCBA 1992
2 ss164 and 165 SSCBA 1992
3 s164(2)(c) SSCBA 1992
4 s164(2)(a) SSCBA 1992
5 s164(2)(b) SSCBA 1992
6 ss171ZA(2) and (3), 171ZB(2) and (3), 171ZC and 171ZE(4)-(7) SSCBA 1992; regs 3(1), 4 and 11 SPPSAP(G) Regs; reg 4(2)(b) and (c) PAL Regs
7 Regs 4 and 11 SPPSAP(G) Regs; reg 2 PAL Regs
8 s171ZL(2)-(4) SSCBA 1992; reg 3(2) SPPSAP(G) Regs
9 ss171(1), 171ZJ(1) and 171ZS(1) SSCBA 1992; reg 17 SMP Regs; reg 32 SPPSAP(G) Regs
10 ss164(6) and (7), 171ZF and 171ZO SSCBA 1992
11 Regs 2 and 5 SMP(PAM) Regs; regs 3, 5 and 6 SPPSAP(PAM) Regs; reg 3 SPP(A)&SAP(AO)(PAM) Regs
12 Reg 17(3) SMP Regs; reg 32(3) SPPSAP(G) Regs
13 ss164(2)(a) and 171ZA(2)(b) SSCBA 1992
14 s171ZA(2)(d) and (3) SSCBA 1992
15 Reg 4(2)(a) SMP Regs; reg 5 SPPSAP(G) Regs
16 Reg 11(4) SMP Regs
17 ss171ZB(2)(b), (d) and (3) and 171ZL(2)(b) and (3) SSCBA 1992
18 ss171ZB(2) and (3) and 171ZL(2) and (3) SSCBA 1992; reg 2(2) SPPSAP(G) Regs
19 Reg 33(4) SPPSAP(G) Regs
20 Reg 11(1) SMP Regs; reg 33 SPPSAP(G) Regs
21 Reg 11(3A) SMP Regs; reg 33(3) SPPSAP(G) Regs
22 Reg 14 SMP Regs; reg 36 SPPSAP(G) Regs
23 Reg 12 SMP Regs; reg 34 SPPSAP(G) Regs
24 ss164(2)(b), 171(4), 171ZA(2)(c), 171ZB(2)(c), 171ZJ(6)-(8), 171ZL(2)(d) and 171ZS(6)-(8) SSCBA 1992
25 Reg 4(2)(b) SMP Regs; reg 5(b) SPPSAP(G) Regs
26 Reg 20 SMP Regs; reg 39 SPPSAP(G) Regs
27 Reg 21(7) SMP Regs
28 Reg 21B SMP Regs
29 *Alabaster v Woolwich plc and Secretary of State for Social Security* [2002] EWCA Civ 211; *Alabaster v Woolwich plc and Secretary of State for Social Security* C-147/02 [2004] ECJ
30 Reg 40(7) SPPSAP(G) Regs
31 Reg 21 SMP Regs; reg 40 SPPSAP(G) Regs
32 Reg 21(5) and (6) SMP Regs; reg 40(5) and (6) SPPSAP(G) Regs
33 CA29, *Statutory Maternity Pay Manual for Employers*, April 2002, para 27
34 ss165(4) and (5), 171ZE(5) and (6) and 171ZN(3) and (4) SSCBA 1992
35 ss165(6), 171ZE(7) and 171ZN(5) SSCBA 1992; reg 8(2) SMP Regs; regs 17(1) and 26(1) SPPSAP(G) Regs
36 s165(6) SSCBA 1992; reg 8(2) SMP Regs
37 Reg 8(1) SMP Regs; regs 10, 16 and 25 SPPSAP(G) Regs
38 Reg 24 SMP Regs; regs 17(2) and (3) and 26(2) and (3) SPPSAP(G) Regs

2. The rules about your age

39 ss171, 171ZJ(2) and 171ZS(2) SSCBA 1992

4. The amount of benefit

40 s166 SSCBA 1992
41 Regs 2 and 3 SPPSAP(WR) Regs
42 s165 SSCBA 1992; reg 2 SMP Regs
43 Reg 2(4) SMP Regs; regs 1(2) and 2(5) Social Security, Statutory Maternity Pay and Statutory Sick Pay (Miscellaneous Amendments) Regs 2002 No.2690
44 Reg 2(6) SMP Regs
45 s171ZE(2) SSCBA 1992; regs 6(3) and 12(3) SPPSAP(G) Regs
46 s171ZE(3) SSCBA 1992; regs 8 and 14 SPPSAP(G) Regs
47 Regs 6 and 12 SPPSAP(G) Regs
48 s171ZN(2) SSCBA 1992; reg 21 SPPSAP(G) Regs
49 Reg 21(3) and (4) SSPSAP(G) Regs
50 Reg 29 SPPSAP(G) Regs
51 Reg 22 SPPSAP(G) Regs

52 ss164(3), 171ZD(1) and 171ZM(1) SSCBA 1992; reg 18 SMP Regs; reg 38 SPPSAP(G) Regs
53 s35(1)(d) SSCBA 1992

5. **Special rules for special groups**
54 Reg 9 SMP Regs; regs 18(c) and 27(1)(c) and (2) SPPSAP(G) Regs
55 Regs 2, 2A, 7 and 8 SMP(PAM) Regs; regs 3, 4, 8 and 9 SPPSAP(PAM) Regs
56 Reg 3 SMP(PAM) Regs; reg 17(3) SMP Regs; reg 2 SPPSAP(PAM) Regs; reg 32(3) SPPSAP(G) Regs
57 ss164(2)(a) and (8), 171ZA(2)(b), 171ZB(2)(b), 171ZD(2), 171ZL(2) and 171ZM(2) SSCBA 1992; regs 2(6) and 3(1) SMP Regs; regs 29 and 30 SPPSAP(G) Regs
58 Reg 3 SMP Regs; regs 20 and 30 SPPSAP(G) Regs
59 Reg 23(4)&(5) SMP Regs; reg 29 SPPSAP(G) Regs
60 ss171(1) and 171ZA(5) SSCBA 1992
61 ss171(1), 171ZA(4), 171ZB(6) 171ZL(5) SSCBA 1992
62 Reg 4 SPP(A)&SAP(AO)(No.2) Regs
63 s171ZB(2) and (3)and 171ZL(2) and (3) SSCBA 1992 as modified by regs 2 and 3 and Schs 1 and 2 Social Security Contributions and Benefits Act 1992 (Application of Parts 12ZA and 12ZB to Adoptions from Overseas) Regulations 2003 SI No.499
64 s171ZB(2) and (3)and 171ZL(2) and (3) SSCBA 1992 as modified by regs 2 and 3 and Schs 1 and 2 Social Security Contributions and Benefits Act 1992 (Application of Parts 12ZA and 12ZB to Adoptions from Overseas) Regulations 2003 SI No.499; reg 40 SPPSAP(G) Regs, as modified by reg 3 SPP(A)&SAP(AO)(No.2) Regs
65 Regs 10 and 16 SPP(A)&SAP(AO)(No.2) Regs
66 s171ZE(2) and (3), as modified by reg 2 and Sch 1 Social Security Contributions and Benefits Act 1992 (Application of Parts 12ZA and 12ZB to Adoptions from Overseas) Regulations 2003 SI No.499; regs 6 and 8 SPP(A)&SAP(AO)(No.2) Regs
67 Reg 12 SPP(A)&SAP(AO)(No.2) Regs
68 Reg 17 SPP(A)&SAP(AO)(No.2) Regs
69 Reg 9 SPP(A)&SAP(AO)(No.2) Regs
70 Reg 15 SPP(A)&SAP(AO)(No.2) Regs
71 Regs 7, 14 and 15(1)(c) SPP(A)&SAP(AO)(No.2) Regs
72 Reg 11 SPPSAP(A) Regs as modified by reg 3(4) and (5) Statutory Paternity Pay (Adoption) and Statutory Adoption Pay (Adoptions from Overseas) (Administration) Regulations 2003 SI 2003 No.1192

6. **Claims and backdating**
73 Regs 22(4) and 23(3) SMP Regs; reg 47 SPPSAP(G) Regs
74 ss164(4) and (5) SSCBA 1992
75 Reg 22 SMP Regs
76 Reg 2 SMP(ME) Regs
77 Reg 23 SMP Regs
78 Reg 22(1) and (2) SMP Regs
79 171ZC(1) and (2) SSCBA 1992; regs 9 and 15 SPPSAP(G) Regs
80 Regs 7(1) and 13(1) SPPSAP(G) Regs
81 Regs 7(2) and 13(2) SPPSAP(G) Regs
82 s171ZL(6) and (7) SSCBA 1992; regs 23 and 24 SPPSAP(G) Regs
83 Reg 23 SPPSAP(G) Regs
84 Reg 31 SMP Regs; reg 46 SPPSAP(G) Regs

7. **Getting paid**
85 Reg 27 SMP Regs; reg 41 SPPSAP(G) Regs
86 ss171ZG(2)and 171ZP(5) and Sch 13 para 3 SSCBA 1992
87 Reg 27 SMP Regs; reg 41 SPPSAP(G) Regs
88 Reg 7(3) SMP Regs; reg 43(2) SPPSAP(G) Regs
89 Reg 44 SPPSAP(G) Regs
90 Reg 24 SMP Regs; regs 17(2) and 26(2) SPPSAP(G) Regs

8. **Challenging your employer's decision**
91 s15(2) SSAA 1992
92 Reg 11 SPPSAP(A) Regs
93 Reg 11 SPPSAP(A) Regs
94 s11(1) and (2) Employment Act 2002; s113A SSAA 1992 as inserted by s9 National Insurance Contributions and Statutory Payments Act 2004; reg 14 SPPSAP(A) Regs
95 Reg 47 SPPSAP(G) Regs

10. **Tax, tax credits and other benefits**
96 s4(1)(a)(ii)-(iv) SSCBA 1992
97 Reg 15(bc) and (c) JSA Regs
98 Regs 15(1)(p)-(r) and 17A(2) SPC Regs
99 Regs 18(a) and 27(1)(a) SPPSAP(G) Regs
100 Reg 14 SS(IFW) Regs
101 Sch 13 para 1 SSCBA 1992; reg 7A(4) and 7B(4) SS(IB) Regs

Chapter 24

Statutory sick pay

This chapter covers:

Statutory sick pay (SSP) is a benefit which is paid to employees for up to 28 weeks of incapacity for work. If you are not an employee you do not qualify for SSP. If you are unemployed or self-employed you should consider claiming incapacity benefit and income support instead. SSP is administered and paid by your employer. Your contract of employment may mean that your employer must also pay you occupational sick pay. But SSP is a legal minimum and, if you qualify for it, your employer is not allowed to pay you less.

It is not necessary for you to have paid national insurance contributions to qualify for SSP and your entitlement is not affected by any savings that you have.

1. Who can claim statutory sick pay

You qualify for statutory sick pay (SSP) if:[1]

- you are an employee (see p594); *and*
- you are incapable of work (see p594); *and*
- you are within a period of incapacity for work (see p595); *and*
- you are within your period of entitlement to SSP (see p596); *and*
- the day is a qualifying day (see p599); *and*
- you are aged 16 or over and under 65 years old (but see p600); *and*
- your normal earnings are equal to or more than the lower earnings limit (see p598).

There are some groups of claimants to whom special rules apply (see p602). Certain people do not qualify for SSP – see p597.

Employees

To be entitled to SSP you must be an employee.[2] This does not mean that you must have a written contract of employment. It is the fact that you are employed that matters rather than any documents (though documents are useful for evidence in case of a dispute). Your right to SSP cannot be taken away by any document, whether you sign it or not,[3] and if your employer sacks you to avoid paying SSP, then they are still liable to pay it after your contract has ended (see below).[4] To be considered an employee you must be aged at least 16.[5] The question of whether you are an employee for SSP purposes is similar to the question of whether you are an 'employed earner' under the industrial injuries scheme (see p320).

However, even if you are an employee, your employer does not have to pay you SSP if they are neither resident nor present in Great Britain (GB), or do not have a place of business in GB, or if they are exempt from the social security legislation because of an international treaty.[6]

See p597 for details of employees who are not entitled to SSP.

Dismissal from work

If your employer dismisses you solely or mainly to avoid having to pay you SSP they are still liable to pay you SSP. In these circumstances your employer should continue to pay you SSP until whichever of the following occurs first:[7]

- your period of entitlement to SSP ends; *or*
- until your contract would have ended had you not been dismissed.

Incapable of work

In order to qualify for SSP you must be 'incapable of work'. However, the usual tests of incapacity for work (see Chapter 30) do not apply to SSP.[8]

To be **'incapable of work'** for SSP purposes, you must either be:[9]

- incapable of doing work which you could reasonably be expected to do under the terms of your contract because you have a specific disease (see p771) or bodily or mental disablement; *or*
- treated as incapable of such work (see p595).

The Revenue relies on employers to administer SSP, but if your employer doubts that you are incapable of work they can ask the Revenue's medical service (MS) to arrange an examination. Your employer can also ask for the Revenue's help in deciding whether you are capable of work. This can only be done with your consent but, since your employer could simply refuse payment, you are unlikely to gain much by not consenting.

Employers are advised that they may wish to seek such help if you have been off work for longer than would be expected, given the condition that you have, or if you have been off sick for less than a week (and so have not submitted a doctor's certificate) four times within the last 12 months. If the Revenue does help, a doctor from the MS contacts your doctor and you may be asked to attend an examination. Your employer is then simply given the MS doctor's view on whether you are capable of work, but is not given any medical report or other explanation. It is still for your employer to decide whether to pay SSP.

Treated as incapable of work

Even if you are not actually incapable of work, your employer (or the Revenue – see p608) has the discretion to treat you as incapable of work if:[10]

- you have been given a certificate by a medical officer for environmental health which excludes you from work because either:
  - you are under medical observation for being a carrier of an infectious disease; *or*
  - you have been in contact with someone with an infectious disease; *or*
- you are under medical care in connection with a specific disease or bodily or mental disablement; *and*
  - a doctor has stated that you should not work as a precautionary measure or in order to convalesce; *and*
  - you do not work for your normal employer.

If you are incapable of work for just part of a day you must be treated as incapable of work for the whole day as long as you do not do any work on that day. If you are a shift worker and do some work on a particular day you should still be treated as incapable of work if you only finish a shift that began the day before or if you do not do any work on a shift that starts on one day and ends the next.

Period of incapacity for work

For SSP to be paid to you, you must also be within a 'period of incapacity for work'. A **'period of incapacity for work'** is defined as four or more consecutive days of incapacity for work (see p594).[11] This means that you can only qualify for SSP if you are incapable of work (or can be treated as incapable of work) for at least four days in a row. Every day of the week (including Sunday[12]) counts for this purpose even if it is not a day on which you would normally work. If you are incapable of work on a day that falls before or after the period covered by your contract, such days can still be included in your period of incapacity for work (but see p599 if you have not started work yet).[13]

Two periods of incapacity for work can be 'linked' and treated as a single period if they are separated by eight weeks or less (see p597).[14]

For incapacity benefit (IB) purposes, a period of incapacity for work can be two or more days in any week if you are receiving certain types of regular treatment such as dialysis (see p265). For SSP, this rule does not apply. If this prevents you getting SSP and you are receiving one of these forms of treatment, you may qualify for IB instead (see Chapter 12).

Period of entitlement to statutory sick pay

You only qualify for SSP if you are within 'a period of entitlement'. In certain circumstances a period of entitlement cannot arise and so you will not qualify for SSP (see p597).

When entitlement to statutory sick pay starts

A period of entitlement to SSP starts on the first day of your period of incapacity for work, unless your contract of employment starts either during your period of incapacity for work or between two linked periods of incapacity for work.[15]

When entitlement to statutory sick pay ends

A period of entitlement to SSP ends (and so your SSP will stop) when *any* of the circumstances detailed below apply to you:[16]

- when your incapacity for work ends;
- when you reach your maximum 28 weeks' entitlement to SSP from a particular employer (see p602);[17]
- when your contract of employment ends (unless it has been brought to an end by your employer solely or mainly to avoid liability to pay SSP – see p594);
- in certain circumstances, when you are pregnant or have just had a baby (see p603);
- when you reach the third anniversary of the start of the period of entitlement (see below);
- when you are imprisoned or detained in legal custody (see p732).

Periods of entitlement with the same employer and in some circumstances with different employers (see p602), separated by eight weeks or less, are linked and treated as a single period.[18] This is why it is possible not to have exhausted your 28 weeks' entitlement to SSP before the third anniversary of the beginning of your period of entitlement.

If your period of entitlement to SSP ends and you are still incapable of work you should claim IB (see Chapter 12) and, if you qualify for it, income support (IS – see Chapter 13) or pension credit (PC – see Chapter 18). If you have at least one dependent child you may qualify for child tax credit (CTC – see Chapter 49). See p1349 for circumstances when it may also be possible for you to qualify for working tax credit (WTC). If your period of entitlement to SSP ends and you are still incapable of work, you are not entitled to SSP again until your current period of incapacity ends and a new one arises. In practice, this means that more than eight weeks must elapse between the date you recover and the date when you fall ill again.

If your employer stops paying you SSP on the grounds that they consider that your period of entitlement has ended, they should provide you with a statement (on an SSP1 form or on their own computerised form which they should provide with the SSP1 form) giving you the reasons for this. There are time limits for providing such information.[19] If your employer knows that your period of entitlement will end soon, and you are likely to continue to be incapable of work, they should normally give you the SSP1 at least six weeks before your period of entitlement ends. Otherwise your employer normally has to give you the SSP1 within seven days of the end of your period of entitlement, although if they cannot reasonably do this, they should give it to you by your next normal payday after this.

If you do not agree with your employer's decision to stop paying you SSP, see p607.

When statutory sick pay will not be paid

In certain circumstances a period of entitlement to SSP cannot arise. As a result, you will not qualify for any SSP during your period of incapacity for work.[20]

A period of entitlement cannot arise if:

- you are 65 or over (but see p600); *or*
- your period of entitlement to SSP would have begun before 1 October 2002 and your employment contract lasts for three months or less[21] (but see p541 of CPAG's *Welfare Benefits Handbook* 2002/2003 for possible grounds for arguing that your contract is not a short-term one); *or*
- your normal weekly earnings are below the lower earnings limit (see p598); *or*
- at some time during the 57 days before the date on which your period of entitlement would have started you qualified for either:
  - IB, or you would have qualified for IB had you satisfied the contribution conditions; *or*
  - severe disablement allowance (SDA).

  In order to have qualified for these benefits you would have had to have claimed them. SDA was abolished on 6 April 2001 (see Chapter 20 for details of who can still receive it); *or*
- you are a 'welfare to work' beneficiary (see p769), but only if you were getting IB or SDA and your period of entitlement would have started within your 52-week linking period (see p770). In these circumstances you should be able to qualify for either IB or SDA again while you are incapable of work (see p265);[22] *or*
- at the time when your period of entitlement would have begun there is a strike at your workplace (but see p741); *or*
- you have not yet started work under your contract of employment (unless you had an earlier contract with the same employer which ended within the last eight weeks); *or*

- at the time when your period of entitlement would have begun you are within a maternity pay period (see p588) or maternity allowance (MA) period (see p456) because you are pregnant or have just given birth (see p603); *or*
- you are not entitled to statutory maternity pay (SMP) or MA and you are within the period immediately before and after you give birth (see p603); *or*
- you are in prison or legal custody (see p732).

If your employer decides not to pay you SSP on any of the above grounds, they should provide you with a statement (on an SSP1 form or on their own computerised form which they should provide with the SSP1 form) giving you the reasons for this.[23] This statement should be provided within the seven days that fall after the fourth day of your period of incapacity for work. If your employer cannot reasonably provide the statement within this time they should provide it on or before your next normal payday. If you do not agree with your employer's decision see p607.

If you are not entitled to SSP you may qualify for IB (see Chapter 12) or, if you are under 60, IS (see Chapter 13). Even if you do not qualify for these benefits, you should normally still send medical certificates to your local JobCentre, Jobcentre Plus or Department for Work and Pensions office to claim national insurance (NI) credits (see p838). If you were in full-time paid work before becoming sick and you qualify for IS, lower rate short-term IB or NI credits, you may also qualify for WTC (see Chapter 50 and p1349). If you have at least one dependent child you may also qualify for CTC. If you are 60 or over you may qualify for PC.

People with low earnings

You cannot get SSP if your 'normal weekly earnings' are less than the lower earnings limit, currently £82 a week (see p827).

It is your gross earnings (ie, before tax and NI contributions are deducted) which are relevant.[24]

As well as your wages, your gross earnings include:[25]

- SMP, statutory paternity pay and statutory adoption pay;
- maternity pay;
- arrears of pay following reinstatement or re-engagement in your job or a continuation of a contract of employment under the Employment Rights Act 1996;
- payment of a protective award under the Trade Union and Labour Relations (Consolidation) Act 1992;
- payment under the Temporary Short-Time Working Compensation Scheme;
- SSP.

Payments made to you because you take part in an employment zone scheme are ignored.[26]

Your **'normal weekly earnings'** are calculated by averaging your gross earnings over the period which runs between:[27]

- your last normal payday before your period of entitlement to SSP began (see below); *and*
- the day after the last normal payday which falls at least eight weeks before this.

Only payments actually made during the eight weeks count.[28] If, on average, you receive less than £82 a week, you do not qualify for SSP even if, in theory, you should have been paid more.

If you have not been employed sufficiently long to have been paid wages over this eight-week period, but you have received at least one wage packet, your earnings are averaged over the period covered by the wages that you have received.[29] If you have not received any pay before your period of entitlement to SSP starts, your normal weekly earnings are based on the amount you should be paid according to your contract.[30]

Example

Ernesto works part time and is paid £96 a week. He is going on holiday and his employer pays him two weeks' holiday pay in advance which he receives during week one. He goes on two weeks' annual leave (weeks two and three). He falls ill in week ten. His SSP is based on the average wages received in weeks two to nine, so the total is £576, not £768. This is divided by eight to give £72. As this is below the lower earnings limit Ernesto gets no SSP.

See p601 if you have more than one job.

People who have not yet started work

If you have agreed to work for an employer but have not started work when you fall ill you are not entitled to SSP from that employer for any day during the same period of incapacity for work, unless:

- you were employed by the same employer previously; *and*
- not more than eight weeks have passed since your last contract ended.[31]

Qualifying days

To be entitled to SSP, the days on which you are incapable of work must not only fall within a period of incapacity for work (see p595) and be within your period of entitlement to SSP (see p596), but must also be 'qualifying days'.[32] **'Qualifying days'** are simply days on which you qualify for payment of SSP, although SSP is not paid for the first three qualifying days. These are called 'waiting days' (see p600).[33]

Qualifying days are usually those days of the week on which you would normally work if you were not sick. However, other days may be selected as qualifying days by agreement between you and your employer if that would provide a better reflection of your contract of employment (eg, if you work a complicated shift pattern).

For this purpose a week begins on Sunday and there must be a minimum of one qualifying day in each week.[34] You and your employer can agree that the qualifying days are those normally worked, so there may be a different number in each week depending on your shift arrangements. Alternatively, you can average these out to give a constant pattern – eg, five days a week for two weeks, and four days a week for another two weeks.

If there is no agreement about which days are qualifying days, or if the only agreement is to treat days of incapacity or days that fall in a period of incapacity for work or a period of entitlement as qualifying days, such an agreement is ignored and the qualifying days are presumed to be:

- the days on which it is agreed that you are required to work; *or*
- Wednesday, if it is agreed that you are required to work no days in that week – eg, offshore oil-workers, who may work two weeks 'on' and then two weeks 'off'; *or*
- if you cannot agree on which days you are or are not required to work, every day in the week, except days on which you and your employer agree that no employee works (if you can agree at least to that extent).[35]

'Required to work' means required by the terms of your contract of employment.[36] Days when you can choose whether or not to work do not count – eg, voluntary overtime shifts.

Waiting days

SSP is not paid for the first three qualifying days (see p599) in a period of entitlement.[37] These three days are called **'waiting days'**. As the waiting days must be qualifying days, they will not necessarily be the first three days of your sickness.

If you become incapable of work within eight weeks of an earlier period of incapacity you do not have to serve the three waiting days again, but become entitled to SSP from the first qualifying day. This is because two periods of incapacity for work are linked and treated as one if they are separated by eight weeks or less.

2. The rules about your age

You must be 16 or over to get statutory sick pay (SSP). If you are aged 65 or over, you cannot get SSP unless your period of entitlement (see p596) began before your 65th birthday and has not yet ended.

3. Claiming for others

You cannot receive an increase in statutory sick pay for any dependants that you have.

4. The amount of benefit

Statutory sick pay (SSP) is not paid for the first three qualifying days in a period of entitlement (see p600).[38] After that it is payable at a rate of **£68.20** a week.[39]

SSP is a daily benefit and so it can be paid for periods of less than a week. The daily rate is calculated by dividing the weekly amount of SSP by the number of qualifying days you have in that week (a week for these purposes runs from Sunday to Saturday).[40] The weekly rate of SSP is below the lower earnings limit (see p827) so, if you are not receiving any occupational sick pay, you do not have to pay national insurance (NI) contributions.

You are entitled to Class 1 NI credits for each week that you are entitled to SSP (see p838).[41] You should claim them from your local NI contributions office (part of the Revenue). You can obtain the address of your local NI contributions office by telephoning any local office of the Revenue – the details will be in the telephone directory. It is important that you do this because if you do not:

- you may lose your entitlement to incapacity benefit (IB) unless you qualify for IB on the basis of your incapacity for work in youth; *and*
- your entitlement to a retirement pension in the future may be reduced.

People with more than one job

If you cannot work, you are entitled to SSP from any job for which you fulfil the qualifying conditions. So, you could get payments of SSP for each of two contracts with the same employer (eg, if you are both a daytime teacher and an evening tutor with an education authority), or payments from two separate employers. However, if the earnings from any of your different jobs are added together when calculating your liability to pay Class 1 NI contributions (which usually means you contribute less than if they had been treated separately – see p832) you can only receive a total of £68.20 from those jobs and your employer's liability to pay you SSP is apportioned accordingly.[42]

It is possible for you to be unable to work on one contract and be entitled to SSP, but at the same time be able to work on a different contract – if, for example, you perform quite different tasks for each.

Maximum entitlement to statutory sick pay

You are entitled to a maximum of 28 weeks' SSP from any one employer in one period of incapacity for work. Twenty-eight weeks' entitlement is equal to 28 times the weekly rate of SSP.[43]

In calculating the 28-week period, previous periods of entitlement to SSP under the same contract with the same employer are linked to your current one if they are separated by eight weeks or less.[44]

Periods of entitlement with different employers cannot usually be linked. However, on leaving a job you should be given a leaver's statement on Form SSP1(L) which includes the details of the SSP you have been paid. Provided that you give or post this to your new employer within the period required by your employer, or within the period of seven days after your first qualifying day (see p599), whichever is later, the two periods can be linked as long as they are separated by no more than eight weeks.[45] The time limit for giving your employer an SSP1(L) can be extended if you can show good cause for the delay in providing the statement and you provide it not later than the 91st day after your first qualifying day (see p599). Linking periods of entitlement in this way allows you to transfer to IB (see Chapter 12) earlier, if you satisfy the NI contribution conditions for IB or if you qualify for IB on the basis of your incapacity for work in youth.

If you are still incapable of work after you have received your maximum 28-week entitlement to SSP you may qualify for IB. You may also qualify for income support (see Chapter 13) if you are under 60, or pension credit (see Chapter 18) if you are 60 or over. You should consider whether you qualify for working tax credit (see Chapter 50). If you have at least one dependent child you may qualify for child tax credit (see Chapter 49).

5. Special rules for special groups

There are some groups of claimants to whom special rules apply. These are covered below and in Chapters 26 and 28. Special rules apply to:

- people outside Great Britain (GB) (see below);
- women who are pregnant or who have recently given birth (see p603);
- people involved in a trade dispute (see p741);
- people in prison or detention (see p732).

People outside Great Britain

Your entitlement to statutory sick pay (SSP) is not affected by any absence from GB as long as you count as an employee and you meet the other conditions of entitlement to SSP. If you are employed abroad you count as an employee if:[46]

- your employer is required to pay Class 1 national insurance contributions for you; *or*
- you are employed in another European Economic Area country and, had you been employed in GB, you would have been considered an employee and the UK is the competent state under European Community legislation (see Chapter 26); *or*
- you are a continental-shelf worker or, in certain circumstances, a mariner or an airwoman or airman.

However, you do not count as an employee if your employer is not present or resident in GB, or does not run a business in GB, or is exempt from the social security legislation by international treaty.[47]

Women who are pregnant or who have recently given birth

If you are entitled to statutory maternity pay (SMP – see p566) or maternity allowance (MA – see p456) you cannot get SSP during the maternity pay period or the MA period.[48] Within the limits set out on pp574 and 456 (and unless your baby is born early – see pp456 and 574) you have a right to choose when your maternity pay or MA period begins. So, for example, your employer cannot insist that you claim MA at the earliest possible date in order to limit the period for which they have to pay SSP.

Even if you are not entitled to SMP or MA:

- you cannot get SSP (because a period of entitlement cannot arise) if your period of incapacity for work started at some time during the 18 weeks which run from the first of the following dates:
  - the beginning of the week in which you are incapable of work wholly or partly because of your pregnancy, if this falls on or after the beginning of the fourth week before your 'expected week of childbirth' (see p464); *or*
  - the week in which you had your baby (but see below);[49]
- if SSP is already being paid to you (because your period of entitlement started before the above period, or because your incapacity for work was not initially linked to your pregnancy), your SSP will stop from the first of the following dates:[50]
  - the first day falling on or after the beginning of the fourth week before your 'expected week of childbirth' when you are incapable of work wholly or partly because of your pregnancy; *or*
  - the date on which you have your baby.

If your baby is stillborn before 24 weeks of pregnancy you qualify for SSP if you satisfy the other conditions of entitlement.

6. Claims and backdating

You must claim statutory sick pay (SSP) from your employer rather than from the Department for Work and Pensions or the Revenue. The rules for claiming are described below. It may be possible to get your claim backdated (see p605).

Making a claim

In order to claim SSP you must inform your employer that you are sick (see below). It is for your employer to decide whether to pay you SSP. Employers are given detailed guidance on the SSP scheme in leaflet CA30, *Employer's Manual on SSP*.

Telling your employer that you are sick

Your employer will decide – possibly in negotiation with you or your trade union – how they require you to notify them that you are sick. Employers can decide both the way you should tell them and the time limits for notifying them of your sickness. However, your employer cannot insist that you notify them of your sickness in the following ways:[51]

- earlier than the first qualifying day (which does not necessarily correspond with your first day of sickness – see p599), or by a specific time on the first qualifying day;
- personally;
- by providing medical evidence;
- more than once a week;
- on a document provided by them;
- on a printed form.

Your employer must take reasonable steps to inform you of how and when they require you to notify them of your absence from work.[52] If they have not taken reasonable steps to inform you, or if they have made no arrangements about the notification they require, you must notify your employer of your incapacity for work in writing on or before the seventh day after your first qualifying day (see p599). This seven-day time limit, or your employer's time limit, can be extended by one month if you have good cause for the delay in informing your employer. If it is not practical for you to inform your employer within that time, the time limit can be extended further as long as you have notified them as soon as is reasonably practicable and you have notified them on or before the 91st day after your first qualifying day.

Notice sent in a properly addressed pre-paid letter is treated as having been given on the day the letter was posted.[53]

Information to support your claim

Your employer can require you to provide 'such information as may reasonably be required' for the determination of your claim for SSP.[54]

Medical evidence

For the first seven days of your incapacity for work your employer cannot insist that you obtain a medical certificate, as you are only required to provide a self-certificate as evidence of your incapacity for work.[55] After the first seven days an employer would normally expect you to provide medical certificates from a doctor. If you provide a certificate from someone else, such as an osteopath or chiropractor, this can be accepted if your employer considers it sufficient to show that you are incapable of work. Whatever type of medical evidence you provide, it is up to your employer to decide whether to accept it. See p607 if your employer does not accept that you are incapable of work and you want to challenge this decision.

Who should claim

As your employer cannot insist that you notify them of your incapacity for work personally, someone else can notify them on your behalf.

If you are not well enough to be able to deal with your own affairs, the Revenue can appoint someone else to act for you. This person is your 'appointee' (see p1075). An application for someone to act as your appointee should be made to the national insurance contributions office.

If you claim the wrong benefit

A claim for another benefit cannot be treated as a claim for SSP. However, if you claim SSP but you are not entitled to it, your claim may be treated as a claim for incapacity benefit (see Chapter 12) or severe disablement allowance (SDA) instead.[56] (SDA was abolished from 6 April 2001, but see Chapter 20 for details of who can still qualify for it.)

Backdating your claim

In order to claim SSP you must notify your employer of your sickness (see p604). If you have not notified your employer of your sickness promptly your claim can be backdated in the following circumstances:

- If you notify your employer of your sickness within the time arranged with your employer (or, if your employer has not arranged any time limit for notifying them, within seven days of your first qualifying day – see p599) your SSP should be paid from your fourth qualifying day. (It is not paid for the first three qualifying days, called waiting days, unless your period of incapacity for work is linked to an earlier one – see p600.)
- If you do not notify your employer within the above time limits, but notify them within one month of these time limits and you have good cause for the delay in informing your employer of your sickness, your claim can be treated as if it had been made on your first qualifying day, and SSP will be backdated if you satisfy the other qualifying conditions. What amounts to 'good cause' is

not defined in the regulations, but you would have to show that your failure to notify your employer was reasonable given the circumstances. Employers are advised that there may be good cause if an employee lives alone, has no telephone and cannot get out, or if the employee has a serious accident, a heart attack or a stroke. These are just examples – there may be other situations that would amount to good cause.

- If you are unable to notify your employer within that month, but you notify them of your sickness within 91 days of your first qualifying day, your SSP claim can be backdated to your first qualifying day if it was not practical for you to inform your employer of your incapacity for work earlier and you have notified them as soon as you reasonably could.[57]

If you claim SSP late, but your claim cannot be backdated, your entitlement is just delayed. You are still entitled to a total of 28 weeks' payment of SSP (see p602) from the date your entitlement begins if you are off work for that long.[58]

7. Getting paid

Statutory sick pay (SSP) is a daily benefit, which means that if you qualify for it, it can be paid for a period of less than a week. SSP is usually paid in the same way as your normal wages or salary. If you have some form of contractual sick pay arrangement with your employer, SSP forms part of your weekly pay. Any payment of SSP goes towards discharging your employer's liability to pay you contractual sick pay for the same period.[59]

Your employer cannot pay you SSP by making a payment in kind or by providing board and lodging, a service or some other facilities.[60]

Deductions that can be made from your wages – such as deductions for union subscriptions – can also be made from your SSP.[61]

Delays and complaints

If your entitlement to SSP has been decided by a Revenue officer or by tax appeal commissioners (see p609) your employer may be required to pay your SSP within a certain time (see p611).

See p611 for details of when payment of SSP can be made by the Revenue if your employer cannot or will not pay you SSP.

Change of circumstances

You should notify your employer of any change in your circumstances that might affect your entitlement to SSP.

Overpayments

The rules on overpayments and recovery of overpaid benefit described in Chapter 41 do not apply to SSP. However, if your employer pays you SSP and later decides that you were not entitled to it, they may attempt to recover the sum they consider overpaid by making a deduction from your wages. If this happens you should seek advice. You may be able to challenge your employer's decision to make deductions from your wages.

See below if you wish to challenge your employer's decision that you are not entitled to SSP.

If your employer decides that you have been paid SSP in error, you should consider claiming incapacity benefit (IB). If you qualify for IB and you make your claim within three months of your employer's decision that you were not entitled to SSP, your IB claim may be backdated to the date of your claim for SSP.[62]

8. Challenging a statutory sick pay decision

The information which follows in this section also applies to challenging decisions on your entitlement to statutory maternity pay, statutory paternity pay and statutory adoption pay.

Remember that not all employees have the right to claim unfair dismissal. Winning a dispute with your employer about your entitlement to statutory sick pay (SSP) may be of little comfort if you find that you do not have a job to return to when you have recovered from your sickness.

If your employer will not pay you SSP or stops paying you SSP you should claim incapacity benefit (IB – see Chapter 12) and, if you qualify for it, income support (IS – see Chapter 13) or pension credit (PC – see Chapter 18). You should also consider whether you may be entitled to working tax credit (WTC – see Chapter 50) and child tax credit (CTC – see Chapter 49).

Information your employer should give you

If your employer has refused to pay you SSP or is going to stop paying you SSP they should give you a statement (on an SSP1 form, or on their own computerised form which they should provide with the SSP1 form) explaining why. There are time limits for providing such a statement.[63]

You also have the right to request the following information from your employer:[64]

- the days for which your employer considers you are entitled to SSP;
- the reason why SSP is not payable for other days;
- the daily rate of SSP.

If your request is reasonable your employer must give you this information, in writing, in respect of the period before your request, within a reasonable time.

Involving the Revenue

If you are dissatisfied with your employer's decision, or they have failed to make a decision, you can request that the Revenue makes a decision on your entitlement to SSP.[65] You do this by completing an SSP14 form which you can obtain from your local national insurance (NI) contributions office. You can get the address of your local NI contributions office by telephoning any local office of the Revenue – the details will be in the telephone directory. The SSP14 form should be returned to your local NI contributions office. The Revenue has the discretion to accept an application in writing even if it is not on this form. Your application asking the Revenue to make a decision on your SSP entitlement should contain the period in respect of which SSP is at issue and the grounds (if any) on which your employer is refusing payment.[66]

Your employer should provide you with an SSP1 form explaining why they are not paying you SSP, or why they are stopping payment of your SSP. If possible you should send a copy of the SSP1 form to the NI contributions office with your application for a decision on your entitlement. However, do not delay your application if your employer has not given you an SSP1 form. The application for a decision by the Revenue must be made within six months of the earliest date for which your entitlement to SSP is in dispute.[67]

While you are asking the Revenue to decide whether you are entitled to SSP from your employer, it is advisable to also claim IB (see Chapter 12) and, if you will qualify for it, IS (see Chapter 13) or PC (see Chapter 18) from the DWP. This is because the process of getting a final decision on your claim for SSP can be lengthy and you may not be awarded SSP at the end of it. You can find the address of your local DWP or Jobcentre Plus office in your local telephone directory. You will need to send your SSP1 form, if your employer has given you this, with your claim for benefit and you should explain that you have made an application for the Revenue to make a decision on your entitlement to SSP. You should also consider applying for CTC, if you have at least one dependent child, and WTC.

The Revenue may seek further information and try to negotiate between you and your employer to try to settle the dispute prior to making a decision on your entitlement to SSP. The Revenue's decision is legally binding on the employer (see p611 for the time limits for complying with a decision). However, both you and your employer have a right to appeal against the Revenue's decision (see p609).

Varying or superseding a decision

The Revenue can change one of its own decisions by varying or superseding the decision.[68] It can **vary** its decision if it believes that the decision was wrong at the time it was made. The new decision may take effect from the date that the original decision would have had effect if the reason for the variation had been known. If you or your employer have appealed against a decision, the Revenue may vary that decision at any time before the appeal is determined. If the Revenue varies its decision it must notify you and your employer of the new decision in writing.

The Revenue can **supersede** an earlier decision if the decision has become incorrect for any reason – eg, if your circumstances have changed. The new decision will take effect from the date of your change in circumstances.

If the Revenue varies or supersedes an earlier decision either you or your employer can appeal against the new decision (see below).

Appealing against a Revenue decision

Both you and your employer have the right to appeal to the tax appeal commissioner if you do not agree with the Revenue's decision.[69] Your appeal should be made in writing and should include your reasons for appealing.[70] It should reach the Revenue within 30 days of the date the decision was issued.[71] This time limit can be extended if there is a reasonable excuse for you not having made your appeal within the time limit[72] and your appeal was made without unreasonable delay. If the Revenue does not accept that a reasonable excuse exists, it must refer the application to a tax appeal commissioner. If the tax appeal commissioner refuses the application, that decision can only be challenged by judicial review (see p1253).

The Revenue can try to settle the appeal through consent of all the parties at any time before the determination of the tax appeal commissioner. If, before the appeal is decided, an agreement is reached between the Revenue and you (if you have appealed), or your employer (if your employer has appealed), the appeal will lapse.[73]

You can withdraw your appeal at any time before it is decided by notifying the Revenue and your employer that you wish to do so. Your employer and the Revenue have 30 days to object to your request and if no objection is made your appeal will lapse.[74]

Your appeal will normally be decided by general commissioners (see below). You can ask for the appeal to be heard by special commissioners instead – eg, if you think there are complex legal issues involved (see p610). The appeal can be transferred to (or from) the special commissioners if both you and your employer agree, or if the commissioners themselves decide that is appropriate.[75] 'Legal help' (ie, help with the cost of legal representation) is not generally available for appeals to either the general or special commissioners.

Appeals to the general commissioners

If your appeal is dealt with by general commissioners it will be decided by a minimum of two, but normally three, lay people assisted by a clerk, who is usually a solicitor. They hear appeals arising within a geographical tax division. Your appeal can be dealt with in the tax division in which you work or live – you should state which you would prefer when you make your appeal.[76]

Appeals to the special commissioners

The special commissioners are full-time, legally qualified adjudicators who hear cases in London or Manchester (for England and Wales), Edinburgh (for Scotland) and Belfast (for Northern Ireland). However, you can apply to the clerk for the case to be heard locally – eg, on the grounds of a disability or sickness.

Appealing further

You, your employer and the Revenue have the right to appeal against the decision of the tax appeal commissioners to the High Court (or the Court of Session in Scotland) on a point of law (ie, on the grounds that the commissioners have interpreted the law incorrectly).[77]

The time limits for making such applications differ depending on whether you are appealing against a decision of the general commissioners or a decision of the special commissioners. If you are appealing against a decision of the general commissioners you should appeal within 30 days of the date on the notification of the general commissioners' decision. If you were told the decision at the hearing of your appeal, the 30-day period runs from the date you were told rather than the date of the notice.

If you are appealing against the decision of special commissioners you should make your appeal within 56 days of the date on the notification of the decision (42 days in Scotland or Northern Ireland) or, if you were told the decision at the hearing, within 56 days of the date of the hearing (42 days in Scotland or Northern Ireland).

There is a fee for lodging an appeal against the decision of the general or special commissioners. You can get further information on the appeals procedure in the leaflet *Tax Appeals: A guide to appealing against decisions of the Inland Revenue on tax and other matters* produced by the Department for Constitutional Affairs. You can obtain a copy of this leaflet from any NI contributions office or tax office, or from the Court Service's website (www.courtservice.gov.uk/tribunals/gcit).

If you are considering appealing against the decision of a tax appeal commissioner you should seek advice from a solicitor, law centre or legal advice centre.

If you win your appeal

If it is decided that your employer should pay you SSP, your employer should pay you within the time limits detailed on p611 unless they have appealed against the decision. Your employer does not have to pay you SSP until a final decision is given on appeal.

Time limits for payment

When it is decided by the Revenue or a tax appeal commissioner that you are entitled to SSP and no appeal against this decision has been made (or the matter has been finally determined), your employer should pay you on or before the first payday after either:[78]

- the day on which the employer is notified that the appeal has been disposed of; *or*
- the day the employer receives notification that leave to appeal has been refused, and there is no further opportunity to apply for leave; *or*
- in any other case, the day the time limit for appeal expires.

If, because of your employer's payroll methods, it is not practical for you to be paid at this time your employer should pay you on or before your next payday after this date.

If your employer does not pay

If your employer does not pay you within the above time limits then the Revenue should pay you SSP.[79] You should write to your local National Insurance Contributions Office. The Revenue should also pay your SSP if your employer was liable to pay you but is insolvent.[80]

9. Tax, tax credits and other benefits

Statutory sick pay (SSP) is treated like any other earnings and you pay tax and (if you also receive earnings and/or occupational sick pay in the same week) national insurance (NI) contributions by Pay As You Earn in the normal way.[81]

Tax credits

If you have at least one dependent child you may qualify for child tax credit (CTC – see Chapter 49). If you are getting SSP you may still be entitled to working tax credit (WTC) even though you are off work. If you were in full-time paid work (see p1342) immediately before your SSP started you count as still being in full-time paid work for tax credit purposes while on SSP. It is not necessary for you to have claimed WTC before you became ill, so if you are not getting WTC, perhaps because your income was too high before you went on SSP, check whether you can claim it now (see Chapter 50). If you have been entitled to SSP for 140 days and you satisfy the additional conditions detailed on p1357 you may qualify for the disability element within your WTC. If you qualify for a disability element, on your return to work you can count as in full-time paid work for WTC purposes if you work at least 16 hours a week (see p1343).[82]

For WTC and CTC, any SSP that you receive during the course of the tax year is taken into account as employment income (see Chapter 53).

Means-tested benefits

If you have a low income, as well as SSP you may be entitled to means-tested benefits such as income support (IS – see Chapter 13) if you are under 60, or pension credit (PC – see Chapter 18) if you are 60 or over. You may also be entitled to housing benefit (HB – see Chapter 10) and council tax benefit (CTB – see Chapter 6) in addition to your SSP. If your partner is not in full-time paid work s/he may qualify for jobseeker's allowance (JSA – see Chapter 15). If you are a member of a 'joint-claim couple' for JSA (see p394) you will not be required to be available for work, actively to seek work or to enter into a jobseeker's agreement while you receive SSP (see p350). Alternatively, if you are getting SSP and were working for 16 hours a week or more immediately before you became incapable of work, your partner can qualify for JSA without you needing to make a joint claim with her/him (see p396).

Any of these benefits can be paid in addition to your SSP. However, your net SSP payment (ie, your SSP minus any deductions made for tax, Class 1 NI contributions, and half of any contribution you make towards a personal or occupational pension scheme) counts in full as your income when calculating your entitlement to IS and income-based JSA and is taken into account as earnings when calculating your entitlement to PC. This means that a certain amount of your SSP may be disregarded when calculating your PC.[83]

SSP is treated as earnings for HB and CTB and a certain amount of it can be disregarded when calculating your entitlement to those benefits (see p963). If you pay for childcare and you were working for at least 16 hours a week immediately before your SSP started, you may also qualify for a deduction from your earnings for certain childcare charges when calculating your entitlement to HB and CTB, see p965 for details. In some circumstances your earnings and any WTC and CTC you receive can be added together before applying this deduction.

If you live in a pilot area, you may be entitled to a 52-week return to work credit of £40 a week if you start working for 16 hours or more a week and your earnings are £15,000 a year or less. To qualify you must have been getting incapacity benefit (IB) and have been getting SSP for at least 13 weeks before qualifying for IB (or have been on IB for three months).

Non-means-tested benefits

You cannot get IB while you are entitled to SSP.[84] However, if your SSP has run out and you qualify for IB you do not need to serve another three waiting days before your IB is paid.[85] If you satisfied the contribution conditions for IB (see p844) while getting SSP, the time you are on SSP counts towards the 196 days you need to qualify for the higher rate of short-term IB and the 364 days you need to qualify for long-term IB (see p274).[86] If you are claiming IB on the grounds of being incapable of work in youth (see p267), days when you are in receipt of SSP can count towards the 196 consecutive days that you must have been incapable of work in order to qualify for IB.[87]

You cannot qualify for contribution-based JSA, maternity allowance, statutory maternity pay, statutory paternity pay or statutory adoption pay while you are getting SSP.[88]

SSP counts as earnings for carer's allowance (Chapter 4), increases in non-means-tested benefits for dependants (Chapter 31) and reduced earnings allowance (p334) and so may affect your entitlement to those benefits.

Payment of SSP does not affect your entitlement to other non-means-tested benefits.

Passports and other sources of help

If you are on a low income, you might be entitled to certain health service benefits, such as free prescriptions (see Chapter 9). You may also qualify for other sources of help (see Chapter 1), a social fund payment (see Chapters 21 and 22) or free school meals (see p18).

Notes

1. **Who can claim statutory sick pay**
 1 ss151, 152, 153, 154 and 155 and Schs 11 and 12 SSCBA 1992
 2 ss151 and 163(1) SSCBA 1992; reg 16 SSP Regs
 3 s151(2) SSCBA 1992
 4 Reg 4 SSP Regs
 5 s163(1) SSCBA 1992
 6 Reg 16(2) SSP Regs
 7 Reg 4 SSP Regs
 8 s171G(1)(b) SSCBA 1992
 9 s151(4) SSCBA 1992
 10 Reg 2 SSP Regs
 11 s152(2) SSCBA 1992
 12 s152(5) SSCBA 1992
 13 s152(6) SSCBA 1992
 14 s152(3) SSCBA 1992
 15 s153(2), (7) and (8) SSCBA 1992
 16 s153(2) and (12) SSCBA 1992; reg 3(1), (3) and (4) SSP Regs
 17 ss153(2)(b) and 155 SSCBA 1992
 18 Reg 3A SSP Regs
 19 Reg 15(1A), (3) and (4) SSP Regs
 20 s153(3) and Sch 11 SSCBA 1992; reg 3 SSP Regs
 21 Sch 11 paras 2(b) and 4 SSCBA 1992, as amended by reg 11 and Sch 2 paras 1 and 4 Fixed Term Employees (Prevention of Less Favourable Treatment) Regulations 2002 SI No.2034
 22 Reg 3(2A) SSP Regs
 23 Reg 15(2) SSP Regs
 24 s163(2) SSCBA 1992; reg 17 SSP Regs
 25 Reg 17 SSP Regs
 26 Reg 17 SSP Regs
 27 Reg 19 SSP Regs
 28 CSSP/2/1984; CSSP/3/1984
 29 Reg 19(7) SSP Regs
 30 Reg 19(8) SSP Regs
 31 Sch 11 para 6 SSCBA 1992
 32 s154 SSCBA 1992
 33 s155(1) SSCBA 1992
 34 s154(3) SSCBA 1992
 35 Reg 5(2) and (3) SSP Regs
 36 R(SSP) 1/85
 37 s155(1) SSCBA 1992

4. **The amount of benefit**
38 s155(1) SSCBA 1992
39 s157 SSCBA 1992
40 s157(3) SSCBA 1992
41 Reg 8B(2)(iii) SS(Cr) Regs
42 Regs 20 and 21 SSP Regs
43 s155(2)-(4) SSCBA 1992
44 Reg 3A SSP Regs
45 Reg 3A SSP Regs

5. **Special rules for special groups**
46 s151(1) SSCBA 1992; reg 16(1) SSP Regs; regs 5 and 5A SSP(MAPA) Regs
47 Reg 16 SSP Regs
48 s153(2)(d) and (12) SSCBA 1992
49 Reg 3(5) SSP Regs
50 Reg 3(4) SSP Regs

6. **Claims and backdating**
51 Reg 7(1), (4) and (5) SSP Regs
52 Reg 7(1) and (4) SSP Regs
53 Reg 7(3) SSP Regs
54 s14(1) SSAA 1992
55 Reg 2(2) Statutory Sick Pay (Medical Evidence) Regulations 1985 SI No.1604
56 Reg 10(1) and (2) SS(C&P) Regs
57 Reg 7(1) and (2) SSP Regs
58 s156(3) SSCBA 1992

7. **Getting paid**
59 Sch 12 para 2 SSCBA 1992
60 Reg 8 SSP Regs
61 s151(3) SSCBA 1992
62 Reg 10(1) and (2) SS(C&P) Regs

8. **Challenging a statutory sick pay decision**
63 Reg 15 SSP Regs
64 s14(3) SSAA 1992
65 s8 SSC(TF)A 1999
66 Reg 3 SSP&SMP(D) Regs
67 Reg 3 SSP&SMP(D) Regs
68 s10 SSC(TF)A 1999; regs 5 and 6 SSC(DA) Regs
69 s11(2)(a) SSC(TF)A 1999
70 s12(3) SSC(TF)A 1999
71 s12(1) SSC(TF)A 1999
72 Reg 9 SSC(DA) Regs; s49 TMA 1970
73 Reg 11 SSC(DA) Regs
74 Reg 11(5) SSC(DA) Regs
75 s44(3) TMA 1970
76 Reg 7 SSC(DA) Regs
77 Reg 12 SSC(DA) Regs
78 Reg 9 SSP Regs
79 s151(6) SSCBA 1992; reg 9A SSP Regs
80 Reg 9B SSP Regs

9. **Tax, tax credits and other benefits**
81 s4(1) SSCBA 1992
82 Regs 6 and 9 WTC(EMR) Regs
83 Regs 35(2)(b) and 40(4) and Sch 9 paras 1, 4 and 4A IS Regs; regs 98(2)(c) and 103(6) and Sch 7 paras 1, 4 and 5 JSA Regs; regs 17(9) and (10) and 17A(2)(h) and (4A) SPC Regs
84 Sch 12 para 1 SSCBA 1992
85 Sch 12 para 4 SSCBA 1992
86 s30D(3) SSCBA 1992; reg 7 SS(IB) Regs
87 Reg 4A SS(IB) Regs
88 s153(2)(d) SSCBA 1992; s1 JSA 1995; reg 55(4) JSA Regs; regs 18 and 27 SPPSAP(G) Regs

Part 3

Special benefit rules for special groups

Chapter 25

Studying and claiming benefits

This chapter covers:

Studying full or part time can have a major impact on your entitlement to benefits if you are aged under 60. For people who are 60 or over who are (or whose partner is) not in receipt of income support or income-based jobseeker's allowance, more generous rules on studying and claiming benefits apply (see p618). The rules about studying are different for each benefit. This means you may not be entitled to some benefits, but other benefits are not affected by your study. If you are already claiming a benefit your entitlement may be affected if you start studying. If you are not able to claim benefit while studying, someone else may be able to claim for you.

Scotland has a different education system from England and Wales. The same terms are often used within the education systems of all three countries, but they can have different technical meanings – eg, further, higher and advanced education. Within benefit rules, terms are used to define different levels of education (eg, relevant, non-advanced and advanced) which have a technical meaning for benefit purposes. However, these are terms which are not generally used by education institutions.

Students, or students with a partner, aged 60 or over

If you are a student aged 60 (or if you are a student aged under 60 but have a partner aged 60 or over), you (or your partner) may be eligible for pension credit (PC – see Chapter 18); income support (IS – see Chapter 13) or jobseeker's allowance (JSA – see Chapter 15). Because students are not excluded from PC and any income from student financial support is treated more generously under PC, you should check to see if you would be better off if you (or your partner) were to claim PC rather than IS or JSA. If you, or your partner, receive PC the more generous rules for calculating housing benefit and council tax may also apply (see p633).

Students from overseas

Most overseas students cannot claim benefits because they are subject to immigration control (see p661). Even if you are entitled, a successful claim for benefit could affect your right to stay in this country and it is best to get immigration advice before making a claim.

Partners of overseas students

If you are not eligible for benefit, but there are no restrictions on your partner, either as a student or as a person subject to immigration control, s/he may be able to claim instead (see p811). However, if s/he receives benefit and you are a 'person subject to immigration control' (see p653) this may affect your right to remain in the UK under the immigration rules.

1. Studying and claiming income support or jobseeker's allowance

If you are treated as attending 'relevant education' (see below) or as a 'full-time student' (see p621) then usually you cannot qualify but there are some exceptions. There are different rules if you are studying part time (see p627).

Relevant education

You count as in **'relevant education'** if you are under 19 and attending a full-time non-advanced course.

- **Full time** means that you attend your course for more than 12 hours a week in normal term time. If your course is for 12 hours or less it does not count as relevant education.[1] You will count as a part-time student instead. See p627 to see if you can claim income support (IS) or jobseeker's allowance (JSA) as a part-time student.
- A **non-advanced course** means any course which leads to a qualification below the standard of a degree, NVQ level 4, Higher National Diploma, Diploma of Higher Education, a teaching qualification or similar. See pp87 for examples of non-advanced courses.

If you are in relevant education you can only claim IS in some circumstances (see below). You cannot claim JSA.[2]

When you reach your 19th birthday you are no longer treated as in relevant education even if you have not completed your course. From your 19th birthday you are treated as a 'full-time student' (see p621) and you can only receive IS if you are in one of the categories of full-time student who can claim (see p624). This may mean you cannot qualify for IS from your 19th birthday even if you qualify up to that date under the rules below.

If you cannot claim IS or JSA, your parents (or person acting in their place) may be able to claim benefits and tax credits for you (see p620). You should note that the term 'relevant education' does not apply for housing benefit (HB) or council tax benefit (CTB) purposes (see p630).

Care leavers in relevant education

If you are a care leaver aged 16 or 17 (see p713) you can only claim IS or JSA while you are in relevant education in the following circumstances:[3]

- if you are a lone parent and treated as responsible for a child; *or*
- you are so severely disabled that you are unlikely to get a job in the next 12 months.

Qualifying for income support while in relevant education

You can get IS while in relevant education (see p618) if:[4]

- you are the parent of a child for whom you are treated as responsible (see p90);
- you are so severely disabled that you are unlikely to get a job in the next 12 months;
- you are an orphan and have no one acting as your parent;
- you have left local authority care and of necessity you have to live away from your parents and any person acting in their place (see below);
- you have to live away from your parents and any person acting in their place (see below) because:
  - you are estranged from them; *or*
  - you are in physical or moral danger; *or*
  - there is a serious risk to your physical or mental health.

  The physical or moral danger does not have to be caused by your parents. Therefore, a young person who is a refugee and cannot rejoin her/his parents can claim IS while at school;[5]
- you live apart from your parents and any person acting in their place and they are unable to support you, *and*:
  - they are in prison; *or*
  - they are unable to come to Britain because they do not have leave to enter under UK immigration law;[6] *or*
  - they are chronically sick or are mentally or physically disabled. This covers people who could get a disability premium or higher pensioner premium, or have an armed forces grant for car costs because of disability, or are substantially and permanently disabled;
- you are a refugee learning English (see p298).

A **person acting in place of your parents** includes a local authority or voluntary organisation if you are being cared for by them, or foster parents but only until you leave care.[7] It does not include a person who is your sponsor under the immigration laws.[8]

Estrangement implies emotional disharmony,[9] where you have no desire to have any prolonged contact with your parents or they feel similarly towards you. It is possible to be estranged even though your parents are providing some financial support or you still have some contact with them. If you are in care, it is also possible to be estranged from a local authority. If you are, then you could qualify for IS if you have to live away from accommodation provided by a local authority.[10]

Qualifying for jobseeker's allowance while in relevant education

You cannot get JSA while in relevant education.[11] You may be able to claim IS instead if you fit into one of the groups who can claim while in relevant education (see p619) or your parents (or a person acting in their place) may be able to claim benefit and tax credits for you (see below).

When somebody else can claim benefits for you while you are in relevant education

If you cannot claim IS or JSA because you are in relevant education somebody else may be able to claim child benefit, child tax credit (CTC) and working tax credit (WTC) because they are treated as 'responsible' for you (see pp798 and 1316).

In some circumstances you may count as both a person who can claim IS while in relevant education and as a person for whom someone else can claim child benefit, CTC and WTC. You should seek advice about which option would mean you are better off financially.

Claiming income support or jobseeker's allowance when you leave relevant education

If you leave school before the legal minimum school-leaving date, you are treated as having stayed on until that date.

Once you have left relevant education you might be able to claim IS or JSA if you satisfy the rules for getting those benefits (see Chapters 13 and 15). However, when you have reached the official leaving date at the end of your course you continue to be treated as in relevant education during the vacation that follows. The day on which you cease to be treated as in relevant education is called the 'terminal date' (see p89). While you continue to be treated as in relevant education, you are only entitled to IS in the circumstances outlined on p619 or from your 19th birthday if it falls after your official leaving date but before the appropriate terminal date.[12]

From the Monday following your terminal date, there are three possibilities:

- You might get IS if you fit into one of the groups of people who can claim – see Chapter 13.

- You might get JSA if you satisfy the qualifying conditions – see Chapter 15 (if you are 16 or 17 you have to satisfy special rules – see p382).
- If you do not get IS or JSA in your own right and you are aged under 18, your parents might be able to go on claiming child benefit for you during the 'child benefit extension period' (see p88).

Calculating income and capital if you are in relevant education

The normal rules for assessing your income and capital apply (see Chapters 38 and 39), except there are special rules for assessing the amount of money available from grants, loans and other financial support for young people in education (see p636). Note that for the purposes of these special rules you are treated in the same way as a student.

Full-time students

If you are a full-time student you cannot usually claim IS or JSA for the duration of your course, including vacations. See p624 for exceptions to this rule. See p624 if you give up, change or take time out of your course and p627 if you are studying part time.

You count as a full-time student if:[13]

- you are under 19 and on a full-time course of 'advanced education'. **'Advanced education'** means degree or postgraduate level qualifications, teaching courses, diplomas of higher education, HND or HNC of the Business Technology Education Council or the Scottish Vocational Education Council and all other courses above advanced GNVQ or equivalent, OND, A-levels, a Scottish national qualification (higher or advanced level). See p622 for what counts as a full-time course;
- you are 19 or over but under pension age (currently 60 for women, 65 for men) and on a full-time course of study. If your course is full time you are treated as a full-time student regardless of the level of the course. See below for what counts as a full-time course.

You are treated as a student until either the last day of your course or until you abandon or are dismissed from it.[14] The **'last day of the course'** is the date on which the last day of the final academic year is officially scheduled to fall.[15] For HB and CTB, guidance to decision makers says that if you are a postgraduate student the end of your course is the date on which you complete attending or undertaking the course. Any time you spend 'writing up' your thesis, which is done totally independently from your course, is not counted as part of your course. However, a decision on whether you are regarded as a full-time student during this 'writing up' period should be made with regard to the amount of work you undertake during this time and all other circumstances of your case. A decision should not be based on the fact that your course was full time.[16]

Full-time courses[17]

If your course is funded by the Learning and Skills Council for England or the National Council for Education and Training in Wales ('the Councils') or Scottish Ministers (SMs) (see below), the definition of 'full time' applies to your personal pattern of attendance on the course. For all other courses, the term 'full time' applies to the course as a whole, not your personal pattern of attendance. However, for such courses the rules contain no definition of when it is classed as a full-time course.

Courses funded by 'the Councils' or Scottish Ministers

In **England and Wales** your course counts as full time and you will be treated as a full-time student if:

- it is totally or partly funded by the Councils and your personal 'learning agreement' involves more than 16 hours of 'guided learning' each week. Courses funded by the Councils include academic or vocational courses leading to a recognised qualification. The Councils also fund basic literacy and numeracy courses, English as a Second Language programmes, access and similar courses which prepare you to move on to qualification-bearing courses, and courses developing independent living skills for people with learning difficulties. The number of guided learning hours you do each week is set out in your learning agreement. This is signed by you and the college. The Department for Work and Pensions (DWP) uses this agreement to decide whether or not you are on a full-time course;[18]
- it is not funded by the Councils and is a 'full-time course of study'.

In **Scotland** your course counts as full time and you will be treated as a full-time student if:[19]

- it is totally or partly funded by SMs at a college of further education, is not higher education *and* your personal learning document states that your course:
  - involves more than 16 hours a week of classroom-based or workshop-based programmed learning under the guidance of a teacher; *or*
  - involves more than 21 hours study a week, 16 hours or less of which involve classroom-based or workshop-based programmed learning and the rest of which involve using structured learning packages with the help of a teacher.

  The number of hours of 'learning' you do each week is set out in your learning document. This is signed by you and the college. The DWP uses this document to decide whether or not you are on a full-time course;
- it is a course of higher education which is funded in whole or in part by SMs;
- it is not funded by SMs and is a full-time course of study.

Sandwich courses

A sandwich course may be classed as a full-time course. A sandwich course[20] (excluding a course of initial teacher training) is one that consists of alternate periods of study at your education institution and periods of industrial, professional or commercial placement or work experience organised such that, taking the course as a whole, you attend the periods of study at your education institution for an average of not less than 18 weeks a year (19 weeks in Scotland). If your periods of full-time study and work experience alternate within any week of your course the days of full-time study are aggregated with any weeks of full-time study to determine the number of weeks of full-time study in each year. If your course includes the study of one or more modern languages for at least half of the time spent studying and a period of residence in the country whose language is part of your course, then any period of residence overseas during which you are employed counts as a period of work experience.

Health-related courses

If you attend a health-related course (including Project 2000 nurses[21]) for which you are entitled to receive an NHS bursary (see p639) you will be treated as attending a full-time course.

Modular courses

A modular course is one that consists of two or more modules and your college or university requires you to complete successfully a specific number of modules before it considers that you have completed the course.[22] You will be treated as a full-time student if you are currently attending a part of a modular course that would be classed as a full-time course.[23] You will be treated as a full-time student for the period beginning on the day that your course is defined as a full-time course and ending on the last day on which you are registered with your college or university as attending or undertaking that part of your course. This includes any vacations in that period, or the vacation immediately following that part of your course, unless that vacation follows the last day on which you are required to attend or undertake your course, or on such earlier date that you finally abandon or are dismissed from that part of the course.[24]

If you have failed examinations or failed to complete successfully a module relating to a period when the course was classed as a full-time course, any period in which you attend or undertake the course in order to re-take those examinations or modules will be classed as part of the full-time course and you will be treated as a full-time student (even if your college or university registers you as a part-time student during your re-sit period).[25]

Because the rules provide no definition of what is a full-time course (unless funded by the Councils or SMs – see p622) you may be able to argue that you are not attending a full-time course, even if:[26]

- you are currently attending or undertaking a modular course on a full-time basis;
- you have transferred to part-time attendance due to exam or module failure; *or*
- you are taking time out of the course (see p625).

Other courses

In England, Wales and Scotland if your course does not automatically count as full time under the rules above, whether it counts as a 'full-time course of study' depends on the college or university. Definitions are often based on local custom and practice within education institutions, or determined by the demands of course validating bodies, or by the fact that full-time courses can attract more resources. The college or university's definition is not absolutely final, but if you want to challenge it you will have to produce a good argument showing why it should not be accepted.[27] If your course is only for a few hours each week, you should argue that it is not full time. However, a course could be full time even though you only have to attend a few lectures a week.[28]

Full-time students who can claim income support

Even if you are a full-time student, you can claim IS if you are:[29]

- a lone parent, including a lone foster parent, of a child under 16; *or*
- a student from abroad and entitled to an urgent cases payment because you are temporarily without funds for a period up to six weeks (see p664); *or*
- a disabled student[30] and you satisfy one of the following conditions:
  - you qualify for the disability premium or severe disability premium (see pp886 and 891);
  - you have been incapable of work (see p263) for 28 weeks. Two or more periods when you are incapable of work are joined to form a single period if they are separated by less than eight weeks;
  - you qualify for a disabled students allowance because you are deaf; *or*
- one of a couple who are both full-time students; *and*
  - you fit into one of the groups of people who can claim IS (see Chapter 13); *and*
  - either one or both of you are responsible for a child or young person (see p90); *and*
  - it is the summer vacation.

  Note: There is a different rule for HB and CTB (see p631); *or*
- a refugee learning English (see p298).

If you are a student who cannot claim IS, check to see if you can claim JSA or pension credit (PC) instead. If you have a partner who is not a full-time student, s/he might be able to claim IS, JSA or PC for you.

Full-time students who can claim jobseeker's allowance

Even if you are a full-time student you can claim JSA if you are:

- one of a couple who are both full-time students and either or both of you is responsible for a child (see p90). This exception only applies during the summer vacation and if you are actually available for work;[31] *or*

- on an employment-related course of up to two weeks which has been approved in advance by the DWP[32] or a Venture Trust training programme of up to four weeks.[33] In either case, only one course is allowed in any 12-month period; *or*
- aged 25 or over and on an approved employment-related course including one under the New Deal for up to nine months; *or*
- waiting to go back to your course, having taken approved time out of your course because of an illness or caring responsibility that has now come to an end (see below).

If you are a student who cannot claim JSA, check to see if you can claim IS or PC instead. If you have a partner who is not a full-time student, s/he might be able to claim PC, IS or JSA for you.

Giving up, changing or taking time out of your course

If you are in any of the circumstances below you should seek specialist advice.

If you abandon your course or are dismissed from it you can claim IS or JSA from the day after that date so long as you satisfy the other rules for getting those benefits (see Chapters 13 and 15).

If you complete one course and start a different course you are not treated as a student in any period between the courses.[34]

If you are on a sandwich course (see p622), or your course includes a compulsory or optional period on placement, you count as a full-time student during the sandwich or placement period even if you have been unable to find a placement or your placement comes to an end prematurely.[35]

If you attend a course at an education institution which provides training or instruction to enable you to take examinations set and marked by an entirely different and unconnected body (ie, a professional institution) and you abandon or take time out from it because you fail the examinations set by the other body (or you finish the course at the education institution but fail the exams) you may be able to argue that you are not a student from the date you left the course at your education institution even if you intend to re-sit the examinations set by the other body at a later date.[36]

If you are taking time out of your course for any other reason (including to study for and re-sit exams – but see above) and for however long a period, you cannot claim IS or JSA during your period of absence[37] except in the limited circumstances below (however, if you are taking time out from a modular or similar course see also p623).

You may also retain entitlement to some student support on a statutory or discretionary basis, for example, through student loans or hardship funds. You should seek specialist advice.

Changing from full-time to part-time attendance

If you have to change from full-time to part-time attendance on a 'traditional' full-time course for personal reasons, you may be able to argue that you have abandoned your full-time course and are registered on a part-time course and, therefore, that you are not a full-time student.[38]

If, due to exam failure or any other reason, you change to a different course, or your college requires you to change the level of course (eg, from A-level to GCSE) and this involves a change from full-time to part-time study you should argue that you are a part-time student (see below).[39]

However, changing your attendance may affect your entitlement to any student support you may be receiving. You should seek advice on this before acting.

Time out because of caring responsibilities

You cannot get IS or JSA while you are caring for someone. However, you can claim JSA, HB and CTB, but not IS, when your caring responsibilities have come to an end. Note that the rules do not provide a definition of caring responsibilities or when they can be said to have come to an end. You can then claim for a maximum period of one year until whichever is the earlier of:

- the day you rejoin your course; *or*
- the first day from which your education institution has agreed that you can rejoin your course,

provided that you are not eligible for a student grant or loan during this period. This means that you may not qualify for benefit for the whole of the period after your caring responsibilities end until the date you actually rejoin your course.

Time out because of illness

You cannot get IS or JSA while you are ill. However, you might be able to claim IS once you count as a 'disabled student' (see p624) – ie, when you have been ill for 28 weeks and are treated as 'incapable of work'. Once your illness has ended you can claim JSA, HB and CTB, but not IS. The rules are the same as for when caring responsibilities have ended – see above.

Time out because of pregnancy

If you are not a student who can claim IS/JSA and you have to take time out because you are pregnant, the rules say you cannot claim IS until you have given birth and become responsible for a child (see p90). The Court of Appeal[40] has decided that, for JSA, this provision does not *directly* discriminate against women under European Community (EC) law. If you are refused IS/JSA/HB/CTB in these circumstances, it may be possible to argue that the decision *indirectly* discriminates against women under EC law or that it is incompatible with the Human Rights Act (see p1290) – you should seek specialist advice.

Housing costs – maintaining two homes

In some cases, if you qualify for IS, income-based JSA or HB, you may be entitled to help with the costs of more than one home if you have to live away from your normal home in order to attend a course. For further details, see pp203 and 910.

Calculating a student's income and capital

The normal rules for assessing the income and capital of part-time and full-time students apply (see Chapters 38 and 39), except that there are special rules for assessing the amount of money available from grants, loans and other types of financial support for students (see p636).[41] These rules do not apply to PC, where income from a student grant or loan does not count as income (see p636).

Part-time students

If you are studying but are not in relevant education (see p618) or attending a full-time course (see p622) then you will be treated as attending a part-time course and classed as a part-time student.

Claiming income support while studying part time

You can get IS while studying part time if you are not on a full-time course, and you satisfy the other rules for getting IS (see Chapter 13).

If you are currently studying part time on a course you previously attended full time, or if you are attending a modular or similar course (see p622) on a part-time basis, the DWP may argue that you are attending a full-time course and should, therefore, be treated as a full-time student. It may be possible to challenge this interpretation.[42] You should seek specialist advice if you are in this situation.

Claiming jobseeker's allowance while studying part time

You count as a part-time student if your course is not full time.[43] In effect, your course is part time if:

- you are under 19 and are not treated as in relevant education (see p618) – ie, you spend 12 hours or less a week in non-advanced education;[44] *or*
- you are on a course funded by the Councils or SMs (see p622) and have a learning agreement (learning document in Scotland) from your course stating that your course is for 16 guided learning hours or less (note the slight variation in Scotland); *or*
- it is not a full-time course of study (see p622).

You can qualify for JSA while studying part time if you meet the labour market conditions (ie, you are available for work, actively seeking work and you have a valid jobseeker's agreement – see Chapter 15). If you have agreed restrictions with the DWP on the hours that you are available for work there are special rules that can help you claim JSA and study part time (see p629).

When you claim JSA, in addition to the JSA claim form and the 'Helping you Back to Work' form you may be asked to fill in a 'student questionnaire'. Your answers are taken into account when deciding whether you are available for and actively seeking work. The DWP needs to be satisfied that you are genuinely available for and actively seeking work while you are studying part time.

Availability for work and part-time study

Your availability for work should not be affected by your part-time course if your hours of study or training are at times outside your agreed pattern of availability (see p363) – ie, they do not clash with the times that you are willing and able to work. If the hours of your course *do* clash with the times that you say you are available for work (as set out in your jobseeker's agreement – see p369) you will only be accepted as available for work if either:[45]

- you are able to rearrange the hours of the course or study to fit around your job; *or*
- you are willing and able to give up the course should a job become available.

If you are under 19 and complete or leave a part-time course, you are not treated as leaving relevant education (see p618) and you, therefore, qualify for benefit straightaway as long as you satisfy the normal rules of entitlement (see p347).

If you are attending an employment-related course as part of the New Deal you can be treated as available for and actively seeking work (see Chapter 15).

Factors when deciding whether you are available for work

The guidance for decision makers states that a number of factors should be considered when deciding whether you are available for work while you are studying part time. If, for example, it appears that you are not willing or able to give up your course or that you cannot confine your study to times that would fit in with employment, you are treated as not being available for work. The factors that may be relevant include:[46]

- where you are studying or training and, if it is away from home, whether you can be contacted if a job becomes available;
- the extent of your efforts to find employment;
- how important the successful completion of the course is to your future career, including whether it will enhance your chances of finding employment;
- whether you gave up a job or training to do the course;
- the days and hours that you are required to attend the course;
- whether the times of attendance could be altered to fit in with any job you might obtain or whether successful completion of the course is possible if you miss some of the scheduled attendances;
- the duration of the study or training;
- whether a fee was paid and, if so, the amount and whether any of the fee could be refunded or transferred if you abandoned or interrupted your studies. If you have paid a fee it may be more difficult (depending on the amount) to convince the DWP that you are prepared to abandon the course;
- whether you received a grant and, if so, the source, the amount and whether you would have to repay any or all of it if you interrupted or abandoned the course.

The guidance for decision makers states that where a number of claimants are following the same course some may be able to show that they are available, but others may not.[47] The DWP should not operate a blanket policy of treating all students on the same course as not being available (equally, you cannot assume that you will be treated as available if other people on your course are getting JSA). Each claim should be considered individually. The DWP assumes that you may be less willing to leave a course if you are near the end of the course or as the chance of obtaining a qualification approaches.[48]

Restricted availability for work and part-time study

There are special rules which can help you to qualify for JSA if you are a part-time student. These say that in certain circumstances the fact that you are on your course will be ignored when deciding whether you are available for work if the hours of your course fall wholly or partially within the times that you say you are available for work. (However, you still have to be available for and actively seeking work during the rest of the week when you are not on your course.)

These rules apply to you if you are a part-time student, and you are willing and able to rearrange the hours of your course to take up a job, and restrictions on your hours of availability have been agreed with the DWP for one of the following reasons:[49]

- your physical or mental condition (see p361); *or*
- your caring responsibilities (see p363); *or*
- you are working short time (see p380); *or*
- your restrictions leave you available for work for at least 40 hours a week (see p362).

You must also satisfy one of two conditions:

- for the three months immediately before the date you started the course you were unemployed and getting JSA, or incapable of work and getting IS or incapacity benefit (IB – see Chapter 12), or you were on a course of 'training'; *or*
- in the six months before you started the course, you were unemployed and getting JSA, or incapable of work and getting IS or IB for a total of three months altogether, or on a course of 'training' for a total of three months, *and*, sandwiched between these spells, you were working full time or earning too much to qualify for benefit.

The three-month and six-month periods can only begin after you have reached your terminal date and are treated as having ceased to be in relevant education (see p89).

'Training' means training for which young people aged under 18 are eligible, or for which a person aged 18–24 may be eligible, that is provided or arranged by the Learning and Skills Council for England or the National Council for Education and Training in Wales or in Scotland a Local Enterprise Council.

2. Studying and claiming housing benefit and council tax benefit

Whether you can claim housing benefit (HB – see Chapter 10) or council tax benefit (CTB – see Chapter 6) depends on whether you are classed as:

- a full-time student; *or*
- a part-time student.

Additional rules apply to claiming and calculating HB. These rules are outlined in this section.

If you have reached the qualifying age for pension credit (PC) (currently 60 for men and women) and neither you nor your partner are in receipt of IS or income-based JSA, the student rules for HB and CTB do not apply and there are no restrictions on you studying and claiming HB/CTB.[50]

Full-time students

If you are a full-time student (see p621) you cannot usually qualify for HB or CTB, but there are some exceptions (see p631).

The rules for deciding if you are a full-time student are the same as for income support (IS) and jobseeker's allowance (JSA) – see p621. Unlike IS and JSA, there is no separate rule in HB/CTB if you are in 'relevant education' (see p618). If you are attending relevant education you are treated as a full-time student for HB/CTB. This means that you may be able to claim HB/CTB while in relevant education even if you cannot claim IS or JSA.

Part-time students

You may be able to claim if you are studying part time. The rules for deciding if you are a part-time student are the same as for IS and JSA (see p627).

Partners of students

If your partner is not a student s/he can claim HB/CTB if s/he meets the qualifying rules.[51] The claim is assessed in the normal way, except that (for HB) the rules about being away from term-time accommodation (see p632) apply to the partner's claim.[52] Additionally, the special rules for assessing any income you receive from grants, loans and other types of financial support for students will apply (see p636).

Giving up, changing or taking time out of your course

If you abandon or are dismissed from your course, or you alter or have to take time out of your course, the rules are the same as for IS and JSA (see p625).

Students and second adult rebate

Full-time students are not precluded from getting second adult rebate and should be assessed in the normal way (see p118).

Studying, council tax and council tax benefit

If you are living in halls of residence predominantly provided to accommodate students, or in a dwelling wholly occupied by students or other 'relevant persons' (there are variations in Scotland), these two classes of accommodation are exempt from council tax. Therefore, in effect, you cannot claim CTB because you will not be liable to pay the tax. See CPAG's *Council Tax Handbook* for more details.

Full-time students who can claim housing benefit and council tax benefit

Note: Even if you meet one of the criteria below there are some circumstances in which you still cannot receive HB (see p632). You can claim if:[53]

- you are on IS or income-based JSA;
- you are under 19 and not following a course of higher education (higher education includes degree courses, teacher training, HND, HNC and postgraduate courses);[54]
- you and your partner are both full-time students and either or both of you are responsible for a child or young person. Note that, unlike IS and JSA, this provision applies throughout the year;
- you are a lone parent with a dependent child or young person aged under 19;
- you are a lone foster parent where the child has been formally placed with you by a local authority or voluntary agency;
- you meet the conditions for the disability premium (see p886), or would do if you were not disqualified from incapacity benefit (see p272);
- you have been incapable of work (see p263) for 28 weeks. Two or more periods when you are incapable of work are joined to form a single period if they are separated by less than eight weeks;
- you meet the conditions for the severe disability premium (see p891);
- you qualify for a disabled students allowance because you are deaf;
- you are waiting to go back to your course, having taken approved time out of your course because of an illness or caring responsibility that has now come to an end (see p626).

If you are a full-time student who fits one of the exception categories on p631, you still cannot receive HB if any of the circumstances under the following two headings apply to you.

Being away from your term-time accommodation

If you are a full-time student who is eligible for HB (see p631) and your main reason for occupying your home is to enable you to attend your course, you cannot get HB on that home for any full week when you are absent from it outside your period of study (see p640).[55]

This rule does not apply if:

- you are away from home because you are in hospital;[56]
- the main reason for occupying your home is *not* to enable you to attend your course but for some other purpose – eg, to provide a home for your children or for yourself if you do not have a normal home elsewhere.[57] If this applies, any absences outside your period of study are dealt with under the temporary absence rules (see p202).

Accommodation rented from an educational establishment

The following rules apply from academic year 2004/05.[58] For a previous academic year see the appropriate edition of this *Handbook*.

Subject to the two exceptions below, if you are a full-time student who can claim HB (see p631), you can receive HB even if you rent your accomodation from your educational establishment. If you are a part-time student this rule applies if you would be able to claim housing benefit if you were treated as a full-time student.

You cannot get HB if you are a:

- full-time student and you are waiting to go back to your course, having taken approved time out of your course because of illness or caring responsibilities (see p626); or
- part-time student receiving IS or JSA.

However, the two exceptions above do not apply if:

- your education establishment itself rents the accommodation from a third party other than on a long lease or where the third party is an education authority providing the accomodation as part of its functions; *or*
- the accommodation is owned by a separate legal body – eg, a company established under the Business Expansion Scheme to build halls of residence.

However, you cannot receive HB if the local authority decides that your educational establishment has arranged for your accommodation to be provided by a person or body other than itself in order to take advantage of the HB scheme.

Living in different accommodation during term time

The rules about claiming HB for two homes are explained on p203.

If you are one of a couple and receive HB for two homes, the assessment of HB for each home is based on your joint income and your applicable amount as a couple.

Calculating a student's housing benefit

If you or your partner get IS, income-based JSA, the guarantee credit of PC or a training allowance you will be entitled to maximum HB (see Chapter 10).

If you do not get IS, JSA, the guarantee credit of PC or a training allowance but you or your partner are eligible for HB, your entitlement is calculated in the same way as for other claimants (see p216), apart from the additional rule below.

Your HB entitlement is calculated differently during your period of study (see p640) than outside it – eg, during most of the summer vacation. For example, your grant or loan income may be taken into account for a different period (see p636 for the treatment of grant and loan income). You may find, therefore, that your HB entitlement is higher, or that you are only entitled to HB, outside your period of study and that you need to make a new claim or check that your entitlement is reviewed at that time. If you start your course at another time of year, for example in January, it is not clear how this rule should apply because your longest vacation may be at some time other than the summer.

Assessing your income and capital

The normal rules apply for assessing the income and capital of both full-time and part-time students (see Chapters 37, 38 and 39), except that there are special rules assessing the amount of money available from grants, loans and other types of financial support for students (see p636).

Payments

Students are covered by all the normal rules on the administration and payment of HB (see Chapter 10). However, there are two provisions which can apply specifically to students.

The local authority has the discretion to decide how long your benefit period (see p225) should last.

The local authority may decide to pay a rent allowance once each term, although students have the same right as other claimants to insist on fortnightly payments if their entitlement is more than £2 a week (see p229).

3. Studying and claiming other benefits and tax credits

Pension credit

There are no restrictions on claiming pension credit (PC – see Chapter 18) and studying either full time or part time. For income support (IS) there are restrictions if you are under pensionable age (60 for women, 65 for men). The less restrictive rules for PC, therefore, benefit men who are studying full time and are aged between 60 and 65. Additionally, the more generous income and capital rules for PC will benefit men and women aged 60 or over who are students or whose partners are students (regardless of their partner's age) as student grants and loans are not taken into account as income (see p636).[59]

Incapacity benefit

You cannot claim incapacity benefit (IB – see Chapter 12) if you are under 19 and in full-time education. Full time means attending a course for 21 hours or more a week.[60] In calculating the 21 hours, any special education or tuition designed for those with a physical or mental disability is ignored (see p270). Temporary interruptions of education are disregarded. Periods of private study are also not included in the 21-hour limit. If you cannot claim IB because you are in full-time education, somebody else may be able to claim benefits for you if you are in 'relevant education' (see p618).

If you are under 25 there are special rules (called the age exception) that may help you get IB, without having to satisfy the national insurance contributions conditions, if you have now completed a course of full-time advanced or secondary education, or vocational or work-based training, which you started at least three months before your 20th birthday (see p268).

It is worth noting that you cannot be treated as capable of work (see Chapter 29) simply because you are studying on either a full-time or part-time course.

Carer's allowance

You cannot claim carer's allowance (CA – see Chapter 4) if you are in full-time education.[61] If you are attending a university, college or school for 21 hours a week or more you will be treated as being in full-time education. In calculating the 21 hours you include only hours spent in 'supervised study'. You ignore any time spent on meal breaks or unsupervised study undertaken on or off the premises of the educational establishment.[62]

The Court of Appeal has decided[63] that for 'supervised study' to count it does not depend on whether your supervisor (ie, teacher, tutor, lecturer) is present with you. If your study is directed to your course of education and the curriculum of your course and your study is undertaken to meet the reasonable requirements of your course it will normally count as supervised study. It will count regardless of whether that study is undertaken on or off the premises of the education institution you attend.

'Unsupervised study' means work beyond the reasonable requirements of your course. In assessing your hours of attendance, evidence from your education institution about the amount of time for which you are expected to study to complete your course will be important. However, your hours of attendance should be judged by the facts in your individual case. You may be able to argue that you intend, expect or actually devote less time to your studies than your education institution considers is necessary to meet the reasonable requirements of the course. However, guidance to decision makers suggests that they should be very slow to accept that you spend less time on supervised study than your education institution expects of you. Equally a decision maker should be very slow to conclude that you receive full-time education because you devote considerably more time to the course than is expected of you.[64]

You will be treated as still being in full-time education during vacations and any temporary interruption of the course, but not if you have abandoned the course or been dismissed from it.

Child benefit

Child benefit (see Chapter 5) can be claimed for a person who is under 19 and in full-time non-advanced education or during the 'child benefit extension period' (see p88).

Working tax credit and child tax credit

You are not excluded from claiming a tax credit simply because you are a full-time student. However, special rules apply to calculating your income from a grant, loan or other financial support for students (see p1383).

NHS benefits

You are not excluded from claiming NHS benefits (see Chapter 9) while you are studying.

Other benefits

Only those benefits covered in this chapter are potentially affected if you are studying.

National insurance credits

You can receive Class 1 national insurance credits (see Chapter 33) for any week of a full-time course.

4. Calculating income from grants and loans

The rules in this section apply *only* to the calculation of income support (IS), income-based jobseeker's allowance (JSA), housing benefit (HB) and council tax benefit (CTB). They apply if you are a part-time or a full-time student.

Some income from a grant, a loan and certain other forms of financial support for students is taken into account when calculating your benefit entitlement under the special rules set out below.

Grant and loan income does not affect any contribution-based JSA that you are entitled to claim. These rules do not apply to HB/CTB claimants who are (or whose partner is) aged 60 or over because any student income you have from a grant or loan is not taken into account as income.[65]

The following information applies to the academic year 2004/05.
For the treatment of grant and loan income for previous academic years see the relevant edition of this *Handbook*.

The DWP has issued guidance to decision makers concerning the treatment of various types of financial support to students. Often that guidance only covers some of the benefits to which this section refers. For example, guidance may have been issued for HB/CTB purposes but no equivalent guidance has been issued for JSA/IS. It is not clear if the guidance issued concerning specific benefits also applies to the other benefits covered in this section. Additionally, the legislation and guidance may not cover all sources of student support across England, Wales and Scotland, particularly as new sources of support are introduced. You should check the current position.

Student support in England, Wales and Scotland

There are many types of financial support available to students attending a course at school, sixth form college, further education, undergraduate (including certain courses below degree level) or postgraduate level which are paid in the form of either a grant or a loan. Some types of grant or loan are available to all students who meet the conditions of entitlement, others are only available on a discretionary basis. The support available to students varies, depending on whether you live in England, Wales or Scotland.

Student support in schools, sixth form colleges and further education

England and Wales

Local education authorities (LEAs) or schools and colleges administer various funds. Whether you can apply for any of these payments may depend on your age, your circumstances or if you normally live in England or Wales. These funds include:

- schools access funds;
- care to learn;
- education maintenance allowance (England);
- learner support fund (England);
- adult learning grant (England);
- assembly learning grant (Wales);
- passport to study grant (Wales);
- financial contingency fund (Wales).

An education maintenance allowance, care to learn payment, assembly learning grant or passport to study grant is disregarded when calculating the grant income of a young person or her/his parents. An adult learning grant is taken into account as grant income (see p640). Payments from the learner support fund and financial contingency fund are treated in the same way as access funds (see p648).

Scotland

Financial support for students in further education includes:

- bursary maintenance allowance;
- dependants' allowance;
- other allowances for books and equipment, travel, study expenses;
- education maintenance allowance;
- further education hardship fund;
- young students retention fund;
- childcare fund.

An education maintenance allowance, other allowances for books and equipment, travel, study expenses (elements for books, equipment and travel only) are disregarded when calculating the grant income of a young person or her/his parents. Payments from the childcare fund, a dependants' allowance and a bursary maintenance allowance is treated as grant income (see p640). Payments from the further education hardship fund and young students retention fund are treated in the same way as access funds (see p648).

Student support in higher education

Higher education student support changed in 1998. This book deals with support under the new system and does not consider support for students who started their course before 1 September 1998 or others still covered under the old student support system. See the 2000/01 edition of the *Welfare Benefits Handbook* for details of how student support under the old system is treated.

Student support for full-time undergraduates is different in Scotland from England and Wales.

Student loans

In England, Wales and Scotland, the main source of financial support to undergraduate students who started their course in or after the 1998/99 academic year is a means-tested **student loan** paid under the Education (Student Support) Regulations (and the equivalent Scottish Regulations). In Scotland, more of the student loan is means tested. Your eligibility for a student loan is assessed by your LEA; in Scotland, by the Student Awards Agency for Scotland (SAAS), but paid by the Student Loan Company (SLC). A student loan is treated in a different way to all other types of loan in the calculation of your benefit. In addition to a student loan, other types of loan, such as a career development loan (see p647) may be available.

Student grants

Full-time undergraduate and part-time initial teacher training students in England and Wales, who start their course in the 2004/05 academic year, may be eligible for a means-tested **higher education grant**. It will be disregarded as grant income because it is paid to cover the costs of books and equipment, travel and childcare.

Additional support

In addition to a basic student loan, intended to meet your daily living expenses, you may also be able to apply for additions (called **supplementary allowances**) to cover other costs – eg, because you have a child or a disability. Supplementary allowances are paid as a 'grant' and are not repayable. Some of them are treated as grant income for benefit purposes. Special rules apply to supplementary allowances that are paid for purposes other than living costs – eg, childcare costs or costs related to your disabilities. Note that for disabled students' allowances and childcare grants, allowances are both assessed and paid by the LEA/SAAS. Supplementary allowances differ between England, Scotland and Wales.

English, Welsh and Scottish undergraduate students may also qualify for additional means-tested grants to cover either living and/or course costs. Some of these are statutory (eg, Welsh Assembly learning grants, Scottish young persons' bursaries) and some are discretionary (eg, English opportunity bursaries and access bursaries, Scottish mature students' bursaries). They are treated as grant income.

Scottish students may qualify for additional supplementary allowances including dependants' allowance, school meals grant, lone parents' grant, two-homes grant, disabled students' allowance and travel grant. These allowances are treated as grant income.

Career-specific support

If you are attending a health-related course you may be entitled to an **NHS bursary**. There are two types of NHS bursary. A non-means-tested bursary is available for nursing and midwifery diploma courses. Diploma students are not eligible to apply for a student loan, therefore no notional loan income (see p643) should be taken into account. Means-tested bursaries are available for some other health-related courses. Students attending such courses are also eligible to apply for a student loan, but at a lower rate. Only this lower rate should be taken into account as notional loan income (see p643).[66]

If you are studying for an undergraduate diploma or degree in social work in England or Wales you may be eligible for a non-means-tested bursary administered by the General Social Care Council or Care Council for Wales. The bursary counts in full as grant income.

For HB/CTB, guidance to decision makers[67] says that an **incentive payment to teachers** (known as 'training bursaries' or 'golden hellos') are treated as income over the period for which they are paid, or as capital depending on how they are paid – ie, in instalments or as a lump sum. No disregard should be applied. No information is available on how they should be treated for JSA/IS.

For HB/CTB, guidance to decision makers[68] says that **lump-sum payments to NHS diploma students** (nursing and midwifery courses) made when they sign a contract of employment with the NHS are to be treated as capital. No information is available on how they should be treated for JSA/IS.

Allowances are paid to **'return to practice'** healthcare professionals to attend refresher training before returning to work in the NHS. It is run by the Workforce Development Confederation and so may vary in the way in which it is provided and funded. If you are undertaking refresher training by attending a course of study provided at an educational establishment you are classed as a student. Therefore, for HB/CTB, guidance to decision makers[69] says that any allowance you receive that is intended for general costs or for books, travel and equipment should be treated as grant income. It is taken into account over your period of study after applying the disregards for travel, books and equipment (to the total allowance payable) regardless of whether the allowance is paid on a weekly, monthly or lump-sum basis. However, any allowance paid for childcare costs is taken into account in full unless it is paid direct to the childcare provider. Any payment of the allowance paid after you have completed your refresher training should not be taken into account during your period of study. No information is available on how these allowances should be treated for JSA/IS.

Grants

The term **'grant'**[70] includes any kind of educational grant or award, bursary (such as those paid by the NHS for certain health-related courses – see above), scholarship, studentship or exhibition, as well as a grant, supplementary allowance or award from an LEA or the SAAS. It does not include any payment from access funds (see p648) or education maintenance allowance (or equivalent in Scotland and Wales).

You are treated as having a parental or partner's contribution to your grant whether or not it has been paid to you. However, if you are (for IS only) a lone parent, a lone foster parent or (for IS and JSA only) a disabled student, only the amount of any contribution that you actually receive counts.[71]

Your grant income (or that of your partner) is taken into account as income but is subject to special rules and disregards. How your grant is treated depends on its source, what it is expected to cover and the period for which it is payable.

Calculating grant income – general rule

In most cases, your grant income will be assessed over a period starting from the 'benefit week' which coincides with, or immediately follows, the first day of your 'period of study' (see below) and ends with the benefit week, the last day of which coincides with, or immediately precedes, the last day of your period of study. In this context, **'benefit week'** means the week corresponding to the week in respect of which benefit is paid.[72]

This means your grant income will be apportioned over the number of complete benefit weeks within your period of study and any part weeks at the beginning or end of that period will be ignored. **Note:** this rule does not apply to an NHS bursary (see p641).

Your grant income is apportioned as follows:[73]

- if it is payable for your period of study, unless you are attending a sandwich course (see below), over the number of benefit weeks within your period of study; *or*
- if it is payable for a period other than your period of study, over the number of benefit weeks within the period for which it is payable.

'Period of study' means:[74]

- for a course of one year or less, from the start of the course to the last day of the course;
- for a course of more than one year, in the first and subsequent years (but not the final year):
  - where the grant is payable at a rate appropriate to study throughout the year, from the start of your academic year and ending with the day before the start of your next academic year; *or*
  - in any other case, from the start of your academic year to the last day of your academic year and excluding your normal summer vacation;

- in the final year of a course lasting more than one year, from the start of the academic year and ending with the last day of the course.

In deciding whether or not your grant is payable at a rate appropriate to study throughout the year (as in the second category above), any supplementary allowances paid in your grant or loan (eg, for dependants) are ignored.[75]

Calculating grant income – specific types of grant income

If you are attending a **sandwich course** (see p622) your grant income is taken into account over a different period. Any periods spent on placement or work experience within your period of study are excluded and your grant is apportioned over the remaining 'benefit weeks' within your period of study.[76] Note that this only applies if your grant is payable for your period of study. If your grant is payable for a different period, your grant is taken into account over the number of benefit weeks within the period for which it is payable but excluding any periods spent on placement or work experience.

Postgraduate awards made by research councils and the British Academy are apportioned over the number of benefit weeks within the period for which they are payable (usually a calendar year).

NHS bursaries paid to students in England and Wales are paid in monthly instalments. The bursary (including any supplementary allowances for an adult dependant) should be taken into account over 52 or 53 weeks (benefit weeks sometimes run to 53 weeks, including part weeks).[77] HB/CTB guidance to decision makers says that, for health-related courses in Scotland, NHS bursaries (including any allowance for an adult dependant) should be taken into account over the period for which they are paid.[78]

If you receive a **supplementary allowance** for an adult dependant as part of a student loan (or you could have received one had you taken reasonable steps to apply for one) under the Education (Student Support) Regulations (or the equivalent Scottish Regulations) the allowance is apportioned over the same period as a student loan (see p643). Similarly, if you receive an adult dependant's allowance from any other source (but see p642) and you also receive a student loan (or could have received one had you taken reasonable steps to apply for one) the allowance is apportioned over the same period as a student loan (see p643).[79] However, if you receive a supplementary allowance for an adult dependant as part of an NHS bursary, or under the Education (Mandatory Awards) Regulations or the equivalent Scottish Regulations (including an allowance because you are an older student), these allowances are apportioned over 52 or 53 weeks (benefit weeks sometimes run to 53 weeks, including part-weeks).[80] This includes the final year of your course[81] – ie, you are treated as having this income for a period after the last day of your course. Arguably, for IS/JSA only, they should still be ignored once you have completed your course (see p649).

Note: Students on health-related courses, except nursing and midwifery diploma courses, may be eligible for supplementary allowances for an adult dependant under both an NHS bursary and (reduced rate) student loan. These separate allowances for an adult dependant will be taken into account over different periods (see p641).

If you receive a supplementary allowance from any other source, but you do not receive a student loan (or could not have received one even if you had taken reasonable steps to apply for one) it will be apportioned over the same period as 'basic' grant income (see p640).

A **care leaver's grant** of up to £100 a week towards accommodation paid during the long vacation can be made under the Education (Student Support) Regulations (or the equivalent Scottish regulations) if you are a student and were aged 21 or under at the start of your course and had been in the care or custody of a local authority. This payment will be taken fully into account for each week for which it is paid.

The **Scottish young person's bursary** is treated in the same way as the student loan (see p643).

A **Scottish mature student's bursary** is taken into account as grant income except an amount paid for childcare.

Calculating grant income – grant income which is ignored

These disregards apply only to the grant you receive for your period of study and not to any supplementary allowances for dependants you may receive during the long vacation.[82]

The following grant income is ignored:[83]

- a fixed sum of £352 for books and equipment (2005/06 academic year). If your grant includes a specific amount to cover the costs of books and equipment, the specific amount will be disregarded in addition to the fixed amount;
- a fixed amount of £280 for travelling expenses (2005/06 academic year). If your grant includes a specified sum for travel this is disregarded in addition to the fixed amount.[84] If your actual travel costs are higher than the fixed amount (plus a specific sum if paid) no additional amount will be disregarded.[85]
  Note: If you also receive a student loan, the above two fixed sum disregards will be allowed against your student loan income rather than your grant income (see p643);[86]
- any allowance for tuition and examination fees;
- disabled students' allowance;
- any allowance to meet the cost of attending a residential course away from your normal student accommodation during term time;
- any allowance for the cost of your normal home (away from college) but, for IS and JSA, only if your rent is not met by HB;
- any amount for a partner or child abroad;

- for IS/JSA only, any amount intended for the maintenance of a child dependant;
- any amount intended for the childcare costs of a child dependant;
- parents' learning allowance;
- a grant for travel, books and equipment (up to a maximum of £510);[87]
- the Higher Education Grant;[88]
- if you receive any payment, apart from your grant, to help you with certain expenses which are disregarded from your grant and these payments are greater than the amount for those expenses disregarded from your grant income, the excess amount is also ignored;[89]
- if you have been required to make a contribution to your own grant (eg, because you have other income, such as maintenance), an amount equivalent to that contribution is disregarded.[90] In the case of a couple, the amount of any contribution that one member has been assessed to pay to her/his partner who is a student is disregarded from the non-student's income;[91]
- an education maintenance allowance or an equivalent payment in England, Wales or Scotland.

If you abandon or are dismissed from your course

For IS and JSA, if you leave or are dismissed from your course before it finishes, any grant you have received is taken into account as if you were still a student until whichever is the earlier:[92]

- you repay the grant; *or*
- the academic term or vacation in which you ceased to be a student ends; *or*
- the end of the period covered by the last instalment of your grant.

For HB/CTB it will be taken into account until the date you are asked to repay it by the grant provider.[93]

Loans

A loan is treated as income but is subject to special rules and disregards. Note that some supplementary allowances paid under the student loan provisions are paid as non-repayable grants and are treated as grant income (see p640).

Calculating income from a student loan

For full-time students, how your, or your partner's, student loan[94] is treated depends on whether your course lasts for one year or less, or for a longer period. The maximum amount of available loan is taken into account even if you do not apply for a loan or for the maximum amount.[95]

A student loan paid to a student on a postgraduate certificate of education (PGCE) course is treated in the same way as student loans and supplementary allowances for undergraduate students. If you receive an NHS bursary (see p623) for a nursing or midwifery diploma course no loan income should be taken into account. If you are on another health-related course only the lower maximum loan rate should be taken into account.

Your loan (including any additional week's allowance[96]) will be treated as explained below. For the treatment of supplementary allowances for dependants, see p638.

Academic year

The rules give a definition of an 'academic year' for the purposes of calculating student loan income. This definition may be different from the actual academic year of the education institution you attend.

'Academic year' means a period of 12 months beginning on 1 January, 1 April, 1 July or 1 September according to whether your course begins in the winter, the spring, the summer or the autumn respectively. But if you are required to begin attending your course during August or September (as is the case for most students) and to continue attending through the autumn, the academic year of your course will be treated as beginning in the autumn rather than summer term' – ie, from 1 September.[97]

'Quarter' means one of the periods from 1 January to 31 March, 1 April to 30 June, 1 July to 31 August, or 1 September to 31 December.[98]

Benefit weeks

Loan income will be apportioned over a period of 'benefit weeks' (see p643).

The first appropriate benefit week may fall before the start of your actual academic year and the last benefit week may fall either before or after the last day of your academic year (academic years vary between education institutions). This may mean your benefit is recalculated several times depending on when your actual academic year falls in relation to the relevant benefit weeks. You will need to make a new claim or check that your entitlement is revised at these times.

If you are required to start attending your course in August, or your course is for less than one academic year, the period will begin with the benefit week which coincides with or immediately follows, the first day of the course.[99]

If your academic year starts other than on 1 September, your loan payable for that academic year will be apportioned equally between the benefit weeks within the period beginning with the first day of that academic year and ending with the last day of that academic year. Excluded from that are any benefit weeks falling entirely within the quarter during which, in the opinion of the decision maker, your longest vacation falls.

But in the first, or only, year of your course your loan income (calculated under the rules below) will be ignored for each benefit week that falls before the start of your 'period of study' (the first day of the first term).[100] This is because you cannot be treated as a student until you actually start your course.

Loan income that is ignored

The following loan income is ignored:[101]

- if your loan includes a specific amount to cover the costs of books and equipment, the specific amount will be disregarded. If it does not include a specified amount, a fixed sum of £343 from the total loan amount is ignored (2004/05 academic year);
- a fixed amount of £2[illegible] from the total loan amount for travelling expenses (2004/05 academic year). Guidance to IS decision makers says that if your loan includes a specified sum for travel this is disregarded in addition to the fixed amount.[102] If your actual travel costs are higher than the fixed amount (plus a specific sum if paid) no additional amount will be disregarded.[103]
  Note: If you also receive a grant, the above two elements are disregarded from your loan income rather than from your grant income;
- £10 weekly disregard on loan income, although it may overlap with other disregards on income from certain war pensions (see p970) and charitable or voluntary payments (see p973). With charitable or voluntary payments, a combined maximum weekly disregard of £20 is allowed;[104]
- hardship loan;[105]
- loans to part-time students – some students taking part-time courses of undergraduate higher education may be able to apply for a student loan of up to £500. This payment is ignored because it is less than the standard disregards for travel, books and equipment;[106]
- if you receive any payment apart from your loan to help you with certain expenses which are disregarded from your loan, and these payments are greater than the amount for those expenses disregarded from your loan income, the excess amount is also ignored;[107]
- if you have been required to make a contribution to your own loan (eg, because you have other income, such as maintenance), an amount equivalent to that contribution is disregarded as income.[108] In the case of a couple, the amount of any contribution that one member has been assessed to pay to her/his partner who is a student is disregarded from the non-student's income.[109]

Period over which loan income is taken into account

A course lasting for one academic year or less

Your loan will be apportioned over the benefit weeks beginning with the benefit week, the first day of which coincides with or follows the first day of the academic year and ending with the benefit week, the last day of which coincides with or immediately follows last day of the course.

A course lasting for more than one academic year

Unless it is your final year (see p646) your loan will be taken into account from whichever is the earlier of:

- the first benefit week in September; *or*

- the first benefit week the first day of which coincides with, or immediately follows, the first day of the autumn term,

and ending with the benefit week which coincides with or immediately precedes the last day of June.[110]

Final year of a course

Your loan will be taken into account over the period beginning with either:

- where the final academic year starts on 1 September, the benefit week, the first day of which coincides with, or immediately follows, the earlier of 1 September or the first day of the autumn term; *or*
- the first benefit week, the first day of which coincides with, or immediately follows, the first day of the academic year,

and ending with the benefit week which coincides with, or immediately precedes, the last day of the course.[111]

If you abandon or are dismissed from your course

If you abandon or are dismissed from your course before it finishes there are special rules about how your student loan will be treated.

If you abandon your course before you have received the final instalment of your student loan, it is taken into account using the formula:[112]

$$\frac{A-(B \times C)}{D}$$

A = the maximum amount of student loan available to you (see p643) – including any amount, paid as a grant, intended for the maintenance of your dependants – that you would have received had you remained a student until the last day of the academic term in which you abandoned or were dismissed from your course, less any disregards that apply (see p645). This amount is the 'relevant payment'.

B = the number of benefit weeks immediately following that which includes the first day of your 'academic year' (see p644) to the benefit week immediately before that which includes the day on which you abandoned or were dismissed from your course.

C = the weekly amount of student loan for the 'academic year' which would have been taken into account to calculate your benefit under the normal rules (see p643) but without applying the £10 a week disregard (see p645). This applies regardless of whether you were actually receiving benefit before you abandoned, or were dismissed, from your course.

D = the number of benefit weeks beginning with the benefit week which includes the day on which you abandoned or were dismissed from your course and ending with the benefit week which includes the last day of the last 'quarter' (see p647) for which your 'relevant payment' (see A) would have been payable to you had you remained on your course.

Example

Bhavna abandons her three-year degree course at a university outside London on 1 November 2004 during the first term of her second year. Her assumed maximum loan income would have been taken into account for 42 weeks (first complete benefit week in September to last complete benefit week in June).

Step A Calculate the relevant payment

Loan instalment paid for first term	£1,365.00
less deduction for books and travel	£618.00
Total taken into account	**£747.00**

Step B Calculate the benefit weeks prior to leaving the course

1.9.04 to 31.10.04	**equals 8 weeks**

Step C Calculate maximum loan for the academic year

Maximum loan	£4,095
less deductions for books and travel	£618
Total loan	£3,477
Weekly amount £3,477 divided by 42 weeks	**£87.78 pw**

Step D

Calculate complete benefit weeks from the benefit week including the date of abandonment to the end of the benefit week including the end of the quarter

1.11.04 to 2.1.05	**equals 9 weeks**

Calculation

$$\frac{747.00 - (8 \times 87.78)}{9} = £4.97 \text{ pw}$$

Therefore, £4.97 pw will be taken into account for the period from 1.11.04 to 2.5.05 (9 weeks) and nothing thereafter.

Note: This formula can result in a nil loan income figure depending on the exact date in your term that you abandon, or are dismissed from, your course.

If you voluntarily repay your student loan, for JSA/IS you are treated as still having that loan income[113] calculated under the above rules. However, guidance to decision makers says you should not be treated as having any loan income if the Student Loan Company demand that you repay the loan instalment immediately.[114]

Calculating income from other types of loan

Career development loans paid under section 2 of the Employment and Training Act 1973 are taken into account as income.[115] For IS and JSA, the weekly income is calculated by dividing the loan by the number of weeks of education or training for which the loan was paid.[116] However, for all means-tested benefits, this income is ignored – except where it is paid for, and is used to meet, 'daily living expenses' (which has the same meaning as for access funds – see p648).[117]

For JSA and IS, financial support (other than a student loan or a career development loan) which is paid by way of a loan, including a loan received from an overseas source, does not count as a student loan or a grant,[118] but is nevertheless taken into account as 'other income' (see p1006). The rules do not say how this income should be treated for HB/CTB but, presumably, the same principle applies.

Payments from access funds

Access funds[119] (which include learner support funds available to some students in the further education sector, financial contingency funds provided by the National Assembly for Wales, and hardship funds offered by higher education institutions in England) are administered by colleges and universities. Individual educational institutions may call all or part of these funds by other names – ie, access bursary, mature students' bursary and childcare support. From September 2004, it is intended that these discretionary funds will be called 'access to learning funds' in English higher education institutions.[120] Payments from access funds should be distinguished from payments with similar names from other sources – ie, hardship loans.

How a payment from access funds is treated depends on whether it is paid as a single lump-sum payment, in instalments or to bridge the period before you start your course or receive a student loan payment.

A single lump-sum payment[121]

A single lump-sum payment will be treated as capital (see Chapter 39) immediately you receive it. However, if it is intended and used for one of the items, expenses or charges (called 'daily living expenses') listed below, which you or your partner may incur or be liable for, it will be disregarded for 52 weeks from the date it is paid:

- food;
- ordinary clothing or footwear (which means that used for normal daily use, but does not include school uniforms or that used solely for sporting activities);
- household fuel;
- (for JSA/IS only) rent for which HB is payable;
- (for JSA/IS only) housing costs – see Chapter 36;
- (for JSA/IS only) accommodation charges for residential nursing or care – see Chapter 36;
- council tax;
- water charges.

If the payment is intended but not used for these items or charges, it will count as capital immediately you receive it.

Payment made in instalments[122]

Payment made in instalments will be treated as income but it will be disregarded in full. However, if the payment is intended and used for expenses or charges in the list above it will be taken into account as income for each week it is intended to cover, but the first £20 a week will be disregarded. The disregard may overlap with other disregards on loan income (see p645), certain war pensions (see p970) and charitable or voluntary payments (see p973). A combined maximum disregard of £20 is allowed.[123]

Payments made before the start of a course or before receipt of a student loan[124]

A payment (whether paid as a single payment or in instalments) made on or after whichever is the earlier of:

- 1 September; *or*
- the first day of your course,

which is intended to bridge the gap before you receive payment of your student loan, or made in anticipation of your becoming a student, is ignored as both income and capital even if it is for an item, expense or charge in the list above.

Treatment of student financial support once you have completed your course

For IS/JSA only, any grant income, student loan, assessed contribution made by a parent or spouse as part of the loan or grant, or career development loan which you received no longer counts as income once you have completed the course.[125]

However, as most (but not all) types of student support are not taken into account for a period after your course is due to end it should also be ignored as income for HB/CTB once you have completed the course.

Presumably, for IS/JSA/HB/CTB any student financial support you have left once you have completed your course will count as capital (see Chapter 39) as there are no provisions to disregard it under the rules about capital.

Notes

1. **Studying and claiming income support or jobseeker's allowance**
   1 Reg 12(1) IS Regs; reg 54 JSA Regs; reg 5 CB Regs
   2 s124(1)(d) SSCBA 1992; s1(2)(g) JSA 1995
   3 Reg 2(1)(b)(i)&(ii) C(LC)SSB Regs; reg 13(2)(a) and (b) IS Regs; Memo JSA/IS 04 para 14

4 Regs 4ZA and 13(2)(a)-(e) IS Regs
5 R(IS) 9/94
6 R(IS) 9/94
7 CIS/11766/1996
8 R(IS) 9/94
9 R(SB) 2/87
10 CIS/11441/1995
11 s1(2)(g) JSA 1995; reg 54 JSA Regs
12 **IS** Reg 12 IS Regs
JSA Reg 54(1) and (2) JSA Regs
Both s142 SSCBA 1992; reg 7 CB Regs
13 **IS** Reg 61(1) IS Regs, definition of 'full time student'
JSA Reg 1(3) JSA Regs, definition of 'full time student'
14 **IS** Reg 2(1) IS Regs, definition of 'period of study'
JSA Reg 1(3) JSA Regs, definition of 'period of study'
HB Reg 46(2)(b) HB Regs
CTB Reg 38(2)(b) CTB Regs
15 **IS** Reg 61(1) IS Regs, definition of 'last day of the course'
JSA Regs 1(3) and 15(1)(a) JSA Regs, definitions of 'full-time student'
HB Reg 46 HB Regs, definition of 'last day of the course'
CTB Reg 38 CTB Regs, definition of 'last day of the course'
16 HB/CTB circulars A31/2001 para 4.1 and A39/2001 para 15
17 **IS** Reg 61(1) IS Regs, definitions of 'full-time course of advanced education' and 'full-time course of study'
JSA Reg 1(3) JSA Regs, definition of 'full-time student' – the definition of 'full-time course' is found within that definition
18 para 30110-1114 DMG
19 **IS** Reg 61 IS Regs definitions of 'full-time course of advanced education' and 'full-time course of study'; para 30107 – 30108 DMG
JSA Reg 1(3) JSA Regs, definition of 'full-time student' – the definition of 'full-time course' is found within that definition
20 **IS** Reg 61(1) IS Regs
JSA Reg 1(3) JSA Regs
HB Reg 46 HB Regs
CTB Reg 38 CTB Regs
All definition of 'sandwich course'
21 R(IS) 19/98
22 **IS** Reg 61(4) IS Regs
JSA Reg 1(3C) JSA Regs
HB Reg 46(4) HB Regs
CTB Reg 38(4) CTB Regs
23 **IS** Reg 61(2)(a) IS Regs
JSA Reg 1(3A)(a) JSA Regs
HB Reg 46(2)(a) HB Regs
CTB Reg 38(2)(a) CTB Regs
24 **IS** Reg 61(3)(b) IS Regs
JSA Reg 1(3B)(b) JSA Regs
HB Reg 46(3)(b) HB Regs
CTB Reg 38(3)(b) CTB Regs
25 **IS** Reg 61(3)(a) IS Regs
JSA Reg 1(3B)(a) JSA Regs
HB Reg 46(3)(a) HB Regs
CTB Reg 38(3)(a) CTB Regs
26 R(IS) 15/98; R(IS) 7/99; CJSA/836/1998; R(IS) 1/00; memo AM(AOG) 121
27 R(SB) 40/83; R(SB) 41/83
28 **IS** Reg 61 IS Regs, definitions of 'full-time course of advanced education' and 'full-time course of study'
JSA Reg 1(3) JSA Regs, definition of 'full-time student' – the definition of 'full-time course' is found within that definition
29 Reg 4ZA and Sch 1B IS Regs
30 Sch 1B paras 10, 11 and 12 IS Regs
31 Reg 15(a) JSA Regs
32 Reg 14(1)(a) JSA Regs
33 Reg 14(1)(k) JSA Regs
34 R(IS) 1/96
35 CIS/368/1992; R(IS) 6/97
36 R(JSA) 2/02
37 R(IS) 7/99
38 HB/CTB Circular A32/2000 para 32; paras 30134-138 DMG
39 CIS/152/1994; R(IS) 15/98
40 R(JSA) 3/02
41 s15 SPCA 2002; reg 15 SPC Regs
42 CIS/152/1994; R(IS) 15/98; CJSA/836/1998; R(IS) 1/00; memo AM(AOG) 121
43 Reg 1(3) JSA Regs, definition of 'part-time student'
44 Reg 54(3) JSA Regs
45 para 21239-241 DMG
46 para 21242 DMG
47 para 21243 DMG
48 para 21244 DMG
49 Reg 11 JSA Regs

2. Studying and claiming housing benefit and council tax benefit

50 Reg 9(a) HB&CTB(SPC) Regs
51 **HB** Reg 6(1)(e) HB Regs
CTB Reg 51(3) and (4) CTB Regs
52 Reg 52 HB Regs
53 **HB** Reg 48A(2) HB Regs
CTB Reg 40(3) CTB Regs
54 **HB** Reg 48A(3) HB Regs
CTB Reg 40(4) CTB Regs
55 Reg 48(1) HB Regs

56 Reg 48(2) HB Regs
57 para C5 140-144 GM
58 Reg 50 HB Regs, as amended by Reg 7 SS(SIIRB)(Amdmt) Regs 2004

3. **Studying and claiming other benefits and tax credits**

59 s15 SPCA 2002; reg 15 SPC Regs
60 Reg 17 SS(IB) Regs; CS/20/1986
61 Reg 5 SS(ICA) Regs
62 Reg 5(2) SS(ICA) Regs
63 R(G) 2/02
64 Memo DMG Vol 10 05/02

4. **Calculating income from grants and loans**

65 **HB** Reg 25 HB Regs
CTB Reg 17 CTB Regs
as substituted by regs 7 and 8 HB&CTB(SPC) Regs
66 HB/CTB Circular A31/2001 paras 3.1-3.2
67 HB/CTB Circular A31/2001 para 5.2
68 HB/CTB Circular A31/2001 para 5.3
69 HB/CTB Circular A39/2001 paras 23-27
70 **IS** Reg 61(1) IS Regs
JSA Reg 130 JSA Regs
HB Reg 46(1) HB Regs
CTB Reg 38(1) CTB Regs
All definition of 'grant'
71 **IS** Reg 61(1) IS Regs
JSA Reg 130 JSA Regs
HB Reg 46(1) HB Regs
CTB Reg 38(1) CTB Regs
All definition of 'grant income'
72 Sch 7, para 4 SS(C&P)Regs
73 **IS** Reg 62(3) IS Regs
JSA Reg 131(4) JSA Regs
HB Reg 53(3) HB Regs
CTB Reg 42(4) CTB Regs
74 **IS** Reg 61(1) IS Regs
JSA Reg 1(3) JSA Regs
HB Reg 46 HB Regs
CTB Reg 38 CTB Regs
All definition of 'period of study'
75 para C5.43 GM
76 **IS** Reg 62(4) IS Regs
JSA Reg 131(6) JSA Regs
HB Reg 53(4) HB Regs
CTB Reg 42(5) CTB Regs
77 **IS** Reg 62(3A) IS Regs
JSA Reg 131(5) JSA Regs
HB Reg 53(3A) HB Regs
CTB Reg 42(4A) CTB Regs
78 HB/CTB Circular A31/2001 para 3.5
79 **IS** Reg 62(3B) IS Regs
JSA Reg 131(5A) JSA Regs
HB Reg 53(3B) HB Regs
CTB Reg 42(4B) CTB Regs
80 **IS** Reg 62(3A) IS Regs
JSA Reg 131(5) JSA Regs
HB Reg 53(3)(b) HB Regs
CTB Reg 42(4)(b) CTB Regs
81 R(IS) 15/95
82 CIS/91/1994
83 **IS** Reg 62(2) and (2B) IS Regs
JSA Reg 131(2) and (3A) JSA Regs
HB Reg 53(2) and (2B) HB Regs
CTB Reg 42(2) and (3A) CTB Regs
84 Joint IS/JSA Bulletin 18/00 para 1.10; Memo DMG Vol 6 3/00 para 22
85 R(IS) 7/95
86 **IS** Reg 62(2A) IS Regs
JSA Reg 131(3) JSA Regs
HB Reg 53(2A) HB Regs
CTB Reg 42(3) CTB Regs
87 Paid under reg 15(8) Education (Student Support) Regulations 2002, SI 2002 No.195
88 **HB/CTB** Circular A26/2004 para 14
IS/JSA Memo DMG JSA/IS 64 para 65
89 **IS** Reg 66(1) IS Regs
JSA Reg 135(1) JSA Regs
HB Reg 57 HB Regs
CTB Reg 46 CTB Regs
90 **IS** Reg 67A IS Regs
JSA Reg 137A JSA Regs
HB Reg 58A HB Regs
CTB Reg 48A CTB Regs
91 **IS** Reg 67 IS Regs
JSA Reg 137 JSA Regs
HB Reg 58(1) HB Regs
CTB Reg 48 CTB Regs
92 **IS** Reg 32(6A) IS Regs
JSA Reg 97(7) JSA Regs
93 R(IS) 5/99
94 **IS** Reg 61(1) IS Regs
JSA Reg 130 JSA Regs
HB Reg 46(1) HB Regs
CTB Reg 38(1) CTB Regs
All definition of 'student loan'
95 **IS** Reg 66A(3) IS Regs
JSA Reg 136(3) JSA Regs
HB Reg 57A(3) HB Regs
CTB Reg 47(3) and (4) CTB Regs
96 HB/CTB Circular A31/2001 para 2.8
97 **IS** Reg 61(1) IS Regs
JSA Reg 130 JSA Regs
HB Reg 46(1) HB Regs
CTB Reg 38(1) CTB Regs
All definition of 'academic year'

Notes

98 **IS** Reg 66A(2)(aa) IS Regs
JSA Reg 136(2)(aa) JSA Regs
HB Reg 57A(2)(aa) HB Regs
CTB Reg 47(2)(aa) CTB Regs
99 **IS** Reg 66A(2)(a) IS Regs
JSA Reg 136(2)(a) JSA Regs
HB Reg 57A(2)(a) HB Regs
CTB Reg 47(2)(a) CTB Regs
100 Memo DMG Vol JSA/IS 19 para 16; HB/CTB Circular A31/2001 para 2.4
101 **IS** Reg 66A(5) IS Regs
JSA Reg 136(5) JSA Regs
HB Reg 57A(5) HB Regs
CTB Reg 47(5) CTB Regs
102 IS Bulletin 99/99 para 2.6
103 R(IS) 7/95
104 **IS** Sch 9 para 36 IS Regs
JSA Sch 7 para 38 JSA Regs
HB Sch 4 para 33 HB Regs
CTB Sch 4 para 33 CTB Regs
105 **IS** Reg 66A(1) and (1A) IS Regs
JSA Reg 136(1) and (1A) JSA Regs
HB Reg 57(1) and (1A) HB Regs
CTB Reg 47(1) and (1A) CTB Regs
106 HB/CTB Circular A32/2000 para 18
107 **IS** Reg 66(1) IS Regs
JSA Reg 135(1) JSA Regs
HB Reg 57 HB Regs
CTB Reg 46 CTB Regs
108 **IS** Reg 67A IS Regs
JSA Reg 137A JSA Regs
HB Reg 58A HB Regs
CTB Reg 48A CTB Regs
109 **IS** Reg 67 IS Regs
JSA Reg 137 JSA Regs
HB Reg 58(1) HB Regs
CTB Reg 48 CTB Regs
110 **IS** Reg 66A(2)(c) IS Regs
JSA Reg 136(2)(c) JSA Regs
HB Reg 57A (2)(c) HB Regs
CTB Reg 47(2)(c) CTB Regs
111 **IS** Reg 66A(2)(b) IS Regs
JSA Reg 136(2)(b) JSA Regs
HB Reg 57A(2)(b) HB Regs
CTB Reg 47(2)(b) CTB Regs
112 **IS** Reg 40(3A)(3AA) and (3AB) IS Regs
JSA Reg 103(5)(5ZA) and (5ZB) JSA Regs
HB Reg 33(3A),(3B) and (3C) HB Regs
CTB Reg 24(4),(4A) and (4B) CTB Regs
113 Reg 6(6)(a) SS&CS(DA) Regs
114 **IS**/JSA memo DMG Vol 6 2/01 paras 17-18; HB/CTB Circular A31/2001 para 6.2
115 **IS** Reg 41(6) IS Regs
JSA Reg 104(5) JSA Regs
HB Reg 34(4) HB Regs
CTB Reg 25(4) CTB Regs
116 **IS** Reg 29(2A) IS Regs
JSA Reg 94(2A) JSA Regs
117 **IS** Sch 9 para 59 IS Regs
JSA Sch 7 para 57 JSA Regs
HB Sch 4 para 63 HB Regs
CTB Sch 4 para 63 CTB Regs
118 R(IS) 16/95
119 **IS** Reg 61(1) IS Regs
JSA Reg 130 JSA Regs
HB Reg 46 HB Regs
CTB Reg 38 CTB Regs
All definition of 'access funds'
120 DfES Press Notice 2002/0226, editor's notes, para 5
121 **IS** Reg 68 IS Regs
JSA Reg 138 JSA Regs
HB Reg 59 HB Regs
CTB Reg 49 CTB Regs
122 **IS** Reg 66B IS Regs
JSA Reg 136A JSA Regs
HB Reg 57B HB Regs
CTB Reg 47A CTB Regs
123 **IS** Sch 9 para 36 IS Regs
JSA Sch 7 para 38 JSA Regs
HB Sch 4 para 33 HB Regs
CTB Sch 4 para 33 CTB Regs
124 **IS** Reg 66B IS Regs
JSA Reg 136A JSA Regs
HB Reg 57B HB Regs
CTB Reg 47A CTB Regs
125 **IS** Sch 9 paras 60 and 61 IS Regs
JSA Sch 7 paras 58 and 59 JSA Regs

Chapter 26

Coming from and going abroad: benefits

This chapter contains all the rules about claiming benefits when you either come from or go abroad. It covers:

This chapter deals with the rules relating to social security benefits, with only some brief references to tax credits. For full details of the immigration rules that apply to tax credits, see Chapter 59.

1. Immigration status

It is important to know your immigration status before making a claim for benefit. This is because your immigration status determines your right to social security benefits and a claim for benefit can sometimes affect your right to remain in the UK. If you are unsure about your immigration status you should seek specialist advice.

Most people, apart from British citizens, are subject to immigration control. This means that you cannot freely enter the UK, but will be subject to scrutiny by the immigration authority. The degree of control varies according to your nationality – for example, European Economic Area (EEA) nationals do not need leave to enter or remain and therefore enjoy much greater freedom to enter by virtue of European Community law. If you are subject to immigration control you require leave, or permission, to enter or remain. Such leave can be:

- limited leave to enter or remain;
- indefinite leave to enter or remain;
- exceptional leave to enter or remain.

If you have limited leave you are only permitted to remain in the UK for a limited period of time. Certain conditions are frequently attached to a grant of limited leave. For example, a restriction may be made on you working or claiming benefits. If you breach these conditions you may put your right to remain in the UK at risk.

The interrelationship between immigration and social security law is extremely complex and your immigration status may not always be clear. There are close links between the benefit authorities and the Home Office. Making a claim for benefit could alert the immigration authorities to the fact that you are here unlawfully, or that you have broken your conditions of entry by claiming 'public funds'. It is vitally important, therefore, to get specialist advice before claiming if you are unsure about your position. You can get advice from your local law centre, citizens advice bureau or other advice agency which deals with immigration problems.

Immigration status and benefit entitlement

Benefits affected by immigration status[1]

Attendance allowance
Carer's allowance
Child benefit
Council tax benefit
Disability living allowance
Housing benefit
Incapacity benefit for incapacity in youth[2]
Income-based jobseeker's allowance
Income support
Pension credit
Severe disablement allowance
Social fund payments

Entitlement to social security benefits is increasingly linked to your immigration status. The law defines certain people as a 'person subject to immigration control'. This phrase has a special meaning for benefit purposes. If you fall within the definition you can be excluded from entitlement to the above benefits unless you fall within certain exempt categories. For details about who is exempt, see p660 for non-contributory benefits and p661 for means-tested benefits.

You are defined as a **'person subject to immigration control'** if you are not an EEA national and:

- you require leave to enter or remain but do not have it;
- you have leave to enter or remain with a public funds restriction (see below);
- you have leave to enter or remain and are the subject of a formal undertaking (see p662);
- you are appealing a decision about your immigration status.

People eligible to claim any benefit

You do not fall within the definition of a 'person subject to immigration control' and therefore cannot be excluded on grounds of immigration status if you are:

- a British citizen;
- a person with right of abode/certificate of patriality;
- a British national with right of re-admission;
- an EEA national (see p672);
- a family member of an EEA national;
- a Swiss national (see p673);
- a refugee (see p669);
- a person with exceptional leave to remain (see p662);
- a person granted humanitarian protection or discretionary leave (see p662);
- a person from Northern Ireland, the Channel Islands or the Isle of Man (see p692);
- a person with indefinite leave to enter/remain (but if you are the subject of a formal undertaking you can be excluded from some means-tested benefits – see p662).

In addition there are some people who come within the general definition of a 'person subject to immigration control' but who are nevertheless eligible for some benefits because regulations exempt them from the definition of a 'person subject to immigration control'. The exemptions vary according to the benefit involved. For details about who can qualify, see p660 for non-contributory non-means-tested benefits and means-tested benefits and p664 for urgent cases payments of income support (IS) and income-based jobseeker's allowance (JSA). There are also some transitional Regulations that provide entitlement to some claimants. For details about tax credits see Chapter 59.

However, EEA and Swiss nationals and their family members may be subject to the habitual residence test and the right to reside test for certain benefits.

Public funds

Most people admitted to the UK with limited leave, such as spouses or visitors, are given limited leave to stay here on condition that they do not have recourse to 'public funds'. If you have recourse to public funds in breach of your permission to stay (your 'leave conditions') you could be liable to deportation, refusal of further leave and prosecution. You should therefore always seek advice before claiming. This is particularly important if your spouse is applying for leave to remain, as leave could be refused.

'Public funds' is defined in the immigration rules as:[3]

- attendance allowance (AA);
- carer's allowance (previously invalid care allowance);
- child benefit;
- child tax credit (CTC);
- council tax benefit (CTB);
- disability living allowance (DLA);
- housing benefit (HB);
- IS;
- income-based JSA;
- pension credit (PC);
- severe disablement allowance;
- social fund payments;
- working tax credit (WTC).

Only the benefits that appear on the list are public funds.

If you are a British citizen or have settled status and you have a partner who is a 'person subject to immigration control', you may claim benefits for yourself but you should not claim any additional benefit for your partner. The rules for tax credits are different (see p1459). Some benefits provide for this situation. For IS and income-based JSA if you have a partner who is a 'person subject to immigration control' you will be paid benefit at the single person rate rather than the couple rate. You are, however, still treated as a couple when income or capital is assessed. Therefore, no additional payment of benefit is paid because of the presence of a partner who is a person subject to immigration control. Equally, because of the structure of some other benefits it will be possible to claim because no extra benefit is paid for another person. This would apply to AA and DLA.

The position with PC is slightly different. For PC, a partner who is a 'person subject to immigration control' does not count as a part of your household. Therefore, you get no PC for her/him but equally her/his income and capital do not affect your benefit.[4]

For HB and CTB, the position is more complicated. No additional benefit is payable for your partner if you receive IS, income-based JSA or the guarantee credit of PC because you are already receiving maximum HB or CTB. If you do not receive these benefits, the calculation for HB and CTB includes allowances for all members of the family and, therefore, could result in an additional amount of benefit being paid for the 'person subject to immigration control'.

Once your spouse is here and has been given limited leave (for the trial two-year period), s/he should receive a letter from the Home Office explaining that the

British, or settled, spouse can claim any benefit to which they are entitled in their own right.

You should also always seek advice before claiming a 'public funds' benefit. This is particularly important if your spouse is applying for leave to remain, as leave could be refused if you are unable to maintain yourselves without recourse to 'public funds'. It would be wise to avoid claiming a public funds benefit at a time when seeking to extend or vary leave because the receipt of benefits indicates that you are unable to maintain your partner.

Limited leave and public funds

'Limited leave' means that you only have permission to enter, or remain in, the UK for a specified period of time, but see p662 if you have been given exceptional leave to enter or remain for a specific period.

Having recourse to 'public funds' in breach of your leave conditions could render you liable to deportation, refusal of further leave and prosecution. See p655 for further information. Claiming urgent cases payments of IS or JSA if you qualify, however, is safe.

Nationals of EEA states (see p672) do not require leave to enter or remain in the UK, and are not 'persons subject to immigration control'.[5] This principle extends to family members of the EEA and Swiss nationals, whatever their nationality.[6] In practice, a non-EEA family member will need to obtain an EEA residence permit in order to enter the UK, but this is simply an administrative process and there is no limit on the period of their stay and no conditions can be placed on their entry.[7] Swiss nationals have the same rights of freedom of movement as EEA nationals and do not require leave to enter or remain.[8] However, your right to claim certain benefits may be affected by the habitual residence test and the right to reside test. For further information on the rights of EEA nationals, see p672.

2. National insurance numbers and contributions

In order to claim most social security benefits it is now necessary to satisfy the national insurance (NI) number requirement. You satisfy this requirement if you:

- provide an NI number together with evidence to show that the number is yours; *or*
- provide evidence or information to enable your NI number to be traced; *or*
- apply for an NI number and provide sufficient information or evidence for one to be allocated.

If you do not satisfy the NI number requirement you are not eligible for benefit. This requirement applies both to the claimant and any person for whom you are claiming benefit except any child or young person for whom you may be claiming. An application for an NI number can be made at a local social security office on form CA5400 and it must be accompanied by sufficient documentary evidence of identity. This might include, for example, a birth or marriage certificate, a passport or an identity card. It could also include a letter from your solicitor or adviser, or a statement from someone who knows you. A person without sufficient documentation should be interviewed to establish whether an NI number should be issued. This can take several weeks.

Despite apparently neutral criteria, the NI number requirement appears to have had a disproportionate effect on black and minority ethnic claimants. Benefit authority staff appear in practice to work to a set list of documents that will be accepted in terms of establishing identity. Many people from abroad cannot produce these documents, yet reasonable alternatives are often rejected.

A further problem arises where couples have different immigration status. A person who is not a 'person subject to immigration control' is likely to be refused benefit if her/his partner does not have an NI number.

Tactics for obtaining a national insurance number

- Provide the benefit authority with as much documentary evidence of your identity as you can. This could include passports, identity cards, birth or marriage certificates or Home Office documents. If you do not have any of these formal types of documents, think about what else you can provide which will help to prove your identity. For example, a letter from your solicitor or a statement from a teacher, doctor or advice worker.
- If you are having difficulty obtaining your documents or confimation of your identity from the Home Office, consider making a request under the Data Protection Act. If you do this the Home Office must comply within a fixed period of time. There is, however, a small charge.
- If the benefit authority refuses to accept the evidence that you have provided, ask for written reasons for the refusal and information about what evidence would be acceptable – this may lead to a reconsideration of the decision and can be useful for later complaints or legal action.
- If you have provided sufficient evidence of your identity but the benefit authority refuses to allocate an NI number or refuses to interview you for one, you should take legal advice about the possibility of seeking a judicial review.
- Consider making a complaint (see p1300) and pursue this through to the Ombudsman if necessary. However, this can take many months, so you should not delay in taking any legal action against the authority.
- It is not possible to appeal against a refusal of an NI number but it is possible to appeal the decision refusing you benefit.[9] However, you may have to wait several months for an appeal hearing. It may, therefore, be wise to also consider a judicial review of the refusal of the NI number.

- If you have been refused benefit because your partner is a 'person subject to immigration control' and has not been able to obtain an NI number, you may be able to appeal on the basis that you do not need to provide an NI number for your partner because you are not claiming for her/him. This is because certain benefits, such as IS, exclude you from receiving benefit for a partner who is a 'person subject to immigration control'.
- The refusal of benefit to a couple because one of them is unable to obtain an NI number does raise questions as to whether there are breaches of Article 8 of the Human Rights Act (right to respect for family life) because arguably the only way in which the person who is not a 'person subject to immigration control' can qualify for benefit is if s/he separates from her/his partner.
- In some circumstances it may be possible to get an interim payment of benefit (see p1108).
- Consider making a complaint to the Commission for Racial Equality on the basis that the current application of the NI number requirement discriminates against black and minority ethnic claimants. If it receives sufficient complaints it may well decide to investigate.
- Complain to your MP.
- In all cases that CPAG is aware of, when threatened with judicial review, the DWP has eventually allocated an NI number.

National insurance contributions

If you have recently arrived in the UK you may not have paid sufficient NI contributions to qualify for certain benefits. However, if you have worked in another EEA country, you can rely on any contributions that you have paid in those countries in order to qualify for UK benefits.[10] Contributions can also be taken into account if they have been paid in a country with which the UK has a reciprocal agreement.[11]

If you have returned from abroad you could ask the DWP for a copy of your contributions record. In some cases it is possible to make up a shortfall in your record by making voluntary contributions.

There are residence and presence conditions attached to NI contributions and you can remain liable for payment in some cases even if you go abroad to work (see p828).

3. Non-means-tested benefits

Contributory benefits

Your immigration status does not, by itself, prevent you from getting contributory benefits, but in practice you may have paid insufficient contributions (see p828) to be entitled. Moreover, to qualify for contributory benefits (see p831), you will normally have had to have worked in the UK. However, if you are a European Economic Area (EEA) or Swiss national, contributions paid in other member states can be used to help you qualify for contributory benefits in the UK.

Non-contributory benefits

You should be aware of your immigration status before claiming non-contributory benefits (see p5) – ie, attendance allowance (AA), child benefit, disability living allowance (DLA) and carer's allowance. These are public funds (see p655). A claim could have serious consequences for your immigration status. Incapacity benefit for incapacity in youth is not listed as a public funds benefit but some people subject to immigration control are excluded from access to it.

Certain in-work benefits are not affected by your immigration status but may be difficult to access because you need to work in order to qualify. These are industrial injuries benefits, maternity allowance, statutory maternity pay, statutory adoption pay, statutory paternity pay and statutory sick pay.

Attendance allowance, child benefit, disability living allowance, carer's allowance and non-contributory incapacity benefit

You are not excluded from getting these benefits by your immigration status if:[12]

- you come within one of the groups on p655;
- you are a person with indefinite leave to remain and you are subject to a formal undertaking (see p662);
- you are a family member of an EEA national regardless of your nationality or whether or not your partner is a 'worker' (see p672);
- you are a family member of a Swiss national;[13]
- you, or if you are living with them a member of your family, are lawfully working (see p685) in Great Britain and are a citizen of a state with which the European Community has an agreement concerning equal treatment in social security. This applies to citizens of Algeria, Morocco, Slovenia, Tunisia and Turkey (see p684) and could apply to asylum seekers from these countries;
- in the case of AA/DLA and child benefit you are covered by a reciprocal arrangement;
- you are a person who is protected by the 1996 transitional rules relating to asylum seekers (see p667) and others with limited leave.

---

4. Means-tested benefits

You should be aware of your immigration status before claiming means-tested benefits. Most of the benefits in this section, apart from pension credit (PC), are listed in the immigration rules as public funds (see p655). Claiming additional public funds could affect your right to stay in the UK.

Income support, income-based jobseeker's allowance, housing benefit, council tax benefit, the social fund and pension credit

You are not excluded from getting these benefits by your immigration status if:[14]

- you are a person who comes within one of the groups listed on p655;
- you are a family member of an European Economic Area (EEA) national or a Swiss national who is a 'worker' or a person covered by EC Regulation 1408/71 (this applies even where you are separated and in some cases divorced from the EEA or Swiss national);
- you are a person with indefinite leave and are the subject of a formal undertaking that was given five or more years ago and you have been in the UK for five years or more (see p662);
- you are the subject of a formal undertaking given within the past five years but the person who gave the undertaking has died;
- you have limited leave and there is a 'public funds' restriction attached to your stay and your funds from abroad are temporarily disrupted (see p655);
- you are an asylum seeker who has transitional protection (see p667). In some cases this can include the separated partner or grown-up children of the asylum seeker;
- for PC, you are an asylum seeker who, prior to reaching pension age, was entitled to income support (IS). (**Note:** if you are in this position and you have dependent children, there is no provision for any additional sum for your children. Instead, PC claimants who are protected asylum seekers are entitled to child tax credit for children for whom they are responsible);
- you are a national of a country that has ratified the European Convention on Social and Medical Assistance or the Council of Europe Social Charter (1961) (Croatia or Turkey) and you are lawfully present (see below). These rights do not stem from European Community (EC) law and consequently do not override any 'public funds' restriction attached to your stay. Therefore, any claim for benefit could affect your right to remain in the UK.
- for the social fund, you are lawfully working in Great Britain and are a national of Algeria, Morocco, Tunisia or Turkey.

If you qualify for benefit it is usually paid at the normal rate. However, if you qualify for IS or income-based jobseeker's allowance (JSA) on the basis that funds from abroad are disrupted, your sponsor has died or because you are an asylum seeker with transitional protection, you receive benefit at the urgent cases rate (see p664). If you qualify for PC it will be paid at the normal rate.

Lawfully present

The Court of Appeal[15] has ruled that an asylum seeker with temporary admission could not be 'lawfully present' and therefore could not benefit from the above agreements. The case concerned access to housing rather than social security benefits. However, the commissioners[16] have now considered the point in respect of IS and have followed the reasoning of the Court of Appeal. Consequently, only asylum seekers who entered the UK in some 'lawful' capacity (such as a visitor or student) will be able to rely on the agreements.

Sponsorship and undertakings

Many people who enter the UK are admitted on the condition that they can maintain and accommodate themselves without recourse to public funds. A relative or friend in the UK can act as a sponsor to help satisfy this condition.

In some cases, sponsors are required to give a written undertaking under the terms of the Immigration Act 1971 (on a special form – RON 112 or SET (F)), that they will provide maintenance and accommodation. Such undertakings are only usually required for dependent elderly relatives and *not* for spouses. They may be required for children over 16. Other sorts of voluntary or informal sponsorships which are commonly used to support applications to enter the UK are *not* undertakings (this distinction is often misunderstood by the DWP).

'Formal undertakings' affect entitlement to means-tested benefits. If you have been resident in the UK and were admitted subject to a mandatory sponsorship undertaking, you are not entitled to benefit for the first five years unless your sponsor dies within that period. In the case of IS or income-based JSA the amount payable is the urgent cases rate of benefit. PC is paid at the normal rate. After five years you qualify for all means-tested benefits in the ordinary way, and in the case of IS and income-based JSA it is paid at the ordinary rate. The five-year period does not have to be one continuous period. If you go abroad for a temporary period you may be able to add together periods towards the five-year limit.[17] Formal undertakings do not affect non-means-tested benefits.

If you are an EEA national, whether or not you have worker status, you are not excluded from benefit even if you are subject to a sponsorship undertaking.[18] If you are a family member of an EEA national, but you are not an EEA national, and you are subject to an undertaking you can override the restriction to benefit only if your partner has worker status or is covered by EC Regulation 1408/71 (see p672).

'Leave outside the rules' – exceptional leave, humanitarian protection or discretionary leave

In some circumstances, you may not fit within the immigration rules but the Home Office will grant you leave to remain in the UK outside the rules. This could be by granting 'exceptional leave' to enter or remain or, for asylum seekers, humanitarian protection or discretionary leave. Leave outside the rules is granted on humanitarian grounds and could be because of poor health or needing to care for a relative. The DWP sometimes wrongly refuses benefit to people with exceptional leave because it mistakenly thinks they have limited leave (see p653). **Exceptional leave** may initially be given for a year but this does not count as 'limited leave'. A person applying for an extension of her/his exceptional leave continues to be treated as a person with exceptional leave, provided her/his application was made before their original leave had expired.[19]

Some asylum seekers who are refused refugee status are nonetheless allowed to remain in the UK by the Home Office because the Home Office accepts that conditions in their country of origin and/or the individual's circumstances warrant them being granted leave to remain. In the past, asylum seekers were granted exceptional leave, usually for four years, after which an application for indefinite leave could be made. However, on 1 April 2003 the Home Office introduced two new types of leave to replace exceptional leave for asylum seekers. Exceptional leave will continue for non-asylum cases.

Humanitarian protection is granted for three years or less. It is awarded to people who have been refused refugee status but who the Home Office believes cannot be returned to their country of origin as they face a serious risk to life or person because of the death penalty, unlawful killing, torture, inhumane or degrading treatment or punishment. After three years the case will be reviewed and if there is still a risk to the person s/he can be granted indefinite leave.

Discretionary leave is also awarded to people who are refused refugee status, but who do not fulfil the criteria for humanitarian protection. The Home Office intends to award it in very limited circumstances. It will be granted for three years and then reviewed. At this point a further three years may be granted and after six years of discretionary leave the person can apply for indefinite leave.

Until 2007 there will continue to be asylum seekers who have been granted exceptional leave as well as asylum seekers who have been granted the new type of status. For benefit purposes a person with exceptional leave, humanitarian protection or discretionary leave is not excluded from entitlement to any benefits or tax credits.

If you are granted exceptional leave to enter or remain in the UK, humanitarian protection or discretionary leave, you are entitled to claim IS, income-based JSA or PC under the normal rules. You do not have to satisfy the 'habitual residence' test (see p702).[20] There is normally no prohibition on claiming 'public funds' (see p655) if you are granted exceptional leave to remain.

Couples and families

The following rules apply where one or more members of your family (see Chapter 31) are 'persons subject to immigration control'.

- If you are a 'person subject to immigration control', you are not entitled to IS, JSA, housing benefit (HB), council tax benefit (CTB) or PC for yourself or for any members of your family, unless you qualify under one of the exemptions above (see p661).[21]
- Foreign fiancé(e)s and spouses who are admitted for settlement on the condition that they can maintain and accommodate themselves, count as

'persons subject to immigration control' and are not entitled to IS/JSA and PC until they are granted indefinite leave to remain in the UK.

- If you are not a 'person subject to immigration control' but your partner is, you can claim IS/JSA under the normal rules but you do not receive any benefit for your partner.[22] You are still treated as a couple (see p811) , so your joint resources are taken into account. For HB and CTB you receive benefit at the couple rate, but there may be public funds implications.
- For PC the rules are similar to IS/income-based JSA in that couples with different immigration status can receive benefit paid at the single person rate. However, there is one important difference – for PC, a 'person subject to immigration control' is treated as not being a member of the household.[23] Therefore, any income or work undertaken will not affect the benefit entitlement of the person who is not subject to immigration control.
- Claimants who are 'subject to immigration control' cannot claim benefit for children, even if the children are not 'subject to immigration control'.
- If one member of a couple is a 'person subject to immigration control' but the other is not, the person who is not a 'person subject to immigration control' can claim child benefit for a child.
- Where a child is a 'person subject to immigration control' but her/his parent(s) are not, the parent can claim IS/income-based JSA for her/him. The child's immigration status does not affect the parent's entitlement to benefit; it is the parent's immigration status that is important.
- A person can qualify for JSA without having to satisfy the joint claims rules (see p394) if her/his partner is a 'person subject to immigration control'.

5. **Urgent cases payments**

Urgent cases payments are payments of income support (IS) and income-based jobseeker's allowance (JSA) at a reduced rate. There is no equivalent of urgent cases payments for pension credit (PC). A 'person subject to immigration control' who qualifies for PC receives it at the full rate.

If you are not entitled to normal rate IS or income-based JSA because you are a 'person subject to immigration control' (see p654), you may be entitled to urgent cases payments if:

- you have 'limited leave' to remain in the UK on the condition that you do not have recourse to 'public funds' (see p655), but you are temporarily without money; *and*
  - you have supported yourself without recourse to public funds during your limited leave; *and*
  - you are temporarily without funds because remittances from abroad have been disrupted; *and*

  - there is a reasonable expectation that your supply of funds will be resumed;[24] *or*
- you have been in the UK subject to a sponsorship undertaking for less than five years and your sponsor has died (see p662); *or*
- you are an asylum seeker entitled to benefit under transitional protection rules (see p667).

How to claim

There is no special procedure for claiming urgent cases payments. You claim IS or income-based JSA in the normal way (see p390). You do not have to make a separate claim for an urgent cases payment. In practice, you may need to request the urgent cases payment and should not rely on the DWP to decide automatically whether you are entitled.

Amount of the payment

Urgent cases payments of IS and income-based JSA are paid at a reduced rate. Your 'applicable amount' (see p876) is:

- a personal allowance for you and possibly your partner.[25] It is paid at 90 per cent of the personal allowance that would have been paid had you qualified for benefit in the normal way; *plus*
- full personal allowances for your children (see p879); *plus*
- premiums (see p882) and housing costs (see Chapter 36) or residential allowance (see p882).

Income

All of your income counts, but the following is ignored:[26]

- any tariff income from capital (see p977). However, as all capital is taken into account this concession is of very little assistance;
- any arrears of urgent cases payments of IS or income-based JSA;
- concessionary urgent cases payments of IS or income-based JSA;
- any housing benefit (HB) and/or council tax benefit;
- any payment made to compensate you for the loss of entitlement to HB;
- social fund payments;
- any payment from any of the Macfarlane Trusts, the Eileen Trust, the Fund, or the Independent Living Funds;
- payments made by people with haemophilia to their partners or children out of money originally provided by one of the Macfarlane Trusts. If the person with haemophilia has no partner or children, payments made to a parent, step-parent or guardian are also disregarded, but only for two years. These payments are also disregarded if the person with haemophilia dies and the money is paid out of the estate;

- payments arising from the Macfarlane Trusts which are paid by a person to a partner who has haemophilia, or to their child(ren).

Certain income is treated as capital if you get IS under the normal rules (see p1030). However, if you apply for an urgent cases payment the following capital is treated as income:[27]

- any lump sum paid to you not more than once a year for your work as a part-time firefighter, part-time member of a lifeboat crew, auxiliary coastguard or member of the Territorial Army;
- any refund of income tax;
- holiday pay which is not payable until more than four weeks after your job ended;
- any irregular charitable or voluntary payment.

Capital

Your capital is calculated in the usual way (see Chapter 39) but the usual disregards do not apply to urgent cases payments. Any capital taken into account affects your urgent cases payment, not just that over the capital limit (see p1031). However, arrears of urgent cases payments are disregarded.

6. Asylum seekers and refugees

You are treated as an 'asylum seeker' while you are waiting for a Home Office decision on an application for refugee status (see p669). If you apply for asylum when you arrive in the UK, you normally are given 'temporary admission' while your case is considered (although you can be detained or removed in certain circumstances). You may also have applied for asylum while you were in the UK with limited leave or as an illegal entrant or overstayer. If your application for asylum is refused you have the right of appeal. It can take a long time before your application is finally decided, although the Government has now introduced quicker procedures and curtailed appeal rights for many asylum seekers.

An asylum seeker will usually be issued with an application registration card (ARC). This is a new identity document confirming that the person has claimed asylum. However, many asylum seekers will have a standard acknowledgement letter (SAL), the previously used identity document. Some asylum seekers who are granted temporary admission are issued with an IS96 rather than an ARC.

Claiming income support (IS), jobseeker's allowance (JSA) or other 'public funds' benefits (see p655) will not affect your application for asylum because asylum seekers are not subject to any condition not to claim 'public funds'. However, in most cases, you are excluded from entitlement by the benefit rules (see p667). See p669 if you have been recognised as a refugee.

The system of support for asylum seekers was the subject of radical reform on 3 April 2000.[28] Prior to this date the type of assistance available depended on where an application for asylum was made. Those claiming asylum at the port of entry or 'on arrival' continued to qualify for the main means-tested benefits, whereas those claiming asylum 'in-country' could receive assistance from the local authority under the National Assistance Act if they were destitute. For further details see CPAG's *Welfare Benefits Handbook* 1999/2000. The system for asylum seekers is now very complicated. You may be supported:

- under the National Asylum Support Service (NASS). This was phased in from 3 April 2000 and now covers most asylum seekers unless they were the responsibility of the local authority before 3 April 2000; *or*
- by interim arrangements through your local authority; *or*
- by a local authority social services department;[29] *or*
- by qualifying for benefit because of transitional protection; *or*
- by qualifying for benefit because, although you are seeking asylum, the Regulations do not exclude you.

Benefit transitional protection

There are two types of transitional protection:

- the first applies to those who are protected because they were entitled to benefit on 4 February 1996, or 6 October 1996 for child benefit ('the 1996 rules');
- the second applies to those who are protected because they applied for asylum on or before 2 April 2000 ('the 2000 rules').

The 1996 rules

Non-means-tested benefits[30]

You are protected by the 1996 transitional rules if you were in receipt of benefit on 4 February 1996 (or 6 October 1996 for child benefit). Protection continues until the first unfavourable decision on the asylum claim or until the decision is revised or superseded.[31] If you break your claim, you will lose entitlement to benefit.[32]

If you were in receipt of child benefit on 6 October 1996 you retain entitlement to that benefit until the claim is revised or superseded by a decision maker. This can only be done if there are grounds for a revision or supersession – eg, a relevant change of circumstances. If you were in receipt of child benefit on 6 October 1996 and you claim child benefit for another child after that date – eg, following the birth of the child or the arrival of a child to join the household, the existing claim for child benefit should not be revised or superseded. Entitlement to that child benefit should continue to be paid and you should receive child benefit for the additional child for whom you are caring. This is because the claim for 'additional child benefit' is in fact a new and separate claim for benefit.[33]

Means-tested benefits

You are entitled to means-tested benefits under the transitional protenction rules if you were entitled to benefit on 4 February 1996 and you have not yet had an adverse decision on your claim. As a result of a Court of Appeal decision a break in your benefit claim does not bring your protection to an end.[34] Protection extends to your spouse, partner or other dependant who was part of your family on 5 February 1996.[35] This could apply even if you were not living together as a couple on this date as long as s/he can be considered to be part of your household.[36]

The 2000 rules[37]

These rules apply to IS, income-based JSA, housing benefit (HB) and council tax benefit (CTB). You are covered by this transitional protection if you applied for asylum on or before 2 April 2000 and either you claimed asylum 'on arrival' or you claimed asylum following a declaration by the Government that your country was in a state of 'significant upheaval'. Only two such declarations have been made to date: Zaire on 16 May 1997 and Sierra Leone on 1 July 1997. 'On arrival' means that the application for asylum has been made either before, or at, immigration control or before you left the port of entry.[38]

Under the 2000 rules, a gap in your claim will not affect entitlement to benefit, but a break in your claim may mean that you lose benefit for your partner (see p663). If this happens, you should get specialist advice. These rules do not offer any specific protection for other family members to claim in their own right. However, the crucial factor for this transitional protection is the date you claimed asylum rather than receipt of benefit. Therefore, a family member who wants to claim benefit in their own right – eg, an adult child, should be protected as long as they were included in the asylum application prior to 3 April 2000. You continue to be protected and therefore eligible for benefit under these rules until you receive a decision about your asylum application. If the decision is positive and you are granted either refugee status or exceptional leave to remain you can claim benefit under the normal rules. You will need to sign on for income-based JSA unless you fall within a category eligible for IS – eg, a lone parent or pensioner. If you are granted refugee status you can make a backdated claim for arrears of benefit to the date when you first claimed asylum (see p669). If you are refused asylum you will no longer be eligible for any social security benefit, unless you qualify for another reason – eg, under European Community (EC) law.

Other help available

If you are no longer entitled to benefit you may be eligible for asylum support either from NASS or your local authority. You will only qualify for support if you are destitute. If you are not eligible for asylum support or benefits you should ask your local authority for help. If you have children, support can be provided by social services departments under the Children Act 1989. If you are sick or disabled you can ask for help under the National Assistance Act 1948. If you need help with rent, the local authority may be able to provide help with deposits or rent under s2 of the Local Government Act 2000.

The Nationality Immigration and Asylum Act 2002 excludes from entitlement to some social services support:[39]

- European Economic Area (EEA) nationals who are not 'workers';
- people who have been granted refugee status in another EEA state, but who are not EEA nationals;
- people who have been refused asylum and who have failed to comply with removal directions or have exhausted all appeal rights.

However, the Act makes clear that a local authority is *not* prevented from supporting one of the above groups where there would otherwise be a breach of EC law or where a refusal of support would lead to a breach of any rights under the European Convention on Human Rights. Therefore, a refusal of support, particularly where children are involved, may well be challengable. Equally the provisions regarding EEA nationals indirectly discriminate against non-British EEA nationals and consequently may be in breach of EC law. In such circumstances you should seek legal advice.

In some circumstances a couple who are both asylum seekers will be in the situation where one of the couple is on urgent cases payments (see p664) and the other is receiving asylum support. They may, however, qualify for urgent cases payments paid at the couple rate (see p665). Asylum support is taken into account as income in respect of any HB and CTB that your partner receives, but it is not taken into account for IS or income-based JSA. However, any IS or income-based JSA that you receive is taken into account as income for asylum support purposes.

Refugees

The UK is a signatory to the 1951 United Nations Convention on the Status of Refugees which gives refugees certain rights in a foreign country, including the right to public relief and assistance. A refugee is defined under the Convention as someone who is unable or unwilling to return to his own country because of a '... well-founded fear of persecution for reasons of race, religion, nationality, membership of a particular social group or political opinion ...'

If the Home Office accepts that you are a refugee, you and your family are entitled to remain in the UK and claim IS or income-based JSA and any other benefits under the normal rules and at the full rate (see Chapters 13 and 15) from the date you are recorded as a refugee by the Secretary of State.[40] You do not have to satisfy the 'habitual residence' test (see p702).

Backdating benefit

Note: The Goverment has introduced legislation allowing for the removal of the backdating of benefit to refugees. It appears that the power to end backdating only extends to IS, HB and CTB.[41] However, at the time of writing there was no date specified by which the changes come into effect. The Government intends to replace the backdating provision with a new system of discretionary loans. However, this appears to be part of a wider programme of intergration. It will be part of a Goverment initiative called Strategic Upgrade of National Refugee Integration Services (Sunrise). This scheme is to be piloted in 2005 and therefore it would seem unlikely that benefit would be withdrawn before the pilot. Therefore refugees should be encouraged to claim backdated benefit until such time as the law changes. Once the new rules take effect it may be possible to challenge the withdrawal of backdating. If you have such a case please contact CPAG.

If you are granted refugee status you or your partner may be able to claim child benefit, child tax credit/working tax credit, IS and HB/CTB backdated to the date that you first claimed asylum (see p666). You cannot, however, get payments of benefit for any period prior to 5 February 1996 and you must submit your claim on the usual claim form within 28 days (three months for child benefit and tax credits) of being notified that you have been accepted as a refugee. The normal restrictions on backdating for these benefits do not apply.[42] As many asylum seekers have to wait years for a decision on their status, substantial benefit arrears can be claimed. It is therefore crucial that you act promptly and submit a claim on a claim form within the 28-day time limit. The 28-day time limit applies from the date that you are notified of your refugee status. If you are outside the time limit there is no scope for backdating, but you should get advice as you may have a compensation claim against your solicitor or adviser. If you have a solicitor who is acting on your behalf in the asylum claim, the Home Office may notify your solicitor of its decision. In these circumstances the 28-day time limit will start from the point the solicitor is notified of the decision.[43]

Income support

It is not necessary for you to fit into a category of person eligible for IS, such as lone parent, in order to qualify for this backdated benefit, although if you worked during this period this may exclude you from entitlement. If you applied for asylum on or after 3 April 2000 then IS is paid at the normal rate. If you were receiving asylum support during this period it will be offset against any arrears of benefit due. If you applied for asylum before 3 April 2000 the backdated payment is made at the urgent cases rate. Any IS or essential living expenses from asylum support already paid to you or your partner for the backdated period is offset against the amount you get. You cannot get backdated payments for any week in which you were receiving contribution-based JSA.[44] If your partner has been recognised as a refugee and was not getting contribution-based JSA, s/he could claim instead. Only IS, and not income-based JSA, can be backdated when you are granted refugee status. If you are only entitled to income-based JSA on becoming a refugee, you must submit a separate claim for backdated IS within the 28-day time limit to receive your arrears of benefit. The claim should be made on a claim form; it is not sufficient to write to the DWP asking for backdating.[45] The arrears are disregarded as capital for 52 weeks from the date of receipt.[46] Some refugees have experienced problems obtaining backdated benefit because they have been wrongly advised by DWP staff. If this happens you should ask for an ex-gratia payment (see Chapter 47).

Pension credit

The Pension Credit Act[47] does provide power for backdating and it was the DWP's intention to draft legislation in similar terms to that of IS. However, this backdating has now been blocked. Therefore a refugee who is a pensioner is discriminated against in terms of backdating.

Housing benefit and council tax benefit

In order to qualify for backdated HB and CTB you need to have been liable for rent and council tax. You must make a claim for retrospective HB/CTB within 28 days of the date you are notified by the Secretary of State that you have been recorded as a refugee.[48] You must claim on a claim form within the time limit, as a late claim cannot be backdated.[49] If you have lived in more than one local authority area, you should make your claim to the local authority in whose area you last lived before being granted refugee status.[50]

HB/CTB can be paid for the whole or part of the period from the date the claim is treated as made until the date you were notified of your refugee status. Any HB/CTB which has already been paid to you or your partner over this period is deducted from your award.[51]

How your claim is assessed

You must provide any evidence and information you have or could reasonably get which the local authority may reasonably require to determine your entitlement.[52] The authority can ask for information from your landlord, from the person to whom you pay rent, from any person who paid the rent on your behalf, or from another local authority.[53]

You must notify the local authority of any change of circumstances which might be relevant to your HB/CTB entitlement over the period for which you are claiming (see p225).[54] Where you are unable to provide the necessary evidence, the local authority must determine your claim on the basis of the information you have been able to provide.[55]

Your HB claim is assessed using the rules for rent and rent restrictions as they stood on 1 January 1996.[56] In particular, this means that the rent officer's assessment of the appropriate rent for your home is not conclusive (see p245).

Payment of benefit

Once the local authority decides you are entitled to retrospective HB/CTB it must make payment within 14 days.[57] CTB is paid into your council tax account if there is any outstanding council tax liability for the period covered by the award. Any remaining CTB is paid to you. If your rent has not been paid, part or all of your HB award can be paid direct to the landlord. If your landlord was a local authority, any eligible rent owing to it is deducted from your award and only the balance paid to you.[58] Otherwise, HB can be paid to your landlord where the local authority considers it reasonable to do so.[59] The landlord must show that you have not paid your rent for part or all of the period of your award and the local authority must give you an opportunity to give reasons why payment should not be made to the landlord.

Child benefit

If you are recognised as a refugee you can claim child benefit backdated to the date of your asylum claim. You must make the claim within three months of being notified that you have been granted refugee status.

7. European Economic Area nationals

Introduction

Social security benefits are not governed by British law alone. There are also laws made by the European Community (EC) which apply directly in the UK and throughout the European Economic Area (EEA). EC law plays an important role in the UK benefit system and has been a useful tool in many of the legal challenges involving social security. Since the introduction of the 'right to reside test' it has become necessary for advisers to develop a much greater understanding of the various instruments of EC law. Most EEA nationals have enhanced rights under EC law but the exact nature of those rights vary according to the activity of the EEA national. Equally certain restrictions apply to eight of the new members to the EU (see p683).

Most UK social security rules now take account of your EC rights. Therefore, EEA nationals are usually entitled to social security benefits under UK rules. However, EC law can enhance your rights under UK rules and help override rules that may be discriminatory. If there is a conflict between rights given in EC law and the UK social security system, EC law takes precedence.[60]

EEA nationals are in a far better position than other non EEA migrants. They do not require leave to enter or remain in the UK and therefore there is no leave to curtail. Any attempt to deport or remove an EEA national is subject to a set procedure and subject to appeal. Furthermore any such removal would not be indefinite. Therefore an EEA national who wants to claim benefits does not put their immigration position at risk.

EC law can also help to give your family members who are not themselves EEA nationals rights – in particular, to enter and reside in the UK and to qualify for benefits. Such rights can be retained if a couple separate and, in some circumstances, if you divorce. EC law helps to override or reduce the impact of the residence and presence test. It allows you to qualify for contribution-based benefits on the basis of contributions paid elsewhere in the EEA and to claim certain benefits for family members even if they are not living with you in the UK.

If you are a national of any of the EEA states, you and your dependants, even if they are non-EEA nationals, have rights under EC law. These rights stem from the EC Treaty and subsequent amending treaties but these rights are expanded upon by a variety of Regulations, Directives and caselaw.

Which countries are in the European Economic Area

The EEA now consists of 27 member states and Switzerland. Nationals from Austria, Belgium, Cyprus, Denmark, Finland, France, Germany, Greece, Iceland, the Irish Republic, Italy, Liechtenstein, Luxembourg, Malta, the Netherlands, Norway, Portugal, Spain, Sweden and the UK have full EC rights. Full rights are also extended to Swiss nationals from June 2002.

Nationals from the following EU States (referred to as EU Accession State Nationals) do not have full EC rights: Czech Republic, Estonia, Hungary, Latvia, Lithuania, Poland, Slovakia and Slovenia. For further details see p683.

EC Law

EC law is complex and it is impossible in a handbook such as this to deal comprehensively with the subject. However, this section aims to highlight the main areas of EC law that affect social security and tax credits. For further detail please contact CPAG.

The EC Treaty

All EC rights stem from the EC Treaty, the primary legislation of the EU, and these are expanded upon in a variety of Regulations and Directives.

Article 12 of the EC Treaty

Article 12 of the EC Treaty specifies that there must be no discrimination on grounds of nationality. This is a general statement of non-discrimination which applies to any matter that falls within the scope of the Treaty, including social security benefits and tax credits. There is now a growing body of caselaw from the European Court of Justice (ECJ) in which the Court has held that EEA nationals who are living lawfully in a member state are entitled to be treated equally with nationals of that state in respect of access to benefits. In the case of *Martinez Sala*[61] the Court decided that a Spanish national who was living in Germany and who was economically inactive could not be denied a social security benefit paid to German nationals because to do so would be in breach of Article 12 of the EC Treaty. The Court took the view that Martinez Sala may not have had a right of residence under EC law[62] but she was living in the member state lawfully and could therefore rely on the anti-discrimination provision in Article 12. It was also significant that in this case the claimant was a national of a state which was a signatory to the European Convention on Social and Medical Assistance. This specifies that a person cannot have their right of residence withdrawn simply because they claim benefits.

In the case of *Grzelczyk*[63] the ECJ considered whether a French national who was a student in Belgium was entitled to a Belgium social security benefit. Belgium law stipulated that non-Belgium EU nationals were only entitled to benefit if they were workers. Mr Grzelczyk was not a worker, he was a student whose right of residence appeared to be governed by EC Directive 93/96 (see p682) which provides a right of residence where a student is self-supporting. Despite this requirement the Court held that Mr Grzelczyk did have rights to benefit. The Court held that a Belgium national in the same situation as Mr Grzelczyk would be entitled to benefit, therefore a denial of benefit was contrary to Article 12 of the Treaty.

A similar approach was taken in the case of *Trojani*[64] where the Court found that a person who was not economically active may not have a right to reside under Article 18 of the EC Treaty but nonetheless was entitled to claim social security benefits under Article 12. The Court ruled that while member states may make residence of a citizen of the EU who is not economically active conditional on her/him having sufficient resources, that does not mean that such a person cannot, during her/his lawful residence in the host member state, benefit from the fundamental principle of equal treatment as laid down in Article 12. The Court went on to say that a person who is not economically active may rely on Article 12 where s/he has been lawfully resident in the host member state for a period of time or where s/he possesses a residence permit.

EEA nationals entering the UK do not require leave to enter or remain in the UK. It is therefore arguable that they are living here lawfully and consequently will have rights to be treated in the same way as British citizens in respect of access to benefit. EEA nationals have better protection than other migrants because any attempt to remove them is more difficult than with other migrants. Furthermore, any removal does not prevent an EU national from subsequently returning to the UK.

Article 17 of the EC Treaty

Article 17 of the EC Treaty states that every person holding nationality of a member state shall be a citizen of the EU and shall enjoy the rights conferred by the Treaty.

Article 18 of the EC Treaty

Article 18 of the EC Treaty gives every citizen of the EEA the right to move and reside freely within the territory of the member states, subject to the limitations and conditions laid down in the Treaty. The question as to what these limits and conditions might be remains unclear. It has been argued that this means the condition to be self-supporting. However, the ECJ has held that those limits and conditions must comply with EC law. In particular, this requires the principle of proportionality to be applied. This means that any national laws must be necessary and appropriate to attain the objective pursued. The ECJ held in *Grzelczylc*[65] that it was a disproportionate measure to deny benefit simply because he was not self-supporting. In the case of *Baumbast*[66] the Court held that a citizen of the EU who no longer enjoys a right of residence as a migrant worker in the host member state can, as a citizen of the EU, enjoy a right of residence by direct application of Article 18.

Article 39 of the EC Treaty

Article 39 of the EC Treaty provides the basic free movement provisions. The Treaty does not provide any detail as to the basic right of free movement, instead these are spelled out in various regulations and directives. However, the developing caselaw of the ECJ[67] shows that Article 39 itself provides EU nationals with a right of residence within the EU and that the right to non-discrimination is not limited only to those who have worked in a member state. Anyone, apart from A8 nationals (see p683), who signs on for jobseeker's allowance (JSA) should be treated as having a right of residence.[68]

EC Regulation 1408/71

EC Regulation 1408/71 is a detailed Regulation that is intended to co-ordinate the various social security systems of the EEA. It was recognised that migrant workers who choose to exercise the right of free movement may find themselves at a disadvantage in respect of social security benefits – eg, if they should fall ill or become unemployed while working in another EEA state. EC Regulation 1408/71 tries to alleviate this potential problem by co-ordinating the various social security systems. It:

- allows you to override residence conditions attached to benefits and to therefore claim any benefits covered by the regulation immediately;
- prohibits discrimination on nationality grounds, in terms of access to or the rate of payment of benefits covered;
- allows you to rely on periods of employment, residence and contributions paid in one EEA country towards entitlement to benefit in others. For example, contributions paid in another EEA state could be used to allow an EEA national who had worked only briefly in the UK to claim contribution-based JSA or incapacity benefit (IB);
- allows you to take certain benefits abroad with you to another EEA state (this is called the 'principle of exportation');
- allows you to claim family benefits for family members living elsewhere in the EEA.

Who is covered by Regulation 1408/71

In order to rely on Regulation 1408/71 you must be an EEA national, a refugee or a stateless person. EU Accesion State nationals (see p683) are fully covered by this regulation. You must also be an employed or self-employed person. This is not the same as the term 'worker' for other areas of EC law. You will be treated as an employed or self-employed person if you are insured under a national social security scheme. In the UK this means that you pay, have in the past paid, or ought to pay national insurance contributions. If you are covered by the Regulation, members of your family are also covered, whatever their nationality. Refugees and stateless people are only covered if they have moved within the EEA.

Benefits covered by Regulation 1408/71

Regulation 1408/71 applies to state benefits which are designed to protect against certain risks. Each member state must declare which benefits fall within these risks. In the UK the relevant benefits are:

Risk	*UK benefit*
Sickness and maternity	Incapacity benefit, maternity allowance, statutory sick pay, statutory maternity pay, statutory adoption pay, statutory paternity pay
Invalidity	Incapacity benefit, severe disablement allowance
Old age	Retirement pension, graduated retirement pension, Christmas bonus (probably pension credit, but see below)
Survivors' benefits and death grants	Bereavement benefits (but see below)
Accidents at work and occupational diseases	Industrial disablement benefit, reduced earnings allowance
Family benefits	Child benefit, guardian's allowance, child dependency increases, child tax credit
Unemployment	Jobseeker's allowance (probably income-based JSA, but see below)

Bereavement benefits are not included in the declaration – only widows' benefits are – but it should be assumed that they will fall into the same category as widows' benefits.

Income-based JSA is listed by the Government as a special non-contributory benefit but there is an increasing body of caselaw which would suggest that it should be treated as an unemployment benefit for EC purposes.[69]

Pension credit is not within the UK declaration. The Government is likely to argue that it is a special non-contributory benefit, but there are strong grounds for arguing that it is an old-age benefit and, therefore, fully exportable.

Special non-contributory benefits

In addition, since 1992 Regulation 1408/71 has been extended to include 'special non-contributory benefits'.

The UK Government states that the following are special non-contributory benefits:

- attendance allowance (AA);
- carer's allowance (CA);
- disability living allowance (DLA);
- income support (IS);
- income-based JSA.

Special non-contributory benefits cannot be exported (see below) but they do attract all the other rights contained in the Regulation, such as non-discrimination. You receive these benefits from the state in which you are resident rather than where you last worked. Under EC law **'resident'** means the place where you are 'habitually resident' (see p706). This is significant because you may be able to rely on the Regulation to overcome residence tests such as the right to reside test or the past presence tests for DLA and AA. Therefore you would be able to claim special non-contributory benefits immediately. The ECJ considered the issue of habitual residence in the context of this Regulation in *Di Paolo*. The Court held that account had to be taken of factors such as the nature of a person's occupation, the reasons for moving to another state to work, and the length of residence before the person moved. The Court also held that stable employment could outweigh other factors in determining habitual residence.[70] In *Swaddling* the ECJ adopted a similar approach, with the exception that there was much less emphasis on stable employment.[71]

Exporting benefits

Under EC law certain benefits can be 'exported'. This means that you can continue to receive the benefit at the full rate while living in another member state, for as long as you continue to satisfy the conditions for that benefit. However, only certain benefits can be fully exported to another member state. These are for 'invalidity, old age or survivors, pensions for accidents at work or occupational diseases and death benefits'. For other benefits, such as for unemployment and sickness, there are only limited rights to export. Also, the DWP sometimes disputes that certain benefits fall within an exportable category.

Benefits that are fully exportable:

- long-term IB;

- retirement pension;
- graduated retirement pension;
- Christmas bonus;
- cold weather payments;
- bereavement benefits;
- industrial injuries benefits.

Benefits with limited exportability:

- AA;
- DLA;
- child benefit;
- guardian's allowance;
- child tax credit (CTC);
- JSA;
- statutory sick pay;
- short-term IB;
- statutory maternity pay;
- maternity allowance.

Benefits about which there is a dispute on exportability:

- income-based JSA;
- AA;
- DLA;
- PC.

Unemployment benefits can be exported but only for a maximum period of three months. You must register as unemployed for at least four weeks before you leave the state in which you are living and must register in the second EEA country within seven days. At present the UK government considers that only contribution-based JSA can be exported. However, a commissioner, and the Court of Appeal, have held that income-based JSA is an 'unemployment benefit' for the purposes of EC law.[72] These cases relate to a different area of EC law[73] but they do give grounds for challenging a refusal by the DWP to allow you to export income-based JSA.

Maternity and sickness benefits. EC law allows these benefits to be exported if you move to live in another member state. It is also payable during a temporary absence provided that your condition requires immediate medical attention or you have authorisation to go aroad for treatment. If you fall sick while claiming exportable unemployment benefits, you can be paid sickness benefits for the balance of the three months. It is, however, often possible to get these benefits without recourse to EC law – eg, you can get UK IB for temporary absences provided the Secretary of State agrees it is consistent with the proper administration of the benefit system and you satisfy certain other conditions.

Family benefits cannot be exported, but they can be paid for family members living in another member state. For example, you may be able to get child benefit for a child who is not living with you but is residing elsewhere in the EEA. You may also be able to get dependants' additions of benefits even though your partner is living elsewhere in the EEA. It has recently been argued before a commissioner that the additional amount of IS paid for a child is a family benefit and, therefore, payable for a child living away from the family in another EEA state. The commissioner did not accept that IS was a family benefit under EC Reg 1408/71, but he nevertheless held that denial of benefit for children was potentially discriminatory under EC Reg 1612/68. Consequently it would be possible to receive IS for children living in other EEA states.[74]

AA, DLA and CA. Prior to 1 June 1992 AA, DLA and CA were fully exportable, but since that date the Government has listed these benefits as special non-contributory benefits, with the effect that they are not exportable. However, there is some transitional protection and if you were receiving AA, DLA or CA prior to 1 June 1992 and you are an insured person by virtue of having worked in the UK, you retain the right to take your AA/DLA/CA to another EEA state. DWP guidance on this point has been wrong in the past and some people may have been misadvised about their right to export benefit. There may also be scope to argue that both these benefits fall within the category of an invalidity benefit and remain fully exportable.

PC. The DWP considers that PC is a special non-contributory benefit and has issued guidance wrongly stating that it is listed as such. Listing PC as a special non-contributory benefit, which would make it non-exportable, requires an amendment to EC law and this has not been done. It is highly arguable that PC is an old-age benefit and, therefore, is fully exportable.

Overcoming residence tests

One of the practical effects of Regulation1408/71 is that if you or a family member is covered by the regulation you are able to override any residence tests. The way in which this is achieved varies according to the benefit involved. Generally, if you have last worked in the UK you should be entitled to be paid any of the benefits covered immediately without having to satisfy any residence tests.

If a person has worked elsewhere in the EEA but has not worked in the UK s/he can become eligible for UK benefits and override residence conditions, but again the rules vary according to the benefit involved. For any of the special non-contributory benefits, you are entitled if you are resident in the UK. This is an EC concept which has been defined by the ECJ in *Di Paolo*.[75] The Court held that account had to be taken of factors such as the nature of a person's occupation, the reasons for moving to another state to work, and the length of residence before the person moved. The Court also held that stable employment could outweigh other factors in determining habitual residence.[76] In *Swaddling* the ECJ adopted a similar approach, with the exception that there was much less emphasis on stable employment.[77]

Aggregating contributions

Another aspect of the rights contained in Regulation 1408/71 is that it allows you to rely on contributions paid elsewhere in the EEA in order to qualify for benefit. This applies even where the contributions were paid prior to the State joining the EU.[78]

EC Regulation 1612/68

Regulation 1612/68 applies to people who are employed or who have been employed. EEA nationals who are covered by this Regulation:

- are exempt from the habitual residence test;[79]
- are exempt from the right to reside test (see p703);
- have a right to claim all benefits with no discrimination;[80]
- retain a right to reside if they are no longer working but their children are in education.[81]

EC law allows for freedom of movement to enter and take up employment, be self-employed, or provide or receive a service in any member state. If you are economically active in one of the above ways you are commonly referred to as a 'worker' and you are entitled to the same tax, housing and social advantages as offered to nationals of the member state. The courts have ruled that this term applies to social security benefits, including means-tested benefits such as IS. Therefore, if you are a 'worker' you cannot be denied a benefit such as income-based JSA on the basis of your nationality, and your worker status allows you to override any residence tests (see Chapter 27). In order to be a 'worker', you or a family member must have worked in the member state in which you seek to claim benefit, but this can be for a short period and includes part-time work.

The term 'worker' is not defined in EC legislation and there is no precise length of time that you must work before being considered to be a worker. It is clear, however, that many people who are not actually working or who are working part time are still classed as 'workers'.[82]

EEA nationals who have never worked in the UK ('workseekers') do not have the same rights under this regulation as those who have worked. However, workseekers may be able to rely on the Treaty to assert rights to benefit (see p705). If you have worked in any EU country you may be classified as an employed person and therefore have rights under Regulation 1408/71 (see p675).[83] Equally, a workseeker does not have a right to reside under this regulation but may have a right to reside under the Treaty (see p703).

Workers under Regulation 1612/68

You should be treated as a **'worker'** for the purposes of Regulation 1612/98 if you fall into any of the following categories.

- You are working in the UK, whether full or part time. Any 'genuine' and 'effective work' should count, so long as it is not so irregular and limited that it is a purely marginal and ancillary activity.[84]
- You have worked in the UK (at any time and even for a short period) but have become involuntarily unemployed or temporarily incapable of work.[85]
- You have worked in the UK, have become involuntarily unemployed and must take up occupational retraining to compete in the job market.[86]
- You have voluntarily given up work in the UK to take up vocational training linked to your previous job.[87]
- You have voluntarily given up work for other reasons and you have remained in the labour market, and are therefore available for, and actively seeking, employment.[88]
- You have been temporarily laid off and are seeking to return to work with the same employer in the UK.[89]
- If you have given up work but you have children in education you retain the right to reside by virtue of your children.[90]

Workers under Regulation 1251/70

Regulation 1251/70 allows certain incapacitated or retired workers to remain in the state where they have worked.

You are a **'worker'** for the purposes of the Regulation if you fall into one of the following categories:

- You have given up work in the UK because of permanent incapacity *and either*:
  - you had resided continuously in the UK for at least two years when you gave up work; *or*
  - your incapacity resulted from an industrial injury or disease (see p321) which entitles you to a disability benefit or IB (see Chapters 7 and 12); *or*
  - your spouse is (or was before marrying you) British.[91]
- You retired on or after pension age *and either*:
  - you had resided continuously in the UK for at least three years and were employed in the UK for at least 12 months immediately before retiring; *or*
  - your spouse is (or was before marrying you) British.[92]

Notes[93]

- Absences from the UK of up to three months a year (or longer for military service) are ignored when calculating your period of residence.

- Periods of unemployment recorded by the JobCentre/Jobcentre Plus and absences from work because of illness or accident are ignored when calculating your period of employment.
- Periods of employment as a 'frontier worker' in another EEA state can count if you returned to your home in the UK at least once a week.

EC Directive 68/360

EC Directive 68/360 applies to people who are exercising rights under Regulation 1612/68. It deals with the administrative arrangements for residence for migrant workers and their families. You have the right to reside in the UK under the Directives if you are a 'worker' for the purposes of EC Regulation 1612/68 (see p681).[94] This right of residence is not lost if you are temporarily unemployed or incapable of work.[95] The Directive also gives a right of residence to family members of an EEA worker. 'Family member' includes your spouse and children but can also include dependent parents or grandparents or other dependent relatives.

Your right to reside in the UK is confirmed by the issue of a residence permit but the lack of a permit does not negate that right.[96] Permits are normally issued for five years on confirmation of employment.

EC Directive 73/148

This Directive sets out the administrative arrangements for people who are self-employed or who wish to receive or provide services in another member state. You are covered by the Directive if:

- you are self-employed or provide a service on a commercial basis in the UK;[97] *or*
- you are receiving commercial services in the UK.[98] These could include tourism, private education or health care and business or professional services;[99] *or*
- you are a member of the family of any of the above. This covers spouses, children under 21, or older children if dependent, parents, grandparents and other dependent relatives.[100]

A person must be allowed time to undertake preparatory steps before trading.[101]

EC Directive 93/96 (Students)

An EU student has a right of residence for the duration of his/her studies and is entitled to a residence permit also valid for the period of study. However, Directive 93/96 specifies that the student is required to have sufficient resources to avoid becoming a burden on the social security system of that state. In one case, however, the ECJ has held that even though the Directive required the student to be self-supporting s/he is not precluded from claiming benefits if a national of that state in the same situation would be eligible. To do so would be discriminatory and contrary to Article 12 of the Treaty.[102]

EC Directives 90/364 and 90/365

These Directives provide a right of residence to people who do not enjoy this right under any other provision of EC law – eg, economically inactive EU nationals. In order to rely on this directive you must have sufficient resources to avoid becoming a burden on the social security system of the particular member state. You would be covered if another person was supporting you.[103] However, the developing caselaw of the ECJ is moving away from this position to the view that EU nationals who are not economically active may still have a right to residence and entitlement to benefit under articles 12 and 18 of the Treaty. The arguments on this area are complicated and will depend on the facts of the individual case. For further advice contact CPAG.

Family members of EEA nationals

EC law may also assist you even if you are not an EEA national – eg, if you are a family member of an EEA national. Family members of EEA nationals generally do not require leave to remain in the UK and are, therefore, admitted without a public funds restriction. This is the case whatever the nationality of the family member. Therefore, they do not fall into the definition of a 'person subject to immigration control' and consequently are not excluded from claiming any benefits. Family members include your spouse, children under 21, other children and granchildren if they are dependent, dependent parents, grandparents and great-grandparents.

In some circumstances you will find that a family member does have limited leave and or a public funds restriction attached. This could be, for example, because s/he was in the UK with another status such as asylum seeker or visitor and s/he has recently married the EEA national. In such circumstances you can argue that her/his right to reside stems from her/his status as an EEA dependant and that this overrides any UK restrictions. Furthermore, EC Regulation 1408/71 gives entitlement to benefits for an EEA national and her/his family members, whatever the nationality of the family member(s). A non-EEA spouse of an EEA national will not lose her/his rights to rely on EC law even if the couple separate.[104] Following a number of cases at the ECJ, UK law was amended from 1 April 2003 to allow these rights to continue after divorce. This applies where the divorced non-EEA spouse is the primary carer of the couple's children who are under the age of 19, and in some circumstances to age 21, and who are attending an educational course in the UK. This will also apply if the EEA national has left the UK and the divorced spouse is left behind to care for the children.[105]

EU accession state nationals

On 1 May 2004 10 countries joined the existing 15 members of the EU. Eight of the 10 new member states (Czech Republic, Estonia, Hungary, Latvia, Lithuania, Poland, Slovakia and Slovenia) are referred to as accession states or A8 states.

The rules for certain benefits have been changed to coincide with the EU accession. Entitlement to IS, housing benefit, council tax benefit, child benefit and CTC is now dependent on a person having a right to reside. For details of the right to reside, see p703.

A8 nationals are excluded from access to some EC provisions. These restrictions, or derogations, are limited to certain areas of EC law and are specific. The intention of the derogations is to limit access to the labour market. Consequently, an A8 national does not have complete freedom to take up employment, instead certain procedures have to be complied with. Once this is done an A8 national should have access to all EC provisions affecting social security.

Unlike other EU nationals, an A8 national who is a workseeker (see p705) does not automatically have the right to reside in the UK. An accession state national who becomes employed must apply to the Home Office within one month of taking up employment to have that work registered.[106] Once employed and registered, A8 nationals in effect gain worker status and have the same rights as nationals from other EU states. However, UK rules specify that if the A8 national becomes unemployed before s/he has worked continuously for 12 months s/he loses the right of residence in the UK and the right to worker status. In CPAG's view this approach contravenes EC law because the UK Regulations go further than the derogations allowed by EC law. EC law allows a derogation only from articles 1–6 of EC Regulation 1612/68. It is Article 7 of Regulation 1612/68 which gives the right to the same 'tax and social advantage' as nationals. A person who has worked in the UK should be treated as a worker and therefore should not be denied access to benefit. The Government does not accept this point and therefore it is important that cases are taken to tribunal and Commissioners.

It is also important to remember that the restrictions that apply to A8 nationals are limited to only certain EC provisions. There may be other areas of EC law that can assist an A8 national. An A8 national who is self-employed is covered by EC Directive 73/148. This gives them the right to reside under EC law and entitlement to all social security benefits. It also provides these rights to the family members of the self-employed person.

A8 nationals can rely on EC Regulation 1408/71 in order to access benefits.

Association and co-operation agreements

The EC has made agreements with a number of countries outside the EEA which specify that there should be equal treatment in social security. The agreements are very similar to EC Regulation 1408/71 and are often referred to as association or co-operation agreements. Such agreements exist with Algeria, Morocco, Slovenia, Tunisia and Turkey.

In order to be covered by these agreements you must be lawfully working in a member state. In one decision a commissioner held that a Turkish asylum seeker who had worked in the UK, was covered by the Turkish association agreement.[107] In this case the claimant had been denied benefit under UK rules on the basis that, as an asylum seeker, he was not eligible. However, the commissioner held that the benefit in question – family credit – was a family benefit for the purposes of the agreement and as a person within the scope of the agreement he could not be denied the benefit. In another case a commissioner found that a Moroccan man was able to claim a dependant's addition to his invalidity benefit for his wife who had remained living in Morocco.[108]

The benefits covered by the agreements are the same as those under EC Regulation 1408/71. There is, however, some debate as to whether the 'special non-contributory benefits' which include IS and possibly income-based JSA are covered by the agreements. There is some positive caselaw which suggests that benefits such as IS are covered.[109] However, in another decision, Commissioner Mesher chose to distinguish the Turkish agreement and held that IS was not within its scope.[110] The position of income-based JSA is much stronger because there is a growing body of caselaw which holds that income-based JSA is an unemployment benefit for EC purposes. However, these mainly relate to EC Directive 79/7 (see p1283).[111] The Directive differs from EC Regulation 1608/71 because there is no concept of special non-contributory benefits. The ECJ has held that where a member state declares a benefit to be a special non-contributory benefit it must be accepted as a special non-contributory benefit.[112]

The Government has recently ended the concession that allowed asylum seekers to take up work if their application for asylum was still outstanding after six months. This means that it will become increasingly difficult for asylum seekers to rely on the association agreements.

Lawfully working

The DWP considers that a person is lawfully working in Great Britain (GB) if s/he is:

- working in GB; *and*
- has been given permission to enter GB; *and*
- does not have restrictions on taking employment in GB.

Furthermore, the DWP guidance also states that a person will continue to be treated as covered by the association agreements if s/he:

- has retired from work in the UK on or after pension age; *or*
- has given up work in the UK because of sickness or invalidity; *or*
- has given up work in the UK because of pregnancy; *or*
- has given up work in the UK because of widowhood; *or*
- has given up work in the UK because of an accident at work or an industrial disease; *or*
- has become unemployed after working in the UK; *or*
- has given up work in the UK to look after children.

8. Benefits when you go abroad

Many benefits have residence and presence conditions which mean that if you go abroad the particular benefit is no longer payable. Some benefits have no residence and presence conditions, and may always be payable abroad – eg, some retirement pensions. Despite being subject to residence and presence conditions, it may be possible to receive some benefits during temporary absences. Other benefits can be paid once you return from a temporary absence abroad. The rules in this section relate to UK law only. If you are a European Economic Area (EEA) national and you are travelling to another EEA state, see p697.

Whether an absence is temporary is a question which depends on the circumstances of each individual case. An absence does not cease to be temporary because no date is fixed for your return, but the absence must be for a limited period only.[113] If you spend longer abroad than the permitted periods you may no longer satisfy the residence condition for your benefit. The residence conditions for benefits are described on pp699–701. For the meaning of presence, residence, and ordinarily resident, see pp696–698.

Payment of benefit while you are abroad

It is not usually possible to have your British benefits paid to you while you are abroad, unless you can rely on either a reciprocal agreement (see p691) or European Community (EC) law (see p673). The lack of uprating for benefits was the subject of a legal challenge relying on the Human Rights Act but the case did not succeed.[114] However, there are some circumstances in which UK rules do allow for payment while you are abroad. This is only possible in the circumstances listed below.

Bereavement benefits, retirement pensions and guardian's allowance

These are payable while you are abroad, but your benefit is not normally uprated each year once you have ceased to be 'ordinarily resident' (see p698) in Great Britain (GB) unless you can rely on reciprocal agreements of EC law.[115] You cannot 'de-retire' (see p490) while abroad.[116]

In the case of bereavement payment (see p24) there are two further conditions:[117]

- you or your spouse must have been in GB when your spouse died; *or*
- the contribution conditions for widowed parent's allowance, widow's pension or bereavement benefit are satisfied (see p23).

Attendance allowance, disability living allowance and carer's allowance

As long as you remain 'ordinarily resident' (see p698) in GB, a temporary absence does not affect your entitlement to disability living allowance (DLA), attendance allowance or carer's allowance and you can continue to receive benefit for up to 26 weeks. However, on your return you may experience difficulties re-qualifying for benefit if your absence has been for more than 26 weeks. This is because you must have been present in GB for 26 out of the last 52 weeks in order to satisfy the residence conditions (see p698). In some circumstances you can be treated as being present in GB even though you are abroad (see p698).

Disablement benefit, reduced earnings allowance and retirement allowance

Disablement benefit (except constant attendance allowance and exceptionally severe disablement allowance) and retirement allowance are unaffected while you are abroad[118] (see also below for information on severe disablement allowance (SDA) abroad).

Constant attendance allowance and exceptionally severe disablement allowance are payable during a temporary absence for up to six months, or such longer period as the Secretary of State may allow.[119]

Reduced earnings allowance (REA) is payable during a temporary absence if:[120]

- you have been away for less than three months, or such further period as the Secretary of State shall allow; *and*
- your absence is not for work purposes; *and*
- you claim before you go; *and*
- you are entitled before you go.

REA has now been abolished, and if you break your claim you will no longer be eligible for benefit.

Incapacity benefit and severe disablement allowance

Incapacity benefit (IB – see Chapter 12) and SDA (see Chapter 20) are payable during the first 26 weeks of any temporary absence if the Secretary of State has certified that payment would be 'consistent with the proper administration of the Act' and:[121]

- your absence from GB is for the specific purpose of being treated for an illness or industrial injury (see p321) which began before you left this country; *or*
- when you left this country you had been continuously incapable of work (see p764) for six months and you have been continuously incapable since your departure.

If you are due to have a medical examination this can be arranged abroad.

Note: SDA was abolished for new claimants in April 2001. A person who is getting SDA and who goes abroad for more than 26 weeks will not re-qualify on her/his return to GB. You may qualify for IB for incapacity in youth (see p272) but you will have to re-satisfy the residence test before qualifying.

Maternity allowance

Maternity allowance (MA – see p456) can be paid to you abroad. You should tell the DWP before you go.

The rules for remaining entitled to MA while abroad are identical to those for IB (see above) except that MA is currently only payable for a period of 26 weeks.

Statutory sick pay, statutory maternity pay, statutory paternity pay and statutory adoption pay

There are no longer any requirements of presence or residence for statutory sick pay (see Chapter 24) or statutory maternity pay (see Chapter 23). You remain entitled if you are abroad for as long as you meet the normal entitlement rules.[122] The same applies for statutory paternity pay and statutory adoption pay.[123]

Child benefit

If you are claiming child benefit (see Chapter 5), your benefit could be affected if you spend more than eight weeks abroad or the child spends more than 12 weeks abroad (see p699).

Income support

Once you have established your right to income support (IS) in GB, it is possible to claim during temporary absences abroad. GB means England, Scotland and Wales only, therefore a trip to Northern Ireland counts as going abroad. If you are going to Northern Ireland for more than four weeks you should claim under the Northern Ireland social security system.

Benefit can continue indefinitely if:[124]

- you were entitled to IS immediately before going abroad;
- your absence is temporary, and that period of temporary absence is for the purpose of receiving NHS treatment at a hospital or other institution outside Great Britain (this does not apply in Scotland).

You can get IS for up to **four weeks** if:

- you were entitled to IS immediately before going abroad;
- your absence is temporary;
- the temporary absence is unlikely to exceed 52 weeks;
- you continue to satisfy the other rules for getting IS described in Chapter 13 while you are away;

and you fall within one of the following groups:[125]

- you are going to Northern Ireland;
- you and your partner are both abroad and your partner qualifies for a pensioner, enhanced pensioner, higher pensioner, disability or severe disability premium (see p891);
- you are incapable of work (see p764); *and*

  - you have been continuously incapable for the previous 28 weeks and you are terminally ill or receiving the highest rate of DLA care component; *or*
  - you have been continuously incapable for 364 days.

  Two or more periods when you are incapable of work are joined together to form a single period if they are separated by less than eight weeks;
- you are incapable of work (see p764) and are going abroad specifically for treatment of the incapacity from an appropriately qualified person. Before you go you should check that the DWP accepts that this rule applies to you;
- you fit into one of the groups of people who can claim IS (see p294). However, you must *not* be:
  - in 'relevant education' (see p618);
  - involved in a trade dispute, or in the first 15 days after you have returned to work following the dispute (see p735);
  - receiving an urgent cases payment of IS (see p664);
  - incapable of work for less than 28 weeks or appealing a decision of the DWP not to treat you as incapable of work (see p787).

You can get IS for up to **eight weeks** if:
- you were entitled to IS immediately before going abroad;
- your absence is temporary, and the temporary absence is unlikely to exceed 52 weeks;
- you continue to satisfy the other rules for getting IS described in Chapter 13 while you are away;
- you are taking a child abroad specifically for medical, physiotherapy or similar treatment from an appropriately qualified person. The child must count as part of your family (see p818).

Your partner is abroad

If your partner is abroad temporarily you may still be treated as a couple for IS purposes (see p816).[126] This can apply even if you have not lived together in the UK, because the rules relate to absence from each other, not absence from home. You will not be treated as a couple if:
- you do not intend to resume living together; *or*
- your absence from one another is likely to be for 52 weeks or more.

If your partner is waiting for entry clearance to come to the UK, you can argue that because this is a lengthy process and refusal rates are high, your separation is likely to exceed 52 weeks, so you should not be treated as a couple (see p816).[127] Alternatively, you can argue that you should not be treated as a couple because your intention to live together depends on entry clearance being granted.[128]

Payment of income support while abroad

If you qualify for IS under the four- or eight-week rule, your benefit is normally paid to you on your return, but if you are a member of a couple and you are the claimant you can ask for it to be paid to your partner during your absence instead. If you are not entitled to IS while abroad or you have already used up your four- or eight-week entitlement, your partner has to make a claim in her/his own right (see p306).

If it is your partner who goes abroad, your benefit is reduced after four weeks (eight weeks if your partner is taking a child abroad for medical treatment). You are then paid as if you were a single claimant or lone parent, but your joint income and capital counts.[129]

Housing benefit and council tax benefit[130]

While you are temporarily out of the country, you may be entitled to housing benefit to cover your rent, and council tax benefit towards your council tax (see pp202 and 112). If your IS stops, you must notify the local authority. You can be treated as temporarily absent for up to 13, and in some cases 52, weeks. For further details of the rules on temporary absence, see p202.

If your partner goes abroad temporarily you will continue to be treated as a couple unless:

- you do not intend to resume living together; *or*
- your absence from one another is likely to exceed 52 weeks.

Jobseeker's allowance[131]

You cannot normally get jobseeker's allowance (JSA) if you are not in GB. However, JSA can be paid when you are temporarily absent absent from GB:

- **indefinitely** if you are entitled to JSA immediately before going abroad and your absence is for NHS treatment at a hospital or other institution outside of GB (this does not apply in Scotland);
- for up to **four weeks** if you satisfy the conditions for being treated as available for work (see p357) and your partner satisfies the conditions for one of the pensioner premiums, a disability premium or a severe disability premium (see p882) or you are in Northern Ireland;
- for up to **eight weeks** if you are taking a child or young person abroad for treatment if that child or young person is a member of your family (see p818);
- for up to **seven days** if you are attending a job interview;
- for up to **three months** if you are unemployed and looking for work in another EEA country (see p673).

Pension credit

In order to qualify for pension credit (PC) you must be present in GB.[132] However, Regulations allow for entitlement to continue during periods of temporary absence from GB and set out situations in which a person can be treated as being present or not present in GB.[133] In addition, there are strong grounds to argue that PC is an 'old age' benefit for EC law purposes (see p676) and, therefore, fully exportable.

In order to satisfy the presence test you must be 'habitually resident' (see p702).[134] You are exempt from the test if you are:
- an EEA 'worker' (see p681);
- a refugee;
- a person with exceptional leave to remain;
- a person who has been deported or expelled from another country to the UK.

You can be treated as satisfying the presence test for PC during certain temporary absences. These are:
- for a period of **four weeks** if the absence is unlikely to exceed 52 weeks and while absent from GB the claimant continues to satisfy the other conditions of entitlement to PC;
- for a period of **eight weeks** if the period of absences is unlikely to exceed 52 weeks and the claimant continues to satisfy the other conditions of entitlement to PC and the claimant is accompanying a young person solely in connection with arrangements for the treatment of that person for a disease or bodily or mental disablement and those arrangements relate to treatment:
  - outside GB;
  - during the period while the claimant is temporarily absent from GB;
  - by, or under supervision of, a person appropriately qualified to carry out that treatment.

If you or your partner are receiving treatment in a hospital or other institution outside GB and the treatment is being provided under certain NHS provisions you can be treated as being present in GB for as long as the treatment continues.[135] However, this only applies where you satisfied the conditions for entitlement to PC immediately before you or your partner left GB. This does not apply in Scotland.

A person is treated as not being a member of the same household as the claimant if s/he is living away from the claimant *and*:
- s/he does not intend to resume living with the claimant; *or*
- her/his absence is likely to exceed 52 weeks.

Returning to Great Britain

On your return to GB you will probably have to show that you are still 'habitually resident' here if you want to claim means-tested benefits (see p702).

9. Reciprocal agreements

There are several countries with which Great Britain (GB) has reciprocal agreements. These mean that you receive some British benefits while in the other country and vice versa.

Each reciprocal agreement is different from the others. For further details of a particular agreement see CPAG's *Migration and Social Security Handbook* or contact CPAG.

Special rules for people from Northern Ireland, the Isle of Man and the Channel Islands

Technically, the rules described in this *Handbook* apply only to GB. GB consists of England, Wales and Scotland. It does not include Northern Ireland, the Isle of Man or the Channel Islands, which have their own social security legislation.

However, because of the close links between GB, Northern Ireland and the Isle of Man, you do not lose any non-means-tested benefit by moving between them[136] and national insurance contributions (see p825) paid in one of those jurisdictions count as though they were paid in each of the others. For most practical purposes the systems in GB, Northern Ireland and the Isle of Man may be treated as identical.

The Channel Islands, Jersey and Guernsey (including Alderney, Herm and Jethou), have their own social security systems but there is a reciprocal agreement under which you can receive some British benefits (see DWP leaflet SA4, from the Overseas Branch).[137] You also remain entitled to benefits (other than jobseeker's allowance) under British legislation while in any part of the Channel Islands.[138]

Notes

1. Immigration status

1 s115 IAA 1999
2 Reg 16 SS(IB) Regs
3 Immigration Rules para 6 HC 395, as amended by para 1 HC 324
4 Regs 3 and 5(1)(h) SPC Regs
5 s115(9) IAA 1999
6 EC Regs 1408/71 and 1612/68
7 Reg 10 Immigration (European Economic Area) Regulations 2000, SI No.2326
8 The EC-Swiss Agreement gives Swiss nationals the right to free movement and to the same social security rights as EEA nationals. It came into force on 1 June 2002.

2. National insurance numbers and contributions

9 CIS/3692/2001
10 EC Reg 1408/71
11 s179 SSAA 1992

3. Non-means-tested benefits

12 s115(9) IAA 1999; regs 2 and 12 and Sch Part II SS(IA)CA Regs; reg 16(1)(b) SS(IB)(MA) Regs
13 Since June 2002 Swiss nationals have the same rights as EEA nationals in respect of free movement and access to social security benefits

4. Means-tested benefits

14 s115(9) IAA 1999; regs 2 and 12 and Sch Part I SS(IA)CA Regs
15 *Kaya v LB Haringey* [2001] EWCA Civ 677, 1 May 2001
16 CIS/2091/01 and joined cases CIS/4727/01 and CIS/4728/01
17 CIS/1077/1999; CIS/6608/1999
18 s115(9) IAA 1999
19 s3(c) IA 1971
20 s115(9) IAA 1999
21 s115(1) and (9) IAA 1999; reg 21(3)and Sch 7 para 16A IS Regs
22 Sch 7 para 16A IS Regs
23 Reg 5(1)(h) SPC Regs

5. Urgent cases payments

24 Reg 2 SS(IA)CA Regs
25 Since April 2000 the DWP interpretation of the Regulations is that you can claim for a partner who was living with you prior to April 2000, but if you are joined by a partner after that date you will not be eligible
26 Reg 72(1) IS Regs; reg 149(1) JSA Regs
27 Reg 72(1)(c) IS Regs; regs 149(1)(c) and 110(1)-(3) and (9) JSA Regs

6. Asylum seekers and refugees

28 IAA 1999
29 It is possible to receive help under s21a NAA 1965 if you are in need of care of attention because of disability or illness, s21(b) if you are a nursing mother, ss17 and 20 CA 1989 if you have children, s2 LGFA 1992 if you need help to pay for accommodation. Unaccompanied child asylum seekers up to the age of 18 should be accommodated and supported by the authority under s20(3) CA. This requires more than simply placing them in a B&B. The Nationality, Immigration and Asylum Act excluded from entitlement to many social services provisions asylum seekers who have been served with a deportation notice or who have exhausted all their appeal rights and people granted refugee status in another EEA member state.
30 Reg 2(4) SS(IA)CA Regs
31 Reg 12(10)(a) SS(IA)(CA) Regs
32 In M (a Minor) v Secretary of State for Social Security [2001] UKHL 35, *The Times*, 5 July 2001, the House of Lords upheld a Court of Appeal decision that a break in claim leads to a loss of benefit
33 CF/1015/1995
34 *Yildiz v Secretary of State for Social Security*, 28 February 2001, unreported (CA)
35 Reg 12(1) SS(PFA)MA Regs 1996
36 s137 SSCBA 1992, definition of 'members of your household'
37 Regs 2(5) and (6), 6, 7, 12 and Sch part 1 SS(IA)CA Regs
38 CIS/4439/1998 (*73/99); CIS/259/1999 (*50/99); CIS/43/2000; CIS/2702/2000
39 Sch 3 Nationality, Immigration and Asylum Act 2002
40 Reg 21ZB IS Regs
41 s12 Asylum and Immigration (Treatment of Claimants, etc.) Act 2004
42 Regs 21ZA and 21ZB IS Regs; Sch A1 HB Regs; Sch A1 CTB Regs
43 This is because a solicitor instructed to act in a particular issue becomes the agent of her/his client; CIS/3797/2003
44 s124(1)(f) SSCBA 1992
45 Reg 4 SS(C&P) Regs requires a claim to be made on a properly completed claim form
46 Sch 10 para 49 IS Regs; Sch 8 para 12(b) JSA Regs
47 Sch 2 para 42 SPCA 2002
48 Sch A1 para 2A(4) HB Regs; Sch A1 para 2A(4) CTB Regs
49 Sch A1 para 2(5) HB Regs; Sch A1 para 2(5) CTB Regs, as amended by SS(IA)CA Regs
50 Sch A1 para 2(1) HB Regs; Sch A1 para 2(1) CTB Regs
51 Sch A1 para 9 HB Regs; Sch A1 para 8 CTB Regs
52 Sch A1 para 5(1) HB Regs; Sch A1 para 4(1) CTB Regs
53 Sch A1 paras 4 and 5(2) HB Regs; Sch A1 para 4(2) and (4) CTB Regs
54 Sch A1 para 6 HB Regs; Sch A1 para 5 CTB Regs
55 Sch A1 para 5(3) HB Regs; Sch A1 para 4(3) CTB Regs
56 Reg 7B(1)(b) HB Regs; reg 10(5A) HB(Amdt) Regs, as amended
57 Sch A1 para 8(1) HB Regs; Sch A1 para 7(1) CTB Regs
58 Sch A1 para 8(5) HB Regs
59 Sch A1 para 8(4) HB Regs

7. European Economic Area nationals

60 s2 ECA 1972
61 *Martinez Sala* Case C-85/96 [1988] ECR I-2691; *Trojani v Centre public d'aide sociale de Bruxelles* ECJ Case C-456/02 7 September 2004, unreported (ECJ);

Baumbast and another v Secretary of State for the Home Department Case C-413/99 [2002] (ECJ)

62 Signatories to ECSMA are Belgium, Denmark, Estonia, France, Germany, Greece, Iceland, Ireland, Italy, Luxembourg, Malta, Netherlands, Norway, Portugal, Spain, Sweden, Turkey, United Kingdom

63 *Grzelczyk v Centre public d'aide sociale d'Ottignies-Louvain-la-Neuve* C-184/99 [2001] (ECJ)

64 *Trojani v Centre public d'aide sociale de Bruxelles* ECJ Case C-456/02 7 September 2004, unreported (ECJ)

65 *Grzelczyk v Centre public d'aide sociale d'Ottignies-Louvain-la-Neuve* C-184/99 [2001] (ECJ)

66 *Baumbast and another v Secretary of State for the Home Department* Case C-413/99 [2002] (ECJ)

67 *Collins v Secretary of State for Work and Pensions* C-138/02 [2004] (ECJ)

68 *Collins v Secretary of State for Work and Pensions* C-138/02 [2004] (ECJ)

69 In *Hockenjos v Secretary of State for Social Security* [2001] EWCA Civ 624, 2 May 2001, the Court of Appeal decided that for the purposes of EC Directive 79/7 income-based JSA should be an unemployment benefit. The same approach has been adopted by commissioners in R(JSA)/3/02.

70 *Di Paulo v Office National de l'Emploi* C-76/76 [1977] ECR 315, but see also R(U) 8/88 which provides a useful analysis

71 *Swaddling v Adjudication Officer* C-90/97 [1999] (ECJ)

72 R(JSA) 3/02; *Hockenjos v Secretary of State for Social Security* [2001] EWCA Civ 624, 2 May 2001 (CA)

73 The cases deal with the question of whether income-based JSA is an 'unemployment benefit'. There are some difficulties in reading this argument across but there is still the basis of an argument.

74 CIS/825/2001. The Secretary of State has sought leave to appeal in this case.

75 *Di Paulo v Office National de l'Emploi* C-76/76 [1977] ECR 315, but see also R(U) 8/88 which provides a useful analysis

76 *Di Paulo v Office National de l'Emploi* C-76/76 [1977] ECR 315, but see also R(U) 8/88 which provides a useful analysis

77 *Swaddling v Adjudication Officer* C-90/97 [1999] (ECJ)

78 Art 94(2) EC Reg 1408/71

79 Reg 21(3) IS Regs; reg 85(4) JSA Regs; reg 7A(4) HB Regs; reg 4A(4) CTB Regs; reg 2 SPC Regs

80 Art 7(2) EC Reg 1612/68

81 Art 12 EC Reg 1612/68

82 *Levin* C-53/81 [1982] ECR 1035; EC Reg 1251/70

83 *Lebon* C-316/85 [1989] ECR 2811

84 *Levin* C-53/81 [1982] ECR 1035; *Kempf* C-139/85 [1986] ECR 1741; *Raulin* C-357/89 [1992] ECR 1027

85 *Scrivner* C-122/84 [1985] ECR 1027; Art 7 I(EEA)O; CIS/12909/1996

86 *Lair* C-39/86 [1988] ECR 3161; *Raulin* C-357/89 [1992] ECR 1027; Art 7(2) EC Reg 1612/68

87 *Raulin* C-357/89 [1992] ECR 1027; Art 7(2) EC Reg 1612/68

88 para 071916 DMG

89 *Lair* C-39/86 [1988] ECR 3161; Art 7(1) EC Reg 1612/68

90 Art 12 EC Reg 1612/68

91 Art 2(b) EC Reg 1251/70

92 Art 2(a) EC Reg 1251/70

93 Arts 2(c) and 4 EC Reg 1251/70

94 Arts 1 and 4 EC Dir 68/360

95 Art 7 EC Dir 68/360

96 *Roye* [1976] ECR 497; *Echternach and Moritz v Minister van Onderwijs* C-389 and C-390/87 [1989] ECR 723; *Raulin* C-357/89 [1992] ECR 1027

97 Arts 1 and 4 EC Dir 73/148

98 Art 1(b) EC Dir 73/148

99 *Cowan* C-186/87 [1989] ECR 195; *Humbel* C-263/86 [1988] ECR 5365; *Luisi* C-286/82 [1988] ECR 5365

100 Art 1 EC Dir 68/360; Art 10 EC Reg 1612/68; Art 1 EC Dir 73/148

101 CIS/3559/97

102 *Grzelczyk v Centre public d'aide sociale d'Ottignies-Louvain-la-Neuve* C-184/99 [2001] (ECJ)

103 *Zhu and Chen v Secretary of State for the Home Department* C-200/02 [2004] (ECJ)

104 *Diatta* C-267/83 established that EC rights are not lost if a couple separate. More recent caselaw has held that where children are involved EC rights may continue even after divorce. See *Baumbast and another v Secretary of State for the Home Department* Case C-413/99 [2002] (ECJ) and *Carpenter v Secretary of State for the Home Department* C-60/00 [2002] (ECJ)

105 Immigration (European Economic Area) (Amendment) Regulations 2003 SI No.549
106 Accession (Immigration and Worker Registration) Regulations 2004 SI No.1219
107 R(FC) 1/01
108 R(S) 1/00
109 See in particular *Babahenini* C-113/97 [1998] EC 1998, I-183; R(JSA) 7/02
110 CIS/5707/1999
111 The position of Directive 79/7 is different because there is no concept of special non-contributory benefits. The UK government has declared income-based JSA to be a special non-contributory benefit and the ECJ held that where such declarations exist benefits will be special non-contributory benefits because the declaration forms part of the Regulation itself.
112 See *Snares* C-20/96 [1997] (ECJ) and *Partridge* C-297/96 [1998] (ECJ) in which the ECJ held that the listing of a benefit in Annexe IIa must be accepted as establishing the nature of that benefit

8. **Benefits when you go abroad**
113 *Akbar, The Times*, 6 November 1992
114 *R(Carson) v Secretary of State for Work and Pensions* [2002] EWHC 978 (Admin), 22 May 2002
115 Reg 4(2A) SSB(PA) Regs
116 Reg 6 SSB(PA) Regs
117 Reg 4(2)(a) SSB(PA) Regs
118 Reg 9(3) SSB(PA) Regs
119 Reg 9(4) SSB(PA) Regs
120 Reg 9(5) SSB(PA) Regs
121 Reg 2 SSB(PA) Regs
122 Reg 10 SSP(MAPA) Regs; reg 2A SMP(PAM) Regs
123 SPPSAP(PAM) Regs
124 Reg 3A IS Regs
125 Reg 4(2)(c) IS Regs
126 Reg 16 IS Regs
127 CIS/13805/1996
128 CIS/508/1992; CIS/13805/1996
129 Sch 7 paras 11 and 11A IS Regs
130 Reg 5 HB Regs
131 Reg 50 JSA Regs
132 s1(2) SPCA 2002
133 s5(5) SPCA 2002
134 Reg 2 SPC Regs
135 This applies where treatment is provided under ss3 or 23 NHSA 1977 or para 13 Sch 2 NHSCCA 1990

9. **Reciprocal agreements**
136 Reg 2 and Sch 1 SS(NIRA) Regs; Art 2 and Sch 1 SS(IoM)O
137 Sch 1 SS(J&G)O
138 Reg 12(1) SSB(PA) Regs

Chapter 27

Residence conditions and benefits

This chapter covers the rules on residence that apply to certain benefits. It covers:

1. Present, resident and ordinarily resident (below)
2. Residence tests and benefits (p699)
3. The habitual residence test and the right to reside test (p702)

Many benefits have residence conditions. Generally such conditions mean that you have to live in the UK for a period of time before you can get that benefit or that you will have to show that you have a right of residence. Equally, if you go abroad the particular benefit is usually no longer payable. The rules are complicated and vary according to the benefit involved. However, there are often exceptions to the general rules or you may be able to rely on enhanced rights under European Community law or on reciprocal arrangements.

There are residence conditions for the following benefits:

- attendance allowance (see p699);
- carer's allowance (see p699);
- child benefit (see p699);
- disability living allowance (see p699);
- guardian's allowance (see p700);
- Category D retirement pension (see p701);
- income support, income-based jobseeker's allowance, pension credit, housing benefit and council tax benefit (see p701);
- incapacity benefit for incapacity in youth (see p699).

For the rules on tax credits, see Chapter 59.

1. Present, resident and ordinarily resident

The type of residence condition varies according to the type of benefit claimed, but you may be required to be:

- present;

- resident;
- ordinarily resident; *or*
- habitually resident.

Present

To be **'present'**, you must prove that you were present throughout any day in question – ie, from midnight to midnight.[1] **'Absent'** is the opposite of present. If the decision maker seeks to disqualify you because you are absent from Great Britain (GB), the burden is upon her/him to prove that you were absent throughout any day in question.[2]

For the purpose of satisfying the presence conditions for attendance allowance, disability living allowance, carer's allowance and incapacity benefit for incapacity in youth you still count as being in GB if you are:[3]

- a member of the armed forces serving abroad; *or*
- a spouse, son, step-son, daughter, step-daughter, parent, parent-in-law or step-parent of a member of the armed forces serving abroad and living with her/him; *or*
- a master, member of crew or other person employed on board a ship under a contract entered into in the UK; *or*
- a pilot or member of crew or other person employed on board an aircraft under a contract entered into in the UK; *or*
- a person employed on an oil or gas rig on the continental shelf.

European Community (EC) law can assist European Economic Area (EEA) nationals and their families to meet the condition of presence. If you have worked in an EEA state, the time that you have spent elsewhere within the EEA can count towards presence in the UK. You do not necessarily have to have worked throughout the period abroad but you must have worked somewhere in the EEA.

The EC also has social security agreements with a number of countries outside the EEA. The agreements are similar but not identical to those of EC Regulation 1408/71 (see p673). They can help those covered by the particular agreement to meet residence conditions and to receive benefit for family members who are not living in the UK. For example, it is possible to receive child benefit for children who are residing in another member state and, where benefits include a dependant's addition, it is possible to claim benefit for your spouse who is living in another member state or in the country with which the agreement has been made.[4]

EC law effectively treats your family as if they are residing with you in the UK. The same principle applies to the association agreements. Therefore, a commissioner held that a Moroccan who worked in the UK but whose wife remained in Morocco was entitled to receive a dependant's addition in his invalidity benefit in respect of his wife.[5] The full rights provided for in EC

Regulation 1408/71 are not included within the association agreements. In particular, the agreement with Turkey only allows for non-discrimination in benefits rather than the complete rules of co-ordination allowed in EC Regulation 1408/71. The non-discrimination principle, however, does remain important. For example, a commissioner held that a Turkish asylum seeker who worked in the UK was covered by the EC agreement with Turkey and therefore was able to qualify for family benefits.[6] Therefore a Turkish national, or a national from one of the other agreement countries, should be able to get any family benefits such as child benefit. As a part of EC law these agreements are important as they will override any rules which exclude a person from entitlement to benefit on the basis of nationality. The EC has such agreements with Algeria, Morocco, Slovenia, Tunisia and Turkey (see p684).

A worker on an oil or gas rig on the continental shelf is not disqualified from benefit if s/he is in the area of an oil or gas field or is travelling to it from another such area or from an EEA state (see p672).[7]

Resident and ordinarily resident

You are usually **'resident'** in the country where you have your home for the time being.[8] It is possible to be resident in more than one place at a time but it is unusual.[9] You can remain resident in a place during a temporary absence but this depends on the circumstances.[10] So if you go abroad to work on one particular project of limited duration, intending to return on its completion, you remain resident in GB. But if you go abroad for a considerable period, you may not remain resident in GB even if you do expect to return eventually. Important factors in deciding the issue are where the rest of your family live, the sort of accommodation you have (eg, a hotel does not suggest residence) and where your furniture and other personal effects are kept. If you move intending to settle at your new address, you are regarded as resident there from the very first day.

You are **'ordinarily resident'** if there is a degree of continuity about your residence so that it can be described as settled.[11] So if you live mostly in GB but also live elsewhere from time to time, you remain ordinarily resident in GB throughout the shorter periods of residence elsewhere.

The burden of proof lies on you to show that you are or were resident in GB at the relevant time if you are claiming benefit.[12]

Residence in another EEA country (see p673) may count as residence in GB. Some reciprocal agreements with other countries (see p692) contain similar rules.

2. **Residence tests and benefits**

Attendance allowance, disability living allowance, carer's allowance and incapacity benefit for incapacity in youth

To qualify for attendance allowance (AA), disability living allowance (DLA), carer's allowance (CA) and incapacity benefit for incapacity in youth you must:[13]

- be ordinarily resident in Great Britain (GB – see p698); *and*
- be present in GB (see p696); *and*
- have been present in GB for a total of 26 weeks in the last 12 months.

People claiming DLA or AA on the basis that they are terminally ill (see p149) are exempt from the rule that they have to have been present in GB for a total of 26 weeks in the last 12 months.[14] There are exemptions from the presence tests for, among others, serving members of the armed services and their families, mariners and off-shore workers.[15] If claims are made for DLA for babies who are less than 6 months old they only have to have been present for 13 out of 26 weeks.[16]

For DLA and AA, you are treated as being present during any temporary absence of less than 26 weeks, and during any further absence for the purpose of treatment if you obtain a certificate from the Secretary of State to the effect that the further absence is reasonable.[17]

For CA, you are treated as being present during any temporary absence of up to four weeks. You are also treated as present during any temporary absence for the purpose of caring for a person, provided of course that the person's DLA care component, AA or constant attendance allowance is still payable.[18]

Child benefit

In order to claim child benefit you and the child for whom you are claiming must be present in the UK and must also be ordinarily resident. Since 1 May 2004, in addition to the residence and ordinary residence conditions, your entitlement to child benefit will depend upon you having a right of residence (see p703).

Residence conditions for the claimant

You will be treated as not present and therefore not eligible for child benefit if:

- you are not ordinarily resident in GB;[19]
- you do not have a right to reside (see p703) in the UK and your claim for child benefit was made after 1 May 2004;
- you are out of the country for longer than the permitted periods.

Regulations treat you as satisfying the presence test if you are:[20]

- a Crown servant, or a partner of a Crown servant, posted overseas; *and*
  - immediately prior to your posting abroad you were ordinarily resident in the UK; *or*

  - immediately prior to your posting you were in the UK in connection with that posting; *or*
- a person who is in the UK as a result of you having been deported or legally removed from another country.[21]

If you remain ordinarily resident in the UK and your absence is unlikely, from the start of the absence, to exceed 52 weeks, child benefit continunes to be paid during:[22]

- the first eight weeks of any temporary absence; *or*
- the first 12 weeks of any period when you are temporarily absent from the UK if that absence, or any extension to that period of absence, is in connection with:
  - the treatmentof an illness or disability of you, your partner, a child for whom you are responsible, or another relative of either you or your partner; *or*
  - the death of your partner, a child for whom you are responsible, or another relative of you or your partner.

Residence conditions for the child

Generally, in order to claim child benefit the child for whom you are claiming must be present in the UK. However, a child will be treated as present if her/his absence abroad is temporary, during:

- the first 12 weeks of any period of absence; *or*
- any period during which the child is absent for the specific purpose of being treated for an illness or physical or mental disability which commenced before her/his absence began; *or*
- any period when s/he is in Northern Ireland; *or*
- any period during which the child is absent only because:
  - s/he is receiving full-time education at a recognised educational establishment in another European Economic Area (EEA) member state (including A8 States) or in Switzerland; *or*
  - s/he is engaged in an educational exchange or visit made with the written approval of the recognised educational establishment which s/he normally attends.

If a child is born outside the UK during a period in which the mother would be treated as present in the UK, the child will also be treated as present.[23]

Guardian's allowance

Entitlement to guardian's allowance depends on entitlement to child benefit, so the above conditions must be satisfied.

A further condition of entitlement to guardian's allowance is that at least one of the child's parents must have been born in the UK or have, at some time after reaching the age of 16, spent a total of 52 weeks in any two-year period in the UK.[24]

Maternity allowance

There is no residence or presence test as such because entitlement is based on past employment.

Bereavement payments

Bereavement payments are payable even if you go abroad. However, uprating of the benefit applies only to those who are ordinarily resident in GB. People living in the EEA can also qualify for full uprating under European Community (EC) law. You cannot qualify for a bereavement payment if your spouse was not in GB when s/he died unless:[25]

- you were in GB on the date of your spouse's death; *or*
- you returned to GB within four weeks of her/his death; *or*
- your spouse's national insurance contribution record is sufficient for you to satisfy the contribution conditions for widowed parent's allowance and bereavement allowance; *or*
- your spouse died while abroad in another EEA state (see p672).

Category D pension

You are only entitled to Category D pension if you are over 80 and are not entitled to any other pension in excess of the present rate of this pension.[26] The residence conditions are:[27]

- you must have been resident (see p698) in GB for at least 10 years in any continuous period of 20 years ending on or after your 80th birthday; *and*
- you were ordinarily resident (see p698) in GB either on the day you reached the age of 80, or on the date of the claim.

Income support, income-based jobseeker's allowance, housing benefit and council tax benefit

For all of these benefits you must be present in GB, habitually resident in the 'common travel area' (see p702) and you must have the right to reside (see p703). In some circumstances if you go abroad these benefits can be payable for short periods (see Chapter 26).

Pension credit

In order to qualify for pension credit (PC) you must be present in GB.[28]

In order to satisfy the presence test you must be habitually resident and from 1 May 2004 you must also have a right to reside (see p702).[29]

However, regulations allow for entitlement to continue during periods of temporary absence from GB and set out situations when you can be treated as being present or not present in GB. You can be treated as satisfying the presence test for PC during certain temporary absences. These are:

- for a period of **four weeks**, where the absence is unlikely to exceed 52 weeks and while absent from GB you continue to satisfy the other conditions of entitlement to PC;
- for a period of **eight weeks**, where the absence is unlikely to exceed 52 weeks, you continue to satisfy the other conditions of entitlement to PC and you are accompanying a young person solely in connection with arrangements for the treatment of that person for a disease, or bodily or mental disablement, and those arrangements relate to treatment:
  - outside GB;
  - during the period while you are temporarily absent from GB;
  - by or under supervision of a person appropriately qualified to carry out that treatment.

If you or your partner are receiving treatment at a hospital or other institution outside GB and the treatment is being provided under certain NHS provisions you can be treated as being present in GB for as long as the treatment continues.[30] However, this only applies where you satisfied the conditions for entitlement to PC immediately before you or your partner left GB.

3. The habitual residence test and the right to reside test

For some benefits you must satisfy the 'habitual residence test' and the 'right to reside' test. The benefits affected by the habitual residence test are:

- income support (IS);
- income-based jobseeker's allowance (JSA);
- pension credit (PC);
- housing benefit (HB);
- council tax benefit (CTB).

The benefits affected by the right to reside test are:

- IS;
- income-based JSA;
- PC;
- HB;
- CTB;
- child benefit;
- child tax credit (CTC).

You are not entitled to IS, income-based JSA, PC, HB or CTB unless you are habitually resident, or are treated as habitually resident, in the '**common travel**

area' which comprises the Republic of Ireland, the Channel Islands, the Isle of Man and the UK. If you do not satisfy the habitual residence test, you are classed as a 'person from abroad' and like those 'subject to immigration control' you become ineligible for benefit.[31]

There are now two stages in the habitual residence test:

- establishing whether or not a person has a right to reside;
- establishing whether or not a person is habitually resident.

If a decision maker decides that you do not have a right to reside, you will fail the habitual residence test. If it is decided that you do have a right to reside, the decision maker will go on to decide if you satisfy the habitual residence test.

The habitual residence test is applied to all claimants of these benefits (but not partners or dependants), including British citizens. The habitual residence test should only apply to you if you have been resident in the country for two years or less. The following people, however, are automatically treated as habitually resident in the UK and are therefore exempt from the test:[32]

- European Economic Area (EEA) nationals who are classed as 'workers'[33] in European Community (EC) law, and their dependants – see p681 for details;
- EEA nationals who have a right to reside under EC Directives 68/360 or 73/148. However, a person only gains the right to reside under these Directives if s/he is a 'worker' (see p681);[34]
- refugees or people who have been granted leave outside the immigration rules. This includes 'exceptional leave to enter or remain' in the UK, humanitarian protection or discretionary leave (see pp654 and 662);
- people in Great Britain who left Montserrat after 1 November 1995 because of a volcanic eruption there;
- people who have been deported, expelled or compulsorily removed from another country to the UK. However, this exemption does not apply to people subject to immigration control;
- for HB and CTB purposes, people who are entitled to IS, income-based JSA or PC.[35]

If you are entitled to urgent cases rates of IS or income-based JSA, you are not usually subjected to the habitual residence test, but you are not specifically exempt by legislation.

The right to reside

The right to reside test was introduced on 1 May 2004 for certain social security benefits and tax credits. The new test requires that claimants have a right of residence in order to be entitled to benefit. However, there is no statutory definition of the term and whether or not a person has a 'right of residence' is a complex matter. The right of residence is a matter of law and fact which is dependent on a person's immigration status and nationality – s/he may have a right to reside under UK rules or EC law or because s/he is a British citizen.

The new test is likely to have the greatest impact on European Union (EU) nationals and in particular, nationals of eight of the new member states, referred to as 'A8 nationals'. The **'A8 nationals'** are nationals of Czech Republic, Estonia, Hungary, Latvia, Lithuania, Poland, Slovakia and Slovenia. Although nationals from these countries are now EU nationals and can have access to EC law, they do not have full EC rights. In particular, A8 nationals do not have complete freedom of movement to take up employment in the way that other EU nationals do. A8 nationals are not excluded from the protection of EC Regulation 1408/71 and therefore may have access to benefits under this Regulation (see below).

Benefits affected

The benefits affected by the right to reside test are:

- IS;
- income-based JSA;
- PC;
- HB;
- CTB;
- child benefit;
- CTC.

For child benefit[36] and CTC[37] the test operates as part of the existing presence test for those benefits. For all of the other benefits the requirement to reside forms part of the habitual residence test.[38] Therefore the exemptions that apply to the habitual residence test will also apply to the right to reside test. Equally, the habitual residence test is only applied to claimants who entered the common travel area within the last two years.

A8 nationals

There are no restrictions on an A8 national entering or living in the UK. However, for benefit purposes unless you are working and have registered that work you will be treated as not having the right to reside and therefore will not qualify for certain benefits.

If you want to work as an employee you have to comply with certain conditions under the Workers Registration Scheme.[39] You must apply for your work to be registered within one month of taking up employment. The following A8 nationals are not required to register:

- a person who is from a state that has ratified the European Convention on Social and Medical Assistance or the European Social Charter (Croatia and Turkey);
- anyone who had leave to enter or remain in the UK on 30 April 2004 which was not subject to any condition restricting employment;

- anyone who, on 30 April 2004, had been working legally for a continuous period of 12 months;
- anyone who has been working legally for a continuous period of 12 months, either partly or wholly after 30 April 2004;
- anyone who has been registered for 12 months or more.

Other European Economic Area nationals

Workers

If you are from one of the established EEA states or from Malta or Cyprus and you have worked in the UK or have been economically active in some other way you have worker status (see p681) and have a right to reside in the UK. Consequently you have full access to benefits. Your worker status should not be lost purely because of a temporary interruption of work due to ill health. Equally, the fact that you are now unemployed should not affect your rights as long as you remain in the labour market. This will usually be achieved by signing on for JSA.

Workseekers

You have the right to reside if you are looking for work (apart from A8 nationals).[40] The Department for Work and Pensions (DWP) sometimes tries to argue that a person seeking work will only have EC rights for a period of six months. This stems from a ruling by the European Court of Justice (ECJ) in the case of *Antonissen*.[41] The Court held that the six-month limit contained in UK immigration rules at the time did not breach EC law. However, the Court went on to say that if a person showed that s/he had a genuine chance of finding work, s/he could not be required to leave that member state.

European Economic Area nationals who are not economically active

If you have never worked and are not seeking work, unless you are the family member of a worker or workseeker you have far fewer rights under EC law. The Government takes the position that you do not have the right to reside unless you are self-supporting. In some cases this will be challengeable, in particular because the ECJ appears to be moving towards a general principle of non-discrimination towards EU citizens rather than simply to workers. However, this is unlikely to be resolved quickly and it will always be better for an EU national to try to become economically active, as this will give better rights. This does not necessarily mean that s/he must undertake full-time employment. It could equally apply to someone registering with the Revenue as self-employed or to someone working a few hours a week.

British and Irish nationals and Commonwealth citizens with right of abode

British citizens, Irish nationals and Commonwealth citizens have rights to reside under UK immigration rules and therefore should not be affected by the right to reside test. However, some people may have some difficulty in proving their status.

Non-EEA nationals

Non-EEA nationals living in the UK may have a right to reside under UK law – eg, if they have indefinite leave to remain. People with a grant of temporary leave such as that given to a spouse or student also have a right to reside, but in most cases these groups are excluded from access to benefits as they are defined as being subject to immigration control (see p655).

Transitional protection

If you were entitled to one of the affected benefits on the day the new rules came into force (1 May 2004) you are protected against the new rules. This transitional protection appears to be lost if there is a break in your period of claiming. However, simply retaining entitlement to any of the affected benefits such as HB or CTB means that you retain entitlement to any of the other benefits.

Habitually resident

The term 'habitually resident' is not defined in the benefit regulations, but it has now been the subject of a substantial body of caselaw. The leading decision is that of *Nessa*[42] by the House of Lords. Also significant is the judgment by the ECJ in *Swaddling*.[43] However, there are also numerous commissioners' decisions on the term which remain significant and DWP guidance now reflects this caselaw. What has emerged from the caselaw is that there is no absolute definition or list of factors which determines a person's habitual residence. Whether a person is habitually resident is a question of fact to be decided by looking at all the circumstances in each case. This means that it is very important for claimants and advisers to put in detailed submissions to the DWP, local authority or tribunal.

To be habitually resident in a country, you must have a **'settled intention'** to reside, which means that you intend to make your home here for a temporary or permanent period. Events subsequent to your arrival can help confirm that your intentions were settled from the outset. You must show some evidence of your intention to reside – eg, by bringing possessions, doing everything necessary to establish residence before coming, having a right of abode, seeking to bring family, 'durable ties' with the country of intended residence.[44] These are only examples and other factors may be relevant to your case. Cutting your links with your previous country of residence may help – eg, travelling on a one-way ticket or selling a home abroad.

You must, unless you are able to rely on EC law, be actually resident for an 'appreciable period of time' before you become habitually resident. What counts as an appreciable period of time depends on the facts of each case. There is no minimum period, although it would appear that, in general, habitual residence cannot be immediately acquired. There is no set time limit after which you establish habitual residence; it could be as little as two or three weeks, but the longer you are here the easier it will be to show that you are habitually resident.

If you go abroad for a temporary period, you may retain your habitual residence in the UK, so that you will be habitually resident from the first day of your return. Other people who are re-establishing ties in the UK may be able to resume their habitual residence immediately. Other claimants may have enhanced rights because they are able to rely on EC law. The way in which you might challenge a decision that you are not habitually resident very much depends on your circumstances.

It is always worth checking whether you fall into one of the categories of people who are exempt, such as EEA workers, refugees, those with exceptional leave to enter or remain, humanitarian protection or discretionary leave (see p653).

European Economic Area nationals

EEA nationals who are 'workers' (including British citizens who have worked in another EEA state – see p672) are automatically treated as satisfying the habitual residence test (see p680).

EEA nationals who do not fall into the category of 'worker' may nonetheless be able to rely on EC Regulation 1408/71 to claim IS, income-based JSA or PC (see p673). HB and CTB do not fall under the scope of EC Regulation 1408/71. However, UK HB rules exempt from the test a person who is entitled to IS, income-based JSA or PC.[45] EEA nationals relying on Regulation 1408/71 must have worked in an EEA state, but not necessarily the UK. To be eligible under this category you have to show that you have strong ties with the UK and that you have a settled intention to reside here.[46] This would almost certainly include most British citizens who have returned to the UK, but would also apply to other EEA nationals who may or may not have lived in the UK but nonetheless have ties – eg, other family or friends within the UK. The *Swaddling* judgment was concerned with a British citizen but the principles established apply equally to other EEA nationals.

Returning residents

If you have lived in the UK in the past and you are resuming your residence you may be able to be treated as habitually resident immediately.

In a decision issued post-*Nessa* and *Swaddling* a commissioner held that in order to establish whether a person is resuming a previous residence it is necessary to conduct a three-stage inquiry.[47] This involves looking at:

- the circumstances in which the claimant's earlier habitual residence was lost;
- the links between the claimant and the UK while abroad;
- the circumstances of the claimant's return to the UK.

The commissioner explained that the fact that a person's absence was only temporary, albeit for a long time, may be a point in favour of the claimant resuming habitual residence immediately on return. On the other hand, if the claimant left the UK with no intention of returning, that may be a point against resuming habitual residence on return. If the person remained abroad for longer than anticipated because of circumstances outside her/his control, that also might be a feature in favour of resuming habitual residence. The ties and contacts retained or established by the claimant while abroad must also be considered. The person must also show that s/he intends resettling in the UK for the time being. Where the intention to settle is very strong, the period of actual residence becomes shorter. It is also clear that if you have previously lived in the UK and are now returning to live here for the foreseeable future, you can be treated as habitually resident immediately.

By contrast, in a later case[48] another commissioner considered the position of returning residents and held that it is necessary for a claimant to be habitually resident for an appreciable period even where the claimant is resuming residence. The case involved a British citizen who had worked in Britain for many years and who had spent no more than 11 months in Britain in the five years before the claim for benefit. The commissioner found that although the claimant had once been habitually resident, he had ceased to be so over that five-year period. A claim for benefit had been made three days after his arrival in the UK. On that basis, the commissioner held that he had not become habitually resident by the time of the claim. The commissioner found, however, that the claimant was habitually resident some five weeks after arrival.

Returning after a temporary absence

If you have been abroad for a temporary period and prior to your absence you were habitually resident, you do not lose your habitual residence.[49] The distinction between the categories of temporary absence and returning resident is not entirely clear and there is some overlap. Temporary absence is more likely to cover short periods of absence – eg, for holidays or to visit relatives or to work. As a returning resident you may have been abroad for a longer period.

People coming to the UK for the first time

People in this situation will have to satisfy the habitual residence test. This means showing that you have been resident for an appreciable period of time, that you have a settled intention to remain and that you have durable ties with the country of intended residence. The period, however, can be very short and in family caselaw it has been held that as little as a month may constitute an appreciable period.

Tactics

- If you are refused benefit because of the habitual residence test, you can request a revision, supersession, or appeal to a tribunal (see p1187 and p1218). You can ask for an expedited hearing of your appeal if you are suffering hardship.

Always ask for an oral hearing, so that you can explain your circumstances in person.

- Always check to see if you fall into one of the categories that are exempt from the test (see p702).
- Only the claimant is subject to the habitual residence test. If you cannot satisfy the test, your partner could be the claimant if s/he would satisfy the test (eg, s/he has been in the UK longer than you) or would be exempt (eg, as an EEA worker – see p672).
- Since the habitual residence test operates to exclude you from IS, income-based JSA, PC, HB and CTB, the onus of proof lies with the DWP or local authority to establish that you are *not* habitually resident.[50] It is vital, nevertheless, that you produce as much evidence as possible to show that you *are* habitually resident, taking into account the above points on the meaning of the term. You should prepare your case thoroughly before attending a DWP or local authority interview or a tribunal.
- A local authority should make its own decision as to whether you are habitually resident. Therefore, even if you are refused a benefit by the DWP under the habitual residence test the local authority should not simply follow that decision.
- Where a claimant is in receipt of IS, income-based JSA or PC a local authority should not apply the habitual residence test.[51]
- If you fail the test, you may be able to satisfy it at a later date, particularly if there is a change in your circumstances, or simply through the passage of time. You will need to make repeated claims, perhaps every two to four weeks. This is now essential because tribunals cannot take into account circumstances between the date of the appeal hearing and the date of the original decision (see p1238). Repeated claims for benefit can highlight your determination to remain in the UK, as well as the unfairness of the test. Some local offices are refusing to accept repeat claims if there is an appeal pending. This is wrong – the local office should accept the claim and make a decision.
- If you have no money to live on because you have failed the habitual residence test, you could:
  - if you have children, apply to your local social services department for support under the Children Act;
  - if you do not have children but are in need of 'care and attention', for example because of ill-health, ask your local authority for help under the National Assistance Act;
  - if you need help with rent or a deposit, ask the local authority to provide financial assistance under section 2 of the Local Government Act 2000;
  - apply for a social fund crisis loan (see p538). Although you have to be able to repay a loan, if you are likely to be counted as habitually resident in the near future you will then qualify for benefit and will be in a position to repay the loan.

- The Nationality, Immigration and Asylum Act 2002 excludes the following people from some social services support:[52]
  - EEA nationals who are not 'workers';
  - people who have been granted refugee status in another EEA state, but who are not EEA nationals;
  - a person who has been refused asylum and who has failed to comply with removal directions.

  Note: the Act makes clear that a local authority is *not* prevented from supporting one of the above groups where there would otherwise be a breach of EC law or where a refusal of support would lead to a breach of any rights under the European Convention on Human Rights. Therefore, a refusal of support, particularly where children are involved, may well be challengeable. Equally, the provisions regarding EEA nationals indirectly discriminate against non-British EEA nationals and consequently may be in breach of EC law. In such circumstances you should seek legal advice.

Notes

1. Present, resident and ordinarily resident

1 R(S) 1/66
2 R(S) 1/66
3 Reg 2(2) SS(AA) Regs; reg 2(2) SS(DLA) Regs; reg 6(2) SS(GA) Regs; reg 9(3) SS(ICA) Regs; reg 3(2) SS(SDA) Regs; reg 16 SS(IB) Regs
4 These rights stem from the co-ordination provisions of EC Regulation 1408/71 and apply to all of the association agreements apart from Turkey. The Turkish Agreement does not allow for co-ordination of social security but does prevent discriminatory treatment in respect of social security.
5 R(S) 1/00
6 R(FC) 1/01
7 EC Reg 1408/71; reg 11 SSB(PA) Regs as amended
8 R(P) 1/78
9 R(G) 2/51
10 CG/204/1949
11 R(P) 1/78
12 R(G) 2/51

2. Residence tests and benefits

13 Reg 2(1) SS(AA) Regs; reg 2(1) SS(DLA) Regs; reg 9(1) SS(ICA) Regs; reg 16 SS(IB) Regs
14 Reg 2(4) SS(DLA) Regs
15 Reg 2(2) SS(AA) Regs; reg 2(2) SS(DLA) Regs
16 Reg 2(5) SS(DLA) Regs
17 Reg 2(2)(d) and (e) SS(AA) Regs; reg 2(2)(d) and (e) SS(DLA) Regs
18 Reg 9(2) SS(ICA) Regs
19 'Ordinary residence' means the place that you have made your place of abode
20 Regs 30 and 31 CB Regs
21 Regs 24(1) and 28(1) CB Regs
22 Reg 22 CB Regs
23 Reg 24(2) and 28 CB Regs
24 Reg 9 SS(GA) Regs
25 WRP(PABWW) Regs. These Regulations did not come into force until 20 August 2001, but anyone who was refused a payment because their spouse died outside GB may be able to receive an ex gratia payment.
26 s78(3) SSCBA 1992
27 Reg 10 SS(WB&RP) Regs

28 s1(2) SPCA 2002
29 Regs 2 and 3 SPC Regs
30 This applies where treatment is provided under ss3 or 23 of NHSA 1977 or para 13 of Sch 2 NHSCCA 1990

3. The habitual residence test and the right to reside test

31 Reg 21(3) IS Regs; reg 85 JSA Regs; reg 7A(4)(e) HB Regs; reg 4A(4)(e) CTB Regs
32 Reg 21(3) and (3F) IS Regs; reg 85(4) and (4A) JSA Regs; reg 7A(4)(e) and (5) HB Regs; reg 2 SPC Regs
33 UK legislation refers to 'workers' under EC Regulations 1612/68 and 1251/70. These Regulations cover employees and former employees. However, under EC law the term 'worker' is used to mean a person who is economically active. This includes not only employees but the self-employed and people who receive or provide services.
34 These Directives allow a person covered by EC Regulation 1612/68 as an employee or who is a person who is self-employed to apply for a residence permit
35 Reg 7A(5)(d) and (e) HB Regs
36 The Child Benefit (General)(Amendment) Regulations 2004 SI No.1244
37 The Tax Credits (Residence)(Amendment) Regulations 2004 SI No.1243
38 The Social Security (Habitual Residence) Amendment Regulations 2004 SI No.1232
39 The Accession (Immigration and Worker Registration) Regulations SI No.1219
40 The right to reside is by virtue of Article 39 EC Treaty
41 *R v IAT ex parte Antonissen* [1991] ECR 1-745
42 *Nessa v CAO* [1994] 4 All ER 677 21 October 1999 (HL)
43 *Swaddling* ECJ Case C-90/97 25 February 1999, unreported (ECJ)
44 *Nessa v CAO* [1999] 4 All ER 677 21 October 1999 (HL)
45 Reg 7A HB Regs 1987
46 Art 10a EC Reg 1408/71; *Di Paolo* ECJ Case C-76/76 17 February 1977, unreported (ECJ); *Swaddling* ECJ Case C-90/97 25 February 1999, unreported (ECJ)
47 CIS/1304/1997 and CJSA/5394/1998
48 CIS/376/2002
49 R(IS) 6/96
50 R(IS) 6/96 para 15
51 Reg 7A(5) HB(Gen) Regs
52 ss17, 23C, 24A and 24B CA 1989; s2 Local Government Act 2000; ss21 and 29 NAA 1948

Chapter 28

Other special groups and benefits

This chapter covers the special rules which affect the benefit entitlement of the following groups of claimants:

People coming from or going abroad are covered in Chapter 26. People who are studying are covered in Chapter 25.

1. 16/17-year-olds

Special rules may affect your entitlement to some benefits if you are aged 16 or 17. This section identifies the rules and where appropriate, refers you to other parts of the *Handbook* for more details.

Means-tested benefits

Income support

You are eligible for income support (IS) in your own right if you fall into one of the categories of people who can claim (see p293). Note, however, that if you are in non-advanced 'relevant education', you can only claim IS in specified circumstances (see p619). If you are or were in local authority care, see p713.

Income-based jobseeker's allowance

You are only entitled to income-based jobseeker's allowance (JSA) in specified circumstances. Note that in some cases, you will only qualify for 'severe hardship payments' and that special rules apply to the labour market conditions and sanctions (see p438). If you are or were in local authority care, see p713.

Housing benefit and council tax benefit

You can claim housing benefit (HB) if you are liable to pay rent and satisfy the other conditions of entitlement (see Chapter 10). The amount you get, however, may be restricted under the 'single room rent' rule (see p247). You are not liable to pay council tax.

If you are or were in local authority care, see p713.

Social fund payments

You are entitled to a Sure Start maternity grant or a funeral expenses payment if you satisfy the normal rules (see Chapter 22).

You may be eligible to claim a community care grant or a budgeting loan if you are receiving IS or income-based JSA (see pp517 and 529). You can claim a crisis loan, unless you are in 'relevant education' and not entitled to IS/income-based JSA (see p539).

Health benefits

You are entitled to most health benefits without charge if you are in full-time education. Otherwise you can qualify for free help if you receive a qualifying benefit (or are a member of the family of someone getting a qualifying benefit), or on the grounds of low income. You also qualify if you are being maintained by a local authority after leaving care. See Chapter 9 for full details.

If you are or were in local authority care

Subject to the exceptions below, you are excluded from IS, income-based JSA and HB in England and Wales (see p714 for Scotland) if:

- you are aged 16 or 17; *and*
- you were looked after by a local authority (ie, subject to a care or supervision order, or provided with accommodation under sections 20, 23 or 23A of the Children Act 1989) on or after 1 October 2001; *and*
- you were looked after for at least 13 weeks after the age of 14 and were still being looked after when you reached 16.[1]

The exclusion continues even if you are no longer being looked after by a local authority. It also applies if you are not subject to a care order, but you were in hospital, or detained in a remand centre, or a young offenders or similar institution when you became 16 and immediately before that you were looked after by a local authority for at least 13 weeks since your 14th birthday.[2]

The 13 weeks referred to above do not have to be continuous. Pre-planned short-term placements of four weeks or less, after which you return to the care of your parent, or person acting as your parent, do not count towards the 13 weeks.[3]

If the above conditions apply, you are also not treated as a member of the family of a person claiming IS, income-based JSA, HB or council tax benefit.[4]

If you are excluded from benefit under the above rules, your local authority (social services) is under a duty to assess and meet your needs for maintenance, accommodation and support.[5] Local Department for Work and Pensions and social services offices should liaise to ensure any disputes about who is responsible are quickly resolved. If you are refused both benefit and social services support, you should seek specialist advice.

Similar rules apply in Scotland, with effect from 1 April 2004, although they are worded slightly differently.[6] Subject to the exceptions set out below, you are excluded from IS, income-based JSA and HB in Scotland if:

- you are aged 16 or 17; *and*
- you were looked after by a local authority (ie, subject to a care or supervision order, or provided with accommodation under section 17(6) of the Children (Scotland) Act 1995) for at least 13 weeks after the age of 14; *and*
- you stopped being looked after by a local authority on or after April 2004 and the local authority is obliged to provide you with after-care services under section 29(1) of the above Act; *and*
- you are not living with your family or another person who has parental responsibility for you (unless you are receiving regular financial assistance from the local authority under section 29(1) of the Act).

The 13 weeks are calculated in the same way as they are for England and Wales (see above). Note that the rules do not apply if you left care (in Scotland, England or Wales) prior to 1 April 2004 and are now living in Scotland.

Exceptions

- You are not excluded from IS or income-based JSA (but are from HB) if you are in one of the following groups who are eligible to claim IS (see p293):
  - lone parents;
  - single foster parents;
  - people incapable of work or appealing against an incapacity for work decision;
  - disabled workers;
  - disabled or deaf students;
  - blind people;
  - young people in 'relevant' education who are lone parents or severely disabled and unlikely to get employment in the next 12 months.[7]
- You are not excluded from IS, income-based JSA or HB if you have been in a family placement for at least six months, and:
  - you are still in local authority care in Wales; *or*
  - you have left local authority care in England or Wales (unless, in England only, the placement has broken down).[8]

Non-means-tested benefits

Disability and incapacity benefits

- You are entitled to disability living allowance, industrial injuries benefits and carer's allowance under the normal rules (see Chapters 7, 14 and 4). If you are a young carer, you can get advice from Carers UK (telephone: 0808 808 7777).
- You can claim incapacity benefit if you have been continuously incapable of work for 28 weeks (see p263). You do not have to satisfy national insurance (NI) contribution conditions.

Other benefits

- You will rarely be able to qualify for contribution-based JSA because of the NI contribution conditions (see p825).
- You may qualify for statutory maternity pay, statutory sick pay or maternity allowance if you have been working (see Chapters 23, 24 and 17).
- You are entitled to Class 3 NI 'starting credits' and Class 2 education and training credits in specified circumstances (see p839).

2. Hospital inpatients

Your benefit may be reduced after you or your dependants have been receiving free NHS-funded maintenance and treatment as an inpatient in a hospital or 'similar institution' for the periods specified below. The rules apply to anyone who is not a fee-paying private patient.[9] Those affected are referred to in this section as 'inpatients'.

Hospitals include all NHS hospitals, armed forces hospitals and special hospitals such as Broadmoor and Rampton. Prison hospital wings, however, do not count as hospitals.[10] What constitutes a 'similar institution' to a hospital is not defined in the legislation but could include some care homes, hospices and rehabilitation units that provide medical or nursing care.[11] You should not count as an inpatient, however, if your maintenance and treatment are not fully funded by the NHS, or if your placement was arranged by a local authority (even if the NHS is contributing to the cost of your nursing care).[12] If a primary care trust decides that you have been receiving 'continuing NHS care' in a care home, which should be provided without charge, you should only be treated as an inpatient from the day of the decision.[13]

Not all benefits are affected by the inpatient rules and in most cases benefit is not reduced until somebody has been an inpatient for 52 weeks (note, however, that attendance allowance (AA) and disability living allowance (DLA) normally stop after four weeks – see p716). You should always inform the benefit authorities promptly if your benefits may be affected by the rules below, to avoid being overpaid or underpaid benefit. You can do this in writing or by telephone (it is always best, where possible, to notify the benefit authorities in writing and keep a copy in case of a dispute).

If you are receiving jobseeker's allowance (JSA) when you become an inpatient, you can only be treated as satisfying the 'labour market conditions' (see Chapter 15) for up to two weeks (you are allowed two such periods in each year of your jobseeking period (see p348).[14] After that, you can claim incapacity benefit (IB) or income support (IS) instead. A hospital can issue medical certificates as evidence of your incapacity for work.

If necessary, you can arrange for somebody else to collect your benefit while you are in hospital. If you are unable to manage your affairs, another person or a hospital can act as your appointee (see p1075). See Chapter 9 for details of how to get help with the cost of your fares to and from hospital. If you are visiting somebody in hospital, you may be able to claim a community care grant to cover the cost of your fares (see p517).

Separate periods as an inpatient that are 28 days or less apart are linked together when calculating the periods specified below.[15] For most benefits you do not count as an inpatient on the day you enter hospital (or a similar institution) but you do count as an inpatient on the day you are discharged.[16] For AA and DLA, however, neither day counts.[17]

After four weeks

Attendance allowance and disability living allowance

If you become entitled to AA or DLA while you are an inpatient, payment cannot begin until you are discharged.[18]

If you are already entitled to AA (including constant attendance allowance – see p333) or DLA when you become an inpatient, payment normally stops after you have been an inpatient for 28 days.[19] Note, however, that:

- any DLA you are getting for a child continues to be paid until s/he has been an inpatient for 12 weeks (see p718);
- you can continue to get the mobility component of DLA if:
  - you had a Motability agreement (see p164) when you became an inpatient, but only until the agreement ends (unless you immediately renew an agreement under the Wheelchair Scheme); *or*
  - you have been an inpatient since 31 July 1995 (other than under 'section' under the Mental Health Acts), in which case your mobility component is paid at the lower rate;[20]
- you can continue to get AA or DLA while you are in a hospice which is not provided by the NHS, if you are terminally ill;[21]
- the 28-day 'linking rule' (see p726) means that your AA or DLA will stop immediately, or before 28 days, if you are re-admitted as an inpatient within 28 days of a previous stay;
- periods spent in prescribed accommodation (eg, a care home) during which AA and the DLA care component are not payable (see p725) link with periods

spent as an inpatient if they are 28 days or less apart (this means that you will not normally be entitled to AA or the DLA care component if you enter hospital from a care home).[22]

You can requalify for AA or DLA from the payday following your discharge as an inpatient.[23] If you expect to be readmitted within 28 days, you can be paid at a daily rate from the day of your discharge.

Carer's allowance

Although carer's allowance (CA) can continue to be paid for up to 12 weeks while you or the person you are looking after are an inpatient, your entitlement to CA will stop when the person you are looking after loses her/his entitlement to AA or DLA. This will normally happen after s/he has been an inpatient for 28 days (see p716). The carer's premium/addition paid with means-tested benefits can continue to be paid for up to eight weeks after CA stops (see p73). If the person you are caring for is discharged for part of a week and receives AA or the DLA care component, you can reclaim CA if you satisfy the 35-hour rule (see p73).

Severe disability premium/addition

Once your AA or DLA stops, you are no longer entitled to the severe disability premium of IS, income-based JSA, housing benefit (HB) and council tax benefit (CTB) or the severe disability addition of pension credit (PC – see p469). If, however, you are a member of a couple and one or both of you are inpatients, the severe disability premium/addition is paid at the single person's rate.[24]

If your IS, income-based JSA, or PC stops because of the loss of the severe disability premium/addition, your HB and CTB will also stop and you will need to submit a new claim.

The loss of the severe disability addition of PC can also affect the amount of savings credit payable (see p472).

Entitlement to the disability, enhanced disability, higher pensioner or disabled child premiums of IS, income-based JSA, HB and CTB are not affected by the withdrawal of AA or DLA because you or your partner are an inpatient.[25]

After 12 weeks

Carer's allowance

You remain entitled to CA for up to 12 weeks in any period of 26 weeks while you, or the person you are caring for, are an inpatient. Your CA will stop, however, when the person you are caring for is no longer entitled to AA or DLA, which will normally happen after s/he has been an inpatient for 28 days (see p717). If you lose your CA because you are an inpatient, the person you were caring for may become entitled to the severe disability premium/addition (see p891). The carer's premium/addition paid with means-tested benefits stops eight weeks after CA stops. The loss of the carer's addition paid with PC can affect the amount of savings credit payable (see p472).

Benefit for children who are inpatients

- DLA for a child under 16 stops after s/he has been an inpatient for 12 weeks.[26]
- The personal allowance for a child or young person paid with IS or income-based JSA is reduced to £16.40 after s/he has been an inpatient for 12 weeks.[27] Child-related premiums remain payable with IS, income-based JSA, HB and CTB. The disabled child premium continues to be paid after DLA stops, as long as the child or young person remains a member of your family.[28] **Note:** Personal allowances and premiums for children paid with IS and income-based JSA are being phased out from April 2004 (see p303).
- Child benefit, guardian's allowance and child dependency additions paid with non-means-tested benefits stop after a child has been an inpatient for 12 weeks, unless you continue to regularly incur expenditure in respect of her/him.[29]

After 52 weeks

Income support and pension credit

Single claimants

If you are a single claimant, your IS applicable amount (see p876) and the standard minimum guarantee of PC for guarantee credit purposes (see p469) are reduced to £16.40 after you have been an inpatient for 52 weeks. You are not entitled to any IS premiums and will no longer qualify for the severe disability or carer's additions of the guarantee credit of PC.[30] You are also no longer entitled to any housing costs payable with IS or the guarantee credit of PC once you are likely to be absent from your home for substantially more than 52 weeks, or you have actually been absent for more than 52 weeks (see p907). Housing costs can be paid to another person if s/he can be treated as liable to pay them (see p905).

Note also the following rules:

- There is no reduction in the standard minimum guarantee of PC for the purposes of calculating entitlement to savings credit. The loss of any additions still being paid for housing costs, severe disability and carers, however, can affect the amount of savings credit payable (see p472).[31]
- Your IS applicable amount can be reduced to less than £16.40 if you have an appointee and your IS is being paid to the hospital or institution you are in as your appointee, or at the request of your appointee, and your doctor has certified that some or all of your IS cannot be used for you. The views of the hospital staff and any relatives must be taken into account when deciding the amount necessary for your personal use.[32]

Couples

You can no longer be treated as a member of a couple for IS or PC purposes once you are likely to be separated from your partner for substantially more than 52 weeks.[33] This may happen before or after you or your partner have been an inpatient for 52 weeks. You will then need to claim IS or PC (including the savings credit of PC) as a single claimant and your benefit will be reduced as above, after you have been an inpatient for 52 weeks.

If you are still treated as a couple when one of you has been an inpatient for 52 weeks (this would only apply if you or your partner are likely to return home in the near future), your IS applicable amount or the standard minimum guarantee of PC is reduced *by* (not *to*) £16.40.[34] If you have both been inpatients for 52 weeks and expect to resume living together in the near future, your IS applicable amount is reduced to £41.00, plus, if applicable, personal allowances and premiums for your children, and the standard minimum guarantee of PC is reduced by £32.80.[35] The rules about housing costs are the same as for single claimants (see p718).

Lone parents

You are no longer treated as a lone parent for IS purposes once you are likely to be separated from your children for substantially more than 52 weeks.[36] You will then need to claim IS as a single claimant and your benefit will be reduced as above, after you have been an inpatient for 52 weeks.

If you are still treated as a lone parent when you have been an inpatient for 52 weeks (this would only apply if you are likely to return home in the near future), your applicable amount is reduced to £20.50, plus, if still applicable, personal allowances and premiums for your children.[37] The rules about housing costs are the same as for single claimants (see p718).

Non-dependants

Non-dependant deductions from housing costs paid with IS and PC (see p924) are no longer made in respect of a non-dependant who has been an inpatient for 52 weeks.[38]

Income-based jobseeker's allowance

You can only continue to qualify for income-based JSA for up to two weeks while you are an inpatient (see p715). After your partner has been an inpatient for 52 weeks, your applicable amount is reduced *by* (not *to*) £16.40.[39] You can no longer claim for a partner, however, as soon as you are likely to be separated from her/him for substantially more than 52 weeks.[40]

Non-dependant deductions from housing costs paid with income-based JSA are no longer made in respect of a non-dependant who has been an inpatient for 52 weeks.[41]

Housing benefit and council tax benefit

You are not entitled to HB or CTB once you are likely to be continuously absent from your home for substantially more than 52 weeks, or you have actually been continuously absent for 52 weeks. In the case of CTB, however, you may be able to argue that you remain entitled to CTB for as long as your home remains your sole or main residence (see p112). If you are no longer entitled to HB because you are an inpatient, another person may be able to claim benefit as a liable person (see p196).

If you are still entitled to HB/CTB after you have been an inpatient for 52 weeks (eg, because you have not yet been continuously absent from your home for 52 weeks), your HB/CTB applicable amount (see p876) is reduced as follows:

- If you are a single claimant, your HB/CTB applicable amount is reduced to £20.50 if you are aged under 60, or £16.40 if you are aged 60 or over.[42]
- If you are still treated as a lone parent (see p719), your applicable amount is reduced to the above amounts, plus, if still applicable, personal allowances and premiums for your children.[43]
- If you are still treated as a member of a couple (see p719), your applicable amount is reduced *by* (not *to*) £16.40 if one of you is an inpatient. If both of you are inpatients, your applicable amount is reduced to £41.00, plus personal allowances and premiums for any children you remain responsible for.

Note: if you are receiving other benefits such as IS, PC, IB and retirement pension, which are also reduced after 52 weeks, the reduction in your HB/CTB applicable amount may not affect your entitlement.

Note also: non-dependant deductions from HB and CTB are no longer made in respect of a non-dependant who has been an inpatient for 52 weeks.[44]

Non-means-tested benefits

The following benefits are reduced after you have been an inpatient for 52 weeks:

- retirement pension (all categories);
- IB;
- severe disablement allowance;
- bereavement and widows' benefits (apart from the lump-sum bereavement payment – see p24);
- unemployability supplement and industrial death benefit.

The basic weekly rates of the above benefits are reduced to £16.40.[45] If you have a dependant, you can opt for the remainder of your normal weekly entitlement (including any dependants' increases), less £31.20, to be paid to her/him, or another person approved by the Secretary of State (you should be sent a form for this purpose shortly before you have been an inpatient for 52 weeks).[46]

The £16.40 paid for you can be reduced further if you have an appointee and your benefit is being paid to the hospital or institution you are in as your appointee, or at the request of your appointee, and your doctor has certified that some or all of your benefit cannot be used for your personal comfort or enjoyment.[47]

Any increase of a non-means-tested benefit you are receiving for a spouse is reduced to £16.40 after s/he has been an inpatient for 52 weeks.[48]

3. People in care homes

Care homes are local authority, NHS and independent (ie, private or voluntary sector) homes which provide personal and/or nursing care for residents. Most care homes are required to be 'registered' by the relevant regulatory body.[49]

Most benefits are payable as normal if you are in a care home. The following benefits, however, may be affected, or not payable:

- income support (IS) and income-based jobseeker's allowance (JSA) (see p724);
- pension credit (PC) (see p724);
- housing benefit (HB) (see p725) and council tax benefit (CTB) (see p725);
- attendance allowance (AA) and the care component of disability living allowance (DLA) (see p725);
- winter fuel payments (see p559), cold weather payments (see p558) and crisis loans (see p539).

You should also note that if your place in a care home is arranged and funded by the NHS, you may count as an inpatient, in which case your benefits will be affected in accordance with the rules outlined in the previous section (see p715).

See p97 for how child benefit is affected if a child is in local authority care. See p712 if you are aged 16 or 17 and were in local authority care. You are entitled to free health benefits if you are a permanent resident in a care home and your place is being funded by a local authority (see Chapter 9).

Funding arrangements

The following is a brief overview of the funding arrangements for adults in care homes. The rules and issues arising are extremely complex and you should always seek specialist and independent financial advice about your situation if you are unsure about anything. Further details about the funding system and how it interacts with the benefit system can be found in CPAG's *Paying for Care Handbook*. Note that placements of children under the age of 18 in care homes are funded without charge.[50]

Sources of funding

If you need help to find or pay for a place in a care home, you should contact your local authority social services or social work department. Your local authority has a duty to arrange a suitable placement in a care home for you if you need it because of your age, disability, or other reasons.[51] It can do this by placing you in one of its own homes, or by funding a placement in an independent (ie, private or voluntary) home, by entering into a contract with the provider. In either case, you will be required to pay a means-tested weekly charge to the authority (see p722). You should note that the local authority is only obliged to provide sufficient funding to secure a suitable placement in an independent home. If you choose to live in a more expensive home than you require, you will have to meet the shortfall in fees from your own resources (this is only allowed in prescribed circumstances[52]), or arrange for a third party to pay the difference (eg, a charity or relative).

The NHS can also arrange and fund a place in a care home which provides nursing care (whether provision is the responsibility of the NHS or the local authority depends on your healthcare needs and local eligibility criteria[53]). The NHS is also responsible for funding the cost of any registered nursing care you receive in a care home in England (there are three levels of weekly payment, depending on your assessed needs). In Wales, the NHS pays a fixed weekly payment for registered nursing care if you are self-funding.[54]

In Scotland, local authorities contribute a fixed weekly amount for any nursing care you receive, plus a further fixed payment towards your personal care if you are aged 65 or over.[55]

What you will have to pay

If your place in a care home is fully funded by the NHS, you will not have to pay any fees. You also cannot be charged for accommodation and care provided as 'after care services' in England and Wales following a period of compulsory detention in a hospital under the Mental Health Act 1983.[56]

In other circumstances, unless your placement is funded by your local authority, you will have to pay the full fees to the provider (net of any contribution for registered nursing care in England and Wales and nursing/personal care in Scotland referred to above).

If you are in a local authority home, or the local authority is funding your place in an independent home, you are required to pay a means-tested weekly charge to the authority.[57]

The rules governing charges are laid down in national Regulations.[58] Guidance on the Regulations is set out in the *Charging for Residential Accommodation Guide*, issued by the Department of Health.

If you have capital in excess of £20,000 in England, £19,500 in Scotland, or £20,500 in Wales, your weekly charge is equivalent to the full cost of your placement. If your capital falls below these levels, your weekly charge is your total weekly income less a personal expenses allowance of at least £18.80 in England and Scotland, or £18.40 in Wales, which you must be left with.

Your capital and income are assessed in a similar way as they are for IS (see Chapters 38 and 39), with the following important differences:

- Your partner's capital and income must not be taken into account.
- The capital value of your former home is disregarded for the first 12 weeks you are permanently resident in a care home. After that there is no disregard, on the basis that the property is up for sale, but any property which is occupied (eg, by a relative or former carer) can be disregarded at the discretion of the local authority. A home occupied by your ex-partner is disregarded if s/he is a lone parent. The value of your normal home must be disregarded if you are temporarily in a care home for a period which is unlikely to exceed (or substantially exceed) 52 weeks.
- In addition to the normal notional capital rules (see p1039), if you deprive yourself of property or other capital in the six months prior to entering a care home, the recipient of the capital can be made liable for your weekly charge.[59]
- Your income includes IS, PC and most other benefits but there is a disregard of up to £4.65 (£4.85 in Scotland and £4.75 in Wales) for a single claimant, or £6.95 for a couple (£7.20 in Scotland), if you qualify for the savings credit of PC, or would do but for your income being too high (see p472). This means that you will have to pay most of your benefit income to the local authority to meet your weekly charges. AA and the care component of DLA count as income if you are permanently resident in a care home, but are ignored if you are a temporary resident. The mobility component of DLA is always disregarded. Arrears of most benefits are disregarded for 52 weeks.
- Tariff income from capital is calculated as for means-tested benefits (see p977) but the threshold is £12,250 in England, £13,500 in Wales and £12,000 in Scotland.

If you are in a care home on a temporary basis for up to eight weeks (eg, for respite care), the local authority can disregard the means test and impose a reasonable standard charge.[60] In the case of all temporary placements of up to 52 weeks, the local authority should take into account your continuing home expenses by making appropriate disregards from your income.

If you are unable to pay your full weekly charge because your assessed capital is tied up in your property, the local authority can place a legal charge on the property and fund your placement until the property is sold.[61] You will be required to pay a weekly charge based on your income and other capital and will have to refund the balance of the charges you owe when the property is sold. The above arrangement can be put into effect through a written 'deferred payment agreement' between you and the local authority, which can continue in force until your death.[62]

You should use the local authority complaints procedure if you want to challenge any of the authority's decisions relating to the provision or funding of your care.

Income support and income-based jobseeker's allowance

Your IS/income-based JSA is subject to the normal conditions of entitlement and is calculated in the normal way (see Chapter 35).

You should, however, note the following points:

- The capital and tariff income rules are more generous if you are a permanent resident in most types of care homes (see p1023 for details). The capital limit is £16,000 and the tariff income threshold is £10,000. The higher limits mean that you may become entitled to IS or income-based JSA when you become a permanent resident in a care home.
- If you or your partner permanently enter a care home, you will no longer count as a couple for IS/income-based JSA purposes.[63] This should also apply if you are both permanently in care homes, even if you are in the same home and the same room.[64]
- If you or your partner are temporarily in a care home, you still count as a couple if you have not been apart for substantially longer than 52 weeks but your applicable amount is calculated in a special way (see p816). You will normally receive the amount applicable to two single claimants. This can include the severe disability premium in respect of either or both of you, as if you were single claimants, even if you are not normally entitled to it at home.[65]
- If your AA or DLA care component stops because you are in a care home, you will no longer be entitled to a severe disability premium (see p891). If you remain entitled to AA or DLA care component, however, you may become entitled to a severe disability premium if, for example, you are no longer treated as living with a non-dependant or a partner.
- Housing costs are payable for up to 52 weeks if you are temporarily in a care home (eg, for respite care) or for up to 13 weeks if you are in a care home on a trial basis (see p908 for details).

Pension credit

PC is subject to the normal rules of entitlement if you are in a care home (see Chapter 18). You should, however, note the following points:

- If you or your partner are permanently resident in most types of care home (disregarding absences of up to 52 weeks), you no longer count as a couple and the capital limit above which tariff income applies is £10,000, rather than the normal £6,000.[66]
- If you are temporarily in a care home, you still count as a couple if you have not been apart for substantially more than 52 weeks and housing costs remain payable under the same rules as apply to IS (see above).[67]
- If your AA or DLA care component stops because you are in a care home, you will no longer be entitled to a severe disability addition (see p891). If you remain entitled to AA or DLA care component, however, you may become

entitled to a severe disability addition if, for example, you are no longer treated as living with a partner or a non-dependant.

Housing benefit

People in local authority homes

You are not entitled to HB if you live in a care home owned or managed by a local authority and you pay an inclusive charge for accommodation and meals.[68] Even if meals are not included, you are excluded from HB if you were living in such a home on 31 March 1993.[69]

People in independent homes

You are not entitled to HB if you live in an independent care home,[70] unless you fall into one of the following categories:

- you were entitled to HB in respect of an independent home on 29 October 1990. You remain eligible for HB in any independent home without time limit;[71]
- you were entitled to HB on 31 March 1993 and you were *either*:
  - in remunerative work; *or*
  - paying a commercial rent to a non-resident close relative (see p199); *or*
  - living in an unregistered home with less than four residents.

  You remain eligible for HB as long as you do not break your claim and you continue to live in the same home, disregarding temporary absences of up to 13 or 52 weeks (see p202).[72]

Temporary residents

You remain entitled to HB for your normal home while you are *temporarily* in a care home for:

- up to 13 weeks, if you are in care for a trial period; *or*
- up to 52 weeks, if you are temporarily in care, you intend to return home and your period of absence is unlikely to substantially exceed 52 weeks.[73]

Council tax benefit

The rules are the same as for HB if you are temporarily living in a care home[74] (see above) but you may be able to argue you are entitled to CTB as long as your normal home remains your sole or main residence (see p112).[75] If you become a permanent resident in a care home, you will not be liable for council tax for your place in the home. If your home in the community is unoccupied you can apply for it to be exempt from council tax (see CPAG's *Council Tax Handbook* for details).

Attendance allowance and disability living allowance care component

Subject to the exceptions on p727, AA and the DLA care component are not payable after you have been in the following types of prescribed accommodation for 28 days or 84 days if you are aged under 16 (note the 28-day linking rule set out below):[76]

- accommodation provided under Part III of the National Assistance Act 1948, Part IV of the Social Work (Scotland) Act 1968 or section 7 of the Mental Health (Scotland) Act 1984; *or*
- accommodation, the cost of which (see below) is borne wholly or partly from public or local funds under the above Acts, or any other Acts relating to people with disabilities, or (in the case of DLA), young people, or people in education or training. The cost of the accommodation does not include the cost of:[77]

- domiciliary services provided to people in a private dwelling;
- improvements to the accommodation;
- furniture or equipment;
- social and recreational activities outside the accommodation;
- the purchase or running of motor vehicles used in connection with the accommodation;
- NHS services, including the fixed payments for nursing care, referred to on p722.

The scope and application of the rules is discussed in more detail on p727.

Note:

- AA and the care component of DLA are not payable for the first 28 days in the above types of accommodation if your entitlement begins when you are already in such accommodation.[78]
- If the person you are caring for loses her/his AA or the DLA care component because of the above rules, your carer's allowance (CA) (see Chapter 4) will stop. The carer's premium/addition paid with means-tested benefits can continue for a further eight weeks (see p896).

28-day linking rule

Different periods spent in the above types of accommodation which are separated by 28 days or less link together for the purpose of calculating the 28 days for which you can continue to be paid AA or the care component of DLA. Periods spent as an inpatient in a hospital or similar institution (see p715) also count towards the 28-day limit on payment, if they are separated from periods spent in the above types of accommodation by 28 days or less.[79] Days spent away from the above types of accommodation, including the days you enter and leave the accommodation, are normal days of entitlement, for which you can be paid AA and the care component of DLA.

It can be important to plan periods of respite care in the light of the linking rules so that you can retain your entitlement to AA and the care component of DLA for as long as possible (which will also enable your carer to keep her/his CA). You can, for example, go into respite care every Friday and return every Monday for 14 weeks without losing benefit. If you then enter care on Saturday and return home on Sunday for a further four weeks, the 28-day link will be broken and you can return to the previous pattern for another 14 weeks without losing benefit.

'Self-funding' and other exceptions

You remain entitled to AA and the care component of DLA after 28 days in the prescribed accommodation listed on p721 if you are 'self-funding' – ie, you are meeting the whole cost of the accommodation from your own resources, or with the assistance of another person or a charity.[80] Note that:

- this applies whether you are in an independent or local authority home;
- your own resources include benefits such as IS, PC, AA and DLA – ie, claiming benefits does not stop you from counting as self-funding;
- you count as self-funding if a local authority has arranged and contracted to pay for your placement in a care home but you are paying the full cost of the accommodation in weekly charges to the local authority;
- you count as self-funding if a local authority is temporarily funding your placement while you sell your property, as long as you are liable and able to repay the local authority in full when the property is sold (ie, you are 'retrospectively self-funding').[81] This would apply if you have entered into a 'deferred payment agreement' with the local authority (see p723). Note, however, that the value of your home is disregarded for the first 12 weeks you are permanently in a care home. If a local authority is providing funding during this period, you are not liable to repay it and are not, therefore, entitled to AA or the care component of DLA beyond the first 28 days on the basis of being retrospectively self-funding.

You also remain entitled to AA and the care component of DLA after 28 days in the accommodation listed on p721 if:

- you are terminally ill and are in a non-NHS hospice, whose primary function is to provide palliative care for terminally ill people;[82] *or*
- in the case of DLA, you are a student and the cost of your accommodation (eg, in a hall of residence) is wholly or partly met from a student grant or loan, or from a grant made to education institutions (eg, from funding councils) under prescribed legislation;[83] *or*
- you are under 18 and are receiving local authority care or services because of your age or health and have been placed (fostered) by the local authority in a private dwelling, or a local authority is funding your accommodation outside the UK under specified legislation (eg, at the Peto Institute in Hungary or the Higashi School).[84]

Scope and application of the rules

Subject to the above exceptions, you will normally be caught by the rules if you reside in most types of care homes and your placement is partly or wholly funded by a local authority. This is because the primary power to provide and fund placements in independent and local authority care homes derives from Part III of the National Assistance Act 1948 or Part IV of the Social Work (Scotland) Act 1984.

There is a wide range of residential and supported accommodation and funding arrangements, however, and it is not always clear whether your placement was provided or is funded under the prescribed legislation. The Department for Work and Pensions (DWP) often sends out enquiry forms to care homes (form BDB26) and local authorities or health authorities (forms DBD46LA or DBD46HA) to find out what type of accommodation you are in, how it is funded and under what legislation it is provided. The forms are not always accurately completed and you may be wrongly denied benefit as a result. If you are unsure whether the accommodation you are in is affected by the rules, you should always seek specialist advice and, if necessary, appeal against the refusal to pay AA or the care component of DLA (the view of a local authority is not binding on tribunals[85]).

Note, in particular, the following points:

- Not all accommodation which offers personal and nursing care is provided under the legislation set out on p725. Local authorities also have powers to provide accommodation under housing legislation and the Local Government Act 1972, which is not caught by the rules.[86] NHS funding does not normally count as accommodation costs (see p725) but if you are treated as a hospital inpatient, your AA and DLA stops after four weeks (see p716).
- The rules should only apply if the actual cost of your placement is being wholly or partly met from public or local funds.[87] The mere involvement of social services in helping to place you in a home should not trigger the rules and you can still be treated as self-funding if the local authority has contracted to pay the home, as long as you are meeting the full cost in weekly charges (see p722).
- If your place in a care home in England and Wales is provided without charge as 'aftercare services' under s117 of the Mental Health Act 1983, a Commissioner has decided that you are caught by the rules and not entitled to AA or DLA care component after 28 days.[88]
- If you are aged 65 or over and living in a care home in Scotland, the DWP is likely to stop your AA after 28 days, on the basis that the contributions made to your personal care costs by the local authority count as public funds. You may be able to argue, however, that these payments are not made towards the cost of your accommodation and are not, therefore, caught by the rules on p725 (you will need to appeal until a test case has decided the issue).

4. Prisoners

Special rules apply to most social security benefits in relation to prisoners. Most benefits are not payable while you are in prison, although in certain circumstances payment is only suspended and arrears may be payable on your release. It is important that you inform the relevant benefit authorities as soon as you, or a member of your family, enter or leave prison to avoid any underpayment or overpayment of benefit. Note particularly that if your income support (IS), guarantee credit of pension credit or income-based jobseeker's allowance (JSA) stops, you will need to make a fresh claim for housing benefit (HB). If you are being held on remand, it is important to notify the benefit authorities as soon as you are sentenced.

For details of benefits on release and help with travelling expenses, see p733.

Note that you may be subject to benefit sanctions if you are convicted of two benefit offences in three years, or if you breach a community service order (in pilot areas only). See Chapter 42 for full details.

Income support

You count as a prisoner for IS purposes if:[89]

- you are detained in custody (eg, prison or young offenders' institution) following a sentence of imprisonment; *or*
- you are detained in custody 'on remand' (eg, in a prison or remand centre) awaiting trial or sentence; *or*
- you are released on temporary licence (this does not include parole licence).

You do not count as a prisoner if:[90]

- you are released on licence or parole; *or*
- you are on bail or in a bail or probation hostel; *or*
- you are detained in hospital under the Mental Health Act 1983 or Scottish equivalent; *or*
- you are released under a home detention curfew (electronic tagging).

If you count as a prisoner, you are not entitled to any IS, apart from housing costs (see p907), which are only payable for up to 52 weeks while you are on remand, awaiting trial or sentence.[91]

A prisoner is not a member of the family for IS purposes (see p816).[92] If you are a prisoner, your partner can claim benefit as a single person or lone parent. If your partner or child is a prisoner, you can no longer claim IS for her/him. If you and your partner are temporarily separated because one of you is in a bail or probation hostel, you still count as a couple for IS purposes and your applicable amount is calculated at either the couple rate or double the single rate, whichever is the greater.[93]

Pension credit

If you are a prisoner as defined for IS purposes (see above), you are not entitled to the guarantee credit or the savings credit (see Chapter 18).[94] If you are on remand, awaiting trial or sentence, you are entitled to housing costs for up to 52 weeks[95] and you may be entitled to arrears of the severe disability addition if you do not receive a sentence of imprisonment and you are awarded arrears of attendance allowance or disability living allowance on your release (see p733).[96]

You are no longer treated as a member of a couple if you or your partner are in prison.[97]

Income-based jobseeker's allowance

You are not entitled to income-based JSA while you are detained in custody or released on temporary licence, as you are not able to satisfy the labour market conditions.

A prisoner no longer counts as a member of the family for income-based JSA purposes.[98] If you are a prisoner (see p816), your partner can claim income-based JSA or IS as a single claimant or lone parent. If your partner or child is a prisoner, you can no longer claim income-based JSA for her/him. If one of you is temporarily in a bail or probation hostel, the rules are as for IS (see p729).[99]

Housing benefit

If you are detained in custody pending trial (on remand) or sentence, or are required to live away from home in a bail hostel or other accommodation as a condition of bail, you remain entitled to HB on your normal home for up to 52 weeks, as long as you intend to return home and your absence from home is unlikely to substantially exceed 52 weeks.[100] If you are serving a custodial sentence, you are entitled to HB for up to 13 weeks, as long as your absence from home is unlikely to exceed 13 weeks.[101] If you are serving a sentence of more than 13 weeks, you may still be entitled to HB, as prisoners serving short sentences are often released early under a home detention curfew (electronic tagging). This means that it is possible for a prisoner serving a sentence of up to a year to be released within 13 weeks. You are treated as serving a custodial sentence during periods of temporary release (unless you are released under an Intermittent Custody Order).[102] These periods, therefore, count towards the 13 weeks for which HB is payable. Also, you can continue to get HB for up to four weeks if you still have to pay rent and you could not reasonably have avoided that.[103] If your partner is working then s/he may be able to have childcare costs deducted from her/his earnings (see p965).

If you are no longer entitled to IS or income-based JSA, you will need to make a new claim for HB.

If you are no longer entitled to HB, your partner or other person occupying your home may be able to claim benefit as a liable person (see p196). A prisoner continues to count as a member of the claimant's family as long as s/he is unlikely to be away for substantially longer than 52 weeks.[104] Non-dependant deductions are not made in respect of a non-dependant who is a prisoner.[105]

Council tax benefit

The rules are the same as for HB,[106] except that you remain entitled to council tax benefit as long as your home remains your sole or main residence.[107] Also, a prisoner remains a member of the claimant's family, so long as s/he is only temporarily absent.[108] If your home is unoccupied while you are a prisoner, you can apply for it to be exempt from council tax, as long as you are not in prison for non-payment of a fine or council tax. See CPAG'S *Council Tax Handbook* for details.

Social fund payments

Most prisoners are excluded from getting a crisis loan (see p538) and a winter fuel payment (see p559) and are unlikely to be receiving a qualifying benefit for the purposes of other social fund payments (see Chapters 21 and 22). If you are released on temporary licence, a person caring for you may be able to claim a community care grant to help with living expenses (see p528).

Non-means-tested benefits

Most non-means-tested benefits are not payable while you are a prisoner, but see below for exceptions.

You count as a prisoner for the purpose of non-means-tested benefits if you are in prison or detained in legal custody (in the UK or abroad), in connection with criminal proceedings.[109] If you are in prison for a civil offence, the following rules do not apply and you remain entitled to all benefits, provided you satisfy the normal rules of entitlement. You do not count as a prisoner if you are released on parole, temporary licence or under a home detention curfew (electronic tagging).

If you receive a sentence of imprisonment or detention and are transferred to hospital because of a mental disorder, you are treated as a prisoner until the date you are expected to be released from prison.[110] After that, you are treated as a hospital inpatient (see p715).

Benefits disqualified or suspended

If you are serving a sentence of imprisonment or detention you are disqualified from receiving the following benefits:[111]

- incapacity benefit and severe disablement allowance ;
- attendance allowance, disability living allowance and carer's allowance ;
- retirement pension and bereavement benefits;
- maternity allowance;
- reduced earnings allowance and retirement allowance .

You are also disqualified from receiving an increase in the above benefits for a spouse who is a prisoner.[112]

If you are a remand prisoner awaiting trial or sentence, payment of the above benefits is suspended. An increase in benefit for your spouse is also suspended while s/he is on remand. If you subsequently receive a sentence of imprisonment or detention[113] (including a suspended sentence[114]), you will be disqualified from receiving the above benefits for the whole period you are in prison. An increase of benefit for your spouse is similarly disqualified if s/he is sentenced to imprisonment or detention.

If you (or your spouse) do not receive a sentence of imprisonment or detention or your conviction is quashed, full arrears of any benefit and national insurance (NI) contributions which have been withheld are payable when you are released.[115]

Note that arrears are only payable if the normal conditions of entitlement for benefit were met while you (or your spouse) were a remand prisoner. You should be treated as still 'residing with' your spouse while s/he is in prison, unless your marriage has broken down and your separation is likely to be permanent.[116]

Other benefits not payable

- You are not entitled to statutory sick pay, statutory maternity pay (SMP), statutory adoption pay (SAP) or statutory paternity pay (SPP) while you are detained in legal custody or sentenced to a term of imprisonment (except where the sentence is suspended).[117] You remain disentitled to SMP and SPP for the whole of your maternity or paternity period (see p588), even if you are released from prison during it. You are entitled to SAP, however, for any period during which you are detained in custody if you are subsequently released without charge or after being found not guilty, or you are convicted but do not receive a custodial sentence.
- You will not be able to satisfy the labour market conditions for contribution-based JSA while you are in prison.
- You are not entitled to an increase in benefit for an adult caring for a child (see p795) if the adult or child is a prisoner.[118]

Benefits payable

- You remain entitled to disablement benefit (but not to the increases listed on p333) while you are a prisoner (see p731), but payment is suspended until you are released and you can only be paid a maximum of 12 months' arrears[119] (if you are in prison for more than a year, you should be paid for the 12-month period which gives you the most benefit[120]). In addition, you are entitled to full arrears for any period you were on remand, if you are not subsequently sentenced to imprisonment or detention.[121]
- You remain entitled to child benefit[122] and guardian's allowance[123] while you are a prisoner. You must continue to be 'responsible' for the child (see p90). If

you are in prison for some time, you may want to arrange for child benefit to be paid to the person looking after the child (see p92). If your child is a prisoner (see p97), child benefit will stop after eight weeks.[124] Full arrears are payable at the end of any period of remand, however, if the child is not sentenced to imprisonment or detention.[125] Once child benefit stops, guardian's allowance and increases in other benefits in respect of the child will also stop.[126]

Benefits on release

- If you are released on temporary licence, somebody caring for you can claim a community care grant (CCG) for living expenses (see p528).
- When you are permanently released, you should claim any benefits to which you are entitled as soon as possible (discharge form B79 can help you prove your identity and claim benefits quickly). As IS and income-based JSA are generally paid in arrears, you may need to apply for an interim payment or a social fund crisis loan to meet your initial expenses (see p538). You can also apply for a CCG if you are, or expect to be, in receipt of IS or income-based JSA (see p517). You may receive a discharge grant from the Prison Department, which counts as capital for IS/income-based JSA purposes.[127] Under the 'Freshstart' initiative, a jobseeker's interview can be pre-arranged prior to your release and you are treated as satisfying the labour market conditions for income-based JSA for the first seven days after your release.[128]
- If you are aged 16 or 17, you should contact the Connexions or Careers Service when you are released.
- If you are released without being sentenced to imprisonment or detention, you should receive any arrears of non-means-tested benefits to which you are entitled (see p5). You should also check that you have been credited with any NI contributions to which you are entitled (see p837).
- If you are released following the quashing of a conviction you are entitled to NI credits for the period you were wrongly imprisoned.

Help with travelling expenses

- The Prison Department can help you with travelling expenses when you are temporarily or permanently released from prison.
- The Prison Department can also help a partner or close relative with the cost of visiting you in prison (including the cost of an overnight stay where necessary) if s/he is receiving IS, income-based JSA, tax credits or has a low income. Application forms are available from the Department for Work and Pensions. For more details contact the Assisted Prison Visits Unit, PO Box 2152, Birmingham B15 1SD (telephone 0845 300 1423 or textphone 0845 304 0800).

5. People without accommodation

Income support/income-based jobseeker's allowance

If you are a person 'without accommodation' you are entitled to the normal income support (IS)/income-based jobseeker's allowance (JSA) personal allowances for yourself and your partner (see p877). You are not, however, entitled to any premiums.[129] This may be challengeable under the Human Rights Act (you will need specialist advice to do this).

The term '**accommodation**' is not defined in law and should be interpreted widely and flexibly. Department for Work and Pensions (DWP) guidance describes it as: 'An effective shelter from the elements which is capable of being heated; and in which occupants can sit, lie, cook and eat; and which is reasonably suited for continuous occupation. The site of the accommodation may alter from day to day, but it is still accommodation if the structure is habitable'.[130] This would cover tents, caravans and other substantial shelters. Cardboard boxes, bus shelters, sleeping bags[131] and cars[132] would not qualify as accommodation.

If you are temporarily absent from the accommodation you occupy as your home and are living a lifestyle as though you have no accommodation (eg, you are sleeping rough) you should be treated as having accommodation.[133]

If the DWP thinks that you have an unsettled way of life, it may refer you to a voluntary project centre. This should only be done with your consent and if a place is available. IS/income-based JSA should not be refused or delayed if you are unwilling to take the advice being offered, or are not interested in being resettled.[134]

Payment

If you are known in an area, you should receive your benefit in the normal way (see p312), but if you are likely to move on or mis-spend your money you may be required to collect your benefit on a daily or part-weekly basis.[135]

Availability for and actively seeking work

You must be available for and actively seeking work to get JSA (see Chapter 15). You can be available for work if you do not have accommodation but it must be possible for you to be contacted at short notice if you are to satisfy the requirement that you are willing and able to take up any job immediately, or at 24 or 48 hours' notice (see p355). You may satisfy this requirement by daily visits to the JobCentre, or a drop-in centre or support group where a message can be left for you.

Being homeless may, of course, reduce your prospects of finding work but personal circumstances which reduce your chances of being employed should not prevent you getting JSA, unless you are placing unreasonable restrictions on your availability. The fact that you are homeless should be taken into account when deciding whether you are taking reasonable steps to find work – eg, it may not be reasonable to expect you to write to employers if you have no address for them to reply to. The DWP should also recognise that you may need time to find accommodation, and that this will leave you with less time to find work (see p365).

Other benefits and sources of help

Your entitlement to other benefits, including pension credit and all non-means-tested benefits, is unaffected if you do not have accommodation. If you are getting contribution-based JSA, you must be available for and actively seeking work (see above).

If you become homeless and have no money, you may initially need a social fund crisis loan (see p538) or an interim payment (see p230). If you set up home as part of a resettlement programme after you have been homeless, you may be entitled to a community care grant (see p525).

If you are homeless, the local authority may have a duty to assist you with accommodation under the Housing Acts, or, arguably, under the National Assistance Act 1948, particularly if you are destitute and your health is at risk.[136] A child or young person may be entitled to help from social services under the Children Act. If you are aged 16 or 17 and were in local authority care, see p713.

6. People involved in a trade dispute

Special rules may stop or reduce the payment of some benefits if you or your partner are involved in a trade dispute. Benefits not referred to below are payable as normal during a trade dispute.

A 'trade dispute' is any dispute between employers and employees or between employees and employees about terms or conditions of employment, or the employment/non-employment of anyone.[137]

You are treated as being involved in a trade dispute if:[138]

- you are not working because of a 'stoppage of work' caused by a trade dispute at your 'place of work' (see below); *or*
- you withdraw your labour in furtherance of a trade dispute.

The **'stoppage of work'** could be due to a strike, lock-out or any other stoppage caused by a trade dispute. The stoppage does not have to involve everybody,[139] or stop all work.[140] There is no 'stoppage' if normal work continues through the employment of replacement workers.[141] You are treated as involved in the trade dispute until the stoppage ends, even if you are not a party to the dispute or your contract has been terminated as part of the dispute (but see p736).[142]

Your **'place of work'** means the place or premises where you are employed but it does not include a separate department carrying out a separate branch of work, which is commonly undertaken as a separate business elsewhere (a colliery canteen worker, for example, laid off during a miners' strike was not 'involved in a trade dispute at her place of work'[143]). It is often difficult, however, to establish that separate branches are commonly separate businesses and not part of integrated activities.[144]

You are treated as being involved in a trade dispute if you withdraw your labour, whether or not there is a stoppage of work at your place of work.[145]

You are not treated as being involved in a trade dispute in the following circumstances:

- You can prove you are not directly interested in the dispute[146] – ie, you will not be affected by its outcome. This could apply if your terms and conditions will not be affected by the outcome of the dispute or your employment has permanently ended and you will not gain anything from the dispute.[147]
- You can prove that during a stoppage of work:[148]
  - you have been made redundant; *or*
  - you have become genuinely employed elsewhere (ie, not just to avoid the trade dispute rules[149]); *or*
  - you genuinely resume employment with your employer and then leave for a reason other than the trade dispute (note that you may be sanctioned if you voluntarily leave – see p419).

Whether or not you are involved in a trade dispute is a complex area of law. If there is any doubt, you should seek specialist advice from your trade union or an advice or law centre. Decisions are subject to appeal.

Income support

If you or your partner are involved in a trade dispute:

- you are treated as being in remunerative work and are, therefore, not entitled to income support (IS) for the first seven days either of you is so involved[150] (if the dispute causes a series of stoppages, the rule only applies for seven days from the start of the first stoppage[151]); *and*
- after that, you are not treated as being in remunerative work[152] but the amount of IS you are entitled to is reduced, sometimes to nil (see p737).

You should also note the following rules:

- You can be treated as being involved in a trade dispute, pending a decision as to whether you are actually so involved.[153] A tribunal cannot decide an appeal until a decision is made.
- You do not count as being involved in a trade dispute during:[154]
  - a 'period of incapacity for work' (four or more days of incapacity – see p771); *or*
  - a 'maternity period' (six weeks before the expected week of confinement and seven weeks after the week of confinement).

- You are no longer treated as being involved in a trade dispute from the day you return to work with the same employer (even if the dispute is continuing or you are doing a different job).[155]
- You are entitled to claim IS while you are involved in a trade dispute and for the first 15 days after you return to work (see p298).[156] If you are not involved in a trade dispute but your partner is, you can only claim IS if you fall into one of the other groups of eligible claimants listed on p294.

Amount payable

Special rules reduce the amount of IS payable if you and/or your partner are involved in a trade dispute. If you are entitled to IS of less than £5 a week, you will only be paid if you are receiving another benefit with which IS can be paid.[157]

Applicable amount

Your applicable amount is calculated as follows:[158]

- If you are a single claimant, or member of a childless couple, both involved in a trade dispute, your applicable amount is nil.
- If you are a lone parent, you are only entitled to:
  - personal allowances for your children (where still applicable);
  - the family and disabled child premiums (where still applicable);
  - housing costs (see below).

  You are not entitled to a personal allowance or any premiums payable in respect of yourself.
- If you are a member of a couple and one of you is involved in a trade dispute, you are eligible for:
  - half the normal personal allowance for a couple;
  - half of any premiums paid at the couple rate;
  - any premiums payable solely in respect of the person not involved in the trade dispute (eg, carer's premium, lower rate of severe disability premium);
  - personal allowances and the family and disabled child premiums for any children (where still applicable);
  - housing costs (see below).

  You are not entitled to any premiums payable solely for the person involved in the trade dispute (eg, carer's premium, lower rate severe disability premium).

Amounts are rounded down to the nearest lower 5 pence.

Housing costs are payable unless all members of your family are involved in a trade dispute. Those members not involved are treated as responsible for the costs.[159]

Actual and assumed strike pay

Any payments you or your partner actually receive from a trade union in excess of £30.50 a week count as income. Payments of up to £30.50 are ignored. If you and your partner are both involved in a trade dispute, only £30.50 in total is ignored.[160]

Whether or not you actually receive any payments, £30.50 is deducted from your IS as 'assumed strike pay'. If you and your partner are both involved in a trade dispute, £30.50 is still deducted.[161] This deduction may extinguish your entitlement to IS.

Example

Cliff is on strike. He and his partner Bernice have no children. Their only income is £35 a week strike pay.

Applicable amount:	£44.05 (half normal amount)
less income:	£4.50 (strike pay over £30.50)
=	£39.55
Less	£30.50 (assumed strike pay)
= IS payable	£9.05

If their strike pay was £45, their income of £14.50 (actual strike pay), plus £30.50 (assumed strike pay) would equal £45, which would extinguish their entitlement to IS.

Other income and capital

Other income and capital is treated as normal except that the following payments are taken into account in full as income:

- any repayment of income tax paid or due;[162]
- any payment received or due because the person involved in the trade dispute is not working (eg, a loan or grant from social services);[163]
- payments made under the Children Act 1989 or Children (Scotland) Act 1995 to promote the welfare of children;[164]
- charitable or voluntary payments (whether regular or irregular, with no £20 disregard for regular payments – see p974), except any payments from the Macfarlane Trusts, the Eileen Trust, the Fund or the Independent Living Funds;[165]
- payment in kind (except payments from the above trusts or funds) paid to the person involved in the trade dispute or to a third party (unless it is used for items allowable under the notional income/capital rules – see pp983 and 1045);[166]
- holiday pay payable more than four weeks after your employment is terminated or interrupted (subject to an earnings disregard);[167]
- an advance of earnings or a loan from an employer (subject to any earnings disregard).[168]

Benefit loans on return to work

If you return to work with the same employer, whether or not the trade dispute has ended, you can receive IS for the first 15 days back at work, in the form of a loan.[169] You are not treated as being in remunerative work for this period.[170] If you are a member of a couple you are not entitled to IS if your partner is in full-time work.[171]

Your income and capital are calculated as if you were still involved in the trade dispute, except that the rules about actual and assumed strike pay do not apply.[172]

Any IS that you are awarded is paid in advance.[173]

Repayment of the loan

Any IS paid during your first 15 days back at work can be recovered by deductions from your earnings.[174] If this is not practical (eg, because you are currently unemployed) it can be recovered directly from you.[175]

The amount deducted from your earnings is worked out by comparing your protected earnings with your available earnings.

Your '**protected earnings**' are:

- your applicable amount excluding housing costs; *plus*
- £27; *less*
- child benefit.[176]

Your '**available earnings**' are the whole of your earnings, including sick pay, after all 'lawful' deductions have been made.[177] These include tax and national insurance contributions, trade union subscriptions and any amount being deducted under a court order or, for instance, a child support deduction from earnings order. Any bonus or commission, if paid on a different day, is treated as paid on your next normal payday.[178]

If your available earnings are less than £1 above your protected earnings, there can be no deduction. If they are £1 or more above, your employer will deduct half of the difference between your protected and available earnings. If you are paid monthly, your protected earnings are multiplied by five. If your monthly available earnings are less than £5 above this level, no deduction is made. Otherwise, half the excess is deducted. If you are paid daily, the amount of your protected earnings and the £1 figure are divided by five to determine the amount (if any) of the deduction. The calculation can be adjusted as appropriate where your wages are paid at other intervals.[179] If you are paid more than one amount of earnings on a payday, your protected earnings and the £1 figure are multiplied to reflect this.[180]

A deduction notice is sent to your employer by the Department for Work and Pensions (DWP) setting out your protected earnings and the amount of IS to be recovered.[181] If you have not actually received IS, no deduction should be made.[182] Your employer *can* begin making the deductions from the first payday after receiving the notice and *must* start doing so one month after getting it.[183]

A deduction notice ceases to have effect if:

- it is cancelled or replaced; *or*
- you stop working for that employer; *or*

- your IS loan has been repaid; *or*
- 26 weeks have passed since the date of the notice.[184]

If you stop work, another deduction notice can be sent if you get another job and part of your IS loan is still outstanding.[185]

You must tell the DWP within 10 days if you leave a job or start another while part of your IS loan remains unpaid.[186] If you fail to do so you can be prosecuted.[187] It is a criminal offence for your employer to fail to keep records of deductions and supply the DWP with these.[188] If your employer fails to make a deduction which should have been made from your pay, the DWP can recover the amount from your employer instead.[189]

Jobseeker's allowance

You are not entitled to contribution-based or income-based jobseeker's allowance (JSA) (including hardship payments) for the whole of any week (seven days from Sunday[190]) if you are involved in a trade dispute (see p735) for one or more days during that week.[191] You may, however, be entitled to IS (see p736). Weeks of disentitlement do not count towards your 26 weeks' entitlement to contribution-based JSA.[192]

Your partner can claim income-based JSA if you are involved in a trade dispute and s/he is not,[193] but:

- you are treated as being in remunerative work precluding any entitlement to income-based JSA for the first seven days you are involved in a trade dispute unless s/he was already entitled when you became involved[194] (if the dispute causes a series of stoppages, the rule only applies for seven days from the start of the first stoppage[195]); *and*
- after that, you are not treated as being in remunerative work[196] but the amount of income-based JSA to which your partner is entitled is reduced (see below).

If you are a 'joint-claim couple' (see p394), you remain entitled to claim JSA if one of you is involved in a trade dispute.[197] The above rules about remunerative work and your applicable amount apply as they do to other couples.[198]

If your partner is claiming income-based JSA, the following rules also apply, as for IS (see p736):

- you can be treated as involved in a trade dispute pending a decision;[199]
- you are not treated as involved in a trade dispute:
  - during a period of incapacity for work; *or*
  - during a maternity period;[200] *or*
  - after you return to work with your employer.[201]

Unlike IS, no special rules apply for the first 15 days after you return to work and you are not entitled to a benefit loan of JSA during that period.

Amount payable

You are not entitled to claim JSA for any week in which you are involved in a trade dispute (see p735).

If your partner claims income-based JSA while you are involved in a trade dispute, as in the case of IS, the following rules reduce the amount payable.

- The applicable amount is reduced in the same way as for IS, where one member of a couple is involved in a trade dispute (see p737).[202]
- As with IS, the special rules relating to actual and assumed strike pay and other income and capital apply (see p737).[203]

Benefit is payable to your partner for part of a week if you are only involved in a trade dispute for part of a week.[204] The amount payable and the amount of assumed strike pay is worked out on a daily, pro rata basis.[205]

Housing benefit and council tax benefit

You remain entitled to housing benefit (HB) and council tax benefit (CTB) while you or your partner are involved in a trade dispute. If your IS/income-based JSA stops because you are involved in a trade dispute, you must make a fresh claim for HB/CTB (see pp216 and 217). You may become entitled to HB/CTB as a result of a drop in income because of a trade dispute.

When assessing your earnings in connection with a claim for HB/CTB, the local authority should take into account any reduction in your income because of a trade dispute and not just consider your pre-strike earnings.[206] The local authority can average out your earnings over a different period than normal, if this results in a more accurate estimate of your earnings (see p988).

Statutory sick pay

You are not entitled to statutory sick pay (SSP) if your period of entitlement would begin when there is a stoppage of work due to a trade dispute at your place of work, unless you can show you did not have a prior direct interest in the dispute.[207] See p735 for the meaning of the terms used. An overtime ban or working to grade does not count as stoppage of work.[208] You remain disentitled throughout your period of sickness, even if the trade dispute ends. You can, however, claim incapacity benefit (IB) and/or IS (see Chapters 12 and 13).

You remain entitled to SSP if your entitlement began before the trade dispute.

Statutory maternity pay, statutory paternity pay and statutory adoption pay

For the purposes of the 26-week 'continuous employment rule' (see p567) for statutory maternity pay, statutory paternity pay and statutory adoption pay:[209]

- any week in which you are not working because of a stoppage of work due to a trade dispute at your place of work (see p735) does not break your continuity of employment; *but*
- any such week does not count towards the total of 26 weeks and if you are dismissed during the stoppage your continuity of employment is broken,

unless, in either case, you can show that you at no time had a direct interest in the trade dispute (see p736).

Increases for dependants

You are not entitled to an increase of IB, severe disablement allowance, carer's allowance, maternity allowance or retirement pension (Category A) for an adult dependant who is involved in a trade dispute (see p735).[210] If the adult dependant returns to work, you should reclaim the increase for her/him.

Social fund payments

Involvement in a trade dispute has no effect on entitlement to a funeral expenses, cold weather or winter fuel payment (see p549).

Sure Start maternity grant

If you or your partner are involved in a trade dispute (see p735), you are only entitled to a Sure Start maternity grant (see p549) if:[211]

- you or your partner are receiving IS or income-based JSA and the trade dispute has been going on for at least six weeks when you claim a maternity grant; *or*
- you or your partner are receiving child tax credit paid at a rate higher than the family element (see p1354) or working tax credit which includes the disability or severe disability element (see pp1357 and 1358) which you claimed before the trade dispute began.

You are not treated as being involved in a trade dispute during a 'period of incapacity for work' (see p595) or a 'maternity period' (see p587).[212]

Community care grants

If you or your partner are involved in a trade dispute, you are not eligible for a community care grant (CCG) other than for travel expenses to visit somebody who is ill and then only in the following circumstances:

- You are involved in a trade dispute and are visiting:
  - your partner in a hospital or similar institution; *or*
  - a dependant in a hospital or similar institution (but only if you have no partner living with you who could get a CCG under these provisions or if your partner is also in hospital); *or*
  - a close relative (not defined) or a member of your household who is critically ill (whether or not s/he is in hospital).

- You are not involved in a trade dispute, but your partner is, and you are visiting:
  - a close relative who is in a hospital or similar institution or who is critically ill; *or*
  - someone else in hospital or critically ill, who was a member of your household before going into hospital or getting ill.[213]

Budgeting loans

You are not eligible for a budgeting loan if you or your partner are involved in a trade dispute (see p735).[214]

Crisis loans

If you or your partner are involved in a trade dispute, you are only eligible for a crisis loan for:[215]

- expenses arising from a disaster; *and*
- the cost of items needed for cooking (including cooking utensils) or space heating (including fireguards).

Notes

1. 16/17-year-olds

1 s6 C(LC)A 2000; regs 3 and 4 C(LC)(E) Regs and C(LC)(W) Regs
2 Reg 4(1) and (2) C(LC)(E) Regs and C(LC)(W) Regs
3 Regs 3(3) and 4(3) C(LC)(E) Regs; reg 3(2) C(LC)(W) Regs
4 C(LC)AO No.2
5 C(LC)A 2000; C(LC)(E) Regs; C(LC)(W) Regs
6 C(LC)SSB(S) Regs
7 Reg 2 C(LC)SSB Regs
8 Reg 4(5-7) C(LC)(E) Regs; regs 3 and 4 C(LC)(W) Regs

2. Hospital inpatients

9 Reg 2(2) SS(HIP) Regs; NHSA 1977; NHS(S)A 1978; NHSCCA 1990
10 Paras 24335 and 18041 DMG
11 *White v CAO, The Times,* 2 August 1993 (CA); *Botchett v CAO, The Times,* 8 May 1996, 2 CCLR 121 (CA); *R v North and East Devon Health Authority ex parte Coughlan* [1999] 2 CCLR 285 (CA); paras 24332-24351 DMG
12 Paras 18059 and 24363 DMG
13 DMG Memo Vol 3 08/04
14 Regs 14(1)(l), 19(1)(l) and 55 JSA Regs
15 Reg 21(2) IS Regs; reg 18(3) HB Regs; reg 10(3) CTB Regs; reg 17(4) SS(HIP) Regs; reg 8(2) SS(AA) Regs; regs 10(5)(a) and 12B(3) SS(DLA) Regs; Sch 3 para 2(6) SPC Regs
16 Reg 2(2A) SS(HIP) Regs
17 Reg 6(2A) SS(AA) Regs; regs 8(2A) and 12(2A) SS(DLA) Regs
18 Reg 8(3) SS(AA) Regs; regs 10(3) and 12B(2) SS(DLA) Regs
19 Regs 6 and 8(1) SS(AA) Regs; regs 8, 10(1), 12A and 12B(1)(a) SS(DLA) Regs
20 Regs 12B(3)-(8) and 12C(1) and (2) SS(DLA) Regs

21 Reg 8(4)-(7) SS(AA) Regs; regs 10(6)-(9) and 12B(9A) and (12) SS(DLA) Regs
22 Reg 8(2) SS(AA) Regs; reg 10(5) SS(DLA) Regs
23 Reg 16(2) SS(C&P) Regs
24 **IS** Sch 2 paras 13(3A) and 15(5) IS Regs
JSA Sch 1 paras 15(5) and 20(6)(b)(i) JSA Regs
PC Sch 1 para 1(2)(b) SPC Regs
HB Sch 2 paras 13(3A) and 15(5) HB Regs
CTB Sch 1 paras 14(3A) and 19(6) CTB Regs
25 **IS** Sch 2 paras 12(1)(d), 13A(1) and 14(b) IS Regs
JSA Sch 1 paras 14(1)(g)(ii), 15A(1) and 16(b) JSA Regs
HB Sch 2 paras 12(1)(a)(iii), 14(b) and 14ZA(3) HB Regs
CTB Sch 1 paras 13(1)(a)(iii), 15(b) and 16(3) CTB Regs
26 Regs 8 and 10(2) SS(DLA) Regs
27 **IS** Sch 7 para 3 IS Regs
JSA Sch 5 para 2 JSA Regs
28 **IS** Sch 2 para 14(b) IS Regs
JSA Sch 1 para 16(b) JSA Regs
HB Sch 2 para 14(b) HB Regs
CTB Sch 1 para 15(b) CTB Regs
29 s143 SSCBA 1992; reg 4 CB(Gen) Regs; reg 13 SS(HIP) Regs
30 **IS** Sch 7 para 2 IS Regs
PC Schs 1 and 3 para 2(2)(a) SPC Regs
31 Sch 3 para 2(5) SPC Regs
32 Sch 7 para 2 IS Regs
33 **IS** Reg 16(2) IS Regs
PC Reg 5(1)(a) SPC Regs
34 **IS** Sch 7 para 1(c)(i) IS Regs
PC Sch 3 para 2(2)(b) SPC Regs
35 **IS** Sch 7 para 1(c)(ii) IS Regs
PC Sch 3 para 2(2)(c) SPC Regs
36 Reg 16(2) IS Regs
37 Sch 7 para 1(b) IS Regs
38 **IS** Sch 3 para 18(7)(g) IS Regs
PC Sch 2 para 14(7)(e) SPC Regs
39 Schs 5 para 1and 5A para 1 JSA Regs
40 Reg 78(2)(b) JSA Regs
41 Sch 2 para 17(7)(g) JSA Regs
42 **HB** Regs 16(2) and (3)(a) and 18(1)(a) HB Regs
CTB Regs 8(2) and (3)(a) and 10(1)(a) CTB Regs
43 **HB** Regs 16(2) and (3)(a) and 18(1)(a) HB Regs
CTB Regs 8(2) and (3)(a) and 10(1)(a) CTB Regs
44 **HB** Reg 63(7)(e) HB Regs
CTB Reg 52(7)(d) CTB Regs
45 Regs 4 and 6 SS(HIP) Regs
46 Regs 6(1) and (5), 10, 11(3) and 12 SS(HIP) Regs
47 Reg 16 SS(HIP) Regs
48 Reg 11(1)(b) SS(HIP) Regs

3. **People in care homes**

49 National Care Standards Commission in England; Care Standards Inspectorate in Wales; Scottish Commission for the Regulation of Care
50 CA 1989; C(S)A 1995
51 Part III NAA 1948; Part IV SW(S)A 1968
52 NA(RA)(APAR)(A)(E) Regs; NA(RA)(APARCAR)(W) Regs; s4 CCH(S)A 2002
53 *R v N & E Devon ex parte Coughlan* [1999] 2 CCLR 285 (CA)
54 s49 HSCA 2001; Health Services Circular 2001/17
55 CCH(S)A 2002
56 s117 MHA 1983; *R v Manchester City Council ex parte Stennett*, 25 July 2002 (HL)
57 s21 NAA 1948
58 NA(AR) Regs; National Assistance (Sums for Personal Requirements) (England) Regulations 2005; National Assistance (Sums for Personal Requirements) (Scotland) Regulations 2005 No.84; National Assistance (Sums for Personal Requirements) (Wales) Regulations 2005
59 s21(1) NAA 1948
60 s22(5A) NAA 1948
61 s22 HSS&SSA 1983; s55 HSCA 2001
62 NA(RA)(RC)(E) Regs; s6 CCH(S)A 2002
63 **IS** Reg 16(3)(c) IS Regs
JSA Reg 78(3)(d) JSA Regs
64 Appendix to CIS/4934/1997; CIS/4965/1997; CIS/5232/1997; CIS/3767/1997
65 CIS/1544/2001; DMG letter 05/02
66 Regs 5(1)(b) and 15(6) SPC Regs
67 Reg 5(1)(a)and Sch 2 para 4(8), (11)(c)(ix) and (12) SPC Regs
68 Reg 8(2)(b) HB Regs
69 Reg 8(2ZA) and (2ZB) HB Regs
70 Regs 7(1)(k) and (3)and 8(2)(a) HB Regs
71 Reg 7(2)(c) and (d) HB Regs
72 Reg 7(4)-(12) HB Regs
73 Reg 5(7B), (7C), (8B) and (8C) HB Regs
74 Reg 4C(1), (2), (4) and (5) CTB Regs
75 s131(3) SSCBA 1992
76 Regs 7(1) and 8(1) SS(AA) Regs; regs 9(1) and 10(1) SS(DLA) Regs
77 Reg 7(5) SS(AA) Regs; reg 9(6) SS(DLA) Regs
78 Reg 8(3) SS(AA) Regs; reg 10(3) SS(DLA) Regs

79 Reg 8(2) SS(AA) Regs; reg 10(5) SS(DLA) Regs
80 Reg 8(6) SS(AA) Regs; reg 10(8) SS(DLA) Regs; *Steane v CAO and Secretary of State*, 24 July 1996 (CA)
81 CA/2937/1999 and CA/2604/1998; see also *CAO v Creighton and others*, 15 December 1999 (N. Ireland Court of Appeal)
82 Reg 8(4) SS(AA) Regs; reg 10(6) SS(DLA) Regs
83 Reg 9(1A) SS(DLA) Regs
84 Reg 9(2) and (2A) SS(DLA) Regs
85 CA/2985/1997
86 CDLA/1465/1998; CDLA/2127/2000
87 *Steane v CAO and Secretary of State*, 20 July 1996 (HL)
88 CDLA/870/2004

4. **Prisoners**
89 Reg 21(3) IS Regs
90 Reg 21(3) IS Regs
91 Schs 3 para 3(11)(c)(i) and (12) and 7 para 8 IS Regs
92 Reg 16(3)(b) and (5)(f) IS Regs
93 Sch 7 para 9 IS Regs
94 Regs 1(2), 6(3)(a) and 7(3)(a) SPC Regs
95 Regs 6(3)(b) and (6)(c) and 7 and Sch 2 para 4(11)(c)(i) SPC Regs
96 Reg 6(3)(b) and (4) SPC Regs
97 Reg 5(1)(c)(ii) SPC Regs
98 Reg 78(3)(b) and (5)(i) JSA Regs
99 Schs 5 para 5 and 5A para 4 JSA Regs
100 Reg 5(8B)(c)(i) HB Regs
101 Reg 5(8) HB Regs
102 Reg 5(8A) HB Regs; R(IS) 17/93; HB Circular A22/2004
103 Reg 5(5A)HB Regs; HB/CTB Circular A29/2005
104 Reg 15(2) HB Regs
105 Reg 63(7)(e) HB Regs
106 Regs 4C(3), (4) and (5) and 52(8)(b) CTB Regs
107 s131(3)(a) SSCBA 1992; CH/2111/2003
108 Reg 7(1) CTB Regs
109 s113(1)(b) SSCBA 1992; reg 2(9) and (10) SS(GB) Regs; R(S) 8/79
110 Reg 2(3) and (4) SS(GB) Regs
111 s113(1)(b) SSCBA 1992; reg 2 SS(GB) Regs
112 s113(1)(b) SSCBA 1992
113 Reg 2(2) and (8)(c) SS(GB) Regs
114 R(S) 1/71
115 Reg 3 SS(GB) Regs
116 CS/541/1950
117 Reg 3(1) SSP Regs; reg 9 SMP Regs; regs 18(c) and 27(1)(c) SPPSAP(G) Regs
118 Reg 10(2)(d) and Sch 2 para 7(b)(ii) SSB(Dep) Regs
119 Reg 2(6) and (7) SS(GB) Regs
120 Reg 2(7) SS(GB) Regs
121 Reg 2(2) and (7) SS(GB) Regs
122 s113(1)(b) SSCBA 1992
123 Reg 2(5) SS(GB) Regs
124 Sch 9 para 1(a) SSCBA 1992; reg 16(6) SS(GB) Regs
125 Reg 16(2) CB Regs; reg 3(1)(b) SS(GB) Regs
126 s80 SSCBA 1992
127 **IS** Reg 48(7) IS Regs
JSA Reg 110(7) JSA Regs
128 Regs 14(1)(h) and 19(1)(h) JSA Regs

5. **People without accommodation**
129 **IS** Sch 7 para 6 IS Regs
JSA Sch 5 para 3 JSA Regs
130 paras 24503-504 DMG
131 para 24504 DMG
132 CIS/16772/1996
133 para 24506 DMG
134 para 15 HC Handbook
135 para 42 HC Handbook
136 s12 NAA 1948; *R v Hammersmith and Fulham LBC and Others, The Times*, 19 February 1997 (CA)

6. **People involved in a trade dispute**
137 s35(1) JSA 1995
138 s14(1) and (2) JSA 1995
139 R(U) 7/58
140 R(U) 1/87
141 para 32107 DMG
142 R(U) 1/65; paras 32121-25 and 32160-61 DMG
143 CU/66/1986(T)
144 R(U) 4/62; R(U) 1/70
145 s14(2) JSA 1995
146 s14(1) JSA 1995
147 *Presho v Insurance Officer* [1984] (HL) (see R(U) 1/84); *Cartlidge v CAO* [1986] 2 All ER 1 (CA); R(U) 1/87; para 32210 DMG
148 s14(3) JSA 1995
149 R(U) 6/74
150 Reg 5(4) IS Regs
151 para 32678 DMG
152 Reg 6(e) IS Regs
153 Reg 13(2)(i) SS&CS(DA) Regs
154 s126(1) and (2) SSCBA 1992
155 s127(a) SSCBA 1992
156 Sch 1B para 20 IS Regs
157 Reg 26(4) SS(C&P) Regs
158 s126(3) and (4) SSCBA 1992
159 Sch 3 para 2(2) IS Regs
160 Sch 9 para 34 IS Regs

161 s126(5)(b) and (7) SSCBA 1992
162 s126(5)(a)(ii) SSCBA 1992; reg 48(2) IS Regs
163 s126(5)(a)(i) SSCBA 1992
164 Reg 41(3) and Schs 9 para 48 and 10 para 17 IS Regs
165 Reg 48(9), (10)(a) and (c) and Schs 9 paras 15 and 39 and 10 para 22 IS Regs
166 Reg 42(4) and Sch 9 para 21 IS Regs
167 Reg 35(1)(d) IS Regs
168 Reg 48(5) and (6) IS Regs
169 s127 SSCBA 1992; Sch 1B para 20 IS Regs
170 Reg 6(e) IS Regs
171 s127(b) SSCBA 1992
172 s127(a) SSCBA 1992; regs 35(1)(d), 41(3) and (4), 42(4) and 48(6) and (10) and Sch 9 paras 15, 21, 28 and 39 IS Regs
173 para 32790 DMG
174 s127(c) SSCBA 1992; reg 18 SS(PAOR) Regs
175 Reg 26 SS(PAOR) Regs
176 Reg 19(3), (4) and (5) SS(PAOR) Regs
177 Reg 18(2) SS(PAOR) Regs
178 Reg 22(2) SS(PAOR) Regs
179 Reg 22(3) SS(PAOR) Regs
180 Reg 22(4) SS(PAOR) Regs
181 Reg 20(1) and (2) SS(PAOR) Regs
182 Reg 22(5)(a) SS(PAOR) Regs
183 Reg 22(6) SS(PAOR) Regs
184 Reg 21(1) SS(PAOR) Regs
185 Reg 25 SS(PAOR) Regs
186 Reg 28 SS(PAOR) Regs
187 Reg 29 SS(PAOR) Regs
188 Regs 27 and 29 SS(PAOR) Regs
189 Reg 27(5) SS(PAOR) Regs
190 s35(1) JSA 1995
191 s14 JSA 1995
192 s5 JSA 1995
193 s15 JSA 1995
194 Reg 52(2) JSA Regs
195 paras 32677-78 DMG
196 Reg 53(g) JSA Regs
197 s15A JSA 1995; reg 3D and Sch A1 para 17 JSA Regs
198 s15A JSA 1995; regs 52(2A) and 53(gg) JSA Regs
199 Reg 15(a)(i) SS&CS(DA) Regs
200 Reg 171(a) JSA Regs
201 s15 JSA 1995
202 s15(2)(a) and (b) JSA 1995; Sch 2 para 2(2) JSA Regs
203 s15(2)(c) and (d) JSA 1995; regs 98(1)(c), 104(3), 105(10) and 110(5), (6), (9) and (10)(a) and (c) and Schs 7 paras 15, 22, 29, 36 and 41 and 8 paras 22 and 27 JSA Regs
204 s15(5) JSA 1995
205 Reg 155 JSA Regs
206 *R v HBRB London Borough of Ealing ex parte Saville* [1986] HLR 349
207 Sch 11 paras 2(g) and 7 SSCBA 1992
208 R(SSP) 1/86
209 Reg 13 SMP Regs; reg 35 SPPSAP(G) Regs
210 s91 SSCBA 1992
211 Reg 6 SFM&FE Regs
212 Reg 3(1) SFM&FE Regs; s126(1) and (2) SSCBA 1992
213 SF Dir 26
214 SF Dir 8(1)(b)
215 SF Dir 17(a) and (f)

Part 4

Common benefit rules

Chapter 29

Work and benefits

This chapter covers:

Entitlement to many benefits is affected by issues to do with work and employment. Most of these rules are specific to the benefit and are included in the relevant chapter in this *Handbook* (see below). This chapter covers the work rules for income support, jobseeker's allowance, pension credit, housing benefit and council tax benefit.

Statutory sick pay, statutory maternity pay, statutory paternity pay and statutory adoption pay	These benefits are linked to you being employed (not self-employed) and in some cases you can get them even if your employment ends (see pp594 and 567).
Industrial injuries benefits	You must have been an employed earner when you had an accident or contracted a disease to be entitled (see p320).
Carer's allowance	You cannot qualify if you are gainfully employed. You count as gainfully employed if you earn more than a set amount each week (see p73).
Incapacity benefit	You cannot qualify for benefits based on your incapacity for work in any week you actually do any work unless this is work you may do while claiming (see p765).
Maternity allowance	There are several rules relating to work for the purposes of claiming maternity allowance (see p456).
Retirement pension, widows' benefits and bereavement benefits, disability living allowance and attendance allowance	Work and income do not affect your entitlement to these benefits.

Adult dependants	You cannot receive an adult dependant addition with incapacity benefit, retirement pension or bereavement benefits for a partner who earns more than that addition.
Child benefit, guardian's allowance and allowances for children	You do not qualify for child benefit or guardian's allowance, or for an allowance in your housing benefit or council tax benefit for a child who is aged 16 or over who does paid work for 24 hours a week or more (see p822).

Deciding whether you are an employed earner or self-employed also affects both your national insurance contributions (see p825) and the way your income from earnings is assessed (see pp939, 942, 955 and 962).

This chapter covers the rules about full-time paid work (the Department for Work and Pensions calls this 'remunerative work') for:

- income support (see Chapter 13);
- jobseeker's allowance (see Chapter 15);
- pension credit (see Chapter 18);
- housing benefit (see Chapter 10); *and*
- council tax benefit (see Chapter 6).

Tax credits

Full-time paid work also affects working tax credit (WTC). See Chapter 51 for the rules on full-time paid work for WTC purposes. Whether or not you are in full-time paid work, you might be able to claim child tax credit (see Chapter 49).

1. The full-time paid work rule

If you work full time and are paid for the work, you count as being in what the Department for Work and Pensions (DWP) calls **'remunerative work'**. This is called 'full-time paid work' in this *Handbook*. See p752 for what counts as paid work and how your hours are calculated. 'Work' includes self-employment and work which is done from home.

In some circumstances you may be treated as not in full-time paid work even if you are (see p757). In others, you may be treated as if you are in full-time paid work when you are not (see p756).

Full-time paid work affects income support (IS), jobseeker's allowance (JSA), housing benefit (HB), council tax benefit (CTB) and pension credit (PC) in different ways:

- Your eligibility for **IS** and **JSA** is affected if you or your partner are in full-time paid work. If neither of you is in full-time paid work, you can claim IS or JSA.
- Work does not affect your eligibility for **HB, CTB** or **PC**. For HB and CTB, however, if you are in full-time paid work, this can affect the way your income is calculated – eg, payments at the end of employment (see p959) and whether you can get an additional full-time earnings disregard (see p965) or a childcare costs disregard (see p965).
- If you have a **non-dependant living with you**, a non-dependant deduction can be made from your IS, JSA or PC housing costs and from your HB and CTB. If your non-dependant is in full-time paid work, the amount of the non-dependant deduction can be affected (see pp924, 115 and 211).

Remember that whether or not you are in full-time or part-time paid work, income from employment or self-employment affects your entitlement to means-tested benefits (see pp955 and 962). This means that although your (or your partner's) hours of work are low enough for you to qualify or it does not matter how many hours you work, you might not satisfy the means test.

Full-time work for income support and jobseeker's allowance

You cannot usually get IS or JSA if you are in full-time paid work.[1] Your partner's working hours do not affect your entitlement to *contribution-based* JSA, but you cannot get IS or *income-based* JSA if your partner is in full-time paid work.

For IS and JSA purposes, you count as in full-time paid work if you work 16 hours or more a week.[2] For IS and income-based JSA, your partner counts as in full-time paid work if s/he works 24 hours or more a week. For joint-claim JSA, your partner does not have to claim JSA with you if s/he works 16 or more but less than 24 hours a week (see p396).[3]

Your non-dependant counts as in full-time paid work if s/he works 16 hours or more a week.

If you or your partner *are* in full-time paid work you might be able to claim working tax credit (WTC). You might be able to choose whether to claim IS/JSA or WTC. In some situations, you might be able to claim both IS/JSA and WTC (eg, if you are a 'term-time only' worker or you are off sick and getting statutory sick pay). This is because different rules for what counts as full-time paid work apply for IS/JSA and WTC. See p759 for information about what you should consider.

Full-time work for housing benefit and council tax benefit

For HB and CTB purposes, you (or your non-dependant) count as in full-time paid work if you work 16 hours or more each week.[4] Note, however, that you and your partner may have to work more hours to benefit from an additional full-time earnings disregard (see p965).

Full-time work for pension credit

For PC purposes, your non-dependant counts as in full-time work if s/he works 16 hours or more each week.[5] See below for how the hours are calculated and for what counts as paid work.

What counts as paid work

Paid work includes work for which you are paid or expect to be paid. This means you expect to get payment for the work you are doing, now or at some date in the future, even if no payment is finally made.[6] Some of the initial work necessary to set up a business may not count if it is preparatory work done in the hope of leading to further work that will be paid, rather than in any expectation of any payment for the initial work itself.[7] The question of whether or not you are paid for work or working in expectation of payment has to be decided at the time the work is done, not, for example, at the end of the year or accounting period.[8]

You must have a real likelihood of getting payment for your work, not just a hope or desire to make money – eg, a self-employed writer who has never sold a manuscript and has no publication agreement may be working without real expectation of payment and so is not treated as being in full-time paid work even if s/he spends a lot of time writing.[9]

If you set up a business but it is not yet making money or has ceased to make a profit, you may count as working in expectation of payment if you are making drawings against future profit or if the business is likely to yield profit in the future. Ultimately, it depends on how viable your employment really is.[10] If there is no realistic possibility of your business yielding a profit, the decision maker is likely to want to know why you are working for nothing.[11]

Paid work includes work for which you receive payment in kind (such as free meals or accommodation or free produce for farmworkers).[12] Note that payments in kind are generally not treated as 'earnings' but as other income which may be disregarded.

How your hours are calculated

The way your hours are calculated depends on the benefit. The rules for IS and JSA are covered below. The rules for HB, CTB and PC are covered on p753.

Income support and jobseeker's allowance

In calculating your hours, include all the hours you actually work for which you are paid or which you do in expectation of payment. Your total hours from more than one job are added together. Paid lunch hours and breaks count towards the total hours you work.[13] If you routinely do paid overtime, those hours are included. For JSA, the hours that you or your partner spend caring for someone in the circumstances that allow you to claim IS as a carer (see p297) are ignored unless you are employed and are being paid to act as a carer.[14]

Where your **hours fluctuate**, an average of your weekly hours is calculated. Your hours are averaged as follows:

- If you have a regular pattern of work, the average hours worked throughout each work 'cycle' is used – eg, if you regularly work three weeks on and one week off, your hours are the average over the four-week period.[15]
- If you have a recognisable cycle of work that lasts for a year with periods where you are not required to work (eg, in an educational establishment):
  - for **IS**, the average of hours in periods where you are actually working is used to decide whether you are in full-time work for the whole year;[16]
  - for **JSA**, the average hours over the whole cycle, including periods of no work but disregarding other absences (eg, holidays) are used to decide whether you are in full-time work for the whole year.[17]

  See p754 for more information about 'term-time only' workers.
- If you do not have a recognisable cycle of work, the average over the five weeks immediately before the date of your claim is used, or over a longer or a shorter period if this would be more accurate.[18] The five-week period may not be appropriate if the average is distorted because, for example, you have done a short period of overtime that is not typical or you have been off sick.[19]
- If you have just started work and no pattern of work is yet established or your working arrangements have changed and your previous work cycle no longer applies, the number of hours or average of hours you are expected to work each week is used.[20] The decision can be revised or superseded when there is sufficient evidence to calculate the average of the actual hours you have been working.

If you are unsure if you are in full-time paid work, see p755. You should lodge an appeal if you think your average hours have been calculated unfairly (see Chapter 44) and this means you cannot claim the benefit or tax credit you want. You should work out first whether you are better off claiming IS/JSA or WTC (see p759). Likewise, you should appeal if your non-dependant's hours have been calculated unfairly and the DWP is making a non-dependant deduction that is too high.

Pension credit, housing benefit and council tax benefit

For PC, HB and CTB, the rules do not say how to calculate the hours of work unless these fluctuate (see p754). For PC, the DWP says to count only the hours for which you are paid or expect to be paid, including overtime, but not including paid breaks (eg, lunch or tea breaks).[21] It says to accept the word of the person who is doing the work unless there is reason for doubt.[22]

For HB, CTB and PC, where hours fluctuate, the average hours are calculated as follows:

- If you have a regular pattern of work, the average hours worked throughout each work 'cycle' is used — eg, if you regularly work three weeks on and one week off, the hours are the average over the four week period.[23]
- If you have a recognisable cycle of work that lasts for a year (eg, in a school or an educational establishment, where you have periods of school holidays or similar vacations where you are not required to work), the 'term-time only' worker rule applies (see below). The rule is the same as for IS.[24]
- If you do not have a recognisable cycle of work, the average over the five weeks immediately before the date of your claim is used, or over a longer or a shorter period if this would be more accurate.[25]
- If you have just started work and no pattern of work is yet established, the number of hours or average of hours you are expected to work each week is used.[26]

You should lodge an appeal if you think your (or your non-dependant's) hours have been calculated unfairly (see Chapter 44).

'Term-time only' workers

If you have a recognisable cycle of work that lasts for a year (eg, in a school or an educational establishment, where you have periods of school holidays or similar vacations where you do not work), the 'term-time only' worker rule applies. How the rule works depends on if you are claiming IS or JSA. If you are not considered to be in full-time paid work and you satisfy the other qualifying conditions you might qualify for IS or JSA. The 'term-time only' worker rule for PC, HB and CTB is the same as for IS (see below).

Sometimes it might not be clear whether you have a cycle of work that lasts a year — eg, if you have only started your job recently or have a fixed-term contract that finishes at the end of the school term or are employed on a casual or relief basis.[27] It takes time before it can be said that you have a yearly cycle of work.[28] However, if you have an indefinite contract to work in term-time only, the decision maker is likely to say that you have a yearly work cycle from the start.[29]

Income support

For IS if you only work for part of a year, it is the average of the hours of work you do during term-time which determines whether you are in full-time paid work throughout the year.[30] Many people who work for schools, colleges or similar institutions and have long periods in which they do not work, find themselves caught by this rule.

In practice, if the average hours of work you do during term-time means you are in full-time paid work during term-time, you also count as being in full-time paid work over the school holidays, even if you do no work and are not paid. This means:

- if you or your partner count as in full-time paid work, you cannot claim IS during the school holidays. However, you might be able to claim JSA (see below). You should be able to claim WTC if you normally work sufficient hours each week (see Chapter 51);[31]
- if your non-dependant counts as in full-time paid work, higher rate non-dependant deductions are applicable.

Jobseeker's allowance

For JSA if you only work for part of a year, the average hours over the whole cycle, including periods of no work, are used to decide whether you are in full-time work for the whole year.[32] However, you disregard weeks when you are:

- on paid holiday;
- absent from work because you are off sick or on maternity, paternity or adoption leave;
- absent from work without 'good cause' (see p756).

In practice, if the average hours of work you do over the whole cycle means you are not in full-time paid work, you can claim JSA. However, you may only qualify for income-based JSA during periods when your income is sufficiently low (eg, during unpaid summer holidays). Because the 'term-time only' worker rule is different for WTC, you could also claim WTC if you work sufficient hours each week during term-time (see Chapter 51).

Example

Sheila is a school dinner worker. She works 20 hours a week, 38 weeks of the year. She gets four weeks' paid holiday, but otherwise is not paid when she is not working at the school.

Her average hours are calculated as follows:

20 hours x 38 weeks = 760 hours. 52 weeks – 4 weeks' paid holiday = 48 weeks.

760 hours divided by 48 weeks = 15.84 average hours a week.

Sheila is not in full-time paid work and can claim JSA if her income is low enough. She might also qualify for WTC.

If you are unsure whether you are in full-time paid work

For IS and JSA, if you are unsure whether you are working for 16/24 hours or more **at the date of your claim**, you should make a further claim in a week when you are more certain. A claim for IS or JSA can only be backdated in limited circumstances (see p1087). If you wait to make a second claim until your first claim is decided, you could lose out.

Alternatively, if you are refused WTC because you or your partner do not count as in full-time paid work for WTC purposes and within 14 days of that decision you claim IS or JSA, your claim for IS or JSA can be backdated to the date you claimed WTC.[33]

If your **circumstances change** while you are claiming IS or JSA you may be uncertain about whether you now count as in full-time paid work (eg, your weekly hours change or you are now getting regular overtime). If it appears that you are now working 16/24 hours or more each week, report this to the DWP to avoid an overpayment of IS or JSA. You should also check to see if you qualify for WTC (see Chapter 49).

If your non-dependant's circumstances change while you are claiming HB or CTB (or help with IS, JSA or PC housing costs), report this to the local authority (or DWP) to enable your non-dependant deduction to be adjusted.

2. People treated as in full-time paid work

You or your partner are treated as being in full-time work if:

- you or your partner normally work full time, but you are off work because of a recognised, customary or other holiday and there is a common intention that your employment will be resumed once the holiday is over.[34] Whether you count as on holiday depends on your contractual or legal entitlement to holiday. You can argue that you only count as on holiday if you are paid for the holiday.[35] However, for jobseeker's allowance (JSA), even if you do not count as in full-time paid work because you are on unpaid leave, you are likely to have difficulty persuading the Department for Work and Pensions that you are available for and actively seeking work (see Chapter 15).
  Remember that for income support (IS), pension credit, housing benefit and council tax benefit, if you are a full-time 'term-time only' worker and your cycle of work lasts a year, you are treated as in full-time work during the school holidays (see p754);
- you or your partner are away from full-time paid work without 'good cause'.[36] What constitutes 'good cause' for these purposes is not defined in the regulations but all of your circumstances should be taken into account. Whether or not your employer has authorised the absence is not conclusive, although if it is authorised it is likely that you have a good reason;
- for **IS** and **JSA**, you or your partner have stopped full-time paid work but you are still within the period covered by earnings received from your full-time paid work. You are treated as in full-time paid work during any period for which you receive:[37]
  - payment in lieu of wages; *or*
  - pay in lieu of notice; *or*
  - holiday pay from your last job. However, unless you are involved in a trade dispute (see p735), you are not treated as in full-time paid work for any period for which you receive holiday pay if this is due to be paid more than four weeks after you left your job; *or*
  - certain other payments in recognition of loss of employment.

See p959 for details on final payments;

- for **income-based JSA** (not including joint-claim JSA), your partner is involved in a trade dispute and s/he is not entitled to JSA in her/his own right because of this, unless you were receiving income-based JSA when your partner became involved in the trade dispute (for up to seven days).[38] You cannot get JSA if you are the person involved in a trade dispute (see p740);
- for **joint-claim JSA**, you or your partner are involved in a trade dispute , unless you were receiving joint-claim JSA when you or your partner became involved in the trade dispute (for up to seven days);[39]
- for **IS**, you or your partner are involved in a trade dispute (for up to seven days).[40]

3. People treated as not in full-time paid work

Even if you are working, there are situations when you are treated as not in full-time paid work. For income support (IS) and jobseeker's allowance (JSA), see below. For housing benefit (HB), council tax benefit (CTB) and pension credit (PC), see p758.

Income support and jobseeker's allowance

You or your partner are treated as *not* being in full-time paid work if:[41]

- you or your partner are on maternity, paternity or adoption leave or are absent from work because you are sick[42], even if you normally work 16/24 hours or more each week. You might also be able to claim working tax credit (see Chapter 51);
- you or your partner are working on a government training scheme and are being paid a training allowance;
- you or your partner are a volunteer or are working for a charity or voluntary organisation and are giving your services free (except for your expenses);
- you or your partner are providing care for someone who is staying with you but who is not normally a member of your household and you receive payments from a health authority, local authority or voluntary organisation for caring for them;
- you or your partner are disabled and because of this:
  - your earnings are 75 per cent or less than a person without your disability would reasonably expect to earn, working the same hours in that job, or in a comparable one in the area; *or*
  - you work 75 per cent or less hours than those a person without your disability would reasonably be expected to work in that job or in a comparable job in the area;

- you or your partner are a foster parent receiving a payment for fostering a child from a local authority, voluntary organisation or a care authority (in Scotland);
- you or your partner work as a part-time firefighter, auxiliary coastguard, member of the Territorial Army or reserve forces, or member of a lifeboat crew;
- you or your partner are performing duties as a local authority councillor;
- you or your partner are working while living in a care home. This also applies during temporary absences from the home. You must need care because of your age, disability, terminal illness or past or present mental disorder, alcohol or drug dependency;
- for **IS**, you qualify for mortgage interest run-on (see p62 and Chapter 36);
- for **JSA**, your partner (you or your partner in the case of joint-claim JSA) has been involved in a trade dispute for more than seven days (see p740);
- for **IS**, you or your partner have been involved in a trade dispute for more than seven days (see p736). This also applies for the first 15 days following your return to work after having been involved in a trade dispute. You can claim if you satisfy the other rules for getting IS described in Chapter 13;
- for **IS**, you or your partner are caring for someone (see p297). Any hours of work that you do are ignored, not just the hours that you spend caring;
- for **IS**, you or your partner are working as a childminder in your home;
- the work you do is studying in connection with your course of education as a student;[43]
- the only payment you receive, or expect to receive, is a sports award from a Sports Council;
- you are receiving assistance in pursuing self-employment while on an employment zone programme or a programme under s2 of the Employment and Training Act 1973 or s2 of the Enterprise and New Towns (Scotland) Act 1990.

Housing benefit, council tax benefit and pension credit

You (and your non-dependant) are treated as *not* being in full-time paid work if:[44]

- you (or your non-dependant) are on sick, maternity, paternity or adoption leave, even if you normally work 16 hours or more each week. However, for HB and CTB, you (or your non-dependant) *can* count as in full-time paid work on such leave to enable you to get an earnings disregard for childcare costs (see p965);
- the only payment you (or your non-dependant) receive is a sports award from the Sports Council.

In addition, you (and your non-dependant) are treated as *not* being in full-time paid work in a benefit week, if in that week you (or your non-dependant) are on IS or income-based JSA for more than three days.[45]

4. Self-employed people

The full-time paid work rule applies to self-employed as well as employed earners. If you simply invest in a business and do not help to run it you are not treated as self-employed.[46]

A problem for some self-employed people is that they work long hours for little financial reward, sometimes even making a loss. Nevertheless, if you are in full-time work and the work is done in expectation of payment, it counts as full-time paid work. The Department for Work and Pensions counts payments from your business to meet living expenses, whether in cash or in kind, as payment for work unless the drawings are from the business capital.[47]

In calculating the number of hours that you work each week, the decision maker counts all the hours necessary to run your business, including time you spend visiting potential customers, advertising or canvassing, bookkeeping and trips to wholesalers and retailers.[48] You count not only the hours spent on services for which you are paid, but also other time which is essential for your business – eg, preparation time or unsuccessfully soliciting new customers.[49] The decision maker should accept your statement about the hours you work unless there is a reason to doubt what you say.[50] The hours your partner spends helping you in your business do not affect your entitlement to *contribution-based* jobseeker's allowance (JSA), but if your partner works 24 hours a week or more you are not entitled to income support or *income-based* JSA.

5. Working tax credit, income support and jobseeker's allowance

Sometimes it is difficult to show that you count as in full-time paid work and the distinction between working tax credit (WTC) and out-of-work benefits (income support (IS) or jobseeker's allowance (JSA)) is not absolute. You may be refused both WTC and IS or JSA because of different rules or because decision makers at the local Department for Work and Pensions office and the Revenue interpret the rules, on the same facts, differently. If this happens, appeal against both decisions and ask for the appeals to be heard consecutively so a tribunal can decide which benefit or tax credit is appropriate. In the meantime you could apply for interim payments of IS or JSA (see p1108).

You might be able to claim WTC or IS/JSA if you have a partner and s/he works for 16 hours or more a week. This is because your partner can work up to 24 hours a week if you are getting IS or income-based JSA.[51] There is no limit on the number of hours your partner can work if you are getting contribution-based JSA. In some situations you might be able to claim both IS or income-based JSA and WTC (eg, if you are a 'term-time only' worker or are off sick and getting statutory sick pay). However, whether you can be paid IS or JSA with WTC depends on your income.

Remember that:

- WTC counts in full as income for IS and income-based JSA;
- only taxable JSA counts as income for WTC. Otherwise, IS and JSA are disregarded.[52]

Choosing which benefit or tax credit to claim

Where you can choose whether to claim IS, JSA or tax credits, remember to consider the following:

- If you are a childminder working from home you are not treated as in full-time work for the purposes of IS (see p758). You may therefore be able to claim either IS or WTC if you work 16 hours or more a week. There are also generous rules on the calculation of income (see p963).
- Child maintenance you receive does not affect WTC and child tax credit (CTC).
- There is no capital limit for WTC and CTC. Instead, income from capital (eg, taxable interest) is taken into account. The first £300 of the total of your income from capital and notional capital, pension income and foreign or notional income is disregarded (see Chapter 53).
- Your WTC and CTC awards are not affected by rises in your income of £2,500 or less per year (see p1374).
- If you and your partner are responsible for any children and one of you works at least 16 hours per week, your hours are added together to work out if you can get a 30-hour element in calculating your WTC (see p1356).
- You can get help with your childcare costs if you claim WTC, but not if you claim IS or JSA.
- You can get help with your housing costs if you claim IS or income-based JSA (see Chapter 36).
- You get free school meals if you claim IS or income-based JSA or are entitled to CTC based on an annual income of £13,910 or less and are not getting WTC.
- You should check which passported benefits you lose or gain (see p10).
- If you finish full-time paid work and are getting WTC, you might be able to claim IS or income-based JSA to top this up. WTC counts as income for IS and JSA purposes (see p968).

Notes

1. The full-time paid work rule

1 s124(1)(c) SSCBA 1992; s1(2)(e) JSA 1995
2 **IS** Reg 5 IS Regs
JSA Reg 51 JSA Regs
3 Reg 3E(2)(g) JSA Regs
4 **HB** Reg 4(1) HB Regs
CTB Reg 4(1) CTB Regs
5 Sch 2 para 2(1) SPC Regs
6 R(IS) 5/95; *Fiore v CAO*, 20 June 1995
7 *Kevin Smith v CAO*, 11 October 1994 (CA), reported as R(IS) 21/95
8 *CAO v Ellis*, 15 February 1995 (CA), reported as R(IS) 22/95; CTC/626/2001
9 R(IS) 1/93
10 *CAO v Ellis*, 15 February 1995 (CA), reported as R(IS) 22/95; CIS/434/1994
11 *CAO v Ellis*, 15 February 1995 (CA), reported as R(IS) 22/95
12 CFC/33/1993; R(FIS) 1/83
13 **IS** Reg 5(7) IS Regs
JSA Reg 51(3)(a) JSA Regs
14 Reg 51(3)(c) JSA Regs
15 **IS** Reg 5(2)(b)(i) IS Regs
JSA Reg 51(2)(b)(i) JSA Regs
16 Reg 5(2)(b)(i) and (3B) IS Regs; *Stafford and Banks v CAO* [2001] UKHL 33 (HL), reported as R(IS) 15/01
17 Reg 51(2)(b)(i) JSA Regs; reg 51(2)(c) JSA Regs disapplied in R(JSA) 4/03; R(JSA) 5/03
18 para 20322 DMG
IS Reg 5(2)(b)(ii) IS Regs
JSA Reg 51(2)(b)(ii) JSA Regs
19 CFC/2963/2001
20 **IS** Reg 5(2)(a) IS Regs
JSA Reg 51(2)(a) JSA Regs
All R(IS) 8/95
21 Ch78 App 5 paras 21, 23 and 47 DMG
22 Ch78 App5 para 30 DMG
23 **PC** Sch 2 para 2(4) SPC Regs
HB/CTB Reg 4(2)(a) HB Regs; reg 4(2)(a) CTB Regs
24 **PC** Sch 2 para 2(3) SPC Regs
HB/CTB Reg 4(2A) HB Regs; reg 4(2A) CTB Regs
25 **PC** Sch 2 para 2(2)(b) SPC Regs
HB/CTB Reg 4(2)(b) HB Regs; reg 4(2)(b) CTB Regs
26 **PC** Sch 2 para 2(4) SPC Regs
HB/CTB Reg 4(3) HB Regs; reg 4(3) CTB Regs
27 R(JSA) 8/03
28 CIS/914/1997; CJSA/2759/1998
29 R(JSA) 5/02
30 **IS** Regs 2(2)(b)(i) and 5(3B) IS Regs
PC Sch 2 para 2(3) SPC Regs
HB/CTB Reg 4(2A) HB Regs; reg 4(2A) CTB Regs
All *Stafford and Banks v CAO* [2001] UKHL 33 (HL), reported as R(IS) 15/01
31 Reg 7 WTC(EMR) Regs
32 Reg 51(2)(b)(i) JSA regs; reg 51(2)(c) JSA Regs disapplied in R(JSA) 4/03; R(JSA) 5/03
33 Reg 6(28) SS(C&P) Regs

2. People treated as in full-time paid work

34 **IS** Reg 5(3) IS Regs
JSA Reg 52(1) JSA Regs
PC Sch 2 para 2(5) SPC Regs
HB/CTB Reg 4(4) HB Regs; reg 4(4) CTB Regs
All R(U) 1/62
35 R(JSA) 5/03; paras 20309 and 20410 and Ch78 App 5 paras 73 and 74 DMG
36 **IS** Reg 5(3) IS Regs
JSA Reg 52(1) JSA Regs
PC Sch 2 para 2(5) SPC Regs
HB/CTB Reg 4(4) HB Regs; reg 4(4) CTB Regs
37 **IS** Reg 5(5) IS Regs
JSA Reg 52(3) JSA Regs
38 Reg 52(2) JSA Regs
39 Reg 52(2A) JSA Regs
40 Reg 5(4) IS Regs

3. People treated as not in full-time paid work

41 **IS** Regs 5(3A) and 6 IS Regs
JSA Regs 52(1) and 53 JSA Regs
42 CIS/621/2004
43 R(FIS) 1/86; CDWA/1/1992
44 **PC** Sch 2 para 2(7) and (8) SPC Regs
HB/CTB Reg 4(6) and (7) HB Regs; reg 4(6) and (7) CTB Regs
45 **PC** Sch 2 para 2(6) SPC Regs
HB/CTB Reg 4(5) HB Regs; reg 4(5) CTB Regs

4. **Self-employed people**
46 CIS/649/1992
47 para 20237 DMG
48 para 20265 DMG
49 R(FIS) 6/85; *Kazantzis v CAO* [1999], reported as R(IS) 13/99
50 para 20267 DMG

5. **Working tax credit, income support and jobseeker's allowance**
51 **IS** Reg 5(1A) IS Regs
JSA Reg 51(1)(b) JSA Regs
52 Reg 7(3) Table 3 paras 13, 16 and 17 TC(DCI) Regs

Chapter 30

Incapacity for work and benefits

This chapter covers:

This chapter explains how the Department for Work and Pensions (DWP) assesses whether you are incapable of work for the purposes of qualifying for the following benefits:[1]

- incapacity benefit (IB);
- severe disablement allowance;
- income support (IS), if you are claiming this on the basis of being incapable of work;
- the disability premium within IS, housing benefit (HB) and council tax benefit (CTB) if your entitlement to the premium depends on you showing that you have been incapable of work;
- national insurance credits for incapacity.

A determination that you are capable or incapable of work for one of the above benefits also applies to claims for all the others.[2] A determination that you are capable of work also applies to a claim for jobseeker's allowance (JSA – see Chapter 15).[3]

The way your incapacity for work is assessed for the purpose of statutory sick pay (SSP) is explained in Chapter 24. The rules described in this chapter do not apply to SSP or to the assessment of your incapacity for work for the purpose of industrial injuries benefits (see Chapter 14).

If you are making a claim for a non-means-tested benefit, such as IB, on the basis of your incapacity for work you should also consider applying for IS, HB and CTB. If you qualify for them, these benefits may be paid in addition to your non-means-tested benefit, although any IB you receive will be treated as income when calculating your entitlement to IS, HB, or CTB. As it may take the DWP some time to decide whether you qualify for a non-means-tested benefit, you should also claim IS if you can, in case your application for IB is refused.

If you are claiming IS on the basis of being incapable of work, or a disability premium within your IS, HB, or CTB and you are not receiving SSP, the DWP or local authority expect you to complete a claim form for IB (an SC1 or SSP1 form – see p282) and submit it to your local DWP office with a medical certificate so that you can be assessed as to whether you are incapable of work. You should do this even if you know that you will not qualify for IB.

Changes during 2005

The Government is introducing a number of changes to the way in which benefits for incapacity for work are claimed. None of these changes concern the rules on incapacity for work itself. The main changes, which were introduced in certain areas from October 2003, and will apply to more areas during 2005, involve more compulsory work-focused interviews (see p1092) and increased support for rehabilitation and job-seeking activities. The new schemes are known as 'Pathways to Work'. See CPAG's *Welfare Rights Bulletin* 175 and 177 for more details on the schemes.

1. Incapacity for work

For all benefits, except statutory sick pay (SSP) and industrial injuries benefits, the question of whether you are incapable of work is determined by one of two tests:

- the 'own occupation test', which applies for the first 28 weeks of your claim if you have a regular occupation when you fall ill (see p772); *or*
- the 'personal capability assessment', which applies after 28 weeks, or from the start of your claim if you do not have a regular occupation when you fall ill.

DWP's Medical Service

The Department for Work and Pensions (DWP) has contracted a private company (referred to in this *Handbook* as the Medical Service (MS)) to provide a medical service for benefit purposes. The MS carries out medical examinations of claimants and provides advice on medical questions relating to incapacity and disability benefits. You may be asked whether you agree to details of your medical condition and history being given to the MS. It is not likely to be in your best interest to refuse to give your authorisation for this as decision makers rely heavily on the MS doctor's assessment of your condition when determining whether you are incapable of work and the MS doctor's assessment may be incomplete if s/he has not been able to obtain information about your medical situation.

In addition, if you refuse to attend a medical examination by an MS doctor, a decision maker can treat you as capable of work, unless you have good cause for your refusal (see p784). An unwillingness to be examined by a doctor from the MS would be unlikely, by itself, to be considered good cause for not attending.

The MS and the DWP must ensure that any information they obtain about you remains confidential.

Treated as incapable of work

In certain circumstances you are treated as incapable of work without having to satisfy the own occupation test or the personal capability assessment.

In particular, you may be:

- deemed to be incapable of work (see p768); *or*
- exempt from the personal capability assessment (see p773); *or*
- treated as incapable of work after failing to satisfy the personal capability assessment because of 'exceptional circumstances' (see p778).

Work you may do while claiming

The general rule is that you cannot work and be incapable of work at the same time. With certain exceptions, even if it has been determined that you are incapable of work, you are treated as capable of work for any week (starting on a Sunday) in which you actually *do* work. (Note that this also applies if you work while appealing against a decision on your incapacity.) You are treated as capable of work for the whole week even if you do not work for the whole week. This applies whether or not you are paid for the work.[4]

However, you will only be treated as capable of work on the actual days that you work, rather than for the whole week, if you work:

- during the first week of your claim; *or*
- during the last week that you were incapable of work; *or*
- during any week when you are undergoing plasmapheresis, parenteral chemotherapy, or radiotherapy treatment, or regular weekly renal dialysis or total parenteral nutrition treatment.[5]

If the amount of work you do is so minimal that it can be regarded as trivial or negligible, you should not be treated as capable of work.[6] For example, a man who occasionally helped his florist wife to cut or pack a few flowers was not treated as capable of work as the work he did was considered negligible.[7]

In addition, the following kinds of work are allowed:[8]

- 'approved work' (ie, work on a trial basis for which you are not paid) that has been arranged in writing by the DWP and you are getting incapacity benefit (IB), income support (IS), severe disablement allowance (SDA), or any other benefit or increase (including a disability premium) or national insurance credits, on the basis of incapacity for work;
- the care of a spouse, a partner (if you are a member of an unmarried couple), a grandparent, grandchild, uncle, aunt, nephew, niece or a 'close relative'

(parent, parent-in-law, son, son-in-law, daughter, daughter-in-law, step-parent, step-son, step-daughter, brother, sister, or the spouse or partner of any of the preceding persons[9]);
- domestic work (ie, cooking and cleaning) in your own home;
- work which you do only to protect someone or prevent serious damage to property or livestock during an emergency;
- work as a local councillor;
- work (for a maximum of one day a week) as a member of an appeal tribunal, if you have been appointed because of your experience of disability issues (see p1244), or of the Disability Living Allowance Advisory Board;
- voluntary work if the work is not for a 'close relative' (see above) and if the only payment you receive for the work is to cover your reasonable expenses (but note that the mere fact that you do not accept a wage will not necessarily mean that you are a volunteer);[10]
- 'permitted' work (see below).

Permitted work[11]

Note: you must inform the DWP if you are doing this work. **'Permitted work'** is work of any kind, which you can do:
- as part of a **treatment programme** done under medical supervision while you are in hospital or regularly attending hospital as an outpatient, as long as you do not earn more than £78 a week; *or*
- for an unlimited period, as long as you do not earn more than £20 a week. This is called **permitted work lower limit** (in practice, because of the minimum wage the DWP will expect you to be working under five hours a week); *or*
- for an unlimited period, as long as you do not earn more than £78 a week and you are in 'supported work' (see p767). This is called **supported permitted work**; *or*
- for up to 26 weeks, as long as you work on average for less than 16 hours a week and do not earn more than £78 a week. This is called **permitted work higher limit**.

For the 16-hour rule see p767. For how your earnings are assessed see Chapter 37.

The Government plans to change the rules on permitted work.[12] The intention is to allow more people to undertake such work, and to allow permitted work higher limit to be undertaken for longer periods. However, people doing permitted work will also have to sign up to an 'action plan' under which they will consider the prospects of a move into full-time employment. At the time of writing, it was not known when these changes were to be introduced. See CPAG's *Welfare Rights Bulletin* for updates.

Permitted work higher limit

Initially, you can do this for up to 26 weeks. (If you work for a few weeks and then stop, you can start again as long as this is within the 26-week period.) You can have a 26-week extension added straight away, if there is evidence that extending the period will improve your capacity to undertake full-time work.

The evidence about improving your capacity for work can come from anyone, including you, but in practice the DWP will usually expect you to have the support of a job broker, personal adviser or disability employment adviser, and will choose the 'most reliable' evidence if there is a conflict.

After the 26-week extension, there must then be a gap period of 52 weeks in which you do not do permitted work higher limit before you can have further 52 week extensions. Again, there must be evidence (usually from a job broker, etc.) that the work will improve your capacity to undertake full-time work. There must always be gap periods of at least 52 weeks between further extension periods of permitted work higher limit. Otherwise, if you work you will be treated as capable of work, unless you move down to permitted work lower limit (earning up to £20 a week) or to supported permitted work (earning up to £78 a week).

If you actually come off benefit for any reason – eg, to try full-time work, a gap of over eight weeks in your benefit claim will mean that your time allowed on permitted work higher limit starts again – ie, it is for 26 weeks initially. If the gap in your claim is eight weeks or less, then you return to the situation you were in before you came off benefit – eg, having to wait 52 weeks before your next period of permitted work higher limit can start.

Informing the DWP

For work done in a treatment programme, permitted work lower limit and supported permitted work, you (or someone acting on your behalf) must inform the DWP in writing that you are working at some point before you stop doing it.

For the permitted work higher limit, you (or someone acting on your behalf) must inform the DWP in writing that you are working within six weeks of starting it.

Note: if the particular activities you carry out in your work suggest to the DWP that you might be capable of work, it may re-assess this.

Note also: there are special rules on how your earnings are assessed – see Chapter 37.

Supported work

This means work which is supervised by someone employed by a public or local authority, or by a voluntary organisation, whose job it is to find work for people with disabilities. This could include work in a sheltered workshop or with help from social services. The DWP says that you do not have to have the person actually working alongside you, although the support should be ongoing and regular.

16-hour rule

Permitted work (see p766) may sometimes only be disregarded if you do such work for less than 16 hours a week.[13]

It is the average number of hours that you work which is important. Even if you work more than 16 hours in a week you are not treated as capable of work in that week if the average number of hours which you normally work is less than 16. If you work for 16 hours or more in a week the decision maker should consider your average hours:

- if you have a normal work cycle, over the period of that cycle;
- otherwise, over the week in question and the four weeks before it.[14]

Only the hours you actually work (as opposed to the hours you are contracted to work) and weeks in which you actually do any work (as opposed to weeks of sickness or holiday) should count.[15]

Although you will not be considered to be capable of work simply because you are doing any of the above types of work, if you are claiming IS the type of work that you do and any earnings you receive may still affect your entitlement. If the work is done for payment or in expectation of payment and you work for 16 hours or more a week, you will not qualify for IS (see p752), unless you can be treated as not being in full-time work (see p752). See p955 for details of how earnings may affect your entitlement to IS.

Deemed incapacity

When either the own occupation test or the personal capability assessment applies to you (see pp771 and 772) you are deemed to be incapable of work in the following circumstances:[16]

- if you are under medical observation as a possible carrier of an infectious or contagious disease (or you have been in contact with a person with such a disease), and a medical officer for environmental health has given you a certificate excluding you from work; *or*
- if you are receiving inpatient treatment (including nursing) at a hospital or in a 'similar institution'; *or*
- on days when you are receiving plasmapheresis, parenteral chemotherapy, or radiotherapy treatment or regular weekly renal dialysis or total parenteral nutrition treatment; *or*
- on days when you are pregnant and there would be a serious risk to your health or your baby's health:
  - when the own occupation test applies to you, if you continue to work in your own occupation; *or*
  - when the personal capability assessment applies, if you work in any occupation;[17] *or*
- if you are pregnant or have recently had a baby; *and*
  - you would not be entitled to either maternity allowance or statutory maternity pay were you to make a claim; *and*
  - you are within the period beginning with the first day of the sixth week before the expected week of childbirth (see p464) or beginning with the

actual day of childbirth if that is earlier, and ending on the 14th day after the date you had the baby; *and*
  - you have a medical certificate giving your expected date of childbirth or your actual date of childbirth;[18] *or*
- if you are a 'welfare to work' beneficiary (see below), in which case you can be treated as incapable of work without having to satisfy the own occupation test or personal capability assessment for up to 91 days if:
  - in your last period of incapacity for work (see p265) you were either assessed under the personal capability assessment (or all-work test) and found to be incapable of work, or you were exempt from the personal capability assessment (or all-work test) for one of the reasons described on pp773–774 (but not for the reasons given in the first two bullet points in that section); *and*
  - you submit a medical certificate to the DWP confirming that you are incapable of work; *and*
  - the days fall within your 52-week linking period or within the first 13 weeks after the end of the 52-week linking period.

  The 91 days do not need to be consecutive and so can be separated by days when you work or are not incapable of work. If you are incapable of work for more than 91 days within the above period you will have to satisfy the own occupation test or the personal capability assessment from the 92nd day of your incapacity for work (unless you can be treated as incapable of work for another reason).[19]

'Welfare to work' beneficiary

You are a 'welfare to work' beneficiary if you satisfy all of the following rules:

- you have stopped receiving a benefit (except SSP) to which you were entitled on the basis of being incapable of work (see p770) after being incapable of work for a period of more than 196 days – known as your 'last period of incapacity for work' (you do not have to have been receiving benefit for all of the 196 days). The 196 days do not need to fall consecutively, as two or more periods of incapacity for work can be linked if they are separated by eight weeks or less – the days within each period of incapacity count towards the 196-day total; *and*
- your benefit stopped on or after 5 October 1998; *and*
- you are within the 52-week period which runs from the first day after the end of that period of incapacity for work (called the 52-week linking period); *and*
- within a week of your entitlement to benefit stopping you start a training course for which you receive a training allowance, or you start work and you are paid for that work or you expect to be paid; *and either*
  - within a month of your entitlement to benefit stopping you notify the DWP that you have started work or training (you should keep a copy of your written notification and make a note of the date of a verbal notification and the name of the person you told); *or*

- you have successfully appealed against an incapacity for work decision and as a result you have been incapable of work for more than 196 days (in this situation you do not have to notify the DWP that you have started work or training and you only have to start work or training within one week of your entitlement to benefit ending, not within a week of the decision that you were capable of work).

Even if you satisfy these conditions you will not be a 'welfare to work' beneficiary if:

- your 'last period of incapacity for work' (see p265) ended because you were found to be capable of work and either you did not appeal against this or you appealed but did not win your appeal; *or*
- when your most recent period of incapacity for work ended, less than 28 weeks had passed since the end of a previous 52-week linking period; *or*
- the work that you have started within a week of your benefit stopping is work that you can do while still being considered incapable of work (see p766).

You will have been receiving benefit based on your incapacity for work if you were receiving IB, SDA, IS on the basis of your incapacity for work, national insurance credits for incapacity for work (see p838), or a disability premium within your IS, housing benefit or council tax benefit paid on the grounds that you are incapable of work.[20]

The 52-week linking period

You are only a 'welfare to work' beneficiary for a fixed 52-week period running from the day after the end of your last 'period of incapacity for work' (see p265). This 52-week period is not affected by whether you subsequently stop work or training or whether or not you have periods of incapacity for work within it.

If you are a 'welfare to work' beneficiary as well as being treated as incapable of work for up to 91 days in the circumstances described on p769, you can immediately return to the same benefit and the same level of benefit that you were receiving before you started work or training, as long as you become incapable of work again within your 52-week linking period. Once your 52-week linking period ends you are no longer considered to be a 'welfare to work' beneficiary. You can only become a 'welfare to work' beneficiary again if at least 28 weeks have passed since the day your last 52-week linking period ended and you satisfy the other conditions described on p769. You will therefore have to have been incapable of work for a further 196 days. In calculating the 196 days, days within two or more periods of incapacity for work can be linked if they are separated by eight weeks or less. So, although your 52-week linking period will have ended more than 196 days ago, it may be possible to count days of incapacity for work within it when calculating whether you have been incapable of work for 196 days.

2. The own occupation test

If you cannot be deemed to be incapable of work (see p768), your incapacity for work will be determined by the 'own occupation test' for the first 28 weeks of your incapacity for work if you have a regular occupation when you become ill or disabled (see below). The **'own occupation test'** is a test of:

> whether [you are] incapable by reason of some specific disease or bodily or mental disablement of doing work which [you] could reasonably be expected to do in the course of the occupation in which [you were] engaged.[21]

'Specific disease' means a disease that has been identified by medical science.[22] A disease is a departure from health capable of identification by its signs and symptoms.[23] If you do not have a specific disease, you may still satisfy the own occupation test if your incapacity for work arises from a bodily or mental disablement.

When the own occupation test applies

The own occupation test applies to you if you have a regular occupation when you become incapable of work. You have a regular occupation if, in the 21 weeks immediately before the start of your period of incapacity for work, you did paid work for more than eight weeks in at least one occupation, for at least 16 hours a week.[24] Paid work includes work done in expectation of payment even if no payment is received.

The own occupation test applies for the first 196 days of your period of incapacity for work (see below). When calculating this 196-day period you only count days:[25]

- when you were incapable of work; *or*
- when you are treated as incapable of work; *or*
- when you were entitled to statutory sick pay (SSP); *or*
- which fall within a maternity allowance period (see p456).

A **'period of incapacity for work'** in this context means four or more consecutive days of incapacity (unless you are undergoing certain forms of treatment such as renal dialysis – see p768 – when the period of incapacity means two or more days of incapacity in any seven consecutive days).

Any two periods of incapacity for work are linked together if they are separated by a period of eight weeks or less. Your days of incapacity in your earlier period of sickness are added to those in your current period of sickness.

After the first 196 days of incapacity for work, the personal capability assessment applies (see p772). The Medical Service (MS) may start the process of a personal capability assessment (see p772) even while your incapacity still falls to be assessed under the own occupation test. This could be up to 10 weeks before the own occupation test ceases to apply to you. The intention is to ensure that a decision can be made under the personal capability assessment as soon as it applies to you.[26]

Evidence of incapacity for the own occupation test

For the first seven days of your incapacity for work the Department for Work and Pensions (DWP) usually accepts a self-certification of your sickness. After seven days you are required to provide a medical certificate (Med 3 or 5) from your doctor. If it is unreasonable to expect you to provide a medical certificate, the DWP should accept other evidence if this is sufficient to show that you should not work because of some specific disease or bodily or mental disablement.[27] The decision maker (see p1180) also has the right to request additional information relating to your incapacity for work in your own occupation if this is reasonable.[28]

Either the decision maker or the MS doctor can ask you to attend a medical examination. If you fail to attend, without good cause, you can be treated as capable of work. In these circumstances, if no decision has been made on your claim, it will be refused. If you are already receiving benefit on the basis of incapacity for work your entitlement to benefit will be revised or superseded and your benefit will stop – see p784.

3. The personal capability assessment

After 196 days of incapacity for work, or from the start of your claim if the own occupation test does not apply to you, your incapacity for work is determined by the 'personal capability assessment'. The **'personal capability assessment'** is an assessment of:

> the extent to which a person who has some specific disease or bodily or mental disablement is capable of performing prescribed activities, or is incapable of performing them because of that specific disease or bodily or mental disablement.[29]

See p771 for the meaning of 'specific disease'.

Apart from being deemed incapable of work (see p768), there are three main ways of being incapable of work under the personal capability assessment:

- being **exempt** from the assessment;
- satisfying the assessment by **scoring sufficient points**;
- being treated as satisfying the assessment because an **'exceptional circumstance'** applies.

The assessment is carried out by the Medical Service (MS) but the decision as to whether you are incapable of work is taken by a decision maker from the Department for Work and Pensions (DWP). You will normally be required to be examined by an MS doctor who will prepare an incapacity report for the decision maker. The report gives details of your ability to carry out the prescribed activities.

Satisfying the personal capability assessment prior to your assessment

You are treated as incapable of work until the assessment is carried out, as long as you continue to provide medical certificates.[30] However, if in the last six months you have been found to be capable of work under the own occupation test or the personal capability assessment, you are only treated as incapable of work while waiting for your personal capability assessment if:

- you have a specific disease or physical or mental disability which you did not have when it was decided that you were capable of work; *or*
- your condition has significantly worsened since you were found to be capable of work; *or*
- you were treated as capable of work because you failed to return the incapacity for work questionnaire (see p780) and you have since returned it.

If you cannot be treated as incapable of work while waiting for a personal capability assessment to be carried out, you can claim benefit again on the basis of your incapacity for work but the DWP can delay payment until you have been assessed again and found to be incapable of work. The DWP should not say that you cannot claim again, and they must arrange for another assessment.[31] You may be sent another questionnaire to complete and you may be required to attend another medical, unless the decision maker considers that there is already sufficient evidence to show that, on the balance of probabilities, you are still not incapable of work.[32]

Exempt from the personal capability assessment

You are exempt from the personal capability assessment if one of the following applies to you:[33]

Exemption under transitional rules

- you were aged 58 or over on 13 April 1995; *and*
  - between 1 December 1993 and 13 April 1995 you had not been capable of work for more than eight continuous weeks; *and*
  - you continue to submit medical certificates to the DWP; *and either*:
    - you were entitled to invalidity benefit on both 1 December 1993 and 12 April 1995; *or*
    - you were entitled to income support (IS), housing benefit or council tax benefit on 1 December 1993 and had been incapable of work for at least

28 weeks prior to that date, and, on 12 April 1995, were getting a disability premium with one of those benefits because of your own incapacity for work.

People in some of the above categories may also be entitled to receive transitional rather than ordinary incapacity benefit (IB) (see p279);

- you were receiving severe disablement allowance (SDA) on 12 April 1995 and your spell of incapacity for work has continued since then and you continue to send medical certificates to the DWP.

Exemption for a severe condition

- you are assessed as at least 80 per cent disabled for the purposes of SDA (see Chapter 20);
- you receive the highest rate of the care component of disability living allowance (see p137);
- you are terminally ill (see p134);
- you are registered as blind;
- you have tetraplegia, paraplegia (including uncontrollable involuntary movements or ataxia which render you functionally paraplegic), dementia or are in a persistent vegetative state;
- you are getting disablement benefit (see p331) based on an assessment of at least 80 per cent disablement;
- you are getting constant attendance allowance paid at a rate which is higher than the 'lower weekly rate' (see p333);
- there is 'medical evidence' (see p775) to show that you have:
  - a severe learning disability involving severe impairment of intelligence and social functioning caused by the arrested or incomplete physical development of the brain or severe brain damage;
  - a severe and progressive neurological or muscle wasting disease;
  - an active and progressive form of inflammatory polyarthritis;
  - progressive impairment of cardio-respiratory function which severely and persistently limits effort tolerance;
  - dense paralysis of the upper limb, trunk and lower limb on one side of the body;
  - severe irreversible motor sensory and intellectual deficits from the multiple effects of impairment of function of the brain or nervous system;
  - a severe and progressive immune deficiency state characterised by the occurrence of severe constitutional disease, opportunistic infections or tumour formation;
  - a severe mental illness which severely and adversely affects your mood or behaviour and which severely restricts your social functioning or your awareness of your immediate environment.

The '**medical evidence**' could be:

- evidence from an MS doctor (see p764); *or*
- evidence from any other doctor, a hospital or a similar institution; *or*
- parts of such evidence which is most reliable in the circumstances.[34]

See p768 for other circumstances in which you can be treated as incapable of work under the personal capability assessment.

Scoring points

If you are not exempt, and you cannot be deemed to be incapable of work in the circumstances detailed on p768, you have to satisfy the personal capability assessment in order to be considered incapable of work. This usually means **scoring sufficient points** (although some people who do not can still be treated as incapable of work – see p778).

You are awarded points according to the level of difficulty you have in performing certain physical and mental activities. You are assessed as incapable of work if you score sufficient points in total. The assessment is carried out without reference to any job and does not take into account your education and training, or any language or literacy problems.

The assessment of your incapacity for work under the personal capability assessment is a test of your ability to perform certain activities. There are two lists of activities: one physical and the other mental. The test is set out in full in Appendix 4.

Under each activity, there is a further list of what are called 'descriptors'. These are designed to measure the level of difficulty you have performing the activities to which they relate. Each descriptor has a number of points allocated to it.

For example, the descriptors and points relating to the activity of walking up and down stairs are:

Descriptor	Points
Cannot walk up and down one stair	15
Cannot walk up and down a flight of 12 stairs	15
Cannot walk up and down a flight of 12 stairs without holding on and taking a rest	7
Cannot walk up and down a flight of 12 stairs without holding on	3
Can only walk up and down a flight of 12 stairs if going sideways or one step at a time	3
No problem in walking up and down stairs	0

To satisfy the test by scoring points, you have to score either:[35]

- 15 points from the physical activities list; *or*
- 10 points from the mental activities list; *or*

- 15 points if you are combining scores from both the mental and physical activities lists (but see p777).

When calculating your score:

- you can only score points in respect of **one** descriptor within each physical activity (the one you score highest on) but you can score points for every mental descriptor you satisfy, regardless of whether they relate to the same activity;[36]
- you cannot score points in respect of both physical activities 1 (walking) and 2 (walking up and down stairs) – only the highest descriptor you score on from either activity counts.[37]

Physical and mental health problems

The physical descriptors can only apply if your difficulty in performing the activities arises from a specific bodily disease or disablement.[38] The mental health descriptors can only apply to you if your difficulty in performing the activities arises from a mental illness or disablement.[39] However, if your incapacity has a mental origin but results in a specific bodily disablement that restricts your physical functions, you may score points for that under the physical descriptors.[40]

Aids and appliances

Your ability to perform any of the activities is assessed as if you were wearing any prosthesis or other aid or appliance that you normally wear or use.[41] So, for example, if you have an artificial leg and have no problem climbing stairs when you are wearing it, you will score 0 for that activity even though without it you may not be able to climb stairs at all.

Example

Andreas has angina and:

– cannot walk more than 400 metres (Activity 1, Descriptor (e));

– cannot walk up and down a flight of 12 stairs without holding on and taking a rest (Activity 2, Descriptor (c));

– cannot stand without the support of another person or the use of an aid (other than a walking stick) for more than 30 minutes without needing to sit down (Activity 4, Descriptor (d)).

Descriptor	*Points*
1(e)	3
2(c)	7
4(d)	7
Total score	14

Only the descriptor with the highest score from activities 1 and 2 is counted. In this case

Andreas scores more for descriptor 2(c) than descriptor 1(e) so his total score would be 14. As his total is less than 15 he is assessed as not being incapable of work.

Combining scores from physical and mental activities lists

If you score points in both lists, you can combine your points. When you are combining points in this way, the calculation of the points for mental activities is adjusted so that:

- a score of between 6 and 9 points (inclusive) from the mental activities list counts as 9;
- a score of less than 6 from the mental activities list is completely disregarded.

Example

Carolyn has arthritis in her hands and cannot turn a tap or control knobs on a cooker with one hand (Activity 7, Descriptor (f)). For this she scores 6 points.

In addition she has a depressive mental illness which means that she:

– needs encouragement to get up and dress (Activity 16, Descriptor (a) – 2 points);

– does not care about her appearance and living conditions (Activity 16, Descriptor (d) – 1 point);

– avoids carrying out routine activities because she is convinced they will prove too tiring or stressful (Activity 17, Descriptor (c) – 1 point);

– is unable to cope with changes in daily routine (Activity 17, Descriptor (d) – 1 point).

Carolyn's total score for mental activities is 5. Because this is less than 6, and she is combining scores from both the physical and mental activities lists, her score from the mental activities list is ignored for the purposes of the assessment and her total score is the 6 points she scored for her physical disability. Carolyn is not incapable of work according to the assessment.

Suppose, however, that in addition she feels too frightened to go out on her own (Activity 18, Descriptor (f) – 1 point). Her total score for mental activities is now 6 but because it is to be added to her score from the physical activities list it counts as 9. Her total score is therefore 15 (9 for mental activities + 6 for physical activities). She is incapable of work.

Interpretation of the descriptors

None of the words used in the descriptors are defined and so should be given their ordinary, everyday meaning. Some of the descriptors, however, have been the subject of appeals to the social security commissioners (see p1245) and their interpretations are binding on decision makers and tribunals. For the latest caselaw, see Volume 1 of Sweet & Maxwell's *Social Security: Legislation*, CPAG's *Welfare Benefits and Tax Credits CD-ROM* and CPAG's *Welfare Rights Bulletin* (see Appendix 3).

Good and bad days, pain and tiredness

If your condition fluctuates, so that on good days you 'can' perform an activity but on bad days you 'cannot', the decision maker (or appeal tribunal – see p1235) should adopt a broad and reasonable approach rather than a literal one, considering your normal capacity to perform an activity. So, if you normally cannot walk up and down a flight of 12 stairs when called to do so this descriptor applies to you even if you could on occasion manage to do so. It is your normal ability to perform the activities with reasonable regularity, taking account of limitations imposed by pain and fatigue, which is important.

Your ability to perform an activity should be considered in the light of your ability over a period of time that gives a true and fair picture of your condition,[42] not just on a day-by-day approach.[43]

A descriptor should apply to you if you cannot perform the activity most of the time. But whether you have more bad than good days is not the only consideration. Also relevant is the severity of your condition on your good and bad days, the frequency of your good and bad days, and the unpredictability of the bad days. So, if in a normal week you would have three bad days when you would meet a particular descriptor and four good days when you would nearly meet it, that descriptor may apply to you, especially if your condition is very bad on the bad days.[44]

If you have long periods of remission you may be considered capable of work during those periods. Whether this is the correct approach will depend on the severity of your condition and the length of your periods of ill-health and your periods of remission.[45] If your periods of remission are short, for example, you could argue that your ability to perform the activities should be considered across a period of time that is representative of your situation as a whole.

In deciding whether you can normally perform an activity, matters such as pain, fatigue and the increasing difficulty you may have performing an activity on a repeated basis compared with someone in good health should be taken into account.[46] 'Pain' might include nausea and dizziness.[47] The decision maker or tribunal should consider whether you could perform the activity without too much discomfort and whether you can repeat the activity within a reasonable time.[48]

Any risk to your health in performing an activity should be considered, particularly if carrying out the activity is against medical advice. If the risk to your health is sufficiently serious you may be considered incapable of the activity.[49]

Exceptional circumstances

Even if your points score is not sufficiently high, you can still be treated as incapable of work in certain **'exceptional circumstances'**. You are treated as incapable of work if you have:[50]

- a severe uncontrolled or uncontrollable life-threatening disease, and you have medical evidence to show this. There must be a reasonable cause for it not to be controlled by a recognised therapeutic procedure; *or*
- a previously undiagnosed, potentially life-threatening condition (eg, cancer or ischaemic heart disease) which is discovered for the first time by the MS doctor; *or*
- medical evidence stating that you are likely to undergo a major operation or other major therapeutic procedure within three months of the date of the medical examination carried out by an MS doctor for the purpose of the personal capability assessment (see below).

In addition, a court case[51] has established that, from 8 November 2002, you are also treated as incapable of work in the following 'exceptional circumstance':

- if there would be a substantial risk to the mental or physical health of any person were you to be found capable of work.

The 'substantial risk' referred to is that which would arise from the sort of work you would be required to be available for were you to be claiming jobseeker's allowance. This means with reference not only to your state of health, but also your qualifications, skills and experience. But the risk can arise from broad factors such as, in mental disablement cases, apprehension caused by the need to look for work, and need not arise only from the details of an individual job description.[52]

The personal capability assessment procedure

The questionnaire

Unless you are exempt (see p773) or you are deemed to be incapable of work (see p768), you are sent an incapacity for work questionnaire (an IB50 form) to complete. When the personal capability assessment is first applied to you during your period of incapacity for work you are also asked to get a form Med 4 from your GP, which you should return with the questionnaire. Although it is advisable, returning the Med 4 form is not compulsory. Even if you do not return it the decision maker can still proceed with the personal capability assessment.[53]

If the information on your original claim form, or your medical certificates, suggests that you have mental health problems, the DWP will write to your own doctor before sending you a questionnaire to try to assess whether those problems are severe. If they are severe, you should be exempt from the personal capability assessment. If the decision maker decides that you are exempt, you are not sent a questionnaire. If your mental health problems are thought to be mild or moderate, a questionnaire is issued in the normal way.

Completing and returning the questionnaire is very important. If you do not fill it in and send it back you are assessed as capable of work and your benefit stops unless you are considered to have good cause for not returning it (see p780).

Failing to return the questionnaire

You have six weeks from the date the questionnaire is sent to you to return it. If you have not returned it, a reminder must be sent to you at least four weeks after the questionnaire was sent. You must then be given a further two weeks from the date the reminder was sent to return the questionnaire. If the DWP follows this procedure and you still have not returned the questionnaire in time you are treated as capable of work unless you can show that you had good cause for not returning it.[54] If you are treated as capable of work the DWP will revise or supersede the decision on your entitlement to benefit, and your benefit will normally stop.

When deciding whether you have 'good cause' the decision maker must consider all of the circumstances, including:[55]

- whether you were outside Great Britain at the relevant time;
- your state of health;
- the nature of your disability.

If your benefit stops because you are treated as capable of work as a result of your failure to return the questionnaire, but you have a good reason for not having done so, write to the DWP asking it to revise the decision (see p1189) . You should send the completed questionnaire and explain why you were unable to send it in time. You should also make a fresh claim for benefit. If the decision maker decides that you did not have good cause you can appeal – see Chapter 44.

If you are exempt (see p773), or you are deemed to be incapable of work (see p768), you are not required to complete a questionnaire. In addition, if the decision maker has sufficient information to determine whether you are incapable of work then a questionnaire is not required.[56] Guidance issued to decision makers states that if you have been diagnosed as having mental health problems and you have not returned the questionnaire, it is not appropriate to decide that you are capable of work. Instead, the decision maker may refer your case directly to the MS (see p782) for a medical examination.[57]

Completing the questionnaire

- Read the notes on the form before answering the questions. It may be helpful to draft your answers on a separate sheet of paper first.
- Some of the descriptors are relevant to your ability to complete the questionnaire. If, for example, you do have difficulty in writing and have asked someone else to fill in your questionnaire, or have only been able to complete it slowly and with pain, you should explain this on the questionnaire.[58]
- Include details of why you cannot perform particular activities to allow the decision maker to fully understand your condition and how it affects you.
- Try to mention everything which may be relevant. Anything you forget to mention at this stage may make a difference to the decision. If you have to appeal, the appeal tribunal may be less likely to believe you have symptoms

which you have raised for the first time only after the decision maker's decision went against you. It may be worth letting someone who knows you well check your answers.

- If you have 'good' and 'bad' days (see p778) you should explain this. Answer the question on the basis of what you can do on your bad days and then give a fuller answer in the space provided, explaining about the good days too. If necessary, give a rough estimate of how often you would be able to perform the activity and how often you would not.
- Compare the draft of your answers with the list in Appendix 4 and work out your score. If your score suggests that you fail the assessment, it will be very difficult for you to persuade the MS doctor, the decision maker or an appeal tribunal that you should pass it. Your answers should not be exaggerated, but you should check that you have not underestimated any of your problems and that you have given all the detail you can in the space provided.
- If you have difficulties with English or with reading or writing it is vital that you get independent help (ie, from someone who is not connected to the DWP) before you submit the form.
- Always make a copy of your answers before you return the original questionnaire to the DWP.

On receiving your completed questionnaire the decision maker considers whether your answers or the information on the Med 4 form which your doctor has completed (see p779) indicate that you are exempt from the personal capability assessment (see p778). The DWP may request further information from your doctor about this. If you do not appear to be exempt the decision maker provisionally assesses your score on the personal capability assessment from the information you have given. If your score indicates that you are not incapable of work, your case is referred to the MS (see p782) for a medical examination to be arranged. If your score indicates that you are incapable of work, your case is referred to the MS for 'medical scrutiny'. If it appears that any of the mental health descriptors apply to you, you are asked to attend a medical examination.

Medical scrutiny

'Medical scrutiny' merely involves a doctor from the MS (see p764) considering the answers you have given on your questionnaire and any other medical evidence that is held. If the MS doctor decides that your answers are consistent with the medical evidence and that you score sufficient points to be considered incapable of work, s/he can refer your case back to the decision maker without examining you. If the medical evidence cannot confirm your level of disability you are asked to attend a medical examination.

Medical examinations

If you have to attend a medical examination, an appointment is made for you to be examined by an MS doctor. The booking for the appointment may be made by telephone. Bear in mind the following:

- Keep the appointment if at all possible. If you fail to attend an examination without having good cause you are treated as capable of work (see p784).
- If you cannot attend the medical examination, you should immediately contact the MS to explain why and to ask for another appointment.
- If you are too ill to travel, you should ask to be examined at home. It is a good idea to confirm in writing any arrangements that you make by telephone.
- You can claim your travel expenses for going to the medical examination. If you have to attend by taxi or minicab (eg, because you are too ill to travel in any other way or there is no public transport available) the DWP will not pay your fares unless you get permission before you travel.
- You can take a friend or adviser to the medical examination with you.

In order to complete a report on your incapacity for work, the doctor asks you about your condition and assesses whether, in her/his opinion, you are incapable of work. S/he considers your degree of incapacity in each of the specific areas of activity set out in Appendix 4. The doctor is supposed to consider all the information and reach her/his own judgement on the basis of:

- your answers to the questions on the incapacity for work questionnaire (see p779);
- what you tell her/him;
- the results of the examination and any tests s/he may carry out;
- your appearance and behaviour during the assessment. This does not just mean during the examination itself. For example, when the doctor comes to greet you in the waiting area, s/he is also able to assess your ability to walk and to rise from a chair. S/he may watch how you manage to put on or take off your clothes during the examination and consider the length of time that you have been sitting without apparent discomfort. How you interact with the doctor is relevant to her/his opinion of your ability to communicate with other people.

The doctor asks about your 'typical' day and uses the information you give to assess your ability to perform activities relevant to the personal capability assessment. If you talk about doing your shopping the doctor may form an opinion on your ability to lift and carry, or if you discuss doing the cleaning this will be relevant to the doctor's assessment of your ability to bend and reach. For this reason, if it is painful for you to do such tasks, or you have to use special equipment, you should explain this to the doctor.

The MS doctor has to complete an incapacity report indicating which descriptors s/he thinks apply to you. The report is then returned to the decision maker dealing with your claim.

MS doctors are told to carry out mental health assessments when:

- you have a mild or moderate mental health problem;
- you are taking medication which impairs your cognitive function;
- you have an alcohol or drug dependency problem which significantly impairs your mental function;
- you have certain physical or sensory disabilities which impair your cognition and/or your mental function – eg, tinnitus;
- you have mild or moderate learning difficulties;
- a previously unidentified mild or moderate mental health problem is discovered during the assessment.

At the medical examination:

- Tell the MS doctor in as much detail as possible exactly what is wrong with you and how it affects you. If you do not do so, something important may be missed and if you have to appeal, the tribunal may be less willing to accept that you have symptoms which you did not mention to the doctor.
- Be sure to take with you the medicines and other aids which you are taking or using. This may lead the doctor to ask questions which s/he would not otherwise have thought of.
- If you suffer from pain and you anticipate that attending the examination will increase that pain, you may be tempted to take additional painkillers to see you through. If possible it is better not to do this as it may mask your true condition and not allow the doctor to see you as you are when you are on your normal dosage of medication. If you have to take additional painkillers you should explain this to the doctor, and you should explain what you can and cannot do when on your normal dosage of medication.[59]
- The place where you are examined is likely to be a very artificial environment and there is only limited time for the doctor's tests. This may affect the doctor's judgement of your abilities. For example, you may be able to bend once or twice on the doctor's request without pain but you know that if you bend for lengthy periods, or repeatedly, you suffer intense discomfort. If so, tell the doctor.
- Similarly, if you have good and bad days and the doctor is seeing you on a good day, be sure to explain how you are on a bad day.
- When asked about the activities you perform on a 'typical day' be sure to explain how your condition affects your ability to carry out day-to-day activities, such as going shopping, doing the chores, washing and dressing, sitting to watch the TV, etc.
- If you are not fluent in English, it is vital that someone with a good knowledge of English goes with you to see the doctor. Alternatively, the MS should be able to provide an interpreter if you request one.[60]

If, after you have seen the MS doctor, you are unhappy with the way the examination went, write down what the doctor said and did and what you are unhappy about before your memory fades. This may be helpful for your adviser if there has to be an appeal. If you feel you were treated unfairly or rudely at the examination, you can make a complaint (ask the MS for a copy of its leaflet on this).

Failing to attend a medical examination

You must be sent notice of the date and time of your medical examination at least seven days beforehand, unless you have agreed to receive less notice than this. If, after being given such notice you fail to attend, you are treated as capable of work unless you can show that you had 'good cause' for not attending.[61]

In deciding whether you have good cause the decision maker must consider all the circumstances including those detailed on p780. Good cause may also include having been too ill or distressed to be examined on that day, or wishing to be examined by a doctor of the same gender as you when none was available. You may also be able to show that you had good cause if your refusal to attend was based on a firm religious conviction.[62]

If you are treated as capable of work because you fail to attend the medical examination without good cause, your benefit is stopped. You should write to the DWP asking it to revise its decision (see p1189) explaining why you were unable to attend the examination. In case the decision maker does not accept that you had good cause you should also submit a fresh claim for benefit. If the decision maker does not accept that you had good cause you should consider appealing – see Chapter 44.

The decision maker's decision

The report prepared by the MS doctor on your incapacity for work is sent to the DWP decision maker. It is the decision maker, and not the MS doctor, who makes the decision on whether you are incapable of work.[63] The decision maker is free to disagree with the MS doctor, although this is rare.

The decision maker considers the information in the incapacity report from the MS doctor, the information you have given on your questionnaire, the information given by your doctor, and any other related evidence. Using this information s/he assesses your score under the personal capability assessment.

If you pass the personal capability assessment

If you are found to be incapable of work under the personal capability assessment, the DWP notifies you of this. You are informed that you do not need to send in further medical certificates from your doctor, but you may be asked to undergo a further personal capability assessment at a later date.

The MS doctor includes in her/his report a suggested date when your incapacity for work should be considered again. There are no detailed guidelines about when individuals should be reassessed.

If you fail the personal capability assessment

If you do not score enough points the decision maker considers whether you can be treated as incapable of work (see p778). If not, you are notified that the DWP considers that you are capable of work. The decision on your entitlement to IB, SDA or IS will be revised or superseded and your benefit will stop. However, your IS should not be stopped if you can still qualify for it for a reason other than your incapacity for work (see p294).

If you have previously passed the personal capability assessment and the DWP is now reassessing you, you should remember that IS, SDA and IB are normally awarded for an indefinite period.[64] If the award is indefinite the decision maker can only stop your benefit by carrying out a revision or supersession in the circumstances detailed on pp1190 and 1199.

If you think you are well enough to work

If you think that you are well enough to work but you do not have a job to return to you should either:

- sign on at your nearest JobCentre (or Jobcentre Plus office) and claim jobseeker's allowance (JSA) (see Chapter 15); *or*
- claim IS if you are entitled to it (see Chapter 13). If you do want to claim IS, you may also want to consider if your national insurance record will continue to be protected (see p837).

Remember the following:

- The rules on linking periods of incapacity for work (see p265) mean that if you try to go back to work but discover that your health does not permit it, you go straight back on to the same rate of IS, SDA or IB as you were previously getting, as long as you give up work within eight weeks and the DWP accepts that you are incapable of work again.
- For IB and SDA, that eight-week period is extended to two years in certain circumstances (see p265).
- You may be able to get your JSA or new IS claim backdated if your claim is delayed because there was a delay in notifying you of the decision to stop your IS or IB (see p1087). However, this is not automatic so you should claim as soon as possible.

If you do not think you are well enough to work

If you think that you are not well enough to work, you can challenge the decision maker's decision on your entitlement to benefit on the basis of your incapacity for work, either on revision or on appeal. You must act quickly because the time limits for requesting a revision or appealing against a decision are short (see pp1190 and 1184). You may also be able to claim IS or JSA while appealing. There are advantages and disadvantages with each option:

- If you ask the DWP decision maker to revise the decision, you are only likely to get the decision changed if you provide further evidence to support your argument that you are incapable of work, or if there has been an obvious mistake. See p1190 for details of requesting a revision.
- If you ask for a revision of the decision then, unless you qualify for IS for a reason other than your incapacity for work, you will not be able to get IS while waiting for a new decision to be made. If you are in any doubt about whether to ask for a revision, or to appeal, you should appeal.
- If you appeal against the decision, you may qualify for IS while waiting for the appeal to be heard (see p296).[65] Claiming IS while appealing means that you are not required to sign on as available for and actively seeking work.
- However, if you would only qualify for IS on the basis of incapacity for work, you are not entitled to IS again until you have actually appealed, and even then it is paid at a reduced rate. Your IS is reduced by 20 per cent of the personal allowance for a single claimant of your age (see p296 for the rule and p878 for the personal allowance). Your IS is not reduced if this is the first time that your incapacity for work has been tested, and on 12 April 1995 you had been off work sick for 28 weeks or were entitled to invalidity benefit or SDA.[66] So it is worth checking to see if you would be entitled to IS on any other ground (see Chapter 13). You do not have to send in medical certificates while waiting for your appeal to be heard.
- Unless you qualify for IS in the week immediately after the week in which you were found capable of work, you will need to make a fresh claim for IS, even if you had previously been getting it on the basis of incapacity for work.[67] As backdating of an IS claim is not automatic (see p1087) this could result in a gap in entitlement. For this reason, it is worth considering appealing and claiming IS on that basis straight away.
- Alternatively, you can appeal against the decision on your entitlement to benefit, and claim JSA. This does involve you having to be available for and actively seeking work (see Chapter 15). However, JSA is not paid at a reduced rate during the appeal, claiming it will not jeopardise your appeal, and it is one way of protecting your national insurance contribution record while you are waiting for your appeal to be heard. See p790 for more detail.
- If you want to claim on the basis of being incapable of work again, special rules apply if you claim again within six months of failing the personal capability assessment – see p773.

4. Appealing against a decision on your incapacity for work

Once a decision maker has determined that you are not incapable of work, the decision on your entitlement to benefit will be revised or superseded and your benefit will normally stop. If you consider that you are incapable of work you should seek advice (see Appendix 2) about appealing against the decision on your benefit entitlement to an appeal tribunal. See Chapter 44 for detailed advice about appealing.

The decision on your incapacity for work

A *determination* that you are not incapable of work is not, in itself, a decision that is subject to appeal.[68] However, determinations on incapacity for work should then be incorporated into a decision on benefit or national insurance (NI) credit entitlement, and you can challenge the determination on your capacity for work by appealing against that decision. If you are claiming income support (IS) on the basis of incapacity for work, you will usually be issued two separate decisions once you have been found capable of work. One will state that you are not entitled to NI credits for the relevant period. The other will state that you are not entitled to IS for the same period. It is important to appeal against the first (usually the credits) decision because an incapacity determination for one benefit is binding on other benefits relating to the same period.[69]

Other things to do when you appeal

Consider seeking advice (see Appendix 2). You should immediately request a copy of the medical evidence that the Department for Work and Pensions (DWP) holds on your file, including a copy of the Medical Service (MS) doctor's incapacity report. Local DWP offices have been advised that they must provide a copy of the MS doctor's report as soon as possible after it has been requested. If you appeal, a copy of the MS doctor's incapacity report should be included in the appeal papers the DWP sends to you and the tribunal service.

Go and see your own doctor to discuss your capacity for work. In practice, it can be very difficult to win an appeal if you cannot get your GP or consultant to support you. If you have to wait for an appointment with your doctor, and the time limit for appeal is approaching, appeal anyway. You can always withdraw your appeal later if you choose to. If your GP and consultant agree with the decision maker, you should seriously consider your position, as your chance of winning the appeal is not good. But remember that, if you are successful, claiming benefit on the basis of incapacity for work is usually more advantageous to you than claiming alternative benefits.

Remember that there are only certain circumstances in which you can work and still be regarded as incapable of work (see p765). So, if you work while you are appealing, you may lose entitlement to benefit even if you actually win your appeal.

The appeal

The appeal tribunal

When one of the issues which is to be considered by an appeal tribunal is whether or not you are incapable of work under the personal capability assessment, the tribunal must be made up of at least one legally qualified person and one medically qualified person.[70]

The question for the tribunal is usually whether you score enough points to be assessed as incapable of work. If relevant, however, it should also consider if you should be exempt from the personal capability assessment or if you should be treated as incapable of work because one of the exceptional circumstances applies.

The tribunal can only take into account your circumstances at the time of the decision that you are appealing against.[71] It is not restricted, however, to considering only the evidence that the decision maker considered.[72] Any fresh evidence which you can provide that supports your appeal may increase your chances of success, but you should try to ensure that your evidence is about your incapacity at the time of the decision under appeal. If you previously satisfied the personal capability assessment and you have stated that your condition and capabilities remain unchanged, or you have a variable condition, the tribunal should usually consider all the details and evidence relating to your previous assessment.[73]

The tribunal can only consider your circumstances at the date of the decision maker's decision. Any deterioration in your condition which occurs after that date cannot be taken into account. You should make a fresh claim for benefit on the basis of your incapacity for work each time your condition deteriorates and appeal if these claims are rejected. Doing so will ensure that you do not lose out if the tribunal decides that the original decision that you were capable of work was correct, but that following a subsequent deterioration in your condition you are incapable of work. See p773 for details of how any fresh claim will be dealt with.

The tribunal does not have to consider any issue that is not raised by your appeal (see p1236).[74] It is, therefore, important to include details of your condition and all of the descriptors that you think apply to you when you appeal.

Appeal tribunal tactics

- It is best to request an oral hearing of your appeal as this will give the tribunal the opportunity of hearing from you first-hand about how your condition affects you.
- The tribunal has to decide the case at least partially on its own assessment of you, although they do not conduct a medical. Therefore, your appearance and

behaviour are important. The tribunal may need to be convinced that you are not exaggerating your situation.

- Although not formally required, it is often important that you get medical evidence to support your appeal. This could be from your GP or your consultant if you have one, or from both of them. You should consider which descriptors you think apply to you and ask your doctor to refer in her/his letter to your ability in relation to these descriptors, making the letter as detailed as possible. If your doctor has been treating you on a regular basis for many years, then s/he should say so specifically, so that there can be no doubt that s/he is fully aware of your medical history.
- If you are getting IS or income-based jobseeker's allowance (JSA), or if your income is very low, and you are being advised by a solicitor, legal advice centre or law centre, it may be possible to get payment for a medical report through the legal help scheme (see Appendix 2).
- If you have not been able to obtain a medical report in any other way, you can ask the chair of the tribunal to obtain one. This is a discretionary decision for the tribunal. You are not charged, but you do not have any control over who does the medical, and the report is the tribunal's rather than yours.[75] The chair cannot obtain a medical report in advance of the hearing, so there will have to be an adjournment if the tribunal agrees. Tribunals have been reminded by the commissioners of their power to obtain reports where claimants cannot afford them,[76] but you should not rely on them doing so, and they do not normally do so if your GP and the MS doctor agree on the diagnosis and disagree only on the effect of your condition on your capacity to work.
- When your appeal concerns your incapacity for work the tribunal cannot carry out its own examination of you.[77] However, it may observe your conduct in the tribunal room – eg, how you walk, sit, etc.
- There is no rule that says the decision maker or appeal tribunal has to agree with the MS report if this conflicts with what you, your GP or consultant says. On the contrary, the decision maker or tribunal should make a reasoned decision based on all the evidence – medical and non-medical. If necessary, point out that the tribunal is at liberty to prefer your own or your doctor's evidence to that of the MS doctor.[78]
- Similarly, your own view or the view of a relative, friend or colleague who has observed you trying to perform the activities on a daily basis may be just as informative as a doctor's. If there is a dispute, the tribunal has to decide whose evidence it accepts.
- It is often useful for a person who lives with you or who knows you well to attend the hearing to describe to the tribunal the day-to-day problems you have.

- You should bring a list of any medication you are taking to the tribunal hearing.

For more about tribunal hearings, see p1235.

Protecting your income and national insurance credits while waiting for an appeal

Incapacity benefit (IB) and severe disablement allowance (SDA) are not paid while your appeal is waiting to be heard. If you have appealed you can still qualify for IS but it may be paid at a reduced rate (see p296). You may qualify for either IS or JSA (see Chapters 13 and 15) while waiting for your appeal to be decided and you will need to consider which benefit you would be better off claiming. Remember:

- Claiming JSA may be preferable as your JSA is not reduced and a successful claim for JSA means that you receive Class 1 NI credits (see p837) while your appeal is waiting to be heard, whatever the outcome.
- If you only claim IS (except in the rare case that you qualify for credits on some other basis) you do not have to sign on as available for and actively seeking work. You get NI credits for the period if you eventually win your appeal, but not if you lose. IS may be reduced while you are waiting for your appeal to be heard (see p296). A complete NI contribution record may be important to ensure that you get the maximum pension when you retire and to protect your spouse's entitlement to bereavement benefits should you die.

To be eligible for JSA you have to be capable of work (see p352).[79] Although, logically, it may seem that you would not qualify for JSA as you are saying in your appeal that you are incapable of work, the decision maker's decision on capacity for work is binding on the JobCentre (or Jobcentre Plus office).[80] This also applies if you later win your appeal and are found to be incapable of work. Your claim for JSA should not influence the decision on your appeal about your incapacity for work. However, remember that there are only certain circumstances in which you can actually work and still be regarded as incapable of work (see p765). So, if you work while you are appealing, you may lose entitlement to benefit even if you actually win your appeal.

To get JSA you must convince the decision maker at the JobCentre (or Jobcentre Plus office) that you are available for and actively seeking work (see pp354 and 365). To qualify for JSA you will need to be prepared to accept any reasonable work within your limitations. You will not qualify if you say that you are really too sick to work but have been told you have to sign on. You can place restrictions on your availability for work if these are reasonable in the light of your physical or mental condition without you having to show that you have a reasonable prospect of obtaining work (see p361). In deciding if you are actively seeking work your physical or mental condition should be taken into account (see p366).

As the decision on your incapacity for work is binding on the JobCentre/Jobcentre Plus office, if you later win your appeal on your incapacity for work it will mean that the decision on your entitlement to JSA should be revised or superseded and you will not qualify for JSA. If the amount of IS, IB or SDA you would have been entitled to would have been more than the JSA you received, you should qualify for arrears amounting to the difference.

The following points are also relevant:

- The contribution conditions for contribution-based JSA are stricter than for IB. You are not necessarily entitled to the former just because you were getting the latter.
- You may not be entitled to IS (or income-based JSA) if you do not pass the means test (eg, if you have savings or other income) or if, for example, you have a partner who works for 24 or more hours a week. If so, you may have no alternative but to claim contribution-based JSA.

If your condition worsens

If your condition has significantly worsened since the decision maker's decision, or you have a specific disease or disability which was not considered by the decision maker, you should make a fresh claim for IS or IB based on your incapacity for work. In such situations you should be assessed under the personal capability assessment again and should be treated as incapable of work until such an assessment is carried out (see p773).

Notes

1 ss171A(1) and 171G(1) SSCBA 1992
2 s17 SSA 1998; reg 10 SS&CS(DA) Regs
3 Sch 1 para 2 JSA 1995

1. **Incapacity for work**

4 s171D SSCBA 1992; reg 16 SS(IFW) Regs
5 Regs 13(2) and 16(3) SS(IFW) Regs
6 CIB/5298/1997
7 CS/5/1954
8 ss171D and 171F SSCBA 1992; regs 10A, 16 and 17 SS(IFW) Regs
9 Reg 2(1) SS(IFW) Regs
10 Reg 2(1) SS(IFW) Regs
11 Reg 17 SS(IFW) Regs
12 2004 Pre-Budget Report, para 4.26
13 Reg 17(2)(b) and (3) SS(IFW) Regs
14 Reg 17(3) SS(IFW) Regs
15 CIB/1723/2000
16 s171D SSCBA 1992; regs 11-14 SS(IFW) Regs
17 Reg 14(a) SS(IFW) Regs
18 Reg 14(b) SS(IFW) Regs
19 Reg 13A(4) SS(IFW) Regs
20 Reg 13A(4) SS(IFW) Regs

2. **The own occupation test**

21 s171B(2) SSCBA 1992
22 CS/57/1982
23 CS/221/1949
24 s171B(1) SSCBA 1992; reg 4(1) SS(IFW) Regs

Notes

25 s171B(3) and (4) SSCBA 1992
26 House of Commons *Hansard*, Written Answers 22 July 2002, col 1566W
27 Regs 2 and 5 SS(ME) Regs
28 Reg 6(1)(c) SS(IFW) Regs

3. The personal capability assessment

29 s171C(2)(a) SSCBA 1992; reg 24 SS(IFW) Regs
30 s171C(3) SSCBA 1992; reg 28 SS(IFW) Regs
31 CIB/3106/2003
32 Reg 6 SS(IFW) Regs
33 Reg 31(3), (4) and (5) SS(IB)(T) Regs; reg 10 SS(IFW) Regs
34 Reg 2(1) SS(IFW) Regs
35 Reg 25(1) SS(IFW) Regs
36 Reg 26(4) SS(IFW) Regs
37 Reg 26(2) SS(IFW) Regs; CIB/14516/1996
38 Reg 25(3)(a) SS(IFW) Regs; CIB/1446/1996
39 Reg 25(3)(b) SS(IFW) Regs
40 CIB/5435/2002
41 Reg 25(2) SS(IFW) Regs
42 CIB/15231/1996
43 CIB/14534/1996
44 CIB/14534/1996
45 CIB/2620/2000
46 CIB/14587/1996; CIB/14722/1996; CIB/13161/1996; CIB/13508/1996
47 CIB/14722/1996
48 CIB/14587/1996
49 CSIB/12/1996
50 Reg 27 SS(IFW) Regs
51 *Howker v Secretary of State for Work and Pensions and the Social Security Advisory Committee* 8 November 2002 (CA), reported as R(IB) 3/03
52 CIB/26/2004; CSIB/33/2004
53 CIB/15325/1996
54 Reg 7 SS(IFW) Regs
55 Reg 9 SS(IFW) Regs
56 Reg 6(2) and (3)(b) SS(IFW) Regs
57 para 13232 DMG
58 CSIB/17/1996
59 CIS/16182/1996
60 www.dwp.gov.uk/medical/ibh/ibh.pdf – para 4.1.2
61 Reg 8 SS(IFW) Regs
62 R(S) 9/51
63 Reg 11 SS&CS(DA) Regs
64 Reg 17 SS(C&P) Regs; R(S) 1/92
65 Reg 4ZA and Sch IB para 24 IS Regs
66 Reg 22A(3) IS Regs
67 Reg 4ZA IS Regs

4. Appealing against a decision on your incapacity for work

68 CIB/2338/2000
69 CIB/2338/2000
70 s7 SSA 1998; reg 36(2)(a)(i) SS&CS(DA) Regs
71 s12(8) SSA 1998
72 CSIB/9/1996
73 CIB/1972/2000; CIB/2338/2000; CIB/3179/2000; CIB/3985/2001
74 s12(8) SSA 1998
75 s20 SSA 1998; reg 41 SS&CS(DA) Regs; R(S) 3/84
76 R(S) 1/88
77 s20 SSA 1998; reg 52 SS&CS(DA) Regs
78 CIB/407/1998; CIB/1149/1998; R(M) 1/93; CIB/3074/2003
79 s1 JSA 1995
80 Reg 10 SS&CS(DA) Regs; Sch 1 para 2 JSA 1995

Chapter 31

Claiming for others: non-means-tested benefits

This chapter explains who can be included in your non-means-tested benefit claim. It covers:

1. Increases for your adult dependant

Under current rules, if you are receiving a non-means-tested benefit it may be possible to claim an increase only for a dependent 'spouse' or for an adult who looks after your child, but not for both. However, the Government is also to include 'civil partners' as adult dependants for whom you can claim an increase.[1] (This will be relevant to you if you have a partner of the same sex who is registered as your civil partner.) At the time of writing the change was expected to take effect on 5 December 2005. See CPAG's *Welfare Rights Bulletin* for updates and further details.

Increases for adult dependants can be included in the following benefits:

- incapacity benefit (IB) paid at the long-term or short-term rate (see Chapter 12);
- severe disablement allowance (SDA) (see Chapter 20);
- carer's allowance (CA) (see Chapter 4);
- Category A or C retirement pensions (see Chapter 19);
- maternity allowance (MA) (see Chapter 17).

However, whether or not you can get an increase for an adult is determined by which of these benefits you are receiving.

Note: if you make a claim for an adult dependant who is your partner, and your benefit would be increased because of that, your partner may be required to attend a work-focused interview as a condition of you getting the full amount of benefit. See p1094 for details.

You can choose not to claim an increase in your non-means-tested benefit for a dependant but if you are entitled to an increase and are also receiving a means-tested benefit, see p806.

You *cannot* get an increase for an adult dependant in the following benefits:

- statutory sick pay;
- statutory maternity pay;
- statutory paternity pay;
- statutory adoption pay;
- bereavement allowance;
- widow's pension;
- widowed parent's allowance;
- widowed mother's allowance;
- disability living allowance;
- attendance allowance;
- contribution-based jobseeker's allowance;
- Category B retirement pension (see p487);
- industrial injuries benefits (unless you are receiving a disablement pension which includes unemployability supplement, a benefit which you only get if you qualified for it before 26 April 1987).

Increase for your spouse

Your '**spouse**' is your husband or wife. You may be entitled to an increase for your spouse if her/his earnings are not too high (see p797). An increase can be paid even if your spouse is not living with you, as long as you are contributing to her/his maintenance. (See p31 for details of who can be recognised as married for these purposes, and p801 if your marriage is polygamous.)

You cannot qualify for an increase in your benefit for your spouse if you are receiving an increase for an adult who cares for your child (see p795).

Who can claim

You qualify for extra money for your wife or husband if:[2]

- you make a separate claim for the increase (see p802);[3] *and*
- your spouse's earnings, or the payments s/he receives from an occupational or personal pension, are not too high (see p797 for details of this earnings rule); *and*
- you are not getting an increase for a dependent adult who is looking after your child (see p795); *and either*
  - you are residing with your spouse (see p800); *or*
  - you are 'contributing to the maintenance' of your spouse (see p800) at a weekly rate of at least the amount of the increase (see p798).

Additional conditions for specific benefits

You will only qualify for an increase in your **IB** or **SDA** for your wife or husband if, in addition to the above conditions, *either*:

- your spouse is 60 or over; *or*
- your spouse is under 60, and you are 'residing with' (and not merely 'contributing to the maintenance' of) her/him and entitled to child benefit.[4] See p800 for the meaning of 'residing with'.

If you are getting **CA** you must reside with (see p800) your spouse to get the increase. You cannot qualify just by contributing to her/his maintenance.[5]

If you are a woman and you are entitled to a **Category A retirement pension** you can only get an increase for your husband if, in addition to the general conditions of entitlement detailed above:

- immediately before you became entitled to the Category A retirement pension you were entitled to IB, including an increase for an adult dependant; *and*
- since then you have not stopped residing with (see p800) your husband or stopped contributing to his maintenance at a rate at least equal to the rate of the increase and your husband's earnings have not been higher than the rate of the increase.[6]

This rule discriminates directly against women, but the discrimination is not unlawful because it falls within an exception to the Equal Treatment Directive (see Chapter 46).[7]

You may not be entitled to an increase for your spouse if your husband or wife is claiming an earnings-replacement benefit (see p1102) in her/his own right. This is a frequent source of overpayment and it is very important that when you complete the claim form you give full details of any benefits that your spouse is receiving.

See p798 for the amount of the increase you receive for your spouse.

Increase for someone who cares for a child

If you are not claiming an increase in your benefit for your spouse you may get an increase for an adult dependant who is looking after a child for whom you are responsible.

Most people who benefit under these rules are unmarried partners living together as husband and wife, where one partner stays at home to look after the child.

But other people can benefit as well. For example, same sex (gay or lesbian) couples may be entitled, as may two people with children who live together for mutual support. You may even get an increase for someone you employ to care for your child.

Who can claim

You qualify for extra money for an adult dependant (who is not your spouse) if:[8]

- you make a separate claim for the increase (see p802);[9] *and*
- your dependant's earnings, or any payments s/he receives from an occupational or personal pension, are not too high (see p797 for details of this earnings rule); *and*
- your dependant has care of a child;

and either:

- if you are claiming an increase to **CA**, **MA** or **retirement pension**, you are entitled to child benefit (or you are treated as entitled to child benefit) for that child (see p799). In some circumstances, even if you are receiving child benefit you will be treated as if you are not (see p799); *or*
- if you are claiming **IB** or **SDA** you are entitled to an increase in that benefit for the child (or you are treated as entitled to such an increase) (see p795);

and either:

- you reside with your dependant (see p800); *or*
- you contribute to the maintenance (see p800) of your dependant at a rate equal to at least the rate of the increase; *or*
- you employ your dependant at a cost to you of at least the standard rate of the increase and the employment started before you became unemployed, incapable of work or retired (whichever applies to you) unless the need for you to employ your dependant arose afterwards; *and*
- you do not also get an increase for your husband or wife; *and*
- your dependant is not absent from Great Britain (GB), unless s/he is residing with you outside GB and you still qualify for benefit.

If you are getting **CA** you must reside with (see p800) your dependant to get the increase. You cannot qualify just by contributing to her/his maintenance or employing her/him.[10]

If you are a man whose wife is entitled to a **Category B or C retirement pension** on the basis of your national insurance contribution record, you are not entitled to an increase in your Category A or C retirement pension for an adult dependant who is caring for a child.[11]

As for increases for dependent wives and husbands, there is an earnings rule (see p797) which means that you may not qualify for the increase if your dependant has earnings or payments from an occupational or personal pension.

You may not be entitled to the increase if your dependant is claiming an earnings-replacement benefit (see p1102) in her/his own right. This is a frequent source of overpayment and it is very important that you give full details of any benefits received by your dependant when you complete the claim form.

The earnings rules

You are not entitled to an increase in your benefit for a spouse or for a dependent adult who cares for your child if her/his earnings are too high (but see below if you employ your dependant).

If you are claiming an increase in your **IB** for your spouse or adult dependant and s/he is treated as incapable of work while doing 'approved work' (see p768), then any payment made to her/him for this work will be ignored.[12]

Otherwise, if you are residing with (see p800) an adult dependant and are claiming an increase in **long-term IB**, **SDA** or **Category A or C retirement pension**, your increase is not paid if, in the previous week, your dependant earned more than £56.20.[13]

This limit does not apply if you have been continuously entitled to an increase in the same benefit[14] since 14 September 1985. For further details see p209 of the 17th edition of CPAG's *Rights Guide to Non-Means-Tested Benefits*.

In any other case (ie, if you are not residing with your dependant or if you are claiming an increase in any other non-means-tested benefit), your increase is not paid if your dependant's earnings in the previous week were more than the standard rate of the increase which you have claimed.[15]

Earnings include any payments received from an occupational or personal pension scheme (see p948).[16]

If you are claiming an increase for an adult dependant who is not your spouse but is looking after a child (see p795), your dependant's earnings do not affect your entitlement to an increase if s/he is employed by you but is not residing with you. If s/he is residing with you (see p800) and you are employing her/him to care for a child, the wages that you pay to her/him for this work are ignored.[17]

Because the earnings rule is more generous for long-term than for short-term IB, you may not be entitled to an increase during the first year of your entitlement to IB but qualify after you transfer to long-term IB. It is then necessary to make a separate claim for the increase.

For how earnings are calculated, see p937.

If your dependant's earnings fluctuate, you do not automatically lose your entitlement to the increase every time s/he earns too much in a particular week (although you have no right to be paid the increase during the following week if that happens).[18] This means that you do not have to make a fresh claim every time your dependant's earnings exceed the limit (although you do have to keep the Department for Work and Pensions informed of any such changes). It also means that if you were claiming on 14 September 1985 you can continue to benefit from the more generous earnings rules that were in force before that date, despite fluctuations in your dependant's earnings.

Amount of increase for an adult dependant

Increases for spouses and adult dependants who are caring for a child are paid as follows:[19]

	£pw
Short-term IB (claimant not over pension age)	35.65
Short-term IB (claimant over pension age)	43.95
Long-term IB	45.70
SDA	27.50
MA	35.65
CA	27.30
Category A retirement pension	49.15

If you are over pension age, an increase in your retirement pension or short-term IB may be reduced if your contribution record is incomplete (see p847).[20]

2. Increases for child dependants

You cannot now make a new claim for an increase for a child dependant. These increases have been replaced by child tax credit.

However, you will remain entitled to an increase for a child dependant if you were entitled to one on 5 April 2003 (or claimed an increase after 6 April 2003 and your entitlement was backdated to include 5 April).

You will lose this transitional protection if:

- your entitlement to an increase for a child dependant ceases; *or*
- your increase stops being paid for 58 days or more. If the benefit you are paid the increase with is terminated, your increase will also stop. However, you keep your transitional protection as long as the benefit is awarded to you again and you reclaim the increase within three months of the date the benefit is re-awarded on revision, supersession or appeal.[21]

Earnings limit[22]

If you are living with your spouse or you are living with someone as husband and wife, your partner's earnings affect your entitlement to an increase for a child. You do not get an increase for your first child for any week if in the previous week your partner earned £170 or more. After that you lose entitlement for another child for each complete £22 a week your partner earns in addition to £170.

Amount of increase for a child dependant

The basic rate of the increase is £11.35 for each child.[23] However, if you are in receipt of child benefit at the only or eldest child rate for the same child, the £11.35 is reduced to £9.40, or to £8.85 if you get the lone parent rate of child benefit for the child.

For all other rules on increases for child dependants see pp746–48 of CPAG's *Welfare Benefits Handbook* 2002/2003.

---

3. Definition of terms

The following definitions apply for the purposes of entitlement to increases for adult dependants.

Who counts as a child

The rules are the same as for child benefit (see p86).

Treated as entitled to child benefit

In order to qualify for an increase for an adult who is not your spouse but is caring for a child, you must either be entitled to child benefit or be treated as entitled to child benefit for that child.

If you do not receive child benefit for a child yourself, you are still treated as doing so if:[24]

- you are residing with your husband or wife and s/he is entitled to child benefit for the child;[25] *or*
- you are residing with (see below) a parent of the child who is receiving child benefit for the child and the child is living with you; *and either*
  - you are also a parent of the child; *or*
  - you are 'wholly or mainly maintaining' the child; *or*
- you or your spouse, if you are residing with your spouse (see p800), would have been entitled to child benefit for that child had s/he been born at the end of the week before the week in which s/he was born.[26] (As child benefit is normally only paid from the Monday after you become entitled to it, this rule ensures that you do not have to wait a further week to qualify for an increase in a weekly non-means-tested benefit); *or*
- you are in Great Britain and would have been entitled to child benefit if you (or your spouse if you are residing with your spouse – see p800) had not been receiving a family benefit from another country.[27]

Treated as not entitled to child benefit

Even if you are getting child benefit for a child, you are treated as if you are not if you are not the child's parent and:[28]

- the child lives with one of her/his parents and is not living with you; *or*
- the child lives with you and one of her/his parents, but you are not 'wholly or mainly maintaining' the child.

In these circumstances you will not qualify for an increase for an adult dependant if you are claiming this on the grounds that s/he is caring for the child.

Residence and maintenance

'Residing with'

The term **'residing with'** should be given its ordinary meaning. You and your husband, wife or other adult dependant will normally be considered to be residing with each other if you share a home. The arrangement has to have some degree of permanence so you should not be considered to be residing with someone who has come to stay with you for a short while.

Temporary absences do not stop two people from being treated as residing with each other.[29] For the purpose of qualifying for an increase for an adult dependant, you are treated as residing with your husband or wife when either or both of you are in hospital, even if the stay in hospital is likely to be permanent.[30]

'Residing with' does not mean the same as 'living with' (see p801) and the rules on whether a couple are residing with each other for the purposes of dependency increases are not the same as for child benefit (see p93).

'Contributing to the maintenance'

If you are not residing with an adult dependant you may still qualify for a dependant's increase for her/him if you are contributing to her/his maintenance at a weekly rate of at least the amount of the increase.

You only qualify for an increase for an adult dependant on this basis if:[31]

- when you were employed, or not incapable of work (see p764), or not a pensioner (whichever applies to you) you were making contributions at this rate, unless the adult only became your dependant later. If you are claiming incapacity benefit (IB), and within a month of you becoming entitled to the increase for an adult dependant the rate of that increase changes (because you reach pension age or start to receive long-term IB), you are treated as satisfying this condition if you were contributing at least the level of the initial increase; *and*
- if the increase is payable at a reduced rate (eg, because of insufficient national insurance contributions – see p847), you continue to contribute at least the amount of the increase which is paid.

'Contributing to the maintenance' means that you are making payments to or on behalf of a person. A weekly payment covers you for the week after it is made, and a monthly payment for the following month etc.[32] Payments may be in kind, so money spent on clothing or an outing for a child, for example, can be counted.[33]

If you make payments for a spouse and one or more children, the total payment is allocated between those dependants in the way that is most advantageous to you (even if you pay under a court order which specifies the amounts in respect of each person).[34] However, a contribution for a spouse can only be treated as a contribution for a child and vice versa if your spouse is entitled to child benefit for that child. If the payment includes an element of arrears the amount for arrears is ignored.[35]

If you have stopped maintaining a person, you cannot later cover yourself by making a payment in arrears.[36] However, a broad view is taken of an interruption in otherwise regular payments.[37] If you are not paying enough, but think you are, a payment of arrears may be taken into account.[38]

You are treated as though you are making the required contributions if you give a written undertaking to make the contributions as soon as the increase is paid. If on receiving the increase you do not make the contributions, the decision to award the increase can be revised.[39]

Note: the conditions of entitlement for the increases mean that it is never necessary to prove that you are contributing to the maintenance of an adult dependant if you are residing with her/him.

'Living with'

'Living with' has the same meaning as it does in relation to child benefit claims (see p90).

4. Special rules for special groups

There are some groups of claimants to whom special rules apply. These are covered below and in Chapters 25, 26 and 28. Special rules apply to:

- people who are in hospital or whose dependants are in hospital (see p715);
- people who are in prison or detention, or whose dependants are in prison or detention (see p729);
- adult dependants involved in trade disputes (see p735);
- people whose marriage is polygamous (see below).

However, it is important to note that your increase may not be affected in the same way as your basic benefit.

Polygamous marriage

You will only qualify for an increase in your non-means-tested benefit for your spouse if you are recognised as having a valid marriage under UK law (see p31 for a discussion of who can be recognised as married). You will not normally be treated as having a valid marriage unless your marriage is a monogamous one.[40] This means if your marriage is polygamous (ie, if you have more than one spouse or your husband or wife has more than one spouse) you will not generally be entitled to an increase in your benefit for your spouse.[41] However, if your marriage was formerly polygamous and currently is not (ie, if either you or your husband or wife have had other spouses in the past but all such spouses have now died or been divorced) you can qualify for an increase.

It is important to remember that even if your marriage is polygamous the law may not consider it to be so (see p32). You should, therefore, seek advice about your entitlement to an increase for your spouse if you are in this situation.

Even if you do not qualify for an increase in your non-means-tested benefit for your spouse because your marriage is polygamous, you may still qualify for an increase for her/him if s/he is caring for a child – see p795.

5. Claims, backdating and getting paid

You must make a claim for an increase for a dependant[42] – a claim for basic benefit is not counted as a claim for an increase in that benefit. The rules are described in brief below. This section should be read in conjunction with Chapter 40, which explains the rules in more detail.

Making a claim

A claim for an increase should be made on the appropriate claim form, although the Department for Work and Pensions (DWP) decision maker may accept a written application which is not on the appropriate form if it is sufficient in the circumstances (see p1079).[43]

Note: if you make a claim for an adult dependant who is your partner, and your benefit would be increased because of that, your partner may be required to attend a work-focused interview as a condition of you getting the full amount of benefit. See p1094 for details.

Claim forms for the relevant benefits contain claims for increases to those benefits for dependants.

Information to support your claim

If you are claiming an increase in your non-means-tested benefit for an adult dependant you will normally be asked to supply her/his national insurance (NI) number.[44] This requirement is called the NI number requirement – see p1083.

When you claim an increase in your non-means-tested benefit for a dependant you may be asked to supply 'certificates, documents, information and evidence' considered relevant to your claim.[45] This may include information about your adult dependant's earnings, for example.

If you are asked to provide evidence or documents which you do not have, ask what other evidence would be acceptable. Ask the DWP to explain what is required and why, and complain if you feel any requests for information are unreasonable.

See p1082 for further details of evidence that may be required to support your claim.

Who should claim

You must normally claim benefit (including increases for dependants) on your own behalf. However, if your benefit is being claimed by another adult on your behalf because you are not able to act for yourself (called your 'appointee'), the increase in that benefit should also be claimed by your appointee (see p1075 for further details).

The date of your claim

The date of your claim for an increase in your non-means-tested benefit for a dependant is normally the date it is received at the DWP office.[46] A claim can be counted as having been received at the DWP office even on a day when the office is closed if that is the day it would have normally been delivered.[47] If you posted your claim it should be accepted as having been delivered unless it is proved not to have been.[48] However, in these circumstances you would have to convince the DWP that the claim was posted.

If the claim you submit is incomplete or not on the correct form you may be asked to provide further information or to complete the correct form. As long as this additional information or form is returned within a month of it being sent back to you (or longer if the decision maker thinks that the delay is reasonable), your claim is treated as being made on the date the initial claim was received at the DWP office.[49]

If you reclaim carer's allowance (CA) after a qualifying benefit was awarded to the person you care for in the circumstances described on p78, your claim for an increase in CA can also be treated as having been made on the date you first claimed the increase or the date from which the qualifying benefit was awarded, if that was later.[50]

Remember that you can only qualify for an increase in your benefit for a dependant if you are entitled to the benefit concerned.

It may be possible to claim in advance or your date of claim may be backdated (see p804).

If you claim the wrong benefit

If you make a claim for an increase of severe disablement allowance this may be treated as a claim for an increase of incapacity benefit instead, and vice versa.

If someone has claimed benefit for her/himself (other than a claim for child benefit) and is not entitled to it, but you are entitled to an increase in your non-means-tested benefit for that person, her/his claim can be treated as a claim for an increase in your benefit.[51]

When someone else has claimed an increase in a benefit for an adult dependant but is not entitled to it, that claim may be treated as a claim for an increase in your non-means-tested benefit for the same adult.[52]

If a claim for another benefit is treated as a claim for an increase in your benefit for an adult dependant, this may allow you to backdate your claim for the increase for more than the usual three months (see below). If you satisfy the qualifying conditions for the increase and for the benefit to which the increase applies you can get the increase backdated for up to three months before the date of the claim for the other benefit.

See p1084 for more details on interchanging claims in this way.

Claiming in advance

You can claim an increase in your **retirement pension** up to four months before you expect to qualify for it.[53]

You can claim an increase in your **maternity allowance** (MA) for an adult dependant up to 14 weeks before your expected week of childbirth (see p464 for the meaning of this term) but only if you would have qualified for the increase at the time you make the claim, had MA been in payment.[54]

You can claim an increase for a dependant in any **other non-means-tested benefit** up to three months before you expect to qualify for it.[55]

It is helpful to claim in advance if you can, as it will give the DWP time to gather the information that it may need, and to decide your claim in good time.

Backdating your claim

Claims for dependants' increases can be backdated for up to three months from the date you make your claim if you satisfy the conditions of entitlement to the benefit and to the dependant's increase over that period.[56] You do not have to show reasons why your claim was late to qualify for backdated benefit.

If you might have qualified for an increase in your benefit for a dependant earlier but did not claim because you were given the wrong information or were misled by the DWP you could:

- ask for an ex gratia payment (see p1304); *or*
- complain to the Ombudsman via your MP (see p1302).

See p804 for details of whether you can be treated as having claimed an increase in your benefit for a dependant on the basis of your (or someone else's) claim for another benefit.

See p803 if you have previously claimed CA but your earlier claim was refused.

See p1085 for more details about the backdating of claims.

Getting paid

If you are claiming an increase in your non-means-tested benefit for your dependants, that increase is included in the payments of the benefit concerned, and is paid in the same way and on the same day as that benefit. See the relevant benefit chapters for details.

Change of circumstances

It is your duty to report any change in your circumstances which might affect your right to, or the amount of, your benefit, including your right to increases for your dependants.[57] You should, for example, inform the DWP of a change in your adult dependant's earnings.

You should do this promptly in writing or by telephone to the office handling your claim (although in individual cases notification might be accepted in a form other than in writing or by telephone). In some cases, however, the decision maker might say that you must report changes in writing. In any case, you might want to report the change in writing and keep a copy, in case of a dispute in the future. If you do not promptly report any change which you are required to notify, any resulting overpayment may be recoverable from you (see Chapter 41). If you are considered deliberately to have acted falsely or dishonestly, you may also be guilty of an offence (see Chapter 42).

6. Tax, tax credits and other benefits

Increases of retirement pensions, carer's allowance and incapacity benefit (IB), apart from the lower rate of short-term IB and transitional IB (see p279) for adult dependants, are taxable.[58] Other increases are not.

Tax credits

For the rules on how entitlement to child tax credit and working tax credit may affect your entitlement to free school meals for your children, community care grants or budgeting loans from the social fund, free milk and vitamins if you are pregnant or have a child under five, and maternity and funeral expenses payments from the social fund, see Chapters 49 and 50. For the 'notional income' rules for tax credits see Chapter 53.

Means-tested benefits

If you have a low income you may also be entitled to means-tested benefits such as income support (IS – Chapter 13), housing benefit (HB – Chapter 10), council tax benefit (CTB – Chapter 6), income-based jobseeker's allowance (JSA – Chapter 15) or pension credit (PC – Chapter 18).

Your entitlement to means-tested benefits will include benefit for your partner and, apart from PC and depending on which of the other benefits you are claiming, may include any dependent children who are members of your household (see Chapter 32). This is your family for the purpose of means-tested benefits. The increases you receive to your non-means-tested benefit may be for dependants who are not part of this family. If so, any increase in your non-means-tested benefit for a dependant who is not part of your family will be ignored when calculating your entitlement to means-tested benefits. However, any increase in your non-means-tested benefit for a member of your family will be treated as income for means-tested benefits (see p968), although some of your widowed parent's allowance can be ignored when calculating your entitlement to IS, income-based JSA, PC, HB and CTB (see p970).

If you are receiving a means-tested benefit you may not be better off by claiming an increase in your non-means-tested benefit for an adult dependant. If the increase is for a member of your family it will affect the amount of means-tested benefit you receive and may mean that your income is too high for you to qualify for that means-tested benefit. If you then lose your entitlement to IS, income-based JSA or PC you may also lose your entitlement to free school meals for your children, community care grants or budgeting loans from the social fund, and free milk and vitamins if you are pregnant or have a child under five. Your entitlement to HB and CTB may also be reduced. In addition, if you no longer qualify for IS, income-based JSA, PC, HB or CTB you will not qualify for maternity and funeral expenses payments from the social fund.

Losing your entitlement to these benefits may therefore make you worse off than you would have been had you not claimed an increase in your entitlement to a non-means-tested benefit for your dependant.

However, if you fail to claim an increase in your non-means-tested benefit for an adult dependant to which you are entitled, you may still be treated as receiving the increase for the purpose of calculating your entitlement to IS, income-based JSA, HB or CTB. This is because you can be treated as if you are receiving income (called 'notional income') which you fail to apply for if you would be entitled to it without having to satisfy further conditions (see p984). You should only be treated as having notional income if your entitlement to an increase is straightforward. If you would have to satisfy further conditions to qualify for the increase you should not be treated as receiving it. You should not be treated as having notional income if the increase would not be for a member of your 'family' for means-tested benefits purposes.

Non-means-tested benefits

The overlapping benefit rules apply to increases in non-means-tested benefits for dependants. These rules mean that you may not be entitled to an increase in more than one benefit for the same child or adult and that you may not qualify for an increase if someone else is receiving an increase for your dependants. You also may not be entitled to an increase for an adult dependant if s/he is claiming an earnings replacement benefit in her/his own right.

See p1102 for details of the overlapping benefit rules.

Notes

1. **Increases for your adult dependant**

1 CPA 2004
2 ss82-84, 86A and 90 SSCBA 1992; regs 8 and 12 and Sch 2 SSB(Dep) Regs; regs 9 and 10 SS(IB-ID) Regs
3 Regs 2(3) and 19(2) and (3) SS(C&P) Regs
4 s86A SSCBA 1992; reg 9(1) SS(IB-ID) Regs
5 Sch 2 para 7 SSB(Dep) Regs; s90 SSCBA 1992
6 s84 SSCBA 1992
7 *Bramhill v CAO,* ECJ Case C-420/92, 7 July 1994 (ECJ) – the discrimination will end in April 2010 as part of the programme to equalise the rules on pension age and retirement pensions; Sch 4 para 2 PA 1995
8 ss82(4), 85 and 90 SSCBA 1992; regs 10 and 12 and Sch 2 SSB(Dep) Regs; regs 9, 10 and 14 SS(IB-ID) Regs
9 Regs 2(3), 4 and 19(2) and (3) SS(C&P) Regs
10 Sch 2 para 7 SSB(Dep) Regs
11 s85(3) SSCBA 1992
12 Reg 9(2A) SS(IB-ID) Regs
13 Regs 8(2), (3) and 12 SSB(Dep) Regs; reg 10 SS(IB-ID) Regs
14 R(P) 4/93
15 ss82 and 83(2)(b) SSCBA 1992; reg 12 and Sch 2 para 7 SSB(Dep) Regs; reg 10(1) SS(IB-ID) Regs
16 s89 SSCBA 1992; Sch 2 SSB(Dep) Regs
17 Reg 10 and Sch 2 para 7 SSB(Dep) Regs; reg 10 SS(IB-ID) Regs
18 s92 and Sch 7 para 8 SSCBA 1992
19 Sch 4 SSCBA 1992
20 Reg 6(3) SS(WB&RP) Regs; reg 13 SS(IB-ID) Regs

2. **Increases for child dependants**

21 Art 3 Tax Credits Act 2002 (Commencement No.3 and Transitional Provisions and Savings) Order 2003 SI No.938
22 s80(4) SSCBA 1992; Sch 2 para 2B SSB(Dep) Regs
23 Sch 4 SSCBA 1992

3. **Definition of terms**

24 Reg 4A SSB(Dep) Regs; reg 6 SS(IB-ID) Regs
25 s122(4) SSCBA 1992
26 Reg 4A(1)(b) SSB(Dep) Regs; reg 6(1)(b) SS(IB-ID) Regs
27 Reg 4A(4) SSB(Dep) Regs; reg 6(2) SS(IB-ID) Regs
28 Reg 4B SSB(Dep) Regs; reg 7 SS(IB-ID) Regs
29 Reg 2(4) SSB(PRT) Regs
30 Reg 2(2) SSB(PRT) Regs
31 Reg 11 SSB(Dep) Regs; reg 12 SS(IB-ID) Regs
32 R(S) 3/74
33 R(U) 3/66
34 Reg 3 SSB(Dep) Regs; reg 3 SS(IB-ID) Regs
35 R(U) 25/58
36 R(S) 3/74
37 R(U) 14/62

38 R(S) 1/59
39 Reg 5 SSB(Dep) Regs; reg 8 SS(IB-ID) Regs

4. **Special rules for special groups**
40 *Hyde v Hyde* [1886]
41 Reg 2 SSFA(PM) Regs

5. **Claims, backdating and getting paid**
42 s1 SSAA 1992
43 Reg 4(1) SS(C&P) Regs
44 s1(1A) and (1B) SSAA 1992
45 Reg 7(1) SS(C&P) Regs
46 Reg 6(1) SS(C&P) Regs
47 R(SB) 8/89
48 CSIS/48/1992; CIS/759/1992
49 Regs 4(7) and 6(1) SS(C&P) Regs
50 Reg 6(29) SS(C&P) Regs
51 Reg 9(4) SS(C&P) Regs
52 Reg 9(5) SS(C&P) Regs
53 Reg 15 SS(C&P) Regs
54 Reg 14 SS(C&P) Regs
55 Reg 13 SS(C&P) Regs
56 Reg 19(2) and (3) SS(C&P) Regs
57 Reg 32(1) SS(C&P) Regs

6. **Tax, tax credits and other benefits**
58 s617 ICTA 1988

Chapter 32

Claiming for others: means-tested benefits

This chapter explains who can be included in your claim for any of the means-tested benefits. It covers:

The phrase '**means-tested benefits**' refers to:

- income support (see Chapter 13);
- income-based jobseeker's allowance (JSA – see Chapter 15);
- housing benefit (see Chapter 10); *and*
- council tax benefit (see Chapter 6).

In this chapter, unless otherwise stated, references to income-based JSA are intended also to refer to joint-claim JSA.

Note: pension credit does not include amounts for children.

This chapter does not deal with the non-means-tested benefits you can and cannot claim for others, as the rules for non-means-tested benefits are different. You should check Chapter 31 to see whether the rules for those benefits apply to any of the other people you may wish to claim for. This chapter also does not deal with who can be included in claims for child tax credit and working tax credit. For those rules, see Chapters 49 and 50 respectively.

1. Who is included in your claim

A claim for any of the means-tested benefits will include yourself and, if you have one, your family. Your '**family**' means your partner and your dependent children.

Couples

Your 'family' includes your partner, if you have one – ie, where you are a couple. Under current rules, a **'couple'** only includes a wife, husband or cohabitee of the opposite sex. The Government is also to include 'civil partners' and cohabitees of the same sex in the definition of couples (see p811). This will mean that same sex partners can count as a couple for benefit purposes. At the time of writing this change was expected to take place on 5 December 2005. See CPAG's *Welfare Rights Bulletin* for updates and further details.

Children

The rules below are about when **dependent children** can count as part of your family regarding *who can be included in your claim for means-tested benefits*. However, even where your child cannot be included in your claim, there are other circumstances in which it may still be important that you are regarded as being responsible for a child living in your household, or having a child as part of your 'family'. This applies particularly to child benefit (see p90), income support (IS – see p300), income-based jobseeker's allowance (JSA – see p374) and in some cases housing costs (see p917).

For all benefits, to count as part of your family the children must be members of your household, but even then certain 16/17-year-old local authority care home leavers are excluded (see p713).[1]

If you are making a new claim for any of the means-tested benefits on or after 6 April 2004, or you did not have a dependent child included in the claim until on or after that date, your family only includes dependent children for **housing benefit** (HB) and **council tax benefit** (CTB).[2]

From 6 April 2004, if you make a new claim for **income-based JSA or IS** ~~and~~ or you did not have a dependent child included in the claim until 6 April or after, then dependent children cannot be included in the claim.[3]* Children continue to be included in the HB or CTB claim. Dependent children cannot be included in any claim for pension credit (PC). In this situation, if you have dependent children you have to claim child tax credit (see Chapter 49) for them instead of having them included in any claim for IS, income-based JSA or PC.

If you are not making a new claim for IS or income-based JSA, and:

- your entitlement to either of those benefits began before 6 April 2004; *and*
- you had a dependent child or children included in the claim,

see p818.

When your benefit is worked out, the needs of your partner and any children included are usually added to yours and so are your partner's income and capital. There are special rules for the treatment of the income and capital of included dependent children (see pp953 and 1026).

If one member of your family is claiming a means-tested benefit, no other member can claim the same benefit for the same period.[4] For IS/income-based

* But see the note in CPAG's Welfare Rights Bulletin 186, p12 for possible doubts about this. The DWP attempted to clarify the rules from 8 September 2005.

JSA/HB/CTB, partners can choose which of them should be the claimant.[5] The same rule applies to PC, but the claimant must be aged 60 or over to qualify for this benefit.[6] **Note:** for JSA when you are required to be a 'joint-claim couple', both you and your partner will need to be available for and actively seeking work.

For details about how to claim see p306 (IS), p390 (JSA), p475 (PC), p216 (HB) and p120 (CTB).

2. **Couples**

For means-tested benefits, you and your partner are considered to be a **'couple'** if you are:

- both 16[7] or over, *and*:[8]
- married and living in the same household; *or*
- not married but 'living together as husband and wife' in the same household.

In these circumstances, you must claim as a couple. Your partner's income and capital are counted when assessing your entitlement to means-tested benefits. For means-tested benefits you receive the amount of benefit for couples.

Special rules apply if either partner is under 18 (see pp712 and 879).

Note: for pension credit (PC) only, if your partner is not habitually resident in the UK (see p702) or is a person subject to immigration control (see p655), you are treated as not being members of the same household,[9] and so cannot count as a couple.

Same sex couples

If you are same sex (lesbian or gay) partners, then under current rules you cannot count as a couple and must claim as single people. This situation will change in the future. This is because the Government is to introduce rules under which same sex couples will have to claim benefit as a couple.[10] This will be done in two ways. First, same sex partners who are registered in a 'civil partnership' and living in the same household will be treated in the same way as different sex partners who are married and living in the same household. Second, same sex partners who are not registered in a civil partnership, but live together 'as if they were civil partners' in the same household will be treated in the same way as different sex partners who are unmarried, but live together 'as if they were husband and wife' in the same household. The rules on living together in the same household were expected to apply in much the same way as described below. At the time of writing these changes were expected to be introduced on 5 December 2005. See CPAG's *Welfare Rights Bulletin* for updates and further details.

Married

Being married to someone does not necessarily mean that you cannot be treated as part of a couple with someone else instead.[11]

You count as '**polygamously married**' if you are married to more than one person and your marriages took place in a country which permits polygamy.[12] There are special rules if you are polygamously married (see p32).[13] Essentially, these specify that any income and capital of a polygamous partner will be taken into account, but an increased sum is allowed to take their needs into account.

Living in the same household

The idea of sharing a household is central to whether you include a child or a partner in your claim. However, the term 'household' is not defined. Whether two people should be treated as members of the same household is very much a question of fact. A house can contain a number of separate households and if one person has exclusive occupation of separate accommodation from another s/he will not be considered to be living in the same household. Physical presence together is also not in itself conclusive. There must be a 'particular kind of tie' binding two people together in a domestic establishment. This could, in appropriate circumstances, include a household within, for example, a hotel or boarding house.[14] However, it must also involve two or more people living together as a unit and, as such a unit, enjoying a reasonable level of independence and self-sufficiency. It has been held that a married couple sharing a room in a residential home – because they needed someone else to help with organising their personal care and domestic activities – were not self-sufficient and could not be said to live in a domestic establishment, and therefore did not share a household.[15]

You and another person may be regarded as members of the same household when you think you should not be. If this occurs it is important to try to show that, although you both live in the same house, you maintain separate households.

A separate household might exist if there are:

- independent arrangements for the storage and cooking of food;
- independent financial arrangements;
- separate eating arrangements;
- no evidence of family life;
- separate commitments for housing costs, even if the liability is to another person in the same premises.

You cannot be a member of more than one household at the same time.[16] If two people can be shown to be maintaining separate homes, they cannot be said to be sharing the same household.[17] Even if you have the right to occupy only part of a room, you may have your own household.[18]

Living together as husband and wife

If it is decided that you are 'living together as husband and wife' (cohabiting), only one of you is able to claim a means-tested benefit. (When the Government introduces rules that same sex partners can count as couples, the test will be whether they are 'living together as civil partners', but will otherwise be the same. At the time of writing this change was expected to take effect on 5 December 2005. See CPAG's *Welfare Rights Bulletin* for updates.)

The amount of benefit for a couple is usually less than that for two single people, so it is important to dispute a decision that you are cohabiting if you believe you are not. If you are awarded income support (IS)/income-based jobseeker's allowance (JSA) (and, arguably, PC), the local authority should not make a separate decision about whether you are cohabiting when considering your claim for housing benefit (HB)/council tax benefit (CTB).[19] However, where fraud is concerned, the local authority can find fraudulent a claim for IS/income-based JSA/PC on which your HB/CTB claim is founded, and therefore find that you are not entitled to HB/CTB.[20] Also, if you have not been awarded IS, income-based JSA, or PC, the local authority has a duty to give its own consideration to whether you are cohabiting and may reach a different conclusion from that of the Department for Work and Pensions (DWP).

The factors considered below are used as 'signposts' in determining whether or not you are cohabiting.[21] No one factor need in itself be conclusive, as it is your 'general relationship' as a whole which is of paramount importance[22] and, just as relationships between couples may often vary considerably, so each case depends on all its own particular facts and circumstances.

Decision makers have often applied too narrow an interpretation of the test. There is no rule, for example, that if your partner stays with you for three nights or more a week you are *automatically* to be treated as a couple who are living together.

Cohabitation – signposts

1. Do you live in the same household?
2. Do you have a sexual relationship?
3. What are your financial arrangements?
4. Is your relationship stable?
5. Do you have children?
6. How do you appear in public?

Living in the same household

In all cases you must spend the major part of your time in the same household (see p812 for a discussion of 'household'). If one of you has a separate address where you usually live, you should not be considered to be cohabiting. You cannot be a member of more than one household at the same time so, if you are a member of one couple, you cannot also be treated as part of another.

Even if you *do* share a 'household', you may not be cohabiting. It is essential to look at *why* two people are in the same household.[23] For example, where a couple were living in the same household for reasons of 'care, companionship and mutual convenience' they were not 'living together as husband and wife'.[24]

Separated couples living under the same roof should not be treated as couples if they are maintaining separate households.[25] Where a relationship has only recently broken down, continuing financial support and shared responsibilities and liabilities may be particularly inconclusive, especially where there is evidence of active steps being taken to live apart. The way people live and their attitude of mind may be more significant. Any 'mere hope' of a reconciliation is not a 'reasonable expectation' where at least one partner has accepted that the relationship is at an end.[26]

However, note that for couples who are still married all that has to be shown is that they are living in the same 'household', and in this type of case a shared attitude of mind that the relationship is at an end may not be enough to show that there is no shared household.[27]

Being in a sexual relationship

In practice, decision makers may not ask you about the existence of a sexual relationship, in which case they will only have the information if you volunteer it. If you do not have a sexual relationship, you should make this known (and perhaps offer to show your separate sleeping arrangements).

Having a sexual relationship is not sufficient by itself to prove you are cohabiting. If you have never had a sexual relationship there is a strong (but not necessarily conclusive) presumption that you are not cohabiting.[28]

A couple who abstain from a sexual relationship before marriage on grounds of principle (eg, religious reasons) should not be counted as cohabiting until they are formally married.[29]

Even if the initial decision makers do not go into the question of whether or not there is a sexual relationship, any tribunal (see p1233) has a duty to ask such questions in order to determine whether or not you are cohabiting.[30]

Your financial arrangements

If one partner is supported by the other or household expenses are shared, this may be treated as evidence of cohabitation. However, it is important to consider how they are shared. There is a difference between, on the one hand, paying a fixed weekly contribution or rigidly sharing bills 50/50 and, on the other hand, a free common fund attributable to income and expenditure. The former does not imply cohabitation, the latter might.

The financial relationship between lodger and landlady/landlord often comes under scrutiny. Decision makers sometimes claim that the payments are too high or too low and so indicate that the relationship is not purely financial. It is important to explain how payments came to be as they are. However low or high the charge may appear, it is the reasoning which led to it at the time which is important. There may be many motives for having a lodger apart from purely commercial ones or cohabitation. It may be that the relationship is entered into so that there is another adult in the house – for company or security, perhaps. Friendship between a lodger and landlady/landlord does not mean that they are cohabiting.

A stable relationship

Marriage is expected to be stable and lasting. It follows that an occasional or brief association should not be regarded as cohabiting. However, the fact that a relationship is stable does not make it cohabitation – eg, you can have a stable landlord/lodger relationship but not be cohabiting.

It is important to remember that many stable relationships are not necessarily relationships where the partners are living together as husband and wife – eg, relationships between housemates or landlords and lodgers may be stable but the parties are not cohabiting. The way you spend your time together, the activities you do together and the things you do for each other are relevant, so questions such as how you spend your holidays, how you organise the shopping, the laundry and cleaning may be important.

Children

If you have had a child together and live in the same household as the other parent, there is a strong (but not conclusive) presumption of cohabitation.

Your appearance in public

Decision makers may check the electoral roll and claims for national insurance benefits to see if you present yourselves as a couple. Many couples retain their separate identity publicly as unmarried people. They should, however, be aware that they may be regarded as cohabiting.

Challenging a 'living together' decision

Sometimes benefit is stopped or adjusted because someone regularly stays overnight, even though you might have none of the long-term commitments generally associated with marriage. But couples with no sexual relationship who live together (eg, as landlord/lodger, tenant or housekeeper, or as flat-sharers) also sometimes fall foul of the rule. People who provide mutual support and share household expenses are not necessarily cohabiting.[31] This is also the case, for example, where friends share a home.

If you are at all unhappy with a decision that you are cohabiting, you should challenge the decision (see Chapters 43 and 44), and carefully consider what evidence to gather and submit in relation to each of the six questions on p813 and any other matters that you consider relevant. Possibilities include evidence of the other person having another address[32] (eg, a rent book and other household bills), receipts for board and lodging, statements from friends and relatives or, where you have been married, evidence of a formal separation or divorce proceedings.

On an initial application for benefit it is not for you to prove that you are not cohabiting,[33] though you are required to provide the decision maker with any information reasonably required to decide your claim.[34] Neither party has the burden of proof in this situation – a decision should simply be made on all the evidence available.[35] By contrast, if your benefit as a single person is stopped because it is alleged that you are cohabiting, the burden of proof is on the decision maker to prove that you are cohabiting.[36]

If your benefit is stopped because you are cohabiting, you should challenge the decision and/or reapply immediately if your circumstances change. You should also apply immediately for any other benefits for which you might qualify – eg, HB/CTB, where the local authority may reach a different decision to that of the DWP.[37] You should apply on the basis of low income for other benefits which you previously qualified for automatically if you were on IS or JSA – eg, health benefits (see Chapter 9).

If you are still entitled to a means-tested benefit, even though it is decided that you are cohabiting, you should be paid as a couple.

If your IS, income-based JSA or PC stops and you have diverted a maintenance order to the DWP (see p852), contact the magistrates' (or, in Scotland, sheriff) court immediately to get payments sent direct to you. If the Child Support Agency is collecting a child maintenance assessment for you (see p854), ask it to start paying the money to you.

If you have no money at all, you may be able to get a social fund crisis loan (see p538).

Couples living apart

If you separate *permanently* you can claim as a single person immediately. However, you continue to be treated as a couple while you and your partner are *temporarily* apart.[38] Your former household need not have been in this country.[39] The following rules apply in determining whether you still count as a couple:

- For **CTB**, you will continue to count as a couple as long as you both remain liable for the council tax at your address. Note that the rules for establishing a couple's liability for council tax are not the same as the rules for establishing their entitlement to CTB (see CPAG's *Council Tax Handbook*).
- For **IS, income-based JSA, PC and HB**, you count as a couple, even if you or your partner are temporarily living away from your family, unless you:[40]
  - have no intention of resuming living together; *or*

- are likely to be separated for more than 52 weeks. However, you can still be treated as a couple if you are likely to be separated for more than 52 weeks provided it is not 'substantially' longer and there are exceptional circumstances such as a stay in hospital, or if there is no control over the length of the absence.

- For **IS, income-based JSA and PC**, you no longer count as a couple if any of the following apply to either of you:[41]
  - you are in custody;
  - you are released on temporary licence from prison;
  - you are a compulsory patient detained in hospital under the mental health provisions;
  - you are staying permanently in local authority residential accommodation, or a care home;
  - the claimant is abroad and does not qualify for IS, income-based JSA or PC (see Chapter 26). However, where your partner is temporarily abroad you continue to be treated as a couple, but after four weeks (eight if s/he has taken a child abroad for medical treatment) the amount of IS, income-based JSA or PC you receive is that for a single claimant or, for IS and income-based JSA only, a lone parent.[42] You can get IS without signing on if you have children under 16.[43] Your partner's income and capital continue to be treated as yours for as long as the absence is held to be temporary.

  If you are no longer treated as a couple for the purposes of calculating your IS or income-based JSA, you may still be liable to maintain your partner (see p851).
- For **PC only**, you no longer count as a couple if you or your partner are not in Great Britain (GB) and cannot be treated as being in GB because you are not receiving treatment provided for by the NHS at a hospital or similar institution abroad.[44]
- For **IS and income-based JSA only**, you are still treated as a couple if you are temporarily living apart and the following applies: one of you is at home or in hospital, or in local authority residential accommodation or in a care home, and the other is:[45]
  - resident in a nursing home, but not counted as a patient; *or*
  - staying in a residential care home; *or*
  - in a home for the rehabilitation of alcoholics or drug addicts; *or*
  - in Polish resettlement accommodation; *or*
  - on a government training course and has to live away from home (see below for your right to housing costs for more than one home); *or*
  - in a probation or bail hostel.

Although your income and capital are calculated in the normal way for a couple, your applicable amount is calculated as if each of you were single claimants if this comes to more than your usual couple rate. If you have children, one of you is treated as a lone parent. If you have housing costs (see Chapter 36), your applicable amount includes these as well as any costs of the temporary accommodation of the partner away from home. If you are both away from home, the costs of both sets of temporary accommodation and the family home may be met.[46] If both homes are rented, see p203 for when HB can be paid for more than one home at a time. If you own your home and your partner is staying in rented accommodation, you may get your housing costs met by IS or income-based JSA and your partner can claim HB.

Additional points

- Where questions of 'intention' are involved (eg, in deciding whether you or your partner intend to resume living with your family), the intention must be unqualified – ie, it must not depend on some factor over which you have no control (eg, the right of entry to the UK being granted by the Home Office[47] or the offer of a suitable job[48]).
- See p909 if one of you lives away from home as a student or on a government training course and you have to pay for two homes.
- See p907 if your child is in hospital and you have to stay in lodgings to be nearby.
- See p907 if one or both of you are temporarily in local authority residential accommodation.

3. Claiming for children

From 6 April 2004, a child can only be included in your claim in the following circumstances:[49]

- you are claiming **housing benefit** (HB) or **council tax benefit** (CTB); *or*
- you are claiming **income support** (IS) or **income-based jobseeker's allowance** (JSA); *and*
  - your current claim for IS or income-based JSA began before 6 April 2004; *and*
  - you had a dependent child or children included in that claim before 6 April 2004 but you have not yet been awarded child tax credit (CTC). However, see also CPAG's Welfare Rights Bulletin 186 p12

In all other circumstances, a child cannot be included in your claim. Instead, you will need to claim CTC for the child (see p1316).

Note: even where your child cannot be *included in your claim*, there are circumstances in which it may still be important that you are regarded as being responsible for a child living in your household, or having a child as part of your 'family'. This applies particularly to child benefit (see p90), IS (see p300), income-based JSA (see p374) and in some cases housing costs (see p917).

Income support and income-based jobseeker's allowance

Even if you were on IS or income-based JSA before 6 April 2004 and your claim included a dependent child before that date, it will cease to include amounts for a child at some point – see below. If you were awarded CTC before 6 April 2004, then your IS/income-based JSA award will have ceased to have included amounts for a child from that date.[50] Any new claim for IS or income-based JSA will not include an amount for a child.

If you were on IS or income-based JSA before 6 April 2004, your claim included a dependent child before that date and you were not awarded CTC before that date, then your benefit claim will cease to include an amount for a child at some point. The key is the date at which you become entitled to CTC.[51] The date your IS/income-based JSA claim will cease to include an amount for a child will be the earliest of:

- the point you make a claim for and are awarded CTC; *or*
- the point the claim for your child is automatically transferred to a CTC claim.

The Department for Work and Pensions (DWP) and the Revenue refer to the process of automatic transfer to CTC claims as 'migration'. At the time of writing, the timetable for this process was not confirmed, but was expected to begin sometime in 2005 – see CPAG's *Welfare Rights Bulletin* for updates.

Entitlement to amounts for a child

You do not have to be a parent to receive IS, income-based JSA (where this is still possible – see above), HB or CTB amounts for a child, but you must be 'responsible' for a child who is living in your household.[52] You can claim for any child under 16, or under 19 if s/he is still in full-time 'relevant' education[53] (see p618 for what this means). **Note:** certain 16/17-year-olds who left local authority care on or after 1 October 2001 do not count as members of your family and so you cannot claim for them (see p713).

Where the same benefit is involved, a child can only be the responsibility of one person in any week.[54] There is no provision allowing benefit to be split between parents where a child divides her/his time equally between the homes of two parents. There is a rule which allows all or part of the benefit paid to one person to be paid to another person in respect of any child or dependant who the benefit is meant to be for,[55] but this is an exceptional measure which only applies if the person paid the benefit is not using it for the child or dependant or is otherwise squandering it.[56] On a claim for HB, rent restrictions will apply so as to limit the amount of HB you may claim for the size of the accommodation you may need for a child if someone else is considered to be 'responsible' for the child (see p246).[57]

See p822 for when a child no longer counts as your dependant.

Note: as you cannot claim joint-claim JSA if you have children, the references to income-based JSA below do not include joint-claim JSA.

Responsibility for a child

The rules are different for different benefits. Even though you may be sharing actual responsibility for a child, you may still be denied benefit because the rules may not treat you as 'responsible' for the child. See below for more detail on individual benefits.

You claim IS or income-based JSA, HB or CTB for a child for whom you are 'responsible'. (However for IS and income-based JSA, children can in any case *only* be included in certain claims made before 6 April 2004 – see p818). You are treated as 'responsible' for a child if:

- For **income-based JSA**, either you get child benefit for the child, or if no-one gets child benefit for the child, the child is 'usually living' with you or you are the only person who has applied for the child benefit. However, if you share actual responsibility for the child (eg, you share responsibility with your ex-partner), then a recent court decision means that even if you do not get child benefit for the child, you should be regarded as responsible for the child if you are the **'substantial minority carer'** – ie, you have the child with you for at least 104 nights a year.[58] However, the DWP are contesting this decision and may not pay you if you do not get child benefit.[59] Seek advice (see Appendix 2) and see CPAG's *Welfare Rights Bulletin* for updates.
- For **HB** and **CTB**, the child is 'normally living' with you.[60] This means that s/he spends more time with you than with anyone else.[61] For HB and CTB only, where it is unclear whose household the child lives in, or where s/he spends an equal amount of time with two parents in different homes (this may not mean literally three and a half days with each parent[62]), you are treated as having responsibility if:[63]
  - you get child benefit for the child (see Chapter 5);
  - no one gets child benefit, but you have applied for it;
  - no one has applied for child benefit, or both of you have applied, but you appear to have the most responsibility.

  However, if you are a **substantial minority carer** (see the bullet above), then following a recent court decision it may be arguable that you should be regarded as responsible for the child even if you do not get child benefit.[64] Seek advice and see CPAG's *Welfare Rights Bulletin* for updates.
- For **IS only**, you get child benefit for the child (see Chapter 5).[65] Where no one gets child benefit you are 'responsible' if you are the only one who has applied for it. In all other cases the person 'responsible' is the person with whom the child *usually lives*.[66] However, if you are a **substantial minority carer** (see the first bullet above), then following a recent court decision it may be arguable

that you should be regarded as responible for the child even if you do not get child benefit. Seek advice and see CPAG's *Welfare Rights Bulletin* for updates.[67] Where a child for whom you are 'responsible' gets child benefit for another child, you are also 'responsible' for that child.[68]

For HB and CTB, it is important to look at who gets child benefit only where it is unclear whose household the child *normally* lives in. For IS, it is essential to look first at who gets child benefit, and only where this is not decisive is it relevant to look at where the child *usually* lives. This difference may mean that in some situations one parent may be able to claim IS for a child while the other parent can claim income-based JSA, HB or CTB for the same child at the same time.

Living in the same household[69]

These rules apply mainly to HB and CTB. For the purpose of deciding when children can be included in your claim, they also apply only to those IS and income-based JSA claims where it is still possible to have an amount for a child included – see p818.

If you are counted as responsible for a child, then that child is usually treated as a member of your household despite any temporary absence. (For a discussion of what 'household' means, see p812.) However, s/he does *not* count as a member of your household if s/he:

- For **IS, income-based JSA, HB** and **CTB**:
  - is being fostered by you under a specific statutory provision. However, you can claim benefit for a child you are fostering privately or where social services has made a less formal arrangement for the child to live with you;
  - is living with you prior to adoption , and has been placed with you by social services or an adoption agency;
  - is boarded out or has been placed with someone else prior to adoption;
  - is in the care of, or being looked after by, the local authority and not living with you. You should receive IS or income-based JSA for her/him for the days when s/he comes home – eg, for the weekend or a holiday.[70] Make sure you tell the decision makers in good time so you can be paid the extra money without delay. The local authority can also increase your applicable amount to include the child for HB and CTB for all of that week whether the child returns for all or only part of it.[71]
- For **IS and income-based JSA**:
  - has been in hospital or a local authority home for more than 12 weeks, and you or other members of your household have not been in regular contact with her/him. The 12 weeks run from the date s/he went into the hospital or home, or from the date you claim IS/income-based JSA, if later.[72] However, if you were getting income-based JSA immediately before your claim for IS, or if you were getting IS immediately before your claim for income-based JSA, the 12 weeks run from the date s/he went into the hospital or home;[73]

– is in custody. You should receive IS or income-based JSA for any periods your child spends at home;[74]
– has been abroad for more than four weeks, or for more than eight weeks if the absence abroad is to get medical treatment for the child.[75] The four- or eight-week periods run from the day s/he went abroad or from the day you claim IS/income-based JSA, if later. However, if you were getting income-based JSA immediately before your claim for IS, or if you were getting IS immediately before your claim for income-based JSA, the four- or eight-week periods are calculated from the day after the child went abroad;[76]
– is living with you and away from her/his parental or usual home in order to attend school. The child is not treated as a member of your family, but remains a member of her/his parent's household.[77]

When to stop claiming for a child

Note: even in those cases where it still possible to have amounts for a child included in a claim for IS or income-based JSA, that will cease at the point you become entitled to CTC.

Otherwise, you stop claiming for a child for whom you are no longer responsible or who is no longer a member of your household or who is no longer treated as a child (see below).

- For **IS**, you stop claiming for a child as soon as someone else starts receiving child benefit for her/him.
- For **HB** and **CTB**, you stop claiming as soon as the child starts normally living elsewhere.
- For **IS, income-based JSA, HB** and **CTB**, you claim for a child until s/he is 16, or 19 if s/he is in 'relevant education' (see p618). Children count as in relevant education until the 'terminal date' (see p89), or until they get a full-time job if that is earlier. 'Full-time' work for dependent children means at least 24 hours a week.[78]

  A 16/17-year-old who has left school or college may continue to be counted as part of your family for a few months after the terminal date. You get benefit for him/her during the child benefit extension period (see p88 for details and dates) provided the following apply:[79]
  – you were entitled to child benefit for that child immediately before the child benefit extension period started; *and*
  – you have made a fresh claim for child benefit in writing for the child benefit extension period; *and*
  – s/he has registered for work/Work-Based Learning for Young People at the JobCentre (or ONE office if you live in a scheme area) or Careers Office; *and*
  – s/he is not in full-time work.

If s/he loses the job or leaves Work-Based Learning before the end of the child benefit extension period (see p88), s/he becomes your dependant again and you can claim for her/him as long as the above conditions are satisfied.

Some 16/17-year-olds can get IS or income-based JSA in their own right before they are 18 (see p712) and you cannot claim for them.[80]

Notes

1. Who is included in your claim

1 s137(1) SSCBA 1992; s35(1) JSA 1995; reg 14(2)(c) IS Regs; reg 76(2)(d) JSA Regs; reg 13(2)(c) HB Regs; reg 5(2)(c) CTB Regs
2 Reg 1 SS(WTCCTC)(CA) Regs
3 Reg 1(4) and (8) SS(WTCCTC)(CA) Regs
4 s134(2) SSCBA 1992; s3(1)(d) JSA 1995; s4(1) SPCA 2002
5 **IS** Reg 4(3) SS(C&P) Regs
JSA Reg 4(3B) SS(C&P) Regs
HB Reg 71(1) HB Regs
CTB Reg 61(1) CTB Regs
6 s1(2)(b) and (6) SPCA 2002

2. Couples

7 CFC/7/1992
8 s137(1) SSCBA 1992; s35(1) JSA 1995; s17(1) SPCA 2002
9 Reg 5(1)(g) and (h) SPC Regs
10 CPA 2004 (at the time of writing the social security provisions of this Act were not due to come into force until late 2005)
11 R(SB) 8/85
12 **IS** Reg 2(1) IS Regs
JSA Reg 1(3) JSA Regs
PC s12 SPCA 2002
HB Reg 2(1) HB Regs
CTB Reg 2(1) CTB Regs
13 **IS** Regs 18 and 23 IS Regs
JSA Regs 84 and 88(4) and (5) JSA Regs
PC Reg 8 and Sch 3 SPC Regs
HB Regs 17 and 19 HB Regs
CTB Regs 9 and 11 CTB Regs
14 *Santos v Santos* [1972] 2 All ER 246; CIS/671/1992; CIS/81/1993
15 CIS/4935/1997
16 R(SB) 8/85
17 R(SB) 4/83
18 CSB/463/1986
19 *R v Penwith District Council HBRB ex parte Menear* 24 HLR 120, 11 October 1991
20 *R v South Ribble Borough Council HBRB ex parte Hamilton*, 24 January 2000 (CA)
21 *Crake and Butterworth v SBC* [1982] 1 All ER 498
22 R(SB) 17/81; R(G) 3/71; CIS/87/1993
23 *Crake and Butterworth v SBC*, quoted in R(SB) 35/85
24 R(SB) 35/85
25 para 11046 DMG
26 CIS/72/1994
27 CIS/2900/1998
28 CIS/87/1993
29 CSB/150/1985
30 CIS/87/1993; CIS/2559/2002
31 CSSB/145/1983
32 R(SB) 13/82
33 CIS/317/1994
34 **IS** Reg 7(1) SS(C&P) Regs
JSA Reg 24 JSA Regs
HB Reg 73 HB Regs
CTB Reg 63 CTB Regs
35 CIS/317/1994
36 R(I) 1/71
37 R(H) 9/04
38 **IS** Reg 16(1) IS Regs
JSA Reg 78(1) JSA Regs
PC Reg 5(2) SPC Regs
HB Reg 15(1) HB Regs
CTB Reg 7(1) CTB Regs
39 CIS/508/1992
40 **IS** Reg 16(1) and (2) IS Regs
JSA Reg 78(2) JSA Regs
PC Reg 5(1)(a) SPC Regs
HB Reg 15(1) and (2) HB Regs
41 **IS** Reg 16(3) IS Regs
JSA Reg 78(3) JSA Regs
PC Reg 5(1)(b)-(d) and (f) SPC Regs

42 **IS** Sch 7 paras 11 and 11A IS Regs
JSA Sch 5 paras 10 and 11 JSA Regs
43 Sch 1B para 23 IS Regs
44 Regs 5(1)(e) and 4 SPC Regs
45 **IS** Sch 7 para 9 IS Regs
JSA Reg 85 and Sch 5 para 5 JSA Regs
46 **IS** Sch 7 para 9 col (2) IS Regs
JSA Reg 85 and Sch 5 para 5 col (2) JSA Regs
47 CIS/508/1992; CIS/13805/1996
48 CIS/484/1993

3. **Claiming for children**

49 Reg 1 SS(WTCCTC)(CA) Regs
50 Reg 1(2) and (6) SS(WTCCTC)(CA) Regs
51 Reg 1(3) and (7) SS(WTCCTC)(CA) Regs
52 s137 SSCBA 1992; s35 JSA 1995; reg 77 JSA Regs
53 **IS** Reg 14 IS Regs
JSA s35 JSA 1995; regs 1(3) and 76 JSA Regs
HB Reg 13 HB Regs
CTB Reg 5 CTB Regs
54 **IS/HB/CTB** s134(2) SSCBA 1992
IS Reg 15(4) IS Regs
JSA s3(1)(d) JSA 1995; reg 77(5) JSA Regs
HB Reg 14(3) HB Regs
CTB Reg 6(3) CTB Regs
55 Reg 34 SS(C&P) Regs
56 *Barber v Secretary of State for Work and Pensions* [2002] EWHC Admin 1915, 17 July 2002, unreported
57 *R v Swale Borough Council, ex parte Marchant, The Times*, 17 November 1999 (CA)
58 Reg 77 JSA Regs, as applied in *Hockenjos v Secretary of State for Social Security*, EWCA Civ 1749 (21 December 2004)
59 DMG Letter 01/05 (January 2005). This implies that the DWP intends to apply the JSA rule without applying either *Hockenjos v Secretary of State for Work and Pensions*, or the earlier decision in CJSA/4890/1998.
60 **HB** Reg 14(1) HB Regs
CTB Reg 6(1) CTB Regs
61 CFC/1537/1995
62 CFC/1537/1995
63 **HB** Reg 14(2) HB Regs
CTB Reg 6(2) CTB Regs
64 *Hockenjos v Secretary of State for Social Security* [2004] EWCA Civ 1749 applies only to JSA. However it may support arguments concerning HB/CTB based on the Human Rights Act.
65 **IS** Reg 15(1) IS Reg
JSA Reg 77(1) JSA Regs
66 **IS** Reg 15(2) IS Regs
JSA Reg 77(3) JSA Regs
67 *Hockenjos v Secretary of State for Social Security* [2004] EWCA Civ 1749 applies only to JSA. However it may support arguments concerning IS based on the Human Rights Act.
68 **IS** Reg 15(1A) IS Regs
JSA Reg 77(2) JSA Regs
69 **IS** Reg 16 IS Regs
JSA Reg 78(1) JSA Regs
HB Reg 15 HB Regs
CTB Reg 7 CTB Regs
70 **IS** Regs 15(3) and 16(6) IS Regs
JSA Regs 77(4) and 78(7) JSA Regs
71 **HB** Reg 15(5) HB Regs
CTB Reg 7(4) CTB Regs
72 **IS** Reg 16(5)(b) IS Regs
JSA Reg 78(5)(c) JSA Regs
73 **IS** Reg 16(5A) IS Regs
JSA Reg 78(6) JSA Regs
74 **IS** Regs 15(3) and 16(6) IS Regs
JSA Regs 77(4) and 78(5)(l) and (7) JSA Regs
75 **IS** Reg 16(5a) and (aa) IS Regs
JSA Reg 78(5)(a) and (b) JSA Regs
76 **IS** Reg 16(5A) IS Regs
JSA Reg 78(6) JSA Regs
77 **IS** Reg 16(7) IS Regs
JSA Reg 78(8) JSA Regs
78 Regs 1(2), definition of 'remunerative work', and 7 CB Regs
79 **IS** Reg 15(1) IS Regs
JSA Reg 77(1) JSA Regs
HB Reg 13 HB Regs
CTB Reg 5 CTB Regs
All Reg 7D(1) CB Regs
80 s134(2) SSCBA 1992

Chapter 33

National insurance contributions and benefits

This chapter covers:

1. Introduction

Many of the benefits described in this *Handbook* are financed from the national insurance (NI) fund, which is made up of payments from the Treasury and social security contributions made by employees, their employers, the self-employed and other people who choose to pay them.

Entitlement to those benefits – and in some cases the amount paid – depends upon the contribution record of the claimant or, in the case of bereavement benefits and Category B retirement pensions, of the claimant's spouse. For the contribution conditions for benefits, see p843.

A percentage of social security contributions goes to the NHS. The rest is paid into the NI fund.[1]

Contributions are collected for the Department for Work and Pensions by the Revenue.

Classes of contribution

There are six different classes of contribution.[2] The class you pay depends upon whether you are an employee, self-employed or a voluntary contributor. Not all classes of contribution count for all benefits.[3]

Class of contribution	*Payable by*	*Giving entitlement to*
Class 1	Employed earners and their employers	All benefits with contribution conditions
Class 1A	Employers of employed earners	No benefits
Class 1B	Employers of employed earners	No benefits
Class 2	Self-employed earners	All benefits with contribution conditions except contribution-based jobseeker's allowance (see p843)
Class 3	Voluntary contributors	Widows' and bereavement benefits and retirement pensions
Class 4	Self-employed earners	No benefits

The amount of Class 1 or 4 contributions you pay depends on your earnings. You do not necessarily gain more benefit by paying higher contributions.

Employed earners and self-employed earners

The distinction between being employed and self-employed is usually clear but there are sometimes grey areas.

An **'employed earner'** is defined as 'a person who is gainfully employed in Great Britain either under a contract of service, or in an office (including elective office) with general earnings'.[4] In other words, if income tax is, or should be, deducted from your earnings before you receive them under the Pay As You Earn scheme, you are an 'employed earner'.

A **'self-employed earner'** is anyone 'gainfully employed in Great Britain otherwise than in employed earner's employment'.[5] If you have two jobs it is possible to be both employed and self-employed.

There is not usually much dispute over whether you hold an office or not. Office-holders include judges, company directors and registrars of births, deaths and marriages.

The usual area of dispute is whether you are employed under a *contract of service* (in which case you are an employee) or a *contract for services* (in which case you are self-employed). This can be a complicated question and the decision maker must take into account a number of factors, including how closely your work is supervised, whether you can employ a substitute to do your job for you, the method of payment, whether the contract is for a fixed period, whether you have to provide your own equipment, where you work and the amount of freedom you have to decide when you work and how much work you must do. No one criterion is conclusive and different aspects may have different weight attached to them in different cases.[6]

Certain people are deemed to be employed earners.[7] These are office cleaners, many agency workers, people employed by their spouse for the purposes of their spouse's employment, lecturers, teachers and instructors (but not if the instruction is for no more than three days in any three months or is given as public lectures) and most ministers of religion. Conversely examiners, moderators and invigilators are deemed to be self-employed.[8]

You do not have to pay contributions if you are employed:[9]

- in your home by a close relative if you both live in the home and the employment is not for the purposes of any trade or business carried on there. **'Close relatives'** are a parent, grandparent, step-parent, son, daughter, grandson, granddaughter, step-son, step-daughter, brother, sister, half-brother or half-sister;
- by your spouse if it is not for the purposes of your spouse's employment;
- as a self-employed earner if you are not ordinarily self-employed;
- as a returning officer at an election;
- by certain international organisations or foreign armed forces (but only in certain circumstances).

Upper and lower earnings limits

Contributions are paid for the tax year (ie, 6 April to 5 April).[10] For each tax year there is an upper and a lower earnings limit. Prior to April 2000 employees were liable to pay Class 1 contributions on weekly earnings between those limits. From April 2000 employees earning below a 'primary threshold' no longer pay NI contributions. However, those with earnings between the lower earnings limit and the primary threshold will be treated as if they had paid NI contributions on those earnings.[11] The earnings limits for the years from 2002/03 to 2005/06 are as follows:

Year	*Lower earnings limit*	*Primary threshold*	*Upper earnings limit*
2002/03	£75	£89	£585
2003/04	£77	£89	£595
2004/05	£79	£91	£610
2005/06	£82	£94	£630

A list of the earnings limits for each year since the present system was adopted in 1975/76 can be found in Appendix 9.

Earnings factors

Payment of Class 1, 2 and 3 contributions gives rise to an 'earnings factor' which is used to calculate your entitlement to contributory benefits (including the additional pension payable under the additional state pension scheme – see p499).

For Class 1 contributions, the earnings factor is the amount of earnings, excluding those earnings above the upper earnings limit, upon which those contributions have been paid. Each Class 2 and Class 3 contribution gives rise to an earnings factor equal to that year's lower earnings limit.[12]

How decisions are made

Most decisions on NI contributions are made by an officer of the Board of the Revenue. If you appeal against such decisions, your appeal will be decided by tax appeal commissioners.[13] The process is the same as appealing to a tax appeal commissioner over a statutory sick pay decision (see p609).

If you appeal against a decision on your entitlement to credited contributions or home responsibilities protection your appeal will be decided by an appeal tribunal (see Chapter 44).

2. Payment of contributions

Age limits

Contributions are intended to be paid during a normal working life. They are not, therefore, payable by those under the minimum school-leaving age of 16,[14] nor by those over pension age (60 for women, 65 for men, but see p841 for details of credited contributions for men over 60).[15] The Revenue National Insurance Contributions Office (NICO) should send you a certificate of age exemption when you reach 60/65. Ask at your local NICO if it does not. Employers of employees over pension age still have to pay their contributions at the full (contracted-in) rate.

These rules discriminate againstmen (and in some circumstances also against women) on the grounds of gender. However, the European Court of Justice ruled that the fact that a man is required to pay contributions over a longer period to qualify for the same amount of basic retirement pension as a woman, and that a man who is working is required to pay contributions between the ages of 60 and 65 whereas a woman is not, did not contravene the principle of equal treatment in European Community (EC) law (see p1285).[16]

Residence and presence in Great Britain

Class 1 contributions must usually be paid by employees who are employed in Great Britain (GB)[17] and who are resident, present (except for temporary absence) or ordinarily resident in GB at the time.[18]

However, if you are employed by an overseas employer and are not ordinarily resident or employed in the UK, you are not liable for Class 1 contributions until you have been resident in GB for a year.[19] This also applies to certain foreign students and apprentices.[20]

If you are working abroad, you must still pay Class 1 contributions for the first year if your employer has a place of business in GB, you were resident in GB before your employment started and you are still ordinarily resident in GB.[21] After that year you are entitled, but not obliged, to pay Class 3 contributions.[22]

Class 2 contributions are compulsory if you are self-employed in GB and are either ordinarily resident in GB, or have been resident here for at least 26 weeks during the last year.[23] If you are present in GB, they may be paid voluntarily if you are not required to pay them.[24] If you are self-employed outside GB, you may pay Class 2 contributions if you wish, provided you were employed or self-employed immediately before you left GB and, *either*:

- you have been resident in GB for a continuous period of at least three years at some time in the past; *or*
- you have paid contributions producing an earnings factor of at least 52 times the lower earnings limit in each of three years in the past. Each set of 52 flat-rate contributions paid before April 1975 counts as satisfying that condition in respect of one year.[25]

You may also pay Class 2 contributions if you are a volunteer development worker resident in GB but employed outside GB and not liable to pay Class 1 contributions. These are paid at a special rate and give entitlement to contribution-based jobseeker's allowance (JSA), but are payable only if the Secretary of State certifies that it would be consistent with the proper administration of the legislation to allow you to do so.[26]

Class 3 contributions are always voluntary. They may be paid if you are resident in GB throughout the course of the year in respect of which you wish to pay the contributions or if:

- you arrived in GB in the year for which you want to pay contributions and either you were liable to pay Class 1 or 2 contributions earlier that year or you have been ordinarily resident for at least part of the year; *or*
- you arrived in GB in the year for which you want to pay contributions, or in the previous year, and you have been in GB for a continuous period of 26 weeks.

They may be paid while you are abroad if you satisfy either of the conditions which would allow you to pay Class 2 contributions, but you do not need to have been employed or self-employed before you left GB. You may also pay them if you have been paying Class 1 contributions while abroad.[27]

Class 4 contributions are payable only if you are resident in the UK for income tax purposes.[28]

If you pay Class 2 or 3 contributions, the NICO sends a bill each quarter or you can pay by direct debit. If you wish to pay contributions while abroad, obtain leaflet NI38 which contains an application form.

When you return to GB, notify the Revenue so that you can be told of any deficiency in your contribution record that you can remedy, and so that your future contribution record is accurately tied in with your past record.

The meaning of the terms **'resident'** and **'present'** are explained on p696. Members of the armed forces are deemed always to be present in GB and there are special rules for aircrew, mariners, share fishermen and offshore workers on the continental shelf.

For the factors which are taken into account in deciding where you are **'ordinarily resident'** see p698.

It should also be noted that Northern Ireland and Isle of Man contributions count towards British benefits, as do contributions paid in other countries in some circumstances. In particular, this may apply if you have paid contributions in the European Economic Area – see p673. You may also be entitled to benefits from other countries while you are in this country (see Chapter 26).

Reduced liability for married women and widows

Women who were married or widowed on 6 April 1977 could choose to pay a reduced Class 1, or no Class 2, contribution, but they had to apply to do so before 12 May 1977.[29] Women who had done so could choose to continue payment at this reduced level. The disadvantages are that the reduced contributions do not entitle you to contributory benefits and there is no right (except for widows and those entitled to starting credits – see p839) to receive credits when these would otherwise be made – eg, during sickness or unemployment.[30] Also, a year in which a woman has elected to have reduced liability for contributions cannot be a year of home responsibilities protection (see p842).

A married woman whose husband dies while she is taking advantage of this provision can normally continue with her reduced liability for as long as she is entitled to a widow's or a bereavement benefit. Otherwise, the right is lost at the end of the tax year in which her husband dies, or at the end of the next tax year if he dies after 30 September.[31]

The right to opt for reduced liability is also automatically lost in other situations including:[32]

- on divorce or annulment of marriage;
- at the end of the tax year in which she stops receiving a widow's benefit;
- after two consecutive tax years with no earnings from self-employment or on which she has had to pay Class 1 contributions.

It is worth thinking carefully about your position if you are considering giving up your reduced liability. Once lost, the right cannot be reclaimed.

On the one hand, if you continue with the reduced liability, you are not accumulating entitlement to contributory benefits. On the other hand, you can still receive widows' benefits and Category B retirement pension based on your husband's record, non-contributory benefits (such as attendance allowance or disability living allowance) and means-tested benefits (such as income support). The following considerations are relevant:

- Take account of the extent to which your pension entitlement would be improved by paying contributions now (see p846).
- Although you could gain an additional pension under the additional state pension scheme if you started to pay full Class 1 contributions, it might be better to continue to pay reduced contributions and put the money into a private scheme instead. This is a point on which you will probably need advice from a financial adviser, but remember that many financial advisers only advise on certain products and may have a vested interest because of the commission they will receive. It is always a good idea to ask how much commission your adviser will get if you follow her/his advice; s/he is obliged to disclose this information if you ask for it.
- If you are looking after a disabled person or a child(ren) for whom you receive child benefit, home responsibilities protection (see p842) is only available if you revoke the election to pay the reduced amount.
- If your earnings are below the primary threshold but above the lower earnings limit (see p827) you will normally be treated as having paid Class 1 contributions on those earnings for the purpose of entitlement to contributory benefits. However, if you have elected to pay reduced contributions you will only be treated as having paid a reduced rate of contribution on those earnings and so will not build up entitlement to contributory benefits.[33]
- You may be entitled to credited contributions (see p837) if you revoke the election – eg, if you are unemployed or too ill to work.

It is very difficult to give general advice. Much depends on individual circumstances, such as the amount you earn, the security of your employment, your state of health, your age and whether you are sufficiently well off not to be entitled to means-tested benefits. Ask your union or local Citizens Advice Bureau for advice.

To revoke your election, complete the form in Revenue leaflet CA13 for married women or CA09 for widows.

Class 1 contributions

Class 1 contributions are paid both by employed earners (see p826 – known as primary contributors) and their employers (secondary contributors).[34] Both your own and your employer's liability depend upon the amount of your earnings in relation to the lower and upper earnings limits and to the 'primary threshold' (see p827).[35] If your earnings are monthly, the earnings limits are multiplied by four and one-third to give monthly equivalents.[36]

If you are not contracted out of the additional state pension scheme (see p501), the rate of your contribution is 11 per cent of your earnings between the primary threshold and upper earnings limits plus 1 per cent of the earnings you have above the upper earnings limit.[37]

Example

If your weekly earnings are £167 your Class 1 contribution is:

£167 – £94 = £73

11% x £73 = £8.03

If you are contracted out of the additional state pension scheme (see p499), the rate of the contribution you pay on your earnings between the primary threshold and the upper earnings limit is 9.4 per cent.[38]

Although your contributions to the national insurance (NI) fund are lower if you are contracted out, you will probably pay more than 2 per cent of your earnings into your occupational pension scheme instead.

If you are a member of an appropriate personal pension or stakeholder pension scheme (see p501), you pay Class 1 contributions at the contracted-in rate but the Revenue will then pay a rebate of contributions, together with tax relief on your share of the rebate, directly into your pension scheme.[39]

If you are a married woman or widow with reduced liability for contributions (see p830), you pay 4.85 per cent of your earnings between the primary threshold and the upper earnings limit plus 1 per cent of your earnings above the upper earnings limit, but your employer pays at the usual rate.[40]

Your employer should deduct your Class 1 contributions from your earnings and pay them with its own contributions to the Revenue.[41] See p835 for what happens if your employer does not do this.

Employer's contributions

Your employer's liability is calculated in a similar way to yours. The contribution your employer pays is calculated as a percentage of the amount of your earnings which are above the secondary threshold (currently £94 a week).[42]

If you are in an occupational pension scheme which is contracted out of the additional state pension scheme your employer's contributions are reduced,[43] and there are **special rates** for the employers of certain mariners employed on foreign-going ships.[44]

More than one job

If you have more than one job, the basic rule is that your liability to pay Class 1 contributions is calculated for each job as if the other(s) did not exist.[45]

Example

Mary earns £60 a week working part time serving dinners at a school and £70 a week working behind the bar of a pub in the evenings. Although her total earnings are £130 a week neither she nor her employers pay any Class 1 contributions because her earnings in each job are below the lower earnings limit. As a result, Mary is not earning any entitlement to contribution-based JSA, incapacity benefit or a Category A retirement pension.

This rule is subject to two exceptions:

- If you have more than one job, you can claim a refund if, during a contribution year, you pay more than the annual maximum.[46]
- If you have two different jobs for the same employer or employers who carry on business in association with each other, your earnings from those jobs are normally added together and you have to pay NI contributions based on your total earnings.[47] This is to stop employers avoiding the liability to pay contributions.

Class 1A contributions[48]

Class 1A contributions are paid by employers. They are paid on certain benefits in kind that you receive from your employer which are taxable but for which no Class 1 contributions are paid, such as the use of a company car.

Class 1B contributions

Class IB contributions are paid by employers who enter into a Pay As You Earn Settlement Agreement with the Revenue.

Class 2 contributions

Class 2 contributions must be paid by self-employed earners (see p826) unless you have a certificate of exemption on the grounds that your income is below a certain level (£4,345 a year in 2005/06).[49]

You must apply for a certificate as soon as possible because it can only be backdated for up to 13 weeks before the date of application,[50] although repayment of contributions is possible. The application form is included in leaflet CA02. It is sometimes possible to have the calculation of your earnings deferred until the end of the year, so you could wait until then to see if you have sufficiently low earnings. Usually your earnings are estimated; they will be estimated as below the minimum level if they were below that level in the previous year and there has been 'no material change of circumstances'. Expenses are deducted when calculating earnings.[51]

You must pay contributions unless you have a certificate; you may pay them even if you do have a certificate.[52] Married women and widows with reduced liability for contributions (see p830) are not liable for Class 2 contributions.[53]

Class 2 contributions are payable at a flat rate.[54] The current and recent rates are:

2002/03	£2.00 a week
2003/04	£2.00 a week
2004/05	£2.05 a week
2005/06	£2.10 a week

Volunteer development workers overseas (see p829) and share fishermen pay contributions at special rates which count towards contribution-based JSA, unlike other Class 2 contributions.[55]

If you are self-employed part of the time and also have a job as an employed earner you pay both Class 1 and Class 2 contributions, subject to a maximum.[56]

If you have paid Class 2 contributions, you can apply to have them repaid to you if your earnings in that year were, in fact, sufficiently low to entitle you to an exemption from liability. The application must be made in writing after the end of the relevant tax year (ie, on or after 6 April) and must be made no later than the 31 January following the end of the relevant tax year.[57]

Class 3 contributions

Class 3 contributions are purely voluntary.[58] They give entitlement only to bereavement benefits and retirement pensions and are not payable if your earnings factor is otherwise sufficient in that tax year to meet the second contribution condition for those benefits (see p846).[59] Any accidental overpayment of contributions should be refunded if you make a written application.[60]

Class 3 contributions are paid at a flat rate. The current and recent rates are:[61]

2002/03	£6.85 a week
2003/04	£6.95 a week
2004/05	£7.15 a week
2005/06	£7.35 a week

The introduction of home responsibilities protection (see p842) lessened the need to pay Class 3 contributions. However, if your contribution record for long-term benefits would otherwise be incomplete (eg, because you have been abroad or in prison) you may still consider it a good idea to pay them. Ask at your local Department for Work and Pensions office if you are in doubt.

Class 4 contributions

Class 4 contributions are paid by self-employed earners (see p826) when their profits in a tax year rise above a certain level. They are paid in addition to Class 2 contributions, but give no extra entitlement to benefit.[62] For the tax year 2005/06, Class 4 contributions are paid on profits above £4,895. The amount paid is 8 per cent of profits between £4,895 and £32,760 plus 1 per cent of profits above £32,760. In the tax years prior to 2003/04 there was a maximum as well as a minimum level of profits on which Class 4 contributions were levied, and Class 4 contributions were only payable on profits between these figures (see below). The current and recent rates are:

Year	*%*	*On profits between*	*%*	*On profits above*
2002/03	7	£4,615 and £30,420		
2003/04	8	£4,615 and £30,940	1	£30,940
2004/05	8	£4,745 and £31,720	1	£31,720
2005/06	8	£4,895 and £32,760	1	£32,760

The profits are those on which income tax under Schedule D is payable, and Class 4 contributions are usually collected with your income tax by the Revenue. You may apply for permission to defer payment for a specified period if the amount to be paid has not yet been established.[63]

If you are liable to pay Class 1, and/or Class 2 and Class 4 contributions, the total payable is subject to a maximum.[64]

Pre-1975 contributions

The present contribution system was introduced on 6 April 1975. Between 5 July 1948 and 5 April 1975 there were no Class 4 contributions, and Class 1 contributions were paid by a 'flat-rate stamp' in the same way as Class 2 and Class 3 contributions. Graduated contributions giving entitlement to graduated retirement benefit (see p488) were introduced in 1961, but were collected separately.

Before 6 April 1975, contribution years were not the same as tax years, as they are now. Instead, each person was allocated a contribution year which might have begun in December, March, June or September depending on the last letter of your NI number. There were complicated transitional arrangements in both 1948 and 1975 so that you may well have had a contribution year which was not 12 months long. That may explain what would otherwise be anomalies in your contribution record.

Non-payment or late payment of contributions

It is an offence to deliberately not pay contributions that you are liable for (unless they are voluntary).[65] As far as Class 1 contributions are concerned, it is your employer's responsibility to make sure that contributions are deducted from your earnings and then paid to the Revenue. But if you connive with your employers in order to avoid paying contributions, you too could be prosecuted. In practice, the Revenue is usually more interested in collecting the appropriate contributions than in prosecuting people.

All employees have the right to receive an itemised pay statement from their employer every time they are paid.[66] The statement must show all the deductions which have been made, including income tax and NI contributions. If you are not given a pay-slip which complies with these rules, you can take your employer to an employment tribunal, which can award you compensation if money has been deducted without your knowledge.[67]

If your employer has deducted Class 1 contributions from your earnings, but has failed to pay them to the Revenue, you are treated as though they had been paid unless you have been negligent, or consented to or connived in that arrangement.[68]

Class 2 contributions are usually paid by quarterly bill or direct debit.[69] At the end of the tax year you will know whether or not it is necessary to pay Class 3 contributions to fill any gap in your record.

Contributions can still count for benefit purposes if paid late, provided they are paid within two years (Class 1) or six years (Class 2 or Class 3) after the end of the tax year in which they were due (but see below).[70] Students, apprentices, trainees and prisoners may pay Class 3 contributions to cover their period of education, apprenticeship or imprisonment at any time before the end of the sixth complete tax year after that period finished.[71] However, late-paid contributions cannot apply to benefit entitlement for a period before the date on which they were actually paid (and, in the case of contribution-based JSA or incapacity benefit, late-paid contributions cannot count for benefit entitlement unless they were either paid before the start of the relevant benefit year – see p844 – or, if they were paid after the start of the relevant benefit year, until six weeks after they have been paid).[72] In very limited circumstances, Class 1, 2 or 3 contributions paid after the above time limits may count for benefit purposes.[73]

Note: the Revenue has extended the deadline for payment of Class 3 contributions for the tax years from 1996/97 to 2001/02 for people who did not receive notice before 1 November 2003 that they were entitled to pay such contributions. This is because it was late in sending out annual notifications informing people that they had paid insufficient contributions in a year for it to count as a qualifying year for retirement pension. If you:

- reached pension age before 24 October 2004 you have until 5 April 2010 to pay;
- reach pension age on or after 24 October 2004 you have until 5 April 2009 to pay the contributions.[74]

If you do not pay Class 3 contributions within the normal six-year time limit but you pay them for any of the tax years from 1996/97 to 2001/02 by the above

deadline then, for benefit purposes, those contributions can be treated as if they were paid on the following dates:[75]

- if you reach pension age between 6 April 1998 and 23 October 2004 (both dates inclusive), on 1 October 1998 or on the day you reach pension age (if that is later);
- if you reach pension age between 24 October 2004 and 5 April 2008 (both dates inclusive), on the day of payment or on the day you reach pension age (if that is earlier);
- if you reach pension age on or after 6 April 2008, on the day on which they were paid.

Voluntary contributions may be paid on behalf of a contributor after her/his death provided they are paid no later than s/he would have been allowed to pay them.[76] This may be useful to gain entitlement to, or increase the rate of, widowed parent's allowance or bereavement allowance (see pp25 and 29).

3. Credits and home responsibilities protection

If you do not pay national insurance (NI) contributions, there will be gaps in your contribution record. However, in many circumstances you will be 'credited' with a contribution. A credited contribution is usually known simply as a 'credit'.

Credits help you satisfy the second contribution condition for benefits with two contribution conditions – ie, contribution-based jobseeker's allowance (JSA), incapacity benefit (IB), Category A and B retirement pensions, widowed parent's allowance and bereavement allowance. It is important to note that credits cannot help you to satisfy the first contribution condition for such benefits or to qualify for a bereavement payment, which has a single contribution condition.

In practice, this means that in order to benefit from the rules on credits, at least a full year's contributions must actually have been paid.[77] The number of years of paid contributions which are necessary to qualify for the above benefits depends on the benefit claimed (see p843).

You are credited with an amount of earnings equal to the lower earnings limit (except 'starting credits', which give you a Class 3 credit). You receive only sufficient credits in any tax year to meet the minimum contribution condition.[78]

Married women currently opting for reduced liability for contributions (see p830) are not entitled to credits other than starting credits (see p839) and those for a bereaved spouse (see p840).[79]

Home responsibilities protection (see p842) helps you satisfy the second contribution condition for long-term benefits by reducing the number of years for which you would otherwise have to satisfy the contribution condition.

Credits for unemployment or incapacity for work

You can get a credit for a week in which you are signing on as unemployed or covered by a medical certificate. You get one Class 1 credit[80] for *either*:

- each complete week (ie, the seven days from Sunday to Saturday) for which you receive JSA (or where you would receive it but for the loss of benefit for benefit offences rules – see p1169); *or*
- each complete week for which you have (either from the first day you claim or within a reasonable period of time) made a written claim for credits and provided the Department for Work and Pensions (DWP) with evidence that you satisfy (or satisfied) the following qualifying conditions for JSA (see Chapter 15) – ie, that you are:
  - available for work; *and*
  - actively seeking work; *and*
  - not engaged in remunerative work; *and*
  - not in relevant education; *and*
  - capable of work; *and*
  - under pension age;

  or you would have been but for being incapable of work (see Chapter 30); *or*
- each complete week in which you would have satisfied the above conditions for JSA except that you are being treated as in remunerative work because you received a compensation payment – eg, pay in lieu of notice (see p756); *or*
- each complete week during which you were incapable of work or could be treated as incapable of work for incapacity benefit (IB) purposes – see p264 – or during which you were entitled to statutory sick pay. You cannot qualify for credits for days on which you were (or would have been, had you otherwise been entitled to IB) treated as not incapable of work for IB purposes (see p264). However, you do not need to have actually made a claim for IB or maternity allowance to be counted as incapable of work for credits purposes.

Credits for incapacity for work must be claimed before the end of the benefit year (see p844) following the tax year in which you are entitled to the credit. So, for example, if you are incapable of work at any time between 6 April 2005 and 5 April 2006 the deadline for claiming credits is Monday 31 December 2007. This time limit can be extended if it is considered reasonable to do so, given your circumstances.[81]

Entitlement to credits is one reason why you might continue to sign on at the JobCentre or Jobcentre Plus office, even though you are getting no immediate benefit from doing so. Therefore, if you do not have a good enough contribution record to claim contribution-based JSA or your entitlement to contribution-based JSA has run out and you are unable to claim income-based JSA or income support (IS) in your own right, you should consider whether it is still worth signing on to protect your right to benefits.

However, you will not get credits for unemployment for weeks in which:[82]

- you would not have been entitled to JSA (whether or not you actually claimed it) because you are involved in a trade dispute; *or*
- you are not getting JSA because you have been 'sanctioned' (eg, because you left or failed to take a job without a good reason – see p415), or you are receiving hardship payments (a reduced rate of JSA – see p443); *or*
- if you are a member of a joint-claim couple, you are not getting JSA or your JSA is reduced because of a sanction, or you are receiving hardship payments; *or*
- you are a 16/17-year-old and are receiving JSA severe hardship payments (see p384).

Credits for caring for a disabled person

You receive a Class 1 credit for each week in which you receive carer's allowance (CA, formerly called invalid care allowance – see Chapter 4) or would receive it, but for the loss of benefit for benefit offences rules (see p1169).[83] You also receive credits if the only reason that you do not receive CA is because you are receiving a bereavement benefit instead.

If you are looking after a disabled person but are not entitled to credits under these provisions, you may receive home responsibilities protection instead (see p842).

Starting credits

You receive Class 3 credits for the tax year in which you were 16 and for the next two years if you would otherwise have an insufficient contribution record for long-term benefits.[84]

This is intended to help those who have stayed on at school after the minimum school-leaving age. No credits are made under this provision for years before 6 April 1975.

Education and training credits

You receive Class 1 credits, for contribution-based JSA and IB purposes only, for either one of the two complete tax years which fall before the benefit year in which your period of incapacity for work (see p265) or your jobseeking period (see p348) started if, for any part of those tax years, you were on:

- a course of full-time training, including training to acquire occupational or vocational skills (or, if you are disabled, part-time – at least 15 hours a week); *or*
- a course of full-time education; *or*
- an apprenticeship.

You are only entitled to these credits if:

- in the other tax year in which you must satisfy the second contribution condition for the benefit (see p845), you have an earnings factor of 50 times the lower earnings limit without recourse to this provision; *and*
- you are at least 18, or will become 18 during the tax year in question; *and*

- you were under 21 when the course started; *and*
- your course of education, training or apprenticeship has finished.[85]

You also receive Class 1 credits for all benefits for each week in which you are undertaking an approved training course provided that:[86]

- the training is full time, unless either you are disabled, when it must be for at least 15 hours a week, or it is an introductory course; *and*
- the training is not part of your job; *and*
- the training is intended to last for one year or less (except in certain circumstances if it is a course for disabled people); *and*
- you were 18 or over at the beginning of the tax year in which the week falls.

All courses run by the DWP count. Other courses are considered on their merits.

Credits for the maternity pay and adoption pay period

You are entitled to a Class 1 credit for each week of the maternity pay period (see p574) for which you receive statutory maternity pay (SMP), and for each week of the adoption pay period for which you receive statutory adoption pay (SAP).[87] This will be important only if you are receiving SMP or SAP at a rate less than the lower earnings limit (currently £82 a week). You must claim these credits in writing before the end of the 'benefit year' (see p844) following the tax year in which the week falls, but this time limit may be extended if it is reasonable to do so.

Credits for jury service

You are entitled to a Class 1 credit for each week after 6 April 1988 during which you spend at least part of the week on jury service, unless you are self-employed.[88] You must claim these credits in writing before the end of the 'benefit year' (see p844) following the tax year in which the week falls (or such further period as is reasonable).

Credits for a bereaved spouse

If you are a bereaved spouse you may receive credits to enable you to satisfy the second contribution condition for contribution-based JSA or IB.[89]

If you were receiving bereavement benefit but you stopped getting that benefit for a reason other than remarriage or cohabitation, you will receive Class 1 credits for each year up to and including the one in which your bereavement benefit stopped. For the purpose of satisfying the second contribution condition for IB only, you were also entitled to Class 1 credits for each year up to and including the one in which your entitlement to widow's allowance (abolished in April 1988) or widowed mother's allowance ceased, unless those benefits stopped because you remarried or started cohabiting.[90]

Credits for people aged 60 or over

Women are not entitled or required to pay contributions once they are 60 or over. A man aged over 60 must continue to pay contributions if he is liable even if his contribution record is already sufficient to qualify for a full Category A retirement pension (see p828).

You can receive Class 1 credits for the tax year in which you turn 60 and for the next four years.[91] This means that if you are a man and you take early retirement at 60 you will still have the last five years of your 'working life' counted in full towards satisfying the second contribution condition for your retirement pension when you reach 65. These are sometimes known as 'autocredits'. You cannot qualify for these credits for any year in which you were abroad for more than 182 days. Also, if you are self-employed you must *either*:

- be liable to pay at least one Class 2 contribution in any of the above tax years; *or*
- have a small earnings exception (see p833) for at least one week in any of the above tax years,

to qualify for credits for the other weeks in those years.

Credits for tax credits

You are entitled to a Class 1 credit for the purpose of satisfying the second contribution condition for any benefit, for each week for any part of which you receive the disability element or severe disability element of working tax credit (WTC).

Alternatively, for Category A or B retirement pension, widowed parent's allowance, bereavement allowance, widowed mother's allowance or widow's pension purposes, a Class 1 credit is given for each week for which WTC is paid to you. In this case, if WTC was paid to you as a member of a couple but only one of you has earnings, the credits will be awarded to that person, otherwise they are awarded to the person to whom WTC is paid.

You will only qualify for such credits during any week in which *either*:[92]

- you were employed and earning less than the lower earnings limit for that year; *or*
- you were self-employed but had been granted an exemption from paying Class 2 contributions because your earnings were below the small earnings limit (see p833).

This provision also existed for working families' tax credit (WFTC) and disabled person's tax credit (DPTC), which were abolished in April 2003 (see CPAG's *Welfare Benefits Handbook* 2002/2003) and for family credit and disability working allowance which pre-dated WFTC and DPTC (see CPAG's *Welfare Benefits Handbook* 1999/2000).

Credits for a quashed conviction

If you were imprisoned or detained in legal custody after being convicted of an offence, and that conviction has subsequently been quashed by the courts, you may be entitled to sufficient credits to qualify for benefit.[93]

You must apply in writing to be awarded the credits. If awarded, you will get credits for each week during at least part of which you were imprisoned or detained.

Home responsibilities protection

A year of home responsibilities protection is a tax year throughout which:[94]

- you receive child benefit for a child aged under 16; *or*
- you get IS on the basis that you are looking after a disabled person; *or*
- you spend at least 35 hours a week looking after someone who, for at least 48 weeks in that tax year, is receiving either the higher or middle rates of disability living allowance care component (see p136), attendance allowance (see p147) or constant attendance allowance (under the industrial injuries scheme or war pensions scheme);
- you are an approved foster parent or foster carer (this only applies for the tax years 2003/04 onwards).

A year should automatically be recorded as a year of home responsibilities protection if you qualify because you receive child benefit or you receive IS while caring for a disabled person. If you qualify only on the third or fourth of the above grounds, or you qualify for part of the year on one ground and the rest on another, you must apply to the Revenue, using form CF411. From April 2002 onwards, if your application is made on the third of the above grounds, you must make your application within three years of the end of the tax year in which you were looking after the disabled person.[95]

Although to qualify for home responsibilities protection for a year on the first of the above grounds, child benefit must have been paid *throughout* a tax year, there are two circumstances when it may be possible to qualify for home responsibilities protection even if your claim for child benefit is not made at the start of the year.

First, if your child benefit is backdated to the start of the tax year – as child benefit can normally be backdated for up to three months this means you will have to have made your claim within three months of the start of the tax year to get home responsibilities for that year.

Second, for tax years from 2004/05 onwards, if child benefit cannot be backdated because someone else was previously receiving it for the same child, you may still be able to qualify for home responsibilities protection if that person's child benefit claim had priority over yours (see p92), but s/he notified the child benefit office that s/he wanted to give up her/his claim so that you could qualify for it, and this notification took effect at some time within the first three months of a tax year. In this circumstance you will be treated as if you were entitled to child benefit for each of the weeks in the tax year prior to the notification if you would have otherwise been entitled to it for those weeks.[96]

If you live with your partner and s/he receives child benefit, and s/he is working and earning enough to pay NI contributions, but you are not working, or you are not earning enough to pay NI contributions, it may be beneficial for the child benefit claim to be transferred into your name as this would entitle you to home responsibilities protection. If you decide to do this, your partner should withdraw her/his claim when you make your child benefit claim. It is not enough for you to say that your name is, or should be, on the child benefit order book together with your partner's.

A year in which a woman has elected to have reduced liability for contributions cannot be a year of home responsibilities protection.[97] It may, therefore, be worth considering whether to revoke such an election (see p830).

No year before 6 April 1978 can be a year of home responsibilities protection.

Home responsibilities protection helps towards satisfying the second contribution condition for long-term benefits (but see p846). Years of home responsibilities protection in which you do not satisfy the contribution conditions are deducted from the requisite number of years for which you would otherwise have to satisfy the contribution conditions.[98]

Example

Florence left school at age 16 in 1976. Because she was born after 6 April 1955, she will reach pension age at 65 (see p491) – ie, in 2025. Her working life for retirement pension purposes is 49 years and the number of years in which she would normally have to satisfy the second contribution condition is 44 (see below). She gets home responsibilities protection for 10 complete years during which time she looked after her children, and for three years when she looked after her disabled mother. This reduces the requisite number of years in which she must satisfy the contribution conditions for a retirement pension on the basis of her own contributions to 31 (ie, 44 – 13).

However, home responsibilities protection can only reduce the requisite number of years to 20, or half what it would otherwise be, whichever is lower.[99]

4. Contribution conditions for benefits

Contributory benefits, except a bereavement payment, have two contribution conditions. To help satisfy the second condition, you may be credited with contributions to fill gaps in your contribution record (see p837). However, the first contribution condition must always be satisfied by contributions which have actually been paid.

If you are covered by EC Regulation 1408/71 it may be possible for you to rely on the contributions you have paid in other European Economic Area states to qualify for contributory benefits (see p673).

Contribution-based jobseeker's allowance and incapacity benefit

The first condition

To qualify for contribution-based jobseeker's allowance (JSA) or incapacity benefit (IB) (apart from IB for people incapable of work in youth, which has no contribution conditions – see p267) you must have actually paid, in one tax year, the appropriate class of contributions producing an earnings factor (see p827) at least 25 times that year's lower earnings limit (eg, £2,050 in 2005/06 – 25 times £82),[100] or 25 flat-rate contributions paid before 6 April 1975.[101] The contributions must be paid before a claim for contribution-based JSA or IB is made.

The first condition and incapacity benefit

For IB, the contributions may be either Class 1 or 2.[102] They must have been paid in one of the last three complete tax years before the relevant 'benefit year' but this rule is relaxed, so that sufficient contributions paid in any one year will be enough, if you were:[103]

- entitled to carer's allowance (CA) (even if it was not paid because of the overlapping benefit rules – see p1102) in the last complete tax year before the benefit year (see below) in which you became incapable of work (CA used to be called invalid care allowance);
- working and entitled to disability working allowance or disabled person's tax credit (DPTC) for more than two years immediately before becoming incapable of work (disability working allowance and DPTC have now been abolished);
- working for more than two years and entitled to the disability element or the severe disability element of working tax credit immediately before becoming incapable of work;
- receiving IB at some time in the last complete tax year before the benefit year of the new claim;
- entitled to credited contributions because you had been in prison or a detention centre and your conviction was subsequently quashed by the courts.

Benefit years are almost the same as calendar years and run from the first Sunday in January.[104] The **'relevant benefit year'** for IB is the year in which the period of incapacity for work (see p265) begins.[105] However, if you have been discharged from the Forces and are able to count days when you were on sickness absence from duty as days on which you were entitled to short-term IB, the relevant benefit year for IB is the year in which your claim for IB starts.[106]

For IB, a widow who loses her entitlement to widowed mother's allowance for a reason other than remarriage or cohabitation (ie, because her children grow up) will be deemed to have satisfied this contribution condition (and will be credited with contributions to satisfy the second condition – see p840).[107] But this help with the first contribution condition does not extend to widows or widowers who lose entitlement to bereavement benefits.

The first condition and contribution-based jobseeker's allowance

The contributions must be Class 1 contributions for contribution-based JSA (unless you are a share fisherman or volunteer development worker – see p829).[108] The contributions must have been paid in one of the last two complete tax years before the 'relevant benefit year'.[109] The **'relevant benefit year'** (which runs from the first Sunday in January) for contribution-based JSA is the benefit year in which the jobseeking period (see p348) begins.[110]

The second condition

This condition is that you must have either paid or been credited with contributions producing an earnings factor (see p827) equal to 50 times the lower earnings limit in each of the last two complete tax years ending before the relevant benefit year.[111]

Credited contributions will not always help you fulfil the second contribution condition. However, for both IB and JSA, a widow or widower who loses her/his entitlement to bereavement benefits for a reason other than marriage or cohabitation will be credited with contributions to satisfy this condition.[112]

In rare cases, the rules about when contributions must have been paid in order to satisfy the second contribution condition may mean that you should delay a claim for contribution-based JSA so that you can draw on a different year's contribution record. This is because the relevant tax year for contribution-based JSA depends on the benefit year in which the first day of your jobseeking period (see p348) falls. Thus, if you claim before Sunday 2 January 2005 the relevant contribution years for contribution-based JSA purposes will be 2001/02 and 2002/03, whereas if you claim on or after Sunday 2 January 2005 they would be 2002/03 and 2003/04.

Any day for which you do not claim does not count as part of your jobseeking period (see p348),[113] so it is easy to postpone when that period begins. However, if you claim and are refused benefit because the contribution conditions are not satisfied, your jobseeking period will have started. You would then normally have to wait for more than 12 weeks to make a fresh claim. The 12-week gap would break the jobseeking period.

Bereavement payment

The only contribution condition for a bereavement payment is that your spouse must actually have paid, in any one tax year before s/he reached pension age (or before her/his death, if s/he died before reaching pension age) contributions of Classes 1, 2 or 3 producing an earnings factor (see p827) of at least 25 times the lower earnings limit (eg, £2,050 in 2005/06 – (25 x £82)).[114]

The sum of any contributions paid in any year may be counted if s/he only became liable to pay contributions in either the last complete tax year before the benefit year in which s/he reached pension age or in which s/he died (if s/he died before reaching pension age), or in the tax year before that.

The contribution condition for bereavement payment is treated as satisfied if your late spouse had ever successfully claimed and met the first contribution condition for maternity allowance (MA) or IB.

Note: MA no longer has contribution conditions, although it did for women whose expected week of childbirth fell before 20 August 2000.[115]

The payment of 25 flat-rate contributions in a contribution year prior to 6 April 1975 also satisfies this condition.[116]

Widowed parent's allowance, bereavement allowance, widowed mother's allowance, widow's pension and Category A and B retirement pensions

The first condition

The contributor – ie, you for Category A retirement pensions (or your late spouse or former spouse if you are divorced), your late spouse for widowed parent's allowance or bereavement allowance, your spouse or your late spouse for Category B retirement pension, or your late husband for widowed mother's allowance or widow's pension – must actually have paid in any one tax year before death or pension age, contributions of Class 1, 2 or 3 with an earnings factor of 52 times that year's lower earnings limit (eg, £4,264 in 2005/06 – (52 x £82)).[117]

This condition is deemed to be satisfied if the contributor was receiving long-term IB either in the year in which s/he died (if s/he died before reaching pension age) or in which s/he reached pension age, or in the preceding year.[118] Fifty flat-rate payments at any time before 6 April 1975 also satisfy this condition.[119]

The second condition

The contributor must have paid or been credited with contributions with an earnings factor of at least 52 times that year's lower earnings limit for each of the requisite number of years.[120]

The requisite number of years you need to satisfy this condition depends on the length of your 'working life'. This is the period inclusive of the tax year in which you reach the age of 16 up to but exclusive of the year in which you reach pension age or in which you die (if earlier).[121]

If you were over 16 on 5 July 1948, your working life is taken as having started either on 6 April 1948 or on 6 April of the year between 1936 and 1948 that you first started paying contributions, if you paid contributions before 5 July 1948.[122]

A year of home responsibilities protection looking after a child or a disabled person does not count as a year of your working life unless your earnings factor in that year was at least 52 times the lower earnings limit (see p827 for exactly how this works).

The requisite number of years is then calculated as follows:[123]

Length of 'working life'	*Requisite number of years*
1–10 years	Length of working life minus 1
11–20 years	Length of working life minus 2
21–30 years	Length of working life minus 3
31–40 years	Length of working life minus 4
41–50 years	Length of working life minus 5

Since contributions paid before 6 April 1975 do not produce an earnings factor (see p827), the number of years before that date in which the contribution condition is satisfied is calculated by adding together all the contributions paid or credited before 6 April 1975, and dividing the answer by 50. If that does not produce a whole number the result is rounded up, as long as that would not produce a number greater than the number of years of the working life before 6 April 1975.

Widows, widowers and divorcees may be able to combine their own contribution records with those of their late or former spouses in order to claim a Category A retirement pension (see p487).

Insufficient contributions

Benefits are paid at a reduced rate if the second contribution condition is not satisfied for the requisite number of years, provided it is satisfied in at least 25 per cent of the requisite number. The benefit is paid at a percentage of the amount which would otherwise be paid. The percentage is calculated by expressing the number of years in which the condition is satisfied as a percentage of the requisite number of years and rounding it up to the nearest whole number.[124] Thus, if you are a widow and your husband's working life was 12 years, so that the requisite number of years is 10, and if he only satisfied the condition in 8 years, you receive 80 per cent of the standard rate of widowed parent's allowance or bereavement allowance.

Increases for adult dependants are reduced in the same proportion, but increases for children are always paid in full. Note that increases for children have been abolished from 6 April 2003, although people entitled to such increases before that date may continue to qualify for them (see p798).[125]

It may be possible for you to pay Class 3 contributions (see p834) to bring the number of years in which the second contribution condition is satisfied up to the 25 per cent figure needed for a minimum pension or to enhance the rate at which the pension will be paid. This can be very worthwhile. For example, if you are only one year short of the minimum number of years, payment of £382.20 (52 Class 3 contributions at £7.35 each) may secure you a pension of £20.51 a week (£82.05 x 25 per cent) uprated annually for the rest of your life. You will get your money back in a little over 18 weeks.

Notes

1. **Introduction**

1 s1(1) SSCBA 1992; s162 SSAA 1992
2 s1(2) SSCBA 1992
3 s21(1) and (2) SSCBA 1992
4 s2(1)(a) SSCBA 1992
5 s2(1)(b) SSCBA 1992
6 *Ready Mixed Concrete South East Ltd v Ministry of Pensions and National Insurance* [1968] 2 QB 497 (QBD); *Global Plant v Secretary of State for Health and Social Security* [1971] 3 All ER 385 (QBD)
7 Sch 1 paras 1-5 SS(CatE) Regs
8 Sch 1 para 6 SS(CatE) Regs
9 Sch 1 paras 7-12 SS(CatE) Regs
10 s21(5)(d) SSCBA 1992
11 ss5(1) and 6A SSCBA 1992
12 Sch 1 SS(EF) Regs
13 s11 SS(TF)A; Part III SSC(DA) Regs

2. **Payment of contributions**

14 ss6(1)(a), 11(1) and 13(1) SSCBA 1992; reg 93 SS(Con) Regs
15 ss6(3)and 11(2) SSCBA 1992; regs 49(e) and 91 SS(Con) Regs
16 *Equal Opportunities Commission v Secretary of State for Social Security*, ECJ Case C-9/91 [1992] 3 CMLR 233. Although a recent commissioner's decision, CIB/4497/2002, indicates that there may be an argument that, in respect of establishing entitlement to other contributory benefits, the differing age limits for liability for payment of contributions may not be lawful.
17 ss2(1)(a) and 6 SSCBA 1992
18 Reg 145(1)(a) SS(Con) Regs
19 Reg 145(2) SS(Con) Regs
20 Reg 145(3) SS(Con) Regs
21 Reg 146 SS(Con) Regs
22 Reg 146(2)(b) SS(Con) Regs
23 ss2(1)(b)and 11 SSCBA 1992; reg 145(1)(d) SS(Con) Regs
24 Reg 145(1)(c) SS(Con) Regs
25 Regs 147 and 148 SS(Con) Regs
26 Regs 149 and 151 SS(Con) Regs
27 Regs 145(1)(e), 146(2)(b), 147 and 148 SS(Con) Regs
28 Reg 91(b) SS(Con) Regs
29 Reg 127 SS(Con) Regs
30 s22(4) SSCBA 1992; regs 7(3), 7A(2), 7B(3), 7C(4), 8(2), 8A(5), 8B(3), 9B(3), 9C(4) and 9D(4) and (5) SS(Cr) Regs
31 Reg 130 SS(Con) Regs
32 Reg 128(1) SS(Con) Regs
33 Reg 6 SSC(NPPC1C) Regs
34 ss6 and 7 SSCBA 1992
35 ss6A, 8 and 9 SSCBA 1992
36 Reg 11(2)(b) SS(Con) Regs
37 s8(1) and (2) SSCBA 1992
38 ss8 and 41 PSA 1993
39 ss43(1) and 45(1) PSA 1993
40 s19(4) SSCBA 1992; reg 131 SS(Con) Regs
41 Sch 1 para 3 SSCBA 1992
42 s9 SSCBA 1992
43 ss41(1B) and 42A PSA 1993; para 2(b) SS(C1CCP)O
44 Reg 119 SS(Con) Regs
45 Regs 13, 14, 15 and 21 SS(Con) Regs
46 Reg 21 SS(Con) Regs
47 Sch 1 para 1 SSCBA 1992; regs 13, 14, 15 and 21 SS(Con) Regs. There are also special rules which affect some people who work for agencies and for barristers' clerks and some ministers of religion.
48 ss1(2) and 10 SSCBA 1992

49 s11 SSCBA 1992; reg 46 SS(Con) Regs
50 s11(5) SSCBA 1992
51 Reg 45 SS(Con) Regs
52 Reg 46 SS(Con) Regs
53 Reg 127(1) SS(Con) Regs
54 s11(1) SSCBA 1992
55 Regs 125, 149, 151 and 152 SS(Con) Regs
56 Reg 21 SS(Con) Regs
57 Reg 47 SS(Con) Regs
58 s13 SSCBA 1992
59 s14 SSCBA 1992
60 Reg 56 SS(Con) Regs
61 s13(1) SSCBA 1992
62 s15(1) and (3) SSCBA 1992
63 Regs 95-99 SS(Con) Regs
64 Reg 100 SS(Con) Regs
65 s114 SSAA 1992
66 s8 ERA 1996
67 s13 ERA 1996. However, as with all disputes with your employer, you should remember that not all employees have a right not to be unfairly dismissed and that, even if you have that right, compensation for unfair dismissal may be a poor second to keeping your job.
68 Reg 60 SS(Con) Regs
69 Regs 89and 90 SS(Con) Regs
70 Reg 4 SS(CTCNIN) Regs
71 Reg 48(3)(b) SS(Con) Regs
72 Reg 4(7) and (8) SS(CTCNIN) Regs
73 Regs 50and 61 SS(Con) Regs; reg 6 SS(CTCNIN) Regs
74 Reg 50A SS(Con) Regs; reg 6A SS(CTCNIN) Regs
75 Reg 6A SS(CTCNIN) Regs
76 Reg 62 SS(Con) Regs

3. **Credits and home responsibilities protection**

77 More accurately, contributions with an earnings factor of at least 52 times the lower earnings limit for the year in question (or 50 flat-rate pre-1975 contributions). This does not apply if the contributor was receiving long-term IB in the year s/he reached pensionable age (or died) or the preceding year. See Sch 3 para 5(6) SSCBA 1992.
78 Reg 3 SS(CR) Regs
79 Regs 7(3), 7A(2)(b), 7B(3), 7C(4), 8(2)(b), 8A(5)(e), 8B(3), 9B(3), 9C(4) and 9D(4) SS(CR) Regs
80 Regs 8Aand 8B SS(Cr) Regs
81 Reg 8B(4) SS(Cr) Regs
82 Reg 8A(5) SS(Cr) Regs
83 Reg 7A SS(Cr) Regs
84 Reg 4 SS(Cr) Regs
85 Reg 8 SS(Cr) Regs
86 Reg 7 SS(Cr) Regs
87 Reg 9C SS(Cr) Regs
88 Reg 9B SS(Cr) Regs
89 Reg 8C SS(Cr) Regs
90 Reg 3(1)(b) SSB(MW&WSP) Regs
91 Reg 9A SS(Cr) Regs
92 Regs 7Band 7C SS(Cr) Regs
93 Reg 9D SS(Cr) Regs
94 Reg 2(2) and (3) SSP(HR) Regs
95 Reg 2(5)(b) and (c) SSP(HR) Regs
96 Reg 6A SS(CTCNIN) Regs
97 Reg 2(5)(a) SSP(HR) Regs
98 Sch 3 para 5(7) SSCBA 1992
99 Sch 3 para 5(7) SSCBA 1992

4. **Contribution conditions for benefits**

100 s21 and Sch 3 para 2 SSCBA 1992; ss1(2)(d) and 2 JSA 1995
101 Reg 15 SS(STB)(T) Regs
102 s21(1) and (2) SSCBA 1992
103 Reg 2B SS(IB) Regs
104 s21(6) SSCBA 1992
105 Sch 3 para 2(6) SSCBA 1992
106 Sch 3 para 2(6) SSCBA 1992, as modified by reg 4 Social Security Contributions and Benefits Act 1992 (Modifications for Her Majesty's Forces and Incapacity Benefit) Regulations 2003, SI 2003 No.737
107 Reg 3(1) SSB(MW&WSP) Regs
108 s2 JSA 1995; regs 158 and 167 JSA Regs
109 s2(1) JSA 1995
110 s2(4) JSA 1995
111 s21 and Sch 3 para 2 SSCBA 1992; s2 JSA 1995
112 Reg 8C SS(Cr) Regs
113 Reg 47(3)(a) JSA Regs
114 s21and Sch 3 para 4 SSCBA 1992
115 Sch 3 para 7 and 9 SSCBA 1992
116 Reg 13(1) SS(STB)(T) Regs
117 Sch 3 para 5 SSCBA 1992
118 Sch 3 para 5(6) SSCBA 1992
119 Reg 6 SS(WBRP&OB)(T) Regs
120 Sch 3 para 5(3) SSCBA 1992
121 Sch 3 para 5(8) SSCBA 1992
122 Reg 7(7) SS(WBRP&OB)(T) Regs; s20 and Sch 3 para 5(5) SSCBA 1992
123 Sch 3 para 5(5) SSCBA 1992
124 Reg 6 SS(WB&RP) Regs
125 s60(4)-(6) SSCBA 1992; reg 6(3) SS(WB&RP) Regs

Chapter 34

Maintenance and benefits

This chapter is about maintenance and how it affects your entitlement to benefit. It covers:

Some of the provisions affect sponsors who have signed undertakings to maintain people coming from abroad; the implications for them are dealt with on p851.

This chapter also covers the benefits you might get if you are contributing to the maintenance of a child or a person caring for a child (see p872).

On 3 March 2003 the new child support scheme was introduced. This means that some parents will be dealt with under the new scheme, which we call the 'new rules', while others may continue to be dealt with under the old scheme, which we call the 'old rules'. At the time of writing it was unclear when all old cases will convert to the new scheme. Where appropriate, the differences between the schemes are highlighted. For more information on child support maintenance, see CPAG's *Child Support Handbook*.

1. Getting maintenance

If you have separated from your partner or from the other parent of your child(ren) you might be able to get maintenance. You are entitled to maintenance payments for your child(ren). You might be entitled to maintenance for yourself if you are or were married. You are treated as applying for child support maintenance if you make a claim for income support (IS) or income-based jobseeker's allowance (JSA), unless you opt out (see p857). The maintenance you get affects your IS, pension credit, income-based JSA (see p865), housing benefit (HB) and council tax benefit (CTB) (see p871).

For information on the rules about maintenance for children under the child support scheme, see p854. These are covered where they affect your right to benefit or the amount to which you are entitled. For further information about the child support scheme, see CPAG's *Child Support Handbook*.

Payments of maintenance for yourself can be made on a voluntary basis or under a court order. Detailed advice about maintenance orders is beyond the scope of this *Handbook*. You should see a solicitor for advice about these. If you are on a low income you could qualify for free legal advice.

While you are on IS or income-based JSA, certain people are 'liable to maintain' you or your children (see below). In some cases, the DWP can take action to obtain maintenance from them on your behalf (see p854).

If you are on IS, income-based JSA, HB or CTB, voluntary payments from your former partner or the parent of your child(ren) are dealt with under the maintenance rules in this chapter and *not* under the normal rules on charitable and voluntary payments (see p973).[1]

If you have been getting child maintenance under an old rules maintenance assessment and you or your partner start working full time (see p750) or increase your earnings and stop getting IS or income-based JSA, you might be able to get a **child maintenance bonus** (see p54).

Some parents who receive maintenance may be better off claiming child tax credit (see Chapter 49) rather than IS or income-based JSA. Parents who are considering this should always have a careful better-off calculation completed before making this decision.

Who is liable to maintain you while you are on income support or income-based jobseeker's allowance

If someone is 'liable to maintain' you or your child(ren), s/he must pay maintenance. The Secretary of State can take proceedings against anyone who has a liability to maintain you or your child(ren) while you are on IS or income-based JSA. If that person fails to maintain you or your child(ren), s/he can be prosecuted (see p852).

While you are on IS or income-based JSA:[2]

- you must be maintained by your spouse, if you are married or separated. If you have to live apart from your spouse because you need care or treatment (eg, in hospital or in a care home) you may be assessed and paid as separate individuals for benefit purposes (see p816). However, your spouse is still liable to maintain you and may be asked to make a financial contribution towards your care.

While you are on IS:[3]

- your child(ren) must be maintained by both their parents. A parent is not liable to maintain children over 16 who are independent or any children over the age of 19;

- if you are the subject of a formal sponsorship/undertaking you must be maintained by a sponsor who has given an undertaking to support you (see p662). This includes your ex-spouse after you are divorced.

Unless you are the subject of a formal sponsorship/undertaking (see above) your right to claim benefit is not affected by the fact that the DWP can get money back from someone who is liable to maintain you. You should not, therefore, be refused IS or income-based JSA while maintenance is being pursued. However, maintenance that is recovered might affect your benefit (see p865).

Note: a parent who does not live with the person who is looking after her/his child(ren) is expected to pay child support maintenance on a regular basis.[4] If you are the parent looking after the child(ren) and claim IS or income-based JSA you are treated as applying for this maintenance unless you opt out (see p857). However, if you opt not to apply for maintenance without good cause your benefit may be paid at a reduced rate (but see p859 before you decide to do this).

Prosecution

A person who is liable to maintain you or your child(ren) (see p851) can be prosecuted if IS or income-based JSA is paid as a result of her/his persistently refusing or neglecting to maintain you. You can even be prosecuted for failing to maintain yourself (this rarely, if ever, happens). Although the power remains in respect of children, it is very unlikely to be used given that child maintenance is dealt with by the Child Support Agency (CSA – see p854). In either case, the maximum penalty is three months' imprisonment or a fine of £2,500, or both.[5] If you are charged with such an offence, see a solicitor. You might qualify for free advice and assistance or even free representation.

Maintenance orders

While you are on IS or income-based JSA, the Secretary of State can take proceedings against anyone who is liable to maintain you or your child(ren) (see p851) if s/he fails to do so. This enables the DWP to pursue maintenance while you are on IS or income-based JSA. These rules are not used to seek maintenance for your child(ren). Instead, you can be required to apply for child support maintenance (see p854).

The magistrates' court can make an order telling the person who is liable what s/he has to pay.[6] The fact that there was an agreement that you would not ask for maintenance is not a bar to an order being made,[7] although all the circumstances must be taken into account.[8] The court is entitled to refuse to make an order for maintenance if you have been cruel or deserted your spouse, or committed adultery.[9]

Since 5 April 1993, the courts have not had the power to make new orders for maintenance for children except in limited circumstances.[10] Instead, you can apply for child support maintenance (see p854).

Amount of maintenance

A new child support scheme was introduced on 3 March 2003.[11] The new scheme includes new rules on calculating child support maintenance, but initially applies, in most cases, only to child support calculations that come into effect on or after 3 March 2003. We call the new scheme the 'new rules' and the old scheme the 'old rules' – these are the names used by the CSA. Most existing cases before 3 March 2003 will convert to the new rules at a future date, known as 'C Day', though some may convert earlier. At the time of writing no date had been announced for C Day. It was anticipated that the date would need to be before 6 April 2005, given the scheme's relation to the abolition of child allowances and premiums. However, as these continue to be in force in relation to IS and income-based JSA cases which have not migrated onto CTC, then no guidance on the date of conversion can be given. See CPAG's *Welfare Rights Bulletin* for updates. Some existing old rules cases may convert earlier than this – see CPAG's *Child Support Handbook* for more details.

Under the new rules, maintenance can be calculated at one of four rates depending on the circumstances and income of the non-resident parent. There are provisions to reflect shared care and there may be variations to the calculation in certain circumstances. Under the old rules, the CSA uses a rigid formula for calculating child support maintenance. However, departures from the formula may be allowed in certain circumstances, for example, where you or a non-resident parent have a disabled child or where a non-resident parent's travel costs to see your child(ren) are expensive or if a parent's lifestyle is more extravagant than her/his declared income allows. See CPAG's *Child Support Handbook* for more details of both schemes.

There is more flexibility about how much maintenance your spouse is required to pay for you (rather than the child(ren)). S/he can negotiate with the DWP to pay an amount s/he can afford, given her/his outgoings. As a starting point for negotiations, the DWP compares your spouse's net income with the total of:[12]

- the IS personal allowances and premiums s/he would qualify for if s/he were entitled to IS (see Chapter 35);
- household expenses, including rent, mortgage and council tax (excluding arrears);
- 15 per cent of her/his net wage (to cover expenses for work);
- the balance of any other expenses exceeding the 15 per cent margin that are considered essential.

If your spouse has a new partner, two calculations are performed – one as if s/he were single and the other using their joint income. The lower figure is used as the basis for negotiation.

If the DWP believes your spouse is not paying sufficient maintenance it can take her/him to court (see p852).

Collection of maintenance by the DWP

While you are on IS or income-based JSA, if maintenance is payable through a magistrates' court (including via orders made in the county court or High Court but registered in the magistrates' court) it can be paid direct to the DWP.[13] In return, the DWP pays you the amount of IS or income-based JSA you would receive if no maintenance were being paid. The DWP does not usually accept this sort of arrangement unless payments have actually been missed, but may if you have a good reason for wanting it done and you explain why.

Collection of child support maintenance by the Child Support Agency

Child support maintenance can be paid to the CSA or direct to you as the person looking after the child(ren). If you claim IS or income-based JSA you will not be given the option of direct payments on the claim form,[14] but direct payments can be requested and made if you can persuade the decision maker to do so.[15] Payment via the CSA is useful where maintenance payments are likely to be irregular or unreliable, or where you do not want to be located by the other party. If the CSA is collecting the payments for you, it should take action automatically when a payment is missed. Where payment should be made direct to you, it is up to you to contact the CSA and the DWP when a maintenance payment does not arrive.

If you are on IS or income-based JSA and your child(ren)'s other parent is making payments to the CSA, the CSA retains the payments made by the non-resident parent. If the CSA does not receive your child support maintenance payment, you can still cash the full amount of IS or income-based JSA.

2. Child support maintenance

You should look at this section if you do not live with your child(ren)'s other parent and are claiming (or thinking about claiming):

- income support (IS); *or*
- income-based jobseeker's allowance (JSA).

Much of what we say below does not apply if you are not claiming either of these benefits. If you are not on IS or income-based JSA, see CPAG's *Child Support Handbook* for more information on child support maintenance.

Note: if you are not on these benefits, you do not have to use the Child Support Agency (CSA) for child support maintenance, and any you do receive is ignored as income for the purposes of working tax credit and child tax credit (CTC). Some parents who get maintenance may, therefore, be better off claiming CTC rather than IS or income-based JSA. Parents considering this should always have a careful better-off calculation completed before making this decision.

If you are on IS or income-based JSA and move onto pension credit (PC) any maintenance you receive will be treated differently. Child maintenance is ignored. However, spousal maintenance counts as income,[16] but it does not count as qualifying income for the savings credit of PC (see p468). When you move from IS or income-based JSA onto PC you will no longer be treated as applying for child support maintenance. This is because there is no provision for this in the Act.

Maintenance for children is dealt with by the CSA and is called 'child support maintenance'. If your child(ren) live with you but their other parent lives elsewhere, and you claim or are paid IS or income-based JSA, the general rule is that the CSA will make a child support maintenance calculation for the child(ren). That calculation requires the other parent (the 'non-resident' parent) to pay child support. This requirement to pay child maintenance also applies to assessments made under the old rules.

If you want to apply for child support maintenance, or are on IS or income-based JSA and have not been approached by the CSA, you can phone the CSA to make an application or ask for a child maintenance application form.

The new rules and the old rules

A new child support scheme was introduced on 3 March 2003. This means that currently there are two child support schemes in operation.

We call the old scheme the 'old rules' and the new scheme the 'new rules' – these are the terms used by the CSA. The new rules have some important differences from the old rules. Where these differences occur, we highlight these below. The Government plans to transfer all cases to the new rules at some point, but at the time of writing there was no date set for this transfer – see CPAG's *Child Support Handbook*.

When the old rules apply and when the new rules apply

The scheme which applies to you depends, in most cases, on when your child support maintenance calculation (new rules) or assessment (old rules) was due to take effect (this date is called the 'effective date'), as follows:[17]

- Effective date before 3 March 2003: old rules apply.
- Effective date on or after 3 March 2003: new rules apply.

The effective date is usually set at the date that the non-resident parent is contacted by the CSA to notify her/him of the child support application and gather information.

There are some exceptions to the main rule. For example, if you apply for child support after 3 March 2003, but had an assessment under the old rules in force within the previous 13 weeks regarding the same child and non-resident parent, then the new application will be assessed under the old rules.[18] If you had a child support assessment under the old rules, but make a new application for a different child with a different non-resident parent after 3 March 2003, then the new rules will apply to both cases; this means that the existing assessment will be converted to the new rules early.

If you would have come under the old rules but had no child support maintenance assessment – eg, because the 'harm or undue distress' rule (see p857) applied or there was a reduced benefit direction in force (see p859) – then if maintenance is to be worked out after 3 March 2003, you will have a calculation made under the new rules.

See CPAG's *Child Support Handbook* for full details.

Applications (old and new rules)

Under the new rules, you are taken to have applied for a maintenance calculation when you apply for benefit, unless you opt out. If you opt out, unless you can show good cause for doing this, your benefit may be reduced (see p857). **'Good cause'** means that there is a 'risk of harm or undue distress' to you or a child living with you (see p857).

Under the old rules you would have been required to authorise pursuit of maintenance by the CSA when you claimed benefit, unless good cause applied. You may have refused to authorise the CSA to act, in which case your benefit may already have been reduced. Even if a maintenance assessment is currently in force you may opt out – ie, ask for this to cease (see p857). However, if you do this without good cause your benefit may be reduced (see p859).

For claimants under the new rules, up to £10 of weekly maintenance is disregarded. This is known as the 'child support premium' (see p972). For claimants under the old rules, maintenance you receive counts in full as income when calculating your benefit. However, you may accrue a child maintenance bonus (see p54).

Your benefit claim should not be held up by the CSA, but opting out (or failure to authorise pursuit of maintenance under the old rules before 3 March 2003) without good cause could affect the amount of benefit you receive (see p858). The CSA may collect other types of maintenance at the same time as child support maintenance.[19]

A child must be maintained by both parents (see p851). If you are a child's non-resident parent and are on IS or JSA, a deduction can be made from your benefit towards your child's maintenance (see p862).

When you are on IS or income-based JSA, regardless of whether the new or old rules apply, the CSA maintenance overrides any previous maintenance agreement you have for your child(ren), including a court order.

Providing information (old and new rules)

Unless you or your child(ren) would be at risk of 'harm or undue distress' (see below), as well as providing authorisation (in old rules cases) you must provide information to enable the CSA to trace your child(ren)'s non-resident parent and to work out and collect child support maintenance.[20] If you come under the new rules, the information you must provide also includes details that will enable the non-resident parent to be identified. This means that you can be required to submit yourself or your child to a DNA test to establish parentage.[21] See CPAG's *Child Support Handbook* for more details of the information the CSA can expect you to provide.

Opting out

You can ask the CSA not to act at any time, regardless of whether you are a new claimant or have an old rules maintenance assessment in force.[22] This is known as 'opting out'.

If you request the CSA not to act, then it cannot proceed with the child support maintenance calculation (or old rules assessment).[23] But, unless the DWP agrees that you or your child(ren) would be at risk of 'harm or undue distress', your IS or income-based JSA may be paid at a reduced rate. Those benefits may also be reduced, under the new rules, if you withhold information from the CSA that is needed to make the calculation (see p856) or if you refuse to take a DNA test with regard to establishing parentage, unless it agrees that you or your child(ren) would be at risk of harm or undue distress.[24] (Under the old rules, benefit could be reduced for failure to provide information as well as refusal to authorise pursuit of maintenance.[25])

If the DWP agrees that you or your child(ren) would be at risk of harm or undue distress, you should be notified in writing, and your benefit should not be paid at a reduced rate. However, where you have requested the CSA not to act, and it has been accepted that you have good cause it can from time to time ask you to re-state your reasons, and reconsider them.[26] This reconsideration can only happen to decisions accepting good cause made on or after 3 March 2003.

Harm or undue distress

When you claim benefit, if you think that you or your child(ren) would be put at risk of suffering harm or undue distress if a child support assessment/calculation were to be made or continues in force, you should say so, give details of your situation, and request that the CSA does not act – ie, you opt out. This is then followed up by the DWP. See CPAG's *Child Support Handbook* for further details.

There is no legal definition of harm or undue distress.[27] It certainly covers situations where there is a possibility of violence or where there has been rape, sexual abuse, threats or other harassment. There does not need to have been a history of actual violence – fear of violence is enough. The DWP decides if a fear of violence is reasonably held.

There are many other situations in which you might find it distressing to pursue maintenance. Examples are where:

- you have not had any contact with the other parent for many years;
- you had a clean-break divorce;

- the other parent is threatening to contest who the child lives with;
- you chose to have the child against the father's wishes;
- you believe that seeking child support maintenance would threaten the arrangement between the child(ren) and their other parent.

You have to persuade the DWP that you or your child(ren) would suffer harm or undue distress. Each case is decided on its merits. Your word should be accepted without any supporting evidence unless you contradict yourself or what you say is improbable.[28]

Harm and undue distress are also considered if you fail to co-operate by not providing information (old and new rules) or refuse a DNA test (new rules).

The procedure

The DWP will want to interview you to gather information to make a decision. Under the new rules it will give you a four-week period to provide reasons to show there is a risk or undue harm or distress if you:

- do not give reasons for opting out; *or*
- refuse to withdraw your request for the CSA not to act, to provide information or submit to a DNA test; *or*
- give reasons, but the DWP does not believe that there is a risk of harm or undue distress.

You are warned in writing that your benefit could be paid at a reduced rate (see p859) unless there is a risk of harm or undue distress. You are given the four-week period either to withdraw your request to opt out, co-operate or supply your reasons for not complying. This applies to new cases and situations where a parent with an existing maintenance assessment opts out.

You can submit supporting letters – eg, from friends and relatives, your doctor, child's school, or other helpful organisations – if you wish.

It is important to explain the harm or undue distress which could arise. Make it clear that this is why you do not wish to co-operate (if you come under the old rules) or why you do not want the CSA to act, or to provide information or submit to a DNA test (if you come under the new rules). You do not have to reply in writing – a telephone call is acceptable, for example. However, you must provide a response in writing if the CSA insists that you do.[29] Nor do you have to provide evidence to prove that you would be under threat. Your word should be accepted,[30] although it is always useful to point to specific examples of problems which have occurred in the past or reasons why you believe they might occur in the future, to help illustrate what effect your co-operation might have. If there are reasonable grounds for believing that you or your child(ren) would suffer harm or undue distress were maintenance pursued, information given or, under the new rules, a DNA test taken, no further action is taken and you are advised of this.[31]

Under the new rules this decision to accept good cause may be reconsidered in the future.[32]

If it is not accepted that there would be a risk of harm or undue distress the DWP decides whether to pay your benefit at a reduced rate (see below). You do not have a right of appeal until the end of the procedure. See CPAG's *Child Support Handbook* for more details about the procedure.

Payment of benefit at a reduced rate

Your IS or income-based JSA can be paid at a reduced rate if:

- under the old rules, you refused to provide authorisation or information to enable the CSA to pursue child support maintenance for your child(ren); *or*
- under the new rules, you refuse to provide information to the CSA or to submit to a DNA test (see p856); *or*
- you refuse to withdraw the request for the CSA not to act; *and*
- the DWP does not accept that there is any risk of harm or undue distress to you or your child(ren) (see p857).

If this is the case, the DWP makes a '**reduced benefit decision**' under the new rules.[33] Under the old rules this was known as a 'reduced benefit *direction*'. Any reduced benefit *direction* in force on 3 March 2003 will now be treated as if it were a reduced benefit decision made under the new rules.[34]

The rest of this section will, therefore, refer to reduced benefit decisions.

When deciding whether to issue a reduced benefit decision, the DWP must consider whether the welfare of any child involved would be adversely affected – eg, because of her/his age or state of health, or that of her/his parents.[35] See p860 for more information about the amount by which your benefit can be reduced.

A reduced benefit decision cannot be issued if IS or income-based JSA paid to you or your partner includes a disabled child premium, a disability premium or a higher pensioner premium, or if a CTC award for you or your partner includes the element for a child/young person with a disability see pp886, 886 and 890.[36] (This applies even if it is your partner who has the disability.) If you are awarded a relevant premium or element of CTC after the reduced benefit decision is imposed this will not stop the reduction. You have a right of appeal to an appeal tribunal against a reduced benefit decision but only if one is actually imposed.[37]

The reduced rate of benefit

Your benefit should be paid in full until a decision is issued; it is then adjusted.

Benefit can be paid at a reduced rate even if it does not include an amount for the child(ren) for whom maintenance is being claimed.[38] However, the reduction is suspended if you are getting IS or income-based JSA while in hospital or a care home.[39]

Only one reduced benefit decision can be in operation at a time even if you refuse to co-operate in seeking maintenance for children from different relationships.[40] However, if another child is born or joins your household you can be treated as applying for maintenance and have to provide information in relation to that additional child. A second reduced benefit decision could be issued if you again fail to opt out, fail to co-operate or fail to allow a DNA test. The second decision replaces the original one, which ceases even if it would otherwise have run for several more months.[41]

The amount by which benefit is reduced and how long this lasts

If a reduced benefit decision is issued, unless it ends early (see below), your benefit is reduced by a percentage of your personal allowance. In 2005/06 this means your benefit will be reduced by £22.48 a week. The reduced benefit decision lasts for three years.[42] If the reduction would take your IS or income-based JSA to below 10p, a lower reduction is made so that you are left with this minimum amount of benefit.[43] When benefit rates are increased in April the amount of the reduction also increases.[44]

The three-year period begins on the first day of the second benefit week after your claim has been reviewed.[45] At the end of the three-year period, if you still opt out or refuse to co-operate, another reduced benefit decision can be issued (see below).

Second reduced benefit decisions

If a second reduced benefit decision is made against you because you opt out or refuse to co-operate in relation to an additional child without good cause, the original decision lapses and the reduction under the new decision lasts for a fresh three years.[46]

Example 1

Paula has been paid benefit at a reduced rate for seven months because she refused to sign a maintenance application form for her first child under the old rules. She has now requested the CSA not to pursue maintenance for her new baby. The first reduced benefit decision (remember that old rules reduced benefit directions are treated as decisions) ends early. However, she is penalised for a further three years under a new reduced benefit decision.

If the second reduced benefit decision terminates, the original decision can be brought back into operation for the balance of the three-year period. This can only be done if you are still refusing to co-operate in relation to the original child support maintenance application.[47]

Example 2

After a second reduced benefit decision has been in operation for one year, Paula has decided to seek child support maintenance for her baby. However, she still does not want to seek maintenance for her first child. The original reduced benefit decision (remember that an old rules reduced benefit direction is treated as a decision) had been in place for seven months. It is reinstated for one year and five months.

3 years – 1 year (second reduced benefit decision) – 7 months (original reduced benefit decision) = 1 year and 5 months.

When a reduced benefit decision ends early

The reduced benefit decision **terminates** if:[48]

- you withdraw the request for the CSA not to act, or you provide information or submit to a DNA test; *or*
- the DWP decides that you do not have to withdraw the request for the CSA not to act, or provide information or to submit to a DNA test; *or*
- in Scotland only, your child(ren) successfully apply to the CSA for a maintenance calculation.

It can also be terminated if the decision to issue a reduced benefit decision is revised or superseded or if you appeal (see pp1189, 1199 and 1217).

A reduced benefit decision is **suspended** if:

- you stop getting IS or income-based JSA.[49] However, if you claim one of these benefits again within 52 weeks, the reduced benefit decision is reinstated for the remainder of the three-year period if you continue to opt out. The DWP will send you notice that unless you opt in or provide reasons to support good cause within 14 days the reduced benefit decision will be reinstated.[50] The reinstated decision will only run for the balance of the three years that was not used up on the previous claim. If you make your new claim more than 52 weeks after you last received IS or income-based JSA, the decision is no longer valid. However, if you opt out when you re-claim benefit, the DWP will again investigate to decide whether or not to impose a reduced benefit decision in the normal way. A new reduced benefit decision could be made that would run for three years;
- either you stop providing a home and caring for your child(ren), or your child(ren) cease(s) to be eligible for maintenance because they are over 16 and have left non-advanced education (see p86), or are 19 or over. If you resume your role as a carer, or they become eligible again (eg, because they return to full-time education) the reduced benefit decision can be reinstated for the balance of the three years;[51]
- you are paid IS or income-based JSA at a special rate because you are in hospital or a care home (see Chapter 28). Initially the reduced benefit decision is suspended, but if you stay there for more than 52 weeks it ceases completely.[52]

You should be notified if a reduced benefit decision ceases.[53]

A reduced benefit decision will also cease when a parent moves from IS or income-based JSA onto PC. This is because you are not treated as applying for maintenance when you claim PC.

Challenging a reduced benefit decision

If you disagree with a reduced benefit decision, you can:

- seek a revision or a supersession. The situations when a decision can be revised or superseded are similar to those for social security benefits (see pp1189 and 1199). For full details of the rules see CPAG's *Child Support Handbook*;
- appeal to an appeal tribunal. Your appeal must be made against the reduced benefit decision, not against the actual reduction in your benefit.[54] You must appeal within one month of the decision being sent to you (one month plus 14 days if you ask for written reasons for the decision where these have not already been provided – see p1223). A late appeal can be accepted in certain circumstances.[55] The rules on late appeals are the same as those for social security benefits (see p1261).

The reduced benefit decision is imposed in the meantime.

Child support maintenance paid by non-resident parents on benefit (old and new rules)

If you are a non-resident parent (known under the old rules as an 'absent parent') you are liable to maintain your child(ren) (see p851). From 3 March 2003 a new child support scheme was introduced. This means you may be having deductions made from your benefit:

- under the old rules, because you have a maintenance assessment in force; *or*
- under the new rules, because you have a maintenance calculation in force.

Deductions for arrears of child support maintenance can be made from your contribution-based JSA (see p864) under both the old and new rules. Under the new rules deductions may also be made from other benefits prescribed for the flat-rate maintenance calculation other than IS, income-based JSA or PC.[56]

Old rules

If you are on IS or income-based JSA, deductions of £5.70 a week can be made from your benefit as a contribution towards the maintenance of your child(ren).[57] This does not apply if you:[58]

- are aged under 18;
- qualify for a family premium or have day-to-day care of any child (see CPAG's *Child Support Handbook* for details of 'day-to-day care');
- receive incapacity benefit (IB), maternity allowance (MA), statutory sick pay, statutory maternity pay, severe disablement allowance (SDA), attendance allowance, disability living allowance, carer's allowance (CA), industrial

injuries disablement benefit, a war disablement pension or a payment from either of the Independent Living Funds. If this benefit is not paid solely because of overlapping benefit rules or an inadequate contribution record, you are still exempt from deductions.

If you are an absent parent on IS or income-based JSA and have children from two or more different relationships, only one deduction can be made and the £5.70 is apportioned between the people who care for the children.[59] If deductions for other debts are being made from your benefits (see p1109), half of the deduction is made – ie, £2.85.

New rules

If you or your partner are on IS or income-based JSA, the flat-rate maintenance calculation applies, in which case a deduction of £5 a week is made. If you are in receipt of any of the following benefits, the flat-rate deduction of £5 can be made:[60]

- bereavement allowance;
- retirement pension;
- IB;
- CA;
- MA;
- SDA;
- industrial injuries benefit;
- widowed mother's allowance;
- widowed parent's allowance;
- widow's pension;
- contribution-based JSA;
- a training allowance (other than Work-Based Learning for Young People);
- war disablement or war widow's pension;
- PC.

However, no deduction will be made if you:[61]

- are a student, child or prisoner;
- are a 16/17-year-old receiving IS or income-based JSA, or your partner is;
- receive an allowance for Work-Based Learning for Young People;
- are in a care home and receive bereavement allowance, retirement pension, IB, CA, MA, SDA, industrial injuries disablement benefit, widowed mother's allowance, widowed parent's allowance, widow's pension, contribution-based JSA, a training allowance (other than Work-Based Learning for Young People), war disablement pension or war widow's pension, or have the whole or part of the cost of your accommodation met by the local authority;
- are a patient in hospital on IS who has been a patient for more than six weeks;

- are a patient in hospital who is on PC and has been a patient for at least 13, but no more than 52, weeks;
- are a patient in hospital in receipt of one of the benefits in the above bullet points who has been in hospital for 52 weeks or more; *or*
- are a person with a net income of less than £5 a week.

If you are a non-resident parent and your current partner is also a non-resident parent with a child support maintenance application in force, and either you or your partner get IS or income-based JSA, then you pay half the flat rate.[62]

If you are a non-resident parent, you or your partner are on benefit and you are regarded as having 'shared care' of your child(ren), then a nil rate calculation will apply and your benefit will not be reduced.[63] For what counts as 'shared care', see CPAG's *Child Support Handbook*.

Transitional amount

You may have deductions made at a different rate (eg, £2.50 or £1.50 depending on your circumstances) if your old maintenance assessment converts to a new maintenance calculation. This may occur where previously you were exempt from paying maintenance but under the new rules you are now due to pay maintenance. For more information on conversion and transitional amounts, see CPAG's *Child Support Handbook*.

Challenging a decision to make deductions

If you think that a decision to make deductions from your IS or income-based JSA is wrong, you can apply in writing to the DWP for a revision or a supersession, or you can appeal. The situations when a decision can be revised or superseded are similar to those for social security benefits (see pp1189 and 1199). For full details of the rules, see CPAG's *Child Support Handbook*.

If you want to appeal, you must do this within one month of the decision being sent to you (one month plus 14 days if you ask for written reasons for the decision where these have not already been provided – see p1223).[64] A late appeal can be accepted in certain circumstances.[65] The rules on late appeals are the same as those for social security benefits (see p1261).

Contribution-based jobseeker's allowance

Deductions for arrears of child support maintenance can be made from your *contribution-based* JSA.[66] You must have been served with a notice that you are in arrears of maintenance before a deduction can be made. The decision maker generally only applies for a deduction to be made from your benefit if the payment of child support maintenance cannot be obtained by other means. Your consent is not needed.

Under the old rules the maximum amount that can be deducted depends on your age – ie, 25 per cent of your applicable amount. Under the old rules, no deduction can be made if deductions are already being made for community charge arrears, a fine or council tax arrears (see p1109).[67]

Under the new rules a deduction of £1 may be made towards arrears, regardless of what other deductions are being made.[68] Deductions may also be made from other prescribed benefits for the flat rate except IS, income-based JSA and PC.

If you disagree with the decision by the DWP to make deductions, you have a right to apply for a revision or a supersession (see pp1189 and 1199) or to appeal to an appeal tribunal (see Chapter 44).

3. How maintenance affects your income support, income-based jobseeker's allowance, pension credit and tax credits

The following are taken into account in working out the amount of income support (IS) or income-based jobseeker's allowance (JSA) to which you are entitled:

- child support maintenance (see below);
- other maintenance payments made by 'liable relatives' (see p866).

Different rules apply if you are claiming housing benefit or council tax benefit. For these rules, see p871.

Note: maintenance is not taken into account when working out the amount of *contribution-based* JSA to which you are entitled.

Child maintenance is ignored for **pension credit** (PC). However, spousal maintenance is taken into account as income,[69] but it does not count as qualifying income for the savings credit of PC (see p468).

Maintenance is not taken into account for tax credits (see p1389). From April 2004 claimants on IS or income-based JSA who have child allowances and child-related premiums will be migrated onto child tax credit.

Child support maintenance

If you come under the old rules, all payments of child support maintenance are treated as income and are taken into account in full on a weekly basis.[70] If you come under the new rules, up to £10 a week of child support maintenance is ignored as income.[71] Where payments are made monthly, multiply by 12 and divide by 52 to obtain a weekly amount. Where regular payments are made at intervals other than each week or month, the payments are spread over the period, including any part-week. It is the actual payments made, and not the amount due under the Child Support Agency (CSA) calculation, which are taken into account in this way.[72]

The DWP should not calculate IS or income-based JSA on the assumption that child support maintenance payments are being made where this has not been happening. So a parent who would lose entitlement to IS or income-based JSA if payments were made can continue to receive it if the child support maintenance is not received. If there is a delay in obtaining increased or reinstated IS or income-based JSA you should seek advice.

Child support maintenance can be paid direct to the CSA or to you. See p854 for further details.

Arrears at the beginning of the child support assessment/calculation

Arrears of child support maintenance have usually accrued by the time an assessment/calculation is made. Usually these arrears are paid to, and retained by, the CSA if you are on IS or income-based JSA. However, if the payment is made to you, the IS or income-based JSA which has been overpaid to you can be recovered by the DWP.[73]

Arrears due during a claim

The CSA is responsible for collecting arrears of child support maintenance if you are on IS or income-based JSA. The CSA retains an amount equal to the IS or income-based JSA you were paid because the maintenance was not paid when it was due.[74]

Arrears paid for a period before the claim

Only child support maintenance both due for and received in the weeks of the claim can be taken into account by the DWP. A payment of child support maintenance due before, but paid after, you claim IS or income-based JSA is treated as paid in the week in which it was due.[75]

Other maintenance payments made by liable relatives

If someone who is a liable relative (see p867) makes maintenance payments to you that are not child support maintenance (see p854), these are dealt with in a special way.[76] To find out how child support maintenance affects your IS and income-based JSA, see p865, and child tax credit, see p1389.

How such a payment affects your benefit depends on whether it:

- counts as a liable relative payment, and is *either*:
  - a regular payment – known as a 'periodical payment' (see p867); *or*
  - a lump sum (in one go or by instalments) treated as income or capital (see p869); *or*
- does not count as a liable relative payment (see p870).

You and your solicitor should look at these rules carefully *before* negotiating payments from your former partner.

Most payments by liable relatives (see below) count as liable relative payments. These are usually treated as income and are taken into account fully to reduce your IS or income-based JSA. If you are receiving IS or income-based JSA, it is usually not a good idea to have a lump sum instead of periodical payments (see below). This is because a lump sum is usually treated as income (see p869), which is spread over a period at a sufficiently high level to disqualify you from benefit altogether. This happens even if the total amount is well below the usual capital limit (see p1023).

For information about lump sums that can be treated as capital, see p869.

Liable relative payments

Unless it is a payment that does not count (see p870), payments from the following people (known as **'liable relatives'**) count as liable relative payments:[77]

- a husband or wife. This includes one from whom you are separated or divorced;
- a parent of a child or young person under 19 for whom you are claiming (this could include a step-parent);
- a parent of a young person under 19 who is claiming IS or JSA in her/his own right (this could include a step-parent);
- a person who has been living with and maintaining a child or young person under 19 or maintaining a young person under 19 who is claiming IS or JSA in her/his own right and can therefore reasonably be treated as her/his parent;
- if you are the subject of a formal sponsorship/undertaking, a sponsor who has given an undertaking to support you financially (see p662).

There are special rules about how payments to you or to someone else on your behalf by one of the people above are taken into account (see below). However, it is important to note that not all of them are legally liable to maintain you (see p851). The Secretary of State can only pursue those who are liable to maintain you (see p852).

Periodical payments

'Periodical payments' are any of the following payments made by liable relatives (see above):[78]

- any payment made, or due to be made, regularly, whether voluntarily or under a court order or other formal agreement;
- any other small payment no higher than your weekly IS or income-based JSA;
- any payment made instead of one or more regular payments due under an agreement (whether formal or voluntary), either as payment in advance or arrears. This does not include any arrears due before the beginning of your entitlement to IS or income-based JSA (see p868).

Periodical payments which are received on time are each spread over a period equal to the interval between them – eg, monthly payments are spread over a month. Payments are converted to a weekly amount – eg, monthly payments are multiplied by 12 and divided by 52 to produce a weekly income figure.[79]

Arrears of periodical payments due during your claim

When a payment arrives during a claim and it includes a lump sum for arrears (or in advance), the payment is spread over a period calculated by dividing it by the weekly amount of maintenance you should have received.[80]

Example

Tia should receive maintenance of £80 a month. It is not paid for three months and she then receives £200.

£80 a month is treated as producing a weekly income of:

$$\frac{£80 \times 12}{52} = £18.46$$

The £200 is taken into account for:

$$\frac{£200}{£18.46} = 10.83 \text{ weeks}$$

Tia is assumed to have an income of £18.46 for the next 10 weeks and six days. The maintenance payments due are still two weeks and one day in arrears (£40).

If a payment is specifically identified as being arrears of maintenance for a particular period, the DWP can:

- take it into account for a forward period from the week you report you have received it; *or*
- attribute it to the past period which it was intended to cover, unless it is 'more practicable' to choose a later week.[81] In this case the Secretary of State can recover the full amount of extra benefit paid to you while maintenance was not being received.[82] This can still be done when you receive a payment, after your claim ends, which is for arrears of maintenance that should have been paid while you were still claiming.

It is important to work out how you would be better off financially. You should then argue for the payment to be spread over whichever period is more advantageous to you. This depends on the amount of IS or income-based JSA you would otherwise receive, the amount of the payment and whether any other periodical payments (see p867) are being made. You should appeal if your argument is not accepted.

Arrears of periodical payments due before your claim

If arrears of maintenance are paid for a period before the date of your claim they do not count as periodical payments (see p867).[83] The DWP deals with such payments as lump sums treated as income (see below). This means that they are spread over a future period.

Lump-sum payments

Lump-sum payments of maintenance are ignored for those receiving maintenance along with working tax credit (WTC) and child tax credit (CTC) (see p1389).

Child maintenance is ignored for PC. However, spousal maintenance is taken into account as income,[84] but it does not qualify as income for the savings credit of PC (see Chapter 38).

However, for IS and income-based JSA, in general the rules ensure that you usually do not benefit financially from receiving lump-sum payments of maintenance. Unless they do not count as 'liable relative payments' (see p870) or can be treated as capital (see p870), lump sums are treated as income (see below).[85] They are spread over a period so as to disqualify you from IS or income-based JSA for as long as possible.

It is only to your advantage to get a lump-sum payment if it can be treated as capital (see below). Lump-sum payments that count as capital do not affect your IS or income-based JSA unless they take your capital over £3,000 (£6,000 if you or your partner are aged 60 or over; £10,000 if you live in a care home). See Chapter 39 for more information about the capital rules.

A lump sum is treated as capital if you are already getting 'periodical payments' (see p867) equal to the IS or income-based JSA you would otherwise receive.[86] If you stop getting periodical payments (see p867) or these decrease, any of the lump sum you still have is taken into account as income (see below).[87]

Unless it can be treated as capital, a lump sum is treated as income as follows. It is divided:[88]

- by the weekly IS or income-based JSA you would otherwise receive, plus £2; *or*
- if you have not migrated onto child tax credit and the lump sum is just paid for your child(ren), by the aggregate of the prescribed amounts – ie, personal allowances for you, personal allowances for your child(ren), and family and child-related premiums (only counting children for whom you receive the maintenance). However, if your weekly IS or income-based JSA entitlement plus £2 would be less than this amount, the lower amount is used. This means that the lump sum disqualifies you from IS or income-based JSA for a longer period.

The lump sum is then treated as paid over the corresponding number of weeks. You are disqualified from getting IS or income-based JSA for a period beginning on the first day of the benefit week in which the lump-sum payment is received. The period can start in a later week if that is more practical.[89]

If you are being paid periodical payments as well as a lump-sum payment and these vary or stop, the calculation is done again, taking the balance of the lump sum into account.[90]

See Chapter 38 for further information about how your IS or income-based JSA is calculated.

If you receive a lump sum that is treated as income, and are disqualified from receiving IS or income-based JSA under the rules described above, you should ask the DWP to recalculate the period of your disqualification whenever:

- your circumstances change so that your entitlement to IS or income-based JSA would be higher; *or*
- benefit rates increase (April of every year).

Payments that do not count as liable relative payments

Certain types of payment from 'liable relatives' (see p867) do not count as liable relative payments.[91] They are therefore dealt with under the normal income and capital rules (see Chapters 37 and 38) and you are usually better off. You should ensure that your solicitor takes account of this when negotiating payments with your former partner. For example:

- some payments can be disregarded as income or capital (see pp951 and 1031);
- some payments made to someone else for the benefit of you or a member of your family (or paid to you or a member of the family to pay to someone else – see p870) do not count as your income or capital (see pp952 and 1031 for more information about 'notional income' and 'notional capital' that do not affect your IS or income-based JSA).

If you receive a payment which does not count as a liable relative payment, it is usually better if it can be treated as capital. If it is treated as capital it does not affect your benefit if it does not take your capital over £3,000 (£6,000 if you are aged 60 or over, £10,000 if you live in a care home). If the payment is more than the capital limit (see p1023), you will not receive any means-tested benefit whether it is capital or a lump sum treated as income (see p1039), but you might be able to reclaim sooner if it is capital.

The following types of payment from liable relatives (see p867) do not count as liable relative payments:[92]

- any payment arising from a 'disposition of property' (see p871) in consequence of your separation, divorce or the nullity of your marriage;
- any gifts not exceeding £250 in any period of 52 weeks (and not so regular as to amount to periodical payments – see p867);
- payments made after the liable relative has died;
- any payment in kind;
- any payment made to someone else for the benefit of you or a member of your family (such as mortgage capital payments), or paid to you or a member of your family to pay to someone else, which it is unreasonable to take into account – you can appeal to a tribunal which may take a different view from the DWP about what is reasonable;

- any payment to, or for, a child or young person who does not count as a member of your household;
- money from a liable relative which has already been taken into account under a previous claim, or which has already been recovered out of overpaid IS or income-based JSA;
- any payment which you have used before the DWP makes its decision, provided that you did not use it for the purpose of gaining entitlement to IS or income-based JSA. It should not be taken into account if you have used it to clear debts, such as your solicitor's bill.

Disposition of property

Any payment arising from a 'disposition of property' does not count as a liable relative payment (see p870). It is, therefore, vital to distinguish between payments that arise from a disposition of property and those that do not. **'Property'** is not confined to houses and land, but includes any asset such as the contents of your former home or a building society account. There is a **'disposition'** when those contents are divided up or your former partner buys out your interest.[93] Therefore, any lump sum which is paid in settlement of a claim to a share in any property does not count as a liable relative payment. It is only those lump sums which are paid instead of income that are liable to be treated as income.[94] It is important to take this into account in any negotiations with your former partner. You should make sure your solicitor knows about this rule.

It is best that court orders are drawn up to make it clear that any lump sum is in settlement of a claim to an interest in property. However, this is not essential and the DWP should accept a letter from your solicitor explaining why a lump sum was asked for and agreed.

Note: the proceeds of the sale of your former home may be disregarded altogether for a period of time (see p1031). Other capital, such as the home itself and its contents, may also be disregarded. There is therefore an advantage, while you are on benefit, to ask for a greater share of the home and accept less in the way of income or capital which would be taken into account to reduce your benefit.

4. How maintenance affects your housing benefit and council tax benefit

The following are taken into account when working out the amount of housing benefit (HB) or council tax benefit (CTB) to which you are entitled:

- child support maintenance;
- other maintenance paid for a member of your family (see p809 for who counts as your 'family').

How payments are taken into account depends on whether they are treated as income or capital (see below). It is important to remember that some payments made to someone else for the benefit of you or a member of your family (or paid to you or a member of the family to pay to someone else) do not always count as your income or your capital (see pp983 and 1039 for more information about notional income and capital that does not affect your HB or CTB).

If someone is paying your child(ren)'s school fees, see p954.

The rules which say who is 'liable to maintain' you or your child(ren) and about 'liable relatives' payments' if you are claiming income support (IS) and income-based jobseeker's allowance (JSA) (see p851) do not apply to HB and CTB.

Different rules apply if you are claiming IS or income-based JSA. For these rules, see p865.

Disregarded maintenance

If you are a lone parent, or a couple with a child, £15 of any maintenance payment made by your former partner, or your partner's former partner, or the parent of any child in your family is disregarded when working out the amount of your benefit. If you receive maintenance from more than one person, only £15 of the total is disregarded.[95] See Chapter 38 for further information about the income rules.

How maintenance is taken into account

If you are claiming HB or CTB, there are no special rules for how child support maintenance or other maintenance is taken into account. If you are receiving payments regularly, they are taken into account as income. If you are paid irregularly or in lump sums, they are taken into account as capital. See Chapters 37 and 38 for information about the income and capital rules. See pp983 and 1039 for information about notional income and capital that does not affect your HB or CTB.

You are usually better off if maintenance can be treated as capital. If it is treated as capital, it does not affect your benefit if it does not take your capital over £3,000 (£6,000 if you or your partner are aged 60 or over, £10,000 if you live in a care home).

Maintenance paid to or for your dependent child counts as yours.[96]

5. Benefits if you are contributing to someone's maintenance

If you are 'contributing to the maintenance' of someone, you might qualify for an increase of a non-means-tested benefit even if you are not living with her/him.

See Chapter 31 for details of the rules. You might also qualify for child benefit (see Chapter 5) or guardian's allowance (see Chapter 8).

From April 2003 it is no longer possible to qualify for an increase for a child dependant. This has been replaced by child tax credit. Claimants entitled to an increase on 5 April 2003 get transitional protection (see p798).

You might qualify for an increase for your spouse or someone who cares for a child (see pp794 and 795) with your:

- incapacity benefit (any rate);
- severe disablement allowance;
- carer's allowance;
- Category A or C retirement pension;
- maternity allowance.

Contributing to the maintenance of someone on income support or income-based jobseeker's allowance

There are special rules that allow the DWP to recover money from you if you are meant to be 'contributing to the maintenance' of someone who is claiming income support (IS) or income-based jobseeker's (JSA) but fail to do so. If you do not pay what you are meant to pay, that person's IS or income-based JSA might be increased to make up the difference. The IS or income-based JSA that would not have been paid to her/him had you paid the maintenance can be recovered from your child benefit, guardian's allowance or the increases in the benefits listed above.[97]

Notes

1. **Getting maintenance**

1 **IS** Sch 9 para 15(3) IS Regs
JSA Sch 7 para 15(3) JSA Regs
HB Sch 4 para 13(3) HB Regs
CTB Sch 4 para 13(3) CTB Regs
2 ss78(6)-(9) and 105(3) and (4) SSAA 1992
3 ss78(6)-(9) and 105 SSAA 1992
4 s1 CSA 1991
5 s105(1) SSAA 1992
6 **IS** s106 SSAA 1992
JSA s23 JSA 1995
7 *NAB v Parkes* [1955] 2 QBD 506 (QBD); *Hulley v Thompson* [1981] 1 WLR 159
8 **IS** s106(2) SSAA 1992
JSA s23 JSA 1995; reg 169 JSA Regs
9 *NAB v Parkes* [1955] 2 QBD 506 (QBD)
10 s9 CSA 1991
11 CSPSSA 2000
12 Residual Liable Relative and Proceedings Guide, paras 1630-42
13 **IS** s106(4)(a) SSAA 1992
JSA s23 JSA 1995; reg 169 JSA Regs
14 s6(3)(b)CSA 1991, as substituted by s3 CSPSSA 2000
15 s29(3) CSA 1991; regs 2 and 6 CS(C&E) Regs

2. **Child support maintenance**
16 Reg 15(5)(d) SPC Regs
17 CSA Press Release, 27 January 2003; CSPSSA 2000
18 Reg 28 CS(TP) Regs, as amended by reg 8 CS(MA) Regs
19 s30(1) CSA 1991; CS(CEOFM) Regs
20 s6(9) CSA 1991 (old rules); regs 2 and 3 CS(IED) Regs
21 s6(7)(a) CSA 1991, as substituted by s3 CSPSSA 2000; reg 31(4) CS(MCP) Regs
22 s6(5)CSA 1991, as substituted by s3 CSPSSA 2000; reg 31(4) CS(MCP) Regs
23 s6(5) CSA 1991, as substituted by s3 CSPSSA 2000
24 s46 CSA 1991, as substituted by s19 CSPSSA 2000
25 s46 CSA 1991 (old rules)
26 s46(4) and (6) CSA 1991, as substituted by s19(6) CSPSSA 2000 (new rules)
27 s6(2) CSA 1991
28 Vol 1 App 14 IS GAP
29 s46(10) CSA 1991; s46(9) CSA 1991, as substituted by s19 CSPSSA 2000 (new rules)
30 R(SB) 33/85
31 s46(3) and (4) CSA 1991 (old rules); s46 (3) and (4), as substituted by s19 CSPSSA 2000
32 s46(4) and (6) CSA 1991, as substituted by s19 CSPSSA
33 s46(5) CSA 1991(old rules): s46(5), as substituted by s19 CSPSSA 2000
34 Reg 31(6) CS(MCP) Regs
35 s2 CSA 1991; Ch 11 App 1 IS GAP; Circular 2/2000; CCS/1037/1995
36 Reg 35A CS(MAP) Regs, as amended by reg 5 CS(MA) Regs 2003 (old rules); reg 10 CS(MCP) Regs, as amended by reg 7(3) CS(MA) Regs 2003 (new rules)
37 s20 CSA 1991(old rules); s20 CSA 1991, as substituted by s10 CSPSSA 2000 (new rules)
38 s6(8) CSA 1991 (old rules); s6(6) CSA 1991, as substituted by CSPSSA 2000 (new rules)
39 Regs 40 and 40ZA CS(MAP) Regs (old rules); reg 14 CS(MCP) Regs (new rules)
40 Reg 36(8) CS(MAP) Regs (old rules); reg 11(8) CS(MCP) Regs (new rules)
41 Reg 47(1) CS(MAP) Regs (old rules); reg 17(1) CS(MCP) Regs (new rules)
42 Reg 36(2) CS(MAP) Regs (old rules); reg 11(2) CS(MCP) Regs (new rules)
43 Reg 37 CS(MAP) Regs (old rules); reg 12 CS(MCP) Regs (new rules)
44 Reg 36(7) CS(MAP) Regs (old rules); reg 11(7) CS(MCP) Regs (new rules)
45 Reg 36(4) CS(MAP) Regs (old rules); reg 11(3) CS(MCP) Regs (new rules)
46 Reg 47(2) CS(MAP) Regs (old rules); reg 11(4) CS(MCP) Regs (new rules)
47 Reg 47(4) and (5) CS(MAP) Regs (old rules); reg 17(4) CS(MCP) Regs (new rules)
48 Reg 41 CS(MAP) Regs (old rules); reg 16 CS(MCP) Regs (new rules)
49 Reg 38 CS(MAP) Regs (old rules); reg 13 CS(MCP) Regs (new rules)
50 Reg 13(6) CS(MCP) Regs
51 Reg 48 CS(MAP) Regs (old rules); reg 18 CS(MCP) Regs (new rules)
52 Regs 40 and 40ZA CS(MAP) Regs (old rules); regs 14 and 15 CS(MCP) Regs (new rules)
53 Reg 49 CS(MAP) Regs (old rules); reg 19 CS(MCP) Regs (new rules)
54 s46(7) CSA 1991 (old rules); s20(1)(c) CSA 1991, as amended by CSPSSA 2000 (new rules)
55 Reg 32 SS&CS(DA) Regs
56 Sch 9B para 3(1) SS(C&P) Regs, as inserted by reg 2 SS(C&P) Regs, amended by reg 14(3) SPC(CTMP) Regs
57 s43 CSA 1991; regs 13 and 28 CS(MASC) Regs; Sch 9 para 7A SS(C&P) Regs
58 Reg 28(1) and Sch 4 CS(MASC) Regs, the latter as amended by reg 6(8) CS(MA) Regs
59 Reg 28(3) CS(MASC) Regs
60 Sch 1 para 4 CSA 1991; reg 4 CS(MCSC) Regs, as amended by reg 3 and Sch 2 para 3 SSA(CA) Regs and reg 27(3) SPC(CTMP) Regs
61 Regs 4 and 5 CS(MCSC) Regs, the former as amended by reg 3 and Sch 2 para 3 SSA(CA) Regs and reg 27(3) SPC(CTMP) Regs and the latter as amended by reg 27(4) SPC(CTMP) Regs
62 Reg 4(3) CS(MCSC) Regs
63 Sch 1 CSA 1991, as substituted by Sch 1 para 8 CSPSSA 2000
64 s43(3) and Sch 4C CSA 1991 (old rules); s43, as substituted by s21 CSPSSA 2000 (new rules)
65 Reg 32 SS&CS(DA) Regs
66 Sch 9 para 7B SS(C&P) Regs (old rules)
67 Sch 9 para 7B(4) SS(C&P) Regs (old rules); Sch 9B SS(C&P) Regs, as inserted by reg 2 SS(C&P)A Regs
68 Sch 9B para 3(1) SS(C&P) Regs, as inserted by reg 2 SS(C&P)A Regs (new rules) and amended by reg 14(3) SPC(CTMP) Regs

3. How maintenance affects your income support, income-based jobseeker's allowance, pension credit and tax credits

69 Reg 15(5)(d) SPC Regs
70 **IS** Reg 60B IS Regs
JSA Reg 126 JSA Regs
71 SS(CMPMA) Regs, as amended by the Social Security (Child Maintenance Premium and Miscellaneous Amendments) Amendment Regulations 2003, SI 2003 No.231
72 **IS** Reg 60C IS Regs
JSA Reg 128 JSA Regs
73 s74(1) SSAA 1992; reg 7 SS(PAOR) Regs
74 s41(2) CSA 1991; reg 8 CS(AIAMA) Regs
75 **IS** Reg 60D(1)(aa) IS Regs
JSA Reg 129(1)(aa) JSA Regs
76 **IS** Regs 54-60 IS Regs
JSA Regs 117-124 JSA Regs
77 **IS** Reg 54 IS Regs
JSA Reg 117 JSA Regs
78 **IS** Reg 54 IS Regs, definition of 'periodical payment'
JSA Reg 117 JSA Regs, definition of 'periodical payment'
Both Bo*lstridge v CAO*
79 **IS** Reg 58 IS Regs
JSA Reg 122 JSA Regs
80 **IS** Reg 58(4) IS Regs
JSA Reg 122(4) JSA Regs
81 **IS** Reg 59(1) IS Regs
JSA Reg 123(1) JSA Regs
82 s74(1) SSAA 1992; reg 7(1) SS(PAOR) Regs
83 **IS** Reg 54 IS Regs, definition of 'periodical payment'
JSA Reg 117 JSA Regs, definition of 'periodical payment'
84 Reg 15(5)(d) SPC Regs
85 **IS** Regs 54, definition of 'payment', as amended by reg 2 Sch 1 para 14 SS(WTCCTC)(CA) Regs, and 55 IS Regs
JSA Regs 117, definition of 'payment', as amended by reg 3 and Sch 2 para 14 SS(WTCCTC)(CA) Regs, and 118 JSA Regs
86 **IS** Reg 60 IS Regs
JSA Reg 124 JSA Regs
87 **IS** Reg 60(2) IS Regs
JSA Reg 124(2) JSA Regs
88 **IS** Reg 57(1) and (2) IS Regs, as amended by reg 2 and Sch 1 para 15 SS(WTCCTC)(CA) Regs
JSA Reg 121(1) and (2) JSA Regs, as amended by reg 3 and Sch 2 para 15 SS(WTCCTC)(CA) Regs
89 **IS** Regs 57(4) and 59(2) IS Regs
JSA Regs 121(4) and 123(2) JSA Regs
90 **IS** Reg 57(3) IS Regs
JSA Reg 121(3) JSA Regs
91 **IS** Reg 54 IS Regs, definition of 'payment', as amended by reg 2 and Sch 1 para 14 SS(WTCCTC)(CA) Regs
JSA Reg 117 JSA Regs, definition of 'payment', as amended by reg 3 and Sch 2 para 14 SS(WTCCTC)(CA) Regs
92 **IS** Regs 54, definition of 'payment', as amended by reg 2 and Sch 1 para 14 SS(WTCCTC)(CA) Regs, 55 and 60(1) IS Regs
JSA Regs 117, definition of 'payment', as amended by reg 3 and Sch 2 para 14 SS(WTCCTC)(CA) Regs, 118 and 124(1) JSA Regs
93 CSB/1160/1986; R(SB) 1/89
94 R(SB) 1/89

4. How maintenance affects your housing benefit and council tax benefit

95 **HB** Sch 4 paras 13(3) and 47 HB Regs
CTB Sch 4 paras 13(3) and 46 CTB Regs
96 s136(1) SSCBA 1992

5. Benefits if you are contributing to someone's maintenance

97 s74(3) SSAA 1992; reg 9 SS(PAOR) Regs

35

Chapter 35

Applicable amounts and means-tested benefits

This chapter explains the different amounts allowed for meeting your needs when calculating your entitlement to income support, income-based jobseeker's allowance (JSA), housing benefit and council tax benefit. It covers:

In this chapter, unless otherwise stated, references to income-based JSA are intended also to refer to joint-claim JSA.

Pension credit

The rules for assessing entitlement to pension credit (PC) are, for the most part, completely different, and are dealt with in Chapter 18. However, the additional amounts in the guarantee credit of PC for claimants who are **severely disabled** or are **carers** have rules which are similar to those for the severe disability premium and carer's premium, and are dealt with in this chapter – see pp891 and 896.

1. What is the applicable amount?

The applicable amount is a figure representing your weekly needs, for the purpose of calculating your income support (IS), income-based jobseeker's allowance (JSA), housing benefit (HB) and council tax benefit (CTB). For IS/income-based JSA, your applicable amount is the amount you are expected to live on each week. For HB/CTB, it is the amount used to see how much help you need with your rent or council tax. This chapter explains how you work out your applicable amount for those benefits. For the way benefit payable is calculated, see p303 for IS, p377 for income-based JSA, p205 for HB and p112 for CTB.

What is included in your applicable amount

For IS, income-based JSA, HB and CTB, your applicable amount is made up of:
- **personal allowances:** the amount the law says you need for living expenses (see p878);
- **premiums:** the amount given for certain extra needs you or your family may have (see p882);
- for IS and income-based JSA only, **housing costs** (see Chapter 36).

Your applicable amount is reduced if, for IS/income-based JSA/HB/CTB, you are:
- receiving an urgent cases payment (see p664);
- a long-stay patient in hospital (see p715);
- a 16/17-year-old, in certain circumstances (see p712);
- involved in a trade dispute (see p735);
- a couple, one of whom is a 'person subject to immigration control' (see p663);
- without accommodation (see p734);
- a prisoner (see p729);
- for IS only, appealing against a decision that you are not incapable of work under the personal capability assessment[1] (see p296 for entitlement to IS in this situation and p772 for more information on the personal capability assessment);
- for income-based JSA only, you are getting JSA on hardship grounds (see p443);
- for income-based JSA only, if you are required to be a 'joint-claim couple', you or your partner are subject to a sanction (see Chapter 16).

When your benefit might be paid at a lower rate

There are a number of other reasons why your benefit might be reduced, such as:
- for IS/income-based JSA, you are subject to a benefit penalty for refusing to co-operate with the Department for Work and Pensions (DWP) regarding a child support maintenance assessment/calculation (see p854);
- you are repaying an overpayment of benefit (see p1142);
- you are subject to a benefit sanction after being convicted of a benefit offence (see p1169);
- for IS/income-based JSA, you are repaying a social fund loan (see p534);
- for IS/income-based JSA, the DWP is making direct payments from your benefit in respect of housing costs, fuel debts, council tax and community charge arrears, fines or child support maintenance (see p1109).

For IS and income-based JSA the amount of your benefit may also be reduced, or not paid at all, if you or your partner are required to attend a work-focused interview and fail to do so (see p1092).

2. Personal allowances

The amount of your personal allowance for income support (IS), income-based jobseeker's allowance (JSA), housing benefit (HB) and council tax benefit (CTB) depends on your age and whether you are claiming as a single person or a couple. For HB and CTB, and in some circumstances for IS and income-based JSA, you also get an allowance for each dependent child (but see below if your child has capital).

If you are polygamously married (see p811) you receive an extra amount for each additional partner in your household. However, for IS and income-based JSA, where any additional partner is under the age of 18, you only receive an extra amount if s/he is responsible for a child (see p820) or would otherwise meet the special conditions for qualifying for JSA as a 16/17-year-old[2] (see p712).

Personal allowances for children

For when children can be included in your claim, see p818. HB and CTB include personal allowances and premiums for dependent children. From 6 April 2004, new claims for IS and income-based JSA do not include such allowances or premiums.

If you already get IS or income-based JSA and have a child tax credit (CTC) award, from 6 April 2004 your benefit is adjusted to remove allowances and premiums for children. However, you may be entitled to continue having them included in your claim for IS or income-based JSA for a time, in certain circumstances. This will apply if:

- you have a claim which began before 6 April 2004; *and*
- you had a dependent child or children included in the claim before 6 April 2004; *and*
- you have not yet been awarded CTC.

In these circumstances, if you are entitled to them the personal allowance and premiums will continue to be included in your claim until such point as you are awarded CTC. It is expected that IS/income-based JSA claims that include amounts for families and children (including premiums) will have those amounts automatically converted (or 'migrated') to a CTC claim at some point in 2005. See p818 for what details were available at the time this *Handbook* was written.

If your child has capital

Even if you are still entitled to amounts for children in your IS/income-based JSA, if a child has over £3,000 capital you do not get any allowance or premium for that child, except for a family premium. See p953 for how a child's income affects benefit. For HB and CTB, your child's income and capital do not affect your benefit.

Rates of personal allowances (ages 18 and over)[3]

Since 6 October 2003 HB/CTB personal allowance amounts for people aged 60 or over who are not claiming IS or income-based JSA are higher (because they include amounts formerly included in the pensioner premium).[4] If you and/or your partner (if any) are aged 16 or 17, the rates for IS/income-based JSA may be different to the rates for HB/CTB (see p881).

	IS/JSA/HB/CTB	*HB/CTB only – claimant or partner aged 60 or over and not claiming IS or income-based JSA*
Single claimant:		
Aged 18–24	£44.50	
Aged 25 or over	£56.20	
Aged 60–64		£109.45
Aged 65 or over		£125.90
Lone parent:		
Aged 18 or over	£56.20	
Couple:		
Both aged 18 or over	£88.15	
One or both aged 60–64		£167.05
One or both aged 65 or over		£188.60
One aged under 18 (some IS/JSA cases – see p881 – and all HB/CTB cases)	£88.15	
One aged under 18 (other IS/JSA cases only – see p881):		
either	£56.20	
or	£44.50	
Polygamous marriages, each additional qualifying partner living in the same household:[5]		
Any age	£31.95	
All partners aged under 65 with one aged at least 60		£57.60
One or more aged 65 or over		£62.70

Rates of personal allowances (16/17-year-olds)

Special rates of IS and income-based JSA personal allowances are paid if you are aged 16 or 17. These depend partly on your age and partly on your partner's age, if you have one. For HB, if you or your partner or both of you are under 18, your personal allowance is the same as the rate for 18–24-year-olds (see p879). However, most 16/17-year-olds who left local authority care on or after 1 October 2001 (England and Wales) or 1 April 2004 (Scotland) cannot claim IS/JSA or HB (see p713). CTB is not payable for single people under 18, or for couples if both of you are under 18 because you cannot be liable to pay council tax at that age (see p112). If one of you is 18 or over you will get the same personal allowance as for all couples aged 18 to 24 (see p879).

Single people and lone parents (income support and income-based jobseeker's allowance)

There are two levels of payment:[6]

Lower rate	£33.85
Higher rate	£44.50

You are paid at the higher rate if:[7]

- you qualify for the disability premium (see p886); *or*
- you are an orphan with no one acting as your parent (which includes foster parents, a local authority or a voluntary organisation if you are in care or are being looked after by them, or any other person with parental responsibility for you); *or*
- you are living away from parents and any person acting as your parent, and immediately before you were 16 you were in custody, or being looked after by a local authority who placed you with someone other than a close relative (see p895); *or*
- you are living away from parents and any person acting as your parent, and instead are living elsewhere:
  - as part of a programme of resettlement or rehabilitation under the supervision of the probation service or a local authority; *or*
  - to avoid physical or sexual abuse; *or*
  - because you need special accommodation due to mental or physical illness or handicap; *or*
- you are living away from your parents and any person acting as your parent, they are unable to support you financially and they are:
  - in custody; *or*
  - unable to enter Great Britain (eg, because of the immigration rules); *or*
  - 'chronically sick or mentally or physically disabled'; *or*
- you have to live away from your parents and any person acting as your parent, because:
  - you are estranged from them (see p620); *or*
  - you are in physical or moral danger; *or*
  - there is a serious risk to your physical or mental health; *or*

- for income-based JSA only, you qualify for JSA either because you are claiming during or after the child benefit extension period or because you are entitled to a special hardship payment (see p384).

Couples (income support and income-based jobseeker's allowance)[8]

The amount paid to couples depends on your ages and whether one or both of you are or would be eligible for IS or income-based JSA (including JSA discretionary severe hardship payments – see p384) if you were a single person. For some couples the amount may be no more than that for a single person.

One partner aged 18 or over and the other under 18 *and* entitled to IS or income-based/discretionary JSA (or would be if not a member of a couple)	£88.15
Both under 18 *and both* entitled to IS or income-based/discretionary JSA (or would be if not a member of a couple)	£67.15
Both under 18 and one is responsible for a child	£67.15
For IS, the claimant, or for JSA, either partner is aged 25 or over and the other under 18 *and* not entitled to IS or income-based/discretionary JSA (even if s/he were not a member of a couple)	£56.20
For IS, the claimant, or for JSA, either partner is aged 18–24 and the other under 18 *and* not entitled to IS or income-based/discretionary JSA (even if s/he was not a member of a couple)	£44.50
Both under 18 and one is entitled to IS or income-based/discretionary JSA at the higher rate for single under-18s	£44.50
Both under 18 and one is entitled to IS or income-based/discretionary JSA at the lower rate for single under-18s	£33.85

Children

Note: For IS and income-based JSA, you are only entitled to personal allowances for children in limited circumstances (see p878).

The rate for your dependent children is the same for IS, income-based JSA, HB and CTB, and is not affected by your (or your partner's) age.

Note, however, that this rate does not apply to joint-claim JSA, as you cannot claim this type of JSA if you have children.

Under 19	£43.88

3. Premiums

Premiums are added to your basic personal allowances and are intended to help with extra expenses caused by age, disability or, in some circumstances, children. They are:

- family premium (see p884);
- disabled child premium (see p886);
- disability premium (see p886);
- enhanced disability premium (see p888);
- pensioner premium (see p889);
- higher pensioner premium (see p890);
- severe disability premium (a similar allowance applies to the guarantee credit of pension credit (PC) – see p891);
- carer's premium (a similar allowance applies to the guarantee credit of PC – see p896); *and*
- bereavement premium (see p897).

See p897 for information about backdating of premiums. See the table on p883 for the premium rates.

Premiums for families with children

For when children can be included in your claim, see p818. Housing benefit (HB) and council tax benefit (CTB) include premiums for families with dependent children. These premiums are the family premium, disabled child premium and the child rate of the enhanced disability premium. From 6 April 2004, new claims for income support (IS) and income-based jobseeker's allowance (JSA) do not include these premiums.

If you already get IS or income-based JSA and have a child tax credit (CTC) award, from 6 April 2004 your IS or income-based JSA no longer includes those premiums. However, you may be entitled to continue having them included in your claim for IS or income-based JSA for a time, in certain circumstances. This will apply if:

- you have a claim which began before 6 April 2004; *and*
- you had a dependent child or children included in the claim before 6 April 2004; *and*
- you have not yet been awarded CTC.

In these circumstances, if you are entitled to them, the premiums will continue to be included in your claim until you are awarded CTC. It is expected that IS/ income-based JSA claims that include amounts for families and children (including premiums) will have those amounts automatically converted (or 'migrated') to a CTC claim at some point in 2005. See p818 for the details that were available at the time this *Handbook* was written.

If your child has capital

Even if you are still entitled to amounts for children in your IS/income-based JSA, if a child has over £3,000 capital you do not get any allowance or premium for that child, except for a family premium. See p953 for how a child's income affects benefit. For HB and CTB, your child's income and capital do not affect your benefit.

Rates

The rates of premiums are the same for all claimants (even if you are under 18 or under 25) of all benefits, except for the family premium if you have a child aged under one, and the lone parent increase of the family premium. This lone parent increase is higher for HB and CTB, if you are aged under 60, than it is for IS and income-based JSA.

Note: If you are aged 60 or over and not claiming IS or income-based JSA then no lone parent increase is payable in your HB or CTB.

Note also: Since 6 October 2003, if you or your partner (if any) are aged 60 or over and not claiming IS or income-based JSA, only the family, disabled child, enhanced disability for a child, severe disability and carer's premiums can be included in your HB or CTB.[9] This is because the pensioner premium has been incorporated into the personal allowance amount.

Premium rates

Where payable, the following premiums can be paid on top of any other premiums, except that the enhanced disability premium cannot be paid on top of the pensioner premium or higher pensioner premium[10] (but see p888):

Family premium	
Ordinary rate	£16.10
Higher rate where one child under 1 year old (for HB and CTB only)	£26.60
Disabled child premium (for each qualifying child)	£43.89
Severe disability premium	
Single (or one partner qualifying)	£45.50
Couple (both partners qualifying)	£91.00
Carer's premium	
Single (or one partner qualifying)	£25.80
Couple (both partners qualifying)	£51.60
Enhanced disability premium	
Child rate (for each qualifying child)	£17.71
Single	£11.70
Couple (one or both partner(s) qualifying)	£16.90

We understand that, where appropriate, the Department for Work and Pensions (DWP) will pay the enhanced disability premium for a child on top of any of the pensioner premiums.

Only one of the following premiums can be paid; if you qualify for more than one you get whichever is the highest:[11]

Family premium for HB/CTB (lone parent increase)	
HB/CTB	£6.10
Disability premium	
Single	£23.95
Couple	£34.20
Pensioner, enhanced pensioner and higher pensioner premium (see p889)	
Single	£53.25
Couple	£78.90
Bereavement premium	£25.85

Entitlement to some premiums depends on receipt of other benefits. Once you have qualified for a premium, if you or your partner cease to receive a qualifying benefit because of the overlapping benefit rules (ie, because you are receiving another benefit at the same or a higher rate – see p1102), or because you or your partner are on an employment training course or getting a training allowance, you continue to receive the relevant premium.[12] In addition, you or your partner (if any) must be getting the benefit for yourself (or for your partner), and not on behalf of someone else – eg, as an appointee (see p1075).[13]

Sometimes, you may be able to get payment of a premium backdated (see p897).

Family premium[14]

Note: For IS and income-based JSA you will only be entitled to a family premium for a time and in certain circumstances (see p882).

You are entitled to a family premium if your family includes a child (see p818). It is paid even if you are not the parent of the child and even if you do not receive a personal allowance in your IS/income-based JSA for any child because s/he has capital over £3,000.

Only one family premium is payable regardless of the number of children you have. A **higher amount is paid in HB and CTB** if at least one child in your family is under 1 year old.[15] For the purpose of this rule, the child will be treated as having reached the age of 1 on the Monday following her/his first birthday if the birthday does not fall on a Monday, or on the Monday if the birthday falls on that day. This higher amount is payable to both couples and lone parents, and the additional amount for a lone parent (see below) is paid on top of the higher amount.

Where a child who is in the care of or being looked after by a local authority or who is in custody comes home for part of a week, your IS or income-based JSA includes a proportion of the premium, according to the number of days the child is with you.[16] For HB and CTB you may be paid the full premium if your child who is in care or being looked after by a local authority is part of the household for any part of the week – if the local authority thinks it is reasonable given how often and for how long the child is at home with you.[17]

Lone parents[18]

Prior to 6 April 1998, a higher rate of the family premium was payable to lone parents than to couples (unless they were also entitled to the disability premium or one of the pensioner premiums, which would be payable instead). The lone parent rate of the family premium is now only payable under the following circumstances.

IS and income-based JSA:

- you were both a lone parent and entitled to IS or income-based JSA on 5 April 1998, *or*, if you were not, you were on any day within 12 weeks before or after that date and you have not ceased to be both a lone parent and entitled to IS or income-based JSA for more than 12 weeks in this time; *and*
- you do not subsequently cease to be both a lone parent and entitled to IS or income-based JSA, although any periods of less than 12 weeks during which you may cease to be either a lone parent or entitled to IS or income-based JSA, or both, are ignored.

HB and CTB:

- you were entitled or treated as entitled to HB/CTB and the lone parent increase on 5 April 1998; *and*
- you do not cease to be a lone parent; *and*
- you do not cease to be entitled or treated as entitled to HB/CTB; *and*
- you do not become or cease to be entitled to IS or income-based JSA; *and*
- the disability premium (see p886) or one of the pensioner premiums (see below) does not become payable instead.

You are treated as entitled to HB and CTB on 5 April 1998 if you were entitled to the other benefit (ie, CTB or HB) as a lone parent from 5 April 1998 to the day before you eventually claim it. You are also treated as entitled to HB during any rent-free weeks.

Unlike IS and income-based JSA, there are no linking periods for HB and CTB, so if you lose the increase, even for a short period, you will not be able to claim it back (although a change of address does not break your entitlement).[19]

If you have been getting the lone parent rate of the family premium with IS/ income-based JSA continuously since 5 July 1998 (or if you have been getting a pensioner or disability premium as a lone parent since 5 April 1998) and you do not already get the lone parent rate of child benefit, you will still be able to claim that benefit as long as you claim within one month of your entitlement to IS/ income-based JSA ending (see p95).

If you lose your entitlement to the lone parent increase for IS, income-based JSA, HB or CTB, you may still be entitled to the ordinary rate of the family premium instead.

Disabled child premium[20]

Note: For IS and income-based JSA you will only be entitled to a disabled child premium for a time and in certain circumstances (see p882).

You are entitled to a disabled child premium for each child in your family who gets disability living allowance (DLA) or who is blind.

A child is treated as blind if s/he is registered as blind and for the first 28 weeks after s/he has been taken off the register on regaining her/his sight.[21] If DLA stops because the child has gone into hospital, see p718. If your child is in local authority care or in custody for part of the week, this premium is affected in the same way as the family premium. For how to qualify for DLA, see Chapter 7.

For IS and income-based JSA, if your child has over £3,000 capital, you do not get this premium.[22] Your child's capital does not affect your HB or CTB.[23]

If your child dies

If your child dies, for HB and CTB only, you may be able to continue receiving the disabled child premium for eight weeks.[24] This will apply if:

- you get child benefit for the child following her/his death (see p104); *and*
- you were getting the disabled child premium included in your applicable amount for that child immediately before her/his death.

Disability premium[25]

The way in which you can get a disability premium differs depending on whether you have a partner or not (see p811). In either case, the person who satisfies the qualifying conditions set out below has to be aged under 60. If you or your partner are aged 60 or over you may instead get the higher pensioner premium. **Note:** with the introduction of PC from 6 October 2003, you will only be able to qualify for the higher pensioner premium for IS if your partner is aged 60 or over.[26] **Note also:** the disability premium cannot be included in your HB or CTB if you or your partner are aged 60 or over and not claiming IS or income-based JSA.

You qualify for a disability premium if:

- you, or your partner (if any), are getting a qualifying benefit. These are:

- DLA (see Chapter 7) or an equivalent benefit paid to meet attendance needs because of an injury at work (see Chapter 14) or a war injury;[27]
- war pensioner's mobility supplement;
- the disability element or severe disability element of working tax credit (WTC);
- severe disablement allowance (SDA) (see Chapter 20);
- incapacity benefit (IB) paid at the long-term rate (see Chapter 12);
- special short-term rate of IB because you are terminally ill (see p274).[28]

Extra-statutory payments to compensate you or your partner for not getting these benefits also count.[29]

You must be getting the benefit in question for yourself, not on behalf of someone else – eg, as an appointee (see p1075). The same applies if it is your partner who gets the benefit.[30]

Once you qualify for the premium, you, or your partner, are treated as still getting a qualifying benefit you no longer in fact get, if you would have got it but for the overlapping benefit rules (see p1102);[31]

- you, or your partner, are registered as blind with a local authority. If you, or your partner, regain your sight you still qualify for 28 weeks after being taken off the register;[32]
- you, or your partner, have an NHS invalid trike or private car allowance because of disability;[33]
- you, or your partner, were getting IB paid at the long-term rate (or at the short-term rate because of terminal illness) which stopped at pension age[34] or when retirement pension became payable, since when you have been continuously entitled to IS/income-based JSA/HB/CTB.[35] If it is your partner who began receiving a retirement pension, s/he must still be alive (IS/income-based JSA),[36] or still be a member of your family (HB/CTB).[37] In the case of IS or income-based JSA only, you or your partner (if any) must have previously qualified for a disability premium;[38]
- you, or your partner, were getting attendance allowance (AA) or DLA but payment of that benefit was suspended when one of you became a hospital in-patient.[39] In the case of IS and income-based JSA only, you or your partner must have previously qualified for a disability premium;
- for IS/HB/CTB, but not for income-based JSA, the DWP has decided that you are 'incapable of work' or you are treated as incapable or (for IS only) you are entitled to statutory sick pay (SSP) and you have been so entitled, incapable of work or treated as incapable of work for a continuous qualifying period of:[40]
  - 196 days if you have been certified as 'terminally ill' – ie, it can reasonably be expected that you will die within six months as a consequence of a progressive disease;[41]
  - 364 days in all other cases.

Incapacity for work

To establish your incapacity for work (unless you get SSP), you should claim IB, whether you are entitled to it or not.

Breaks in entitlement/incapacity of up to 56 days (or 52 weeks if you are a 'welfare to work' beneficiary[42]) are ignored for the qualifying period above. See p594 for more details about SSP and 'incapacity for work'.

If you consider you have been incapable of work for 364/196 days or more, but you have not previously been certified or assessed as incapable of work, you should claim IB (see Chapter 12). You do not have to be awarded IB, you only have to show that you have been incapable of work. You should supply a medical certificate covering the whole period. This and other evidence of your incapacity can be accepted even though it relates to a past period.[43] Even if you have not yet been incapable of work for 364/196 days, it is advisable to claim IB as soon as possible so that the disability premium can be awarded to you as soon as you reach the end of the qualifying period.

Couples

If you are a couple, you get the disability premium at the couple rate provided that one of you meets one of the above qualifying conditions, except in the case of the condition concerning SSP and incapacity for work. In that case, you do not get the premium at all unless the person who qualifies is the claimant of the IS/HB/CTB paid to you as a couple.[44] You may, therefore, need to swap who is the claimant of your IS/HB/CTB (see pp811 and 1074). This does not apply to income-based JSA because you cannot claim JSA while you are incapable of work. If your partner is incapable of work s/he should probably claim IS instead of your claim for JSA so that you may benefit from the disability premium. **Note:** If your partner is in receipt of long-term IB the disability premium can be included in your claim for JSA.[45]

Training

If you go on a government training course such as Work-Based Training for Adults or Work-Based Learning for Young People, or for any period you receive a training allowance, you keep the disability premium even though you may cease to receive one of the qualifying benefits, or cease to be entitled to SSP or be incapable of work during the course, as long as you continue to be entitled to IS, income-based JSA, HB or CTB. After the course, the premium continues (except for income-based JSA) if you remain entitled to SSP (for IS only), are still incapable of work, or are getting a qualifying benefit.[46]

Enhanced disability premium[47]

Note: For IS and income-based JSA you will only be entitled to the child rate of this premium for a time and in certain circumstances (see p882).

This premium does not replace the disability or severe disability premiums, and can be paid in addition to either or both of these premiums where those premiums are payable (see p883). For more details of which premiums the enhanced disability premium can and cannot be paid on top of, see p883.

You qualify for one enhanced disability premium for each child who receives DLA highest rate care component and who is a member of your family (see Chapter 32 for the meaning of 'family').

You are also entitled to an enhanced disability premium for an adult (at the single or couple rate) if you or your partner receive DLA highest rate care component and are aged under 60.

Once you or your partner reach the age of 60 you will be paid the pensioner premium instead, or, for HB/CTB, the higher personal allowance. **Note:** for HB and CTB only, if you or your partner are aged 60 or over and not claiming IS or income-based JSA, you cannot get an enhanced disability premium for yourself or your partner.

The DWP has stated that it will pay the enhanced disability premium in respect of a child on top of any of the pensioner premiums.

In most cases, you (or the family member) will be treated as receiving the highest rate of DLA care component during any period when DLA is suspended while you are in hospital. The exception is where you are in one of the groups of people listed below who cannot qualify for the premium.

The following people cannot qualify:

- for IS and income-based JSA only, children or young people with more than £3,000 in capital;
- a claimant who has been a hospital inpatient for more than 52 weeks;
- either member of a couple (polygamous or otherwise), where each member of the couple has been a hospital inpatient for more than 52 weeks.

Pensioner premiums[48]

There are three pensioner premiums, but they are all paid at the same rate, which is either a single person's rate or a couple rate. The premiums are:

- **pensioner premium** if you or your partner are aged 60–74 inclusive;
- **pensioner premium** (sometimes referred to as **enhanced pensioner premium**) if you or your partner are aged 75–79 inclusive;
- **higher pensioner premium** if you or your partner are 80, or certain other conditions are satisfied (see p890).

For **IS** you will only qualify for any of the pensioner premiums if your partner satisfies the age requirements.[49]

Note: For **HB** and **CTB** only, if you or your partner are aged 60 or over and not claiming IS or income-based JSA, no pensioner premiums can be included in your HB or CTB. However, you do not lose out because the amount of the pensioner premium is now included as part of your personal allowance.

Qualifying for the higher pensioner premium may still be important, for example because it qualifies you for a £20 earnings disregard (see p964), or because it meets one of the qualifying conditions for the disability element of WTC (see p1357).

The couple rate for either is paid even if only one partner fulfils the condition. You are paid the highest rate which may apply to you (or your partner). If you or your partner are sick or disabled check to see if you could get the higher pensioner premium instead (see below).

Higher pensioner premium

You qualify for the higher pensioner premium if one of the following applies:[50]

- for income-based JSA, HB and CTB either you or your partner are 80 or over, or for IS your partner is aged 80 or over;
- for IS your partner is aged 60–79, for income-based JSA, HB and CTB you or your partner are aged 60–79 and either of you receives a qualifying benefit (as for the disability premium – see p886 – but including AA), or are registered blind, or have an NHS trike or a private car allowance.

  If your AA or DLA stops because you go into hospital, see p716. If you stop getting IB, or if you are getting SDA, see below;
- you were getting a disability premium as part of your income-based JSA, HB or CTB before you were 60 and you have continued to claim that benefit since reaching that age. You must have been getting a disability premium at some time during the eight weeks (or 52 weeks if you are a 'welfare to work' beneficiary[51]) before you were 60, and have received that benefit continuously since you reached 60.[52] But you can have a period off that benefit of up to eight (or 52) weeks and still qualify;
- for IS, you were getting a disability premium before your partner was 60, and continued to get IS since s/he reached 60.

For HB and CTB, if you were entitled to a higher pensioner premium for one benefit in the previous eight (or 52) weeks you will get a higher pensioner premium with the other if you then qualify or requalify for that benefit.[53] Previous entitlement to a premium while on HB or CTB does not help you qualify for the higher pensioner premium when you claim IS or income-based JSA, and vice versa, but whereas previous entitlement while on IS helps you qualify when you claim income-based JSA,[54] the reverse does not apply.

In the case of couples, the person who was the claimant for that benefit before s/he was 60 must continue to claim after that, but it is not necessary for the claimant to have been the person who qualified for the disability premium.

If you stop getting incapacity benefit

If you (for IS/HB/CTB), or your partner (for IS/income-based JSA/HB/CTB), stop getting IB (or if in the past you stopped getting invalidity benefit) because you reach pension age[55] or get retirement pension instead, you still get a higher pensioner premium with your IS, income-based JSA, HB or CTB, if you remain continuously entitled (apart from breaks of eight weeks – or 52 weeks if you are a 'welfare to work' beneficiary – or less) to the same benefit.[56] In the case of HB and CTB, if you were entitled to a higher pensioner premium for one of these benefits in the previous eight or 52 weeks, you get a higher pensioner premium with the other if you then qualify or requalify for that benefit.[57] Previous entitlement within this period to the higher pensioner premium with IS will also count when you claim income-based JSA, but the reverse will not apply.[58] If it is your partner who had changed to a retirement pension, s/he must still be alive (in the case of IS/income-based JSA), or still be a member of your family (HB and CTB).[59] In the case of IS and income-based JSA, the higher pensioner premium or a disability premium must also have been applicable to you or your partner.[60] So, if, up to the time your IB (or invalidity benefit) ceased, your applicable amount was calculated by a method that did not include premiums (eg, because you were in a hostel prior to 9 October 1989, or you lived in a care home before 31 March 1993), you are not able to qualify in this way.[61]

If you are getting severe disablement allowance

If you are getting SDA by the time you reach 65, you will be awarded it for life even if you no longer satisfy the incapacity or disability conditions. You will therefore continue to qualify for the higher pensioner premium.[62] This also applies even if it ceases to be paid because you get retirement pension at a higher rate.[63]

Severe disability premium and pension credit additional amount[64]

You qualify for a severe disability premium, or for the additional amount for severe disability in the guarantee credit of PC, if all of the following apply to you:

- you receive a **qualifying benefit**. This is either AA, the middle or higher rate care component of DLA, constant attendance allowance, exceptionally severe disablement allowance (or the equivalent war pension),[65] or extra-statutory payments to compensate you for not receiving any of these benefits;[66]
- for **couples**, both partners must be getting a qualifying benefit, or else one must be getting a qualifying benefit while the other is registered blind or treated as blind because s/he came off the register in the last 28 weeks. If one partner is blind, the other partner who gets the qualifying benefit must be the claimant to get the premium in IS, income-based JSA, HB or CTB. For PC, either partner can be the claimant.[67] You and your partner are treated as getting the qualifying benefit while either or both of you are still in hospital, but this is only where you are claiming the amount for severe disability on the basis that both you and your partner are receiving a qualifying benefit.[68] For IS, income-based JSA, HB and CTB, the qualifying benefit must be paid in respect of

yourself/selves, receipt of benefit for someone else (eg, a child) does not count,[69] and it is probably intended that the same rule should apply to PC;

- **no non-dependant aged 18 or over is 'normally residing with you'** (see p893) – eg, a grown-up son or daughter or your parents. It does not matter whose house it is, yours or the non-dependant's.[70] For IS, income-based JSA, PC and HB, someone is only counted as living with you if you share accommodation apart from a bathroom, lavatory or a communal area such as a hall, passageway or a room in common use in sheltered accommodation. If s/he is separately liable to make payments for the accommodation to the landlord, s/he does not count as living with you.[71] This is not explicitly stated in the rules for CTB, although the same test may in practice be applied;
- **no one gets carer's allowance (CA) for looking after you,** or if you are a couple, no one gets CA for both of you (but see below for an exception when you and/or your partner go into hospital). For couples, if a person is getting CA for one (but not both) of you then you can get the amount for severe disability, but only at the single person's rate. Only actual receipt of CA counts[72] (except where it is not paid because of the loss of benefit rules – see p1169), so no account is taken of any underlying entitlement to CA where it is awarded but not paid because of the overlapping benefit rules, or of any extra-statutory payments to compensate for it not being paid. Similarly, no account is taken of any backdated payments or arrears of CA.[73] You should also argue that no account should be taken of any CA which has been overpaid, and that if you have been denied the premium because of a CA overpayment, it should be repaid to you (see p896).

Couples

Couples get the couple rate only if both of you are getting a qualifying benefit and no one gets CA for either of you. However, if your partner does not get a qualifying benefit but is registered blind (or treated as blind), or if CA is paid for one of you, you still get the single rate. (In polygamous marriages the single rate is awarded in respect of each eligible partner who gets a qualifying benefit while CA is not paid.)

Note: for couples only, you and/or your partner are treated as getting AA (or the higher or middle rate care component of DLA), even though it has stopped because you/your partner have been in hospital for more than four weeks but the severe disability premium is paid at the single rate only. Similarly, for couples only, where the benefit is IS, income-based JSA, HB or CTB, a person is treated as receiving CA even if the qualifying benefit of the person for whom s/he is caring has stopped because that person has been in hospital for more than four weeks.[74]

Note also: for IS and JSA only, for couples, if you (or your partner) temporarily move into an independent care home (see p721), although you remain members of the same household,[75] your applicable amount is the greater of:

- the normal amount for you as a couple; *or*

- the total of the applicable amounts for each of you as if you and your partner were each a single claimant (or lone parent) living in your present accommodation.[76] This means that if the person who stays at home gets a qualifying benefit, then totalling the applicable amounts separately will enable a severe disability premium to be included for her/him, even though the person in the care home cannot get the premium once his/her AA or DLA care component stops.

For PC, if you (or your partner) temporarily move into a care home, you still count as a couple if you have not been apart for substantially more than 52 weeks (see p724). So for PC, once the person in the care home loses her/his AA or DLA care component, no severe disability premium can be paid for either member of the couple even if the person at home gets a qualifying benefit.

Non-dependants[77]

The following people who live with you do *not* count as non-dependants.

For IS, income-based JSA, PC, HB and CTB:

- anyone aged under 18;
- anyone else who receives a qualifying benefit;[78]
- anyone who is registered blind (or treated as blind);[79]
- anyone staying in your home who normally lives elsewhere. In deciding whether someone normally lives with you or elsewhere it may be relevant to consider: why the residence started; the relationship and its history, if any, between those concerned; the motivations involved; the purpose for which residence has been taken up; its duration; and whether there is any other home in which residence is or could be taken up;[80]
- any person (and, for IS, income-based JSA and PC only, her/his partner) employed by a charitable or voluntary body as a resident carer for you or your partner if you pay a charge for that service (even if the charge is only nominal).[81] **Note:** these rules do not apply to live-in carers employed directly by you (even if, for example, you are paying them from payments made to you by social services for that purpose under the Community Care (Direct Payments) Act 1996). For such a person to be disregarded as a non-dependant you would either have to pay a charitable or voluntary body to employ her/him for you, or prove that s/he normally lives elsewhere.

For IS, income-based JSA, HB and CTB:

- any member of your family (see p809 for who counts as part of your family). This may include any child up to the age of 19 (see p818) as well as your partner, although your partner must be getting a qualifying benefit (or would be if s/he were not in hospital), or be registered or treated as blind (see p295) if you are to be paid the severe disability premium (see p891).

For IS, income-based JSA and PC:

- any person (or her/his partner) who jointly occupies (see p895) your home and is either the co-owner with you or your partner, or jointly liable with you or your partner to make payments to a landlord in respect of occupying it. If this person is a close relative (see p895), however, s/he *will* count as a non-dependant *unless* the co-ownership or joint liability to make payments to a landlord existed either before 11 April 1988 or by the time you or your partner first moved in (but, for IS only, see transitional provisions below);
- any person (or any member of her/his household) who is liable to pay you or your partner on a commercial basis (see p895) in respect of occupying the dwelling (eg, tenants or licensees), unless s/he is a close relative of you or your partner (but, for IS only, see transitional provisions below);
- any person (or any member of her/his household) to whom you or your partner are liable to make such payments on a commercial basis, unless s/he is a close relative (see p895) of you or your partner (for IS only, see below).

In any of these situations, for IS only the presence of close relatives (see p895) does *not* prevent you from continuing to get the severe disability premium if you fall within the scope of the transitional provisions which applied to IS claimants entitled to this premium before 21 October 1991. These were set out in the 22nd edition of CPAG's *National Welfare Benefits Handbook* (1992/93).

Note also that, for IS, income-based JSA and PC, if someone comes to live with you in order to look after you (or your partner), and has not lived with you before, your severe disability premium or amount for severe disability remains in payment for the first 12 weeks after the carer moves in, even if s/he would otherwise count as a non-dependant.[82] After that, you lose the premium (or get a lower rate premium) or the amount for severe disability. The carer should then consider claiming CA (see Chapter 4).).

For HB only:[83]

- any person who jointly occupies your home and is either the co-owner with you or your partner, or liable with you or your partner to make payments in respect of occupying it. A joint occupier who was a non-dependant at any time within the previous eight weeks counts as a non-dependant if the local authority thinks that the change of arrangements was created to take advantage of the HB scheme;
- any person who is liable to pay you or your partner on a commercial basis in respect of occupying the dwelling unless s/he is a close relative (see p895) of you or your partner, or if the local authority thinks that the rent or other agreement has been created to take advantage of the HB scheme (but this cannot apply if the person was otherwise liable to pay rent for the accommodation at any time during the eight weeks before the agreement was made);

* From 5 December 2005, 'step' and 'in-law' relations of a civil partner can also count as close relatives.

- any person, or any member of her/his household, to whom you or your partner are liable to make payments in respect of your accommodation on a commercial basis unless s/he is a close relative of you or your partner.

For CTB only:[84]

- any person who is jointly and severally liable (see p895) with you to pay council tax. If s/he was a non-dependant at any time within the eight weeks before s/he became liable for council tax, s/he counts as a non-dependant if the local authority thinks that the change of arrangements was created to take advantage of the CTB scheme;
- any person who is liable to pay you or your partner on a commercial basis in respect of occupying the dwelling unless s/he is a close relative (see below) of you or your partner, or if the local authority thinks that the liability to make payments has been created to take advantage of the CTB scheme (but this cannot apply if the person was otherwise liable to pay rent for the accommodation at any time during the eight weeks before that liability arose).

Definitions

'Close relative' means parent, parent-in-law, son, son-in-law, daughter, daughter-in-law, step-parent, step-son, step-daughter, brother, sister, or partners of any of these.[85] *

'Jointly occupies' has a technical meaning. It is a legal relationship involving occupation by two or more persons (whether as owner-occupiers or as tenants or licensees), with one and the same legal right.[86] It does not exist if people merely have equal access to different parts of the premises (as had previously been decided by a commissioner[87]).

'Commercial basis' has no technical meaning, and there is no requirement that there need be any intention to make a profit.[88] It may be sufficient if a 'reasonable' charge is made, even if this does not fully cover the cost of the accommodation and meals being provided.[89] The reasonableness of the charge made should be judged solely against the cost of occupying the dwelling, disregarding the additional costs of providing food, clothing and care for the claimant.[90] A useful, but not conclusive, test to apply is to consider whether the same arrangement *might* have been entered into with a lodger rather than with the claimant.[91] It is not relevant to the question of whether the arrangement is on a commercial basis to consider either whether the non-dependant depends financially on the charge being paid or if s/he would take action against the claimant if s/he did not pay.[92] However, these last two matters are relevant to whether there is a *liability* (see below).

'Liability' means a legal or contractual liability (as distinct from a moral or ethical obligation), although this can always be inferred from the circumstances, there being no requirement that any arrangements need be evidenced in writing.[93] It has been held, however, that even though a landlord may have expected relatives of a liable person to share her/his home in order to provide care, it cannot be inferred that they are also liable. Nor can it be assumed that someone is owed a liability in recompense merely for allowing another person to occupy her/his home, particularly if the gains (eg, when someone depends on another person for her/his care) exceed any possible loss.[94] Any liability must arise from the costs of occupying the home. People with no contractual capacity (eg, people with very severe learning disabilities) cannot establish liability under English law. However, there is always a presumption that capacity exists and the test of capacity may not be very stringent. In any case, a commissioner has urged a consistency of approach for England and Scotland, where the law is different in that a liability can exist even where contractual capacity is not established.[95]

Carer's premium and pension credit additional amount[96]

You qualify for this if you or your partner are entitled to, or are treated as getting, CA (see Chapter 4).

- You are treated as getting CA even if you do not receive it but:
  - you would get it but for the overlapping benefit rules (see p1102) (eg, you get long-term IB or retirement pension instead);[97]
  - you are awarded an extra-statutory payment to compensate you for non-payment of invalid care allowance (ICA) or CA.[98]
- If you stop getting, or being treated as getting, CA, or the person you are getting the CA for dies, your entitlement to a carer's premium will continue for a further eight weeks, even if you first claim IS, income-based JSA, HB or CTB in this time.[99]
- A double premium is awarded where both you and your partner satisfy the conditions for it.

Carers and severe disability

Before claiming CA, you should consider how your claim may affect the entitlement to the severe disability premium, or the amount for severe disability in the guarantee credit of PC (see p891), of the disabled person you are caring for – particularly where the only financial advantage to you as the carer is the amount of the carer's premium, which may be worth considerably less than the severe disability premium (but see p891 for the rules on notional income).

Any backdated award of CA does not affect a disabled person's entitlement to the severe disability premium or the amount for severe disability in the guarantee credit of PC.[100] There may therefore be scope for careful planning to take advantage of this rule so that carers can be paid CA or the carer's premium for the same period that the disabled person has already received the severe disability premium or the amount for severe disability in PC.

Although the severe disability premium or amount for severe disability is not payable throughout any period during which a carer is entitled to, and receiving, CA, if it is later decided that CA has been overpaid (ie, that the carer was not in fact entitled to receive CA) you should ask for any decision denying you entitlement to the severe disability premium or the amount for severe disability to be revised. Until 9 March 2000, you could, strictly, have been denied the severe disability premium solely because ICA was in fact being paid, even if it was incorrectly paid, although in practice the DWP agreed that the severe disability premium would remain payable for any period during which ICA was overpaid.[101] Since that date, however, the rules have been changed to make it clear that the carer must be both entitled to *and* in receipt of ICA or CA for the severe disability premium not to be payable.[102]

Bereavement premium[103]

You qualify for this premium if:

- you were aged 55 or over but under 60 on 9 April 2001; *and*
- you were previously in receipt of a bereavement allowance (see p29) following the death of your husband or wife on or after 9 April 2001, but are no longer entitled to that allowance; *and*
- you are claiming IS, income-based-JSA, HB or CTB as a single claimant and you claimed this benefit within eight weeks of ceasing to be entitled to the bereavement allowance.

Note: a bereavement premium cannot be included in your HB and CTB if you or your partner are aged 60 or over and not claiming IS or income-based JSA.

For IS and income-based JSA, if you cease to be a single claimant or stop getting IS or income-based JSA, you will only requalify for the bereavement premium if you claim either IS or income-based JSA as a single claimant within eight weeks of ceasing to get IS/income-based JSA or ceasing to be a single claimant.[104]

Similarly, for HB/CTB, if you cease to be a single claimant or stop getting HB/CTB, you will only requalify for the bereavement premium if you claim HB/CTB as a single claimant within eight weeks of ceasing to get HB/CTB or ceasing to be a single claimant.[105]

In addition, for HB and CTB only, because of the way the rules have been written, it is arguable that entitlement to the bereavement premium in your HB or CTB claim eight weeks prior to a claim for the other benefit (ie, CTB or HB) should automatically qualify you for the bereavement premium in the claim for the other benefit, even if by the time of that claim you are no longer single.[106]

The bereavement premium will only be available until 10 April 2006. By that date all people eligible for this premium will have reached the age of 60 and be able to claim one of the pensioner premiums (or higher personal allowances) instead, which are worth more than the bereavement premium and cannot be paid on top of it in any event.

4. Backdating of premiums

To qualify for the disability premium, enhanced disability premium, higher pensioner premium, severe disability premium, disabled child premium, carer's premium and/or bereavement premium, you and/or a member of your family usually have to have been awarded the qualifying benefit which applies to each premium. The date you may begin to get your premium may therefore depend on the date from which your qualifying benefit is awarded. However, because of the time it may take to deal with your claim for the qualifying benefit, or because your claim is backdated (see p1085), or because it is initially refused but awarded some time later after a revision (see p1189), supersession (see p1199) or appeal (see p1217), you may not get your premium straight away and you may have to apply for it to be backdated.

If you are already getting benefit

If you are already getting income support (IS), income-based jobseeker's allowance (JSA), housing benefit (HB) or council tax benefit (CTB), you should ask for your award of this benefit either to be revised or superseded and for your premium to be backdated either to the same date that your qualifying benefit is awarded from, or to when you first got (or claimed) IS, income-based JSA, HB or CTB if that is later. In such circumstances there is no limit to the period for which arrears can be paid to you.[107]

If you were refused benefit

If you have previously claimed IS or income-based JSA but your claim was refused because you or a member of your family did not at that time get the qualifying benefit for the premium, you should make another IS or income-based JSA claim once the qualifying benefit is awarded. To get full backdating you should have claimed the qualifying benefit before, or no later than 10 days after, the first IS or income-based JSA claim. You must then make your second claim for IS or income-based JSA within three months of the decision awarding the qualifying benefit. The second claim is backdated, including the premium, to the date of the first IS or income-based JSA claim or to the date from which the qualifying benefit was awarded, if that is later.[108] If the qualifying benefit is initially refused, or awarded at a lower rate than you need for the premium, but is later decided in your favour, to get full backdating you must make your second IS or income-based JSA claim within three months of the date the qualifying benefit is decided in your favour on revision, supersession or appeal.[109]

If you lose entitlement to benefit

If you lose your existing **IS** or **income-based JSA** as a result of having your or a member of your family's qualifying benefit stopped or reduced, and that qualifying benefit is then reinstated on a revision, supersession or appeal, you should make a new claim for IS or income-based JSA. Provided you claim within three months of the favourable decision on the qualifying benefit, your IS or income-based JSA is fully backdated to the date entitlement had previously ended, or to the date from which the qualifying benefit is payable if that is later.[110]

If you lose your **HB** or **CTB** because you lose entitlement to a qualifying benefit, the decision ending your HB/CTB can be revised if the qualifying benefit is reinstated. Your HB/CTB can be fully backdated in this situation. You need to tell the local authority that you have got back your qualifying benefit, but you do not need to make a fresh claim for HB/CTB.[111]

Backdating and arrears

If your premium has been missed out on an earlier refused claim or on your current claim, because your entitlement to the premium has been overlooked or because of some other error in assessing your entitlement, you can also apply for your claim to be revised in order to get your claim backdated. In such circumstances there is no limit to the period for which IS/income-based JSA arrears can be paid to you and although the rules may limit any arrears of any new or increased entitlement to HB or CTB to 12 months,[112] you may be able to get compensation for any longer period (see p1304).

For the rules on backdating of claims, see Chapter 40.

Additional points to note

- Although a later award of carer's allowance may entitle you to have your carer's premium backdated, this will not affect the severe disability premium of the person you are looking after (see p891).
- For HB and CTB, if you are one of a couple and the person who is incapable of work is not the claimant, you can swap the claimant role and s/he can apply to backdate a new claim if s/he has 'good cause' (see pp221 and 121). In this way you can get the disability premium backdated for up to 12 months.[113] For IS/income-based JSA, it will not be possible to backdate your claim unless one of the specified reasons for making a late claim applies (see p1088).

Backdating of pension credit

For backdating of pension credit see p477.

Notes

1. **What is the applicable amount?**
   1 Reg 22A IS Regs

2. **Personal allowances**
   2 **IS** Reg 18(2) IS Regs
   JSA Reg 84(2) JSA Regs
   3 **IS** Sch 2 Part I IS Regs
   JSA Sch 1 paras 1 and 2 JSA Regs
   HB Sch 2 Part I HB Regs
   CTB Sch 1 Part I CTB Regs
   4 **HB** Sch 2A para 1 HB Regs
   CTB Sch 1A para 1 CTB Regs
   5 **IS** Reg 18(1)(b) IS Regs
   JSA Reg 84(1)(b) JSA Regs
   HB Reg 17(b) HB Regs
   CTB Reg 9(b) CTB Regs
   HB/CTB paras C4.05-06 GM
   6 **IS** Sch 2 para 1(1)(a), (b) and (c) and (2)(a), (b) and (c) IS Regs
   JSA Sch 1 para 1(1)(a)-(c) and (2)(a)-(c) JSA Regs
   7 **IS** Sch 2 paras 1(1)(b) and (c), (2)(b) and (c) and 1A IS Regs
   JSA Sch 1 para 1(1)(b)-(c) and (2)(b)-(c) JSA Regs
   8 **IS** Sch 2 para 1(3) IS Regs
   JSA Sch 1 para 1(3) JSA Regs

3. **Premiums**
   9 **HB** Sch 2A paras 3 and 6-9 HB Regs
   CTB Sch 1A paras 3 and 6-9 CTB Regs
   Both as substituted by regs 6 and 15 HB&CTB(SPC) Regs
   10 **IS** Sch 2 para 6(2) IS Regs
   JSA Sch 1 paras 7(2) and 20C(2) JSA Regs
   HB Sch 2 para 6(2) HB Regs
   CTB Sch 1 para 6(2) CTB Regs
   11 **IS** Sch 2 para 5 IS Regs
   JSA Sch 1 para 6 JSA Regs
   HB Sch 2 para 5 HB Regs
   CTB Sch 1 para 5 CTB Regs
   12 **IS** Sch 2 para 7 IS Regs
   JSA Sch 1 para 8 JSA Regs
   HB Sch 2 para 7 HB Regs
   CTB Sch 1 para 7 CTB Regs
   13 **IS** Sch 2 para 14B IS Regs
   JSA Sch 1 para 19 JSA Regs
   HB Sch 2 para 14B HB Regs
   CTB Sch 1 para 18 CTB Regs
   See also R(IS) 10/94
   14 **IS** Sch 2 para 3 IS Regs
   JSA Sch 1 para 4 JSA Regs
   HB Sch 2 para 3 HB Regs
   CTB Sch 1 para 3 CTB Regs
   For people aged 60 or over:
   HB Sch 2A para 3 HB Regs
   CTB Sch 1A para 3 CTB Regs
   15 **HB** Sch 2 para 3(1A) HB Regs
   CTB Sch 1 para 3(1A) CTB Regs
   16 **IS** Regs 15(3) and 16(6) IS Regs
   JSA Regs 74(4) and 78(7) JSA Regs
   17 **HB** Reg 15(4)-(5) HB Regs
   CTB Reg 7(3)-(4) CTB Regs
   18 **IS** Sch 2 para 3 IS Regs
   JSA Sch 1 para 4 JSA Regs
   HB Sch 2 para 3 HB Regs
   CTB Sch 1 para 3 CTB Regs
   19 para C4/4.74 GM
   20 **IS** Sch 2 paras 14 and 15(6) IS Regs
   JSA Sch 1 para 16 JSA Regs
   HB Sch 2 paras 14 and 15(6) HB Regs
   CTB Sch 1 paras 15 and 19(7) CTB Regs
   21 **IS** Sch 2 paras 12(1)(a)(iii) and (2) and 14(c) IS Regs
   JSA Sch 1 para 14(1)(h) and (2) JSA Regs
   HB Sch 2 paras 12(1)(a)(v) and (2) and 14(c) HB Regs
   CTB Sch 1 paras 13(1)(a)(v) and (2) and 15(c) CTB Regs
   22 **IS** Sch 2 para 14(a) IS Regs
   JSA Sch 1 para 16(a) JSA Regs
   23 **HB** Sch 2 para 14 and Sch 2A para 8 HB Regs
   CTB Sch 1 para 15 and Sch 1A para 8 CTB Regs
   24 Sch 2 para 14 HB Regs; Sch 1 para 15 CTB Regs
   25 **IS** Sch 2 para 11 IS Regs
   JSA Sch 1 paras 13 and 14 JSA Regs
   HB Sch 2 para 11 HB Regs
   CTB Sch 1 para 12 CTB Regs
   26 Reg 29(5) SPC(CTMP) Regs
   27 **IS** Reg 2(1) IS Regs
   JSA Reg 1(3) JSA Regs
   HB Reg 2(1) HB Regs
   CTB Reg 2(1) CTB Regs
   All Definition of 'attendance allowance'

28 **IS** Sch 2 para 12(6) IS Regs
JSA Sch 1 para 14(1)(d) JSA Regs
HB Sch 2 para 12(7) HB Regs
CTB Sch 1 para 13(6A) CTB Regs
29 **IS** Sch 2 para 14A IS Regs
JSA Sch 1 para 18 JSA Regs
HB Sch 2 para 14A HB Regs
CTB Sch 1 para 17 CTB Regs
30 **IS** Sch 2 para 14B IS Regs
JSA Sch 1 para 19 JSA Regs
HB Sch 2 para 14B HB Regs
CTB Sch 1 para 18 CTB Regs
See also R(IS) 10/94
31 **IS** Sch 2 para 7(1)(a) IS Regs
JSA Sch 1 para 8(1)(a) JSA Regs
HB Sch 2 para 7(1)(a) HB Regs
CTB Sch 1 para 7(1)(a) CTB Regs
32 **IS** Sch 2 para 12(1)(a)(iii) and (2) IS Regs
JSA Sch 1 para 14(1)(h) and (2) JSA Regs
HB Sch 2 para 12(1)(a)(v) and (2) HB Regs
CTB Sch 1 para 13(1)(a)(v) and (2) CTB Regs
33 **IS** Sch 2 para 12(1)(a)(ii) IS Regs
JSA Sch 1 para 14(1)(e) and (f) JSA Regs
HB Sch 2 para 12(1)(a)(iv) HB Regs
CTB Sch 1 para 13(1)(a)(iv) CTB Regs
34 R(IS) 7/02
35 **IS** Sch 2 para 12(1)(c)(i) IS Regs
JSA Sch 1 para 14(1)(g)(i) JSA Regs
HB Sch 2 para 12(1)(a)(ii) HB Regs
CTB Sch 1 para 13(1)(a)(ii) CTB Regs
36 **IS** Sch 2 para 12(1)(c)(i) IS Regs
JSA Sch 1 para 14(1)(g)(i) JSA Regs
37 **HB** Sch 2 para 12(1)(a)(ii) HB Regs
CTB Sch 1 para 13(1)(a)(ii) CTB Regs
38 **IS** Sch 2 para 12(1)(c) IS Regs
JSA Sch 1 para 14(1)(g) JSA Regs
39 **IS** Sch 2 para 12(1)(c)(ii) IS Regs
JSA Sch 1 para 14(1)(g)(ii) JSA Regs
HB Sch 2 para 12(1)(a)(iii) HB Regs
CTB Sch 1 para 13(1)(a)(iii) CTB Regs
40 **IS** Sch 2 para 12(1)(b) IS Regs
HB Sch 2 para 12(1)(b) HB Regs
CTB Sch 1 para 13(1)(b) CTB Regs
41 s30B(4) SSCBA 1992
42 **IS** Sch 2 para 12(1A) IS Regs
JSA Sch 1 para 12(3) JSA Regs
HB Sch 2 para 12(8) HB Regs
CTB Sch 1 para 13(8) CTB Regs
43 R(IS) 4/04
44 **IS** Sch 2 paras 11(b) and 12 IS Regs
HB Sch 2 paras 11(b) and 12 HB Regs
CTB Sch 1 paras 12(b) and 13 CTB Regs
45 Sch 1 para 14(d) JSA Regs
46 **IS** Sch 2 paras 7(1)(b) and 12(5) IS Regs
JSA Sch 1 para 8(1)(b) JSA Regs
HB Sch 2 paras 7(1)(b) and 12(5) HB Regs
CTB Sch 1 paras 7(1)(b) and 13(5) CTB Regs
47 **IS** Sch 2 para 13A IS Regs
JSA Sch 1 paras 15A and 20IA JSA Regs
HB Sch 2 para 13A HB Regs
CTB Sch 1 para 14A CTB Regs
For people aged 60 or over:
HB Sch 2A para 7 HB Regs
CTB Sch 1A para 7 CTB Regs
48 **IS** Sch 2 paras 9 and 9A IS Regs
JSA Sch 1 paras 10 and 11 JSA Regs
HB Sch 2 paras 9 and 9A HB Regs
CTB Sch 1 paras 9 and 10 CTB Regs
49 Sch 2 para 10 IS Regs
50 **IS** Sch 2 para 10 IS Regs
JSA Sch 1 para 12 JSA Regs
HB Sch 2 para 10 HB Regs
CTB Sch 1 para 11 CTB Regs
51 **IS** Sch 2 para 10(4) IS Regs
JSA Sch 1 para 12(3) JSA Regs
HB Sch 2 para 10(4) HB Regs
CTB Sch 1 para 11(4) CTB Regs
52 **IS** Sch 2 para 10(1)(b)(ii) and (3) IS Regs
JSA Sch 1 para 12(2) JSA Regs
HB Sch 2 para 10(1)(b)(ii) and (3) HB Regs
CTB Sch 1 para 11(1)(b)(ii) and (3) CTB Regs
53 **HB** Sch 2 para 10(3)(c) HB Regs
CTB Sch 1 para 11(3)(c) CTB Regs
54 Sch 1 para 12(1)(a)(ii) JSA Regs
55 R(IS) 7/02
56 **IS** Sch 2 para 12(1)(c)(i) and (1A) IS Regs
JSA Sch 1 paras 14(1)(g)(i) and 12(3) JSA Regs
HB Sch 2 para 12(1)(a)(ii) and (8) HB Regs
CTB Sch 1 para 13(1)(a)(ii) and (8) CTB Regs
57 **HB** Sch 2 para 10(3)(c) HB Regs
CTB Sch 1 para 11(3)(c) CTB Regs
58 Sch 1 para 12(2) JSA Regs
59 **IS** Sch 2 para 12(1)(c)(i) IS Regs
JSA Sch 1 para 14(1)(g)(i) JSA Regs
HB Sch 2 para 12(1)(a)(ii) HB Regs
CTB Sch 1 para 13(1)(a)(ii) CTB Regs
60 **IS** Sch 2 para 12(1)(c) IS Regs
JSA Sch 1 para 14(1)(g) JSA Regs
61 CIS/458/1992
62 CIS/458/1992
63 **IS** Sch 2 para 7(1)(a) IS Regs
JSA Sch 1 para 8(1)(a) JSA Regs
HB Sch 2 para 7(1)(a) HB Regs
CTB Sch 1 para 7(1)(a) CTB Regs

64 **IS** Sch 2 para 13 IS Regs
JSA Sch 1 para 15 JSA Regs
PC Reg 6(4) and Sch 1 paras 1-2 SPC Regs
HB Sch 2 para 13 HB Regs
CTB Sch 1 para 14 CTB Regs
For people aged 60 or over:
HB Sch 2A para 6 HB Regs
CTB Sch 1A para 6 CTB Regs
65 **IS** Reg 2(1) IS Regs
JSA Reg 1(3) JSA Regs
PC Reg 1(2) SPC Regs
HB Reg 2(1) HB Regs
CTB Reg 2(1) CTB Regs
66 **IS** Sch 2 para 14A IS Regs
JSA Sch 1 para 18 JSA Regs
PC Sch 1 para 1(2)(a)(ii) SPC Regs
HB Sch 2 para 14A HB Regs
CTB Sch 1 para 17 CTB Regs
67 **IS** Sch 2 para 13(2A) IS Regs
JSA Sch 1 para 15(3) JSA Regs
PC Sch 1 para 1(b) and (c) SPC Regs
HB Sch 2 para 13(2A) HB Regs
CTB Sch 1 para 14(2A) CTB Regs
68 **IS** Sch 2 para 13(3A)(a) IS Regs
JSA Sch 1 paras 15(5)(a) and 20I(4)(a) JSA Regs
PC Sch 1 para 2(b) SPC Regs
HB Sch 2 para 13(3A)(a) HB Regs
CTB Sch 1 para 14(3A)(a) CTB Regs
69 **IS** Sch 2 para 14B IS Regs
JSA Sch 1 para 19 JSA Regs
HB Sch 2 para 14B HB Regs
CTB Sch 1 para 18 CTB Regs
See also R(IS) 10/94, upheld in *Rider v CAO, The Times*, 30 January 1996 (CA)
70 *Bate v CAO* [1996] 2 All ER 790 (HL)
71 **IS** Reg 3(4) and (5) IS Regs
JSA Reg 2(6) and (7) JSA Regs
HB Reg 3(4) HB Regs
72 **IS** Sch 2 para 13(2)(a)(iii) and (b) IS Regs
JSA Sch 1 para 15(1)(c) and (2)(d) JSA Regs
HB Sch 2 para 13(2)(a)(iii) and (b) HB Regs
CTB Sch 1 para 14(2)(a)(iii) and (b) CTB Regs
73 **IS** Sch 2 para 13(3ZA) IS Regs
JSA Sch 1 para 15(7) JSA Regs
PC Sch 1 para 2(c) SPC Regs
HB Sch 2 para 13(4) HB Regs
CTB Sch 1 para 14(4) CTB Regs
74 **IS** Sch 2 para 13(3A) IS Regs
JSA Sch 1 para 15(5) JSA Regs
PC Reg 6(5) and Sch 1 para 1(2)(b) SPC Regs
HB Sch 2 para 13(3A) HB Regs
CTB Sch 1 para 14(3A) CTB Regs
75 **IS** Reg 16(1) IS Regs
JSA Reg 78(1) JSA Regs
76 **IS** Sch 7 para 9 IS Regs
JSA Sch 5 para 5 IS Regs and R(IS) 9/02
77 **IS** Reg 3 and Sch 2 para 13 IS Regs
JSA Reg 2 and Sch 1 para 15 JSA Regs
PC Sch 1 para 2 SPC Regs
HB Reg 3 and Sch 2 para 13 HB Regs
CTB Reg 3 and Sch 1 para 14 CTB Regs
78 **IS** Sch 2 para 13(3)(a) IS Regs
JSA Sch 1 para 15(4)(a) JSA Regs
PC Sch 1 para 2(2)(a) SPC Regs
HB Sch 2 para 13(3)(a) HB Regs
CTB Sch 1 para 14(3)(a) CTB Regs
79 **IS** Sch 2 para 13(3)(d) IS Regs
JSA Sch 1 para 14(1)(h) and (2) JSA Regs
PC Sch 1 para 2(2)(b) and (c) SPC Regs
HB Sch 2 para 13(3)(c) HB Regs
CTB Sch 1 para 14(3)(c) CTB Regs
80 CIS/14850/1996 para 10
81 **IS** Reg 3(2)(c) and (d) IS Regs
JSA Reg 2(2)(c) and (d) JSA Regs
PC Sch 1 para 2(d) and (e) SPC Regs
HB Reg 3(2)(f) HB Regs
CTB Reg 3(2)(f) CTB Regs
82 **IS** Sch 2 para 13(3)(c) and (4) IS Regs
JSA Sch 1 para 15(4)(b) and (5) JSA Regs
PC Sch 1 paras (3)-(4) SPC Regs
83 Regs 3 and 7(1) HB Regs
84 Reg 3 CTB Regs
85 **IS** Reg 2(1) IS Regs
JSA Reg 1(3) JSA Regs
HB Reg 2(1) HB Regs
CTB Reg 2(1) CTB Regs
All Definition of 'close relative'
86 *Bate v CAO* [1996] 2 All ER 790 (HL)
87 CIS/180/1989
88 R(IS) 11/98 (Tribunal of Commissioners)
89 CSIS/43/1989
90 CIS/754/1991 and R(IS) 11/98 para 12
91 R(IS) 11/98 para 8
92 R(IS) 11/98 paras 10 and 11
93 CIS/754/1991
94 CSIS/641/1995
95 CIS/754/1991, referring to CSIS/28/1992 and CSIS/40/1992
96 **IS** Sch 2 para 14ZA IS Regs
JSA Sch 1 para 17 JSA Regs
PC Reg 6(6)(a) and Sch 1 para 4 SPC Regs
HB Sch 2 para 14ZA HB Regs
CTB Sch 1 para 16 CTB Regs
For people aged 60 or over:
HB Sch 2A para 9 HB Regs
CTB Sch 1A para 9 CTB Regs

97 CIS/367/2003
IS Sch 2 para 14A IS Regs
JSA Sch 1 para 18 JSA Regs
PC Sch1 para 5 SPC Regs
HB Sch 2 para 14A HB Regs
CTB Sch 1 para 17 CTB Regs
98 **IS** Sch 2 para 14A IS Regs
JSA Sch 1 para 18 JSA Regs
PC Sch 1 para 5 SPC Regs
HB Sch 2 para 14A HB Regs
CTB Sch 1 para 17 CTB Regs
99 **IS** Sch 2 paras 7 and 14ZA(3) IS Regs
JSA Sch 1 paras 17(3) and 20(3) JSA Regs
HB Sch 2 paras 7 and 14ZA(3) HB Regs
CTB Sch 1 paras 7 and 16(3) CTB Regs
100 **IS** Sch 2 para 13(3ZA) IS Regs
JSA Sch 1 para 15(7) JSA Regs
PC Sch 1 para 1(2)(c) SPC Regs
HB Sch 2 para 13(4) HB Regs
CTB Sch 1 para 14(4) CTB Regs
101 Correspondence from the ICA Unit to the Carers National Association (24 July 1999) and to Wolverhampton Social Services (6 January 2000)
102 Sch 1B para 4(b) IS Regs
103 **IS** Sch 2 para 8A IS Regs
JSA Sch 1 para 9A JSA Regs
HB Sch 2 para 8A HB Regs
CTB Sch 1 para 8A CTB Regs
104 **IS** Sch 2 para 8A(3) IS Regs
JSA Sch 1 para 9A(3) JSA Regs
105 **HB** Sch 2 para 8A(3) HB Regs
CTB Sch 1 para 8A(3) CTB Regs
106 **HB** Sch 2 para 8A(5) HB Regs
CTB Sch 1 para 8A(5) CTB Regs

4. **Backdating of premiums**
107 **IS/JSA** Regs 3(7) and 6(2)(e) SS&CS(DA) Regs
HB Reg 79 HB Regs
CTB Reg 69 CTB Regs
108 Reg 6(16)-(18) SS(C&P) Regs
109 Reg 6(26) SS(C&P) Regs
110 Reg 6(19)-(20) SS(C&P) Regs
111 Reg 4(7C) HB&CTB(DA) Regs
112 **IS/JSA** Reg 3(7) SS&CS(DA) Regs
HB Reg 79 HB Regs
CTB Reg 69 CTB Regs
113 CSIS/66/1992; CIS/706/1992

Chapter 36

Housing costs for means-tested benefits

This chapter covers the rules for getting income support (IS), income-based jobseeker's allowance (JSA) and pension credit (PC) to cover your housing costs. It contains:

If you own or are buying your home, IS, *income-based* JSA or PC can include a variety of payments for your housing costs. Housing costs are not included as part of *contribution-based* JSA, but if you satisfy the means test you can claim income-based JSA to top this up.

If you are a tenant you can get IS, income-based JSA or PC for some types of housing costs, but not for your rent.[1] This is covered by housing benefit (HB) instead (see Chapter 10). If you live in a care home permanently, you cannot get help with housing costs for your former home.[2] However, if you are only staying in a care home temporarily, you might get help with the housing costs on your normal home (see p907).

You cannot get extra help with your housing costs if you are claiming working tax credit (see Chapter 50). However, you can get HB to help you with your rent (see Chapter 10).

If your entitlement to IS or income-based JSA ends because you start work, or increase your hours or your pay, you may be entitled to mortgage interest run-on. See p62 for further information.

In this chapter, unless otherwise stated, references to income-based JSA also refer to joint-claim JSA.

1. When you can get help with housing costs

You can get help with your housing costs if:[3]

- the type of housing costs can be met by income support (IS), income-based jobseeker's allowance (JSA) or pension credit (PC) (see below);
- for IS and income-based JSA, you, or someone in your family, are liable to pay the housing costs (see below). See p906 for who counts as your 'family';
- for PC, you or your partner are liable to pay the housing costs (see p905);
- the housing costs are for the home in which you normally live (see p906).

There are some situations in which you might not get help with housing costs. These are:

- For IS and JSA only, for the first few weeks after you claim you cannot get any help with housing costs (see p926). You are expected to rely on mortgage protection payments, or other income or savings initially.
- Where you become liable for or increase a loan while you are entitled to IS, JSA or PC or during a period of 26 weeks between two claims, in some cases you cannot get any help with housing costs. In others, you *can* get help but the amount you can be paid is restricted. See p911for further information.

If your housing costs are too high the amount you are paid can be restricted (see p921).

Which housing costs can be met

Your IS, income-based JSA and PC can include help with the following housing costs:[4]

- payments towards the interest on mortgages and other loans for house purchase. This includes money borrowed under a hire purchase agreement taken out to buy your home. See p910 for further information;
- payments towards the interest on loans used to pay for certain repairs and improvements or to meet a service charge for repairs and improvements (see p916);
- 'other housing costs' (see p918):
  - rent or ground rent (feu duty in Scotland) if you have a lease of more than 21 years. If you have a lease of 21 years or less you might get housing benefit instead. **Note:** from 28 November 2004 feu duties (other than arrears of these) are no longer payable;[5]
  - service charges (though some are excluded – see p919);
  - rentcharge payments;
  - payments under a co-ownership scheme;
  - rent if you are a Crown tenant (minus any water charges);
  - payments for a tent and its pitch if that is your home.

Are you liable to pay housing costs?

You count as liable to pay housing costs (see above for the types that can be met) if:[6]

- you, or your partner, are **liable** to pay them. You do not have to be legally liable.[7] However, you do not count as liable to pay housing costs if you pay these to someone who is a member of your household (see p812 for the meaning of 'household'). If you or your partner share liability with someone, you might only get help with your share of the housing costs (see p915);
- you are **treated as liable** to pay them. You are treated as liable if:
  - you share the costs with other members of your household (see p812 for the meaning of 'household'); *and*
  - at least one of those with whom you share is liable.

  In this case, you can be paid for your share,[8] as long as those you share with are not 'close relatives' of yourself or your partner and it is reasonable to treat you as sharing. (**'Close relative'** means a parent, parent-in-law, son, son-in-law, daughter, daughter-in-law, step-parent, step-son, step-daughter, brother, sister or the partner of any of these.* **'Sister'** or **'brother'** includes a half-sister or half-brother. An adopted child ceases to be related to her/his natural family on adoption and becomes the relative of her/his adoptive family[9]);
- **someone else is liable to pay them but is not paying** so you have to meet the cost yourself in order to continue to live in your home. You must show that it is reasonable for you to pay instead of her/him – eg, if you have given up your home to live with and care for someone and s/he has now gone into a care home, or if you have separated from your partner (even if you have not lived in the home continuously since your partner left[10]).

If you are not required to pay any housing costs currently (eg, if under the terms of your mortgage you do not have to pay interest) you cannot receive IS, income-based JSA or PC for housing costs. This applies to special mortgage schemes for pensioners where the mortgage is repaid from your estate when you die rather than by regular monthly payments.[11]

For IS and income-based JSA only, if you are on strike, a member of your family (see below) who is not affected by the strike is treated as liable for your housing costs.[12]

Member of the family

For IS and income-based JSA purposes, member of the **'family'** means your partner (see p811) and any child or young person who lives in your household and for whom you count as 'responsible' (see pp300 and 374).[13]

Are the costs for the home in which you normally live?

Housing costs are paid for the home in which:[14]

- for IS and income-based JSA, you and your 'family' (see above) normally live;
- for PC, you and your partner normally live.

* From 5 December 2005, 'step' and 'in-law' relations of a civil partner can also count as close relatives.

You cannot usually be paid for any other home. If you are liable to pay the mortgage on a property but have no immediate intention of living there you cannot get help with the cost.[15]

Your '**home**' is defined as the building, or part of the building, in which you live. This includes any garage, garden, outbuildings and other premises and land which it is not reasonable or practicable to sell separately.[16] You can argue that a home can consist of more than one building if you occupy more than one dwelling, for example because your family is too large for one.[17]

There are special rules if:

- you have just moved into your home (see below);
- you are temporarily away from home (see below);
- you are liable to pay housing costs on more than one home (see p909).

Moving home

If you have just moved into your home but were liable to pay housing costs before moving in, your IS, income-based JSA or PC can include these costs for a period of up to four weeks before your move if your delay in moving was reasonable, you claimed IS, JSA or PC before moving in, *and*:[18]

- you were waiting for adaptations to be finished to meet the disability needs of:
  - for IS and income-based JSA, you or a member of your family (see p906 for who counts as your family); *or*
  - for PC, you, your partner, or someone under 19 for whom you or your partner are responsible ('responsible' is not defined in the rules);
- you became responsible for the housing costs while you were in hospital or a care home; *or*
- you were waiting for a social fund payment to help you set up home – eg, for help with removal costs or furniture and bedding (see Chapter 21). For IS and JSA only, you must have a child of five or under, or qualify for a pensioner, enhanced pensioner, higher pensioner, disability, severe disability or disabled child premium (see p882). **Note:** this rule has not been amended. You cannot qualify for a disabled child premium when your IS or JSA no longer includes allowances and premiums for your children (see p818). See CPAG's *Welfare Rights Bulletin* for updates.

The amount for housing costs is not actually paid until you move in. If the earlier IS, JSA or PC claim you made before you moved was turned down you must claim again within four weeks of moving in to qualify.

Temporary absence from home

If you are temporarily away from home but are still entitled to IS, income-based JSA or PC, have not rented out your home and intend to return, your housing costs continue to be paid for a period. You can try to argue that you count as temporarily absent from home even if you have not yet stayed there – eg, you move your furniture and belongings in but then have to go into hospital.[19]

You can get housing costs for up to **13 weeks** while you are away, whatever the reason. You must be unlikely to be away for longer than this.[20]

You can get housing costs for up to **52 weeks** if you are unlikely to be away for longer than this (or in exceptional circumstances, unlikely to be away for substantially longer than this) and you are:[21]

- in hospital. If you are claiming JSA, you must be treated as capable of work during a two-week period of sickness – see p352. If you are sick for longer than this you should claim IS or PC;
- receiving care (approved by a doctor) in the UK or abroad, as long as this is not in a care home;
- receiving medical treatment or convalescing in the UK or abroad (approved by a doctor) or your partner or a dependent child (or for PC only, a dependant under 19) is, as long as this is not in a care home;
- attending a 'training course' away from home in the UK or abroad. Your training course counts if it is provided by, or on behalf of, or by arrangement with, or approved by a government department, the Secretary of State, Scottish Enterprise or Highlands and Islands Enterprise;
- required to live in a bail hostel or an address away from your normal home as a condition of bail;
- for IS and PC only, in prison on remand pending trial or sentence. If you were claiming JSA before going into prison you must claim IS or PC instead to cover your housing costs;
- in a care home for short-term or respite care. However, if you are in the home for a trial period to see if you wish to move there permanently, you can only get your housing costs met for 13 weeks.[22] You must intend to return home if the accommodation is not suitable; once you decide to become a permanent resident, this rule no longer applies.[23] If the home does not suit your needs you can have further trial periods in other homes, so long as you are not away from home for more than 52 weeks in total;
- providing care for someone living in the UK or abroad (approved by a doctor);
- caring for a child (or for PC only, someone under 19) whose parent or guardian is receiving medical treatment or care (approved by a doctor) away from home;
- away from home through fear of violence (see below if you need to claim for two homes and for what counts as violence);
- a full-time student (see p621); *and*
  - living apart from your partner but cannot get housing costs for two homes (see p910); *or*
  - a single claimant or a lone parent who is liable to pay housing costs on both a term-time and a home address.

Whether or not you are unlikely to be away for longer than 13/52 weeks should be considered initially based on the circumstances on the date you leave your home.[24] If at any time after that date it becomes likely that you will be away from home for more than the 13/52 weeks, your entitlement can be reconsidered.

There is no linking rule with these provisions, which means that a new period can start if you return home even for a short stay – eg, a day or a weekend.[25]

If you have to live in temporary accommodation while essential repairs are done to your normal home and you only have to pay for housing costs for one of the homes, your IS, income-based JSA or PC covers these costs.[26] This is not subject to the normal limits on temporary absence from home.[27] If you have to pay housing costs for both homes, you may be able to claim IS, income-based JSA or PC for both for up to four weeks (see p909). After that you are only paid for one home. This could be your normal home if you are unlikely to be away for more than 13/52 weeks (see p907) or your temporary home if you will be away for longer.

Housing costs for more than one home

In most cases you can only be paid housing costs for one home (but see p907). However, if you have to pay housing costs for two homes you can get IS, income-based JSA or PC for both:[28]

- for up to **four weeks** if you have moved into a new home and cannot avoid having to pay for the other one as well;
- **indefinitely** if you left your home through fear of violence. So long as you left home because of this and are still away from home because of this, it does not matter if you were away from home for some other reason during this period – eg, because you were in prison.[29] You have to show that it is reasonable for you to get payment for two homes. Thus, if you do not intend to return home or someone else is paying the mortgage, you might not get IS, income-based JSA or PC for both homes.

  'Violence' means violence against you and not caused by you.[30] For the purpose of these rules, it must be fear of violence:[31]
  - in your old home. Remember that your garden and garage, for example, count as your home. Fear of a racial attack should be covered provided the attack would take place in your home (see p907 for what counts as your 'home'); *or*
  - for IS and income-based JSA, from a former member of your family. See p906 for who counts as your 'family'; *or*
  - for PC, from a close relative (see p906) or former partner;
- **indefinitely** if you are one of a couple and you or your partner are a full-time student or on a training course and living away from your home (see p910).

If you have to live in temporary accommodation while essential repairs are done to your normal home, see above.

If you have to live away from your normal home because you are a **full-time student** (see p621) or on a training course (see p908) IS, income-based JSA or PC can cover the housing costs as follows:

- if you are one of a couple and have to live apart, you can get IS, income-based JSA or PC for both of your homes if it is reasonable for you to get help with both;[32]
- if you are a single person or lone parent and are having to pay housing costs for *either* your normal home *or* your term-time accommodation but not both, you can get IS, income-based JSA or PC, for the home for which you pay.[33]

If neither of the above applies you may only get help with your usual home for up to 52 weeks during a temporary absence (see p907).[34]

If you are getting IS, income-based JSA or PC for your term-time accommodation and you stop living there during a vacation, you cannot get housing costs unless you are away because you are in hospital.[35]

2. Mortgages and loans

An amount for home loan payments can be included in your income support (IS) or income-based jobseeker's allowance (JSA) applicable amount (see p303 and p379). An additional amount for home loan payments can be included in your pension credit (PC) appropriate minimum guarantee (see p469).

You must have a home loan.[36] The term **'home loan'** refers to, for example, a mortgage, a hire purchase agreement or some other loan to help you buy your home.

It is important to remember that:

- not all loans qualify for help;
- restrictions might be made – eg, if your total housing costs are thought to be too high (see p921) or if you took out or increased your loan while entitled to IS, JSA or PC or during a period between claims (see p911);
- your IS, income-based JSA or PC for housing costs does not cover all of your loan(s). You only get help towards the interest payments on your loan(s) and the amount you are paid is calculated in a special way (see p915);
- for IS and JSA only, you might not get your full housing costs met initially (see p926);
- deductions can be made if other people live in your home (see p924);
- payment is usually made directly to the lender.

Loans that qualify

You are only paid if your loan qualifies. If your loan was taken out to pay for repairs or improvements, see p916. If you have other housing costs, see p918.

Your loan qualifies if it was:[37]

- **taken out to buy the home in which you live.** Loans taken out to buy an existing property as well as those to pay for materials and labour to build your own home are covered. If all or part of your loan was not taken out with the immediate intention of paying for your home (eg, it was to buy a car or set up a business) you cannot get help with the cost even if the loan is secured on your home (but see p929);[38]
- **taken out to buy an additional interest in the home in which you live,** for example:[39]
  - by buying out your ex-partner's share in your home after you separated. However, where your ex-partner has registered a right to occupy your home (what is known as a 'Class F land charge') you cannot get help with a loan to pay her/him to remove it;[40]
  - by purchasing the freehold on a leasehold property;[41]
  - by buying your partner's share back from a trustee in bankruptcy if s/he is bankrupt;[42]
  - by buying out sitting tenants;[43]
- **taken out to repay a loan which itself would have qualified.** However, if the second loan is also for things that do not qualify for help (eg, to pay debts or to pay for a holiday) you only get help with the amount of the original loan.

Example

Mr Clay took out a new mortgage of £60,000. £45,000 was to pay off the mortgage he took out to buy his home and £15,000 was to pay off business debts. He gets help with the loan for £45,000.

Loans taken out for any costs necessary to help you buy the home or the additional interest are covered.[44] These could include things like search or valuation fees, legal fees and stamp duty.

Note: even if your entire loan qualifies, you might not get help if you took it out or increased it while entitled to IS, JSA or PC or during a period between claims (see below). Where your home is used for both business and domestic purposes and neither part can be sold off separately, you can only get help with the loan for the part where you live.[45]

Taking out or increasing loans while entitled to income support, jobseeker's allowance or pension credit

Even if your loan qualifies (see p910) you cannot usually get IS, income-based JSA or PC to help you pay the cost if you became liable for it or increased it during a period (called a **'relevant period'**):

- **for IS:**[46]
  - when you were entitled to IS or income-based JSA; *or*

- when you were living as a member of the family with someone who was entitled to IS or income-based JSA (see p906 for who counts as your 'family'); *or*
- of up to 26 weeks between two of either of the types of period listed above;

- **for JSA:**[47]
  - when you were entitled to IS or JSA; *or*
  - when you were living as a member of the family of someone who was entitled to IS or JSA (see p906 for who counts as your family); *or*
  - of up to 26 weeks between two of either of the types of period listed above.

  Note: Official guidance suggests that the DWP might only apply this rule if you (or the person you were living with) was entitled to IS or *income-based* JSA.[48]
- **for PC:**[49]
  - when you were entitled to IS, income-based JSA or PC; *or*
  - if you had a partner, when your partner was entitled to IS, income-based JSA or PC; *or*
  - of up to 26 weeks between two of either of the types of period listed above.

Remember that if you become liable for the loan during a period of 26 weeks or more between two claims, you *can* get help with the cost.

You and your partner are treated as entitled to IS, income-based JSA or PC when you are on one of the New Deal programmes or schemes listed on p931, even if as a result you:[50]

- count as in full-time paid work (see p750); *or*
- have too much income to qualify for IS, JSA or PC.

The DWP might say that you count as in a relevant period if you are treated as entitled to IS, JSA or PC even if you were not actually entitled to it, if the rules described on pp930–933 apply.[51]

Getting help with a new or increased loan

Even if you became liable for your loan during a 'relevant period', you may still be able to get IS, income-based JSA or PC for your housing costs. See below, p913 and p914.

General rules

You can get IS, income-based JSA or PC for housing costs even if you became liable for your loan during a 'relevant period' (see p911) if this was before 2 May 1994:[52] *or*

- for IS and PC if:
  - you became liable for your loan between 2 May 1994 and 7 October 1995 and you got IS for it in one or more of the 26 weeks before 2 October 1995 under the rules that then applied; *or*

- you became liable for your loan in the 26 weeks before 2 October 1995, *and*:
  - at the time you became liable, you were not entitled to IS; *and*
  - neither you nor your partner became entitled to IS or income-based JSA after 1 October 1995 within 26 weeks of your IS ceasing; *or*
- for JSA if:
  - you became liable for your loan between 2 May 1994 and 7 October 1996 and you got IS for it in one or more of the 26 weeks before 7 October 1996 under the rules that then applied; *or*
  - you became liable for your loan in the 26 weeks before 7 October 1996, *and*:
    - at the time you became liable, you were not entitled to IS, *and*
    - neither you nor your partner became entitled to IS or JSA after 6 October 1996 within 26 weeks of your IS ceasing.

Other rules

You can get IS, income-based JSA or PC for housing costs even if you became liable for your loan during a 'relevant period' (see p911) if:

- you have taken out, or increased, your loan to buy a home which is better suited than your former home to the needs of a disabled person.[53] There is no time limit in the rule that says, for example, that you must buy the home or take out the loan within a certain time before or after the disabled person moves in.[54] However, the person has to qualify as disabled at the time the loan is taken out.[55] S/he does not have to be a member of your family nor to have previously lived with you. A **'disabled person'** is:[56]
  - for IS and income-based JSA, anyone for whom you or someone living with you is getting a disabled child, disability, enhanced pensioner or higher pensioner premium (see p882) as well as other people living in your home who would get one of these premiums if they were on IS or JSA. **Note:** this rule has not been amended. You cannot qualify for disabled child premium when your IS or JSA no longer includes allowances and premiums for your children (see p818). See CPAG's *Welfare Rights Bulletin* for updates;
  - for PC only:
    - anyone under 19 for whom you or your partner are responsible who gets disability living allowance or who is registered blind (in Scotland, certified blind. 'Responsible' is not defined in the rules); *or*
    - anyone living in your home who is aged at least 75, or who would qualify for a disability or higher pensioner premium if s/he were on IS;

  It also includes a person who is sick, but, under the incapacity rules, is either disqualified from receiving benefit or is treated as capable of work (see p272); *or*
- for IS or JSA, you have a boy and a girl aged 10 or over, or for PC, you are looking after a boy and a girl who live with you and are aged 10 or over but under 19, and you increased your loan and moved to a new home because you needed to provide them with separate bedrooms.[57] You can argue that this

should apply if one of the children is aged 10 or over and the other will be 10 in the reasonably near future.[58]

When you can get restricted housing costs

If you became liable for your loan during a 'relevant period' (see p911), and cannot get housing costs under the other rules described above, you can sometimes get IS, income-based JSA or PC for your housing costs but the amount you get might be restricted to your former housing costs. This applies if:

- you re-mortgaged your home to pay off your original house purchase loan;[59] *or*
- you sold your previous home, paid off an original loan which you took out to buy a home or pay for repairs or improvements, and have now taken out a new loan for a new property, even if this is some time later.[60]

  The original loan must have qualified (see pp910 and 917) and be one for which you can get IS, income-based JSA or PC even when taken out during a 'relevant period' (see p911). Unless the loan was to buy a home for a disabled person or to provide separate bedrooms for a boy and girl aged 10 or over (see p913) you cannot get help with any increase in your housing costs. Thus, if your original mortgage was £30,000 and you took out a new loan for £35,000 to buy a new home, you can only get housing costs on £30,000 of the second loan.

  It seems that the rule *is* intended to apply if, following divorce or separation, you buy out your former partner's share of your home – you will not get help with the mortgage in relation to that share. Similarly, if you take out a loan or increase an existing loan to buy a home after separation, the rule will in principle apply. However, where couples on IS, income-based JSA or PC separate, it can be argued that each should be entitled to housing costs up to the amount of the loan they were liable to pay when they were together.[61] So, for example, if you were liable to pay a mortgage of £50,000 when you were together, you can argue that you should each be entitled to housing costs on a mortgage of up to £50,000 when you separate;
- you buy your home and immediately beforehand you were in rented accommodation and getting housing benefit (HB – see Chapter 10). Your housing costs are restricted to the amount of HB you were entitled to plus any 'other housing costs' (see p918) you were already getting.[62] You get any subsequent increases in the standard rate of interest (see below) or the 'other housing costs' and do not lose these if the interest rate or costs go down again;[63]
- you were only getting 'other housing costs' (see p918) paid with your IS, income-based JSA or PC (eg, as a Crown tenant) and you then buy a home.[64] To begin with you only get the amount you had been getting for those other costs. You get any subsequent increases in the standard rate of interest or the 'other housing costs' and do not lose these if the interest rate or costs go down again.

A bank overdraft which you arrange to pay for the repairs or improvements counts as a loan.[74]

It is important to remember that:

- not all loans for repairs and improvements qualify for help;
- for IS and JSA only, you might not get your full costs met initially (see p926);
- the amount you are paid might be restricted if your total housing costs are thought to be too high (see p921);
- deductions can be made if other people live in your home (see p924);
- your IS, income-based JSA or PC does not cover all of your loan(s) and there is a special way the amount you can be paid is calculated (see p915);
- payment is usually made directly to the lender.

Repairs and improvements that qualify

You can only get help with loans for repairs or improvements to maintain your current home,[75] or any part of the building in which it is contained, in a habitable condition. Loans towards the cost of necessary survey work should also be included.[76] You can get help towards the interest payments on a loan for any of the following:

- provision of a bath, shower, toilet, wash basin and the necessary plumbing and hot water;
- repairs to your heating system;
- damp-proof measures (you can argue this includes repairs to a roof[77]);
- provision of ventilation and natural lighting;
- provision of drainage facilities;
- facilities for preparing and cooking food (but not for storing it[78]);
- home insulation;
- provision of electric lighting and sockets;
- storage facilities for fuel or refuse;
- repairs of unsafe structural defects;
- adaptations for a disabled person (see p913 for who counts);
- providing separate bedrooms for children of different sexes:
  - for IS and income-based JSA, aged 10 or over who are part of your family (see p906 for who counts as your family); *or*
  - for PC, aged 10 or over but under 19 for whom you or your partner are responsible and who live with you. 'Responsible' is not defined in the rules.

  You can argue that this should apply if one of the children is aged 10 or over and the other will be 10 in the reasonably near future.[79]

If your loan is also for other repairs and improvements, you are only paid housing costs for the proportion which relates to any of the items listed above. If your loan is for the right sort of repairs or improvements the amount payable is calculated as for mortgages:

- for IS and JSA only, you do not get your charges paid in full when you first claim (see p926); *and*
- the standard rate of interest is used (see p915).

If you or your partner share the costs with someone, you might only get your share (see p915). The restriction on taking out loans while entitled to IS, JSA or PC does not apply to those taken out for repairs and improvements.

The rules for help with loans for repairs and improvements changed on 2 October 1995. If you took out your loan before that date, you might be able to get help under the old, more favourable rules (see p928).

4. Help with other housing costs

You are paid the normal weekly charge for all **'other housing costs'** covered by income support (IS), income-based jobseeker's allowance (JSA) and pension credit (PC).[80] These are:

- service charges (see p919);
- rent or ground rent (feu duty in Scotland) if you have a lease of more than 21 years. If your lease is of 21 years or less, the ground rent might be met by housing benefit (HB) instead (see p195). **Note:** from 28 November 2004, feu duties (other than arrears of these) are no longer payable;
- rentcharge payments;
- payments under a co-ownership scheme;
- rent if you are a Crown tenant (minus any water charges[81]);
- payments for a tent and its pitch if that is your home.

Where you pay your other housing costs annually or irregularly, the weekly amount is worked out by dividing what is payable for the year by 52.[82]

It is important to remember that:

- for IS and JSA only, you might not get your full costs met initially (see p926);
- some charges cannot be met (see p919);
- the amount you are paid might be restricted if your total housing costs are thought to be too high (see p921).

If your other housing costs have been waived because you or your partner (or for IS and income-based JSA only, a member of your family – see p906 for who counts as your family) have paid for repairs or redecoration which are not your responsibility, you can still get IS, income-based JSA or PC for them for up to eight weeks.[83]

If you or your partner share the costs with someone, you might only get your share.[84] If the other person is not paying her/his share you can argue that you should get help with all the other housing costs you pay.[85]

Charges that cannot be met

The following charges cannot be met:[86]

- Fuel, where this is included in your 'other housing costs'. If there is no specific charge for fuel, set deductions are made as follows:

Heating	£10.55	Lighting	£0.85
Hot water	£1.25	Cooking	£1.25

- Repairs and improvements listed on p917. You are expected to take out a loan to pay for these and can claim help with this.[87]
- Ineligible services listed on p209. These are the same as for HB.[88]

Service charges

A **'service'** is something which is agreed and arranged on your behalf and for which you are required to pay. So, for example, if you own a flat and the lessor arranges the exterior painting of the building for which you have to pay a share of the cost, your IS, income-based JSA or PC includes this as a service charge. Some service charges are specifically excluded (see p209). Some service charges only count if they relate to the provision of 'adequate accommodation' (see p209).[89]

If you normally pay service charges annually you may want to ask if you can make weekly payments.

You should bear the following in mind:

- Service charges to cover minor repairs and maintenance are covered. However, repairs and improvements listed on p917 are not covered.[90]
- Payments you make for support services are not eligible service charges. Instead, you can get help with these via your local authority's 'supporting people team'. See p210 for further information. Note that you continue to be passported to full council tax benefit entitlement if you or your partner lost your entitlement to IS or income-based JSA on or before 5 April 2003 because your housing costs no longer included help with charges for support services.[91]
- House insurance paid under the terms of your lease can be a service charge, but insurance required by a building society as a condition of your mortgage is not.[92]
- Services provided by an outside authority which you arrange yourself are not covered. Thus charges for water and sewerage paid to a water board are not met.[93]

5. The amount of housing costs you get

Once you have worked out which housing costs can be met by income support (IS), income-based jobseeker's allowance (JSA), or pension credit (PC) you need to:

- calculate the weekly amount of:
  - housing costs for home loans (see p910);
  - housing costs for loans for repairs and improvements (see p916);
  - other housing costs (see p918);
- add these amounts together;
- deduct any restrictions being made because your housing costs are too high (see below);
- deduct any amounts for other people living in your home (known as non-dependants – see p924).

For IS and income-based JSA only, a reduced amount might also be paid for the early weeks of your claim (see p926).

If your housing costs are not met in full

If you do not have enough money to pay your housing costs you may be in danger of losing your home, particularly if you are on IS, JSA or PC for a long time. You should inform your lender and discuss with them how to resolve the situation. Your lender may be prepared to accept interest-only payments for a while. It is important to discuss this with them so that you do not fall into arrears and risk losing your home. You should also seek independent debt advice.

If you have to make payments towards the shortfall:

- you may be able to increase your income by taking in lodgers. See p976 for how this affects your IS, income-based JSA or PC;
- some payments made direct to the lender by relatives, friends or a charity towards the capital repayments can be ignored in calculating your entitlement to IS or income-based JSA;[94]
- you could try finding a part-time job and benefit from an earnings disregard (see p963).

Ultimately, you may have to sell your home and buy somewhere cheaper. If you move out and put your house up for sale the capital value of your house can be disregarded for a period while you take reasonable steps to sell it (see p1031).[95] For IS and income-based JSA, if you also rent it out while trying to sell, the income from any tenants can be disregarded up to the value of any mortgage outgoings which you have on the property.[96] For PC, most actual income from capital is ignored (see p1002).

Restrictions if your housing costs are too high

Your housing costs can be restricted if:

- your loans exceed an upper limit (see p921); *or*
- your total housing costs are thought to be excessive (see p921).

Your housing costs can also be restricted if you take out or increase a loan while entitled to IS, JSA or PC or in a period between claims (see p911).

The upper limit

If your loans amount to more than £100,000 in total, your housing costs might not be met in full.[97] This includes all mortgages taken out to buy your home and also any loans for repairs and improvements. The restriction is applied proportionately to each loan. If a loan was taken out to adapt your home for a disabled person (see p913 for who counts), it is ignored when working out if your loans exceed the upper limit. If you are getting housing costs on more than one home (see p909) you can be paid up to the limit for each.[98]

Upper limits for loans have only existed since 2 August 1993 and have changed twice since that date. The limit has been £100,000 since 10 April 1995. However:

- your limit is £125,000 if you have been entitled to IS or income-based JSA since 11 April 1994;
- your limit is £150,000 if you have been entitled to IS or income-based JSA since 2 August 1993;
- there is no limit if you have been entitled to IS or income-based JSA from before 2 August 1993.

If you are getting IS or income-based JSA without an upper limit or with one greater than £100,000, but you then claim PC you should not lose out. Check to see if you qualify for a transitional amount as part of your appropriate minimum guarantee (see p469).

If you or your partner are a 'welfare to work' beneficiary (see p769) you can be treated as entitled to IS or income-based JSA for up to 52 weeks. This means your old upper limit applies if you have to claim IS or income-based JSA again within that period.[99]

If you are uncertain about which limit applies to you, you should seek advice. If you are considering increasing your mortgage or loan, see p911.

Excessive housing costs

Whether your loan is higher or lower than the upper limit (see above), your housing costs can be restricted if:[100]

- your home (excluding any part which you let) is too big for:
  - for IS and income-based JSA, you and your family (see p906 for who counts as your family) and any of your non-dependants (see p924) or foster children;

- for PC, you and your partner, anyone under 19 living with you and any other non-dependants (see p924).

When deciding if your home is too big, a comparison is made with other accommodation which would be suitable given the size of your household. Everyone's needs must be considered. For example, if a member of your family needs extra space because of a disability or you have a child or elderly relative in care who regularly comes to stay with you, your need for a large home may be justified;

- the area in which you live is more expensive than other areas where there is accommodation suitable for your needs. An area is 'something more confined, restricted and compact than a locality or district ... It might consist of ... a number of roads, refer to a neighbourhood and even to a large block of flats.'[101] The area should not be chosen on too wide a basis – ie, you should not be expected to move to a completely different part of the country;
- the outgoings on your home which are met by IS, income-based JSA or PC housing costs (see pp910, 916 and 918) are higher than on other properties in the area which are suitable for your needs.

The capital value of your home cannot be taken into account.[102]

When no restriction should be made

No restriction should be made, even if suitable accommodation is available, if it is not reasonable for you and your family (for IS and income-based JSA) or you and your partner (for PC) to look for cheaper accommodation. Account should be taken of:[103]

- the general level of housing costs in the area and whether suitable accommodation is available. This means that property must be generally available, not necessarily available to you personally;[104]
- your family circumstances (for IS and income-based JSA) or your circumstances and those of the people who live with you (for PC) – eg, your employment prospects, the age and state of health of your family members and whether the move would have a detrimental effect on a child's or young person's education if s/he were to change schools.

These are not the only situations which count.[105] A move may not be reasonable where:

- the size of your family would make it difficult to find accommodation;
- you need to be near relatives or friends to provide (or receive) care or support;
- you have moved a number of times recently;
- it would be difficult to sell your property,[106] you have negative equity, or selling would cause you financial hardship;[107]

- you have lived in your home for many years and it is now too large because you are separated or divorced, your children have left home, or your partner has died;
- prior to your claim you were advised by the Department for Work and Pensions (DWP) that your housing costs would not be restricted;[108]
- you could not get another mortgage on a property.[109]

Even if it is reasonable for you to move, your housing costs should not be restricted in certain circumstances (see below). If it *is* appropriate to restrict your IS, income-based JSA or PC housing costs, these are limited to help with the amount of loan you would need in order to get suitable alternative accommodation.[110] This must be assessed in practical and realistic terms. Any loans that are repayable on the sale of your home which would leave you with less money to purchase another home should be taken into account.[111] However, if the equity in your property was sufficient to buy a new home outright, without a loan, your housing costs could be nil.[112]

Income support and income-based jobseeker's allowance

For IS and income-based JSA, your housing costs cannot be restricted for 26 weeks if you, or a member of your family (see p906), were able to meet these costs when they were first taken on.[113] Your housing costs are not restricted for a further 26 weeks if you are trying to find cheaper accommodation. If full payment is made but later, following a supersession, your housing costs are restricted, the 26-week periods begin from the date you are informed of the intention to restrict your costs under these provisions.[114] Periods of 12 weeks or less when you stop getting IS or income-based JSA are included when calculating these periods. Periods when your partner was in receipt of IS or income-based JSA count towards the 26-week periods if:[115]

- you have only recently become one of a couple or separated from your partner and you make a new claim within 12 weeks;
- your partner was getting or treated as getting IS or income-based JSA for you both and you have taken over the claiming role;
- you or your partner were on one of the New Deal programmes or schemes listed on p931, your partner was claiming IS or income-based JSA (but not joint-claim JSA) for you immediately before this and you claim IS or income-based JSA (but not joint-claim JSA) immediately after.

Periods when someone who was not your partner was claiming IS or income-based JSA while you and a child or young person counted as a member of her/his family (see p906), count towards the 26-week periods. This only applies if you claim IS or income-based JSA yourself, that child or young person becomes a member of *your* family and you claim within 12 weeks of this (52 weeks if you are a 'welfare to work' beneficiary (see p769) or qualify for a longer linking period – see p932).

Pension credit

For PC, your housing costs cannot be restricted during the first 26 weeks of any period when you are entitled to PC (or IS or income-based JSA if this was immediately before 6 October 2003 or before you or your partner turned 60), nor the next 26 weeks if:[116]

- you or your partner were able to meet these costs when they were first taken on; *and*
- you are trying to find cheaper accommodation.

If full payment is made but later, following a 'review', your housing costs are restricted, the 26-week periods begin from the date of the 'review'.[117] You and your partner are treated as entitled to PC during any period:[118]

- of 12 weeks or less when you stop getting PC (or IS or income-based JSA if this was immediately before 6 October 2003 or before you or your partner turned 60); *and*
- before 6 October 2003 when you or your partner were entitled to IS or income-based JSA.

Deductions for other people living in your home

If other people normally live with you and your partner and dependent children in your home (they are called **'non-dependants'**) a set deduction is usually made from your housing costs.[119] This is because it is assumed the non-dependant makes a contribution towards your outgoings, whether or not s/he does so. Examples of non-dependants are adult sons or daughters, or elderly relatives who share your home. You may therefore need to ask your non-dependant(s) for a contribution.

A person can only be treated as living with you if s/he shares rooms with you. This includes the kitchen (unless it is only used by someone else to prepare food for her/him[120]), but not a bathroom, toilet or common access areas.[121] A person who is separately liable to pay rent to a landlord is not counted as living with you.

When no deduction is made

No deduction is made from your housing costs if **the person living with you is not treated as a non-dependant** (though any rent or lodging charges s/he pays to you affect the amount of your IS, income-based JSA or PC – see p976). People who do not count as non-dependants are:[122]

- someone who is liable to pay you, or your partner, in order to live in your home – eg, a sub-tenant, licensee or boarder along with other members of her/his household. This does not apply if the person is a close relative of you or your partner (see p906).

The payment must be on a commercial basis. A low charge does not necessarily mean that the arrangement is not commercial. Nor do you have to make a profit. An arrangement between friends can be commercial;[123]

- for IS and income-based JSA only, someone other than a close relative (see p906) to whom you, or your partner, are liable to make payments on a commercial basis (ie, as a sub-tenant, licensee or boarder) in order to live in her/his property. Other members of her/his household do not count as non-dependants either;
- someone who jointly occupies your home and is a co-owner or joint tenant with you or your partner. Your joint occupier's partner is also not a non-dependant. For IS and income-based JSA only, close relatives (see p906) who jointly occupy your home *are* treated as non-dependants unless they had joint liability prior to 11 April 1988 or joint liability existed on or before the date you first lived in the property (or your partner did if s/he is the joint owner/tenant). However, no non-dependant deduction is made for them even though they are non-dependants (see below);
- someone who is employed by a charitable or voluntary organisation as a resident carer for you, or your partner, and you pay for that service (even if the charge is nominal). If the carer's partner also lives in your home s/he does not count as a non-dependant.

Even **if you do have a non-dependant** in your home no deduction is made if you (or your partner):[124]

- are blind or treated as blind;
- get attendance allowance (AA) (or equivalent benefits paid because of injury at work or a war injury) or the care component of disability living allowance (DLA).

In addition, no deduction is made for a non-dependant:[125]

- who is staying with you but who normally lives elsewhere;
- who is 16 or 17 years old;
- for IS and income-based JSA only, for whom a deduction is already being made from your HB (see p211);
- who is under 25 years old and getting IS or income-based JSA;
- who is getting PC;
- who gets a Work-Based Learning for Young People allowance;
- who is a full-time student (see p621). Unless you are getting PC and you or your partner are 65 or over, this only applies during the summer vacation if the student is not in full-time paid work (see p750);
- who is not living with you at present because s/he:
  - has been in hospital for more than 52 weeks. Separate stays in hospital which are not more than 28 days apart are added together when calculating the 52 weeks;

– is in prison;
- for IS and income-based JSA only, who is a close relative (see p906) and a co-owner or joint tenant with you, or your partner. For PC, no deduction is made because co-owners and joint tenants do not count as non-dependants, even if they are close relatives.

The amount of the deduction

If you have a non-dependant living with you who is 18 or over, a fixed amount is usually deducted from your housing costs, whatever s/he pays you. If your non-dependant is in full-time paid work, the amount depends on her/his weekly gross income as follows:[126]

Gross weekly income	*Weekly non-dependant deduction*
£322 or more	£47.75
£258–£321.99	£43.50
£194–£257.99	£38.20
£150–£193.99	£23.35
£101–£149.99	£17.00
Less than £101	£7.40

In all other cases, a £7.40 deduction is made per week. However, see p924 for situations when no deduction is made.

For further information about who counts as in full-time paid work for IS, income-based JSA and PC, see Chapter 29.

Gross income includes wages before tax and national insurance are deducted plus any other income the non-dependant has (but not AA, DLA or certain payments from the Macfarlane Trusts, the Eileen Trust, the Fund or the Independent Living Funds (for IS and JSA this includes the Skipton Fund) – see p973 – or for PC only, payments in kind).[127]

A deduction is made for each non-dependant in your home. However, if you have a non-dependant couple and a non-dependant deduction applies to both members, only one deduction is made – the highest applicable. The couple's joint income counts.

If you are a joint owner with someone other than your partner, any deductions are shared proportionally between you and the other owner(s).

Reduced payment of income support/income-based jobseeker's allowance during the first weeks of your claim

Even if you are entitled to IS or income-based JSA to cover your housing costs, the amount for your housing costs is not usually paid until you have been claiming for a number of weeks – known as a **'waiting period'**.[128] This applies to all types of housing costs. You can get help with your housing costs sooner if you are treated as entitled to IS or JSA for certain weeks prior to your claim even though you were not actually entitled to it (see p930).

You can be paid straight away if:[129]

- you have already been entitled to IS or JSA for the relevant number of weeks in your waiting period when you agree to pay your loan or other housing costs (but see p911 for the rules restricting housing costs if you take out or increase a loan while entitled to IS or JSA);
- you were getting help with your housing costs when your IS or JSA ceased because:
  - you became a 'welfare to work' beneficiary (see p769); *or*
  - you started full-time paid work or training for work, or increased your hours or your pay (so long as you qualify for a 'longer linking period' – see p932).

  This only applies if you claim IS or income-based JSA again within 52 weeks;
- you or your partner are 60 or over. Remember: if you are 60 or over, you cannot claim IS. Instead you can claim PC;
- you are claiming for payments as a Crown tenant, under a co-ownership scheme or for a tent.

In addition, if you reclaim IS or income-based JSA within 26 weeks of a previous claim during which you were getting housing costs and you have been receiving payments under an employment insurance policy which has since run out, periods when you were getting those payments are ignored in calculating the waiting periods.[130] This means that you can requalify for housing costs sooner.

All other claimants get a reduced amount of help initially. How long your waiting period is depends on when you agreed to pay your mortgage or loan or other housing costs and how long you have been entitled to (or treated as entitled to) IS or JSA (see p930). You are expected to use mortgage payment protection policy payments, savings or disregarded income to meet any shortfall. If you do not have enough to pay the shortfall you should approach your lender to discuss how you can protect your home.

Remember: if you claim PC, there are no waiting periods for housing costs. You can get help with your housing costs straightaway.

The 26-week waiting period

If you agreed to pay your loan or other housing costs before 2 October 1995 (the DWP calls these 'existing housing costs') you get:[131]

- nothing for the first eight weeks of your claim;
- 50 per cent of your housing costs for the next 18 weeks;
- full housing costs after you have been entitled to IS or JSA for 26 weeks.

This 26-week waiting period can also apply if you agreed to pay a loan after 2 October 1995, provided it replaces a loan you agreed to pay before that date. You must have been liable for the housing costs under both the old and the new agreements and the new loan must be for the same amount (or lower) as the earlier loan.

The 39-week waiting period

If you agreed to pay your loan or other housing costs after 1 October 1995 (the DWP calls these 'new housing costs') you get:[132]

- nothing for the first 39 weeks of your claim;
- full housing costs after you have been entitled to IS or JSA for 39 weeks.

However, if the loan replaces another loan you agreed to pay before 2 October 1995, see above.

Certain claimants are exempt from this 39-week waiting period. Instead, the 26-week waiting period applies. This is the case if you:[133]

- are a lone parent and have claimed IS or JSA because your partner has abandoned you[134] or died, unless you become one of a couple again. This includes where you have been 'constructively abandoned' – eg, your partner's behaviour was such as to give you little reasonable option but to leave her/him or require her/him to leave you;[135]
- are claiming IS or JSA; *and*
  - you are a carer getting carer's allowance; *or*
  - you are caring for someone getting AA or DLA higher or middle rate care component (see Chapter 7); *or*
  - you care for someone who has been awarded AA or the highest or middle rate of DLA care component on an advance claim but it has not yet gone into payment; *or*
  - you are caring for someone who has claimed AA or DLA. This applies for 26 weeks from the date of that claim or until it is decided if this is sooner; *or*
  - for IS only, it is not more than eight weeks since you have ceased to meet those conditions or have stopped being a carer;
- are claiming IS and are in prison awaiting trial or sentence;
- have been refused payments under a mortgage payment protection policy due to a pre-existing medical condition or because you are HIV positive.[136]

If you have two loans or agreements to pay other housing costs and one was agreed before and one after 1 October 1995, the relevant waiting periods apply to each.[137]

Transitional protection

The rules on payment of housing costs changed on 2 October 1995. However if you were getting help with your housing costs when the rules changed, there are two types of 'transitional protection' which ensure that you should be no worse off than you were under the old rules.

Note: If you are claiming PC, you should not be worse off than you were on IS or income-based JSA. See p469 to see if you qualify for a transitional amount as part of your appropriate minimum guarantee.

Types of housing costs that are no longer paid

You can continue to get certain types of housing costs which could be paid with IS before 2 October 1995, but which can no longer be paid by IS or income-based JSA. These are:[138]

- accumulated arrears of interest;
- interest on a secured loan which was not for house purchase, taken out when you were one of a couple, where your partner had left and could not or would not pay the cost, or had died;
- interest on a loan for repairs and improvements under the pre-2 October 1995 rules.

You can continue to get these if they were included in your housing costs before 2 October 1995, if you fulfil the qualifying conditions *and* you remain on (or are treated as being on) IS or income-based JSA. You are treated as being on IS or income-based JSA during the periods described on p930. See CPAG's *National Welfare Benefits Handbook*, 1995/96 edition, pp30–32 for more details on how these costs were assessed.

Higher housing costs under the old rules

If you were on IS both on and after 1 October 1995 and the amount of IS or income-based JSA housing costs to which you are now entitled is less because of the rules since 2 October 1995, you can get an extra payment to make up the loss.[139] This payment is called an 'add-back' and is equal to the difference between your IS housing costs in the week including 1 October 1995 and your entitlement in the next week. Where you have more than one loan, the add-back for each is calculated separately.

You continue to be paid the add-back so long as you remain entitled to IS or income-based JSA. However, you lose the add-back if you stop being entitled to (or being treated as entitled to – see below) IS or income-based JSA for more than 12 weeks (52 weeks if you or your partner are a 'welfare to work' beneficiary – see p769) or if you cease to qualify for housing costs. If you lose the add-back but your partner makes a claim for you within 12 weeks (52 weeks if you are a 'welfare to work' beneficiary – see p769), s/he can continue to get the add-back to which you were entitled.

The add-back reduces if your entitlement to housing costs (ignoring the add-back) increases above the amount which was payable to you in the week after the week including 1 October 1995.[140] However, it does not increase if your entitlement to housing costs goes down. You lose the add-back when your entitlement equals what you used to get under the old rules.

If you are on a fixed-rate mortgage, where your interest rate stays the same throughout, the way the add-back rule is applied means you lose out if the standard rate of interest used to calculate your housing costs goes down. However, although the rule is unfair, it is lawful.[141]

Treated as entitled to income support or jobseeker's allowance

You are treated as entitled to and receiving IS or JSA for certain periods prior to your claim even though you were not actually entitled to or receiving it. These are sometimes known as 'linking rules'. They can:

- help you get full housing costs earlier. Periods when you are treated as entitled to IS or JSA can count towards your waiting period (see p926);
- allow you to continue to receive help with certain types of housing costs that are no longer met (see p929) if there is a break in your claim.

General rules

You are treated as entitled to and getting IS for any period when you were entitled to or getting JSA.[142] You are treated as entitled to income-based JSA for any period when you were entitled to or getting IS.[143] In addition, you are treated as entitled to and getting IS or JSA:[144]

- for any period where you were **getting JSA as a 'joint-claim couple'** (see p394);
- during a period of 12 weeks (52 weeks if you or your partner are a 'welfare to work' beneficiary – see p769 – or if you qualify for a longer linking period – see p932) or less **between two periods** when:
  - you were entitled to or getting or treated as getting IS or JSA; *or*
  - you were treated as entitled to IS or JSA while your income or capital were too high in the circumstances described on p931.

  The period of 12 weeks is extended to 26 weeks if you were getting full housing costs but stopped getting IS or income-based JSA because you received child support maintenance, and this has now reduced as a result of child support rule changes in April 1995 or because an interim maintenance assessment has been replaced or terminated (see CPAG's *Child Support Handbook*, 2003/04 edition for details);[145]
- during any period for which you are awarded IS or JSA after a **revision, supersession or an appeal** (see pp1189, 1199 and 1217).

Couples and former couples

You are treated as entitled to and getting IS or income-based JSA:[146]

- during the time when your **ex-partner was getting or treated as getting** IS, income-based JSA (but not joint-claim JSA) or PC for you both, provided you claim IS or income-based JSA within 12 weeks of separating (52 weeks if you are a 'welfare to work' beneficiary (see p769) or qualify for a longer linking period – see p932);

- during the time when your **partner was getting or treated as getting** IS or income-based JSA on her/his own, provided you make a claim for IS or income-based JSA within 12 weeks of becoming a couple (or a 'joint-claim couple' – see p394). Unless you are a joint-claim couple, the time limit is 52 weeks if you or your partner are a 'welfare to work' beneficiary (see p769) or you qualify for a longer linking period (see p932);
- during the time when your **partner was getting or treated as getting** IS or income-based JSA (but not joint-claim JSA) for you both, if you take over the claiming role.

Employment schemes and training

You are treated as entitled to and getting IS or income-based JSA:[147]

- during the time when you or your partner were on one of the **New Deal programmes or schemes** listed below, so long as your partner was claiming IS or income-based JSA (but not joint-claim JSA) for you immediately before this and you claim IS or income-based JSA (but not joint-claim JSA) immediately after;
- during periods when you stop getting IS or income-based JSA because you or your partner are:
  - doing an **employment training rehabilitation course**;
  - on one of the **New Deal programmes or schemes** listed below, or an **employment zone programme** and as a result count as in full-time paid work (see p750), or have too much income (see Chapter 38);
- during any period when you were **getting contribution-based JSA** immediately before starting on one of the New Deal programmes or schemes listed below.

New Deal programmes and schemes

The self-employed employment option of the New Deal for young people
The voluntary sector option of the New Deal for young people
The environment task force option of the New Deal for young people
The 'intensive activity period' for people aged 25 or over but under 50
The 'intensive activity period' for people aged 50-plus

Other

You are treated as entitled to and getting IS or income-based JSA during the time when **someone who was not your partner was entitled** to IS or income-based JSA and you and a child or young person counted as a member of her/his family.[148] You must claim within 12 weeks of that child or young person becoming a member of *your* family (52 weeks if you are a 'welfare to work' beneficiary (see p769) or qualify for a longer linking period – see p932). See p906 for who counts as a member of your family.

You are treated as entitled to IS or income-based JSA for up to 39 weeks where you were not entitled to IS or income-based JSA only **because your income was too high or your capital was over £8,000** (including where your contribution-based JSA was the same as or higher than your income-based JSA applicable amount);[149] *and*

- you have been entitled to contribution-based JSA, statutory sick pay or incapacity benefit (or credits for unemployment or incapacity). A claim for IS or *income-based* JSA is not required;[150] *or*
- for IS only, you are treated as getting IS or income-based JSA; *or*
- you are a lone parent or for IS, a carer (see p296) or for JSA, a carer who is allowed to restrict the hours you are available for work (see p363) and you, or someone claiming on your behalf, has previously claimed and been refused IS or JSA. This does not apply if you or your partner count as in full-time paid work (see p751), or you are a full-time student who cannot claim IS or JSA (see p621), or are temporarily absent from Great Britain and not entitled to IS or JSA (see pp688 and 690).

However, where the above applies and you were not entitled to IS or income-based JSA only because your *income* was too high and you were getting payments under a mortgage payment protection policy, you are treated as entitled to IS or income-based JSA for *any* period for which the payments were made.[151] This could be longer than 39 weeks.

Longer linking periods

The 12-week periods when you can be treated as entitled to or getting IS or income-based JSA are extended to 52 weeks in some cases. These 52-week periods are referred to in this *Handbook* as 'longer linking periods'. You qualify for a longer linking period if you stop getting IS or JSA because:[152]

- you or your partner:
  - start work or increase your hours; *or*
  - are taking steps to get work under certain training for work schemes; *or*
  - are on one of the New Deal programmes or schemes listed on p931, the full-time education and training option of the New Deal for people aged 18 or over but under 26, or an employment zone programme; *or*
  - are getting assistance in pursuing self-employment while on a training course funded by or on behalf of the Secretary of State for Education and Employment, the National Assembly for Wales, Scottish Enterprise, or Highlands and Islands Enterprise; *and*
- as a result, you or your partner count as in full-time paid work (see p750) or your earnings or your income are too high.

You only qualify for a longer linking period if, immediately before the day your entitlement to IS or income-based JSA ceased, you had served enough of your waiting period (see p926) that housing costs:[153]

- were included in your IS or income-based JSA (in full or in part); *or*
- would have been included but for a non-dependant deduction (see p924).

You can also qualify for a 52-week linking period if you are a 'welfare to work' beneficiary. See p769 for further information.

Notes

1 **IS** Sch 3 para 4(1) IS Regs
JSA Sch 2 para 4(1)(a) JSA Regs
PC Sch 2 para 5(1)(a) SPC Regs
2 **IS** Sch 3 para 4(1)(b) IS Regs
JSA Sch 2 para 4(1)(b) JSA Regs
PC Sch 2 para 5(1)(b) SPC Regs

1. When you can get help with housing costs

3 **IS** Sch 3 para 1 IS Regs
JSA Sch 2 para 1 JSA Regs
PC Sch 2 para 1 SPC Regs
4 **IS** Sch 3 paras 15-17 IS Regs
JSA Sch 2 paras 14-16 JSA Regs
PC Sch 2 paras 11-13 SPC Regs
5 CH/3110/2003
6 **IS** Sch 3 para 2 IS Regs
JSA Sch 2 para 2 JSA Regs
PC Sch 2 para 3 SPC Regs
7 CSB/213/1987
8 **IS** Sch 3 para 5(5) IS Regs
JSA Sch 2 para 5(5) JSA Regs
PC Sch 2 para 6(5) SPC Regs
All R(IS) 4/95
9 **IS** Reg 2(1) IS Regs
JSA Reg 1(3) JSA Regs
PC Reg 1(2) SPC Regs
HB Reg 2(1) HB Regs
All R(SB) 22/87
10 *Ewens v Secretary of State for Social Security*, reported as R(IS) 8/01
11 CIS/636/1992, confirmed by the Court of Appeal in *Brain v CAO*, 2 December 1993
12 **IS** Sch 3 para 2(2) IS Regs
JSA Sch 2 para 2(2) JSA Regs
13 **IS** s137(1) SSCBA 1992
JSA s35(1) JSA 1995
14 **IS** Sch 3 para 3(1) IS Regs
JSA Sch 2 para 3(1) JSA Regs
PC Sch 2 para 4(1) SPC Regs
15 CIS/297/1994
16 s137(1) SSCBA 1992, definition of 'dwelling'; reg 2(1) IS Regs; reg 1(3) JSA Regs and reg 1(2) SPC Regs, definition of 'dwelling occupied as the home'
17 *Secretary of State for Work and Pensions v Mohamed Miah*, reported as R(JSA) 9/03; Memo DMG JSA/IS 48
18 **IS** Sch 3 para 3(7) IS Regs
JSA Sch 2 para 3(7) JSA Regs
PC Sch 2 para 4(7) SPC Regs
19 CH/2957/2004
20 **IS** Sch 3 para 3(10) IS Regs
JSA Sch 2 para 3(10) JSA Regs
PC Sch 2 para 4(10) SPC Regs
21 **IS** Sch 3 para 3(11) and (12) IS Regs
JSA Sch 2 para 3(11) and (12) JSA Regs
PC Sch 2 para 4(11) and (12) SPC Regs
22 **IS** Sch 3 para 3(8) and (9) IS Regs
JSA Sch 2 para 3(8) and (9) JSA Regs
PC Sch 2 para 4(8) and (9) SPC Regs
23 CH/1854/2004
24 CH/1237/2004
25 *R v Penwith District Council ex parte Burt*
26 **IS** Sch 3 para 3(5) IS Regs
JSA Sch 2 para 3(5) JSA Regs
PC Sch 2 para 4(5) SPC Regs
27 CIS/719/1994
28 **IS** Sch 3 para 3(6) IS Regs
JSA Sch 2 para 3(6) JSA Regs
PC Sch 2 para 4(6) SPC Regs
29 CIS/543/1993

30 CIS/339/1993
31 **IS** Sch 3 para 3(6)(a) IS Regs
JSA Sch 2 para 3(6)(a) JSA Regs
PC Sch 2 para 4(6)(a) SPC Regs
32 **IS** Sch 3 para 3(6)(b) IS Regs
JSA Sch 2 para 3(6)(b) JSA Regs
PC Sch 2 para 4(6)(b) SPC Regs
33 **IS** Sch 3 para 3(3) IS Regs
JSA Sch 2 para 3(3) JSA Regs
PC Sch 2 para 4(3) SPC Regs
34 **IS** Sch 3 para 3(11)(c)(viii) IS Regs
JSA Sch 2 para 3(11)(c)(viii) JSA Regs
PC Sch 2 para 4(11)(c)(viii) SPC Regs
35 **IS** Sch 3 para 3(4) IS Regs
JSA Sch 2 para 3(4) JSA Regs
PC Sch 2 para 4(4) SPC Regs

2. **Mortgages and loans**

36 CIS/14483/1996
37 **IS** Sch 3 para 15 IS Regs
JSA Sch 2 para 14 JSA Regs
PC Sch 2 para 11 SPC Regs
38 R(IS) 14/01
39 R(IS) 11/94
40 R(IS) 4/95
41 R(IS) 7/93
42 R(IS) 6/94
43 R(IS) 24/95
44 R(IS) 11/94
45 **IS** Sch 3 para 5 IS Regs
JSA Sch 2 para 5 JSA Regs
PC Sch 2 para 6 SPC Regs
46 Sch 3 para 4(2) and (4) IS Regs; reg 32 IS(JSACA) Regs
47 Sch 2 paras 4(2) and (4) and 18(1)(c) JSA Regs
48 para 23466 DMG
49 Sch 2 para 5(2) and (4) SPC Regs
50 **IS** Sch 3 para 4(4A) IS Regs
JSA Sch 2 para 4(4A) JSA Regs
PC Sch 2 para 5(5) SPC Regs
51 para 23466 DMG
52 **IS** Sch 3 para 4(2) and (4) IS Regs
JSA Sch 2 para 4(2) and (4) JSA Regs
PC Sch 2 para 5(2) and (4) SPC Regs
All paras 23481 and 23486-87 DMG, definition of 'relevant period'; *Saleem v Secretary of State for Social Security*, reported as R(IS) 5/01
53 **IS** Sch 3 paras 1(3) and (4) and 4(9) IS Regs
JSA Sch 2 paras 1(3) and (4) and 4(9) JSA Regs
PC Sch 2 para 1(2)(a) and (3) and 5(10) SPC Regs
54 CIS/3295/2003
55 R(IS) 20/98
56 **IS** Sch 3 para 1(3) and (4) IS Regs
JSA Sch 2 para 1(3) and (4) JSA Regs
PC Sch 2 para 1(2)(a) and (3) SPC Regs
57 **IS** Sch 3 para 4(10) IS Regs
JSA Sch 2 para 4(10) JSA Regs
PC Sch 2 para 5(11) SPC Regs
All *Saleem v Secretary of State for Social Security* reported as R(IS) 5/01; CIS/1068/2003
58 CIS/14657/1996
59 **IS** Sch 3 para 4(6)(a) IS Regs
JSA Sch 2 para 4(6)(a) JSA Regs
PC Sch 2 para 5(7)(a) SPC Regs
60 **IS** Sch 3 para 4(6)(b) IS Regs
JSA Sch 2 para 4(6)(b) JSA Regs
PC Sch 2 para 5(7)(b) SPC Regs
All R(IS) 20/98
61 CIS/11293/1995
62 **IS** Sch 3 para 4(8) IS Regs
JSA Sch 2 para 4(8) JSA Regs
PC Sch 2 para 5(9) SPC Regs
All CIS/4712/2002
63 R(IS) 8/94
64 **IS** Sch 3 para 4(11) IS Regs
JSA Sch 2 para 4(11) JSA Regs
PC Sch 2 para 5(12) SPC Regs
65 **IS** Sch 3 para 10 IS Regs
JSA Sch 2 para 9 JSA Regs
PC Sch 2 para 7(1) SPC Regs
66 **IS** Sch 3 para 12 IS Regs
JSA Sch 2 para 11 JSA Regs
PC Sch 2 para 9 SPC Regs
67 **IS** Sch 3 para 5(5) IS Regs
JSA Sch 2 para 5(5) JSA Regs
PC Sch 2 para 6(5) SPC Regs
68 R(IS) 4/00
69 **IS** Sch 3 paras 6(1A) and (1B) and 8(1A) and (1B) IS Regs
JSA Sch 2 paras 6(2) and 7(2)-(2B) JSA Regs
PC Sch 2 para 7(2) and (4C) SPC Regs
70 **IS** Sch 3 para 1A(2) IS Regs
JSA Sch 2 para 1A(2) JSA Regs
PC Sch 2 para 7(5) SPC Regs
71 Reg 7(14), (17A), (18) and (23) and Sch 3A paras 12 and 13 SS&CS(DA) Regs
72 Reg 7(17B) and (17C) SS&CS(DA) Regs

3. **Loans for repairs and improvements**

73 **IS** Sch 3 para 16 IS Regs
JSA Sch 2 para 15 JSA Regs
PC Sch 2 para 12 SPC Regs
74 R(IS) 22/98
75 R(IS) 5/96
76 CIS/14657/1996
77 CIS/2132/1998
78 R(IS) 16/98
79 CIS/14657/1996

4. **Help with other housing costs**
80 **IS** Sch 3 para 17(1) IS Regs
JSA Sch 2 para 16(1) JSA Regs
PC Sch 2 para 13(1) SPC Regs
81 **IS** Sch 3 para 17(5) IS Regs
JSA Sch 2 para 16(5) JSA Regs
PC Sch 2 para 13(5) SPC Regs
82 **IS** Sch 3 para 17(3) IS Regs
JSA Sch 2 para 16(3) JSA Regs
PC Sch 2 para 13(3) SPC Regs
83 **IS** Sch 3 para 17(4) IS Regs
JSA Sch 2 para 16(4) JSA Regs
PC Sch 2 para 13(4) SPC Regs
84 **IS** Sch 3 para 5(5) IS Regs
JSA Sch 2 para 5(5) JSA Regs
PC Sch 2 para 6(5) SPC Regs
85 R(IS) 4/00
86 **IS** Sch 3 para 17(2) IS Regs
JSA Sch 2 para 16(2) JSA Regs
PC Sch 2 para 13(2) SPC Regs
87 CIS/15036/1996
88 **IS** Sch 3 para 17(2)(b) IS Regs
JSA Sch 2 para 16(2)(b) JSA Regs
PC Sch 2 para 13(2)(b) SPC Regs
All Sch 1 para 1 HB Regs
89 R(IS) 3/91; R(IS) 4/91; CIS/1460/1995
90 **IS** Sch 3 para 17(2)(c) IS Regs
JSA Sch 2 para 16(2)(c) JSA Regs
PC Sch 2 para 13(2)(c) SPC Regs
91 Sch 4 para 4B CTB Regs
92 R(IS) 4/92; R(IS) 19/93
93 CIS/4/1988

5. **The amount of housing costs you get**
94 **IS** Reg 42(4)(a)(ii) IS Regs
JSA Reg 105(10(a)(ii) JSA Regs
95 **IS** Sch 10 para 26 IS Regs
JSA Sch 8 para 6 JSA Regs
PC Sch 5 para 7 SPC Regs
96 **IS** Sch 9 para 22 IS Regs
JSA Sch 7 para 23 JSA Regs
97 **IS** Sch 3 para 11(4) and (5) IS Regs
JSA Sch 2 para 10(3) and (4) JSA Regs
PC Sch 2 para 8(1) and (2) SPC Regs
98 **IS** Sch 3 para 11(6) IS Regs
JSA Sch 2 para 10(5) JSA Regs
PC Sch 2 para 8(3) SPC Regs
99 **IS** Sch 3 para 14(3AA) IS Regs
JSA Sch 2 para 13(4A) JSA Regs
100 **IS** Sch 3 para 13 IS Regs
JSA Sch 2 para 12 JSA Regs
PC Sch 2 Para 10 SPC Regs
101 R(IS) 12/91
102 **IS** Sch 3 para 13(2) IS Regs
JSA Sch 2 para 12(2) JSA Regs
PC Sch 2 para 10(2) SPC Regs
103 **IS** Sch 3 para 13(4) and (5) IS Regs
JSA Sch 2 para 12(4) and (5) JSA Regs
PC Sch 2 para 10(4) and (5) SPC Regs
104 R(SB) 7/89
105 R(SB) 6/89; R(SB) 7/89
106 R(IS) 10/93
107 CIS/347/1992
108 CSB/617/1988. This case has been reported as R(SB) 4/89, but the reported version omits the relevant paragraphs.
109 R(SB) 7/89
110 **IS** Sch 3 para 13(3) IS Regs
JSA Sch 2 para 12(3) JSA Regs
PC Sch 2 para 10(3) SPC Regs
111 CJSA/2683/2002
112 R(IS) 9/91; CJSA/2536/2000
113 **IS** Sch 3 para 13(6) and (7) IS Regs
JSA Sch 2 para 12(6) and (7) JSA Regs
Both *Secretary of State for Social Security v Julien*, reported as R(IS) 13/92; R(SB) 7/89; CIS/104/1991
114 CJSA/2536/2000
115 **IS** Sch 3 para 13(9) IS Regs
JSA Sch 2 para 12(9) JSA Regs
116 Sch 2 para 10(6) and (10) SPC Regs; *Secretary of State for Social Security v Julien*, reported as R(IS) 13/92; R(SB) 7/89; CIS/104/1991
117 The term 'review' is used in Sch 2 para 10(6) SPC Regs, not the term 'revision' or 'supersession'
118 Sch 2 para 10(7) and (9) SPC Regs
119 **IS** Sch 3 para 18 IS Regs
JSA Sch 2 para 17 JSA Regs
PC Sch 2 para 14 SPC Regs
120 CSIS/185/1995
121 **IS** Reg 3(4) and (5) IS Regs
JSA Reg 2(6) and (7) JSA Regs
PC Sch 2 para 1(8) and (9) SPC Regs
122 **IS** Reg 3 IS Regs
JSA Reg 2 JSA Regs
PC Sch 2 para 1(4)-(7) SPC Regs
123 CSB/1163/1988
124 **IS** Sch 3 para 18(6) IS Regs
JSA Sch 2 para 17(6) JSA Regs
PC Sch 2 para 14(6) SPC Regs
125 **IS** Sch 3 para 18(7) IS Regs
JSA Sch 2 para 17(7) JSA Regs
PC Sch 2 para 14(7) SPC Regs
126 **IS** Sch 3 para 18(1) and (2) IS Regs
JSA Sch 2 para 17(1) and (2) JSA Regs
PC Sch 2 para 14(1) and (2) SPC Regs
127 **IS** Sch 3 para 18(8) IS Regs
JSA Sch 2 para 17(8) JSA Regs
PC Sch 2 para 14(8) SPC Regs
128 **IS** Sch 3 paras 6 and 8 IS Regs
JSA Sch 2 paras 6 and 7 JSA Regs

129 **IS** Sch 3 para 9 IS Regs
JSA Sch 2 para 8 JSA Regs
130 **IS** Sch 3 paras 14(8) and (9) IS Regs
JSA Sch 2 paras 13(10) and (11) JSA Regs
131 **IS** Sch 3 paras 1(2), definition of 'existing housing costs', and 6 IS Regs
JSA Sch 2 paras 1(2), definition of 'existing housing costs' and 6 JSA Regs
Both CJSA/2028/2000
132 **IS** Sch 3 paras 1(2) definition of 'new housing costs', and 8 IS Regs
JSA Sch 2 paras 1(2) definition of 'new housing costs', and 7 JSA Regs
Both CJSA/2028/2000
133 **IS** Sch 3 para 8(2) and (3) IS Regs
JSA Sch 2 para 7(3)-(6) JSA Regs
134 CIS/5177/1997; R(IS) 12/99; CIS/2790/1998; CIS/3303/1998
135 R(IS) 2/01; CIS/2816/2003
136 CJSA/679/2004
137 **IS** Sch 3 para 11(2) IS Regs
JSA Sch 2 para 10(1) JSA Regs
138 Reg 3 IS(AT) Regs
139 **IS** Sch 3 para 7 IS Regs
JSA Sch 2 para 18 JSA Regs
140 CIS/672/2004
141 s16 IA 1978; CIS/1939/1997
142 Sch 2 para 18(1)(c) JSA Regs
143 Reg 32 IS(JSACA) Regs
144 **IS** Sch 3 para 14(1)(a) and (3A) IS Regs
JSA Sch 2 para 13(1)(a), (2A) and (4) JSA Regs
145 **IS** Sch 3 para 14(2) IS Regs
JSA Sch 2 para 13(2) JSA Regs
146 **IS** Sch 3 para 14(1)(c), (d) and (e), (3A) and (14) IS Regs
JSA Sch 2 para 13(1)(c), (d), (dd) and (e), (4) and (16) JSA Regs
147 **IS** Sch 3 para 14(1)(ee), (3), (3ZA), (3A) and (3B) IS Regs
JSA Sch 2 para 13(1)(ee), (3), (3A) and (4) JSA Regs
148 **IS** Sch 3 para 14(1)(f) and (3A) IS Regs
JSA Sch 2 para 13 (1)(f) and (4) JSA Regs
149 **IS** Sch 3 para 14(4), (5), (5A) and (5B) IS Regs
JSA Sch 2 para 13(5), (6), (7) and (8) JSA Regs
Both Reg 32 IS(JSACA) Regs; CIS/621/2004
150 CJSA/4631/2001
151 **IS** Sch 3 para 14(6) IS Regs
JSA Sch 2 para 13(9) JSA Regs
152 **IS** Sch 3 para 14(11) and (12) IS Regs
JSA Sch 2 para 13(13) and (14) JSA Regs
153 **IS** Sch 3 para 14(13) IS Regs
JSA Sch 2 para 13(15) JSA Regs

Chapter 37

Income: non-means-tested benefits

This chapter explains the income rules for non-means-tested benefits. It covers:

1. Earnings-related income for non-means-tested benefits (except contribution-based jobseeker's allowance) (p937)
2. Earnings-related income for contribution-based jobseeker's allowance (p947)

The term **'earnings-related income'** is used in this chapter to cover both earnings from employment and self-employment (see pp939 and 942) as well as payments from occupational and personal pension schemes (see p946).

This chapter explains which benefits are affected, what counts as earnings and pension payments, how they are calculated, and how they affect your entitlement. However, the rules on how your pension payments affect your entitlement to incapacity benefit are dealt with in Chapter 12.

No other forms of income you, or any member of your family, or anyone else receives affect your entitlement to any non-means-tested benefit you may be able to claim for yourself or anyone else.

1. Earnings-related income for non-means-tested benefits

The rules in this section apply to all non-means-tested benefits except contribution-based jobseeker's allowance (JSA). For the rules on contribution-based JSA, see p947.

Most non-means-tested benefits are not affected by income. However, some non-means-tested benefits are intended as earnings replacement benefits and they may be affected by earnings-related income. There is a list of non-means-tested benefits on p5.

Benefits affected by earnings-related income

You are not entitled to any of the following benefits if you earn more than a certain amount:

- carer's allowance (CA);
- incapacity benefit (IB);
- severe disablement allowance (SDA).

Payment of an increase for an adult dependant may be affected by the earnings of your dependant, and payment for a child dependant may be affected by the earnings of your partner.

Carer's allowance

You are not entitled to CA if your earnings are above £82 a week.[1] Earnings of £82 a week or less do not affect the amount you are entitled to. Only your own earnings count, not those of a partner. Any pension payments you get do not affect your benefit. See below for how earnings are worked out. For more about the earnings limit, and when all your earnings can be ignored, see p73.

Incapacity benefit

Your IB can be affected by the following income:

- **Earning from permitted work.** If you are entitled to IB while doing 'permitted work' (see p766) the amount you get is not reduced by your earnings but you can only be allowed permitted work if your earnings do not go above certain limits. The permitted work lower limit is £20 a week. The permitted work higher limit is £78 a week. Only your own earnings count towards these limits. Pension payments do not count.
- **Pensions.** If you get certain kinds of pension payments, these can affect the amount of IB you are entitled to. See p277 for which pensions count and how they reduce your IB.
- **Councillors' allowances.** IB is paid at a reduced rate if you are a local councillor and your net allowances are more than £78 in a week. A basic allowance and special responsibilities allowance is converted into a weekly amount in a set way (eg, if paid monthly, multiply by 12 and divide by 52).[2] Ignore any payments for expenses and, from the allowances, deduct any other expenses incurred in the relevant week in connection with your council duties,[3] but do not deduct any tax or national insurance.[4] Your IB in that week is reduced by the amount by which the net allowances exceed £78.[5]

Severe disablement allowance

Your SDA can be affected by the following income:

- **Earnings from permitted work.** If you are entitled to SDA while doing 'permitted work' (see p766), the amount of SDA you get is not reduced by your earnings but you can only be allowed permitted work if your earnings do not

go above certain limits. You can continue to get SDA while doing 'permitted work' (see p766). The permitted work lower limit is £20 a week. The permitted work higher limit is £78 a week. Only your own earnings count towards these limits.
- **Councillors' allowances.** As for IB, your SDA in any week is reduced by the amount by which your net councillors' allowance exceeds £78. See p938 for details.

Any pension payments you get do not affect the amount of SDA to which you are entitled.

Increases for dependants

You may not be entitled to an increase in CA, IB, maternity allowance, retirement pension or SDA for an **adult dependant** if her/his earnings-related income is over the relevant earnings limit. Your adult dependant's earnings (see p939) and any pension payments s/he gets (see p946) count towards the limit. For the amount of the earnings limits and more details of how entitlement is affected, see p797.

Increases for **child dependants** in non-means-tested benefits were abolished from 6 April 2003. Those already entitled can continue to get the increase for as long as they remain entitled. Payment of the increase stops if your partner's earnings-related income is over the earnings limit. Your partner's earnings (see p939) and any pension payments s/he gets (see p946) count towards the limit. If payments stop for more than eight weeks then entitlement is lost altogether. See p798 for more details.

Earnings

It is important to distinguish between 'earnings' and other types of income because, apart from the rules for contribution-based JSA (see p948) and the rules on how pension payments you receive can affect your IB (see p290), only your earnings and the earnings and pension payments of adult dependants (see p946) can affect your entitlement to non-means-tested benefits.

Earnings are what you get in return for working as opposed to, for example, interest on your savings or social security benefits. What counts as earnings depends on whether you are an employee or self-employed.

Employees

If you are employed by someone else (including employment by a limited company in which you have shares) **'earnings'** means 'any remuneration or profit derived from ... employment'. The main type of income which counts as earnings is, therefore, your wages. But the following are also included:[6]
- any bonus or commission (including tips);
- holiday pay (but not if it is payable more than four weeks after your job ends or is interrupted);

- any payment in lieu of notice;
- any payment in lieu of remuneration (eg, loss of earnings payment to a councillor);
- compensation for unfair dismissal and certain other types of compensation under the Employment Rights Act 1996 or under trade union legislation;[7]
- other compensation payments paid on termination of employment (eg, ex-gratia payments) if you have waived or not received some or all pay in lieu of notice due:[8]
  - for part-time employment the whole payment counts (taken into account over one week);
  - for full-time employment, take into account the nearest multiple of £280 (from February 2005, amounts go up each February) on or below the amount of the compensation payment, and ignore the remainder. For example, for compensation of £600 take into account £560 in total over two weeks (or, if shorter, over any unworked notice period not covered by pay in lieu). If compensation is less than £280 it is ignored;[9]
- any payments made by your employer for expenses not 'wholly, exclusively and necessarily' incurred in carrying out your job, including any travel expenses to and from work, and any payments made to you for the cost of arranging care for members of your family;
- a retainer fee (eg, you may be paid during the school holidays if you work for the school meals service) or a guarantee payment (ie, payment for a workless period under the Employment Rights Act 1996);[10]
- maternity pay, paternity pay, adoption pay and sick pay.[11]

Note: it is the pay you actually receive which should be taken into account rather than what you may be legally entitled to,[12] so if you receive less than the national minimum wage then it is that lesser amount that counts as your 'earnings'.

The following do not count as earnings:

- periodic payments made as part of a redundancy scheme;[13]
- payments towards expenses that are 'wholly, exclusively and necessarily' incurred in the performance of your employment, such as travelling expenses during the course of your work.[14] In appropriate circumstances these could, for example, include:
  - tools or work equipment;
  - special clothing or uniform;[15]
  - telephone costs (including rental);[16]
  - postage;
  - fuel costs (including standing charges);
  - secretarial expenses;[17] *and*
- the costs of running a car (including petrol, tax, insurance, repairs and maintenance and rental on a leased car).[18]

Where any expenditure serves a dual purpose for both business and private use it should be apportioned as appropriate to the circumstances (and any determination by the Revenue should normally be followed).[19]

Calculating net earnings from employment

For the earnings rules for the non-means-tested benefits in this *Handbook* (other than contribution-based JSA – see p947), your 'earnings' are your net earnings. **'Net' earnings** are your 'gross' earnings (calculated as set out on p939) less any deductions made for income tax, Class 1 national insurance (NI) contributions (but not Class 3 voluntary contributions[20]) and half of any contribution you make towards a personal or occupational pension scheme.[21] It is the amount of your earnings calculated on a weekly basis which is important.[22] So, for example, if you are paid monthly, this figure will be multiplied by 12 and divided by 52 to arrive at a weekly figure.[23] If you are paid for a period of less than a week, this payment will be treated as a payment for a week.[24]

If your earnings fluctuate and have changed more than once, or your employment is such that you do not work every week, your weekly earnings may be averaged as follows:[25]

- if you have a regular pattern of work, over one complete 'cycle' of work. This includes periods where you do no work if this forms part of your regular pattern of work (eg, if you regularly work three weeks on and one week off, your earnings will be averaged over four weeks); *or*
- in any other case, over five weeks, or whatever other period will enable your weekly earnings to be assessed more accurately.[26]

The date from when earnings from employment are counted

You are usually treated as having received earnings on the first day of the benefit week in which they are due to be paid.[27] The **'benefit week'** is the seven days corresponding to the week for which the particular benefit you are claiming is paid (see the relevant chapter for the benefit you are claiming).[28]

The exception to this is if you are claiming:

- an increase in maternity allowance or CA for an adult dependant (see p793); *or*
- an increase in your Category A retirement pension for an adult dependant who does not live with you (see p793),

in which case earnings are treated as having been paid on the first day of the benefit week after the week in which they are due to be paid.[29]

The date that a payment is due may well be different from the date of actual payment. Earnings are due on the employee's normal payday. If your contract of employment does not reveal the date of due payment and there is no evidence to suggest differently, the date the payment was received should be taken as the date it was due.[30] If your contract of employment is terminated without proper notice, outstanding wages, wages in hand, holiday pay and any pay in lieu of notice are due on the last day of employment and are treated as paid on that day, even if this does not happen.[31] If an employment tribunal awards you compensation for loss of earnings, for example, for being dismissed in circumstances constituting sex discrimination, the relevant date is the date when the earnings in question were due to be paid, not when the compensation was awarded.[32]

The period covered by earnings from employment

Once it has been calculated, your earnings count for a future period. The length of that period is worked out as follows:

- Where a payment of income is made in respect of an identifiable period, it is taken into account for a period of equal length.[33] For example, a week's part-time earnings are taken into account for a week.
- If the payment does not relate to a particular period, the amount of the payment is divided by the amount of the weekly earnings limit (see pp797 and 937) plus one penny and then rounded down to the nearest whole number. If part of the payment should be disregarded (see p943), the weekly earnings limit is increased (for the purpose of this calculation only) by the amount of the appropriate disregard (see p943). The result of this calculation is the number of full weeks for which you will not get benefit.[34]

Example

Bob receives a Category A retirement pension with an increase for his wife who lives with him. She receives £700 net earnings for work which cannot be attributed to any specific period of time. The £700 figure includes a tax refund of £150 paid through the PAYE system.

The earnings limit for the dependant's increase is £56.20.

The £150 tax refund is disregarded.

The period over which the income is taken into account is

£700 ÷ (£56.20 + £0.01 + £150) =

£700 ÷ 206.21 = 3.39 weeks

This means that Bob is not entitled to his dependency increase for three weeks.

Self-employed people

If you are self-employed, your weekly earnings – see p943 – (including any allowance from a DWP scheme to assist you with your business[35]) are averaged over a period of a year unless:

- you have recently become self-employed; *or*
- there has been a change which is likely to affect the normal pattern of your business,

in which case, your earnings are averaged over whatever other period the decision maker considers will give the most accurate figure.[36] This means that when you first claim, the decision maker will need you to provide an up-to-date set of accounts. If you receive royalties or payments from copyrights, the period for which these payments will count is calculated in a similar way to payments made for unspecified periods to employees.[37]

The figure used for your earnings is your 'net profit' from self-employment or, if you are a member of a partnership or a share fisherman, your share of the net profit. Unless you are a childminder (in which case, see below) your **'net profit'** is calculated taking your earnings over the period and deducting:[38]

- expenses incurred during the period wholly and exclusively for the purposes of the business. Where a car or telephone, for example, is used partly for business and partly for private purposes, the costs of it can be apportioned and the amount attributable to business use can be deducted.[39] Certain expenses cannot be deducted, including business entertainment, repayment of capital on a business loan, capital expenditure and depreciation;
- income tax and NI contributions;[40] *and*
- half of any contributions you have made during the period towards a personal pension scheme or retirement annuity contract.

Childminders are always treated as self-employed. If you are a childminder, your net profit is deemed to be one-third of your earnings less income tax, your NI contributions and half of certain pension contributions (see p941).[41] The rest of your earnings are completely ignored.

Disregarded earnings

Some of your income which might otherwise be classed as earnings is specifically disregarded and does not affect your benefit. Some care and childcare costs can also be disregarded. The same earnings disregards apply whether you are an employee or self-employed (and, if you are a childminder, they apply in addition to the other disregards explained above).

Earnings which can be disregarded are:[42]

- any payment made to you by someone who normally lives with you on an informal or non-contractual basis as part of her/his contribution towards shared living expenses;
- the first £4 of any income you receive each week for renting out room(s) in your home. This disregard is increased to £13.25 a week if your tenant(s) pays for her/his heating as part of the rent rather than, for example, through a separate electricity meter;
- the first £20 of any income you receive each week for providing board and lodging in your home. If you receive more than £20 a week, then 50 per cent of the excess is also disregarded. This disregard applies to each person who lodges with you so, for example, if you are providing bed and breakfast accommodation and in one week five different people each stay for one night and pay £20 each, then the full £100 is disregarded;
- payments from a local authority or voluntary organisation for fostering or accommodating a child under formal arrangements, or payments from a

health authority or local authority or voluntary organisation for providing temporary care;
- refunds of Schedule D income tax or what was formerly Schedule E income tax and now comes under IT(EP)A 2003;
- if you are an employee, any loan or advance of earnings from your employer;
- certain bounty payments made to part-time firefighters, auxiliary coastguards, members of the territorial or reserve armed forces and part-time lifeboat crews;
- unless you are abroad yourself, earnings payable abroad which cannot be brought into Great Britain (eg, because of exchange control regulations);
- unless you are abroad yourself, if your earnings are paid in another currency, any bank charges for converting them into sterling.

Childcare costs[43]

In addition to the earnings disregards, certain childcare costs may also be deducted from earnings. The following rules apply to claims for those benefits and dependency increases listed on p938 except that different rules (see p945) apply to the treatment of childcare costs if you are claiming CA (although the following rules do apply to CA dependency increases).

An allowance of up to a maximum of £60 a week may be deducted from your earnings if:
- you are a lone parent; *or*
- you are a member of a couple and both you and your partner are working (full or part time); *or*
- you are a member of a couple and your partner is incapacitated (see below).

This will only apply if you have any child(ren) in your family under the age of 11 for whom you are paying charges for childcare (not counting charges paid by you to your partner or by your partner to you, or charges in respect of compulsory education) which is provided:
- by a registered childminder or other registered childcare provider (such as a nursery or after-school club for the under-8s); *or*
- for children aged 8 or over but under 11, by a school on school premises or by a local authority (eg, an out-of-hours or holiday play scheme); *or*
- by a childcare scheme operating on Crown property; *or*
- in schools or establishments exempt from registration.[44]

Your partner counts as '**incapacitated**' if:[45]
- s/he is getting long-term IB, SDA, attendance allowance, disability living allowance (or an equivalent award under the war pensions or industrial injuries schemes), or would have been if s/he were not a hospital inpatient; *or*
- s/he is provided with an invalid carriage or other vehicle by the NHS; *or*
- you or your partner are getting housing benefit or council tax benefit and either childcare costs have been allowed for under the rules applying to claims

for those benefits (see p965) or else a disability premium or higher pensioner premium in respect of your partner has been awarded.

As childcare costs are likely to vary considerably between term time and holiday periods, a formula is used to assess the costs that will be taken into account.

Where charges are paid monthly, the amount will be:

- if the charge is for a fixed amount, that amount multiplied by 12 and divided by 52; *or*
- if the charge is variable, 1/52 of the aggregate of charges over the previous 12 months.

Where charges are paid other than monthly, the amount will be either:

- 1/52 of the aggregate of:
  - the average weekly charge in the four most recent complete weeks falling in term time, multiplied by 39; *and*
  - the average weekly charge in the two most recent complete weeks falling out of term time, multiplied by 13; *or*
- if your child does not yet attend school, the average weekly charge in the four most recent complete weeks.

However, if there is no, or insufficient, information available to calculate your childcare costs in these ways (eg, you have just started to use a childminder), an estimate will be made based on the information provided by the childcare provider or, if that is not available, by the claimant.[46]

Notes on childcare costs

- Childcare allowances apply separately to each individual in respect of whom benefit is claimed. For example, the childcare costs you and your partner pay may be deducted from your earnings on your own IB, as well as on your award of an adult dependency increase of IB in respect of your partner's earnings.
- Similarly, the same childcare costs may apply to a claim for CA for yourself, as well as on a claim for a CA dependency increase. Because different rules apply on the treatment of childcare costs, however, the same childcare costs may be allowed on one claim but not on the other (eg, if your child is over 11, your costs may be deducted from your earnings on a claim for yourself, but will not be deducted from your partner's earnings on a claim for a dependency increase).
- Whether or not childcare costs are taken into account on a claim for a non-means-tested benefit, different rules apply on claims for any means-tested benefit (see p965).

Care costs and carer's allowance[47]

If you are getting CA and because of your work you have to pay for someone (other than a 'close relative') to look after the severely disabled person you care for or to look after a child or children under 16 for whom you or your partner are getting child benefit then (in addition to any disregarded earnings), those care costs can be deducted when your earnings are calculated. The maximum deduction is 50 per cent of the figure which would otherwise be your net earnings. Any disregarded income is deducted from your net earnings before calculating the 50 per cent figure. **'Close relative'** means a parent, son, daughter, brother, sister, husband, wife or partner of you or the severely disabled person you care for. There is, therefore, no restriction on charges paid to someone who is only a close relative of the child being looked after (eg, the parent of the child if you are not married and s/he is not also your partner).

Notional earnings

You will be deemed to have notional earnings only if[48] it is not possible to work out your earnings when your claim is decided. This may apply if, for example, you have just started employment and your pay will depend on your performance, or you have just started a business and there is no way of calculating what profits you will make. If so, you will be treated as earning such amount as is considered reasonable taking into account the number of hours you work and the earnings paid for comparable work in the area.

Estimates of the appropriate deductions for income tax and NI contributions, and half of any occupational or personal pension contributions, are deducted from your notional earnings, as are any earnings disregards or allowances for childcare or care costs.

Pension payments

For all claims for dependency increases, certain pension payments count as earnings.[49] There is an exception for those covered by the 'transitional protection' rules described on p873 of the 2001/2002 edition of CPAG's *Welfare Benefits Handbook* which apply to those getting an increase since at least 1989.

All the following periodical payments of an occupational or personal pension which are made in connection with the ending of a person's employment count as earnings if they are paid:

- out of money provided wholly or partly by or under arrangements made by an employer; *or*
- under an approved personal pension, contract or trust scheme; *or*
- under a statutory scheme.[50]

This covers most pension payments, including early retirement schemes for those who retire early on health grounds or for other reasons,[51] or, in some cases, those who volunteer for redundancy.[52]

However, it does not include lump-sum or redundancy payments which are not related to a specific period, even if you have chosen to receive a lump sum

- a personal pension scheme; *or*
- a pension connected with the ending of your employment as an earner under an occupational pension scheme or a public service pension scheme.

Although the meaning of pension payments is slightly different than that applying to other non-means-tested benefits, it should still cover most periodical pension payments (including contractual redundancy/early retirement payments[66]) as explained on p946, and identical rules apply to the calculation of weekly pension payments.[67] **Note:** lump-sum payments may still count as pension payments for the purposes of JSA if they are calculated on the basis of a weekly or monthly entitlement.[68]

The amount of your pension payments may mean that you are not paid any JSA. However, unless your earnings also exceed the prescribed amount (see p948) you remain *entitled* to contribution-based JSA even though it is not paid because your pension payments are too high (so long as you also satisfy the other conditions for getting JSA – see p347). Any day on which you are entitled to JSA even if it is not paid counts towards your 182 days' entitlement to contribution-based JSA (see p377). A combination of earnings and pension payments may also mean that you are not paid any JSA, even though you may remain entitled to it.

Any payments you receive under a personal, occupational or public pension scheme because of the death of the person who was a member of the pension scheme are ignored when calculating your contribution-based JSA.[69] For example, if your late partner was a member of a scheme, any payment made to you following her/his death does not affect your contribution-based JSA.

Any pension payment you receive is counted from the first day of the benefit week in which the payment is actually made to you.[70]

Example

Brian claims JSA and is entitled to contribution-based JSA from Wednesday 5 May 2004. His benefit week begins on a Friday (his signing-on day is Thursday). He starts receiving a personal pension of £68 a week from Monday 10 May 2004. £18 a week is deducted from his contribution-based JSA (£68 – £50) from the benefit week starting Friday 7 May 2004.

If your pension is increased when you are on contribution-based JSA, the change should be taken into account from the first day of the benefit week in which the increase is paid.[71]

Notes

1. Earnings-related income for non-means-tested benefits

1 Reg 8 SS(ICA) Regs
2 Reg 9 SS(IB) Regs
3 s30E(3) SSCBA 1992
4 R(IB) 3/01
5 s30E(1) SSCBA 1992; reg 8 SS(IB) Regs
6 Reg 9 SSB(CE) Regs
7 Reg 9(1)(g) and (h) SSB(CE) Regs
8 Reg 9(1)(i) and (4) SSB(CE) Regs
9 Reg 6(6), (7), (8) and (9)1)(i), (2) and (4) SSB(CE) Regs
10 CIS/743/1992
11 Reg 9(1)(j) SSB(CE) Regs
12 CIB/1650/2002
13 Reg 9(1)(b) SSB(CE) Regs
14 Reg 9(3) SSB(CE) Regs; *Parsons v Hogg* [1985] 2 All ER 897 (CA), also reported as an appendix to R(FIS) 4/85
15 R(FC) 1/90
16 CFC/26/1989
17 R(FIS) 4/85
18 R(IS) 13/91; R(IS) 16/93; CFC/26/1989
19 R(U) 2/72; R(FIS) 4/85; R(FC) 1/91; R(IS) 13/91
20 CIS/521/1990
21 Reg 10(4) SSB(CE) Regs
22 Reg 6(1) SSB(CE) Regs
23 Reg 8(1)(b)(i) SSB(CE) Regs
24 Reg 8(1)(a) SSB(CE)Regs
25 Reg 8(3) SSB(CE) Regs. This Regulation applies as much to IB as it does to other non-means-tested benefits. CIB/4090/1999, which held that the claimant's earnings could not be averaged, must therefore be read as concluding that, on the facts of that particular case, the earnings should not be averaged, rather than saying earnings in IB cases cannot be averaged as a rule of law.
26 See CG/4941/2003 for how averaging can work
27 Reg 7(b) SSB(CE) Regs
28 Reg 2(1) SSB(CE) Regs
29 Reg 7(a) SSB(CE) Regs
30 R(SB) 33/83
31 R(SB) 22/84; R(SB) 11/85
32 CIS/590/1993
33 Reg 6(2)(a) SSB(CE) Regs
34 Reg 6(2)(b) SSB(CE) Regs
35 Reg 12(1) SSB(CE) Regs
36 Reg 11(1) SSB(CE) Regs
37 Reg 11(2) SSB(CE) Regs
38 Reg 13(1)(a) and (b), (4) and (5) SSB(CE) Regs
39 R(IS) 13/91; R(FC) 1/91; CFC/26/1989
40 See also reg 14 SSB(CE) Regs
41 Reg 13(10) SSB(CE) Regs
42 Sch 1 SSB(CE) Regs
43 Regs 10(2) and 13(2) and Sch 2 SSB(CE) Regs
44 Sch 2 para 2 SSB(CE) Regs
45 Sch 2 para 8 SSB(CE) Regs
46 Sch 2 paras 4-7 SSB(CE) Regs
47 Regs 10(3) and 13(3) and Sch 3 SSB(CE) Regs
48 Reg 4(1) and (3) SSB(CE) Regs and CIB/1650/2002, disapplying reg 4(2) of these Regs
49 s89 SSCBA 1992; Sch 2 para 9 SSB(Dep) Regs
50 s122(1) SSCBA 1992
51 CP/7/1987
52 CU/66/1993
53 R(U) 5/85
54 para 15283 DMG
55 R(U) 8/83
56 R(U) 4/83; para 15286 DMG
57 Reg 9A SSB(Dep) Regs; paras 15290-91 DMG
58 para 15285 DMG

2. Earnings-related income for contribution-based jobseeker's allowance

59 Reg 80 JSA Regs
60 Regs 99(3) and 101(3) and Sch 6 JSA Regs
61 Reg 80 JSA Regs
62 s2(1)(c) JSA 1995; reg 56(1) and (2) JSA Regs
63 s4(1) JSA 1995
64 Reg 81(1) JSA Regs
65 s35(1) JSA 1995
66 R(JSA)1/01
67 Reg 81 JSA Regs; para 23931 DMG
68 R(JSA)6/02, though R(U)5/85 was not referred to in that decision and note the doubts expressed in CJSA/1542/2000
69 Reg 81(2)(c) JSA Regs
70 Reg 81(1A) JSA Regs
71 Reg 81(1B) JSA Regs

Chapter 38

Income: means-tested benefits

This chapter explains the rules for working out your weekly income for income support (IS), income-based jobseeker's allowance (JSA), pension credit (PC), housing benefit (HB) and council tax benefit (CTB). It covers:

1. **Income: aged under 60** (p952)
   This part applies to IS, income-based JSA and, if you and your partner (if you have one) are aged under 60, to HB and CTB. It looks at:
   - whose income counts (p952);
   - what counts as income (p954);
   - working out weekly income (p987).
2. **Income: aged 60 or over** (p992)
   This part applies to PC and, if you or your partner (if you have one) are aged 60 or over, to HB and CTB. It looks at:
   - whose income counts (p992);
   - what counts as income (p992);
   - working out weekly income (p1006).

In this chapter, unless otherwise stated, references to income-based JSA are intended also to refer to joint-claim JSA.

Your entitlement to IS, income-based JSA, PC, HB and CTB and the amount you receive depends on how much income you have. **Note:** if you get IS, income-based JSA or the guarantee credit of PC you do not need to work out your income again for HB or CTB purposes (see pp112 and 206).[1]

In each case some of your income may be completely ignored, *or* partially ignored, *or* counted in full. Some income may be treated as capital (see p1030) and some capital may be treated as income (see p978). There are some important differences in the rules on income for urgent cases payments under the IS and income-based JSA schemes. These are set out on p665.

The rules described in this chapter about *earnings* for income-based JSA (as opposed to other forms of income) are also relevant when applying the earnings rules for contribution-based JSA. However, for contribution-based JSA, only the claimant's earnings are relevant, and never the earnings of other members of her/

his family.[2] For further information about the earnings rules for contribution-based JSA, see p947.

For information about the earnings rules for certain other non-means-tested benefits, see Chapter 37.

For the treatment of earnings and other income on claims for certain health benefits, see p188.

For the rules on income for tax credits, see Chapter 52.

1. Income: aged under 60

This part applies to:

- income support (IS) – including those over 60 with a partner under 60 claiming IS;
- income-based JSA – including men aged 60 to 64;
- housing benefit (HB) and council tax benefit (CTB) if you and your partner (if you have one) are aged under 60.

The rules for IS, JSA, HB and CTB are very similar. Where there are differences these are indicated.

In this part, whenever HB or CTB is referred to, this only applies to the rules for people aged under 60.

Whose income counts

Income of a partner

If you are a member of a couple (see p811), your partner's income is added to yours.[3]

Note: for HB and CTB if you or your partner (if any) are getting IS or income-based JSA all of your (and your partner's) income is ignored.[4]

If, for IS/income-based JSA, you receive the reduced rate of the normal personal allowance for a couple because your partner is under 18 and not eligible for IS or income-based JSA (see p879), an amount of her/his income equivalent to the reduction is ignored.[5]

Example

Kalid is 19. His partner, Kate, is 17 and is not able to claim IS or income-based JSA. Kalid's personal allowance is £44.50 (the rate for a single person aged 18–24). If Kate was eligible for IS or income-based JSA, their personal allowance would be £88.15. Up to £43.65 (£88.15 – £44.50) of any income that Kate has is ignored.

Income of a dependent child

The income of a dependent child does *not* affect the following benefits:

- IS or income-based JSA[6] – unless you have been getting benefit since before 6 April 2004 with a child included in your claim and you do not yet have a child tax credit (CTC) award (see below);
- HB and CTB – from 4 April 2005, children's income is no longer taken into account;[7]
- any benefit – for income of certain 16- and 17-year-olds who leave local authority care on or after 1 October 2001 in England and Wales or, in Scotland, on or after 1 April 2004. They do not count as members of your family so their income is not counted in with yours.[8]

Although in the above cases a dependent child's income does not affect your benefit, if the child has left school/college and is working 24 hours a week or more, you cannot get benefit for her/him any more (see p822).

Maintenance paid to or for a child counts as your income (see p865) but some may be disregarded (see p972).

IS and income-based JSA (no CTC award): The income of a dependent child *does* affect IS and income-based JSA, but only if you have been getting benefit since before 6 April 2004 with a child included in your claim and you do not yet have an award of CTC. Once CTC is awarded, amounts for children are no longer included in your IS or income-based JSA and any income of a dependent child is ignored.

Even when you still have a child included in your IS or JSA claim, if your child has capital of over £3,000, you do not get benefit for her/him[9] (although you can still get a family premium) and her/his income is not counted as yours.[10] If your child has capital of £3,000 or less, any income is treated as yours but may be disregarded as follows:[11]

- Earnings of a dependent child at school/college are ignored.
- Earnings from part-time work (less than 16 hours a week) of a dependent child are ignored even if s/he has left school.
- If a child has left school/college and is working 24 hours or more a week, you do not get benefit for her/him and her/his earnings do not count with yours. If s/he is working 16 hours or more but less than 24 hours a week, earnings are treated as your income while you are still entitled to claim for that child (eg, during the summer holidays). Ignore £5 a week and any earnings above the child's personal allowance.
- If you get a disabled child premium for your child, earnings are still treated as your income as described above, but you ignore £20 a week and any earnings above the the child's personal allowance, disabled child premium and any enhanced disability premium. All your disabled child's earnings are ignored if

her/his earnings capacity is less than 75 per cent of what it would be if s/he was not disabled.[12]

- Income other than earnings and maintenance is taken into account up to the level of the child's personal allowance, and any disabled child premium and enhanced disability premium. Income above that level is ignored.[13]

School fees

School fees paid by someone other than you or your partner are dealt with differently for each benefit.

IS and income-based JSA (general rule): For IS and income-based JSA, the general rule is that your child is not included in your claim and your benefit is not affected by school fees paid direct to the school by someone other than you or your partner.[14] The exception is where you do not yet have a CTC award in the circumstances described below.

IS and income-based JSA (no CTC award): If you have been getting IS or income-based JSA since before 6 April 2004 with a dependent child included in your claim, but you do not yet have an award of CTC, the rules below apply. Once CTC is awarded, the general rule above applies instead.

Your entitlement to IS or income-based JSA is not affected if someone is paying school fees directly to the school,[15] except that any payments for the child's living expenses at a boarding school count as the child's income (up to the amount of the child's personal allowance and, if applicable, the disabled child premium and enhanced disability premium) for the period that the child is there.[16] If your child comes home for part of the week, you receive full benefit for the child for the days s/he is at home and any payments towards the child's living expenses are averaged over the period the child is at school.[17] If your child spends a night with you s/he does not count as at the boarding school on that day.[18]

If your child goes away to school and this is paid for by the local education authority, the child is treated as having income equal to the amount of her/his IS or income-based JSA child's personal allowance (and, if applicable, the disabled child premium and enhanced disability premium) for the days s/he is at school.[19] You are entitled to full benefit for the child for the days s/he spends at home.

HB and CTB: Boarding school fees met by, for example, a child's grandparents should be ignored[20] if treated as the child's income under the rules for payments made to someone else on your behalf (see p985).

What counts as income

All income is taken into account for IS and income-based JSA except for income that is specifically disregarded.

If you get IS or income-based JSA, all your income is ignored for HB and CTB. If you do not get IS or income-based JSA, all income is taken into account for HB and CTB other than income that is specifically disregarded.

The way income from employment and self-employment is treated is explained on pp955 and 962. Some of your earnings are disregarded (see p963). Most other types of income are taken into account, less any tax due on them.[21] For HB and CTB, changes in tax and national insurance (NI) rates and in the maximum rate of CTC or working tax credit (WTC) may be ignored for up to 30 weeks,[22] as for earnings (see p988).

Income will only count if it is paid to you for your own use, and will not count if you cannot prevent it being paid to a third party – eg, under an attachment of earnings order – although other payments for you made to a third party might count.[23]

Income is converted into a weekly amount (see p989).

Income or capital?

The difference between income and capital is not defined. Payments of income are normally made in respect of a specified period or periods and form, or are intended to form, part of a regular series of payments.[24] In this way, payments of income can usually be distinguished from payments of capital. However, some income is treated as capital (see p1030) and some capital is treated as income (see p978).

Earnings of employed earners

This section explains how any earnings received by you or anyone for whom you are claiming (see p809) are treated for any claim for IS, income-based JSA and, if you and your partner are aged under 60, for HB and CTB. The same rules apply to your (but not your partner's or child's) earnings if you are claiming contribution-based JSA (for further information, see p947). For the rules on earnings for non-means-tested benefits, see Chapter 37.

To work out how earnings are taken into account:

- check whether payments count as earnings (see p957). In some cases payments are treated as capital, or as income other than earnings, or ignored altogether;
- calculate net earnings (see below);
- work out weekly earnings (see p987);
- deduct the appropriate weekly earnings disregard of £5, £10, £20 or £25 (see p963) and, for HB and CTB, if you qualify, the additional earnings disregard (see p965) and disregard for childcare costs (see p965);
- for HB and CTB, the amount worked out as above is your weekly income from earnings in the benefit assessment. For IS and income-based JSA, work out the period covered by payments of earnings (see p990). Normally a payment counts from the date it is due to be paid, for the length of time it has been paid

for – eg, a month's wages count for a month, starting from the day they are due, at the weekly rate as calculated (see p987).

There are special rules for how payments affect benefit when you leave a job (see p959).

Calculating net earnings from employment

Both your 'gross' earnings and 'net' earnings need to be calculated so that a proper assessment can be made of your income from employment.

'Gross' earnings means the amount of earnings received from your employer less deductions for any expenses wholly, necessarily and exclusively incurred by you in order to carry out the duties of your employment.[25] For example, deductions could be made for:

- tools or work equipment;
- special clothing or uniform;[26]
- telephone costs (including rental);[27]
- postage;
- fuel costs (including standing charges);
- secretarial expenses;[28]
- running a car (including petrol, tax, insurance, repairs and maintenance and rental on a leased car);[29]
- armed forces local overseas allowance (for extra overseas living expenses),[30] but not lodgings allowances if you are stationed in the UK,[31] and probably not rent allowances for police officers;[32]
- professional expenses for membership fees to an approved body if also deducted for income tax.[33]

Where any expenditure serves a dual purpose for both business and private use it should be apportioned as appropriate to the circumstances (and any Revenue determination normally followed).[34]

'Net' earnings means your gross earnings less any deductions made for:

- income tax;
- Class 1 NI contributions (but not Class 3 voluntary contributions[35]);
- half of any contribution you make towards a personal or occupational pension scheme.[36]

For HB and CTB, if your earnings are estimated the authorities estimate the amount of tax and NI you would expect to pay on those earnings, and deduct this plus half of any pension contribution you are paying.[37]

For HB and CTB, the local authority has the discretion to ignore changes in tax or NI contributions and the maximum rate of WTC or CTC for up to 30 benefit weeks. This can be used, for example, where Budget changes are not reflected in your actual income until several months later. When the changes are eventually taken into account and your benefit entitlement is either increased or reduced accordingly, you are not treated as having been underpaid or overpaid benefit during the period of the delay.[38]

What counts as earnings

'Earnings' means 'any remuneration or profit derived from ... employment'.

As well as your wages, this includes:[39]

- any bonus or commission (including tips);
- holiday pay. However, if your job ends, it counts as capital if your contract provides for it to be payable more than four weeks after termination of employment. If the contract does not provide for this (and it usually does not), holiday pay counts as earnings whenever it is actually paid.[40] If your job is interrupted, holiday pay counts as capital unless it is due to be paid within four weeks of the interruption. If you are involved in a trade dispute, holiday pay always counts as earnings, not as capital, for IS and income-based JSA and for IS only, it always counts as earnings if you go back to work after a trade dispute.[41] For more detail on payments at the end of a job, see p959;
- for HB and CTB, any statutory sick pay (SSP) or contractual sick pay.[42] For IS and income-based JSA all sick pay is treated as income other than earnings and therefore does not attract an earnings disregard and is counted in full less any tax, Class 1 NI contributions and half of any pension contributions;[43]
- for HB and CTB, any statutory maternity pay (SMP), statutory paternity pay (SPP) or statutory adoption pay (SAP), or any other pay made to you by your employer while you are on maternity, paternity or adoption leave.[44] For IS and income-based JSA all maternity, paternity or adoption pay is treated as income other than earnings and therefore does not attract an earnings disregard and is counted in full less any tax that is payable, Class 1 NI contributions and half of any pension contributions;[45]
- any payments made by your employer for expenses not 'wholly, exclusively and necessarily' incurred in carrying out your job, including any travel expenses to and from work, and any payments made to you for looking after members of your family;
- a retainer fee (eg, you may be paid during the school holidays if you work for the school meals service[46]) or a guarantee payment (eg, if you are working short time or laid off);[47]
- compensation payments in respect of the termination of your employment including:
  - an employment tribunal award as compensation for loss of earnings due to unfair dismissal,[48] or sex or race discrimination,[49] or for loss of maternity pay if an employer becomes insolvent, or for arrears of pay in respect of a reinstatement order, or because of a 'protective' award when an employer fails to comply with redundancy procedures;[50]

- pay in lieu of notice[51] and, except for periodic payments following a redundancy (which count instead as other income), pay in lieu of wages.[52] For HB/CTB, however, pay in lieu of notice only counts in so far as it represents loss of income (and not, therefore, any ex gratia award). **Note:** for IS/income-based JSA any pay in lieu of wages or notice will count for the period for which the payment relates so that you will be treated as if you are still in work in that period and may not be entitled to benefit (see p959). For how redundancy pay is treated, see p959;
- for income-based JSA, employment tribunal awards in respect of guaranteed payments, pay while suspended from work on medical or maternity grounds, or compensatory awards in respect of trade union activity, and certain other awards.[53]

For IS/JSA, compensatory refunds of contributions to an occupational scheme[54] and lump-sum payments made under the Iron and Steel Re-adaptation Benefits Scheme[55] are not treated as earnings;

- any payment of a non-cash voucher which is liable for Class 1 NI contributions.[56] Non-cash vouchers that are *not* liable for contributions are classed as payments in kind (see below).[57]

Examples of payments not counted as earnings:

- Payments in kind (eg, petrol) are ignored[58] unless you are on IS or income-based JSA and involved in a trade dispute (see p735), but the notional income rules may be applied instead (see p983).[59] Although non-cash vouchers which are liable for Class 1 NI contributions are not treated as payments in kind, vouchers which are not liable for contributions (eg, certain childcare and charitable vouchers) are treated as payments in kind and these are disregarded.[60]
- The value of any accommodation provided as part of your job is ignored for IS and income-based JSA.[61] For CTB, and for HB where job-related accommodation is in addition to the normal home, you should argue that this is payment in kind[62] and should be disregarded.
- An advance of earnings or a loan from your employer. This is treated as capital[63] (although it is still treated as earnings for IS or income-based JSA if you or your partner are involved in a trade dispute, or have been back at work after a dispute for no longer than 15 days).[64]
- Payments towards expenses that are 'wholly, exclusively and necessarily' incurred, such as travelling expenses during the course of your work.[65]
- If you are a local councillor, travelling expenses and subsistence payments are (and basic allowances may be[66]) ignored as expenses 'wholly, exclusively and necessarily' incurred in your work.
- Earnings payable abroad which cannot be brought into Britain – eg, because of exchange control regulations.[67] If your earnings are paid in another currency, any bank charges for converting them into sterling are deducted before taking them into account.[68]

- Any occupational pension.[69] This counts as income other than earnings and the net amount is taken into account in full.[70] See p948 for the occupational pension rules for contribution-based JSA.

Payments at the end of a job

Redundancy payments are normally treated as capital. However, for IS/JSA, if an employer makes a redundancy payment in excess of the statutory amount, the excess will be treated as earnings for the period it covers (see p960).[71]

Some redundancy schemes make periodic payments after leaving work; these are treated as income other than earnings.[72]

Other payments can cause problems, and are dealt with separately for each benefit.

Income support and income-based jobseeker's allowance

In most cases, when you finish a job you need to claim income-based JSA rather than IS. However, if you are not expected to be available for work, you may need to claim IS instead.

Leaving a full-time job

If you retire from a full-time job (16 hours or more a week) and you are aged at least 60 (women) or 65 (men), any payments counted as earnings (eg, final wages, holiday pay, etc.) that you receive are disregarded in full for IS and JSA.[73] You are not treated as being in full-time work for any period covered by those earnings after the end of your job. **Note:** if you have reached 60 you will have to claim pension credit (PC) instead of IS unless you have a partner aged under 60 who can claim IS for both of you. If you are a man aged between 60 and 65 you can choose to claim income-based JSA or PC.

In all other cases, only the following final payments that you receive when you leave a *full-time* job affect your right to IS or income-based JSA (because you will still be treated as if you are still in that job for the period for which these payments are made):[74]

- holiday pay which counts as earnings (see p957);
- pay in lieu of notice;
- pay in lieu of wages;
- for IS, any other compensation payments in respect of that job, but only if you have not had any or all of the pay in lieu of notice due to you, and not counting any compensation payments that are counted as if they are or are not earnings. In practice, this will mean redundancy pay in excess of the statutory amount, any ex gratia payments or payments in settlement of a claim to an employment tribunal. Any payment is divided by the maximum payable under the statutory redundancy scheme (usually uprated yearly). The result is the number of weeks the payment will cover up to a maximum of your notice period, whether statutory, contractual or customary.[75] If the amount is less

than the statutory maximum for one week or if the calculation creates a fraction, these are treated as capital.[76] If the ex gratia payment is not compensation but a gift (eg, a 'golden handshake'), you should argue that it should be treated as capital, not income;

- for income-based JSA, any other compensation payments in respect of that job including redundancy pay in excess of statutory redundancy pay, except for any awards payable by an employment tribunal which are treated as earnings, refunds of pension contributions or any payments in respect of wages earned before you lost your job. Do not count as compensation a periodic sum paid for redundancy (this counts as other income) or any occupational pension, expenses payment, sick pay or maternity pay.

Period in which the payments are taken into account
You are treated as being in full-time work (and therefore ineligible for IS/JSA) for the number of weeks covered by these payments after your employment ended.[77] These payments are taken into account consecutively and in the following order:

- any pay in lieu of wages or in lieu of notice; *then*
- payments of compensation for loss of employment; *then*
- holiday pay.[78]

The period for which you are treated as being in full-time work starts on the earliest date that any of these payments are due to be paid.[79]

Example
Mary leaves her full-time job with a final week's wages, a week in hand and one week's holiday pay. All three amounts are due to be paid on 30 May. Only the holiday pay will be taken into account, starting from 30 May. Mary will not be entitled to IS/income-based JSA for one week.

If you receive an award of compensation for unfair dismissal or certain other awards of pay from an employment tribunal, these are taken into account as earnings in calculating the amount of your IS or income-based JSA from when the award is made.

If your employment is interrupted (eg, you are laid off), any holiday pay which is treated as your earnings affects your right to IS/income-based JSA; all other payments are disregarded except that any retainer you are paid is taken into account as earnings in calculating the amount of your IS/income-based JSA.[80] If you have been suspended, any payment you receive is taken into account and affects your right to IS/income-based JSA.

Leaving a part-time job

If you were working part time (less than 16 hours a week) before you claimed IS, any payments you receive, except any retainer, when the job ends or is interrupted (unless you have been suspended) are ignored and do not affect your IS. For income-based JSA payments are ignored except for a retainer, any compensation payments, holiday pay or awards payable by an employment tribunal which are treated as earnings (see p957).[81]

If, however, you were claiming IS or income-based JSA while you were in part-time work, any payments made to you when that job ends are taken into account as earnings in the normal way except that, for IS only, a payment of compensation is taken into account for a period of one week only.[82] Your wages, including any final wages, are counted first (for both IS and income-based JSA), then (for IS only) any pay in lieu of wages or notice, then (for IS/income-based JSA) any compensation paid by your employer for loss of employment, and then any holiday pay.[83] Once the period covered by payments at the end of a full- or part-time job has ended, any money remaining is treated as capital.[84]

Because sick pay does not count as earnings for IS/income-based JSA, any arrears of sick pay you receive when a job ends will be treated as income from when it is paid for the same length of time covered by the arrears.[85]

Housing benefit and council tax benefit

If you leave a full-time job for any reason other than retirement, any payments you receive should be disregarded except:[86]

- holiday pay which counts as earnings (see p957);
- pay in lieu of wages (except for periodical redundancy payments);
- pay in lieu of notice or other compensation for loss of employment, but only in so far as it represents loss of income;
- an award of compensation for unfair dismissal, or certain other awards of pay from an employment tribunal (see p957);
- any retainer fee.

Pay is disregarded in this way only if your employment ends before you claim HB/CTB.

If your work is interrupted before you claim HB/CTB, your earnings are disregarded except for holiday pay which counts as earnings (see p957), sick pay, maternity pay, paternity or adoption pay and any retainer paid to you.[87]

Where you were in part-time work (ie, less than 16 hours a week) before claiming HB or CTB, any earnings paid when your job ended or was interrupted are disregarded, *except* where that payment is a retainer or sick pay, maternity pay, paternity or adoption pay.[88] This disregard does not apply to earnings paid when your job ends if you are already getting HB/CTB.

Earnings from self-employment

Even if you are an employee, any other earnings from work you do as a self-employed person are assessed under the following rules.

Calculating net earnings

Your **'net profit'** over the period before your claim must be worked out. This consists of your self-employed earnings, including any allowance from a Department for Work and Pensions (DWP) scheme to assist you with your business (unless, for IS and JSA, paid during a period of test trading to those undertaking the self-employment option of the New Deal, including the New Deal for Lone Parents),[89] *minus*:[90]

- reasonable expenses (see p962); *and*
- income tax and NI contributions; *and*
- half of any premium paid in respect of a personal pension scheme or a retirement annuity contract which is eligible for tax relief.[91] For IS and income-based JSA, if you or your partner (if any) are aged 60 or over, you must supply certain information about the scheme or annuity contract to the relevant authority if requested.[92]

If you receive payments for board and lodging charges these do not count as earnings[93] but as other income (less any disregards, see p976).

Reasonable expenses

Expenses must be reasonable and 'wholly and exclusively' incurred for the purposes of your business.[94] This involves similar considerations to those that apply in the allowances permitted in the assessment of 'gross' earnings of employed earners. Where a car or telephone, for example, is used partly for business and partly for private purposes, the costs of it can be apportioned and the amount attributable to business use can be deducted.[95]

Reasonable expenses include:[96]

- repayments of capital on loans for replacing equipment and machinery;
- repayment of capital on loans for, and income spent on, the repair of a business asset except where this is covered by insurance;
- interest on a loan taken out for the purposes of the business;
- excess of VAT paid over VAT received.

Reasonable expenses do not include:[97]

- any capital expenditure;
- depreciation, although the normal accountancy practice in valuing stock should be applied so that the 'cost of sales' (the cost of any opening stock plus purchases less any closing stock) should be set against actual sales;[98]
- money for setting up or expanding the business – eg, the cost of adapting the business premises;

- any loss incurred before the beginning of the current assessment period. If the business makes a loss, the net profit is nil. The losses of one business cannot be offset against the profit of any other business in which you are engaged, or against your earnings as an employee[99] (although where two businesses or employments share expenses these may be apportioned and offset);[100]
- capital repayments on loans taken out for business purposes;
- business entertainment expenses;
- for HB and CTB (if you and your partner are aged under 60), debts (other than proven bad debts) – but the expenses of recovering a debt can be deducted.

Working out average earnings from self-employment

For **IS and income-based JSA**, the weekly amount is the average of earnings:[101]

- over a period of any one year (normally the last year for which accounts are available);
- over a more appropriate period where you have recently taken up self-employment or there has been a change which will affect your business or for any other reason if a different period may enable any part or all of your income and expenditure to be calculated more accurately.[102]

If your earnings are royalties or copyright payments, the amount of earnings is divided by the weekly amount of IS or income-based JSA which would be payable if you had not received this income plus the amount which would be disregarded from those earnings.[103] You are not entitled to IS/income-based JSA for the resulting number of weeks.

For **HB/CTB** the amount of your weekly earnings is averaged out over an 'appropriate' period (usually based on your last year's trading accounts) which must not be longer than a year.[104]

Childminders

Childminders, in practice, are always treated as self-employed. Your net profit is deemed to be one-third of your earnings less income tax, your NI contributions and half of certain pension contributions (see p962).[105] The rest of your earnings are completely ignored.

Disregarded earnings

Some of your earnings from employment or self-employment are disregarded and do not affect your benefit. The amount of the 'disregard' depends on your circumstances. The three main levels of disregard are £25 or £20 or £5/£10. For HB and CTB there is an additional disregard depending on the hours you work and a childcare costs disregard (see p965). These disregards are explained below.

For the amount of disregarded earnings for contribution-based JSA, see p947.

£25 disregard

Lone parents on HB or CTB have £25 of their earnings ignored.[106] This does not apply to anyone claiming IS or income-based JSA.

£20 disregard

£20 of your earnings (including those of your partner, if any) is disregarded if:

- for IS or income-based JSA, you are a lone parent;[107]
- you or your partner qualifies for a disability premium (see p886).[108] For IS and income-based JSA, you are treated as qualifying for the premium if you would do so but for being in hospital or a care home;
- you or your partner qualifies for a carer's premium (see p896). The disregard applies to the carer's earnings. For a couple, if both partners get the carer's premium, £20 is disregarded from their combined earnings. If you are the carer and you are the claimant and your earnings are less than £20, the remainder of the disregard can be used up on your partner's earnings as an auxiliary coastguard, etc. (see below), or up to £5 (for HB and CTB up to £10) of it can be used up on your partner's earnings from another job but the total disregard cannot be more than £20;[109]
- you or your partner are an auxiliary coastguard, part-time firefighter, part-time member of a lifeboat crew or member of the Territorial Army.[110] If you earn less than £20 for doing any of these services you can use up to £5 (for HB and CTB up to £10 if you have a partner) of the disregard on another job[111] or on a partner's earnings from another job;[112]
- you are a member of a couple, your benefit would include a disability premium but for the fact that one of you qualifies for the higher pensioner premium (see p890), and one of you is under 60 and either of you are in employment. For IS and income-based JSA, you are treated as qualifying for the higher pensioner premium if you would do so but for being in hospital or a care home;[113]
- you or your partner qualifies for the higher pensioner premium (see p890) and, immediately before reaching age 60, you or your partner were in employment (part time for IS and income-based JSA) and you were entitled to a £20 disregard because of qualifying for a disability premium. Since reaching 60, you or your partner must have continued in employment (part time for IS and income-based JSA), although breaks of up to eight weeks when you were not getting IS or income-based JSA (or HB/CTB where you claim either of these benefits) are ignored. For IS and income-based JSA you are treated as qualifying for the higher pensioner premium even if you are in hospital or a care home.[114]

If you qualify under more than one category you still have a maximum of only £20 of your earnings disregarded.

Basic £5 or £10 disregard

If you do not qualify for a £25 or £20 disregard, £5 of your earnings is disregarded if you are single. If you claim as a member of a couple, £10 of your total earnings is disregarded – whether or not you are both working.[115]

Additional earnings disregard for housing benefit and council tax benefit[116]

For **HB/CTB only**, whichever earnings disregard applies is increased by £14.50 if:

- you or your partner (if any) receive the 30-hour element as part of your (or your partner's) WTC (see p1356); *or*
- you or your partner are aged 25 or over and work 30 hours a week or more on average; *or*
- you or your partner work 16 hours or more a week on average and your HB/CTB includes the family premium (see p884); *or*
- you are a lone parent and work 16 hours or more a week on average; *or*
- you or your partner (if any) work 16 hours or more a week on average and your HB/CTB includes the disability or higher pensioner premium (see p886). For couples, the partner for whom the premium is awarded must be working 16 hours a week or more on average; *or*
- you or your partner (if any) get a 50-plus element in WTC, or would qualify for one if you applied for WTC (see p1358).

This additional earnings disregard is based on the qualifying conditions for the 30-hour element in WTC but extends it to include many people working 16 hours a week. The additional earnings disregard does not apply where your total earnings are less than the total of £14.50 plus any earnings disregard (see above) and childcare costs disregard (see below). In that case, £14.50 is disregarded from any WTC which is awarded to you or your partner, but the earnings disregard is not increased.

Note: as with the ordinary earnings disregards, only one additional disregard can be allowed from your (or your partner's) earnings.

Childcare costs for housing benefit and council tax benefit

For **IS and income-based JSA**, no allowance is made for any childcare charges you may have to pay.

For **HB/CTB**,[117] an allowance of up to £175 a week for one child, or up to £300 a week for two or more children, can be deducted from your (or your partner's) earnings (from employment or self-employment) in respect of childcare costs if you are:

- a lone parent working 16 hours a week or more; *or*

- a couple and both of you work 16 hours a week or more, or else one of you works 16 hours a week or more and the other is 'incapacitated' (see p967) or in hospital or prison.

Lone parents and couples can still make this deduction for childcare costs if they are off work sick, although for lone parents it stops after 28 weeks (see p967 for details).

If you or your partner (if any) also get WTC or CTC, in some circumstances your earnings (and, if applicable, those of your partner) and the WTC/CTC are added together before the deduction for childcare costs is made. This applies where your earnings, once other HB/CTB deductions have been taken off, are less than the deduction for childcare costs.[118]

The childcare allowance only applies if you have any child(ren) in your family under the age of 15 (or 16 if s/he is 'disabled' – see p968) for whom you are paying charges for childcare which is provided:[119]

- by a registered childminder or other registered childcare provider (such as a nursery or local authority daycare service); *or*
- out of school hours for children between the ages of 8 and 15/16, by a school on school premises or a local authority – eg, an out-of-hours or holiday play scheme; *or*
- by a childcare scheme operating on Crown property; *or*
- in schools or establishments exempt from registration; *or*
- by 'approved providers' who are not required to register but who operate out-of-hours or breakfast clubs for children aged 8 to 15/16; *or*
- by a foster parent for a child other than the one fostered; *or*
- in the child's own home, by someone registered as a domiciliary care worker or approved under the Home Care Providers Scheme who is not a relative of your child.

Note: a child is not treated as having reached the age of 15/16 until the day before the first Monday in September *following* her/his 15th/16th birthday.[120]

You cannot include charges for care provided by a relative of the child in the child's own home even if s/he is a registered childminder, nor charges paid by you to your partner or by your partner to you for a child in your family. Charges for compulsory education do not count.

If you or your partner (if any) are on maternity, paternity or adoption leave you will be treated as *working*, and so be able to deduct childcare charges if you or your partner (if any):[121]

- were working and paying childcare charges that qualify (see above) in the week immediately before the maternity, paternity or adoption leave began; *and*
- are entitled to SMP, SPP, SAP or maternity allowance (MA) (see Chapter 17), or are getting IS because you are on paternity leave.

You are no longer treated as working and thus cannot get childcare charges deducted any longer when:

- the maternity, paternity or adoption leave comes to an end; *or*
- if you are not receiving the childcare element of WTC, you or your partner stop getting SMP, SPP, SAP or MA, or IS because you are on paternity leave; *or*
- if you are receiving the childcare element of WTC when you stop getting SMP, SPP, SAP or MA or IS because you are on paternity leave, you stop getting the childcare element of WTC.

You can deduct charges for childcare for the new child in your family while you are still on maternity, paternity or adoption leave.

Childcare costs and ill health or disability

As long as you were working at least 16 hours a week immediately before you started getting one of the following benefits, you can still deduct charges for childcare while off work sick for the first 28 weeks while you are getting:[122]

- SSP;
- short-term lower rate incapacity benefit (IB);
- IS on incapacity grounds;
- NI credits for incapacity.

After 28 weeks, lone parents who are off work sick can no longer deduct childcare charges but couples can do so if one of them is treated as 'incapacitated'.

You (or your partner) are treated as **'incapacitated'** if:[123]

- you get short-term (higher rate) or long-term IB (see Chapter 12); *or*
- you get severe disablement allowance (SDA) (see Chapter 20); *or*
- you get attendance allowance (AA), disability living allowance (DLA) or constant attendance allowance (or an equivalent award under the war pensions or industrial injuries schemes) or you would receive one of these benefits but for the fact that you (or your partner) are in hospital; *or*
- you have an invalid carriage or similar vehicle; *or*
- your HB and CTB includes (or would include, but for a disqualification of up to six weeks for misconduct) a disability or higher pensioner premium (see Chapter 35) for the incapacity. **Note:** this particular rule only applies to HB and CTB if you and your partner (if any) are aged under 60; *or*
- you (but not your partner) have been treated as incapable of work for a continuous period of 196 days or more (disregarding any break of up to 56 days, or 52 weeks if you are a 'welfare to work' beneficiary); *or*
- you are aged 80 or over, or are aged less than 80 and satisfy the qualifying conditions for the disability or higher pensioner premiums (or would qualify but for you being treated as capable of work). **Note:** this particular rule only applies to HB and CTB if you or your partner are aged 60 or over.

A child is defined as **'disabled'** if s/he is:[124]

- in receipt of DLA (or payment has been suspended because s/he is a hospital in-patient);
- registered as blind or was taken off the register in the last 28 weeks.

Calculating childcare costs[125]

The costs to be taken into account are estimated over whatever period, not exceeding a year, that will give the best estimate of the average weekly charge based on information to be provided by the childminder or care provider.

Points to note

- These rules do *not* apply to IS or JSA and *only* apply to HB and CTB. There are also separate childcare costs rules for non-means-tested benefits (see p944).
- £175 is the maximum amount that can be deducted for one child even if the actual cost of your childcare is more. £300 is the maximum even if you have to pay for childcare for more than two children and even if the actual cost is more.
- The costs of any childcare provided by a relative or friend (other than your partner – but a former partner, who may even be the child's parent, is not excluded) may be allowed so long as s/he is a registered childminder.
- It is not necessary for the childcare to be provided only while you are at work, nor for it to be in any way work-related, and there is no requirement for the charges to be reasonable (so the £175/£300 charge could be incurred for only one hour of childcare).

Income other than earnings

As well as income from earnings, most other forms of income are taken into account in full less any tax due. To work out the weekly income to take into account, check whether the payment can be disregarded in part or in full (see below), deduct any tax due and work out the weekly amount (see p987). Where a taxable benefit or other unearned income is not taxed at source and you have not yet had a tax assessment, ask the Revenue for a forecast of tax due on that income, otherwise the DWP itself needs to calculate how much tax to deduct.[126]

Benefits and tax credits

Benefits and tax credits that count in full:

- carer's allowance (CA);
- child benefit is taken into account:
  - in full for HB/CTB;
  - for IS and income-based JSA, but only if you have been getting IS or income-based JSA since before 6 April 2004 with a child already included in your claim (ie, you still have amounts for children in your IS/income-based JSA)

and you do not yet have an award of CTC. In this case, child benefit continues to be taken into account in IS/income-based JSA until your CTC award begins.[127] £10.50 a week is ignored if you are getting child benefit for a child under 1 year old;[128]

- CTC counts in full for HB and CTB but is disregarded for IS and income-based JSA. See p971 if your CTC is reduced to recover a tax credit overpayment;
- child's special allowance and war orphan's pension;
- contribution-based JSA;
- IB and SDA;
- industrial injuries benefits, except constant attendance allowance and exceptionally severe disablement allowance which are disregarded;
- MA;
- retirement pensions;
- SSP, SMP, SPP and SAP count for IS and income-based JSA only, less any Class 1 NI contributions and half of any pension contributions and any tax.[129] These are treated as earnings for HB and CTB and therefore may benefit from an earnings disregard (see p963);[130]
- widow's pension, bereavement allowance and industrial death benefit;
- WTC counts in full for IS and income-based JSA. For HB and CTB, WTC is taken into account in full (but see p971 if a tax credit overpayment is being deducted) except for those whose earnings are too low to use the whole £14.50 additional full-time earnings disregard (see p965). In this case, £14.50 is disregarded from your WTC instead of your earnings. You must satisfy the conditions for the additional earnings disregard and have earnings of less than £14.50 plus whichever other earnings disregard applies plus any childcare costs disregard.[131]

Benefits that are ignored completely:[132]

- AA;[133]
- child benefit is ignored for IS and income-based JSA[134] unless you have a child included in a pre-6 April 2004 claim and do not have a CTC award (see p968). It counts in full for HB and CTB;
- CTC is ignored completely for IS and income-based JSA.[135] CTC is taken into account in full for HB and CTB;
- constant attendance allowance, exceptionally severe disablement allowance or severe disablement occupational allowance paid because of an injury at work or a war injury;[136]
- DLA care component and mobility component;[137]
- guardian's allowance;[138]
- mobility supplement under the War Pensions Scheme;[139]
- pensioner's Christmas bonus (see Chapter 3);[140]
- any extra-statutory payment made to you to compensate for non-payment of IS, income-based JSA, mobility allowance, mobility supplement, AA or DLA;[141]
- social fund payments.[142] They are also disregarded as capital indefinitely;[143]

- HB, CTB or, formerly, community charge benefit;[144]
- certain special war widows' payments[145] and any special or supplementary payments to pre-1973 war widows or widowers;[146]
- any increase for adult or child dependants who are not members of your family (see p809), where you are getting IB, MA, SDA, widowed mother's allowance, widowed parent's allowance, retirement pension, industrial injuries benefits (including unemployability supplement), CA or a service pension;[147]
- IS and income-based JSA are ignored for HB and CTB.[148] There are special HB and CTB rules for IS and income-based JSA claimants (see pp112 and 206);
- resettlement benefit paid to certain patients who are discharged from hospital and who had been in hospital for more than a year before 11 April 1988;[149]
- any transitional payment made to compensate you for loss of benefit due to the changes in benefit rules in April 1988, except for income-based JSA;[150]
- any payment made to the Secretary of State to compensate for the loss of HB (whether due to the 1988 changes in benefit rules or not);[151]
- any payment in consequence of a reduction in liability for council tax (or, formerly, community charge).[152]

Benefits that have £15 ignored:

- for HB/CTB only, widowed mother's allowance and widowed parent's allowance.[153]

Benefits that have £10 ignored:

- for IS and income-based JSA only, widowed mother's allowance and widowed parent's allowance;[154]
- war disablement pension[155] (including any tax-free service invaliding pension or 'service attributable pension'[156]);
- war widow's or widower's pension;[157]
- widow's or widower's pension payable to a spouse of a member of the Royal Navy, Army or Royal Air Force who was disabled or died as a result of service in the armed forces;[158]
- an extra-statutory payment made instead of the above pensions;[159]
- similar payments made by another country;[160]
- a pension from Germany or Austria paid to the victims of Nazi persecution.[161]

Even if you have more than two payments which attract a £10 disregard, only £20 in all can be ignored.[162] However, the £10 disregard allowed on these war pensions is additional to the total disregard of any mobility supplement or AA (ie, constant attendance allowance, exceptionally severe disablement allowance and severe disablement occupational allowance) paid as part of a war disablement pension.

The £10 disregard may overlap with other disregards on student loans (see p645) and charitable, voluntary or personal injury payments (see p973) when a combined maximum of £20 is allowed.

Local authorities are given a limited discretion to increase the £10 disregard on war disablement, war widows' or widowers' pensions and the pension payable to widows or widowers of members of the Royal Navy, Army or Royal Air Force, when assessing income for HB and CTB.[163] Some local authorities disregard the full amount of these pensions, and some do not increase the disregard at all, so you should check your own local authority's policy on this issue. It has been held that a local authority must at least consider the nature and purpose of such pensions when deciding whether or not to disregard them, and the courts have indicated that it may be appropriate to apply a disregard to retrospective awards.[164]

Benefit delays

Problems can arise where a decision maker tries to take into account a benefit you are not receiving (such as child benefit), that has been delayed. In such a case, the benefit should not be treated as income possessed by you. For IS and income-based JSA, you should get your full benefit and leave the DWP to deduct the difference from arrears of the delayed benefit when it is eventually awarded.[165]

For the treatment of payments of arrears of certain benefits and CTC and WTC, see p1035.

Tax credit payments and overpayments

For **HB and CTB**, where a tax credit overpayment from a previous year is being recovered from the current year's tax credit award, it is the amount of your tax credit award less any reduction to recover the overpayment that is taken into account.[166] Guidance advises local authorities not to treat you as having been underpaid HB or CTB for the earlier period when tax credits were being overpaid, so your HB/CTB award is not revised for that period.[167]

The situation where you have been overpaid in the same year as your tax credit award and your tax credits are reduced accordingly is similar. This is because it is the actual amount of the tax credit award still due to be paid to you that is taken into account, instalment by instalment. For example, if paid weekly or four-weekly, each tax credit instalment is taken into account for the 7 or 28 days ending on the day on which the instalment is due to be paid.[168] If the Revenue gives you an additional payment (eg, because your reduced tax credit award leaves you in hardship), local authorities count this as income for HB and CTB.[169]

For **IS and income-based JSA**, the rules are less clear, however the intention is to take into account the actual award paid – eg, after any overpayment has been deducted or additional payment added. WTC is taken into account from the start of the WTC award, if you already get IS or income-based JSA, at a weekly amount averaged over the whole period of the award. If you already get WTC when you make your IS/JSA claim, WTC counts as income from the start of the IS/JSA claim at a weekly amount averaged over the period of the WTC award left to run.[170]

Maintenance payments

There are special rules about the treatment of any payments of maintenance or child support maintenance which you or your partner receive for yourself/selves or any child(ren) in your family. These are explained in Chapter 34.

Most maintenance counts in full while you are claiming **IS or income-based JSA** (but see p54 for the rules on entitlement to a child maintenance bonus) but there is a £10 a week disregard (called a child maintenance premium) in the following cases:[171]

- you get child maintenance under the 'new rules' child support scheme in respect of a child or young person who is a member of your family;
- you get child maintenance under an agreement or court order first paid on or after 3 March 2003;
- you get voluntary child maintenance payments (eg, pending an assessment) and you claimed IS or income-based JSA on or after 16 February 2004;
- you are already on IS or income-based JSA on 16 February 2004 and on or after that date you begin to receive voluntary child maintenance payments. You will not get the £10 disregard if you were previously getting voluntary maintenance while on IS or income-based JSA.[172]

For **HB and CTB**, £15 of any maintenance payments made by your or your partner's former partner or the parent of any child in your family is disregarded, but only if you are a lone parent or a couple with a child.[173]

If you pay maintenance

If you *pay* maintenance to a former partner or a child not living with you, your payments are not disregarded for the purpose of calculating your income for any benefits.[174] Even if you are on IS or income-based JSA you may still have to pay child support maintenance (see p862).

Student loans and grants

There are special rules on the treatment of student grants and loans, career development loans and Access Fund payments paid to students. These are explained in Chapter 25.

Adoption, fostering, guardianship and residence order payments

Adoption allowance

An adoption allowance is disregarded in full for IS and income-based JSA unless your benefit still includes amounts for children as described below.[175]

An adoption allowance is taken into account for:

- IS and income-based JSA if you have been getting benefit since before 6 April 2004 with a child included in your claim and do not yet have an award of CTC;[176]

- HB and CTB.

In the two cases above, the adoption allowance is taken into account in full up to the level of the adopted child's personal allowance and any disabled child premium.[177] Above that level it is ignored. For IS and income-based JSA, if the child has capital over £3,000, you get no benefit for that child and all the adoption allowance is disregarded.[178] However, if the adoption allowance is paid for a child or young person who is not a member of your family (eg, because s/he is in custody), it is fully disregarded in England and Wales[179] but, in Scotland, only the amount you spend on the child is disregarded, while any you keep or use for yourself is taken into account.[180]

Fostering allowance

The way a fostering allowance is treated depends on whether the arrangement is official or private. If a child is placed or boarded out with you by the local authority or a voluntary organisation under specific legal provisions,[181] the child is not counted as a member of your family (see p821) so you are not entitled to any benefit for her/him, but any fostering allowances you receive while the child is placed with you should be ignored altogether.[182] If the fostering arrangement is a private one, any money you receive from the child's parent(s) is counted as maintenance (see p851). If the money you receive is not from the child's parent(s), you should probably be treated as a childminder (see p963).

Residence order

If you are paid a residence order allowance by the local authority, this is treated in the same way as an adoption allowance (see p972).[183] If not disregarded altogether under the rules above, arrears of residence order allowances are treated as capital for IS and income-based JSA.[184] Any payments made by the biological parents count as maintenance (see p851).

Special guardianship allowance

A special guardianship allowance (payable in England and Wales) is treated in the same way as an adoption allowance.[185] However, for IS and income-based JSA, note that guidance suggests that this would be ignored completely even for those who still have child personal allowances included in their benefit.[186]

Charitable, voluntary and personal injury payments

Payments from the Macfarlane and similar trusts

Any payments, including payments in kind, from the Macfarlane Trust, the Macfarlane (Special Payments) Trust, the Macfarlane (Special Payments) (No.2) Trust, the Fund, the Eileen Trust or either of the Independent Living Funds are disregarded in full.[187]

The Macfarlane Trusts make payments to people with haemophilia. The Fund was set up on 24 April 1992 for people who do not have haemophilia who contracted HIV through blood or tissue transfusions. The Skipton Fund is for people infected with hepatitis C through NHS blood products.

If you have, or had, haemophilia, or have received a payment from the Fund, the Skipton Fund or the Eileen Trust, the following payments from money that originally came from any of the three Macfarlane Trusts, the Fund, the Skipton Fund or the Eileen Trust are also disregarded in full:[188]

- any payment made by you, or on your behalf, to, or for the benefit of:
  - your partner, or former partner from whom you are not estranged or divorced;
  - any child who is a member of your family (see p818) or who was but is now a member of another family; *or*
- if you have no partner or former partner (other than one from whom you are estranged or divorced), or children, any payment made by you (or from your estate in the event of your death) to:
  - your parent or step-parent; *or*
  - your guardian if you have no parent or step-parent and were a child (see p86) or student at the date of the payment (or at the date of your death).

  In the case of a payment to a parent, step-parent or guardian, this is only disregarded until two years after your death;
- any payment made by your partner, or former partner from whom you are not estranged or divorced, or on her/his behalf, to, or for the benefit of:
  - you;
  - any child who is a member of your family, or who was and is now a member of another family.

Any income or capital that derives from any such payment is also disregarded.

Other payments

Most other charitable or voluntary payments that are made irregularly and are intended to be made irregularly are treated as capital and are unlikely to affect your claim unless they take your capital above the limit.[189] However, if you are on IS or income-based JSA it counts as income:

- if you are involved in a trade dispute, and for IS only, for the first 15 days following your return to work after a dispute (see p735);[190] *or*
- where payments made to a child's boarding school are treated as the child's notional income (see p954).[191]

Payments made on a regular basis

Charitable, voluntary or certain personal injury payments made, or due to be made, regularly are completely ignored if they are intended and used for:[192]

- anything *except* food, ordinary clothing or footwear, household fuel, council tax, water charges and rent (less any non-dependant deductions) for which HB could be payable; *and*
- for IS and income-based JSA only, housing costs which could be met by IS or income-based JSA. Where the local authority has placed you in a care home that is more expensive than normal for a person of your needs because you preferred that home, a charitable or voluntary payment towards the *extra* cost is ignored for IS and income-based JSA.[193]

A **'voluntary payment'** is one given without getting anything back in return.[194]

School uniform and sportswear are examples of clothing and footwear that are not ordinary.

If not ignored altogether, charitable, voluntary or personal injury payments have a £20 disregard, although this disregard may overlap with other disregards for certain war pensions and widows' benefits (see p970) or student loans (see p645) when a combined maximum of £20 is allowed.[195] **Note:** this is a weekly disregard so payments spread over different or successive benefit weeks attract a £20 disregard for each.

From 3 October 2005, all charitable, voluntary and personal injury payments from a trust fund will be disregarded for HB and CTB.[196]

For HB and CTB, discretionary grants to Canadian war veterans or their widows settled in the UK should also be treated as voluntary payments and attract a £20 disregard.[197] It is arguable that this disregard should also apply to IS and income-based JSA, and to any other discretionary grants paid to any other overseas war veterans (or their widows) who are settled in the UK.

For IS and income-based JSA, these rules do not apply where you are involved in a trade dispute and, for IS only, for the first 15 days following your return to work after a trade dispute.

Payments from a former partner, or the parent of your child, are dealt with as maintenance (see p867).

The **personal injury payments** which qualify under the above rules are:[198]

- payments from a trust fund set up out of money paid because of any personal injury to you, and which are not charitable or voluntary payments; *or*
- payments under an annuity purchased either under an agreement or court order set up because of any personal injury to you, or from money paid because of any personal injury to you; *or*
- payments you get under an agreement or court order because of any personal injury to you.

For the treatment of sports awards made by the Sports Council out of National Lottery funds, see p982.

See also: payments made to someone else on your behalf (p985) and payments disregarded under miscellaneous income (p982).

For the treatment of concessionary coal or cash in lieu of payments, see p908 of CPAG's *Welfare Benefits Handbook* 2001/02.

Income from tenants and lodgers

Lettings without board

If you let out room(s) in your home to tenants, sub-tenants or licensees under a formal contractual arrangement, £4 of your weekly charge for each tenant, sub-tenant or licensee (and her/his family) is ignored, plus an extra £10.55 if the charge covers heating costs.[199] The balance counts as income.

If someone shares your home under an informal arrangement, any payment made by her/him to you for her/his living and accommodation costs is ignored,[200] but a non-dependant deduction may be made from any HB/CTB or housing costs paid with IS/income-based JSA (see pp212, 115 and 924).

Boarders

If you have a boarder(s) on a commercial basis in your own home, and the boarder or any member of her/his family is not a close relative of yours, the first £20 of the weekly charge is ignored and half of any balance remaining is then taken into account as your income.[201] (With HB and CTB, there is no specific reference to non-commercial arrangements or close relatives, but the rules on contrived tenancies could possibly apply – see p199.) This applies for each boarder you have. The charge must normally include at least some meals.[202] If you have a business partner, even though your gross income includes just your share of the weekly charge to boarders, you still get the full disregard of £20 plus half the excess for each boarder.[203]

Note: whether you let part of your home to a tenant, sub-tenant, licensee or to a boarder, any income left after applying the above disregards may be considered to be intended to be used to meet any housing costs of your own which are not met by IS, income-based JSA, PC or HB, and may therefore be offset accordingly (see p981).[204]

Tenants in other properties

If you have a freehold interest in a property other than your home and you let it out, the rent is treated as capital.[205] This rule also applies if you have a leasehold interest in another property which you are sub-letting. There is disagreement between commissioners as to whether it is the gross rent which should be taken into account, or only the sum left after deducting expenses.[206]

Income from capital

In general, actual income generated from capital (eg, interest on savings) is ignored as income[207] but counts as *capital*[208] from the date you are due to receive

Mortgage and insurance payments

The following income is ignored:

- for IS and income-based JSA only, payments you receive under a mortgage protection policy which you took out, and which you use, to pay the housing costs which are not being met by the DWP in your IS or income-based JSA[238] (for restrictions on housing costs see p921). However, if the amount you receive exceeds the total of:
  - the interest you pay on a qualifying loan which is not met by the DWP;
  - capital repayments on a qualifying loan; *and*
  - any premiums you pay on the policy in question and any building insurance policy,

  then the excess is counted as your income;
- for IS and income-based JSA only, and as long as you have not already used insurance payments for the same purpose, *any* money *you* receive which is given, and which *you* use to make:[239]
  - payments under a secured loan which do not qualify under the housing costs rules (see Chapter 36);
  - interest payments which are not met under the housing costs rules, even though some interest payments under the loan in question are met;
  - capital repayments on a qualifying loan;
  - payments of premiums on an insurance policy which you took out to insure against the risk of not being able to make the payments in the above three categories, and premiums on a building insurance policy;
  - payment of any rent that is not covered by HB (see Chapter 10);
  - payment of the part of your accommodation charge in a care home that exceeds that payable by a local authority;
- for HB and CTB (see above for IS/income-based JSA), payments you receive under an insurance policy you took out to insure against the risk of being unable to maintain payments on a loan secured on your home. However, anything you get above the total of the following counts as your income:
  - the amount you use to maintain your payments; *and*
  - any premium you pay for the policy; *and*
  - any premium for an insurance policy which you had to take out to insure against loss or damage to your home;[240]
- for IS, income-based JSA, HB and CTB, payments you receive under an insurance policy you took out to insure against the risk of being unable to maintain hire purchase or similar payments or other loan payments – eg, credit card debts. However, anything you get above the amount you use to make your payments and the premium for the policy counts as your income.[241]

Social services, community care and supporting people payments

The following payments are ignored:

- a payment from a social services department under sections 17, 23B, 23C or 24A of the Children Act 1989, or, in Scotland, a payment from a social work department under section 12 of the Social Work (Scotland) Act 1968 or under sections 29 or 30 of the Children (Scotland) Act 1995 – ie, payments from social services to assist children in need or young people who have been in care or been looked after by them.[242] For IS and income-based JSA, if you have been getting benefit since before 6 April 2004 with a child included in your claim and do not yet have a CTC award, such payments are not ignored if you or your partner are involved in or, for IS only, have returned to work after a trade dispute (see p735);
- any community care direct payments. Local authorities pay these to disabled people or carers to buy their own services instead of providing services directly;[243]
- any payment you receive for looking after a person temporarily in your care if it is paid under community care arrangements by a health authority, primary care trust, local authority, voluntary organisation or by the person being looked after;[244]
- if the local authority makes a lump-sum payment to enable you to make adaptations to your home for a disabled child, this is treated as capital and ignored;[245]
- payments by a local authority for support services to help you live independently (ie, under the supporting people programme) are ignored indefinitely.[246] Landlords receiving such payments for providing the services do not benefit from this disregard, although other disregards may apply (see p976).

Miscellaneous income

The following income is ignored:

- education maintenance allowances (or corresponding payments).[247] These are paid to young people staying on at school or other non-advanced education beyond school leaving age;
- any payment to cover your expenses if you are working as an unpaid volunteer, or working unpaid for a charity or voluntary organisation;[248]
- payments in kind (unless, for IS or income-based JSA, you or your partner are involved in a trade dispute, see p735).[249] These may include food, fuel, cigarettes,[250] clothing, holidays, gifts, accommodation, transport, or nursery education vouchers[251] (but see p983 for the rules on notional income and p958 for the rules on non-cash vouchers paid as earnings)*. Items for essential living

* But payments to a third party which are then used to provide benefits in kind to you are taken into account.

needs provided from the National Asylum Support Service to an asylum-seeking partner are ignored;

- a payment (other than a training allowance) to a disabled person under the Disabled Persons (Employment) Act 1944 to assist her/him to obtain or retain employment;[252]
- any discretionary payment made to you by an employment zone contractor while you are taking part in an employment zone scheme;[253]
- any payments, other than for loss of earnings or a benefit, made to jurors or witnesses for attending at court;[254]
- Victoria Cross or George Cross payments or similar awards;[255]
- income paid outside the UK which cannot be transferred here;[256]
- if income is paid in another currency, any bank charges for converting the payment into sterling;[257]
- fares to hospital;[258]
- payments instead of milk tokens and vitamins;[259]
- payments to assist prison visits;[260]
- for HB and CTB, if you make a parental contribution to a student's grant, an equal amount of any 'unearned' income you have for the period the grant is paid is ignored.[261] If your 'unearned' income does not cover the contribution, the balance can be disregarded from your earnings.[262] If you are a parent of a student under 25 in advanced education who does not get a grant (or who only gets a smaller discretionary award) and you contribute to her/his living expenses, the amount of your 'unearned' income that is ignored is the amount equal to your contribution up to a maximum of £44.50 (less the weekly amount of any discretionary award the student has).[263] This is only ignored during the student's term. Again, any balance can be disregarded from your earnings;[264]
- any payment of a sports award made by the Sports Council out of National Lottery funds *except* for any part of any award which is made for 'ordinary living expenses'.[265] The definition of ordinary living expenses which applies differently to each benefit is the same as that which applies to the rules about charitable and voluntary payments (see p973) *except that*, for sports awards, the rules expressly state that food does not include vitamins, minerals or other special dietary supplements intended to enhance performance;
- any discretionary housing payments paid by a local authority.[266]

Notional income

You may, in certain circumstances, be treated as having income although you do not possess it, or have used it up.

Deprivation of income to claim or increase benefit

If you deliberately get rid of income in order to claim or increase your benefit, you are treated as though you are still in receipt of the income.[267] The basic issues involved are the same as those for the deprivation of capital (see p1040). **Note:** the rule can only apply if the purpose of the deprivation is to gain benefit for *yourself* (or your family). It should not apply if, for example, you stop claiming CA solely so that another person (who is not a member of your family) can become entitled to the severe disability premium (see p891).[268] However, if you do not claim a benefit which would clearly be paid if you did, it may be argued that you have failed to apply for income (see p984).

A deliberate decision to 'de-retire' and give up your retirement pension (in the expectation of achieving an overall increase in benefit in the future) currently can come within this deprivation rule.[269] For an explanation of de-retirement, see p490.

Failing to apply for income

If you fail to apply for income to which you are entitled without having to fulfil further conditions, you are deemed to have received it from the date you could have obtained it.[270]

This does not include income from:

- a discretionary trust; *or*
- a trust set up from money paid as a result of a personal injury; *or*
- funds administered by a court as a result of a personal injury or the death of a parent of someone under 18; *or*
- a rehabilitation allowance made under the Employment and Training Act 1973; *or*
- if you are under 60, a personal pension scheme or retirement annuity. However, if you are 60 or over, you are treated as receiving income in certain circumstances if you fail to purchase an annuity;[271] *or*
- WTC and CTC;[272] *or*
- the lone parent element of child benefit – but only for IS and income-based JSA if you have been on benefit since before 6 April 2004 including amounts for a child and you do not yet have a CTC award.

For other income or benefits it must still be certain that it would be paid upon application (and the rule ceases to apply as soon as a claim is made[273]). It may, therefore, be difficult to establish that there is 'no doubt' that CA, for example, would be paid to a carer who does not wish to claim it because of the effect on another person's severe disability premium (see p891).[274]

Any such income must also be available to *you* (or your family) *for your own benefit*. For example, income could not be attributed to the leaseholder of a shop he was forced to sublet to tenants in order to meet his liabilities to the landlord. Although their rents were technically available to him, they were immediately passed on to the landlord so no profit was ever available.[275]

Income due to you that has not been paid

This applies to IS and income-based JSA only.[276] You are treated as possessing any income owing to you. Examples of when this rule *may* apply could include:

- when wages are legally due to you but are not paid. However, guidance for HB/CTB states that it should not be automatically assumed that you should be receiving the national minimum wage, which is currently £4.85 an hour, or £4.10 an hour if you are under 22;[277] *or*
- an occupational pension payment that is due but has not been received. However, this does not apply where an occupational pension has not been paid, or fully paid, because the pension scheme has insufficient funds.[278]

This rule should *not* apply if:

- any social security benefit has been delayed; *or*
- you are waiting for a late payment of a pension under the Job Release Scheme, a government training allowance or a benefit from a European Economic Area country; *or*
- money is due to you from a discretionary trust, or a trust set up from money paid as a result of a personal injury; *or*
- you are owed earnings when your job has ended due to redundancy but these have not been paid to you.[279]

As above, the income must be due to *you* (or your family) and *for your own benefit*.[280]

If this rule is applied, an urgent cases payment should be considered (see p664).[281]

Unpaid wages

This applies to IS and income-based JSA only. If you have wages due to you, but you do not yet know the exact amount or you have no proof of what they will be, you are treated as having a wage similar to that normally paid for that type of work in that area.[282] If your wages cannot be estimated you might qualify for an interim payment (see p1108).[283]

Income paid to someone else on your behalf

If money is paid to someone on your behalf (eg, the landlord for your rent) this can count as notional income. See p1045 for a description of these 'third party' rules – the notional income rules are the same as those for notional capital.

Payments made to a third party of an occupational pension or from a personal pension scheme in respect of you count as yours regardless of whether the payments are used or intended to be used for ordinary living expenses or not. The only exceptions are:

- such payments are disregarded if you (or the member of your family on whose behalf the payments are made) are bankrupt (or the subject of a sequestration order), *and* the payment is made to the trustee or other person acting on your creditors' behalf, *and* you (and your partner) have no other income other than the payment made;[284] *and*

- payments which do nothing to actually support you financially (and therefore do not reduce or remove your need to be supported by IS, income-based JSA, HB or CTB) – eg, deductions from an occupational pension made under an attachment of earnings order.[285]

For IS and income-based JSA (but not for HB and CTB), payments of income in kind are ignored, unless you or your partner are involved in a trade dispute, but even then they are ignored if they are from the Macfarlane Trusts, the Fund, the Eileen Trust or either of the Independent Living Funds (see p973) or in the form of concessionary coal under the Coal Industry Act 1994, or if they are paid in respect of participation in a government training scheme or a New Deal programme.[286]

For the treatment of school fees paid for your child(ren) by someone else, see p954.

Income paid to you for someone else[287]

If you or your partner get a payment for somebody not in the 'family' (see p809 – eg, a relative living with you) it counts as your income if you keep any of it yourself or spend it on yourself or your partner.

If you have been on IS or income-based JSA since before 6 April 2004 with a dependent child included in your claim and you do not yet have a CTC award, income paid to your dependent child for someone not in the family also counts as yours in the same way as it would if it were paid to you or your partner.

The payment does not count as yours in this way if it is from the Macfarlane Trusts, the Fund, the Eileen Trust or either of the Independent Living Funds or is in the form of concessionary coal under the Coal Industry Act 1994, or if it is a grant for participating in an approved employment-related course of education, or in a New Deal programme.[288]

Note: the same exception for payments in kind applies for IS and income-based JSA as for income payments made to someone else on your behalf.

Cheap or unpaid labour

If you are helping another person or an organisation by doing work of a kind which would normally command a wage, or a higher wage, you are deemed to receive a wage similar to that normally paid for that kind of job in that area.[289] In the similar context of child support law, this rule has been held to apply to a person who chose to offer his services through personal service companies he set up himself so that he could control the payments he received for his work.[290]

The burden of proving that the kind of work you do is something for which an employer would pay, and what the comparable wages are, lies with the decision maker.[291]

The rule does not apply if *one* of the following is the case:

- for IS only, you are a lone parent taking part in work experience under the New Deal for lone parents;[292] *or*
- for IS, income-based JSA, HB and CTB, you are on a government employment or training programme for at least three days a week and for which no training allowance is paid, or you or your partner are on a government employment or training programme for which no allowance is payable, or is only for travelling or meal expenses.[293] This rule can, however, apply to you where you are taking part in the 'intensive activity period' of the New Deal or the 'intensive activity period' of the New Deal for those aged 50 or over;[294] *or*
- you can show that the person ('person' in this context includes a limited company[295]) cannot, in fact, afford to pay, or pay more; *or*
- you work for a charitable or voluntary organisation or as a volunteer, and it is accepted that it is reasonable for you to give your services free of charge.[296] A **'volunteer'** in this context is someone who, without any legal obligation, performs a service for another person without expecting payment.[297]

Sometimes it may also be reasonable to do a job for free out of a sense of community duty, particularly if the job would otherwise have remained undone, and there would be no financial profit to an employer.[298] Even if you are caring for a sick or disabled relative or another person, it may be considered reasonable for her/him to pay you from her/his benefits, unless you can bring yourself within these exceptions.[299] There are, however, many arguments which carers can rely on to show that it would not be reasonable for them to be expected to be paid. It has been held, for example, that it may be more reasonable for a close relative to provide services free of charge out of a sense of family duty,[300] particularly if a charge would otherwise break up a relationship.[301] Whether it is reasonable to provide care free of charge depends on the basis on which the arrangement is made, the expectations of the family members concerned, the housing arrangements and the reasons (if appropriate) why a carer gave up any paid work. The risk of a carer losing entitlement to CA if a charge were made should also be considered,[302] as should the likelihood that a relative being looked after would no longer be able to contribute to the household expenses.[303] If there is no realistic alternative to the carer providing services free to a relative who simply will not pay, this may also make it reasonable not to charge.[304] It may also be worth arguing that carers should not charge because they will otherwise lose their statutory right to an assessment of their needs by social services.[305]

Working out weekly income

For HB and CTB, to assess your current normal weekly income:

- average your earnings over a past period (see p988 for earnings from employment and p963 for self-employed earnings);

- estimate income other than earnings (see p968 for what income counts) by looking at an appropriate period of up to 52 weeks. The period chosen must give an accurate assessment of your income.[306] CTC and WTC are taken into account instalment by instalment – eg, if paid weekly or four-weekly, each instalment counts for the 7 or 28 days ending on the day it is due to be paid;
- for earnings from employment and income other than earnings, convert income into a weekly amount if necessary (see p989);
- deduct appropriate earnings disregard/s (see p963).

For IS and income-based JSA, as well as working out weekly income, you also need to know the period that payments cover. These rules apply to earnings from employment and income other than earnings (see p963 for how self-employed earnings are assessed):
- work out the period covered by income (see p990);
- work out the date from which to start taking the income into account (see p991);
- convert income into a weekly amount if necessary (see p989). There are special rules covering variable income, payments for less than a week and overlapping payments (see below).

Averaging earnings for housing benefit and council tax benefit

For HB and CTB, earnings as an employee are usually averaged out over:
- the previous five weeks if you are paid weekly; *or*
- two months if you are paid monthly.[307]

Where your earnings vary, or if there is likely to be or has recently been a change (eg, you usually do overtime but have not done so recently, or you are about to get a pay rise), the local authority may average them over a different period where this is likely to give a more accurate picture of what you are going to earn.[308]

If you are on strike, the local authority should not take into account your pre-strike earnings and average them out over the strike period.[309]

If you have only just started work and your earnings cannot be averaged over the normal period (ie, five weeks or two months) an estimate is made, based on any earnings you have been paid so far if these are likely to reflect your future average wage. Where you have not yet been paid or your initial earnings do not represent what you will normally earn, your employer must provide an estimate of your average weekly earnings.[310] Where your earnings change during your award, your new weekly average figure is estimated on the basis of what you are likely to earn over whatever period (up to 52 weeks) best allows an accurate estimate.[311] Where averaging does not result in a weekly figure, the amount is converted (see p989).

Converting income into a weekly amount

IS, income-based JSA, HB and CTB are all calculated on a weekly basis so your earnings and other income have to be converted into a weekly amount if necessary.

The following rules apply to income from employment and income other than earnings.[312] For income from self-employment, see p962.

To convert income to a weekly amount:

- if the payment is for less than a week, it is treated as the weekly amount;
- if the payment is for a month, multiply by 12 and divide by 52;
- for IS and income-based JSA, multiply a payment for three months by 4 and divide by 52;
- for IS and income-based JSA, divide a payment for a year by 52;
- for all four benefits, for any other period, divide the payment by the number of days in the period then multiply by 7.

If you work on certain days but are paid monthly, it is necessary to decide whether the payment is for the days worked or for the whole month. This generally depends on the terms of your contract of employment,[313] but may depend on how your employer has arranged to make payments to you.[314]

Variable income

For IS and income-based JSA, where your income fluctuates or your earnings vary because you do not work every week, your weekly income may be averaged over the cycle, if there is an identifiable one; or, if there is not, over five weeks, or over another period if this would be more accurate.[315] If the cycle involves periods when you do no work, those periods are included in the cycle, but not other absences – eg, holidays, sickness.

Example

Ahmed works a cycle of two weeks on and one week off. He works 20 hours a week in the weeks he works for which he is paid £105. In the third week he is paid a retainer of £30. He claims income-based JSA in the third week. His average weekly earnings are £80 a week (£105 + £105 + £30 = £240 ÷ 3 = £80) which will be taken into account in calculating his income-based JSA entitlement.

Part-week payments

For IS and income-based JSA, there are rules about the calculation of income for part-weeks. They are:

- Where income covering a period up to a week is paid before your first benefit week (normally the seven days ending with your payday for IS, or your signing-on day for JSA), and part of it is counted for that week; *or* if, in any case, you are paid for a period of a week or more, and only part of it is counted in a particular benefit week – multiply the whole payment by the number of days it covers in the benefit week, then divide the result by the total number of days covered by the payment.[316]

- Where any payment of MA, IB or SDA falls partly into the benefit week, only the amount paid for those days is taken into account. For any payment of IS or JSA, that amount is the weekly amount multiplied by the number of days in the part-week and divided by seven.[317]

Overlapping payments

For IS or income-based JSA, where you have regularly received a certain kind of payment of income from one source, and in a particular benefit week you receive that payment and another of the same kind from the same source (eg, where your employer first pays you sick pay in arrears and this then overlaps with a payment in advance), the maximum amount to be taken into account is the one paid first.[318]

This does not apply if the second payment was due to be taken into account in another week, but the overlapping week is the first in which it could practically be counted (see p991).

The period covered by income for income support and jobseeker's allowance

For IS or income-based JSA, there are special rules for deciding the length of the period for which and the date from which payments of earnings and other income count. These rules are designed to give a clearer indication of how you are expected to make use of any earnings or other income you receive for each week of your claim for IS/income-based JSA. These rules do not, however, apply to self-employed earnings (see p962).

- Where a payment of income is made in respect of an identifiable period, it is taken into account for a period of equal length.[319] For example, a week's part-time earnings are taken into account for a week.
- If the payment does not relate to a particular period, the amount of the payment is divided by the amount of the weekly IS or income-based JSA to which you would otherwise be entitled. If part of the payment should be disregarded, the amount of IS or income-based JSA is increased by the appropriate disregard. The result of this calculation is the number of weeks that you are not entitled to IS or income-based JSA.[320]

Example

Conor receives £800 net earnings for work which cannot be attributed to any specific period of time. He and his partner are both aged 28. Their rent and council tax are met by HB or CTB. Conor's income-based JSA is £88.15. As a couple they are entitled to a £10 earnings disregard.

£800 ÷ (£88.15 + £10 = £98.15) = 8 with £14.80 left over.

This means that Conor is not entitled to income-based JSA for eight weeks and the remaining £14.80 (less a £10 earnings disregard, leaving £4.80) is taken into account in calculating his benefit for the following week.

Payments made on leaving a job are taken into account for a forward period (see p959).

The date from when a payment is counted

For IS and income-based JSA, the date from which a payment of earnings and/or other income counts depends on when it was due to be paid. If it was due to be paid before you claimed IS or income-based JSA, it counts from the date on which it was due to be paid.[321] Otherwise it is treated as paid on the first day of the benefit week in which it is due, or on the first day of the first benefit week after that in which it is practicable to take it into account.[322]

Payments of IS, JSA, MA, IB or SDA are treated as paid on the day they are officially due.[323] Payments of WTC are treated as paid on the first day of the first benefit week on or after the start of the WTC award – or from the first benefit week at the start of the IS or income-based JSA award if you are already getting WTC when your IS or JSA starts – until the last day of the last benefit week on or after the last day of the WTC award.[324] In other words, WTC is not counted instalment by instalment but rather over the whole period of the award.

The '**benefit week**' is normally the seven days ending with the signing-on day for JSA or the payday for IS. It often overlaps two calendar weeks.[325]

The date that a payment is due may well be different from the date of actual payment. Earnings are due on the employee's normal payday. If the contract of employment does not reveal the date of due payment, and there is no evidence pointing in another direction, the date the payment was received should be taken as the date it was due.[326] If your contract of employment is terminated without proper notice, outstanding wages, wages in hand, holiday pay and any pay in lieu of notice are due on the last day of employment and are treated as paid on that day, even if this does not happen.[327]

If you receive compensation for, say, being dismissed in circumstances constituting sex discrimination, the relevant date is the date when the earnings in question were due to be paid, not when the compensation was awarded.[328]

If income due to you has not been paid, you may be entitled to an urgent cases payment (see p664) or a crisis loan from the social fund (see p538).

For the treatment of payments at the end of a job, see p959.

2. Income: aged 60 or over

This part applies to:
- pension credit (PC);
- housing benefit (HB) and council tax benefit (CTB) if you or your partner are aged 60 or over and not getting income support (IS) or income-based jobseeker's allowance (JSA). If you do get IS or income-based JSA, all your income is ignored for HB and CTB.

If you are under 60, or you have a partner and both of you are under 60, this part does not apply. See section 1, 'Income: aged under 60' instead (p952). If you or your partner get IS or income-based JSA, section 1 explains how your income is treated.

The rules for PC and, if you or your partner (if any) are aged 60 or over, for HB and CTB, are very similar. Where there are differences, they are indicated.

In this part, whenever HB or CTB are referred to, this only applies to the rules for people aged 60 or over.

Whose income counts

If you are a member of a couple (see p811), your partner's income is added to yours.[329]

The income of a dependent child does *not* affect:
- PC;
- HB or CTB – if you or your partner are aged 60 or over.[330]

If someone other than you or your partner pays school fees for your child direct to the school, these should be ignored.[331]

What counts as income

Pension credit

For PC, **'income'** means:
- earnings (see pp994 and 996);
- certain benefits and tax credits, including state retirement pensions and war pensions (see p999);
- maintenance (see p1001);
- income from tenants and lodgers (see p1002);
- income from capital (see p1002);
- other specified miscellaneous income, including occupational and personal pensions (see pp1003 and 1004);
- notional income (see p1005);
- any income paid in lieu of the above.

For each type of income, some income is taken into account and some is ignored in the assessment of PC. The details are explained in this chapter. If the rules do not specify a type of income as being included in the assessment, then it is ignored and does not affect your benefit.

For the rules on 'qualifying income' for the savings credit and the 'assessed income period', both of which only apply to PC, see Chapter 18.

Housing benefit and council tax benefit

How your income affects your entitlement to HB and CTB if you or your partner are aged 60 or over depends on whether you are getting PC and, if you are, which type of PC.

If you get pension credit guarantee credit

If you (or your partner) are getting the guarantee credit of PC, all of your (and your partner's) income is ignored.[332] This is because entitlement to PC guarantee credit acts as a passport to maximum HB and CTB.

If you get pension credit savings credits

If you (or your partner) are only getting the savings credit of PC, your income for HB and CTB purposes is the income (and capital) figure used by the DWP to work out your PC, *plus*:[333]

- the amount of savings credit of PC;
- any income (and capital) of your partner which was not taken into account in the PC calculation (eg, where a partner abroad is no longer included for PC but is for HB/CTB); *and*
- any income of a non-dependant, but only where her/his income can be treated as yours under the HB rules (see p215);[334]

minus[335]

- any childcare charges earnings disregard;
- the higher amount disregarded, where applicable, for:
  - lone parent earnings;
  - payments of maintenance made by your former partner (or your partner's former partner), or payments of maintenance made by the parent of a child or young person who is a member of your family, as long as that parent is neither yourself nor your partner;
  - any additional full-time earnings disregard (see p999);
  - any discretionary increase to the £10 disregard for war pensions, and war widows' and widowers' pensions.

If you do not get pension credit

If you or your partner are aged 60 or over and are not getting the guarantee or savings credit of PC, or IS or income-based JSA, income is defined in the same way as for PC (see p992).[336] As for PC, some income is taken into account and some disregarded but the rules on how this happens are not always the same as for PC. Any differences are explained in each relevant section.

Net weekly income

The income that is taken into account is the amount after deducting any tax or national insurance (NI) contributions.[337]

For HB and CTB, the local authority may ignore changes (eg, Budget changes) in tax or NI contributions and the maximum rate of tax credits for up to 30 benefit weeks. When the changes are eventually taken into account, you are not treated as having been underpaid or overpaid benefit during the period of the delay.[338]

Once you have worked out what income should be taken into account, this is converted into a weekly amount (see p1006) and the total taken into account in the benefit assessment (see p1007 for the date from when a payment is counted). Chapters 10 and 18 explain how income affects the amount of HB, CTB or PC you get.

Earnings of employed earners

This section explains how any earnings received by you or your partner (see p809) are treated for PC and, if you or your partner are aged 60 or over, for HB and CTB.

Calculating net earnings from employment

It is your net earnings that are taken into account in the assessment. See p1006 for how earnings are converted into a weekly amount. **'Net earnings'** means your 'gross earnings' (see below) *minus*:

- any deductions made for income tax; *and*
- Class 1 NI contributions; *and*
- half of any contribution you make towards a personal or occupational pension scheme.[339]

If your earnings are estimated for HB or CTB, the authorities estimate the amount of tax and NI you would expect to pay on those earnings, and deduct this plus half of any pension contribution you are paying.[340]

For HB and CTB, the local authority has the discretion to ignore changes in tax or NI contributions for up to 30 benefit weeks. When the changes are eventually taken into account, you are not treated as having been underpaid or overpaid benefit during the period of the delay.[341]

'Gross earnings' means the amount of earnings received from your employer less deductions for any expenses 'wholly, necessarily and exclusively incurred' by you in order to carry out the duties of your employment.[342] A range of deductions may be made (see p956 – the provisions are the same as those for people aged under 60).

What counts as earnings

'Earnings' means 'any remuneration or profit derived from ... employment'.

As well as your wages, this includes:[343]

- any bonus or commission (including tips);
- holiday pay - but this is ignored if your employment ends before your PC entitlement starts;
- statutory sick pay (SSP) and contractual sick pay,[344] statutory maternity pay (SMP), statutory paternity pay (SPP) or statutory adoption pay (SAP) or any other pay made to you by your employer while you are on maternity leave;[345]
- any payments made by your employer for expenses not 'wholly, exclusively and necessarily' incurred in carrying out your job, including any travel expenses to and from work, and any payments made to you for looking after members of your family;
- pay in lieu of notice, or pay in lieu of remuneration except for periodic payments following redundancy. However, all earnings – including pay in lieu – are ignored if your employment ends before your PC entitlement starts;
- a retainer fee (eg, you may be paid during the school holidays if you work for the school meals service[346]) or a guarantee payment;[347]
- any payment of a non-cash voucher which is liable for Class 1 NI contributions.[348] Non-cash vouchers that are *not* liable for contributions (eg, certain childcare and charitable vouchers) are classed as payments in kind and ignored.[349]

Examples of payments not counted as earnings:

- If you become entitled to HB, CTB or PC after your employment ends, all earnings are disregarded (see p997) except certain royalties.[350]
- Payments in kind (eg, petrol) are ignored.[351]
- An advance of earnings or a loan from your employer – this is treated as capital, according to PC guidance.[352]
- The value of free accommodation provided as part of your job is ignored, according to PC guidance.[353]
- Payments towards expenses that are 'wholly, exclusively and necessarily' incurred, such as travelling expenses during the course of your work, are ignored.[354]
- If you are a local councillor, travelling expenses and subsistence payments are (and basic allowances may be[355]) ignored as expenses 'wholly, exclusively and necessarily' incurred in your work.
- If your earnings are paid in another currency, any bank charges for converting them into sterling are deducted before taking them into account.[356]
- Any occupational pension[357] – although not counted as earnings (and therefore having no earnings disregard), the net amount is still taken into account in full.[358]

- Any compensation payments made by an employment tribunal for unfair dismissal or unlawful discrimination do not count as earnings.[359]
- Any lump-sum payments made under the Iron and Steel Re-adaptation Benefits Scheme are not treated as earnings.[360]

Payments at the end of a job

Redundancy payments are treated as capital.[361]

If you leave a job, any earnings should be disregarded except[362] certain copyright royalties, payments for patents, trademarks or under the Public Lending Right Scheme.

However, these rules only apply if you leave your job before you claim benefit. If you are already getting HB/CTB or PC when you leave your job, your earnings are not disregarded for that benefit. If you are already getting HB/CTB but not PC, your earnings are disregarded for PC.

For PC, any final payment is treated as paid on the date your next regular payment of earnings would have been paid and taken into account for the same period unless the final payment is higher than the normal amount. If it is higher, the final payment is taken into account over the corresponding multiple of the regular payment period with any remainder counting for a further payment period.[363]

Example

Sandra has been getting PC and working part time. She earned £25 a week paid on a Friday. She finishes work on Wednesday 4 August and on that day is given £35 made up of £15 final wages and £20 holiday pay. This £35 is treated as paid on Friday 6 August and taken into account for two benefit weeks – £25 in the first week and the remaining £10 in the second week.

Earnings from self-employment

Even if you are an employee, any other earnings from work you do as a self-employed person are assessed under the following rules for PC and, if you or your partner are aged 60 or over, for HB and CTB.

Calculating net earnings

Your '**net profit**' over the period before your claim must be worked out. This consists of your self-employed earnings, including any allowance from a Department for Work and Pensions (DWP) scheme to assist you with your business *minus*:[364]

- reasonable expenses (see p962 – the rules are the same as those for people under age 60); *and*
- income tax and NI contributions; *and*
- half of any premium paid in respect of a personal pension scheme or a retirement annuity contract which is eligible for tax relief.[365] For PC, you must

supply certain information about the scheme or annuity contract to the relevant authority if requested.[366]

If you receive payments for board and lodging charges, these do not count as earnings[367] but as other income (less any disregards – see p1002).

Working out average earnings from self-employment

The weekly amount is the average of earnings:[368]

- over a period of one year (normally the last year for which accounts are available);
- over a more appropriate period where you have recently taken up self-employment or there has been a change which will affect your business.

Childminders

Childminders, in practice, are always treated as self-employed. Your net profit is deemed to be one-third of your earnings less income tax, your NI contributions and half of certain pension contributions (see p996).[369] The rest of your earnings are completely ignored.

Disregarded earnings

Some of your earnings from employment or self-employment are disregarded and do not affect your PC or, if you or your partner are aged 60 or over, your HB or CTB. The amount of the 'disregard' depends on your circumstances. The three main levels of disregard are £25 or £20 or £5/£10, but additional disregards may apply in special circumstances. These are explained below.

For the treatment of childcare costs for claims for HB/CTB, see p999.

Full disregard

For HB and CTB only:

The amount (or the balance of the amount) of the student parental contribution which is not disregarded under other income (see p1006) is ignored.[370]

For PC, HB and CTB:

- All earnings (except royalties or other payments of earnings made for the use of, or the right to use, any copyright, patent, trademark or book registered under the Public Lending Right Scheme if you or your partner (if any) are the first owner of the copyright, patent or trademark or are the author of the book) derived from employment which ended before you claimed PC, HB or CTB are ignored.[371]
- Any banking charges or commission payable for converting your earnings into Sterling if you are paid in a currency other than Sterling are deducted.[372]

£25 disregard

Lone parents on HB or CTB have £25 of their earnings ignored.[373] This does not apply to PC.

£20 disregard

£20 of your earnings (including those of your partner, if any) is disregarded if:

- for PC, you are a lone parent;[374]
- you or your partner (if any) are in receipt of long-term incapacity benefit (IB), severe disablement allowance (SDA), attendance allowance (AA), disability living allowance (DLA), any mobility supplement or the disability or severe disability element of WTC;[375]
- you or your partner (if any) are registered or certified as blind;[376]
- for HB and CTB only, you or your partner (if any) are, or are treated as, incapable of work and have been, or have been treated as, incapable of work for a continuous period of 196 days in the case of a person who is terminally ill, or 364 days in any other case;[377]
- you or your partner (if any) qualify for a carer's premium (see p896). For a couple, if both partners get the carer's premium, £20 is disregarded from their combined earnings;[378]
- you or your partner (if any) previously had an earnings disregard of £20 in (for PC) your IS or income-based JSA or in (for HB/CTB) your HB or CTB, *and* that previous award of IS, income-based JSA, HB or CTB was not more than eight weeks before (for PC) the date you or your partner (if any) first became entitled to PC or (for HB/CTB) you or your partner reached the age of 60, *and* the employment which the earnings disregard applied to continues after the end of the previous award of IS, income-based JSA or HB/CTB.[379] This £20 disregard will continue so long as there is no break of more than eight weeks in either your claim for PC or HB/CTB or in employment. Only one £20 disregard can apply, even if both you and your partner could qualify for a £20 disregard under this rule;
- for PC only, you or your partner (if any), immediately before reaching pensionable age, had a £20 disregard under an award of PC because you or your partner were in receipt of long-term IB or SDA.[380] This £20 disregard will continue so long as there is no break of more than eight weeks in your claim for PC. Only one £20 disregard can apply, even if both you and your partner could qualify for a £20 disregard under this rule;
- you or your partner (if any) are an auxiliary coastguard, part-time firefighter, part-time member of a lifeboat crew or member of the Territorial Army.[381] If your, or your partner's, earnings from any of these jobs come to less than £20 a week, what is left over of the £20 disregard can be used against your, or your partner's, earnings from any other employment.

If you qualify under more than one category you still have a maximum of only £20 of your earnings disregarded.

Basic £5 or £10 disregard

If you do not qualify for a £25 or £20 disregard, £5 of your earnings is disregarded if you are single. If you claim as a member of a couple, £10 of your total income is disregarded, whether or not you are both working.[382]

Additional earnings disregard for housing benefit and council tax benefit[383]

For **HB/CTB only**, whichever earnings disregard applies is increased by £14.50 if:

- you or your partner (if any) receive the 30-hour element as part of your (or your partner's) WTC (see p1356); *or*
- you or your partner are aged 25 or over and work 30 hours a week or more on average; *or*
- you or your partner work 16 hours or more a week on average and your HB/CTB includes the family premium (see p884); *or*
- you are a lone parent and work 16 hours or more a week on average; *or*
- you or your partner (if any) work 16 hours or more a week on average and one or both of you get long-term IB, SDA, AA, DLA, mobility supplement, WTC disability or severe disability element, are registered blind or have been incapable of work for 364 days (196 days if terminally ill). For couples, the partner who is disabled is the one who must be working 16 hours a week or more on average; *or*
- you or your partner (if any) get a 50-plus element in WTC, or would qualify for one if you claimed WTC (see p1358).

The only exception is where your total earnings are less than the total of £14.50 plus any earnings disregard (see above) and childcare costs disregard (see below). In that case £14.50 is disregarded from any WTC that is awarded to you or your partner, but the earnings disregard is not increased.

Note: as with the ordinary earnings disregards, only one additional disregard can be allowed from your (or your partner's) earnings.

Childcare costs for housing benefit and council tax benefit

For **HB/CTB**,[384] an allowance of up to £175 a week for one child, or up to £300 a week for two or more children, can be deducted from your (or your partner's) earnings (from employment or self-employment) in respect of childcare costs in certain circumstances. The rules are the same as those for people aged under 60 (see p965). There is no allowance for childcare costs for PC.

Benefits and tax credits

For PC and, if you or your partner are aged 60 or over, for HB and CTB, some benefits and tax credits are taken into account as income and others are disregarded wholly or partly.

Benefits and tax credits that count in full:

- carer's allowance (CA);
- child's special allowance (it counts for HB/CTB but is ignored for PC[385]) and war orphan's pension;
- contribution-based JSA;
- IB and SDA;
- industrial injuries benefits, except constant attendance allowance and exceptionally severe disablement allowance which are disregarded;
- maternity allowance (MA);
- retirement pensions (including payments from the Financial Assistance Scheme);
- SSP, SMP, SPP and SAP are treated as earnings and therefore may benefit from an earnings disregard (see p963);[386]
- widow's pension, bereavement allowance and industrial death benefit;
- WTC counts for PC, and for HB and CTB. For HB and CTB if your earnings are too low to use the whole £14.50 additional full-time earnings disregard (see p999), £14.50 is disregarded from your WTC instead of your earnings.[387] If a tax credit overpayment is being recovered from your WTC award, it is the amount of the WTC award less the overpayment that is taken into account for PC, HB and CTB;
- foreign social security benefits which are similar to the benefits listed above.[388]

Benefits that are ignored completely:[389]

- AA;[390]
- bereavement payments are ignored as income,[391] however they would be taken into account as capital;
- child benefit;[392]
- CTC is ignored for PC and, from 4 April 2005, for HB and CTB;[393]
- constant attendance allowance, exceptionally severe disablement allowance or severe disablement occupational allowance paid because of an injury at work or a war injury;[394]
- DLA care component and mobility component;[395]
- guardian's allowance;[396]
- mobility supplement under the War Pensions Scheme;[397]
- pensioner's Christmas bonus (see Chapter 3);[398]
- social fund payments;[399]
- HB, CTB or, formerly, community charge benefit;[400]
- certain special war widows' payments[401] and any special or supplementary payments to pre-1973 war widows or widowers;[402]
- increases for child dependants are ignored. Increases for adult dependants are only ignored if the dependant is not your partner.[403]

Benefits that have £15 ignored:

- for HB/CTB only, widowed mother's allowance and widowed parent's allowance.[404]

Benefits that have £10 ignored:

- for PC only, widowed mother's allowance and widowed parent's allowance;[405]
- war disablement pension;[406]
- war widow's or widower's pension;[407]
- widow's or widower's pension payable to a spouse of a member of the Royal Navy, Army or Royal Air Force who was disabled or died as a result of service in the armed forces;[408]
- an extra-statutory payment made instead of the above pensions;[409]
- similar payments made by another country;[410]
- a pension from Germany or Austria paid to the victims of Nazi persecution.[411]

The £10 disregard allowed on these war pensions is additional to the total disregard of any mobility supplement or AA (ie, constant attendance allowance, exceptionally severe disablement allowance and severe disablement occupational allowance) paid as part of a war disablement pension.

Local authorities have discretion to increase the £10 disregard on war disablement, war widows' or widowers' pensions and the pension payable to widows or widowers of members of the Royal Navy, Army or Royal Air Force, when assessing income for HB and CTB.[412] Some local authorities disregard the full amount of these pensions, and some do not increase the disregard at all, so you should check your own local authority's policy on this issue. It has been held that a local authority must at least consider the nature and purpose of such pensions when deciding whether or not to disregard them, and the courts have indicated that it may be appropriate to apply a disregard to retrospective awards.[413]

Benefit delays

If you have made a claim for benefit but have not yet been paid, the benefit should not be treated as income possessed by you. For PC, you should get your full benefit and leave the DWP to deduct the difference from arrears of the delayed benefit when it is eventually awarded.[414]

For the treatment of payments of arrears of certain benefits and CTC and WTC, see p1057.

Maintenance payments

For **HB and CTB** (if you or your partner are aged 60 or over), if you have a family premium included in your HB/CTB, £15 of any maintenance payments for you or your partner made by your, or your partner's, spouse or former spouse is disregarded.[415] If you receive maintenance from more than one person, only £15 of the total is disregarded. Other kinds of maintenance (eg, for a child) do not count as income and are ignored completely.[416]

For **PC**, any maintenance payments for you or your partner made by your, or your partner's, spouse or former spouse count in full as income. Maintenance for a child is ignored completely.[417]

If you *pay* maintenance to a former partner or a child not living with you, your payments are not disregarded for the purpose of calculating your income for PC, HB or CTB.[418] Even if you are on PC you may still have to pay child support maintenance (see p862).

Income from tenants and lodgers

For PC and, if you or your partner are aged 60 or over, for HB and CTB, how income from tenants is treated depends on whether or not you live in the same property.

Lettings without board

If you are the owner of a property (or the tenant of it), you live in part of the property and you have an agreement with another person allowing her/him to occupy another part of the property for which s/he pays you rent, then all the rent paid to you is ignored if the rent is less than £20 a week. If the rent is £20 a week or more, £20 of the rent is ignored.[419]

Boarders

If you have a boarder(s) in your own home, the first £20 of the weekly charge is ignored and half of any balance remaining is then taken into account as your income.[420] (If the boarder is a close relative or not staying on a commercial basis, the rules on contrived tenancies could possibly apply – see p199.) This applies for each boarder you have. The charge must normally include at least some meals.[421] If you have a business partner, even though your gross income includes just your share of the weekly charge to boarders, you still get the full disregard of £20 plus half the excess for each boarder.[422]

Tenants in other properties

Rent from a property other than your home is not taken into account as income.[423] Instead, the value of the property is treated as producing a 'deemed income' (see p1003).

Income from capital

For PC and, if you or your partner are aged 60 or over, for HB and CTB, the general rule is that capital (unless disregarded) is assumed to provide a set rate of income called 'deemed income' (see p1003). Actual income generated from capital is ignored as income[424] with the exception of the following types of capital. In these cases any actual income (but no deemed income) is taken into account.[425] **Note:** for HB and CTB it is only taken into account in these cases if the total capital listed below is worth more than £6,000 or, if you live in a care home, £10,000.[426]

Actual income from the following capital is taken into account:

- the value of the right to receive a payment in the future of:
  - income under a life interest or life rent;

- rent, unless you only have a reversionary (ie, future) interest in the property (for the way actual rent is treated, see p1002);
- the surrender value or income under an annuity;
- property held in a trust, including a discretionary trust, but not charitable trusts or, for PC, trusts set up out of payments from personal injury to you or your partner or, for HB/CTB, from the Independent Living Funds, Macfarlane Trusts, the Fund, the Eileen Trust or the Skipton Fund.

Where deemed income is taken into account, actual income from the same capital is ignored.

Example

Frank, aged 72, has savings in the bank of £12,000. Deemed income is taken into account for PC, HB and CTB of £12 a week for each benefit. Any interest from the savings is ignored as income.

There are no rules that treat capital of any kind as though it were income.

Deemed income

There is no upper capital limit for PC. If you have capital above £6,000 (or £10,000 if you live in a care home), you will be treated as having an assumed income of £1 for every £500, or part of £500, by which your capital exceeds £6,000 (or £10,000).[427]

For HB and CTB (if you or your partner are aged 60 or over) the following apply:

- If you or your partner are getting the guarantee credit of PC then all of your (and your partner's) capital is ignored.[428]
- In any other case, there is a capital limit of £16,000.[429] If you have capital above £6,000 (or £10,000 if you live in a care home), you will be treated as having an assumed income of £1 for every £500, or part of £500, by which your capital exceeds £6,000 (£10,000) but does not exceed £16,000.[430]

For PC, HB and CTB, you are not treated as having deemed income on capital that is disregarded (see p1054).

Occupational and personal pensions

The following income is taken into account for PC and, if you or your partner are aged 60 or over, for HB and CTB:[431]

- an occupational pension;
- income from a personal pension;
- income from a retirement annuity contract (including an annuity purchased for you or transferred to you from an ex-husband or ex-wife);

- payments from a former employer for early retirement on the grounds of ill health or disability, unless this was under a court order or settlement of a claim;[432]
- overseas pension;
- Civil List Act pension;[433]
- payment under an equity release scheme.[434] This provides regular payments by way of a loan secured on your home. For some home income plans, interest on the loan can be disregarded (see p1004).

Some charitable trusts provide discretionary income to people retired from specific occupations. This would be ignored for PC, HB and CTB.[435]

Specified miscellaneous income

For PC and, if you or your partner are aged 60 or over, for HB and CTB, the following rules apply.

Income counted in full:

- Copyright royalties, payments for patents, trademarks or under the Public Lending Right Scheme – add these payments to your earnings (if any) if you are the first owner of the copyright or patent or author of the book and deduct the appropriate earnings disregards on p997.[436]

Income that is ignored:

- Income paid outside the UK which cannot be transferred here.[437]
- If income is paid in another currency, any bank charges for converting the payment into Sterling.[438]
- Income from an annuity is normally taken into account. However, an amount equal to the interest payable on the loan with which the annuity was bought is ignored if the following conditions are met:[439]
  - you used at least 90 per cent of the loan made to you to buy the annuity; *and*
  - the annuity will end when you and your partner die; *and*
  - you or your partner are responsible for paying the interest on the loan; *and*
  - you, or both your partner and yourself, were at least 65 at the time the loan was made; *and*
  - the loan is secured on a property which you or your partner owns or has an interest in, and the property on which the loan is secured is your home or that of your partner.

  If the interest on the loan is payable after income tax has been deducted, it is an amount equal to the net interest payment that is disregarded, otherwise it is the gross amount of the interest payment.
- Any discretionary payment made to you by trustees is ignored altogether, *except* where the payment is for the purpose of:
  - obtaining food, ordinary clothing or footwear or household fuel; *or*

  - paying rent, council tax or water charges for which you or your partner (if any) are liable. **'Rent'** means eligible rent under the HB rules, less any non-dependant deductions; *or*
  - meeting housing costs which could be met by the PC rules,

  in which case £20 of the payment is disregarded, or if the payment is less than £20 the whole of the payment is disregarded.[440] If this disregard overlaps with certain other disregards (eg, certain war pensions) then a combined maximum of £20 is allowed.[441] **Note:** this is a weekly disregard so payments spread over different or successive benefit weeks attract a £20 disregard for each.

  School uniform and sportswear are examples of clothing and footwear that are not ordinary.
- Periodic payments made to you or your partner (if any) under an agreement entered into in settlement of a claim for any injury to you or your partner.[442] Any payment ordered by a court to be made to you or your partner (if any) because of an accident, injury or disease suffered by you or your partner (or, for HB and CTB only, your child).[443]

Notional income

You may, in certain circumstances, be treated as having income although you do not possess it or have used it up in the PC assessment and, if you or your partner are aged 60 or over, in HB and CTB.

If you are working but earning less than the going rate, there are no rules to treat you as though your wages were higher than those you actually get, as there are for IS.

Deprivation of income to claim or increase benefit

If you deliberately get rid of income in order to claim or increase your benefit, you are treated as though you are still in receipt of the income.[444] The basic issues involved are the same as those for the deprivation of capital (see p1059). **Note:** the rule can only apply if the purpose of the deprivation is to gain benefit for *yourself* (or your partner). It should not apply if, for example, you stop claiming CA solely so that another person (who is not your partner) can become entitled to the severe disability premium (see p891).[445] However, if you do not claim a benefit which would clearly be paid if you did, it may be argued that you have failed to apply for income (see p1005).

Failing to apply for income

You will be treated as receiving:[446]

- the amount of any retirement pension (including a Category A, B, C or D state pension, age additions, graduated retirement benefit and any shared additional pension paid on divorce) you expect to be entitled to, but for which you have not made a claim (but not where you have deferred your pension – see p489);

- income from any occupational pension scheme which you elected to defer; *and*
- income in certain circumstances if you fail to purchase an annuity under an occupational or personal pension scheme or retirement annuity contract.

Income paid to someone else on your behalf

Any money paid to someone on your behalf is normally treated as being yours. The exception is for payments of income made under an occupational or personal pension scheme if you or your partner (if any) are bankrupt (or the subject of a sequestration order). In this case, if the payment is made to the trustee or other person acting on your creditors' behalf and you (and your partner) have no other income other than the payment made, then it is not treated as being yours.[447]

Other income

For PC and, if you or your partner are aged 60 or over, for HB and CTB, only income that is specified in the rules can affect your benefit. That income is listed on p992 and described above. Any other kind of income is ignored. Below are some examples of income that is ignored and does not affect your benefit:

- **Student loans and grants** are disregarded for PC and, if you or your partner are aged 60 or over, for HB and CTB.[448]
- For HB and CTB only, there is a specific disregard if you make a **parental contribution** to a student's grant or loan. An equal amount of income you have for the period the grant or loan is paid is ignored.[449] If you are a parent of a student under 25 in advanced education who does not get a grant or loan (or who only gets a smaller discretionary award) and you contribute to her/his living expenses, your contribution up to a maximum of £44.50 (less the weekly amount of any discretionary award the student has) is ignored from your income during term time.[450]
- **Adoption allowances, fostering allowances and residence order payments** are disregarded in full.[451]
- **Charitable and voluntary payments** are not taken into account as income, so if a charity or a person gives you voluntary payments, that does not reduce your benefit. Note that maintenance payments can affect your benefit (see p1001).

Working out weekly income

To assess your weekly income:

- work out whether income is taken into account or fully or partly disregarded (see p992);
- if income varies, work out average income (see p1007);
- convert into a weekly amount if necessary (see p1007);
- add any deemed weekly income from capital (see p1003);

- for HB and CTB if you are working and eligible for a childcare cost disregard, deduct the eligible childcare charges (see p999).

Variable income

Where your earnings vary because you do not work the same hours every week, your weekly income may be averaged over the cycle, if there is an identifiable one.[452] Where you do not work a recognisable cycle or your income fluctuates, your income is worked out on the basis of:

- the last two payments before your claim was made or treated as made (or, where applicable, before your claim was superseded), if those payments are at least one month apart; *or*
- the last four payments before your claim was made or treated as made (or, where applicable, before your claim was superseded), if the last two payments are less than a month apart; *or*
- calculating (or estimating for HB or CTB) any other payments that would give a more accurate figure for your average weekly income.[453]

In all cases, if the cycle involves periods when you do no work, those periods are included in the cycle, but not other absences – eg, holidays, sickness.

If you are entitled to receive:

- royalties or other sums in respect of the use of any copyright, patent or trademark; *or*
- payments in respect of any book registered under the Public Lending Right Scheme 1982; *or*
- payments made on an occasional basis,

the payment is treated as if made for a period of a year.[454]

Converting income into a weekly amount

PC, HB and CTB are calculated on a weekly basis so your earnings and other income have to be converted into a weekly amount if necessary.

The following rules apply to income from employment and other income.[455] For income from self-employment, see p996.

- If the payment is for less than a week, it is treated as the weekly amount.
- If the payment is for a month, multiply by 12 and divide by 52.
- Multiply a payment for three months by 4 and divide by 52.
- Divide a payment for a year by 52.
- Multiply payments for any other periods by 7 and divide by the number of days in the period.

The date from when a payment is counted

For PC, at the start of a claim or a new 'assessed income period' (see p480), the total weekly income is taken into account from the first day of the first 'benefit week' or new assessed income period.[456] A **'benefit week'** is the seven days starting on the day PC is payable.[457]

The general rule is that social security benefits are treated as paid on the first day of the PC benefit week in which the benefit is payable.[458] Some benefits are treated slightly differently. Contribution-based JSA, IB, SDA and MA are treated as paid on the day that benefit is payable.

For other types of income, the general rule is that changes to income take effect from the first day of the benefit week in which the change takes place.[459] If that is not practicable, the change is put into effect from the start of the next benefit week. However, where there is a change to the amount of deemed income from capital or an increase in WTC, the change is put into effect from the benefit week that starts on or after the change takes place.[460]

Notes

1 **HB** Sch 3 para 10 and Sch 4 para 4 HB Regs
CTB Sch 3 para 10 and Sch 4 para 4 CTB Regs
For people aged 60 or over:
HB Reg 22 HB Regs
CTB Reg 14 CTB Regs
as substituted by regs 8 and 17 HB&CTB(SPC) Regs

2 Reg 80(2) JSA Regs

1. Income: aged under 60

3 **IS/HB/CTB** s136(1) SSCBA 1992
JSA s13(2) JSA 1995

4 **HB** Sch 3 para 10 and Sch 4 para 4 HB Regs
CTB Sch 3 para 10 and Sch 4 para 4 CTB Regs

5 **IS** Reg 23(4) IS Regs
JSA Reg 88(3) JSA Regs

6 **IS** Reg 23(2) IS Regs
JSA Reg 88(2) JSA Regs

7 **HB** Reg 19(4) HB Regs
CTB Reg 11(4) CTB Regs

8 **IS** Reg 14(2)(c) IS Regs
JSA Reg 76(2)(d) JSA Regs
HB Reg 13(2)(c) HB Regs
CTB Reg 5(2)(c) CTB Regs

9 **IS** Reg 17(b) IS Regs
JSA Reg 83(b) JSA Regs

10 **IS** Reg 44(5) IS Regs
JSA Reg 106(5) JSA Regs

11 **IS** Sch 8 para 15 IS Regs
JSA Sch 6 para 18 JSA Regs

12 **IS** Sch 8 paras 14 and 15 IS Regs
JSA Sch 6 paras 17 and 18 JSA Regs

13 **IS** Reg 44(4) IS Regs
JSA Reg 106(4) JSA Regs

14 **IS** Reg 42(4) and Sch 9 para 25A IS Regs
JSA Reg 105(10) and Sch 7 para 26A JSA Regs
as amended by Schs 1 para 10 and 2 para 10 SS(WTCCTC)(CA) Regs

15 **IS** Reg 42(4)(a)(ii) IS Regs
JSA Reg 105(10) JSA Regs

16 **IS** Reg 44(2)(a) and (4) IS Regs
JSA Reg 106(2)(a) JSA Regs

17 **IS** Reg 44(2)(b) IS Regs
JSA Reg 106(2)(b) JSA Regs

18 **IS** Reg 44(9) IS Regs
JSA Reg 106(9) JSA Regs

19 **IS** Reg 44(3) IS Regs; CIS/164/1994
JSA Reg 106(3) JSA Regs

20 **HB** Reg 19(4) HB Regs
CTB Reg 11(4) CTB Regs

21 **IS** Reg 40 and Sch 9 para 1 IS Regs
JSA Reg 103(1) and (2) and Sch 7 para 1 JSA Regs
HB Reg 33 and Sch 4 para 1 HB Regs
CTB Reg 24 and Sch 4 para 1 CTB Regs

22 **HB** Reg 26 HB Regs
CTB Reg 18 CTB Regs
23 R(IS) 4/01
24 *R v SBC ex parte Singer* [1973] 1 WLR 713
25 *Parsons v Hogg* [1985] 2 All ER 897 (CA), appendix to R(FIS) 4/85
26 R(FC) 1/90
27 CFC/26/1989
28 R(FIS) 4/85
29 R(IS) 13/91; R(IS) 16/93; CFC/26/1989
30 CCS/318/1995 (applying the identical provisions in child support law)
31 CCS/5352/1995
32 R(CS) 2/99, following CCS/10/1994 and R(CS) 10/98, and CCS/2561/1998, but see CCS/12769/1996 for a contrary view
33 CCS/3882/1997
34 R(U) 2/72; R(FIS) 4/85; R(FC) 1/91; R(IS) 13/91
35 CIS/521/1990
36 **IS** Reg 36(3) IS Regs
JSA Reg 99(1) and (4) JSA Regs
HB Reg 29(3) HB Regs
CTB Reg 20(3) CTB Regs
37 **HB** Regs 22(2) and 29(4) HB Regs
CTB Regs 14(2) and 20(4) CTB Regs
38 **HB** Reg 26 HB Regs
CTB Reg 18 CTB Regs
HB/CTB paras C3.30-34 GM
39 R(SB) 21/86
IS Reg 35(1) IS Regs
JSA Reg 98(1) JSA Regs
HB Reg 28(1) HB Regs
CTB Reg 19(1) CTB Regs
40 **IS** Reg 48(3) IS Regs
JSA Reg 110(3) JSA Regs
HB Reg 40(3) HB Regs
CTB Reg 31(3) CTB Regs
R(SB) 15/82, R(SB) 33/83, R(SB) 11/85
41 **IS** Regs 35(1)(d) and 48(3) IS Regs
JSA Regs 98(1)(c) and 110(3) JSA Regs
42 **HB** Reg 28(1)(i)-(j) HB Regs
CTB Reg 19(1)(i)-(j) CTB Regs
43 **IS** Regs 35(2)(b) and 40(4) and Sch 9 paras 1, 4 and 4A IS Regs
JSA Regs 98(2)(c) and 103(6) and Sch 7 paras 1, 4 and 5 JSA Regs
44 **HB** Reg 28(1)(i)-(j) HB Regs
CTB Reg 19(1)(i)-(j) CTB Regs
45 **IS** Regs 35(2)(b) and 40(4) and Sch 9 paras 1, 4 and 4A IS Regs
JSA Regs 98(2)(c) and 103(6) and Sch 7 paras 1, 4 and 5 JSA Regs
46 **IS** Reg 35(1)(e) IS Regs
JSA Reg 98(1)(d) JSA Regs
HB Reg 28(1)(e) HB Regs
CTB Reg 19(1)(e) CTB Regs
47 R(IS) 9/95
48 **IS** Reg 35(1)(g) IS Regs
JSA Reg 98(1)(f) JSA Regs
HB Reg 28(1)(g) HB Regs
CTB Reg 19(1)(g) CTB Regs
49 CIS/590/1993
50 **IS** Reg 35(1)(h) IS Regs
JSA Reg 98(1)(b) JSA Regs
HB Reg 28(1)(h) HB Regs
CTB Reg 19(1)(h) CTB Regs
51 **IS** Reg 35(1)(c) IS Regs
JSA Reg 98(1)(b) JSA Regs
HB Reg 28(1)(c) HB Regs
CTB Reg 19(1)(c) CTB Regs
52 **IS** Reg 35(1)(b) IS Regs
JSA Reg 98(1)(b) and (2)(b) JSA Regs
HB Reg 28(1)(b) HB Regs
CTB Reg 19(1)(b) CTB Regs
53 **JSA** Reg 98(1)(f), (ff) and (g) JSA Regs
54 **IS** Reg 35(3)(iv) IS Regs
JSA Reg 98(3)(d) JSA Regs
55 **IS** Reg 35(2)(e) IS Regs
JSA Reg 98(2)(g) JSA Regs
56 **IS** Reg 35(1)(j) IS Regs
JSA Reg 98(1)(h) JSA Regs
HB Reg 28(1)(k) HB Regs
CTB Reg 19(1)(k) CTB Regs
57 **IS** Reg 35(2A) IS Regs
JSA Reg 98(2A) JSA Regs
HB Reg 28(3) HB Regs
CTB Reg 19(3) CTB Regs
58 **IS** Reg 35(2)(a) and Sch 9 para 21 IS Regs
JSA Reg 98(2)(a) and Sch 7 para 22 JSA Regs
HB Reg 28(2)(a) and Sch 4 para 21 HB Regs
CTB Reg 19(2)(a) and Sch 4 para 22 CTB Regs
59 CIS/11482/1995
60 C3.96 GM
61 **IS** Reg 35(2)(a) IS Regs
JSA Reg 98(2)(a) JSA Regs
Both para 26043 DMG
62 **HB** Reg 28(2)(a) HB Regs
CTB Reg 19(2)(a) CTB Regs
63 **IS** Reg 48(5) IS Regs
JSA Reg 110(5) JSA Regs
HB Reg 40(5) HB Regs
CTB Reg 31(5) CTB Regs
64 **IS** Reg 48(6) IS Regs
JSA Reg 110(6) JSA Regs
65 **IS** Reg 35(2)(c) IS Regs
JSA Reg 98(2)(d) JSA Regs
HB Reg 28(2)(b) HB Regs
CTB Reg 19(2)(b) CTB Regs
66 CIS/77/1993; CIS/89/1989

67 **IS** Sch 8 para 11 IS Regs
JSA Sch 6 para 14 JSA Regs
HB Sch 3 para 11 HB Regs
CTB Sch 3 para 11 CTB Regs
68 **IS** Sch 8 para 12 IS Regs
JSA Sch 6 para 15 JSA Regs
HB Sch 3 para 12 HB Regs
CTB Sch 3 para 12 CTB Regs
69 **IS** Reg 35(2)(d) IS Regs
JSA Reg 98(2)(e) JSA Regs
HB Reg 28(2)(c) HB Regs
CTB Reg 19(2)(c) CTB Regs
70 **IS** Reg 40(4) and Sch 9 para 1 IS Regs
JSA Reg 103(6) and Sch 7 para 1 JSA Regs
HB Reg 33(4) and Sch 4 para 1 HB Regs
CTB Reg 24(5) and Sch 4 para 1 CTB Regs
71 **IS** Regs 35(1)(i) and (3) and 5(5) IS Regs
JSA Regs 98(1)(b) and 52(3) JSA Regs
72 **IS** Regs 35(1)(b) and 40(1) IS Regs
JSA Regs 98(2)(b) and 103(1) JSA Regs
HB Regs 28(1)(b) and 33(1) HB Regs
CTB Regs 19(1)(b) and 24(1) CTB Regs
73 **IS** Sch 8 para 1(A) IS Regs
JSA Sch 6 para 1(a)(i) JSA Regs
74 **IS** Regs 5(5) and 35(1)(b)-(e) and (g)-(i) and Sch 8 para 1(a)(ii) IS Regs
JSA Regs 53(3) and 98(1)(b), (c), (f) and (g) and Sch 6 para 1(a)(ii) JSA Regs
75 Reg 29(4B) and (4D)(b) IS Regs
76 Regs 35(1)(i), 35(1A) and 48(11) IS Regs
77 **IS** Regs 5(5) and 29(3)(a) IS Regs
JSA Regs 52(3) and 94(3)(a) JSA Regs
78 **IS** Reg 29(4) IS Regs
JSA Reg 94(4) JSA Regs
79 **IS** Reg 29(3)(b) IS Regs
JSA Reg 94(3)(b) JSA Regs
80 **IS** Reg 5(5) and Sch 8 para 1(b) IS Regs
JSA Reg 52(3) and Sch 6 para 1(b) JSA Regs
81 **IS** Sch 8 para 2 IS Regs
JSA Sch 6 para 2 JSA Regs
82 Regs 29(4C) and 32(7) IS Regs
83 **IS** Reg 29(4) and (4C) IS Regs
JSA Reg 94(4) JSA Regs
84 R(IS) 3/93; CIS/104/1989
85 *Owen v CAO*, 29 April 1999 (CA), reported as R(IS) 8/99
86 **HB** Sch 3 para 1(aa) HB Regs
CTB Sch 3 para 1(aa) CTB Regs
87 **HB** Sch 3 para 1(b) HB Regs
CTB Sch 3 para 1(b) CTB Regs
88 **HB** Sch 3 para 2 HB Regs
CTB Sch 3 para 2 CTB Regs
89 **IS** Reg 37(1) IS Regs
JSA Reg 100(1) JSA Regs
HB Reg 30 HB Regs
CTB Reg 21 CTB Regs
90 **IS** Reg 38(3) IS Regs
JSA Reg 101(4) JSA Regs
HB Reg 31(3) HB Regs
CTB Reg 22(3) CTB Regs
91 **IS** Reg 2(1) IS Regs
JSA s35(1) JSA 1995
HB Regs 2(1) and 31(11)-(12) HB Regs
CTB Regs 2(1) and 22(11)-(12) CTB Regs
92 Reg 32(3) SS(C&P) Regs
93 **IS** Reg 37(2)(a) IS Regs
JSA Reg 100(2)(a) JSA Regs
HB Sch 4 para 42 HB Regs
CTB Sch 4 para 21 CTB Regs
94 **IS** Reg 38(3)(a), (4), (7) and (8)(a) IS Regs
JSA Reg 101(4) and (8) JSA Regs
HB Reg 31(3)(a), (4), (7) and (8)(a) HB Regs
CTB Reg 22(3)(a), (4), (7) and (8)(a) CTB Regs
95 R(IS) 13/91; R(FC) 1/91; CFC/26/1989
96 **IS** Reg 38(6) and (8)(b) IS Regs
JSA Reg 101(7) and (9) JSA Regs
HB Reg 31(6) and (8)(b) HB Regs
CTB Reg 22(6) and (8)(b) CTB Regs
97 **IS** Reg 38(5) IS Regs
JSA Reg 101(6) and (8) JSA Regs
HB Reg 31(5) HB Regs
CTB Reg 22(5) CTB Regs
98 R(FC) 1/96 (formerly CFC/41/1993), following CFC/19/1993 and disagreeing with CFC/22/1989, CFC/19/1992 and CFC/10/1993
99 **IS** Reg 38(11) IS Regs
JSA Reg 101(12) JSA Regs
HB Reg 31(10) HB Regs
CTB Reg 22(10) CTB Regs
See also R(FC) 1/93
100 CFC/836/1995
101 **IS** Reg 30 IS Regs
JSA Reg 95 JSA Regs
102 **IS** CIS/166/1994; CIS/14409/1996
JSA Regs 95(1)(b) and 101(11) JSA Regs
103 **IS** Reg 30(2) IS Regs
JSA Reg 95(2) JSA Regs
104 **HB** Regs 23(1) and 25(2) HB Regs
CTB Regs 15(1) and 17(2) CTB Regs
105 **IS** Reg 38(9) IS Regs
JSA Reg 101(10) JSA Regs
HB Reg 31(9) HB Regs
CTB Reg 22(9) CTB Regs
106 **HB** Sch 3 para 4 HB Regs
CTB Sch 3 para 4 CTB Regs

107 **IS** Sch 8 para 5 IS Regs
JSA Sch 6 para 6 JSA Regs
108 **IS** Sch 8 para 4(2) IS Regs
JSA Sch 6 para 5(1) and (2) JSA Regs
HB Sch 3 para 3(2) HB Regs
CTB Sch 3 para 3(2) CTB Regs
109 **IS** Sch 8 paras 6A and 6B IS Regs
JSA Sch 6 paras 7 and 8 JSA Regs
HB Sch 3 paras 4A and 4B HB Regs
CTB Sch 3 paras 4A and 4B CTB Regs
110 **IS** Sch 8 para 7(1) IS Regs
JSA Sch 6 para 9(1) JSA Regs
HB Sch 3 para 6(1) HB Regs
CTB Sch 3 para 6(1) CTB Regs
111 **IS** Sch 8 para 8 IS Regs
JSA Sch 6 para 10 JSA Regs
HB Sch 3 para 7 HB Regs
CTB Sch 3 para 7 CTB Regs
112 **IS** Sch 8 para 7(2) IS Regs
JSA Sch 6 paras 9-10 JSA Regs
HB Sch 3 para 6(2)(b) HB Regs
CTB Sch 3 para 6(2)(b) CTB Regs
113 **IS** Sch 8 para 4(3) IS Regs
JSA Sch 6 para 5(3) JSA Regs
HB Sch 3 para 3(3) HB Regs
CTB Sch 3 para 3(3) CTB Regs
114 **IS** Sch 8 para 4(4) IS Regs
JSA Sch 6 para 5(4) JSA Regs
HB Sch 3 para 3(4) HB Regs
CTB Sch 3 para 3(4) CTB Regs
115 **IS** Sch 8 paras 6 and 9 IS Regs
JSA Sch 6 paras 11-12 JSA Regs
HB Sch 3 paras 5 and 8 HB Regs
CTB Sch 4 paras 5 and 8 CTB Regs
116 **HB** Sch 3 para 16 HB Regs
CTB Sch 3 para 16 CTB Regs
117 **HB** Regs 21(1)(c) and 21A HB Regs
CTB Regs 13(1)(c) and 13A CTB Regs
For people aged 60 or over:
HB Reg 26(1)(c) HB Regs
CTB Reg 18(1)(c) CTB Regs
as substituted by regs 8 and 17 HB&CTB(SPC) Regs
118 **HB** Reg 21(1ZA) HB Regs
CTB 13(1ZA) CTB Regs
For people aged 60 or over:
HB Reg 26(2) HB Regs
CTB Reg 18(2) CTB Regs
as substituted by regs 8 and 17 HB&CTB(SPC) Regs
119 **HB** Reg 21A(2ZA)-(2ZC) HB Regs
CTB Reg 13A(2ZA)-(2ZC) CTB Regs
For people aged 60 or over:
HB Reg 27(3)-(5) HB Regs
CTB Reg 19(3)-(5) CTB Regs
as substituted by regs 8 and 17 HB&CTB(SPC) Regs
120 **HB** Reg 21A(2ZA) HB Regs
CTB Reg 13A(2ZA) CTB Regs
For people aged 60 or over:
HB Reg 27(3) HB Regs
CTB Reg 19(3) CTB Regs
as substituted by regs 8 and 17 HB&CTB(SPC) Regs
121 **HB** Reg 21A(7) HB Regs
CTB Reg 13A(7) CTB Regs
For people aged 60 or over:
HB Reg 27(11) HB Regs
CTB Reg 19(11) CTB Regs
as substituted by regs 8 and 17 HB&CTB(SPC) Regs
122 **HB** Reg 21A(1A)-(1C) HB Regs
CTB Reg 13A(1A)-(1C) CTB Regs
For people aged 60 or over:
HB Reg 27(1A)-(1C) HB Regs
CTB Reg 19(1A)-(1C) CTB Regs
as substituted by regs 8 and 17 HB&CTB(SPC) Regs
123 **HB** Reg 21A(4) HB Regs
CTB Reg 13A(4) CTB Regs
For people aged 60 or over:
HB Reg 27(8) HB Regs
CTB Reg 19(8) CTB Regs
as substituted by regs 8 and 17 HB&CTB(SPC) Regs
124 **HB** Reg 21A(6) HB Regs
CTB Reg 13A(6) CTB Regs
For people aged 60 or over:
HB Reg 27(10) HB Regs
CTB Reg 19(10) CTB Regs
as substituted by regs 8 and 17 HB&CTB(SPC) Regs
125 **HB** Reg 21A(3) HB Regs
CTB Reg 13A(3) CTB Regs
For people aged 60 or over:
HB Reg 27(7) HB Regs
CTB Reg 19(7) CTB Regs
as substituted by regs 8 and 17 HB&CTB(SPC) Regs
126 CIS/1067/2004
127 **IS** Reg 7(4) and (5) SS(WTCCTC)(CA) Regs
JSA Reg 8(3) and (4) SS(WTCCTC)(CA) Regs
128 **IS** Reg 7(6) SS(WTCCTC)(CA) Regs
JSA Reg 8(5) SS(WTCCTC)(CA) Regs
129 **IS** Reg 35(2) and Sch 9 para 4 IS Regs
JSA Sch 7 para 5 JSA Regs
130 **HB** Reg 28(1)(i) HB Regs
CTB Reg 19(1)(i) CTB Regs
131 **HB** Sch 4 para 58 HB Regs
CTB Sch 4 para 57 CTB Regs

132 **IS** Sch 9 IS Regs
JSA Sch 7 JSA Regs
HB Sch 4 HB Regs
CTB Sch 4 CTB Regs
133 **IS** Sch 9 para 9 IS Regs
JSA Sch 7 para 10 JSA Regs
HB Sch 4 para 8 HB Regs
CTB Sch 4 para 8 CTB Regs
134 **IS** Sch 9 para 5B(2) IS Regs
JSA Sch 7 para 6B(2) JSA Regs
135 **IS** Sch 9 para 5B(1) IS Regs
JSA Sch 7 para 6B(1) JSA Regs
136 **IS** Sch 9 para 9 IS Regs
JSA Sch 7 para 10 JSA Regs
HB Sch 4 paras 5 and 8 HB Regs
CTB Sch 4 paras 5 and 8 CTB Regs
137 **IS** Sch 9 paras 6 and 9 IS Regs
JSA Sch 7 paras 7 and 10 JSA Regs
HB Sch 4 para 5 HB Regs
CTB Sch 4 para 5 CTB Regs
138 **IS** Sch 9 para 5A(1) IS Regs
JSA Sch 7 para 6A(1) JSA Regs
HB Sch 4 para 50 HB Regs
CTB Sch 4 para 49 CTB Regs
139 **IS** Sch 9 para 8 IS Regs
JSA Sch 7 para 9 JSA Regs
HB Sch 4 para 7 HB Regs
CTB Sch 4 para 7 CTB Regs
140 **IS** Sch 9 para 33 IS Regs
JSA Sch 7 para 35 JSA Regs
HB Sch 4 para 31 HB Regs
CTB Sch 4 para 32 CTB Regs
141 **IS** Sch 9 paras 7 and 8 IS Regs
JSA Sch 7 paras 8 and 9 JSA Regs
HB Sch 4 paras 6 and 7 HB Regs
CTB Sch 4 paras 6 and 7 CTB Regs
142 **IS** Sch 9 para 31 IS Regs
JSA Schs 7 para 33 and 8 para 23 JSA Regs
HB Sch 4 para 30 HB Regs
CTB Sch 4 para 31 CTB Regs
143 **IS** Sch 10 para 18 IS Regs
JSA Sch 8 para 23 JSA Regs
HB Sch 5 para 19 HB Regs
CTB Sch 5 para 19 CTB Regs
144 **IS** Sch 9 paras 5, 45 and 52 IS Regs
JSA Sch 7 paras 6, 44 and 51 JSA Regs
HB Sch 4 paras 40 and 51 HB Regs
CTB Sch 4 paras 36 and 50 CTB Regs
145 **IS** Sch 9 para 47 IS Regs
JSA Sch 7 para 46 JSA Regs
HB Sch 4 para 43 HB Regs
CTB Sch 4 para 42 CTB Regs
146 **IS** Sch 9 paras 54-56 IS Regs
JSA Sch 7 paras 53-55 JSA Regs
HB Sch 4 paras 53-55 HB Regs
CTB Sch 4 paras 52-54 CTB Regs
147 **IS** Sch 9 para 53 IS Regs
JSA Sch 7 para 52 JSA Regs
HB Sch 4 para 52 HB Regs
CTB Sch 4 para 51 CTB Regs
148 **HB** Sch 4 para 4 HB Regs
CTB Sch 4 para 4 CTB Regs
149 **IS** Sch 9 para 38 IS Regs
JSA Sch 7 para 40 JSA Regs
HB Sch 4 para 37 HB Regs
CTB Sch 4 para 39 CTB Regs
150 **IS** Sch 9 paras 40-42 IS Regs
HB Sch 4 paras 35, 36 and 48 HB Regs
CTB Sch 4 paras 37, 38 and 47 CTB Regs
151 **IS** Sch 9 para 40 IS Regs
JSA Sch 7 para 42 JSA Regs
HB Sch 4 para 35 HB Regs
CTB Sch 4 para 37 CTB Regs
152 **IS** Sch 9 para 46 IS Regs
JSA Sch 7 para 45 JSA Regs
HB Sch 4 para 41 HB Regs
CTB Sch 4 para 41 CTB Regs
153 **HB** Sch 4 para 14A HB Regs
CTB Sch 4 para 14A CTB Regs
154 **IS** Sch 9 para 16 IS Regs
JSA Sch 7 para 17 JSA Regs
155 **IS** Sch 9 para 16 IS Regs
JSA Sch 7 para 17 JSA Regs
HB Sch 4 para 14 HB Regs
CTB Sch 4 para 14 CTB Regs
156 R(IS) 3/99
157 **IS** Sch 9 para 16 IS Regs
JSA Sch 7 para 17 JSA Regs
HB Sch 4 para 14 HB Regs
CTB Sch 4 para 14 CTB Regs
158 **IS** Sch 9 para 16 IS Regs
JSA Sch 7 para 17 JSA Regs
HB Sch 4 para 14 HB Regs
CTB Sch 4 para 14 CTB Regs
159 **IS** Sch 9 para 16 IS Regs
JSASch 7 para 17 JSA Regs
HB Sch 4 para 14 HB Regs
CTB Sch 4 para 14 CTB Regs
160 **IS** Sch 9 para 16 IS Regs
JSA Sch 7 para 17 JSA Regs
HB Sch 4 para 14 HB Regs
CTB Sch 4 para 14 CTB Regs
161 **IS** Sch 9 para 16 IS Regs
JSA Sch 7 para 17 JSA Regs
HB Sch 4 para 14 HB Regs
CTB Sch 4 para 14 CTB Regs
162 **IS** Sch 9 para 36 IS Regs
JSA Sch 7 para 38 JSA Regs
HB Sch 4 para 33 HB Regs
CTB Sch 4 para 34 CTB Regs
163 ss134(8) and 139(6) SSAA 1992
164 *R v South Hams District Council, ex parte Ash, The Times*, 27 May 1999

165 s74(2) SSAA 1992
166 **HB** Reg 33(3AA) HB Regs
CTB Reg 24(3A) CTB Regs
167 para C3.644 GM; although there is guidance on this issue, the law itself is unclear
168 **HB** Reg 24A HB Regs as amended
CTB Reg 16A CTB Regs as amended
For people aged 60 or over:
HB Reg 27A HB Regs as amended
CTB Reg 19A CTB Regs as amended
as substituted by regs 8 and 17. HB&CTB(SPC) Regs
169 para C3.657GM
170 **IS** Regs 29, 31(3), 32 and 40 IS Regs
JSA Regs 94, 96(3), 97 and 103 JSA Regs
171 **IS** Sch 9 para 73 IS Regs
JSA Sch 7 para 70 JSA Regs
172 Reg 1(3) Social Security (Child Maintenance Premium) Amendment Regulations 2004 SI No.98
173 **HB** Sch 4 paras 13(3) and 47 HB Regs
CTB Sch 4 paras 13(3) and 46 CTB Regs
174 CIS/683/1993
175 **IS** Sch 9 para 25(1)(a) and (1A) IS Regs
JSA Sch 7 para 26(1)(a) and (1A) JSA Regs
176 Reg 1 and Schs 1 para 23(c) and 2 para 23(c) SS(WTCCTC)(CA) Regs
177 **IS** Sch 9 para 25(1)(a) and (2)(b) IS Regs
JSA Sch 7 para 26(1)(a) and (2)(b) JSA Regs
HB Sch 4 para 23(1)(a) and (2)(b) HB Regs
CTB Sch 4 para 24(1)(a) and (2)(b) CTB Regs
178 **IS** Sch 9 para 25(2)(a) IS Regs
JSA Sch 7 para 26(2)(a) JSA Regs
179 **IS** Sch 9 para 25(1A) IS Regs
JSA Sch 7 para 26(1A) JSA Regs
HB Sch 4 para 23 (1A) HB Regs
CTB Sch 4 para 24(1A) CTB Regs
180 **IS** Reg 42(4)(b) IS Regs
JSA Reg 105(10)(b) JSA Regs
HB Reg 35(3)(b) HB Regs
CTB Reg 26(3)(b) CTB Regs
181 That is, under ss23(2)(a) or 59(1)(a) CA 1989 or (in Scotland) s26 Children (Scotland) Act 1995 or reg 9 Boarding Out and Fostering of Children (Scotland) Regulations 1985
182 **IS** Sch 9 para 26 IS Regs
JSA Sch 7 para 27 JSA Regs
HB Sch 4 para 24 HB Regs
CTB Sch 4 para 25 CTB Regs
183 **IS** Sch 9 para 25(1)(c) and (2) IS Regs
JSA Sch 7 para 26(1) JSA Regs
HB Sch 4 para 23(1)(b) and (2) HB Regs
CTB Sch 4 para 24(1)(b) and (2) CTB Regs
184 **IS** Reg 48(8) IS Regs
JSA Reg 110(8) JSA Regs
185 **IS** Sch 9 para 25(1)(e) IS Regs
JSA Sch 7 para 26(1) JSA Regs
HB Sch 4 para 23(1)(d) HB Regs
CTB Sch 4 para 24(1)(d) CTB Regs
186 para 12 Memo DMG JSA/IS 76
187 **IS** Sch 9 para 39 IS Regs
JSA Sch 7 para 41(1) JSA Regs
HB Sch 4 para 34 HB Regs
CTB Sch 4 para 35 CTB Regs
188 **IS** Sch 9 para 39 IS Regs
JSA Sch 7 para 41(2) JSA Regs
HB Sch 4 para 34 HB Regs
CTB Sch 4 para 35 CTB Regs
189 **IS** Reg 48(9) IS Regs
JSA Reg 110(9) JSA Regs
HB Reg 40(6) HB Regs
CTB Reg 31(6) CTB Regs
190 **IS** Reg 48(10)(a) IS Regs
JSA Reg 110(10) JSA Regs
191 **IS** Reg 48(10)(b) IS Regs
JSA Reg 110(10)(b) JSA Regs
192 **IS** Sch 9 para 15 IS Regs
JSA Sch 7 para 15 JSA Regs
HB Sch 4 para 13 HB Regs
CTB Sch 4 para 13 CTB Regs
All See *Secretary of State for Work and Pensions v Perkins and Ryedale District Council* [2004] EWCA Civ 1671, 17 November 2004, unreported (EWCA) if it is not clear what the payments are intended or used for
193 **IS** Sch 9 para 15A IS Regs
JSA Sch 7 para 16 JSA Regs
194 CH/3013/2003 explains the difference between a loan and a voluntary payment
195 **IS** Sch 9 paras 15(4) and 36 IS Regs
JSA Sch 7 paras 15(4) and 38 JSA Regs
HB Sch 4 paras 13(4) and 33 HB Regs
CTB Sch 4 paras 13(4) and 34 CTB Regs
196 **HB** Sch 4 para 13(2A) HB Regs
CTB Sch 4 para 13(2A) CTB Regs
197 HB/CTB Circular A17/97
198 **IS** Sch 9 para 15(5A) IS Regs
JSA Sch 7 para 15(5A) JSA Regs
HB Sch 4 para 13(6) HB Regs
CTB Sch 4 para 13(6) CTB Regs
199 **IS** Sch 9 para 19 IS Regs
JSA Sch 7 para 20 JSA Regs
HB Sch 4 para 20 HB Regs
CTB Sch 4 para 20 CTB Regs

200 **IS** Sch 9 para 18 IS Regs
JSA Sch 7 para 19 JSA Regs
HB Sch 4 para 19 HB Regs
CTB Sch 4 para 19 CTB Regs
201 **IS** Sch 9 para 20 IS Regs
JSA Sch 7 para 21 JSA Regs
HB Sch 4 para 42 HB Regs
CTB Sch 4 para 21 CTB Regs
202 **All** Definition of 'board and lodging accommodation'
IS Reg 2(1) IS Regs
JSA Reg 1(3) JSA Regs
HB Sch 4 para 42(2) HB Regs
CTB Sch 4 para 21(2) CTB Regs
203 CIS/521/2002
204 CIS/13059/1996
205 **IS** Reg 48(4) IS Regs
JSA Reg 110(4) JSA Regs
HB Reg 40(4) HB Regs
CTB Reg 31(4) CTB Regs
All *CAO v Palfrey and Others, The Times*, 17 February 1995, R(IS) 26/95
206 R(IS) 26/95
207 **IS** Sch 9 para 22(1) IS Regs
JSA Sch 7 para 23 JSA Regs
HB Sch 4 para 15(1) HB Regs
CTB Sch 4 para 15(1) CTB Regs
208 **IS** Reg 48(4) IS Regs
JSA Reg 110(4) JSA Regs
HB Reg 40(4) HB Regs
CTB Reg 31(4) CTB Regs
209 **IS** Sch 9 para 22(1) IS Regs
JSA Sch 7 para 23(2) JSA Regs
HB Sch 4 para 15(1) HB Regs
CTB Sch 4 para 15(1) CTB Regs
210 CFC/13/1993
211 **IS** Sch 9 para 22(2) IS Regs
JSA Sch 7 para 23(2) and (3) JSA Regs
HB Sch 4 para 15(2) HB Regs
CTB Sch 4 para 15(2) CTB Regs
212 **IS** Reg 53 IS Regs
JSA Reg 116 JSA Regs
HB Reg 45 HB Regs
CTB Reg 37 CTB Regs
213 **IS** Reg 32(1B) SS(C&P) Regs
JSA Reg 24(7) JSA Regs
214 **HB** Reg 75 HB Regs
CTB Reg 65 CTB Regs
215 **IS** Reg 41(1) IS Regs
JSA Reg 104(1) JSA Regs
216 **HB** Reg 34(1) HB Regs
CTB Reg 25(1) CTB Regs
217 **IS** Reg 29(2)(a) IS Regs
JSA Reg 94(2)(a) JSA Regs
HB Reg 25 HB Regs
CTB Reg 17 CTB Regs
218 **IS** Reg 44(1) and (5) IS Regs
JSA Reg 106(1) and (5) JSA Regs
HB Reg 36(2) and (5) HB Regs
CTB Reg 27(2) and (5) CTB Regs
219 **IS** Reg 32(1) IS Regs
JSA Reg 97(1) JSA Regs
HB Reg 25(1) HB Regs
CTB Reg 17(1) CTB Regs
220 **IS** Reg 41(2) IS Regs
JSA Reg 104(2) JSA Regs
HB Reg 34(2) HB Regs
CTB Reg 25(2) CTB Regs
221 **IS** Reg 41(6) IS Regs
JSA Reg 104(5) JSA Regs
HB Reg 34(4) HB Regs
CTB Reg 25(4) CTB Regs
222 Regs 41(4) and 48(2) IS Regs
223 **IS** Reg 41(3) IS Regs
JSA Reg 104(3) JSA Regs
224 **IS** Reg 41(7) IS Regs
JSA Reg 104(6) JSA Regs
HB Reg 34(5) HB Regs
CTB Reg 25(5) CTB Regs
225 *R v SBC ex parte Singer* [1973] 1 All ER 931; *R v Oxford County Council ex parte Jack* [1984] 17 HLR 419; *R v West Dorset DC ex parte Poupard* [1988] 20 HLR 295; para C3.118 GM
226 paras C2.09(xix) and 3.118 GM
227 *R v West Dorset DC ex parte Poupard* [1988] 20 HLR 295
228 **IS** Sch 10 para 20 IS Regs
JSA Sch 8 para 25 JSA Regs
HB Sch 5 para 21 HB Regs
CTB Sch 5 para 21 CTB Regs
229 **IS** Reg 48(2) IS Regs
JSA Reg 110(2) JSA Regs
HB Reg 40(2) HB Regs
CTB Reg 31(2) CTB Regs
230 **IS** s126(5) SSCBA 1992
JSA s5(2)(c) JSA 1995
231 Regs 41(4) and 48(2) IS Regs
232 **IS** Sch 9 para 13 IS Regs
JSA Sch 7 para 14 JSA Regs
HB Sch 4 para 11 HB Regs
CTB Sch 4 para 11 CTB Regs
233 **IS** Sch 9 para 64 IS Regs
JSA Sch 7 para 62 JSA Regs
HB Sch 4 para 66 HB Regs
CTB Sch 4 para 66 CTB Regs
All Reg 18 SS(NDP) Regs
234 **HB** Reg 40(7) HB Regs
CTB Reg 31(7) CTB Regs
235 **IS** Regs 39C and 39D IS Regs
JSA Regs 102C and 102D JSA Regs

236 **IS** Reg 40(4) IS Regs
JSA Regs 103(6) and 98(2)(e) JSA Regs
HB Reg 33(4) HB Regs
CTB Reg 24(5) CTB Regs
All Definition of 'occupational pension' in reg 2(1) of each of those Regs
237 **IS** Reg 41(2) and Sch 9 para 17 IS Regs
JSA Reg 104(2) and Sch 7 para 18 JSA Regs
HB Reg 34(2) and Sch 4 para 16 HB Regs
CTB Reg 25(2) and Sch 4 para 16 CTB Regs
238 **IS** Sch 9 para 29 IS Regs; para 28240 DMG
JSA Sch 7 para 30 JSA Regs
239 **IS** Sch 9 para 30 IS Regs
JSA Sch 7 para 31 JSA Regs
Both R(IS) 13/01
240 **HB** Sch 4 para 28 HB Regs
CTB Sch 4 para 29 CTB Regs
241 **IS** Sch 9 para 30ZA IS Regs
JSA Sch 7 para 31A JSA Regs
HB Sch 4 para 28 HB Regs
CTB Sch 4 para 29 CTB Regs
242 **IS** Sch 9 para 28 IS Regs
JSA Sch 7 para 29 JSA Regs
HB Sch 4 para 26 HB Regs
CTB Sch 4 para 27 CTB Regs
243 **IS** Sch 9 para 58 IS Regs
JSA Sch 7 para 56 JSA Regs
HB Sch 4 para 67 HB Regs
CTB Sch 4 para 62 CTB Regs
244 **IS** Sch 9 para 27 IS Regs
JSA Sch 7 para 28 JSA Regs
HB Sch 4 para 25 HB Regs
CTB Sch 4 para 26 CTB Regs
245 **IS** Sch 10 para 8(b) IS Regs
JSA Sch 8 para 13(b) JSA Regs
HB Sch 5 para 9(b) HB Regs
CTB Sch 5 para 9(b) CTB Regs
246 **IS** Sch 9 para 76 IS Regs
JSA Sch 7 para 72 JSA Regs
HB Sch 4 para 75 HB Regs
CTB Sch 4 para 74 CTB Regs
247 **IS** Sch 9 para 11 IS Regs
JSA Sch 7 para 12 JSA Regs
HB Sch 4 para 10 HB Regs
CTB Sch 4 para 10 CTB Regs
248 **IS** Sch 9 para 2 IS Regs
JSA Sch 7 para 2 JSA Regs
HB Sch 4 para 2 HB Regs
CTB Sch 4 para 2 CTB Regs
249 **IS** Sch 9 para 21 IS Regs
JSA Sch 7 para 22 JSA Regs
HB Sch 4 para 21 HB Regs
CTB Sch 4 para 22 CTB Regs
250 para C3 Annex B para 13 GM
251 HB/CTB Circular A17/97
252 **IS** Sch 9 para 51 IS Regs
JSA Sch 7 para 50 JSA Regs
HB Sch 4 para 49 HB Regs
CTB Sch 4 para 48 CTB Regs
253 **IS** Sch 9 para 72 IS Regs
JSA Sch 7 para 69 JSA Regs
HB Sch 4 para 73 HB Regs
CTB Sch 4 para 72 CTB Regs
254 **IS** Sch 9 para 43 IS Regs
JSA Sch 7 para 43 JSA Regs
HB Sch 4 para 38 HB Regs
CTB Sch 4 para 40 CTB Regs
255 **IS** Sch 9 para 10 IS Regs
JSA Sch 7 para 11 JSA Regs
HB Sch 4 para 9 HB Regs
CTB Sch 4 para 9 CTB Regs
256 **IS** Sch 9 para 23 IS Regs
JSA Sch 7 para 24 JSA Regs
HB Sch 4 para 22 HB Regs
CTB Sch 4 para 23 CTB Regs
257 **IS** Sch 9 para 24 IS Regs
JSA Sch 7 para 25 JSA Regs
HB Sch 4 para 32 HB Regs
CTB Sch 4 para 33 CTB Regs
258 **IS** Sch 9 para 48 IS Regs
JSA Sch 7 para 47 JSA Regs
HB Sch 4 para 44 HB Regs
CTB Sch 4 para 43 CTB Regs
259 **IS** Sch 9 para 49 IS Regs
JSA Sch 7 para 48 JSA Regs
HB Sch 4 para 45 HB Regs
CTB Sch 4 para 44 CTB Regs
260 **IS** Sch 9 para 50 IS Regs
JSA Sch 7 para 49 JSA Regs
HB Sch 4 para 46 HB Regs
CTB Sch 4 para 45 CTB Regs
261 **HB** Sch 4 para 17 HB Regs
CTB Sch 4 para 17 CTB Regs
262 **HB** Sch 3 para 9 HB Regs
CTB Sch 3 para 9 CTB Regs
263 **HB** Sch 4 para 18 HB Regs
CTB Sch 4 para 18 CTB Regs
264 **HB** Sch 3 para 9 HB Regs
CTB Sch 3 para 9 CTB Regs
265 **IS** Sch 9 para 69 IS Regs
JSA Sch 7 para 67 JSA Regs
HB Sch 4 para 71 HB Regs
CTB Sch 4 para 70 CTB Regs
266 **IS** Sch 9 para 75 IS Regs
JSA Sch 7 para 71 JSA Regs
HB Sch 4 para 74 HB Regs
CTB Sch 4 para 73 CTB Regs
267 **IS** Reg 42(1) IS Regs
JSA Reg 105(1) JSA Regs
HB Reg 35(1) HB Regs
CTB Reg 26(1) CTB Regs

268 paras 28608-16 DMG; see also CIS/15052/1996
269 CSIS/57/1992
270 **IS** Reg 42(2) IS Regs
JSA Reg 105(2) JSA Regs
HB Reg 35(2) HB Regs
CTB Reg 26(2) CTB Regs
271 **IS** Reg 42(2A) IS Regs
JSA Reg 105(3) JSA Regs
HB Reg 35(2A) HB Regs
CTB Reg 26(2A) CTB Regs
272 **IS** Reg 42(2)(e)-(f) IS Regs
JSA Reg 105(2)(d) JSA Regs
HB Reg 35(2)(f)-(g) HB Regs
CTB Reg 34(2)(f)-(g) CTB Regs
273 CIS/16271/1996
274 paras 28608-16 DMG
275 CIS/15052/1996, para 11
276 **IS** Reg 42(3) IS Regs
JSA Reg 105(6) JSA Regs
277 para C3.273 GM
278 **IS** Reg 42(3A) and (3B) IS Regs
JSA Reg 105(7)(a), (8) and (9) JSA Regs
279 **IS** Reg 42(3C) IS Regs
JSA Reg 105(7)(d) JSA Regs
280 CIS/15052/1996, para 10
281 **IS** Reg 70(2)(b) IS Regs
JSA Regs 147-149 JSA Regs
282 **IS** Reg 42(5) IS Regs
JSA Reg 105(12) JSA Regs
283 Reg 2 SS(PAOR) Regs
284 **IS** Reg 42(4)(a)(ia) and (4ZA)(d) IS Regs
JSA Reg 105(10)(a)(ia) and (10A)(d) JSA Regs
HB Reg 35(3)(za) and (3A)(d) HB Regs
CTB Reg 26(3)(za) and (3A)(d) CTB Regs
285 R(IS) 4/01
286 **IS** Reg 42(4) and (4ZA) IS Regs
JSA Reg 105(10) and (10A) JSA Regs
287 **IS** Reg 42(4ZA) IS Regs
JSA Reg 105(10A) JSA Regs
HB Reg 35(3A) HB Regs
CTB Reg 26(3A) CTB Regs
288 **IS** Reg 42(4)(b) IS Regs
JSA Reg 105(10)(b) JSA Regs
HB Reg 35(3)(b) HB Regs
CTB Reg 26(3)(b) CTB Regs
289 **IS** Reg 42(6) IS Regs; CIS/191/1991
JSA Reg 105(13) JSA Regs
HB Reg 35(5) HB Regs
CTB Reg 26(5) CTB Regs
290 CCS/4912/1998
291 R(SB) 13/86
292 Reg 42(6A)(c) IS Regs
293 **IS** Reg 42(6A)(b) IS Regs
JSA Reg 105(13A)(b) JSA Regs
HB Reg 35(5A)(b) HB Regs
CTB Reg 26(5A)(b) CTB Regs
294 R(SB) 13/86
295 **IS** Reg 42(6A)(a) IS Regs
JSA Reg 105(13A)(a) JSA Regs
HB Reg 35(5A)(a) HB Regs
CTB Reg 26(5A)(a) CTB Regs
296 R(IS) 12/92
297 **IS** Reg 42(6A)(b)(i) IS Regs
JSA Reg 105(13A)(b)(i) JSA Regs
HB Reg 35(5A)(b)(i) HB Regs
CTB Reg 26(5A)(b)(i) CTB Regs
298 CIS/147/1993
299 *Sharrock v CAO*, 26 March 1991 (CA); CIS/93/1991
300 CIS/93/1991
301 CIS/422/1992
302 CIS/701/1994
303 CIS/422/1992
304 CIS/701/1994
305 s1(3)(a) Carers (Recognition and Services) Act 1995 excludes those who care 'by virtue of a contract of employment or other contract' which, according to policy guidance issued by the Department of Health, means 'anyone who is providing personal assistance for payment either in cash or in kind'
306 **HB** Reg 24 HB Regs
CTB Reg 16 CTB Regs
307 **HB** Reg 22(1)(a) HB Regs
CTB Reg 14(1)(a) CTB Regs
Both para C3.53 GM
308 **HB** Reg 22(1)(b) HB Regs
CTB Reg 14(1)(b) CTB Regs
Both para C3.53 GM
309 *R v HBRB of the London Borough of Ealing ex parte Saville* [1986] 18 HLR 349
310 **HB** Reg 22(2)(a)-(b) HB Regs
CTB Reg 14(2)(a)-(b) CTB Regs
Both para C3.19 GM
311 **HB** Reg 22(3) HB Regs
CTB Reg 14(3) CTB Regs
312 **IS** Reg 32(1) IS Regs
JSA Reg 97 JSA Regs
HB Reg 25 HB Regs
CTB Reg 17 CTB Regs
313 R(IS) 3/93
314 R(IS) 10/95
315 **IS** Reg 32(6) IS Regs
JSA Reg 97(6) JSA Regs
316 **IS** Reg 32(2) and (3) IS Regs
JSA Reg 97(2) and (3) JSA Regs
317 **IS** Reg 32(4) IS Regs
JSA Reg 97(4) JSA Regs

318 **IS** Reg 32(5) and Sch 8 para 10 IS Regs
JSA Reg 97(5) and Sch 6 para 13 JSA Regs
319 **IS** Reg 29(2)(a) IS Regs
JSA Reg 94(2)(a) JSA Regs
320 **IS** Reg 29(2)(b) IS Regs
JSA Reg 94(2)(b) JSA Regs
321 **IS** Reg 31(1)(a) IS Regs
JSA Reg 96(1)(a) JSA Regs
322 **IS** Reg 31(1)(b) IS Regs
JSA Reg 96(1)(b) JSA Regs
323 **IS** Reg 31(2) IS Regs
JSA Reg 96(2) JSA Regs
324 **IS** Reg 31(3) IS Regs
JSA Reg 96(3) JSA Regs
325 **IS** Reg 2(1) IS Regs
JSA Reg 1(3) JSA Regs
326 R(SB) 33/83
327 R(SB) 22/84; R(SB) 11/85
328 CIS/590/1993

2. **Income: aged 60 or over**
329 **HB/CTB** s136(1) SSCBA 1992
PC s5 SPCA 2002
330 **HB** Reg 19(4) HB Regs
CTB Reg 11(4) CTB Regs
331 **PC** Reg 24 SPC Regs
HB Reg 37 HB Regs
CTB Reg 29 CTB Regs
as substituted by regs 8 and 17 HB&CTB(SPC) Regs
all of which only refer to payments made to a third party in respect of the 'claimant', not any member of her/his family
332 **HB** Reg 21 and 22 HB Regs
CTB Regs 13 and 14 CTB Regs
as substituted by regs 8 and 17 HB&CTB(SPC) Regs
333 **HB** Reg 23(4) HB Regs
CTB Reg 15(4) CTB Regs
as substituted by regs 8 and 17 HB&CTB(SPC) Regs
334 **HB** Reg 20 HB Regs
335 **HB** Reg 23(4)(b)(iii) and (c) HB Regs
CTB Reg 15(4)(b)(iii) and (c) CTB Regs
as substituted by regs 8 and 17 HB&CTB(SPC) Regs
336 **HB** Reg 25 HB Regs
CTB Reg 17 CTB Regs
as substituted by regs 8 and 17 HB&CTB(SPC) Regs
337 **PC** Reg 17(10) SPC Regs
HB Reg 28(11) HB Regs
CTB Reg 20(11) CTB Regs
as substituted by regs 8 and 17 HB&CTB(SPC) Regs
338 **HB** Reg 29 HB Regs
CTB Reg 21 CTB Regs
as substituted by regs 8 and 17 HB&CTB(SPC) Regs
339 **PC** Regs 17(10) and 17A(4A) SPC Regs
HB Reg 31(2) and (4) HB Regs
CTB Reg 23(2) and (4) CTB Regs
as substituted by regs 8 and 17 HB&CTB(SPC) Regs
340 **HB** Reg 31(5) HB Regs
CTB Reg 23(5) CTB Regs
as substituted by regs 8 and 17 HB&CTB(SPC) Regs
341 **HB** Reg 29 HB Regs
CTB Reg 21 CTB Regs
as substituted by regs 8 and 17 HB&CTB(SPC) Regs
342 *Parsons v Hogg* [1985] 2 All ER 897 (CA), appendix to R(FIS) 4/85
343 **PC** Reg 17A(2) SPC Regs
HB Reg 30(1) HB Regs
CTB Reg 22(1) CTB Regs
as substituted by regs 8 and 17 HB&CTB(SPC) Regs
344 **PC** Reg 17A(h) and (k) SPC Regs
HB Reg 30(1)(h) and (k) HB Regs
CTB Reg 22(1)(h) and (k) CTB Regs
as substituted by regs 8 and 17 HB&CTB(SPC) Regs
345 **PC** Reg 17A(h)-(k) SPC Regs
HB Reg 30(1)(h)-(k) HB Regs
CTB Reg 22(1)(h)-(k) CTB Regs
as substituted by regs 8 and 17 HB&CTB(SPC) Regs
346 **PC** Reg 17A(2)(e) SPC Regs
HB Reg 30(1)(e) HB Regs
CTB Reg 22(1)(e) CTB Regs
as substituted by regs 8 and 17 HB&CTB(SPC) Regs
347 R(IS) 9/95
348 **PC** Reg 17A(2)(g) SPC Regs
HB Reg 30(1)(g) HB Regs
CTB Reg 22(1)(g) CTB Regs
as substituted by regs 8 and 17 HB&CTB(SPC) Regs
349 **PC** Reg 17A(4) SPC Regs
HB Reg 30(3) HB Regs
CTB Reg 22(3) CTB Regs
as substituted by regs 8 and 17 HB&CTB(SPC) Regs
350 **PC** Sch 6 para 6 SPC Regs
HB Sch 3A para 8 HB Regs
CTB Sch 3A para 8 CTB Regs
351 **PC** Reg 17A(3)(a) SPC Regs
HB Reg 30(2)(a) HB Regs
CTB Reg 22(2)(a) CTB Regs
as substituted by regs 8 and 17 HB&CTB(SPC) Regs

352 para 86055 DMG
353 para 86054 DMG
354 **PC** Reg 17A(3)(b) SPC Regs
HB Reg 30(2)(b) HB Regs
CTB Reg 22(2)(b) CTB Regs
as substituted by regs 8 and 17
HB&CTB(SPC) Regs
355 CIS/77/1993; CIS/89/1989
356 **PC** Sch 6 para 7 SPC Regs
HB Sch 3A para 10 HB Regs
CTB Sch 3A para 10 CTB Regs
357 **PC** Reg 17A(3)(c) SPC Regs
HB Reg 30(2)(c) HB Regs
CTB Reg 22(2)(c) CTB Regs
as substituted by regs 8 and 17
HB&CTB(SPC) Regs
358 **PC** s15(1)(c) SPCA 2002
HB Reg 25(1)(c) HB Regs
CTB Reg 17(1)(c) CTB Regs
as substituted by regs 8 and 17
HB&CTB(SPC) Regs
359 **PC** Reg 17A(3)(e) SPC Regs
HB Reg 30(2)(e) HB Regs
CTB Reg 21(2)(e) CTB Regs
as substituted by regs 8 and 17
HB&CTB(SPC) Regs
360 **PC** Reg 17A(3)(d) SPC Regs
HB Reg 30(2)(d) HB Regs
CTB Reg 22(2)(d) CTB Regs
as substituted by regs 8 and 17
HB&CTB(SPC) Regs
361 para 86162 DMG
362 **PC** Sch 6 para 6 SPC Regs
HB Sch 3A para 8 HB Regs
CTB Sch 3A para 8 CTB Regs
363 Reg 17ZA SPC Regs
364 **PC** Reg 17B(5) SPC Regs; reg 13(1) and (4) SSB(CE) Regs
HB Reg 34(1)-(3) HB Regs
CTB Reg 26(1)-(3) CTB Regs
as substituted by regs 8 and 17
HB&CTB(SPC) Regs
365 **PC** Reg 17B(1) SPC Regs; regs 2 and 13(4) SSB(CE) Regs
HB Regs 2(1), 34(2) and (11) HB Regs
CTB Regs 2(1), 26(2) and (11) CTB Regs
as substituted by regs 8 and 17
HB&CTB(SPC) Regs
366 Reg 32(3) SS(C&P) Regs
367 **PC** Reg 17B(4)(b) SPC Regs; reg 12(2) SSB(CE) Regs
HB Reg 33(2)(a) HB Regs
CTB Reg 25(2)(a) CTB Regs
as substituted by regs 8 and 17
HB&CTB(SPC) Regs
368 **PC** Reg 17B SPC Regs; reg 11(1) SSB(CE) Regs
HB Reg 32(1) HB Regs
CTB Reg 24(1) CTB Regs
as substituted by regs 8 and 17
HB&CTB(SPC) Regs
369 **PC** Reg 17B(5)(b) SPC Regs; reg 13(10) SSB(CE) Regs
HB Reg 34(8) HB Regs
CTB Reg 26(8) CTB Regs
as substituted by regs 8 and 17
HB&CTB(SPC) Regs
370 **HB** Sch 3A para 6 HB Regs
CTB Sch 3A para 6 CTB Regs
371 **PC** Sch 6 para 6 SPC Regs
HB Sch 3A para 8 HB Regs
CTB Sch 3A para 8 CTB Regs
372 **PC** Sch 6 para 7 SPC Regs
HB Sch 3A para 10 HB Regs
CTB Sch 3A para 10 CTB Regs
373 **HB** Sch 3A para 2 HB Regs
CTB Sch 3A para 2 CTB Regs
374 **PC** Sch 6 para 1 SPC Regs
375 **PC** Sch 6 para 4(1)(a) SPC Regs
HB Sch 3A para 5(1)(a) HB Regs
CTB Sch 3A para 5(1)(a) CTB Regs
376 **PC** Sch 6 para 4(1)(b) SPC Regs
HB Sch 3A para 5(1)(b) HB Regs
CTB Sch 3A para 5(1)(b) CTB Regs
377 **HB** Sch 3A para 5(1)(c) HB Regs
CTB Sch 3A para 5(1)(c) CTB Regs
378 **PC** Sch 6 paras 3 and 4A SPC Regs
HB Sch 3A para 4 HB Regs
CTB Sch 3A para 4 CTB Regs
379 **PC** Sch 6 para 4(2) SPC Regs
HB Sch 3A para 5(2) HB Regs
CTB Sch 3A para 5(2) CTB Regs
380 Sch 6 para 4(3) SPC Regs
381 **PC** Sch 6 para 2 SPC Regs
HB Sch 3A para 3 HB Regs
CTB Sch 3A para 3 CTB Regs
382 **PC** Sch 6 para 5 SPC Regs
HB Sch 3A para 7 HB Regs
CTB Sch 3A para 7 CTB Regs
383 **HB** Sch 3A para 9 HB Regs
CTB Sch 3A para 9 CTB Regs
384 **HB** Reg 26(1)(c) HB Regs
CTB Reg 18(1)(c) CTB Regs
as substituted by regs 8 and 17
HB&CTB(SPC) Regs
385 Reg 15(1)(f) SPC Regs
386 **PC** Reg 17A(2)(h)-(j) SPC Regs
HB Reg 30(1)(h)-(j) HB Regs
CTB Reg 22(1)(h)-(j) CTB Regs
as substituted by regs 8 and 17
HB&CTB(SPC) Regs

387 **PC** s15(1)(b) SPCA 2002
HB Sch 4A para 21 HB Regs
CTB Sch 4 para 21 CTB Regs
388 **PC** Reg 15(2) SPC Regs
HB Reg 25(1)(i) HB Regs
CTB Reg 17(1)(i) CTB Regs
as substituted by regs 8 and 17 HB&CTB(SPC) Regs
389 **PC** Reg 15(1) SPC Regs
HB Reg 25(1)(h) HB Regs
CTB Reg 17(1)(h) CTB Regs
as substituted by regs 8 and 17 HB&CTB(SPC) Regs
390 **PC** Reg 15(1)(b) SPC Regs
HB Reg 25(1)(h)(ii) HB Regs
CTB Reg 17(1)(h)(ii) CTB Regs
as substituted by regs 8 and 17 HB&CTB(SPC) Regs
391 **PC** Reg 15(1)(n) SPC Regs
HB Reg 25(1)(h)(xii) HB Regs
CTB Reg 17(1)(h)(xii) CTB Regs
as substituted by regs 8 and 17 HB&CTB(SPC) Regs
392 Reg 15(1)(j) SPC Regs
393 **PC** s15 SPCA 2002
394 **PC** Reg 15(1)(c) and (e) and Sch 4 para 2 SPC Regs
HB Reg 25(1)(h)(iii) and (v) and Sch 4A para 2 HB Regs
CTB Reg 17(1)(h)(iii) and (v) and Sch 4A para 2 CTB Regs
as substituted by regs 8 and 17 HB&CTB(SPC) Regs
395 **PC** Reg 15(1)(a) SPC Regs
HB Reg 25(h)(i) HB Regs
CTB Reg 17(h)(i) CTB Regs
396 **PC** Reg 15(1)(g) SPC Regs
HB Reg 27(1)(h)(vi) HB Regs
CTB Reg 17(1)(h)(vi) CTB Regs
as substituted by regs 8 and 17 HB&CTB(SPC) Regs
397 **PC** Sch 4 para 3 SPC Regs
HB Sch 4A para 3 HB Regs
CTB Sch 4A para 3 CTB Regs
398 **PC** Reg 15(1)(k) SPC Regs
HB Reg 25(1)(h)(ix) HB Regs
CTB Reg 17(1)(h)(ix) CTB Regs
as substituted by regs 8 and 17 HB&CTB(SPC) Regs
399 **PC** Reg 15(1)(i) SPC Regs
HB Reg 25(1)(h)(viii) HB Regs
CTB Reg 17(1)(h)(viii) CTB Regs
as substituted by regs 8 and 17 HB&CTB(SPC) Regs
400 **PC** Reg 15(1)(l) and (m) SPC Regs
HB Reg 25(1)(h)(x) and (xi) HB Regs
CTB Reg 17(1)(h)(x) and (xi) CTB Regs
as substituted by regs 8 and 17 HB&CTB(SPC) Regs
401 **PC** Sch 4 para 17 SPC Regs
HB Sch 4A para 22 HB Regs
CTB Sch 4A para 22 CTB Regs
402 **PC** Sch 4 paras 4-6 SPC Regs
HB Sch 4A paras 4-6 HB Regs
CTB Sch 4A paras 4-6 CTB Regs
403 **PC** Reg 15(1)(h) SPC Regs
HB Reg 25(1)(h)(vii) HB Regs
CTB Reg 17(1)(h)(vii) CTB Regs
as substituted by regs 8 and 17 HB&CTB(SPC) Regs
404 **HB** Sch 4A paras 7 and 8 HB Regs
CTB Sch 4A paras 7 and 8 CTB Regs
405 Sch 4 paras 7 and 7A SPC Regs
406 **PC** Sch 4 para 1(a) SPC Regs
HB Sch 4A para 1(a) HB Regs
CTB Sch 4A para 1(a) CTB Regs
407 **PC** Sch 4 para 1(b) SPC Regs
HB Sch 4A para 1(b) HB Regs
CTB Sch 4A para 1(b) CTB Regs
408 **PC** Sch 4 para 1(c) SPC Regs
HB Sch 4A para 1(c) HB Regs
CTB Sch 4A para 1(c) CTB Regs
409 **PC** Sch 4 para 1(d) SPC Regs
HB Sch 4A para 1(d) HB Regs
CTB Sch 4A para 1(d) CTB Regs
410 **PC** Sch 4 para 1(e) SPC Regs
HB Sch 4A para 1(e) HB Regs
CTB Sch 4A para 1(e) CTB Regs
411 **PC** Sch 4 para 1(f) SPC Regs
HB Sch 4A para 1(f) HB Regs
CTB Sch 4A para 1(f) CTB Regs
412 ss134(8) and 139(6) SSAA 1992
413 *R v South Hams District Council, ex parte Ash*, *The Times*, 27 May 1999
414 s74(2) SSAA 1992
415 **HB** Sch 4A para 20 HB Regs
CTB Sch 4A para 20 CTB Regs
416 **HB** Reg 25(1)(m) HB Regs
CTB Reg 17(1)(m) CTB Regs
as substituted by regs 8 and 17 HB&CTB(SPC) Regs
417 Reg 15(5)(d) SPC Regs
418 CIS/683/1993
419 **PC** Sch 4 para 9 SPC Regs
HB Sch 4A para 10 HB Regs
CTB Sch 4A para 10 CTB Regs
420 **PC** Sch 4 para 8 SPC Regs
HB Sch 4A para 9 HB Regs
CTB Sch 4A para 9 CTB Regs

421 **All** Definition of 'board and lodging accommodation'
PC Sch 4 para 8(2) SPC Regs
HB Reg 2(1) HB Regs
CTB Reg 2(1) CTB Regs
as substituted by regs 3 and 13 HB&CTB(SPC) Regs
422 CIS/521/2002
423 **PC** s15(1)(i) SPCA 2002
HB Reg 25(1)(g) HB Regs
CTB Reg 17(1)(g) CTB Regs
as substituted by regs 8 and 17 HB&CTB(SPC) Regs
424 **PC** Sch 4 para 18 SPC Regs
For **HB/CTB** the Regulations do not explicitly disregard actual income from capital but it is seemingly implied by reg 25(2) HB Regs and reg 17(2) CTB Regs, which treat capital only as producing deemed income except in the limited cases listed
425 **PC** s15(1)(i) SPCA 2002; reg 15(6) and Sch 4 para 18 SPC Regs
HB Reg 25(1)(g) HB Regs
CTB Reg 17(1)(g) CTB Regs
as substituted by regs 8 and 17 HB&CTB(SPC) Regs
426 **HB** Sch 4A para 23 HB Regs
CTB Sch 4A para 23 CTB Regs
427 s15(2) SPCA 2002; reg 15(6) SPC Regs
428 **HB** Regs 21 and 22 HB Regs
CTB Regs 13 and 14 CTB Regs
as substituted by regs 8 and 17 HB&CTB(SPC) Regs
429 **HB** Reg 38 HB Regs
CTB Reg 30 CTB Regs
as substituted by regs 8 and 17 HB&CTB(SPC) Regs
430 **HB** Reg 25(2) HB Regs
CTB Reg 17(2) CTB Regs
431 **PC** ss15(1)(c) and 16(1)SPCA 2002; reg 16 SPC Regs
HB Reg 25(1)(c) HB Regs
CTB Reg 17(1)(c) CTB Regs
as substituted by regs 8 and 17 HB&CTB(SPC) Regs
432 **PC** Reg 16 SPC Regs
HB Reg 25(1)(q) HB Regs
CTB Reg 17(1)(q) CTB Regs
433 **PC** Reg 16 SPC Regs
HB Reg 25(1)(r) HB Regs
CTB Reg 17(1)(r) CTB Regs
as substituted by regs 8 and 17 HB&CTB(SPC) Regs
434 **PC** Reg 16 SPC Regs
HB Reg 25(1)(u) HB Regs
CTB Reg 17(1)(u) CTB Regs
435 para 85136 DMG
436 **PC** Reg 17(9) SPC Regs
HB Reg 28(8) HB Regs
CTB Reg 20(8) CTB Regs
as substituted by regs 8 and 17 HB&CTB(SPC) Regs
437 **PC** Sch 4 para 15 SPC Regs
HB Sch 4A para 16 HB Regs
CTB Sch 4A para 16 CTB Regs
438 **PC** Sch 4 para 16 SPC Regs
HB Sch 4A para 17 HB Regs
CTB Sch 4A para 17 CTB Regs
439 **PC** Sch 4 para 10 SPC Regs
HB Sch 4A para 11 HB Regs
CTB Sch 4A para 11 CTB Regs
440 **PC** Sch 4 para 11 SPC Regs
HB Sch 4A para 12 HB Regs
CTB Sch 4A para 12 CTB Regs
441 **PC** Sch 4 para 11(3)(b) SPC Regs
HB Sch 4A paras 12(3) HB Regs
CTB Sch 4A paras 12(3) CTB Regs
442 **PC** Sch 4 para 14 SPC Regs
HB Sch 4A para 15 HB Regs
CTB Sch 4A para 15 CTB Regs
443 **PC** Sch 4 para 13 SPC Regs
HB Sch 4A para 14 HB Regs
CTB Sch 4A para 14 CTB Regs
444 **PC** Reg 18(6) SPC Regs
HB Reg 36(6) HB Regs
CTB Reg 28(6) CTB Regs
as substituted by regs 8 and 17 HB&CTB(SPC) Regs
445 paras 28608-16 DMG; see also CIS/15052/1996
446 **PC** Reg 18(1)-(5) SPC Regs
HB Reg 36(1)-(5) HB Regs
CTB Reg 28(1)-(5) CTB Regs
as substituted by regs 8 and 17 HB&CTB(SPC) Regs
447 **PC** Reg 24 SPC Regs
HB Reg 37 HB Regs
CTB Reg 29 CTB Regs
as substituted by regs 8 and 17 HB&CTB(SPC) Regs
448 The rules do not include grants and loans in the definition of 'income'
449 **HB** Sch 3A para 6 and Sch 4A para 18 HB Regs
CTB Sch 3A para 6 and Sch 4A para 18 CTB Regs
450 **HB** Sch 4A para 19 HB Regs
CTB Sch 4A para 19 CTB Regs
451 **PC** s15 SPCA 2002; reg 15 SPC Regs
HB Reg 25 HB Regs
CTB Reg 17 CTB Regs
as substituted by regs 8 and 17 HB&CTB(SPC) Regs

452 **PC** Reg 17(2)(b)(i) SPC Regs
HB Reg 28(2)(b)(i) HB Regs
CTB Reg 20(2)(b)(i) CTB Regs
as substituted by regs 8 and 17
HB&CTB(SPC) Regs
453 **PC** Reg 17(2)(b)(ii) SPC Regs
HB Reg 28(2)(b)(ii) HB Regs
CTB Reg 20(2)(b)(ii) CTB Regs
as substituted by regs 8 and 17
HB&CTB(SPC) Regs
454 **PC** Reg 17(4) SPC Regs
HB Reg 28(4) HB Regs
CTB Reg 20(4) CTB Regs
as substituted by regs 8 and 17
HB&CTB(SPC) Regs
455 **PC** Reg 17(1) SPC Regs
HB Reg 28(1) HB Regs
CTB Reg 20(1) CTB Regs
as substituted by regs 8 and 17
HB&CTB(SPC) Regs
456 para 85030 DMG
457 Reg 1(2) SPC Regs
458 Reg 13B SPC Regs
459 para 2 Sch 3B SS&CS(DA) Regs
460 paras 3 and 1(b) Sch 3B SS&CS(DA) Regs

Chapter 39

Capital and means-tested benefits

This chapter explains how capital affects your entitlement to any means-tested benefit. It covers:

1. Capital: aged under 60 (p1023)

This part applies to income support (IS), income-based jobseeker's allowance (JSA) and, if you and your partner (if you have one) are aged under 60, to housing benefit (HB) and council tax benefit (CTB). It looks at:

- the capital limits (p1023);
- whose capital counts (p1026);
- what counts as capital (p1026);
- disregarded capital (p1031);
- notional capital (p1039);
- how capital is valued (p1046).

2. Capital: aged 60 or over (p1050)

This part applies to pension credit (PC) and, if you or your partner (if you have one) are aged 60 or over, to HB and CTB. It looks at:

- how is capital taken into account (p1050);
- the capital limits (p1051);
- whose capital counts (p1052);
- what counts as capital (p1052);
- disregarded capital (p1054);
- notional capital (p1059);
- how capital is valued (p1060).

In this chapter, unless otherwise stated, references to income-based JSA are intended also to refer to joint-claim JSA.

How much capital you have may affect your entitlement to any of the means-tested benefits. The phrase 'means-tested benefits' is used to refer to:

- IS;
- income-based JSA;
- PC;

- HB;
- CTB.

Similar rules on the treatment of capital, and different capital limits, apply to social fund payments (see Chapter 22), grants and loans (see Chapter 21) and certain health benefits (see Chapter 9). The different rules are explained in those chapters.

There are no capital rules for any of the non-means-tested benefits. Your entitlement to any non-means-tested benefit is therefore not affected by any capital you may have.

1. Capital: aged under 60

This part applies to:

- income support (IS) – including those over 60 whose partner is claiming for them;
- income-based jobseeker's allowance (JSA) – including men aged 60 to 64;
- housing benefit (HB) and council tax benefit (CTB) if you and your partner (if you have one) are aged under 60.

If you get **IS or income-based JSA**, you do not need to work out your capital again for HB and CTB purposes because you receive your maximum HB or CTB,[1] less any deductions for non-dependants (see pp115 and 211).

In this part, whenever HB or CTB are referred to, this only applies to the rules for people aged under 60.

The capital limits

Different capital limits apply depending on what benefit is involved, whether you or your partner are aged 60 or over, and if you are living permanently in a care home or similar accommodation.

Whichever capital limit applies, some capital is disregarded (see p1031), but you may also be treated as having some capital which you do not actually possess (see p1039).

Income support and income-based jobseeker's allowance

For IS and income-based JSA, if both you and your partner are aged under 60:

- the lower limit is £3,000;
- the upper limit is £8,000.

If you have over £8,000[2] you are not entitled to benefit. The first £3,000 is ignored and does not affect your weekly benefit at all. If you have between £3,000.01 and

£8,000 you may be entitled to benefit but some income from your capital is assumed.[3] This is 'tariff income' (see p977), which is assumed to be £1 for every £250, or part of £250 of your capital within those limits. The limits are different if you live in a care home (see p1024).

There are some important differences in the rules on capital for urgent cases payments under the IS and income-based JSA schemes (see p666).

If you or your partner are aged 60 or over:

- the lower limit is £6,000;
- the upper limit is £12,000.

The rules on capital for IS and income-based JSA are modified as follows:

- For IS only, if you are aged under 60 but your partner is aged 60 or over, the capital limit is increased to £12,000 (unless you are in residential accommodation – see p1025). The first £6,000 is ignored. The tariff income rules apply to capital between £6,000.01 and £12,000.[4] **Note:** you cannot get IS at all if you are aged 60 or over.
- For income-based JSA only, if you are aged under 60, but your partner is aged 60 or over, or if you are a man aged between 60 and 65, the capital limit is increased to £12,000 (unless you are in residential accommodation – see below). The first £6,000 is ignored. The tariff income rules apply to capital between £6,000.01 and £12,000.[5] **Note:** you cannot get JSA at all if you are of pension age or above – 60 for a woman, 65 for a man.

Housing benefit and council tax benefit

For HB and CTB, if both you and your partner are aged under 60:

- the lower limit is £3,000;
- the upper limit is £16,000.

The basic rule is that if you have over £16,000 you are not entitled to benefit (but for CTB, see p118 for second adult rebate). However, the first £3,000 is ignored and does not affect your weekly benefit at all. If you have between £3,000.01 and £16,000 you may be entitled to benefit but some income from your capital is assumed.[6] This is 'tariff income' (see p977). The limits are different if you live in a care home (see below).

Care homes

There are higher capital limits if you live permanently in a care home or similar accommodation:

- the lower limit is £10,000;
- the upper limit is £16,000.

Tariff income starts at above £10,000.

You cannot claim **CTB** if you are permanently in a care home because you will not then be liable for council tax so these limits do not apply to CTB.

For **HB**,[7] the higher limits apply if you live permanently in one of the limited categories of care home for which HB is payable, referred to on p725. Some temporary absences (see p202) are ignored.

For **IS and income-based JSA**[8] the higher limits apply if you live permanently in:

- a residential care or nursing home and in either case you are given board and personal care because of:
  - old age;
  - disablement;
  - past or present dependence on alcohol or drugs;
  - past or present mental disorder; *or*
- residential accommodation (see below); *or*
- an Abbeyfield Society home; *or*
- a home provided under the Polish Resettlement Act in which you are receiving personal care because of:
  - old age;
  - disablement;
  - past or present dependence on alcohol or drugs;
  - past or present mental disorder;
  - a terminal illness.

A **'residential care home'** is a home which is:[9]

- registered or deemed to be registered under the Registered Homes Act 1984 or the Social Work (Scotland) Act 1968 (all homes providing board and personal care are required to be registered); *or*
- run by a body established by Royal Charter or Act of Parliament (other than a local authority) and which provides board and personal care; *or*
- a housing association registered with Scottish Homes which provides residential care.

A **'nursing home'** is a home which is:[10]

- registered as a nursing home under the Registered Homes Act 1984 or the Nursing Homes Registration (Scotland) Act 1938 or the Mental Health (Scotland) Act 1984; *or*
- run by a body established by Royal Charter or special Act of Parliament.

You are in **'residential accommodation'** if:[11]

- the home is owned or managed by a local authority; *and*
- the accommodation is provided under sections 21 and 24 of Part III of the National Assistance Act 1948 or sections 13B and 59 of the Social Work (Scotland) Act 1968 or section 7 of the Mental Health (Scotland) Act 1984.

If you were living in residential accommodation provided by a local authority on 31 March 1993, you may count as living in residential accommodation even if it does not fit the above definition.[12] This should not apply, however, if you were moved from a local authority to an independent home.[13] If you are living in residential accommodation which transferred from the local authority to become a residential care home (after 11 August 1991, for IS) while you were there, you are treated as still living in residential accommodation.[14]

Note: you are treated as living permanently in one of these homes for periods of absence of up to 13 weeks.

Whose capital counts

Your partner's capital

Your partner's capital is added to yours – ie, it counts as yours.[15]

Your child's capital

Your child's capital is not added to yours.[16] However, there are certain circumstances in which your child's capital can affect your claim.

For **IS and income-based JSA**, the general rule is that, if you are not entitled to have benefit for children included in your claim, then your child's capital does not affect your claim in any way.[17]

You are not entitled to have amounts for your children included in your claim for IS or income-based JSA if that claim began on or after 6 April 2004, or once you have been awarded child tax credit (CTC) – see p818 for further details.

If you are entitled to have benefit for children included in your claim (ie, you have a claim that includes a child that began before 6 April 2004 and you have not yet been awarded CTC), then if your child's capital is over £3,000 you will still not get benefit included for that child[18] (although the ordinary or lone parent rate of the family premium is still payable – see p884). If that applies, any income of the child will not be counted as yours either.[19]

For **HB and CTC**, your child's capital does not affect the amount of benefit included for your child even if it is over £3,000.[20]

What counts as capital

The term 'capital' is not defined. In general, it means lump-sum or one-off payments rather than a series of payments[21] – eg, it includes savings, property and redundancy payments.

Capital payments can normally be distinguished from income because they are not payable in respect of any specified period or periods, and they do not form, nor are intended to form, part of a regular series of payments[22] (although capital can be paid by instalments).

However, some capital is treated as income (see p978), and some income is treated as capital (see p1030).

Savings

Your savings generally count as capital – eg, cash you have at home, premium bonds, stocks and shares, unit trusts and money in a bank account or building society.

Your savings from past earnings can only be treated as capital when all relevant debts, including tax liabilities, have been deducted.[23] Savings from other past income (including social security benefits – see p1035) will be treated as capital after the period for which the income was paid has lapsed (so that, for example, a weekly payment of child benefit will become capital a week after it is paid and a monthly occupational pension will become capital after a month).[24] There is no provision for disregarding money put aside to pay bills.[25] If you have savings just below the capital limit, it may be best to pay bills for gas, electricity, telephone, etc. by monthly standing order, or by use of a budget account, to prevent your capital going above the limit.

Fixed-term investments

Capital held in fixed-term investments counts. However, if in reality it is presently unobtainable, it may have little or no value. If you can convert the investment into a realisable form, sell your interest, or raise a loan through a reputable bank using the asset as security, its value counts. If it takes time to produce evidence about the nature and value of the investment, you may be able to get an interim payment for IS, JSA or HB[26] (see p230) or a crisis loan from the social fund (see p538).

Property and land

Any property or land that you own counts as capital. Many types of property are disregarded (see p1031). See also 'proprietary estoppel' – p1028.

Loans

A loan usually counts as money you possess. However, a loan granted on condition that you only use the interest but do not touch the capital should not be counted as part of your capital because the capital element has never been at your disposal.[27] Where you have been paid money to be used for a particular purpose on condition that the money must be returned if not used in that way, it should not be treated as part of your capital.[28] Where you have bought a property on behalf of someone else who is paying the mortgage,[29] or where you are holding money in your bank account on behalf of another person which is to be returned to them at a future date,[30] the capital should not count as yours.

For HB and CTB, some loans might be treated as income even if they were paid as a lump sum (see p978).

Trusts

A trust is a way of owning an asset. In theory, the asset is split into two notional parts: the legal title owned by the trustee, and the beneficial interest owned by the beneficiary. A trustee can never have use of the asset, only the responsibility of looking after it. An adult beneficiary, on the other hand, can ask for the asset at any time. Anything can be held on trust – eg, money, houses, shares, etc.

If you are the adult beneficiary of:

- a non-discretionary trust, you can obtain the asset from the trustee at any time. You effectively own the asset, and so its market value counts as your capital;
- a discretionary trust, you cannot insist on receiving payments from the trust. Payments are at the discretion of the trustee within the terms of the trust. Any payments made are treated in full as income or capital depending on the nature of the payment. The trust asset itself would not normally count as your capital because you cannot demand payment (of either income or capital);
- a trust which gives you the right to receive payments in the future – eg, on reaching 25. This is a right that has a present capital value, unless disregarded (see p1035).

If you have a life interest (or, in Scotland, a life rent) only in an asset (ie, if you have the right to enjoy an asset in your lifetime, but the asset will pass on to someone else when you die), the value of your right to receive income is disregarded[31] (see p1035), but not the income itself if you get any.

If the beneficiary is under 18, even with a non-discretionary trust, s/he has no right to payment until s/he is 18 (or later if that is what the trust stipulates). Her/his interest may nevertheless have a present value.[32]

If you hold an asset as a trustee, it is not part of your capital. You are only a trustee either if someone gives you an asset on the express condition that you hold it for someone else (or use it for their benefit), or if you have expressed the clearest intention that your own asset is for someone else's benefit, and renounced its use for yourself[33] (assets other than money may need to be transferred in a particular way to the trust).

It is not enough to only intend to give someone an asset. However, in the case of property and land, **'proprietary estoppel'** may apply. This means that if you lead someone to believe that you are transferring your interest in some property to her/him, but fail to do so (eg, it is never properly conveyed), and that person acts on the belief that s/he has ownership (eg, s/he improves or repairs it, or takes on a mortgage), it would then be unfair on her/him were s/he to lose out if you insisted that you were still the owner.[34] In this case, you can argue the capital asset has been transferred to her/him, and you are like a trustee. Thus, you can insist that it is not your capital asset, but the other person's, when claiming benefit.

If money (or another asset) is given to you to be used for a special purpose, it may be possible to argue that it should not count as your capital. This is called a **'purpose trust'**.[35]

Payments of personal injury compensation

Where a trust fund has been set up out of money paid because of a personal injury, the value of the trust fund is ignored.[36] The rules refer to 'personal injury to the claimant' only. Because of this wording it is doubtful if the capital value of a trust fund will be ignored if the money was paid in respect of a family member other than yourself; it will not be ignored if it was paid in respect of someone who is no longer a member of your family (eg, because s/he is dead).[37]

It is not necessary for the trust to be set up by a formal deed. For these purposes, personal injuries compensation held by the Court of Protection (because the injured person is incapable of managing her/his own affairs) and administered by that Court and/or the Public Trustee is treated in the same way as a trust.[38] The important point is that the person who is awarded the compensation should not be able to have any direct access to it.

In this context, **'personal injury'** includes not only accidental and criminal injuries, but also any disease and injury suffered as a result of a disease. Therefore a trust fund for a child who has had both legs amputated following meningitis and septicaemia could be disregarded for the purposes of the parent's claim.[39]

Note: the notional income and capital rules (see pp983 and 1039) cannot apply to trusts or funds administered by the Court which, in either case, have been set up as a result of a personal injury.

Note also: if there is no trust, or until one can be set up, the whole of the compensation payment counts as capital for IS, income-based JSA, HB or CTB. However, there are plans to ignore all personal injury payments for HB and CTB from October 2005. See CPAG's *Welfare Rights Bulletin* for updates.[40]

Trust funds administered by the court[41]

The value of a trust fund is also ignored where damages are awarded in respect of personal injury (or, for minors under the age of 18, as compensation for the death of one or both parents), and the money paid into a special fund to be administered by, and at the discretion of, the court (eg, the Court of Protection). Payments out of funds administered by the court should usually be treated as capital.[42] The exception is where they are periodic payments made under the terms of an agreement or court order, in which case they will be treated as income.[43]

Payments from trust funds

Any payments actually made to you from trusts (other than court-administered trusts – see above) may count in full as income or capital depending on the nature of the payment.[44] However, trustees may have a discretion to use such funds to purchase items that would normally be disregarded as capital, such as personal possessions (see p1034) – eg, a wheelchair, car, new furniture – or to arrange payments that would normally be disregarded as income – eg, for IS, income-based JSA, HB and CTB, ineligible housing costs. Similarly, they may have discretion to clear debts or pay for a holiday, leisure items, or educational or medical needs. See p973 for the treatment of voluntary payments and pp973 and 985 for the treatment of payments made to third parties.

Money held by your solicitor

Money held by your solicitor will normally count as your capital, including compensation payments before a trust fund has been set up.[45] Where the money is being held by your solicitor pending quantification of any statutory charge due to the Legal Services Commission it does not count as your capital, as it is not possible to identify the capital which belongs to you until any statutory charge has been quantified and deducted.[46]

Income treated as capital

Certain payments which appear to be income are nevertheless treated as capital. These are:[47]

- an advance of earnings or loan from your employer;*
- holiday pay which is not payable until more than four weeks after your employment ends or is interrupted;*
- income tax refunds;*
- income from capital (eg, interest on a building society account) and income from rent on property let to tenants (see p976). However, income from the first five disregarded property bullet points listed on p1031, income from the home of a partner, former partner or relative in the circumstances described on p1033, income from the home you normally live in and income from business assets or personal injury trusts counts as income not capital;
- a lump sum or 'bounty' paid to you not more than once a year as a part-time firefighter or part-time member of a lifeboat crew, or as an auxiliary coastguard or member of the Territorial Army;
- irregular (one-off) charitable or voluntary payments;*
- for IS only, the part, or the whole, of a compensation payment for loss of employment that is treated as capital under the IS rules;[48]
- for IS and income-based JSA only, a discharge grant paid on release from prison;
- for IS and income-based JSA only (where these are still taken into account, see p973), arrears of residence order payments from a local authority;
- for HB and CTB only, any arrears of CTC or working tax credit (WTC)[49]
- arrears of subsistence allowance paid as a lump sum. The arrears are ignored (as capital) for 52 weeks.[50] A 'subsistence allowance' is an allowance paid by an employment zone contractor to a person participating in the employment zone programme, and is equivalent to the weekly amount of income-based JSA which would be payable to that person less 50p.[51]
- for HB and CTB, the gross receipts from work carried out under the self-employment route of the New Deal.

* Except:
- for IS, in the case of people involved in, or returning to work after, a trade dispute; *or*
- for income-based JSA, when it is paid to someone involved in a trade dispute or, if paid in consequence of the dispute, to a member of her/his family (see p735).

Disregarded capital

Your home

If you own the home you normally live in, its value is ignored.[52]

The value of your home

Your **'home'** includes any garage, garden, outbuildings and land, together with any premises that you do not occupy as your home but which it is impractical or unreasonable to sell separately – eg, croft land.[53] This disregard applies to any home you are treated as normally living in (eg, because you are only temporarily living away from it – see p907), although if you own more than one property, only the value of the one normally occupied is disregarded under this rule.[54] Although the home may consist of more than one unit of accommodation,[55] both units will only count as the home if the claimant (as opposed to any member of her/his family) normally has to occupy both units (ie, where one unit is treated as an extension or annexe of the other).[56]

Disregards

The value of the property can be disregarded even if you do not normally live in it in the following circumstances.

- **If you have left your former home following a marriage or relationship breakdown**, the value of the property is ignored for six months from the date you left. It may also be disregarded for longer if any of the steps below are taken. If it is occupied by your former partner who is a lone parent its value is ignored as long as s/he lives there.[57]
- **If you have sought legal advice or have started legal proceedings in order to occupy property** as your home, its value is ignored for six months from the date you first took either of these steps.[58] The six months can be extended, if it is reasonable to do so, where you need longer to move into the property.
- **If you are taking reasonable steps to dispose of any property**, its value is ignored for six months from the date you *first* took such steps.[59] This may include a period before you claimed benefit.[60] The definition of **'property'** here includes land on its own, even if there are no buildings on it.[61] Putting the property in the hands of an estate agent or getting in touch with a prospective purchaser should constitute 'reasonable steps',[62] as might taking ancillary relief proceedings to resolve financial issues in a divorce before putting a property up for sale.[63] The test for what constitutes 'reasonable steps' is an

objective one. Any period when the house is advertised at an unrealistic sale price would not count.[64] But if you need longer to dispose of the property, the disregard can continue for years if it is reasonable – eg, where a husband or wife attempts to realise her/his share in a former matrimonial home but the court orders that it should not be sold until the youngest child reaches a certain age.

- **If you are carrying out essential repairs or alterations** which are needed so that you can occupy a property as your home, the value of the property is ignored for six months from the date you first began to take steps to carry them out.[65] **'Steps'** may include applying for planning permission or a grant or a loan to make the property habitable, employing an architect or finding someone to do the work.[66] If you cannot move into the property within that period because the work is not finished, its value can be disregarded for as long as is necessary to allow the work to be carried out.
- **If you have acquired a house or flat for occupation** as your home but have not yet moved in, its value is ignored if you intend to live there within six months of acquisition.[67] If you cannot move in by then the value of the property can be ignored for as long as seems reasonable.
- **If you sell your home** and intend to use the money from the sale to buy another home, the capital is ignored for six months from the date of the sale.[68] This also applies even if you do not actually own the home but, for a price, you surrender your tenancy rights to a landlord.[69] If you need longer to complete a purchase, the authorities can continue to ignore the capital if it is reasonable to do so. You do not have to have decided within the six months to buy a *particular* property. It is sufficient if you intend to use the proceeds to buy *some* other home within the six-month (or extended) period,[70] although your 'intention' must involve more than a mere 'hope' or 'aspiration'.[71] There must be an element of 'certainty' which may be shown by evidence of a practical commitment to another purchase, although this need not involve any binding obligation.[72] If you intend to use only part of the proceeds of sale to buy another home, only that part is disregarded even if, for example, you have put the rest of the money aside to renovate your new home.[73]
- **If your home is damaged or you lose it altogether**, any payment in consequence of that, including compensation, which you intend to use for its repair, or for acquiring another home, is ignored for a period of six months, or longer if it is reasonable to do so.[74]
- If you have taken out a **loan or been given money for the express purpose of essential repairs and improvements** to your home, it is ignored for six months, or longer if it is reasonable to do so.[75] If it is a condition of the loan that the loan must be returned if the improvements are not carried out, you should argue that it should be ignored altogether.[76]
- If you have **deposited money with a housing association as a condition of occupying your home**, this is ignored indefinitely.[77] If money which was deposited for this purpose is now to be used to buy another home, this is

ignored for six months, or longer if reasonable, in order to allow you to complete the purchase.[78]

- **Grants made to local authority tenants to buy a home or do repairs/alterations** to it can be ignored for up to 26 weeks, or longer if reasonable, to allow completion of the purchase or the repairs/alterations.[79]

Is it reasonable to extend the disregard? When considering whether to increase the period of any disregard, as provided for under some of the rules above, all the circumstances should be considered – particularly your and your family's personal circumstances, any efforts made by you to use or dispose of the home[80] (if relevant) and the general state of the market (if relevant). In practice, periods of around 18 months are not considered unusual.

It is possible for property to be ignored under more than one of the above paragraphs in succession.[81]

Some income generated from property which is disregarded is ignored (see p976).

The home of a partner, former partner or relative

The value of a home (see p1031) is also ignored if it is occupied wholly or partly as her/his home by:[82]

- *either*
  - your partner[83] – ie, your husband/wife, provided you are both still treated as living in the same household (see p811) or your cohabitee, provided you are still treated as living together as husband and wife (see p813); *or*
  - a relative of yours, or any member of your family,

  who in either case, is aged 60 or over or is incapacitated (see below);
- your former partner from whom you are not estranged or divorced. This means your husband/wife where you are not still treated as living in the same household or your former cohabitee where you are not still treated as living together as husband and wife;
- your former partner from whom you are estranged or divorced if s/he is a lone parent. If your former partner is not a lone parent, the value of the home is ignored for 26 weeks from the date you ceased to live in the home.[84]

It has been held that this disregard only applies to a property which you previously occupied yourself.[85]

Note: when the Civil Partnership Act 2004 comes into force in December 2005, this disregard will also apply to same sex couples (see p811).

'**Incapacitated**' is not defined, but guidance suggests it refers to someone who is getting an incapacity or disability benefit, or who is sufficiently incapacitated to qualify for one of those benefits.[86] However, you should argue for a broader interpretation, if necessary.

'**Relative**' includes: a parent, son, daughter, step-parent/son/daughter, or parent/son/daughter-in-law; brother or sister; or a partner of any of these people; or a grandparent or grandchild, uncle, aunt, nephew or niece.[87] It also includes half-brothers and sisters and adopted children.[88]

Personal possessions

All personal possessions, including items such as jewellery, furniture or a car, are ignored.[89] Personal possessions are not ignored if you have bought them in order to be able to claim or get more benefit (in which case the sale value, rather than the purchase price, is counted as actual capital, and the difference is treated as notional capital[90] – see p1039).

Compensation for damage to or the loss of any personal possessions, which is to be used for their repair or replacement, is ignored for six months, or longer if reasonable.[91]

Business assets

If you are self-employed, your business assets are ignored for as long as you continue to work in that business.[92] Guidance for IS and income-based JSA suggests that as little as half an hour's work a week may be sufficient.[93] If you cannot work because of physical or mental illness, but intend to work in the business when you are able, the disregard operates for 26 weeks from the date of claim, or for longer if reasonable in the circumstances.[94] If you stop working in the business, you are allowed a reasonable time to sell these assets without their value affecting your benefit. It is sometimes difficult to distinguish between personal and business assets. The test is whether the assets are 'part of the fund employed and risked in the business'.[95] Where the assets of a business partnership (eg, plant and machinery) have been sold but the partnership has not yet been dissolved, the proceeds of sale can still count as business assets.[96] **Note:** letting out a single house does not constitute a business.[97] For the treatment of business assets if you are taking part in the self-employment route under the employment option of the New Deal, see p1039.

Tax rebates

Tax rebates for the tax relief on interest on a mortgage or loan obtained for buying your home or carrying out repairs or improvements are ignored.[98]

Personal pension schemes and retirement annuity contracts

The value of a fund held under a personal pension scheme or retirement annuity is ignored.[99]

Insurance policy and annuity surrender values

The surrender value of any life assurance or endowment policy is ignored.[100] **Note:** the life assurance aspect need not be the sole or even the main aspect of the policy (although the other features of any policy may still be considered under the actual or notional income and capital rules – see pp1039 and 1042). The surrender value of any annuity is also ignored (see pp977 and 1023). Any actual income the surrender value generates for you, and which is not disregarded as income, can be taken into account as income.[101] Any payment under the annuity counts as income[102] (but see p982 for when this is ignored).

Future interests in property

A future interest in most kinds of property is ignored.[103] A **'future interest'** is one which will only revert to you, or become yours for the first time, when some future event occurs.

However, this does not include a freehold or leasehold interest in property which has been let *by you* to tenants. If you did not let the property to the tenant (eg, because the tenancy was entered into before you bought the property), then your interest in the property should be ignored as a future interest in the normal way. In addition, a commissioner has suggested that if you grant someone an *'irrevocable* licence' to occupy property, your interest in that property is a future one and should be ignored.[104]

An example of a future interest is where someone else has a life interest in a fund and you are only entitled after that person has died.

The right to receive a payment in the future

If you know you will receive a payment in the future, you could sell your right to that payment at any time so it has a market value and therefore constitutes an actual capital resource. The value of this is ignored where it is a right to receive:

- income under a life interest or, in Scotland, a life rent;[105]
- an occupational or personal pension;[106]
- any rent if you are not the freeholder or leaseholder.[107] Any actual income which the right to receive such rent in the future generates for you, and which is not disregarded as income, can be taken into account as income;
- any payment under an annuity (see p982).[108] Any actual income generated by the right to receive income from an annuity in the future, and which is not disregarded as income, can be taken into account as income;
- any earnings or income that is ignored because it is frozen abroad;[109]
- any outstanding instalments where capital is being paid by instalments;[110]
- any payment under a trust fund that is disregarded.[111]

Benefits and other payments

Arrears of benefits and tax credits

The general rule is that arrears of specified benefits, CTC and other payments (see below) are ignored for:[112]

- 52 weeks after they are received by you; *or*

- the remainder of your (or your partner's) award (or awards if each award follows on immediately from the previous award) of IS, income-based JSA, HB and CTB if that is a longer period than 52 weeks, but only if the arrears amount to £5,000 or more, are received in their entirety during the period of your award and on or after 14 October 2001, and were paid in order to rectify or compensate for an official error (see p1193).[113] For the purposes of this rule and awards which immediately follow a previous award, awards of IS and income-based JSA are interchangeable.

Note: for **HB and CTB** regarding tax credit arears, this rule applies only where the payment of arrears is made as a result of a change of circumstances.

The benefit arrears that are ignored under the general rule described above are:

- attendance allowance (AA), mobility supplement, disability living allowance (DLA), income-based JSA, IS, HB, CTB, CTC, WTC and discretionary housing payments (as well as the former supplementary benefit, family income supplement, family credit, working families' tax credit, disabled person's tax credit and mobility allowance), or concessionary payments instead of any of these;
- arrears of certain war widows' and war widowers' payments,[114] and refunds on council tax (or, formerly, community charge) liability are also ignored, but only for 52 weeks from the date you receive the arrears;[115]
- for IS, any backdated payments of IS, HB and CTB made once the Home Office has accepted you are a refugee (see p669) are ignored for 52 weeks from the date of receipt.[116] The same rule also applies in relation to backdated payments of IS and HB (for HB)[117] and IS and CTB (for CTB).[118] For special capital rules and urgent cases, see p664;
- for HB and CTB only, any child maintenance bonus (see p54) is ignored for 52 weeks from the date you receive it;[119]
- the following payments are ignored for 52 weeks from receipt:
  - fares to hospital;[120]
  - payments in place of milk tokens or vitamins;[121]
  - payments to assist prison visits.[122]

Other payments

The following payments are ignored:

- social fund payments are ignored indefinitely;[123]
- a payment to a disabled person under the Disabled Persons (Employment) Act 1944 (other than a training allowance or training bonus) to assist with employment, or a local authority payment to assist blind homeworkers;[124]
- any payments made to holders of the Victoria or George Cross ;[125]
- compensatory payments made by the Secretary of State for the loss of entitlement to HB, or to supplementary benefit or housing benefit supplement

as a consequence of the 1988 changes to the means-tested benefits scheme, are ignored indefinitely;[126]

- payments by a local authority or the National Assembly for Wales for support services to help you live independently from the Supporting People team are ignored indefinitely;[127]
- for the treatment of payments for taking part in the New Deal programme, see p1039;
- lump-sum payments to HB claimants through the under-occupation pilot scheme are ignored for 52 weeks.[128]

Second World War compensation payments

There are two different ways in which such compensation payments may be disregarded.

- **Former Japanese prisoners of war:** any £10,000 ex gratia payment(s) made by the Secretary of State in consequence of the imprisonment or internment by the Japanese during World War II of you, your partner, your deceased spouse or your partner's deceased spouse is indefinitely ignored.[129]
- **Victims of World War II:** any payment (except for a war pension) made to compensate for the fact that, during World War II, you, your partner, your deceased spouse or your partner's deceased spouse was a slave or forced labourer, lost property or suffered a personal injury, or was the parent of a child who died, is ignored for an indefinite period.[130]

Creutzfeldt-Jakob disease payments

Payments made out of trust funds established from funds provided by the Secretary of State for people with variant Creutzfeldt-Jakob disease (CJD) are ignored as capital for varying periods.[131] This disregard applies to any claimant who has the disease, her/his partner (or who was her/his partner at the date of the claimant's death), her/his parent (or person acting in place of her/his parents) or a dependent child (or who was a dependent child at the date of the claimant's death). Where trust payments are made to the claimant or her/his partner, they are ignored up to the date that person dies. Where trust payments are made to the claimant's parent, they are ignored for two years from the date the first payment is made. Where trust payments are made to another member of the claimant's family, they are ignored for two years from the date the first payment is made or the date when that person leaves full-time education or reaches 19, whichever is the latest.

Similar disregards apply to payments made by a person to whom such a trust payment has been made (or out of her/his estate), where the payments are made by that person (or her/his estate) to either a claimant or a member of her/his family and the claimant or family member is *either*:

- the partner of a person with CJD (or was the partner at the date of the person's death); *or*

- the parent of a person with CJD (or a person who is acting – or was acting at the time of the person with CJD's death – in place of the person with CJD's parents); *or*
- another member of the family of the person with CJD (or who was a member of the family at the date of the person with CJD's death).[132]

Charitable payments

Any payment in kind by a charity is ignored.[133]

All payments from the Macfarlane Trusts, the Fund, the Skipton Fund, the Eileen Trust and either of the Independent Living Funds (see p973) are ignored.[134] Payments from the Macfarlane Trusts, the Fund, the Skipton Fund or the Eileen Trust do not have to be declared for HB and CTB at all, or for all other benefits, if they are kept separately from the claimant's other capital and income.[135] Certain payments from money that originally came from any of the three Macfarlane Trusts, the Fund, the Skipton Fund or the Eileen Trust are also ignored – the rules are the same as for income (see p973).

Any sports award made by the Sports Council out of National Lottery funds, *except for* any part of the award which is made in respect of ordinary living expenses (for definition see p983), is disregarded for 26 weeks.[136]

There are plans to ignore all voluntary and charitable payments for HB and CTB from October 2005. See CPAG's *Welfare Rights Bulletin* for updates.[137]

Payments in other currencies

Any payment in a currency other than sterling is taken into account after disregarding banking charges or commision payable on conversion to sterling.[138]

Payments by social services[139]

A payment under s17 of the Children Act 1989 from a social services department or, in Scotland, a payment from a social work department under s12 of the Social Work (Scotland) Act 1968 is ignored. Payments made by local authorities to young people who have previously been in care or been looked after by social services (in England and Wales under ss23C, 24, 24A or 24B of the Children Act 1989, in Scotland under ss29 or 30 of the Children (Scotland) Act 1995) are also ignored. But if you or your partner are involved in a trade dispute or, for IS, it is paid during the first 15 days following your return to work after the dispute, it counts as income for IS and income-based JSA.

Also ignored indefinitely are:

- community care direct payments;[140]
- special guardianship allowances (payable in England and Wales);[141]
- payments under para 3 of Schedule 4 to the Adoption and Children Act 2002.[142]

Payments to jurors and witnesses

Any payments made to jurors or witnesses for attending at court are ignored, except for payments for loss of earnings or of benefit.[143]

Employment and training programme payments

A payment under s2 of the Employment and Training Act 1973 or s2 of the Enterprise and New Towns (Scotland) Act 1990 is ignored,[144] but only for a year from the date it is received.

Employment zone payments

A payment made by an employment zone contractor to a person taking part in an employment zone scheme[145] is ignored for 52 weeks. Payments to help you in self-employment are treated in the same way as described below for the New Deal.

Education maintenance allowances

An education maintenance allowance is ignored indefinitely.[146]

New Deal payments

Any sum of capital acquired for the purpose of participating under the 'self-employment route' of the New Deal is ignored for 52 weeks,[147] and any capital assets acquired for such purposes will be ignored for as long as you are receiving assistance for taking part in the programme[148] and, after you have ceased trading, for as long as is reasonable in order to dispose of the assets.[149]

For the treatment of payments under the New Deal as income, notional income and notional capital, see pp979, 983 and 1039.

Age-related payments

Payments made to you under the Age-related Payments Scheme are ignored indefinitely.[150]

Capital treated as income

Some payments which appear to be capital are treated as income. See p978 for the detailed rules.

Any capital treated as income is ignored as capital.[151]

Notional capital

In certain circumstances, you are treated as having capital which you do not, in fact, possess. This is called **'notional capital'**.[152] There is a similar rule for notional income (see p983). Notional capital counts in the same way as capital you actually do possess except that a 'diminishing notional capital rule' (see p1042) may be applied so that the value of the notional capital you are treated as having will be considered to reduce over time.

Depending on the benefit involved, there are five circumstances in which you will be treated as having notional capital:

- where you deliberately deprive yourself of capital in order to claim or increase benefit (see p1040);
- where you fail to apply for capital which is available to you (see p1044);
- where someone else makes a payment of capital to a third party on your behalf or on behalf of a member of your family (see p1045);
- where you (or a member of your family) receive a payment of capital on behalf of a third party and, instead of handing it on, you (or the member of your family) use or keep the capital (see p1046);
- where you are a sole trader or a partner in a business which is a limited company (see p1046).

Note: the 'diminishing notional capital rule' (see p1042) can only apply where you are treated as having notional capital under the first circumstance.

Deprivation of capital in order to claim or increase benefit

If you deliberately get rid of capital in order to claim or increase your benefit, you are treated as still possessing it.[153] You are likely to be affected by this rule if, at the time of using up your money, you know that you may qualify for benefit (or more benefit) as a result, or qualify more quickly. It should not be used if you know nothing about the effect of using up your capital (eg, you do not know about the capital limit for claiming benefit),[154] or if you have been using up your capital at a rate which is reasonable in the circumstances. Knowledge of capital limits can be inferred from a reasonable familiarity with the benefit system as a claimant,[155] but if you fail to make enquiries about the capital limit, this does not constitute an intention to secure benefit. This is because you cannot form the required intention if you do not know about the capital rules.[156]

Why was the capital got rid of?

Even if you do know about the capital limits, it still has to be shown that you intended to obtain, retain or increase your benefit.[157] For example, where a claimant, facing repossession of his home, transferred ownership to his daughter (who, he feared, would otherwise be made homeless), in spite of having been warned by Department for Work and Pensions (DWP) staff that he would be disqualified from benefit if he did so, it was held that, under the circumstances, he could not be said to have disposed of the property with the intention of gaining benefit.[158] The longer the period that has elapsed since the disposal of the capital, the less likely it is that it was for the purpose of obtaining benefit.[159] However, no matter how long it has been since you may have disposed of an asset, there is no set 'safe' period after which it may be said that benefit can be claimed without the need for further enquiry.[160]

A person who uses up her/his resources may have more than one motive for doing so. Even where qualifying for benefit is only a subsidiary motive for your actions, and the predominant motive is something quite different (eg, ensuring your home is in good condition by spending capital to do necessary repairs and improvements) you may still be counted as having deprived yourself of a resource in order to gain benefit.[161]

Examples of the kinds of expenditure that could be caught by the rule are an expensive holiday and putting money in trust.[162] (For IS and income-based JSA, putting money in trust for yourself does not constitute deprivation if the capital being put in trust came from compensation paid for any personal injury.[163]) But the essential test is not the kind of item that the money has been spent on but the *intention* behind the expenditure.

Gifts and paying off debts

If you pay off a debt which you are required by law to repay immediately, then you may well not be counted as having deprived yourself of money in order to gain benefit.[164] But it is the facts of your case which are most important: if you paid off an immediately repayable debt when the facts show you thought it would not actually be called in for some time, it may be that you will be held to have deprived yourself of money in order to get benefit. However, even if you pay off a debt which you are not required by law to repay immediately, it is still for the decision maker to prove that you did so in order to get benefit – again, it is the facts of your case which are important.[165]

Intention to get benefit

In practice, arguing successfully that you have not deprived yourself of capital to get or increase benefit may boil down to whether you can show that you would have spent the money in the way you did (eg, to pay off debts or reduce your mortgage), regardless of the effect on your benefit entitlement. Where this is unclear, the burden of proving that you did it in order to get benefit lies with the decision maker.

In one case a man lost over £60,000 speculating on the stock market. Due to his wife's serious illness which affected his own health and judgement, he did not act to avoid losses when the stock market crashed. It was held that the decision maker had not proved that this had been done to obtain IS.[166] In another case, a council house was bought at a discount (under the right-to-buy legislation) using a loan from a relative secured by a trust deed over the property. In effect, the relative was being given the value of the discount. When the owner fell ill he had to be rehoused so that the relative acquired the property. A claim for HB was initially refused on the grounds that the claimant had deprived himself of the value of the property he had bought. A court later rejected this decision on the grounds that there was no evidence of intention, as it was clear that the sole purpose of the arrangement was so that the relative would be gifted the discount value.[167]

Calculation of notional capital

If you are treated as possessing notional capital, it is calculated in the same way as if it were actual capital[168] and the same disregards usually apply. The only possible exception is that you may not be able to rely on the disregard for the 26 weeks (or longer) you would otherwise be allowed to take steps to dispose of a property, even if the new owner is trying to sell it. However, there is conflicting caselaw on this.[169]

Note: where a disposal of capital is not effective (eg, where there is a disposal between the serving of a bankruptcy notice and the appointment of a trustee in bankruptcy) the notional capital rules will not apply (but the actual capital rules will apply if you still own the asset in question).[170] If, on the other hand, a person acting on your behalf as your attorney has misspent your money for her/his own benefit, the amount spent cannot be notional capital (because the disposal was unlawful) or actual capital (because you no longer have it), but your right to recover the money may still have an actual capital value.[171]

Other points on deprivation of capital

It has been held that deprivation for the purposes of obtaining supplementary benefit could not be said to have been deprivation for the purposes of obtaining IS,[172] because IS did not exist at the time of the deprivation. It should also, therefore, be argued that there could have been no deprivation for the purposes of obtaining CTB prior to April 1993, as it did not come into existence until that date.

The only exception is that a deprivation for the purposes of gaining IS may be treated as a deprivation for the purposes of gaining income-based JSA (but not vice versa).

Where an intentional deprivation has been found for the purposes of obtaining IS, for example, it does not necessarily follow that there has also been any intention to gain HB and CTB.

Each decision maker must reach her/his own decision on each benefit. Even decisions on deprivation for HB must be made independently of decisions for CTB.[173] This may result in different conclusions being drawn on any disposal for each benefit. And even where intent is found in two different benefits, there may be different views about the amount of capital that has been intentionally disposed of.[174]

However, where you are held to have deprived yourself of capital for the purposes of claiming HB and CTB, and you then submit a successful claim for IS, the notional capital rules for HB and CTB should be put in abeyance for as long as IS remains in payment.[175]

The diminishing notional capital rule

This rule provides a calculation for working out how your notional capital may be treated as *spent*.[176] It only applies if you have deliberately deprived yourself of capital.[177] Prior to 1 October 1990 there was a different rule (see p1044). The rule starts to operate from the first week or part-week after the week in which it is first decided that the notional capital is to be taken into account. The rule provides that:

- **Where your benefit has been refused altogether** because of your notional capital, the amount of your notional capital is reduced by the weekly total of any of the following benefits (or the additional amounts of the benefits, unless it is IS or income-based JSA) that you would have been entitled to but for the notional capital rule for:

IS	IS, HB and CTB
Income-based JSA	Income-based JSA, HB and CTB
HB	IS, income-based JSA, HB and CTB
CTB	IS, income-based JSA, HB and CTB
Pension credit (PC)	PC, HB and CTB

  In order to ensure that account is taken of as many other benefits as possible, it is important (where you are not already doing so) to make a claim for any of the other benefits (where appropriate) as soon as the notional capital rule has been applied. Any notice you are then given of any amounts of benefits you have 'lost' can then be supplied as evidence of the total weekly aggregate that should be taken into account.

- **Where your means-tested benefit is reduced because of tariff income from your notional capital**, that capital is diminished by the amount of that reduction each week (or part-week). For example, if your notional capital is £3,750, giving a tariff income of £3 a week, the reduction is £3 a week until it reaches £3,500, when it will be £2 and so on.

  For HB and CTB, the amount of your notional capital is also reduced by the weekly aggregate of the following benefits (or any additional amounts of these benefits, unless it is IS or income-based JSA) which you would have been entitled to but for the notional capital rule for:

HB	IS, income-based JSA, and CTB
CTB	IS, income-based JSA, and HB

- **The reduction in your notional capital is calculated on a weekly basis.** However, where your benefit has been stopped altogether because of the notional capital rule, the amount is fixed for a period of at least 26 weeks. Even if the amount you would have been entitled to increases during this period, there will be no change in the amount by which the capital is reduced (except for HB and CTB where guidance[178] states that in circumstances not related to capital – eg, you have married or a baby has been born – a new assessment can be made). The aggregate of your benefit entitlement can, however, be recalculated from the end of this 26-week period when you reclaim benefit, and is increased if it is more than it was before, but it stays the same as in the earlier assessment if it is unchanged or less. You do not have to reclaim at the end of every 26-week period but there can be no recalculation unless and until you do. However, you cannot renew a claim until at least 26 weeks (IS, income-based JSA, HB and CTB) have passed since the last assessment. Once the amount of reduction has been recalculated in this way, it is again fixed for the same period.

For IS, PC or income-based JSA, you should ask the DWP for a forecast of when your notional capital will reduce to a point where a further claim might succeed, but the onus will be on you to reclaim when it is to your advantage to do so[179] – ie, when you may qualify for an increased assessment, or because you have requalified for benefit. Timing will be important. If you delay you may lose out as new assessments cannot take effect before you reclaim. However, if you reclaim too soon you have to wait until the fixed periods have lapsed before you can apply for a fresh determination.

- **Where you have both actual and notional capital**, you may have to draw on your actual capital to meet your living expenses, which may include (and will probably exceed) amounts equivalent to benefits you have 'lost'. There is no reason why this should affect the amount by which your notional capital is diminished, even if this effectively results in double-counting. Any reduction in your actual capital should be taken into account in calculating any tariff income arising from your combined actual and notional capital, unless, of course, you have spent it at such a rate and in such a way that it raises questions of intent, when you may find that the notional capital rules are applied all over again.

Note: it has been decided that these rules on how your capital was *spent* only apply from 1 October 1990. Prior to that date, any reasonable living and other expenditure was counted, which was far more generous.[180] Any notional capital you have been held to possess until 30 September 1990 is reduced under the earlier rules, and any notional capital carried forward to 1 October 1990 and onwards is reduced under the current rules.[181] Note that the current rules apply to deprivation of capital only; the earlier rules still apply to other forms of notional capital.

Failing to apply for capital[182]

The benefit rules treat you as having capital you could get if you applied for it. Examples of failure to apply could be where money is held in court which would be released on application, or even an unclaimed premium bond win. However, this does not include money held by your solicitor pending quantification of any statutory charge due to the Legal Services Commission, as until any statutory due has been quantified it is impossible to identify what part of the capital will remain yours.[183] You are only treated as having such capital from the date you could obtain it.

This rule does not apply if you fail to apply for:

- capital from a discretionary trust; *or*
- capital from a trust (or fund administered by the court[184]) set up from money paid as a result of a personal injury; *or*
- capital from a personal pension scheme or retirement annuity contract; *or*
- a loan which you could only get if you gave your home or other disregarded capital (see p1031) as security; *or*
- for HB and CTB only, CTC or WTC.[185]

Capital payments made to a 'third party' on your behalf

If someone else pays an amount to a 'third party' (eg, an electricity company or a building society) for you or a member of your family (if any), this may count as your capital.[186] It counts if the payment is to cover certain of your or your family's normal living expenses – ie, food, household fuel, council tax or ordinary clothing or footwear. (School uniforms and sportswear are not ordinary clothing;[187] nor are, for example, special shoes because of a disability.[188])

It also counts if it is to cover:

- rent for which HB could be payable (less any non-dependant deductions) or water charges;
- **for IS and income-based JSA only**, housing costs which could be met by IS or income-based JSA.

If the payment is for other kinds of expenses – eg, children's school fees (see p954), a TV licence, accommodation charges above the IS/income-based JSA limit, or mortgage capital repayments – it does not count. Payments from the Macfarlane Trusts, the Fund, the Skipton Fund, the Eileen Trust or either of the Independent Living Funds do not count, whatever their purpose.

Payments for participating in any of the employment, education or training options of the New Deal also do not count, whatever they are for, including payments from the 'intensive activity period' of the New Deal for those aged 50 or over.[189]

Payments made for the food, etc. of any member of the family count as the capital of the member of the family in respect of whom they are paid. Since a child's capital is not counted as belonging to the claimant, a payment to, for example, a clothes shop for your child, should count as the child's notional capital and not yours.

Payments of an occupational pension or from a personal pension scheme to a third party count as yours regardless of whether or not the payments are used or intended to be used for ordinary living expenses.[190] The only exception is that such payments are disregarded if you (or the member of your family on whose behalf the payments are made) are bankrupt (or the subject of a sequestration order), *and* the payment is made to the trustee or other person acting on your creditors' behalf, *and* you (and your family) have no other income other than the payment made.[191]

For IS and income-based JSA only, payments *derived* from certain social security benefits (including war disablement pensions and war widows' pensions) and paid to a third party count:

- as yours, if you are entitled to the benefit; *and*
- as a member of your family's, if it is the family member who is entitled to the benefit.[192]

For IS and income-based JSA, there are different rules if you could be liable to pay maintenance as a liable relative (see p851).

Capital payments paid to you for a 'third party'[193]

If you or a member of your family get a payment for someone not in your family (eg, a relative who does not have a bank account) it only counts as yours if it is kept or used by you. Payments from the Macfarlane Trusts, the Fund, the Skipton Fund, the Eileen Trust or either of the Independent Living Funds, or any of the New Deal payments referred to on p1046 do not count at all.

Companies run by sole traders or a few partners

You will also be treated as possessing notional capital if, as a sole trader or a small partnership, you have registered your business as a limited company. For IS and income-based JSA, the value of your shareholding is ignored but you are treated as possessing a proportionate share of the capital of the company.[194] This does not apply while you are doing any work on the company's business.[195] Even if you work for the company for, say, only half an hour a week, this will suffice.[196] It has, however, been held that a 'sleeping partner' in a business managed and worked exclusively by others may not benefit from this disregard. As well as having a financial commitment to the business you must also be involved or engaged in it in some practical sense as an earner.[197]

For HB and CTB, the local authority has a discretion whether to apply the same rules as for IS and income-based JSA, but if it decides to, it must apply them all.[198]

How capital is valued

Market value

Apart from National Savings certificates (see p1047), your capital is valued at its current market or surrender value.[199] This means the amount of money you could raise by selling it or raising a loan against it. The test is the price that would be paid by a willing buyer to a willing seller on a particular date.[200] So if an asset is difficult or impossible to realise, its market value should be very heavily discounted or even nil.[201]

In the case of a house, an estate agent's figure for a quick sale is a more appropriate valuation than the District Valuer's figure for a sale within three months.[202]

It is not uncommon for an unrealistic assessment to be made of the value of your capital. You should consider challenging any decision you disagree with (see Chapters 43 and 44).

Expenses of sale

If there would be expenses involved in selling your capital, 10 per cent is deducted from its value for the cost of sale.[203]

Debts

Deductions are made from the 'gross' value of your capital for any debt or mortgage secured on it.[204] If a creditor (eg, a bank) holds the land certificate to your property as security for a loan and has registered notice of deposit of the land certificate at the Land Registry, this counts as a debt secured on your property.[205] Where a single mortgage is secured on a house and land, and the value of the house is disregarded for benefit purposes, the whole of the mortgage can be deducted when calculating the value of the land.[206]

If you have debts which are not secured against your capital (eg, tax liabilities), these cannot be offset against the value of your capital.[207] However, once you have paid off your debts your capital may well be reduced. You can be penalised if you deliberately get rid of capital in order to get benefit (see p1040).

National Savings

For IS and income-based JSA, a certificate bought from an issue which ceased before the 1 July before your claim is decided, or your benefit is first payable (whichever is earlier), or the date of any subsequent supersession, has the value it would have had on that 1 July if purchased on the last day of the issue. For HB and CTB, it is the 1 July before your claim is made or treated as made or when your benefit is reviewed. In any other case, the value is the purchase price.[208] DWP guidance contains a convenient valuation table for each issue.[209]

Capital that is jointly owned under a joint tenancy

If you jointly own any capital asset (except as a partner in a company when the rules explained on p1046 will apply instead) under a joint tenancy you are treated as owning an equal share of the asset with all other owners.[210] For example, if two of you own the asset, then you will each be treated as having a 50 per cent share of it. This rule does not apply, however, if you jointly own the capital asset as tenants in common.[211]

The key differences between a joint tenancy and a tenancy in common are that with a joint tenancy each co-owner owns the whole of the capital asset jointly and severally and if one of the joint tenants was to die then her/his interest in the asset would pass automatically to the other joint tenant(s), whereas with a tenancy in common each co-owner owns a discrete share in the asset and this share can be passed on by the deceased on her/his death to whoever s/he wishes.

If the rule does apply, the value of your deemed share should be calculated in the same way as your actual capital. However, it is only the value of your deemed share looked at in isolation which counts, and this will usually be worth rather less than the same proportion of the value of the whole asset. If the asset is a house, for example, the value of any deemed share may be very small or even worthless, particularly if the house is occupied and there is a possibility that the sale of the property cannot be forced. This is because even a willing buyer could not be expected to pay much for an asset s/he would have difficulty making use of or selling on to someone else.[212] Whether a sale can be forced will depend on individual circumstances, and valuations should take into account legal costs and the length of time it could take to gain possession of the property.[213] Valuations often fail to take into account official guidance on a range of factors relevant to the assessment of jointly-owned properties.[214] A proper valuation should set out details of the valuer's expertise (where relevant), describe the property in sufficient detail to show that all factors relevant to its value have been taken into account, and should state any assumptions on which it is based.[215] You may need to challenge any decision (see Chapters 43 and 44) based on an inadequate valuation.

The rule applies regardless of whether the capital asset in question is in the UK or abroad[216] (see p1049 for the particular valuation rules which also apply to assets abroad).

If the rule does not apply to you because you jointly own the capital asset under a tenancy in common then it is your actual share in the asset which has to be valued.

Treatment of assets after a relationship breakdown

When partners separate, assets such as their former home or a building society account may be in joint or sole names. For example, if a building society account is in joint names, under the rule about jointly-owned capital, you and your former partner are treated as having a 50 per cent share each (see p1047). But if your former partner is claiming sole ownership of the account, DWP guidance which used to apply to working families' tax credit and disabled person's tax credit stated that your interest in the account should count as having a nil value until the question of ownership is settled.[217] Arguably, the same should apply to IS, income-based JSA, PC, HB and CTB. The guidance dealt only with a marriage breakdown, but there is no reason why the same should not apply if you were not married. If your former partner puts a stop on the account, in effect freezing it, the account should be disregarded until its ownership is resolved.

On the other hand, a former partner may have a right to some or all of an asset that is in your sole name – eg, s/he may have deposited most of the money in a building society account in your name. If this is established, then you may well, depending on the circumstances, be treated as not entitled to the whole of the account but as holding part of it as trustee for your former partner.[218] The point made in the DWP guidance referred to above should logically apply equally here, so you should not be treated as owning half the capital (or indeed any of it) unless or until it is established that you do own at least some share of it, and the value of your interest can be assessed.

You cannot be treated as having any interest in a capital asset (eg, the former matrimonial home) under the Matrimonial Causes Act 1973 unless and until an Order (eg, a decree of divorce) has actually been made under that Act.[219]

Shares

Shares are valued at their current market value less 10 per cent for the cost of sale[220] and after deducting any 'lien' held by brokers for sums owed for the cost of acquisition and commission. Market value should be calculated in accordance with guidance from the Revenue, which is based on the bid price plus a quarter of the difference between this and the offer price (rather than *Financial Times* figures, which rely on the mean between the bid and offer prices).[221] Fluctuations in price between routine reviews of your case are normally ignored. Where a claimant has a minority holding of shares in a company, the value of the shares should be based on what the claimant could realise on them, and not by valuing the entire share capital of the company and attributing to the claimant an amount calculated according to the proportion of shares held.[222] Although there may be some practical difficulties in selling shares held by children, there are no obstacles to sale that cannot be overcome by courts, if necessary. They would, therefore, still have a value, even though allowance would have to be made for some inducement to overcome the reluctance of stockbrokers, registrars and potential purchasers in contracting with minors for an immediate sale.[223]

Unit trusts

These are valued on the basis of the 'bid' price quoted in newspapers. No deduction is allowed for the cost of sale because this is already included in the 'bid' price.[224]

The right to receive a payment in the future

The value of any such right that is not ignored (see p1035) is its market value – what a willing buyer will pay to a willing seller.[225] For something which is not yet realisable this may be very small.

Overseas assets

If you have assets abroad, and there are no exchange controls or other prohibitions that would prevent you transferring your capital to this country, your assets are valued at their current market or surrender value in that country.[226] If there are problems getting benefit because it is difficult to get the assets valued, you may be able to get an interim payment of IS, PC or income-based JSA (see p1108), or a 'payment on account' of HB (see p230).

If you are not allowed to transfer the full value of your capital to this country, you are treated as having capital equal to the amount that a willing buyer in this country would give for those assets.[227] It seems likely that the price such a person (if there is one) would be willing to pay may bear little relation to the actual value of the assets.

The same deductions of 10 per cent if there are expenses of sale, and for any debts or mortgage secured on the assets abroad, are made. If the capital is realised in a currency other than sterling, charges payable for converting the payment into sterling are also deducted.[228]

2. Capital: aged 60 or over

This part applies to:

- pension credit (PC);
- housing benefit (HB) and council tax benefit (CTB) if you or your partner (if you have one) are aged 60 or over and not getting income support (IS) or income-based jobseeker's allowance (JSA).
  If you get **IS or income-based JSA**, you do not need to work out your capital again for HB and CTB purposes because you receive your maximum HB or CTB,[229] less any deductions for non-dependants (see pp211 and 115).

This part does not apply to IS or income-based JSA even if you or your partner are over 60. If you get IS or income-based JSA, see p1023 for the rules on how your capital is treated.

In this part, whenever HB or CTB are referred to, this only applies to the rules for people aged 60 or over.

How is capital taken into account

Unlike other benefits, for **PC** there is no upper limit on your capital beyond which you are excluded from benefit. Instead, your capital above the lower limit (see p1051) is taken into account in the assessment as follows:

- actual income from capital (eg, interest or regular payments) is only taken into account for some specific kinds of capital.[230] This includes the value of the right to receive certain kinds of payment in the future, and capital in a trust unless the trust is set up out of personal injury payments to you or your partner or is a charitable trust (see p1002);

- any other capital, unless it is specifically disregarded, is assumed to provide you with a set rate of income called 'deemed income' (see p1003). Some capital can be ignored for a time or ignored permanently. This part explains which payments can be disregarded. If deemed income is taken into account, then any actual income, such as interest, is ignored.[231]

If any actual income is taken into account – eg, payments from a trust – then the capital is ignored when working out how much deemed income to include.

For **HB and CTB** there is an upper capital limit. If your capital is over £16,000 you are not eligible for HB or CTB unless you get PC guarantee credit. Capital between the lower limit (see below) and the upper limit is taken into account in the assessment in the same way as described above for PC.

The capital limits

Different capital limits apply depending on which benefit you claim and on whether you are living in a care home. The rules below apply to PC and, if you or your partner are aged 60 or over, to HB and CTB.

Pension credit

For PC:

- there is no upper capital limit;
- the lower limit is £6,000 (£10,000 if you live in a care home, see below).

Capital of £6,000 or less is ignored altogether. If you have capital above £6,000 (or £10,000 if you are in a care home), you will be treated as having a deemed income of £1 for every £500, or part of £500, by which your capital exceeds £6,000 (£10,000 if you are in a care home).[232]

Housing benefit and council tax benefit

- If you or your partner are getting the guarantee credit of PC, all of your (and your partner's) capital is ignored.[233] This means that you can get HB or CTB even if your capital is above £16,000.
- If you or your partner get IS or income-based JSA, you do not need to work out your capital again for HB or CTB because you get maximum HB or CTB.
- In any other case, there is a capital limit of £16,000,[234] but capital of £6,000 or less (£10,000 if you live in any of the care homes listed below) is ignored altogether. If you have capital above £6,000 (or £10,000 if you are in a care home), you will be treated as having a deemed income of £1 for every £500, or part of £500, by which your capital exceeds that amount.[235]

Care homes

There are higher capital limits if you live permanently in a care home or similar accommodation.

For **PC**, as usual there is no upper limit. However, deemed income starts at above £10,000 instead of £6,000[236] if you live permanently in:

- a care home (as defined in the Care Standards Act 2000); *or*
- an Abbeyfield Society home; *or*
- a home provided under the Polish Resettlement Act in which you receive personal care; *or*
- accommodation in a home owned or managed by a local authority, provided under sections 21 to 24 of the National Assistance Act 1948 or sections 13B or 59 of the Social Work (Scotland) Act or section 7 of the Mental Health (Scotland) Act 1984.

For **HB** the upper limit remains at £16,000. Also, deemed income starts at above £10,000 (instead of £6,000). You cannot claim CTB if you are permanently in a care home because you will not then be liable for council tax. For HB,[237] the higher limits apply if you live permanently in one of the limited categories of care home for which HB is payable, referred to on p725. Some temporary absences (see p202) are ignored.

Whose capital counts

Your partner's capital is added to yours – ie, it counts as yours.[238]

The capital of any dependent child will not affect your PC as you cannot claim for any children in your PC (see p468).

For HB and CTB, your child's capital is not added to yours[239] and does not affect your claim. You can get benefit included for your child, including premiums, even though her/his capital is over £3,000.

What counts as capital

The term 'capital' is not defined. In general, it means lump-sum or one-off payments rather than a series of payments[240] – eg, it includes savings, investments and property. The rules below apply to PC and, if you or your partner are aged 60 or over, to HB and CTB.

Savings

Your savings generally count as capital – eg, cash you have at home, premium bonds, stocks and shares, unit trusts, and money in a bank account or building society.

Savings from past income (including social security benefits – see p1057) will be treated as capital after the period for which the income was paid has lapsed. There is no provision for disregarding money put aside to pay bills.[241] If you have savings just below the capital limit, it may be best to pay bills for gas, electricity, telephone, etc by monthly standing order, or by use of a budget account, to prevent your capital going above the limit.

Fixed-term investments

Capital held in fixed-term investments counts. However, if in reality it is presently unobtainable, it may have little or no value. If you can convert the investment into a realisable form, sell your interest, or raise a loan through a reputable bank using the asset as security, its value counts. If it takes time to produce evidence about the nature and value of the investment, you may be able to get an interim payment of PC (see p1108) or HB[242] (see p230) or a crisis loan from the social fund (see p538).

Property and land

Any property or land that you own counts as capital. Many types of property are disregarded (see p1054). See also 'proprietary estoppel' – p1028.

Loans

A loan usually counts as money you possess. However, in some limited cases you can argue that a loan should be disregarded (see p1027).

Trusts

Money or property held in a trust for the benefit of you or your partner is ignored when working out deemed income – ie, you are not assumed to have a fixed income from the trust.[243] This applies to both discretionary and non-discretionary trusts. However, payments actually made from the trust can be taken into account. If made regularly, payments are treated as income. For discretionary trusts, regular payments are either disregarded in full or in part (see p1004). If payments are not made regularly they would be taken into account as capital.

The rules are different if the trust is set up out of personal injury payments (see below). Payments made from certain charitable trusts are specifically ignored (see pp1058 and 1058).

Payments of personal injury compensation

Any money paid because of a personal injury is ignored whether or not it has been placed into a trust.[244] Neither deemed income nor actual income from the fund is taken into account. The rules refer to 'personal injury to the claimant or, if the claimant has a partner, to the partner'. Because of this wording it is doubtful if the capital value of a trust fund will be ignored if the money was paid in respect of a family member other than yourself or your partner; it will not be ignored if it was paid in respect of someone who is no longer a member of your family (eg, because s/he is dead).[245]

Trust funds administered by the court[246]

The value of a trust fund is also ignored where damages are awarded in respect of personal injury and the money paid into a special fund to be administered by, and at the discretion of, the court (eg, the Court of Protection). Payments out of funds administered by the court are ignored completely both as capital and income.[247]

Disregarded capital

Some kinds of capital are ignored in the assessment of PC and, if you or your partner are aged 60 or over, of HB and CTB.

Your home

If you own the home you normally live in, its value is ignored.[248] The value of your home is disregarded for the purposes of the deemed income rule.[249]

The value of your home

Your **'home'** includes any garage, garden, outbuildings and land, together with any premises that you do not occupy as your home but which it is impractical or unreasonable to sell separately – eg, croft land.[250] This disregard applies to any home you are treated as normally living in (eg, because you are only temporarily living away from it – see p907), although if you own more than one property, only the value of the one normally occupied is disregarded under this rule.[251] Although the home may consist of more than one unit of accommodation,[252] both units will only count as the home if the claimant (as opposed to any member of her/his family) normally has to occupy both units (ie, where one unit is treated as an extension or annexe of the other).[253]

Disregarding property

The value of the property can be disregarded even if you do not normally live in it in the following circumstances.

- **If you have left your former home following a marriage or relationship breakdown,** the value of the property is ignored for six months from the date you left. It may also be disregarded for longer if any of the steps below are taken. If it is occupied by your former partner who is a lone parent its value is ignored as long as s/he lives there.[254]
- **If you have sought legal advice or have started legal proceedings in order to occupy property** as your home, its value is ignored for six months from the date you first took either of these steps.[255] The six months can be extended, if it is reasonable to do so, where you need longer to move into the property.
- **If you are taking reasonable steps to dispose of any property**, its value is ignored for six months (which may start before you claimed benefit) from the date you *first* took such steps.[256] The steps you take must be objectively 'reasonable' so, for example, advertising at an unrealistic sale price would not count. Placing the property with an estate agent or contacting a possible buyer should count,[257] as might taking ancillary proceedings to resolve financial issues in a divorce.[258] The disregard can continue beyond six months, even for years if it is reasonable – eg if a husband or wife cannot sell because a court

orders that the former matrimonial home should not be sold until the children grow up.

- **If you are carrying out essential repairs or alterations** which are needed so that you can occupy a property as your home, the value of the property is ignored for six months from the date you first began to take steps to carry them out.[259] 'Steps' may include applying for planning permission or a grant or a loan to make the property habitable, employing an architect or finding someone to do the work.[260] If you cannot move into the property within that period because the work is not finished, its value can be disregarded for as long as is necessary to allow the work to be carried out.
- **If you have acquired a house or flat for occupation** as your home but have not yet moved in, its value is ignored if you intend to live there within six months of acquisition.[261] If you cannot move in by then, the value of the property can be ignored for as long as seems reasonable.
- **Any amounts paid to you or deposited in your name for the sole purpose of buying a home for you to live in or carrying out essential repairs or alterations to your home or the home you intend to occupy** are ignored for a year from the date you were paid them, or for PC only, until the end of the assessed income period (p480), if there is one, if this is longer.[262]
- **Any compensation paid under an insurance policy because of loss or damage to your home** is ignored for a year from the date it is paid to you, or for PC only, until the end of the assessed income period, if there is one, if this is longer.[263]

When considering whether to increase the period of any disregard, all the circumstances should be considered – particularly your and your family's personal circumstances, any efforts made by you to use or dispose of the home[264] (if relevant) and the general state of the market (if relevant). In practice, periods of around 18 months are not considered unusual.

It is possible for property to be ignored under more than one of the above paragraphs in succession.[265]

The home of a former partner or relative

The value of a home (see p1054) is also ignored if it is occupied wholly or partly as her/his home by:[266]

- a relative of yours or your partners[267] who is aged 60 or over or is incapacitated (see p1056);
- your former partner from whom you are not estranged or divorced. This means your husband/wife where you are not still treated as living in the same household or your former cohabitee where you are not still treated as living together as husband and wife;

- your former partner from whom you are estranged or divorced if s/he is a lone parent. If your former partner is not a lone parent, the value of the home is ignored for 26 weeks from the date you ceased to live in the home.[268]

It has been held that this disregard only applies to a property which you previously occupied yourself.[269]

Note: when the Civil Partnership Act 2004 comes into force in December 2005, this disregard will also apply to same sex partners (see p811).

'Incapacitated' is not defined, but guidance suggests it refers to someone who is getting an incapacity or disability benefit, or who is sufficiently incapacitated to qualify for one of those benefits.[270] However, you should argue for a broader interpretation, if necessary.

'Relative' includes: a parent, son, daughter, step-parent/son/daughter, or parent/son/daughter-in-law; brother or sister; or a partner of any of these people; or a grandparent or grandchild, uncle, aunt, nephew or niece.[271]* It also includes half-brothers and sisters and adopted children.[272]

Personal possessions

All personal possessions, including items such as jewellery, furniture or a car, are ignored.[273]

Compensation paid under an insurance policy for damage to or loss of your personal possessions is ignored for a year from the date you were paid the compensation or, for PC only, until the end of the assessed income period (if there is one) if that is longer.[274]

Business assets

If you are self-employed, your business assets are ignored for as long as you continue to work in that business.[275] If you cannot work because of physical or mental illness, but intend to work in the business when you are able, the disregard operates for 26 weeks from the date of claim, or for longer if reasonable in the circumstances.[276] For more about this, see p1056.

Insurance policy and annuity surrender values

The surrender value of any life assurance or endowment policy is ignored.[277] **Note:** the life assurance aspect need not be the sole or even the main aspect of the policy (although the other features of any policy may still be considered under the actual or notional income and capital rules – see p1005).

The surrender value of any annuity is also ignored for the purposes of the deemed income rule (see p1003). Any actual income the surrender value generates for you, and which is not disregarded as income, can be taken into account as income.[278] Any payment under the annuity counts as income[279] (but see p1004 for when this is ignored).

* From 5 December 2005, 'step' and 'in-law' relations of a civil partner can also count as relatives.

Future interests in property

A future interest in most kinds of property is ignored.[280] A **'future interest'** is one which will only revert to you, or become yours for the first time, when some future event occurs. For more about this, see p1057.

The right to receive a payment in the future

If you know you will receive a payment in the future, you could sell your right to that payment at any time so it has a market value and therefore constitutes an actual capital resource. The value of this is ignored where it is a right to receive:

- income under a life interest or, in Scotland, a life rent.[281] However, it is only ignored for the purposes of the deemed income rule (see pp1003 and 1050);
- an occupational or personal pension;[282]
- any rent if you are not the freeholder or leaseholder.[283] However, it is only ignored for the purposes of the deemed income rule (see pp1003 and 1050). Any actual income which the right to receive such rent in the future generates for you, and which is not disregarded as income, can be taken into account as income;
- any payment under an annuity (see p1004).[284] However, that is only ignored for the purposes of the deemed income rule (see pp1003 and 1050). Any actual income generated by the right to receive income from an annuity in the future, and which is not disregarded as income, can be taken into account as income.
- any payment under a retirement annuity contract.[285]

Benefits and other payments

The general rule is that arrears of specified benefits, child tax credit (CTC) and other payments (see below) are ignored for:[286]

- 52 weeks after they are received by you or, for PC only, until the end of the assessed income period (if there is one) if that is longer; *or*
- any payment of £5,000 or more for arrears or late payment of a 'specified benefit' (see below), which was made to rectify or compensate for an official error, and which you received in full since becoming entitled to PC, HB or CTB. If you got the compensation before then, it is still disregarded if your current award follows on immediately from a previous award of IS, income-based JSA, HB or CTB (or PC for current awards of HB and CTB) in which the compensation was disregarded, or it is still being disregarded in an award of one of those benefits.

The compensation is ignored for as long as the award of benefit lasts. The **specified benefits** are those listed below.

The benefit arrears that are ignored under the general rule described above are:

- AA, DLA, income-based JSA, IS, PC, HB, CTB, CTC, constant attendance allowance, exceptionally severe disablement, and for PC only, child benefit

and social fund payments – or concessionary payments (ie, compensation) made instead of any of these or payments made in lieu of any of these benefits;
- payments made by a local authority under section 91 of the Local Government Act 2003 (the 'Supporting People' scheme) or under section 91 of the Housing (Scotland) Act 2001.

Lump-sum payments to HB claimants through the under-occupation pilot scheme are ignored for 52 weeks, but this rule does not apply to PC.[287]

World War II compensation payments

There are two different ways in which such compensation payments may be disregarded.

- **Former Japanese prisoners of war:**
  - £10,000 is ignored indefinitely if you received an ex gratia payment from the Secretary of State because during World War II the Japanese imprisoned or interned you, your partner, your deceased spouse or your partner's deceased spouse.[288] Arguably the £10,000 disregard can be set against other capital if the payment itself has been spent;
- **Victims of World War II:**
  - any payment (except for a war pension) made to compensate for the fact that, during World War II, you, your partner, your deceased spouse or your partner's deceased spouse was a slave or forced labourer, lost property or suffered a personal injury, or was the parent of a child who died, is ignored for an indefinite period.[289]

Creutzfeldt-Jakob disease payments

Payments made out of trust funds established from funds provided by the Secretary of State for people with variant Creutzfeldt-Jakob disease (CJD) are ignored as capital for varying periods.[290] See p1037 for details.

Funeral plan payments[291]

The value of any funeral plan contract is ignored indefinitely.

A funeral plan contract is a contract under which:

- you make at least one payment to another person;
- that person undertakes to provide, or ensure you are provided with, a funeral in the UK on your death; *and*
- the sole purpose of the plan is to provide, or ensure that you are provided with, a funeral on your death.

Charitable payments

All payments from the Macfarlane Trusts, the Skipton Fund, the Fund, the Eileen Trust and either of the Independent Living Funds are ignored.[292] Certain payments from money that originally came from any of the three Macfarlane Trusts, the

Fund, the Skipton Fund or the Eileen Trust are also ignored – the rules are the same as for income (see p973).

Payments in other currencies

Any payment in a currency other than sterling is taken into account after disregarding banking charges or commission payable on conversion to sterling.[293]

Age-related payments

Payments made to you under the Age-related Payments Scheme are ignored indefinitely.[294]

Notional capital

In certain circumstances, you are treated as having capital which you do not, in fact, possess. This is called **'notional capital'**.[295] There is a similar rule for notional income (see p1005). Notional capital counts in the same way as capital you actually do possess except that a 'diminishing notional capital rule' (see p1060) may be applied so that the value of the notional capital you are treated as having will be considered to reduce over time.

For PC and, if you or your partner are aged 60 or over, for HB and CTB, there are two circumstances in which you will be treated as having notional capital:

- where you deliberately deprive yourself of capital in order to claim or increase benefit (see p1059);
- where you are a sole trader or a partner in a business which is a limited company (see p1060).

Note: the 'diminishing notional capital rule' (see p1060) can only apply where you are treated as having notional capital under the first circumstance.

Deprivation of capital in order to claim or increase benefit

If you deliberately get rid of capital in order to claim or increase your benefit, you are treated as still possessing it.[296] You are likely to be affected by this rule if, at the time of using up your money, you know that you may qualify for benefit (or more benefit) as a result, or qualify more quickly. It should not be used if you know nothing about the effect of using up your capital (eg, you do not know about the capital limit for claiming benefit),[297] or if you have been using up your capital at a rate which is reasonable in the circumstances. Knowledge of capital limits can be inferred from a reasonable familiarity with the benefit system as a claimant,[298] but if you fail to make enquiries about the capital limit, this does not constitute an intention to secure benefit. This is because you cannot form the required intention if you do not know about the capital rules.[299]

Why was the capital got rid of?

Even if you do know about the capital limits, it still has to be shown that you intended to obtain, retain or increase your benefit.[300] For examples of this, see p1040.

Gifts and paying off debts

You will be treated as not having deprived yourself of capital if:

- you pay off or reduce a debt which you owe; *or*
- you pay for goods or services if the purchase of those goods or services was reasonable in the circumstances of your case.[301]

Intention to get benefit

You may need to show that you would have spent the money in the way you did regardless of how that affected your benefit. For more information about this, see p1041.

Calculation of notional capital

If you are treated as possessing notional capital, it is calculated in the same way as if it were actual capital[302] and the same disregards usually apply. For more information about this, see p1042.

Diminishing notional capital

So that the full amount of notional capital does not continue to affect your benefit indefinitely, there is a rule for working out how to reduce it over time. This is described on p1042.

Companies run by sole traders or a few partners

You are also treated as possessing notional capital if, as a sole trader or a small partnership, you have registered your business as a limited company. The value of your shareholding is ignored but you are treated as possessing a proportionate share of the capital of the company.[303] This does not apply while you are doing any work on the company's business.[304] Even if you work for the company for, say, only half an hour a week, this will suffice.[305] It has, however, been held that a 'sleeping partner' in a business managed and worked exclusively by others may not benefit from this disregard. As well as having a financial commitment to the business you must also be involved or engaged in it in some practical sense as an earner.[306]

How capital is valued

There are a number of issues to consider when valuing capital.

- **Market value.** Except for National Savings certificates (see p1061), capital is valued at its current market or surrender value,[307] which could be very low if it is difficult to sell. See p1046 for more information (the rules are the same as those for people under age 60).

- **Expenses of sale.** If there would be expenses involved in selling your capital, 10 per cent is deducted from its value for the cost of sale.[308]
- **Debts.** Deductions are made from the 'gross' value of your capital for any debt or mortgage secured on it.[309] For more information, see p1047 (the rules are the same as those for people aged under 60).
- **National savings.** For PC, a certificate bought from an issue which ceased before the 1 July before your claim is decided, or your benefit is first payable (whichever is earlier), or the date of any subsequent supersession, has the value it would have had on that 1 July if purchased on the last day of the issue. For HB and CTB it is the 1 July before your claim is made or treated as made or when your benefit is reviewed. In any other case, the value is the purchase price.[310] DWP guidance contains a convenient valuation table for each issue.[311]
- **Capital that is jointly owned under a joint tenancy.** If you jointly own any capital asset (except as a partner in a company when the rules explained on p1060 will apply instead) under a joint tenancy you are treated as owning an equal share of the asset with all other owners.[312] For example, if two of you own the asset, then you will each be treated as having a 50 per cent share of it. This rule does not apply, however, if you jointly own the capital asset as tenants in common.[313] For more information, see p1047.
- **Treatment of assets after a relationship breakdown.** There are no specific rules about this, but there is some guidance and caselaw. For information, see p1048, the information there applies equally to people aged 60 or over.
- **Shares.** Shares are valued at their current market value less 10 per cent for the cost of sale[314] and after deducting any 'lien' held by brokers for sums owed for the cost of acquisition and commission. See p1049 for more details (the rules are the same as those for people aged under 60).
- **Unit trust.**These are valued on the basis of the 'bid' price quoted in newspapers. No deduction is allowed for the cost of sale because this is already included in the 'bid' price.[315]
- **The right to receive a payment in the future.** The value of any such right that is not ignored (see p1057) is its market value – what a willing buyer will pay to a willing seller.[316] For something which is not yet realisable this may be very small.
- **Overseas assets.** If you have assets abroad, and there are no exchange controls or other prohibitions that would prevent you transferring your capital to this country, your assets are valued at their current market or surrender value in that country.[317] If you are not allowed to transfer your capital, you are treated as having capital equal to the amount that a willing buyer in this country would give (which might not be very much).[318] Deduct any debts or mortgage secured on the assets, 10 per cent for any expenses of sale and anycharges for converting the payment into sterling.[319]

Notes

1. Capital: aged under 60

1 **HB** Sch 5 para 5 HB Regs
CTB Sch 5 para 5 CTB Regs
2 **IS** Reg 45 IS Regs
JSA s13(1) JSA 1995; reg 107(a) JSA Regs
3 **IS** Reg 53(1) IS Regs
JSA Reg 116(1) JSA Regs
4 Reg 45(aa) IS Regs
5 Regs 107(aa) and 116(1ZA) JSA Regs
6 **HB** Regs 37 and 45(1) HB Regs
CTB Regs 28 and 37(1) CTB Regs
7 **IS** Regs 45 and 53(1A), (1B), (1C) and (4) IS Regs
JSA Regs 107(b) and 116(1A) JSA Regs
8 **IS** Reg 2(1) IS Regs
JSA Reg 1(3) JSA Regs
9 **IS** Reg 2(1) IS Regs
JSA Reg 1(3) JSA Regs
10 **IS** Regs 21(3) and 53(4) IS Regs
JSA Regs 85(4) and 116(4) JSA Regs
11 **IS** Reg 21(3B)-(3E) IS Regs
JSA Reg 85(5)(b) JSA Regs
12 CIS/16440/1996
13 **IS** Reg 21(3A) IS Regs
JSA Reg 85(5)(a) JSA Regs
14 Regs 7(2), (5) and (7) and 45(1A), (1B), (1C), (4) and (5) HB Regs
15 **IS/HB/CTB** s136(1) SSCBA 1992
JSA s13(2) JSA 1995
16 **IS** Reg 47 IS Regs
JSA Reg 109 JSA Regs
HB Reg 19(4) HB Regs
CTB Reg 11(4) CTB Regs
17 **IS** Regs 23, 41, 44, 48 and 51 and Sch 10 IS Regs
JSA Regs 88, 104, 106, 110 and 113 and Sch 8 JSA Regs
Both as amended by reg 1 and Schs 1 and 2 SS(WTCCTC)(CA) Regs
18 **IS** Reg 17(1)(b) IS Regs
JSA Reg 83(b) JSA Regs
19 **IS** Reg 44(5) IS Regs
JSA Reg 106(5) JSA Regs
20 **HB** reg 19(4) HB Regs
CTB reg 11(4) CTB Regs
21 para C2.21 GM; para 29020 DMG
22 *R v SBC ex parte Singer* [1973] 1 WLR 713
23 R(SB) 2/83; R(SB) 35/83; R(IS) 3/93
24 R(IS) 3/93
25 R(IS) 3/93 para 22
26 **IS/JSA** Reg 2 SS(PAOR) Regs
HB Reg 91(1) HB Regs
27 R(SB) 12/86
28 R(SB) 53/83; R(SB) 1/85
29 R(SB) 49/83
30 R(SB) 12/86
31 **IS** Sch 10 para 13 IS Regs
JSA Sch 8 para 18 JSA Regs
HB Sch 5 para 14 HB Regs
CTB Sch 5 para 14 CTB Regs
32 *Peters v CAO*, reported as an appendix to R(SB) 3/89
33 R(IS) 1/90
34 R(SB) 23/85
35 *Barclays Bank v Quistclose Investments Ltd* [1970] AC 567; R(SB) 49/83; CFC/21/1989
36 **IS** Sch 10 para 12 IS Regs
JSA Sch 8 para 18 JSA Regs
HB Sch 5 para 13 HB Regs
CTB Sch 5 para 13 CTB Regs
37 R(IS) 3/03
38 **IS** Sch 10 paras 44 and 45 IS Regs
JSA Sch 8 paras 42 and 43 JSA Regs
HB Sch 5 paras 46 and 47 HB Regs
CTB Sch 5 paras 46 and 47 CTB Regs
All CIS/368/1994
39 R(SB) 2/89
40 2004 Pre-Budget Report, para 4.59
41 **IS** Sch 10 paras 44 and 45 IS Regs
JSA Sch 8 paras 42 and 43 JSA Regs
HB Sch 5 paras 46 and 47 HB Regs
CTB Sch 5 paras 46 and 47 CTB Regs
42 CIS/4037/1999
43 **IS** Reg 41(7) IS Regs
JSA Reg 104(6) JSA Regs
HB Reg 34(5) HB Regs
CTB Reg 25(5) CTB Regs
44 **IS** Regs 40 and 46 IS Regs
JSA Regs 103 and 108 JSA Regs
HB Regs 33 and 38 HB Regs
CTB Regs 24 and 29 CTB Regs
All CIS/559/1991
45 *Thomas v CAO*, appendix to R(SB) 17/87
46 CIS/984/2002
47 **IS** Reg 48 IS Regs
JSA Reg 110 JSA Regs
HB Reg 40 HB Regs
CTB Reg 31 CTB Regs

48 Reg 48(11) IS Regs
49 **HB** Reg 40(9) HB Regs
CTB Reg 31(9) CTB Regs
50 **IS** Sch 10 para 59 IS Regs
JSA Sch 8 para 54 JSA Regs
HB Sch 5 para 62 HB Regs
CTB Sch 5 para 62 CTB Regs
51 **All** Reg 2(1) IS/JSA//HB/CTB Regs
52 **IS** Sch 10 para 1 IS Regs
JSA Sch 8 para 1 JSA Regs
HB Sch 5 para 1 HB Regs
CTB Sch 5 para 1 CTB Regs
53 **IS** Reg 2(1) IS Regs, meaning of 'dwelling occupied as the home'; R(SB) 3/84; CIS/427/1991 and R(IS) 3/96
JSA Reg 1(3) JSA Regs, meaning of 'dwelling occupied as the home'
HB Sch 5 para 1 HB Regs
CTB Sch 5 para 1 CTB Regs
54 **IS** Sch 10 para 1 IS Regs
JSA Sch 8 para 1 JSA Regs
HB Sch 5 para 1 HB Regs
CTB Sch 5 para 1 CTB Regs
55 R(JSA) 9/03
56 R(SB)10/89
57 **IS** Sch 10 para 25 IS Regs
JSA Sch 8 para 5 JSA Regs
HB Sch 5 para 24 HB Regs
CTB Sch 5 para 24 CTB Regs
58 **IS** Sch 10 para 27 IS Regs
JSA Sch 8 para 7 JSA Regs
HB Sch 5 para 26 HB Regs
CTB Sch 5 para 26 CTB Regs
59 **IS** Sch 10 para 26 IS Regs
JSA Sch 8 para 6 JSA Regs
HB Sch 5 para 25 HB Regs
CTB Sch 5 para 25 CTB Regs
All CIS/6908/1995; R(IS) 4/97
60 CIS/562/1992
61 R(IS) 4/97
62 R(SB) 32/83
63 CIS/1846/2004
64 R(IS) 4/97, para 22
65 **IS** Sch 10 para 28 IS Regs
JSA Sch 8 para 8 JSA Regs
HB Sch 5 para 27 HB Regs
CTB Sch 5 para 27 CTB Regs
66 *R v London Borough of Tower Hamlets Review Board ex parte Kapur*, 12 June 2000, unreported
67 **IS** Sch 10 para 2 IS Regs
JSA Sch 8 para 2 JSA Regs
HB Sch 5 para 2 HB Regs
CTB Sch 5 para 2 CTB Regs
68 **IS** Sch 10 para 3 IS Regs
JSA Sch 8 para 3 JSA Regs
HB Sch 5 para 3 HB Regs
CTB Sch 5 para 3 CTB Regs
69 R(IS) 6/95
70 R(IS) 7/01
71 CIS/685/1992
72 CIS/8475/1995; CIS/15984/1996
73 R(SB) 14/85
74 **IS** Sch 10 para 8(a) IS Regs
JSA Sch 8 para 13(a) JSA Regs
HB Sch 5 para 9(a) HB Regs
CTB Sch 5 para 9(a) CTB Regs
75 **IS** Sch 10 para 8(b) IS Regs
JSA Sch 8 para 13(b) JSA Regs
HB Sch 5 para 9(b) HB Regs
CTB Sch 5 para 9(b) CTB Regs
76 *Barclays Bank v Quistclose Investments Ltd* [1970] AC 567; CSB/975/1985
77 **IS** Sch 10 para 9(a) IS Regs
JSA Sch 8 para 14(a) JSA Regs
HB Sch 5 para 10(a) HB Regs
CTB Sch 5 para 10(a) CTB Regs
78 **IS** Sch 10 para 9(b) IS Regs
JSA Sch 8 para 14(b) JSA Regs
HB Sch 5 para 10(b) HB Regs
CTB Sch 5 para 10(b) CTB Regs
79 **IS** Sch 10 para 37 IS Regs
JSA Sch 8 para 9 JSA Regs
HB Sch 5 para 37 HB Regs
CTB Sch 5 para 36 CTB Regs
80 para 29578 DMG
81 CIS/6908/1995
82 **IS** Sch 10 para 4 IS Regs
JSA Sch 8 para 4 JSA Regs
HB Sch 5 para 4 HB Regs
CTB Sch 5 para 4 CTB Regs
83 **IS** Reg 2(1) IS Regs
JSA Reg 1(3) JSA Regs
HB Reg 2(1)HB Regs
CTB Reg 2(1) CTB Regs
All definition of 'partner'
IS/HB/CTB s137(1) SSCBA 1992;
JSA s35 JSA 1995, definition of 'married couple' and 'unmarried couple'
84 **IS** Sch 10 para 25 IS Regs
HB Schs 5 para 24 and 5ZA para 6 HB Regs
CTB Schs 5 para 24 and 5ZA para 6 CTB Regs
85 R(IS) 3/96
86 para 29432 DMG
HB/CTB para C2.Annex A, A2.00 GM
87 **IS** Reg 2(1) IS Regs, definition of 'relative'
JSA Reg 1(3) JSA Regs, definition of 'relative'
HB Reg 2(1) HB Regs, definition of 'relative'
CTB Reg 2(1) CTB Regs, definition of 'relative'

88 CSB/209/1986; CSB/1149/1986; R(SB) 22/87
89 **IS** Sch 10 para 10 IS Regs
JSA Sch 8 para 15 JSA Regs
HB Sch 5 para 11 HB Regs
CTB Sch 5 para 11 CTB Regs
90 CIS/494/1990
91 **IS** Sch 10 para 8(a) IS Regs
JSA Sch 8 para 13(a) JSA Regs
HB Sch 5 para 9(a) HB Regs
CTB Sch 5 para 9(a) CTB Regs
92 **IS** Sch 10 para 6(1) IS Regs
JSA Sch 8 para 11(1) JSA Regs
HB Sch 5 para 7(1) HB Regs
CTB Sch 5 para 7(1) CTB Regs
93 **IS/JSA** para 29375 DMG
94 **IS** Sch 10 para 6(2) IS Regs
JSA Sch 8 para 11(2) JSA Regs
HB Sch 5 para 7(2) HB Regs
CTB Sch 5 para 7(2) CTB Regs
95 R(SB) 4/85
96 CIS/5481/1997
97 CFC/15/1990
98 **IS** Sch 10 para 19 IS Regs
JSA Sch 8 para 24 JSA Regs
HB Sch 5 para 20 HB Regs
CTB Sch 5 para 20 CTB Regs
99 **IS** Sch 10 para 23A IS Regs
JSA Sch 8 paras 28 and 29 JSA Regs
HB Sch 3 para 39A HB Regs
CTB Sch 5 para 30A CTB Regs
100 **IS** Sch 10 para 15 IS Regs
JSA Sch 8 para 20 JSA Regs
HB Sch 5 para 16 HB Regs
CTB Sch 5 para 11 CTB Regs
All R(IS) 7/98
101 **IS** Sch 10 para 11 IS Regs
JSA Sch 8 para 16 JSA Regs
HB Sch 5 para 12 HB Regs
CTB Sch 5 para 12 CTB Regs
102 **IS** Reg 41(2) IS Regs
JSA Reg 104(2) JSA Regs
HB Reg 34(2) HB Regs
CTB Reg 25(2) CTB Regs
All *Beattie v Secretary of State for Social Security* [2001] EWCA Civ 498, *The Times*, 3 May 2001, upholding CIS/114/1999, reported as R(IS) 10/01
103 **IS** Sch 10 para 5 IS Regs
JSA Sch 8 para 10 JSA Regs
HB Sch 5 para 6 HB Regs
CTB Sch 5 para 6 CTB Regs
104 CIS/635/1994
105 **IS** Sch 10 para 13 IS Regs
JSA Sch 8 para 18 JSA Regs
HB Sch 5 para 14 HB Regs
CTB Sch 5 para 14 CTB Regs
106 **IS** Sch 10 para 23 IS Regs
JSA Sch 8 para 28 JSA Regs
HB Sch 5 para 30 HB Regs
CTB Sch 5 para 30 CTB Regs
107 **IS** Sch 10 para 24 IS Regs
JSA Sch 8 para 30 JSA Regs
HB Sch 5 para 31 HB Regs
CTB Sch 5 para 31 CTB Regs
108 **IS** Sch 10 para 11 IS Regs
JSA Sch 8 para 16 JSA Regs
HB Sch 5 para 12 HB Regs
CTB Sch 5 para 12 CTB Regs
109 **IS** Sch 10 para 14 IS Regs
JSA Sch 8 para 19 JSA Regs
HB Sch 5 para 15 HB Regs
CTB Sch 5 para 15 CTB Regs
110 **IS** Sch 10 para 16 IS Regs
JSA Sch 8 para 21 JSA Regs
HB Sch 5 para 17 HB Regs
CTB Sch 5 para 17 CTB Regs
111 **IS** Sch 10 para 12 IS Regs
JSA Sch 8 para 17 JSA Regs
HB Sch 5 para 13 HB Regs
CTB Sch 5 para 13 CTB Regs
112 **IS** Sch 10 para 7 IS Regs
JSA Sch 8 para 12 JSA Regs
HB Sch 5 para 8 HB Regs
CTB Sch 5 para 8 CTB Regs
113 **IS** Sch 10 para 7(2) IS Regs
JSA Sch 8 para 12(2) JSA Regs
HB Sch 5 para 8(2) HB Regs
CTB Sch 5 para 8(2) CTB Regs
114 **IS** Sch 10 para 41 IS Regs
JSA Sch 8 para 39 JSA Regs
HB Sch 5 para 8 HB Regs
CTB Sch 5 para 37 CTB Regs
115 **IS** Sch 10 para 36 IS Regs
JSA Sch 8 para 35 JSA Regs
HB Sch 5 para 36 HB Regs
CTB Sch 5 para 35 CTB Regs
116 Sch 10 paras 47-49 IS Regs
117 Sch 5 paras 50-51 HB Regs
118 Sch 5 paras 50-51 CTB Regs
119 **HB** Sch 5 paras 49 and 52 HB Regs
CTB Sch 5 paras 49 and 52 CTB Regs
120 **IS** Sch 10 para 38 IS Regs
JSA Sch 8 para 36 JSA Regs
HB Sch 5 para 39 HB Regs
CTB Sch 5 para 38 CTB Regs
121 **IS** Sch 10 para 39 IS Regs
JSA Sch 8 para 37 JSA Regs
HB Sch 5 para 40 HB Regs
CTB Sch 5 para 39 CTB Regs
122 **IS** Sch 10 para 40 IS Regs
JSA Sch 8 para 38 JSA Regs
HB Sch 5 para 41 HB Regs
CTB Sch 5 para 40 CTB Regs

123 **IS** Sch 10 para 18 IS Regs
JSA Sch 8 para 23 JSA Regs
HB Sch 5 para 19 HB Regs
CTB Sch 5 para 19 CTB Regs
124 **IS** Sch 10 paras 42 and 43 IS Regs
JSA Sch 8 paras 40 and 41 JSA Regs
HB Sch 5 paras 43 and 44 HB Regs
CTB Sch 5 paras 42 and 43 CTB Regs
125 **IS** Sch 10 para 46 IS Regs
JSA Sch 8 para 44 JSA Regs
HB Sch 5 para 48 HB Regs
CTB Sch 5 para 48 CTB Regs
126 **IS** Sch 10 paras 31-33 IS Regs
JSA Sch 8 para 33 JSA Regs
HB Sch 5 paras 28-29 and 42 HB Regs
CTB Sch 5 paras 28-29 and 41 CTB Regs
127 **IS** Sch 10 para 66 IS Regs
JSA Sch 8 para 59 JSA Regs
HB Sch 5 para 68 HB Regs
CTB Sch 5 para 68 CTB Regs
128 **IS** Sch 10 para 60 IS Regs
JSA Sch 8 para 55 JSA Regs
HB Sch 5 para 63 HB Regs
CTB Sch 5 para 63 CTB Regs
129 **IS** Sch 10 para 61 IS Regs
JSA Sch 8 para 56 JSA Regs
HB Sch 5 para 64 HB Regs
CTB Sch 5 para 64 CTB Regs
130 **IS** Sch 10 para 65 IS Regs
JSA Sch 8 para 58 JSA Regs
HB Sch 5 para 67 HB Regs
CTB Sch 5 para 67 CTB Regs
131 **IS** Sch 10 para 64 IS Regs
JSA Sch 8 para 57 JSA Regs
HB Sch 5 para 66 HB Regs
CTB Sch 5 para 66 CTB Regs
For people aged 60 or over:
PC Sch 5 para 13 SPC Regs
HB Sch 5ZA para 14 HB Regs
CTB Sch 5ZA para 14 CTB Regs
132 **IS** Sch 10 para 64(3) and (4) IS Regs
JSA Sch 8 para 57(3) and (4) JSA Regs
HB Sch 5 para 66(3) and (4) HB Regs
CTB Sch 5 para 66(3) and (4) CTB Regs
For people aged 60 or over:
PC Sch 5 para 13(3) and (4) SPC Regs
HB Sch 5ZA para 14(3) and (4) HB Regs
CTB Sch 5ZA para 14(3) and (4) CTB Regs
133 **IS** Sch 10 para 29 IS Regs
JSA Sch 8 para 31 JSA Regs
HB Sch 5 para 32 HB Regs
CTB Sch 5 para 32 CTB Regs
134 **IS** Sch 10 para 22 IS Regs
JSA Sch 8 para 27 JSA Regs
HB Sch 5 para 23 HB Regs
CTB Sch 5 para 23 CTB Regs
135 **IS** para 29460 DMG
HB Reg 73(1) and (3) HB Regs
CTB Reg 63(1) and (3) CTB Regs
136 **IS** Sch 10 para 56 IS Regs
JSA Sch 8 para 51 JSA Regs
HB Sch 5 para 59 HB Regs
CTB Sch 5 para 59 CTB Regs
137 2004 Pre-Budget Report, para 4.59
138 **IS** Sch 10 para 21 IS Regs
JSA Sch 8 para 26 JSA Regs
HB Sch 5 para 22 HB Regs
CTB Sch 5 para 22 CTB Regs
139 **IS** Sch 10 para 17 IS Regs
JSA Sch 8 para 22 JSA Regs
HB Sch 5 para 18 HB Regs
CTB Sch 5 para 18 CTB Regs
140 **IS** Sch 10 para 67 IS Regs
JSA Sch 8 para 60 JSA Regs
HB Sch 5 para 69 HB Regs
CTB Sch 5 para 69 CTB Regs
141 **IS** Sch 10 para 68A IS Regs
JSA Sch 8 para 61A JSA Regs
HB Sch 5 para 70A HB Regs
CTB Sch 5 para 70A CTB Regs
142 **IS** Sch 10 para 68 IS Regs
JSA Sch 8 para 61 JSA Regs
HB Sch 5 para 70 HB Regs
CTB Sch 5 para 70 CTB Regs
143 **IS** Sch 10 para 34 IS Regs
JSA Sch 8 para 34 JSA Regs
HB Sch 4 para 38 HB regs
CTB Sch 4 para 40 CTB Regs
144 **IS** Sch 10 para 30 IS Regs
JSA Sch 8 para 32 JSA Regs
HB Sch 5 para 33 HB Regs
CTB Sch 5 para 33 CTB Regs
145 **IS** Sch 10 para 58 IS Regs
JSA Sch 8 para 53 JSA Regs
HB Sch 5 para 61 HB Regs
CTB Sch 5 para 61 CTB Regs
146 **IS** Sch 10 para 63 IS Regs
JSA Sch 8 para 52 JSA Regs
HB Sch 5 para 60 HB Regs
CTB Sch 5 para 60 CTB Regs
147 **IS** Sch 10 para 52 IS Regs
JSA Sch 8 para 47 JSA Regs
HB Sch 5 para 55 HB Regs
CTB Sch 5 para 55 CTB Regs
148 **IS** Sch 10 para 6(3) IS Regs
JSA Sch 8 para 11(3) JSA Regs
HB Sch 5 para 7(3) HB Regs
CTB Sch 5 para 7(3) CTB Regs
149 **IS** Sch 10 para 6(1) IS Regs
JSA Sch 8 para 11(1) JSA Regs
HB Sch 5 para 7(1) HB Regs
CTB Sch 5 para 7(1) CTB Regs
150 s6 Age-related Payments Act 2004

151 **IS** Sch 10 para 20 IS Regs
JSA Sch 8 para 25 JSA Regs
HB Sch 5 para 21 HB Regs
CTB Sch 5 para 21 CTB Regs
152 **IS** Reg 51(6) IS Regs
JSA Reg 113(6) JSA Regs
HB Reg 43(6) HB Regs
CTB Reg 34(6) CTB Regs
153 **IS** Reg 51(1) IS Regs
JSA Reg 113(1) JSA Regs
HB Reg 43(1) HB Regs
CTB Reg 34(1) CTB Regs
154 CIS/124/1990; CSB/1198/1989
155 R(SB) 9/91
156 CIS/124/1990
157 CIS/40/1989
158 CIS/621/1991
159 CIS/264/1989
160 R(IS) 7/98, para 12(3)
161 R(SB) 38/85
162 para 29817 DMG
163 **IS** Reg 51(1) IS Regs
JSA Reg 113(1) JSA Regs
164 R(SB) 12/91; *Verna Jones v Secretary of State for Work and Pensions* [2003] EWCA Civ 964, 10 July 2003, unreported (CA)
165 CIS/2627/1995; *Verna Jones v Secretary of State for Work and Pensions* [2003] EWCA Civ 964, 10 July 2003, unreported (CA)
166 CIS/236/1991
167 *R v Caerphilly CBC HBRB ex parte Jones*, 1 February 1999, unreported
168 CIS/634/1992
169 CIS/12403/1996
170 **IS** Reg 51(6) IS Regs
JSA Reg 113(6) JSA Regs
HB Reg 43(6) HB Regs
CTB Reg 34(6) CTB Regs
171 CIS/30/1993, but other commissioners have taken a different view (see for example, CIS/25/1990 and CIS/81/1991)
172 R(IS) 14/93
173 para C2.69 GM
174 para C2.97 GM
175 para C2.92 GM
176 **IS** Reg 51A IS Regs
JSA Reg 114 JSA Regs
PC Reg 22 SPC Regs
HB Reg 43A HB Regs
CTB Reg 35 CTB Regs
For people aged 60 or over:
HB Reg 43 HB Regs
CTB Reg 35 CTB Regs
as substituted by regs 8 and 17 HB&CTB(SPC) Regs
177 **IS** Reg 51A(1) IS Regs
JSA Reg 114(1) JSA Regs
HB Reg 43(1) HB Regs
CTB Reg 35(1) CTB Regs
For people aged 60 or over:
HB Reg 43(1) HB Regs
CTB Reg 35(1) CTB Regs
as substituted by regs 8 and 17 HB&CTB(SPC) Regs
PC Reg 22(1) SPC Regs
178 para C2.84 GM
179 R(IS) 9/92
180 R(IS) 1/91; R(IS) 9/92
181 R(IS) 9/92
182 **IS** Reg 51(2) IS Regs
JSA Reg 113(2) JSA Regs
HB Reg 43(2) HB Regs
CTB Reg 34(2) CTB Regs
183 CIS/984/2002
184 CIS/368/1994
185 **HB** Reg 43(2) HB Regs
CTB Reg 34(2) CTB Regs
186 **IS** Reg 51(3)(a)(ii) and (8) IS Regs
JSA Reg 113(3)(a)(ii) JSA Regs
HB Reg 43(3)(a) and (7) HB Regs
CTB Reg 34(3)(a) and (7) CTB Regs
187 **IS** Reg 51(8) IS Regs
JSA Reg 113(8) JSA Regs
HB Reg 43(7)(b) HB Regs
CTB Reg 34(7) CTB Regs
188 **IS/JSA** para 29866 DMG
189 **IS** Reg 51(3A) IS Regs
JSA Reg 113(3A) JSA Regs
HB Reg 43(3A) HB Regs
CTB Reg 34(3A) CTB Regs
190 **IS** Reg 51(3)(a)(ia) IS Regs
JSA Reg 113(3)(a)(ia) JSA Regs
HB Reg 43(3)(za) HB Regs
CTB Reg 34(3)(za) CTB Regs
191 **IS** Reg 51(3A)(c) IS Regs
JSA Reg 113(3A)(c) JSA Regs
HB Reg 43(3A)(c) HB Regs
CTB Reg 34(3A)(c) CTB Regs
192 **IS** Reg 51(3)(a)(i) IS Regs
JSA Reg 113(3)(a)(i) JSA Regs
193 **IS** Reg 51(3)(b) IS Regs
JSA Reg 113(3)(b) JSA Regs
HB Reg 43(3)(b) HB Regs
CTB Reg 34(3)(b) CTB Regs
194 **IS** Reg 51(4) IS Regs
JSA Reg 113(4) JSA Regs
195 **IS** Reg 51(5) IS Regs
JSA Reg 113(5) JSA Regs
HB Reg 43(5) HB Regs
CTB Reg 34(5) CTB Regs
196 **IS/JSA** para 29375 DMG; see also R(IS) 13/93
197 R(IS) 14/98

198 **HB** Reg 43(4) HB Regs
CTB Reg 34(4) CTB Regs
199 **IS** Reg 49(a) IS Regs
JSA Reg 111(a) JSA Regs
HB Reg 41(a) HB Regs
CTB Reg 32(a) CTB Regs
200 R(SB) 57/83; R(SB) 6/84
201 R(SB) 18/83
202 R(SB) 6/84
203 **IS** Reg 49(a)(i) IS Regs
JSA Reg 111(a)(i) JSA Regs
HB Reg 41(a)(i) HB Regs
CTB Reg 32(a)(i) CTB Regs
204 **IS** Reg 49(a)(ii) IS Regs
JSA Reg 111(a)(ii) JSA Regs
HB Reg 41(a)(ii) HB Regs
CTB Reg 32(a)(ii) CTB Regs
205 CIS/255/1989
206 R(SB) 27/84
207 R(SB) 2/83; R(SB) 31/83
208 **IS** Reg 49(b) IS Regs
JSA Reg 111(b) JSA Regs
HB Reg 41(b) HB Regs
CTB Reg 32(b) CTB Regs
209 **IS/JSA** Chapter 29 Appendix 3 DMG
HB/CTB para C2.Annex B GM; HB/CTB Circular A20/99 (July 1999)
210 **IS** Reg 52 IS Regs
JSA Reg 115 JSA Regs
HB Reg 44 HB Regs
CTB Reg 36 CTB Regs
211 *Hourigan v Secretary of State for Work and Pensions* [2002] EWCA Civ 1890 reported as R(IS) 4/03
212 CIS/15936/1996; CIS/263/1997; CIS/3283/1997 (joint decision); R(IS) 26/95
213 R(IS) 3/96
214 Memo AOG JSA/IS 35, October 1998
215 R(JSA) 1/02
216 CIS/2575/1997
217 **HB/CTB** para 2.42 GM
218 R(IS) 2/93
219 R(IS) 1/03
220 **IS** Reg 49(a) IS Regs
JSA Reg 111(a) JSA Regs
HB Reg 41(a) HB Regs
CTB Reg 32(a) CTB Regs
221 R(IS) 18/95
222 R(SB) 18/83; R(IS) 2/90
223 R(IS) 13/95
224 **IS/JSA** para 29681 DMG
HB/CTB para C2.34 GM
225 *Peters v CAO* (appendix to R(SB) 3/89)
226 **IS** Reg 50(a) IS Regs
JSA Reg 112(a) JSA Regs
HB Reg 42(a) HB Regs
CTB Reg 33(a) CTB Regs
227 **IS** Reg 50(b) IS Regs
JSA Reg 112(b) JSA Regs
HB Reg 42(b) HB Regs
CTB Reg 33(b) CTB Regs
228 **IS** Sch 10 para 21 IS Regs
JSA Sch 8 para 26 JSA Regs
HB Sch 5 para 22 HB Regs
CTB Sch 5 para 22 CTB Regs

2. **Capital: aged 60 or over**
229 **HB** Sch 5 para 5 HB Regs
CTB Sch 5 para 5 CTB Regs
230 **PC** s15 SPCA 2002, Sch 5 paras 24-28 SPC Regs
HB reg 25(1(g) and Sch 5ZA paras 26-30 HB Regs
CTB reg 17(1)(g) and Sch 5ZA paras 26-30 CTB Regs
as substituted by regs 8 and 17 HB&CTB(SPC) Regs
231 **PC** Sch 4 para 18 SPC Regs
HB reg 25(2) HB Regs
CTB reg 17(2) CTB Regs
as substituted by regs 8 and 17 HB&CTB(SPC) Regs
232 s15(2) SPCA 2002; reg 15(6) SPC Regs
233 **HB** Regs 21 and 22 HB Regs
CTB Regs 13 and 14 CTB Regs
as substituted by regs 8 and 17 HB&CTB(SPC) Regs
234 **HB** Reg 38 HB Regs
CTB Reg 30 CTB Regs
as substituted by regs 8 and 17 HB&CTB(SPC) Regs
235 **HB** Reg 25(2) HB Regs
CTB Reg 17(2) CTB Regs
as substituted by regs 8 and 17 HB&CTB(SPC) Regs
236 Reg 15(6) SPC Regs
237 Reg 25(2) and (5) HB Regs
238 **PC** s5 SPCA 2002
HB/CTB s136(1) SSCBA 1992
239 **HB** Reg 19(4) HB Regs
CTB Reg 11(4) CTB Regs
240 para C2.09 GM; para 29020 DMG
241 R(IS) 3/93
242 **PC** Reg 2 SS(PAOR) Regs
HB Reg 91(1) HB Regs
243 **PC** 5 para 28 SPC Regs
HB Sch 5ZA para 30 HB Regs
CTB Sch 5ZA para 30
CTB Regs
244 **PC** Sch 5 para 16(1) SPC Regs
HB Sch 5ZA para 17(1) HB Regs
CTB Sch 5ZA para 17(1) CTB Regs
245 R(IS) 3/03

246 **PC** Sch 5 para 16(2)(a) and (b) SPC Regs
HB Sch 5ZA para 17(2)(a) and (b) HB Regs
CTB Sch 5ZA para 17(2)(a) and (b) CTB Regs
247 **PC** Schs 4 paras 13 and 14 and 5 para 16(2) SPC Regs
HB Schs 4A paras 14 and 15 and 5ZA para 17(2) HB Regs
CTB Schs 4A paras 14 and 15 and 5ZA para 17(2) CTB Regs
248 **PC** Sch V para 1A SPC Regs
HB Sch 5ZA para 25(A) HB Regs
CTB Sch 5ZA para 25(A) CTB Regs
249 **PC** Reg 17(8) SPC Regs
HB Reg 28(10) HB Regs
CTB Reg 20(10) CTB Regs
as substituted by regs 8 and 27 HB&CTB(SPC) Regs
250 **PC** reg 1(2) SPC Regs
HB reg 2(1) HB Regs
CTB reg 2(1) CTB Regs
under the definition of 'dwelling'
251 **PC** Sch 5 para 1A SPC Regs
HB Sch 5ZA para 25A HB Regs
CTB Sch 5ZA para 25A CTB Regs
252 R(JSA) 9/03
253 R(SB)10/89
254 **PC** Sch 5 para 6(1) SPC Regs
HB Sch 5ZA para 6(1) HB Regs
CTB Sch 5ZA para 6(1) CTB Regs
255 **PC** Sch 5 para 2 SPC Regs
HB Sch 5ZA para 2 HB Regs
CTB Sch 5ZA para 2 CTB Regs
256 **PC** Sch 5 para 7 SPC Regs
HB Sch 5ZA para 7 HB Regs
CTB Sch 5ZA para 7 CTB Regs
All CIS/6908/1995; R(IS) 4/97
257 R(SB) 32/83
258 CIS/1846/2004
259 **PC** Sch 5 para 3 SPC Regs
HB Sch 5ZA para 3 HB Regs
CTB Sch 5ZA para 3 CTB Regs
260 *R v London Borough of Tower Hamlets Review Board ex parte Kapur*, 12 June 2000, unreported
261 **PC** Sch 5 para 1 SPC Regs
HB Sch 5ZA para 1 HB Regs
CTB Sch 5ZA para 1 CTB Regs
262 **PC** Sch 5 paras 17 and 19 SPC Regs
HB Sch 5ZA paras 18 and 20 HB Regs
CTB Sch 5ZA paras 18 and 20 CTB Regs
263 **PC** Sch 5 paras 17 and 18 SPC Regs
HB Sch 5ZA paras 18 and 19 HB Regs
CTB Sch 5ZA paras 18 and 19 HB Regs
264 para 29578 DMG
265 CIS/6908/1995
266 **HB** Sch 5ZA para 4 HB Regs
CTB Sch 5ZA para 4 CTB Regs
PC Sch 5 para 4 SPC Regs
267 See definition of 'close relative' in:
PC Reg 1(2) SPC Regs
HB Reg 2(1) HB Regs
CTB Reg 2(1) CTB Regs
268 **HB** Sch 5ZA para 6 HB Regs
CTB Sch 5ZA para 6 CTB Regs
PC Sch 5 para 6 SPC Regs
269 R(IS) 3/96
270 para 84444 DMG
HB/CTB para C2.Annex A, A2.00 GM
271 **PC** Sch 5 para 4)a) and Reg 1(2) SPC Regs, definition of 'close relative'
HB Reg 2(1) HB Regs, definition of 'relative'
CTB Reg 2(1) CTB Regs, definition of 'relative'
272 CSB/209/1986; CSB/1149/1986; R(SB) 22/87
273 **PC** Sch 5 para 8 SPC Regs
HB Sch 5ZA para 8 HB Regs
CTB Sch 5ZA para 8 CTB Regs
274 **PC** Sch 5 paras 17 and 18 PC Regs
HB Sch 5ZA paras 18 and 19 HB Regs
CTB Sch 5ZA paras 18 and 19 CTB Regs
275 **PC** Sch 5 para 9 SPC Regs
HB Sch 5ZA para 9 HB Regs
CTB Sch 5ZA para 9 CTB Regs
276 **PC** Sch 5 para 9A SPC Regs
HB Sch 5ZA para 10 HB Regs
CTB Sch 5ZA para 10 CTB Regs
277 **PC** Sch 5 para 10 SPC Regs
HB Sch 5ZA para 11 HB Regs
CTB Sch 5ZA para 11 CTB Regs
All R(IS) 7/98
278 **PC** Sch 5 para 26 SPC Regs
HB Sch 5ZA para 28 HB Regs
CTB Sch 5ZA para 28 CTB Regs
279 **PC** s15(1)(d) SPCA 2002
All R (IS)10/01
HB Reg 25(1)(d) HB Regs
CTB Reg 17(1)(d) CTB Regs
as substituted by regs 8 and 17 HB&CTB(SPC) Regs
280 **HB** Sch 5ZA para 5 HB Regs
CTB Sch 5ZA CTB Regs
PC Sch 5 para 5 SPC Regs
281 **PC** Sch 5 para 24 SPC Regs
HB Sch 5ZA para 26 HB Regs
CTB Sch 5ZA para 26 CTB Regs
282 **PC** Sch 5 para 22 SPC Regs
HB Sch 5ZA para 23 HB Regs
CTB Sch 5ZA para 23 CTB Regs

283 **PC** Sch 5 para 25 SPC Regs
HB Sch 5ZA para 27 HB Regs
CTB Sch 5ZA para 27 HB Regs
284 **PC** Sch 5 para 26 SPC Regs
HB Sch 5ZA para 28 HB Regs
CTB Sch 5ZA para 28 CTB Regs
285 **PC** Sch 5 para 23 SPC Regs
HB Sch 5ZA para 24 HB Regs
CTB Sch 5ZA para 24 CTB Regs
286 **PC** Sch 5 paras 17, 20 and 20A SPC Regs
HB Sch 5ZA paras 18, 21 and 21A HB Regs
CTB Sch 5ZA paras 18, 21 and 21A CTB Regs
287 **HB** Sch 5ZA para 25 HB Regs
CTB Sch 5ZA para 25 CTB Regs
288 **PC** Sch 5 para 12 SPC Regs
HB Sch 5ZA para 13 HB Regs
CTB Sch 5ZA para 13 CTB Regs
289 **PC** Sch 5 para 14 SPC Regs
HB Sch 5ZA para 15 HB Regs
CTB Sch 5ZA para 15 CTB Regs
290 **PC** Sch 5 para 13 SPC Regs
HB Sch 5ZA para 14 HB Regs
CTB Sch 5ZA para 14 CTB Regs
291 **PC** Sch 5 para 11 SPC Regs
HB Sch 5ZA para 12 HB Regs
CTB Sch 5ZA para 12 CTB Regs
292 **PC** Sch 5 para 15 SPC Regs
HB Sch 5ZA para 16 HB Regs
CTB Sch 5ZA para 16 CTB Regs
293 **PC** Sch 5 para 21 SPC Regs
HB Sch 5ZA para 22 HB Regs
CTB Sch 5ZA para 22 CTB Regs
294 s6 Age related Payments Act 2004
295 **PC** Reg 21 SPC Regs
HB Reg 42 HB Regs
CTB Reg 34 CTB Regs
as substituted by regs 8 and 17 HB&CTB(SPC) Regs
296 **PC** Reg 21(1) SPC Regs
HB Reg 42(1) HB Regs
CTB Reg 34(1) CTB Regs
as substituted by regs 8 and 17 HB&CTB(SPC) Regs
297 CIS/124/1990; CSB/1198/1989
298 R(SB) 9/91
299 CIS/124/1990
300 CIS/40/1989
301 **PC** Reg 21 SPC Regs
HB Reg 42(2) HB Regs
CTB Reg 34(2) CTB Regs
as substituted respectively by regs 8 and 17 HB&CTB(SPC) Regs
302 **PC** Reg 21(5) SPC Regs
HB Reg 42(5) HB Regs
CTB Reg 34(5) CTB Regs
as substituted by regs 8 and 17 HB&CTB(SPC) Regs
303 **PC** Reg 21(3) SPC Regs
HB Reg 42(3) HB Regs
CTB Reg 34(3) CTB Regs
as substituted by regs 8 and 17 HB&CTB(SPC) Regs
304 **PC** Reg 21(4) SPC Regs
HB Reg 42(4) HB Regs
CTB Reg 34(4) CTB Regs
as substituted by regs 8 and 17 HB&CTB(SPC) Regs
305 para 29375 DMG; see also R(IS) 13/93
306 R(IS) 14/98
307 **PC** Reg 19(a) SPC Regs
HB Reg 40(a) HB Regs
CTB Reg 32(a) CTB Regs
as substituted by regs 8 and 17 HB&CTB(SPC) Regs
308 **PC** Reg 19(a)(i) SPC Regs
HB Reg 40(a)(i) HB Regs
CTB Reg 32(a)(i) Regs
as substituted by regs 8 and 17 HB&CTB(SPC) Regs
309 **PC** Reg 19(a)(ii) SPC Regs
HB Reg 40(a)(ii) HB Regs
CTB Reg 32(a)(ii) Regs
as substituted by regs 8 and 17 HB&CTB(SPC) Regs
310 **PC** Reg 19(b) SPC Regs
HB Reg 40(b) HB Regs
CTB Reg 32(b) CTB Regs
as substituted by regs 8 and 17 HB&CTB(SPC) Regs
311 **PC** Chapter 84 Appendix 1 DMG
HB/CTB para C2.Annex B GM; HB/CTB Circular A20/99 (July 1999)
312 **PC** Reg 23 SPC Regs
HB Reg 44 HB Regs
CTB Reg 36 CTB Regs
as substituted by regs 8 and 17 HB&CTB(SPC) Regs
313 R(IS) 4/03 (upholding CIS/5906/1999 and affirming CIS/7097/1995)
314 **PC** Reg 19(a) SPC Regs
HB Reg 40(a) HB Regs
CTB Reg 32(a) CTB Regs
as substituted by regs 8 and 17 HB&CTB(SPC) Regs
315 **PC** para 84771DMG
HB/CTB para C2.34 GM

316 *Peters v CAO* (appendix to R(SB) 3/89)
317 **PC** Reg 20(a) SPC Regs
HB Reg 41(a) HB Regs
CTB Reg 33(a) CTB Regs
as substituted by regs 8 and
17 HB&CTB(SPC) Regs
318 **PC** Reg 20 SPC Regs
HB Reg 41(b) HB Regs
CTB Reg 33(b) CTB Regs
as substituted by regs 8 and
17 HB&CTB(SPC) Regs
319 **PC** Sch 5 para 21 SPC Regs
HB Sch 5ZA para 22 HB Regs
CTB Sch 5ZA para 22 CTB Regs

Part 5

Benefit claims, decisions and challenges

Chapter 40

Claims, backdating and getting paid: benefits

This chapter covers:

This chapter deals with benefits administered by the DWP, and with child benefit and guardian's allowance administered by the Revenue. (For tax credits administered by the Revenue, see Chapter 54.) This chapter does not cover statutory sick pay (see Chapter 24), statutory adoption pay, statutory maternity pay or statutory paternity pay (see Chapter 17), bonuses (see Chapter 3), the health benefits discussed in Chapter 9 or payments from the social fund (see Chapters 21 and 22).

This chapter does not cover the main rules for housing benefit (HB) or council tax benefit (CTB). For those rules, see Chapters 10 and 6. However, the rules on the national insurance number requirement and suspensions are the same for HB and CTB as for other benefits. Therefore, the description of those rules here also applies to HB and CTB.

You should look at this chapter if you are claiming:

- attendance allowance (AA);
- child benefit;
- CTB – but only regarding the national insurance number requirement and suspensions (otherwise see Chapter 6);
- disability living allowance (DLA);

- guardian's allowance;
- HB – but only regarding the national insurance number requirement and suspensions (otherwise see Chapter 10);
- incapacity benefit;
- income support;
- industrial injuries benefits;
- carer's allowance (CA);
- jobseeker's allowance (JSA);
- maternity allowance;
- pension credit;
- retirement pension;
- widows' benefits or bereavement benefits.

Most of the benefits listed above are administered by your local DWP office (this is usually the Jobcentre Plus office). However, there are exceptions:

- HB and CTB are administered by your local authority in its own local offices.
- All claims for certain benefits are processed centrally:
  - child benefit is administered by the Revenue (see Appendix 1);
  - JSA is administered by the DWP but claims are dealt with at local JobCentres and payments are made from a central computer;
  - AA and DLA claims are administered initially by regional disability centres and then by the Disability Benefits Unit in Blackpool;
  - CA claims are administered by a central unit in Preston.

You can find your appropriate local benefit office by looking in the telephone directory for business and service numbers. See Appendix 1 for the addresses of the central units. For information about who makes the decisions when you claim, see Chapter 43. To find out about challenging a decision, see Chapters 43 and 44.

1. Who should claim

Generally, you claim benefit for yourself. If you cannot do so, another person can claim on your behalf – eg, an appointee (see p1075) or your parent if you are a child claiming disability living allowance.

Couples and children

If you are part of a couple, then for some benefits you may be assessed as a couple, but still only one of you actually makes the claim. You can sometimes choose which one of you claims income support for both of you.[1] Couples can also choose which one of them claims pension credit.[2] For housing benefit (HB) and council tax benefit (CTB), see p218. Check to see how the decision on which one of you claims makes you better or worse off. In the case of jobseeker's allowance (JSA), there are special provisions for joint claims by couples (see below).

If you have children, you can claim child benefit, but other people might also be entitled (see p92). If you cannot decide who should claim, a decision maker can decide for you (see p92).

Appointees

A decision maker (or in child benefit and guardian's allowance cases, the Revenue) can authorise someone else (eg, a friend or relative) called an 'appointee' to act on your behalf if you cannot claim for yourself – eg, you are mentally ill.[3] This is not necessary if a court has already appointed someone to look after your affairs. The appointee takes on all your rights and responsibilities as a claimant. For example, s/he must notify changes in your circumstances. Normally this only applies from the date the appointment is agreed, but if someone acts on your behalf before becoming your official appointee her/his actions can be validated in retrospect by her/his appointment.[4] To become an appointee, a person must normally apply in writing. However, if s/he has already been made an appointee by the local authority for HB or CTB purposes, the DWP can by agreement make them an appointee without a written application, and vice versa.[5] S/he must be over 18.

If you are an appointee for a claimant who dies, you must re-apply for appointee status in order to settle any outstanding benefit matters.[6] An executor under a will can also pursue an outstanding claim or appeal on behalf of a deceased claimant even if the decision was made before the formal grant of probate.[7]

Joint claims for jobseeker's allowance

Where appropriate, both members of a couple are subject to the labour market conditions for entitlement to JSA (see Chapter 1).

These rules only apply to couples who are not receiving child benefit for, or are looking after, a child, and where at least one member of the couple was born after 28 October 1957.[8] There are a wide variety of exceptions to the requirement (see p396). They apply only where the couple is receiving income-based JSA, whether on its own or in combination with contribution-based JSA.[9]

Where a joint claim is made, the Secretary of State may require either member of the couple to provide information and evidence[10] and may notify either of any information relating to the claim.[11] A joint claim is treated as being made on the day on which the first member of the couple notifies an intention to claim[12] unless they both infringe the requirement to attend for an interview, in which case the claim is treated as being made on the day that the first member attends for an interview with an employment officer.[13]

2. How to make a claim

In almost all circumstances, to qualify for a benefit you must make a claim.[14] There are exceptions to this rule. However, where there is a delay in making a claim, you may be able to get an **interim payment** of benefit (see p1108). You do not have to make a claim for retirement allowance (see p338) and certain retirement pensions, if you are already receiving certain other retirement pensions or widows' benefits (see p498).[15]

Getting your claim started

You usually need to make your claim on an official claim form (see p1077). A claim in writing on something other than a claim form can sometimes be accepted. If you are claiming income support (IS) or jobseeker's allowance (JSA), that *must* be claimed on an official claim form.[16]

In practice, however, if you live in a Jobcentre Plus area (see below), then for most benefits the DWP usually encourages you to get your claim started by making a telephone call to a contact centre. If you are aged 60 or over, or do not live in a Jobcentre Plus area, then you may still need to start your claim by filling in an official claim form and sending it in to the address given with the form.

If you live in a Jobcentre Plus area

The basic process described here only applies to some benefit claims. If you are claiming:

- attendance allowance (AA);
- disability living allowance (DLA);
- child benefit;
- guardian's allowance;
- pension credit (PC);
- retirement pension; *or*
- you are aged 60 or over,

then the process is the same as if you are living outside a Jobcentre Plus area (see p1077). If you are aged 60 or over, see also p1078.

Otherwise, if you do live in a Jobcentre Plus area, the basic process is usually as follows, if you are claiming:

- IS;
- JSA;
- incapacity benefit (IB);
- bereavement benefits;
- carer's allowance (CA);
- industrial injuries benefits; *or*
- maternity allowance.

You will usually be asked to start your claim by telephoning a contact centre. Your local Jobcentre Plus office (see the telephone book or the Jobcentre Plus website at www.jobcentreplus.gov.uk for details) will have this number, and it may also be displayed in local libraries, post offices and advice centres. The contact centre will take your basic details, and will then either:

- phone you back to take more detailed information, then send you a 'written statement' for you to confirm the details (IS, JSA and IB claims only); *or*
- send you a claim form (claims for other benefits).

The contact centre will also arrange for your first jobseeker's interview if you are claiming JSA (see p393) or your initial work-focused interview, where that applies (see p1092). If you are sent a written statement, then you are asked to bring that along to the work-focused interview where it will be finalised and signed, and so become your written claim. (If no work-focused interview is considered appropriate, then you are asked to confirm the statement and return it by post.) If you are sent a claim form, then you are asked to complete it and return it to the address given with the form.

There is no rule that says that you must get your claim started by making a telephone call. For example, Jobcentre Plus offices can still accept your claim if it is made on a claim form and sent in the post. However, in practice it is best to make your claim in the way that the DWP prefers you to. If starting your claim by telephone is either impractical or impossible for you, tell the Jobcentre Plus office this and ask to claim in an alternative way. If necessary, a face-to-face interview can be arranged to gather your details. If this request is refused, complain and seek further advice.

If you do not live in a Jobcentre Plus area

Most benefits should be claimed by completing and sending in a claim form to the relevant DWP office – the address will come with the form. You can get claim forms from your local DWP office. You may also be able to download forms via the DWP website at www.dwp.gov.uk. Child benefit and guardian's allowance are administered by the Revenue so claim forms for these can be requested from the Revenue. You may also be able to download forms from the Revenue website at www.inlandrevenue.gov.uk. See the 'Claims and backdating' section of the relevant chapter of this *Handbook* for more detail on the benefit you are claiming. This also applies if you are aged 60 or over, but if you are then see also p1078.

Claims using the internet or telephone and in person

Child benefit and **CA** can also be claimed using the internet – see p101 for child benefit and p78 for CA.

Apart from starting a claim by calling a contact centre in Jobcentre Plus areas, a claim for **JSA** must be made in person at a JobCentre, unless the decision maker tells you otherwise.[17]

Claims for **PC** can be made in writing (usually on a form), by telephone or in person at a DWP office. They can also be made in writing at a local authority HB office or an 'alternative office' (see below). PC only has to be claimed in writing if the DWP so decides.[18]

Claims for **retirement pension** (and graduated retirement benefit) may be made by telephone, unless the DWP specifies that it must be in writing.[19]

Where to claim

If you live in a Jobcentre Plus area and are aged under 60, then for **most benefits** except those listed below you will normally be expected to start your claim by telephoning a contact centre. Depending on the benefit you are claiming, you may then need to fill in and return a claim form (see above for details).

If you do not live in a Jobcentre Plus area, are aged 60 or over or are claiming:

- AA;
- DLA;
- child benefit;
- guardian's allowance;
- PC; *or*
- retirement pension,

then you will usually – but not always – be expected to send in a claim form to the relevant office. For information about where you should get and return your claim form, see the chapter in this *Handbook* about the benefit you are claiming. If you are aged 60 or over, see also the section below.

If you are aged 60 or over

If you are aged 60 or over, you can claim certain benefits not only from the relevant DWP office, but also at designated local authority HB/CTB offices, and at other 'alternative offices'.[20] You do not have to use the local authority or alternative office, but if you want to you can claim there in writing or by attending in person, although for **PC** the claim must be in writing. Even if you do not make your claim at the local authority office, you can give information and evidence relating to the claim, and get advice about it there (but you cannot do this at alternative offices). Alternative offices had not been widely introduced at the time of writing, but were expected to increase in number during 2005.

The alternative offices are expected eventually to include some local advice centres and local authority HB offices identified by the DWP.

The offices can deal with claims for the following benefits:

- AA;
- bereavement benefits;
- CA;

- DLA;
- IB;
- PC;
- retirement pension;
- winter fuel payments;
- IS.

When to claim

You should claim as soon as you think you might be entitled to the benefit, even if it might take you time to collect all the information required on the form. See p1084 for further information about your date of claim.

Very occasionally, it may be in your interests to wait for the next calendar year to claim JSA on the basis of a better record of national insurance contributions. In some limited circumstance your claim can be backdated (see p1085). The rules are very strict.

Amending or withdrawing your claim

You can **amend** your claim by writing to the office handling your claim.[21] If your letter is received before a decision is made, the decision maker can treat your claim as being amended from the date it was initially made.

You can **withdraw** your claim at any time before a decision is made.[22] Once a decision is made, the claim may not be withdrawn in respect of a period before the date of the decision; but it may be possible to withdraw it in respect of a future period even if you have ongoing entitlement.[23]

Making sure your claim is valid

You cannot get benefit until you make a valid claim. For most benefits, for the claim to be valid your claim must be in writing and should normally be made on the appropriate claim form. Exceptions are:

- PC does not have to be claimed in writing unless you are specifically required to do so;
- for IS and JSA, there is an additional 'evidence requirement' (see p1080).

For claims other than for IS and JSA, the decision maker may decide to treat any letter or other written communication as being a valid claim.[24] Claims for IS and JSA must *always* be made on the appropriate form – this includes the 'written statement' that is sent to you if you start your claim by telephone in a Jobcentre Plus area.

If your claim is valid, it is referred to a decision maker (see p1180) to decide if you are entitled to benefit. The decision maker can ask you to provide further information to support your claim (see p1082) or even ask you to attend a medical examination before s/he makes a decision (see pp772 and 782). This should not prevent a decision being made on your claim (but see below). If you are asked to provide information after a decision has been made on your claim, see p1106.

A valid claim can be backdated for up to three months in certain circumstances, or longer if you are reclaiming following the award of a 'qualifying benefit' (see p1085).

If your claim is not accepted as valid

If your claim is not accepted as valid, the decision maker will not make a decision on your entitlement to benefit. The DWP or the Revenue may tell you that the claim is not valid, and give you some time to return a properly completed claim form (though except for IS, PC not claimed in advance, and JSA, it does not have to).[25] The time allowed for this is one month but, except for PC, can be extended.

In any case, if the DWP or the Revenue does not accept that your claim is valid, you should still be given a decision saying so. You have the right of appeal against such decisions.[26] If your claim is accepted as valid, the decision maker must make a decision on your entitlement to benefit.[27]

Work-focused interviews

The Government is introducing schemes that make entitlement to certain benefits dependent on attending interviews about work. In these schemes, the general rule is that you will not be regarded as having made a claim unless you attend a 'work-focused interview' with an adviser. Also, you usually have to attend further such interviews. If you are part of a couple, then in some cases your partner may have to attend a work-focused interview as well. Some lone parents claiming IS are also required to attend work-focused interviews. See p1092 for further information about the schemes.

Evidence requirement for income support and jobseeker's allowance

It is your responsibility to:[28]

- complete your claim form fully and correctly; *and*
- produce information and evidence to verify your claim.

This is known as the 'onus of proof' rule or 'evidence requirement'. See p394 (for JSA) and p307 (for IS) for the information you can be asked to provide.

If you do not fill in the form properly or provide all the information and evidence required, the DWP should notify you that your claim is defective and contact you to put things right.[29] It might telephone or write to you or, in the case of IS, visit you to get the information or evidence. But it might simply return your claim form. You should provide the information or evidence or complete the form and return it to your local office within one month of your initial contact (or that of someone contacting the DWP on your behalf). If you do not, you might lose benefit (see p1085 for information about when your claim can be backdated).

In any case, if the DWP does not accept that your claim is valid, you should be given a decision saying so, and you have the right of appeal against that decision.[30]

Exemptions from the evidence requirement

You are exempt from the evidence requirement if:[31]

- you could not complete the form or get the information or evidence required because of a physical, mental, learning or communication difficulty. You must also show that it is not reasonably practicable for you to find someone to help you complete the form or get the proof on your behalf. However, you can argue that someone else is not expected to take the initiative in offering you assistance;[32] *or*
- the information or evidence required does not exist; *or*
- you could not get the information or evidence required without serious risk of physical or mental harm. You must also show that it is not reasonably practicable to get it in another way; *or*
- you could only get the information or evidence required from a third party and it is not reasonably practicable to get it from her/him; *or*
- the decision maker thinks sufficient proof has been provided to show that you are not entitled to IS or JSA (eg, because your capital or income is too high) so it would be inappropriate to require further information or evidence.

If you are unable to complete your claim form or provide the required information or evidence for one of the reasons listed above, you should give your local office notice of this as soon as possible, ideally by explaining this on the claim form or by ringing or visiting the benefit office or JobCentre. The DWP says that such notice must be given within one month of the date when you first contacted it. Explain your circumstances fully. You can provide supporting letters – eg, from a social worker or a solicitor. If the DWP accepts that you are exempt from the evidence requirement, it might:

- help you to fill in the form; *or*
- give you longer to complete it; *or*
- collect evidence or information on your behalf; *or*
- tell you that you do not have to provide the information after all.

If you are claiming JSA, you are normally required to attend an interview at which a properly completed claim form is handed in. Your claim is then treated as being made on the date you first notified your intention to claim (usually when you picked up the form and made the appointment for the interview), or the first date in respect of which your claim is made if this is later.[33] If you fail to attend the interview or hand in a properly completed form you might lose benefit.

Remember that the decision maker can ask you for further information or evidence even after s/he has accepted your claim as valid. However, this should not change the date from which you can be paid. If s/he eventually decides you are entitled to benefit you should still be paid from your date of claim. See pp1084 and 1085 for more information about your date of claim.

Other benefits

For benefits other than IS or JSA if you just write a letter or send the wrong form, you can be sent the appropriate form to fill in. Similarly, if you do not fill in the form properly, it can be returned to you. If you subsequently return it correctly filled in within a month, you count as having made a valid claim on the date of your first letter or form.[34] The decision maker can extend this one-month period if s/he thinks this is reasonable – eg, because you were ill. For PC, there is no provision for extending the one-month period although you always have one month from when the decision maker last drew attention to the defect.[35] See p1085 for other situations when your claim can be backdated.

Example

Geraldine was claiming JSA and wrote to the DWP office to say that her husband had died. She was unaware that she could claim a bereavement payment. Two years later, she finds out about bereavement payment. She can ask the decision maker to treat her letter as being a claim for bereavement payment. She should write to her local DWP office and argue that she should have been given proper advice two years ago.

Remember that the decision maker can ask you for further information or evidence even after s/he has accepted your claim as valid (see below). However, this should not change the date from which you can be paid. If s/he eventually decides you are entitled to benefit (or tax credit) you should still be paid from your date of claim. See the chapter in this *Handbook* about the benefit you are claiming for more information about your date of claim.

Providing information to support your claim

Once your claim has been accepted as valid, you may be required to provide additional documentation and evidence relevant to your claim and you can be asked for an interview to discuss your circumstances if this is reasonable.[36] You may be able to claim travelling expenses for this.[37]

In the case of IS and JSA, you might not count as having made a valid claim until you provide all the information and evidence required on the claim form (see p1080).

To find out what information and evidence you are required to provide, see the chapter in this *Handbook* about the benefit you are claiming.

You are also usually required to satisfy the national insurance (NI) number requirement (see p1083). To establish that you satisfy this requirement, you could also be asked to provide proof of your identity (see p1083).

The national insurance number requirement

When you claim benefit (including HB and CTB) you must usually satisfy the NI number requirement:[38]

- by providing an NI number and information or evidence to show that it is yours; *or*
- by providing evidence or information to enable the DWP (or, in child benefit and guardian's allowance cases, the Revenue) to trace your NI number, if you do not know it; *or*
- by applying for an NI number if you do not have one and providing enough information and evidence to allow one to be allocated to you.

If you cannot satisfy the NI number requirement straight away, you may be able to claim an **interim payment** of benefit (see p1108). If you are refused an NI number, you have the right of **appeal** against that decision, including where you are refused benefit as a result.[39]

Are you exempt?

You are exempt from the NI number requirement if:

- you are under 16 and the benefit is DLA;[40]
- the benefit is statutory adoption pay, statutory maternity pay, statutory paternity pay, statutory sick pay or social fund payments;
- you made your claim before the test was introduced for the particular benefit in question. See p1059 of the *Welfare Benefits Handbook 2000/01* for a list of dates;
- the benefit is HB and you live in a hostel.[41]

Members of your family and the national insurance number requirement

If you are claiming a means-tested benefit as a couple (see p811), your partner must also satisfy the NI number requirement unless the claim was made or treated as made prior to 5 October 1998.[42]

The same applies if you are claiming extra benefit for an adult dependant with your non-means-tested benefit (see p793), in relation to that dependant.[43]

A child under the age of 16 does not need to satisfy the NI number requirement.[44]

Proof of identity

In addition to requiring you to satisfy the NI number requirement, you may be asked to produce further documents or evidence that prove your identity. If you are claiming for your partner or an adult dependant (see p793) you must also prove her/his identity.

You can prove your identity with a passport, a national identity card issued by an European Economic Area member state, or a letter issued by the Home Office acknowledging your application for asylum (known as a SAL). However, there are many other things that can help you to prove who you are. Examples include your birth certificate, full driving licence, a travel pass with a photograph, a local council rent card or tenancy agreement or even paid fuel or telephone bills. Remember:

- it is important to provide details of any other people who can confirm what you have stated – eg, your solicitor or other representative, or a support group or official organisation;
- you should not be refused benefit simply because you do not have any documents, especially where it is unreasonable for you to have or obtain them. Ask the decision maker to make a decision on your claim and you can then appeal.

In some cases the decision maker may refuse to accept evidence that you are who you say you are. Some claimants may have particular difficulty supplying evidence, or feel that they have been discriminated against. Press the decision maker to be clear about what is required and why, and complain if you feel any requests for information are unreasonable (see p1299). You may also wish to approach your local race equality council if you feel that you have experienced race discrimination.

3. The date of your claim

You are not usually entitled to benefit for any day before your date of claim. See the chapter in this *Handbook* about the benefit you are claiming for information about this. In addition, remember:

- you might be able to claim in advance if you know you are not entitled now but will be later – eg, you are coming out of hospital (see the chapter in this *Handbook* about the benefit you are claiming);
- your claim might be backdated in certain circumstances (see p1085);
- if you claim the wrong benefit, your claim can be treated as one for the right benefit (see below).

If you claim the wrong benefit

If you have claimed the wrong benefit but are in fact entitled to another benefit, your original claim can sometimes be treated as a claim for the right benefit.[45] This might be a way around the strict backdating rules (see p1085). To find out which claims can interchange, see p1085. See also the section 'If you claim the wrong benefit' in the chapter about the benefit you should have claimed.

Interchange of claims[46]

Benefit claimed:	*May be treated as a claim for:*
Incapacity benefit	Severe disablement allowance; maternity allowance
Severe disablement allowance	Incapacity benefit; maternity allowance
Maternity allowance	Incapacity benefit; severe disablement allowance
Widows' benefits; bereavement benefits	Retirement pension
Retirement pension	Widows' benefits; bereavement benefits
Income support	Carer's allowance
Attendance allowance	Disability living allowance
Disability living allowance	Attendance allowance

In addition, a claim for:

- child benefit can be treated as a claim for guardian's allowance and vice versa;[47]
- attendance allowance (AA) or disability living allowance (DLA) can be treated as a claim for an increase in disablement pension where constant attendance is needed (see p333) and vice versa.

If you claim a non-means-tested benefit (other than child benefit) but are not entitled to it, your claim may be treated as a claim by someone else for an increase in her/his benefit for you (see p804).

If you claim an increase of a non-means-tested benefit for an adult dependant but are not entitled to it, the claim may be treated as a claim by someone else who is entitled.[48] An increase of incapacity benefit (IB) can be treated as an increase of severe disablement allowance (SDA) and vice versa.

The decision maker does not have to accept your claim for one benefit as a claim for another but usually decides in your favour if it should have been realised from your claim that you had made a mistake. You cannot appeal if this is refused. Your only remedy is to seek a judicial review (see p1253).

In addition, for all benefits except income support (IS) and income-based jobseeker's allowance (JSA) there is a general power to treat any written document as a claim for benefit.[49] You may be able to argue that the claim form for the wrong benefit should be treated in that way. Again, if the relevant office refuses to do so, you cannot appeal and your only remedy is to seek a judicial review (see p1253).

Backdating your claim

There are strict time limits for claiming benefits.[50] However, if you miss the time limit for claiming, your claim can sometimes be backdated for up to three months (12 months for pension credit (PC)) or, for most benefits, longer if you are reclaiming following the award of a 'qualifying benefit' (see p1090).

In general:

- if you want your claim to be backdated you must ask for this to happen or it will not be considered;[51]
- some benefits can be backdated without special reasons for up to three months (see p1087);
- claims for IS and JSA can only be backdated in limited circumstances (see p1087);
- special rules apply if you are claiming backdated JSA because your entitlement ceased when you failed to attend an interview or sign on (see p405);
- extra backdating of most benefits is allowed after awards of qualifying benefits (see p1090);
- claims for AA and DLA can never be backdated;[52]
- different rules apply to housing benefit (HB) and council tax benefit (CTB) (see p221);
- if you claim the wrong benefit, your claim can sometimes be treated as a claim for the benefit you should have claimed (see p1084).

For exceptions to the rules, see the chapter in this *Handbook* about the benefit you are claiming.

If you are prevented from receiving backdated benefit due to an error on the part of the DWP (or, in child benefit and guardian's allowance cases, the Revenue) you should try to persuade it to meet its moral obligation and make an ex gratia payment or extra-statutory payment to you, as compensation (see p1304). To do this, simply write and ask. The intervention of an MP or the Ombudsman (see p1302) may help in these circumstances.

If you satisfy the conditions for getting benefit it should be paid from your date of claim. If backdating is refused you have a right to appeal (see Chapter 44). Payment should not be held up because you are challenging the decision on backdating.

The rules on backdating changed in April 1997. Even if you would have been entitled prior to that date on making a claim, you cannot now rely on the old rules.[53]

Benefits that can be backdated without special reasons

Claims for the following benefits can be backdated without the need for special reasons for up to three months:[54]

- IB (Chapter 12);
- industrial injuries benefits (Chapter 14);
- child benefit (Chapter 5);
- guardian's allowance (Chapter 8);
- increase of non-means-tested benefit for an adult (Chapter 31);
- retirement pension (Chapter 19);
- bereavement benefits, except for bereavement payment which can be backdated for 12 months (Chapter 2). The time limit can be extended in some cases – eg, when you did not know your partner had died (see p42);

- maternity allowance (p456); *and*
- carer's allowance (CA) (Chapter 4).

A claim for PC can be backdated without the need for special reasons for up to 12 months.[55]

If you want backdated benefit for a period before your actual date of claim (see p1084) you must show that you would have qualified for the benefit had you claimed at the time. For example, if you want to claim three months' backdated IB, you must show that you have been incapable of work (see p764) for the past three months.

You can only ask for benefit to be backdated for up to three months (12 months for PC). If you ask for backdating for a longer period, the decision maker must treat the request as if it were for the maximum possible.[56]

Example

Glenn is self-employed. He has been off sick for six months but did not realise he could claim IB. He makes a claim and asks for it to be backdated. He qualifies for IB and is paid three months' arrears.

There are exceptions to the rules. If you miss the time limit for claiming disablement benefit for occupational deafness (prescribed disease A10) or occupational asthma (prescribed disease D7) (see p325) or bereavement payment (see p24), you may lose your right to benefit altogether.

Backdating income support and jobseeker's allowance

If you want to claim IS or JSA for a period before your date of claim, your claim can be backdated:

- for up to one month if you can show that it was not reasonable to expect you to claim before you did and your delay was for one or more of the reasons given on p1088; *or*
- for up to three months if you can show that it was not reasonable to expect you to claim before you did and your delay was for one or more of the reasons set out on p1088; *or*
- for longer periods where your original claim was refused because you were not entitled to a 'qualifying benefit', that qualifying benefit has now been awarded and you reclaim in time (see p1090).

If you are claiming backdated IS after you are awarded refugee status the backdating rules do not apply (see p670).

If you are claiming benefit late, it is important to explain why. If you can, provide evidence or information that backs this up – eg, a copy of the letter from your adviser or information from your employer which misled you (see p1089).

If you have been misled, misinformed or given insufficient advice by an officer of the DWP, explain how and when this happened and where possible, give the name and a description of the officer concerned. Where relevant, you should explain why there is no one else who could help you make your claim.

One month's backdating of income support or jobseeker's allowance[57]

The decision maker is required to backdate your IS or JSA claim for up to one month, if one or more of the following applies (or has applied) and because of which you could not reasonably have been expected to make your claim any earlier:

- your claim is late because the office where you are supposed to claim was closed (eg, due to a strike) and there were no other arrangements for claims to be made;
- you could not get to the DWP office due to difficulties with the type of transport you normally use and there was no reasonable alternative;
- there were adverse postal conditions – eg, bad weather, a postal strike, or the post office failed to act under its agreement to deliver under-stamped mail to the DWP;[58]
- you (or your partner) stopped getting another benefit but you (or your partner) were not informed before your entitlement ceased so you could not claim IS or JSA in time;
- you claimed IS or JSA in your own right within one month of separating from your partner;
- a close relative of yours died in the month before your claim. **'Close relative'** in these circumstances means your partner, parent, son, daughter, brother or sister.

Three months' backdating of income support or jobseeker's allowance

Your claim for IS or JSA can be backdated for up to three months if you can show that it was not reasonable to expect you to claim earlier than you did for one or more of the following specified reasons.[59] If more than one reason applies to you, the combined effect of all of them must be considered in deciding whether it was reasonable to expect you to claim earlier.[60]

- You were given information by an officer of the DWP and as a result thought your claim would not succeed. This covers situations where:
  - you were given incorrect information or the wrong claim form and this led you to claim the wrong benefit – eg, you were advised to claim IB although you did not qualify and you should have claimed IS instead;[61] *or*
  - someone with authority to act on your behalf was given incorrect information;[62] *or*
  - you were told your claim would not be accepted;[63] *or*
  - you were told you did not have to fill in a claim form;[64] *or*

  - the refusal of an earlier claim for the same[65] or a different[66] benefit led you to believe that you were not entitled; *or*
  - the information was incomplete in that it failed to include advice to claim where it should have done.[67]

  '**Officer**' includes anyone carrying out public functions at the benefit office (eg, a security guard).[68] It does not matter if the information you received was correct or reasonable on the basis of any information that you gave to the officer about your circumstances, as long as the officer's advice caused you to think that a claim would fail.[69]

- You were given advice in writing by a Citizens Advice bureau or other advice worker, a solicitor or other professional adviser (eg, an accountant), a doctor or a local authority and as a result thought your claim would not succeed. 'Advice in writing' includes advice in the form of leaflets or electronic communication such as emails[70] or information on a website, provided it is directed at claimants in your position. Your claim should be backdated if you are given written confirmation of advice that was originally given to you orally,[71] provided that this is done before the decision maker decides whether you are entitled to backdating.[72] The written advice must also be given to you and so it will not be enough if your adviser records a note of oral advice unless you are provided with a copy.[73]
- You or your partner were given written information about your income or capital by your employer or former employer or a bank or building society and as a result you thought your claim would not succeed.
- You could not get to the DWP office because of bad weather.

In addition, you can have your claim backdated if you comply with any of the following conditions *and* it was not 'reasonably practicable' for you to seek help to make your claim from anyone else.[74] Where you are mentally ill, that will not necessarily mean that you cannot be expected to seek assistance.[75] However, another person is not expected to take the initiative in offering assistance.[76] The conditions are:

- you have learning, language or literacy difficulties; *or*
- you are deaf or blind *or* were sick or disabled (but not if you are claiming JSA); *or*
- you were caring for someone who is sick or disabled; *or*
- you were dealing with a domestic emergency which affected you.

Even if one of these applies, you might be paid less than three months' arrears if you claim because of a new interpretation of the law (see p1211).

If a person has been formally appointed by a court or the DWP to act on your behalf, it is your appointee (see p1075), not you, who must show that it was not reasonable to expect her/him to claim sooner than s/he did for one of the reasons listed above.[77] If someone is informally acting on your behalf, you must show this. You must also show that it was reasonable for you to delegate responsibility for your claim and that you took care to ensure the person helping you did it properly.[78]

Extra backdating after awards of qualifying benefits

Most benefits, if refused on an original claim, can be backdated if they are then reclaimed after the award of a 'qualifying benefit'. A **'qualifying benefit'** means, in general, any benefit which gives you entitlement to another benefit, or makes another benefit payable at a higher rate.[79] For example, depending on the facts in your case, you may not be entitled to IS until you also become entitled to DLA.

The rules apply to most benefits covered by this chapter, including IS and JSA. They do not apply to backdating a claim for HB or CTB.

The general rule is that you can get backdating where the following happens:

- your original claim (eg, for IS, JSA, etc.) is refused while you (or your dependent child or, if you are a member of a couple, your partner) are waiting to hear about a qualifying benefit (eg, DLA); *and*
- you claimed that qualifying benefit no later than 10 days after your original claim; *and*
- the qualifying benefit is then awarded; *and*
- you then make a further claim (eg, for IS, JSA, etc.), within three months of the decision awarding the qualifying benefit and you are now entitled (because of the award of the qualifying benefit) to IS, JSA, etc.

In these circumstances, benefit is backdated to the date of your original claim or the date on which the qualifying benefit was first payable, whichever is later.[80] Note the following:

- When trying to backdate CA under these rules, your original claim must have been refused because the person you care for had not yet been awarded AA or DLA middle or higher rate care component.
- When trying to backdate **SDA** under these rules, your original SDA claim must have been refused because you were not yet regarded as 80 per cent disabled.[81]
- When trying to backdate **IB** under these rules, they only apply where you have stopped being entitled to IB because you were no longer incapable of work, at that time you had made a claim for a qualifying benefit, that claim is subsequently decided in your favour and you reclaim IB within three months of being awarded the qualifying benefit.[82]
- The rule also applies where the claim for the qualifying benefit was originally refused, but you were awarded it later on revision, supersession or appeal.
- Where you lost entitlement to benefit (eg, CA) because your award of a qualifying benefit (eg, DLA) was terminated, your benefit is backdated if you reclaim within three months of the reinstatement of your qualifying benefit.[83]

An additional qualifying benefit rule applies for **IS** and **income-based JSA** only. Where you have been awarded either of these benefits but that award is terminated, then further claims for IS/income-based JSA will be backdated either to the date of the termination, or the date when a qualifying benefit was first awarded (whichever date is the later) if:

- you or a member of your family (or, where applicable, the person being cared for) claim a qualifying benefit within 10 working days of the IS/JSA award coming to an end; *and*
- you make a further claim for IS/income-based JSA within three months of the qualifying benefit being awarded.[84]

What if you lose out?

If you still lose out because a decision maker made an unfavourable decision on your original claim, when s/he could have decided in your favour if s/he had put off making a decision until your claim for a qualifying benefit was decided, you can try to argue that the decision maker's failure to delay making a decision on your original claim was an 'error of law'.[85] This is, therefore, grounds for an 'any time' revision (see p1196). However, if the error of law was only shown to be an error of law because of a decision by a commissioner or court, it cannot count as an 'official error'.[86]

Even if you are already entitled to some IS or JSA, you might only be entitled to it at a higher rate once you or another member of your family becomes entitled to another benefit. See p1209 for information about what you must do to get extra backdating in this situation.

4. How your claim is dealt with

If your claim is not accepted as valid

If your claim is not accepted as valid, you should get a decision saying so. You have the right of appeal against that decision.[87]

If your claim is accepted as valid

Once your claim is accepted as valid, a decision maker (see p1180) makes a decision on your entitlement to benefit.[88] If you are asked for additional information or evidence but do not provide it, or you do not attend an interview, a decision should still be made on your claim.[89] However, the decision maker, and the tribunal if you appeal, can only make a decision on the available evidence. This is unlikely to be in your favour if you fail to provide evidence which would help to show you are entitled to benefit. You should make sure that the decision maker has all the relevant evidence.

If benefit is awarded, it is awarded:

- for a set or indefinite period if the benefit is attendance allowance, disability living allowance or disablement benefit (see pp159 and 331); *or*
- for a fortnight at a time if the benefit is jobseeker's allowance (JSA); *or*
- in all other cases, for as long as you continue to be entitled to benefit.[90]

Your award may be superseded if your circumstances change or if you cease to satisfy the conditions for entitlement (see p1189).

If you disagree with a decision on your claim, you can seek a revision or a supersession (see Chapter 43). You can also appeal (see Chapter 44). If you are unhappy about how your claim has been dealt with you can make a complaint or even seek compensation (see Chapter 47).

Change of circumstances after you claim

It is your duty to report any change in your circumstances which you might reasonably be expected to know might affect your right to, the amount of, or the payment of, your benefit.[91] The DWP/the Revenue should inform you of the kind of changes this includes.

You should notify changes promptly to the office handling your claim. This can be done in writing or, except for housing benefit, council tax benefit and JSA, by telephone. However, in individual cases notification in writing might be required, or notification in some other form may be accepted. In any case, it is always best to notify changes in writing. For child benefit and guardian's allowance, the rules say that the office handling your claim includes the Revenue child benefit office (see Appendix 1) or any Revenue enquiry centre and any DWP Jobcentre Plus office.[92] It is always best to check that the child benefit office has been notified. If you do not promptly report any change which it is your duty to notify, any resulting overpayment may be recoverable from you (see Chapter 41). If you are considered deliberately to have acted falsely or dishonestly, you may also be guilty of an offence (see Chapter 42).

If you do report a change orally, confirm what was said in writing. Keep a copy of any letters you send reporting changes. If you hand the original in person to an officer, ask her/him to stamp your copy to confirm s/he has received the original.

5. Work-focused interviews and benefit

The Government is introducing schemes, mostly for people making new claims for benefit, that make entitlement to certain benefits conditional on attendance at 'work-focused interviews'. The interviews are supposed to help and encourage you to keep in contact with the employment market, and eventually to begin full-time work. At the interview, job opportunities, training, rehabilitation, etc. are discussed. The main scheme is the **Jobcentre Plus** scheme. That is gradually replacing the ONE scheme, and is expected to cover the whole country by 2006. There are two other main schemes: **Pathways to Work**, for people claiming benefits for incapacity for work, and a **lone parent** scheme for lone parents claiming income support (IS).

The basic process is similar in all the work-focused interview schemes. There are three basic stages:

- Initial contact, where you indicate that you want to claim benefit, forms are issued and basic information is taken.
- Initial work-focused interview – this is a part of the benefit claim.
- Repeat work-focused interviews at various times (called 'trigger points') during your claim.

Jobcentre Plus scheme

This scheme is administered by Jobcentre Plus, an agency of the Department for Work and Pensions (DWP), which administers benefits for people of working age. The scheme is run from Jobcentre Plus offices. If you are a member of a couple, similar but not identical rules may apply to your partner (see p1094). In the Jobcentre Plus scheme for claimants, those of working age who make a new claim for benefit are required to attend work-focused interviews with a personal adviser as a condition of receiving the following benefits:[93]

- IS;
- incapacity benefit (IB);
- severe disablement allowance (SDA – though new claims are no longer possible);
- bereavement benefits;
- carer's allowance (CA).

You do not have to attend an interview if you are:

- in remunerative work (that is, of at least 16 hours a week); *or*
- claiming jobseeker's allowance (JSA); *or*
- aged 60 or over.[94]

At the interview, you first see a benefits specialist (called a 'financial assessor') who deals with your benefit claim and queries, before the actual work-focused interview which is conducted by the personal adviser.

You can be required to take part in an interview as part of your ongoing entitlement to benefit if you have already had a work-focused interview, are an existing claimant of one of the benefits set out above and certain conditions (called 'trigger points') are fulfilled.[95] These are:

- if you are a lone parent aged at least 18 and are not on IB or SDA, six months have passed since your last interview or you were last due to have one;
- in any other case, any of the following applies:

- you have been found incapable of work under the personal capability assessment;
- you are no longer entitled to CA, but are still entitled to another of the benefits listed on p1093;
- you have stopped or started part-time work (ie, any work which does not count as full-time work);
- you have stopped education or training that was arranged by your personal adviser;
- you have reached the age of 18 and have had a work-focused interview before;
- you have not been required to take part in an interview for three years.

Work-focused interviews for partners

If you are a member of a couple and are entitled to benefit in a Jobcentre Plus area, your partner may be required to take part in a work-focused interview (as well as you where you are required to do so). This will apply if:[96]

- you and your partner are both aged 18 or over but under 60; *and*
- you are getting one of the benefits listed below from a Jobcentre Plus office; *and*
- you have been continuously entitled to the benefit for 26 weeks or more; *and*
- the benefit is paid to you at a higher rate because of your partner (this includes where you get an increase for an adult dependant).

However, your partner does not have to take part in an interview under these rules if s/he is entitled to one of the benefits listed below as a claimant in her/his own right.[97]

The benefits that the work-focused interviews for partners rules apply to are:

- IS;
- income-based JSA (but not joint-claim JSA);
- IB;
- SDA;
- CA.

If these rules apply, your partner has to take part in work-focused interviews as a condition of you receiving the full amount of the benefit. There is no specified time or 'trigger points' at which further such interviews must take place.[98]

The interviews themselves and the consequences of failing to take part are much the same as for the work-focused interviews that apply to you as a claimant (see p1093). The main differences are:[99]

- the only consequence for your partner failing to take part in an interview is a reduction in your benefit (of £11.24 a week);

- if your benefit is reduced because you partner fails to take part in an interview, income-based JSA is the first benefit in the list to be reduced, and SDA is reduced before CA; *and*
- both you and your partner are notified of and have the right of appeal against the decision on failure to take part and on 'good cause' for not taking part.

Pathways to Work – incapacity

This scheme is being introduced in various parts of the country. It is aimed at people claiming benefit for incapacity for work. The Government intends to apply the scheme to more areas during 2005. You will come under the scheme if:[100]

- you live in a Pathways to Work area; *and*
- you are aged 18 or over but under 60; *and*
- you make a new claim for IB, SDA or IS on the basis of incapacity for work.

In addition, from 7 February 2005 you may be affected by Pathways to Work even if you are not making a new claim for benefit. We call this the **'Pathways to Work extension scheme'** in this *Handbook*. You will come under this scheme if:

- you live in a Pathways to Work area; *and*
- you are aged 18 or over but under 60 on 7 February 2005; *and*
- you are not exempt from the personal capability assessment on the basis of a severe condition (see p773); *and*
- you made a successful claim for IB, SDA or IS on the basis of incapacity for work at some point in the two years before the Pathways to Work pilot scheme was introduced in your area, and are still on the benefit. (Depending on your area, this means you claimed on or after 27 October 2001 but before 27 October 2003, on or after 5 April 2002 but before 5 April 2004.)

The work-focused interviews in the Pathways to Work scheme are much the same as in the main Jobcentre Plus work-focused interviews, as described on p1093. (See CPAG's *Welfare Rights Bulletin* 177 for full details.) The most important differences are:

- the first work-focused interview takes place eight weeks after your claim (or when the personal adviser determines, if you come under the Pathways to Work extension scheme). You must then attend an additional five interviews at monthly intervals (or two additional interviews if you come under the Pathways to Work extension scheme);
- after that, you must attend further interviews whenever you are again assessed as being incapable of work, if you stop being entitled to CA, if you start or stop part-time work, or if you have been on DWP-arranged education, training or rehabilitation and that comes to an end;
- you must draw up an 'action plan' with your adviser, which records your discussion with her/him about your employability and any steps to improve

your job prospects which it is agreed are reasonable and that you would be prepared to take (although there is nothing to say that you actually have to take them);

- the only sanction for failing to take part in an interview (that includes not drawing up an action plan) is a reduction in your benefit of £11.24 a week.

The Pathways to Work pilots also include a 'return to work credit' of £40 a week, payable for 52 weeks for certain people returning to work and earning less than £15,000 a year, and grants to help with work expenses. If you are in the Pathways to Work extension scheme (see p1095) then you can also be offered a 'job preparation premium' of £20 a week if you actually carry out some of the steps set out in your action plan. See CPAG's *Welfare Rights Bulletin* 175 and 182 for full details.

The Jobcentre Plus scheme areas

The Government is gradually extending work-focused interviews by opening more Jobcentre Plus offices in various parts of the country between 2001 and 2006, by which time the scheme will cover the entire country. The DWP keeps a list of currently opened offices, which is available in a leaflet or on the Jobcentre Plus website at www.jobcentreplus.gov.uk.

Work-focused interviews for lone parents

Certain lone parents have to attend work-focused interviews under the ONE scheme or the Jobcentre Plus scheme (see p1093). However, a similar scheme exclusively aimed at lone parents claiming IS operates on a national basis. In the scheme, entitlement to IS is dependent on attendance at work-focused interviews.

The requirement to attend interviews under the lone parent scheme applies to you if you are a lone parent and:[101]

- you were entitled to IS on 5 April 2004 and were responsible for a child living in your household; *or*
- you become entitled to IS after 5 April 2004.

In most cases, if you come under this scheme you are required to attend a repeat work-focused interview every six months. However, in certain pilot areas of the country (Bradford, Greenwich, Haringey, Leicestershire, Lewisham, Sandwell, Torfaen, Aberdeenshire and Fife) you may be required to attend every 13 weeks (see CPAG's *Welfare Rights Bulletin* 182 for details).[102]

In any case, however, you are not required to attend a work-focused interview under this scheme if you are a lone parent and:[103]

- are aged under 18; *or*
- are aged 60 or over; *or*
- are subject to either the ONE scheme or the Jobcentre Plus scheme.

A Pathways to Work pilot scheme for lone parents will run in five areas (Leicestershire, Dudley and Sandwell, Bradford, South East London and North London) from April 2005. Details were not available at the time of writing. See CPAG's *Welfare Rights Bulletin* for updates.

Work-focused interviews

You will be informed when your interview is to take place. It will normally take place at the office running the scheme, but you can ask your personal adviser to interview you at home if going to the office would cause undue inconvenience or endanger your health.[104] If there is a dispute about where the interview should take place, there is no right to appeal and so you would have to apply for judicial review (see p1253). If you are in this position, seek advice.

Some people may have the requirement to attend an interview 'waived' (ie, cancelled) or 'deferred' (ie, put off to another date), if it is considered that an interview would not be of assistance or would not be appropriate.[105] The interview is defined as one in which you and the adviser look at your prospects of employment and what activities (including training and education) you might undertake to strengthen these.[106]

Failing to comply

After your interview, the decision maker will make a decision as to whether you have taken part in the interview and, if you have not, whether you have 'good cause' for not having done so.[107] If you are over the age of 18, **'taking part'** requires you to do more than just turn up; you must answer questions put to you as well. In the **Pathways to Work** scheme, you must also assist the adviser in drawing up an 'action plan' of the sorts of things that you are willing to do in order to enhance your employment prospects. If there is nothing you reasonably can do, then you will not have failed to comply, and there is nothing which says you actually have to take the steps in the action plan. The Government plans to introduce compulsory action plans for people making new claims for benefit for incapacity for work in the Jobcentre Plus scheme from October 2005.[108] Also, in the Jobcentre Plus scheme, if you are under 18, **'taking part'** requires you to attend an interview with the Careers Service or Connexions.[109]

Consequences of failing to take part in an interview

In most of the schemes (but not the Pathways to Work scheme) when you make a claim for benefit you are required to attend an initial work-focused interview. If the decision maker decides that you did not take part, unless you have 'good cause' for not doing so (see p1098), you will be treated as not having made a claim and hence will not be entitled to benefit.[110] You will have to make a new claim before you can become entitled to benefit.[111]

If you are already getting benefit, then you may be required to attend work-focused interviews, including in the Pathways to Work scheme. If you fail to take part without 'good cause', a benefit reduction of £11.24 will be applied to one of your benefits. In the **lone parent** scheme, only IS can be reduced. In the **Pathways to Work** scheme, only IS, IB and SDA can be reduced (if you are entitled to more than one, they are reduced in that order of priority).[112] In all the schemes, the deduction will continue to apply until you take part in an interview.[113] In the **Jobcentre Plus** scheme, if you are entitled to more than one of the following benefits, the deduction is normally made in the following order of priority, but you must be left with at least 10p per week:[114]

- IS;
- IB;
- any bereavement benefit;
- CA;
- SDA.

The reduction should stop from the point that you do take part in the interview. The consequences also cease to apply if you are no longer required to take part in work-focused interviews of the scheme that you are in (eg, in the lone parent scheme, you cease to be a lone parent), or if you attain the age of 60. In the **Pathways to Work** scheme, the consequences *also* cease to apply if, within a month of the date of the decision that you failed to take part in the interview or that you did not have good cause for not taking part, you:

- notify new facts which show you had good cause, *and*
- you could not reasonably have notified those facts within five working days of the date of the interview.[115]

You have a right of **appeal** against a decision that you did not take part in an interview and that you did not have good cause. However, in order to appeal about whether you had good cause you will need to have tried to show that, within five working days of the date on which the interview was to take place. The decision may also be revised or superseded on normal grounds (see Chapters 43 and 44).[116]

Good cause for failing to take part

To avoid having a penalty imposed, you must show good cause within five working days following the date on which the interview was to take place.[117] However, you may still be able to demonstrate good cause up to a month after the decision that you did not take part was notified to you, if the facts you rely on could not have been brought to the personal adviser's attention within five days.[118]

In deciding whether you have good cause, the decision maker will consider all the circumstances but must take the following circumstances into account:[119]

- any misunderstanding on your part due to learning, literacy or linguistic difficulties or misleading information given by the benefit authority;

- attending a doctor or dentist or accompanying a person for whom you are caring, where the appointment could not reasonably have been rearranged;
- difficulties with transport where no reasonable alternative was available;
- the practice of your religion that prevented you attending at the fixed time;
- attending a job interview;
- the need to work in your business if you are trying to become self-employed;
- if you or a person for whom you are caring had an accident, illness or relapse;
- attending a funeral of a close friend or relative;
- a disability that makes attendance impracticable.

6. Getting paid

The DWP (or in child benefit and guardian's allowance cases, the Revenue) decides how benefit is paid to you.[120] The rules provide that payment can be made in the way that appears to be 'appropriate' in any individual case. In practice, this normally means that you are paid by direct credit transfer ('direct payment') into a bank, building society or similar account. There is no right of appeal about the way in which you are paid. Normally, therefore, it is the decision maker who will have the final say as to how you are paid, although s/he may agree to pay you in the way that you prefer.

Direct payments

The DWP and the Revenue intend that payment by direct credit transfer into a bank account, building society account or similar account will be the normal method of payment on new claims for benefit. The Government calls this **'direct payment'**. The last girocheques and order books for benefit payments were issued in October 2004. If payment by direct payment is not suitable for you, you may be able to get your benefit paid by cheque (see below).

The Government has said that all benefit recipients will, at the appropriate time, be given information setting out the various account options.[121] If you experience difficulty getting your money as a result of these new arrangements, complain to the DWP or the Revenue. You could also contact your MP.

Payment by cheque

The DWP and the Revenue recognise that some people will have difficulty getting or using bank, building society or similar accounts. If you cannot open or manage an account, then it should be possible for you to be paid by a cheque which can be cashed at a post office. However, there are no rules that say that you must be paid in this way. If you cannot open or manage an account, make sure the DWP or the Revenue know this, and ask to be paid by cheque.

Getting your money – account options

When you are paid by direct payment, there are five main options you have regarding the accounts that your benefit is paid into:

- an existing bank or building society account (this is often a current account but may be another sort of account, such as a savings account);
- a new current account at a bank or building society;
- a new 'basic bank account' at a bank or building society (sometimes this is called an 'introductory' or 'starter' account);
- a post office card account; *and*
- in some cases, a credit union account.

All of these accounts (excepting some credit unions) are suitable for direct payment, and you can withdraw cash without charge. But they are not all the same. For example, you cannot access all current accounts at post offices, basic bank accounts and post office card accounts do not offer cheque books or overdrafts, and you cannot pay bills by direct debit with a post office card account. The DWP or the Revenue should write to you with details of your options, including how to get started with opening an account. The DWP publishes a leaflet called 'Any questions? A guide to Direct Payment', and has a Direct Payment Helpline on 0800 107 2000, or you can visit www.dwp.gov.uk/directpayment.

The change to direct payment means that more people will be able to get their benefit in the way they get other money in their account – eg, by cheque or via a cash machine at bank branches and at supermarket checkouts with a 'cashback' facility. If you do want to get your money at a post office, the following will apply to direct payment:

- You may be able to access your bank or building society current account at a post office. You may want to use this method if you do not want to have to use a PIN number at the post office (however, not all bank and building societies have this facility – check with your bank, building society or the DWP/Revenue).
- You can use a PIN number at a post office if you have a basic bank account. At the time of writing, not all banks and building societies offered these accounts – check with your bank, building society or the DWP/Revenue.
- You can use a PIN number at a post office if you have a post office card account. If you have a card account, you can nominate someone else to collect your benefit for you, in which case that person will be issued with a card her/himself.

If someone collects your benefit for you

If you need to have someone you trust collect your benefit for you, then it should be possible to arrange for her/him to be able to access your account in order to so. If you already have a bank or building society account that you want your benefit paid into, or want to open such an account, ask the bank or building society about this. If you use a post office card account, then a second card can be issued to the person who collects your benefit. For more information from the DWP, you can contact the Helpline on 0800 107 2000.

If you forget your PIN

If you use a bank/building society account and you forget your PIN, you need to contact the bank to change the PIN and issue you with a new one as soon as possible. If you cannot access your benefit, contact the benefit office for advice about what to do.

If you use a post office card account and you forget your PIN, you can call the customer service helpline number on 08457 22 33 44 (or textphone 08457 22 33 55). You will get a replacement PIN within four working days. Again, if you cannot access your benefit in the meantime, contact the benefit office for advice.

If all else fails, you may be invited to claim a crisis loan (see p538) while the problem is sorted out. If you cannot get access to your benefit, and the DWP/the Revenue refuses to remedy the situation, seek advice (see Appendix 2).

When you are paid

How, when and how often your benefit is paid depends on what benefit you have claimed.[122] You are sometimes paid in advance and sometimes in arrears. For further information, see the chapter in this *Handbook* about the benefit you are claiming.

Who is paid

Payment is usually made directly to you, but there are some circumstances in which payments can be made to other people or organisations on your behalf:

- If you are unable to manage your own money or if you die, your benefit is paid to a person appointed to act on your behalf (see p1075).[123]
- If it is in the interests of you, your partner or your children, the decision maker can pay your benefit to another person.[124] For example, if your partner is refusing to support you, all or part of her/his benefit can be paid to you. If you are neglecting your children even though benefit is being paid for them, it might be paid to another person to help look after them.
- If you are claiming income support (IS), pension credit (PC) or income-based jobseeker's allowance (JSA) and are getting help with your housing costs (see Chapter 36), these are usually paid directly to your lender on your behalf (see p1111).
- If you are claiming IS, PC or JSA, and are in certain types of debt, payments can be made to your creditors on your behalf (see p1109).[125]

Getting more than one benefit

You can claim a combination of benefits. However, there are rules which deal with situations where you are entitled to more than one non-means-tested benefit at a time or to an increase in your non-means-tested benefit for an adult dependant (see p793) while that person is her/himself entitled to benefit. These are the **'overlapping benefit' rules**. These rules also apply where more than one person is claiming for the same child or adult dependant (see p1104) and where you are getting child benefit or guardian's allowance as well as an increase in your non-means-tested benefit for your child (see p1104).

Remember:

- disability living allowance (DLA) care component and attendance allowance (AA) overlap with constant attendance allowance.[126] Otherwise AA, DLA, disablement benefit (see p331), reduced earnings allowance (see p334) and retirement allowance (see p338) can be received in addition to any of the other benefits described in this *Handbook* – eg, you may receive incapacity benefit (IB), both components of DLA and disablement benefit all at once;
- you might qualify for IS, PC, income-based JSA, housing benefit (HB) or council tax benefit in addition to your non-means-tested benefit, although the non-means-tested benefit is usually taken into account as income (see p968).

Earnings replacement benefits

Some benefits are available to compensate you for your inability to work through unemployment, sickness, pregnancy or old age. These are 'earnings replacement' benefits. You cannot usually receive more than one of the following 'earnings replacement' benefits at a time.

- Contributory benefits:
  - contribution-based JSA;
  - IB;
  - maternity allowance;
  - retirement pension;
  - widow's or bereavement pension;
  - widowed mother's or widowed parent's allowance.
- Non-contributory benefits:
  - severe disablement allowance (SDA);
  - carer's allowance(CA).

Where there is an entitlement to more than one of the benefits above the following rules apply:[127]

- A contributory benefit is paid in preference to a non-contributory benefit. However, this is topped up by any balance of a non-contributory benefit due.
- Weekly benefits are paid and topped up by any balance of daily benefit (unless the claimant makes an application to receive the daily benefit in full) – see the

chapter in this *Handbook* about the benefit you are claiming to see if it is a daily or a weekly benefit.

- The highest rate benefit is paid, or if the rates are the same, one benefit is paid.

Special rules apply if you are entitled to widows' benefits or bereavement benefits and to IB at the same time. See p278 for further information.

Other adjustments

If you are getting a training allowance paid by a government department or training agency, your earnings replacement benefit is reduced by the amount of the training allowance.[128]

If you are getting unemployability supplement under the industrial injuries scheme or war pensions scheme, your earnings replacement benefit – other than maternity allowance – is reduced by the amount of the unemployability supplement.

You cannot usually get more than one retirement pension at a time. However, there are special rules if you are a widow or widower entitled to both a Category A (see p487) and a Category B retirement pension (see p487) and your Category A pension would be paid at a reduced rate because you have not paid enough contributions (see p846). In this situation your basic Category A pension is increased by either:

- the amount of the shortfall between your Category A pension and the full Category A amount of £82.05; *or*
- the amount of your Category B pension,

whichever amount is less.[129]

You are also entitled to an additional pension on your own contribution record and one on your spouse's record up to the maximum additional pension a person could theoretically receive on one contribution record.[130]

Earnings-related additions to non-means-tested benefits

Additional pensions under the additional state pension scheme (see p127) and graduated retirement benefit (see p488) do not overlap with non-means-tested benefits. However, if two or more benefits would otherwise be payable with an additional pension and graduated retirement benefit, only the higher or highest total of additional pension and graduated retirement benefit payable in addition to one of those benefits is due.[131]

There are exceptions to this rule if you are a Category B retirement pensioner whose own contribution records would entitle you to a Category A retirement pension or if you are a widow who receives transitional long-term IB (see p279).

An age addition paid with IB, SDA or retirement pension overlaps with another age addition.[132]

Increases to non-means-tested benefits for adult dependants

Only one person may receive an increase of benefit in respect of the same dependant, except when one of you receives an increase because the dependant is someone employed by you to look after your child(ren) and the dependant does not live with you (in this case, both of you can claim). Equally, you may only receive one increase in respect of an adult dependant. If, apart from those rules, more than one increase would be payable, only the higher or highest total is paid.[133] See p793 for who can claim increases for dependants.

An increase for an adult dependant also overlaps with any of the benefits listed on p1102 or training allowances which are payable to that dependant – eg, you are claiming an increase of retirement pension for your partner, but s/he is claiming IB in her/his own right.[134] If the increase is less than or equal to the benefit payable to your dependant, the increase is not paid. If the increase is greater than the basic benefit, you get the difference. This does not apply if the adult is not residing with you and is employed by you to care for a child.

Child benefit, guardian's allowance and increases to non-means-tested benefits for child dependants

Since 6 April 2003, no increases to non-means-tested benefits for child dependants are payable, although some people already entitled to them on 5 April 2003 will still be paid them (see p798).

If you receive a child dependant addition

Only one person may receive child benefit or an increase to a non-means-tested benefit for a child dependant for the same child (see pp85 and 798).

The standard rate of child benefit (see p95) does not overlap with any other benefit. However, if you receive the higher amount payable for your eldest child (see p95), any other benefit (except guardian's allowance) or increase paid for the same child is reduced by £1.95.[135]

You cannot get the lone parent rate of child benefit if, for the same child, you get an increase in widowed mother's allowance, widowed parent's allowance, disablement benefit, CA or retirement pension.[136] Instead, you get the standard rate of child benefit for the child. Otherwise, increases are reduced by £2.50 a week if you receive the lone parent rate of child benefit for the same child.[137]

All increases for children and child's special allowance overlap with guardian's allowance and industrial death benefit for children and are reduced by the level of guardian's allowance you get for the child.[138]

Missing payments and lost PIN numbers

If you are entitled to benefit you must be paid it.[139] Therefore, if your benefit is not paid into your account or you are not issued with a cheque, then the DWP or the Revenue must rectify that.

What happens where you have lost the PIN number for your account, and so can't access your money, is less clear. The DWP or the Revenue is likely to say that the duty is discharged when the money is credited to your bank account or similar account. In some cases, it may also point to a rule (applying to benefits paid by the DWP) that says that your entitlement to payment is lost 12 months after the date it was due to be paid into your account. However, the rule should only apply where you have actually been allocated benefit, not where you have not been paid it.[140] So if you have forgotten your PIN number and this cannot be rectified, you may not be able to get your benefit. You may need to claim a crisis loan (see p538) while the problem is sorted out. If necessary, seek advice (see Appendix 2).

Getting a replacement giro or order book

During 2004 giros and order books were phased out as ways of paying benefit. If you need to see information about replacing giros and order books, see CPAG's *Welfare Benefits and Tax Credits Handbook* 2004/2005, p1080.

Suspension of payments of benefit

A decision maker can suspend payment of part or all of your benefit in certain circumstances (see below). In some of these circumstances, s/he can ask you to provide further information or evidence or submit to a medical examination to help her/him decide if you are still entitled to benefit (or are getting it at the correct rate). It is very important that you provide the information that is required or submit to the medical examination. Your entitlement to benefit could be terminated if you fail to do so (see p1107).

Local authorities are able to suspend HB in similar circumstances.[141]

Suspension while an appeal is pending

Your benefit can be suspended if the DWP (or, in child benefit and guardian's allowance cases, the Revenue) or local authority is appealing (or considering an appeal) against:[142]

- a decision of a tribunal, commissioner or court to award *you* benefit; *or*
- a decision of a commissioner or court about *someone else's case*, but only if the issue in the appeal could affect your claim (and for HB, only where the other case is about an HB issue).

But, except for HB, s/he must give you written notice of the intention either to request the statement of reasons for the tribunal's decision, to apply for leave to appeal or to appeal, whichever is the first of those that is yet to be done. S/he must do that as soon as is 'reasonably practicable'.[143]

The decision maker must then actually go on to do one of those things within the usual time limits for doing them (see Chapter 44 for the details of time limits). If s/he does not, then the suspended benefit must be paid to you. The suspended benefit must also be paid to you if the decision maker withdraws an application for leave to appeal, withdraws the appeal or is refused leave to appeal and it is not possible for her/him to renew the application for leave to appeal.[144]

Suspension in other circumstances

Your benefit can also be suspended if:[145]

- a question has arisen about your entitlement.[146] In this case, all or part of the benefit due to you can be suspended pending a revision, supersession or appeal of the decision about your entitlement. For example, if you are being paid IS but it is thought that you are in full-time work, your benefit may be suspended while information is gathered about the true situation;
- you have been getting JSA and a question has arisen about whether you are available for or actively seeking work. Your JSA must be suspended until this matter is resolved;[147]
- it looks as though your award of benefit should be superseded or revised;[148]
- the DWP (or, in child benefit and guardian's allowance cases, the Revenue) thinks you are being (or may have been) overpaid.[149] All or part of your benefit may be withheld while the possible overpayment is investigated;
- you are not living at the last address you notified;[150]
- for child benefit and guardian's allowance, the bank account or other account details which you have given to the Revenue are incorrect;[151]
- for HB, a recoverable overpayment may have occurred.[152]

In some cases, your benefit can also be suspended if you fail to provide information or submit to a medical examination (see p1107).

Providing information and evidence

You can be required to supply information or evidence (including evidence of your incapacity for work[153]) if the decision maker needs this to determine whether your award of benefit should be revised or superseded (see pp1189 and 1199). There are different rules for benefits (see below) and for tax credits (see p1198).

You can be required to provide information and evidence if:[154]

- your benefit has been suspended in the circumstances described above; *or*
- you apply for a revision or supersession (see pp1189 and 1199); *or*
- you fail to provide certificates, documents, evidence and other information about the facts of your case as required;[155] *or*
- your entitlement to benefit is conditional on you being incapable of work.

You must be notified in writing if the decision maker wants you to provide information or evidence. Within one month of being sent the request, you must:

- supply the information or evidence.[156] You can be given more time than this if you satisfy the decision maker that this is necessary; *or*
- satisfy the decision maker that the information does not exist or you cannot obtain it.[157]

If the decision maker has not already done so, your benefit can be suspended if you do not provide the information or evidence within one month of the request.[158] To find out if your entitlement to benefit can be terminated, see below.

Medical examinations

Your benefit can be suspended if you fail to submit to a medical examination on two consecutive occasions without 'good cause'.[159] This applies where:

- the decision maker is looking at whether you should still be getting a benefit (or whether you are getting it at the correct rate); *or*
- you apply for a revision or a supersession (see pp1189 and 1199) and the decision maker thinks a medical examination is necessary in order to make a decision.

This rule does not apply where the issue is whether you are incapable of work. For information about the rules on medical examinations when your incapacity for work is being assessed, see p782.

To find out if your entitlement to benefit can be terminated, see below.

Challenging decisions to suspend benefit

Even if the decision maker may legally suspend benefit in your case, that does not mean s/he must always do so. S/he may be willing to continue to pay your benefit, or at least some of it, if you can show that you will suffer hardship otherwise. If you receive a letter telling you that your benefit has been suspended, you can write back explaining how the suspension will affect you and asking the DWP, the Revenue or local authority to reconsider. It may be wise to get advice (see Appendix 2) before writing.

You cannot appeal to a tribunal against the decision to suspend your benefit. The only ways to change the decision are to negotiate to get your benefit reinstated or to challenge the decision in the courts by judicial review (see p1253). Aside from getting the decision changed, you could also ask for an interim payment (see p1108). Seek advice (see Appendix 2).

Termination of entitlement to benefit

Your entitlement to benefit can be terminated if:

- your benefit was suspended *in full* in the circumstances described on p1106 and you are required to provide information or evidence and fail to do so within one month of the request;[160]
- your benefit was suspended *in full* because you failed to provide information in the circumstances described on p1106, but only if it is more than one month since your benefit was suspended.[161]

The termination of entitlement to benefit takes effect from the date payment was suspended (or an earlier date if you ceased to be entitled for another reason).[162]

Your entitlement to benefit can also be terminated if you fail to submit to a medical examination, but only if it is more than one month since your benefit was suspended on this ground.[163] This is discretionary.

Challenging decisions to terminate your benefit

If you disagree with a decision to terminate your benefit you can seek a revision (see p1189) or appeal (see Chapter 44).[164]

Interim payments

If your claim or payment of your benefit is delayed, you can ask for an interim payment. However, you cannot get an interim payment if you have appealed and that has not yet been decided.

An interim payment can be made where it seems that you are or may be entitled to benefit and where:[165]

- there is a delay in your making a claim, including being able to satisfy straight away the national insurance number requirement; *or*
- you have claimed it but not in the correct way (eg, you have filled in the wrong form, or filled in the right form incorrectly or incompletely – see p1080) and you cannot put in a correct claim immediately (eg, because the DWP office is closed); *or*
- you have claimed it correctly, but it is not possible for the claim, or for a revision or supersession which relates to it, to be dealt with immediately; *or*
- you have been awarded benefit, but it is not possible to pay you immediately other than by means of an interim payment.

You cannot appeal to a tribunal if you are refused an interim payment. It may be possible to apply for judicial review (see p1253). If you are refused an interim payment, see Chapter 21 to find out if you can get a crisis loan. You could contact your MP to see if s/he can help to get the decision to refuse you an interim payment reconsidered. You could also try using the emergency service (see p1109).

An interim payment can be deducted from any later payment of benefit and if it is more than your actual entitlement, the overpayment can be recovered.[166] You should be notified of this in advance, unless it is an interim payment of:

- IS made because you have not received child support maintenance (see p854). In this case, any overpayment is recovered from the arrears of maintenance rather than your benefit; *or*
- DLA and you are terminally ill or had an invalid vehicle.

Emergencies

If you have lost all your money or there has been a similar crisis, it is possible to get help at any time. Any local police station should have a contact number for DWP staff on call outside normal office hours.

If you are unable to contact the DWP, your local social services office may be able to help. The police station should have a contact number.

It is important, if you need money urgently, that you provide as much information as you can to support your claim. It may help if you can get an advice agency or third party (such as a health visitor or social worker, doctor or MP) to support you.

7. Deductions from your benefit

Your benefits are usually paid directly to you but there are some circumstances when money can be deducted and paid to a third party on your behalf. The majority of these deductions can only be made from income support (IS), pension credit (PC) and income-based jobseeker's allowance (JSA). They can also be made from contribution-based JSA or from other benefits, but only in limited circumstances.

What deductions can be made

Amounts can be deducted from your IS, PC or *income-based* JSA to pay for:[167]

- housing costs paid to your lender under the mortgage payment scheme (p1111);
- other housing costs (p1112);
- rent arrears (p1112);
- residential accommodation charges (p1113);
- hostel payments (p1113);
- fuel (p1113);
- water charges (p1114);
- council tax arrears (p1114);
- community charge arrears (p1114);
- fines (p1114); *and*
- child support maintenance (p862).

> However, if you are on IS or PC and the amount is not enough to cover the deduction, deductions can also be made from your IB, SDA or SRP if they are paid in combination with your IS or PC. You may also have deductions made for the recovery of social fund loans (p535) and overpayments (p1142).

Deductions from contribution-based jobseeker's allowance

Deductions can be made from your *contribution-based* JSA for the payments listed above (other than child support maintenance – see example on p1110) if you have an 'underlying entitlement' to income-based JSA. This means that if you were not entitled to contribution-based JSA, you would be entitled to income-based JSA of at least the same rate (see example below).

Deductions can also be made from contribution-based JSA if you have no underlying entitlement to income-based JSA, but only for community charge arrears, council tax arrears, fines and child support maintenance arrears.

Example 1

Tina is 27 and receives contribution-based JSA of £56.20 a week. She has no other income and no savings. The amount of the income-based JSA she would receive if she was not getting contribution-based JSA would also be £56.20 a week.

Deductions can be made from Tina's contribution-based JSA as if she were receiving income-based JSA.

Example 2

George is 42. He receives contribution-based JSA of £56.20 a week. His wife works full time. Because of this, if George were not getting contribution-based JSA he would not be entitled to income-based JSA. As he has no underlying entitlement to income-based JSA, deductions can only be made from his contribution-based JSA for community charge or council tax arrears, child support maintenance arrears and fines.

Deductions from other benefits

Deductions may only be made from other benefits to pay child support maintenance that you owe (see p1114).

When deductions can be made

Deductions and direct payments to third parties can only be made if you or your partner are liable to make the payments.[168] If there is a doubt about whether you or your partner are liable, deductions should only be made if there is evidence that you are liable – eg, the bill is in your name or your partner's name.

Do you have to agree to deductions?

You must consent before direct payments are made for housing costs arrears, rent arrears, service charges for fuel and water, fuel costs (including arrears) and water charges (including arrears), if the total to be deducted for these payments exceeds 25 per cent of your family's applicable amount (ie, allowances and premiums – see Chapter 35) or, in the case of PC, 25 per cent of your minimum guarantee (see p469) before housing costs.[169] Any housing costs included in your applicable amount (see Chapter 36) should not be taken into account when calculating the 25 per cent.

The DWP can make deductions without your agreement if they are made for:

- community charge or council tax arrears;
- fines;
- child support maintenance;

- current housing costs;
- current mortgage interest;
- nursing home charges or hostel charges not included in your housing benefit (HB).

Consent is not needed for these deductions even if the total amount deducted exceeds 25 per cent of your applicable amount.[170]

The deductions

Deductions are made at the DWP office before you receive your regular benefit payment. If you want to have deductions made to help you clear any arrears or debts, ask at the DWP office dealing with your claim. If you disagree with a decision about deductions, you can appeal (see Chapter 44).

The mortgage payment scheme

When you claim IS, PC or income-based JSA, you may get help with your housing costs (see Chapter 36). The general rules for payment of housing costs are:

- Once you qualify for help with housing costs the amount for mortgage interest or interest on loans for repairs and improvements is usually paid directly to your lender for each complete week that you are on benefit.[171]
- The main exceptions to this are where your lender is not covered by, or has opted out of, the mortgage payments scheme.[172] The DWP should tell you if this is the case and you must pay your own mortgage.
- Also, if you receive PC, if you are entitled only to the savings credit and not to the guarantee credit, then direct payments will only be made where a written request has been made and the DWP agrees that it is in the best interests of you or your family.[173]

*Your housing costs are deducted from your total IS, PC or income-based JSA entitlement and you get the balance.[174] You have to make up any difference between what the DWP pays to your lender and the amount you owe it. This could include such things as mortgage capital, non-dependant deductions or a restriction due to excessive housing costs. If you get incapacity benefit (IB), severe disablement allowance or retirement pension paid on the same giro or order book as your IS, deductions can be made from these benefits too. If you do not have enough benefit to meet the full cost, all but 10p of your benefit is paid over and you must pay the rest yourself.[175]

Payments are made four-weekly in arrears[176] even if your payments are due on a calendar month basis, so you may appear to be in arrears even though your full mortgage is being met. You might need to explain this to your lender. If the DWP deducts your housing costs from your benefit, but fails to pay these to your lender in time and as a result you have to pay interest on arrears that build up or you lose your home, you should seek advice. You might be able to claim compensation.[177]

*If you are on IS or PC and the amount is not enough to cover the deduction, then deductions can also be made from your IB, SDA or SRP if they are paid in combination with your IS or PC.

If you have more than one type of housing cost or more than one loan, deductions for non-dependants (see p924) and certain restrictions for excessive housing costs are apportioned using a formula (see p1116).[178]

If you are in mortgage arrears, no amount towards the arrears can be deducted from your benefit if your lender is covered by the mortgage payments scheme. If you are in this situation, you should seek financial advice. If you are in arrears and your lender is not covered by the mortgage payment scheme, see p1111.

Except in the case of PC, if you have a mortgage protection policy the amount of mortgage interest paid directly is reduced. The reduction is the amount of income from the insurance policy which is taken into account.[179]

If an overpayment of mortgage interest is paid to your lender, see p1141.

Other housing costs[180]

The IS, PC or income-based JSA for your mortgage interest is usually paid directly to your lender under the mortgage payments scheme (see p1111). If this applies to you (or would if your lender had not opted out of the scheme) then the deductions under this provision only cover payments for other types of housing costs (see p905).[181]

If your current IS, PC or income-based JSA includes money for such housing costs and you are in debt for these costs (excluding payments for ground rent or feu duty unless paid with your service charges or for a tent[182]), deductions can be made from your benefit both to clear the debt and to meet current payments. Deductions are made if it would be 'in the interests' of you or your family to do so.

You only qualify for direct deductions if you owe more than half of the annual total of the relevant housing cost. This condition can be waived if it is in the 'overriding interests' of you or your family that deductions start as soon as possible – eg, repossession of your home is imminent.[183]

In the case of mortgage payments, the decision maker must be satisfied there are arrears.[184] You must have paid less than eight weeks' worth of full payments in the last 12 weeks.[185] The amount of mortgage interest taken into account is the amount after deductions for non-dependants (see p924).

Rent arrears[186]

If you are in arrears with your rent (including any inclusive water, fuel and service charges) while on benefit, an amount can be deducted from your IS, PC or JSA and paid directly to your landlord.

Rent arrears do not include the amount of any non-dependant deductions (see p211), but can cover any water charges or service charges payable with your rent and not met by HB. Fuel charges included in your rent cannot be covered by direct deductions if they change more than twice a year.

To qualify for direct deductions, your rent arrears must amount to at least four times your full weekly rent. If you have not paid your full rent for more than eight weeks, direct deductions can be made automatically if your landlord asks the

DWP to make them.[187] If your arrears relate to a shorter period, deductions can only be made if it is in the overriding interests of your family to do so.[188] In either case, the decision maker must be satisfied that you are in rent arrears. Even if you are, you can ask her/him not to make direct deductions – eg, where you are claiming compensation from your landlord because of the state of repair of your home.[189] Once your arrears are paid off, direct payments can continue for any fuel and water charges inclusive in your rent.[190]

Residential accommodation charges[191]

IS, PC and income-based JSA do not cover charges for your accommodation. The only exception is where you were getting a residential allowance on 7 April 2002, and continue to be entitled to it (see p721). However, deductions can be made from your IS, PC or income-based JSA to meet your accommodation charges if you have failed to budget for the charges and it is considered to be in your interest for deductions to be made. The deductions can be made even if that does not apply if you are in a home run by a voluntary organisation for alcoholics or drug addicts.

Hostel payments[192]

If you (or your partner) live in a hostel *and* you have claimed HB to meet your accommodation costs *and* your payments to the hostel cover fuel, meals, water charges, laundry and/or cleaning of your room, part of your IS, PC or JSA can be paid directly to the hostel for these items. You do not have to be in arrears for this to apply. These costs are all items which cannot be covered by HB (see p207) and which you must meet from your IS, PC or JSA. Fuel costs are not paid directly if the charge varies according to actual consumption, unless the charge is altered less than three times a year.

Fuel debts[193]

If you are in debt, an amount can be deducted from your benefit each week and paid over to the fuel company (mains gas or mains electricity) in instalments – usually once a quarter. This is **'fuel direct'**. In return, the fuel company agrees not to disconnect you. Deductions can be made where:[194]

- the amount you owe is £56.20 or more (including reconnection or disconnection charges if you have been disconnected); *and*
- you continue to need the fuel supply; *and*
- it is in your interest to have deductions made.

An amount is deducted for the fuel you use each week (your current consumption) as well as for the arrears you owe. The amount deducted for current consumption is whatever is necessary to meet your current weekly fuel costs. This is adjusted if the cost increases or decreases. Deductions for current consumption can be continued after the debt has been cleared.[195]

Water charges[196]

If you get into debt with charges for water and sewerage, direct deductions might be made – 'debt' includes any disconnection, reconnection and legal charges. If you pay your landlord for water with your rent, deductions are made under the arrangements for rent arrears (see p1112).[197]

Deductions can be made if you failed to budget and it is in the interests of your family to make deductions.[198] If you are in debt to two water companies you can only have a deduction for arrears made to one of them at a time. Your debts for water charges should be cleared before your debts for sewerage costs, but the amount paid for current consumption can include both water and sewerage charges.[199]

Council tax and community charge arrears[200]

Deductions for council tax or community charge arrears can be made from IS, PC or JSA if the local authority gets a liability order from a magistrates' court (in Scotland, a summary warrant or decree from a sheriff's court) and applies to the DWP for recovery to be made in this way. For community charge purposes, if it wants to recover arrears from both you and your partner the order must be against both of you. Deductions can be made for arrears and any unpaid costs or penalties imposed. Deductions cannot be made for council tax arrears while community charge deductions are being made.

Fines, costs and compensation orders[201]

Magistrates' courts (any court in Scotland) can apply to the DWP for a fine, costs or compensation order to be deducted from your IS, PC or JSA. Only one court application can be dealt with at a time – if a second application is made it is not dealt with until the first debt is paid.

Deductions can only be made if you are 18 or over, on IS, PC or JSA, and you have defaulted on payments. Payments continue until the debt is paid off, or your IS, PC or JSA ceases or is too low to cover the repayments.

Child support maintenance

The rules that apply depend on whether the maintenance is payable under the old rules that applied up to the changeover date of 3 March 2003, or the new rules that apply from that date (see Chapter 34 and CPAG's *Child Support Handbook* for more details).

Under the **old rules**, deductions can be made from an absent parent's IS, PC or income-based JSA as a contribution towards the maintenance of her/his child(ren). Currently, the deduction is £5.70 a week. Deductions can be made from contribution-based JSA for arrears of child support maintenance. Deductions cannot be made in certain circumstances (see p864).[202]

Under the **new rules**, if a non-resident parent is liable to pay child support maintenance at the flat rate – currently set to be £5 a week – deductions for that may be made from the following benefits:[203]

- IB;
- maternity allowance;
- widows' and bereavement benefits;
- retirement pensions;
- industrial injuries benefits;
- IS;
- PC;
- JSA (income-based or contribution-based);
- disablement pension; *or*
- war widow's pension.

The whole of the maintenance may be deducted from one of the benefits listed above.[204] If more than one partner in a couple or polygamous marriage is liable to pay maintenance at the flat rate, £5 is deducted from any IS or income-based JSA s/he is receiving.[205]

Up to £1 a week may be deducted for arrears, except where IS, PC or income-based JSA is payable.[206]

How much can be deducted

Deductions are made to pay off the debt or current weekly costs, or both.[207] Deductions are made from your IS, PC and any IB, retirement pension or severe disablement allowance paid with it in the same giro or order book. They are also made from your JSA. You must be left with at least 10p.[208] Council tax and community charge arrears can be deducted from IS, PC and JSA only.[209]

If deductions are being made from your *contribution-based* JSA for community charge arrears, council tax arrears or fines, where you do not have an underlying entitlement to income-based JSA (see p1109), the maximum deduction is one-third of the weekly amount of JSA for a person of your age.

If deductions are being made from your IS, PC or income-based JSA (or contribution-based JSA where you have an underlying entitlement to income-based JSA – see p1109), maximum deductions are shown below.

Type of arrears	*Deduction for arrears*	*Deduction for ongoing cost*
Mortgage direct payments*	Nil	Current weekly cost
Housing costs*	£2.85 each housing debt (maximum of £8.55 payable)	Current weekly cost
Rent arrears	£2.85	Nil (met by HB)

Fuel	£2.85 each fuel debt (maximum of £5.70 payable)	Estimated amount of current consumption
Water charges	£2.85 (adjusted every 26 weeks)	Estimated costs
Council tax	£2.85	Nil (met by council tax benefit)
Community charge	£2.85 (single person) £4.45 (couple)	Not applicable
Fines	Nil	£2.85
Child maintenance	Nil	£5.00 (new rules) £5.70 (old rules)
Residential accommodation charges	Nil	The accommodation allowance (for those in local authority homes); all but £18.80 of your IS, PC or JSA (for those in private or voluntary homes)
Hostel charges	Nil	Weekly amount assessed by local authority

*If you have more than one type of housing cost and these are not met in full because of a restriction on the amount which can be covered (see p921) or a non-dependant deduction (see p924), the direct payment to meet current weekly costs is reduced as follows:[210]
Multiply the amount of the restriction and/or deduction by the amount of the item of housing costs to be paid directly and then divide by the amount of total housing costs.
This ensures that such reductions are shared proportionately between different items of housing costs.

More than one debt

For **IS**, **PC** and **income-based JSA** deductions for arrears can be made for more than one debt. However:

- the maximum amount that can be deducted from your benefit for arrears (excluding community charge arrears) and a contribution towards child maintenance (under the old rules) is £8.55 a week.[211] The *total* amount deducted from benefit may be more than that if you are having deductions made for current costs as well as for arrears. If the total amount of deductions for arrears would exceed £8.55 a week, the deductions are made in a set order of priority (see p1117);
- if deductions of £5.70 are being made for items of a higher priority than child maintenance (under the old rules), half of the child maintenance deduction is made – ie, £2.85;

- in the case of fuel, rent arrears, water charges and housing costs arrears, if the combined cost of deductions for arrears and current consumption is more than 25 per cent of your total applicable amount (see p877) or, in the case of PC, more than 25 per cent of your minimum guarantee (see p469) before housing costs, the deductions cannot be made without your consent.[212]

Where there is no underlying entitlement to income-based JSA, the maximum amount that can be deducted in total (for debts) from **contribution-based JSA** for community charge or council tax, fines and child support maintenance arrears is one-third of the age-related amount of contribution-based JSA payable to you.

Priority between debts

If you have more debts or charges than can be met within the limits for direct payments (see p1115), they are paid in the following order of priority:[213]
1st – housing costs not covered by the mortgage payment scheme;
2nd – rent arrears (and related charges);
3rd – fuel charges;
4th – water charges;
5th – council tax and community charge arrears;
6th – unpaid fines, costs and compensation orders;
7th – payments for maintenance of children under the old rules. Note that payments due under the new scheme are always payable whatever other deductions are being made.

If you owe both gas and electricity, the DWP chooses which one to pay first, depending on your circumstances. If you have arrears for both council tax and community charge, only one application can be dealt with at a time and the earliest debt should be dealt with first.[214]

If you have been overpaid benefit or given a social fund loan, you may have to repay these too by having deductions from your benefit.[215] You should argue that these deductions should take a lower priority.

8. Sanctions for breach of community orders and for benefit offences

Breach of community orders

From 15 October 2001, a pilot scheme began imposing sanctions on claimants who fail to comply with community orders. The pilot is due to run at least until 2005.[216] What follows is a summary of the main rules; seek further advice (see Appendix 2) if you are affected.

A **'community order'** is a sentence passed by a criminal court requiring you to do community service, undergo probation, or a combination of the two.[217]

The sanctions will be available if the following conditions are complied with:[218]

- a court has decided that you have failed to comply with the requirements of the order without reasonable excuse; *and*
- the Secretary of State is notified of the determination; *and*
- you otherwise satisfy the conditions of entitlement to benefit.

The sanction is that specified benefits will not be payable for a period. The benefits specified are: income support (IS), jobseeker's allowance (JSA), and the training allowances paid with Work-Based Learning for Adults, the employment, voluntary sector, environmental task force, education and training options of the New Deal, and the 'intensive activity period' of the New Deal.[219] However, where you are getting IS, or in some cases joint-claim JSA, only a proportion of your benefit will be withheld.[220]

The pilot scheme only applies to people who are subject to community orders in the following probation areas: Derbyshire, Hertfordshire, Teeside and West Midlands.

Under the rules there is a four-week sanction period in which benefit is not payable. IS will be paid at a reduced rate. So will joint-claim JSA, as long as both members of the couple are not subject to a sanction.

The basic reduction for IS is 40 per cent of the relevant personal allowance for a single person (20 per cent in cases of pregnancy or 'serious illness'). For joint-claim JSA, benefit is reduced to the amount for a single person unless you are considered to be a 'couple in hardship'. If the non-offending member of the couple satisfies the contribution conditions for contribution-based JSA, then s/he will get the single person rate of that benefit.

If you are considered to be a 'person in hardship' or a 'couple in hardship' then you may be entitled to reduced rate income-based JSA or joint-claim JSA. 'Person' and 'couple' 'in hardship' are defined in the rules, and are very similar to the definition of a 'vulnerable group' for JSA (see p446). If the hardship rule applies, the applicable amount for you and your partner is reduced by 40 per cent (20 per cent in cases of serious illness or pregnancy) of the personal allowance for a single person.

Even if you are sanctioned, for housing benefit and council tax benefit you are treated as if you are still in receipt of income-based or joint-claim JSA.[221]

Benefit offences

If you are convicted of one or more benefit 'offences' (ie, in connection with fraud) in two separate proceedings within a three-year period, sanctions may be imposed on certain of your benefits, with the result that they may be paid at a reduced rate or not at all – see Chapter 42.

9. Recovery of benefits from compensation payments

If you are seeking compensation from someone (a defendant) through the courts (eg, because you have been unfairly dismissed or because you have had a personal injury) you might be awarded damages to compensate you for your loss. However, if, as the result of a defendant's action, you have had to claim benefit, the amount of damages to be awarded is reduced by the amount of benefit you received.

Employment cases

In a wrongful or unfair dismissal case, your claim for loss of earnings is reduced by the amount of jobseeker's allowance (JSA) you received.[222] The DWP is able to recover an equivalent sum from your employer if it is an unfair dismissal case dealt with in an industrial tribunal,[223] but not if there is a settlement or it is a wrongful dismissal case dealt with by a court.

Personal injury cases

If you are paid compensation in respect of an accident, injury or disease after 6 October 1997, those compensating you can reduce compensation paid to you when you have received benefit in respect of a particular loss for which the compensation is paid. They must then pay money back to the Compensation Recovery Unit (CRU), which is part of the DWP. It does not matter whether the payment is voluntary, with or without legal proceedings, or by order of a court. A reduction is not made if the compensation is paid for pain and suffering, because benefits are not paid for this. You are, therefore, able to keep all compensation paid for that reason. However, because the right to reduce your compensation can reduce it quite considerably, it is important to be aware of the law governing the CRU's rights of recovery.

The CRU is not entitled to recover all the benefits you have received. It may only recover those listed in the right-hand column of the table on p1121, and only then if you were paid the benefit as a consequence of the accident (see p1120).

Note: the rules described here apply to payments made from 6 October 1997 onwards. The rules that applied under the old scheme are described in CPAG's *Rights Guide to Non Means Tested Benefits*, 20th edition, 1997/98, pp230-32.

Which benefits can be recovered

The recoverable benefit consists of all benefits paid to you 'in consequence' of the injury or disease from which you have suffered during the 'relevant period' (see p1121).

Before you are paid compensation, those compensating you must apply to the DWP for a 'certificate of recoverable benefits'.[224] The certificate tells them which benefits are recoverable.

Those compensating you become liable to pay the DWP for the total amount of recoverable benefit 14 days after the certificate is issued.[225] It is the compensator's obligation, not yours, and so if the compensator fails to pay, the CRU cannot pursue you for the money. The compensator remains liable even if it fails to apply for a certificate.[226]

When benefit is paid 'in consequence'

In many cases it will be obvious that you were paid benefit 'in consequence' of the relevant accident or disease, because you have stopped working. However, you may have another health problem that had an influence on your entitlement to benefits. The following rules apply:

- If both the relevant event (cause A) and some unrelated problem (cause B) led you to be entitled to benefit, then provided that cause A is at least partially to blame for your illness or disability, the benefit is recoverable.[227]
- However, if cause A would not have led you to be entitled to benefit by itself, but cause B did do so, then the benefit is not recoverable.[228]
- It is common, particularly in back injury cases, for doctors to say that you have 'aggravated' or 'exacerbated' pre-existing damage to your body which you may not have been aware of prior to the accident. They often say that after a certain period of time, say two years, you would have been experiencing the same level of pain even had the accident not happened. In such a case, after that period of time the benefit is not being paid in consequence of the accident but as a result of your underlying problem.[229]

The CRU must look at the reality of your state of health when deciding whether benefit was paid 'in consequence' of your accident or illness and may not simply look at the opinions given by DWP doctors at the time of awarding you benefit.[230] It can help if you think about the effects of the CRU scheme on your compensation while the case is still proceeding and get your solicitor to ask appropriate questions of the medical experts in your case. You can then use the evidence of the medical expert if you want to challenge the CRU certificate.

Compensators can argue that you were wrongly paid benefit, and that where this is accepted, the benefit was not 'paid in respect of' an injury, accident or disease. Where that is the case, the money will not be recoverable from the compensator. Also, where the compensator has shown that you were not entitled to benefit, the DWP can consider whether your benefit award should be revised or superseded, and if any overpayment is recoverable from you (see Chapter 41 for overpayments and when they can be recovered).[231] If you are asked to repay an overpayment in this situation, seek advice (see Appendix 2). Although you can argue that money already recovered from the compensator is not also recoverable from you,[232] this may not help you if the compensator has been refunded.

The relevant period

The **'relevant period'** is usually the period of five years from the date:[233]

- of your accident or injury if you are claiming compensation for an accident or injury; *or*
- you first claimed a recoverable benefit because of the disease (see p1120) if you are claiming compensation in respect of a disease.

The relevant period ends if those compensating you make a final payment of compensation or an agreement is made under which compensation already paid is accepted as being in final payment.[234]

Offsetting against your compensation

Before the compensator pays your compensation, it is allowed to deduct the recoverable benefits paid during the relevant period (see above) from certain types of compensation.[235] The type of compensation is shown in the left-hand column and the relevant benefits in the right-hand column of the table below.

Compensation	*Recoverable benefits*
Loss of earnings	Disability working allowance, disablement benefit, incapacity benefit, income support, invalidity pension, jobseeker's allowance, reduced earnings allowance, severe disablement allowance, sickness benefit, statutory sick pay (paid before 6 April 1994), unemployment benefit, unemployability supplement, invalidity allowance
Cost of care	Attendance allowance, disability living allowance care component, disablement benefit paid for constant attendance (see p333) or exceptionally severe disablement (see p333)
Loss of mobility	Mobility allowance, disability living allowance mobility component

Example

Gary receives a £30,000 compensation payment consisting of £15,000 for loss of earnings, £5,000 for pain and suffering, and £10,000 for the cost of care. By the time the award is made he has received £20,000 of incapacity benefit and £5,000 disability living allowance care component. The award for loss of earnings is reduced to nil. Gary will receive the full award for pain and suffering, but his award for the cost of care is reduced by £5,000. The compensator is liable to pay the DWP recoverable benefits of £25,000, and pays Gary a net award of £10,000 (£5,000 pain and suffering + £5,000 care).

Any compensation reduced by this method is treated as being paid to you. Those compensating you must give you a statement showing how the payment has been calculated, even if the recovery of benefits reduces a particular type of compensation to nil. If the recoverable benefit (see above) exceeds the compensation paid to you for a particular loss, those compensating you still have to pay the balance to the DWP.

Exempt payments

Prior to 6 October 1997, compensation payments of under £2,500 were exempt from the rules on recovery of benefits. To date no such figure has been set under the new rules so the recovery rules apply to all claims, no matter how small. However, certain compensation payments are exempt.[236] These include:

- payments under the Fatal Accident Act 1996, the Vaccine Damage Act 1979 and the NHS industrial injury scheme;
- payments under the Pneumoconiosis Compensation Scheme and certain payments for loss of hearing;
- criminal injuries compensation;
- contractual sick pay and redundancy payments;
- payments from insurance companies from policies agreed before the accident; *and*
- payments from certain trusts.

Challenging a recovery decision

A decision maker may look at a certificate of recoverable benefit (see p1120) again if s/he is satisfied that it was issued in ignorance of, or was based on a mistake as to, a material fact or if there was an error in its preparation – eg, a miscalculation.[237] You and those compensating you can both appeal against the certificate but not until the compensation payment has been made and the benefit paid back to the DWP. There are only two possible grounds for appeal:[238]

- that the amount, rate, or period of benefit specified on the certificate is wrong; *or*
- that the benefits specified were not paid because of an accident, injury or disease.

Appeals are heard by an appeal tribunal[239] (see p1217). Further appeals can be made to a commissioner in the usual way (see p1245).[240]

Other sources of information

Details of the procedures to be followed and other advice can be obtained from the CRU (see Appendix 1). A guide to the procedures, called *Social Security Recovery of Benefits: Procedures for Liaison with Compensation Recovery Unit – A Guide for Companies and Solicitors*, is available free from the DWP.

Notes

1. **Who should claim**
   1 Reg 4(4) SS(C&P) Regs
   2 Reg 4D(7) and (8) SS(C&P) Regs
   3 **CB/GA** Reg 28 CB&GA(Admin) Regs
   Other benefits Reg 33 SS(C&P) Regs
   4 R(SB) 5/90
   5 Reg 33(1A) SS(C&P) Regs; Reg 71(5) HB Regs; Reg 61(5) CTB Regs
   6 CIS/642/1994
   7 CIS/379/1992
   8 Reg 3A(1) JSA Regs
   9 s3B JSA 1995
   10 Reg 24(1A) and (5A) JSA Regs
   11 Reg 3G JSA Regs
   12 Reg 6(4ZB)(a) SS(C&P) Regs
   13 Reg 6(4ZB)(b) SS(C&P) Regs

2. **How to make a claim**
   14 s1 SSAA 1992
   15 Reg 3 SS(C&P) Regs
   16 **CB/GA** Reg 5 CB&GA(Admin) Regs
   Other benefits Reg 4 SS(C&P) Regs
   17 Reg 4(6)(a) SS(C&P) Regs
   18 Reg 4D SS(C&P) Regs
   19 Reg 4(11) SS(C&P) Regs
   20 Regs 4(6A)-(6CC) and 4D SS(C&P) Regs; Memo Vol 1 06/03 DMG
   21 **CB/GA** Reg 8 CB&GA(Admin) Regs
   Other benefits Reg 5(1) SS(C&P) Regs
   22 **CB/GA** Reg 8 CB&GA(Admin) Regs
   Other benefits Reg 5(2) SS(C&P) Regs
   23 CJSA/3979/1999
   24 Reg 4 SS(C&P) Regs
   25 Regs 4(7) and 4D(10)-(12) SS(C&P) Regs
   26 CIS/540/2002; from 20 and 21 December 2004 respectively, the SS&CS(D&A) Regs and the CB&GA(D&A) Regs were amended so that there is a right of appeal
   27 s8 SSA 1998
   28 Reg 4(1A) SS(C&P) Regs
   29 Reg 4(7A) SS(C&P) Regs
   30 CIS/540/2002
   31 Reg 4(1B) SS(C&P) Regs
   32 CIS/2057/1998
   33 Reg 6(4A) SS(C&P) Regs
   34 Reg 4(7) SS(C&P) Regs
   35 Reg 4D(11) SS(C&P) Regs
   36 **CB/GA** Reg 7 CB&GA(Admin) Regs
   Other benefits Regs 7 and 8(2) SS(C&P) Regs; reg 23 JSA Regs
   37 s180 SSAA 1992
   38 s1(1A) and (1B) SSAA 1992; reg 2A IS Regs
   39 CIS/345/2003
   40 Reg 1A SS(DLA) Regs
   41 Reg 2B(a) HB Regs
   42 Reg 2A IS Regs; reg 2A JSA Regs
   43 Reg 2A SS(IB) Regs; reg 2A SS(ICA) Regs; reg 1A SS(MA) Regs; reg 1A SS(WB&RP) Regs; reg 2A SS(SDA) Regs
   44 Reg 2A IS Regs; reg 2A JSA Regs; reg 2A SS(IB) Regs; reg 2A SS(ICA) Regs; reg 1A SS(MA) Regs; reg 1A SS(WB&RP) Regs; reg 2A SS(SDA) Regs

3. **The date of your claim**
   45 **CB/GA** Reg 11 CB&GA(Admin) Regs
   Other benefits Reg 9(1) and Sch 1 SS(C&P) Regs
   46 Sch 1 SS(C&P) Regs
   47 Reg 11 CB&GA(Admin) Regs
   48 Reg 9(4) and (5) SS(C&P) Regs
   49 **CB/GA** Reg 5(1)(b) CB&GA(Admin) Regs
   Other benefits Reg 4(1) SS(C&P) Regs
   50 Reg 19 and Sch 4 SS(C&P) Regs
   51 R(SB) 9/84
   52 ss65(4) and (6) and 76 SSCBA 1992
   53 CIS/4354/1999; CI/5151/1999
   54 **CB/GA** Reg 6 CB&GA(Admin) Regs
   Other benefits Reg 19(2) and (3) and Sch 4 SS(C&P) Regs
   55 Reg 19 and Sch 4 SS(C&P) Regs
   56 CJSA/3994/1998
   57 Reg 19(6) and (7) SS(C&P) Regs
   58 CIS/4901/2002
   59 Reg 19(4) and (5) SS(C&P) Regs
   60 CIS/2484/1999
   61 CIS/1721/1998; CIS/3749/1998; CSIS/256/1999
   62 CJSA/4573/1999
   63 CJSA/4066/1998
   64 CIS/610/1998
   65 CIS/4354/1999
   66 CIS/4490/1999
   67 CJSA/0580/2003
   68 CIS/610/1998

69 CIS/3994/1998
70 CIS/5430/1999
71 CJSA/1136/1998
72 CIS/5430/1999
73 CIS/5430/1999
74 Reg 19(5) SS(C&P) Regs; C12/98 (IS)
75 C12/98 (IS)
76 CIS/2057/1998
77 R(SB) 17/83; R(IS) 5/91; CIS/812/1992
78 R(P) 2/85
79 Reg 6(22) SS(C&P) Regs
80 Reg 6(16)-(26) SS(C&P) Regs
81 Reg 6(17) SS(C&P) Regs
82 Reg 6(22)-(25) SS(C&P) Regs
83 Reg 6(19) SS(C&P) Regs
84 Reg 6(30) SS(C&P) Regs
85 CG/1479/1999
86 Reg 1(3) SS&CS(DA) Regs

4. **How your claim is dealt with**

87 Decisions on invalid claims are not excluded from appeal rights: Sch 2 para 5 SS&CS(DA) Regs; Sch 2 para 6 CB&GA(DA) Regs
88 s8 SSA 1998
89 R(SB) 29/83
90 **CB/GA** Reg 15 CB&GA(Admin) Regs
Other benefits Reg 17 SS(C&P) Regs
91 Reg 32(1) SS(C&P) Regs
92 Regs 23(5) and 2 CB&GA(Admin) Regs, definition of 'appropriate office'

5. **Work-focused interviews and benefit**

93 Reg 2(1) SS(JPI) Regs
94 Reg 8 SS(JPI) Regs
95 Reg 4 SS(JPI) Regs
96 s2AA SSAA 1992
97 Reg 7 SS(JPIP) Regs
98 s2AA SSAA 1992; regs 3 and 4 SS(JPIP) Regs
99 Regs 10, 11 and 14 SS(JPIP) Regs
100 Reg 3 SS(IBWFI) Regs 2003
101 Reg 1(3) SS(WFILP) Regs
102 Reg 2 SS(WFILP) Regs; The Social Security (Quarterly Work-focused Interviews for Certain Lone Parents) Regulations 2004 SI No.2244
103 Reg 4 SS(WFILP) Regs
104 Reg 10(2) SS(JPI) Regs; reg 2(3) SS(WFILP) Regs; reg 5(3) SS(IBWFI) Regs
105 Regs 6 and 7 SS(JPI) Regs; regs 5 and 6 SS(WFILP) Regs; regs 6 and 7 SS(IBWFI) Regs
106 Reg 2 SS(JPI) Regs; reg 1 SS(WFILP) Regs; reg 2 SS(IBWFI) Regs
107 Regs 12 and 14 SS(JPI) Regs; regs 3 and 7 SS(WFILP) Regs; regs 10 and 11 SS(IBWFI) Regs
108 Reg 11(2) SS(JPI) Regs; reg 3(2) SS(WFILP) Regs; reg 9(2) SS(IBWFI) regs; DWP press release, 2 December 2004
109 Reg 3(3) SS(JPI) Regs
110 Reg 12(2)(a) SS(JPI) Regs; reg 7(3)(a) SS(WFILP) Regs; reg 10 SS(IBWFI) Regs
111 Reg 12(10) SS(JPI) Regs; reg 7(6) SS(WFILP) Regs
112 Reg 12(2)(c) to (8) SS(JPI) Regs; reg 8 SS(WFILP) Regs; reg 10 SS(IBWFI) Regs
113 Reg 12(9) SS(JPI) Regs; reg 8(3)(c) SS(WFILP) Regs; reg 10(10) SS(IBWFI) Regs
114 Reg 12(3)-(5) SS(JPI) Regs
115 Reg 13 SS(JPI) Regs; reg 10(12) SS(IBWFI) Regs; reg 8(3)(a) and (b) SS(WFILP) Regs
116 Reg 15 SS(JPI) Regs; reg 9 SS(WFILP) Regs; reg 12 SS(IBWFI) Regs
117 Reg 11(4) SS(JPI) Regs; reg 7(1)(b) SS(WFILP) Regs; reg 9(4) SS(IBWFI) Regs
118 Regs 12(12) and 15(1) SS(JPI) Regs; reg 7(2) SS(WFILP) Regs; reg 10(12) SS(IBWFI) Regs
119 Reg 14 SS(JPI) Regs; reg 7(5) SS(WFILP) Regs; reg 11 SS(IBWFI) Regs

6. **Getting paid**

120 **CB/GA** Reg 16 CB&GA(Admin) Regs
Other benefits Reg 20 SS(C&P) Regs
121 House of Commons *Hansard*, Written Answers, 6 November 2002, col 288W
122 **CB/GA** Regs 16-20 CB&GA(Admin) Regs
Other benefits Regs 22-26A SS(C&P) Regs
123 **CB/GA** Regs 27 and 28 CB&GA(Admin) Regs
Other benefits Regs 30 and 33 SS(C&P) Regs
124 **CB/GA** Reg 33 CB&GA(Admin) Regs
Other benefits Reg 34 SS(C&P) Regs
125 Reg 35 SS(C&P) Regs
126 Reg 6 SS(OB) Regs
127 Reg 4(5) SS(OB) Regs
128 Reg 6 SS(OB) Regs
129 s52(2) SSCBA 1992
130 s16(1), (2) and (6) SSCBA 1992; reg 2 SS(MAP) Regs
131 Reg 4(4) SS(OB) Regs
132 Reg 4(3) SS(OB) Regs
133 Reg 9 SS(OB) Regs
134 Reg 10 SS(OB) Regs
135 Reg 8 SS(OB) Regs
136 Reg 2(4)(a) and (5) CB&SS(FAR) Regs
137 Reg 8 SS(OB) Regs
138 Reg 7 SS(OB) Regs

139 **CB/GA** Reg 18 CB&GA(Admin) Regs
Other benefits Reg 20 SS(C&P) Regs
140 Reg 38(1)(bb) SS(C&P) Regs; CDLA/2609/2002 commented on the way a similar rule applied to payment by giro/order book
141 Reg 11 HB&CTB(DA) Regs
142 **HB/CTB** Sch 7 para 13(2) CSPSSA 2000; reg 11(2)(b) HB&CTB(DA) Regs
CB/GA Reg 18(3) CB&GA(DA) Regs
Other benefits ss21(2)(c) and (d) SSA 1998; reg 16(3)(b) SS&CS(DA) Regs
143 **CB/GA** Reg 18(4) and (5) CB&GA(DA) Regs
Other benefits Reg 16(4) SS&CS(DA) Regs
144 **CB/GA** Reg 21 CB&GA(DA) Regs
Other benefits Reg 20(2) and (3) SS&CS(DA) Regs
145 **CB/GA** Reg 18(2) CB&GA(DA) Regs
HB/CTB Sch 7 para 13(2)(a) CSPSSA 2000
Other benefits ss21(2)(a) and (b), 22 and 24 SSA 1998
146 **CB/GA** Reg 18(2)(a) CB&GA(DA) Regs
HB/CTB Reg 11(2)(a)(i) HB&CTB(DA) Regs
Other benefits Reg 16(3)(a)(i) SS&CS(DA) Regs
147 Reg 16(2) SS&CS(DA) Regs
148 **CB/GA** Reg 18(2)(b) CB&GA(DA) Regs
HB/CTB Reg 11(2)(a)(ii) HB&CTB(DA) Regs
Other benefits Reg 16(3)(a)(ii) SS&CS(DA) Regs
149 **CB/GA** Reg 18(2)(c) CB&GA(DA) Regs
HB/CTB Reg 11(2)(c)(i) and (ii) HB&CTB(DA) Regs
Other benefits Reg 16(3)(a)(iii) SS&CS(DA) Regs
150 Reg 16(3)(a)(iv) SS&CS(DA) Regs
151 Reg 18(e) CB&GA(DA)Regs
152 Reg 11(2)(c) HB&CTB(DA) Regs
153 Reg 17(6) SS&CS(DA) Regs
154 **CB/GA** Reg 19 CB&GA(DA) Regs
Other benefits Reg 17(2) SS&CS(DA) Regs
155 As required under reg 32(1) SS(C&P) Regs or for **CB/GA** reg 23 CB&GA(Admin) Regs
156 **CB/GA** Reg 19(2) CB&GA(DA) Regs
HB/CTB Reg 13(4)(a) HB&CTB(DA) Regs
Other benefits Reg 17(4)(a) SS&CS(DA) Regs
157 **CB/GA** Reg 19(2)(b) CB&GA(DA) Regs
HB/CTB Reg 13(4)(b) HB&CTB(DA) Regs
Other benefits Reg 17(4)(b) SS&CS(DA) Regs
158 **CB/GA** Reg 19(5) CB&GA(DA) Regs
Other benefits Reg 17(5) SS&CS(DA) Regs
159 s24 SSA 1998; reg 19(2) SS&CS(DA) Regs
160 **CB/GA** Reg 20(1)(a) CB&GA(DA) Regs
Other benefits Reg 18(1)(a), (2) and (4) SS&CS(DA) Regs
161 **CB/GA** Reg 20(1)(b) CB&GA(DA) Regs
Other benefits Reg 18(1)(b), (3) and (4) SS&CS(DA) Regs
162 **CB/GA** Reg 20(2) CB&GA(DA) Regs
Other benefits Reg 18(1) SS&CS(DA) Regs
163 Reg 19(3) and (4) SS&CS(DA) Regs
164 para 04130 DMG
165 Reg 2 SS(PAOR) Regs
166 Regs 3 and 4 SS(PAOR) Regs

7. **Deductions from your benefit**
167 Regs 34A and 35 SS(C&P) Regs
168 Sch 9 para 2(1) SS(C&P) Regs
169 Sch 9 para 8(2) and (2A) SS(C&P) Regs
170 Sch 9 para 8 SS(C&P) Regs
171 Reg 34A and Sch 9A para 2 SS(C&P) Regs
172 Sch 9A paras 8 and 9 SS(C&P) Regs
173 Regs 34A(1A) and 34B and Sch 9A para 2A SS(C&P) Regs
174 Sch 9A para 3 SS(C&P) Regs
175 Sch 9A paras 1 and 3 SS(C&P) Regs
176 Sch 9A para 6 SS(C&P) Regs
177 *Pazio v Secretary of State for Social Security*, Birmingham County Court, 1996
178 Sch 9A para 3 SS(C&P) Regs
179 Sch 9A para 3(4) SS(C&P) Regs
180 Sch 9 para 3 SS(C&P) Regs
181 Sch 9 para 3(5) SS(C&P) Regs
182 Sch 9 para 1 SS(C&P) Regs
183 Sch 9 para 3(4) SS(C&P) Regs
184 CIS/15146/1996
185 Sch 9 para 3(4) SS(C&P) Regs
186 Sch 9 para 5 SS(C&P) Regs
187 Sch 9 para 5(1)(c)(i) SS(C&P) Regs
188 Sch 9 para 5(1)(c)(ii) SS(C&P) Regs
189 Sch 9 para 5(6) SS(C&P) Regs; R(IS) 14/95
190 Sch 9 para 5(7) SS(C&P) Regs
191 Sch 9 para 4 SS(C&P) Regs
192 Sch 9 para 4A SS(C&P) Regs
193 Sch 9 para 6 SS(C&P) Regs
194 Sch 9 para 6(1) SS(C&P) Regs

195 Sch 9 para 6(4)(b) SS(C&P) Regs
196 Sch 9 paras 1 and 7 SS(C&P) Regs
197 Sch 9 para 7(1) SS(C&P) Regs
198 Sch 9 para 7(2) SS(C&P) Regs
199 Sch 9 para 7(7) SS(C&P) Regs
200 CC(DIS) Regs; CT(DIS) Regs; CIS/11861/1996
201 F(DIS) Regs
202 s43 CSA 1991; Sch 9 paras 7A and 7B SS(C&P) Regs
203 Sch 1 para 4(l)(b) CSA 1991; Sch 9B para 2 SS(C&P) Regs
204 Sch 9B para 2 SS(C&P) Regs
205 Sch 9B paras 4-6 SS(C&P) Regs
206 Sch 9B para 3(1) SS(C&P) Regs
207 Sch 9 SS(C&P) Regs
208 Sch 9 paras 1 and 2(2) SS(C&P) Regs
209 Reg 2 CC(DIS) Regs; regs 2 and 3 CT(DIS) Regs
210 Sch 9 para 3(2A) SS(C&P) Regs
211 Sch 9 para 8(1) SS(C&P) Regs
212 Sch 9 paras 5(5), 5(5A), 6(6), 6(6A), 7(8), 7(9), 8(2) and 8(2A) SS(C&P) Regs
213 Sch 9 para 9 SS(C&P) Regs
214 Reg 4 CC(DIS) Regs; reg 8 CT(DIS) Regs
215 Regs 15 and 16 SS(PAOR) Regs; reg 3 SF(RDB) Regs

8. **Sanctions for breach of community orders and for benefit offences**
216 Child Support, Pensions and Social Security Act 2000 (Commencement No.10) Order 2001 No.2619(C.86); SS(BCO) Regs; DWP Press Release, 5 February 2004
217 s62(8) CSPSSA 2000
218 s62(1) CSPSSA 2000
219 s62(2) CSPSSA 2000; reg 2 SS(BCO) Regs
220 s62(3) and (4) CSPSSA 2000
221 Reg 2(3A)(d) HB Regs and reg 2(3A)(d) CTB Regs

9. **Recovery of benefits from compensation payments**
222 *Nabi v British Leyland (UK) Ltd* [1980] 1 WLR 529 (CA)
223 EP(RUB&SB) Regs
224 s4 SS(RB)A 1997
225 s6(4) SS(RB)A 1997
226 s7 SS(RB)A 1997
227 CCR/5336/1995
228 CCR/5336/1995
229 CCR/4/1993; CCR/2129/1999
230 CCR/12532/1996
231 R(CR) 1/02
232 CSIS/37/1994
233 s3 SS(RB)A 1997
234 s3(4) SS(RB)A 1997
235 s8 and Sch 2 SS(RB)A 1997
236 s1 and Sch 1 SS(RB)A 1997; reg 2 SS(RB) Regs
237 s10 SS(RB)A 1997
238 s11 SS(RB)A 1997
239 s12 SS(RB)A 1997
240 s13 SS(RB)A 1997; reg 13 SS(RB)App Regs

Chapter 41

Overpayments of benefit

This chapter covers all the rules about overpayments of benefit. It contains:

If you are paid more benefit than you are entitled to, then an overpayment occurs. You may have to repay the overpayment – including, in some cases, where there was no fault on your part. If you have been overpaid a social fund payment (see Chapters 21 and 22) you might have to repay that too.

If it is considered that an overpayment was made due to fraud, as well as the overpayment being recovered you may be prosecuted, or you may be offered the option of paying a penalty as an alternative to going to court. You should seek advice before agreeing to pay. See Chapter 42 for further information.

If you were paid too much income support, pension credit or jobseeker's allowance, this could mean that you were also paid too much housing benefit and council tax benefit. If you are in this situation, see p1144.

Note: Working families' tax credit and disabled person's tax credit were abolished on 7 April 2003. For information on overpayments of these tax credits, see the 2002/2003 edition of this *Handbook*. For information on overpayments of the new tax credits introduced in April 2003, see Chapter 56.

1. Ordinary overpayments of benefits

Most overpayments are recoverable only in certain circumstances. We call these 'ordinary overpayments'. However, there are a number of cases in which different rules apply:

- where you have been paid too much income support (IS), income-based jobseeker's allowance (JSA) or pension credit (PC) because other income was paid late (see p1139);

- where too much mortgage interest has been paid direct to your lender (see p1141);
- where too much benefit has been paid into your bank account by mistake (see p1140);
- where you have been paid too much housing benefit (HB) or council tax benefit (CTB) (see pp1144 and 1156).

Which benefits are covered by these rules

This section covers the rules that allow recovery of overpayments of:

- all of the benefits (not tax credits) covered in this *Handbook*, other than HB and CTB. HB and CTB are paid by local authorities and special rules apply to them (see pp1144 and 1156);
- Sure Start maternity grants, funeral expenses, cold weather and winter fuel payments (see pp549, 551, 558 and 559 for the rules of entitlement to these payments);
- payments from the discretionary social fund (see Chapter 21) paid after 5 October 1998. If the payment was made prior to 5 October 1998, it cannot be recovered under these rules at all (though in the case of loans, you are still under the normal obligation to repay them – see p534). The DWP has said that it only intends to exercise these powers if you were overpaid because you fraudulently claimed another benefit. It should not use these rules to recover a payment where:[1]
  - you are given a loan or grant for an item but use the money to buy something else instead; *or*
  - one social fund officer (SFO) decides to give you a loan or grant but, for example following a request for a review, another SFO interprets the guidance (see p514) differently.

Overpayments made before 6 April 1987

The old law still applies if the overpayment which the DWP (or, for child benefit or guardian's allowance, the Revenue) is seeking to recover from you was made before 6 April 1987.[2] For further information regarding most benefits see CPAG's *Rights Guide to Non-Means-Tested Benefits*, 9th edition, 1986/87, p8. However, if the DWP is seeking to recover overpaid supplementary benefit from this period, the law on recovery was in any case very similar to that which applies now: see CPAG's *National Welfare Benefits Handbook*, 1986/87.

From whom an overpayment can be recovered

An overpayment can be recovered from you if you failed to disclose a material fact, or misrepresented a material fact, and that caused the overpayment.[3] This means that an overpayment can be recovered from you even if you are not the claimant, provided that the conditions set out on p1129 are fulfilled. However, a possible consequence of a recent decision is that overpayments may in fact only be recoverable from you if you are the claimant,[4] although this decision is under appeal. See CPAG's *Welfare Rights Bulletin* for updates.

If you are an appointee (see p1075), in general the overpayment can be recovered either from you or the claimant, or both of you. Exactly who the overpayment is recoverable from will depend on the individual facts of the case – ie, who misrepresented or failed to disclose a material fact. The DWP or the Revenue should issue a decision that deals with the liability of both the appointee and the claimant.[5] There are two exceptions to this rule:

- If the overpaid benefit has not been given to the claimant, the overpayment cannot be recovered from the claimant, unless s/he contributed to misrepresentation of or failure to disclose a material fact; *or*
- If the overpayment was caused by misrepresentation of a material fact by an appointee, the overpayment cannot be recovered from the appointee if s/he used 'due care and diligence' in making the representation.

If you have power of attorney, that is not the same as being an appointee. Unless you are an appointee, a benefit overpayment caused by your actions cannot be recovered from the claimant. Depending on the facts, however, such an overpayment may be recoverable from you.[6] You should seek advice if you are in this situation.

An overpayment can be recovered from a claimant's estate if s/he dies.[7] However, no recovery may be made until a grant either of probate (where the claimant has a will) or of letters of administration (where the claimant has no will) has been made.[8]

When an overpayment can be recovered

Before an overpayment can be recovered, a number of conditions must usually have been fulfilled.[9] Unless it can be shown that all of them are present in your case, the benefit cannot be recovered from you.[10] The conditions are:

- the decisions awarding you benefit have been changed (see below); *and*
- you failed to disclose or misrepresented a material fact (see p1130); *and*
- as a result of your failure to disclose, or misrepresentation, the overpayment was made (see p1136); *and*
- the whole amount is in fact recoverable (see p1137).

The decisions awarding you benefit have been changed

In order for you to be paid benefit, a decision maker will have made a decision to award you that benefit. If it later turns out that you have been overpaid benefit, the decision must be changed before the benefit is recoverable.[11] There are, therefore, two decisions. First, there is a decision which alters previous decisions awarding you benefit. Second, there is a decision that the overpayment is recoverable.

If both decisions are not made, then it is not possible to recover the overpayment from you.[12] Moreover, during the period for which you were overpaid, there may have been more than one decision awarding you benefit, and unless they are *all* changed, the overpayment cannot be recovered.[13]

If this rule is not complied with, you should appeal to a tribunal (see p1217) against the second decision. The tribunal should decide that it is of no effect. In this case, the DWP (or, in child benefit or guardian's allowance cases, the Revenue) can try again to recover the overpayment by complying with this formality.[14] However, sometimes a tribunal will go further and say that an overpayment is not recoverable, in which case the tribunal's decision will be final (unless the DWP or the Revenue appeals or the decision can be altered in some other way – see pp1241, 1245 and 1190).

How a decision is changed

A decision to alter your benefit award should have been made by an officer called a 'decision maker'. A decision maker can change a decision by carrying out a revision or a supersession of the decisions to award you benefit (see pp1189 and 1199 for more details).

Special cases

The way in which the decision to award benefit is changed differs in some cases:

- If you are 16 or 17 and have been overpaid discretionary JSA to avoid severe hardship (see p384), the Secretary of State must 'revoke' your award of JSA before you can be asked to repay the overpayment.[15] You cannot appeal against the revocation, which can only be challenged by way of judicial review.[16] If you are in this situation, seek advice.
- Decisions to make awards from the discretionary social fund are made by 'appropriate officers' (see p513). Such officers will make the initial decision to revise the award.[17]

Did you fail to disclose or misrepresent a material fact?

You have a duty to report your circumstances correctly when you first claim, and to notify the DWP (or, in the case of child benefit or guardian's allowance, the Revenue) when they have changed[18] (see p1187 and the section 'Change of circumstances' in the relevant benefit chapter of this *Handbook*).

In deciding whether this condition is fulfilled, it does not have to be established that you were careless or fraudulent. Provided that you failed to disclose or misrepresented a material fact, you can still be required to repay the benefit even if you innocently misrepresented your situation or you failed to tell the relevant office certain facts because you did not understand how the benefit scheme works.[19]

What is a material fact?

Overpayments can only usually be recovered if you failed to disclose (see below) or misrepresented (see p1134) a 'material fact'. A **'material fact'** is one which is relevant to how much benefit you should be paid.[20] Sometimes, where there is a difficult matter of judgement involved, there can be a difference between a statement of your honest opinion and a statement of a material fact.[21] If the decision maker has simply come to a different *conclusion* about the facts than you, you can argue that an overpayment should not be recovered.[22]

Facts	*Conclusions about the facts*
You have arthritis	You are incapable of work
A friend of the opposite sex is sharing your flat	You are living together as husband and wife
You have a bad back	Your mobility is severely restricted most of the time

Failure to disclose

Failure to disclose occurs where you do not give the 'relevant office' material facts – eg, you forget to tell it that you or your partner's working hours or pay have increased. It must be shown:

- that you knew of the material fact (see p1133); *and*
- that you did not inform the relevant office about the material fact by making a **valid disclosure** (see below); *and*
- that not informing the relevant office amounted to a **'failure' to disclose** on your part (see p1133).

Failure to disclose: have you made a valid disclosure?

Generally, to make a valid disclosure you have to disclose to the 'relevant office' the material fact in sufficiently clear terms so that the relevant office can examine how the fact affects your claim.[23] The following points should be borne in mind:

- The **'relevant office'** for these purposes is the one that administers the benefit that you are claiming.[24] That may be a local office (eg, for IS) or a central office (eg, for DLA). If you do not disclose a material fact to the relevant office, you may have failed to disclose. If you are not sure which is the correct office, seek advice. If you are in an area in which your benefits are adminstered under the ONE scheme, disclosure to the ONE office counts.[25] If you are in a Jobcentre Plus area (see p1093) then arguably you should be able to make a disclosure at the Jobcentre Plus office. However the DWP may not accept that you have made a proper disclosure unless you made the disclosure to the office dealing with the claim. Regarding child benefit and guardian's allowance you can disclose changes in your circumstances to the Revenue child benefit office, DWP Jobcentre Plus office or any Revenue enquiry centre.[26] However, the best advice is to ensure that you tell the Revenue, as it, and not the DWP or local authority, administers your claim.

- You should notify changes in your circumstances in writing. You could argue that, if the old test of failure to disclose applies (see p1133), you could give the information over the telephone, or in an office interview, either verbally or by presenting the relevant documents.[27] However, if fraud is suspected (see Chapter 41) you may be prosecuted if you have not notified a change in your circumstances in writing, and anyway it is always best to notify the office in writing and to keep a copy of your letter.
- If you filled in a form while giving information, a tribunal should not just look at what you said on the form, but also consider whether you gave the necessary information in another way.[28] If you fail to fill in a form correctly, but give the relevant information in the wrong place, you have disclosed the facts.[29]
- If you have made a statement in person or over the telephone but the decision maker says there is no record of this, you only have a case to answer once the decision maker has shown, 'on the balance of probabilities', that there would be a record of the conversation at the local office if it had taken place. In order to do this, the decision maker must give a tribunal information on:[30]
  - the instructions which should have applied for recording and attaching information to a claimant's file;
  - whether there were the appropriate administrative arrangements to enable these instructions to be carried out;
  - to what extent *in practice* these instructions are, or are not, carried out.

  Where there is no record of what happened, other than your own statement, then under the old test of failure to disclose (see p1133),the decision maker may not be able to prove that there has been a recoverable overpayment.[31]
- You should usually make the disclosure yourself,[32] unless you have an appointee acting for you (see p1075). Disclosure by someone else on your behalf, to be effective, must be made to the right office with your knowledge and you must think that there is no need to repeat the disclosure yourself. However, if someone else makes the disclosure to a DWP office (or, in the case of child benefit and guardian's allowance, the Revenue) not handling your claim, but s/he reasonably believes that the information will be passed on to the correct office, that may count as disclosure.[33]
- Once you have made a disclosure, you are not normally expected to repeat it.[34] However, if you give the information to the wrong person and subsequently become aware that it has not been acted upon, you are under an obligation to take further steps to make a proper disclosure.[35] A short time may elapse before you can reasonably be expected to realise that the original information has not been acted on.[36] It is still unclear whether, if you make a disclosure at a Jobcentre Plus office but that is not acted upon – eg, the office fails to pass on the information – you are under an obligation to take further steps. Arguably, as disclosure to a Jobcentre Plus office is disclosure to a

'relevant office', you are under no such obligation. However, the DWP may not accept this. If you are in this situation it is safest to write to the office handling your claim and keep a copy of the letter. If you are overpaid and the DWP argues that you did not do enough by disclosing to the Jobcentre Plus office, seek advice and ask your adviser to contact CPAG.

Failure to disclose: have you 'failed' to disclose?

If you did not report a material fact, then the overpayment will be recoverable from you if that amounted to a 'failure' to disclose on your part. Following a recent decision,[37] you will have failed to disclose a fact where you did not report it (you cannot rely on one DWP/Revenue office telling another), and:

- you were clearly told by the DWP or the Revenue (eg, in your benefit award letter) that you needed to disclose the fact; *and*
- you knew about the material fact; *or*
- you were not clearly told of the need to disclose the fact, but:
  - you knew about the fact; *and*
  - the fact was a change in your circumstances; *and*
  - it was reasonable to expect you to know that your benefit might be affected.

You may be able to argue that the test of whether you were clearly informed depends on whether it was reasonable for you to understand the instructions from the DWP or the Revenue. It is possible a challenge will be made in an attempt to re-instate the old test of failure to disclose (see below). See CPAG's *Welfare Rights Bulletin* for updates and seek advice.

If you did not know about the fact, then whether it was a change in your circumstances or not, you have not 'failed' to disclose it.[39] You cannot have failed to disclose something you did not know about unless:

- there is some reason why you should have been aware of it;[40] *or*
- it was reasonable for you to make enquiries which would have revealed the information to you;[41] *or*
- you had been aware of it but simply forgot.[42]

If you were *not* clearly told that you needed to report a certain fact, the overpayment is not recoverable *unless* the fact was a change in your circumstances, and you could reasonably have been expected to know that your benefit might be affected (but see also the old test described below).[43] What was reasonable will depend on the details of your case. But if there is no obvious connection between the fact and the benefit, then you could argue that it was not reasonable to expect you to know that your benefit might be affected.

The test described above may be challenged in an attempt to establish that, in cases where you are alleged to have failed to disclose a material fact, the **old test of failure to discl ose** still applies.

~~disclose still applies~~. This test is simply one of whether it was reasonable to expect you to disclose. It involves looking at more than just whether you should have known that your benefit might be affected, although that question should be included.[44] Under this test, if disclosure was not reasonably to have been expected, then arguably you will not have failed to disclose. Whether or not it was reasonable to expect you to disclose will depend on the facts of your case. In general though the following is relevant:

- It is irrelevant that you did not personally realise the need to tell the DWP (or the Revenue in child benefit and guardian's allowance cases) these facts – the test is whether a reasonable person would have realised that disclosure was required.[45]
- You cannot be expected to understand exactly how the DWP works, so making a disclosure to the office where your claim is being handled and making a specific reference to your claim is enough because you can then reasonably expect the person receiving the information to pass it on to the right person.[46]
- Where you reasonably rely on advice from a lawyer in not disclosing something, then it may be that there is no 'failure' on your part.[47] However, if the DWP (or, in child benefit and guardian's allowance cases, the Revenue) has given you different advice to that of the expert, that should be taken into account.
- The DWP sometimes points to warnings and instructions, for example at the back of your order book, that you should have read.[48] But it should not rely on warnings on forms you were asked to sign if you did not have a proper chance to read them.[49] The same should apply to the Revenue in child benefit and guardian's allowance cases.
- If you were mentally incapacitated, and a reasonable person aware of your circumstances would not have expected you to have made a disclosure, then it is arguable that disclosure was not reasonably to have been expected, and that therefore you did not fail to disclose.[50] If you were so mentally incapacitated that you were 'wholly incapable' of recognising your duty to make a disclosure, then again it is arguable that disclosure was not reasonably to have been expected.[51] It is unclear whether such arguments might apply to other situations – eg, where you did not make a disclosure because of language problems.

Misrepresentation

Misrepresentation occurs where you have provided information which is inaccurate – eg, you gave an incorrect answer to a specific question on the claim form. It will not apply to a failure to give information, unless you do so deliberately and with an intention to mislead.[52] Consider the following:

- It does not matter whether a reasonable person would have also given the information inaccurately. No 'failure' on your part needs to be shown.[53]

- It does not matter if you honestly believed that the information you gave was correct – once it is shown to be incorrect, you have committed a misrepresentation. You would not be guilty of misrepresentation if you add the phrase 'not to my knowledge' to your statement.[54]
- A written misrepresentation may be qualified by an oral one so that, if you fill in a form incorrectly but explain the situation to an officer when handing in the form, the explanation has to be taken into account when deciding whether what is stated on the form amounts to a misrepresentation.[55] Similarly, if you give wrong information in one document but the correct information in another, there may not be a relevant misrepresentation.[56] However, if you have declared a fact on a previous claim but inadvertently give incorrect information on a later claim, you have misrepresented. The decision maker is not required to check back for you.[57]
- If you are incapable of managing your affairs but nevertheless sign a claim form which is incorrectly completed, the Court of Appeal has decided that you cannot argue later that you were not capable of making a true representation of your circumstances to avoid recovery.[58] However, the Court of Appeal did not consider a rule of law called *'non est factum'* ('the deed is not mine') and there cannot be recovery from you on the basis of the misrepresentation if:[59]
  - you had a disability. This may include illiteracy, poor understanding of English or mental incapacity; *and*
  - you thought that you were signing something different from that which you were signing, or you did not understand the effect of your signature; *and*
  - you were not careless in failing to take any precautions that you should have taken to understand what you were signing.

Most overpayments arise due to a failure to disclose facts (see p1131) and it is easier to challenge such a decision than to show that you did not misrepresent anything. Because of this, decision makers often rely on general statements which you have signed to argue that a failure to disclose facts can later become a misrepresentation. This can occur:[60]

- **when you sign the claim form**. Some claim forms end with a statement: 'I declare that the information I have given is correct and complete'. If you gave correct answers but left out relevant information because you were unaware of it, the information is incomplete and you have failed to disclose. You can argue that signing the declaration does not convert this into a misrepresentation as the declaration means 'complete insofar as I have knowledge of the material facts';[61]
- **when you cash a giro or an order book**. Each time you do this you are signing a declaration that you have reported any facts which could affect the amount of your benefit. This is different from a 'failure to disclose'. If you knew a fact but failed to declare it (eg, if you were claiming IS, then start getting incapacity benefit (IB) so became entitled to less IS but did not tell the IS section about

your IB award) you are misrepresenting your circumstances each time you sign the declaration because you are incorrectly declaring that you have reported relevant facts. Arguably, the overpayment is recoverable due to the misrepresentation. However, a court case cast doubt on whether such misrepresentations actually cause the overpayment.[62] This might mean that the overpayment is not recoverable. See CPAG's *Welfare Rights Bulletin* for updates.

However:

- if you did not declare a fact because you were unaware of it, signing the declaration does not amount to a misrepresentation because all you are declaring is that you have correctly disclosed those facts *which were known to you*;[63]
- if you were told by the DWP (or, in the case of child benefit and guardian's allowance, the Revenue) that certain facts are irrelevant to your claim, then signing the declaration cannot be a misrepresentation if you fail to disclose those facts;[64]
- if someone else disclosed a fact to an office not handling your claim but s/he reasonably believed it would be passed on to the correct office, it may be that disclosure has been made, and therefore you signing the declaration does not amount to a misrepresentation.[65]

Did an overpayment result?

Even if there is information you failed to provide or you did misrepresent your circumstances, you might still be able to argue that this was not the cause of the overpayment. If something else caused the overpayment, it should not be recovered. Consider the following:

- If the relevant office has been given the correct information to decide your claim by someone else, but fails to act on it, you could argue that any overpayment did not arise because of your failure.[66] If one office of the DWP fails to inform another about *other* changes in your circumstances (eg, an increase in your earnings), that does not prevent the overpayment resulting from your failure to disclose that to the second office yourself.[67]
- In any case, if you have not actually disclosed a relevant fact to the relevant office and you then sign a declaration on a giro or order book that you have reported the relevant facts, this will be a misrepresentation. Where you are overpaid, the DWP (or in child benefit and guardian's allowance cases, the Revenue) may argue that the misrepresentation caused the overpayment. However, that may not be right as a court case has cast doubt on whether such declarations actually cause the overpayment.[68] See CPAG's *Welfare Rights Bulletin* for updates.
- If what you say on your claim form is obviously incorrect and the decision maker does not check this out, the overpayment is due to official error, not

your misrepresentation, and you do not have to pay it back. For example, if you say you pay ground rent and are a freeholder, the decision maker should recognise that this must be incorrect and check before paying you benefit.[69]

How much is repayable

It is always worth checking how the overpayment has been calculated, as you may be asked to repay too much by mistake. Ask for more information if you need it. To calculate the amount of the overpayment, you should:

- determine the dates between which the overpayment is recoverable;
- work out the total amount of benefit you were paid over the period;
- work out the correct amount of benefit you should have received during the period;
- deduct this from the total amount of benefit you were paid.

No interest charges may be added to the amount of the overpayment.

The amount of the overpayment is the difference between what you were paid and what you should have been paid.[70] The decision maker works out what you should have been paid using the information that you originally gave her/him, plus any facts which you misrepresented or did not disclose.

Except for child benefit and guardian's allowance,[71] the decision maker must consider whether you have also been underpaid IS or income-based JSA (see Chapters 13 and 15) for a past period.[72] S/he should do this even if you have been overpaid a benefit other than IS or income-based JSA.[73] S/he should deduct (offset) from the overpayment any underpaid IS or income-based JSA. Consider the following:

- If your benefit claim contained enough information to alert the decision maker to your potential need, but s/he did not investigate this fully, you can argue that the underpayment should be offset against the overpayment. It does not matter if the overpayment was for a different period, so long as there was sufficient information to alert the decision maker to your need for extra benefit.[74]
- If additional facts are needed to prove you were underpaid IS or income-based JSA, you cannot offset the underpayment of those benefits against the overpayment.[75] However, if you have been getting IS or income-based JSA, you can ask the DWP to revise or supersede your claim (see pp1189 and 1199). It could then withhold any arrears owed to you to reduce the overpayment.

You should claim any other benefits or tax credits to which you may have been entitled and ask for these to be backdated (see p1085 for benefits and p1405 for tax credits) so you can repay the overpayment. You should not delay in making the claims or you could lose out.

Example

Bert has been claiming JSA but was working full time (see p751). The DWP decides he has been overpaid JSA and decides to recover it. Bert is on a low wage and has children, so he should claim tax credits and ensure that they are backdated as far as possible (ie, up to three months).

If you were overpaid a benefit which overlaps with another benefit you claimed but were not being paid (see p1102 for the overlapping benefit rules), you should seek a revision or supersession of that benefit and ask for it to be paid instead (see p1189).

Example

Kathy has been claiming widow's pension but has been living with her new partner. She had also been claiming carer's allowance (CA) but this was not being paid because of the overlapping benefit rules. The DWP decides she has been overpaid widow's pension and that it should be recovered. Kathy should ask the DWP to supersede, or preferably revise, the decision not to pay her CA and offset any arrears she is paid against the overpayment.

If you were overpaid a benefit, but in fact were entitled to another benefit, check whether the claim for the benefit you were overpaid can be treated as a claim for the other (see p1084).

Example

Maxine should not have been receiving IS because her partner is in full-time paid work (see p751). However, she is caring for her aunt who is disabled and receiving AA. Maxine should ask the DWP to treat her claim for IS as a claim for CA and offset arrears of CA against the IS she has been overpaid.

If you were overpaid IS or income-based JSA because you had too much capital (see p1023), the overpayment is calculated taking account of the fact that, had you received no benefit, you would have had to use your capital to meet everyday expenses. For each 13-week period, the DWP assumes that your capital is reduced by the amount of overpaid benefit.[76] This is known as the 'diminishing capital' rule, and if your capital goes below the capital limit any subsequent overpayment will not be recoverable. However, if there are any increases or decreases in your actual capital during the overpayment period these are also taken into account.[77]

Example

Nina received IS of £100 a week for a period of 30 weeks. She has capital of £12,000. After 13 weeks, the rule means that she is treated as having spent 13 x 100 = £1,300 and her capital is deemed to be £10,700. After a further 13 weeks, her capital is deemed to be £9,400.

After 26 weeks of the period, Nina paid £5,000 towards credit card arrears after the credit card company threatened her with court proceedings. Provided that obtaining benefit was not a significant purpose for her making that payment (see the 'notional capital rule' on p1039), her capital is then deemed to be £4,400. The weekly overpayment will be lower from the end of week 26 because she is then entitled to full benefit minus a certain amount of 'tariff income' (see p977).

Although your capital is treated as reducing for these purposes, if you reclaim benefit your full capital counts (see p1042).

Challenging an overpayment decision

Whether or not you are the claimant, you can appeal if you:[78]

- do not agree that an overpayment has occurred; *or*
- disagree that an overpayment can be recovered; *or*
- disagree with the amount to be recovered.

You can also appeal if the decision concerns a payment from the *regulated* social fund (see Chapter 22). If you have been overpaid a payment from the *discretionary* social fund, you can instead seek a review by an SFO and then a further review by the social fund inspector (see pp1272 and 1277).

Do not pay back any of the money until your appeal has been decided. If you do so, and then successfully appeal the decision that the overpayment is recoverable from you, the DWP ought to reimburse you. If it does not do so, you may be entitled to recover the money in court proceedings because you paid the money on the basis of a mistake. You should write to the DWP (or, in child benefit or guardian's allowance cases, the Revenue) and explain that you do not intend to repay any of the money until your appeal has been decided. If the DWP is already making deductions from your benefit (see p535) you should ask it to stop doing this straight away.

The decision actually to recover an overpayment is discretionary, so you can ask that it is not recovered (see p1144).

2. **Late receipt of other income**

This section only applies to payments of:

- income support (IS); *and*
- income-based jobseeker's allowance (JSA); *and*
- pension credit (PC).

Sometimes you receive too much IS, income-based JSA or PC because money which is owing to you does not arrive on time. When you get your arrears, you must repay the IS, income-based JSA or PC which you would not have received if the other income had been paid on time.[79] This is to prevent a **'duplication of payment'**.

The rule applies to any income which affects the amount of your IS, income-based JSA or PC. This includes:

- other social security benefits (remember, though, that arrears of some benefits are treated as capital and ignored for 52 weeks – see Chapter 39);
- arrears of child support maintenance paid to you for the period from your application to the date it is assessed by the Child Support Agency;
- benefits paid by other European Economic Area member states;[80]
- Payments under the Financial Assistance Scheme.

The decision to make you pay back the money is a discretionary decision, and does not carry the right of appeal. You can still ask the DWP not to recover the overpayment, even though it can. See p1144 for further information about how to do this. See p1142 for how the overpayment can be recovered.

However, you are entitled to appeal about whether an overpayment has occurred, and how it has been calculated.[81]

3. Excess benefit credited to your account

Your benefit may be paid by direct credit transfer into a bank or other account – eg, a building society. If you are credited with too much benefit because of the direct credit transfer system itself, the excess benefit can be recovered in certain circumstances (see below).[82] This is the case even if the rules for recovery of ordinary overpayments do not apply.

Recovery under this rule can only happen if the overpayment was caused by the direct credit transfer system itself. Even though you may be paid by direct credit transfer, that does not automatically mean that the overpayment was caused by the system itself.

When excess benefit can be recovered

Excess benefit credited to your bank or other account can only be recovered if:[83]

- you were notified in writing, before you agreed for your benefit to be paid into a bank or other account, that excess benefit could be recovered; *and*
- it has been certified that you were paid excess benefit because of the direct credit transfer system itself.

If excess benefit cannot be recovered under the rules described above, it could still be recoverable under the 'ordinary' overpayment rules (see p1127) or those for recovery following late payment of income (see p1139).

Challenging decisions

You can appeal to a tribunal against a decision to recover excess benefit credited to your bank or other account.[84]

4. Mortgage interest paid to a lender

This section only applies to payments of:

- income support (IS); *and*
- income-based jobseeker's allowance (JSA); *and*
- pension credit (PC).

If you are getting help with your housing costs within your IS, income-based JSA or PC (see Chapter 36) your mortgage interest is usually paid directly to your lender. Any overpayment of mortgage interest which is paid directly to your lender must be sent back to the DWP by that lender if it arose because:[85]

- you ceased to be entitled to IS, income-based JSA or PC, but only if the DWP asks for repayment within four weeks of your entitlement ceasing; *or*
- the DWP failed to reduce your mortgage direct payments, even though you were entitled to less IS, income-based JSA or PC because there was a reduction in:
  - the amount of your outstanding loan; *or*
  - the standard interest rate (see p915); *or*
  - your actual mortgage interest rate. If you have a deferred interest mortgage, the relevant interest rate is the one that you are liable to pay, not the one being charged by your lender (which under the terms of such a mortgage you have to repay later on). If the Secretary of State pays the latter rate by mistake, there is no power to recover.[86]

In this case, your mortgage account should simply be corrected, but where you come off IS, income-based JSA or PC and interest is recovered, you will be in arrears unless you have started to make payments yourself.

In practice, the DWP often stops sending your lender your ongoing housing costs until it has recovered the overpayment, rather than ask a lender to return what was overpaid. However, the DWP should not do this if you are put into arrears as a result.[87] If you are put into arrears, you should seek advice immediately to avoid losing your home.

You can appeal to a tribunal (see p1218) if, for example, you think the rules do not apply to you, or if the DWP has not revised or superseded your IS, income-based JSA or PC properly (see p1217), or if you dispute the amount being recovered.[88] If you are not to blame for the overpayment, or would suffer hardship, you can also ask the Secretary of State to use her/his discretion not to ask your lender to repay the overpayment.

The DWP can also recover overpaid mortgage interest under the rules for 'ordinary' overpayments[89] described on p1127 – eg, if it fails to ask your lender to repay within four weeks of you coming off IS, income-based JSA or PC. If it tries to do this, you should make sure that those rules actually apply.

5. Recovery of overpaid benefit

Note: this section does not apply to recovery of overpayments of housing benefit (HB) or council tax benefit (CTB). For those, see pp1144 and 1156.

Methods of recovery

There are a number of different ways in which overpayments can be recovered.

Deductions from benefit

What deductions are allowed

If an overpayment of benefit must be repaid, it can be done through deductions from most of the benefits in this *Handbook*. However, no deduction can be made from guardian's allowance, child benefit, HB or CTB. Remember that recovery is discretionary (see p1144). Except in the case of income support (IS), income-based jobseeker's allowance (JSA) or pension credit (PC), deductions can only be made from the benefit of the person who has to repay the overpayment (see p1127).

For IS, income-based JSA and PC overpayments, as long as a couple are married or living together as husband and wife, the amount overpaid can be recovered from either partner's IS, income-based JSA or PC.[90]

If an overpayment of IS, income-based JSA or PC occurred because of a duplication of payment, the DWP normally deducts any overpaid IS, income-based JSA or PC from the arrears owing to you.[91] However, if it omits to do so you can still be asked to repay even if you have spent the money.

Maximum deductions from benefit

For some benefits, there is a maximum weekly amount that can be deducted.[92] These benefits are:

- IS;
- income-based JSA; *and*
- contribution-based JSA (but only if you would be entitled to income-based JSA at the same rate); *and*
- PC.

The following are the maximum weekly amounts that can be deducted from IS, PC and income-based JSA:

- £11.40 if you have agreed to pay a penalty (see p1172), admitted fraud or been found guilty of fraud; *or*
- £8.55 in any other case.

The deduction can be increased by half of any:[93]
- earnings subject to the £5, £10 or £15 disregard (see p963); *or*
- charitable income subject to a disregard (see p973); *or*
- benefit subject to a disregard (see p968).

If you have been overpaid *contribution-based* JSA but are not entitled to *income-based* JSA, the maximum deduction is one-third of the personal allowance for someone of your age (see p879).[94] However, this depends on whether you have any other deductions being made from your JSA.

Remember, the above amounts are maximum amounts. The DWP might be persuaded to deduct less, especially if you have other direct deductions made from your benefit.

If you have been overpaid a benefit other than IS, income-based JSA or PC, the rules limiting the maximum payment that can be deducted do not apply. The DWP usually wants to deduct one-third of your weekly benefit. However, you can argue that your rate of repayment should be less than this.

Overpaid benefit cannot be recovered by withholding tax credits.[95]

Other methods of recovery

Benefit may also be recovered by enforcement proceedings in the county courts in England or Wales or the sheriff's courts in Scotland.[96] The DWP (or, in child benefit or guardian's allowance cases, the Revenue) might use these proceedings – for example, if you have gone back to work and are no longer claiming benefit.

Once a decision of a decision maker, tribunal or commissioner is produced, the court has to enforce it unless you persuade the court to delay enforcement (what is known as a 'stay of execution') while you appeal against the relevant decision. If you are in this situation you should seek advice.

Overpayments can also be recovered from arrears of benefit you are owed, except arrears where the benefit has previously been suspended (see p1105).[97]

Recovery under common law

Sometimes the DWP claims to be entitled to recover overpayments of benefit not under the rules described in this chapter, but by relying instead on what it claims are its rights under what is known as the 'common law'. It remains to be seen if the Revenue will adopt a similar approach in child benefit or guardian's allowance cases.

Under 'common law' it is possible for someone to reclaim money through the courts from someone to whom it has been paid as a result of a mistake. If the DWP does retain its common law rights then it would be entitled to use this procedure to recover overpayments even where there has been no misrepresentation (see p1134) or failure to disclose (see p1131) and, indeed, even if the overpayment was entirely caused by its own mistake rather than yours.

If you are in this situation, you should seek urgent advice. You can argue two things:

- The rules about overpayments are in the Social Security Acts. These rules replace the 'common law' as far as overpayments of benefit are concerned.
- The Social Security Acts say it is a decision maker (see p1180) who must decide whether there has been an overpayment and that you have a right to appeal to a tribunal against the decision – on this basis, a court would have no jurisdiction to decide the point.

If the DWP or the Revenue threatens to use the 'common law' in your case, you should get advice from a solicitor immediately. Tactically the best course may be to apply for judicial review of the decision to proceed in this way (see p1253). Alternatively, you may simply wish to defend the action in the county court. There are a number of defences to this type of court action which would not be available to you if the DWP had used the rules described in this chapter. In the past, the DWP has tended to back down if challenged.

The discretion to recover

A tribunal cannot 'write off' part of the overpayment even if there are mitigating circumstances. It can only decide if it is recoverable and, if so, how much is repayable. In a case where you acted in all innocence and hardship is likely to be caused,you can apply to the DWP (or, in child benefit or guardian's allowance cases, the Revenue), which has the discretion to decide whether or not to recover the overpayment. You cannot appeal against a refusal to exercise this discretion in your favour. Your only possible legal recourse is judicial review (see p1253) but it may also help to involve your MP.

If you have been underpaid in the past but cannot now get arrears – for example, because of the rules on backdating (see p1085) – ask the DWP/Revenue to reduce the amount to be recovered by this sum if it will not write it off altogether.

6. Overpayments of housing benefit

Note: This section only applies to housing benefit (HB) or council tax benefit (CTB).

The rules about recovery of overpayments of CTB are generally the same as those for HB. The references given in this section cover both HB and CTB. See p1156 for the exceptions to the rules for CTB.

If you have been overpaid income support (IS) or income-based jobseeker's allowance (JSA) you may also have been overpaid HB. This is because your automatic passport to maximum HB ceases when you are no longer entitled to IS or income-based JSA. If you are in this situation, you should inform the local authority dealing with your HB claim.

To see from whom an overpayment can be recovered, see p1148.

What is an overpayment

An **'overpayment'** is an amount of HB which has been paid, and which the local authority later decides that you were not entitled to under the HB rules.[98] Being **'paid'** includes payment to you, your landlord or somebody else and also includes HB credited to your local authority rent account (see p226).[99]

Arrears of benefits and tax credits

In general, if you are paid arrears of income, including benefit income, then that is treated as if the income was paid at the time when it was due, and that may lead to a decision that you have been overpaid HB.[100] However, remember that arrears of some benefits are treated as capital and ignored for 52 weeks (see p968).

Similarly, arrears of child tax credit and working tax credit are treated as capital, although they are only ignored for 52 weeks if the arrears were paid as a result of a change in circumstances.[101]

So, where your arrears are treated as capital, unless the arrears mean that your capital is increased above a relevant capital limit (see p1023), you will not have been overpaid HB.

When an overpayment can be recovered

An overpayment can only be recovered if the local authority has taken the following five steps. It must:

- decide whether the overpayment is legally recoverable (see below);
- decide whether recovery of the overpayment should be sought, and if so from whom (see p1148);
- work out how much of the overpayment is repayable and for what period (see p1150);
- decide how the overpayment should be recovered and at what rate (see p1151);
- notify you of all the above decisions regarding the overpayment (see p1154) and give you an opportunity to request further information or a review (see p223).

Step one: is the overpayment legally recoverable?

Overpayments can have many causes, but the general rule is that an overpayment is recoverable.[102] However, certain types of overpayment are never recoverable and there are some which are only recoverable in certain circumstances (see below). An overpayment may be recoverable even if it was caused by an innocent mistake on your part or was somebody else's fault. Remember that in most cases, the local authority has the discretion to decide whether or not to recover an overpayment (see p1151).

For the differences for overpayments of CTB, see p1156.

Overpayments that are always recoverable

There are two types of overpayments which are always recoverable:

- an overpayment which is the result of the local authority overestimating your HB when making an interim payment (see p230). When the local authority decides how much HB you should actually get, it is obliged to recover any excess you were paid from future HB payments.[103] However, if you stop getting HB before the local authority decides, this rule does not apply. In this case, the overpayment can only be recovered under the other rules described in this section;
- where an overpayment of HB that relates to a future payment is credited to your rent account. In this case, the overpayment can be recovered even if it was made as a result of an 'official error' (see below).[104] Where an overpayment of HB caused by an official error has been credited to your account for a *past* period, see below to find out if it is recoverable.

Overpayments that are not always recoverable

Overpayments that do not fall into the above category are not recoverable if you can show that:[105]

- the overpayment was caused by an official error (see below); *and*
- no 'relevant person' caused the official error to be made (see p1147); *and*
- no relevant person could reasonably be expected to have realised that an overpayment was being made (see p1148).

An **'official error'** is defined as a mistake, whether in the form of an act or omission, by:

- the appropriate authority; *or*
- an officer of the authority; *or*
- a person acting for that authority. This would include a person employed by a private organisation providing services to the local authority or to a ONE office; *or*
- an officer of the DWP or the Revenue acting as such.[106]

It therefore includes:

- a mistake made by the local authority in calculating your entitlement;
- a failure by the local authority to reduce your HB when you inform it of a change of circumstances. It is always best to notify changes in writing and keep

a copy. If you notify the local authority by telephone there may be a dispute as to whether you actually called or about what you said. In such disputes, what you say should not be rejected solely on the evidence of local authority recording procedures, unless it is accepted that those procedures are infallible;[107]

- a failure by an officer of another department of the local authority, such as a social worker, to pass on details of a change of circumstances, where s/he has promised to do so. This is an official error because the definition does not require the mistake to be made by an officer in the department handling HB. A mistake by any local authority officer will be an official error if it results in an overpayment;
- similar mistakes by somebody carrying out functions relating to HB on behalf of the local authority, for example a private agency to whom work has been contracted;
- a mistake made by the DWP in calculating your entitlement to IS or income-based JSA which results in an incorrect calculation of your entitlement to HB – however, it is not an official error for the local authority to fail to check with the DWP about the correctness of your IS or income-based JSA entitlement, unless it has information that shows the award is wrong or fraudulent;[108]
- a failure by the DWP to pass on information to the local authority;[109]
- wrong advice given to you by an officer of the local authority, the DWP or the Revenue, provided that s/he is acting as an officer at the time (rather than, say, as a friend giving you informal advice).

The list above is not exhaustive. The official error does not have to be the sole cause of the overpayment. However, even if an official error has occurred, if the primary cause of the overpayment was something that you did or failed to do, the overpayment is likely to be recoverable.[110]

No relevant person caused the official error

An official error does not prevent the overpayment being recoverable if the error was partially or wholly caused by a 'relevant person'. You are a relevant person if you are:

- the HB claimant; *or*
- a person acting on the HB claimant's behalf, whether because s/he is unable to deal with her/his affairs or because s/he has asked the authority in writing to deal with you on her/his behalf (see p210); *or*
- a person to whom the payment was made, which would include a different person acting on the HB claimant's behalf or a landlord.

The relevant person must have amended the *error*, not the overpayment.[111]

The local authority might say it only needs to show that *any* relevant person caused the official error but it does not have to pursue that person for the overpayment.[112] If the local authority tries to recover an overpayment from you but it was another person who caused the official error, you should argue that the structure of the rules means that recovery must be sought from the person causing the official error. You could also argue that the authority should exercise its discretion to recover from that person instead (see below). See p1149 for information about who overpayments can be recovered from.

No relevant person realised that an overpayment was being made

Even if the official error was not caused by a relevant person, an overpayment is still recoverable if any relevant person (see p1147) knew, or ought reasonably to have known, that an overpayment had been made. The test is whether or not you could reasonably be expected to *know* (not merely suspect) that an overpayment had occured. Much depends on what could reasonably have been expected of you given the information available to you, in particular the extent to which the local authority has advised you about the scheme or your duties and obligations, particularly about your duty to notify changes of circumstances.[113] You should always argue that, as a claimant, you cannot be expected to know the intricacies of the HB rules and that, unless it was glaringly obvious that a change of circumstances would reduce your HB, you should be given the benefit of the doubt.

If you or some other 'relevant person' could only have realised that there was an overpayment at some point during the period of the overpayment, the overpayment is only recoverable from that date.

Step two: should the overpayment be recovered?

The local authority's discretion

Apart from certain interim payments of HB on account (see p230), the local authority has a **discretion** whether to recover an overpayment.[114] Some recover all recoverable overpayments and others only recover those caused by claimant error.

A policy of always recovering recoverable overpayments could be challenged by judicial review (see p1253).

If you have been overpaid and this was either not your fault or the result of a genuine mistake or oversight on your part, you should consider challenging the decision either by asking for a revision (see Chapter 43) or making an appeal (see Chapter 44). Remember that even if the decision does prove to be recoverable from you, you can still ask the local authority not to recover the overpayment, especially if recovery would cause you hardship.

If the overpayment was caused by someone else, you could suggest that recovery is made from her/him (but where this is your landlord, see p1155).

You may be asked to repay a non-recoverable overpayment on a voluntary basis. You are under no legal obligation to do so.

From whom the overpayment can be recovered

The general rule is that a recoverable overpayment can be required to be paid back by the person to whom it was paid.[115] This may include your landlord (see below).

As well as or instead of that person, an overpayment can be recovered from:[116]

- you (ie, the claimant) or your partner (but see below); *and*
- the person who misrepresented or failed to disclose a material fact (see p1131) where this caused the overpayment, and they were acting for the claimant or any other person who has been paid.

In the event of the death of the person from whom recovery is being sought, local authorities may consider recovering any outstanding overpayment from that person's estate.[117]

For the differences for overpayments of CTB, see p1156.

Recovery from your landlord

Where a recoverable overpayment has been paid to your landlord, then in general s/he can be required to pay it back.

However, the local authority can decide to require you to pay it back instead or as well (see below). You and your landlord can appeal against the decision to recover the overpayment, but only about things like whether an overpayment has actually occurred, if it is an overpayment recoverable from either of you or if there is some legal error in the decision, such as not taking all the relevant evidence into account. You cannot appeal about the mere fact that it has decided to recover from you, or from you rather than the other person.[118]

Also, the overpayment cannot be recovered from your landlord if:[119]

- s/he was receiving the payment; *and*
- s/he wrote to the local authority notifying it of the possible overpayment; *and*
- it appears to the local authority that either there are grounds for action to be taken for fraud (see p1166) or that the overpayment was caused by a deliberate failure to report a relevant change of circumstances; *and*
- s/he has not colluded with you (ie, the claimant) or otherwise contributed to the overpayment.

Recovery from you

Where a recoverable overpayment has been paid to you, then you can be required to pay it back. In addition, the rules say that the local authority can require you to repay a recoverable overpayment instead of or as well as another person, even where it was not paid to you.[120] Note that this might include cases where the overpayment was paid to your landlord (see above).

However, a recent case[121] has indicated that, regarding overpayments that occurred before 1 October 2001, it is unlawful to require you to repay an overpayment where it was not paid to you *unless* you had failed to disclose a material fact, or had misrepresented a material fact (see p1130 for what that means). Arguably, this also applies to overpayments that occured on or after 1 October 2001. If you are affected, you should consider making an appeal including, if necessary, a late appeal in order to avoid the 'anti-test case' rule (see Chapter 44 for appeals and p1211 for the anti-test case rule) . However the law on all these points is not yet settled. If necessary, seek advice and see CPAG's *Welfare Rights Bulletin* for updates.

Step three: how much is repayable and for what period?

Check the amount of an overpayment to ensure the local authority has calculated it correctly. Ask for more information if you need it. The local authority should distinguish between parts of an overpayment that are recoverable and those which are not. To calculate the amount of the overpayment, you should:

- determine the dates between which you have been paid too much benefit;
- identify the period or periods over which the local authority is entitled to recover;
- work out the total amount of HB you were paid over the period(s) during which the local authority can recover;
- work out the correct amount of HB you should have received during the period(s) of recovery. If an overpayment is discovered, the local authority must award you whatever amount of HB you would have received if it was aware of your true circumstances (this applies even where the overpayment occured before the rules were changed in October 2000);[122]
- deduct the HB you should have been paid from what you were paid.[123]

The authority is not allowed to add any interest charges to the amount of the overpayment.[124]

For the differences for overpayments of CTB, see p1156.

Deductions from the overpayment

Besides any amount of HB which you should have been paid (see above), the local authority must deduct other amounts from the overpayment (this is known as **'offsetting'**). These are:

- extra rent paid into your rent account. If you have been getting HB over the overpayment period and, for some reason, have paid more into your rent account than you should have paid according to your original (incorrect) benefit assessment, the extra rent you paid can be deducted from any overpayment made during that period. The local authority might not apply this rule where you paid extra rent to repay rent arrears;[125]
- reductions under the 'diminishing capital rule' (see below).

You are not entitled to have other amounts deducted.

If you were overpaid HB because you had too much capital, the overpayment is calculated taking into account the fact that had you received no HB, you would have used your capital. This is known as the **'diminishing capital rule'**. This only applies if:[126]

- you were overpaid for more than 13 weeks; *and either*
- the overpayment was caused by a 'misrepresentation' of, or a 'failure to disclose', the amount of your capital (see p1130 for the meaning of 'misrepresentation' and 'failure to disclose'); *or*
- the overpayment was caused by an error (other than an 'official error' – see p1146) about your capital (or that of a member of your family – see p809).

For each 13-week period, the local authority assumes that your capital is reduced by the amount of overpaid HB.[127] However, although your capital is treated as reducing for these purposes, if you reclaim benefit your full capital counts (see p1026).

Step four: how should the overpayment be recovered and at what rate?

A local authority can decide how much of a recoverable overpayment it will actually recover. It can ask for the whole amount at once or recover it by instalments. If agreement cannot be reached, there are several different ways in which a local authority can seek to recover an overpayment. When an overpayment is recovered from your landlord, you should take careful note of how that affects your liability to pay rent (see p1155). Overpayments of HB can be recovered:

- from payments of HB (see below);
- from other benefits (see p1152);
- for local authority tenants only, by adjusting your rent account (see p1153);
- through the courts (see p1153).

You should check that the methods used by the authority and the rates of recovery are consistent between groups of claimants. For example, council tenants should not be required to repay overpayments in a lump sum (ie, the whole overpayment is debited to their account) where private tenants can repay by instalment (eg, by weekly deductions made to their HB).

For the differences for overpayments of CTB, see p1156.

Recovery from payments of housing benefit

A local authority is entitled to recover an overpayment by deducting sums from HB payable to any person from whom an overpayment can be recovered (see p1149).[128] As well as yourself, this could be your partner (see p1152) or your landlord (see p1152). Deductions can be made from both future payments of HB and any arrears of HB that are owing.

Recovery from your partner

If you were overpaid HB while you were a claimant, the local authority may recover an overpayment from payments of HB made to your partner but only if:[129]

- the overpayment was made to you, rather than to your landlord or someone acting on your behalf; *and*
- you and your partner were living in the same household (see p812) *both* at the time of the overpayment *and* when the deduction is made. You must have been living together for the whole period of the overpayment, not just for part of it.

Recovery from a landlord

If you have been overpaid HB, the local authority may recover the overpayment from:

- HB paid to your landlord personally, as a claimant;[130]
- HB paid directly to your landlord on your behalf (if the overpayment was paid to her/him on your behalf).[131] The notification of the overpayment (see p1154) should make it clear from whom the authority is recovering;
- HB paid directly to your landlord on behalf of claimants other than you (even if the overpayment was paid to her/him on your behalf).[132]

When HB is recovered from a landlord in this way, there are special rules as to how this affects your liability to pay rent (see p1155).

The rate of recovery

The same weekly rates apply as those for IS and income-based JSA (see p1142).[133] They apply both to any arrears owed to you (eg, payments which have been withheld pending an investigation) and to future entitlement. However, you may argue that the rate will cause you hardship and in your particular circumstances a lesser amount should be recovered. You should also ask the local authority to take into account any other debts, financial commitments or health problems you may have.[134] Complain if the rate of recovery is causing you hardship and suggest an amount you think you can afford.

Recovery from other benefits

The local authority can ask the DWP to recover an overpayment by making deductions from most of the benefits in this *Handbook*. However, deductions cannot be made from child benefit or guardian's allowance. You can argue that deductions to recover an overpayment of HB cannot be made from incapacity benefit.[135] Overpayments of HB cannot be recovered by deductions from CTB (and vice versa).[136]

An overpayment can also be recovered from benefits paid to your landlord personally.[137]

Deductions can only be made if:[138]

- a recoverable overpayment has been made as a result of a misrepresentation or failure to disclose (see p1130) a material fact by you or on your behalf or by or on behalf of some other person to whom HB has been paid; *and*
- the local authority is unable to recover that overpayment from any HB entitlement; *and*
- the person who misrepresented or failed to disclose is receiving enough of at least one of the relevant benefits to allow deductions to be made.

There are no rules limiting the maximum amount that can be deducted. However, you can argue that your rate of repayment should be reasonable. If you are on IS or income-based JSA, you should argue that the weekly maximums for those benefits should apply (see p1142). You should make representations to the DWP if deductions cause hardship.

If deductions stop because you are no longer entitled to a particular benefit, or the amount to which you are entitled is insufficient for deductions to be made, the DWP notifies the local authority which, once again, becomes responsible for any further recovery action.

Adjustment of a rent account

If you are a local authority tenant, the local authority can recover an overpayment by adding it as a debt to your rent account. If a local authority recovers overpaid HB by adjusting your rent account, the overpayment should be separately identified and you should be informed that the amount being recovered does not represent rent arrears.[139]

If the local authority is trying to seek possession of your home on the grounds of rent arrears, you should seek advice. It should not be able to say you owe it rent arrears if you have only been overpaid HB. Local authorities are reminded in DWP guidance that overpayments of HB in respect of their own tenants are not rent arrears and should not be treated as such.[140]

An overpayment cannot be recovered in this way if you have a private or housing association landlord. However, an overpayment can be recovered from your landlord (see p1152). If the local authority recovers from your landlord, you might count as being in rent arrears (see p1134).

Court action

If a local authority cannot use any of the methods of recovery above, and you cannot agree on repayments, it can try to recover the money you owe through the county court (sheriff's court in Scotland) if it thinks you could afford to make repayments. You have one month to ask for a revision or appeal against a decision that an overpayment is recoverable. This should be borne in mind when local authorities are deciding when to start proceedings.

A local authority should not use court proceedings to recover an overpayment if it has not followed the correct procedure (see p1145). The correct procedure has not been followed if, for example, the local authority has not issued the correct notification (see below).[141]

An authority may use one of two means of recovering through the courts. It can:

- sue you for the debt created by the overpayment.[142] If the correct procedure (see p1145) has not been followed, you can use this as a defence to the authority's claim.[143] You may also be able to make a compensation claim in certain circumstances (see p1145). However, you are not allowed to say that you should have received more HB because you must seek a review instead;[144]
- use the special rules to register the overpayment as a debt which can then be recovered using a court procedure.[145] Seek advice if you think the local authority is not entitled to do this.

If the local authority is successful in using court proceedings against you, you may have to pay legal costs and interest as well as the overpayment. Remember that court procedures often require you to take action within a very short period of time. If the local authority is threatening to use court proceedings, seek urgent advice.

Step five: notification of overpayments

If the local authority decides that a recoverable overpayment has occurred, it must write to the person from whom recovery is being sought (see p1149) – within 14 days, if possible – and notify her/him accordingly.[146] This notification must state:[147]

- the fact that there is an overpayment which is legally recoverable;
- the reason why there is a recoverable overpayment;
- the amount of the recoverable overpayment;
- how the amount of the overpayment was calculated;
- the benefit weeks to which the overpayment relates;
- if recovery is to be made from future benefit, how much the deduction will be;
- if recovery is to be made from your landlord by deduction from direct payments of HB of a claimant other than you (if you were overpaid – see p1152), your identity and the claimant whose HB will be deducted from;[148]
- that you have a right to ask for a further written explanation of any of the decisions the local authority has made regarding the overpayment, how you can do this and the time limit for doing so;
- that you have a right to ask the local authority to reconsider any of the decisions it has made regarding the overpayment, how you can do this and the time limit for doing so.

It may also include any other relevant matters.

If you write and ask the local authority for a more detailed written explanation of any of the decisions it has made regarding an overpayment, it must send you this within 14 days or, if this is not reasonably practicable, as soon as possible after that.[149]

If a notification sent to you does not contain the matters set out on p1154, then it will only be valid if the omissions do not cause you any prejudice.[150] If, for example, it does not set out your rights to seek a revision so that you do not do so until it is too late, you will have been prejudiced and so can argue that the overpayment is not recoverable. If you are a landlord from whom overpayments are being recovered and you receive a large number of overpayment notices, the extra administration involved in dealing with defective notices and the confusion it causes you will be sufficient prejudice.[151]

If your local authority does not give proper notification, you should write and point out that the decision to recover the overpayment is not valid until you are given proper notification. No recovery should be sought until after you have been notified and have had a chance to discuss your case or apply for a revision.[152]

The effect of recovery from your landlord

If you are a private or housing association tenant, an overpayment of HB recovered from your landlord (see p1152) could leave your landlord claiming money from you. This could put you in difficulty, particularly if the landlord claims that you are in arrears of rent as a result and seeks possession of your home.

The legal effect of recovery of an overpayment from a landlord has varied from time to time. Whether you are put in rent arrears when an overpayment is recorded depends on when the overpayment was made (see below).

Whether HB was paid directly to your landlord or not, s/he may still try to claim that even if you owe no rent, you nevertheless owe a debt under common law, which is probably not correct. If s/he threatens to sue you, seek advice straight away.

If you are a local authority tenant, these rules do not apply. However, the local authority can recover an overpayment of HB by making deductions from your rent account. To see how these rules might affect you, see p1152.

If you were overpaid HB after 4 November 1997 and HB was paid directly to your landlord, the following rules apply:

- Where you are overpaid, and the local authority recovers the overpayment from your landlord by making deductions from direct payments of **other tenants' HB** (see p1151), the other tenants are treated as having paid the amount of the deduction towards their rent.[153]
- Where you are overpaid, and the local authority recovers the overpayment from your landlord by making deductions from direct payments of **your HB**, you are treated as having paid the amount of the deduction towards your rent where your landlord is convicted of an offence or agrees to pay a penalty (see p1172) in relation to that overpayment.[154]

If the local authority decides to recover under this rule, it must notify both your landlord and you that you are to be treated as having paid your rent.[155]

In these situations, it is clear that your landlord cannot claim that you are in arrears of rent. It is also much easier to argue that your landlord cannot sue you under common law for a debt (see p1155).

The law does not make clear what happens in other cases where deductions are made from your HB. If you are in this position, you could try to argue that the rules do not say what happens in your case, and so the same rules apply as before the law was introduced. If this is right, you should be treated as having paid your rent. However, because there is a risk of you losing your home if your landlord were to seek possession, you should seek advice *immediately*.

If you were overpaid HB before 4 November 1997, see the different rules set out on pp1119-1120 of the *Welfare Benefits Handbook 2000/01* and seek advice.

Challenging an overpayment decision

You can seek a revision or appeal (see Chapters 43 and 44) if you want to do any or all of the following:
- dispute the decision that you have been overpaid;
- dispute the amount of the overpayment;
- dispute the decision that it is a recoverable overpayment.

Note, however, that if it is a recoverable overpayment, then you cannot appeal against the decision actually to recover it from you – eg, instead of or as well as your landlord (see p1149).

Do not pay any of the money back until your challenge has been dealt with. Local authorities have guidance that overpayments should not be recovered while under appeal.[156] If the local authority is already making deductions from your HB (see p1150) or deductions are being made from your other benefits (see p1152) you should ask it to stop this straight away.

If the local authority thinks an overpayment was made due to fraud , as well as recovering the overpayment it can prosecute you or offer you the option of paying a penalty as an alternative to going to court. You should seek advice before agreeing to pay. See Chapter 42 for further information.

7. Overpayments of council tax benefit

An overpayment of council tax benefit (CTB) is called 'excess benefit'.[157] The rules about recovery are the same as for housing benefit (HB) (see p1144), with the following exceptions.

Is the overpayment recoverable?

The criteria for when an overpayment is recoverable are the same as for HB (see p1144), except that the following categories of overpayments are always recoverable:

- an overpayment of CTB credited to your council tax account that relates to a future period, even if it was made as a result of an 'official error' (see p1146);[158]
- an overpayment which has arisen because you were paid CTB, but then your council tax liability was reduced because of a disability reduction, discount, transitional relief or charge-capping (see CPAG's *Council Tax Handbook*);[159]
- an overpayment that results from the local authority changing the levels of council tax for the financial year.[160]

The amount of the overpayment

The amount overpaid is the difference between what you were actually paid and what you should have received. However, there are two possible variations of what should have been paid – either a reduced amount of main CTB (see p110), or a second adult rebate (see p110) if you are eligible for this and it would have been higher than the revised amount of main CTB.

When assessing the amount overpaid, the local authority should do both calculations (see pp112 and 118) and can only recover the balance between the higher of the two figures and the amount which you in fact received. It is always worth checking that the second adult rebate calculation has been done and that the correct amount is being recovered.

From whom benefit can be recovered

Recovery of a CTB overpayment is always from the CTB claimant or the person to whom benefit was paid – eg, your partner or an appointee. There can be no recovery from any other person, even if s/he caused the overpayment.[161]

CTB is recoverable by the same methods as HB (see p1150) with the following exceptions:

- the overpayment can be recovered by increasing your outstanding council tax liability;[162]
- there are no limits for the maximum amount of CTB that can be recovered in each week;[163]
- the local authority cannot use the special court procedures for recovering the overpayment (see p1153). If it wishes to recover through the court, it must sue you instead. It may not start proceedings for 21 days after it notifies you of the amount due.[164]

Notes

1. Ordinary overpayments of benefits

1 paras 8 and 9 *Social Fund Bulletin* 17/98, 9 September 1998
2 *Plewa v CAO* [1995] 1 AC 248 (HL)
3 s71(3) SSAA 1992
4 CIS/4348/2003, which says that overpayments are actually recoverable because of a breach by a claimant of reg 32 SS(C&P) Regs. The decision is under appeal as *B v Secretary of State for Work and Pensions.*
5 CIS/2178/2001. This Tribunal of Commissioners' decision was intended to resolve the conflict between the earlier CIS/332/1993 and R(IS) 5/2000, and preferred the latter.
6 CA/1014/1999; CSDLA/1282/2001
7 *Secretary of State for Social Services v Solly* [1974] 3 All ER 922; R(SB) 21/82
8 CIS/1423/1997
9 s71 SSAA 1992
10 R(SB) 34/83
11 s71(5A) SSAA 1992
12 R(SB) 7/91
13 CSIS/45/1990
14 R(SB) 7/91
15 s71A SSAA 1992
16 Sch 2 para 1 SSA 1998
17 s38(1)(b) SSA 1998
18 Reg 32 SS(C&P) Regs
19 *Page and Davis v CAO, The Times*, 4 July 1991 (CA)
20 CSB/1006/1985
21 CDLA/5803/1999
22 R(S) 4/86; R(I) 3/75
23 R(SB) 15/87
24 R(SB) 15/87; *Hinchy v Secretary of State for Work and Pensions*, 3 March 2005 (HL)
25 CIS/4848/2002; *Hinchy v Secretary of State for Work and Pensions*, 3 March 2005 (HL)
26 Reg 23(5) CB&GA (Admin) Regs
27 Reg 32(1B) SS(C&P) Regs requires written notification. For the old test, see CSB/688/1982; R(SB) 12/84; R(SB) 20/84; R(SB) 40/84
28 R(SB) 18/85
29 CWSB/2/1985
30 CSB/347/1983; R(SB) 10/85
31 R(SB) 33/85; CSB/1195/1984
32 R(SB) 15/87
33 CDLA/6336/1999
34 R(SB) 15/87
35 R(SB) 54/83
36 CSB/393/1985
37 CIS/4348/2003, upheld by the Court of Appeal as *B v Secretary of State for Work and Pensions*
38 CDLA/1823/2004
39 R(SB) 21/82
40 R(SB) 54/83; CSB/296/1985
41 CG/190/1999
42 R(SB) 21/82
43 This part of the test is in reg 32(1B) SS (C&P) Regs, and would appear to be common ground between CIS/4348/2003 and the old test as set out in R(SB) 21/82
44 R(SB) 21/82.
45 R(SB) 21/82; R(SB) 28/83; R(SB) 54/83; R(A) 1/95
46 R(SB) 15/87
47 CSB/510/1987; CIS/545/1992
48 R(G) 2/72
49 R(U) 6/70; CP/20/1990
50 CIS/1769/1999, applying the approach set out in CSB/957/1987. This approach is not applied in some other decisions - eg, R(A) 1/95 and CIS/757/1994. See *Welfare Rights Bulletin* 175, p10, for a full discussion.
51 CIS/12032/1996
52 CIS/5117/1998
53 R(SB) 9/85
54 *Jones and Sharples v CAO* [1994] 1 All ER 225 (CA); R(SB) 9/85
55 R(SB) 18/85
56 R(SB) 2/91
57 R(SB) 3/90
58 *Sheriff v CAO, The Times*, 10 May 1995 (CA), reported as R(IS) 14/96
59 CG/4494/1999
60 *Jones and Sharples v CAO* [1994] 1 All ER 225 (CA); *Franklin v CAO, The Times*, 29 December 1995 (CA); CIS/674/1994; CIS/583/1994
61 CIS/674/1994

62 This was an obiter comment by the Court of Appeal in *Hinchy v Secretary of State for Work and Pensions* [2003] EWCA Civ 138 (CA). The point was not approved or disapproved by the further decision in *Hinchy v Secretary of State for Work and Pensions*, 3 March 2005 (HL).
63 *Franklin v CAO, The Times*, 29 December 1995 (CA)
64 CIS/583/1994
65 CDLA/6336/1999
66 CIS/159/1990; CS/11700/1996; CSIS/7/1994; CG/5631/1999
67 *Duggan v CAO*, The Times, 18 December 1989 (CA); CG/662/1998; CG/4494/1999; Hinchy v Secretary of State for Work and Pensions [2003] EWCA Civ 138 (CA)
68 This was an obiter comment by the Court of Appeal in *Hinchy v Secretary of State for Work and Pensions* [2003] EWCA Civ 138 (CA). It was not approved or disapproved by the House of Lords in *Hinchy v Secretary of State for Work and Pensions*, 3 March 2005 (HL)
69 CIS/222/1991
70 R(SB) 20/84; R(SB) 24/87
71 Reg 43 CB&GA(Admin) Regs
72 Reg 13 SS(PAOR) Regs
73 CP/5257/1999
74 R(IS) 5/92
75 *Commock v CAO*, reported as an appendix to R(SB) 6/90; CSIS/8/1995
76 Reg 14 SS(PAOR) Regs
77 CIS/5825/1999
78 s12 SSA 1998

2. **Late receipt of other income**
79 s74 SSAA 1992
80 R(SB) 3/91
81 See for example, the appeals in R(SB) 28/85 and R(IS) 6/02

3. **Excess benefit credited to your account**
82 s71(4) and (5) SSAA 1992 and reg 11 SS(PAOR) Regs; reg 35 CB&GA(Admin) Regs
83 Reg 11 SS(PAOR) Regs; reg 35 CB&GA(Admin) Regs
84 Sch 2 para 20(d) SS&CS(DA) Regs

4. **Mortgage interest paid to a lender**
85 Sch 9A para 11 SS(C&P) Regs
86 *R v Secretary of State for Social Security ex parte Craigie* [2000] (CA)
87 *R v Secretary of State for Social Security ex parte Golding* [1996] (CA)
88 CIS/5206/1995
89 CIS/5206/1995

5. **Recovery of overpaid benefit**
90 Reg 17 SS(PAOR) Regs
91 s74(2)(b) SSAA 1992
92 Reg 16(4), (4A), (5) and (6) SS(PAOR) Regs
93 Reg 16(6) SS(PAOR) Regs
94 Reg 16(5A) SS(PAOR) Regs
95 There is no provision allowing this
96 s71(10) SSAA 1992
97 Reg 16(3) SS(PAOR) Regs

6. **Overpayments of housing benefit**
98 **HB** Reg 98 HB Regs
CTB Reg 83 CTB Regs
99 **HB** Reg 98 HB Regs
CTB Reg 83 CTB Regs
100 **HB** Reg 68(7) HB Regs
CTB Reg 59(9) CTB Regs
101 **HB** Reg 40(9) HB Regs
CTB Reg 31(9) CTB Regs
102 **HB** Reg 99(1) HB Regs
CTB Reg 84(1) CTB Regs
103 Reg 91(3) HB Regs
104 Reg 99(4) HB Regs
105 **HB** Reg 99(2) HB Regs
CTB Reg 84(2) CTB Regs
106 **HB** Reg 99(3) HB Regs
CTB Reg 84(3) CTB Regs
107 CH/4065/2001
108 CH/571/2003. See also CH/5485/2002, which makes a similar finding.
109 CH/939/2004; see also *R on the application of Sier v Cambridge CC* [2001], unreported (QBD), as upheld by the Court of Appeal [2001] EWCA 1523, 8 October 2001
110 *Duggan v CAO, The Times*, 18 December 1989 (CA); *R on the application of Sier v Cambridge CC* [2001], unreported (QBD), as upheld by the Court of Appeal [2001] EWCA 1523, 8 October 2001; CH/571/2003
111 *R on the application of Sier v Cambridge CC* [2001] (QBD), as upheld by the Court of Appeal, [2001] EWCA 1523, 8 October 2001
112 *Warwick DC v Freeman* [1994] 27 HLR 616 (CA)
113 *R v Liverpool City Council ex parte Griffiths* [1990] 22 HLR 312; CH/2554/2002
114 **HB** s75(1) SSAA 1992
CTB Reg 85 CTB Regs
115 s75(3)(a) SSAA 1992
116 **HB** Reg 101 HB Regs
CTB Reg 86 CTB Regs

117 paras A7.491 GM
118 CH/5216/2001; CH/841/2002; CH/3880/2002
119 Reg 101(1) HB Regs
120 Reg 101(2) HB Regs
121 CH/5216/2001, CH/841/2002 and CH/3880/2002
122 **HB** Reg 104 HB Regs
CTB Reg 90 CTB Regs
Both Adan v London Borough of Hounslow and Secretary of State for Work and Pensions [2004] EWCA Civ 101, 19 February 2004, unreported (CA)
123 **HB** Reg 104(1) HB Regs
CTB Reg 90(1) CTB Regs
124 *R v Kensington and Chelsea RBC ex parte Brandt* [1995] 28 HLR 528 at 537 (QBD)
125 **HB** Reg 104(3) HB Regs
CTB Reg 90(3) CTB Regs
126 **HB** Reg 103 HB Regs
CTB Reg 89(1) CTB Regs
127 **HB** Reg 103(1)(a) and (b) HB Regs
CTB Reg 89(1)(a) and (b) CTB Regs
128 **HB** s75 SSAA 1992; reg 102 HB Regs
CTB s75 SSAA 1992; reg 87(2)(a) CTB Regs
129 **HB** Reg 101(2) HB Regs
CTB Reg 86(2) CTB Regs
130 s75(5)(a) SSAA 1992; reg 2(2)(a) HB(RO) Regs
131 s75(5)(b) SSAA 1992; reg 2(3) HB(RO) Regs
132 s75(5)(c) SSAA 1992; reg 2(3) HB(RO) Regs
133 Reg 102 HB Regs; HB/CTB Circular A42/2000
134 para A7.390 GM
135 Reg 105(1)(a) HB Regs; incapacity benefit is not a benefit payable under the SSA 1975
136 **HB** Reg 105 HB Regs
CTB Reg 91 CTB Regs
137 Reg 2(4) HB(RO) Regs
138 **HB** Regs 102 and 105 HB Regs
CTB Regs 87(3) and 91 CTB Regs
139 *R v Haringey LBC ex parte Azad Ayub* [1992] 25 HLR 566 (QBD)
140 paras A7.360 GM
141 *Warwick DC v Freeman* [1994] 27 HLR 616 (CA)
142 Reg 88 CTB Regs; para A7.361 GM
143 *Warwick DC v Freeman* [1994] 27 HLR 616 (CA)
144 *Plymouth CC v Gigg* [1997] 30 HLR 284 (CA)
145 s75(7) SSAA 1992
146 **HB** Reg 77(1)(b) HB Regs
CTB Reg 67(1)(b) CTB Regs
147 **HB** Sch 6 paras 2, 3, 6 and 14 HB Regs; para A7.222 GM
CTB Sch 6 paras 2, 3, 6 and 16 CTB Regs
148 Reg 4(4) HB(RO) Regs
149 **HB** Reg 77(4) and (5) HB Regs
CTB Reg 67(2) and (3) CTB Regs
150 *Haringey LBC v Awaritefe* [1999] 32 HLR 517 (CA)
151 *R v Thanet DC ex parte Warren Court Hotels Ltd* [2000] 33 HLR 32 (QBD)
152 para A7.230-233 GM
153 s75(6) SSAA 1992
154 s75(6) SSAA 1992; reg 3(1) and (2) HB(RO) Regs
155 Reg 3(3) HB(RO) Regs
156 HB/CTB Overpayments Guide, paras 4.07 and 6.25

7. **Overpayments of council tax benefit**
157 Reg 83 CTB Regs
158 Reg 84(5) CTB Regs
159 Regs 83(a) and 84(4) CTB Regs
160 Regs 83(a) and 84(4) CTB Regs
161 Reg 86(1) CTB Regs
162 Reg 87(2)(b) CTB Regs
163 HB/CTB Circular A42/2000
164 Reg 88 CTB Regs

Chapter 42

Fraud and benefits

This chapter covers the rules about fraud. It contains:

Child benefit and guardian's allowance

The Revenue makes decisions about child benefit and guardian's allowance as well as tax credits. However, references to the Revenue in this chapter only apply to decisions about child benefit and guardian's allowance. For information about tax credit and fraud, see Chapter 57.

When you claim benefit you must give correct and complete information to the DWP, the Revenue or local authority. You might commit an offence if you deliberately mislead them. You are also required to report changes in your circumstances that could affect your entitlement to benefit. You might commit an offence if you fail to notify the relevant office of such changes promptly, or cause or allow another person to fail to do so. We refer to such offences as 'fraud' in this chapter.

If the DWP, the Revenue or the local authority believe you have committed fraud:

- you may be at risk of being prosecuted (see p1166);
- your benefit could be reduced or removed if you are prosecuted for committing an offence twice within a three-year period (see p1169);
- you might be given the option of paying a penalty instead of being taken to court (see p1172);
- for benefits dealt with by the DWP you may be given the option of accepting a formal caution (see p1174).

If you are accused of fraud you should seek urgent advice before taking any action or making any statements.

This chapter does *not* cover:
- child tax credit or working tax credit (for these, see Chapter 57); *or*
- statutory sick pay, statutory maternity pay, statutory paternity pay or statutory adoption pay; *or*
- the benefits in Chapter 9.

1. Investigation of claims

The Department for Work and Pensions (DWP), the Revenue or local authority may start an investigation into your benefit claim for a variety of reasons. It does not have to tell you straight away about the enquiries it is making. It normally waits until it has gathered more information and then asks you to attend an interview to explain matters.

Powers to seek information

Local authorities, the Revenue and the DWP have powers to gather a wide variety of information from other public bodies for the purposes of:
- the prevention, detection, investigation or prosecution of social security offences;
- checking the accuracy of information relating to benefits, contributions or national insurance numbers;
- amending or supplementing such information.

The DWP and the Revenue can seek information from:
- tax authorities;[1]
- government departments (this provision relates in particular to issues about passports, immigration, emigration, nationality and prisoners);[2]
- the registration service, which is under an additional duty to report particulars of deaths to the Secretary of State for social security purposes;[3]
- local authorities.[4]

Local authorities have no specific powers to seek information from the above bodies themselves but are entitled to any information that the DWP or the Revenue hold.[5]

Local authorities, the Revenue and the DWP can seek information about redirected post and have undelivered social security post returned to them.[6]

All information gathered is confidential to the bodies concerned with administration of benefit, including private companies contracted to carry out such functions. Unauthorised disclosure of such information is a criminal offence.[7]

The **Data Protection Act 1998** restricts the use of accessible personal data held on computer or in a relevant filing system in written form. The DWP has a code of practice for data matching which applies to all information held or sought by it.[8] If local authorities, the Revenue or the DWP make a request for information based on either the information-seeking provisions on p1162, or the investigative powers below, which is inappropriate or unreasonable, the matter can be referred to the Data Protection Registrar. The Data Protection Act covers written records but most manual data which was held in a relevant filing system before 24 October 1998 is exempted from full compliance until 2007.

Powers of investigation

The Secretary of State can appoint 'authorised officers' to investigate possible benefit fraud.[9] The head of a local authority's paid service or its chief finance officer can appoint 'authorised officers' from the groups below to investigate housing benefit (HB) or council tax benefit (CTB) fraud.[10]

'Authorised officers' can be:

- officials of any government department (not just the DWP or the Revenue);
- employees of local authorities carrying out HB or CTB functions; *or*
- employees of organisations which perform contracted-out HB and CTB functions.

Authorised officers can carry out investigations, enter premises and seek information and documents for the 'authorised purpose'[11] of:

- establishing whether benefit was payable in a particular case;
- investigating the circumstances of an accident, injury or disease which may give rise to a claim for industrial injury or other benefit in a particular case;
- ascertaining whether social security provisions are being contravened;
- preventing, detecting or gathering evidence about social security offences.

The first two purposes above relate to individual claimants and claims, but the second two apply to cases 'whether by particular persons or more generally'. Therefore, investigators may be able to ask employers to produce classes of information, such as lists of employees and wages. However, information sought in connection with fraud investigation must be 'reasonably required'. In deciding what is reasonable, factors such as confidentiality procedures and the Data Protection Act must be considered.

Authorised officers can write to the following (including by email) to ask for any information or documents that they believe them to hold and which the officer 'reasonably requires' for an 'authorised purpose':[12]

- employers and employees;
- self-employed earners;
- people running agencies offering goods or services through people other than their own employees;
- local authorities acting as grantors of any licence;
- trustees or managers of pension schemes;

- people liable to make compensation payments.

Under these provisions, authorised officers can require people to make copies of documents or extracts of such, or to create documents, such as lists of casual staff, where no such documents currently exist.

For the purpose of obtaining information about specified individuals, authorised officers can also approach:[13]

- banks and the Director of National Savings;
- credit providers;
- insurance companies;
- credit reference agencies;
- fraud agencies;
- money transfer businesses;
- water or sewerage authorities;
- gas suppliers and distributors;
- electricity suppliers and distributors;
- telecommunication services;
- educational establishments and their service providers;
- student loans companies; *or*
- any servant or agent of any of the above.

Authorised officers should have regard to a Code of Practice when obtaining information from any of the above.[14] No information can be requested that is the subject of **'legal privilege'** – ie, confidential communications between a legal adviser and her/his client for the purpose of giving or receiving legal advice.[15]

The information must be required because it is suspected that a person, or a member of her/his family (see p809 for who counts as your family), has committed, is committing or is going to commit a benefit offence.[16] If any of these bodies keep electronic records, they can be required to allow access to those records by an authorised officer.[17]

Although, in general, information must relate to specific persons identified by name or description, authorised officers can:

- require the water, electricity and gas suppliers and distributors to provide information about whether, and in what quantities, these services have been supplied to specified residential premises;[18]
- request **'communications data'** from telecommunications companies, which is information about the use made by a subscriber of that service, as well as any other information held about that subscriber. The actual contents of any communications are excluded from investigation, as is identifying the person, apparatus and location to or from which a communication is sent.[19] However, information can be required from a telecommunication service about the identity and postal address of a person identified solely by reference to a phone number or electronic address.[20]

In addition, you can also be charged with offences under the Theft Act 1968: theft, obtaining property by deception and false accounting.[28]

If you are found guilty of the offence of false representations or dishonest representations, you can be fined or imprisoned, or both. The maximum fine is £5,000, but can be smaller. Remember that any fine that you have to pay is in addition to any overpayment that is found to be recoverable from you (see Chapter 41).

False representations for claiming benefit

False representations for claiming benefit are considered to be the less serious of the benefit offences. You commit these offences if you:

- for the purpose of claiming a benefit or payment for yourself or someone else or for any other purpose relating to the benefit rules:[29]
  - make a statement which you know to be false; *or*
  - give information or produce documents that you know to be false (or knowingly cause or allow someone else to do so).

  It does not have to be shown that you intended to obtain benefit;[30]
- fail to notify the Department for Work and Pensions (DWP), the Revenue or local authority promptly of a change of circumstances which you are required to notify and which you know affects your entitlement to benefit or other payment.[31] This also applies to appointees and other third parties receiving benefit on your behalf. You count as notifying a change promptly if you do so as soon as reasonably practicable after the change occurs;[32]
- cause or allow another person to fail to notify a change of circumstances to the DWP, the Revenue or local authority promptly which is required to be notified and which you know affects her/his entitlement to benefit or other payment.[33]

You do not 'know' something if you are merely careless about whether or not something is true, or if you fail to find out.[34]

The **maximum penalty** for these offences is a £5,000 fine or three months in prison, or both.[35]

Duty to report a change in circumstances

It is your duty to report any changes in your circumstances which might affect your right to, or the amount of, your benefit.[36] You will only be liable to commit an offence if you fail to report a change which you know affects benefit, but, in order to avoid potential allegations of fraud or prosecution, you should report all changes promptly and in writing or by telephone.

Remember, where the benefit affected by the change of circumstances is:

- jobseeker's allowance (JSA), you must notify the DWP in writing or by telephone to the office at which you sign on as available for work;[37]
- housing benefit (HB) or council tax benefit (CTB), you must notify the local authority in writing or by telephone to the office where you make your claim;[38]

- a benefit other than JSA, HB or CTB, you must notify the DWP (or the Revenue if the benefit is child benefit or guardian's allowance) in writing or by telephone to the office that deals with your benefit claim.[39]

In individual cases, notification in a form other than in writing or by telephone may be accepted. However, it will usually be best to notify changes in writing and to keep a copy of your letter.

Advisers and other third parties

Offences can be committed by any person who is required to make statements or notify changes of circumstances, not just the benefit claimant. The offences of allowing or causing a claimant to fail to notify a change of circumstances or knowingly allowing or causing someone to give false information do not place any additional duty on advisers to notify the DWP, the Revenue or local authority of a claimant's change of circumstances. In order for an offence to be committed there must be some sort of implied permission given to the person, under a duty to notify or to give information, not to do so.[40] You do not 'allow' somebody to do something unless you are able to stop them doing it. If you are an adviser you should not be liable if you have advised your client fully of the law and the requirement to notify a change of circumstances and provide truthful information. You should do nothing to help facilitate a misrepresentation or failure to notify a change of circumstances (eg, help complete a claim or review form which you know is inaccurate).

Dishonest representations for claiming benefit

Dishonest representations for claiming benefit are considered to be the more serious of the benefit offences. You commit these offences if:[41]

- you commit any of the acts subject to the offence of false representations for claiming benefit (see p1167); *and*
- you act dishonestly ('knowingly', in Scotland) in doing so. This means that in committing the offence you do something that most people would consider dishonest and that you must have known this was dishonest.[42]

The **maximum penalty** for these offences is:[43]

- if you are convicted in a magistrates' court, a £5,000 fine or six months in prison, or both; *or*
- if you are convicted in the Crown Court, an unlimited fine or seven years in prison, or both.

Will you be prosecuted?

Not all cases where there is evidence to justify a prosecution are taken to court. In some cases you may be given the chance to pay a penalty (see p1173) or accept a formal caution instead (see p1174). In some cases no fraud action is taken at all. The factors that the DWP, the Revenue and local authorities take into account include the strength of the evidence, the amount of benefit involved, whether an offence was planned and your personal circumstances.

There are time limits for prosecutions of the offences of false representations for claiming benefit (see p1167). A prosecution must be started by the *later* of the following dates:[44]

- three months from the date the DWP, the Revenue or local authority thinks that it has enough evidence to prosecute you; *or*
- 12 months from the date you committed the offence.

Prosecutions of the offences of dishonest representations for claiming benefit (see p1168) may be started at any time.

What to do if you are prosecuted

The most important thing to do if you are prosecuted is to get advice. You may be entitled to free legal help from a solicitor and representation in court. You should check carefully that the DWP, the Revenue or local authority is able to prove all the parts of the offence you are charged with. Do not plead guilty until you have obtained advice.

3. Loss of benefit for benefit offences

You can have sanctions imposed on certain benefits known as 'sanctionable' benefits (see p1170) if:[45]

- you are convicted of one or more benefit offences (see p1166) in two separate sets of proceedings; *and*
- the later offence occurs within three years of the date on which you were first convicted of an offence; *and*
- those offences have not previously been taken into account.

The Department for Work and Pensions sometimes refers to this as the 'two strikes' rule.

The benefit offence must have been committed after 1 April 2002:[46]

- in connection with a claim for a 'disqualifying' benefit (see p1170); *or*
- in connection with the receipt or payment of an amount of a 'disqualifying' benefit; *or*
- for the purpose of facilitating the commission (whether or not by the same person) of a benefit offence; *or*
- having consisted of an attempt or conspiracy to commit a benefit offence.

Disqualifying benefits

All social security benefits (including pension credit (PC)) are 'disqualifying' benefits for the purposes on p1169, except statutory sick pay, statutory maternity pay, maternity allowance, working families' tax credit, disabled person's tax credit and war pensions.[47]

Sanctionable benefits

Sanctions can be imposed on sanctionable benefits. These are all the disqualifying benefits except retirement pension, graduated retirement benefit, disability living allowance, attendance allowance, child benefit, guardian's allowance, constant attendance allowance, exceptionally severe disablement allowance, mobility supplement, social fund payments, Christmas bonus and bereavement payments.[48] Joint-claim jobseeker's allowance (JSA) is also not a sanctionable benefit. However, it can still be removed or reduced (see p1171).[49]

The sanctions

If the 'loss of benefit for benefit offences' rules apply, sanctionable benefits are not paid during the sanction period unless the benefit is income support (IS), income-based JSA, joint-claim JSA, PC, housing benefit (HB) or council tax benefit (CTB).[50] Those benefits are instead paid at a reduced rate during the sanction period in some circumstances (see below).

The **sanction period** is 13 weeks and can be applied to any benefit claim for a sanctionable benefit within a three-year period following the later conviction.[51]

While benefits are sanctioned, an underlying entitlement remains in place to ensure the link between benefits and other entitlements (eg, free school meals, free prescriptions, etc.) remains.

Income support

IS is paid at a reduced rate during the sanction period if you or a member of your family (see p809) are the benefit offender.[52] The reduction is:[53]

- 20 per cent of the appropriate IS personal allowance for a single person of the offender's age (see p879) if:
  - you or a member of your family are pregnant or seriously ill; *or*
  - the offender's IS has already been reduced while s/he is appealing against a decision that s/he is capable of work under the personal capability assessment (see p295); *or*
- 40 per cent of the appropriate IS personal allowance for a single person of the offender's age (see p879) in all other cases.

Payment cannot be reduced to below 10p a week. No reduction is made if IS is already being restricted because you breached a community order (see p1117). If the rate of IS to which you are entitled changes, the reduction is recalculated and takes effect from the first day of the first benefit week following the change.

Income-based jobseeker's allowance

Income-based JSA is paid at a reduced rate during the sanction period if:[54]

- you or a member of your family (see p809) are the benefit offender; *and*
- you are what is known as a **'person in hardship'** – ie, you are in a 'vulnerable group' or a decision maker is satisfied that you or your partner would suffer hardship if a payment is not made. The rules for who counts as in a 'vulnerable group' and on deciding hardship are the same as for JSA sanctions (see p447).[55]

If you do not fall into a 'vulnerable group', you are not paid reduced rate JSA until the 15th day of the sanction period.[56]

You do *not* count as a 'person in hardship':[57]

- if you or your partner are entitled to IS or fit into one of the groups of people who can claim IS (see p294). In this case, you or your partner can claim IS instead of JSA; *or*
- during any period when JSA is not payable to you because you have been given an employment-related or a New Deal, training or employment programme-related sanction (see Chapter 16); *or*
- during any week in the sanction period when your benefit has been restricted because you breached a community order (see p1117).

The reduction is:[58]

- 20 per cent of the appropriate JSA personal allowance for a single person of your age (see p879) if you or a member of your family are pregnant or seriously ill; *or*
- 40 per cent of the appropriate JSA personal allowance for a single person of your age (see p879) in all other cases.

Joint-claim jobseeker's allowance

If you are a member of a joint-claim couple, joint-claim JSA is not paid at all where the 'loss of benefit for benefit offences' rules apply to:

- both you and your partner;[59] *or*
- one of you, while:
  - the other has been given an employment-related or a New Deal, training or employment programme-related sanction (see Chapter 16);[60] *or*
  - the other's benefit has been restricted because s/he breached a community order (see p1117).[61]

In other cases, if one of you is sanctioned, the other person is paid at the rate of:

- contribution-based JSA, if s/he satisfies the rules for claiming it (see p349); *or*
- hardship payments, if you and your partner qualify (see p443); *or*

- income-based JSA calculated as if s/he is a single person (see p379), although any income or capital either of you have is taken into account in the calculation (see Chapters 37 and 38).

Housing benefit and council tax benefit

If you or a member of your family (see p809) are entitled to IS or income-based JSA during a sanction period, your HB and CTB, or that of your family member if s/he is the IS or income-based JSA claimant, is unaffected by any sanction.[62] Otherwise, any HB/CTB payable to you is reduced rather than removed during the sanction period if you or a member of your family are the benefit offender. The reduction is:[63]

- 20 per cent of the appropriate personal allowance for a single person of the offender's age (see p879) if you or a member of your family are pregnant or seriously ill; *or*
- 40 per cent of the appropriate personal allowance for a single person of the offender's age (see p879) in all other cases.

If the rate of HB/CTB to which you are entitled changes, the reduction is recalculated and takes effect from the first day of the first benefit week following the change.

Pension credit

PC is paid at a reduced rate during the sanction period if you or a member of your family (see p809) are the benefit offender. The reduction is:[64]

- 20 per cent of the 'relevant amount' below, if you or a member of your family is pregnant or seriously ill; *or*
- 40 per cent of the 'relevant amount' below in all other cases.

The **'relevant amount'** is:

- if a member of your family is the offender, and s/he is under 25, the appropriate IS personal allowance for a single person of her/his age (see p878); *or*
- the IS personal allowance for a single person aged 25 (see p878) in all other cases.

Payment cannot be reduced to below 10p a week. If the rate of PC to which you are entitled changes, the reduction is recalculated and takes effect from the first day of the first benefit week following the change.

4. **Penalties**

The Department for Work and Pensions (DWP), the Revenue or local authority may offer you the option of agreeing to pay a financial penalty, instead of being prosecuted.

The penalty is 30 per cent of the amount of the overpayment that is recoverable from you.[65] The overpayment must have been caused by an offence you committed after 18 December 1997.

The penalty is added to the overpayment of benefit and is recoverable in the same way as the overpayment[66] (see pp1142 and 1151). Guidance from the DWP to local authorities suggests that where an overpayment is being recovered from weekly benefits, deductions to recover the penalty should be instituted after the overpayment is fully recovered.[67]

The option of paying a penalty

You can *only* be offered the option of paying a penalty if:[68]

- an overpayment has been found to be recoverable from you. The DWP, the Revenue or local authority must have gone through the process of revising or superseding your award of benefit and issuing a decision that the overpayment is recoverable; *and*
- the overpayment was due to an act or omission on your part. This act or omission must have occurred after 18 December 1997;[69] *and*
- there are grounds for prosecuting you for an offence relating to the overpayment.

The DWP, the Revenue or local authority issues you with a notice which must set out how the scheme works and give you information about how you agree to pay a penalty or notify your withdrawal of your agreement.[70] If you are not issued with a proper notice, it may not be possible for the DWP, the Revenue or local authority to enforce the penalty.

The notice is sent with an invitation to an interview to discuss accepting the penalty. The interview should not be carried out by the same officer who gave the interview under caution.[71] The interview relates only to the offering of a penalty. You are not able to use it to add to or alter any statement that you made about the alleged offence in an interview under caution. If you are unable to decide whether or not to accept the caution at the interview, you should be allowed five days to make up your mind.[72]

Remember:

- If you agree to pay a penalty you are immune from prosecution for any offence in relation to the overpayment.[73] However, this does not stop you being prosecuted in the future if you commit another offence, or one in relation to a different overpayment.
- If it is found on review or appeal that the overpayment is not due or not recoverable, any penalty that you have paid must be repaid to you.[74] This does not affect the existence of the agreement, so you are still immune from prosecution.
- If the amount of the overpayment is changed on review or appeal, the agreement is cancelled, so you lose your immunity from prosecution and any

penalty you have paid must be repaid to you. However, if you enter into a fresh agreement:
 - you are again immune from prosecution; *and*
 - the amount of penalty you have already paid can be offset against the new penalty rather than being repaid to you.[75]
- If you decline to accept the penalty, the DWP, the Revenue or local authority considers whether to prosecute you.

Changing your mind

If you enter into an agreement to pay a penalty, you are entitled to change your mind so long as you notify the DWP, the Revenue or local authority within 28 days, on a form provided for the purpose as specified on the penalty notice.[76] You lose your immunity, but you do not have to pay the penalty and if you have paid any part of it, it must be refunded to you.

Whether to accept the penalty

It can be difficult deciding whether to accept a penalty or to risk facing prosecution. You should seek advice and consider your options carefully. In considering what to do, bear the following in mind:

- You might be invited to pay a penalty when there is insufficient evidence to prosecute you. If you are offered a penalty, make sure that you are told what evidence the DWP, the Revenue or local authority has against you.
- The fraud officer can only recommend that your case be considered for prosecution. The DWP, the Revenue or local authority legal department decides whether to prosecute (see p1166). You are not automatically prosecuted if you refuse to accept a penalty.
- If you are prosecuted and found guilty, you might be offered community service rather than a fine. On the other hand, you could get a large fine or even a prison sentence.
- A penalty of 30 per cent of the overpayment may be a substantial amount of money. For minor offences, a fine imposed on you could be less than the penalty.

5. Formal cautions

The Department for Work and Pensions (DWP) operates a system of 'cautioning' for social security offences. This system only applies within the DWP, although a few local authorities have similar systems of their own. It does not apply in Scotland where the law does not permit the use of cautions. The cautioning system is not laid down in regulations but is based on guidance modelled on the established guidelines for the police practice of cautioning.

A formal caution can only be offered when you have been interviewed under caution (see p1165), an overpayment has been calculated and the fraud officer believes that there is sufficient evidence to prosecute you for an offence. Cautions are generally only offered in less serious fraud where the value of an overpayment is low.

The procedure is as follows:

- You attend a formal caution interview, where you are asked to sign a record admitting the offence and accepting the caution. If you accept a caution you are immune from prosecution for the offence that you have admitted. This may encompass overpayments of more than one benefit.
- A caution certificate is sent to the DWP headquarters in Leeds and the caution is recorded on a central database. The record is kept initially for five years. It is subject to data protection rules. Information about the caution can be disclosed to other bodies in some circumstances – eg, to local authorities for use in housing benefit (HB) and council tax benefit matters or to the police for use in criminal investigations.
- A properly recorded formal caution may be cited in court if you are successfully prosecuted for a subsequent offence. It may then become part of a criminal record.
- If you refuse to admit the offence and accept a formal caution, your case is considered for prosecution.

Whether to accept a caution

In can be difficult deciding whether to accept a caution or to risk facing prosecution. You should seek advice and consider your options carefully. In considering what to do, bear the following in mind:

- A formal caution may be offered in circumstances where there is insufficient evidence to prosecute you for an offence. You are not necessarily prosecuted just because you refuse to accept a caution. You should not admit to something that you did not do just to avoid the threat of prosecution.
- Accepting a formal caution is an admission of guilt. Once you have accepted a caution you cannot change your mind.
- Although accepting the formal caution means that you are immune from prosecution for offences specified on the caution certificate, you may be prosecuted for related offences not specified, such as an HB overpayment.
- If you are subsequently found guilty of another benefit offence in court, your formal caution could be cited and may mean that you get a stiffer sentence.

6. The effect of fraud investigation on benefit claims

Your benefit cannot be stopped just because of fraud. However, the Department for Work and Pensions (DWP), the Revenue or local authority is entitled to suspend or withhold your benefit in some circumstances (eg, if it has a doubt about whether you are entitled or there is a possibility that you are being overpaid). See p1105 for further information about when payments of benefit can be suspended.

The DWP, the Revenue or local authority can ask you to provide information and evidence about your claim. If you do not do so within a specified time limit, your claim can be terminated (see p1106).[77] If you still believe that you are entitled to benefit, make a new claim.

You may have difficulties in getting your benefit reinstated during a fraud investigation or after you have been prosecuted. However, the DWP, the Revenue or local authority should not withhold your benefit indefinitely without making a decision as to whether or not you are, in fact, entitled. If you think an investigation is taking too long, you should complain (see p1300). If that brings no results, seek legal advice about forcing the DWP, the Revenue or local authority to make a decision.

Being under investigation for fraud can be very distressing. Fraud officers can take your papers away from the DWP, the Revenue or local authority section that normally deals with your claim and it can sometimes be difficult to find out what is happening. You might be put under pressure by the fraud officer to withdraw your benefit claim. You should not do so unless you know that you are not entitled to benefit. Fraud officers cannot make decisions on your entitlement to benefit. They merely pass on evidence to decision makers (some local authority fraud officers may also be decision makers). Always insist on a proper decision from a DWP, Revenue or local authority decision maker.

The decision on whether you should be prosecuted is separate from a decision to recover an overpayment of benefit (see Chapter 41). Whether you are entitled to benefit, and the amount and recoverability of any overpayment, is decided by the DWP, the Revenue or local authority decision maker without regard to dishonesty of intention. These decisions can be appealed, revised or superseded in the usual way (see Chapters 43 and 44). The fraud investigation department decides whether your actions were fraudulent and recommends whether action should be taken to prosecute, award penalties or caution you. The two processes are independent and have different tests. Therefore:

- a decision or appeal relating to your claim should not normally be delayed awaiting the outcome of a criminal prosecution; *and*
- a court-awarded fine does not prevent separate action for overpayment recovery. However, successful prosecution of a fraudulent offence alters the

burden of proof in an overpayment appeal and if a court has awarded compensation to the DWP, the Revenue or local authority it cannot also recover that amount as an overpayment.[78]

Whatever the result of an investigation or prosecution, the DWP, the Revenue or local authority may take more time assessing your future claims because they may check out your circumstances thoroughly. If they take too long to make a decision, you should complain (see p1300). You should not be prevented from making a fresh claim during a fraud investigation if your circumstances have changed. You could also apply for interim payments (see p1108) or help from the social fund (see Chapter 20).

Notes

1. **Investigation of claims**

1 ss122 and 122ZA SSAA 1992
2 s122B SSAA 1992
3 ss124 and 125 SSAA 1992
4 ss122D and 122E SSAA 1992
5 s122C SSAA 1992
6 ss182A and 182B SSAA 1992; Housing Benefit Fraud Circular HB/CTB F5/98
7 s123 and Sch 4 SSAA 1992
8 DWP Code of Practice for Data Matching, August 2000, available free of charge from DWP Public Enquiry Office and the DWP website
9 s109A SSAA 1992
10 s110A SSAA 1992
11 ss109A(2)and 110A(2) SSAA 1992
12 s109B(2) SSAA 1992
13 s109B(2A) SSAA 1992
14 s3(6) SSFA 2001
15 s109B(5)(b) SSAA 1992; s2.11 DWP's Code of Practice on Obtaining Information
16 s109B(2C) SSAA 1992
17 ss109BA and 110AA SSAA 1992
18 s109B(2D) SSAA 1992
19 s109B(2E) SSAA 1992
20 s109B(2F) SSFA 1992
21 s109C SSAA 1992
22 s28(2) Regulation of Investigatory Powers Act 2000
23 ss109B(5) and 109C(6) SSAA 1992
24 s67(9) PACEA 1984
25 s78(1) PACEA 1984; *DHSS v McKee* [1995] 6 Bulletin of NI Law 17 (NI Crown Court)
26 Housing Benefit Fraud Circular HB/CTB F5/97
27 s34 CJPOA 1994

2. **Prosecution of offences**

28 *Osinunga v DPP, The Times*, 26 November 1997 (DC)
29 s112(1) SSAA 1992
30 *Clear v Smith* [1981] 1 WLR 399 (DC)
31 s112(1A) SSAA 1992
32 s112(1C)-(1F) SSAA 1992
33 s112(1B) SSAA 1992
34 *Taylor's Central Garages v Roper* [1951] 115 JPR 445
35 s112(2) SSAA 1992
36 **HB/CTB** Reg 75(1) HB Regs; reg 65(1) CTB Regs
Other benefits Reg 32(1) SS(C&P) Regs
37 Reg 3 SS(NCC) Regs
38 Reg 4 SS(NCC) Regs
39 Reg 5 SS(NCC) Regs
40 *R v Chainey* [1914] 1 KB 137 at 142 (DC)
41 s111A SSAA 1992
42 *R v Ghosh* [1982] QB 1053 at 1064D-G (CA)
43 s111A(3) SSAA 1992
44 s116(2) and (2A) SSAA 1992

nefit for benefit offences

- 7(1) SSFA 2001
- 46 s7(8) SSFA 2001, definition of 'benefit offence'
- 47 s7(8) SSFA 2001, definition of 'disqualifying benefit'
- 48 s7(8) SSFA 2001, definition of 'sanctionable benefit'; reg 19 SS(LB) Regs
- 49 s8 SSFA 2001
- 50 s7(2)-(5) SSFA 2001
- 51 ss7(6) and 8(2) and (3) SSFA 2001; reg 2 SS(LB) Regs
- 52 ss7(3) and 9(3) SSFA 2001
- 53 Reg 3 SS(LB) Regs
- 54 ss7(4) and 9(4) SSFA 2001; regs 6-9 SS(LB) Regs
- 55 Reg 5(1)-(2) SS(LB) Regs
- 56 Reg 7 SS(LB) Regs
- 57 Reg 5(3) SS(LB) Regs
- 58 Reg 10 SS(LB) Regs
- 59 s8(2)(a) SSFA 2001
- 60 s8(2)(b)(i) SSFA 2001; s20A JSA 1995
- 61 s8(2)(b)(ii) SSFA 2001; s62(2) CSPSSA 2000
- 62 s7(5) SSFA 2001; reg 18 SS(LB) Regs
- 63 s7(5) SSFA 2001; reg 17 SS(LB) Regs
- 64 Reg 3A SS(LB) Regs

4. **Penalties**

- 65 s115A(3) SSAA 1992
- 66 s115A(4)(a) SSAA 1992
- 67 para 44(e) and (f) Housing Benefit Fraud Circular F4/98
- 68 s115A(1) SSAA 1992
- 69 s25(7) SSA(F)A 1997; Art 2(1)(b) SSA(F)AO No.5
- 70 s115A(2) SSAA 1992; reg 2(1) and (2) SS(PN) Regs
- 71 para 24 Housing Benefit Fraud Circular F4/98
- 72 para 48 Housing Benefit Fraud Circular F4/98
- 73 s115A(4)(b) SSAA 1992
- 74 s115A(6) SSAA 1992
- 75 s115A(7) SSAA 1992
- 76 s115A(5) SSAA 1992

6. **The effect of fraud investigation on benefit claims**

- 77 paras 17 and 18 SS&CS(DA) Regs
- 78 CIS/683/1994

Chapter 43

Decisions, revisions and supersessions: benefits

Once you have made a valid claim for benefit, a decision must be made by a decision maker.[1] The Department for Work and Pensions calls this an 'outcome decision'. See pp1079 and 216 for what counts as a valid claim.

If you want more information about a decision, you can ask for an explanation (see p1183). In many cases, you can also ask for written reasons for a decision if these have not already been provided (see p1184). If you disagree with the decision, you can ask the decision maker to change it by seeking a revision or a supersession (see pp1189 and 1199). In many cases, you can also challenge a decision by appealing to a tribunal (see Chapter 44). You may also be able to seek a supersession if your circumstances change after a decision is made.

Child benefit and guardian's allowance

The Revenue makes decisions about child benefit and guardian's allowance as well as tax credits. However, references to the Revenue in this chapter only apply to decisions about child benefit and guardian's allowance.

This chapter does *not* cover:

- child tax credit or working tax credit. For these, see Chapters 55 and 58; *or*
- statutory sick pay, statutory maternity pay, statutory adoption pay or statutory paternity pay. For these, see Chapters 23 and 24; *or*
- payments from the *discretionary* social fund. For these, see Chapter 45; *or*
- the benefits in Chapter 9 or on p18; *or*

- discretionary housing payments of housing benefit (HB) and council tax benefit (CTB). For these see p237.

You should look at this chapter if you are claiming any of the other benefits in this *Handbook*, including payments from the *regulated* social fund (see Chapter 22), HB and CTB.

1. Decisions

Decisions about benefits and the social fund (other than child benefit, guardian's allowance, housing benefit (HB) and council tax benefit (CTB)) are made by the Secretary of State for Work and Pensions. In practice, such decisions are made by the Secretary of State's representatives, known as decision makers. Decision makers are civil servants in the Department for Work and Pensions (DWP).

Decisions about child benefit and guardian's allowance are made by officers of the Revenue. They are also known as decision makers.

Decisions about HB and CTB are made by officers of the local authority. References in this chapter to a decision maker can be read as references to a local authority officer.

Employment officers (EOs) work in JobCentres and Jobcentre Plus offices. If you are claiming jobseeker's allowance (JSA), their job is to agree with you the steps you are willing to take to get back to work (see p365), to keep a check on those steps and to offer practical help and advice.

Other officers – sometimes called personal advisers – are involved in work-focused interviews which you (and your partner) may have to attend. See p1092 for further information.

Making a decision

The decision maker might need further information before making a decision. You can be asked to provide this (see pp218 and 1082). In some cases, if you fail to do so, your claim could be suspended or even terminated (see pp1106). In addition, if your claim:

- involves medical issues, the decision maker can refer you to a doctor for a medical examination and a report.[2] The doctor can ask you to submit to a medical examination. If you fail to do so without 'good cause' the decision maker must decide against you.

  Remember that different rules apply if you fail to attend for a medical examination about your incapacity for work (see p784) or if a decision maker requires you to attend for a medical examination to see if a decision to award you benefit should be revised or superseded (see p1107) or if a chair of a tribunal refers you to a doctor for a medical examination (see pp1235–36);

- involves issues about your national insurance contributions, the decision maker can refer these to the Revenue. See below for further information about the special procedure;
- involves a question about the facts where special expertise is needed, the decision maker can get assistance from experts.[3]

If your claim is for income support (IS), JSA, pension credit (PC) or a social fund payment but the decision maker needs more evidence or information to make a decision, s/he can make a decision in the meantime in certain circumstances. A decision is made on the basis that the evidence or information needed is adverse to you, if it is needed to decide:[4]

- for IS, JSA and social fund payments only,
  - whether you should be paid less benefit because you are involved in a trade dispute (see p735); *or*
  - whether you or your child(ren) are in relevant education (see p618);
- for IS and social fund payments only, whether you are entitled to the severe disability premium (see p891);
- for PC only, whether you are entitled to a severe disability additional amount (see p891).

For IS, PC and social fund payments only, if further evidence or information is needed to decide what housing costs you can be paid (see Chapter 36), a decision is made on the basis of the evidence or information the decision maker already has.[5]

If your claim is for IS or JSA, you must be notified if your claim is defective (see p1080). If your claim is for other benefits, if you do not fill in the form properly, you are given time to do so (see pp1082 and 217). In addition, for PC, the decision maker must draw your attention to any defects in your claim.

A decision maker might withhold making a decision if there is a test case pending. See p1212 for further information.

It is not possible to sue a decision maker for negligence in the way s/he decides your claim.[6] Instead, if a decision is wrong, you can seek a revision or supersession or appeal against it. But the position is different if you are given wrong advice by an employee of the DWP, local authority or the Revenue. See p1304 for information about seeking compensation.

Special procedure

Certain questions are dealt with by a special procedure. These are to do with contributions and a person's employment – eg, whether you:[7]

- are an 'employed earner' for the purposes of paying contributions or entitlement to industrial injuries disablement benefit; *or*
- are liable to pay contributions of a particular class; *or*
- have paid contributions for a particular period; *or*

- are the employee or employer of another person; *or*
- satisfy the conditions for receipt of home responsibilities protection.

The decision maker refers contribution issues to the Revenue for a decision.[8] The Revenue either gives an initial decision or a formal decision against which you can then appeal. The decision maker can continue to deal with other issues relating to your claim, but can defer making a decision. The Revenue decision on contributions is binding on the decision maker.

Appeals on most contribution issues are dealt with by tax appeal commissioners (other than home responsibilities protection and whether you can be credited with contributions – you can appeal to a tribunal about these).[9] You must appeal in writing within 30 days after the date on which a decision notice is issued.[10] This time limit can be extended if you have a reasonable excuse for not making your appeal within the time limit and your appeal was made without unreasonable delay.[11]

Appeal tribunals can also refer to the Revenue for decisions on contribution issues which are relevant to a benefit appeal.[12] The Secretary of State may revise the decision on your claim as a result.

Delays

The DWP and the Revenue have target times for dealing with claims. These are available at your benefit office, JobCentre or Jobcentre Plus office. Local authorities must make a decision on your claim for HB or CTB within 14 days, or if that is not reasonably practicable, as soon as possible after that. See p229 for further information.

If you have been waiting more than the relevant target time (or in the case of HB and CTB, more than 14 days) for a decision, contact the DWP, local authority or the Revenue. First check that your claim has been received. If it has not, let the office have a copy of your claim or fill out a new form and refer it to the claim form you sent earlier. If the DWP, local authority or the Revenue does not accept that you made the claim, you may have to claim again and ask for it to be backdated if possible (see pp1085 and 221).

If your claim has been received but not dealt with, ask why. If you are not satisfied with the explanation for the delay, make a complaint (see Chapter 47). In extreme cases, it might be possible to make an application for judicial review (see p1253).

If a decision cannot be made on your claim straight away:

- you should ask the office to make interim payments (see p1108). If the benefit is HB and you are a private or housing association tenant, in most cases you *must* be given an interim payment (see p230);
- if your claim is for a non-means-tested benefit, you may be able to claim IS, income-based JSA or PC in the meantime. The amount of any of these paid to

you may be deducted from arrears of social security benefits which you subsequently receive;[13]

- you may be able to claim a crisis loan from the social fund (see Chapter 21) if you have inadequate resources.

Correcting a decision

Unless the benefit is child benefit or guardian's allowance, if the decision maker makes an accidental error in her/his decision (eg 'a slip of the pen') this can be corrected.[14] You must be sent written notice of the correction as soon as it is practicable. In calculating the time limit for seeking an 'any grounds' revision or appealing against the decision, days before the day on which notice is given of the correction are ignored (see p1191 and 1223).

Information about decisions

You may want to know more about a decision or want a breakdown of how your benefit has been calculated. To find out more about a decision, you can ask for an explanation. In addition, if the decision is one against which you have a right of appeal, you must be given a written statement of reasons for it (see p1184).

Explanations

You can ask for an explanation of any decision maker's decision. This is optional, and is *not* the same as a revision, supersession or appeal. You can ask for an explanation in writing, in person or over the telephone. You should contact the office that made the decision. Ask about anything that is unclear to you and point out any errors you think the decision maker made.

At the end of the explanation, you should be asked whether you are happy with the decision and whether or not you want it to be looked at again. If you are not happy with a decision, say so. The decision maker should then advise you about your right to seek a revision (see p1189) or to appeal (see Chapter 44). S/he may refer to this as a dispute or a request for a reconsideration but you should use the proper term wherever possible.

For **benefits (other than HB or CTB)**, you can ask for a revision there and then. If you do this:

- Make it clear to the decision maker why you disagree with the decision.
- If you ask for a revision orally, make a note of the date, the time and the name of the decision maker.
- Write down what both you and the decision maker said in case you need this later.

For **HB and CTB**, requests for revisions must be made in writing.

Explanations are usually given orally and it can sometimes be difficult to take in or remember what has been said. However, you have a right to a written statement of reasons for a decision if it is one against which you can appeal (see below).

The time limit for seeking a revision or appealing is very strict. It runs from the date you are sent the decision with which you disagree, *not* the date of the explanation (see pp1191 and 1223). You should therefore ensure you seek a revision or appeal within the time limit even if an explanation for the decision has not yet been given to you.

Written reasons for a decision

Whether or not you asked for an explanation (see p1183) you may want to see the reasons for a decision in writing. These are especially useful if you are considering seeking a revision or a supersession or appealing to a tribunal.

You must be given a written notice of a decision against which you have a right of appeal (see p1219). These are sometimes called 'decision notices'. You must be informed of:[15]

- your right to appeal against the decision; *and*
- your right to a written statement of reasons for the decision (if this is not already included).

If the decision is about **HB or CTB**, there is no time limit for asking for a written statement of reasons. However, the time limit for seeking a revision or appealing is very strict. If you want to seek a revision or appeal you should remember to do so within the time limit, even if you decide to ask for a written statement of reasons later. If you ask for a written statement of reasons (where this has not already been provided), the local authority must provide one within 14 days if this is practicable.[16] Days between the date you request the statement and the date on which it is provided to you are ignored when calculating the one-month time limit for seeking a revision and appealing (see pp1191 and 1223).

If the decision is about **other benefits**, you must ask for a written statement of reasons within one month of being sent the decision.[17] The decision maker must then provide one within 14 days or as soon as practicable afterwards. Your time limit for seeking a revision or appealing is automatically extended if you ask for a written statement of reasons, but only where these have not already been provided. See pp1191 and 1223 for further information.

'Month' means a complete calendar month running from the day after the day you have been sent or given a decision.[18] For example, a decision sent on 24 July has a time limit that expires at the end of 24 August.

The DWP says a written statement of reasons for a decision should be provided automatically with a decision about some benefits. In the case of these benefits, the DWP is likely to argue that your time limit for seeking a revision or appealing cannot be extended. The benefits are:

- incapacity benefit;
- severe disablement allowance (now abolished for new claimants);
- maternity allowance;
- bereavement benefits;
- retirement pension;
- Sure Start maternity payments; *and*
- social fund funeral and cold weather payments.

Although *you* may believe a written statement of reasons has not been included with your decision or that what has been provided is inadequate, the DWP, local authority or the Revenue could disagree. If you are in any doubt about the situation, you should presume your time limit for seeking a revision or appealing has *not* been extended. If you miss the time limit in this situation, you should argue that the rules which allow a late application for a revision or a late appeal apply (see pp1192 and 1261).

Remember that the time limit for seeking a revision or appealing is strict.

If you disagree with a decision maker's decision

If you think a decision maker's decision is wrong (eg, because the decision maker got the facts or law wrong, or your circumstances have changed) you can:

- seek a revision of the decision (see p1189); *or*
- seek a supersession of the decision (see p1199).

In many cases, you also have a right to appeal to a tribunal (see Chapter 44). See p1219 for information about the kinds of decisions against which you can appeal.

The time limits for seeking what is known as an 'any grounds' revision or appealing are strict – normally only one month (see pp1191 and 1223). For information about how an application for a revision could affect your appeal rights and the time limit for appealing, see p1227.

You may have sought a revision or a supersession of a decision which you cannot appeal to a tribunal (see p1221). If you are still dissatisfied you should seek advice about whether you can apply for judicial review (see p1253).

Checklist for challenging a decision

1. If you want more information about a decision, ask for an explanation (see p1183) or seek a written statement of reasons (if this has not already been provided – see p1184). This is optional.
2. Decide whether to seek a revision (see p1189) or appeal (see Chapter 44). Get advice as soon as possible if you need this (see Appendix 2).
3. Ensure you keep within the time limit (see p1191 for revisions and p1223 for appeals).

If you disagree with an employment officer's decision

You cannot appeal against an EO's decision to issue a jobseeker's direction (see p423), but if you are sanctioned by a decision maker for failing to comply with it you can appeal against the sanction.

If you cannot reach an agreement with your EO about the terms of your jobseeker's agreement or whether your jobseeker's agreement should be changed you can ask for it to be referred to a decision maker for a decision. See p371 for details of the procedure. If you disagree with the decision maker's decision, you can seek a revision (see p1189) or appeal (see Chapter 44).

2. Contacting benefit offices

Writing to the Department for Work and Pensions (DWP), local authority or the Revenue is nearly always the best way to have your case dealt with. It ensures there is a permanent record of what you said and enables you to cover clearly all the points you want to make. Remember:

- always put your name, address, the date and your national insurance (NI) number at the top of your letter as well as the name of the benefit your letter is about;
- make it clear what it is you want to query, giving the date of the decision if this is relevant;
- always try to make a copy of your letter;
- keep all letters and forms sent to you. Such a record may help you or your adviser to work out later whether any decision can be challenged.

On occasion, it may be necessary to telephone the DWP, local authority or the Revenue. If you telephone an office:

- ask for the relevant section;
- be ready to give your surname, address and NI number;
- try to get the name, title and telephone extension number of the person you speak to as this may be useful in the future;
- make a brief note of what is said, together with the date. If the information is important, follow up the telephone call with a letter confirming what was said so that any misunderstanding can be cleared up. Offices are usually reluctant to write merely to confirm a telephone conversation.

Visiting the DWP or local authority office enables you to have a detailed conversation with an officer. Check the opening times first. Be prepared to wait if you need to see someone. The receptionist should tell you how long it is likely to take. If you want a private interview, this should be provided. Make a note of the name of the officer you speak to. Remember:

- take any relevant documents with you, otherwise you may be asked to make a second visit to provide the additional information;
- follow up any important meeting with a letter confirming the points you or the officer have made or ask the officer to confirm in writing any advice to you;
- take a friend or relative with you if you want to, not only for moral support, but also as a witness to what is said.

If you cannot get to the office (eg, because of your age, health or a disability) an officer may be able to make a home visit if your case cannot be dealt with by telephone. Ask for a visit if you need one. If you are refused and are not satisfied with the reason you are given, ask to speak to a supervisor or the customer services manager.

3. Change of circumstances after a claim

If you are getting benefit and your circumstances change so that you are entitled to more or less benefit, a decision maker can look at your claim again and make a new decision (a supersession – see p1199). If, as a result, your entitlement to benefit ends, you should make a fresh claim if your circumstances change again. You *cannot* seek a supersession instead of making a fresh claim in this situation (unless you are seeking a supersession because there has been a 'recrudescence' of a prescribed disease – see p327).[19] Even if you are appealing against the decision refusing or stopping your benefit, you should make a fresh claim when your circumstances change and appeal if you are still refused. If you do not, you could lose out. This is because if you appeal to a tribunal against a decision refusing benefit or terminating your award, the tribunal cannot take a change of circumstances into account if it happens after the decision with which you disagree (but see p1237).

If you report a change of circumstances that *you* think is relevant, but the decision maker disagrees, s/he might refuse to do a supersession (see p1210).

Note: It is your duty to report any change in your circumstances which might affect your right to, the amount of, or payment of, your benefit. For further information and to find out when a change of circumstances takes effect, see p1204 and the chapter in this *Handbook* about the benefit you are claiming.

4. General information about revisions and supersessions

If you are getting benefit but you cease to satisfy the conditions of entitlement, or the amount of benefit to which you are entitled is reduced or increased, the decision awarding you benefit is changed either by a revision or a supersession. This can only be done if one of the grounds for revision or supersession applies (see pp1190, 1193 and 1199).

Whoever wants a revision or supersession has to show that there are grounds.[20] It is best to ask for a revision or supersession in writing giving the reasons why you think one should take place. For housing benefit and council tax benefit, you *must* ask for a revision or supersession in writing. Claims for benefit or questions about your entitlement can be treated as requests for a revision or a supersession.[21]

After a decision is changed

If a decision is changed in your favour, you can receive arrears of benefit. You usually get more arrears if you ask for a revision than if you ask for a supersession. For this reason it is best to apply for a revision if you can. If you are in any doubt about how you would be better off, you should seek advice. See pp1198 and 1204 for how far back your arrears can be paid.

If you are trying to get arrears going back several years, it can be difficult to identify the grounds for a revision or supersession, particularly where the Department for Work and Pensions (DWP), local authority or the Revenue has destroyed old papers relating to your claim. If you are the one who wants the revision or supersession, the onus is on you to show that there are grounds. You cannot simply rely on the DWP's, local authority's or the Revenue's lack of evidence.[22]

If you were underpaid benefit because of a clear error by the DWP, local authority or the Revenue you could apply for compensation as well as getting arrears owed to you (see p1304).

A possible consequence of a decision not being changed in your favour is that you may have been overpaid. The decision maker decides whether or not to recover the overpayment (see Chapter 41). There is no limit on how far back an overpayment can be recovered.

The risks of revision and supersession

Following a revision or a supersession, the original decision may:

- remain the same; *or*
- be changed either to increase or decrease the amount of your benefit or take away your entitlement altogether.

Thus, your benefit can go down as well as up. If the revision or supersession reduces the amount of benefit to which you are entitled, it may mean that you have been overpaid. See Chapter 41 for information about overpayments and when they can be recovered.

You should seek advice before you seek a revision or supersession if you are concerned about what could happen in your case. However, you must notify changes in your circumstances that could affect your benefit.

People subject to immigration control

You should seek specialist advice before initiating a revision or a supersession if you are a 'person subject to immigration control' (see Chapter 26) who has been getting severe disablement allowance, attendance allowance, disability living allowance (DLA), or carer's allowance (known as invalid care allowance prior to April 2003) since before 5 February 1996, or child benefit since before 7 October 1996. You risk losing your benefit altogether (see p667).

Disability living allowance

As well as the risks described on p1188, you should seek advice if you want to seek a revision or supersession:

- because you have not been awarded one component of DLA (see pp127 and 136) when you are already in receipt of the other; *or*
- of the rate you have been awarded of one component when you are quite satisfied with the rate you have been awarded of the other.

In these circumstances the decision maker may consider the component which is not the subject of the revision or supersession, although s/he does not have to do so.

If you have been awarded one component of DLA for an indefinite period (see p159), the decision maker can reconsider the rate of that component, or the length of time for which it has been awarded. However, you should argue that s/he should not do so, unless you ask for a revision or supersession on that basis.[23]

5. **Revisions**

If you disagree with a decision maker's decision (including a decision superseding an earlier decision), you can seek a revision.[24] If you seek a revision, the decision maker must look at the decision again to see if it can be changed. The Department for Work and Pensions (DWP), local authority and the Revenue often refer to your request as a dispute or a request for a reconsideration. However, you should use the term 'revision' wherever possible. Seeking a revision is only one of the ways of getting a decision changed. See p1222 for help in deciding whether to seek a revision or supersession, or to appeal.

In some cases, you can seek a revision even if the decision was made a long time ago (see p1193). Revisions can therefore be a way around the strict time limit for appealing to a tribunal (see p1223).

Following a revision, your benefit could be increased but it could also be decreased or stopped altogether. See p1188 for what you should consider before seeking a revision.

For information on how to seek a revision, see p1196. To find out how much benefit you can be paid after a revision, see p1198.

When a decision can be revised

You can ask for a decision to be revised or the decision maker can decide to do this.[25] There are two types of revision:

- 'any grounds' revisions where all you have to do is show you disagree with the decision (see below); *and*
- 'any time' revisions where you must show that certain grounds apply (see p1193).

A decision maker can only revise a decision on the basis of your circumstances at the time the decision:[26]

- took effect; *or*
- in the case of advance awards for benefits other than housing benefit (HB) and council tax benefit (CTB), was made.

If your circumstances have since changed, you should instead make a fresh claim or ask for the decision to be superseded (see p1199).

If you want to seek a revision of a decision about attendance allowance (AA) or disability living allowance (DLA) because you (or the person on whose behalf you are claiming) are terminally ill (see p149), you must specify this.[27] If you do not do so, the decision maker cannot revise the decision on this ground.

'Any grounds' revisions

You can ask for a revision on any grounds if you do so within a strict time limit, normally one month.[28] The decision maker may refer to this as the dispute period. You do not have to show specific grounds for a revision, so it is enough if you simply think a decision is wrong. However, you should still explain why you disagree with the decision and provide information and evidence which supports this (see p1196). We call these 'any grounds' revisions in this *Handbook*.

You do not have to seek a revision and can appeal to a tribunal instead. However, if you seek a revision rather than appealing you get two bites at the cherry because if your application for a revision is turned down, you are given a fresh decision. You can then appeal to a tribunal (but see p1198).

If you are uncertain whether your request for a revision of a decision is being acted on, you should remember to appeal against the decision within the time limit (see p1223). However, your appeal could lapse if the decision maker revises the decision, even if you do not get everything you want (see p1227).

Who can seek an 'any grounds' revision?

You can seek a revision of a decision about **benefits (other than child benefit, guardian's allowance, HB or CTB)** if you are a claimant, someone acting on a claimant's behalf (eg, an appointee – see p1075) or someone from whom the decision maker decides to recover an overpayment.[29]

You can seek a revision of a **child benefit or guardian's allowance** decision if you are a claimant, being paid one of these under an award, or a person affected by that decision.[30]

You can seek a revision of an **HB or CTB** decision if you are a person affected by that decision, that is, you are:[31]

- a claimant;
- someone acting for a claimant who is unable to act for her/himself – eg, an appointee (see p1075);
- someone from whom the local authority decides to recover an overpayment (including a landlord);[32] *or*
- a landlord or agent, where the decision concerns whether or not to make a direct payment of HB to you.

In addition, a **decision maker** can decide to revise a decision her/himself on any ground:

- for HB and CTB:[33]
  - within one month of the date you are sent or given a decision, if s/he has information which shows that there was a mistake about the facts of your case or the decision was made in ignorance of relevant facts; *or*
  - if you appeal within the one-month time limit (or make a late appeal) (see pp1223 and 1261) and your appeal has not yet been decided;
- for other benefits, within one month of the date you are sent the decision.[34] Note that the decision maker can do an 'any time' revision if you appeal against a decision and your appeal has not yet been determined (see p1195).

The time limit for seeking an 'any grounds' revision

If you want an 'any grounds' revision you must ask for one:

- in the case of a **Sure Start maternity grant or a social fund funeral expenses payment**, within one month of the date you were sent the decision or within the time limit for claiming the payment (see pp549 and 551) if this is later;[35]
- in the case of **HB and CTB**, within one month of the date you were sent the decision.[36] If a written statement of reasons has not already been included with the decision, days between the date you request the statement and the date on which it is provided to you are ignored when calculating the one month;[37]
- in all **other cases**:[38]
  - within one month of the date you were sent the decision; *or*

- within one month and 14 days of the date you were sent the decision, if you requested a written statement of reasons (see p1184) and it is provided within the month; *or*
- within 14 days of a written statement of reasons being provided, if you requested one within one month of the date you were sent the decision, but it is not provided within that one-month period.

For benefits (other than a Sure Start maternity grant or a social fund funeral expenses payment, child benefit or guardian's allowance), if an accidental error in a decision has been corrected (see p1183), any day falling before the day on which the correction is notified to you is ignored in calculating the one-month period.[39]

Late requests for an 'any grounds' revision

You can ask for an 'any grounds' revision outside the time limit in limited circumstances. You must do so within an absolute time limit of 13 months.[40] However, if you requested a written statement of reasons within one month of the date you were sent the decision:

- for HB and CTB, days between the date you requested the statement and the date on which it was provided are ignored; *or*
- for other benefits, if the statement of reasons is provided:
  - within one month of the date you were sent the decision, the 13 months is extended by 14 days; *or*
  - during a period later than one month after the date you were sent the decision, the 13 months is extended by 14 days, plus the number of days in that period.

Your application must contain:[41]

- enough details about the decision with which you disagree for it to be identified. You should say which benefit you are disagreeing about eg, income support (IS) or HB and the date the DWP, local authority or the Revenue sent you the decision; *and*
- a summary of your reasons for applying for a revision late. You must show that:[42]
  - it is reasonable to grant your request; *and*
  - your application has merit; *and*
  - there are special circumstances which mean that it was not practicable for you to request a revision within the time limit.

The longer you have delayed seeking a revision, the more compelling the special circumstances have to be.[43] See p1263 for information about what might count as a special circumstance.

When deciding whether it is reasonable to grant your application, the decision maker cannot take account of the fact that:[44]

- a court or commissioner has interpreted the law in a different way than previously understood and applied;
- you (or anyone acting for you) misunderstood or were unaware of the relevant law, including the time limits for seeking a revision.

You cannot appeal against the decision maker's refusal or failure to let you seek a revision outside the time limit.[45] The only remedy is judicial review.

'Any time' revisions

If you can show there are specific grounds (see below) you can ask for a revision at any time. We call these 'any time' revisions in this *Handbook*. There is no time limit for seeking an 'any time' revision. In practice, if you ask for a revision and it is within one month of you being sent the decision, the DWP, local authority or the Revenue treats your application as one for an 'any grounds' revision (see p1190).

If a decision maker refuses to do an 'any time' revision, see p1198.

The main grounds for revision

There are a number of grounds for an 'any time' revision. The main ones are where there has been:

- official error (see below);
- a mistake about or ignorance of facts (see p1194);
- an award of a 'qualifying benefit' (see p1194);
- an appeal against a decision (see p1195).

Other grounds for revision are on p1195.

Official error

You can ask for an 'any time' revision if there was an official error.[46] For **benefits, other than child benefit and guardian's allowance**, this means an error made by an officer of the DWP or the Revenue or a local authority or someone acting on behalf of a local authority. It also includes errors made by:[47]

- for HB and CTB, someone providing services relating to HB and CTB to the authority (eg, where HB and CTB have been privatised by the local authority);
- for other benefits, someone acting for or providing services to the DWP.

For **child benefit and guardian's allowance**, it means an error made by the Revenue or a person providing services to the Revenue.[48]

If the official error was made before the Social Security Act 1998 took effect (see CPAG's *Welfare Benefits Handbook* 1999/2000, p2:649) by an officer known as an adjudication officer, you can argue that the decision can be revised.[49]

In all cases, if someone else caused or materially contributed to the error, it does not count as an official error. This certainly includes you, but could include other people – eg, your partner or your representative.

You should argue that the following count as official errors:

- The decision maker made an error of law (see p1245).[50] However, this does not apply if the decision maker was only shown to have made an error of law after a later decision of a commissioner or a court. In this case, you should try to make a late appeal (see p1261). You could also make a fresh claim or ask for a supersession, but the 'anti-test case rule' could apply (see p1211).
- There is specific evidence which the decision maker had, but which s/he failed to take into account even though it was relevant. You should argue this applies even if the evidence does not conclusively prove your entitlement, so long as it raised a strong possibility that you were entitled.
- There is documentary or other written evidence of your entitlement which the DWP, local authority or the Revenue had, but failed to give to the decision maker dealing with your claim when the earlier decision was made.

Mistake about or ignorance of facts

An 'any time' revision can be done if there was a mistake about the facts of your case or the decision was made in ignorance of relevant facts. However, this is only the case if, as a result of the mistake or ignorance about the facts, the decision was more favourable to you than it would have been.[51]

If it is a disability decision about AA, DLA, severe disablement allowance, industrial injuries disablement benefit or a decision about your incapacity for work under the personal capability assessment (see p772) or whether you can be treated as incapable of work or there are exceptional circumstances (see p778), then in addition, it must be shown that at the time of the decision you (or the person being paid the benefit) knew, or could reasonably have been expected to know, about the fact and that it was relevant to your benefit. Note that if the disability benefit is a qualifying benefit for another benefit (see p1209) and revision of the disability decision means your entitlement to the other benefit is affected, the decision about the other benefit takes effect on the same date.[52]

If this ground for revision applies, you will have been overpaid benefit and the decision maker might seek to recover the overpayment (see Chapter 41). Remember that if the mistake about or ignorance of facts means you should be entitled to *more* benefit, a decision can be superseded on this ground (see p1201).

Awards of 'qualifying benefit'

If you are awarded a benefit (eg, IS or HB) and for a period which includes the date that award took effect, you or a member of your family are awarded another benefit (eg, DLA or carer's allowance) – known as a 'qualifying benefit' – or the qualifying benefit is increased, the decision awarding you benefit can be revised.[53] See p1209 for further information.

A decision to end your entitlement to HB or CTB because your or a member of your family's qualifying benefit ceases can also be revised at any time. This only applies if the qualifying benefit is later reinstated following a revision, supersession or appeal.[54]

If you are only entitled to a benefit at all once a qualifying benefit is awarded, see pp1090 and 220.

A decision that has been appealed

For benefits other than HB and CTB, if you appeal against a decision within the time limit or have been allowed a late appeal (see pp1223 and 1261), but the appeal has not yet been determined, the decision maker can look at the decision again and do a revision.[55] **Note:** There is a similar rule for HB and CTB (see p1191).

If you have appealed against a decision and your circumstances then change, the tribunal cannot, in general, take the changes into account (see p1237). Instead, you need to make a fresh claim or seek a supersession. Then, a decision maker can revise the new decision once the appeal against the first decision has been determined. This applies if:

- for benefits other than HB and CTB, you appealed against a decision to a tribunal;[56] *and*
  - a fresh claim is decided or the decision is superseded (see p1199) before your appeal is determined; *and*
  - the tribunal then makes its decision; *and*
  - the decision maker would have made her/his decision differently if s/he had been aware of the appeal decision at the time her/his decision was made;
- for HB and CTB only, you appealed against a decision to a tribunal, a commissioner or court;[57] *and*
  - a fresh claim is decided or the decision is changed (eg, by a supersession – see p1199); *and*
  - the decision maker would have made her/his decision differently if s/he had been aware of the appeal decision at the time her/his decision was made.

Note: If you have appealed a decision, your appeal could lapse if a decision maker revises the decision, even if you do not get everything you want (see p1227).

Other grounds for revision

There are a number of other situations when a decision maker can do an 'any time' revision. These are where:

- for IS or pension credit (PC) only, you have a **non-dependant living with you** (see p893) and since you were awarded IS or PC, your non-dependant has been awarded a benefit – known as a qualifying benefit (eg, AA or DLA) – for a period which includes the date the award took effect, and this means that you are entitled to a severe disability premium (for IS) or a severe disability additional amount (for PC);[58]

- a decision has been made to terminate your IS on the grounds that you are capable of work under the **personal capability assessment**, you have since appealed against the decision and so are entitled to IS at a reduced rate;[59]
- you have been getting IS at a reduced rate while **appealing about the personal capability assessment** and you have since won your appeal;[60]
- a decision has been made that you cannot be paid **jobseeker's allowance** for any period because a **sanction** applies (see Chapter 16);[61]
- you were refused **reduced earnings allowance**(see p334) because of a decision about your entitlement to industrial injuries disablement benefit but this decision was revised by a decision maker or changed on appeal in your favour;[62]
- if you (or your partner) are a person who is required to attend a **work-focused interview** as a condition of getting benefit (see p1092), the decision contains an error and is about you (or your partner) failing to take part in the interview or show good cause for this.[63] **Note:** This rule does not apply to child benefit, guardian's allowance, HB and CTB;
- you were sanctioned because you **failed to comply with a community order** (see p1117), but the order has since been quashed or set aside;[64]
- your benefit was stopped or restricted under the **loss of benefit for benefit offences rules** (see p1169) following your conviction by a court, but the conviction has since been quashed or set aside;[65]
- for HB only, your **maximum rent** (see p250) **has increased** because a rent officer determination (see p245) has been changed;[66]
- the decision is one against which you have **no right of appeal** (see p1221).[67] If you then disagree with the new decision, your only remedy is to apply for judicial review (see p1253).

How to seek a revision

You should apply for a revision to the office that sent you the decision with which you disagree.[68] For benefits (other than child benefit, guardian's allowance, HB and CTB) if you are a person who is required to attend a work-focused interview as a condition of getting benefit, you can also apply to the ONE or Jobcentre Plus office. The DWP, local authority or the Revenue can treat a request for a supersession (see p1199) as a request for a revision.[69]

For **benefits other than HB and CTB**, you do not have to ask for a revision in writing, although it is always best to do so. This ensures that the decision maker understands that you are asking for a revision, not just seeking an explanation or complaining about the rules.

Example

Stan is awarded IS, but the DWP says he is not entitled to help with his housing costs. He telephones the benefit office and complains that he has not got enough money to live on. The benefit office takes no action because it thinks Stan is simply letting off steam, not seeking a revision. Stan should have made it clear he wanted a revision. He can still ask for one (or appeal) but only if he is within the time limit (see pp1191 and 1223).

For **HB** and **CTB**, you *must* apply for a revision in writing.[70] A late application for a revision must also be in writing.[71]

A decision maker does not have to consider any issue not raised by your application for a revision or which caused her/him to act on her/his own initiative.[72] You should therefore ensure you:

- tell the decision maker all the points about the decision with which you disagree;
- provide any information or evidence that supports your case. This includes, for example, medical evidence from a GP or consultant or other health worker (eg, a psychiatric nurse) if this is relevant. If you are claiming AA or DLA, evidence or information from your carer or a diary of your walking, supervision or care needs over a period may be equally useful.

It is worth following up your request for a revision with the DWP, local authority or the Revenue to check that your application has been received. This is to ensure that you do not miss the time limit for seeking a revision or for appealing.

What happens after you seek a revision

A revision should be carried out by a different decision maker from the one who made the original decision.[73] S/he decides what further evidence is needed in order to come to a decision, and how to collect this. You can be asked to have a medical examination (see p1107). Note that for HB and CTB, the local authority *cannot* ask you to have a medical examination.

The decision maker can ask you for more evidence or information if s/he thinks this is needed to consider all the issues raised by your application for a revision.[74] You must provide this information within one month of the request. The decision maker can allow longer than this. If you do not provide the information, your application is decided on the basis of the information and evidence the decision maker already has.

Remember, in some cases if you fail to provide information or to submit to a medical examination, payment of your benefit could be suspended and your entitlement terminated (see p1107).

See p1211 if you are seeking a revision because you think a test case applies to you.

The new decision

After a decision maker carries out a revision s/he makes a new decision. S/he can decide there are:

- grounds for revision and that the original decision was correct; *or*

- grounds for revision and that the original decision should be changed; *or*
- no grounds for revision and refuse to change the original decision.

For information about challenging the new decision, see below.

When a revision takes effect

The date a revision takes effect is important. This is the date from which:
- you are paid arrears, if you are entitled to more benefit;
- you have been overpaid, if you are entitled to less benefit.

A revision takes effect from:
- the date the decision with which you disagree took (or would have taken) effect[75] – eg, your date of claim or the date a decision was superseded; *or*
- the correct date, if the date on which the original decision took effect was found to be wrong;[76]
- in the case of retirement pension only, the later of 1 October 1998 and the date on which you reached pensionable age (where you claimed a category A retirement pension) or your spouse reached pensionable age (if you claimed a category B retirement pension), if:[77]
  - the claim was refused because you or your spouse had not paid enough national insurance contributions in the tax years 1996/97 to 2001/02; *and*
  - you or your spouse were invited by the DWP to make these up by paying voluntary contributions and have since done so.

It is important to make it clear that you want payment for the past period. You might get less backdating if the 'anti-test case rule' applies (see p1211).

Challenging a revision

Following your application for an 'any grounds' revision, a decision maker makes a new decision (see p1197). If a decision is revised or the decision maker refuses to revise a decision, you are notified in writing of this new decision and of your right to appeal. If you disagree with the new decision and the original decision is one against which you have a right of appeal (see p1219) you can appeal to a tribunal. Your time limit for appealing (see p1223) runs from the date you are sent or given the new decision.[78]

If a decision maker refuses to do an 'any time' revision (see p1193) – eg, because s/he does not accept a decision was made due to an official error – you cannot appeal against the refusal.[79] However, you can try for an 'any grounds' revision outside the time limit (see p1191) or try to make a late appeal against the original decision. See p1261 for information about when late appeals to tribunals can be accepted.

In an appeal the tribunal must identify which decision is to be revised and establish whether there are grounds for revision and if so from which date.[80] If you think a revision decision you are appealing about is faulty, see p1237.

6. Supersessions

If your circumstances have changed since a decision was made, you can seek a supersession.[81] You can also seek a supersession if you think a decision is wrong, but you must show there are grounds (see below). You can seek a supersession of an original decision or one superseding an earlier decision.

You can ask for a supersession of a decision of:

- a decision maker; *or*
- an appeal tribunal; *or*
- a commissioner (see p1245).

You can seek a supersession even if the decision was made a long time ago. However, the arrears of benefit you are paid are limited (see p1204). It is usually better to try for a revision or appeal if you can (see p1189 and Chapter 44).

Following a supersession, your benefit could be increased but it could also be decreased or stopped altogether. See p1187 to see what you should consider before seeking a supersession.

For information on how to seek a supersession, see p1203. To find out how much benefit you can be paid after a supersession, see p1204.

When a decision can be superseded

You can ask for a supersession if you can show there are grounds. For the main grounds see below, and for other grounds see p1201.

You can ask for a decision to be superseded or the decision maker can decide on her/his own to do this.[82] A request for a revision can be treated as a request for a supersession.[83] For benefits other than child benefit and guardian's allowance, a notification of a change in circumstances can also be treated as a request for a supersession.

Note: If a decision could be revised (see p1189) it cannot be superseded unless there are grounds for supersession which are not covered by the revisions rules.[84]

The main grounds for supersession

There are a number of grounds for supersession. The main grounds are:

- changes of circumstance (see p1200);
- mistakes about or ignorance of facts (see p1201);
- where a decision is legally wrong (see p1201);

- where a qualifying benefit has been awarded (see p1201).

For other grounds for supersession, see p1201.

Changes of circumstance

A decision can be superseded if, since it had effect (or in the case of advance awards for benefits other than HB and CTB, since it was made), your circumstances have changed or it is anticipated that they will do so and this means the decision is no longer correct.[85] This is what is known as a relevant change of circumstances. If the change means that you could be entitled to more benefit, there is a strict time limit for reporting the change, or to get all the arrears of benefit to which you are entitled (see p1204).

A decision can only be superseded on the basis of a change of circumstances if you are currently entitled to benefit and your situation changes. If you were correctly refused benefit in the past and your circumstances are now different, you must make a fresh claim (unless you are seeking a supersession because there has been what is known as a recrudescence of a prescribed disease – see p327).[86] See p1237 if you are appealing the decision to refuse you benefit.

You should bear the following in mind:

- An amendment to the law counts as a change of circumstances, but a decision of a court or commissioner that the law has been wrongly interpreted does not.[87]
- A new medical opinion is not a change of circumstances, but a new medical report following an examination might give evidence of such a change.[88] See also p1201 regarding incapacity for work medicals.
- For income support (IS) and jobseeker's allowance (JSA), the repayment of a student loan does not count as a relevant change of circumstance.[89]
- For attendance allowance (AA) and disability living allowance (DLA), you or the person claiming on your behalf must specify that you are terminally ill, in the application for a supersession, for this to count as a relevant change of circumstances.[90]
- For housing benefit (HB) and council tax benefit (CTB) you are not required to report some changes in your circumstances (see pp232 and 124). However, those changes will still count as a change of circumstance and so this ground for supersession can still be used.[91]
- In respect of your assessed income period for pension credit (PC), the only change of circumstance that is relevant for these purposes is that the period has ended for one of the reasons listed on p481.[92]

The decision maker might say that a change of circumstances you have reported is not a relevant one and refuse to do a supersession. If this happens, see p1210.

To see when a change of circumstances takes effect, see p1204 and the chapter in this *Handbook* about the benefit you are claiming.

Mistake about or ignorance of facts

A decision can be superseded if there was a mistake about the facts of your case or it was made in ignorance of relevant facts.[93] However, if as a result of this, a decision is more favourable to you than it would have been, a decision maker can, instead, revise it at any time (see p1194).

For HB and CTB, a local authority cannot do a supersession on this ground if the decision can be revised instead.[94] For other benefits, a decision maker cannot do a supersession on this ground unless the time limit for seeking an 'any grounds revision' (or any longer period allowed) has passed (see p1191).[95]

Decisions that are legally wrong

A decision can be superseded if it was made by a decision maker (not a tribunal or commissioner) and was legally wrong.[96] This is what is known as an error of law (see p1245). If you think a tribunal's or commissioner's decision is legally wrong, you need to appeal against it.

For HB and CTB, a local authority cannot do a supersession on this ground if the decision can be revised instead.[97] For other benefits, a decision maker cannot do a supersession on this ground unless the time limit for seeking an 'any grounds revision' (or any longer period allowed) has passed (see p1191).[98]

Awards of qualifying benefit

If you are awarded a benefit (eg, IS or HB) but, from a later date than the entitlement began you or a member of your family become entitled to another benefit (eg, DLA or carer's allowance – known as a qualifying benefit) or the qualifying benefit is increased, the decision awarding you benefit can be superseded.[99] See p1209 for further information and p809 for who counts as your family. If you are only entitled to a benefit at all once a qualifying benefit is awarded, see pp1090 and 220.

Other grounds for supersession

There are a number of other grounds for supersession. These are:

- There has been a decision to award you benefit or national insurance (NI) credits on the basis that you are **incapable of work**, it has been determined that you satisfy the personal capability assessment (see p772), can be treated as incapable of work, or there are exceptional circumstances (see p778), and since the decision:[100]
  - you have been examined by a doctor approved by the Secretary of State; *and*
  - the doctor has provided new medical evidence on your capacity for work.

  However, your benefit (or NI credits) cannot be stopped unless the decision maker considers whether, and shows that, you are no longer incapable of work.[101]

  If you have told the decision maker that your condition has not improved since your last personal capability assessment or you have a variable condition, you can argue that reference should be made to earlier assessments and decisions on your claim.[102]

Note: This ground for supersession is not available for HB and CTB or if you are getting a transitional award of incapacity benefit because you were getting invalidity benefit immediately before 13 April 1995.[103]

- Your IS was terminated because a decision maker decided you were no longer incapable of work, you appealed to a tribunal who confirmed this but another tribunal subsequently decided that you *are* incapable of work.[104]
- For IS or PC only, you have a **non-dependant living with you** (see p893) and since you were awarded IS or PC, your non-dependant has been awarded a benefit – known as a qualifying benefit (eg, AA or DLA) – for a period after the date the award took effect, and this means that you are entitled to a severe disability premium (for IS) or a severe disability additional amount (for PC).[105]
- You appealed to a tribunal while a **test case was pending**, a tribunal or commissioner determines your appeal as if the test case had been decided in the way most unfavourable to you and the test case eventually goes in your favour (see p1232).[106]
- You have been awarded **jobseeker's allowance (JSA)** and a decision maker subsequently decides that this should not be payable because a **sanction** applies (see Chapter 16).[107]
- For benefits other than HB and CTB, child benefit and guardian's allowance, if you (or your partner) are a person who was required to attend a **work-focused interview** as a condition of getting benefit (see p1092), and there has been a decision that you (or your partner) did not take part in such an interview but since then:[108]
  - you moved to an area where the interview requirement does not apply; *or*
  - you turned 60; *or*
  - if your partner was the person required to attend a work-focused interview, s/he no longer has to do so or has ceased to be your partner.
- For HB, the local authority has referred your tenancy to a **rent officer** to make determinations because it has been more than 52 weeks since s/he last did so (see p243).[109]
- For HB, your **maximum rent** (see p250) **has decreased** because a rent officer determination (see p245) has been changed.[110]
- You were awarded IS or JSA, but you have since **failed to comply with a community order** (see p1117).[111]
- Your benefit is to be stopped or restricted under the **loss of benefit for benefit offences rules** (see p1169).[112] An HB or CTB decision which is affected by such a decision can also be superseded.[113]
- You are entitled to PC, the decision maker specified an **assessed income period** (see p480) and that period has ended or is about to end.[114] If the decision maker is unable to set a new assessed income period because you fail

to provide information and evidence within the time limit, s/he can also do a supersession when you eventually provide the evidence or information.[115]
- The decision is one against which you have **no right of appeal** (see p1221).[116] If you then disagree with the new decision, your only remedy is to apply for judicial review (see p1253).

For HB only, if the local housing allowance rules apply to you (see p253), the local authority can also do a supersession when your maximum HB would otherwise expire.[117]

How to seek a supersession

Apply for a supersession to the office that made the decision with which you disagree. The Department for Work and Pensions (DWP), local authority or the Revenue can treat a request for a revision as a request for a supersession.[118] The DWP and local authority can also treat a notification of a change in circumstances as a request for a supersession. Claims for benefit or questions about your entitlement can be treated as requests for a supersession.[119]

For benefits other than HB and CTB, you do not have to ask for a supersession in writing although it is always best to do so. For HB and CTB, you *must* ask the local authority for a supersession in writing.[120]

The decision maker does not have to consider any issue not raised by your application for a supersession or which caused her/him to act on her/his own initiative.[121] You should therefore ensure you:
- tell the decision maker all the points about the decision with which you disagree;
- provide any information or evidence that supports your case. This includes medical evidence from a GP or consultant if this is relevant. If you are claiming AA or DLA, evidence or information from your carer or a diary of your walking, supervision or care needs over a period may be equally useful.

What happens after you seek a supersession

The decision maker decides what further evidence is needed in order to come to a decision, and how to collect this. You can be asked to have a medical examination (see p1107). **Note:** For HB and CTB, the local authority *cannot* ask you to have a medical examination.

A decision maker can ask you for more information or evidence in order to allow her/him to consider all the issues raised by your application for a supersession.[122] If you do not provide the information or evidence within one month (or such longer period as the decision maker allows), your application is considered on the basis of what you have already provided.

Remember, in some cases, if you fail to provide information or to submit to a medical examination, payment of your benefit can be suspended and your entitlement terminated (see p1107).

See p1211 if you are seeking a supersession because you think a test case applies to you.

The new decision

After a decision maker carries out a supersession s/he makes a new decision. S/he can decide that:

- the original decision was correct; *or*
- the original decision should be changed.

For information about challenging a decision, see p1210.

If the decision maker refuses to consider a supersession because s/he says your application is hopeless, see p1211.

When a supersession takes effect

The date a supersession takes effect is important. This is the date from which:

- you are paid arrears, if you are entitled to more benefit;
- you have been overpaid, if you are entitled to less benefit.

When a supersession takes effect depends on the grounds for the supersession. It is important to make it clear that you want payment for the past period. You might get less backdating if the 'anti-test case rule' applies (see p1211).

The general rule

The general rule is that, if a decision is superseded, the new decision takes effect from the date you applied for the supersession or, if the decision maker decides to do one on her/his own, the date the decision is made.[123]

There are a number of situations when the general rule does not apply. These depend on the grounds for supersession. For exceptions to the rules, see below and the chapter in this *Handbook* about the benefit you are claiming.

Note: for some of the exceptions, where the amount of your award of IS or JSA is changed by a supersession, the supersession takes effect from the first day of the benefit week in which the award is changed.[124] For IS only, if you are paid in advance, it takes effect from the date the award is changed if this is the day you are paid benefit; otherwise it takes effect from the next week. If the decision maker certifies that it is not practical for the supersession to take effect on the days outlined above, your IS or JSA is adjusted from the first day of the benefit week following the week in which the award is changed.

Changes in your circumstances

For benefits other than child benefit and guardian's allowance, if the change of circumstances is that there has been a change in the legislation that affects your benefit, the decision takes effect from the date the legislation took effect.[125] Otherwise, the supersession takes effect as set out below.

It is important to remember that if you fail to notify a change of circumstances in time, and the change means you are entitled to less benefit, you will have been overpaid. The DWP, local authority or the Revenue might seek to recover the overpayment (see Chapter 41).

Housing benefit and council tax benefit

If the decision is about HB or CTB, in most cases the new decision takes effect from the start of the benefit week after the one in which the change occurs.[126] This applies whether or not a decision is advantageous to you. For further information about the general rule on when changes in circumstances take effect and exceptions to this rule, see p232.

However, if the change is one you are required to notify to the local authority (other than one relating to you having to take part in a work-focused interview – see p1092) and it is advantageous to you, the change must be notified within one month of it taking place.[127] The one-month period can be extended in certain circumstances (see p1206). If you notify the change outside the one-month period (or any longer period allowed by the local authority) the date you notify the change is treated as if that is the date the change occurred.

Other benefits

If you are claiming a benefit on the basis that you are incapable of work and you are covered by the own occupation test (see p771), the decision maker can anticipate a change in your circumstances as a result of information gathered for a personal capability assessment and do a supersession. The new decision takes effect the day after the day on which the own occupation test ceases to apply to you.[128] Otherwise, when the change takes effect depends on whether or not the new decision is advantageous to you.

If the new decision is **advantageous** to you the supersession takes effect as follows. For examples of when a decision might count as advantageous, see p1227.

- If you apply for the supersession and the decision is about AA or DLA[129] *and*:
  - the change means you are now entitled to a particular rate of benefit, the supersession takes effect from the first benefit payday after you satisfy the conditions of entitlement to that rate. You must notify the DWP of the change within one month of doing so;
  - the change makes a difference to whether benefit is payable to you, the supersession takes effect from the first benefit payday after the change. You must notify the DWP of the change within one month of it taking place.

  In both cases, the one-month period can be extended in certain circumstances (see p1206).

- If you apply for the supersession and the decision is *not* about AA or DLA, the supersession takes effect from the date of the change so long as the DWP or the Revenue is notified of the change within one month of it taking place.[130] The one-month period can be extended in certain circumstances (see below).
- If the decision maker decides to do a supersession her/himself, it takes effect from the date s/he first took action with a view to doing a supersession.[131]

If a decision is **not advantageous** to you (see p1227), the supersession usually takes effect from the date of the change of circumstances.[132] This does not apply to certain disability and incapacity decisions (for which see below).

If a decision is a disability decision about AA, DLA, severe disablement allowance (SDA), industrial injuries disablement benefit or a decision about your incapacity for work under the personal capability assessment (see p772) or whether you can be treated as incapable of work – ie, you are exempt from the test (see p773), or there are exceptional circumstances (see p778), the supersession usually takes effect from the date you notified the decision maker of your change of circumstances or, if the decision maker decides to do a supersession on her/his own, the date the decision is made.[133]

However, the supersession takes effect from the date you (or the person being paid the benefit) ought to have notified the change if you (or the person being paid the benefit) failed to notify the change when you knew that you should have, or could reasonably be expected to have known that you should have done so.[134]

Note: If the benefit is a qualifying benefit (see p1209) and the supersession means your entitlement to another benefit is affected, the decision about the other benefit takes effect on the same date.[135]

Late notification of a change of circumstances

If you fail to notify a change within the one-month periods noted on p1205, you can apply for an extension of time in limited circumstances.[136] You must do so within an absolute time limit of 13 months from the date the change occurs. Your application must contain:[137]

- details of the relevant change of circumstances; *and*
- the reasons why you failed to notify the change in time. You must show that:[138]
  - it is reasonable to grant your request; *and*
  - the change of circumstances is relevant to the decision you want changed; *and*
  - there are special circumstances which mean that it was not practicable for you to notify the change within the time limit.

The longer you have delayed notifying a change, the more compelling the special circumstances have to be. See p1263 for information about what might count as a special circumstance. When deciding whether it is reasonable to grant your application, the decision maker cannot take account of the fact that:[139]

- a court or commissioner has interpreted the law in a different way than previously understood and applied;
- you (or anyone acting for you) misunderstood or were unaware of the relevant law, including the time limits for seeking a supersession.

If your application for an extension of time is refused, the supersession takes effect from:

- for benefits (other than AA, DLA, HB and CTB), when you notified the change;[140] *or*
- for AA or DLA, the date you applied for the supersession;[141] *or*
- for HB and CTB, from the start of the benefit week after the date when you notified the change.[142]

Mistake about or ignorance of facts

Where a tribunal or commissioner made a decision in ignorance of relevant facts or made a mistake about the facts, and as a result the decision was more advantageous to you than it would otherwise have been, the supersession takes effect from the date the tribunal's or commissioner's decision took effect.[143] However, if it is a disability decision about AA, DLA, SDA, industrial injuries disablement benefit or a decision about your incapacity for work under the personal capability assessment (see p772) or whether you can be treated as incapable of work or there are exceptional circumstances (see p778), this only happens if you (or the person being paid the benefit) knew or could reasonably have been expected to know the fact in question and that it was relevant to the decision. If this is not the case, the general rule applies (see p1204).

For HB and CTB, where a decision was made in ignorance of facts or there was a mistake about the facts and the new decision is advantageous to you, the supersession takes effect from the start of the benefit week in which:[144]

- you applied for the supersession; *or*
- where you did not apply for a supersession, the local authority got information sufficient to show that the original decision was wrong.

Other grounds for supersession

There are a number of other exceptions to the general rule:

- If you are entitled to a benefit at a higher rate because you or a member of your family or a non-dependant were awarded a **qualifying benefit**, the supersession takes effect on the date of entitlement to the qualifying benefit or an increase in its rate. See p1209 for further information.[145]
- If a decision about your benefit is being superseded because of a decision by a commissioner or court in another case – a **test case** – the supersession is

effective from the date of the commissioner's or court's decision.[146] See p1211 for further information about the 'anti-test case rule'.

- For benefits other than HB and CTB, if a decision was made on your claim for benefit or to make a revision or a supersession, but your benefit was suspended while a **test case was pending** (see p1105) and the test case is eventually decided against you (in whole or in part), the supersession takes effect from the date of the earlier decision.[147]
- If you appealed to a tribunal while a **test case was pending**, a tribunal or commissioner determines your appeal as if the test case had been decided in the way most unfavourable to you and the test case eventually goes in your favour (see p1232), the supersession takes effect from the date it would have taken effect had the decision maker made it in accordance with the decision in the test case.[148]
- If the decision is to apply a **sanction** to your JSA, it takes effect from the subsequent benefit week, or subsequent payment.[149] If you are 16 or 17, are getting JSA severe hardship payments at a reduced rate due to a sanction but you are later given a 'certificate of good cause' (see p441), the new decision takes effect from the date your JSA was reduced.[150]
- If the decision is that you (or your partner) failed to take part in a **work-focused interview** without good cause (see p1092), it takes effect from the first day of the next benefit week. If that date is five days or less since the decision was made and it is your partner who has failed to take part in the interview, it takes effect from the first day of the next benefit week.[151]
- If the decision is that you are entitled to be paid incapacity benefit (IB) at the long-term rate because you have become entitled to the highest rate of the care component of DLA (see p274), even though you have been incapable of work for less than a year, the supersession takes effect from the date you became entitled to the highest rate of the care component.[152]
- If you are awarded IB or SDA on the grounds that you are **exempt from the personal capability assessment** (see p772) the supersession takes effect from the date from which you are to be treated as incapable of work.[153]
- If your award of IS, PC or JSA is being superseded to include help with **mortgage interest** (see p910) or **interest on a loan for repairs and improvements** (see p916), the supersession can be backdated by up to eight weeks. This can only be done if the supersession could not take place sooner because your lender did not supply the DWP with your mortgage details.[154] For information about when your IS, PC or JSA housing costs are recalculated, see p916.
- For HB, if the local authority has referred your tenancy to the **rent officer** to make determinations (see p243), the new decision takes effect:[155]
  - if the determination is the same or has increased; *and*

  - your rent is payable weekly or in multiples of weeks, from the first day of the benefit week which includes the day after the end of the period covered by the previous determinations; *or*
  - your rent is payable at other intervals, from the day after the end of the period covered by the determinations; *or*
- if the determination has decreased, from the first day of the benefit week after the local authority receives it.

- For HB, if your **maximum rent** (see p250) **has decreased** because a rent officer determination (see p245) has been changed, the new decision takes effect from the start of the benefit week after the date of the determination.[156]
- For IS and JSA, if you are sanctioned because you **failed to comply with a community order** (see p1117), the new decision takes effect from the beginning of the sanction period.[157]
- If benefit has been stopped or restricted under the **loss of benefit for benefit offences rules** (see p1169), the new decision takes effect from the beginning of the disqualification period.[158]
- For PC, if the decision maker specified an **assessed income period** (see p480) and that period has ended or is about to end, the new decision takes effect from the day after your assessed income period ends, if that is the first day of the benefit week. Otherwise, it takes effect from the first day of the next benefit week.[159]
- For PC, if a decision is being superseded because the decision maker was unable to set a **new assessed income period** when you failed to provide information and evidence (see p480) but you have since done so, it takes effect from the date you provided the information and evidence.[160] However, if your circumstances have changed and the decision is:[161]
  - advantageous to you, it takes effect from the day you provide the information and evidence, if this is the first day of the benefit week. Otherwise, it takes effect from the first day of the next benefit week; *or*
  - not advantageous to you, it takes effect from the day after your assessed income period ended.

  For examples of when a decision might count as advantageous to you, see p1227.
- If your IS was terminated because a decision maker decided you were no longer incapable of work, you appealed to a tribunal who confirmed this but another tribunal subsequently decides that you *are* incapable of work, the supersession takes effect from the date your IS was terminated.[162]

After an award of a qualifying benefit

If you, or a member of your family, are awarded another benefit (a 'qualifying benefit') or an increase in its rate, and arrears of the qualifying benefit are payable, your award of IS, JSA, PC, HB or CTB can be increased on a revision or a supersession and arrears paid for the same length of time.[163] See pp906 and 809 for who counts as your family.

This provision helps if you did not get certain premiums or allowances for your children[164] paid with your IS, JSA, HB or CTB (or for PC, additional amounts within your appropriate minimum guarantee) because of delays in assessing entitlement to a qualifying benefit – eg, where a DLA claim took 18 months to be decided and you have missed out on the severe disability premium for this period. You can only ask for a revision or supersession if you are already entitled to IS, JSA, PC, HB or CTB.[165] It is therefore important to make a claim for these at the same time as the claim for a qualifying benefit.

If you only qualify when the qualifying benefit is awarded

If you only qualify for IS, JSA or PC when the qualifying benefit is awarded, you should make a second claim as soon as you hear about the qualifying benefit. See p1090 for further information.

If you only qualify for HB or CTB when the qualifying benefit is awarded, see p220. If you lose benefit because of the way the rules operate, ask the local authority for an extra-statutory payment.

Remember, if you only claim for the first time after you hear about the qualifying benefit:

- for IS or JSA , you can only get arrears if you satisfy the backdating rules on p1087;
- for PC, your claim can only be backdated for 12 months (see p477);
- for HB or CTB, your claim can be backdated for 12 months, but if you are under 60 or either you or your partner are getting IS or income-based JSA, only if you can show 'good cause' for your late claim (see p221).

There are similar rules that help you get extra backdating if your entitlement to IB, SDA or carer's allowance (CA) depends on whether you (or in the case of CA, the person you care for) are entitled to a qualifying benefit. See p1090 for information.

Challenging a supersession

Following your application for a supersession, or a decision maker deciding to do a supersession on her/his own, a new decision is issued in writing. If you do not get all that you wanted from the supersession, you can seek a revision of the decision (see p1189). If the original decision is one against which you have a right of appeal (see p1219) you can appeal to a tribunal. If you have a right of appeal against the decision, you must be told about this.

If you appeal, you have to persuade the tribunal that there were grounds for supersession and also that the original decision was wrong. Where the decision maker has said there are no grounds for a supersession (see p1199), you must show why there are, as well as giving your reasons for disputing the original decision. Where the decision maker has done a supersession but you do not agree that s/he had grounds for this, you should explain why.

In an appeal the tribunal must identify which decision is to be superseded and establish whether there are grounds for supersession and if so from which date.[166] If you think a supersession decision you are appealing about is faulty, see p1237.

If a decision maker refuses to consider a supersession

When you apply for a supersession, a decision maker must, in almost all cases, make a decision. There are two possibilities. Your application for a supersession contains a ground for supersession that is potentially relevant to the amount of benefit you can be paid or the length of time you can be paid it, and:

- the decision maker agrees that there is a reason to change your award – eg, you are claiming child benefit and notify the decision maker that you have had a new baby and so are entitled to more benefit. In this situation, the decision maker does a supersession; *or*
- the decision maker does not think there is a reason to change your award – eg, you are getting DLA care component at the lower rate, feel your condition has deteriorated and want to claim middle rate instead. However, the decision maker thinks you do not qualify for the middle rate. In this situation, the decision maker issues a decision refusing to do a supersession.

In either situation, you can seek a revision of the decision maker's decision or appeal against it.[167] The only situations where a decision maker does not have to make a decision is where an application has not been made properly and therefore cannot possibly lead to a supersession or where there is no potentially relevant ground for supersession. In these cases, there is no decision against which you can seek a revision or appeal.

7. The 'anti-test case rule'

There is a rule – known as the 'anti-test case rule' – which says that some court and commissioners' decisions should be ignored when decision makers are considering a claim, or revising or superseding decisions for periods before they were given. This is intended to prevent you from taking advantage of a test case brought against the Department for Work and Pensions or local authority, but it goes rather wider. If the anti-test case rule applies, you can only get arrears of benefit going back to the date of the decision in the test case.

How the anti-test case rule operates

If a commissioner or court decides that a decision maker in a totally different case (the test case) has made an error of law (see p1245), *your* decision maker must decide any part of *your* claim (or revision or supersession) which relates to the period *before* the test case decision as if that decision had been found by the commissioner or court in question not to have been wrong.[168] The anti-test case rule only applies if the test case is the first authoritative decision on the issue, and not merely a later decision which confirms an earlier decision *and*:[169]

- you make a claim; *or*
- you seek a revision or supersession and this is done on the grounds that the decision in your case was found to be legally wrong by the decision of the commissioner or court in the test case (and not for some other reason).[170]

The test case decision only has to be disregarded for the period before it was made if it found the tribunal to have been wrong, not if it found the tribunal to be right. The anti-test case rule also applies if the High Court (in Scotland, the Court of Session) has found a decision maker to have been wrong on an application for judicial review.

You can avoid the anti-test case rule by appealing rather than seeking a revision or supersession. This means that in cases where the anti-test case rule might apply, it may be better to appeal first (applying for leave to appeal out of time if necessary – see p1261) and only ask for a revision or supersession if you cannot appeal. For further details on revisions, supersessions and appeals, see pp1189 and 1199 and Chapter 44.

What happens while a test case is pending

If a test case is pending, the decision maker can postpone making a decision on your claim or request a supersession or review.[171] This prevents you appealing until a decision is made in the test case. If you already have a decision in your favour, the decision maker can suspend payment of your benefit (see p1105).

If you would be entitled to benefit even if the test case were decided against you, the decision maker can make a decision.[172] This is done on the assumption that the test case has been decided in the way that is most unfavourable to you. However, this does mean that you are at least paid something while you wait for the result of the test case.

If the decision on your claim or request for a revision or supersession is postponed, once a decision has been made in the test case, the decision maker, the tribunal or the commissioner then makes the decision in your case. If the test case goes in your favour, you are paid the extra benefit you are owed.[173] However, if your decision was not postponed, the anti-test case rule applies whether or not you made your claim or sought a revision or supersession before the decision in the test case.[174]

If you have already appealed to a tribunal, see p1232.

Notes

1 R(SB) 29/83; R(SB) 12/89; CIS/807/1992; CH/2155/2003

1. **Decisions**

2 s19 SSA 1998
3 **HB/CTB** Sch 7 para 5 CSPSSA 2000
Other benefits s11(2) SSA 1998
4 Regs 13(2) and (3)and 15 SS&CS(DA) Regs
5 Reg 13(1) SS&CS(DA) Regs
6 *Jones v Department of Employment* [1989] QB 1 (CA)
7 ss8 and 17 SSC(TF)A 1999
8 s10A SSA 1998; reg 11A SS&CS(DA) Regs
9 s11 SSC(TF)A 1999
10 s12(1) SSC(TF)A 1999
11 Reg 9 SSC(DA) Regs; s49 TMA 1970
12 s24A SSA 1998; reg 38A SS&CS(DA) Regs
13 s74 SSAA 1992; regs 7-10 SS(PAOR) Regs
14 **HB/CTB** Reg 10A HB&CTB(DA) Regs
Other benefits Reg 9A SS&CS(DA) Regs
15 **CB/GA** Reg 26(1) CB&GA(DA) Regs
HB/CTB Reg 10(1) HB&CTB(DA) Regs
Other benefits Reg 28(1) SS&CS(DA) Regs
16 Reg 10(2) HB&CTB(DA) Regs
17 **CB/GA** Regs 3 and 26(1)(b) and (2) CB&GA(DA) Regs
Other benefits Regs 2 and 28(1)(b) and (2) SS&CS(DA) Regs
18 R(IB) 4/02

3. **Change of circumstances after a claim**

19 **HB/CTB** Sch 7 para 2 CSPSSA 2000
Other benefits s8(2) SSA 1998; reg 12A SS&CS(DA) Regs

4. **General information about revisions and supersessions**

20 CSB/376/1983; R(I) 1/71; CI/11/1977
21 R(I) 50/56
22 R(IS) 11/92
23 ss9(2) and 10(2) SSA 1998

5. **Revisions**

24 **HB/CTB** Sch 7 para 3 CSPSSA 2000
Other benefits s9 SSA 1998
25 **CB/GA** s9(1) SSA 1998; regs 5, 8, 10 and 11 CB&GA(DA) Regs
HB/CTB Sch 7 para 3(1) CSPSSA 2000; reg 4 HB&CTB(DA) Regs
Other benefits s9(1) SSA 1998; reg 3 SS&CS(DA) Regs
26 **CB/GA** Reg 5(3) CB&GA(DA) Regs
HB/CTB Reg 4(10) HB&CTB(DA) Regs
Other benefits Reg 3(9)(a) SS&CS(DA) Regs
27 Reg 3(9)(b) SS&CS(DA) Regs
28 **CB/GA** Reg 5(2)(b) CB&GA(DA) Regs
HB/CTB Reg 4(1)(a) HB&CTB(DA) Regs
Other benefits Reg 3(1)(b) SS&CS(DA) Regs
29 Reg 1 SS&CS(DA) Regs, definition of 'claimant'
30 Reg 2(1) CB&GA(DA) Regs, definition of 'claimant'
31 Reg 3 HB&CTB(DA) Regs
32 R(H) 3/04
33 Reg 4(1)(b) and (c) HB&CTB(DA) Regs
34 **CB/GA** Reg 5(2)(a) CB&GA(DA) Regs
Other benefits Reg 3(1)(a) SS&CS(DA) Regs
35 Reg 3(3) SS&CS(DA) Regs
36 Regs 2 and 4(1)(a) HB&CTB(DA) Regs
37 Reg 4(4) HB&CTB(DA) Regs
38 **CB/GA** Regs 3 and 5(2)(b) CB&GA(DA) Regs
Other benefits Regs 2 and 3(1)(b) SS&CS(DA) Regs
39 **HB/CTB** Reg 10A(3) HB&CTB(DA) Regs
Other benefits Reg 9A(3) SS&CS(DA) Regs
40 **CB/GA** Reg 6(3)(c) CB&GA(DA) Regs
HB/CTB Reg 5(3)(b) HB&CTB(DA) Regs
Other benefits Reg 4(3)(b) SS&CS(DA) Regs
41 **CB/GA** Reg 5(2)(b) and 6(3)(a) and (b) CB&GA(DA) Regs
HB/CTB Reg 5(3)(a) HB&CTB(DA) Regs
Other benefits Regs 3(1)(b)(iv) and 4(3)(a) SS&CS(DA) Regs

42 **CB/GA** Reg 6(4) CB&GA(DA) Regs
HB/CTB Reg 5(4) HB&CTB(DA) Regs
Other benefits Reg 4(4) SS&CS(DA) Regs
43 **CB/GA** Reg 6(5) CB&GA(DA) Regs
HB/CTB Reg 5(6) HB&CTB(DA) Regs
Other benefits Reg 4(5) SS&CS(DA) Regs
44 **CB/GA** Reg 6(6) CB&GA(DA) Regs
HB/CTB Reg 5(5) HB&CTB(DA) Regs
Other benefits Reg 4(6) SS&CS(DA) Regs
45 CTC/3433/2003
46 **CB/GA** Reg 10(2)(a) CB&GA(DA) Regs
HB/CTB Reg 4(2)(a) HB&CTB(DA) Regs
Other benefits Reg 3(5)(a) SS&CS(DA) Regs
47 **HB/CTB** Reg 1(2) HB&CTB(DA) Regs, definition of 'official error'
Other benefits Reg 1(3) SS&CS(DA) Regs, definition of 'official error'
48 Reg 10(3) CB&GA(DA) Regs
49 R(CS) 3/04; CG/2122/2001
50 para 03257 DMG
51 **CB/GA** Reg 10(2)(b) CB&GA(DA) Regs
HB/CTB Reg 4(2)(b) HB&CTB(DA) Regs
Other benefits Regs 3(5)(b) and (c) and 7A(1) SS&CS(DA) Regs
52 Reg 7A(2) SS&CS(DA) Regs
53 **CB/GA** Reg 11 CB&GA(DA) Regs
HB/CTB Reg 4(7B) HB&CTB(DA) Regs
Other benefits Reg 3(7) SS&CS(DA) Regs
54 Reg 4(7C) HB&CTB(DA) Regs
55 **CB/GA** Reg 8(2) CB&GA(DA) Regs
Other benefits Reg 3(4A) SS&CS(DA) Regs
56 **CB/GA** Reg 8(3) CB&GA(DA) Regs
Other benefits Reg 3(5A) SS&CS(DA) Regs
57 Reg 4(7) HB&CTB(DA) Regs
58 Reg 3(7ZA) SS&CS(DA) Regs
59 Reg 3(7C) SS&CS(DA) Regs
60 Reg 3(7B) SS&CS(DA) Regs
61 Reg 3(6) SS&CS(DA) Regs
62 Reg 3(7A) SS&CS(DA) Regs
63 Reg 3(6A) SS&CS(DA) Regs
64 Reg 3(8A) SS&CS(DA) Regs
65 **HB/CTB** Reg 4(7A) HB&CTB(DA) Regs
Other benefits Reg 3(8B) SS&CS(DA) Regs
66 Reg 4(3) HB&CTB(DA) Regs
67 **CB/GA** Reg 9 CB&GA(DA) Regs
HB/CTB Reg 4(6) HB&CTB(DA) Regs
Other benefits Reg 3(8) SS&CS(DA) Regs
68 **CB/GA** Reg 2(1) CB&GA(DA) Regs, definition of 'appropriate office'
HB/CTB Reg 4(8) HB&CTB(DA) Regs
Other benefits Reg 3(11) SS&CS(DA) Regs
69 **CB/GA** Reg 7(1) CB&GA(DA) Regs
HB/CTB Reg 4(9) HB&CTB(DA) Regs
Other benefits Reg 3(10) SS&CS(DA) Regs
70 Reg 4(8) HB&CTB(DA) Regs
71 Reg 5(2) HB&CTB(DA) Regs
72 **HB/CTB** Sch 7 para 3(2) CSPSSA 2000
Other benefits s9(2) SSA 1998
73 para 03025 DMG
74 **CB/GA** Reg 7(2) and (3) CB&GA(DA) Regs
HB/CTB Reg 4(5) HB&CTB(DA) Regs
Other benefits Reg 3(2) SS&CS(DA) Regs
75 **HB/CTB** Sch 7 para 3(3) CSPSSA 2000
Other benefits s9(3) SSA 1998
76 **CB/GA** Reg 12 CB&GA(DA) Regs
HB/CTB Reg 6 HB&CTB(DA) Regs
Other benefits Reg 5(1) SS&CS(DA) Regs
77 Reg 5(2) SS&CS(DA) Regs
78 **CB/GA** Reg 28(2) CB&GA(DA) Regs
HB/CTB Sch 7 para 3(5) CSPSSA 2000; reg 18(3) HB&CTB(DA) Regs
Other benefits s9(5) SSA 1998; reg 31(2) SS&CS(DA) Regs
79 R(IS) 15/04; *Beltekian v Westminster City Council and Another* [2004] EWCA Civ 1784 (8 December 2004)
80 CIS/714/1991; CDLA/3364/2001;CDLA/4217/2001

6. **Supersessions**

81 **HB/CTB** Sch 7 para 4 CSPSSA 2000
Other benefits s10 SSA 1998
82 **CB/GA** Reg 13(1) CB&GA(DA) Regs
HB/CTB Reg 7(2) HB&CTB(DA) Regs
Other benefits Reg 6(2) SS&CS(DA) Regs
83 **CB/GA** Reg 14(1) CB&GA(DA) Regs
HB/CTB Reg 7(6) HB&CTB(DA) Regs
Other benefits Reg 6(5) SS&CS(DA) Regs
84 **CB/GA** Reg 15 CB&GA(DA) Regs
HB/CTB Reg 7(4) HB&CTB(DA) Regs
Other benefits Reg 6(3) SS&CS(DA) Regs
85 **CB/GA** Reg 13(2)(a) CB&GA(DA) Regs
HB/CTB Reg 7(2)(a) HB&CTB(DA) Regs
Other benefits Reg 6(2)(a) SS&CS(DA) Regs

86 **HB/CTB** Sch 7 para 2 CSPSSA 2000
Other benefits s8(2) SSA 1998; reg 12A SS&CS(DA) Regs
87 *CAO v McKiernon*, 8 July 1993 (CA)
88 *Cooke v The Secretary of State for Social Security* [2001], reported as R(DLA) 6/01; R(S) 4/86; R(IS) 2/98; CIB/7899/1996; CIS/856/1994
89 Reg 6(6)(a) SS&CS(DA) Regs
90 Reg 6(6)(c) SS&CS(DA) Regs
91 Reg 7(3) HB&CTB(DA) Regs
92 Reg 6(8) SS&CS(DA) Regs
93 **CB/GA** Reg 13(2)(b)(i) and (c)(i) CB&GA(DA) Regs
HB/CTB Reg 7(2)(b) and (d) HB&CTB(DA) Regs
Other benefits Reg 6(2)(b)(i) and (c) SS&CS(DA) Regs
94 Reg 7(2)(b)(i) HB&CTB(DA) Regs
95 **CB/GA** Reg 13(2)(b)(ii) CB&GA(DA) Regs
Other benefits Reg 6(2)(b)(ii) SS&CS(DA) Regs
96 **CB/GA** Reg 13(2)(b)(i) CB&GA(DA) Regs
HB/CTB Reg 7(2)(b) HB&CTB(DA) Regs
Other benefits Reg 6(2)(b)(i) SS&CS(DA) Regs
97 Reg 7(2)(b)(i) HB&CTB(DA) Regs
98 **CB/GA** Reg 13(2)(b)(ii) CB&GA(DA) Regs
Other benefits Reg 6(2)(b)(ii) SS&CS(DA) Regs
99 **CB/GA** Reg 13(2)(e) CB&GA(DA) Regs
HB/CTB Reg 7(2)(i) HB&CTB(DA) Regs
Other benefits Reg 6(2)(e) SS&CS(DA) Regs
100 Reg 6(2)(g) SS&CS(DA) Regs and reg 7A(1) SS&CS(DA) Regs, definition of 'incapacity benefit decision' and 'incapacity determination'; CIB/4033/2003; CIB/451/2004
101 CSIB/377/2003; CIB/1509/2004
102 CIB/1972/2000; DMG Letter June 2001; CIB/3179/2000; CIB/3985/2001
103 CSIB/501/2003
104 Reg 6(2)(n) SS&CS(DA) Regs
105 Reg 6(2)(ee) SS&CS(DA) Regs
106 **CB/GA** Reg 13(2)(c)(ii) CB&GA(DA) Regs
HB/CTB Reg 7(2)(d)(ii) HB&CTB(DA) Regs
Other benefits Reg 6(2)(c)(ii) SS&CS(DA) Regs
107 Reg 6(2)(f) SS&CS(DA) Regs
108 Reg 6(2)(h) SS&CS(DA) Regs
109 Reg 7(2ZA) HB&CTB(DA) Regs
110 Reg 7(2)(c) HB&CTB(DA) Regs
111 Reg 6(2)(i) SS&CS(DA) Regs
112 Reg 6(2)(j) and (k) SS&CS(DA) Regs
113 Reg 7(2)(g) and (h) HB&CTB(DA) Regs
114 Reg 6(2)(l) SS&CS(DA) Regs
115 Reg 6(2)(m) SS&CS(DA) Regs
116 **CB/GA** Reg 13(2)(d) CB&GA(DA) Regs
HB/CTB Reg 7(2)(e) HB&CTB(DA) Regs
Other benefits Reg 6(2)(d) SS&CS(DA) Regs
117 Reg 7(2B) and (2C) HB&CTB(DA) Regs
118 **CB/GA** Reg 14(1) CB&GA(DA) Regs
HB/CTB Reg 7(6) HB&CTB(DA) Regs
Other benefits Reg 6(5) SS&CS(DA) Regs
119 R(I) 50/56
120 Reg 7(7) HB&CTB(DA) Regs
121 **HB/CTB** Sch 7 para 4(3) CSPSSA 2000
Other benefits s10(2) SSA 1998
122 **CB/GA** Reg 14(3) CB&GA(DA) Regs
HB/CTB Reg 7(5) HB&CTB(DA) Regs
Other benefits Reg 6(4) SS&CS(DA) Regs
123 **HB/CTB** Sch 7 para 4(5) CSPSSA 2000
Other benefits s10(5) SSA 1998
124 Sch 3A paras 12 and 13 SS&CS(DA) Regs
125 **HB/CTB** Reg 8(10) HB&CTB(DA) Regs
Other benefits Reg 7(9)(a)(ii) and (30) SS&CS(DA) Regs
126 Reg 8(2) HB&CTB(DA) Regs
127 Reg 8(3) HB&CTB(DA) Regs
128 Reg 7(31) and (32) SS&CS(DA) Regs
129 Reg 7(9) SS&CS(DA) Regs
130 **CB/GA** Reg 16(3)(a) CB&GA(DA) Regs
Other benefits Reg 7(2)(a) SS&CS(DA) Regs
131 **CB/GA** Reg 16(4) CB&GA(DA) Regs
Other benefits Reg 7(2)(bb) and (9)(a) SS&CS(DA) Regs
132 **CB/GA** Reg 16(5) CB&GA(DA) Regs
Other benefits Reg 7(2)(c)(iii) SS&CS(DA) Regs, but see CIB/763/2004 for some incapacity decisions where the general rule applies
133 s10(5) SSA 1998
134 Reg 7(2)(c)(ii) SS&CS(DA) Regs
135 Reg 7A(2) SS&CS(DA) Regs
136 **CB/GA** Reg 17 CB&GA(DA) Regs
HB/CTB Reg 9 HB&CTB(DA) Regs
Other benefits Reg 8 SS&CS(DA) Regs
137 **CB/GA** Reg 17(3) CB&GA(DA) Regs
HB/CTB Reg 9(2) HB&CTB(DA) Regs
Other benefits Reg 8(3) SS&CS(DA) Regs

138 **CB/GA** Reg 17(4) CB&GA(DA) Regs
HB/CTB Reg 9(3) HB&CTB(DA) Regs
Other benefits Reg 8(4) SS&CS(DA) Regs
139 **CB/GA** Reg 17(6) CB&GA(DA) Regs
HB/CTB Reg 9(5) HB&CTB(DA) Regs
Other benefits Reg 8(6) SS&CS(DA) Regs
140 **CB/GA** Reg 16(3)(b) CB&GA(DA) Regs
Other benefits Reg 7(2)(b) SS&CS(DA) Regs
141 Reg 7(9)(d) SS&CS(DA) Regs
142 Reg 8(3) HB&CTB(DA) Regs
143 **CB/GA** Reg 16(7) CB&GA(DA) Regs
HB/CTB Reg 8(7) HB&CTB(DA) Regs
Other benefits Reg 7(5) SS&CS(DA) Regs
144 Reg 8(4) HB&CTB(DA) Regs
145 **CB/GA** Reg 16(10) CB&GA(DA) Regs
HB/CTB Reg 8(14) HB&CTB(DA) Regs
Other benefits Reg 7(7) SS&CS(DA) Regs
146 **CB/GA** Reg 16(9) CB&GA(DA) Regs
HB/CTB Reg 8(8) HB&CTB(DA) Regs
Other benefits Reg 7(6) SS&CS(DA) Regs
147 **CB/GA** Reg 16(9A) CB&GA(DA) Regs
Other benefits Reg 7(6A) SS&CS(DA) Regs
148 **CB/GA** Reg 16(8) CB&GA(DA) Reg
HB/CTB Reg 8(11) HB&CTB(DA) Regs
Other benefits Reg 7(33) SS&CS(DA) Regs
149 Reg 7(8) SS&CS(DA) Regs
150 Reg 7(24) SS&CS(DA) Regs
151 Reg 7(25) SS&CS(DA) Regs
152 Reg 7(10) SS&CS(DA) Regs
153 Reg 7(11) SS&CS(DA) Regs
154 Reg 7(12) and (13) SS&CS(DA) Regs
155 Reg 8(6A) HB&CTB(DA) Regs
156 Reg 8(2) and (6) HB&CTB(DA) Regs
157 Reg 7(27) SS&CS(DA) Regs
158 **HB/CTB** Reg 8(9) HB&CTB(DA) Regs
Other benefits Reg 7(28) SS&CS(DA) Regs
159 Reg 7(29) SS&CS(DA) Regs
160 Reg 7(29C) SS&CS(DA) Regs
161 Reg 7(29A) and (29B) SS&CS(DA) Regs
162 **CB/GA** Reg 16(9A) CB&GA(DA) Regs
Other benefits Reg 7(34) SS&CS(DA) Regs
163 **IS/JSA/PC** Regs 3(7), 6(2)(e) and 7(7) SS&CS(DA) Regs
HB/CTB Regs 4(7B) and (7C), 7(2)(i) and 8(14) HB&CTB(DA) Regs
164 CIS/1178/2001; memo DMG Vol 1 01/02
165 **IS/JSA/PC** s8(2) SSA 1998
HB/CTB Sch 7 para 2 CSPSSA 2000
166 CIS/714/1991; CDLA/3364/2001; CDLA/4217/2001
167 *Wood v Secretary of State for Work and Pensions* [2003] EWCA Civ 53, reported as R(DLA) 1/03

7. **The 'anti-test case rule'**
168 **HB/CTB** Sch 7 para 18 CSPSAA 2000
Other benefits s27 SSA 1998
All *CAO and Another v Bate* (HL) [1996] 2 All ER 790
169 R(FC) 3/98; CI/2107/2001; CI/2540/2001
170 *CAO and Another v Woods* 12 December 1997, unreported (CA); CDLA/12045/1996
171 **HB/CTB** Sch 7 para 16 CSPSAA 2000
Other benefits s25 SSA 1998
172 **CB/GA** s25(3) SSA 1998; reg 22 CB&GA(DA) Regs
HB/CTB Sch 7 para 16(3) CSPSAA 2000; reg 15 HB&CTB(DA) Regs
Other benefits s25(3) SSA 1998; reg 21 SS&CS(DA) Regs
173 **HB/CTB** Sch 7 para 18(2) CSPSAA 2000
Other benefits s27(2) SSA 1998
174 **HB/CTB** Sch 7 para 18(5) CSPSAA 2000
Other benefits s27(6) SSA 1998

44

Chapter 44

Appeals: benefits

This chapter covers:

You can appeal to an appeal tribunal if you disagree with certain decisions made by the Department for Work and Pensions, local authorities and the Revenue about the benefits in this *Handbook* or payments from the regulated social fund (see Chapter 22). See p1219 for information about the decisions you can appeal. In addition, you can appeal against some decisions about your national insurance contributions (see p1181).

The Revenue

The Revenue makes decisions about child benefit and guardian's allowance as well as tax credits. However, references to the Revenue in this chapter apply to decisions about child benefit and guardian's allowance and do *not* apply to child tax credit (CTC) and working tax credit (WTC).

The rules for appeals about CTC and WTC are covered in Chapter 58. However, many of the rules for appeals about CTC and WTC are the same as those described in this chapter. Chapter 58 refers you to this chapter where relevant. The footnotes in this chapter contain references to the CTC and WTC legislation where applicable.

This chapter does *not* cover:

- statutory sick pay, statutory maternity pay, statutory adoption pay or statutory paternity pay. For these, you can appeal to the tax appeal commissioners (see p607); *or*
- payments from the *discretionary* social fund. You *cannot* appeal to an appeal tribunal. Instead you can seek a review (see Chapter 45); *or*
- the benefits in Chapter 9 or on p18; *or*

- discretionary housing payments of housing benefit or council tax benefit. For these, see p237.

You can seek a 'revision' (see p1189) prior to appealing against a decision. If you want to seek a revision or appeal you should not delay. The time limit for doing this is very strict (see pp1223 and 1191). For information about the advantages and disadvantages of revisions or appeals, see pp1188 and 1222. Appeals can take time. If your circumstances change while you are waiting for your appeal to be heard, you may need to make a fresh claim for benefit or seek a supersession (see p1238).

1. Appeal rights

You can appeal to an appeal tribunal against some decisions of the Department for Work and Pensions (DWP), local authority or the Revenue. The main rules are:

- There is a strict time limit for appealing – normally only one month (see p1223).
- You must provide certain information when you appeal. If you do not do this, your appeal might not go ahead (see p1224).
- You must appeal in writing and normally on the appropriate form. If you do not use the appropriate form, your appeal can be accepted so long as it is in writing and includes all the information required (see p1225). There is no guarantee of this, so use the form wherever possible.
- The completed appeal form should be sent or delivered to the office that made the decision with which you disagree. The office passes forms or appeal letters to The Appeals Service (TAS – see p1233).
- A decision maker can ask you to provide further information about your appeal, but it is TAS that decides if your appeal is valid, not the DWP, local authority or the Revenue (see p1225).

If you want the tribunal to deal with your appeal quickly, make this plain on your appeal form, explaining why. You could also telephone the DWP, local authority, the Revenue or the clerk to the tribunal at TAS about this.

The make-up of the tribunal which deals with your appeal depends on the issue with which you disagree (see p1244). See p1253 for advice about how to prepare an appeal.

Who can appeal

You can appeal to an appeal tribunal if you are the claimant. However, certain other people can also appeal as follows:

- If you are appealing about a **benefit other than housing benefit (HB) or council tax benefit (CTB)**, you also have a right to appeal if you are:[1]

- an appointee claiming on someone's behalf (see p1075);
- acting on behalf of someone claiming attendance allowance (AA) or disability living allowance (DLA) (even if this is without her/his knowledge) and you are appealing about whether or not s/he is terminally ill (see p149);
- a person from whom an ordinary overpayment of a benefit or social fund payment or a duplication of payment of income support (IS), pension credit (PC) or income-based jobseeker's allowance (JSA) can be recovered. This is the case even if you were not the person who claimed the benefit that was overpaid;[2]
- a person appointed by the DWP or the Revenue to proceed with a claim for benefit made by someone who has since died;
- a person appointed by the DWP or the Revenue to make a claim for (and who has claimed) benefit for someone who has died. This includes claims for industrial injuries disablement benefit or reduced earnings allowance if:[3]
  - the person who died would have been entitled to the benefit if s/he had claimed it in time; *and*
  - you apply to be appointed within six months of a death certificate being issued.

- If you are appealing about **HB** or **CTB**, you also have a right to appeal to a tribunal if you are a person affected by a decision (see p1191).[4] In some cases, this includes landlords.

In all cases, if the person who appealed dies, the DWP, local authority or the Revenue can appoint some other person to proceed with the appeal.[5]

Decisions you can appeal

You can appeal to an appeal tribunal against *most* decisions taken by the Secretary of State, a local authority officer or an officer of the Revenue (known as 'decision makers' – see p1180).[6] You can appeal against an original decision or a decision made after an application for a revision or a supersession (see pp1198 and 1210).

You must be given a written notice of any decision against which you can appeal.[7] The notice must give you information about your right to appeal against the decision and your right to request a written statement of reasons for it if this has not been included (see p1220).

Sometimes, a decision maker refuses to make a decision on your claim. If this happens, it effectively prevents you having the right to appeal. However, a decision maker must make a decision on every valid claim.[8] See pp1079 and 216 for what counts as a valid claim. You can then appeal and it is up to the tribunal to decide whether the decision is correct. Remember, if the decision maker does not accept that your claim is valid, you should be given a decision saying so. You can appeal to a tribunal and ask it to decide if your claim is valid.

Remember that a decision maker can sometimes postpone making a decision if there is a test case pending (see p1212).

Examples of decisions against which you can appeal

Jobseeker's allowance	*All benefits*
Whether a jobseeker's agreement is reasonable.	Whether you are incapable of work.
Whether you are available for work.	Calculation of your earnings.
Whether you are actively seeking work.	Whether benefit can be exported.
Whether you have left a job.	Whether you satisfy the disability conditions for benefit.
Whether you have lost your job through misconduct.	Whether your claim can be backdated.
Whether you have given up or lost your place on a training scheme.	Whether you have been overpaid benefit and if it is recoverable.
Whether your refusal or failure to carry out a jobseeker's direction was reasonable.	Whether you satisfy the habitual residence test.
Whether you should be sanctioned and how long a sanction should last.	Whether your claim has been validly made.
Whether you can be paid hardship payments.	The refusal to allocate you a national insurance number.[9]
	Whether your benefit is payable under the overlapping benefit rules.[10]

If you are uncertain whether you can appeal against a decision, you should seek advice immediately. There is a strict time limit for appealing (see p1223).

You can seek a revision (see p1189) before you appeal, but you do not have to do so. See p1222 before deciding what to do.

Reasons for the decision maker's decision

You can ask why a decision was made, but remember that there is a one-month time limit for making an appeal (see below). For information about explanations, see p1183 and for written statements of reasons for a decision, see p1184. These could help you decide if it is worth challenging the decision.

Sometimes it might not be clear whether you have been given a written statement of reasons with your decision, or in the case of benefits other than HB or CTB you might not receive it before your time limit for appealing expires. In both of these situations, you should appeal within the one-month time limit to protect your position.

On receiving the written statement of reasons, if there are grounds for a revision or supersession (see pp1189 and 1199), you may decide it is worth asking for one of these rather than appealing immediately (but see p1222). In any case, if you appeal, a decision maker may look at the decision again and decide to revise it (see p1226).

Remember, if the decision is about:

- **HB or CTB**, there is no time limit for asking for a written statement of reasons.[11] However, the time limit for appealing is very strict. If you want to appeal you should remember to do so within the time limit, even if you decide to ask for a written statement of reasons later. If you ask for a written statement of reasons, these must be provided by the local authority within 14 days if this is practicable. Days between the date you request the statement and the date on which it is given to you are ignored when calculating the one-month time limit for appealing.[12]
- **Benefits other than HB or CTB**, you must ask for a written statement of reasons within one month of being sent a decision. The DWP or the Revenue must then provide the written statement of reasons within 14 days, but rarely meets this deadline.[13] See p1224 for information about how your time limit is extended if you ask for a written statement of reasons.

Decisions you cannot appeal

You cannot appeal to a tribunal against some decisions made by decision makers.[14] You *can* ask for a revision or a supersession of these (see pp1189 and 1199). You do not have to have specific grounds for the revision or supersession. However, if the decision maker refuses to revise or supersede the decision, your only legal remedy is to apply for judicial review (see p1253).

Examples of decisions against which you cannot appeal

Who should be the claimant when a couple is unable to decide.

How benefit should be paid.

Whether:

– a claim for one benefit can be treated as (or in addition to) a claim for another benefit;
– to demand recovery of an overpayment, and the amount of weekly deductions (subject to the maximum – see p1142);
– to suspend payment of benefit;
– to take action against people who are liable to maintain claimants (see p851);
– to appoint a person as an appointee (see p1075);
– to issue or replace giros and order books;
– to pay an interim payment;
– a school or college is a 'recognised educational establishment'.

If you are uncertain whether you can appeal against a decision, you should seek advice straight away. If a decision maker says you cannot appeal against a refusal to do an 'any time' revision, or to consider a supersession, see pp1198 and 1211. Remember, there is a strict time limit for appealing (see p1223).

Revision, supersession or appeal

Revisions, supersessions and appeals are all ways of getting decisions changed. If you can opt to seek a revision or supersession as well as appealing you need to be careful which one you choose. For more information about revisions and supersessions, see Chapter 43.

Advantages of applying for a revision

Some of the advantages of applying for an 'any grounds' revision include:

- it is simpler to seek a revision than to appeal;
- you could receive a decision more quickly if you seek a revision;
- you get two bites at the cherry because if your application for a revision is turned down you can still appeal against the decision.

You do not have to seek a revision and can appeal straightaway. However, if the decision maker agrees that a decision is wrong, s/he might revise it anyway and your appeal could lapse (see p1227).

Example

Lindsey fails to satisfy the 'personal capability assessment' (see p772) and her incapacity benefit ceases. She asks the DWP to revise the decision to stop her benefit because her GP has told her to refrain from work. The DWP considers the new medical evidence but refuses to revise its decision. Lindsey can still appeal to an appeal tribunal.

The advantage of seeking an 'any time' revision is that there is no time limit for doing so (see p1193). You can ask for an 'any time' revision even if the time limit for appealing has expired. However, see p1198 for information about challenging an 'any time' revision.

Disadvantages of applying for a revision

Before deciding whether to seek a revision or to appeal, there are some important problems to bear in mind:

- The time limit for appealing (one month – see p1223) continues to run while the decision maker considers your application for a revision. You therefore need to make sure the DWP, local authority or the Revenue has actually received your request. Otherwise, you should appeal within the time limit to protect your position.
- The arrears of benefit you get could be limited if the 'anti-test case' rule applies (see p1211).

Disadvantages of applying for a supersession

There is a major disadvantage to applying for a supersession. You may not be paid all the arrears of benefit due to you if you seek a supersession, even if you are successful. See p1204 for information about the arrears of benefit you can be paid following a supersession.

In deciding whether you would want to ask for a supersession or make an appeal, you should take into account all of the factors that might lead to arrears of benefit being limited. These include:

- the length of time since the original decision; *and*
- whether the 'anti-test case' rule (see p1211) applies to you.

If you think there is a risk that you will not obtain all the arrears you are due you should seek a revision (see p1190) or appeal instead of applying for a supersession if you can.

Problems in making an appeal

There is not usually any risk attached to making an appeal. However, if you are appealing about a benefit which can be paid at different rates, for example, your AA, DLA or industrial injuries disablement benefit, and the rate of the benefit you are claiming could go down, you should seek advice before you appeal. Because the tribunal looks at your case afresh, there is a risk you could lose benefit.

When you appeal against a decision, a decision maker looks at it again and could change it. If this happens, your appeal could lapse (see p1227).

There is a strict time limit for appealing (see below). If your appeal is late, you must get permission before you can appeal (see p1261) and this is only given in limited circumstances.

The time limit for appealing

Your appeal, including all the information described on p1225, must arrive at the relevant office within one month of the date the written decision was sent to you.[15] It is very important that you provide all the information required within the time limit. Your appeal is not valid until you do. The time limit can be extended (see p1224) and you can appeal outside the one-month time limit (see p1224) in limited circumstances.

'Month' means a complete calendar month running from the day after the day you have been sent or given a decision.[16] For example, a decision sent on 24 July has an appeal time limit that expires at the end of 24 August.

Remember:

- Unless it is a decision about child benefit or guardian's allowance, if an accidental error in a decision has been corrected (see p1183), any day falling before the day on which the correction is notified to you is ignored in calculating the one-month period.[17]

- It is a legally qualified tribunal member, *not* the DWP, local authority or the Revenue who decides whether your appeal has been made within the time limit.[18]

If the decision maker revises or supersedes a decision or refuses to do so (see pp1198 and 1210), the one-month time limit runs from the date that you are sent the new decision.[19] If the decision maker refuses to do an 'any time' revision or to consider a supersession and says you cannot appeal, you should appeal against the original decision within the time limit if this has not already passed and seek advice.

Extending the time limit

If you ask for a written statement of reasons for a decision where one has not already been given to you (see p1184), your time limit is automatically extended. If the decision is about:

- **HB** or **CTB**, the days between the date you request the statement and the date on which it is given to you are ignored when calculating the one-month time limit;[20]
- **other benefits**, you must appeal within:[21]
  - one month and 14 days of the date you were sent the decision, if you requested a written statement of reasons and it is provided within the month; *or*
  - 14 days of a written statement of reasons being provided, if you requested one within one month of the date you were sent the decision, but it is not provided within that one-month period.

If you miss the one-month time limit

You can appeal outside the one-month time limit in limited circumstances. However, you must appeal within an absolute time limit which is one year from the date the one-month time limit for appealing expired. See p1261 for further information about late appeals.

You could also:

- make a late application for a revision in limited circumstances (see p1191);
- ask for a supersession if you can show there are grounds (see p1199).

How to appeal

You must appeal in writing, preferably using the appropriate appeal form, within the time limit (see p1223).[22] For **HB and CTB**, you should use the form approved by your local authority.[23] For **other benefits** (other than child benefit and guardian's allowance), the appeal form is in leaflet GL24, *If You Think Our Decision is Wrong*. For **child benefit and guardian's allowance**, the appeal form is in leaflet CH24A, *If You Think Our Decision is Wrong*. The leaflets are available at DWP offices, the Revenue, some Citizens Advice Bureaux and advice centres. In addition, the form for child benefit and guardian's allowance is on the Revenue website and the form for other benefits is on the DWP website (see Appendix 1 for the addresses.

You must sign the appeal form. For benefits other than HB and CTB, if you have provided written authority, your representative can sign it on your behalf.[24] You should send or deliver your appeal to the office of the DWP, local authority or the Revenue (the JobCentre if you are appealing about your JSA) which sent you the decision.[25] If you live in a ONE scheme area and the decision concerns a claim you made at a ONE office, you can send or deliver your appeal form to that office.

Making sure your appeal is valid

For your appeal to be valid, it must contain all the information required (see below). If you do not use the correct appeal form, your appeal can still be valid, so long as you provide the information.[26] It is a legally qualified tribunal member who decides if your appeal is valid, not the DWP, local authority or the Revenue (see p1226).

When you appeal you must provide:[27]

- enough details about the decision with which you disagree for it to be identified. For example, the DWP appeal form asks you for:
  - the name of the benefit you are appealing about – eg, IS or incapacity benefit; *and*
  - the date you were sent the decision with which you disagree. You can find this date on the letter notifying you of the decision;
- a summary of your reasons for saying the decision was wrong. You should not simply say you think the decision was wrong, but explain why.

Examples

'The local authority says I have been overpaid housing benefit because I failed to disclose that my wife had started working part time, but I wrote to them as soon as she started work and told them what her take-home pay would be.'

'The decision is that I should not get child benefit for my son because he left school in June. This decision is wrong because my son decided to stay on at school and do his 'A' levels.'

'You say I cannot get DLA care component. This decision is wrong because you have not taken into account the amount of help I need due to my incontinence of the bowel and bladder.'

It is also helpful to include information and evidence which supports your appeal because a decision maker looks at the decision again before the appeal hearing and might revise it (see p1226).

What happens if you do not provide sufficient information

If you do not include sufficient information on your appeal form or letter, a decision maker can send it back to you and ask you to provide the information you left out.[28] You must be given at least 14 days to return this. Be sure to complete the form properly and return it or provide the information required within the time allowed. Otherwise you might not count as having made your appeal within the time limit.

Your one-month time limit for appealing (see p1223) is extended if you are asked to complete your appeal form or provide information. The one-month time limit is extended by:[29]

- 14 days from the date your appeal form is returned to you for completion, if the completed form is received back within 14 days;
- 14 days from the date you are asked for further information, if you provide this within 14 days of the request;
- the length of time you are given to complete a form or provide information, if this is longer than 14 days.

If you fail to complete the form properly or provide the information required in time, your appeal is forwarded to TAS (see p1233). A legally qualified tribunal member then considers whether your appeal is valid and can go ahead.[30] If you complete and return the form or provide the information before the tribunal member makes a decision, any further details you provide must be taken into account.[31]

If your appeal is not accepted as valid, you can try to make a late appeal (see p1261).

What happens after you appeal

After you appeal, the DWP, local authority or the Revenue:

- prepares the appeal papers – known as the decision maker's submission (see p1228) – and sends a copy to you (and your representative if you have one); *and*
- sends you a questionnaire (called an 'enquiry form') asking you whether you want an oral hearing and, if so, when you and your representative (if you have one) are available to attend; *and*
- forwards your appeal to the local TAS office along with a copy of the decision maker's decision. Your appeal should not be held up while the decision maker considers whether s/he should do a revision (see p1227). Following a complaint, an Ombudsman said that the local authority should forward an appeal to TAS within 28 days.[32]

You should be sent a postage-paid envelope in which to return the enquiry form to TAS. You must return it within 14 days (the clerk to a tribunal has discretion to increase this period).[33] Your appeal could be struck out if you fail to return the enquiry form in time (see p1229).

You might find that your appeal is not dealt with if there is a test case pending which deals with the same issues (see p1232).

The effect of a revision on your appeal

After you appeal, a decision maker might look at the decision you are appealing about again and might revise the decision – eg, on the basis of any facts, information or evidence that you provided with your appeal form. If this happens, your appeal could lapse, even if you do not get everything you want, and you will have to appeal again.[34]

Your **appeal lapses** where the new decision is more advantageous to you than the original decision – eg, the decision:[35]

- awards you benefit at a higher rate or for a longer period;
- lifts a refusal or disqualification of benefit or a JSA sanction, either in whole or in part;
- reverses a decision to pay benefit to a third party (see p1109);
- means you gain financially from the revised decision;
- says an overpayment of benefit is not recoverable or that less should be recovered; *or*
- reverses a decision that an accident was not an industrial accident.

If the new decision is not more advantageous to you, your appeal must go ahead, but against the new decision.[36] You have one month from the date the decision is sent to you to make further representations.[37] At the end of that period (or earlier if you agree in writing), your appeal proceeds unless the decision is revised again and is now more advantageous to you (see above).[38]

If your appeal lapses, you must make a fresh appeal. Your time limit for appealing (see p1223) runs from the date the new decision is sent to you.[39]

Oral or paper hearings

If you want an **oral hearing**, you must state this on the enquiry form (see p1226).[40] You are more likely to win your appeal if you attend an oral hearing, particularly where your appeal concerns a medical issue or your disability or where there is an argument about the facts of your case. The DWP, local authority or the Revenue can also ask for an oral hearing. If you (or the DWP, local authority or the Revenue) asks for an oral hearing, you must be given one, unless your appeal has been struck out (see p1229).[41] Even if none of you wants an oral hearing, the chair of the tribunal might decide that one should take place.[42]

If none of you opts for an oral hearing and the chair does not think one is necessary, the tribunal makes its decision by looking at what you said on your appeal form, any evidence or other information you provided to support your appeal, and the decision maker's submission (see p1228). This is known as a **paper hearing.**

You may feel that you would rather not attend an oral hearing – eg, because you are worried about speaking for yourself or would have difficulties getting there. But remember:

- if you attend an oral hearing, you can explain your side of the story to the tribunal and you are more likely to win;
- you can seek advice before you decide what to do;
- you can ask someone to represent you (see Appendix 2). If you take someone with you to an oral hearing your chances of winning are much higher. You can take a friend, relative, adviser or representative with you[43] – you can have more than one person if the chair of the tribunal agrees;[44]
- TAS aims to provide a qualified interpreter if you need one (eg, if English is not your first language). If you do, tell the clerk to the tribunal in advance of the hearing;
- if you or your representative cannot be physically present at an oral hearing (eg, because of a disability you cannot get to where the tribunal is heard), you might be able to be present via a video link if the chair of the tribunal agrees.[45] Contact the TAS office you normally use and see if this can be arranged;
- you, an interpreter (if needed) and any witnesses may be able to get expenses paid – eg, you can claim for travel, meals, loss of earnings and childcare costs.[46]

If you opt for a paper hearing, you should think about what other information and evidence you can get to support your appeal, and send it to the tribunal. You should make sure that everything you want to say in support of your appeal has been put in writing and that there are no other documents which you would like the tribunal to see. You should send this to the clerk to the tribunal as soon as possible (see p1229). See p1253 for information about sorting out the facts and checking the statute law and the caselaw that apply in your case.

The decision maker's submission

The DWP, local authority or the Revenue prepares a detailed explanation of the reasons for its decision – known as the decision maker's submission – and this is sent to you along with a bundle of papers relevant to your appeal. Where your appeal involves a medical issue or one about your disability, a record of medical examinations you have had in connection with your claim is usually included.

If your appeal is to be dealt with at an oral hearing, see p1231 for information about how much notice you must be given.

If you opted for a paper hearing, but decide you want an oral hearing after all, you might be able to change your mind. You must tell the clerk to the tribunal before the tribunal makes its decision.

Providing other information

Once you have seen the decision maker's submission, you might want to provide additional information to support your appeal. For example, you might want to get independent medical evidence or provide supporting statements from witnesses. If your appeal is to be dealt with at a paper hearing, you should provide this information as soon as possible after being sent the decision maker's submission (see p1228). Even if you are going to have an oral hearing, it is important to provide information in advance. See p1253 for further information about how to prepare an appeal.

Information you must provide

A legally qualified tribunal member (see p1233) or clerk to the tribunal might issue directions requiring you or the DWP (or local authority or the Revenue) to provide further information or documents.[47] You or the decision maker can also apply to the clerk to ask a legally qualified tribunal member to issue directions.[48] This can be useful, for example, if you are having trouble getting documents or information from the decision maker. If you are given a direction to provide information or evidence within a specific period, it is important that you comply with it. If you do not, your appeal can be struck out (see below), or the tribunal might conclude that the information or evidence was adverse to you. If you miss the deadline in the directions, try to provide what has been requested as soon as possible. The tribunal should still consider the information or evidence – eg, if you provide it at the hearing.[49]

When your appeal can be struck out

Your appeal can be struck out, but only in certain circumstances. This cancels your appeal and it does not go ahead. This might happen where you fail to provide information or documents that you have been asked to provide by a legally qualified tribunal member or clerk (see above) or you fail to return the tribunal enquiry form (see p1226).

Your appeal can only be struck out if:[50]

- the tribunal does not have what is known as 'jurisdiction' to deal with it (eg, you do not have a right to appeal against the decision – see p1221).[51] You must have been informed that it might be struck out;
- there is want of prosecution (eg, you do not appear to be pursuing it) including where you have not appealed within the absolute time limit (see p1261);
- you fail to comply with a direction given to you by a legally qualified tribunal member or clerk to the tribunal – eg, a request to provide information to support your appeal. You must be told that a failure to do so could lead to your appeal being struck out;
- you fail to notify the clerk to the tribunal whether or not you want an oral hearing within the 14-day time limit (see p1226). You must be told that a failure to do so could lead to your appeal being struck out.[52]

The procedure for striking out an appeal

Your appeal can be struck out by the clerk to the tribunal or by a legally qualified tribunal member. In practice, the clerk to the tribunal only strikes out appeals where you fail to notify her/him whether or not you want an oral hearing. In all other cases, it is a legally qualified tribunal member.[53] If the clerk to the tribunal strikes out your appeal, you must be notified and told how you can apply for your appeal to be reinstated (see below).[54]

Getting your appeal reinstated

If your appeal is struck out, you may be able to get it reinstated. A clerk to the tribunal can reinstate the appeal if:[55]

- it has been struck out because you failed to notify the clerk to the tribunal whether or not you wanted an oral hearing within the 14-day time limit (see p1229); *and*
- the clerk is satisfied that there are reasonable grounds for the appeal to be reinstated.

You must apply in writing to the clerk to the tribunal, within one month of the order to strike out your appeal being issued. You must say why you think your appeal should not have been struck out. If the clerk is not satisfied that there are reasonable grounds for your appeal to be reinstated, your application must be passed to a legally qualified tribunal member to make a decision.

A legally qualified tribunal member can reinstate your appeal if s/he is satisfied that:[56]

- there are reasonable grounds for it to be reinstated. You must apply in writing to the clerk to the tribunal within one month of the order to strike out your appeal being issued, saying why your appeal should not be struck out; *or*
- it is not an appeal which can be struck out (see p1229); *or*
- it is not in the interests of justice for your appeal to be struck out.

If the tribunal member refuses to reinstate your appeal, you might be able to make a fresh appeal.[57] See p1223 for the time limit for appealing and p1261 for late appeals.

Withdrawing an appeal

If you change your mind about appealing, you can withdraw your appeal.[58] If your appeal has not yet been passed to TAS, you should write to the DWP, local authority or the Revenue to say that you do not wish your appeal to go ahead. Your authorised representative can write on your behalf.

If your appeal has been passed to TAS, you must apply in writing to the clerk to the tribunal. S/he must allow you to withdraw your appeal. You can also withdraw your appeal at an oral hearing.

Once an appeal has been withdrawn it cannot be reinstated.[59] However, if you decide that you want to go ahead after all, you could try to make a late appeal (but see p1261).[60]

The oral hearing

You must be sent notice of the oral hearing at least 14 days before it is to take place unless you agree to less notice than this.[61] However, TAS aims to give you six weeks' notice of the oral hearing as soon as it receives your enquiry form (see p1226).

If you have not been given the correct notice (you can argue this includes the decision maker's submission and evidence as well as the time and date of the hearing) the tribunal can only go ahead if you agree.[62] If you give up your right to notice, for example because you want your appeal to be dealt with quickly and are happy for it to be listed at short notice, the tribunal can go ahead with the hearing even if you are not there.[63]

An appeal is heard in public unless the chair thinks it should be in private:[64]

- because it is in the interests of national security, morals, public order or children; *or*
- for the protection of the private or family life of a party to the proceedings; *or*
- in special circumstances, because publicity would prejudice the interests of justice.

If you want your hearing to be in private, you should ask the chair of the tribunal to consider this. In practice, it is extremely rare for members of the public to turn up.

Postponements and adjournments

If the hearing date is inconvenient or you want more time to prepare your case, you can ask for it to be **postponed**. You must apply in writing to the clerk to the tribunal, before the hearing date, saying why you want your appeal to be postponed.[65] You should do this as soon as you decide that you want a postponement. Clerks and tribunal members can postpone your oral hearing even if this is not requested.[66]

TAS is very keen to avoid postponements and you should *not* presume that one will be granted. You should ring before the hearing is due to take place to check if a postponement has been agreed. Be ready to attend the hearing if it goes ahead. If you have a representative, s/he should warn you that your application might not be successful.[67] If you are refused a postponement, you should be given written notice and your request and the refusal is put to the tribunal.[68]

If you do not attend and have not asked for a postponement, the tribunal can hear the appeal without you,[69] and you are less likely to succeed. If you are refused a postponement but do not attend the hearing, the tribunal should consider whether to adjourn the hearing.[70] A hearing should be **adjourned** if:

- there is doubt about whether you received notice of the oral hearing;[71]
- you have advised the tribunal that you cannot attend, have a good reason for not attending and have asked for another hearing date;[72] *or*

- you are unable to attend the hearing (eg, you are in prison) but your evidence could be expected to play an important part in the tribunal reaching its decision;[73] *or*
- you want to be represented at the oral hearing, but your representative is not available on the date it has been listed and has made a reasonable request for a postponement. Your representative should explain why s/he cannot attend and why no one else can represent you in his/her place;[74] *or*
- you need to get a representative – eg, because it is difficult for you to represent yourself, or the decision with which you disagree concerns a large overpayment.[75]

If the tribunal makes a decision in your absence with which you disagree, you can try to appeal to a social security commissioner (see p1245) or you can ask for the decision to be set aside (but see p1242).

Even if an oral hearing is under way, it can be adjourned if you or the DWP, local authority or the Revenue wants this to happen, or if the tribunal itself thinks this is the best course.[76] Your case may be adjourned if, for example, more evidence is required. A tribunal might adjourn your case if there is a test case pending which deals with the same issues as your appeal (see below). You should consider asking for an adjournment if the tribunal says it is going to consider whether you should get a lower rate of benefit than you are getting currently, for example DLA or AA, to allow you to prepare your case and make representations.

You can only appeal against a tribunal's decision to adjourn if it is what is known as a 'final decision' – eg, there are no major issues to resolve or it is inevitable what the tribunal will eventually decide.[77]

What happens if a test case decision is pending

If a test case is pending which deals with issues raised in your case (your appeal is then known as a 'look alike' case), the DWP, local authority or the Revenue can suspend payment of your benefit or even postpone making a decision about your claim (see p1212). This means you will not be able to appeal until a decision is made about the test case.

But what happens if you have already appealed? For benefits other than HB and CTB, where a decision is pending in a test case against a commissioner's or court's decision and you have appealed to a tribunal or commissioner in a 'look alike' case, the decision maker can serve notice requiring the tribunal or commissioner in *your* appeal:[78]

- not to make a decision and to refer your case back to her/him (s/he could then postpone making a decision – see p1212);
- to postpone making a decision until the test case is decided; *or*
- to decide your appeal as if the test case had been decided in the way most unfavourable to you, but only if this is in your interests. If this happens, and the test case eventually goes in your favour, the decision maker has to make a

new decision superseding the decision of the tribunal or commissioner in the light of the decision in the test case.[79]

If the decision on your claim or appeal has been postponed, once a decision has been made in the test case, the decision is made on your claim or appeal. If a decision maker postponed making the decision, see p1212.

The paper hearing

You are not sent notice of a paper hearing. The tribunal makes its decision in your absence and you are then notified of its decision (see p1239).

2. Tribunal procedures

The Appeals Service (TAS) consists of:

- an executive agency headed by a chief executive who is responsible for the administration of appeals; *and*
- an independent panel of tribunal members who are appointed by the Lord Chancellor and headed by the President.

The standards of tribunals are the responsibility of the President of TAS. TAS is divided into regions, with a chair for each region who is responsible for the recruitment and training of tribunal members. The names and addresses of the President and the regional chairs are given in Appendix 1.

The President issues protocols to guide tribunals on how they should conduct themselves. Copies of these can be obtained by contacting one of the TAS offices or on the TAS website (see Appendix 1).

Each region has a panel of tribunal members. The people who hear your appeal are drawn from this panel. For more information about who is likely to deal with your appeal, see p1244. The tribunal's administration is dealt with by clerks.

People present at hearings

The tribunal consists of a **chair** and up to two other **members**. One member of the tribunal is always legally qualified and s/he is normally the chair of the tribunal. The chair makes a note of what is said by you, your representative, the Department for Work and Pensions (DWP) (or local authority or the Revenue) and any witnesses. The chair has to record the tribunal's decision, and the reasons for its decision – known as a 'full decision'. See p1239 for information about decisions. To see who makes up a tribunal, see p1244.

The **clerk to the tribunal** is there in an administrative capacity – eg, to pay expenses. The clerk takes no part in making the decision on your appeal and should not express any views on the case.

A **presenting officer** sometimes attends – eg, when an appeal is considered complicated. S/he represents the decision maker. S/he is seldom the person who made the decision you are appealing about. S/he explains the reasons for the decision, but is not there to defend it at all costs. S/he may provide information which helps your case.[80] Even if there is no presenting officer, the tribunal can consider and decide your appeal, although it might adjourn the hearing and request a presenting officer to attend a new hearing. Note that the DWP has agreed to send a presenting officer to a hearing where directed to do so by the tribunal.[81]

If your appeal raises difficult issues, an **expert** may also be present at the hearing (see p1244).

You can have a **representative** with you at the hearing.[82] S/he can help you understand the procedures, present your case to the tribunal and help to ensure that the tribunal is aware of all the relevant issues and the law.

Procedure at an oral hearing

When the tribunal is ready to hear your case, you (and your representative if you have one) are taken in with the presenting officer (see above). There are no strict rules of procedure. The chair decides how the hearing is conducted.[83]

The chair should start by introducing the members of the tribunal and everyone else who is present. If a presenting officer is at the hearing, s/he is often asked to summarise the decision maker's submission (see p1228) and you are asked to explain your reasons for disagreeing with it. Alternatively, you may be asked to explain your position first. If you think there are mistakes in the tribunal papers, point them out. You can call any witnesses and can ask questions of the presenting officer, and the tribunal members ask questions of you both.[84] See p1253 for information about preparing for your appeal and presenting your case.

The tribunal considers all the facts, evidence, law and caselaw before it makes a decision. See p1254 for information about evidence and p1257 about the law and caselaw. The tribunal should not bargain with you by 'offering' to allow part of your appeal if you agree to drop other parts – eg, by offering you one component of disability living allowance (DLA) if you agree not to argue for the other.[85]

Medical examination at the oral hearing

Tribunals cannot carry out physical examinations unless your appeal is related to the assessment of your disablement for severe disablement allowance (SDA) or industrial injuries disablement benefit or whether you have a prescribed disease or injury.[86] Likewise, there is no 'walking test' for the disability living allowance (DLA) mobility component. However, the tribunal may take its visual observation of you into account. It should not, however, attach undue weight to its observations.[87]

If a physical examination is allowed, this usually takes place after the main hearing. The medical tribunal member(s) usually examines you in a separate room in the absence of everyone else, although you can have someone with you as a chaperone or to help you if you need assistance undressing. When you are examined, make sure you tell the member(s) of the tribunal if you are in pain or suffering discomfort. It is also a good idea to give the tribunal a full list of any medicines you are taking. After the examination, you should be invited to make further representations to the tribunal if you wish.

Appeals about disability or incapacity for work

You should tell the tribunal how your disability or incapacity affects you at work or in your daily life at home. You should be completely straightforward with the tribunal, neither underplaying nor overplaying your symptoms. If you feel better on some days than others, explain in what ways and tell the tribunal whether they are seeing you on a good day or a bad day and how often these occur.

The tribunal listens to you and asks you questions. It considers all of the medical reports and other documents in the tribunal papers and other evidence relevant to your case. It tries to draw out the evidence about your disabilities, perhaps with the help of questioning from the doctor or consultant members. This may confirm the opinions expressed in medical reports with which you disagree, or it may support your view.

The tribunal should not feel restricted to merely accepting the medical evidence about you given in written reports.[88] If there is conflict between what is said in a report and what you have said about your disability or incapacity in writing, for example on your claim form, the tribunal should not accept the evidence in the report without first listening to what you have to say about how your condition affects you.[89]

A chair can adjourn the hearing and refer you to a doctor for a medical examination and report if your appeal concerns:[90]

- whether you are entitled to attendance allowance (AA) or DLA, the appropriate rate of benefit or the period for which you are entitled;
- whether you are entitled to SDA;
- whether you are incapable of work;
- the extent of your disablement for SDA or industrial injuries disablement benefit purposes; *or*
- whether you suffer from a prescribed disease or injury (see p325) or have suffered a loss of faculty as a result of an industrial accident (see p327).

Where you are referred for a medical examination and report, the chair should ensure that this happens promptly. A medical examination may take place in your home or at a DWP medical examination centre. Alternatively, a report may be requested from your GP or other medical adviser. The written decision to adjourn for a report should make clear why the tribunal adjourned and what sort of medical evidence is being sought.[91]

Remember that although you cannot be compelled to undergo a medical examination by the chair, the tribunal might draw negative conclusions if you refuse.

Domiciliary hearings

Because of, for example, your medical condition, you may be unable to attend a tribunal hearing at the appeal venue. It is possible that the hearing could instead be held in your home, or in another venue that you can get to. This is known as a 'domiciliary hearing'. You might be asked to provide a letter from a doctor saying why such a hearing is necessary. You cannot appeal against a decision to refuse to grant you a domiciliary hearing. However, if the refusal meant that your appeal was unfair, you might be able to appeal against the tribunal's decision on your appeal.[92]

TAS does seek to limit the number of domiciliary hearings.[93] Therefore, although it is possible for a regional or full-time chair to decide that a case requires a domiciliary hearing there is often a preliminary hearing to consider whether it is really necessary.

It may be felt that the appeal could go ahead if further information was obtained, even if you were still unable to attend. This could be because someone who knows you could attend and give evidence about your condition, or you or someone who knows you could send in written or recorded evidence, or a report could be sought from a medical adviser. You could also be asked to give fuller details of why you are appealing. TAS can also arrange for an ambulance to bring you to and from the normal tribunal venue if that is feasible.

Note: you might be able to be present via a video link if the chair of the tribunal agrees.[94] Contact the TAS office you normally use to see if this can be arranged.

What the tribunal can consider

Tribunals do not have to consider issues that are 'not raised by' your appeal.[95] You should certainly argue that an issue should be considered if:

- it is in the appeal papers;
- it is raised in any representations you make;
- the evidence before the tribunal should lead it to believe that it is relevant to your appeal.

It does not matter when you raise an issue – eg, you (or the DWP, local authority or the Revenue) can even raise an issue at the hearing.[96] However, the tribunal might then adjourn to give the other side a chance to meet the point. Bear in mind that if you have a representative, the tribunal might decide not to investigate matters that s/he does not raise on your behalf.[97]

The tribunal can consider issues even if neither you nor the DWP, local authority or the Revenue raises them.[98] The tribunal should exercise its discretion fairly.

Difficulties may arise – eg, where you are appealing about not being awarded one component of DLA (see Chapter 7) when you are already in receipt of the other, or against the rate of one component of DLA when you are quite satisfied with the rate you receive of the other, or where you ask for a higher rate of DLA or AA than you are already getting. In these circumstances the tribunal *does not have to* consider issues which are not the subject of your appeal. If it *does* decide to consider both components of DLA, or if it decides to consider whether you should get a lower rate of DLA or AA than you are already getting, it should give you notice of this and a chance to prepare your case and make representations.[99] You should consider asking for the hearing to be adjourned if you need time to do this or want someone to represent you. **Note:** If you are concerned about what might happen in your appeal, you can withdraw it at any time before the tribunal makes its decision (see p1230).

If you have been awarded a component of DLA for an indefinite period (see p159), you should argue that the tribunal *need not* consider the rate of that component, or the length of time for which it has been awarded, unless your appeal is expressly about one of those questions.

Faulty revisions and supersessions

If your appeal involves a revision or a supersession decision which is faulty, the tribunal can correct it.[100] This includes where the decision maker:

- carried out a supersession but failed to state the ground or to identify the correct ground for doing so; *or*
- did a supersession when s/he should have done a revision (and vice versa).

The tribunal must identify a relevant ground for revision or supersession. It can then go on and deal with your appeal. If errors in the decision making are very extensive, you can try to argue that the tribunal should refer the matter back to a decision maker, rather than making any corrections itself.[101]

Changes of circumstances after you appeal

When a tribunal hears your appeal, it considers whether the decision with which you disagree was correct when it was made. If your circumstances change after the decision the tribunal cannot take this into account.[102] This includes where a change occurs between the date a decision is made on a renewal claim for DLA and the date that decision takes effect, unless you are appealing about a revision or supersession of that decision.[103] The tribunal can take a change into account if it is a change a decision maker can take into account because it is almost certain to occur.[104]

Any evidence you get after the decision with which you disagree could still be relevant to your appeal.[105] If the evidence relates to the period before the decision you are disputing was made, or to a past event that was relevant to the decision, it must be taken into account.[106]

Repeat claims

It is important as a *general* rule for you to consider making a fresh claim (or seeking a supersession) every time your circumstances change, and appeal if you are unhappy with the subsequent decision. This is particularly so where your appeal is about:

- whether you are incapable of work (see p765) or qualify for AA or DLA and your condition has worsened;
- whether you satisfy the 'habitual residence test' (see p702); *or*
- how much income or capital you have and this changes.

If you wait until the tribunal makes its decision and this goes against you, you could lose out. You could only get arrears going back to the date your circumstances changed if you make a fresh claim (or seek a supersession) and ask for benefit to be backdated. See pp1085 and 1204 for how far your benefit can be backdated.

Example

Ravi has been getting incapacity benefit (IB) for some time. A decision maker decides he is fit for work and stops his IB. He appeals. While awaiting his appeal hearing, his health deteriorates, he makes a fresh claim and is awarded IB. When the tribunal hears his appeal against the original decision it upholds the decision maker's decision. However, because Ravi made a fresh claim when his circumstances changed, he has not lost out.

Where you make a fresh claim (or seek a supersession), you can ask the decision maker to wait to make a decision until your appeal has been determined. However, if the decision maker decides the fresh claim (or supersession) and you disagree with the decision:

- you can appeal against the new decision and ask for all of the appeals to be heard together by the same tribunal;[107] *or*
- whether or not you appeal against the new decision, you can ask the decision maker to revise it once your first appeal is determined (see p1195).

Example

Ali claims income support (IS) but the decision maker says he does not satisfy the 'habitual residence test' and refuses his claim. He appeals against the decision and makes a fresh claim for IS straight away. The fresh claim is refused on 8 July 2003. Ali wins his appeal. Because he did not appeal the new decision, the tribunal can only award IS up to 8 July 2003. However, the decision maker does an 'any time' revision and awards IS from that date.

In some cases, it might not be a good idea to appeal after making a fresh claim (or seeking a supersession). If you are in any doubt about what to do, you should seek advice.

The decision

Usually you are told of the tribunal's decision at the hearing and you are given a decision notice confirming it. If the tribunal is unable to come to a unanimous decision, it makes a majority decision.

Most appeal venues are computerised, so many decisions are done on computer. The decision notice may include a summary of the tribunal's reasons for its decision. If it is not given at the hearing or you opted for a paper hearing, the decision notice is sent to you later by the clerk. You must be informed of:[108]

- your right to request a statement of reasons for the tribunal's decision – a 'full decision' (see below); *and*
- the conditions for appealing to a commissioner (see p1245).

A decision can be corrected or set aside (see p1241).

The full decision

If you lose your appeal and want to appeal to a commissioner (see p1245) you must generally have a statement of reasons for the tribunal's decision, known as a 'full decision' (but see p1247).[109] A chair may give you a full decision at the hearing or tell you s/he will send one to you later. If not, you have a right to ask the chair for one. This must then be given to you as soon as it is 'practicable'.[110] Your request for a full decision must be in writing.[111] Your request must be received by the clerk to the tribunal within one month (see p1223) of you being sent or given the tribunal's decision notice. If an accidental error in the tribunal's decision is corrected or you applied for the tribunal's decision to be set aside and this has been refused, the one-month period runs from the date you are sent notice of this.[112] However, this does not apply where the decision was not set aside because of a refusal to extend the time limit for applying for one. Late applications can be allowed in limited circumstances (see p1240).

Note:

- If the decision is not unanimous, the full decision must give the reasons why a tribunal member disagreed.[113]
- If you mistakenly ask the chair of the tribunal for permission to appeal to a commissioner (see p1247) instead of asking for a full decision, s/he should treat this as a request for a full decision.[114]
- If the chair fails to provide a full decision, whether or not you ask for it in time, you should see p1246 and seek advice.

The DWP (or local authority or the Revenue) can also ask for a full decision. If this happens, it means the DWP (or local authority or the Revenue) is considering appealing to a commissioner.

A **record of the tribunal proceedings**, made by the chair of the tribunal, is kept by the tribunal clerk for six months from the date of the tribunal's decision, or from the date:[115]

- of any statement of reasons for it; *or*
- of any correction of an accidental error in it; *or*
- of any refusal to set it aside; *or*
- your application for permission to appeal against it is determined; *or*
- any of the above are sent to the commissioners' office in connection with an appeal or an application to appeal against the decision, so long as this is within the six months.

You can apply for a copy within that period. The record must be sufficient to indicate the evidence taken by the appeal tribunal. You must apply in writing. If you are considering an appeal to a commissioner you should definitely ask for a copy. If you foresee disputes about what happened at the hearing, you should make and keep your own notes.

Late applications for a full decision

You can make a late application for a full decision in limited circumstances, but must do so within an absolute time limit of three months.[116] If an accidental error in the tribunal's decision has been corrected or you applied for the tribunal's decision to be set aside (see p1242) and this has been refused, the three-month period runs from the date you are sent notice of this. However, this does not apply where a decision was not set aside because of a refusal to extend the time limit for applying for one.

A late application for a full decision can only be allowed if it is 'in the interests of justice' for it to be allowed late.[117] It can only be in the interests of justice if it was not practicable for you to apply in time because of one of the following special circumstances:[118]

- you, your partner or a dependant has died or had a serious illness;
- you are not resident in the UK;
- normal postal services were disrupted; *or*
- there are other special circumstances.

See p1263 for examples of what might count as a special circumstance.

The longer you have delayed in applying, the more compelling the special circumstances need to be.[119] When deciding if it is in the interests of justice to allow your application, the tribunal member cannot take account of the fact that:[120]

- a court or commissioner has interpreted the law in a different way than previously understood and applied;
- you (or anyone acting for you) misunderstood or were unaware of the relevant law, including the time limits for appealing.

After the hearing

If you have won your appeal, the DWP (or local authority or the Revenue) ought to carry out the tribunal's decision straightaway. It can do this on the basis of the decision notice (see p1239). However, if the DWP (or local authority or the Revenue) disagrees with the decision it might consider seeking permission to appeal against the tribunal's decision to a social security commissioner (see p1245). In this case, you are not normally paid while it decides what to do. See p1105 for details of what the DWP (or local authority or the Revenue) must do before it can suspend your benefit. If the DWP (or local authority or the Revenue) decides to appeal, you are not normally paid until the commissioner hears the case.[121] However, you can ask the DWP, local authority or the Revenue to pay you if you are left in financial hardship. If you are left without any money, you might be able to apply for an interim payment (see p1108) or get a crisis loan (see p538).

If you disagree with the tribunal's decision

A tribunal's decision is final. However:

- if the decision notice contains an accidental error this can be corrected by the clerk to the tribunal or a legally qualified tribunal member. This only applies if it is a genuine error such as a typing or spelling mistake, not an error of law on an important issue in your appeal – eg, a change of the date of onset of an industrial disease;[122]
- it can be superseded in the normal way – eg, where new facts have come to light since the decision was made (see p1199). However, where the tribunal made a mistake about the law you must appeal to a social security commissioner (see below);
- you or the DWP (or local authority or the Revenue) can appeal to a social security commissioner (see p1245). If you want to do so you must generally have a copy of the full decision of the tribunal (but see p1247). See p1239 for information about the time limit for requesting a full decision;
- a decision can be set aside, which means the decision is cancelled and your appeal is heard again (see p1242).

If you are considering an appeal to a social security commissioner remember to ask for the tribunal's full decision within the one-month time limit (see p1239). You should do so even if you are first going to apply for the tribunal's decision to be set aside.

When a decision can be set aside

A tribunal decision can only be set aside in limited circumstances. You must apply, in writing, to the clerk to the tribunal for the decision to be set aside within one month of being sent or given:[123]

- the decision notice (see p1239); *or*
- the full decision (see p1239), if this is later.

The application should be signed by you. If you have provided written authority, your representative can sign it on your behalf. You must include your reasons for applying for the decision to be set aside. You can make a late application in limited circumstances (see p1243).

A legally qualified tribunal member can set aside a decision **if s/he thinks it is just**:[124] *and*

- you, your representative or the DWP (or local authority or the Revenue) or the tribunal that made the decision did not receive appeal papers or other relevant documents, or did not receive them in sufficient time before the hearing; *or*
- you, your representative or the DWP, local authority or the Revenue were not present at the hearing. However, if you or the presenting officer chose not to attend it may not be just to set the decision aside. If you did not ask for an oral hearing the decision cannot be set aside for this reason unless it would clearly be in the 'interests of justice'.

In some circumstances, a tribunal decision can also be set aside when you (or the DWP, local authority or the Revenue) seek the permission of the tribunal chair to appeal to a commissioner (see p1243).

Sometimes there are 'procedural irregularities' which lead to an obvious unfairness. If, as a result, it would be in the 'interests of justice' for a tribunal decision to be set aside, you should argue that there is also a power to do this.[125] If the tribunal refuses to do so, you could try to appeal to a commissioner against the tribunal's original decision on the grounds that there was a breach of the rules of natural justice (see p1245).

Applications for a decision to be set aside are normally decided without a hearing, so make sure you give a full explanation of your reasons when you apply.[126] If the tribunal's decision is set aside, your appeal is then referred back to be heard by another tribunal.

You must be sent a written notice of the decision on your application as soon as it is practicable.[127] The notice must include a statement of the reasons for the decision. If the legally qualified tribunal member refuses to set aside the decision, s/he can treat your application to set aside as an application for a statement of reasons for the decision (a 'full decision'), subject to the usual time limits.[128]

If a decision is wrongly set aside, any subsequent re-hearing by a tribunal is invalid. The second tribunal could thus refuse to re-hear the case if there was no power to set aside the previous decision.[129]

Late applications for a decision to be set aside

The time limit for applying for a decision to be set aside can be extended by up to one year.[130] You must apply in writing. In addition to the reasons for your application, you must explain your reasons for lateness, including details of any special circumstances.[131]

A late application can only be accepted if there is a reasonable chance that the tribunal's decision will be set aside and it is 'in the interests of justice' for the time limit for applying to be extended.[132] It can only be in the interests of justice if it was not practicable for you to apply in time because of one of the following special circumstances:[133]

- you, your partner or a dependant has died or had a serious illness;
- you are not resident in the UK;
- normal postal services were disrupted; *or*
- there are other special circumstances which are 'wholly exceptional'.

See p1263 for examples of what might count as a special circumstance.

The longer you have delayed in applying for a decision to be set aside, the more compelling the special circumstances need to be.[134]

You cannot appeal against the refusal to allow your late application[135] but you can ask the tribunal member to look at it again or you may be able to apply to the High Court for judicial review if the decision is clearly unreasonable.

If the decision is not set aside

You cannot appeal against a refusal to set aside, but you may be able to apply for judicial review (see p1253).[136] You could also try to appeal to a commissioner (see p1245) against the tribunal's original decision. In calculating the time limit for appealing to a commissioner, days before the day you were given notice that your application for the tribunal's decision to be set aside has been refused (see p1242) are ignored.[137] However, the days are not ignored where a decision was not set aside because of a refusal to extend the time limit for applying for one. You must generally have the tribunal's 'full decision' (see p1239) but see p1247.

If you seek permission to appeal to a commissioner

A tribunal decision can also be set aside if:[138]

- you (or the DWP, local authority or the Revenue) seek the permission of the tribunal chair to appeal to a commissioner (see p1247); *and*
- the tribunal chair also thinks that the tribunal made an 'error of law' (see p1245).

The tribunal *must* set aside the tribunal decision if you and the DWP (or local authority or the Revenue) agree that the tribunal made an 'error of law' (see p1245).[139]

If the DWP (or local authority or the Revenue) seeks permission to appeal to the commissioner, a copy of the application must be sent to you by TAS.[140] This gives you the chance to let the tribunal chair know if you agree that the tribunal made an 'error of law'. However, there is no such requirement if *you* seek permission. In this case, if you think that the DWP (or local authority or the Revenue) might agree that the tribunal made an 'error of law', you should send a copy of your application to them.

If the tribunal decision is set aside, you should be given the opportunity to ask for an oral hearing, even if your appeal was originally decided at a paper hearing.[141]

Commissioners have the discretion to set aside decisions in similar circumstances when applications for permission to appeal are made directly to them (see p1248).

3. The tribunal members

Tribunals are made up of one, two or three members.[142] The people who hear your appeal are drawn from a panel of doctors, lawyers, people with an experience of disability and people with financial expertise – eg, accountants. One of the tribunal members must be legally qualified. S/he usually acts as the chair of the tribunal.

The types of tribunal appropriate to hear a particular kind of appeal are set out in the rules.[143] The types of tribunal are as follows:

- A three-member tribunal hears disability living allowance and attendance allowance appeals – a lawyer, a doctor and a person with experience of disability.[144]
- A two-member tribunal (a lawyer and a doctor) hears appeals about whether you are incapable of work under the 'personal capability assessment' (see p772).[145]
- A two-member tribunal (a lawyer and a financial expert) hears appeals involving difficult financial issues, such as profit and loss accounts, balance sheets and the accounts of trust funds. Only complex cases are dealt with in this way.[146]
- A two- or three-member tribunal (a lawyer and one or two doctors) hears appeals about industrial injuries benefits (see Chapter 14) or severe disablement allowance, unless the only issue is whether you had an industrial accident (see p321).[147] If your appeal also involves difficult financial issues (see above), your appeal is heard by a three-member tribunal – a financial expert is substituted for one of the two doctors.
- A one-member tribunal (a lawyer) hears all other appeals.[148]

A doctor *cannot* be a member of your tribunal if s/he has ever attended, advised or prepared a report about you or any other person whose medical condition is relevant to your appeal.[149] You cannot argue that a doctor should not be a member of a tribunal even if s/he regularly provides medical reports about benefit claimants to the Department for Work and Pensions (DWP).[150] Note, however, that a tribunal should not rely on evidence from a DWP doctor who it sits with on tribunals at other times.[151]

If the tribunal feels that your appeal involves a particularly difficult point, it can ask another member of the panel of tribunal members – known as an 'expert' – to assist.[152] The expert can be asked either to attend at the hearing and give evidence or provide a written report. Any written report should be sent to every party to the proceedings. The expert cannot take part in making the decision.

Where a tribunal has more than one member, the chair has the casting vote.[153]

4. Appealing to a commissioner

Both you and the Department for Work and Pensions (DWP) (or local authority or the Revenue) have a further right of appeal to a social security commissioner against a decision of an appeal tribunal. This is only the case, however, if the tribunal has made an 'error of law' (see below).[154] You must first apply for, and obtain, permission to appeal and there is a strict time limit for applying (see p1247).

Commissioners have only very limited powers to deal with questions of fact. However, if you have new evidence, it might enable you to apply for a supersession of the tribunal's decision (see p1199) and you can do that while your appeal is pending.

Error of law

The tribunal made an error of law if:[155]

- it got the **law wrong** or misinterpreted it – eg, it misunderstood the particular benefit rule concerned;
- there is no **evidence** to support its decision. In addition, if a tribunal gave you a physical examination when it was not permitted to do so (see p1234), it made an error of law if its decision is based on evidence obtained from that examination.[156] However, a tribunal has *not* made an error of law if it fails to take account of evidence that was not before it at the hearing – ie, where you (or the DWP, local authority or the Revenue) only produce evidence when your appeal is before a commissioner.[157] Likewise, it has not made an error of law if it accepts evidence that was not challenged at the hearing (eg, where the DWP, local authority or the Revenue chooses not to attend);[158]
- the **facts it found** are such that, had it acted reasonably, and interpreted the law correctly, it could not have made the decision it did. This argument can be used where the facts are inconsistent with the decision – eg, a tribunal finds that a man and a woman live in separate households, but decides they are

living together as husband and wife. The tribunal also made an error of law if it took things into account which it should not have taken into account or refused or failed to take into account things which it should have taken into account;

- there is a **breach of the rules of natural justice**. This includes where:
  - the procedure followed by the tribunal leads to unfairness, for example:
    - you are not allowed to call witnesses to support you; *or*
    - the tribunal refuses a postponement or an adjournment (see p1231) even though you cannot attend for a good reason and have told it so; *or*
    - the standard of interpretation is not adequate and the tribunal does not take appropriate action;[159] *or*
    - the tribunal pressurises you into giving up your right to a fair hearing – eg, it bargains with you by 'offering' you one component of disability living allowance if you agree not to argue for the other;[160] *or*
  - you did not get the 'enquiry form' (see p1226) from the clerk to the tribunal so were unable to ask for an oral hearing;[161] *or*
  - you did not get notice of the hearing and the result is that you lost without having a chance to put your case properly, even if you could have applied for the tribunal's decision to be set aside instead;[162]
  - you (or the DWP, local authority or the Revenue) asked for an oral hearing but one did not take place;[163]
  - you did not receive the decision maker's submission or receive it in sufficient time before the hearing and were not able to read it properly;[164]
- it does not give **proper findings of fact**. The tribunal can rely on the summary of the facts given in the decision maker's submission (see p1228), but only if these are not in dispute and s/he has covered all relevant issues.[165] If you and the DWP (or local authority or the Revenue) disagree about the facts the tribunal must explain which version it prefers and why.

  It is important to remember that a tribunal will not have erred in law simply because a different tribunal or a commissioner might have come to a different conclusion;[166]
- it does not provide **adequate reasons** for its decision (see p1239). If a delay in writing the reasons indicates that they are unreliable as an accurate statement of the tribunal's reasoning, you can argue the reasons are inadequate.[167] The tribunal must not simply say what its decision was. It must put down sufficient reasons so that you can see why, on the evidence, it reached the conclusion it did. If the tribunal sets out the reasons for its decision in the decision notice (see p1239) and these indicate that the tribunal did not apply the law correctly, the decision notice is likely to be a more reliable statement of the tribunal's reasons than a later conflicting explanation in a statement of reasons (a 'full decision' – see p1239).[168] **Note:** a tribunal does not have to give its reasons for refusing to adjourn an appeal hearing.[169]

How to appeal to a commissioner

You must first obtain permission to appeal to a commissioner – sometimes called 'leave to appeal'.[170] This means that you have to show that there has possibly been an error of law (see p1245) and that you have the beginnings of a case. There is a strict time limit for applying for permission to appeal. If you wish to appeal:

- you must generally have the tribunal's 'full decision' (see p1239) – but see below;
- you apply for permission to appeal, in the first instance, to the chair of the tribunal (see below);
- if the chair of the tribunal refuses your application, you can apply for permission direct to a commissioner (see below).

Applying to the chair of the tribunal

You should first apply for permission to appeal to the chair of the tribunal.[171] Your application must be received by the clerk to the tribunal at The Appeals Service (TAS) office within one month (see p1223) of you being sent the 'full decision' of the tribunal.[172] If, after you are sent the 'full decision', an accidental error in the decision notice is corrected or your application for the tribunal's decision to be set aside is refused, the one-month period runs from the date you are sent notice of this. However, this does not apply where a decision was not set aside because of a refusal to extend the time limit for applying for one.

You must apply for permission to appeal in writing.[173] You must sign the application yourself. However, if you have given written authority to your representative, s/he can sign it on your behalf. Your application must contain details of your grounds for appeal and sufficient information about the tribunal's decision for it to be identified. If you are making a late application (see p1248) you must give your grounds for this.

Where the DWP (or local authority or the Revenue) applies for permission to appeal you are sent a copy of the application. You can make comments on the application if you want to, but these do not have to be taken into account.[174] If you and the DWP (or local authority or the Revenue) agree that the tribunal made an 'error of law', the chair of the tribunal must set the decision aside (see p1243).

Outside the one-month time limit, an application for permission to appeal can only be considered if a legally qualified tribunal member thinks there are special reasons for doing so.[175] However, you must apply within an absolute time limit. This is one year from the date the one-month limit expired. See p1261 for further information about late appeals.

If the chair refuses your application

If the chair refuses you permission to appeal or rejects your application – eg, because you did not have a copy of the tribunal's full decision (see p1239) – you may make a fresh application direct to a commissioner. Your application must be sent within one month (see p1223) of the date the refusal (or rejection) was sent to you.[176] You can send your application by post, fax or email. However, you can only send it by email if you have been given written permission in advance.[177]

A late application may be accepted if there are special reasons. This is the case even if you made a late application to the chair so long as you did this within 13 months of the tribunal's decision (or of being sent the tribunal's 'full decision').[178] See p1261 for further information about late appeals.

Your application for permission to appeal must be in writing. You should use form OSSC1. The form is available from your local TAS office, the Office of the Social Security and Child Support Commissioners (see Appendix 1 for the address) or at www.osscsc.gov.uk. Your application must include:[179]

- your details;
- the grounds for your appeal. If your application is late, you must also give your reasons for this;
- copies of the tribunal's decision, the full decision (if you have one – see below) and the notice of the chair's refusal to grant permission.

The commissioner can waive any irregularities in your application for permission to appeal.[180] Therefore, if you do not have a full decision, your application can still be considered. However, you must still show that the tribunal made an error of law (see p1245) without it – ie, if sufficient information was given in the decision notice.[181] The failure of the chair of the tribunal to provide a full decision where s/he has a duty to do so is in itself an error of law.[182]

You are sent a written notice of the commissioner's decision on your application for permission to appeal. This must include the reasons for the decision.[183] You cannot appeal against a commissioner's refusal to grant you permission to appeal but you might be able to apply for the decision to be set aside[184] (see p1251) or for judicial review (see p1253).

What happens when you get permission to appeal

Once you have been given permission to appeal, you must send what is known as a 'notice of appeal' within one month of being sent notice that your permission to appeal has been granted.[185] You are sent a form on which to do this. The time may be extended for special reasons (see p1263).[186] As well as the notice of appeal, you must send a copy of the notice telling you that your application for permission to appeal has been granted, the tribunal decision and the full decision (if you have one), as well as your details and your grounds for appealing against the decision. You may be told that your notice of application has been treated as a notice of appeal – eg, where you have applied for permission to appeal direct to a commissioner on Form OSSC1 (see above). In this case you do not have to send in another.[187]

The DWP (or local authority or the Revenue) might agree with you that the tribunal made an error of law (see p1245). If this happens the commissioner can:[188]

- set aside the tribunal's decision straightaway;
- refer your appeal back to be heard by a different tribunal; *and*
- issue a direction to the tribunal which will hear your appeal again. You or the DWP (or local authority or the Revenue) can ask the commissioner to do this and suggest what the direction should say.

If a test case is pending

If a test case is pending that deals with issues raised in your appeal, you may find that your appeal is delayed. See p1232 for further information.

The written procedure

A bundle of documents is prepared by the decision maker and sent to the commissioners' office where it is added to any submissions from you. The commissioners' office then sends copies of the bundle, including the decision maker's submission, to you. You may find that the decision maker supports your appeal and suggests that the commissioner considers referring it back to be heard by a different tribunal (see p1248).

If your appeal is about:

- benefits other than child benefit, guardian's allowance, housing benefit (HB) and council tax benefit (CTB), the Decision Making and Appeals Unit deals with the DWP's side of the case. See Appendix 1 for the address;
- child benefit or guardian's allowance, the Guidance Team deals with the the Revenue's side of the case. See Appendix 1 for the address;
- HB or CTB, the local authority deals with its side of the case.

You are given one month in which to reply to the decision maker's submission, although the commissioner may extend the time limit.[189] The information on pp1253–61 about how to prepare an appeal also applies to appeals to commissioners.

If you have nothing to add and do not want to reply at any stage, tell the commissioners' office. A commissioner has the power to strike out an appeal that appears to have been abandoned, although you can apply for it to be reinstated.[190]

When the commissioner has all the written submissions, if your appeal is not to be referred back to another tribunal (see p1248), s/he decides whether or not there should be an oral hearing of the appeal. If you ask for an oral hearing, the commissioner holds one unless s/he feels that the case can be dealt with properly without one.[191] Occasionally, the commissioner decides to hold an oral hearing even if you have not asked for one.

If there is no oral hearing, the commissioner reaches a decision on the basis of written submissions and other documents.

Because of the length of time you usually have to wait before your case is dealt with, you should make a fresh claim for benefit (or seek a supersession) if, for example, your circumstances change (but see p1237).

Oral hearings

Oral hearings are usually held at the commissioners' offices in London, Edinburgh or Belfast, or at the law courts in Bury, Cardiff, Doncaster or Plymouth. If you are unable to travel, oral hearings can be held exceptionally at other court centres. You are told the date in good time and your fares are paid in advance if you want to attend.

Unless you are appealing about HB or CTB, you and your representative might be able to participate in the oral hearing via a video conferencing link – eg, where your disability makes it difficult for you to travel, or to avoid travel costs and time.[192] These are currently available in Birmingham, Cardiff, Leeds, London, Manchester, Plymouth, Preston and Winchester.

Usually, one commissioner hears your case. However, if there is a 'question of law of special difficulty', the hearing may be before a tribunal of three commissioners,[193] but the procedure is the same.

The commissioner might ask you to provide a summary of the arguments you are going to make – known as a 'skeleton argument' – in advance of the hearing. If s/he does so, you must provide one.[194] See p1253 for information about how to prepare an appeal.

The hearing is more formal than those before tribunals, but the commissioner lets you say everything you want to. Commissioners usually intervene a lot and ask questions so you need to be prepared to argue your case without your script. A full set of commissioners' decisions (see p1259) and the statute law (see p1256) are available for your use. The DWP (or local authority or the Revenue) is usually represented by a lawyer, so you should consider trying to obtain representation as well.

The commissioner may exclude members of the public if intimate personal or financial circumstances, or matters of public security, are involved.[195] This is not usually necessary because it is rare for anyone not involved in the case to attend.

The decision

The decision is always given in writing.[196] It may be several weeks before it is sent to you.

If the commissioner agrees that an appeal tribunal's decision was wrong, the case is usually sent back to a differently constituted tribunal with directions as to how it should go about reconsidering the issues.[197] However, if the commissioner feels that the record of the decision of the original tribunal contains all the material facts, or s/he feels that it is expedient to make findings on any extra factual issues necessary to the decision, the commissioner makes the final decision.[198] It is unusual for a commissioner not to send a case back to a tribunal if there is a dispute about facts not determined by the original tribunal, unless all the evidence points in one direction.[199]

If you disagree with a commissioner's decision

A commissioner's decision is final. However:

- a commissioner may correct or set aside her/his decision.[200] A decision can be set aside if the commissioner thinks it is just and:
  - you, your representative or the DWP (or local authority or the Revenue) or the commissioner who made the decision did not receive papers or other relevant documents, or did not receive them in sufficient time; *or*
  - you, your representative or the DWP (or local authority or the Revenue) were not present at the hearing.

  You must apply for a decision to be set aside within one month of being given the decision;
- it can be superseded in the normal way – eg, where new facts have come to light since the decision was made (see p1199). However, where the commissioner made a mistake about the law you must appeal to a court (see below);
- you or the DWP (or local authority or the Revenue) can appeal to the Court of Appeal (in Scotland, the Court of Session) – see below.

5. **Appealing to the courts**

There are two situations in which you might consider appealing to a court:

- if you want to appeal against a commissioner's decision (see below);
- if you want to seek a judicial review (see p1253).

Appeals from social security commissioners

You may appeal against a commissioner's decision to the Court of Appeal (in Scotland, the Court of Session). You can only do this if the commissioner made an error of law (see p1245) and you must first obtain permission to appeal.[201] The Department for Work and Pensions (DWP) (or local authority or the Revenue) has the same rights of appeal as you.

The procedure in the Court is strict, formal and far less flexible than the procedure before a tribunal or a commissioner. For an outline of the procedure, see below for England and Wales and p1252 for Scotland.

The DWP (or local authority or the Revenue) will certainly be represented by a barrister at the hearing. You should consider obtaining legal advice from a solicitor before appealing. See p1253 for information about meeting the cost of going to court. **Note:** Before making *any* application, you should seek advice about whether you might be liable for your opponent's costs if you were to lose your case.

England and Wales

In England and Wales, an application for **permission to appeal** to the Court of Appeal must first be made to a commissioner in writing within three months of the date when you were sent the commissioner's decision. If an accidental error in the commissioner's decision has been corrected or you applied for the decision to be set aside (see p1251) and this has been refused, the time limit runs from the date you are sent notice of this.[202] This does not apply where your application for a set aside was refused because it was made outside the time limit for this.

The commissioner may extend the time limit.[203] If you do not apply to the commissioner within the time limit and the commissioner refuses to extend it, the Court of Appeal cannot hear your appeal and you can only proceed by applying to the High Court for judicial review of the refusal to grant a late appeal (see p1253).[204]

If the commissioner refuses to give you permission to appeal (for reasons other than being outside the time limit), you can apply direct to the Court of Appeal.[205] Your notice of application should be lodged with the Civil Appeals Office within six weeks of being sent notification of the commissioner's refusal.[206] The court may extend the time limit.[207]

Generally, the Court of Appeal first considers your application for permission to appeal without an oral hearing. If permission is refused, you may renew your application in open court by writing to the court office but must do this within seven days. Similarly, if permission is granted, the DWP (or local authority or the Revenue) has seven days in which to ask for an oral hearing.[208]

If permission to appeal is granted by a commissioner or the Court of Appeal, you must serve a **notice of appeal** on the relevant parties. There are strict time limits for doing this.[209] Seek advice immediately if you are in this position. The solicitor to the DWP will accept service on behalf of the DWP. The solicitor of the Revenue will accept service on behalf of the Revenue (see Appendix 1 for the addresses). Ask your local authority who will accept service on its behalf.

If the Court of Appeal refuses you permission to appeal after an oral hearing, you cannot appeal further, nor apply for a judicial review.

You cannot appeal to the Court of Appeal against a commissioner's refusal to grant you permission to appeal against a tribunal's decision, but you can apply to the High Court for judicial review of such a decision.[210]

Scotland

In Scotland the procedures for appealing to the Court of Session are similar to those for England and Wales but there are a number of crucial differences.

If the commissioner refuses you permission to appeal to the Court of Session you are allowed six weeks from the date of notification to lodge a further application for permission to appeal with the Court of Session.

The Court of Session hears applications for permission to appeal in open court rather than making the decision simply by reading the papers as in England and Wales. The DWP (or local authority or the Revenue) may agree that the application for permission and the appeal itself are heard at the same time.

Applying for judicial review

Occasionally it is possible to challenge decisions with which you disagree by going to court for a judicial review. Judicial review is a means of challenging the decisions of any form of tribunal, government department or local authority.

For example, you can apply for judicial review of a decision:

- made by a decision maker, if it is a decision against which you do not have a right of appeal (see p1221); *or*
- made by a tribunal chair refusing to grant you permission to appeal to a commissioner; *or*
- made by a social security commissioner refusing to grant you permission to appeal; *or*
- refusing you a payment from the discretionary social fund (see Chapter 21); *or*
- made by a local authority about discretionary housing payments of housing benefit and council tax benefit (see p235).

You cannot usually go to court for a judicial review if you have another independent means of appeal, such as an appeal to a tribunal.

To go for a judicial review, you need the services of a solicitor, law centre or legal advice centre. You must apply to the High Court within three months of the decision you want to challenge. In Scotland, you apply to the Court of Session. There is no time limit but you should make your application as soon as possible.[211] See below for information about meeting the cost of going to court.

Meeting the cost of going to court

Free legal help from a solicitor is available for cases in the Court of Appeal, the High Court and the Court of Session and you should consider obtaining legal advice and representation for these. If you are not eligible for free legal help and you want to be represented by a lawyer, you are likely to have to pay. It may be a worthwhile investment if your claim is worth hundreds of pounds.

Note: Before making *any* application to a court you should seek advice about whether you might be liable for your opponent's legal costs if you were to lose your case.

6. How to prepare an appeal

Appeals are taken on all sorts of issues so the advice given here can only be fairly general.

Appeals may concern disputes about facts or disputes about the law or both. You usually need to think about both the facts and the law because they are connected. The law tells you which facts are relevant and the facts tell you which bits of the law you need to consider. Always try, if possible, to link the facts of your case and your arguments to the rules laid down in the Acts and regulations (see p1256).

Sorting out the facts

You are likely to know more than anyone else about the facts of your case. Your key task is to pass your knowledge (and the knowledge of others who know something about the facts) on to the tribunal. A tribunal is a complete re-hearing of your case, so fresh facts and arguments can be put by either side.

Remember to:

- check through the appeal papers carefully to work out where there are disagreements between you and the Department for Work and Pensions (DWP) (or local authority or the Revenue). This helps you decide what evidence you need to win your case;
- gather evidence to back up what you are saying (see below). If you want to give any evidence or information to the tribunal, send it to the clerk to the tribunal as soon as possible before your oral hearing. Otherwise the tribunal might decide to adjourn your appeal (see p1231). The clerk sends a further copy to the DWP (or local authority or the Revenue) who might then decide to support your appeal;
- ask any witnesses who support your case to attend the hearing. Both you and the DWP (or local authority or the Revenue) can ask witnesses to come and give information. Chairs do have the power to refuse to hear witnesses who are not relevant, but they should always be fair to you and generally allow witnesses to speak, even if it looks like they may have nothing useful to say.[212]

Evidence

Evidence includes:

- oral evidence – what you (and any witnesses or others) actually say at the hearing; *and*
- written evidence – any documents you (or the DWP, local authority or the Revenue) produce.

The tribunal considers all the evidence and decides what weight should be given to it.[213]

The DWP (or local authority or the Revenue) might use video evidence – eg, if you are appealing about entitlement to incapacity benefit or disability living allowance. You cannot prevent the DWP (or local authority or the Revenue) doing so.[214] However, you should insist you are given time to view and consider the evidence in advance of the tribunal hearing.

Oral evidence

You are usually expected to give your own oral evidence at the hearing, if you can. Your representative, if you have one, is generally not allowed to give it for you. However, your representative can assist the tribunal in gathering evidence from you,[215] and can give her/his *own* evidence based on her/his observations.[216] A tribunal cannot dismiss oral evidence without a proper explanation of why it has done so.[217]

Witnesses can also give oral evidence at the hearing. You or the DWP (or local authority or the Revenue) can call witnesses.[218]

If s/he is at the hearing, the presenting officer (see p1234) puts the DWP's (or local authority's or the Revenue's) case but is rarely the person who actually made the decision on your claim. The presenting officer's submissions are not evidence,[219] nor are comments made by another DWP (or local authority or the Revenue) officer if s/he did not make the decision on your claim.[220]

You, your representative and the presenting officer can report what other people have said. This is called hearsay evidence. Tribunals can accept hearsay evidence, but they must carefully weigh up its value as proof, given that the person who originally made the statement is not present at the hearing.[221]

Written evidence

Written evidence includes letters of support, medical and other reports, wage slips, bank statements, birth certificates and anything else which helps to prove the facts. If, for example, the DWP (or local authority or the Revenue) says that you failed to disclose an increase in your earnings and you have been overpaid, you could explain to the tribunal how and when you told it. It is even better to produce a copy of the letter which you sent informing it of the change. It is not unknown for the DWP (or local authority or the Revenue) to fail to include copies of relevant letters from you or other parties in the decision maker's submission. You should check the submission carefully and submit copies of any missing documents to the tribunal as soon as you can.

Most evidence relied on by the DWP (or local authority or the Revenue) is written and you can point out that you have not had the opportunity of questioning the witnesses. You are not entitled to insist on the presence of any particular witness,[222] but you should argue that the tribunal should not place any weight on the written evidence of, say, an interviewing officer if you are disputing the interview or an investigating officer if you dispute what s/he heard or saw.

Medical evidence

If you are getting medical evidence it is essential that it deals with the points in dispute if that is possible and also with the dates that are relevant to the decision with which you disagree. Sometimes, a doctor might not know much about the effect of a disability on your everyday life, in which case your evidence or that of a friend or relative may well be of more use. Where medical evidence might be useful, you can ask your doctor to provide it, or seek help from an advice agency in writing to your doctor. Your doctor may charge for such evidence, but your advice agency or solicitor might be able to get a report free. The tribunal can refer you for an examination and obtain a report if it thinks this is necessary (see p1235). If the lack of a report is causing you difficulties at a tribunal hearing, you could remind the tribunal of this power to obtain one itself.

You may have problems at the hearing if your opinion about the effect of your ill-health or disabilities is contradicted by evidence from an examining doctor or your own GP. The tribunal should weigh all the evidence on its own merits. It should not automatically assume any evidence is the best. If a doctor does not know you or how your condition affects you, including where s/he only gave you a very short examination, that should be taken into account.[223] If the doctor does not know much about your day-to-day living activities or walking abilities you should say so. You should seek further medical evidence in support of your view in advance of the hearing if you foresee any such conflict of evidence.

Note that a tribunal should not rely on evidence from a DWP doctor who it sits with on tribunals at other times.[224]

Checking the law

The DWP (or local authority or the Revenue) does not always get the law right and you should emphasise a point that it has overlooked. If you know what the law says, you know what facts you have to prove.

The primary sources of social security law are statute law and caselaw decided by commissioners and the courts. It is fairly easy to find both sorts of law once you know what you are looking for. The footnotes in this *Handbook* are intended to point you in the right direction. You should also look carefully at the decision maker's submission (see p1228), as that refers to the statute law and caselaw which s/he thinks is relevant. There are also a number of books which can help by explaining the law and referring you to relevant legislation and cases (see Appendix 3).

Statute law

The law consists of Acts of Parliament and regulations. The Acts set out the main framework and empower the Secretary of State to make regulations covering the details. These regulations are known as statutory instruments .

The best way to look up the relevant statute law is to read one of the annotated volumes of legislation, listed in Appendix 3. Remember:

- in rare cases, the books do not contain all the regulations that are relevant. You can purchase regulations individually from The Stationery Office. Many Acts and regulations are also available at www.legislation.hmso.gov.uk;
- the Acts and regulations are amended from time to time, so you must confirm that the rules as contained in the books are up to date.

If you are trying to discover the current state of the law or chase up a reference, unless your appeal is an old one and the law has changed since the relevant time, you can refer to the loose-leaf book, *The Law Relating to Social Security*. This is in 12 volumes – the 'Blue Volumes' or the 'Blue Books'. Most large reference libraries have a copy. Your local DWP office has a copy which you are allowed to look at free of charge.[225] Make sure it is up to date. It is also available at www.dwp.gov.uk/advisers/docs/lawvols/bluevol/index.asp.

Benefit laws are complicated and the staff who administer benefits are issued with guidance manuals and circulars. However, the DWP (or local authority or the Revenue) and tribunals are only bound by what the law says, not by the guidance. Nevertheless, it is sometimes useful to check out the guidance. See Appendix 3 for a list of what is available.

Caselaw

When a commissioner or a court decides an appeal, the decision sets what is known as a precedent. A decision maker or appeal tribunal deciding a similar case must follow that precedent.[226] Unreported decisions must be followed by appeal tribunals in the same way as reported ones.[227]

The decision maker's submission often refers to caselaw. You should also use caselaw to support your appeal if possible. To help you decide which cases to use, see p1258.

Identifying commissioners' decisions

All commissioners' decisions have file numbers – eg, CU/255/1984. The last numbers indicate the year in which the appeal was lodged. The second letter indicates the type of benefit involved in the decision. See below for the full list. An extra 'S' or 'W' after a 'C' denotes a Scottish or Welsh case, as in CWG/3/1978. Significant decisions are highlighted on the internet on the social security commissioners' website (see p1259).

The most important cases are chosen to be reported by the Chief Commissioner. These are called 'reported decisions'. They are given a new number – eg, CU/255/1984 became R(U) 3/86. All reported cases since 1951 begin with an 'R'. Again, the second letter denotes the type of benefit. The last numbers indicate the year in which the case was decided.

Commissioners' decisions references

A	Attendance allowance
CR	Compensation recovery
CS	Child support
DLA	Disability living allowance
DWA	Disability working allowance
F	Child benefit and family allowance
FC	Family credit

FG	Forfeiture – widows' benefits and bereavement benefits
FIS	Family income supplement
FP	Forfeiture – retirement pension
G	General (all benefits not covered in other categories)
H	Housing benefit and council tax benefit
HR	Home responsibilities
I	Industrial injuries benefits
IB	Incapacity benefit
IS	Income support
JSA	Jobseeker's allowance
M	Mobility allowance
P	Retirement pensions
PC	Pension credit
S	Severe disablement allowance, sickness benefit and invalidity benefit
SB	Supplementary benefit
SMP	Statutory maternity pay
SSP	Statutory sick pay
TC	Working tax credit, child tax credit, working families' tax credit and disabled person's tax credit
U	Unemployment benefit
UK	Unknown

Identifying court decisions

Court decisions are identified by the names of the parties involved in the appeal. The first name is usually the party that has appealed and the second name is the other party. In judicial review cases, the case citation begins with 'R'.

Examples of court decisions

Mallinson v Secretary of State for Social Security, 21 April 1994, (HL) is a House of Lords decision on appeal from the Court of Appeal.

R v South Tyneside MBC ex parte Tooley [1997] QBD and *R (Reynolds) v Secretary of State for Work and Pensions* [2002] EWHC Admin 426 are decisions following applications for judicial review.

Which cases to use

Caselaw can seem less precise than statute law (see p1256) and frequently cases seem to contradict each other. Very often there are small differences in the facts of the cases which justify the different results. You need to find cases where the facts are similar to yours. If cases appear to be against you, look at the facts of those cases and see whether any differences justify a different decision in your case. This is known as 'distinguishing' cases. One distinction may simply be that what seemed reasonable in the 1950s does not seem fair in the 2000s.[228] It should also be remembered that most appeals before April 1987 were decided when there was a right of appeal to commissioners on questions of fact as well as law so tribunals may not necessarily be erring in law if they take a different view from a commissioner in an older decision.

Where there is an irreconcilable conflict between two or more decisions, a tribunal has to choose which decision to follow. It normally follows a reported commissioner's decision in preference to an unreported one, and must follow a decision of a tribunal of commissioners in preference to a decision of a single commissioner.[229] Decisions of the House of Lords, the Court of Appeal or of the High Court on an application for judicial review (or, in Scotland, the Court of Session) take precedence over all commissioners' decisions.[230]

Commissioners have more freedom and do not have to follow the decision of another single commissioner if satisfied that the earlier decision was wrong.[231] Where two earlier decisions conflict, the commissioner should follow the latest decision if it fully considers the earlier one, unless satisfied it was wrong.[232] A single commissioner must follow a decision of a tribunal of commissioners although, if s/he thinks it may be wrong, s/he can ask the Chief Commissioner to appoint another tribunal to reconsider the point. A tribunal of commissioners does not have to follow the decision of another tribunal, but usually does so.[233]

Obtaining commissioners' and court decisions

Since September 2000, reported commissioners' decisions have been published in a loose-leaf format, available on subscription. All reported decisions from 1991 onwards are also available on the DWP website (see Appendix 1). Earlier reported decisions were published from time to time in bound volumes which are sometimes available in law libraries. Each local DWP office has a set of reported decisions which you are allowed to look at.

Many unreported decisions are available at www.osscsc.gov.uk. Many older decisions (up to the end of 2001) are available on www.hywels.clara.co.uk/commrs/index.htm.

Reported and unreported commissioners' decisions may be purchased from the Office of the Social Security Commissioners (see Appendix 1).

If an unreported decision is to be used at a tribunal hearing by the DWP (or local authority or the Revenue), a copy should be supplied to you. Similarly, if you wish to use one, you should supply copies to everyone, preferably by sending one to the tribunal clerk in advance of the hearing.

Many court decisions are now available on the internet. A useful link to these is at www.courtservice.gov.uk/judgments/judg_home.htm. In addition, where there has been an appeal against a commissioner's decision, it is usually reported (see above) with the court decision attached.

Summaries of all reported commissioners' decisions, most highlighted decisions and important court decisions are published in CPAG's *Welfare Rights Bulletin*. Many are also available on CPAG's CD-ROM.

It is worth checking the decisions referred to in the decision maker's submission (see p1228). Sometimes they rely on only part of a decision and fail to mention another part which is more favourable to you. To find other cases relevant to your own, you can use the footnotes in this *Handbook* or any of the books listed in Appendix 3.

Debates in Parliament

Where the statute law (see p1256) is ambiguous, the courts – which include tribunals and commissioners – can look at statements made to Parliament by ministers when the law was first made.[234] It may, therefore, be worth checking the House of Commons and House of Lords' official reports (known as *Hansard*) to see what was said in Parliament when the rules were first introduced. If you want help, ring the House of Commons Public Information Office on 020 7219 4272. You can also find *Hansard* at www.parliament.uk/hansard/hansard.cfm.

Presenting your case to the tribunal

Each case is different and hearings are informal so there is no set pattern for presenting cases.

It is a good idea to send in any detailed submissions and medical reports before the hearing. Some claimants like to use a written submission at the hearing and to read directly from it. However, tribunals usually ask questions so it is necessary to be able to talk about your case without the script.

It is helpful to make it clear at the beginning which bits of the decision maker's submission are in dispute. It is, then, usually best to tell the tribunal about the facts first and to call any witnesses before turning to legal arguments.

It is the tribunal's job to help you to say everything you want by putting you at your ease and asking the right questions. If you forget to say something when it is your turn to speak, do not hesitate to add it at the end of the hearing.

Advice and representation

There are a number of agencies which can advise you about social security matters and can help you prepare your case for the tribunal hearing. Some can also represent you at hearings if you feel that someone else can put your case better than you can yourself. See Appendix 2 for more information. Remember that many non-lawyer advisers know more about social security law than lawyers and their advice is usually free.

Meeting the costs of going to a tribunal or the commissioner

You cannot normally get free legal help from a solicitor to cover representation before tribunals. However, if you are on income support, income-based jobseeker's allowance, the guarantee credit of pension credit or have a very low income, you might be able to get free legal advice and assistance that might cover not only advice but also preparatory work for a hearing, such as obtaining medical reports and writing submissions. If you have a solicitor acting for you in an industrial injury claim against your employer, s/he may have medical and other reports and evidence which you can use for your benefit claim. If you are not eligible for free advice and assistance, or you want to be represented by a lawyer at an oral hearing, you are likely to have to pay. It may be a worthwhile investment if your claim is worth hundreds of pounds.

If you are resident in Scotland, free legal help is available for appeals to commissioners. This includes help with preparation for paper as well as oral hearings. If you are resident in England or Wales, free legal help for appeals to commissioners is only available in exceptional cases, at the personal discretion of the Lord Chancellor. If you are granted funding, you must send a copy of the funding notice (in Scotland, the legal aid certificate) to the office of the commissioners.[235] You must also let the other parties involved in your appeal know that you have been granted funding.

7. Late appeals

If you miss the time limit for lodging an appeal, a late appeal can be accepted in certain circumstances by:

- a legally qualified tribunal member or a decision maker, if you are appealing to a tribunal (see below);
- a legally qualified tribunal member or a commissioner, if you are seeking permission to appeal to the commissioner against a tribunal's decision (see p1262);
- a commissioner or the Court of Appeal (in Scotland, the Court of Session), if you are seeking permission to appeal to the Court against a commissioner's decision (see p1251).

The rules for making a late appeal to a tribunal are much more strict.

Late appeals to tribunals

You need permission to appeal – sometimes called 'leave to appeal' – if you miss the time limit (see p1223) and this can be difficult to get. It might be simpler to ask for a revision or supersession of the decision maker's decision instead of making a late appeal, so long as there are grounds for doing this and this would give you everything to which you are entitled (see pp1189 and 1199). However, you often get less arrears of benefit if you seek a supersession (see p1204).

No appeal can be allowed outside an absolute time limit. This is one year from the date your time limit for appealing expired.[236] You must apply in writing. In addition to the information you must provide on your appeal form (see p1224), you must explain your reasons for lateness, including details of any special circumstances (see below).[237]

A late appeal can only be allowed if:[238]

- a decision maker is satisfied that it is in the 'interests of justice'. The decision maker's submission tells you if the decision maker has given you permission to appeal.[239] If the decision maker does not give you permission to appeal, s/he *must* pass your application to The Appeals Service for a legally qualified tribunal member to decide; *or*
- a legally qualified tribunal member:
  - is satisfied that it is in the 'interests of justice'; *or*
  - the appeal has reasonable prospects of success.

It can only be in the interests of justice to allow a late appeal if it was not practicable for you to appeal in time because of one of the following special circumstances:[240]

- you, your partner or a dependant has died or had a serious illness;
- you are not resident in the UK;
- normal postal services were disrupted; *or*
- there are other special circumstances which are 'wholly exceptional'.

See p1263 for ideas about what might count as a special circumstance.

The longer you have delayed appealing, the more compelling the special circumstances need to be.[241] When deciding if it is in the interests of justice to allow your application, account cannot be taken of the fact that:[242]

- a court or commissioner has interpreted the law in a different way than previously understood and applied;
- you (or anyone acting for you) misunderstood or were unaware of the relevant law, including the time limits for appealing.

You must be sent a written summary of the tribunal member's decision as soon as practicable.[243]

You cannot appeal against the refusal to allow your late appeal[244] but you may be able to apply to the High Court (the Court of Session in Scotland) for judicial review if the decision is clearly unreasonable (see p1253).

Late appeals to commissioners

An application to a **tribunal chair** for permission to appeal to the commissioner can only be considered outside the one-month time limit (see p1247) if a legally qualified tribunal member thinks there are 'special reasons' for doing so.[245] No application can be allowed outside an absolute time limit. This is one year from the date the one-month limit expired.

If your application is refused, you can apply direct to a **commissioner** for permission to appeal. If you apply outside the one-month limit (see p1247), your application can be accepted if there are special reasons.[246] This is also the case where you have already made an unsuccessful late application to the tribunal chair, so long as you applied to her/him within 13 months of being given the tribunal's decision (or full decision if this is later).

In this context – and in contrast to late appeals to tribunals – potentially anything can count as a special reason as long as it is special enough. In particular, special reasons do not have to relate to why the appeal was late[247] (although they may do so). See below for information about what might count as a special reason.

The decision whether or not to allow a late appeal must be made bearing in mind the merits of the appeal and the consequences for the claimant (and the Department for Work and Pensions (DWP), local authority or the Revenue). The rules should be interpreted liberally, so you do not suffer unfairly.[248] If you are refused permission for a late appeal to a commissioner, you do not have a right of appeal against the decision. However, if you ask the commissioner to look at it again because there is something which is relevant and which s/he did not consider before, s/he may – but does not have to – do so. The only other possible remedy is judicial review (see p1253).

Special reasons and circumstances

What may or may not be a special reason or circumstance cannot be defined in advance. It depends on the circumstances of each case and the commissioner or tribunal chair (or decision maker) has to make her/his decision on an individual, case-by-case basis.

You should stress reasons or circumstances which are personal to you. Permission to appeal is sometimes refused because the reasons given are general ones – ie, ones which apply in a large number of cases rather than special ones which apply to you specifically.

There are no hard and fast rules about what should be taken into account but the following are obviously relevant.

The reasons for delay

Explaining the delay is an important part of any application for a late appeal. Do not worry if some or all of the delay is your fault. Almost any explanation is better than none at all. The worst situation is where you knew the time limit but simply ignored it; even then it may be possible to say something favourable. Say if things have been difficult at home or you were confused by the rules or just assumed that the DWP (or local authority or the Revenue) were the experts and had got it right. You should suggest there are special reasons or circumstances if:

- you made a reasonable mistake in calculating the time limit;
- you did not receive the decision;
- you posted your appeal in time but it went astray in the post;

- a mistake was made by your advisers. It should not make any difference that you might be able to sue your advisers for negligence. Professional advisers are not normally negligent and if yours does make an error then that is special to your case;
- you were ill. If so, provide medical evidence where possible;
- you were given wrong advice or otherwise misled by the DWP (or local authority or the Revenue). Many claimants are discouraged from appealing by decision makers who advise them incorrectly that an appeal would be doomed to fail. If you have been badly advised by the DWP (or local authority or the Revenue) and lose money because you are refused a late appeal you should consider claiming compensation (see Chapter 47).

The length of the delay

Short delays are likely to be easier to justify than long delays. However, the usual approach is that time limits have to be kept to, and there has to be good reason for not doing so. So even a short delay may be difficult to justify without good reason. Make sure you explain the reasons for the delay as clearly and as fully as possible.

The merits of your appeal

The more likely your appeal is to succeed, the greater the injustice in refusing to allow an extension of time. A strong case is particularly useful if there has been a very long delay and permission is usually granted where there has been a 'clear error' which would have long-term continuing effects unless corrected.[249]

The amount of money at stake

Even if there has been no clear error, permission to appeal may be granted if there is a lot of money at stake.[250]

A decision in a test case

The fact that there has been a decision in a test case which establishes that an earlier decision was incorrect can amount to a special reason, at least in some circumstances.[251] In any case, if there are other reasons why a late appeal should be granted these should be emphasised as well as the decision in the test case. Such appeals often involve large sums of money and (given the test case) a clear error in the decision which is being appealed against. Both of these have been accepted as special reasons in other contexts – usually when it is the DWP (or local authority or the Revenue) which wishes to appeal late rather than you.

Notes

1. **Appeal rights**

1 **CB/GA** Reg 24 CB&GA(DA) Regs
Other benefits s12 SSA 1998; reg 25 SS&CS(DA) Regs
2 s12(4) SSA 1998
3 Reg 30(5) and (6)-(6B) SS(C&P) Regs
4 Sch 7 para 6(3) and (6) CSPSSA 2000; reg 3 HB&CTB(DA) Regs
5 **CB/GA** Reg 33 CB&GA(DA) Regs
HB/CTB Reg 21 HB&CTB(DA) Regs
Other benefits Reg 34 SS&CS(DA) Regs
6 **CB/GA** s12 and Schs 2 and 3 SSA 1998; reg 25(2) CB&GA(DA) Regs
HB/CTB Sch 7 para 6 CSPSSA 2000
Other benefits s12 and Schs 2 and 3 SSA 1998; reg 26 SS&CS(DA) Regs
7 **CB/GA** Reg 26 CB&GA(DA) Regs
HB/CTB Reg 10 HB&CTB(DA) Regs
Other benefits Reg 28 SS&CS(DA) Regs
8 R(SB) 29/83; R(SB) 12/89; CIS/807/1992; CH/2115/2003
9 CIS/0345/2003
10 *Secretary of State for Work and Pensions v Adams* [2003] EWCA Civ 796, 18 June 2003 (EWCA), reported as R(G) 1/03
11 Reg 10(1)(b) and (2) HB&CTB(DA) Regs
12 Reg 18(2) HB&CTB(DA) Regs
13 **CB/GA** Reg 26(1)(b) and (2) CB&GA(DA) Regs
Other benefits Reg 28(1)(b) and (2) SS&CS(DA) Regs
14 **CB/GA** Sch 2 SSA 1998; reg 25 and Sch 2 CB&GA(DA) Regs
HB/CTB Sch 7 para 6(2) CSPSSA 2000; reg 16 and Schedule to HB&CTB(DA) Regs
Other benefits Sch 2 SSA 1998; reg 27 and Sch 2 SS&CS(DA) Regs
15 **CB/GA** Reg 28(1)(a) and (2) CB&GA(DA) Regs
HB/CTB Reg 18(1)-(3) HB&CTB(DA) Regs
Other benefits Reg 31(1)(a) and (2) SS&CS(DA) Regs
16 CIB/3937/2000
17 **HB/CTB** Reg 10A(3) HB&CTB(DA) Regs
Other benefits Reg 9A(3) SS&CS(DA) Regs
18 **CB/GA** Reg 28(3) CB&GA(DA) Regs
HB/CTB Reg 18(4) HB&CTB(DA) Regs
Other benefits Reg 31(4) SS&CS(DA) Regs
19 **CB/GA** Reg 28(2) CB&GA(DA) Regs
HB/CTB Reg 18(3) HB&CTB(DA) Regs
Other benefits Reg 31(2) SS&CS(DA) Regs
20 Reg 18(2) HB&CTB(DA) Regs
21 **CB/GA** Reg 28(1)(b) and (c) CB&GA(DA) Regs
Other benefits Reg 31(1)(b)-(c) SS&CS(DA) Regs
22 **CB/GA** Reg 31(1) CB&GA(DA) Regs
HB/CTB Reg 20(1)(a) HB&CTB (DA) Regs
Other benefits Reg 33(1) SS&CS(DA) Regs
23 Reg 20(1)(a) HB&CTB(DA) Regs
24 **CB/GA** Reg 31(1)(b) CB&GA(DA) Regs
HB/CTB Reg 20(1)(b) HB&CTB(DA) Regs
Other benefits Reg 33(1)(a) SS&CS(DA) Regs
25 **CB/GA** Regs 2(1), definition of 'appropriate office' and 31(1)(c) CB&GA(DA) Regs
HB/CTB Reg 20(1)(c) HB&CTB(DA) Regs
Other benefits Reg 33(1) and (2) SS&CS(DA) Regs
26 **CB/GA** Reg 31(1)(a) CB&GA(DA) Regs
HB/CTB Reg 20(1)(a) HB&CTB(DA) Regs
Other benefits Reg 33(1) SS&CS(DA) Regs
27 **CB/GA** Reg 31(1)(d) and (e) CB&GA(DA) Regs
HB/CTB Reg 20(1)(d) and (e) HB&CTB(DA) Regs
Other benefits Reg 33(1)(c) and (d) SS&CS(DA) Regs
28 **CB/GA** Reg 31 (2)-(6) CB&GA(DA) Regs
HB/CTB Reg 20(2)-(6) HB&CTB(DA) Regs
Other benefits Reg 33(3)-(7) SS&CS(DA) Regs

29 **CB/GA** Reg 31(6) CB&GA(DA) Regs
HB/CTB Reg 20(6) HB&CTB(DA) Regs
Other benefits Reg 33(7) SS&CS(DA) Regs
30 **CB/GA** Reg 31(7) CB&GA(DA) Regs
HB/CTB Reg 20(7) HB&CTB(DA) Regs; paras 05144 and 05146 HB/CTB Circular A18/2001
Other benefits Reg 33(8) SS&CS(DA) Regs; para 06069 DMG
31 **CB/GA** Reg 31(8) CB&GA(DA) Regs
HB/CTB Reg 20(8) HB&CTB(DA) Regs
Other benefits Reg 33(9) SS&CS(DA) Regs
32 The local government Ombudsman Complaint No. 01/C/13400 against Scarborough BC
33 **HB/CTB** Reg 23 HB&CTB(DA) Regs
Other benefits Reg 39(1) and (3) SS&CS(DA) Regs
TC Reg 12(1) and (3) TC(A)(No 2) Regs
34 **HB/CTB** Sch 7 para 3(6) CSPSSA 2000
Other benefits s9(6) SSA 1998
35 **CB/GA** Reg 27(1) and (5) CB&GA(DA) Regs
HB/CTB Reg 17(1) and (2) HB&CTB(DA) Regs
Other benefits Reg 30(1) and (2) SS&CS(DA) Regs
36 **CB/GA** Reg 27(2) CB&GA(DA) Regs
HB/CTB Reg 17(3) HB&CTB(DA) Regs
Other benefits Reg 30(3) SS&CS(DA) Regs
37 **CB/GA** Reg 27(3) CB&GA(DA) Regs
HB/CTB Reg 17(4) HB&CTB(DA) Regs
Other benefits Reg 30(4) SS&CS(DA) Regs
38 **CB/GA** Reg 27(4) CB&GA(DA) Regs
HB/CTB Reg 17(5) HB&CTB(DA) Regs
Other benefits Reg 30(5) SS&CS(DA) Regs
39 **CB/GA** Reg 28(2) CB&GA(DA) Regs
HB/CTB Reg 18(3) HB&CTB(DA) Regs
Other benefits Reg 31(2) SS&CS(DA) Regs
40 **HB/CTB** Reg 23 HB&CTB(DA) Regs
Other benefits Reg 39 SS&CS(DA) Regs
TC Reg 12 TC(A)(No 2) Regs
41 **HB/CTB** Reg 23 HB&CTB(DA) Regs
Other benefits Reg 39(4) SS&CS(DA) Regs
TC Reg 12(4) TC(A)(No 2) Regs
42 **HB/CTB** Reg 23 HB&CTB(DA) Regs
Other benefits Reg 39(5) SS&CS(DA) Regs
TC Reg 12(5) TC(A)(No 2) Regs
43 **HB/CTB** Reg 23 HB&CTB(DA) Regs
Other benefits Reg 49(8) SS&CS(DA) Regs
TC Reg 18(9) TC(A)(No 2) Regs
44 **HB/CTB** Reg 23 HB&CTB(DA) Regs
Other benefits Reg 49(9)(d) SS&CS(DA) Regs
TC Reg 18(10)(d) TC(A)(No 2) Regs
45 **HB/CTB** Reg 23 HB&CTB(DA) Regs
Other benefits Reg 49(7)(b) SS&CS(DA) Regs
TC Reg 18(8)(b) TC(A)(No 2) Regs
All Memo Vol 1 06/02 DMG
46 Sch 1 para 4 SSA 1998
47 **HB/CTB** Reg 23 HB&CTB(DA) Regs
Other benefits Reg 38 SS&CS(DA) Regs
TC Reg 11 Regs
48 **HB/CTB** Reg 23 HB&CTB(DA) Regs
Other benefits Reg 38(2) SS&CS(DA) Regs
TC Regs 7 and 11(2) TC(A)(No 2) Regs
49 CIB/4253/2004
50 **HB/CTB** Reg 23 HB&CTB(DA) Regs
Other benefits Reg 46 SS&CS(DA) Regs
51 **CB/GA** Reg 1(3) SS&CS(DA) Regs, definition of 'out of jurisdiction appeal', as modified by reg 36 CB&GA(DA) Regs; reg 25 CB&GA(DA) Regs
Other benefits Reg 1(3) SS&CS(DA) Regs, definition of 'out of jurisdiction appeal'
All Reg 46(1)(a) SS&CS(DA) Regs
52 **HB/CTB** Reg 23 HB&CTB(DA) Regs
Other benefits Reg 39(2) SS&CS(DA) Regs
53 **HB/CTB** Reg 23 HB&CTB(DA) Regs
Other benefits Reg 46(3) SS&CS(DA) Regs
TC Reg 16(3) TC(A)(No 2) Regs
All *Hansard*, 8 December 2004
54 **HB/CTB** Reg 23 HB&CTB(DA) Regs
Other benefits Reg 46(2) SS&CS(DA) Regs
TC Reg 16(2) TC(A)(No 2) Regs
55 **HB/CTB** Reg 23 HB&CTB(DA) Regs
Other benefits Reg 47(1) SS&CS(DA) Regs
TC Reg 17(1) TC(A)(No 2) Regs
56 **HB/CTB** Reg 23 HB&CTB(DA) Regs
Other benefits Reg 47(2) SS&CS(DA) Regs
TC Reg 17(2) TC(A)(No 2) Regs
57 R(IS) 5/94

58 **CB/GA** Reg 32 CB&GA(DA) Regs
HB/CTB Regs 20(9) and 23 HB&CTB(DA) Regs
Other benefits Regs 33(10) and 40 SS&CS(DA) Regs
59 *Rydqvist v Secretary of State for Work and Pensions* [2002] EWCA Civ 947, 24 June 2002, *The Times* 8 July (CA)
60 R(IS) 5/94
61 **HB/CTB** Reg 23 HB&CTB(DA) Regs
Other benefits Reg 49(2) SS&CS(DA) Regs
TC Reg 18(2) TC(A)(No 2) Regs
62 **HB/CTB** Reg 23 HB&CTB(DA) Regs
Other benefits Reg 49(2) SS&CS(DA) Regs
TC Reg 18(3) TC(A)(No 2) Regs; CH/3594/2002
63 **HB/CTB** Reg 23 HB&CTB(DA) Regs
Other benefits Reg 49(3)-(5) SS&CS(DA) Regs
TC Reg 18(4)-(6) TC(A)(No 2) Regs
64 **HB/CTB** Reg 23 HB&CTB(DA) Regs
Other benefits Reg 49(6) SS&CS(DA) Regs
TC Reg 18(7) TC(A)(No 2) Regs
65 **HB/CTB** Reg 23 HB&CTB(DA) Regs
Other benefits Reg 51(1) SS&CS(DA) Regs
TC Reg 20(1) TC(A)(No 2) Regs
66 **HB/CTB** Reg 23 HB&CTB(DA) Regs
Other benefits Reg 51(3) SS&CS(DA) Regs
TC Reg 20(3) TC(A)(No 2) Regs
67 CDLA/1290/2004
68 **HB/CTB** Reg 23 HB&CTB(DA) Regs
Other benefits Reg 51(2) SS&CS(DA) Regs
TC Reg 20(2) TC(A)(No 2) Regs
69 **HB/CTB** Reg 23 HB&CTB(DA) Regs
Other benefits Reg 49(4) SS&CS(DA) Regs
TC Reg 18(5) TC(A)(No 2) Regs
70 CDLA/3680/1997
71 CDLA/5413/1999
72 CIS/566/1991; CS/99/1993
73 CIS/2292/2000
74 CIS/6002/1997; *R v Social Security Commissioner ex parte Angora Bibi* [HC], 23 May 2000, unreported; CIB/1009/2004; CIB/2058/2004
75 CIS/3338/2001
76 **HB/CTB** Reg 23 HB&CTB(DA) Regs
Other benefits Reg 51(4) SS&CS(DA) Regs
TC Reg 20(4) TC(A)(No 2) Regs
77 CDLA/557/2001
78 s26 SSA 1998
79 s26(5) SSA 1998

2. **Tribunal procedures**
80 para 06234 DMG; para 0524 HB/CTB Circular A18/2001
81 R(IS) 17/04
82 **HB/CTB** Reg 23 HB&CTB(DA) Regs
Other benefits Reg 49(8) SS&CS(DA) Regs
TC Reg 18(9) TC(A)(No 2) Regs
All CIB/1009/2004; CIB/2058/2004
83 **HB/CTB** Reg 23 HB&CTB(DA) Regs
Other benefits Reg 49(1) SS&CS(DA) Regs
TC Reg 18(1) TC(A)(No 2) Regs
84 **HB/CTB** Reg 23 HB&CTB(DA) Regs
Other benefits Reg 49(11) SS&CS(DA) Regs
TC Reg 18(12) TC(A)(No 2) Regs
All CDLA/2014/2004
85 CSDLA/606/2003
86 s20(3) SSA 1998; reg 52 SS&CS(DA) Regs; R(DLA) 5/03
87 CDLA/21/1994, qualified by CM/2/1994
88 CM/527/1992
89 CIB/5586/1999
90 s20(2) SSA 1998; reg 41 SS&CS(DA) Regs
91 ITS President's Circular No.1 para 9, June 1997
92 CIB/2751/2002; CDLA/1350/2004
93 ITS President's Circular No.4, June 1997
94 **HB/CTB** Reg 23 HB&CTB(DA) Regs
Other benefits Reg 49(7)(b) SS&CS(DA) Regs
All Memo Vol 1 06/02 DMG
95 **HB/CTB** Sch 7 para 6(9)(a) CSPSSA 2000
Other benefits s12(8)(a) SSA 1998
96 CH/1229/2002
97 CSDLA/336/2000; CSIB/160/2000; R(H) 1/02
98 CH/1229/2002; CIB/4751/2002; CDLA/4753/2002; CDLA/4939/2002; CDLA/5141/2002
99 CI/531/2000; CDLA/1000/2001; CH/1229/2002; R(IB) 2/04
100 R(IB) 2/04
101 CIS/1675/2004
102 **HB/CTB** Sch 7 para 6(9)(b) CSPSSA 2000
Other benefits s12(8)(b) SSA 1998
TC s12(8)(b) SSA 1998; reg 4(6) TC(A) Regs
103 CDLA/2751/2003; CDLA/3567/2003; CDLA/3725/2003

104 CDLA/4331/2002
105 ITS President's Circular No.15, July 1998
106 R(DLA) 2/01; R(DLA) 3/01; CJSA/2375/2000
107 R(SB) 4/85
108 **HB/CTB** Reg 23 HB&CTB(DA) Regs
Other benefits Reg 53(3) SS&CS(DA) Regs
TC Reg 21(3) TC(A)(No 2) Regs
109 **HB/CTB** Reg 23 HB&CTB(DA) Regs
Other benefits Reg 58(1) SS&CS(DA) Regs
TC Reg 27(1) TC(A)(No 2) Regs
110 **HB/CTB** Reg 23 HB&CTB(DA) Regs
Other benefits Reg 53(4) SS&CS(DA) Regs
TC Reg 22(5) TC(A)(No 2) Regs
All CCS/1664/2001
111 **CB/GA** Reg 3(1)(a) CB&GA(DA) Regs; reg 53(4) SS&CS(DA) Regs
HB/CTB Regs 2(a) and 23 HB&CTB(DA) Regs
Other benefits Regs 2(a) and 53(4) SS&CS(DA) Regs
TC Regs 2(a) and 21(4) TC(A)(No 2) Regs
All CIB/3937/2000
112 **HB/CTB** Reg 23 HB&CTB(DA) Regs
Other benefits Reg 53(4A) SS&CS(DA) Regs
TC Reg 21(4A) TC(A)(No.2) Regs
113 **HB/CTB** Reg 23 HB&CTB(DA) Regs
Other benefits Reg 53(5) SS&CS(DA) Regs
TC Reg 21(6) TC(A)(No 2) Regs
All CDLA/572/2001
114 R(IS) 11/99; CDLA/5793/1997
115 **HB/CTB** Reg 23 HB&CTB(DA) Regs
Other benefits Reg 55 SS&CS(DA) Regs
TC Reg 23 TC(A)(No.2) Regs
116 **HB/CTB** Reg 23 HB&CTB(DA) Regs
Other benefits Reg 54(1) SS&CS(DA) Regs
TC Reg 22(1) TC(A)(No 2) Regs
117 **HB/CTB** Reg 23 HB&CTB(DA) Regs
Other benefits Reg 54(4) SS&CS(DA) Regs
TC Reg 22(4) TC(A)(No 2) Regs
118 **HB/CTB** Reg 23 HB&CTB(DA) Regs
Other benefits Reg 54(5) and (6) SS&CS(DA) Regs
TC Reg 22(5) and (6) TC(A)(No 2) Regs
119 **HB/CTB** Reg 23 HB&CTB(DA) Regs
Other benefits Reg 54(7) SS&CS(DA) Regs
TC Reg 22(7) TC(A)(No 2) Regs
120 **HB/CTB** Reg 23 HB&CTB(DA) Regs
Other benefits Reg 54(8) SS&CS(DA) Regs
TC Reg 22(8) TC(A)(No 2) Regs
121 **HB/CTB** Sch 7 para 13 CSPSSA 2000; reg 11 HB&CTB(DA) Regs
Other benefits s21 SSA 1998; reg 16 SS&CS(DA) Regs
122 **HB/CTB** Reg 23 HB&CTB(DA) Regs
Other benefits Reg 56 SS&CS(DA) Regs
TC Reg 24 TC(A)(No 2) Regs
All CI/3887/1999
123 **HB/CTB** Reg 23 HB&CTB(DA) Regs
Other benefits Reg 57(3) SS&CS(DA) Regs
TC Reg 25(3) TC(A)(No 2) Regs
124 **HB/CTB** Reg 23 HB&CTB(DA) Regs
Other benefits Reg 57 SS&CS(DA) Regs
TC Reg 25 TC(A)(No 2) Regs
125 **HB/CTB** Sch 7 para 19(2) CSPSSA 2000
Other benefits s28(2) SSA 1998
TC s28(2) SSA 1998; reg 11(1) TC(A) Regs
All *Lloyd v McMahon* [1987] AC 625, 702-703
126 CSB/172/1990
127 **HB/CTB** Reg 23 HB&CTB(DA) Regs
Other benefits Reg 57(5) SS&CS(DA) Regs
TC Reg 25(5) TC(A)(No 2) Regs
128 **HB/CTB** Reg 23 HB&CTB(DA) Regs
Other benefits Reg 57(4A) SS&CS(DA) Regs
TC Reg 25(4A) TC(A)(No.2) Regs
129 CI/79/1990; CIS/373/1994
130 **HB/CTB** Reg 23 HB&CTB(DA) Regs
Other benefits Reg 57(6) SS&CS(DA) Regs
TC Reg 25(6) TC(A)(No 2) Regs
131 **HB/CTB** Reg 23 HB&CTB(DA) Regs
Other benefits Reg 57(7) SS&CS(DA) Regs
TC Reg 25(7) TC(A)(No 2) Regs
132 **HB/CTB** Reg 23 HB&CTB(DA) Regs
Other benefits Reg 57(8) SS&CS(DA) Regs
TC Reg 25(8) TC(A)(No 2) Regs
133 **HB/CTB** Reg 23 HB&CTB(DA) Regs
Other benefits Reg 57(9) and (10) SS&CS(DA) Regs
TC Reg 25(9) and (10) TC(A)(No 2) Regs
134 **HB/CTB** Reg 23 HB&CTB(DA) Regs
Other benefits Reg 57(11) SS&CS(DA) Regs
TC Reg 25(11) TC(A)(No 2) Regs

135 **HB/CTB** Reg 23 HB&CTB(DA) Regs
Other benefits Regs 57(12) and 57A(2) SS&CS(DA) Regs
TC Reg 25(12) TC(A)(No 2) Regs
136 **HB/CTB** Reg 23 HB&CTB(DA) Regs
Other benefits Reg 57A(2) SS&CS(DA) Regs
TC Reg 26(2) TC(A)(No 2) Regs
137 **HB/CTB** Reg 23 HB&CTB(DA) Regs
Other benefits Reg 57A(1) SS&CS(DA) Regs
TC Reg 26(1) TC(A)(No 2) Regs
138 **HB/CTB** Sch 7 para 7(2) CSPSSA 2000
Other benefits s13(2) SSA 1998
TC s13(2) SSA 1998; reg 5(1) TC(A) Regs
All CIS/4533/2003
139 **HB/CTB** Sch 7 para 7(3) CSPSSA 2000
Other benefits s13(3) SSA 1998
140 **HB/CTB** Reg 23 HB&CTB(DA) Regs
Other benefits Reg 58(2) SS&CS(DA) Regs
TC Reg 27(2) TC(A)(No 2) Regs
141 CIB/4193/2003

3. **The tribunal members**

142 s7(1) and (2) SSA 1998
143 s7(6) SSA 1998
144 Reg 36(6) SS&CS(DA) Regs
145 Reg 36(2)(a) SS&CS(DA) Regs
146 **HB/CTB** Reg 22(1)(a) HB&CTB(DA) Regs
Other benefits Reg 36(3) SS&CS(DA) Regs
147 Reg 36(2)(b) SS&CS(DA) Regs
148 **HB/CTB** Reg 22(1)(b) HB&CTB(DA) Regs
Other benefits Reg 36(1) SS&CS(DA) Regs
149 Reg 36(8) SS&CS(DA) Regs
150 *Secretary of State for Work and Pensions v Social Security Commissioners & James Gillies* [2003] 292, 28 November 2003 (ScotCS)
151 *Secretary of State for Work and Pensions v Cunningham* [2004] 6 August, ScotCS 211, reported as R(DLA) 7/04
152 **HB/CTB** Reg 23 HB&CTB(DA) Regs
Other benefits Reg 50 SS&CS(DA) Regs; s7(4) and (5) SSA 1998
TC Reg 19 TC(A)(No 2) Regs
153 s7(3) SSA 1998

4. **Appealing to a commissioner**

154 **HB/CTB** Sch 7 para 8(1) CSPSSA 2000
Other benefits s14(1) SSA 1998
TC s14(1) SSA 1998; reg 6(1) and (2) TC(A) Regs
155 R(A) 1/72; R(SB) 11/83; R(IS) 11/99
156 CDLA/433/1999
157 CH/5221/2001; CH/396/2002
158 CIB/2977/2002
159 CDLA/2748/2002
160 CSDLA/606/2003
161 CIB/5227/1999
162 CS/1939/1995; CDLA/5413/1999; CIB/303/1999
163 CDLA/3224/2001
164 CH/3594/2002
165 R(IS) 4/93
166 CDLA/1456/2002; CH/627/2002
167 CJSA/322/2001; R(IS) 5/04
168 CIS/2345/2001; CH/4065/2001
169 *Carpenter v Secretary of State for Work and Pensions* [2003] EWCA Civ 33, reported as R(IB) 6/03
170 **HB/CTB** Sch 7 para 8(1) CSPSSA 2000
Other benefits s14(10) SSA 1998
TC s14(10) SSA 1998; reg 6(1) TC(A) Regs
171 **HB/CTB** Sch 7 para 8(7) CSPSSA 2000
Other benefits s14(10) SSA 1998
All benefits reg 9(1) SSCP Regs
TC s14(10) SSA 1998; reg 6(1) TC(A) Regs; reg 7(1) SSCP(TCA) Regs
172 **HB/CTB** Reg 23 HB&CTB(DA) Regs
Other benefits Reg 58(1) SS&CS(DA) Regs
TC Reg 27(1) TC(A)(No 2) Regs
173 **HB/CTB** Reg 23 HB&CTB(DA) Regs
Other benefits Reg 58(1)(b) SS&CS(DA) Regs
TC Reg 27(1)(b) TC(A)(No.2) Regs
174 **HB/CTB** Reg 23 HB&CTB(DA) Regs
Other benefits Reg 58(2) SS&CS(DA) Regs
TC Reg 27(2) TC(A)(No 2) Regs
175 **HB/CTB** Reg 23 HB&CTB(DA) Regs
Other benefits Reg 58(5) SS&CS(DA) Regs
TC Reg 27(4) TC(A)(No 2) Regs
176 **Benefits** Regs 8 and 9(2) SSCP Regs
TC Regs 6 and 7 SSCP(TCA) Regs
177 **Benefits** Reg 8(2) SSCP Regs
TC Reg 6(2) SSCP(TCA) Regs
178 **Benefits** Reg 9(3) and (4) SSCP Regs
TC Reg 7(3) and (4) SSCP(TCA) Regs
179 **Benefits** Reg 10 SSCP Regs
TC Reg 8 SSCP(TCA) Regs
All CSDLA/1207/2000

180 **Benefits** Reg 27 SSCP Regs
TC Reg 22 SSCP(TCA) Regs
181 R(IS) 11/99; CDLA/5793/1997
182 CCS/1664/2001
183 Undated Practice Memorandum of the Chief Commissioner, 'Tribunals and Inquiries (Social Security Commissioners) Order 1980 and the Social Security Act 1998'
184 Regs 31 and 32 SSCP Regs; CDLA/3432/2001
185 **Benefits** Reg 13(1) SSCP Regs
TC Reg 11(2) SSCP(TCA) Regs
186 **Benefits** Reg 13(2) SSCP Regs
TC Regs Reg 11(3) SSCP(TCA) Regs
187 **Benefits** Reg 11(2) SSCP Regs
TC Reg 9(2) SSCP(TCA) Regs
188 **HB/CTB** Sch 7 para 8(3) CSPSSA 2000
Other benefits s14(7) SSA 1998
TC s14(7) SSA 1998; reg 6(1) TC(A) Regs
All Chief Commissioner's Practice Memorandum, 11 August 1998
189 **Benefits** Regs 18, 19 and 20 SSCP Regs
TC Regs 14, 15 and 16 SSCP(TCA) Regs
190 **Benefits** Reg 5(3) and (4) SSCP Regs
TC Reg 3(3) and (4) SSCP(TCA) Regs
191 **Benefits** Reg 23 SSCP Regs
TC Reg 18 SSCP(TCA) Regs
192 **Benefits** Regs 4(1), definition of 'live television link' and 24(6A) and (6B) SSCP Regs
TC Regs 2(1), definition of 'live television link' and 19(6A) and (6B) SSCP(TCA) Regs
193 **HB/CTB** Sch 7 para 10(5) CSPSSA 2000
Other benefits s16(7) SSA 1998
TC s16(7) SSA 1998; reg 9(1) TC(A) Regs
194 R(I) 1/03
195 **Benefits** Reg 24(5) SSCP Regs
TC Reg 19(5) SSCP(TCA) Regs
196 **Benefits** Reg 28 SSCP Regs
TC Reg 23 SSCP(TCA) Regs
197 **HB/CTB** Sch 7 para 8(5)(c) CSPSSA 2000
Other benefits s14(8)(b) SSA 1998
TC s14(8)(b) SSA 1998; reg 6(1) TC(A) Regs
198 **HB/CTB** Sch 7 para 8(5)(a) CSPSSA 2000
Other benefits s14(8)(a) SSA 1998
TC s14(8)(a) SSA 1998; reg 6(1) TC(A) Regs
199 *Innes v CAO* 19 November 1986, unreported (CA)
200 **Benefits** Regs 30 and 31 SSCP Regs
TC Regs 24 and 25 SSCP(TCA) Regs

5. **Appealing to the courts**

201 **HB/CTB** Sch 7 para 9 CSPSSA 2000
Other benefits s15 SSA 1998
All benefits Reg 33 SSCP Regs
TC s15 SSA 1998; reg 8 TC(A) Regs; reg 27 SSCP(TCA) Regs
202 **Benefits** Reg 33(2) SSCP Regs
TC Reg 27(2) SSCP(TCA) Regs
203 **Benefits** Regs 5(2) and 33(1) SSCP Regs
TC Regs 3(2) and 27(1) SSCP(TCA) Regs
204 *White v CAO* [1986] 2 All ER 905 (CA), also reported as R(S) 8/85
205 **HB/CTB** Sch 7 para 9(2)(b) CSPSSA 2000
Other benefits s15(2)(b) SSA 1998
TC s15(2)(b) SSA 1998; reg 8 TC(A) Regs
206 Practice Direction 52 para 21.5
207 Civil Procedure Rules r.52.6
208 Practice Direction 52 paras 4.11 and 4.14
209 Civil Procedure Rules r.52.4; Practice Direction 52 para 5.1
210 *Bland v CSBO* [1983] 1 WLR 262 (CA), reported as R(SB) 12/83
211 See *Hanlon v Traffic Commission* [1988] SLT 802 and *Perfect Swivel v Dundee District Licensing Board* (No.2) [1993] SLT 112

6. **How to prepare an appeal**

212 R(SB) 6/82
213 CDLA/2014/2004
214 R(DLA) 4/02
215 CIB/2058/2004
216 **HB/CTB** Reg 23 HB&CTB(DA) Regs
Other benefits Reg 49(8) and (11) SS&CS(DA) Regs
All CDLA/1138/2003; CDLA/2462/2003
217 R(SB) 33/85; R(SB) 12/89
218 **HB/CTB** Reg 23 HB&CTB(DA) Regs
Other benefits Reg 49(1) SS&CS(DA) Regs
TC Reg 18(1) TC(A)(No 2) Regs
All CDLA/2014/2004
219 R(SB) 10/86
220 R(IS) 6/91
221 CIS/4901/2002
222 R(SB) 1/81
223 See CPAG's *Welfare Rights Bulletin* 183, pp4-5 for a discussion on tribunals and medical evidence.
224 *Secretary of State for Work and Pensions v Cunningham* [2004] 6 August, ScotCS 211, reported as R(DLA) 7/04
225 s123(2) SSCBA 1992

226 R(I) 12/75
227 R(SB) 22/86
228 *Nancollas v Insurance Officer* [1985] 1 All ER 833 (CA), also reported as R(I) 7/85
229 R(I) 12/75
230 *CSBO v Leary* reported as R(SB) 6/85; see generally CS/140/1991
231 R(G) 3/62; R(U) 4/88
232 R(IS) 13/01
233 R(U) 4/88
234 *Pepper v Hart* [1992] 3 WLR 1032
235 **Benefits** Reg 8A SSCP Regs
TC Reg 6A SSCP(TCA) Regs

7. **Late appeals**
236 **CB/GA** Reg 29(1) CB&GA(DA) Regs
HB/CTB Reg 19(1) and (2) HB&CTB(DA) Regs
Other benefits Reg 32(1) SS&CS(DA) Regs
TC Reg 5(1) TC(A)(No 2) Regs
237 **CB/GA** Reg 29(4) CB&GA(DA) Regs
HB/CTB Reg 19(4) HB&CTB(DA) Regs
Other benefits Reg 32(3) SS&CS(DA) Regs
TC Regs 5(3) and 6 TC(A)(No 2) Regs
238 **CB/GA** Reg 29(5) CB&GA(DA) Regs
HB/CTB Reg 19(5) HB&CTB(DA) Regs
Other benefits Reg 32(4) SS&CS(DA) Regs
TC Reg 5(4) TC(A)(No 2) Regs
239 **HB**/CTB Circular A28/2002, as amended by HB/CTB Circular A31/2002 paras 40-43. It is understood that DWP decision makers have been given similar internal guidance.
240 **CB/GA** Reg 30(1) and (2) CB&GA(DA) Regs
HB/CTB Reg 19(6) and (7) HB&CTB(DA) Regs
Other benefits Reg 32(5) and (6) SS&CS(DA) Regs
TC Reg 5(5) and (6) TC(A)(No 2) Regs
241 **CB/GA** Reg 30(4) CB&GA(DA) Regs
HB/CTB Reg 19(8) HB&CTB(DA) Regs
Other benefits Reg 32(7) SS&CS(DA) Regs
TC Reg 5(7) TC(A)(No 2) Regs
242 **CB/GA** Reg 30(5) CB&GA(DA) Regs
HB/CTB Reg 19(9) HB&CTB(DA) Regs
Other benefits Reg 32(8) SS&CS(DA) Regs
TC Reg 5(8) TC(A)(No 2) Regs
243 **CB/GA** Reg 29(7) and (8) CB&GA(DA) Regs
HB/CTB Reg 19(11) and (12) HB&CTB(DA) Regs
Other benefits Reg 32(10) and (11) SS&CS(DA) Regs
TC Reg 5(10) and (11) TC(A)(No 2) Regs
244 **CB/GA** Reg 29(6) CB&GA(DA) Regs
HB/CTB Reg 19(10) HB&CTB(DA) Regs
Other benefits Reg 32(9) SS&CS(DA) Regs
TC Reg 5(9) TC(A)(No 2) Regs
245 **HB/CTB** Reg 23 HB&CTB(DA) Regs
Other benefits Reg 58(5) SS&CS(DA) Regs
TC Reg 27(4) TC(A)(No 2) Regs
246 **Benefits** Reg 9(3) and (4) SSCP Regs
TC Reg 7(3) and (4) SSCP(TCA) Regs
247 R(M) 1/87
248 *R v Home Secretary ex parte Mehta,* applied to social security law by R(M) 1/87 and R(I) 5/91
249 R(M) 1/87; R(I) 5/91
250 R(M) 1/87
251 CIS/147/1995

Chapter 45

Social fund reviews

This chapter covers:

The social fund (SF) review system only covers decisions relating to the discretionary SF (see Chapter 21) – ie, community care grants (CCGs), budgeting loans (BLs) and crisis loans (CLs). Decisions relating to the regulated SF (see Chapter 22) – ie, funeral, maternity, cold weather and winter fuel payments – can be challenged by revision, supersession or appeal, in the same way as for most other benefits (see p1218).

There is no right of appeal against CCG, BL and CL decisions. There is, instead, a review system, which is divided into two distinct stages:

- First, an internal review is carried out by the Department for Work and Pensions (DWP) office which made the decision.
- Second, an applicant has a right to request a further review by a social fund inspector (SFI). SFIs are part of the Independent Review Service, based in Birmingham (see Appendix 1), which conducts second-tier reviews independently of the DWP.

1. **Internal reviews**

Powers of review

The law relating to internal reviews is set out in legislation and legally binding social fund (SF) directions.[1] All decisions relating to community care grants (CCGs), budgeting loans (BLs) and crisis loans (CLs) made by decision makers are subject to review,[2] including:

- the refusal of a CCG or loan;
- the amount awarded;
- payment to a third party or in instalments;
- refusal to determine a repeat application (see p515);
- refusal to treat an application for a CL as an application for a CCG;
- overpayment decisions (see p1276).

Decisions about the repayment of loans are not subject to review, but can still be challenged (see p535).

Internal reviews are carried out by reviewing officers.[3]

A reviewing officer *must* review a decision if:

- you apply for a review within the time limit (see below);[4] *or*
- a decision was based on a mistake about the law, the directions or a material fact, or was given in ignorance of a material fact; *or*
- in the case of CCGs and CLs only, there has been a relevant change of circumstances since the decision was given; *or*
- in the case of BLs only, there has been a change in the district budget and in the maximum awards set by the district manager (see p533), or a change in your ability to repay a BL (see p534).[5]

In the last three cases, the reviewing officer can conduct a review at any time, with or without an application.

A reviewing officer *may* review a decision:

- if you misrepresented or failed to disclose a material fact, in which case any overpayment is recoverable;[6] *or*
- in such other circumstances as s/he thinks fit.[7]

In both of the above cases, the reviewing officer can conduct a review at any time. The second case offers wide (but discretionary) scope for reviews on any grounds, and at any time (eg, if you have missed the time limit for a mandatory review) with or without an application.

Procedure

Applying for a review

You must apply for a review of a decision by writing to the office where the decision was made within 28 days of the date the decision was issued to you.[8] Your application must include your grounds for requesting a review.[9] If somebody is making an application on your behalf, it must be accompanied by your written authority (unless the person is your appointee – see p1075).[10]

Late applications can be accepted for 'special reasons'.[11] 'Special reasons' are not defined. They could include reasons why the application is late (eg, ill health, domestic crisis, wrong advice) or any other reasons (eg, you will suffer hardship without a review). If the DWP does not accept there are special reasons, get advice. You may have to threaten judicial review if its refusal is unreasonable (see p1253).

If your application is out of time, you can also ask a reviewing officer to conduct a discretionary review (see above).

The DWP can ask you to submit further information in connection with your application if reasonably required.[12]

You can withdraw your application in writing at any time.[13]

See p1276 for reviews relating to overpayment decisions.

Review interviews

If a decision is not wholly revised in your favour, you must be given the opportunity to have an interview with the reviewing officer.[14] The interview should either be conducted in person (at your local Jobcentre Plus office, or in your home if, for example, you are seriously ill or disabled), or by telephone, if you agree to this or if it is not practicable for you to be interviewed in person. You may not be offered an interview if you are given a partial award (although you can request one) or if an award has been refused because you are not in receipt of a qualifying benefit.[15] You have the legal right to be accompanied to an interview by a friend or adviser.[16]

During the interview, you must be given an explanation of the reasons for the review decision and an opportunity to make representations and submit any additional evidence.[17] The reviewing officer must make an accurate written record of the interview, including your representations, which must be agreed with you. You must be sent a copy of the record of your telephone interview with your decision.[18]

Decisions

You are entitled to a written decision on your application for review (whether or not you have had an interview), which must include notification of your right to request a further review by a social fund inspector (SFI).[19] There are no legal time limits for carrying out reviews and notifying decisions. The SF Independent Review Service has stated that all reviews should be carried out within 10 working days, while a review of a crisis loan decision relating to urgent living expenses should be completed on the day the request is received.[20] If there are unreasonable delays, you should complain to the SF manager and, if necessary, ask your MP or an advice agency to assist.

How review decisions are made

Community care grants and crisis loans

When carrying out a review relating to a CCG or CL, a reviewing officer must have regard to all the circumstances of each case, and in particular to:[21]

- the nature, extent and urgency of the need;
- the existence of resources which could meet the need;
- whether any other person or body could wholly or partly meet the need;
- the district budget (see p513);
- the SF directions (see p514);
- national and local guidance (see p514); *and*
- in the case of CLs, the likelihood of repayment and the time it would take.

The High Court has ruled that need and the priority of an application should be assessed before budgeting considerations are taken into account.[22]

The reviewing officer must also:[23]

- check whether the decision was correctly arrived at (eg, sustainable on the evidence and based on all relevant considerations and a correct interpretation of the law);
- check that the decision maker acted fairly and reasonably and exercised discretion properly;
- check that you were given the opportunity to put your case and that there was no bias;
- take into account all the circumstances which existed at the time of the original decision and any new evidence and relevant changes in circumstances since the decision was made.

The reviewing officer does not have to take into account any issue not raised by the application for review.[24]

The above legal duties establish what should be a thorough and exacting system for review. In practice, however, reviewing officers tend to confirm decision makers' decisions unless new evidence comes to light which clearly shows that the decision was wrong. As with original decisions, budget considerations and the guidance on priorities tend to be the major determinants of decision making.

Budgeting loans

When carrying out a review relating to a BL decision, a reviewing officer must have regard to the same factors as decision makers (see p530).[25] This means that s/he is bound by the factual criteria set out in the directions (see p514).

The reviewing officer must also take into account:[26]

- whether the decision was correctly arrived at and whether you had sufficient opportunity to put your case;
- your personal circumstances, which determined the weighting of your application (see p531) when the decision was made, including any new evidence about them;
- any new loan debt you have;
- the district budget and the maximum amounts payable, from the time of the original decision up to the date of the review decision.

The reviewing officer does not have to take into account any issue not raised by the application for review.[27]

The above legal duties and restrictions mean that the scope for revision of a decision is very limited. In practical terms, unless it emerges that the original decision was based on incorrect information relating to the factual criteria, or there has been an increase in the district budget and maximum awards, the decision will merely be confirmed by the reviewing officer.

Overpayments

A decision to award you a CCG or a loan can be reviewed at any time if you misrepresented or failed to disclose a material fact (see p1130). Any resulting overpayment is recoverable. An overpayment decision is most likely to be triggered by a decision that you were not entitled to a qualifying benefit when you applied for a CCG or BL. You are entitled to a written decision of any overpayment and can ask for a further review by a reviewing officer.[28]

The reviewing officer must:[29]

- check whether the decision was correctly arrived at and based on the evidence and law; *and*
- take into account all the circumstances of the misrepresentation or non-disclosure and any new evidence which has been produced.

You will then receive a new decision. If you are still dissatisfied, you can request a further review by an SFI (see p1277).[30]

Tactics

- You should always consider requesting a review if you are dissatisfied with a decision. Although you could end up with a less favourable decision, any CCG you have received is only recoverable if you misrepresented or failed to disclose a material fact (see p1130), while a review decision to award you a lower loan, or no loan, has no practical effect if you have already been paid.
- You should also bear in mind the limited scope for a successful review of a BL decision (see p529). There is little point in requesting a review if the factual criteria were correctly applied in your case unless there is a change in the maximum awards set by the district budget (see Chapter 21 and p533). You could also consider re-applying for a BL, as an alternative to requesting a review.
- Your application for review must be in writing and you should retain a copy. If your application is late, you should give your special reasons why it should be considered out of time (see p1273). Alternatively, you could ask the reviewing officer to conduct a discretionary review (see p1273).
- You should explain, as fully as possible, why you disagree with a decision. CCGs are often refused on the grounds that your application was not for one of the purposes for which a CCG can be given, or because your application was of insufficient priority. You should explain how your application *is* for one of the allowable purposes (see p518) and why it should be given high priority. If you are unhappy about the amount awarded, you should explain and justify the reasonableness of the amount you asked for.

- You should decide whether you want a review interview to be conducted in person or by telephone. The telephone may be more convenient but you may be able to get your case across more effectively in person and can take a friend or representative with you. If you attend an interview, you should ask to be interviewed in a private room and complain if one is not offered. Always insist on an interpreter if you are not familiar with English. You should, of course, make sure that all your evidence and representations are recorded.
- You should be prepared to receive a negative review decision and to pursue your case by requesting a further review by an SFI (see below).

2. Social fund inspector reviews

Powers of review

The law relating to reviews by social fund inspectors (SFIs) is set out in legislation and legally binding SFI directions.[31]

All decisions which have been reviewed by a reviewing officer are subject to further review by an SFI (see below).[32]

The SFIs conduct their reviews independently of the Department for Work and Pensions (DWP). They are part of the Independent Review Service for the social fund, based in Birmingham (see Appendix 1).

SFIs can:[33]

- confirm the decision of the reviewing officer; *or*
- substitute their own decision; *or*
- refer the case back to a reviewing officer at the DWP for re-determination (in practice, this happens in very few cases).

Procedure

Applying for a further review

You must apply for a further review in writing within 28 days of the date the review decision was issued to you.[34] You can apply on Form IRS1 ('How to ask for an Independent Review'), which you can get from your local Jobcentre Plus office, or in a letter. Your application must include your grounds for requesting a further review (see p1279).[35] If somebody is applying on your behalf, you must send your written authority (unless the person is your appointee).[36] You should specifically authorise the person to make an application for further review by an SFI on your behalf. You need to do this even if you supplied written authority when you first applied for an internal review. Late applications can be accepted for 'special reasons' (see p1273).[37]

You must send your application to the office where the decision you are disputing was made, and not directly to the SFI office in Birmingham. The DWP will send your application, together with all relevant papers, to the SFI office in

Birmingham (this should be done within four working days, or, in the case of an urgent crisis loan, on the same day by fax[38]). Decisions about late or incomplete applications must be made by the SFI and not the DWP. The SFI writes to you directly for further information or evidence.

Process

Reviews are almost always conducted on the basis of written information (papers received from the local DWP and any new evidence submitted). You have no right to an oral hearing, although an SFI can interview you, if necessary, at a mutually convenient location.[39]

Within a few days of receiving an application, the SFI dealing with your case should write to you setting out the main issues and facts of the case and any additional information s/he needs. You should also be sent copies of your application form, the decisions made by the social fund (SF) decision maker and reviewing officer and the local guidance on priorities. You will normally be given eight days to make any further comments or supply further information or evidence to the SFI (either by telephone or on the provided reply form). You can request more time if you need it. The SFI will then decide the case.[40]

Decisions

You should receive a detailed written decision from the SFI. The Independent Review Service says it aims to clear all cases within 12 working days (23 days if further investigation is necessary). Crisis loan reviews should be dealt with more quickly (those relating to urgent living expenses should be dealt with within 24 hours).[41] If you are unhappy about an SFI decision, get advice. There is no right of appeal, but you can ask an SFI to reconsider her/his decision – eg, because it is unreasonable or wrong in law.[42] You can also apply for a judicial review of the decision in the High Court (see p1253).

If a case is referred back to the DWP for another internal review, the SFI should identify the factors which need further consideration. A decision maker must re-determine the case and send you a new decision, with a full explanation of how this was reached, taking into account the SFI's comments.[43] If you are dissatisfied with the new decision, you have the right to request a further review by an SFI.

How social fund inspectors' decisions are made

When carrying out a further review, SFIs must take into account the same factors as reviewing officers must when conducting internal reviews (see p1272).[44] This means they must exercise individual discretion in community care grant and crisis loan reviews, but they are bound by the factual criteria in budgeting loan reviews. See p1275 for reviews of overpayment decisions.

The High Court has ruled that it must be clear from the SFI's decision that s/he has taken the Secretary of State's guidance into account.[45] In another case, the

Court ruled that the SFI must apply the law at the time of the SFI decision, not the law at the time of the original SF officer's decision.[46]

SFI decision making tends to be of a much higher standard than reviewing officer decision making. SFIs are more independent and thorough and tend to be less bound by local budgets and guidance. You should note, however, that the SFI is primarily concerned with ensuring that the DWP decision was 'reasonable' rather than 'right' – ie, that discretion was exercised reasonably and in accordance with the law.[47]

Tactics

- You should always consider requesting a further review if you are dissatisfied with a reviewing officer's decision. SFI decision making is more thorough and independent and your application is more likely to be successful than at the internal review stage.
- Your application must be in writing and sent to your local DWP office. It needs to contain the same sort of information as an application for an internal review (see p1273).
- If your case is urgent, state this and explain why. There is a special express procedure if you are seeking a review of a crisis loan decision and you can ask the DWP to fax the decision and papers to the SFI office rather than relying on a courier.
- It is a good idea to contact the SFI office a few days after submitting your application to make sure it has been received. The DWP should send applications to Birmingham by courier on the day they are received, whenever possible. Complain to the district manager and, if necessary, your MP if there are delays.
- When you are sent the papers relating to your case by the SFI, you should look through them carefully and make appropriate comments on the form provided or by telephone.

Notes

1. **Internal reviews**
 1 s38 SSA 1998; SF Dirs 31-39
 2 s66 SSAA 1992; s38 SSA 1998
 3 SF Dir 31(4)
 4 s38(1)(a) SSA 1998
 5 SF Dir 31
 6 s38(1)(b) SSA 1998; s71ZA SSAA 1992; SF Dir 43
 7 s38(1)(c) SSA 1998
 8 Reg 2(1)(a) and (2)(a) SF(AR) Regs
 9 Reg 2(4) SF(AR) Regs
 10 Reg 2(6) SF(AR) Regs
 11 Reg 2(3) SF(AR) Regs

12 Reg 2(5) SF(AR) Regs
13 SF Dir 37
14 SF Dir 33(1)
15 SF Dir 33(2)-(4)
16 SF Dir 33(1)
17 SF Dir 34
18 SF Dir 35
19 SF Dir 36
20 IRS *Journal*, Issue 28, Summer 2004
21 s38 SSA 1998
22 *R v SFI ex parte Taylor* [1998] COD 152 (HC)
23 SF Dirs 32 and 39
24 s38 SSA 1998
25 s66(6)(b) SSAA 1992; s38(7) SSA 1998
26 SF Dirs 32 and 39
27 s66(5A) SSAA 1992; s38(6) SSA 1998
28 SF Dir 44
29 SF Dirs 45 and 46
30 SF Dirs 47 and 48

2. **Social fund inspector reviews**

31 s38 SSA 1998; SFI Dirs
32 s38(3) SSA 1998
33 s38(4) SSA 1998
34 Reg 2(1)(b) and (2)(b) SF(AR) Regs
35 Reg 2(4) SF(AR) Regs
36 Reg 2(6) SF(AR) Regs
37 Reg 2(3) SF(AR) Regs
38 IRS *Journal*, Issue 28, summer 2004
39 para 10105 SFG
40 IRS *Journal*, spring 2002 and summer 2004
41 IRS *Journal*, summer 2004
42 s38(5) SSA 1998
43 SF Dir 38
44 s38 SSA 1998; SFI Dirs 1-5
45 *R v IRS ex parte Connell* 3 November 1994, unreported (HC)
46 *R v SFI ex parte Ledicott* [1995] CO/2492/94 (HC)
47 SF Commissioner's Advice on SFI Directions 1 and 2, 2 January 2002

Chapter 46

Equal treatment and human rights

This chapter looks at European rules which prohibit discrimination between men and women in matters of social security and considers the Human Rights Act and its possible application to social security law. It covers:

1. European law and equal treatment

Social security benefits are not governed by British law alone. There are also Regulations and Directives made by the European Community (EC) which apply directly in the UK and throughout the European Economic Area (EEA) (see p672).

In particular, there are a number of Directives which are designed to ensure that (subject to limited exceptions) social security benefits, occupational pensions, pay and other benefits from employment are received on an equal basis by both men and women.

British courts (including decision makers, tribunals and social security commissioners) are obliged to apply EC law as well as domestic British law and although British law has been amended to take these Directives into account, the EC rules override the British rules where the two still conflict.[1] Cases which involve new points of EC law may be referred to the European Court of Justice (ECJ) in Luxembourg for a ruling. The ECJ is not the same as the European Court of Human Rights (ECtHR), which is an institution of the Council of Europe and operates from Strasbourg.

There has been a vast amount of caselaw in the ECJ and national courts on these anti-discrimination provisions and this *Handbook* cannot begin to cover the subject comprehensively.[2] What follows is an outline of the general principles and a discussion of what these mean in practical terms for people claiming benefits. If you think there is a chance that you may benefit from the principle of equal treatment, there is no substitute for getting proper advice on the particular circumstances of your claim. See Appendix 2 for the names and addresses of organisations which may be able to help you with this.

For social security the most important Directive is the Council Directive 79/7 of 19 December 1978 on the progressive implementation of the principle of equal treatment for men and women in matters of social security.[3] This Directive, which became binding on all member states on 22 December 1984, has direct effect. This means that individual citizens of the EEA countries can rely on it to claim benefits from their governments on a non-discriminatory basis even if those governments have not introduced national legislation putting the Directive into operation or if they have implemented it only in part.

2. The principle of equal treatment

The 'principle of equal treatment' established by Directive 79/7 is that:

> There shall be no discrimination whatsoever on ground of sex either directly, or indirectly by reference in particular to marital or family status.[4]

'Discrimination' simply means treating one person less favourably than another. Indirect discrimination occurs when a rule appears to be neutral but in practice can be complied with by fewer members of one sex than the other and that rule cannot be justified for reasons other than discrimination based on sex.

For example, a rule which said that applicants for a job had to be at least 6'3" tall would be indirectly discriminatory even though it applied equally to women and men. This is because, in practice, fewer women than men would qualify. Such a rule would be unlawful unless the employer could show a good, non-discriminatory, reason for employing only tall people.

It is often necessary to rely on statistical evidence to prove indirect discrimination. Governments may not rely upon purely financial reasons to justify a discriminatory practice.[5]

The principle of equal treatment only prohibits discrimination 'on ground of sex'. It does not prevent a government from discriminating on the ground of marital or family status unless that amounts to a form of indirect discrimination on the ground of sex. So a rule is not necessarily contrary to the Directive just because it differentiates between married (or cohabiting) people and single people.[6] On the other hand, a rule which differentiates between married men and married women or single men and single women is directly discriminatory on grounds of sex.

If the principle of equal treatment applies to you, then your claim for benefit should be decided using the rules which would have applied had you been a member of the opposite sex where those rules would be more favourable.[7]

However, this broad general principle is subject to a number of limitations and to exceptions (known as 'derogations'). In practice, this means that you have to ask three questions before you can know whether the principle of equal treatment applies in your case.

- Is the benefit you are claiming (or your liability to pay contributions) covered by the Directive? Only schemes for benefits which cover certain risks are subject to the principle of equal treatment. This is sometimes referred to as the material scope of the Directive.
- Does the Directive apply to you? You are only entitled to benefit from the principle of equal treatment if you are a member of the working population (see p1284). This is sometimes referred to as the personal scope of the Directive.
- Does the Directive include a derogation which applies in your case? If so, the Government is allowed to discriminate against you even if you are within both the personal and material scope of the Directive.

3. The material scope of the Directive

The Directive applies to schemes for state benefits which are designed to protect against the following risks:[8]

- sickness;
- invalidity;
- old age;
- accidents at work and occupational diseases;
- unemployment.

Most contributory benefits are covered by the Directive. However, whether or not a benefit is contributory is not the crucial factor in deciding whether it falls within the scope of the Directive. Certain non-contributory benefits such as carer's allowance (previously invalid care allowance), severe disablement allowance and industrial injury benefit are within the scope of the Directive.[9]

The Directive can also apply to means-tested benefits (sometimes referred to as 'social assistance') to the extent that they are intended to supplement or replace the schemes referred to above.[10] For example, a commissioner decided that income-based jobseeker's allowance is covered as it is a benefit that protects against the risk of unemployment.[11] A similar approach has been taken by the Court of Appeal.[12]

It could also be argued that pension credit (PC) is covered by the Directive.

The Government considers that PC is not within the scope of the Directive. However, as PC clearly has all the characteristics of an old age benefit, there is considerable scope to challenge this.

Income support, housing benefit and council tax benefit are not within the scope of the Directive.

Certain risks are specifically excluded from the Directive – in particular, positive discrimination for maternity allowances and the different pension ages for men and women. It is also notable that widows' and widowers' benefits are not covered by the Directive. Family benefits such as child benefit and child tax credit are also excluded from the scope of the Directive.

The fact that the Directive applies only to state schemes means that other schemes (such as occupational pension schemes) are beyond its scope. These are, however, covered by a later Directive[13] which is in similar terms.

4. The personal scope of the Directive

The Directive applies to you if you are a member of the working population. There is no requirement to have moved from one member state to another in order to fall within the scope of the Regulation. If you are not a member of the working population then you cannot use the Directive to stop the Government discriminating against you even if the benefit which you are claiming is within the material scope of the Directive.

The **'working population'** is defined as being:[14]

- workers (ie, people in employment);
- the self-employed;
- people seeking employment;
- workers and self-employed people whose jobs have been interrupted by illness, accident or involuntary unemployment;
- workers and self-employed people who have retired or become unable to work because of invalidity.

This means that to be covered by the Directive you must have been either working or actively looking for work when you became affected by one of the risks set out on p1283.[15] So, for example, the Directive does not apply to you if:

- you have been so ill or disabled since before you reached the age of 16 that you have never been able to contemplate working or looking for work; *or*
- you stopped working for a reason which is not included in the list of risks on p1283 (eg, because you were pregnant) and before you began to look for work again you became too ill to work.

It is not, however, necessary for the risks to be suffered by you personally. In one case, a woman who gave up work to look after her severely disabled mother was held to be a member of the working population because her work had been interrupted by invalidity, even though it was the invalidity of her mother and not her own personal invalidity.[16]

5. Exceptions to the principle of equal treatment

The Directive permits member states to adopt or continue discriminatory rules on certain aspects of entitlement to benefits even if they are within its material scope.

The types of discriminatory rule which may be lawful are:[17]

- rules which set a different age for men and women to become entitled to retirement pensions. This derogation also covers rules which deal with the possible consequences for other benefits of having a differential pensionable age;
- rules which allow people who have looked after children to claim retirement pensions and other benefits on advantageous terms. In Britain, this derogation would seem to permit the rules about home responsibilities protection (see p842) which discriminate indirectly against men;
- rules which allow wives to derive entitlement to old age pensions and incapacity benefits on the basis of their husbands' contributions or periods of insurance. This permits the British rules on Category B and C retirement pensions which discriminate directly against men;
- rules which cover increases for a dependent wife of incapacity benefits, retirement pensions and industrial injuries benefits. This allows the discrimination in the different rules for dependency increases in Category A retirement pensions (see p487);
- rules which allow special treatment for people who, before 22 December 1984, have opted 'not to acquire rights or incur obligations under a statutory scheme'. This is intended to cover the British rules on the married woman's reduced national insurance contribution (see p830).

The derogations should not be regarded as carte blanche to discriminate. As part of the progressive implementation of the principle of equal treatment, European Economic Area (EEA) states are supposed to keep these discriminatory rules under review to ensure that they are still justified in the light of social developments,[18] and to notify the European Commission of the measures that they have taken to do so.[19]

Perhaps more importantly, the European Court of Justice (ECJ) has repeatedly held that the elimination of discrimination based on sex is a fundamental right which it has a duty to protect. In the past it therefore scrutinised the validity of rules which rely on the derogations very carefully to ensure that the principle of proportionality was observed.[20]

This meant that it did not follow that a discriminatory rule was lawful just because it had one of the effects allowed by the derogations. In each case it was for the government of the member state which made the rule to establish that the discriminatory means which it adopted were an appropriate way of achieving the ends permitted by the derogation.

One case suggests that the principle of proportionality will not be applied in the future and that where the discrimination is within the wording of the derogation, the principle of proportionality has no application to it.[21] This is contrary to the earlier caselaw and may have been prompted by the particular facts of that case (which the Court saw as threatening the implementation of the principle of equal treatment by making it impossible for states to abolish discrimination in the areas covered by the derogations a little at a time). It therefore remains to be seen what attitude the Court will take on this point in other cases.

6. Equal treatment and social security benefits

The principle of equal treatment has had a significant impact on claimants' entitlement to social security benefits. Even before the Directive came into force, many discriminatory rules about entitlement to benefit were abolished in order to comply with Britain's Community obligations. Since December 1984, the Directive has been used by the European Court of Justice (ECJ) to extend entitlement for many women by overruling many discriminatory laws which still remained.

For British social security law, one of the most important issues has been the scope of the derogation for 'the possible consequences' for other benefits of different retirement ages.[22] What this means is whether it is lawful to withdraw or reduce earnings replacement benefits (eg, contribution-based jobseeker's allowance (JSA), incapacity benefit, severe disablement allowance (SDA), carer's allowance (CA) (previously invalid care allowance) and reduced earning allowance (REA)) when a claimant reaches pensionable age – with the effect, in most cases, that women are denied benefits which would be paid to a man of the same age.

It is clear that not just any connection between a benefit and pensionable age is sufficient for the derogation to apply. To take a far-fetched example, a country could not, for instance, pay contribution-based JSA to women aged over 20 while making men wait until they were 25 and then justify the discrimination against men by claiming that the qualifying age was pensionable age less 40 years. The question is on how close the link must be before it is covered by the derogation.

This question has been the subject of a number of decisions of the ECJ. In the *Thomas*[23] case the Court ruled that different pensionable ages for men and women in non-contributory benefits such as CA and SDA were contrary to EC Directive 79/7 and therefore unlawful. As a result, British law was amended to bring the rules on non-contributory benefits into line with the law as declared by the ECJ.

In the *Equal Opportunities Commission*[24] case, the Court held that inequality with respect to the number of contributions required to be paid in order to gain entitlement to a full retirement pension was justified. Men could be required to pay contributions for 44 years but women only for 39 years for the same amount of benefit.

The decision in the *Graham*[25] case was that the DWP could lawfully:

- reduce invalidity benefit (now abolished) to pension rate at 60 for women and 65 for men;
- take invalidity benefit away altogether from women at 60 and men at 65; *and*
- pay extra benefit to men who became incapable of work between the ages of 55 and 60 and not to women in the same position.

Although the Court's reasoning is unconvincing,[26] there is no appeal against a decision of the ECJ so there can be no doubt that the *Graham* decision is an effective statement of the law. A commissioner has recently considered whether the same discriminatory age rules contravene the Directive.[27] The Commissioner held that there was a possible contravention of the Directive in spite of the ECJ judgment in *Graham*. It was significant in the case before the Commissioner that incapacity had arisen after pension age. This was important because it may not be lawful to limit the contributions that a claimant has paid to those paid before pension age where that age is different for women than for men. However, to enforce that right the claimant would be required to pay outstanding contributions after age 60.

By contrast, in the *Richardson*[28] case it was held that the discriminatory treatment of men in respect of free prescriptions for those over retirement age unlawfully discriminated against men, since there was no necessary or objective link to pensionable ages. The Court followed a similar line in the *Taylor*[29] case where it was held that the refusal of winter fuel payments to men aged between 60 and 64 was in breach of Directive 79/7, as men were unlawfully discriminated against. The combined effect of these cases is that, in order to be covered by the derogation for 'the possible consequences for other benefits' of setting different pensionable ages for men and women, the discriminatory rule must be necessary *either*:

- to avoid disturbing the financial equilibrium of the social security system; *or*
- to ensure coherence between the retirement pension scheme and other benefit schemes.

Applying these tests, the Court has held (in general terms) that for contributory benefits (*Graham*) or the liability to pay national insurance contributions (*EOC*), a discriminatory link to pensionable age is lawful, but for non-contributory benefits (*Thomas*) such discrimination is unlawful. For a list of which benefits are contributory and which are non-contributory see p5.

The ECJ has considered the discriminatory rules in respect of REA. REA is not strictly contributory although the requirement that the claimant must have been an 'employed earner' at the time of the industrial accident or the onset of the prescribed disease means that in practice many REA claimants would actually have been paying, or liable to pay, Class 1 contributions.[30]

Although the Advocate-General gave an opinion that was favourable, the ECJ held that the discrimination within the REA Regulations is objectively justified and therefore exempted from the prohibition on discrimination under Directive 79/7.[31]

Income-based jobseeker's allowance

More recent cases have focused on discrimination within the income-based JSA rules. For example, in one case before the social security commissioners[32] a woman successfully argued that a student who was pregnant and temporarily gave up her course could claim income-based JSA. The UK Regulations which excluded her from benefit were discriminatory as they would have far greater impact on women. However, the decision has subsequently been overturned by the Court of Appeal in a particularly harsh judgment.[33] The Court decided that the JSA Regulations were not directly discriminatory against pregnant women or against women generally and were not, for that reason, in breach of the Directive. The Regulations made no express distinction between men and women, nor did they seek to deal with whether a woman was pregnant or not. What they did was to define student status in such a way that any full-time student who interrupted her/his course was deemed to remain a student, and so was ineligible for JSA until the last day of the course or such earlier date as s/he abandoned it or was dismissed from it. The claimant's ineligibility for JSA derived from the fact that she was a student, not from the fact that she was pregnant.

In another case a commissioner considered whether the requirement to be available for work for 40 hours a week in order to qualify for JSA was indirectly discriminatory. The commissioner found that the rule could not be discriminatory because the JSA Regulations allowed for certain people to be exempt from this condition. In particular, those with caring responsibilities can be exempt from the 40 hours a week requirement provided the restrictions are reasonable.[34]

A more successful outcome was found in a number of joined cases which looked at the discriminatory effect of the JSA rules on part-time staff employed in schools and colleges. The rules meant that this group were treated as working during periods when they received no pay. Consequently, they were unable to claim income-based JSA. The commissioners found this rule to be incompatible with Article 4 of Directive 79/7 and decided that it should be struck down.[35] The same discriminatory rules operate within the income support (IS) Regulations, but as IS is not within the scope of the Directive it is not possible to challenge in the same way.

Shared care

In the case of *Hockenjos* before the Court of Appeal[36] it was argued that the income-based JSA rules discriminated against a man who had shared care of his two children with his separated partner. Although the children spent equal periods of time with each parent, only the mother received an additional amount of income-based JSA for the children because she was the parent who received child benefit for them. For couples, the child benefit Regulations give priority to women claimants. Where a couple subsequently separate, it was argued that the rules favour the person already in receipt of child benefit, therefore the rules for income-based JSA discriminate against men and are contrary to the Directive. The Court of Appeal referred the case back to the commissioners to decide on the discrimination point. The commissioner subsequently held that where a person is able to rely on Directive 79/7, receipt of child benefit should not be the determining factor in deciding who has responsibility for a child.[37] The case was further appealed to the Court of Appeal. The Court has now held that in genuine shared care cases, linking increases in JSA to child benefit for dependent children for whom there is shared responsibility is discriminatory and therefore contrary to Directive 79/7. Consequently, in such cases both parents are entitled to the child addition of income-based JSA for their children. The Court further held that a person would be considered to be sharing the care of her/his child if s/he is caring for 104 nights or more a year.

The Secretary of State is considering applying for leave to appeal to the House of Lords in the *Hockenjos* case and is currently staying all similar appeals until the case is decided or the appeal is abandoned. The DWP has issued guidance instructing decision makers to determine new claims as though the *Hockenjos* case had been unfavourably decided.[38]

In theory, anyone in a similar position to Mr Hockenjos is now entitled to an additional amount of income-based JSA. However, the judgment is unlikely to affect other claimants apart from those with outstanding appeals.

A fresh claim for the addition is not likely to succeed because the child additions for income-based JSA have been abolished for claims made after April 2004. Instead, claimants are expected to claim child tax credit (CTC). In theory, it would be possible to make a similar argument in respect of CTC, but CTC does not fall under this area of EC law and therefore the discrimination argument would have to be made by relying on human rights law. This is more difficult and the Courts have been largely unsympathetic to human rights challenges in social security.

Claimants who are already in receipt of income-based JSA are also unlikely to succeed in a claim. In order to claim the child addition the claimant would need to seek a revision of the original decision. However, in such cases the anti test case rules mean that where an established interpretation of the law is overturned by a decision of a Court or Commissioner, the effect of that decision is retrospective only so far as the individual litigant is concerned. Other claimants can only gain the benefit of such a ruling on a revision or fresh claim with effect from the date of the new decision. As there are no longer any child additions, claimants seeking a revision will not benefit from the judgement.

It might be argued that the anti test case rules cannot operate to deny rights in EC law and they too should be disapplied. Such an approach has been applied by the ECJ. In the case of *Emmott*[39] the ECJ disapplied a national rule on the limitation period for instituting judical review proceedings. However, the ECJ has also considered the UK anti test case provisions in *Johnson*. The case concerned a woman who successfuly argued that the rules which restricted her entitlement to SDA were contrary to Directive 79/7. She sought to challenge the anti test case rules which restricted the amount of backdated benefit that she could receive. The ECJ considered that the anti test case provisions were not in breach of EC law.[40]

The implications of the *Hockenjos* judgement in respect of other benefits such as CTC, HB/CTB and IS is also limited. These benefits are not covered by the Directive so any challenges would have to be made by relying on human rights legislation. However, the Courts have been largely unsympathetic to human rights challenges in respect of social security. See CPAG's *Welfare Rights Bulletin* for updates.

7. The Human Rights Act

Key aspects of the Act

The Human Rights Act 1998 (HRA) came into effect on 2 October 2000. It incorporates into domestic (ie, UK) law most of the Articles of the European Convention on Human Rights.[41] For social security purposes, all of the relevant provisions of the Convention now form part of our domestic law.

An appeal tribunal, social security commissioner or court must take account of any relevant caselaw of the European Court of Human Rights (ECtHR) when deciding an appeal in which a human rights issue arises.[42]

In addition, all legislation must be read and given effect, *so far as it is possible to do so*, in a way which is compatible with the Convention.[43] This duty applies to all social security decision makers (eg, Secretary of State decision makers, appeal tribunals and the commissioners),[44] and applies regardless of whether the legislation in question was made before October 2000 or after. This interpretative obligation is a strong one. It may require words to be 'read into' the statutory provision concerned in order to remove a breach of the Convention (as long as this stops short of creating a new and different legal rule) and decision makers should strive to find a Convention compatible reading of the statute or regulations in issue.[45]

To which decisions does the Act apply?

The HRA only applies to decisions made on or after 2 October 2000.[46] It therefore will not be of any use if you were refused benefit before that date (whether on a fresh claim or a revision or supersession you had applied for, or a revision or supersession which had been instigated by the DWP, the Revenue or a local authority[47]), and cannot be relied on in any challenge (see Chapters 43 and 44) to such a decision. This remains the case even if, for example, the appeal tribunal does not hear your appeal against the refusal of benefit until after 2 October 2000, as what is being challenged is the refusal of benefit and that decision was made before 2 October 2000.[48] However, if an appeal is brought against the appeal tribunal's decision because of the way in which the tribunal came to its (post-2 October 2000) decision, or is about the tribunal's jurisdiction to hear the appeal,[49] arguments relying on the HRA may be applicable.

Example

Rafina claimed income support on 30 August 2000. The claim was refused on 14 September 2000 because she was said to be part of a couple and her alleged partner's income was too high. An appeal was made against the decision. Rafina could not use any arguments relying on the HRA in her appeal against the refusal of benefit. At the appeal hearing, which took place on 28 October 2000, the tribunal refused to allow the alleged partner to give evidence in support of Rafina's appeal. This aspect of the tribunal's procedure may be open to challenge using arguments relying on the HRA on any appeal to the commissioners.

Relevant Articles of the Convention

The Articles of the Convention which are most likely to be relevant in social security are:

- Article 6(1): right to a fair trial;
- Article 8: right to respect for private and family life, home and correspondence;
- Article 1 of the First Protocol: protection of property;
- Article 14: prohibition of discrimination (though not a free-standing right).

In addition, Article 2 of Protocol 1 (right to education) could be relevant.

Note: Article 14 will often be needed in social security cases to supplement the other Articles because of the difficulty of bringing social security within those Articles.

Key aspects of relevant Articles

Article 6(1) provides:

In the determination of his civil rights and obligations or any criminal charge against him, everyone is entitled to a fair and public hearing within a reasonable time by an independent and impartial tribunal established by law.

- This article should cover any social security benefit where there is no element of discretion. Whether the benefit is contributory or non-contributory, or means-tested or non-means-tested, should not matter.[50]
- The discretionary social fund may be excluded, but this is not certain because the discretion which appropriate officers have is very constrained (especially for budgeting loans). However, ex gratia payments made by the Secretary of State and discretionary housing payments are almost certainly excluded.
- Working families' tax credit and disabled person's tax credit fell under Article 6 (though tax disputes generally are excluded), as these tax credits were social security benefits.[51] An issue may arise as to whether the new child tax credit and working tax credit fall within Article 6.
- The term 'fair ... hearing' has been widely interpreted, and means that a claimant must:
  - have real and effective access to a court. Although access to a court or tribunal may be restricted in a particular case or class of cases,[52] any such restriction must not impair the very essence of the right and must both be proportionate and pursue a legitimate aim;[53]
  - have a real opportunity of presenting her/his case;
  - be given a reasoned decision; *and*
  - have 'equality of arms' with her/his opponent.[54] This includes the right to have a representative. In an appropriate case, there may be a right to *paid* representation.[55] However, note that the test here is a broad one. 'Equality of arms' only requires that a claimant is not placed under a *substantial* disadvantage compared to her/his opponent (eg, the Secretary of State or Board of the Revenue).[56] This rule has been held to have been breached when the DWP failed to ensure the attendance of one of its staff as a witness at an appeal hearing[57] and when it failed to provide an appeal tribunal with previous personal capability assessments in respect of the appellant.[58]
- 'Public hearing' includes the concept of a right to an oral hearing, but this will usually be confined to a hearing by a fact-finding body.[59]
- 'Within a reasonable time' has not been interpreted very beneficially as far as social security cases are concerned, with the ECtHR only finding breaches of this criterion with delays of four years and above and the social security commissioners finding delays of seven months[60] and one year[61] for hearing of appeals not unreasonable.[62] However, much will depend on the circumstances and, in particular, the benefit in question.
- 'Independent and impartial tribunal' includes the *appearance* of impartiality. The test of bias is 'real possibility of bias'.[63] This is an objective test based on the circumstances of the case and whether these would lead a fair-minded observer to conclude that there was a real possibility of bias.[64]

Note: a breach of Article 6 may be cured by access to a review or appellate court, if that court itself complies with Article 6.[65]

Article 8 provides:

Everyone has the right to respect for his private and family life, his home and his correspondence.

There shall be no interference by a public authority with the exercise of this right except such as is in accordance with the law and is necessary in a democratic society in the interests of national security, public safety or the economic well-being of the country, for the prevention of disorder or crime, for the protection of health or morals, or for the protection of the rights and freedoms of others.

- This article may impose a positive obligation on the state to ensure effective respect for private or family life – eg, by regulating the conduct of people. At present, this does not extend to an obligation to provide any particular social security benefit.
- Benefits which promote respect for family life or the home may be covered by Article 8 – eg, widowed mother's allowance/widowed parent's allowance.[66] However, the income support and jobseeker's allowance schemes are not, in general, covered by Article 8.[67]
- 'Family life' extends beyond formal and legitimate relationships.[68]
- 'Private life' covers the right to develop personally as well as create relationships with others,[69] and can include protection of a person's physical and psychological integrity.[70] However, it is not a breach of the right to respect for private life to film a disability living allowance claimant in public to check whether s/he is entitled to the benefit.[71] Respect for private life may extend to housing assistance in certain circumstances[72] and it may, therefore, arguably cover housing benefit and other benefits of last resort in certain circumstances. However, the Court of Appeal has rejected arguments that Article 8 imposes an obligation on the state to provide financial assistance towards the payment of housing costs in circumstances where the Regulation in question[73] meant a complete denial of benefit.[74]

Note: wide discretion is given to national governments in deciding how the right in question should be 'respected', and Article 8(2) provides a get-out for governments where there is a *prima facie* breach of Article 8(1).

Article 1 of the First Protocol provides:

Every natural or legal person is entitled to the peaceful enjoyment of his possessions. No one shall be deprived of his possessions except in the public interest and subject to the conditions provided for by law and by the general principles of international law.

The preceding provisions shall not, however, in any way impair the right of a State to enforce such laws as it deems necessary to control the use of property in accordance with the general interest or to secure the payment of taxes or other contributions or penalties.

- This Article will be breached if:
  - the state interferes with the peaceful enjoyment of the claimant's possessions; *or*

  - the claimant has been deprived of possessions by the state; *or*
  - the claimant's possessions have been subjected to control by the state.
- At present, the critical issue in social security is whether benefits constitute 'possessions' under this Article. The answer to this question is dependent on whether the benefit in question is contributory or non-contributory. Contributory benefits are possessions,[75] and it should not matter whether the contributions have been paid by the claimant or her/his spouse.[76] Non-contributory benefits, however, are not possessions.[77]
- However, even if your benefit is a 'possession', this Article provides no general right to be paid the benefit at a particular rate unless the reduction in your benefit is of such a substantial amount that it affects 'the very substance of the right'.[78] In a case relating to the reduction of retirement pension for hospital inpatients, the following factors were listed as helping to determine whether there was deprivation:[79]
  - did the provision in question reduce a benefit previously in payment?
  - was the provision in force throughout the time when the claimant was paying relevant contributions?
  - how close was the link between the benefit and payment of contributions?
  - the amount of the reduction in benefit.

Note: as with Article 8, states have a wide get-out in accordance with the 'public interest' or 'general interest'.

Article 14 provides:
The enjoyment of the rights and freedoms set forth in this Convention shall be secured without discrimination on any ground such as sex, race, colour, language, religion, political or other opinion, national or social origin, association with a national minority, property, birth or other status.

- It is important to note that this Article only comes into play if one of the other Articles applies, though it is not necessary to demonstrate that the other Article has been breached. It includes a long list of different sorts of discrimination, with a catch-all 'or other status'. This covers 'age',[80] 'residence'[81] and sexual orientation,[82] and should also cover discrimination on the grounds of disability.
- It covers indirect as well as direct discrimination.[83]
- However, only different treatment of people 'placed in an analogous situation' falls within Article 14.
- It will be breached if a measure creates differential treatment which does not pursue a legitimate aim, or if it is disproportionate to the aim pursued.[84] Administrative convenience may not amount to a legitimate aim,[85] and very weighty reasons will be needed to justify discrimination based on race or sex.[86]

Article 2 of the First Protocol provides:
No person shall be denied the right to education. In the exercise of any functions which it assumes in relation to education and to teaching, the State shall respect the right of parents to ensure such education and teaching in conformity with their own religious and philosophical convictions.

- This Article has recently been interpreted as applying to both school education and further and higher education, which may provide new scope for arguments in respect of the problems created for students by the income support and housing benefit rules in particular.[87]
- The Article, however, is expressed in the negative, so it probably does not create any duty on a state to subsidise education.

Using the Human Rights Act

For most social security cases, there are no special courts or procedures which need to be used if you want to bring a challenge relying on the HRA. Therefore, HRA arguments can be used in front of appeal tribunals, social fund inspectors and the commissioners, and the ordinary time limits for bringing such challenges will continue to apply (see Chapters 43 and 44).[88] However, such challenges will be expected to be responsible.[89] In addition, guidance has been issued concerning social security (and child support) appeals, which recommends the following:

- any HRA challenges should be raised at as early an opportunity as possible (eg, in the grounds of appeal);
- such grounds of appeal need to:
  - identify the rule, regulation or practice which it is alleged breaches the HRA and the Article(s) of the Convention;
  - set out the Articles of the Convention which it is claimed have been breached, and explain why they have been breached; *and*
  - set out the relevant supporting caselaw (and provide copies of the cases);
- grounds of appeal which fail to do the above and merely state that the decision is in breach of the Convention are unlikely to succeed; *and*
- raising an argument relying on the Convention for the first time at the hearing, when it could have reasonably been raised in advance, will almost certainly lead to an adjournment of the appeal.[90]

The starting point for any appeal tribunal (or other relevant decision-making body) considering an HRA challenge is to decide whether the statute, regulation, rule or practice which is in issue on the appeal is compatible with the relevant Articles of the Convention, or can be read 'so far as it is possible to do so' in such a way to make it compatible with the Convention. However, if the legislation cannot be interpreted in a way which makes it compatible with the Convention,[91] then the following two considerations apply.

- If the legislation is contained in an Act of Parliament, the appeal tribunal, commissioner or social fund inspector has to apply it as it stands.[92] Even the higher courts (High Court, Court of Appeal (Court of Session in Scotland) and House of Lords) are limited to issuing what is termed a 'declaration of incompatibility' in this situation,[93] which does not change the legislation[94] and simply requires the government minister to consider amending the legislation.[95]
- If the legislation in question is contained in a Regulation, then the appeal tribunal, commissioner or social fund inspector may disapply the (incompatible) Regulation,[96] unless the Act under which the Regulation was made is so prescriptive that it required an incompatible Regulation to be made. In this latter case, the appeal tribunal, commissioner or social fund inspector cannot disapply the Regulation,[97] and the remedy here is again limited to seeking a declaration of incompatibility from the higher courts.

Challenges in social security using the HRA and the Convention are difficult and may call for specialist input. In these circumstances, if you have a case in which an HRA argument arises, you should think very seriously about seeking specialist advice (see Appendix 2).

Notes

1. **European law and equal treatment**
   1 s2 ECA 1972
   2 For a detailed account see McCrudden (ed), *Equal Treatment Between Women and Men in Social Security*, Butterworths, 1994
   3 Directive 79/7/EEC (*Official Journal of the European Communities* No. L6, 10 January 1979, p24)

2. **The principle of equal treatment**
   4 Art 4(1) Directive 79/7/EEC
   5 *M.A. De Weerd (nee Roks) & Others v Bestuur van de Bedrijfsvereniging voor de Gezondheid, Geestelijke en Maatschappenlijke Belangen & Others* ECJ Case C-343/92 24 February 1994, unreported (ECJ)
   6 R(SB) 6/91, *Blaik v Department of Health & Social Security* 19 July 1990, unreported (CA)
   7 For example, see *Cotter and McDermott v Minister for Social Welfare and Another* ECJ Case C-286/85 24 March 1987, unreported (ECJ)

3. **The material scope of the Directive**
   8 Art 3(1)(a) Directive 79/7/EEC
   9 *Thomas v Secretary of State for Social Security* ECJ Case C-328/91 30 March 1993, unreported (ECJ)
   10 Art 3(1)(b) Directive 79/7/EEC
   11 CJSA/1920/1999 (*65/00)
   12 *Hockenjos v Secretary of State for Social Security* [2001] EWCA Civ 624 (CA)
   13 Directive 86/378/EEC (*Official Journal of the European Communities* No. L225, 12 August 1986, p40)

4. **The personal scope of the Directive**

14 Art 2 Directive 79/7/EEC
15 *Achterberg-te Riele & Others v Social Verzekeingsbank* C-48/88, C-106-107/88 [1989] (ECJ)
16 *Drake v CAO* ECJ Case 150/85 24 June 1986, unreported (ECJ)

5. **Exceptions to the principle of equal treatment**

17 Art 7(1) Directive 79/7/EEC
18 Art 7(2) Directive 79/7/EEC
19 Art 8(2) Directive 79/7/EEC
20 *Johnston v Chief Constable of the Royal Ulster Constabulary* [1986] ECR 723 (ECJ)
21 *Bramhill v CAO*, ECJ Case C-420/92 7 July 1994, para 23 of judgment

6. **Equal treatment and social security benefits**

22 Art 7(1)(a) Directive 79/7/EEC
23 *Thomas v Secretary of State for Social Security*, ECJ Case C-328/91 30 March 1993, unreported (ECJ)
24 *Graham v Secretary of State for Social Security*, ECJ Case C-92/94 11 August 1995, unreported (ECJ)
25 *Graham v Secretary of State for Social Security*, ECJ Case C-92/94 11 August 1995, unreported (ECJ)
26 It is interesting to compare the Court's decision with the opinion of the Advocate-General in the same case
27 CIB/4497/2002
28 *R v Secretary of State for Health ex parte Richardson*, ECJ Case C-137/94 19 October 1995, unreported (ECJ)
29 *R v Secretary of State ex parte Taylor*, ECJ Case C-382/98 16 December 1999, unreported (ECJ)
30 It is possible to be an employed earner but not liable to pay national insurance contributions if you are in part-time or low-paid work and earn less than the lower earnings limit
31 *Hepple and Others v CAO*, ECJ Case C-196/98 23 May 2000, unreported (ECJ), reported as R(I) 2/00
32 CJSA/1920/1999
33 *Secretary of State for Social Security v Walter* [2001] EWCA Civ 1913 [2002] ICMLR 794, reported as R(JSA) 3/02
34 CJSA/1434/2000; regs 6 and 13(4) JSA Regs
35 R(JSA) 4/03
36 *Hockenjos v Secretary of State for Social Security* [2001] EWCA Civ 624 (CA)
37 CJSA/4890/1998 (decision given 13 January 2003)
38 DMG letter 01/05, Section 25 SSA 1998
39 *Emmott v Minister for Social Welfare* [1991] ECR 1-4569 Case C208/90
40 *Johnson v Chief Adjudication Officer* [1994] ECR I-5483 Case C-410/92

7. **The Human Rights Act**

41 s1(2) HRA 1998
42 s2(1) HRA 1998
43 s3(1) HRA 1998
44 See definition of 'public authority' in s6(3) HRA 1998
45 *Ghaidan v Godin-Mendoza* [2004] UKHL 30, [2004] 3 All ER 411
46 ss7(1)(b) and 22(4) HRA 1998
47 CDLA/3908/2001 ruling that s22(4) HRA 1998 does not apply to supersession instigated by the Secretary of State. See also the House of Lords' decision in *R v Lambert* [2001] UKHL 37, 3 All ER 577 – s22(4) has no application to appeals against decisions.
48 CIS/1077/1999, CSDLA/1019/1999 and CDLA/1388/2002
49 CIS/758/2002
50 *Salesi v Italy* [1998] 26 EHRR 187 (ECtHR); R(IS) 6/04
51 s1 and Sch 1 TCA 1999
52 See for example, the categories of non-appealable decisions in Sch 2 SS&CS(DA) Regs
53 *Tolstoy Miloslavsky v United Kingdom* [1995] 20 EHRR 441 (ECtHR); R(IS) 6/04
54 *Neumeister v Austria* [1968] 1 EHRR 91 (ECtHR); CDLA/5413/1999
55 *Airey v Ireland* [1979] 2 EHRR 305 (ECtHR); see also CJSA/5101/2001 where the commissioner confirmed that there is no general right to (paid) legal representation before an appeal tribunal
56 *De Haes and Gijsels v Belgium* [1997] 24 EHRR 1 (ECtHR)
57 CJSA/5100/2001
58 CIB/3985/2001
59 *Schuler-Zgraggen v Switzerland* [1993] 16 EHRR 405 (ECtHR)
60 R(IS) 1/04
61 R(IS) 2/04
62 *Deumeland v Germany* [1986] 8 EHRR 448 (ECtHR) and *Schouten and Meldrum v Netherlands* [1995] 19 EHRR 432 (ECtHR)
63 *Porter and another v Magill* [2001] UKHL 67, [2002] 1 All ER 465 (HL)

64 In social security this test has been adopted in relation to EMPs sitting on and providing reports to appeal tribunals (see CSDLA/1019/1999 (*Gillies*) and CSDLA/444/2002 - though the challenge in the *Gillies* case failed on a further appeal to the Court of Session)
65 *R v Secretary of State for the Environment, Transport and the Regions ex parte Holding and Barnes plc and others* [2001] 2 All ER 929 (HL); *Runa Begum v LB Tower Hamlets* [2003] UKHL 5, 1 All ER 731 (HL)
66 *R (Hooper and others) v Secretary of State for Work and Pensions* [2003] EWCA Civ 813, [2003] 3 All ER 673, para 18; *Petrovic v Austria* [2001] 33 EHRR 14 (ECtHR); CH/4574/2003 (but contrast CH/663/2003 and see the contrasting views expressed in *Langley v Secretary of State for Work and Pensions* [2004] EWCA Civ 1343, 15 October 2004
67 *R (Reynolds) v Secretary of State for Work and Pensions* [2003] EWCA Civ 797, [2003] All ER 577, para 28
68 *Marckx v Belgium* [1979] 2 EHRR 330 (ECtHR); *X, Y and Z v UK* [1997] 24 EHRR 143 (ECtHR)
69 *Niemitz v Germany* [1992] 16 EHRR 97 (ECtHR)
70 *Botta v Italy* [1998] 26 EHRR 241 (ECtHR)
71 R(DLA)4/02
72 *Marzari v Italy* Application No.36448/97 4 May 1999, unreported (ECtHR)
73 Reg 7(1)(c) and (d) HB Regs
74 *R (Tucker) v The Secretary of State for Social Security* [2001] EWCA Civ 1646, 8 November 2001, unreported
75 *Willis v United Kingdom* Application No.36042/97 11 June 2002, unreported (ECtHR); *R (Reynolds) v Secretary of State for Work and Pensions* [2003] EWCA Civ 797, [2003] 3 All ER 577
76 *Willis v United Kingdom* Application No.36042/97 11 June 2002, unreported (ECtHR), effectively overruling the contrary view in *Hooper and others v Secretary of State for Work and Pensions* [2002] EWHC Admin 191
77 *R (Reynolds) v Secretary of State for Work and Pensions* [2003] EWCA Civ 797, [2003] All ER 577, para 28
78 *Müller v Austria* (Commission) (1975) 3 D and R 25
79 CP/5084/2001
80 *R (Reynolds) v Secretary of State for Work and Pensions* [2003] EWCA Civ 797, [2003] All ER 577, para 28
81 *R(Carson) v Secretary of State for Work and Pensions* [2003] EWCA Civ 797, [2003] 3 All ER 577
82 *Langley v Secretary of State for Work and Pensions* [2004] EWCA Civ 1343, 15 October 2004
83 CH/5125/2002
84 *Belgian Linguistics Case (No. 2)* [1968] 1 EHRR 252 (ECtHR)
85 *Darby v Sweden* [1990] 13 EHRR 774 (ECtHR)
86 *Schmidt v Germany* [1994] 18 EHRR 513 (ECtHR)
87 See *Douglas v North Tyneside Metropolitan Borough Council* [2003] EWCA Civ 1847 [2004] 1 All ER 709 and compare with *O'Connor v CAO* (reported as R(IS) 7/99)
88 s7(5) HRA 1998
89 *R v Perry*, *The Times*, 28 April 2000 (CA) and *Daniels v Walker*, *The Times*, 17 May 2000 (CA)
90 President's Protocol No.6, 'Handling Questions Under the Human Rights Act 1998' (14 July 2000)
91 For example, the pre-April 2000 rules on widows' benefits arguably conflicted with the Convention because the benefits were only available to women who had been widowed, and not men. However, the relevant part of the legislation referred to women and wives (as being entitled), and such specific and deliberate references cannot be interpreted as applying also to men and husbands. *Hooper and others v Secretary of State for Work and Pensions* [2003] EWCA Civ 813, [2003] 3 All ER 673, para 28.
92 s3(2)(b) HRA 1998
93 s4 HRA 1998
94 s4(6) HRA 1998
95 s10(2) HRA 1998
96 On the basis that the Minister acted outside the powers given to him in the Act to made such Regulations (referred to as the *ultra vires* rule), following the House of Lords' decision in *CAO v Foster* [1993] 1 All ER 705 (HL)
97 s3(2)(c) HRA 1998

Chapter 47

Complaints

This chapter covers:

Note: For details of complaints about the Child Support Agency, see CPAG's *Child Support Handbook.*

The procedures for revision, supersession and appeal (see Chapters 43 and 44) allow you to challenge decisions about your entitlement to benefit (including the refusal of benefit). However, in some circumstances you may want to make a complaint simply about the way in which your benefit claim was handled.

The things you might want to complain about could include:

- delay in dealing with your claim;
- poor administration in the benefit office – eg, it keeps losing your papers, or you can never get through on the telephone;
- poor or negligent advice from DWP, the Revenue, local authority or Appeals Service staff;
- the behaviour of members of staff – eg, staff rudeness or sexist or racist remarks.

If you think you have lost out because you were badly advised by an independent adviser, such as a Citizens Advice Bureau or law centre, you should seek legal advice about taking action for negligence.

You should ask your local office for any written information on the standards and levels of service which you can expect. This may include targets for the time it should take to deal with your claim. You can also visit the DWP, the Revenue and The Appeals Service websites (see Appendix 2) for information about standards and complaints. All the agencies should also be able to provide you with written details about how to complain if you are not getting the service you think you should be.

Whenever you write to the DWP, the Revenue, The Appeals Service or local authority you should quote your national insurance number and, if you are not writing to the office which is handling your claim, the name and address of that office. If you are complaining, explain exactly what you are complaining about, any costs that you have incurred as a result of this problem and what you would like to see done to resolve your complaint. Always keep a copy of any letters you send or receive and take the name of anyone you speak to on the phone.

1. Complaining to the Department for Work and Pensions

If you want to complain about how the Department for Work and Pensions (DWP) has dealt with your individual case, as a first step you should speak to the supervisor in the office concerned. If you are still dissatisfied, you can contact the customer services manager. S/he investigates your complaint and should respond within seven days. If this does not solve the problem you should write to the manager of your district office with details of the complaint. If you are still unhappy, you can ask the DWP for an independent review of your complaint.

2. Complaining to the Revenue

If you want to complain about how the Revenue has dealt with your tax credit claim or with your national insurance credits or contributions, it is best to raise the complaint with the officer dealing with your case, or the named contact person on any letters you have received, to ask them to sort the matter out. This can be done verbally or in person but it is advisable to put the complaint in writing. If you are still not satisfied you can write to the customer service manager at the Revenue. If s/he cannot resolve the matter satisfactorily then you can write to the director of that office (see Appendix 1). The customer service manager should provide you with the director's details. S/he should reply to your letter within seven days. The Revenue's complaints procedure is set out in its Code of Practice 'Putting things right', COP1, which is available on their website (see Appendix 2). The Revenue's target for answering correspondence is 15 days.

If you are not happy with the Revenue's reply you can ask the independent Adjudicator to look into it and recommend appropriate action (see p1301).

3. Complaining to the Adjudicator

The Adjudicator's Office was set up in 1993 to investigate complaints about the way in which the Revenue deals with people's tax matters. It now also covers a number of areas, including complaints about tax credits and the Public Guardianship Office (see Appendix 1). The Adjudicator is similar in nature to the Ombudsman (see p1303). Therefore, complaints can be made about delays, inappropriate staff behaviour, misleading advice or any other form of maladministration. The Adjudicator cannot, however, investigate disputes about matters of law. The Adjudicator will only investigate a complaint if you have first exhausted the Revenue's internal complaints procedure. A complaint should be made within six months of the final correspondence with the Revenue.[1]

The Adjudicator can recommend that compensation is paid, and the Revenue has undertaken to follow her/his recommendations in all but exceptional circumstances. The Revenue publishes a leaflet, *How to Complain about the Inland Revenue*, which gives guidance on taking a case to the Adjudicator.

If you are unhappy with the Adjudicator's response to your complaint you can ask your MP to put your complaint to the Ombudsman. As well as looking at your complaint about the Revenue the Ombudsman may also look into the way in which the Adjudicator has investigated your complaint.[2]

4. Complaining to a local authority

Most local authorities have a complaints procedure and you should ask for details of how this works. Where there is no formal procedure, you should begin by writing to the supervisor of the person dealing with your claim, making it clear why you are dissatisfied. If you do not receive a satisfactory reply, you should take the matter up with someone more senior in the department and ultimately the principal officer. Send a copy of the letter to your ward councillor and to the councillor who chairs the council committee responsible for housing benefit/ council tax benefit – local authority officers are always accountable to the councillors. If this does not produce results, or if the delay is causing you severe hardship, you should consider a complaint to the local goverment Ombudsman (see p1303) or court action.

Government departments also monitor local authorities, so you could contact your MP or write to the relevant minister – eg, the Secretary of State for Work and Pensions. One of the things that the minister can do if s/he believes that there is a widespread problem with maladministration in the local authority is to ask the Benefit Fraud Inspectorate to report on the authority's administration.

5. Complaining to The Appeals Service

Complaints about the administration of your appeal

The Appeals Service provides administrative support to appeal tribunals. If you have a complaint about the administration of your appeal you should complain to The Appeals Service. Initially you should raise your complaint with the person who has been dealing with your appeal. Her/his name and telephone number should be on all correspondence that you have received. If you are not satisfied with the response that you receive to your complaint you can ask to be referred to the customer services manager. If you remain dissatisfied you should complain in writing to the Chief Executive of The Appeals Service.

Complaints about the conduct of panel members

If you are unhappy about the way in which you were treated by a tribunal member (eg, because they were discourteous or racist) you should raise the matter initially by writing to the regional chair of the region in which the tribunal was heard. The chair will then investigate the complaint. You should receive an acknowledgement of your complaint within five working days of the complaint being received. The regional chair will contact all of the people involved and then write to you telling you whether or not the complaint is upheld and if so what action is to be taken.[3]

If the complaint is about the conduct of the regional chair it should be made to the President of The Appeals Service. If your complaint is about the President it should be made to the Lord Chancellor.

6. Using your MP

If you are not satisfied with the reply from the officers to whom you have written, the next step is to take up the matter with your MP.

Most MPs have 'surgeries' in their areas where they meet constituents to discuss problems. You can get the details from your local library or Citizens Advice Bureau. You can either go to the surgery or write to your MP with details of your complaint.

Your MP will probably want to write to the benefit authorities for an explanation of what has happened. If you or s/he are not satisfied with the reply, the next stage is to complain to the Ombudsman, via your MP.

7. Complaining to the Ombudsman

The system of the Ombudsman was introduced to the UK in 1967 with the appointment of the Parliamentary Commissioner for Administration (PCA). The role of the Ombudsman is to investigate complaints from members of the public who feel that they have suffered an injustice because of some maladministration by a government department.[4] Maladministration means poor administration and can include avoidable delays, failure to advise about appeal rights, refusal to answer reasonable questions or to respond to correspondence, discourteousness, racism or sexism.

As the name suggests, the PCA is concerned with complaints about central government. In 1974 local government also became subject to the scrutiny of the Ombudsman with the creation of the Commissioner for Local Administration.[5]

The Ombudsman will not usually investigate a complaint unless you have first exhausted the internal complaints procedure. However, if the authority is not acting upon your complaint, or there are unreasonable delays, then this delay may also form part of your complaint. The time limit for lodging a complaint with the Ombudsman is 12 months from the date that you were notified of the matter complained about.

The Parliamentary Commissioner for Administration

The PCA deals with complaints about all central government departments. This includes the Department for Work and Pensions and the Revenue as well as any agencies carrying out functions on behalf of these departments. It also includes both The Appeals Service and the Office of the Social Security and Child Support Commissioners. In order to make a complaint it is necessary to write to your MP, who will then refer the complaint to the Ombudsman. The Ombudsman can only investigate complaints of maladministration and not complaints about entitlement, which should be dealt with by an appeal tribunal. The Ombudsman has extensive powers to look at documents held by the benefit authority on your claim. You may be interviewed to check any facts. The Ombudsman can recommend financial compensation if you have been unfairly treated or suffered a loss as a result of the maladministration.

The Commissioner for Local Administration

If you have tried to sort out your complaint with the local authority but you are still not satisfied with the outcome, you can apply to the Commissioner for Local Administration (more commonly known as the local government Ombudsman). The Ombudsman can investigate any cases of maladministration by local authorities, but not matters of entitlement, which can be dealt with by an appeal tribunal.

You may apply to the Ombudsman by writing to the appropriate local office (see Appendix 1). The Ombudsman has extensive powers to look at documents held by the local authority on your claim. You may be interviewed to check any facts. Straightforward cases can be dealt with in about three months. The Ombudsman can recommend financial compensation if you have been unfairly treated or suffered a loss as a result of the maladministration. A complaint may also make the authority review its procedures, which could be of benefit to other claimants.

8. Compensation payments

You should expect prompt, courteous and efficient service from staff dealing with your claim. If you are dissatisfied with the way your claim has been administered you can seek compensation.

The Department for Work and Pensions (DWP), the Revenue and local authorities sometimes pay compensation if you can show that you have lost out through its error or delay and the loss cannot be made good by a revision, supersession, appeal or backdating a claim (see Chapters 43 and 44). For instance, if you failed to claim guardian's allowance because you were misled by the DWP and you could not have the benefit backdated for more than three months you could claim compensation.

The DWP uses a guide, *Guide to Financial Redress for Maladministration*, to help it decide when and how much compensation (known as an 'extra statutory' or ex gratia payment) should be paid. The guide is available from The Stationery Office or can be obtained from the DWP website (see Appendix 2). The Revenue has a code of practice (COP1), *Putting Things Right When We Make Mistakes*, which sets out when it will make compensatory or consolatory payments.

You should ask for a payment equal to the money you have lost, but you could also ask for additional amounts to cover interest on arrears and extra expenses you had to pay out, and to compensate you for any hardship or distress suffered because of the mistake. Payments are discretionary, so you should stress the DWP, Revenue or local authority error, and the fact that you have suffered as a consequence of official negligence, in order to ensure payment. If your loss was as a clear result of incorrect advice or negligence on the part of the agency, you may be able to bring a court action for damages.[6] You will need the help of an advice agency or solicitor to do this. Tactically it is probably better to pursue a payment under this scheme before making a complaint to the Ombudsman. This is because if the Ombudsman does not uphold your complaint, the particular benefit authority is likely to resist making a compensation payment.

9. Delays

All benefit authorities should act promptly to process a claim. A failure to do so can lead to you making a complaint and possibly obtaining compensation.

Local authorities should process housing benefit claims within 14 days as long as you have given them all the information they have asked for.[7] Most do not. Complaining may be one way to get your claim processed more quickly, although threatening legal action may be more effective. The local government Ombudsman often orders compensation to be paid where there have been long delays which are not your fault.

The Revenue has no official targets for processing tax credit claims. It also has no guidelines for when it will pay compensation. However, many claimants have experienced long delays and errors in their claims and as a consequence have suffered financial hardship. In such cases claimants should consider making a complaint to the Adjudicator (see p1301) and/or the Ombudsman (see p1303).

Department for Work and Pensions (DWP) offices have target times for dealing with claims, but they are not always able to meet these. If there is a long delay (eg, in assessing your entitlement or paying you benefit) you may be entitled to compensation if:[8]

- a significant reason for the delay was DWP error or delay; *and*
- the amount of benefit involved was more than £100; *and*
- the delay in payment was more than a set length of time (known as a 'delay indicator' – see below); *and*
- any compensation would be £10 or more.

Delay indicator	*Benefit*
2 months	Income support, pension credit and bereavement payment
3 months	Jobseeker's allowance, community care grants and budgeting loans
4 months	Incapacity benefit, bereavement allowance and widowed parent's allowance
5 months	Maternity allowance and social fund funeral expenses payments
7 months	Attendance allowance and disability living allowance (two months if claimed under the special rules)
8 months	Retirement pension
9 months	Carer's allowance and renewal claims for disability living allowance
1 year	Industrial injuries disablement benefit

You are not automatically awarded compensation, although the DWP should automatically consider whether it should be paid where you are owed arrears of benefit. You should still write to your local DWP office and ask. If you do not get a sympathetic response you could ask your MP to write on your behalf or to take up your case with the social security minister.

10. Legal action

It is not possible to sue a benefit authority for negligence in the way it decides your claim.[9] Instead, if a decision is wrong, you can seek a revision or supersession or appeal against it. However there are some circumstances in which it is possible to seek compensation through the courts:

- Misadvice – if an employee of a benefit authority or The Appeals Service gives wrong advice which leads to some financial loss for you.
- Unpaid benefit – if your benefit claim has been determined but you have not received payment. This might be, for example, because a giro has gone missing.
- Breach of human rights – since the introduction of the Human Rights Act it may also be possible to sue benefit authorities where there is a breach of human rights.

Although it is possible to seek compensation through the courts it should never be the first course of action and should only ever be considered after seeking legal advice.

If a benefit authority refuses to process your claim you may be able to take action in the courts by way of judicial review. Contact CPAG for further details.

Notes

3. **Complaining to the Adjudicator**
   1 For further details see CPAG's *Welfare Rights Bulletin* 180 'Tax credits, complaints and the Adjudicator'
   2 See also CPAG's *Welfare Rights Bulletin* 180 'Tax credits, complaints and the Adjudicator'

5. **Complaining to The Appeals Service**
   3 President's Protocol 2

7. **Complaining to the Ombudsman**
   4 s5(1)(a) Parliamentary Commissioner Act 1967
   5 ss23 and 24 Local Government Act 1974

8. **Compensation payments**
   6 *Haringey LBC v Cotter* [1996] 29 HLR 682 (CA)

9. **Delays**
   7 Reg 76(3) HB Regs
   8 *Guide to Financial Redress for Maladministration* (2001 version), paras 104-105, Appendix A1

10. **Legal action**
   9 *Jones v Department of Employment* [1989] QB 1 (CA)

Part 6

Tax credits

Chapter 48

Introduction

This chapter covers:

1. Tax credits

On 6 April 2003 two important new tax credits were introduced:

- child tax credit; *and*
- working tax credit.

These tax credits are administered by **the Revenue. Note:** At the time of writing, the Inland Revenue was expected to merge with Customs and Excise to form a new department called Her Majesty's Revenue and Customs. This merger was expected to take place during April 2005. Therefore, references to 'the Revenue' should be taken to mean references to both the Inland Revenue and Her Majesty's Revenue and Customs.

The rules are mainly separate from the benefit rules that are described elsewhere in this *Handbook*, although tax credits can be paid with most benefits. In this chapter we outline the basic rules for the tax credits, describe the special rules that apply to them from April 2004 and during 2005, the way they affect benefits, and the rules on tax credits and passported benefits. Detailed rules on other matters are described in the chapters that follow this one.

Child tax credit[1]

This is an income-based credit for low-income and middle-income families who are in or out of work and who have responsibility for a child(ren) under 16, or under 19 if in full-time non-advanced education (see p87). See Chapter 49 for more details.

Working tax credit[2]

This is an income-based credit for working adults. To be eligible to claim, you or your partner have to fit into one of four categories:

- work 16 hours or more a week; *and*
  - have responsibility for a child; *or*
  - have a disability that puts you at a disadvantage in getting a job; *or*
  - qualify for a 50-plus element (see p1358); *or*
- work 30 hours or more a week; *and*
  - be 25 or over.

See Chapter 50 for more details.

2. Summary of the main features

- Tax credits are payable and assessed on a yearly basis, in line with the tax year (6 April – 5 April) (see p1402).
- Child tax credit is payable whether or not the person claiming it is in or out of work.
- Working tax credit eligibility extends to employees without a child or a disability if they are 25 or over and work 30 hours or more a week (see p1329).
- Tax credits are based on income only and not capital, but actual income from capital counts as income (see p1373).
- Tax credits can be paid in addition to most other benefits. However, they may count as income for some means-tested benefits (not for some income support (IS) or income-based jobseeker's allowance (JSA) claims from 6 April 2004).
- Regarding access to passported benefits, different rules apply to tax credits than the rules for IS and income-based JSA (see p1313).

3. 2004 and after

Amounts for children

From 6 April 2004 amounts for children ceased to be included in new claims for income support (IS) and income-based jobseeker's allowance (JSA), leaving just the amounts for adults and any housing costs included in the claim.[3] For these claims, child tax credit (CTC) will replace the following amounts for children within IS and income-based JSA:

- personal allowances for children;
- family premium;
- enhanced disability premium for children;
- disabled child premium.

Families with children will therefore no longer claim one benefit for the whole family but instead will need to claim IS or income-based JSA or working tax credit (WTC) for themselves and CTC and child benefit for their children.

People with children who have been on IS or income-based JSA since before 6 April 2004 who are not yet in receipt of CTC will have the child part of their claim transferred to CTC at some point during 2005. At the point that the child part of the claim is transferred to CTC, the IS or income-based JSA will cease to include amounts for children. People will be transferred at different dates, but will be paid amounts for children in their benefit up to the point that they are transferred.[4]

4. Impact on benefits

Benefits – general

Tax credits can be paid with the benefits described in this *Handbook*, including child benefit, income support (IS) and income-based jobseeker's allowance (JSA). Child benefit is ignored as income when calculating entitlement to tax credits. However, see Chapter 53 for how benefits count as income when calculating your entitlement to tax credits.

Means-tested benefits

Income support and income-based jobseeker's allowance

From 6 April 2004 the amounts for children within IS and income-based JSA were not included in new claims, leaving only the amounts in respect of adults and housing costs (see p818). If you have children, you will have to claim child tax credit (CTC) as well as child benefit in order to get money for them. You will only have child amounts included in your IS or income-based JSA if your current claim included a child before 6 April 2004 and you have not yet been awarded CTC.

You may be entitled to both CTC and IS or income-based JSA if you are not working 16 hours (or 24 in the case of a partner) or more a week.

If you claim both CTC and IS or income-based JSA, CTC does not count as income for those benefits from 6 April 2004.[5] Working tax credit (WTC) counts as income at all times.

If you are in receipt of IS or income-based JSA that still includes child amounts because you have not yet been transferred onto CTC, any child benefit you receive will count in full as income for IS and income-based JSA (with a £10.50 disregard if you are getting child benefit for a child under one).[6]

Pension credit

This replaced IS for those over 60 from 6 October 2003. If you have responsibility for a child(ren) you will have to claim CTC as well as pension credit (PC). Only

WTC, not CTC, counts as income when claiming PC.[7] For the purposes of calculating any savings credit you may be entitled to, WTC does not count as qualifying income[8] (see Chapter 18).

Housing benefit and council tax benefit

Housing benefit (HB) and council tax benefit (CTB) continue to include amounts for children. You can claim HB and CTB and tax credits at the same time. The local authority is not allowed to take unclaimed or unawarded tax credits into account as income.[9] CTC and WTC count as income for HB and CTB and only from the date they are awarded. However, CTC no longer counts as income for calculating HB and CTB for those aged 60 or over who are, or whose partner is, not in receipt of IS or income-based JSA.

If your award of tax credits includes the 30-hour or 50-plus elements of WTC (or would include the 50-plus element were you to apply for it) or the disability or severe disability element of WTC, £14.50 of your earnings is disregarded when calculating your HB and CTB.[10]

Your HB and CTB are normally based on the amount of tax credits you actually receive. Also, any arrears of tax credits are treated as capital[11] and if the arrears are caused by a change in circumstances, the capital is ignored for 52 weeks.[12]

If your tax credit is reduced in order to recover an overpayment of tax credits, your HB/CTB entitlement is based on that reduced amount (see p968).

Non-means-tested benefits

Child benefit can be paid in addition to CTC and WTC. It is ignored as income for the purposes of calculating CTC and WTC[13] (but child benefit is still taken into account for the purposes of calculating HB and CTB, except for those aged 60 or over who are, or whose partner is, not in receipt of IS or income-based JSA).

Other non-means-tested benefits to which you are entitled can be paid in addition to any tax credits you are getting. Getting certain non-means-tested benefits can help you qualify for or increase an award of WTC or CTC. However, see Chapter 53 for how these benefits may count as income when claiming tax credits.

Example

Merlene is in receipt of disability living allowance (DLA). She starts work for 16 hours or more a week. She may be entitled to WTC as a person with a disability and CTC and child benefit if she has responsibility for a child(ren). If she has a mortgage for her main home she will not qualify for any IS housing costs (as she works over 16 hours a week and so is not entitled to IS), but she might get some CTB.

If she is in rented accommodation she may qualify for HB and/or CTB. She will still get her DLA, as long as she continues to satisfy the conditions of entitlement.

For more details of which benefits and/or tax credits you should claim see p11.

Increases for child dependants

CTC replaced increases for child dependants previously available with some non-means-tested benefits from April 2003 (see p798).[14] However, you can continue to get an increase if you were entitled to an increase for a child dependant on 5 April 2003 (or have claimed an increase after 6 April 2003 and your entitlement is backdated to include 5 April).

This 'transitional protection' will be lost once your entitlement to an increase for a child dependant ceases (or your increase stops being paid for 58 days or more because your partner's earnings exceed the earnings limit). If the benefit you are paid the increase with is terminated, your increase will also stop. You keep your transitional protection, however, as long as you reclaim the benefit and the increase within three months of the date the benefit is re-awarded on revision, supersession or appeal.[15]

5. Passporting

You are automatically entitled to the following benefits if you qualify for one (or more) of the 'passports':

- Sure Start maternity grant (see p549);[16]
- social fund funeral expenses payment (see p551);[17]
- free school meals (see p18);[18]
- health benefits (see p179);[19]
- free milk and vitamins (see p184);[20]
- reduced-cost dried milk (see p185).[21]

Notes

1. **Tax credits**
   1 s8 TCA 2002; regs 3-5 CTC Regs
   2 s10 TCA 2002; reg 4 WTC(EMR) Regs

3. **2004 and after**
   3 Reg 17(1) IS Regs; reg 83 JSA Regs; reg 1 SS(WTCCTC)(CA) Regs
   4 Reg 1(3) and (7) SS(WTCCTC)(CA) Regs

4. **Impact on benefits**
   5 Regs 1and 7 SS(WTCCTC)(CA) Regs
   6 Regs 7(6)and 8(5) SS(WTCCTC)(CA) Regs
   7 s15(1) SPCA 2002
   8 Reg 9 SPC Regs
   9 Reg 35(2)(f) and (g) HB Regs; reg 26(2)(f) and (g) CTB Regs
   10 Sch 3 para 16(3)(c) HB Regs; Sch 3 para 16(3)(c) CTB Regs
   11 Reg 40(9) HB Regs; reg 31(9) CTB Regs
   12 Sch 5 para 8(1)(f) HB Regs; Sch 5 para 8(1)(f) CTB Regs
   13 Reg 7(3) TC(DCI) Regs
   14 s1(3)(e) TCA 2002
   15 Art 3 Tax Credits Act (Commencement No.3 Transitional Provisions and Savings) Order 2003

5. **Passporting**
   16 Reg 5(1) SFM&FE Regs
   17 Reg 7(1)(a)(i) SFM&FE Regs
   18 s5122B(4) Education Act 1996; s53(3) Education (Scotland) Act 1980
   19 NHS (TERC) Regs; NHS (TERC)(S) Regs; NHS(CDA) Regs; NHS(CDA)(S) Regs; NHS(CDA)(W) Regs; NHS (DC) Regs; NHS(DC)(S) Regs; NHS(OCP) Regs; NHS(OCP)(S) Regs; WF Regs
   20 Regs 3 and 4 WF Regs
   21 Reg 7 WF Regs

Chapter 49

Child tax credit

This chapter covers:

Child tax credit (CTC) is paid to families with children. It is paid whether or not you are in full-time paid work. CTC does not count as income for income support, income-based jobseeker's allowance or pension credit purposes and can be paid in addition to those benefits.

CTC is administered by the Revenue.

You do not have to have paid national insurance contributions to qualify for CTC.

1. Who can claim child tax credit

You qualify for child tax credit (CTC) if:[1]

- you (or your partner) have at least one dependent child or qualifying young person for whom you are responsible (see p1316);
- your income is sufficiently low (see p1322);
- you are 'present' and 'ordinarily resident' in the UK. You can be treated as present and ordinarily resident in the UK in some circumstances – eg, if you are temporarily away. You can be treated as not being in the UK if you claim CTC for the first time on or after 1 May 2004 and do not have a legal right to reside there. See Chapter 59 for further information;
- you are not 'subject to immigration control' (see Chapter 59).

2. The rules about your age

You (and your partner) must be aged at least 16 to make a claim for child tax credit.[2] There is no upper age limit.

3. Who is included in your claim

You can only claim child tax credit (CTC) if you are responsible for one or more children. Some young people continue to count as children until they are 19 – see below. When we use the terms 'child' or 'children' in this chapter this includes these qualifying young people. CTC includes elements for each of your children and additional elements if they are disabled (see Chapter 52).

If you are a member of a married or unmarried couple, you must claim CTC jointly with your partner.[3] If you are not a member of a couple, you claim for yourself.[4] For information about who counts as a couple for tax credit purposes, see p1331. See Chapter 54 for further information about joint claims for CTC.

If you are a couple:

- when working out how much CTC you get, your partner's income is added to yours (see Chapter 53);
- CTC is paid to the person who is the main carer for your children (see p1403).

Children

To qualify for CTC, you must be 'responsible' for a child or qualifying young person.[5] You do not have to be the child or young person's parent. You could, for example, be the grandparent, sister or brother. See p1318 for when you count as responsible for a child or young person and p1319 for when you do not count as responsible.

Who counts as a child

Someone counts as a child until the 1st of September following her/his 16th birthday.[6] In some circumstances, a young person aged under 19 also counts as a child. The Revenue refers to her/him as a 'qualifying young person'. When we use the terms 'child' or 'children' in this chapter this includes these qualifying young people.

A young person counts as a child during any period from the 1st of September following her/his 16th birthday to her/his 19th birthday in which s/he is:[7]

- in full-time education (see p1317). This does not apply if it is advanced education or if s/he is getting the education because of her/his own employment; *or*
- under 18, has ceased full-time education and it is not more than 20 weeks since s/he did so. S/he must notify the Revenue within three months of ceasing full-

time education that s/he has registered for work or training with the Careers Service or the Connexions Service. This rule can apply again if s/he goes back into full-time education and ceases again.

You should let the Revenue know if either of the above applies to ensure that you continue to get CTC for your child.

Full-time non-advanced education[8]

'Education' means education at a recognised educational establishment or elsewhere, if the education is recognised by the Secretary of State, the Revenue or the Scottish Ministers. Education counts as **full time** if it is for more than 12 hours a week, on average, in normal term time including instruction or tuition, supervised study, exams, practical work and experiments or projects provided for in the curriculum but excluding meal breaks and unsupervised study. It includes gaps between the end of one course and the start of another so long as the young person enrols on and commences the new course.

For examples of what counts as **non-advanced** education, see p87.

When a young person does not count as a child

A young person cannot count as a child during any period from the 1st of September following her/his 16th birthday to her/his 19th birthday which includes:

- a period in which s/he has ceased full-time education but has not registered for work or training with the Careers Service or Connexions service (see above); *or*
- a week in which, having ceased full-time education, s/he is in full-time paid work.[9] This means work of 24 hours or more per week. For information about:
  - what counts as paid work, see p1343;
  - how the hours are calculated, see p1344;
  - situations when the young person is not treated as in full-time paid work, see p1349.

  The rules for what counts as full-time paid work are the same as for WTC; *or*
- a period in which s/he is on a training programme for which a training allowance can be paid.[10] See below for what counts as a training programme; *or*
- a period in which s/he gets income support or income-based jobseeker's allowance in her/his own right (see Chapters 13 and 15).[11] **Note:** you might not count as *responsible* for a child 16 or over if s/he gets CTC or incapacity benefit in her/his own right (see p1319).

Training programmes

'Training programme' means training:[12]

- under s2 of the Employment and Training Act 1973 or s2 of the Enterprise and New Towns (Scotland) Act 1990; *or*

– secured by the Learning and Skills Council for England or the National Council for Education and Training for Wales under Part 1 and 2 of the Learning and Skills Act 2000; *or*
– for people enlisted in the armed forces for a special term of service under s2 of the Armed Forces Act 1966; *or*
– under corresponding provisions in another European Union member state.

Being responsible for a child

For tax credits purposes, a child can only count as the responsibility of one claimant (or joint-claim couple).[13] You are treated as 'responsible' for a child if:[14]

- s/he normally lives with you.[15] The Revenue calls this the 'normally living with test'; *or*
- you have the main responsibility for her/him.[16] The Revenue calls this the 'main responsibility test'. This test only applies if you and another person (or couple) make competing claims for CTC for the same child.

If a child for whom you are treated as responsible has a child of her/his own who normally lives with her/him, you also count as responsible for that child.[17] This does not apply if your child is 16 or over and is awarded CTC in her/his own right.[18]

The 'normally living with test'

The rules do not define when a child counts as 'normally living with' you. The Revenue says it means that your child 'regularly, usually, typically' lives with you and that this allows for temporary or occasional absences.[19] So if your child counts as normally living with you, s/he should also count as doing so even if s/he is away from home – eg, because s/he is away at school or for a temporary period on holiday or in hospital. You can argue that a child is normally living with you if s/he spends more time with you than with anyone else.[20]

Your child can count as normally living with you even if s/he also lives with someone else or only lives with you for part of the week, and lives for part of the week with someone else (eg, your child's other parent). This means that more than one person could claim CTC for the child. However, CTC can only be paid to one claimant (or joint-claim couple). If more than one claims, see p1319.

The 'main responsibility test'

Even though you may be sharing responsibility for a child and s/he normally lives with you for part of the week, you might not qualify for CTC because the rules might not treat you as having the main responsibility. There is currently no provision for allowing CTC to be split between parents where a child divides her/his time between their homes. However, if you share actual responsibility for the child (eg, you share responsibility with your ex-partner) and are a 'substantial minority carer' (ie, you have the child with you for at least 104 nights a year), then following a recent court decision it may be arguable that you should be regarded as responsible for the child.[21] Seek advice and see CPAG's *Welfare Rights Bulletin* for updates.

Where you (and your partner, if you have one) and at least one other person (or couple) with whom the child also normally lives claim CTC for the same child, you only qualify for CTC for the child if you can show *you* have the 'main responsibility' for her/him. The main responsibility test applies if:[22]

- your child normally lives with *both* you *and*:
  - at least one other person in another household (eg, with you and with the child's other parent from whom you have separated); *or*
  - someone who is not your partner in the same household (eg, with you and with the child's grandparent where you live together).

  It also applies if it is a combination of these situations. 'Household' is not defined. See p812 for ideas about what might count as a household; *and*
- you and at least one of the other people with whom your child normally lives claim CTC.

You and the other CTC claimant(s) can decide which of you should count as having 'main responsibility'. If you cannot agree, a decision maker decides.[23]

'Main responsibility' is not defined in the rules. The decision maker is likely to consider things like:[24]

- whether there are any court orders in existence that set out where your child is to live or who is to care for her/him;
- how many days of the week a child lives with you compared with the number of days s/he lives elsewhere;
- who pays for your child's food and clothes and who is responsible for giving her/him pocket money;
- where your child's clothes and toys are kept;
- who is the main contact or registered address for the school, nursery or child care provider;
- who does the child's laundry;
- who looks after your child when s/he is ill and who takes her/him to the doctor.

When you do not count as responsible for a child

Even if a child normally lives with you or, where the main responsibility test applies, you have the 'main responsibility' for her/him, you do *not* count as responsible for the child and cannot claim CTC for her/him during any period when s/he is:[25]

- provided with or placed in accommodation and the accommodation or the child's maintenance is funded wholly or partly by the local authority under s23 of the Children Act 1989, s26 of the Children (Scotland) Act 1995 or out of other public funds. This includes children staying with foster carers who get foster payments for them from the local authority.

This does not apply if your child is staying in certain forms of residential accommodation and this is only necessary because your child has a disability or because her/his health would be significantly impaired or further impaired if s/he was not staying in the accommodation;[26] *or*

- being looked after by a local authority and has been placed with you because you want to adopt her/him. This only applies if the local authority is paying for the child's accommodation or maintenance or both under s23 of the Children Act 1989 or s26 of the Children (Scotland) Act 1995; *or*
- in custody. This only applies if your child:
  - is serving a life or unlimited sentence; *or*
  - is serving a term of more than four months; *or*
  - has been detained 'during Her Majesty's pleasure'; *or*
- at least 16 and is awarded CTC in her/his own right for a child for whom s/he is responsible; *or*
- at least 16 and entitled to and receiving incapacity benefit (IB) in her/his own right. However, you still count as responsible if your child's incapacity for work began before 6 April 2004: *and*
  - both IB and CTC were payable for the child before that date; *and*
  - CTC has been continuously payable for the child since 5 April 2004.

Note that a young person does not count as a child if s/he gets income support or income-based jobseeker's allowance in her/his own right (see p1317).

Challenging a decision

In some cases the Revenue might say that your child does not normally live with you. In other cases it might say that you are not the person with main responsibility for your child. If you think a decision is wrong and it affects your tax credits, consider appealing. See Chapter 58 for more information about appeals. It is possible that the DWP, local authority and the Revenue might reach different conclusions about whether your child(ren) can be included in your claims. If so you should appeal *all* the decisions with which you disagree.

Whether or not you appeal, you should apply immediately for any other benefits or tax credits for which you might qualify. You may be able to get a social fund crisis loan in the meantime (see p538).

Change of circumstances

If you are entitled to CTC for a child (or would have been had you made a claim) and the child dies, you continue to be entitled to CTC for the child for eight weeks immediately following the death (or to the date your child would have turned 19 if this is earlier).[27] After that period, you may still continue to qualify for CTC – ie, if you are responsible for any other child(ren).

There are other changes of circumstances connected with your child(ren) you may wish to report – eg, to enable your award of CTC to be increased or to avoid overpayment at the end of the year. These include circumstances where your child:

- starts normally living with you or elsewhere;
- becomes your or someone else's 'main responsibility';
- ceases or returns to full-time education;
- claims a benefit or tax credit in her/his own right, gets a place on a training programme or takes up full-time paid work.

Entitlement to CTC ends if:[28]

- you were claiming as a single person and you become part of a married or unmarried couple;
- you cease to be a member of a couple while you are claiming CTC as a couple; *or*
- you or your partner lose your right to reside in the UK or no longer count as resident there (see p1413).

These are changes of circumstances that you must report to the Revenue. If you do not do so, you could incur a recoverable overpayment and a penalty (see Chapters 56 and 57).

For further information about changes of circumstances and whether you should or must report them, see Chapter 54.

Benefits

The rules about who counts as a couple and responsibility for a child are different for income support, income-based jobseeker's allowance, pension credit, housing benefit and council tax benefit. See pp300 and 374, and Chapter 32 for further information.

4. The amount of child tax credit

The amount of child tax credit (CTC) you get depends on:

- your maximum CTC. This is made up of a combination of 'elements' (see below);
- how much income you have; *and*
- the 'income threshold figure' that applies to you.

The elements and thresholds can be increased every April. If you do not qualify for CTC currently, you might qualify if the rates go up.

If you are on income support, income-based jobseeker's allowance or pension credit

Entitlement to income support, income-based jobseeker's allowance or pension credit acts as an automatic passport to maximum CTC.[29] You therefore do not need to work out your income or capital. In these circumstances, CTC = maximum CTC. See p1368 for further information.

If you are not on income support, income-based jobseeker's allowance or pension credit

- Step one: work our your 'relevant period' (see p p1353 and 1364).
- Step two: find your maximum entitlement for the relevant period. This involves working out your maximum CTC for your relevant period (see p1364).
- Step three: find your relevant income (see p1365).
- Step four: compare your income with the 'income threshold figure' for the relevant period – currently £13,910.[30] If your maximum amount of tax credits includes any element of working tax credit as well as elements of CTC, an 'income threshold figure' of £5,220 is used.[31] See p1366 for further information.
- Step five: calculate CTC entitlement for the relevant period (see p1366). If your income is less than the 'income threshold figure', CTC = maximum CTC. If your income exceeds the 'income threshold figure', your maximum CTC is reduced by 37 per cent of the excess. Remember, however, that your maximum CTC is not reduced below the level of the family element (including the baby element if your are entitled to this) unless your annual income is higher than £50,000.

For full details of the calculation, see Chapter 52.

Maximum child tax credit

Your maximum CTC is calculated by adding together all of the elements that apply to you.[32] These are:[33]

- child element (£1,690 a year);
- disability element (£2,285 a year);
- severe disability element (£920 a year);
- family element (£1,090 including the 'baby element' per year; £545 if not).

For details of how you qualify for the above elements, see Chapter 52.

5. Claims and backdating

This section gives an outline of the rules about claims for child tax credit (CTC). For more information about claiming and how your award can be renewed at the end of the year, see Chapter 54.

Making a claim

Your first claim for CTC must be made in writing on Form TC600. You use the same form for CTC and for working tax credit. See p1396 for further information.

Remember:

- You should send the completed form directly to the Tax Credit Office (TCO) of the Revenue in the pre-paid envelope provided with the claim form (or see Appendix 1 for the address). The claim form can also be sent, if necessary, to any JobCentre, DWP office or Revenue enquiry centre office.[34] Keep a copy of your claim form in case queries arise.
- You can make a claim online at the Revenue website (see p1396).
- You can amend or withdraw your claim at any time before the claim has been decided.[35] If your claim has been decided, your award of CTC can be amended in certain circumstances. See Chapter 55 for information about changes in circumstances and when they can affect your CTC claim.

Information to support your claim

When you claim CTC, you must satisfy the national insurance number (NINO) requirement. In most cases this means you must provide your NI number, as well as your partner's. You may also be asked to provide proof of your identity and information to support your claim.[36] See p1398 for further details. It is important that you provide all the information required. If you do not do so, a decision might not be made on your claim.

When you claim CTC you must provide:

- your child benefit reference number. This can be found on your child benefit order book or on any letters about child benefit that you have received;
- details of your income for the previous tax year (see p1398);
- details of a bank or building society account into which CTC can be paid. If you do not have an account, you need to open one within eight weeks of making your claim. See pp1399 and 1404 for further information.

The Revenue might need further information before it makes a decision on your claim. See p1399 for further details on the time you must be given to provide the information and what happens if you fail to do so.

Who should claim

If you are a member of a married or unmarried couple, you must make a joint claim with your partner. If you are not a member of a couple, you claim for yourself. For information about who counts as a couple for tax credit purposes, see p1331.

If, exceptionally, you are unable to claim for yourself, the decision maker may authorise someone else (eg, a friend or relative) to act on your behalf.

See p1395 for further information about who should claim and p1396 for information about appointees.

When to claim

The general rule is that your claim runs from the date it is received by the Revenue.[37] You cannot make a claim in advance of the tax year for which you are claiming. Remember:

- your claim can be backdated for up to three months (see below);
- there is a special backdating rule if you are not paid CTC (ie, you are given a 'nil award') because your child did not receive disability living allowance at the time of your claim (see p1405);
- if your circumstances change after you claim, in some cases, you must report this to the Revenue. In others, you may wish to consider reporting changes to allow your award to be increased, or to avoid an overpayment at the end of the year. See p1413 for further information.

Awards of CTC are always based on annual income (see p1373). The Revenue bases the initial award of CTC on your *previous* tax year's income. If you think your income for the current tax year is likely, eventually, to be low enough for you to qualify for CTC (eg, you know your income is going to fall or has fallen), you may wish to consider making a claim (including a request for your claim to be backdated if relevant), even if you know you will be given what is known as a 'nil award'. This protects your position because you can then ask the Revenue to amend the award on the basis of a change in your income (see p1374). The amended award would then run from your original date of claim (or the date to which your claim was backdated). However, see pp1415-1417 before deciding what to do.

How your claim is dealt with

Once you have claimed CTC and provided all the information required, the Revenue makes a decision on your claim. You receive an award notice telling you how much CTC you are entitled to and when payment will start. See p1402 for further information.

Backdating your claim

It is very important to claim in time. A claim for CTC can be backdated for a maximum of three months.[38] You only need to show that you qualified for CTC during that period. Unlike for most means-tested benefits, you do not have to show any reasons for your delay. See p1405 for further information. Remember that there is an exception to this rule if you were not paid CTC (ie you were given a 'nil award') because your child did not receive disability living allowance at the time of your claim.

Renewal awards

At the end of the tax year in which you claimed CTC, you (and your partner if you are a member of couple), receive a 'final notice' from the Revenue asking you to confirm that your income and/or your household circumstances are as stated for the tax year just passed (see p1410). The Revenue then makes a final decision, based on your actual income during the tax year. It decides whether you were entitled to CTC and if so, the amount of your award. This is known as the 'end of year review'. The Revenue also uses the information about your income and household circumstances for the last tax year to renew your award for the next tax year.[39]

Example

Joe is a lone parent who is in full-time paid work. He claims CTC during the 2004/05 tax year. His initial award is based on his income during the 2003/04 tax year. In May 2005, he is sent a 'final notice'. He sends the Revenue details of his actual income for 2004/05. The Revenue uses this information and works out that his CTC award for 2004/05 was correct. Joe's actual income for 2004/05 is now the previous year's income in respect of a CTC claim for 2005/06. The Revenue uses this income to make an initial decision to award Joe CTC and set payments for 2005/06.

6. Getting paid

This section gives an outline of the rules about payment of child tax credit (CTC). For more information about getting paid, see pp1403-00.

Payments of CTC are usually made directly into the bank or building society account or post office card account of whoever is deemed to be the main carer of your children (see p1403). However, you might be paid by cheque while your account arrangements are finalised. CTC can be paid into the account every week or every four weeks, whichever is the more convenient for you.[40]

If your award of CTC (or the combination of CTC and working tax credit (WTC) the Revenue is paying you) is £2 a week or less, it is paid in a single lump sum into your account to cover the whole year.[41] **Note:** if your entitlement to CTC (or the combination of CTC and WTC) is less than £26 for the whole of the tax year, no award is made and you are not paid at all.[42]

Length of award

Your award of CTC runs from the date your claim is received by the Revenue (or from the date to which your claim can be backdated) to the end of the tax year.[43]

However, changes in your circumstances can be taken into account during the tax year. In some cases, you *must* report changes of circumstances. See below and Chapter 55 for details.

Change of circumstances

Your award of CTC is made on the basis of your previous year's income and your personal circumstances on the date of your claim. If your current year's income or your personal circumstances change, your award of CTC can be amended. Remember:

- there are some changes you *must* report to the Revenue (see p1413). If you fail to do so within three months, you might be given a financial penalty;
- it is optional to report changes that affect your maximum entitlement to CTC – eg, when you have a baby or one of your children leaves school or leaves home (see p1414). However, changes that increase your entitlement to CTC can only be backdated three months from when you notify the Revenue. Changes that decrease your entitlement always take effect from the date of the change so an overpayment can occur if you delay;
- there is a special rule that allows an increase in your entitlement to CTC to be backdated *more* than three months if you were waiting to hear about a disability living allowance (DLA) claim for your child when you claimed CTC, this has now been awarded and the disability or severe disability elements should now be included in your CTC entitlement. You must notify the Revenue within three months of the date the DLA is awarded (see p1415);
- it is optional to report changes in your income (see p1415). These are always taken into account at the end of the tax year, but you may want to consider reporting these sooner to avoid an overpayment or underpayment of CTC.

See Chapter 55 for further information.

Overpayments and fraud

If you are overpaid CTC, you may have to repay it. The rules on overpayments are covered in Chapter 56. In some cases, interest can be added to the overpayment (see p1427). For information on fraud see Chapter 57. In some cases, you can be given a financial penalty (see p1433).

7. Challenging a child tax credit decision

You can apply for a revision of a child tax credit decision or appeal against it (see Chapter 58).

8. Tax, tax credits and benefits

Child tax credit (CTC) does not count as taxable income.

Tax credits

If you are in full-time paid work, you might qualify for working tax credit (WTC). CTC is not taken into account as income for WTC.

Means-tested benefits

If you (and your partner) are not in full-time paid work, you might qualify for income support (IS) or income-based jobseeker's allowance (JSA). If you are 60 or over, whether or not you (or your partner) are in full-time paid work, you might qualify for pension credit (PC). CTC is not taken into account as income for IS, income-based JSA or PC.

If you pay rent or council tax, you might qualify for housing benefit (HB) or council tax benefit (CTB). The amount of CTC you are paid is taken into account as income for HB and CTB. However, if you get arrears of CTC, these count as capital and can be disregarded in some circumstances.

For details of all the income and capital rules for means-tested benefits, see Chapters 38 and 39.

Non-means-tested benefits

CTC can be paid in addition to any non-means-tested benefits to which you (or your partner) are entitled, including child benefit. See Chapter 53 for which of these benefits may be taken into account as income for CTC. If your child qualifies for disability living allowance, you might qualify for the disability or severe disability elements of CTC.

Passports and other sources of help

If you are entitled to CTC you may also qualify for:

- health benefits such as free prescriptions (see Chapter 9).You do not have to satisfy the means test if you are getting CTC and your gross annual income is below a set amount (see p179); *and*
- education benefits such as free school meals. You do not have to satisfy the means test if you are getting CTC (but not working tax credit) and your gross annual income is below £13,910.

You may also qualify for a Sure Start maternity grant or a social fund funeral expenses payment (see Chapter 22).

Notes

1. Who can claim child tax credit

1 ss3(3) and (7), 8 and 42 TCA 2002; regs 3-5 CTC Regs; reg 3 TC(R) Regs; reg 3 TC(Imm) Regs

2. The rules about your age

2 s3(3) TCA 2002

3. Who is included in your claim

3 s3(3)(a), (5) and (6) TCA 2002
4 s3(3)(b) TCA 2002
5 s8(1) TCA 2002
6 s8(3) TCA 2002; regs 2, definition of 'child' and 4 CTC Regs
7 s8(4) TCA 2002; regs 2, definition of 'qualifying young person' and 5(1)-(3) CTC Regs
8 Regs 2(1), definition of 'advanced education'and 5(5) and (6) CTC Regs
9 Regs 2, definition of 'remunerative work and 5(4)(a) CTC Regs
10 Reg 5(4)(b) CTC Regs
11 Reg 5(4)(c) CTC Regs
12 Reg 2, definition of 'relevant training programme' CTC Regs
13 Reg 3(1) rule 2.2 CTC Regs
14 s8(2) TCA 2002; reg 3(1) CTC Regs
15 Reg 3(1) rule 1 CTC Regs
16 Reg 3(1) rule 2 CTC Regs
17 Reg 3(2) CTC Regs
18 Reg 3(1) rule 4, 4.1 Case D CTC Regs
19 para 02201 TCTM
20 CFC/1537/1995
21 *Hockenjos v Secretary of State for Social Security* [2004] EWCA Civ 1749, 21 December 2004, unreported (EWCA) applies only to JSA. However, it may support arguments concerning CTC and WTC based on the Human Rights Act.
22 Reg 3(1) rule 2, 2.1 and 2.2 CTC Regs
23 Reg 3 rule 3, 3.1 CTC Regs
24 para 02201 TCTM
25 Reg 3(1) rule 4, 4.1 CTC Regs
26 Reg 3(1) rule 4, 4.1 Case A CTC Regs; reg 3 CB Regs
27 s8(5) TCA 2002; reg 6 CTC Regs
28 s3(4) and (7) TCA 2002; reg 21 TC(CN) Regs

4. The amount of child tax credit

29 ss7(2)and 13 TCA 2002; reg 4 TC(ITDR) Regs
30 Reg 3(3) TC(ITDR) Regs
31 Reg 3(2) TC(ITDR) Regs
32 s9(2) TCA 2002
33 Reg 7 CTC Regs

5. Claims and backdating

34 Regs 2 and 5 TC(CN) Regs
35 Reg 5(7) TC(CN) Regs; CIS/995/2004
36 Reg 5(3)-(6) TC(CN) Regs
37 s5(2) TCA 2002
38 Reg 7 TC(CN) Regs
39 Regs 11 and 12 TC(CN) Regs

6. Getting paid

40 Regs 8 and 13 TC(PB) Regs
41 Reg 10 TC(PB) Regs
42 Reg 9 TC(ITDR) Regs
43 s5(2) TCA 2002

Chapter 50

Working tax credit

This chapter covers:

Working tax credit (WTC) is paid to low-paid workers. It tops up your wages if you are in 'remunerative work'. We call this full-time paid work in this *Handbook*.

WTC is administered by the Revenue.

You do not have to have paid national insurance contributions to qualify for WTC.

1. Who can claim working tax credit

You qualify for working tax credit (WTC) if:[1]

- you (or your partner) are in full-time paid work (see p1329);
- your income is sufficiently low (see Chapter 53);
- you are 'present' and 'ordinarily resident' in the UK. You can be treated as present and ordinarily resident in the UK in some circumstances – eg, if you are temporarily away. You can be treated as not being in the UK if you claim WTC for the first time on or after 1 May 2004 and do not have a legal right to reside there. See Chapter 59 for further information;
- you are not 'subject to immigration control' (see Chapter 59).

Full-time paid work

You count as in full-time paid work if:[2]

- you (or your partner) are responsible for a child or qualifying young person, and you work at least 16 hours a week (see p1316 for who counts as a child or qualifying young person);

- you have a physical or mental disability that puts you at a disadvantage in getting a job, you qualify for a disability element (see p1357) and you work at least 16 hours a week;
- you are aged 25 years or over and you work at least 30 hours a week;
- you (or your partner) are at least 50, work at least 16 hours a week and qualify for a 50-plus element of WTC (see p1358).

In addition, you must actually be working, or have accepted an offer of work which is expected to start within seven days from the date of your claim, and the work must be expected to last for at least four weeks.

For further information about full-time paid work and when you can be treated as in full-time paid work, see Chapter 51.

2. The rules about your age

You (and your partner) must be aged at least 16 to make a claim for working tax credit.[3] There is no upper age limit.

3. Who is included in your claim

If you are a member of a couple, you must claim working tax credit (WTC) jointly with your partner.[4] If you are not a member of a couple, you claim for yourself.[5] For information about who counts as a couple for tax credit purposes, see below. See Chapter 54 for further information about joint claims. WTC includes elements for you and your partner and for the special needs of either of you (see Chapter 52). When working out how much WTC you get, your partner's income is added to yours (see Chapter 53).

If you are responsible for one or more children or qualifying young people:

- you (or your partner) need only do paid work of 16 hours a week to qualify for WTC (see Chapter 51);
- if you are a couple and one of you works at least 16 hours a week, your hours of work can be added to those of your partner to enable you to qualify for the 30-hour element (see p1356);
- you (and your partner) might qualify for the childcare element of WTC if you pay for childcare (see p1360). The childcare element is paid to the person who is your child(ren)'s main carer (see p1403).

To see who counts as a child, see p1316. The rules are the same as for child tax credit (CTC).[6] Some young people continue to count as children until they are 19. The Revenue calls them 'qualifying young people'. When we use the terms 'child' or 'children' in this chapter this includes these qualifying young people.

To see when you count as responsible for a child see p1318. The Revenue uses the same test as for CTC.[7]

Couples

You and your partner count as a 'couple' if you are:[8]

- married, unless you are separated and this is under a court order or is likely to be permanent (see below); *or*
- not married and 'living together as husband and wife' (see p1332).

If you are a member of a same sex (lesbian or gay) couple, currently you do not count as a couple for tax credit purposes and must claim as a single person. This situation is due to change later in 2005. From then, you and your partner will also count as a couple if you are the same sex as your partner and you are:

- registered as civil partners, unless you are separated and this is under a court order or is likely to be permanent; *or*
- not civil partners but are living together as if you are. This will only apply if you would be regarded as living together as husband and wife if you were a different sex from your partner.

The change was expected to be introduced on 5 December 2005. See CPAG's *Welfare Rights Bulletin* for updates.

Married couples

You must claim tax credits jointly with your partner if you are married to her/him. You continue to count as a couple while you and your partner are **temporarily separated**. It does not matter how long the temporary separation lasts. However, if you or your partner go abroad, either permanently or for more than a set period of time (see p1460), you cease to satisfy the residence conditions. In this case, you must terminate your joint claim. Failure to do this may result in a penalty (see p1433). The person still in the UK may be able to make a new claim as a single person.

If you and your partner are **permanently separated** or are separated under a court order, you can claim tax credits as a single person immediately. This is the case even if you are still living under the same roof and whether or not you are taking steps to divorce your partner. The test is whether you are 'separated in circumstances in which the separation is likely to be permanent' and this depends on your (and your partner's) intentions.[9]

You count as a 'polygamous unit' if you are a member of a couple married under a law which permits polygamy and either you or your partner are also married to another person (unless any of you are separated and this is under a court order or is likely to be permanent).[10]

Special rules apply if you are a member of a 'polygamous unit'.[11] These provide that:

- you must make a claim jointly with *all* your partners and the income of all of these is taken into account;

- an increased maximum award of WTC is allowed to take all your partners' needs into account;
- your entitlement to tax credits ceases if you are a married or unmarried couple and become a member of a polygamous unit or if you are claiming as a polygamous unit and there is any change in the people who are members of that unit.

Living together as husband and wife

You must claim tax credits jointly with your partner if you are 'living together as husband and wife'. If you and your partner stop living together, you can claim tax credits as a single person immediately. However, if you and your partner are only temporarily living apart (eg, one of you is in hospital or in respite care), you may still be treated as a couple. However, if you or your partner go abroad, either permanently or for more than a set period of time (see p1460), you cease to satisfy the residence conditions. In this case, you must terminate your joint claim. Failure to do this may result in a penalty (see p1433). The person still in the UK may be able to make a new claim as a single person.

In determining whether or not you are living together as husband and wife, the Revenue is likely to consider the following:[12]

- whether you live in the same household;
- if you have a sexual relationship;
- your financial arrangements;
- whether your relationship is stable;
- whether you have children;
- how you appear in public;
- if you are living apart from your partner, the length of time you have been doing so.

See p813 for more information about the situations when you might count as living together as husband and wife.

No one factor need in itself be conclusive, as it is your 'general relationship' as a whole which is of paramount importance[13] and, just as relationships between couples may often vary considerably, so each case depends on all its own particular facts and circumstances.

People with no sexual relationship who live together might sometimes still be treated as a couple. People who provide mutual support and share household expenses should not necessarily be treated as a couple – this is also the case where people of the same sex or friends of different sexes share a home.[14]

Decision makers applying similar rules to DWP benefit claims often apply too narrow an interpretation of the test. There is no rule, for example, that if your partner stays with you for three nights or more a week you are *automatically* to be treated as a couple who are living together.

Challenging a decision

In some cases you may have to prove that you are a couple – eg, where you want to claim WTC instead of income support (IS), and you are not in full-time paid work yourself, but your partner is. In other cases you may have to prove that you are not a couple – eg, where your former partner's income is being taken into account in working out your tax credits and not just yours.

If you think a decision about whether or not you count as a couple is wrong and it affects your tax credits, consider appealing. It is possible that the DWP, local authority and the Revenue might reach different conclusions about whether you are a couple. If so you should appeal *all* the decisions with which you disagree.

Whether or not you appeal, you should apply immediately for any other benefits or tax credits for which you might qualify. You may be able to get a social fund crisis loan in the meantime (see p538).

Change of circumstances

Entitlement to WTC ends if:[15]

- you were claiming as a single person and you become part of a married or unmarried couple.
- you cease to be a member of a couple while you are claiming WTC as a couple; *or*
- you or your partner lose your right to reside in the UK or no longer count as resident there (see p1413).

These are changes of circumstances that you must report to the Revenue (see p1413). If you do not do so, you could incur a recoverable overpayment and a penalty (see Chapters 56 and 57).

If you are claiming WTC, and you only qualify for the lone parent element or childcare element because you (or your partner) are responsible for a child, and the child dies, you are paid WTC for a further eight weeks (or to the date your child would have turned 19 if this is earlier) as if this had not happened.[16] This is only the case if you would have continued to qualify for the lone parent or childcare element but for the child's death. After that period, you may still continue to qualify for WTC if you satisfy the rules for entitlement.

For further information about changes of circumstances and whether you should or must report them, see Chapter 55.

Benefits

The rules about who counts as a couple and responsibility for a child are different for income support, income-based jobseeker's allowance, pension credit, housing benefit and council tax benefit. See pp300 and 374, and Chapter 32 for further information.

4. The amount of working tax credit

The amount of working tax credit (WTC) you get depends on:

- your maximum WTC. This is made up of a combination of 'elements' (see p1334);
- how much income you have; *and*
- the 'income threshold figure' that applies to you.

The elements and threshold can be increased every April. If you do not qualify for WTC currently, you might qualify when the rates go up.

If you are on income support, income-based jobseeker's allowance or pension credit

Entitlement to income support (IS), income-based jobseeker's allowance (JSA) or pension credit (PC) acts as an automatic passport to maximum WTC.[17] You therefore do not need to work out your income and capital. In these circumstances, WTC = maximum WTC.

Remember:

- In practice, there are not many situations when you can claim IS or income-based JSA at the same time as WTC. This is because you cannot claim IS or JSA if you or your partner are in full-time paid work for IS and JSA purposes.
- WTC counts in full as income for IS, income-based JSA and PC.

If you are not on income support, income-based jobseeker's allowant or pension credit

- Step one: work out your 'relevant period' (see p1353).
- Step two: find your maximum entitlement for the relevant period. This involves working out your maximum WTC for your relevant period (see p1364).
- Step three: find your relevant income (see p1365).
- Step four: compare your income with the 'income threshold figure' for the relevant period – currently £5,220.[18] Note that the 'income threshold figure' is higher for child tax credit. See p1366 for further information.
- Step five: calculate WTC entitlement for the relevant period (see p1366). If your income is less than the 'income threshold figure', WTC = maximum WTC. If your income exceeds the 'income threshold figure', your maximum WTC is reduced by 37 per cent of the excess.

For full details of the calculation, see Chapter 52.

Maximum working tax credit

Your maximum WTC is calculated by adding together all the elements that apply to you.[19] These are:[20]

- basic element (£1,620 a year);
- disability element (£2,165 a year);
- lone parent/couple element (£1,595 a year);
- 30-hour element (£660 a year);
- severe disability element (£920 a year);
- 50-plus element (£1,110 a year for 16–29 hours work; £1,660 a year for 30 or more hours work);
- childcare element (see Chapter 52 for how this is calculated).

For details of how you qualify for the above elements, see Chapter 52.

5. Claims and backdating

This section gives an outline of the rules about claims for working tax credit (WTC). For more information about claiming and how your award can be renewed at the end of the year, see Chapter 54.

Making a claim

Your first claim for WTC must be made in writing on Form TC600. You use the same form for WTC and for child tax credit. See p1396 for further information. Remember:

- You should send the completed form directly to the Tax Credit Office (TCO) of the Revenue in the pre-paid envelope provided with the claim form (or see Appendix 1 for the address). The claim form can also be sent, if necessary, to any JobCentre, DWP office or the Revenue enquiry centre office.[21] Keep a copy of your claim form in case queries arise.
- You can make a claim online at the Revenue website (see p1396).
- If your circumstances change, you can amend your claim at any time before the claim has been decided.[22] If your claim has been decided, your award of WTC can be amended in certain circumstances. See Chapter 54 for information about changes in circumstances and when they can affect your WTC claim.

Information to support your claim

When you claim WTC, you must satisfy the national insurance number (NINO) requirement. In most cases this means you must provide your national insurance number, as well as your partner's. You may also be asked to provide proof of your identity and information to support your claim.[23] See p1398 for further details. It is important that you provide all the information required. If you do not do so, a decision might not be made on your claim.

When you claim WTC you must provide:

- details of your income for the previous year (see Chapter 52);

- details of the work that you do, including your usual hours of work;
- if you are an employed worker, your employer's name, phone number, pay office address and PAYE reference, as well as your payroll number, for each job that you have;
- if you are a self-employed worker, your tax reference number and the date that you started self-employment;
- if you have childcare expenses that you can claim help with (see Chapter 52), your childcare provider's name, address, phone number, approval or registration details and the average weekly cost;
- details of a bank or building society account into which your WTC can be paid. If you do not have an account, you need to open one within eight weeks of making your claim. See pp1399 and 1404 for further information.

The Revenue might need further information before it makes a decision on your claim. See p1399 for further details on the time you must be given to provide the information and what happens if you fail to do so.

Who should claim

If you are a member of a couple, you must make a joint claim with your partner. If you are not a member of a couple, you claim for yourself. For information about who counts as a couple for tax credit purposes, see p1331.

If, exceptionally, you are unable to claim for yourself, the decision maker may authorise someone else (eg, a friend or relative) to act on your behalf.

See p1395 for further information about who should claim and p1396 for information about appointees.

When to claim

The general rule is that your claim runs from the date it is received by the Revenue.[24] You cannot make a claim in advance of the tax year in which you are claiming. Remember:

- you can claim WTC in advance of starting work, provided that you expect to start work within seven days and will be entitled to WTC within seven days of starting work;[25]
- your claim can be backdated for up to three months (see p1324);
- there is a special backdating rule if you are refused WTC because you do not receive a qualifying benefit (eg, disability living allowance) and make a second claim when the qualifying benefit is awarded (see p1405);
- if your circumstances change after you claim, in some cases, you must report this to the Revenue. In others, you may wish to consider reporting changes to allow your award to be increased, or to avoid an overpayment at the end of the year. See p1413 for further information.

Awards of WTC are always based on annual income (see p1373). The Revenue bases the initial award of WTC on your *previous* tax year's income. If you think your income for the current tax year is likely, eventually, to be low enough for you to qualify for WTC – eg, you know your income is going to fall (or has fallen), you may wish to consider making a claim (including a request for your claim to be backdated if relevant), even if you know you will be given what is known as a 'nil award'. This protects your position because you can then ask the Revenue to amend the award on the basis of a change in your income (see p1374). The amended award would run from your original date of claim (or the date to which your claim was backdated). However, see pp1415-1416 before deciding what to do.

How your claim is dealt with

Once you have claimed WTC and provided all the information required, the Revenue makes a decision on your claim. You receive an award notice telling you how much WTC you are entitled to and when payment will start. See p1402 for further information.

Backdating your claim

It is very important to claim in time. A claim for WTC can be backdated for a maximum of three months.[26] You only need to show that you qualified for WTC during that period. Unlike for most means-tested benefits, you do not have to show any reasons for your delay. See p1405 for further information. **Note:** there is a special backdating rule if you are refused WTC because you do not receive a qualifying benefit (eg, disability living allowance) and make a second claim when the qualifying benefit is awarded (see p1405).

Renewal awards

At the end of the tax year in which you claimed WTC, you (and your partner if you are a member of couple), receive a 'final notice' from the Revenue asking you to confirm that your income and/or your household circumstances are as stated for the tax year just passed (see p1410). The Revenue then makes a final decision, based on your actual income during the tax year. It decides whether you were entitled to WTC and if so, the amount of your award. This is known as the 'end of year review'. The Revenue also uses the information about your income and household circumstances for the last tax year to renew your award for the next tax year.[27]

Example

Louise, aged 37, works 30 hours a week. She claims WTC during the 2004/05 tax year. Her initial award is based on her income during the 2003/04 tax year. In May 2005, she is sent a 'final notice'. She sends the Revenue details of her actual income for 2004/05. The

Revenue uses this information and works out that her WTC award for 2004/05 was correct. Louise's actual income for 2004/05 is now the previous year's income in respect of a WTC claim for 2005/06. The Revenue uses this income to make an initial decision to award Louise WTC and set payments for 2005/06.

6. Getting paid

This section gives an outline of the rules about payment of working tax credit (WTC). For more information about getting paid, see p1403. Remember:

- If you are an employee, payments of WTC are made with your wages by your employer.
- If you are self-employed, WTC is usually paid directly into your bank, building society account, or post office card account.
- Any WTC to which you are entitled towards your childcare expenses is paid to whoever is decided to be the main carer of the child(ren) (see p1403 for how this is worked out). Payments of the childcare element are made directly into the bank, building society or post office card account of the main carer.

Note that the Government says that it intends to amend the rules to make WTC payable by the Revenue, *not* employers. See CPAG's *Welfare Rights Bulletin* for updates.

Where WTC is paid into a bank or other account, it can be paid into the account every week or every four weeks, whichever is the more convenient for you.[28]

If your award of WTC (or the combination of WTC and child tax credit (CTC) the Revenue is paying you) is £2 a week or less, it is paid in a single lump sum into your account to cover the whole year.[29] **Note:** If your entitlement to WTC (or the combination of WTC and CTC) is less than £26 for the whole of the tax year, no award is made and you are not paid at all.[30]

Length of award

Your award of WTC runs from the date your claim is received by the Revenue (or from the date to which your claim can be backdated) to the end of the tax year.[31] However, changes in your circumstances can be taken into account during the tax year. In some cases, you *must* report changes of circumstance. See below and Chapter 55 for details.

Change of circumstances

Your award of WTC is made on the basis of your previous year's income and your personal circumstances on the date of your claim. If your current year's income or your personal circumstances change, your award of WTC can be amended. Remember:

- there are some changes you *must* report to the Revenue (see p1413). If you fail to do so within three months, you might be given a financial penalty;
- it is optional to report changes that affect your maximum entitlement to WTC – eg, when your hours increase to 30 or more so you would qualify for a 30-hour element (see p1414). However, changes that increase your entitlement to WTC can only be backdated three months from when you notify the Revenue. Changes that decrease your entitlement always take effect from the date of the change so an overpayment can occur if you delay;
- there is a special rule that allows an increase in your entitlement to WTC to be backdated *more* than three months if you were waiting to hear about a qualifying benefit claim when you claimed WTC, this has now been awarded and the disability or severe disability elements should now be included in your WTC entitlement. You must notify the Revenue within three months of the date the qualifying benefit is awarded (see p1415);
- it is optional to report changes in your income (see p1415). These are always taken into account at the end of the tax year, but you may want to consider reporting these sooner to avoid an overpayment or underpayment of WTC.

See Chapter 55 for further information.

Overpayments and fraud

If you are overpaid WTC, you may have to repay it. The rules on overpayments are covered in Chapter 56. In some cases, interest can be added to the overpayment (see p1427). For information on fraud, see Chapter 57. In some cases, you can be given a financial penalty (see p1433).

7. Challenging a working tax credit decision

You can apply for a revision of a working tax credit decision or appeal against it (see Chapter 58).

You cannot appeal decisions about which member of a couple is paid WTC.

8. Tax, tax credits and benefits

Working tax credit (WTC) does not affect your tax allowances, tax code or PAYE rate.

Tax credits

If you have dependent children you might qualify for child tax credit (CTC). WTC is not taken into account as income for CTC.

Means-tested benefits

WTC counts as income for income support (IS), pension credit (PC), income-based jobseeker's allowance (JSA), housing benefit (HB) and council tax benefit (CTB). However, for HB and CTB, see below.

For details of all the income and capital rules for means-tested benefits, see Chapters 38 and 39.

Income support or income-based jobseeker's allowance

Sometimes you may be able to claim IS/income-based JSA or WTC. For example, you may be able to claim IS if your partner works more than 16 but less than 24 hours a week. If you have to pay housing costs (see Chapter 36), in some cases you might be better off financially if you claim IS or income-based JSA. You may be able to claim both IS/income-based JSA and WTC at the same time in some circumstances. However, your earnings and WTC are taken into account as income in working out how much IS or income-based JSA you can get.

Pension credit

There is no rule that prevents you or your partner doing full-time paid work while claiming PC. This means that you can claim WTC at the same time as PC. However, your earnings and WTC are taken into account as income in working out how much PC you can get.

Housing benefit and council tax benefit

If you pay rent or council tax you might qualify for HB or CTB. The amount of WTC you are paid is taken into account as income for HB and CTB. However, in some circumstances you get an additional earnings disregard. See pp965 and 999 for details.

If you get arrears of WTC, these count as capital for HB and CTB purposes and can be disregarded in some circumstances (see p1035) .

Non-means-tested benefits

WTC can be paid in addition to any non-means-tested benefits to which you (or your partner) are entitled. See Chapter 53 for which of these benefits may be taken into account as income for WTC. Any WTC you receive does not count as earnings for the purposes of a non-means-tested benefit claim made by you, or for you or your partner or child(ren).

Qualifying for certain non-means-tested benefits means you may also qualify for the disability element or severe disability element of WTC. See Chapter 52 for further information.

Passports and other sources of help

If you are entitled to WTC you may also qualify for health benefits, such as free prescriptions (see Chapter 9).You do not have to satisfy the means test if your gross annual income is below a set amount (see p179) and you are getting:

- WTC which includes a disability element; *or*
- CTC with your WTC.

You may also qualify for a Sure Start maternity grant or a social fund funeral expenses payment (see Chapter 22).

Notes

1. **Who can claim working tax credit**
   1 ss3(3) and (7), 10 and 42 TCA 2002; regs 4-8 WTC(EMR) Regs; reg 3 TC(R) Regs; reg 3 TC(I) Regs
   2 Reg 4 WTC(EMR) Regs

2. **The rules about your age**
   3 s3(3) TCA 2002

3. **Who is included in your claim**
   4 s3(3)(a), (5) and (6) TCA 2002
   5 s3(3)(b) TCA 2002
   6 Reg 2 WTC(EMR) Regs, definition of 'child' and 'qualifying young person'
   7 Reg 2(2) WTC(EMR) Regs
   8 s3(5) and (6) TCA 2002; reg 2 WTC(EMR) Regs, definition of 'couple'
   9 s3(5)(b) TCA 2002
   10 s43 TCA 2002; reg 2 TC(PM) Regs
   11 See the TC(PM) Regs
   12 *Crake and Butterworth v SBC* [1982] 1 All ER 498
   13 R(SB) 17/81; R(G) 3/71; CIS/87/1993
   14 CSSB/145/1983
   15 s3(4) TCA 2002; reg 21 TC(CN) Regs
   16 Reg 19 WTC(EMR) Regs; reg 6 CTC Regs

4. **The amount of working tax credit**
   17 ss7(2) and 13 TCA 2002; reg 4 TC(ITDR) Regs
   18 Reg 3(2) TC(ITDR) Regs
   19 s11 TCA 2002
   20 Regs 3 and 20 and Sch 2 WTC(EMR) Regs

5. **Claims and backdating**
   21 Regs 2and 5 TC(CN) Regs
   22 Reg 5(7) TC(CN) Regs
   23 Reg 5(3)-(6) TC(CN) Regs
   24 s5(2) TCA 2002
   25 Reg 10 TC(CN) Regs
   26 Reg 7 TC(CN) Regs
   27 Regs 11 and 12 TC(CN) Regs

6. **Getting paid**
   28 Regs 8and 13 TC(PB) Regs
   29 Reg 10 TC(PB) Regs
   30 Reg 9 TC(ITDR) Regs
   31 s5(2) TCA 2002

Chapter 51

Work and tax credits

This chapter covers:

Full-time paid work (the Revenue calls this 'remunerative work') affects working tax credit (WTC – see Chapter 50). If you or your partner are in full-time paid work you can claim WTC.[1] This chapter covers the rules about full-time paid work for this purpose. If neither you nor your partner are in full-time paid work you might be able to claim income support (IS) or jobseeker's allowance (JSA). You might be able to choose whether to claim IS/JSA or WTC. In some situations, you might be able to claim both IS/JSA and WTC (eg, if you are a 'term-time only' worker or are off sick and getting statutory sick pay). This is because different rules for what counts as full-time paid work apply for WTC and IS/JSA. See p759 for information about what you should consider.

Whether or not you are in full-time paid work, you might be able to claim child tax credit (CTC – see Chapter 49) or pension credit (see Chapter 18). However, you cannot get CTC for a young person for whom you are claiming for any period that includes a week in which s/he:[2]

- has left full-time education (see p1317); *and*
- is in full-time paid work of 24 hours or more. Even if s/he is, see p1349 to see if s/he can be treated as not being in full-time paid work. The rules are the same as for WTC claimants.

Entitlement to many benefits is affected by issues to do with work and employment. For further information, see Chapter 29.

1. The full-time paid work rule

If you work full time and are paid for the work, you count as being in what the Revenue calls 'remunerative work'. This is called 'full-time paid work' in this *Handbook*. See p1343 for what counts as full-time work and paid work and p1344 for how your hours are calculated. 'Work' includes self-employment and work which is done from home.

In some circumstances you may be treated as not being in full-time paid work even if you are (see p1349). In others, you may be treated as if you are in full-time paid work when you are not (see p1348).

Remember that your income from employment affects your entitlement to working tax credit (WTC – see p1329). This means that although your (or your partner's) hours of work are high enough for you to qualify, you might not satisfy the means test. Although full-time paid work does not affect entitlement to child tax credit, your income from employment and self-employment affects the amount you can be paid.

Full-time work

You can only get WTC if you or your partner are in full-time paid work. For the purpose of WTC, you count as being in full-time paid work if:[3]

- you or your partner are responsible for a child or young person (see p1318), and you work at least 16 hours per week; *or*
- you have a physical or mental disability which puts you at a disadvantage in getting a job, you qualify for a disability element (see p1357) and you work at least 16 hours a week; *or*
- you or your partner are at least 50, work at least 16 hours a week and qualify for a 50-plus element (see p1358); *or*
- you are 25 or over and work at least 30 hours a week.

Note that if you are under 25, you can only claim WTC if you count as being in full-time work under any of the first three categories.

At the date of your claim, you must:[4]

- be working; *or*
- have accepted an offer of work which is expected to start within seven days. In this case, you only count as being in full-time paid work when the work begins.

The work must be expected to continue for at least four weeks after you make your claim (or if you have accepted an offer of work, after the work starts).[5]

If you normally work at least 16 (or 30) hours a week, but are off sick or on maternity, paternity or adoption leave you might be able to claim WTC (see p1348). You might also be able to claim income support (IS) or jobseeker's allowance (JSA).

What counts as paid work

'Paid work' includes work for which you are paid or expect to be paid.[6] See p752 for further information. The information about what counts as paid work for IS, JSA, pension credit (PC), housing benefit and council tax benefit also applies to WTC.

How your hours are calculated

How you calculate your hours depends on if you are employed or self-employed.

You count as **employed** if you are employed under a contract of service or apprenticeship and your earnings are taxable as employment income under certain provisions of the Income Tax (Earnings and Pensions) Act 2003.[7] You count as **self-employed** if you are carrying on a trade, profession or vocation.[8]

To work out whether you are in full-time paid work:[9]

- if you are employed, include all the hours:
  - you normally work under your contract, if you are an apprentice or employee; *or*
  - you normally perform in the office in which you are employed, if you are an office holder; *or*
  - for which you are normally paid by the employment agency with whom you have a contract, if you are an agency worker; *or*
- if you are self-employed, include all the hours you normally do for payment or for which you expect to be paid.

Paid meal and refreshment breaks count towards the total hours you work.[10] Also included is any time allowed for visits to a hospital, clinic or other establishment, but only if this is for the treatment or monitoring of your disability and if you are paid, or expect to be paid, for the time.[11] Your total hours from more than one job are added together.

Periods when you are on a customary or paid holiday from work are ignored in calculating your hours.[12] Likewise, unpaid meal and refreshment breaks are ignored.

Hours you normally work

Whether you are employed or self-employed, the measure for WTC purposes is the number of hours you normally work. 'Normally' is not defined in the WTC rules. The Revenue says it means 'regularly, usually, typically' and that the number of hours you normally work is not necessarily the number of hours specified in your contract of employment.[13] The hours that are relevant are those you *actually* work. If you routinely do paid overtime, try to argue that these are hours you normally work and that they should be included. See p1345 if your hours fluctuate.

Example

Harriet is a cashier in a supermarket. Her partner stays at home to look after their children. She is contracted to work 14 hours a week over a two-day week but does 3.5 hours overtime almost every week. She gets an unpaid half-hour lunch break. When Harriet and her partner claim WTC she has just returned from two weeks' paid holiday.

Harriet normally works 14 + 3.5 = 17.5 hours a week. Unpaid lunch breaks and the time she was on paid holiday are not taken into account. As Harriet and her partner are responsible for children, she need only work 16 hours or more a week. Harriet therefore counts as being in full-time paid work.

In working out your normal hours if you are self-employed, the Revenue says you can include not only the hours you spend providing orders or services but also those that are necessary to your self-employment. These include things like trips to the wholesalers, visits to potential clients, time spent on advertising or canvassing, cleaning the business or vehicles used as part of the business, book-keeping and research work.[14]

If your hours fluctuate

Working out the number of hours you normally work is straightforward if:

- you do the same number of hours each and every week; *or*
- your hours vary, but you always do at least enough hours each week to count as being in full-time paid work (16 or 30, as the case may be).

However, if your weekly hours fluctuate, it can be more complicated. Unless you are a term-time only worker (see p1346), there is no rule to tell you how to average your hours. You should therefore bear the following in mind:

- If you have a recognisable cycle of work that lasts for a year with periods where you are not required to work (eg, in an educational establishment), a special rule applies. See below for further information about 'term-time only' workers; *or*
- If your hours fluctuate:
  - over a regular short-term cycle (eg, you work two weeks on and two weeks off), the Revenue says you can average your hours over that cycle;[15]
  - but there is no regular pattern to your hours, and in some weeks you do not do enough hours each week (16 or 30 as the case may be), working out the number of hours you 'normally' work is a question of judgement.

If you are in any doubt about what your normal hours are, contact the Revenue Tax Credit Office or Helpline and seek advice. If you are unsure if you are in full-time paid work, see p1347.

Examples

Shane works in a residential project. He works three weeks on and one week off. When he is on, he works 40 hours a week. His average hours are 40 x 3 ÷ 4 = 30 hours a week. Shane can try to argue that he normally works 30 hours or more a week. As Shane is aged 45, does not have a physical or mental disability and has no children, he must work at least 30 hours a week. He therefore counts as being in full-time paid work.

Narindar is contracted to do 15 hours a week. However, she gets regular overtime of three hours every other week. Her average hours are 15 + 18 ÷ 2 = 16.5 hours. Narindar can try to argue that she normally works 16 hours or more per week. As Narindar is a lone parent, she need only work 16 hours or more a week. She therefore counts as being in full-time paid work.

You should appeal if you think your average hours have been calculated unfairly (see Chapter 58). You should work out first whether you are better off claiming IS/JSA or WTC (see p759).

'Term-time only' workers

If you have a recognisable cycle of work that lasts for a year (eg, in a school or an educational establishment) where you have periods of school holidays or similar vacations where you do not work, the 'term-time only' worker rule applies.[16] The periods when you are not working are ignored in deciding whether you are in full-time paid work.

In practice, if the hours of work you do during term-time mean you are in full-time paid work during term-time, you also count as being in full-time paid work over the holidays. You should be able to claim WTC during this period if your normal hours of work are 16/30 hours a week during term time. If you are not paid for the holidays, you might also be able to claim JSA during these periods if you satisfy the other qualifying conditions (see p347).

Example

Dee is 35 years old and has no children. She is a cleaner at a local college and works 35 hours a week, 32 weeks of the year. She does not work (and is not paid) when the students are on study leave or on holiday. The periods when Dee does not work are ignored. She is in full-time paid work during term-time because she works 30 hours or more a week. She therefore counts as being in full-time paid work throughout the year and can claim WTC.

Sometimes it might not be clear whether you have a cycle of work that lasts a year – eg, if you have only started your job recently or have a fixed-term contract that finishes at the end of the school term, or are employed on a casual or relief basis.[17] It can take time before it can be said that you have a yearly cycle of work.[18] However, if you have an indefinite contract to work in term-time only, you can argue that you have a yearly work cycle from the start.[19]

Students

You are not excluded from claiming WTC simply because you are a student. However, you must count as in full-time paid work under the rules described in this chapter. So if, for example, you do sufficient hours of paid work (16 or 30 as the case may be) in addition to your studies or during the holidays, you can qualify for WTC. Remember: the work must be expected to last for four weeks.

The Revenue says that any work you do in studying for a degree or other qualification does not count as full-time paid work – any grant or loan you receive is a contribution to your maintenance and is not paid in return for work done on the course. It also says that it does not consider you to be in full-time paid work if you are a student nurse because the NHS Bursary and other grants or loans you get are not payments for work done on the course and do not count as income for tax credit purposes.[20]

However, if you are paid in return for the work you do – eg, you are paid by an employer during a work placement, you can try to argue that you are in full-time paid work.

Remember that there are a number of situations when you do not count as in full-time paid work even if you are – eg, if you are on a government training scheme being paid a training allowance. See p1349 for further information.

When calculating how much WTC you can get, student loans and most other student income is disregarded. See p1383 for information about what income counts.

If you are unsure whether you are in full-time paid work

If you are unsure if the number of hours you normally work are 16/30 hours or more **at the date of your claim**, contact the Revenue Tax Credit Office or Helpline and seek advice. You should consider making a further claim for WTC in a week when you are certain. Bear in mind that a claim for WTC can be backdated for three months automatically (see p1405). This means that there is scope to postpone claiming WTC to see if you are doing enough hours to count as in full-time paid work. If time is running out and you are still uncertain, consider making a claim to protect your position.

If you claim WTC when you should have claimed IS or JSA, the day you claimed WTC counts as your date of claim for IS or JSA if:[21]

- you are refused WTC because neither you nor your partner are in full-time paid work for WTC purposes; *and*
- you claim IS or JSA within 14 days of the decision refusing your claim for WTC.

If your **circumstances change** while you are claiming WTC, consider the following:

- If you are now uncertain about whether you are still in full-time paid work (eg, your weekly hours change or you no longer get regular overtime), keep a record of the hours you work each week. If it appears that you no longer normally work 16/30 hours each week, you are no longer entitled to WTC. You may wish to consider reporting this to the Revenue to avoid an overpayment of WTC at the end of the year. See Chapter 55 for more information on changes of circumstances.

- If you no longer count as being in full-time paid work, check to see if you qualify for IS or JSA and make a claim if this is possible. Remember that claims for IS and JSA can only be backdated in limited circumstances (see p1087).
- If you are 60 or over, whether or not you are in full-time paid work, check to see if you qualify for PC (see Chapter 18). There is no full-time paid work rule for PC, but earnings and WTC count as income.
- If your hours change, but you still count as being in full-time paid work, the amount of WTC to which you are entitled could be affected by:
  - a change in your earnings. If these increase, you may wish to report this to the Revenue to avoid an overpayment at the end of the year (see p1413). If these decrease, you can get increased WTC if you report the change to the Revenue. You may wish to consider waiting until the end of the year. If you do, and have been underpaid, you are given a lump sum. See p1415 for further information;
  - whether or not you are entitled to have a 30-hour element (see p1356) or the lower or higher rate of the 50-plus element (see p1358) included in calculating your WTC. Any increase in your entitlement to WTC can only be backdated three months from the date you notify the Revenue of the change (see p1414). If your entitlement decreases, you may wish to report this to the Revenue to avoid an overpayment at the end of the year.

2. **People treated as being in full-time paid work**

You or your partner are treated as being in full-time paid work:

- during any period when:[22]
  - you are being paid statutory maternity pay (SMP), statutory paternity pay (SPP), statutory adoption pay (SAP) or maternity allowance (MA); *or*
  - you are absent from work during ordinary maternity leave, paternity leave or ordinary adoption leave.

If you are an employee, you are treated as in full-time paid work from the start of the period, so long as you are in full-time paid work for WTC purposes (16 or 30 hours a week as the case may be) immediately before the period begins. However, if this is not the case – eg, you are under 25, or are 25 or over but working less than 30 hours a week and the child you and your partner are having (or adopting) is your first child, you are treated as in full-time paid work from the date of birth (or adoption). You must have been working at least 16 hours a week immediately before the period begins.[23]

If you are self-employed, you count as in full-time paid work during any period when the above would have applied had the work done in the week before the period began been done as an employee.

Remember: if you do not return to work when your SMP, SPP, SAP or MA ceases or your leave ends, you are no longer treated as being in full-time paid work under this rule; *and*

- during any period when:[24]
  - you are being paid statutory sick pay (SSP) or short-term lower rate incapacity benefit (IB); *or*
  - you are being paid income support (IS) because you are incapable of work (including where this is due to pregnancy) or are getting national insurance credits because you are incapable of work. This only applies for 28 weeks.

  You must have been in full-time paid work (16 or 30 hours, as the case may be) immediately before the period began.

  If you are self-employed, you count as in full-time paid work during any period when the above would have applied had the work done in the week before the period began been done as an employee.

  Remember: if you do not return to work when your SSP or short-term lower rate IB ceases (or if you are being paid IS, after 28 weeks), you no longer count as being in full-time paid work under this rule; *and*
- during any period when you are on strike. This only applies if you were in full-time paid work (16 or 30 hours, as the case may be) immediately before the period began. You must not be on strike for longer than 10 consecutive days when you should have been working;[25] *and*
- during any period when you are suspended from work while complaints or allegations against you are investigated. This only applies if you were in full-time paid work (16 or 30 hours, as the case may be) immediately before the period began;[26] *and*
- if you were in full-time paid work within the past seven days.[27] This means you can make a new claim or continue to qualify for WTC – eg, during a short period between jobs or when you are on jury service.

3. People treated as not being in full-time paid work

You or your partner are treated as *not* being in full-time paid work during any period when you are receiving pay in lieu of notice after you stop work.[28] In addition, you and your partner are treated as *not* being in full-time work if:[29]

- you or your partner are a volunteer or are working for a charity or voluntary organisation and are giving your services free (except for your expenses);
- you or your partner are providing care for someone who is staying with you temporarily but who is not normally a member of your household; *and*

- the only payment you receive is from a health authority, a local authority, a voluntary organisation, a primary care trust or from the person her/himself for caring for her/him; *and*
- the payment is disregarded (see p1389);

- you or your partner are working on a government training scheme and are being paid a training allowance (see below), unless the training allowance you are paid is subject to income tax as a profit from work;[30]
- the only payment you receive, or expect to receive, is a sports award from a Sports Council;
- you are participating in the 'intensive activity period' of the New Deal for people aged 25 to 49, unless the money you are being paid by the Department for Work and Pensions is subject to income tax as a profit from work.[31] Note that if you are on any other employment scheme and you are paid for your services, if you do sufficient hours (16 or 30 as the case may be) you *can* count as in full-time paid work;[32]
- you are on an employment zone programme and are only being paid:[33]
  - training premiums; *or*
  - discretionary payments (eg, fees and grants) that are disregarded (see p1388).

A '**training allowance**' is an allowance paid to maintain you or a member of your family:[34]

- paid by a Government department or by or on behalf of the Secretary of State or Scottish Enterprise or Highlands and Islands Enterprise; *and*
- paid for the period or part of a period during which you are on a course provided or approved by or under arrangements made by any of these.

Allowances paid to or in respect of you by a Government department or the Scottish Executive are not included if these are paid because you are a trainee teacher or on a full-time course of education, unless this is under arrangements made under s2 of the Employment and Training Act 1973.

4. Working tax credit, income support and jobseeker's allowance

Sometimes it is difficult to show that you count as being in full-time paid work and the distinction between **working tax credit** (WTC) and **out-of-work benefits** (income support (IS) or jobseeker's allowance (JSA)) is not absolute. In some situations, you may have a choice about whether to claim WTC or out-of-work benefits. In some situations, you might be able to claim both IS or income-based JSA and WTC (eg, if you are a 'term-time only' worker or are off sick and getting statutory sick pay). See p759 for further information.

Notes

1 s10(1) TCA 2002
2 Regs 2, definition of 'remunerative work', and 5(4)(a) CTC Regs

1. **The full-time paid work rule**
3 Reg 4(1) (second condition) WTC(EMR) Regs
4 Reg 4(1) (first condition) WTC(EMR) Regs
5 Reg 4(1) (third condition) WTC(EMR) Regs
6 Reg 4(1) (fourth condition) WTC(EMR) Regs
7 Reg 2(1), definition of 'employed' WTC(EMR) Regs
8 Reg 2(1), definition of 'self-employed' WTC(EMR) Regs
9 Reg 4(3) WTC(EMR) Regs
10 Reg 4(4)(b) WTC(EMR) Regs
11 Reg 4(5) WTC(EMR) Regs
12 Reg4(4)(b) WTC(EMR) Regs
13 TCTM para 02405
14 TCTM para 02405
15 TCTM para 02405
16 Reg 7 WTC(EMR) Regs; *Stafford and Banks v CAO* [2001] UKHL 33 (HL), reported as R(IS) 15/01
17 R(JSA)8/03
18 CIS/914/1997; CJSA/2759/1998
19 R(JSA) 5/02
20 R(FIS) 1/83; R(FIS) 1/86; TCTM para 02403
21 Reg 6(28) SS(C&P) Regs

2. **People treated as being in full-time paid work**
22 Reg 5 WTC(EMR) Regs
23 Reg 5A WTC(EMR) Regs
24 Reg 6 WTC(EMR) Regs
25 Reg 7A WTC(EMR) Regs
26 Reg 7B WTC(EMR) Regs
27 Reg 8 WTC(EMR) Regs

3. **People treated as not being in full-time paid work**
28 Reg 7C WTC(EMR) Regs
29 Reg 4(2) WTC(EMR) Regs
30 Reg 4(2)(c) and (2A) WTC(EMR) Regs
31 Reg 4(2)(d) and (2A) WTC(EMR) Regs
32 TCTM para 02404
33 Reg 4(2)(f) WTC(EMR) Regs only applies to Employment Zone programmes that are subject to the Employment Zone Regulations 2000 No.721, and not to those subject to the Employment Zone Regulations 2003 No.2438
34 Reg 2 WTC(EMR) Regs, definition of 'training allowance'

Chapter 52

The amount of tax credit

This chapter covers:

Main features

The amount of tax credit to which you are entitled depends on your family circumstances and your income. There are no limits on the amount of savings or other capital that you might have.

- If you are entitled to income support (IS), income-based jobseeker's allowance (JSA) or pension credit (PC – guarantee *and/or* savings element), you are automatically entitled to the maximum amount of tax credit that you could receive.
- If you are not entitled to IS, income-based JSA or PC, you may receive less than your maximum amount of tax credit, depending on the level of your income.
- Your maximum amount of child tax credit (CTC) depends on the size of your family, the ages of the children in your family, and whether any child in your family has a disability.
- The amount of working tax credit (WTC) you can get depends on whether you are single with no dependants, a lone parent or a member of a couple, the hours you work, whether you (or your partner if you have one) are disabled, whether you are returning to work aged 50 or above, and whether you have eligible childcare costs.
- If you are entitled to both CTC and WTC, the maximum amount for each is added together to give your total maximum amount. The maximum amount of tax credit you could receive is compared with your income and with one or more of three set amounts (called 'income thresholds').
- If your income is less than the threshold which applies to you, you can receive your maximum amount of tax credit. If you have income in excess of an income threshold, your maximum amount is reduced by a percentage of this

excess income. If your income exceeds the relevant threshold by more than a certain amount, you will not be entitled to any tax credit.

- Your award of CTC and/or WTC is based on entitlement for a whole tax year. If you are entitled to tax credit for a period of less than a year, or if your entitlement changes during the tax year, your annual entitlement will be reduced to cover this shorter period. A period during which your entitlement remains the same is known as a 'relevant period'.

The basic steps

The basic steps in calculating the amount of tax credit are as follows:

- Work out the number of days in your 'relevant period'.
- Work out your 'maximum amount'.
- Work out your 'relevant income'.
- Compare this income with the 'threshold figure'.
- Calculate entitlement.

1. The relevant period

The amount of tax credit you can receive is based on your entitlement during a 'relevant period'. Tax credit awards are calculated by reference to a maximum *annual* amount that you could receive. If you claim at the beginning of the new tax year, your award will usually be calculated on the basis that you will be entitled to tax credit for the whole of that tax year (6 April–5 April), and your relevant period will therefore be one year.[1] Your annual entitlement will be calculated and then paid to you over the course of that year.

If you claim a tax credit after the beginning of a tax year your award will be calculated for a period beginning with the date on which you make your claim and ending at the end of that tax year, unless you are able to have your claim backdated to an earlier period (see p1405). Similarly, if your circumstances change in the course of the year, and your award is amended, a new relevant period will begin. The new relevant period will be calculated on the basis that it will end at the end of the tax year.[2] In both of these cases, you will be entitled to tax credit for less than a year, and so only a proportion of the annual amount can be paid.

In order to work out your maximum amount of tax credit, therefore, you need to know how long your relevant period is. This means that you have to count the number of days in your relevant period.

A **'relevant period'** is:

- for child tax credit (CTC), a period of an award during which your maximum amount remains the same;[3]
- for working tax credit (WTC), a period during which the elements making up your maximum amount of tax credit (apart from the childcare element) remain the same, *and:*

- during which there is no change in the childcare you use; *and*
- your average weekly childcare charge does not change by £10 or more, or reduce to nil.[4]

If you are entitled to both CTC and WTC, a relevant period is one during which both of the above conditions are satisfied.[5]

2. The maximum amount of child tax credit

The maximum amount of child tax credit (CTC) you can get is calculated by adding together each of the 'elements' which apply to you.[6] The amount of each element is set at a yearly rate. If you are entitled to CTC for a period of less than a year, or if your entitlement changes part of the way through the year, the amount of each of these elements is adjusted so that the correct proportion of your annual maximum amount is paid to you.[7] How entitlement is calculated when entitlement changes part of the way through a tax year is explained on p1368.

The elements are:[8]

Element	*Annual rate*
Family element (not including baby element)	£545
Family element (including baby element for child under 1)	£1,090
Child element	£1,690
Disability element (for a child)	£2,285
Severe disability element (for a child)	£920

- A family element is payable for each family, and the amount is not affected by whether you are a single parent or one of a couple. Only one family element is payable for your family (see p1330 for who counts as your family). The basic rate is £545. If your family includes at least one child under the age of 1, you receive an additional 'baby element', which brings your total family element to £1,090. (This higher amount is not increased if your family includes more than one child under the age of 1.)
- You get a child element for each child in your family (see p1316 for when a child or young person can count as a member of your family).
- You get a disability element for any child in your family who gets disability living allowance (DLA), or is registered blind, or who has been taken off the register in the last 28 weeks. The element still applies if DLA has stopped because your child is in hospital.[9] It is paid in addition to the child element for that child.
- You get a severe disability element for each child in your family who gets the highest rate of the care component of DLA. The element still applies if DLA has

stopped because your child is in hospital.[10] It is paid in addition to the child element and disability element for that child.

The Revenue uses the term 'family element' to cover both rates at which the family element is paid, and uses the term 'child element' to cover the child element *plus* any related disability and severe disability element for that child.

Example

Tracy is a single parent with two children aged 5 and 3. The annual elements used when calculating her maximum amount are as follows:

Family element	£545
Child element for 3-year-old child	£1,690
Child element for 5-year-old child	£1,690

3. The maximum amount of working tax credit

The maximum amount of working tax credit (WTC) you get is calculated by adding together each of the elements which apply to you.[11] The amount of each element, with the exception of the childcare element, is set at a yearly rate. The amount of the childcare element is set by reference to your average *weekly* childcare costs.[12] See p1360 for how your childcare element is calculated.

If you are entitled to WTC for a period of less than a year, or if your entitlement changes part of the way through the year, the amount of each of these elements is adjusted so that the correct proportion of your annual maximum amount is paid to you.[13] See p1368 for an explanation of how entitlement is calculated when entitlement changes part of the way through a tax year.

There are eight elements:[14]

Element	*Annual rate*
Basic element	£1,620
Lone-parent element	£1,595
Couple element	£1,595
30-hour element	£660
Disability element	£2,165
Severe disability element	£920
50-plus element	
16-29 hours	£1,110
30+ hours	£1,660

	Weekly rate
Childcare element	
maximum eligible cost for two or more children per week	£300
maximum eligible cost for one child per week	£175
percentage of eligible costs covered	70%

Basic element

One basic element is paid with each award of WTC. To be entitled to this element you must be engaged in 'qualifying remunerative work'. In this *Handbook* we call this 'full-time work'.[15] For the definition of full-time work see Chapter 51. Unless you qualify for the basic element of WTC you cannot qualify for any of the other elements.[16]

Couple element

You get the couple element if you are one of a couple making a joint claim (see p1395) unless:

- either you or your partner are aged 50 or over; *and*
- either you or your partner are entitled to the 50-plus element; *and*
- neither you nor your partner are engaged in full-time work for at least 30 hours a week.[17] However, if either you or your partner are responsible for a child or qualifying young person, or are entitled to the disability element, then you will not be prevented from receiving the couple element simply because you do not work for at least 30 hours a week.[18] This means that if you or your partner are aged 50 or above, and are entitled to the 50-plus element, and are *either*:
  – responsible for a child or qualifying young person; *or*
  – entitled to the disability element,
  you can still have the couple element included in your maximum tax credit.

You cannot get the couple element if your partner is serving a prison sentence of more than 12 months, unless either you or your partner are responsible for a child or qualifying young person.[19] You can only have one couple element included in your maximum amount.[20] For when you count as a couple, see p1331.

Lone parent element

You get the lone parent element if you are a lone parent.[21]

30-hour element

You get a 30-hour element if you are:[22]

- a single claimant who works for at least 30 hours a week; *or*
- making a joint claim and either or both of you work for at least 30 hours a week; *or*

- making a joint claim and at least one of you is responsible for a child or qualifying young person *and*:
  - you are both engaged in remunerative work; *and*
  - at least one of you works for at least 16 hours a week; *and*
  - your joint hours of work total at least 30 hours a week.

You can only have one 30-hour element included in your maximum amount.[23]

Disability element

You get a disability element if you or your partner (in the case of a joint claim) work for at least 16 hours a week *and* have a disability which puts you at a disadvantage in getting a job.[24] This means you must pass a disability test (see Appendix 10).

You must also satisfy one of the following conditions in your current claim for a tax credit. It does not matter that you did not satisfy any of these conditions in any previous claim, or that you are part of the way through an award of tax credit which until now has not included a disability element. If you pass the disability test and meet one of the following conditions, a disability element can be included in your maximum amount in an existing award of tax credit (see p1368), or in a new award of tax credit. The conditions are that you must:[25]

- receive (or for at least one day in the 182 days immediately preceding your claim have been in receipt of):
  - the higher rate of short-term incapacity benefit (IB); *or*
  - long-term IB; *or*
  - severe disablement allowance (SDA); *or*
  - a higher pensioner premium or disability premium paid with income support (IS), income-based jobseeker's allowance (JSA), housing benefit (HB) or council tax benefit (CTB); *or*
- on the date of your claim receive disability living allowance (DLA), attendance allowance (AA) or a mobility supplement or constant attendance allowance payable with a war pension or industrial injuries disablement benefit; *or*
- have an invalid carriage or similar vehicle; *or*
- have received for at least 140 days forming a single period of incapacity for work (see Chapter 30) (the last of which must have fallen within the 56 days of the date of the claim) statutory sick pay (SSP), occupational sick pay, short-term IB at the lower rate, or IS on account of incapacity, or credits for incapacity for a period of 20 weeks; *and*
  - have a disability at the date of the claim which is likely to last for at least six months (or for the rest of your life, if your death is expected within that time); *and*
  - have gross earnings which are less than they were before the disability began by at least the greater of 20 per cent and £15 per week; *or*

- have undertaken 'training for work' for at least one day in the 56 days immediately preceding the claim, *and* are receiving long-term IB, SDA or the higher rate of short-term IB within the 56 days before that training started. For an explanation of what 'training for work' means, see p266.

If there is a break in your claim

If you make a further claim for WTC within 56 days of the day your previous award ended, *and* in that earlier claim you qualified for the disability element *either*:

- because you received (or for at least one day in the 182 days immediately preceding that earlier claim had been in receipt of) the higher rate of short-term IB; long-term IB; SDA, or a higher pensioner premium or disability premium paid with IS, income-based JSA, HB or CTB; *or*
- because you have undertaken training for work for at least one day in the previous 56 days and had received the higher rate of short-term IB, long-term IB or SDA within the 56 days preceding that training; *or*
- because you received for at least 140 days (the last of which must have fallen within the 56 days of the date of the earlier claim) SSP, occupational sick pay, short-term IB at the lower rate, IS, or credits for incapacity for a period of 20 weeks; *and*
  - you had a disability at the date of that earlier claim which was likely to last for at least six months (or for the rest of your life, if your death was expected within that time); *and*
  - you have gross earnings which are less than they were before the disability began by at least the greater of 20 per cent and £15 per week; *and*
  - you continue in qualifying remunerative work for at least 16 hours a week,

you will be treated as though you still met those conditions, and can continue to receive the disability element in your new award.

You can still benefit from this linking rule if your income was too high for you to receive any WTC within the previous 56 days, as long as your maximum amount of WTC would have included the disability element on one of the above grounds.[26]

If both you and your partner meet the above conditions, then two disability elements can be paid.[27]

Severe disability element

You get a severe disability element if you receive the highest rate of the care component of DLA or the higher rate of AA, or if payment of either of these has been suspended because you are in hospital.[28] If you have a partner who meets these conditions, a severe disability element can also be included for them.[29]

50-plus element

You get a 50-plus element if:[30]

- you are aged 50 or over; *and*

- you start qualifying remunerative work; *and*
- you are engaged in full-time work (see Chapter 51) of at least 16 hours a week *and either*:
  - for consecutive periods (that is, periods separated by no more than 12 weeks) which add up to six months and end immediately before you start work, you have been getting at least one of the following: IS, JSA, IB, SDA, state retirement pension plus pension credit, or a training allowance paid under the 'work-based learning for adults' or 'training for work' schemes; *or*
  - for an uninterrupted period of at least at least six months immediately before you started work you have been getting at least one of the following: IS, JSA, IB, SDA, state retirement pension plus pension credit, or a training allowance paid under the 'work-based learning for adults' or 'training for work' schemes; *or*
  - for at least six months immediately before you started work someone else was getting an increase for you in their IS, JSA, IB, SDA, or state retirement pension (which must have been paid with pension credit); *or*
  - for at least six months immediately before you started work you were entitled to be credited with national insurance (NI) contributions or earnings.

  If any of the last three conditions above applies, but for a period of less than six months, you can still qualify for the 50-plus element if immediately before you started satisfying one of those three conditions, you or your partner were getting carer's allowance, bereavement allowance or widowed parent's allowance, and this period, plus one of the last three periods described above, add up to at least six months.

This element is payable for only a 12-month period starting when you return to work. This can be one period of 12 months, or periods separated by 26 weeks or less, adding up to 12 months. A lower rate is payable if you work for between 16 and 29 hours, and a higher rate is paid if you work for 30 hours a week or more. If you have a partner who also meets these conditions, then a 50-plus element can be paid for them too.[31]

Childcare element

If you have 'eligible childcare costs', your maximum amount of WTC can include a childcare element.[32] For the definition of eligible childcare costs, and an explanation of how these are calculated, see pp1361–1363.

Example

Tracy works for 20 hours a week. She has eligible childcare costs of £200 a week, and her childcare element is therefore £7,280 a year. The annual elements used when calculating her maximum amount are as follows:

Basic element	£1,620
Lone parent element	£1,595
Childcare element	£7,280

4. The childcare element of working tax credit

Your maximum amount of working tax credit (WTC) can include a childcare element, to help meet the cost of 'relevant childcare' (see p1361).[33] This element is 70 per cent of actual childcare costs of up to £175 a week for one child, or £300 a week for two or more children (ie, up to £122.50 or £210 a week).[34]

To get the childcare element of WTC, you or your partner must be responsible for at least one child.[35] You do not have to be the child's parent. 'Responsible for' has the same meaning for WTC as it does for CTC (see p1318).[36]

The childcare element is just a part of the maximum WTC calculation, and cannot be claimed on its own, or as part of child tax credit (CTC).[37]

This element can be included to help meet the costs of childcare if you are incurring charges for relevant childcare and you are:[38]

- a lone parent engaged in qualifying remunerative work; *or*
- a member of a married or unmarried couple and *either*
  - you are both engaged in qualifying remunerative work; *or*
  - one of you is engaged in qualifying remunerative work and the other is incapacitated (see below); *or*
  - one of you is engaged in qualifying remunerative work and the other is in hospital or in prison (serving a sentence or remanded in custody).

Incapacitated

You or your partner are treated as incapacitated if:[39]

- you get short-term higher rate or long-term incapacity benefit (IB); *or*
- you get severe disablement allowance (SDA); *or*
- you get attendance allowance (AA), disability living allowance (DLA) (or an equivalent award paid as an increase under the war pensions or industrial injuries disablement scheme) or would be getting it but for the fact that you are in hospital; *or*
- you get industrial injuries disablement benefit with constant attendance allowance; *or*
- you have an award of housing benefit (HB) or council tax benefit (CTB) which includes a disability premium or a higher pensioner premium in respect of incapacity; *or*
- you have an invalid carriage or similar vehicle.[40]

You can claim the childcare element in respect of a new baby while you are on statutory maternity, paternity or adoption leave, as well as for any other children for whom you are responsible.

Relevant childcare charges can be for any child in your family up to the last day of the week in which 1 September falls, following the child's 15th birthday, or their 16th birthday if s/he is disabled.[41] **'Disabled child'** means a child who:[42]

- receives DLA, or whose DLA has been suspended because the child is a hospital inpatient; *or*
- has been registered blind; *or*
- ceased to be registered blind in the 28 weeks immediately preceding the WTC claim.

Relevant childcare

In order to be **'relevant childcare'** the childcare must be provided by:[43]

- a registered childminder; *or*
- other registered childcare providers such as nurseries, after-school clubs and local authorities providing day care services; *or*
- schools or establishments exempt from registration; *or*
- an out-of-hours club on school premises run by the school or the local authority for children up to age 15 (or 16 if the child is disabled). The child counts as 15 (or 16, in the case of a disabled child) up to the last day of the week in which 1 September falls, following the child's 15th birthday, or her/his 16th birthday if s/he is disabled; *or*
- childcare provided by a foster parent or foster carer under specified fostering regulations – but not in respect of a child which is being fostered by that foster parent; *or*
- (in England only) childcare provided in your own home by a person approved to care for children (including, from 6 April 2005, childcare provided by someone approved under the Childcare Approval Scheme), or childcare provided by a domiciliary worker or nurse employed by an agency registered for that purpose; *or*
- (in England only) from April 2005, childcare provided for children over the age of 7 on other domestic premises, by someone approved under the Childcare Approval Scheme. **'Domestic premises'** means any premises used wholly or mainly as a private dwelling.[44] You cannot claim help under this scheme for childcare provided in the home of a relative of your child, where the care is usually provided only for children to whom that childcare provider is a relative;[45] *or*
- (in Wales only) by a domiciliary care worker registered under the Domiciliary Care Agencies (Wales) Regulations 2004; *or*
- (in Scotland only) childcare provided by or arranged through a childcare agency which is required to be registered.

A registered childminder, childcare scheme or nursery, or an approved home childcare provider means one which is registered or approved:

- (in England) by OFSTED, the National Care Standards Commission or, in the case of a childminder approved under the Childcare Approval scheme, by Nestor Primecare Services Ltd;[46]
- (in Wales) by the National Assembly for Wales (via the Care Standards Inspectorate for Wales);
- (in Scotland) by the Scottish Commission for the Regulation of Care;
- (in Northern Ireland) by a Health and Social Services Trust.

Some schemes run on school premises may be approved by local authorities or local education authorities. You can also claim help with the costs of childcare in these schemes.

You cannot claim help with the costs of childcare provided in your own home if that care is provided by a relative of your child. **'Relative'** means parent, grandparent, aunt or uncle, brother or sister, whether related by blood, marriage or affinity. By affinity, we understand that the Revenue means people who are related through partners, rather than husbands or wives. For example, if childcare is provided in your home by your partner's mother, she is related to the child by affinity, even if your partner is not a parent of the child, and so you cannot claim for the cost of paying her.

You can only claim for charges that you are actually paying. If you will not be making payments for childcare until some time after you have claimed WTC, you cannot receive a childcare element for these until you actually start making the payments. If you have made an arrangement with a childcare provider to pay childcare costs, you can claim for these costs up to a week before the childcare is provided.[47]

The amount of the childcare element

The amount of the element is calculated as follows.

Step one: work out your relevant period

Add up the number of days in your relevant period (see p1353). If you are making a claim for tax credit before the beginning of a new tax year, your award will usually be based on entitlement at the same rate for a whole tax year, and your relevant period will be one year. The tax year 2005/06 has 365 days.

Step two: calculate your relevant childcare charge

Your **'relevant childcare charge'** is your average weekly charge. The way in which your average weekly charge is calculated depends on whether you pay for childcare weekly, monthly, or at some other interval, and on whether the amount you pay varies over time.[48]

- If you pay for childcare on a weekly basis and the charge is a fixed weekly amount, add together the charges in the most recent four weeks before the claim and divide by four.
- If you pay for childcare on a weekly basis, have paid for childcare for at least 52 weeks and the charge varies over time, add together the charges in the 52 weeks before the claim and divide by 52.
- If you pay on a monthly basis, and the charge is a fixed monthly amount, multiply that monthly amount by 12 and divide the total by 52.
- If you pay on a monthly basis, and the charge varies from month to month, add together the charges for the last 12 months and divide the total by 52.
- If there is not enough information for the Revenue to establish your average weekly charge by any of the above methods, then the charge will be calculated by the Revenue on the basis of information which you provide about your childcare costs, using any method which in its opinion is reasonable.
- If you have entered into an agreement to pay for childcare, which will be provided during the period of your award, your average weekly childcare costs will be calculated on the basis of your own written estimate of these costs. In practice, you will be providing this estimate on your tax credit claim form.

When you have calculated your average weekly childcare charges by one of these methods, round the figure up to the nearest whole pound.

Step three: calculate the actual childcare costs for the relevant period

The weekly amount found in step two is now converted to an amount covering your relevant period. Multiply the weekly charge by 52 to calculate the annual amount. Divide this figure by the number of days in the current tax year to find the daily rate, and then multiply this daily rate by the number of days in your relevant period. This gives your childcare costs for the relevant period.[49]

Step four: calculate your maximum eligible childcare costs for the relevant period

Divide the maximum eligible weekly childcare cost which applies to you by seven, to find the daily rate. The maximum eligible weekly cost is £175 for one child, and £300 for two or more children. Round this figure up to the nearest penny and then multiply this daily rate by the number of days in the relevant period.

Step five: calculate the childcare element for the relevant period

Take the lower of the two figures found in steps three and four, and calculate 70 per cent of that figure. Round the amount up to the nearest penny. This gives your childcare element for the relevant period.

Example

Tracy paid a fixed amount of £200 every week in eligible childcare costs for her two children during each of the four weeks before her application for tax credits was made. She makes an application for WTC in advance of the new tax year. She will continue to pay £200 a week for the same childcare. Her childcare element for the whole of a tax year is found as follows.

Step one

Tracy's relevant period is one year (365 days).

Step two

Her relevant childcare charge is £200. (This is her average weekly charge.)

Step three

£200 x 52 = £10,400

(£10,400 ÷ 365) x 365 = £10,400

Step four

The maximum weekly eligible childcare cost for Tracy is £300, as she has two children.

The daily rate is £300 ÷ 7 = £42.86 (rounded up to the nearest penny)

The annual rate is £42.86 x 365 = £15,643.90.

Step five

The lower figure from steps 3 and 4 is £10,400.

Childcare element is 70% of £10,400 = £7,280.

Tracy's childcare element for the relevant period (in this case, one whole tax year) is £7,280.

5. How to calculate the amount of tax credit

If you are not receiving income support, income-based jobseeker's allowance or pension credit

The following steps describe how your entitlement is worked out if you are not receiving income support (IS), income-based jobseeker's allowance (JSA) or pension credit (PC).

Step one: work out your relevant period

Add up the number of days in your relevant period (see p1353). If you are making a claim for tax credit at the beginning of a new tax year, your award will be based on entitlement at the same rate for a whole tax year, and your relevant period will be one year. The tax year 2005/06 has 365 days.

Step two: find your maximum entitlement for the relevant period

First, identify the different elements of each tax credit you are eligible for. Take the annual amount of each element *apart from the childcare element of working tax credit (WTC)* and convert each of these amounts to a daily rate.

This is done by dividing the amount of each element by the number of days in the current tax year[50] and then rounding this amount up to the nearest penny.

Example

To find the daily rate of the family element of child tax credit (CTC) in the tax year 2005/06, divide the annual amount (£1,090 where the baby element is included because the family includes a child under one year of age) by 365 and round up to the nearest penny.
£1,090 ÷ 365 = £2.99, rounded up to the nearest penny.

To find the daily rate of the child element of CTC in the tax year 2005/06, divide the annual amount (£1,690) by 365 and round up to the nearest penny.
£1,690 ÷ 365 = £4.64, rounded up to the nearest penny.

For each element, multiply this daily rate by the number of days in the relevant period. Add the adjusted amounts of each element together. Next, calculate your childcare element for the relevant period as described on p1362.

Add the childcare element for the relevant period to the other elements for the relevant period to find your maximum entitlement for the relevant period.

Step three: find your relevant income

The income used in the tax credit calculation is your relevant income (see below).

The usual procedure which the Revenue uses is to base the calculation on your previous tax year's income. (In some cases, it may be to your advantage to have an estimate of your current tax year's income used in the calculation instead – see p1374.)

Divide this income by the number of days in the tax year to which your claim for tax credits relates to find the daily rate, and then multiply this daily rate by the number of days in the relevant period. Round this amount down to the nearest penny. This is your relevant income.

At the end of the tax year, when determining whether your entitlement during that year should have been based on the current year's income or the previous year's income, the Revenue will compare the two amounts, to see whether there is a difference of £2,500 or more between the two.[51]

- If your income in the current tax year exceeds your income in the previous tax year by £2,500 or less, the previous year's income will be used.
- If your income in the current tax year exceeds your income in the previous tax year by more than £2,500, your current year's income minus £2,500 will be used.
- If your income in the current tax year is less than or the same as your income in the previous tax year, your current year's income will be used.

Step four: compare your income with the threshold for the relevant period

Find the annual threshold which applies to you.

- If you are entitled to WTC only, the annual threshold is £5,220.
- If you are entitled to WTC *and* CTC, the annual threshold is £5,220.
- If you are entitled to CTC only, and not to WTC, the annual threshold is £13,910.

Divide the threshold which applies to you by the number of days in the tax year in the current tax year, and then multiply this figure by the number of days in the relevant period. Round this amount up to the nearest penny. This figure is your threshold for the relevant period.

Step five: calculate tax credit entitlement for the relevant period

- If your income is less than the threshold that applies to you, you are entitled to receive the maximum amount of tax credit(s).
- If your income is greater than the threshold which applies to you, subtract the threshold figure from your relevant income to find your excess income. Calculate 37 per cent of this excess income and round this figure down to the nearest penny. Finally, reduce your maximum amount of tax credit(s) by this amount.
- The different elements of your maximum tax credit are tapered away in a set order:
  - First, the elements of WTC except for the childcare element are reduced.
  - Next, the childcare element is reduced.
  - Third, the child elements of CTC plus any disability or severe disability elements for your children are reduced.
  - The family element of CTC will not be reduced unless you have income for a tax year in excess of the second income threshold of £50,000. At this point, the family element will be reduced by £1 for every £15 of income in excess of £50,000 (that is, at a rate of 6.67 per cent).

It is expected that in a small number of cases, a claimant's maximum amount of tax credit will be so high that the child element of CTC will not have been tapered away completely by the time income for the tax year has reached £50,000. In these cases, the child element will continue to be tapered away at a rate of 37 per cent until this element is exhausted, and then the family element will be tapered away at the rate of £1 for every £15 of excess income.

If you are entitled to CTC only, or WTC only, and the calculation results in entitlement of less than £26, no award of tax credit will be made. If you are entitled to both CTC and WTC, and the total entitlement from both adds up to less than £26, no award will be made.[52]

To find out how much your weekly payment will be, divide the total found in Step 5 above by the number of days in your relevant period to find the daily rate and then multiply this daily rate by seven. If your credit is paid four-weekly, multiply the daily rate by 28, to calculate the amount of your payments.

Example

Tracy claims tax credits at the beginning of the tax year 2005/06. During the tax year 2004/05 she worked 20 hours a week and earned £6 an hour, gross. During the tax year 2004/05, she continues to work the same hours, for the same rate of pay. Tracy's entitlement to tax credits is calculated as follows:

Step one: work out relevant period

Tracy's relevant period is 365 days.

Step two: find maximum entitlement for the relevant period

CTC	Family element	£547.50
	Child element for 3-year-old child	£1,693.60
	Child element for 5-year-old child	£1,693.60
WTC	Basic element	£1,620.60
	Lone parent element	£1,595.05
	Childcare element	£7,280.00
Total maximum amount of tax credit		**£14,430.35**

(**Note:** although Tracy's annual period is one year, the figures for each element do not equal the annual amount of each element. For example, the annual amount of the family element is £545.00, but the calculation above shows Tracy's family element during her relevant period of one year as being £547.50. This is because when the annual amount has been divided by 365, the figure produced is *rounded up* to the nearest penny, before being multiplied by the number of days in the tax year. This rounding up has the effect of increasing Tracy's annual maximum amount.)

Step three: find relevant income

Tracy earned £6,257.14 during the tax year 2004/05. (She is paid £6 an hour, gross, and works 20 hours a week.) This total is calculated as follows:
((£6 x 20) ÷ 7) x 365 = £6,257.14
She continues to be paid at the same rate during the tax year 2005/06. During the year in which tax credits are paid (2005/06), her income for the year 2004/05 is used.
Tracy's income for the relevant period is therefore:
(£6,257.14 ÷ 365) x 365 = £6,257.14

Step four: compare income with the threshold for the relevant period

As Tracy will receive both WTC and CTC, her annual threshold figure is £5,220.
The threshold for the relevant period is therefore:
(£5,220 ÷ 365) x 365 = £5,220

Step five: calculate tax credit entitlement for the relevant period

Tracy has excess income of £1,037.14 (income of £6,257.14 minus the threshold figure of £5,220).
Apply the taper of 37 per cent to this excess income:
37% x £1,037.14 = £383.74
Tracy's maximum tax credit (£14,430.35) will be reduced by this amount. Her total tax credit entitlement will be:
£14,430.35 – £383.74 = £14,046.61
The reduction is first applied to the elements of her WTC apart from the childcare element (that is, the basic element of £1,620.60 plus the lone parent element of £1,595.05 = £3,215.65):
£3,215.65 – £383.74 = £2,831.91
Tracy's tax credits for the tax year 2004/05 will therefore be:

WTC (not including childcare element)	£2,831.91
Childcare element	£7,280.00
CTC	£3,934.70
Total tax credits	**£14,046.61**

To find the weekly rate of payment, this figure is divided by 365 (the number of days in Tracy's relevant period) and multiplied by 7.
(£14,046.61 ÷ 365) x 7 = £269.39

If you are receiving income support, income-based jobseeker's allowance or pension credit

If you are entitled to IS, income-based JSA or PC, you are automatically entitled to the maximum amount of CTC or WTC you could receive.[53] You calculate this by adding together the elements of each tax credit you qualify for, over your relevant period, as described above. Your maximum amount is not subject to any reduction during the period you are receiving IS, income-based JSA or PC.

6. Calculating entitlement after a change of circumstances

There are three different ways in which your circumstances can change so as to change your entitlement to tax credits:

- Where your circumstances change in a way that affects your maximum entitlement, a new relevant period begins. For example, if a disability benefit which gives entitlement to a disability element is awarded to you or someone included in your claim, this changes your maximum amount of tax credit, and starts a new relevant period.
- Other changes, such as a change in the number of adults heading your household, will bring your award to an end, and you will have to make a fresh claim for tax credit, if you remain entitled. This will also start a new relevant period.
- Finally, some changes, which do not affect your maximum entitlement and do not bring your existing award to an end, will affect the amount of tax credit which is payable to you. For example, if your existing award has been based on your current tax year's income, and you have a significant rise in your income during that tax year, you may be overpaid tax credit unless you report the change at once, enabling your award to be recalculated.

See p1413 for a description of the changes of circumstances which bring one relevant period to an end and start another, for changes which end your current award, and for changes which will affect the amount of your award.

In any of these circumstances, your tax credit award will need to be recalculated. This is done by working through steps 1 to 5 as described on pp1364–1367, for each relevant period.

Example

Tracy claims disability living allowance (DLA) for her 5-year-old child and this is awarded (middle rate of the care component) from day 201 of the tax year 2005/06. She therefore has two relevant periods during this tax year. The first is 200 days long, and the second, from the date her daughter is awarded DLA, 165 days long.

Her entitlement during the first 200 days is calculated as follows:

Step one: work out the relevant period

The first relevant period is 200 days long.

Step two: find maximum entitlement for the relevant period

Maximum entitlement to all of the elements of tax credits for the relevant period of 200 days, apart from the childcare element, is calculated.

Child tax credit (CTC)	Family element	£300
	Child element for 3-year-old child	£928
	Child element for 5-year-old child	£928
Working tax credit (WTC) (not including childcare element)	Basic element	£888
	Lone parent element	£874

Next, the childcare element for the relevant period is calculated, as described above.

Childcare element	£3,989.05

Tracy's total maximum amount of tax credit for this relevant period is therefore £7,907.05 (£3,918.00 + £3,989.05).

Step three: find relevant income

Tracy's annual income is £6,257.14. This is adjusted for the relevant period by dividing by the number of days in the tax year, and multiplying by the number of days in the relevant period.

(£6,257.14 ÷ 365) x 200 = £3,428.56

Step four: compare income with the threshold for the relevant period

As Tracy receives both WTC and CTC, her annual threshold figure is £5,220. The threshold figure is also adjusted to cover the relevant period.

(£5,220 ÷ 365) x 200 = £2,860.28

Step five: calculate tax credit entitlement for the relevant period

Tracy has excess income of £568.28 (relevant income of £3,428.56 minus the threshold figure of £2,860.28).

Apply the taper of 37 per cent to this excess income:

37% x £568.28 = £210.26

Tracy's maximum tax credit (£7,907.05) will be reduced by this amount. Her total tax credit entitlement will be:

£7,907.05 – £210.26 = £7,696.79

This reduction of £210.26 is first applied to the elements of her WTC apart from the childcare element (ie, the basic element of £888 plus the lone parent element of £878 = £1,762).

£1,762.00 – £210.26 = £1,551.74

Tracy's tax credits for first 200 days will be made up as follows:

WTC (not including childcare element)	£1,551.74
Childcare element	£3,989.05
CTC	£2,156.00
Total tax credits	**£7,696.79**

Tracy's total tax credit entitlement for the first 200 days is therefore £7,696.79.

To find the weekly rate of payment, this figure is divided by 200 and multiplied by 7.

(£7,696.79 ÷ 200) x 7 =£269.38

Her entitlement for the second relevant period is calculated as follows:

Step one: work out relevant period

The second relevant period is 165 days long.

Step two: find maximum entitlement for the relevant period

Maximum entitlement to all of the elements of tax credits for the relevant period of 165 days, apart from the childcare element, is calculated:

CTC	Family element	£247.50
	Child element for 3-year-old child	£765.60
	Child element for 5-year-old child	£765.60
	Disability element for 5-year-old child	£1,034.55
WTC (not including childcare element)	Basic element	£732.60
	Lone parent element	£721.05
Total		**£4,266.90**

Next, the childcare element for the relevant period is calculated, as described above.

	Childcare element	£3,290.96

Tracy's total maximum amount of tax credit for this relevant period is therefore £7,557.86 (£4,266.90 + £3,290.96).

Step three: find relevant income

Tracy's annual income is £6,257.14. This is adjusted for the relevant period by dividing by the number of days in the tax year, and multiplying by the number of days in the relevant period.

(£6,257.14 ÷ 365) x 165 = £2,828.57

Step four: compare income with the threshold for the relevant period

As Tracy receives both WTC and CTC, her annual threshold figure is £5,220. The threshold figure is also adjusted to cover the relevant period.

(£5,220 ÷ 365) x 165 = £2,359.73

Step five: calculate tax credit entitlement for the relevant period

Tracy has excess income of £468.84 (relevant income of £2,828.57 minus the threshold figure of £2,359.73).

Apply the taper of 37 per cent to this excess income.

37% x £468.84 = £173.47

Tracy's maximum tax credit (£7,557.86) will be reduced by this amount. Her total tax credit entitlement will be:

£7,557.86 – £173.47 = £7,384.39

The reduction is first applied to the elements of her WTC apart from the childcare element (ie, the basic element of £732.60 plus the lone parent element of £721.05 = £1453.65).

£1453.65 – £173.47 = £1,280.18

Tracy's tax credits for second 165 days will be made up as follows:

WTC (not including childcare element)	£1,280.18
Childcare element	£3,290.96
CTC	£2,813.25
Total tax credits	**£7,384.39**

Tracy's total tax credit entitlement for the second 165 days is therefore £7,384.39.

To find the weekly rate of payment, this figure is divided by 165 and multiplied by 7.

(£7,384.39 ÷ 165) x 7 = £313.27

Notes

1. **The relevant period**
   1 s5(1) TCA 2002
   2 s5(2) TCA 2002
   3 Reg 8(2) TC(ITDR) Regs
   4 Reg 7(2) TC(ITDR) Regs
   5 Reg 8(2) TC(ITDR) Regs

2. **The maximum amount of child tax credit**
   6 Reg 7 CTC Regs
   7 Regs 7 and 8 TC(ITDR) Regs
   8 Reg 7 CTC Regs
   9 Reg 8(1) and (2) CTC Regs
   10 Reg 8(1) and (3) CTC Regs

3. **The maximum amount of working tax credit**
   11 Reg 20 WTC(EMR) Regs
   12 Reg 15 WTC(EMR) Regs
   13 Regs 7 and 8 TC(ITDR) Regs
   14 Reg 20 WTC(EMR) Regs
   15 Reg 4 WTC(EMR) Regs
   16 Reg 3(2) WTC(EMR) Regs
   17 Reg 11(2) WTC(EMR) Regs
   18 Reg 11 WTC(EMR) Regs
   19 Reg 11 WTC(EMR) Regs
   20 Reg 3 WTC(EMR) Regs
   21 Reg 12 WTC(EMR) Regs
   22 Reg 10 WTC(EMR) Regs
   23 Reg 3 WTC(EMR) Regs
   24 Reg 9 WTC(EMR) Regs
   25 Reg 9(2) WTC(EMR) Regs
   26 Reg 9(8) WTC(EMR) Regs
   27 Reg 3 (3) WTC(EMR) Regs
   28 Reg 17 WTC(EMR) Regs
   29 Reg 3 (3) WTC(EMR) Regs
   30 Reg 18 WTC(EMR) Regs
   31 Reg 3 (3) WTC(EMR) Regs
   32 Reg 13 WTC(EMR) Regs

4. **The childcare element of working tax credit**
   33 Regs 3 and 13 WTC(EMR) Regs
   34 Reg 20(3) WTC(EMR)Regs
   35 Reg 14(1) WTC(EMR) Regs
   36 Reg 14(1) WTC(EMR) Regs
   37 Reg 20 WTC(EMR) Regs
   38 Reg 13(1) WTC(EMR) Regs
   39 Reg 13(4) WTC(EMR) Regs
   40 Reg 13(8) WTC(EMR) Regs
   41 Reg 14(3) WTC(EMR) Regs
   42 Reg 14(4) WTC(EMR) Regs
   43 s12(5) TCA 2002; Reg 14(2) WTC(EMR) Regs
   44 Art 2 TC(ACCP)S
   45 Art 5 TC(ACCP)S
   46 Arts 2 and 3 TC(ACCP)S
   47 Inland Revenue leaflet WTC5
   48 Reg 15 WTC(EMR) Regs
   49 Reg 7(3) TC(ITDR) Regs, steps 7-10

5. **How to calculate the amount of tax credit**
   50 Regs 7(3) and 8(3) TC(ITDR) Regs
   51 s7(3) TCA 2002; reg 5 TC(ITDR) Regs
   52 Reg 9 TC(ITDR) Regs
   53 ss7(2)and 13 TCA 2002; reg 4 TC(ITDR) Regs

Chapter 53

Income: tax credits

This chapter explains how to work out your annual income for child tax credit and working tax credit. It contains:

The amount of tax credit to which you are entitled depends on how much income you have. Chapter 52 explains how income affects the amount of tax credit you get. In general, most taxable income is taken into account in the assessment while non-taxable income is ignored, but there are exceptions. This chapter explains what income is taken into account and what income is disregarded.

For tax credits, your **savings or other capital** are not taken into account in the assessment, although interest or other income earned from savings or capital does count. There is no capital limit as there is for social security benefits. You are eligible for tax credits whatever the level of your capital.

In this chapter, unless otherwise stated, references to income-based jobseeker's allowance (JSA) are intended also to refer to joint-claim JSA.

1. Annual income

The assessment is always based on income over a full tax year – 6 April to 5 April – except during a time when you are getting income support (IS) or income-based jobseeker's allowance (JSA) (see below). If the tax credit award only runs for part of the year, the full year's income is reduced on a *pro-rata* basis as explained on p1365.

At the start of your claim, your tax credit is calculated based on income for the previous tax year (or previous year but one for awards in 2003/04[1]).

At the end of the tax year the Revenue finalises entitlement by comparing income over the year of the award ('current year's income') with that in the previous tax year. If the current year's income is less, final entitlement is based instead on the current year's income. If the current year's income is more than £2,500 higher than in the previous year, final entitlement is based instead on the current year's income less a disregard of £2,500. Thus your final entitlement may be less or more than the award originally made.

The original award can be revised during the year with the calculation based instead on an estimate of your current year's income if you tell the Revenue about the change in income.

Note: while you are on IS or income-based JSA, you are entitled to maximum tax credits without any income test, so the level of your income in the previous year or in the current year is not relevant. When IS or income-based JSA stops, the tax credit award is again based on annual income.

When you claim

When you claim, and you are claiming or reclaiming for all or part of the tax year 6 April 2005 to 5 April 2006, your award is based initially on your income for the year 6 April 2004 to 5 April 2005. This is the case even if you know at the outset that your income during the year of the award will be quite different. If your income in the previous year is too high to qualify for a tax credit, but you satisfy the other qualifying conditions, the decision will be to award a tax credit at a nil rate. If you think your income will be lower or significantly higher in the current year, you can ask for the award, including a nil-rate award, to be revised (see below).

If your income has changed since the previous year

Increases in income of £2,500 or less between the current and previous years do not affect your award and there is no need to tell the Revenue. Larger increases, or decreases however small, affect the level of your final entitlement to tax credit.

If you do not tell the Revenue about your change in income, your award continues at the same rate until the end of the tax year if other circumstances stay the same. At that point you must give full details when the Revenue sends you the Annual Review pack and it will recalculate your final entitlement for that year.

If you tell the Revenue during the year about your change in income, your award can be recalculated straightaway based on an estimate of the current year's income (less a disregard of £2,500 for increases above this level). This is advisable if you want to reduce the risk of overpayments (or underpayments) at the end of the year.

You can phone the Tax Credit Helpline or write to the Tax Credit Office to give them details of your current year's income (or you can pass it to a Revenue Enquiry Centre, Jobcentre Plus or other Department for Work and Pensions office). There is no special form to fill in so you need to take care that you give full details of *all* your (and your partner's) relevant income for the current year.

At the end of the tax year

At the end of the tax year, the Revenue finalises your entitlement. It sends you an Annual Review form to see whether your income in the current year is any different from that in the previous year.

The previous year means the tax year just ended – eg, 6 April 2004 to 5 April 2005 for awards in the tax year 6 April 2005 to 5 April 2006. (When tax credits were introduced, the previous year was taken to be 6 April 2001 to 5 April 2002 for awards in the tax year 6 April 2003 to 5 April 2004.)

Your final entitlement is based on:[2]

- the current year's income, if income in the current year is less than the previous year's income;
- the current year's income less £2,500 if income in the current year has gone up by more than £2,500;
- the previous year's income if income has stayed the same or gone up by no more than £2,500.

Example 1: Award in 2004/05

From 6 April 2003 to 5 April 2004 Izzy worked part time and earned a total of £5,000. Since then she has gone full time and earned £12,500 in the current year of the award from 6 April 2004 to 5 April 2005. Her tax credit award is initially based on income of £5,000. Final entitlement is based on income in the current year of the award less £2,500 – ie, £10,000. If she did not tell the Revenue at the start how much she expected to earn, she will have been overpaid tax credit.

Example 2: Award in 2005/06

From 6 April 2004 to 5 April 2005, Marsha and Bill, who are claiming as a couple, had total income of £16,000. In the current year of the award from 6 April 2005 to 5 April 2006, they earned £16,800. Their tax credit award is initially based on the previous year's income of £16,000. Because their income went up by just £800 in the current year – below the £2,500 threshold – their final entitlement is also based on income of £16,000.

Estimating income

There are no special rules for how to estimate income. Using payslips, benefit award letters etc, work out how much income you have already received in the current year and estimate how much you will receive for the remainder of the year. Tax credits are always worked out using annual income, so you must include all income received or estimated for the whole tax year, 6 April to 5 April, even if you are asking for an award to be adjusted partway through the year.

If you are self-employed, the Revenue's Self-assessment Helpline (0845 9000 444) can advise you how to work out your business profits. You need to estimate your profits for the accounting period relevant to the current tax year. This might be different from your current earnings, particularly if your accounting year-end is early in the tax year.

2. Whose income counts

If you are a member of a couple (see p1316), your partner's income is added to yours.[3] Otherwise, only your own income counts.

If you were part of a couple in the previous tax year but this year are single or a lone parent, only your income counts, not that of your former partner, even where the previous year's income is used in the assessment.

If you were single or a lone parent in the previous tax year but this year are part of a couple, it is your joint income that is assessed, whether entitlement is based on the current or previous tax year.

Children's income

Children's income is ignored. However, if you have transferred money under a trust to your child, income from that trust may still be treated as yours.[4]

3. What income counts

In general, taxable social security benefits are taken into account, and gross earnings (before tax and national insurance (NI)) and business profits are taken into account less your pension contributions. Most other income, such as pensions and interest on savings, is added together and taken into account only to the extent that the total exceeds £300 a year. The rules specify what income must be taken into account and what is disregarded.

If you have some special exemption or immunity from income tax, your income is calculated as though you were liable for tax.[5] People such as foreign military personnel based in the UK, officials of international organisations or consular staff may have such an exemption.

Types of income

Income to be taken into account falls into certain categories and within each category certain amounts may be disregarded. There is also a general list of income that is disregarded (see p1388).

The income taken into account in the assessment is worked out as follows.[6]

Add together your income, or your joint income if you are a couple, from these five categories:

- social security benefits (see p1377);

- income from employment (see p1379);
- taxable profits from self-employment (see p1382);
- student income (see p1383);
- miscellaneous income (see p1384).

Add together your income, or your joint income if you are a couple, from these five categories:

- pension income (see p1384);
- income from investments (see p1385);
- income from property (see p1386);
- foreign income (see p1387);
- notional income (see p1390).

If the total income in the last group of five categories is less than £300 it is ignored completely, otherwise deduct £300 and add the remainder to your income under the first group of five categories. **Note:** couples share one £300 disregard.[7]

This gives you the total income that is taken into account – subject to any disregards described later in this chapter.

Example

Mr and Mrs Killean renew their claim for child tax credit (CTC) and working tax credit (WTC) from April 2005. The Revenue assesses their claim on their joint income for the year 6 April 2004 to 5 April 2005. In 2004/05 Mrs Killean earned £13,500 before tax and NI contributions. Mr Killean received taxable long-term incapacity benefit (IB) totalling £4,500 and an occupational pension of £500. Income taken into account is:

Employment income £13,500

Incapacity benefit £4,500

Occupational pension £200 (ie, £500 less £300 disregard)

Total income £18,200

Benefits

Generally, benefits are taken into account if they are taxable and ignored if they are not. However, increases for child dependants, although not taxable themselves, are nevertheless taken into account if paid with a taxable benefit.

Disregarded benefits

The following benefits are disregarded:[8]

- age-related payment;[9]
- attendance allowance;
- back-to-work bonus;
- bereavement payment;
- child benefit;

- Christmas bonus;
- council tax benefit;
- disability living allowance;
- disabled person's tax credit;
- discretionary housing payment;
- an ex-gratia supplement to IB for those over pension age;
- guardian's allowance;
- housing benefit (HB);
- income support (IS), except to strikers;
- income-based jobseeker's allowance (JSA);
- industrial injuries benefit (except industrial death benefit);
- maternity allowance;
- pension credit (guarantee and savings credit);[10]
- severe disablement allowance;
- short-term lower rate incapacity benefit;
- social fund payments;
- transitional long-term IB (see p279);
- working families' tax credit;
- any payment to compensate you for the loss of IS, JSA or HB;
- any payment in lieu of milk tokens or vitamins;
- increases for a child[11] or adult dependant[12] paid with any of the above.

Tax credits themselves are disregarded. Statutory sick pay (SSP), statutory maternity pay (SMP), statutory adoption pay (SAP) and statutory paternity pay (SPP) are treated as employment income (see p1379). Retirement pensions and war pensions are treated as pension income (see p1384).

Benefits taken into account

Any benefits not in the list above are taken into account in full. This includes the following:

- bereavement allowance;
- carer's allowance (CA);
- contribution-based JSA (amounts above the 'taxable maximum' are ignored. In practice, you are not normally paid above this maximum so all your contribution-based JSA will be taken into account. Your annual statement from the Department for Work and Pensions (DWP) shows how much taxable JSA you have received);[13]
- long-term IB (but the non-taxable transitional long-term IB paid to those who transferred from invalidity benefit in 1995 is not taken into account);
- short-term higher rate IB;
- for the tax year 2001/02, widow's pension, widowed mother's allowance, widowed parent's allowance and industrial death benefit. From April 2003, these are treated as pension income and therefore attract the £300 annual

disregard. Although the Revenue regards widows' benefits paid in 2001/02 as social security income not pension income, arguably they should be treated as pensions;[14]
- increases for a child or adult dependant paid with the above.

It is the amount of benefit payable that is taken into account. Arrears of benefit or any ex-gratia payment in connection with a benefit are taken into account as income for the year in which the payment of arrears is made.[15]

Each year the DWP should give you a statement of the taxable benefits you received in the previous tax year. You can ask the local benefit office for a replacement if you did not get one. If you get any increase for a child dependant paid with CA or IB (or widowed mother's or widowed parent's allowance), this will not be included in the statement but it is taken into account as income so you should include it when completing your tax credit claim form.

Employment income

For tax credits, it is your **'gross'** pay that is taken into account.[16] This means your pay before any income tax or NI contributions are deducted.

Income counts whether received in the UK or elsewhere.[17]

What counts as employment income

'Employment income' means the following income received during the tax year:[18]

- 'any earnings from an office or employment received in the tax year'. This includes:[19]
  - wages;
  - fees;
  - bonuses;
  - commission;
  - overtime pay;
  - tips or gratuities;
  - goods or assets that can be converted into money – eg, gifts of drink, clothes, fuel, etc (the taxable value is shown on Form P9D or P11D which your employer gives you at the end of the tax year);
  - payments made on your behalf – eg, rent paid by your employer direct to your landlord (amounts are shown on Form P9D or P11D from your employer);
- taxable expenses (see p1380 for expenses that do not count as earnings);[20]
- any taxable cash voucher, non-cash voucher or credit token (eg, company credit card).[21] Vouchers that you spend on allowable expenses are ignored.[22] Disregard 15p a day from meals vouchers. (Taxable values are shown on Form P9D or P11D which your employer gives you at the end of the tax year.);[23]

- taxable payments in connection with the termination of your employment or with a change in your duties or wages, including non-statutory and statutory redundancy payments, pay in lieu of notice and employment tribunal awards for unfair dismissal above a total of £30,000. The first £30,000 of the total of such payments is ignored;[24]
- SSP;[25]
- SMP above £100 a week. The first £100 a week is ignored;[26]
- SPP and SAP above £100 a week;[27]
- strike pay from your trade union (even though this is non-taxable);[28]
- the cash equivalent of the benefit of a company car for private use and car fuel benefits if you earn £8,500 or more or you are a company director; these amounts are shown in Form P11D which your employer should give you.[29] Other expenses in connection with the car are ignored.[30] However, if you are a disabled employee with an adapted or automatic company car, the car is exempt from income tax and ignored for tax credits;[31]
- payments for agreeing to restrict your future conduct or activities;[32]
- taxable income from an employee share scheme (from 6 April 2003);[33]
- UK equivalent rate of a Brigade of Gurkhas voluntary settlement.[34]

Payments not counted as earnings

Some payments do not count as earnings and are disregarded in the tax credits assessment. In so far as they are exempt from income tax, ignore the following:[35]

- expenses incurred 'wholly, exclusively and necessarily' in the course of your employment.[36] **Note:** if you are a volunteer with a charity or voluntary organisation, all your expenses are ignored.[37] If you earn less than £8,500 a year, generally all your expenses are ignored. However, any that are taxable would be taken into account – eg, 'round sum' expense allowances payable irrespective of how you might spend it;[38]
- approved mileage allowance;[39]
- fixed-sum deductions for maintaining work tools;[40]
- homeworkers' additional household expenses (from 6 April 2003);[41]
- travel expenses, but not to and from work[42] unless you are a disabled employee or need transport home because of irregular late-night working or disrupted car sharing arrangements;[43]
- the first £8,000 of relocation expenses;[44]
- car parking payments for a space near your work;[45]
- the use of, or voucher for, sports or recreational facilities;[46]
- incidental overnight expenses up to a maximum of £5 a night in the UK (£10 overseas);[47]
- travel and subsistence allowance when public transport is disrupted by industrial action;[48]
- small gifts of goods or vouchers below £250 from a donor (who cannot be your employer) a year;[49]

- childcare voucher or credit token for 'relevant childcare' (see p1361);[50]
- 15p a day of meals vouchers.[51] The taxable value of meals vouchers that is taken into account for tax credits is shown on Form P9D or P11D from your employer. Vouchers for staff canteens are ignored;[52]
- a non-cash long service award of not more than £50 per year of service;[53]
- expenses for personal security;[54]
- an award under a staff suggestion scheme below the taxable limit;[55]
- any fees to approved professional bodies;[56]
- premium payments for professional indemnity insurance or towards liability claims made against you;[57]
- deduct from earnings or from a benefit or pension[58] any charity payments under a payroll giving scheme;[59]
- payment for work-related training or individual learning account training;[60]
- job grant, return to work credit, in-work credit or DWP payment under the Employment Retention and Advancement Scheme or Working Neighbourhoods Pilot;[61]
- payment of retraining course expenses for people leaving their employment (from 6 April 2003);[62]
- amount of salary given up under the Home Computer Initiative (from 6 April 2004);[63]
- travel, accommodation and subsistence costs for work outside the UK, including travel for a spouse and child where your absence lasts at least 60 days;[64]
- travel expenses for work inside the UK if you live outside the UK.[65]

Some groups of workers have special income tax exemptions; the following are ignored as earnings for tax credits:

- armed forces' travel facilities for going to and returning from leave;[66]
- armed forces' food, drink and mess allowances and reserve forces' training allowances;[67]
- free coal to miners, or former miners, or cash in lieu;[68]
- if you are an actor or performer, deduct from earnings the tax-free amount of agents' fees;[69]
- expenses for mainland transfers for offshore oil and gas workers;[70]
- Crown employees' foreign service allowance;[71]
- expenses of a minister of religion, including a rent deduction;[72]
- European Commission daily subsistence allowance to seconded national experts.[73]

Deduct pension contributions

Deduct any contributions you make to a personal or occupational pension that is approved by the Revenue.[74]

If you pay contributions through your employer, your P60 or P45 should show your wages after the contributions have been deducted, so there is no further deduction to make.

If you pay the pension contributions directly, deduct the gross annual contributions. Because tax relief is given on personal pension contributions, your actual contributions are less than the gross amount included in the pension plan. It is the higher gross amount that you should deduct from your employment income. Your pension provider should supply you with annual statements of contributions received.

If you have no income from employment but are still making pension contributions, deduct the contributions from any other income you may have.

Income from self-employment

Your taxable profits from any 'trade', 'profession' or 'vocation' are taken into account for the relevant year.[75] If you have a business partner, it is taxable profits from your share of the business income that count.[76] This includes trading outside the UK. It also includes profits from renting out property if this is conducted as a business. (If property income comes from a 'trade', then income counts without the £300 disregard that would otherwise apply to such income.) If renting property is not conducted as a business, see p1386.

Taxable profits are shown on your tax return for the relevant year. If you have not yet submitted a tax return, the notes that accompany the tax credit claim form (TC600) explain how to work out your profit. You should deduct allowable business expenses from annual turnover to arrive at a profit figure. The Revenue's Self-assessment Helpline (0845 9000 444) should be able to give advice. **Note:** the provision allowing artists, farmers and market gardeners to average out fluctuating profits across two tax years does not apply, and for them it is the actual taxable profit in the relevant year that counts.[77]

Business losses

If your business has made a loss, then your income is nil for that tax year unless you have other income that counts in the assessment. If you do have other income, you should deduct the amount of the loss from that income (from joint income if you are claiming as a couple).[78] If you do not have enough income to offset the full amount of the loss, any amount left over can be carried forward and deducted from profits of the same trade in the next and later tax years.

Deduct pension contributions

Deduct the gross amount of any contributions you make to an approved personal pension scheme or a retirement annuity (see p1381).

Student income

In general, student grants and loans are ignored in the tax credit assessment, with the exception of parts of the supplementary grant for dependants.

Student income taken into account

In England and Wales the following grants are taken into account:[79]

- adult dependants' grant;
- child dependants' grant (but not NHS grants for children) – ignore any additional allowance for the first child of a student eligible for the childcare grant and ignore the allowance for books, travel and equipment;
- lone parents' grant;
- two homes grant.

In Northern Ireland, any grants corresponding to those above are taken into account.

In Scotland, take into account:

- dependants' grant for adults;
- dependants' grant for children;
- lone parents' grant.

Student income disregarded

Apart from the grants above, other kinds of student support are ignored. For example, the following are disregarded:

- student loan;
- any supplementary grant from the local education authority or Student Awards Agency for Scotland (SAAS), except for those listed above;
- postgraduate award from research councils, the British Academy or SAAS;
- access funds;
- adult learners' grant;
- care to learn grant;
- childcare grant;
- career development loan, except any amount applied for or paid in respect of living expenses for the period supported by the loan;[80]
- education maintenance allowance;[81]
- English opportunity bursary;
- hardship funds;
- learner support funds;
- mature student's bursary;
- NHS bursary;
- Northern Irish higher education bursary;
- parents' learning allowance;
- 'scholarship', 'exhibition, bursary or any other similar educational endowment' if you are 'receiving full-time instruction' at an educational institution;[82]

- Scottish Executive Health Department bursary;
- social work bursary;
- Welsh National Assembly learning grant;
- young student's bursary;
- interest paid to you for an amount of student loan recovered then repaid by the Student Loan Company.[83]

Note that, unlike means-tested benefits, no students are excluded from WTC or CTC. So long as you satisfy the eligibility rules, you can qualify. Another key difference from means-tested benefits is that your student loan and most other student income is ignored in the assessment, so if you are eligible you may well qualify for a tax credit throughout the year, not just in the long vacations.

Miscellaneous income

Any income which does not fit into any of the other nine categories is taken into account if it is taxable under the Revenue 'sweep up' provisions found in Case VI of Schedule D of the Income and Corporation Taxes Act 1988.[84] This includes copyright royalties where your writing does not amount to a trade or profession, and certain life annuities arising from contracts made between March 1974 and January 1992.

Pension income

Pension income taken into account

Take into account the following pension income. The first £300 a year is ignored from the total of your pension and any income from savings, investments, property or foreign or notional income.

- **State retirement pensions** and **graduated retirement benefit.**[85] (**Note:** the Christmas bonus, age-related payment and winter fuel payment are ignored.) The Revenue says that as well as your pension, it takes into account any additional state pension, incapacity addition, adult dependant addition and child dependant addition paid with your pension.[86]
- **Personal and occupational pensions.**[87] It is the gross amount before tax is deducted that counts. Your pension provider should give you a certificate each year showing how much pension was paid and how much tax taken off. If you retired because of work-related illness or disability caused by injury on duty, only count the amount of pension that you would have been paid if you had retired on non-work-related ill-health grounds. Any extra amount paid is ignored.[88] Tax-free lump sums paid under a personal pension scheme, retirement annuity contract or tax exempt pension scheme are ignored completely.[89]
- **Widow's pension** and **widowed mother's** and **widowed parent's allowance** from April 2003, including any increases for a child or adult dependant.[90] For

2001/02, the Revenue treats these pensions and allowances as benefit income rather than pension income (see p1378).
- **Industrial death benefit** from April 2003. For 2001/02 this is treated as benefit income (see p1378).[91]

Pension income disregarded

Ignore the following **war pensions**:[92]
- war disablement pension including constant attendance allowance and mobility supplement;
- war widow's or widower's pension;
- annuity or additional pension to holders of the Victoria Cross, George Cross and certain other medals;
- wounds, injury or disablement pensions to members of the armed forces;
- death in service pensions for service in the armed forces or war injuries. If the death in service pension is overlapped by another pension, ignore an equivalent amount from the other pension;
- increase for a non-family dependant paid with a pension under the Service Pensions Order.

Investment income

There is no capital limit in the tax credit assessment as there is with means-tested benefits. The value of your savings is ignored completely. However, taxable *income* from savings and investments is taken into account. For example, the amount of savings in a bank account is ignored, but the interest on those savings is taken into account.

Investment income is taken into account as described below. The first £300 a year is ignored from the total of your investment income and any income from pensions or property, or foreign or notional income.

Investment income taken into account

Take into account the following amounts before tax is deducted:[93]
- interest on invested money, including outside the UK – eg, interest on savings in a bank account;[94]
- dividends from shares of a company resident in the UK (including the tax credit payable by the company with the dividend);[95]
- income from government stocks and bonds;[96]
- taxable payments from a life assurance policy, life annuity contract or capital redemption policy;[97]
- discounts on securities (ie, the profit from trading in securities such as government stocks and bonds);[98]
- payments from a trust;[99]
- payments from the estate of a deceased person;[100]
- interest arising from a debt owed to you.[101]

Investment income disregarded

Certain investment income is disregarded:

- interest, dividend or bonus from an ISA or TESSA;[102]
- any dividend on a PEP. If you have cash held in a PEP (rather than shares) you can withdraw up to £180 interest and this is disregarded. If you withdraw more than this, the whole amount of interest is taken into account;[103]
- interest or bonus from a share option-linked scheme in a certified contractual savings scheme;[104]
- income from savings certificates and tax reserve certificates;[105]
- £70 per tax year of interest on deposits with National Savings and Investments;[106]
- investment income from tax-exempt annual payments – eg, from a covenant;[107]
- winnings from betting, pools, lotteries and games with prizes;[108]
- interest on a £10,000 payment for a prisoner of the Japanese during WWII and interest on a compensation payment for a victim of the Nazis. In both cases the payment must be held alone in a separate account;[109]
- any Restore UK compensation payment for an unclaimed bank or building society account held by a Holocaust victim;[110]
- interest on damages awarded through the courts for personal injuries;[111]
- interest on Thalidomide Trust payments;[112]
- annuity payments under a Criminal Injuries Compensation Scheme award;[113]
- interest on the first £30,000 of a 'home income plan' loan taken out before 9 March 1999 to buy a life annuity;[114]
- interest on compensation to a child under 18 for the loss of a parent;[115]
- payments from the variant Creutzfeldt-Jakob disease government-funded trust, the Macfarlane Trusts, Independent Living Funds and the Eileen Trust. These are disregarded for the lifetime of the recipient, or for two years if paid to the disabled person's parent (or someone acting in place of a parent). If you inherit money from the estate of a disabled person who received such a payment, that inheritance is ignored, up to a maximum of the value of the original trust payment, for your lifetime if you were her/his partner or for two years if you were her/his parent;[116]
- capital element of a purchased life annuity.[117]

Property income

The capital value of the property is ignored but rental income from the property is taken into account unless this is exempt from tax under the 'rent-a-room-scheme'.[118] This scheme allows you to rent furnished accommodation in your own home earning up to £4,250 a year tax free.[119]

If you are not within the rent-a-room scheme – eg, you rent out a property that you do not live in yourself, the amount of rent taken into account is the same as that agreed for income tax purposes. You can deduct from the rent received, expenses wholly and exclusively incurred in running the property – eg, repairs, council tax (if you, rather than your tenant, are liable to pay), water charges, insurance premiums and mortgage interest (but not capital repayments of a mortgage).[120] You can offset any losses against property income in the following tax year.

The first £300 a year is ignored from the total of your property income and any pensions, investment income, foreign or notional income.

If you rent property as a business (eg, running a hotel or guesthouse), count this as income from self-employment (see p1382).[121]

Income from property outside the UK counts as 'foreign income' (see below).

Income from outside the UK

Although earnings from abroad are taken into account in the same way as UK earnings, other 'foreign income' – eg, from pensions, property or investments (other than taxable gains from an overseas insurer, which fall within the definition of 'investment income') – is taken into account subject to the following rules.[122]

The following are disregarded:[123]

- a banking charge or commission for converting currency to pounds sterling;[124]
- social security payments from outside the UK that are equivalent to tax-free UK benefits (see p1377);
- any German or Austrian annuity or pension paid for victims of Nazi persecution;
- one-tenth of the amount of any overseas pension or of a pension payable in the UK by the governments of certain countries;
- tax-free lump-sum payments under an overseas pension scheme;
- personal injury damages from a court outside the UK;
- certain education allowances payable to workers in the public sector of some countries outside the UK;
- property losses in one tax year that can be offset against property income in the following year;[125]
- income that you are prevented from transferring to the UK by law or by the government of the country where the income arises or because you cannot get foreign currency in that country; other income that remains abroad is counted.[126]

The first £300 a year is disregarded from the total of your 'foreign income' and any pensions, investment, property or notional income.

Income from outside the UK is still taken into account even if you would normally have tax relief on that income in the UK to avoid double taxation in both countries (such income is treated as though it were taxable in the UK in the normal way).[127]

Converting currency

If your income is in another currency, the Revenue converts it to pounds sterling using a 12-month average of exchange rates for the tax year in which the income is paid.[128] Where your tax credit award is based on an estimate of current year's income, the rate of conversion will be adjusted once the exchange rate average is available at the end of the tax year. These rates are published on the Revenue's website (see Appendix 1).

General income disregards

All of the following income is disregarded in the tax credit assessment.[129]

Employment and training programmes

Ignore the following income:

- New Deal 50-plus employment credit;[130]
- mandatory top-up payment on a New Deal voluntary sector option, environment task force option or under a written agreement for your participation in the intensive activity period of the New Deal 25 plus (or the pilots) or the preparation for employment programme (where these are not taxable as profits);[131]
- discretionary payment for special needs on a New Deal full-time education and training option;[132]
- childcare expenses while you are participating in training on a New Deal option, or on the intensive activity period of the New Deal pilots for 25 plus or a preparation for employment programme (where these are not taxable as profits);[133]
- travelling expenses, a living away from home allowance and a training grant if you are participating in training under section 2 of the Employment and Training Act 1973 or, in Scotland, under section 2 of the Enterprise and New Towns (Scotland) Act 1990 or, in Northern Ireland, under section 1 of the Employment and Training Act (Northern Ireland) 1950, or attending a course at an employment rehabilitation centre (where these are not taxable as profits);[134]
- if you are aged 25 or over and getting JSA while on a 'qualifying course', a discretionary payment to help meet your special needs;[135]
- a payment to a disabled person under section 2 of the Employment and Training Act 1973 or section 15 of the Disabled Persons (Employment) Act 1944 (or equivalent Northern Ireland Acts) to assist disabled people to get or keep employment;[136]
- education maintenance allowance;[137]
- training premium or discretionary payment paid to you by an employment zone contractor for your participation in an employment zone programme.[138]

See also p1381 for other disregarded credits and payments.

Maintenance and children

Any maintenance you receive from an ex-partner is ignored, whether it is paid under a court order or not. Any child support you receive from your child's other parent (who is not now your partner) is ignored.[139]

If you pay maintenance to your ex-husband or ex-wife and one of you was born before 6 April 1935, you may qualify for tax relief. An amount equal to these qualifying maintenance payments is disregarded from your income in the tax credit assessment.[140]

For income before 6 April 2003, a **fostering allowance** from a local authority, voluntary organisation or care authority is ignored so long as it does not count as taxable profits of a business.[141]

From 6 April 2003, if you foster a child placed with you by a local authority, independent fostering provider or, in Northern Ireland, an HSS trust, all your income from foster care (eg, the fostering allowance) is ignored, provided the annual amount is no more than £10,000 plus £200 a week for each child under 11 and £250 a week for each child aged 11 or over. If fostering income is over this limit, only the taxable amount is taken into account – ie, the amount above this limit or the actual net profit.[142]

Note: a foster child may not count as a member of your family for tax credits, so you may not get CTC for her/him (see p1319).

An **adoption allowance,**[143] **residence order allowance**[144] or special guardianship payment for a child who is a member of your household is ignored completely.

Other income

The following is ignored from your income:

- any contribution you make to an approved personal or occupational pension scheme (see p1381);[145]
- payments for fares to hospital;[146]
- payments to assist prison visits;[147]
- community care direct payments;[148]
- payments under the Supporting People programme;[149]
- payment or voucher for a former asylum seeker or dependant;[150]
- trade union provident benefits – eg, sickness or accident benefit or funeral payment;[151]
- payment for expenses incurred if you are an unpaid volunteer with a charity or voluntary organisation;[152]
- jury or witness payments if this is not compensation for loss of earnings or loss of benefit;[153]
- a payment to you for someone you are caring for temporarily made by a health authority, local authority, voluntary organisation, primary care trust or by the person themselves under the local authority's financial assessment, or, in Northern Ireland,[154] by a training school. This disregard only applies if the

payment would be tax free under the Revenue's 'rent-a-room' scheme which, in brief, allows you to rent a furnished room in your own home for up to £4,250 a year tax free;[155]

- any payment under an insurance policy taken out to insure against the risk of being unable to maintain mortgage repayments or other payments on a loan secured on your home. However, any payment you get above the amount you use to maintain the repayments plus the premiums on that policy or buildings insurance premiums required as a condition of the mortgage counts as your income;[156]
- any payment under an insurance policy taken out to insure against the risk of being unable to maintain repayments under a hire purchase, regulated or conditional sale agreement. However, any payment above the amount you use to maintain the repayments and the premiums on that policy counts as your income;[157]
- the gross amount of any 'gift aid' donation to charity;[158]
- a sports award for anything other than living expenses. Living expenses count as your income. Ignore parts of the award for dietary supplements and living away from home accommodation costs.[159]

4. Notional income

Sometimes you are treated as though you have income that you do not actually have. This is called **'notional income'**.[160] There are four kinds of notional income:

- income you have deprived yourself of to get or increase tax credits;
- income that would be available to you if you applied for it;
- a reasonable rate for work that you have done for less than the going rate;
- income you are treated as having through certain provisions for preventing tax avoidance or when tax law treats capital as income and charges it to income tax.

Deprivation of income

You are treated as having income you have deprived yourself of for the purpose of getting a tax credit or a higher tax credit.[161] See p1040 for details of when this rule might affect you.

Failing to apply for income

You are treated as having income that would become available to you if you applied for it.[162] This does not include:

- income under a trust set up from a personal injury payment;
- income from a personal pension scheme or retirement annuity contract;
- interest on damages awarded through the courts for personal injury;

- a rehabilitation allowance;
- Category A or B retirement pension;
- graduated retirement benefit;
- a deferred shared additional pension.

Cheap or unpaid labour

If you work or provide a service for less than the going rate, you are treated as getting a reasonable rate for the job if the person has the means to pay.[163]

This does not affect you if you are a volunteer and the Revenue is satisfied that it is reasonable for you to provide your services free of charge. Nor does it apply if you are on an employment or training programme under section 2 of the Employment and Training Act 1973 where no training allowance is payable (with the exception of the intensive activity period and preparation for employment programme).

Sometimes carers looking after disabled people have been expected to charge the person they care for under a similar provision affecting means-tested benefits. If you are in this position, see p986 for more details.

Preventing tax avoidance and treatment of capital as income

If income is treated as yours under certain prevention of tax avoidance provisions or where tax law treats capital as income, it also counts as your income for tax credits.[164] In general terms, this includes:

- if you rent property, taxable income when a tenant pays you a lump sum in lieu of rent under the terms of the lease;[165]
- profits from selling a certificate of deposit before maturity;[166]
- if you receive additional shares in lieu of a cash dividend, you are treated as receiving a taxable dividend;[167]
- a loan to you from, and written off by, a small company of which you are a director or in which you have a share or interest;[168]
- income under a trust that you have given to someone else but retained an interest in;[169]
- income under a trust transferred to your child;[170]
- undistributed income built up in a trust and paid out to you as a lump sum;[171]
- income left to you which is taxable during the administration of the will (shown on Revenue Form R185);[172]
- certain income from buying and selling stocks and shares;[173]
- assets transferred outside the UK to avoid tax and of which you will have the benefit;[174]
- certain offshore income gains;[175]
- profit from a tax-avoiding sale of land;[176]
- taxable profit from the discount on a relevant discounted security.[177]

Notes

1. Annual income
 1 Reg 3 TC(CTPA)O
 2 s7(3)(a) and (b) TCA 2002; reg 5 TC(ITDR) Regs

2. **Whose income counts**
 3 s7(5) TCA 2002
 4 Reg 14(2)(vi) TC(DCI) Regs

3. **What income counts**
 5 Reg 3(6) TC(DCI) Regs
 6 Reg 3(1) TC(DCI) Regs
 7 Reg 3(1) Step One TC(DCI) Regs
 8 Reg 7(3) TC(DCI) Regs
 9 s6 Age-Related Payments Act 2004
 10 PC paid under SPCA 2002 is by definition not counted as social security income under reg 7(1) TC(DCI) Regs
 11 Reg 7(4) TC(DCI) Regs
 12 Regulations make no mention of the treatment of increases for adults. However, these are non-taxable if paid with a non-taxable benefit and the intention is that tax credits follow suit. See Inland Revenue Schedule E Manual para 76102.
 13 Taxable maximum for a couple is the portion of the applicable amount that would be included for them if they were paid income-based JSA. For a single person, it is her/his age-related contribution-based JSA amount; s674 IT(EP)A 2003.
 14 Reg 5(1) TC(DCI) Regs is amended from 6 April 2003 by the Tax Credits (Definition and Calculation of Income)(Amendment) Regs 2003 SI No.732 to specify widows' benefits as pension income. However, it is arguable that the amendment should also apply to income from 2001/02.
 15 Reg 7(1)(c) and (d) TC(DCI) Regs
 16 Reg 4 TC(DCI) Regs
 17 Reg 4(1) TC(DCI) Regs
 18 Reg 4 TC(DCI) Regs
 19 Reg 2(2) TC(DCI) Regs; Inland Revenue Schedule E Manual, Vol 1, para SE00520; reg 4(1)(a) TC(DCI) Regs
 20 Reg 4(1)(b) TC(DCI) Regs
 21 Reg 4(1)(c)-(e) TC(DCI) Regs
 22 Reg 4(5) TC(DCI) Regs; ss362 and 363 IT(EP)A 2003; reg 4(4) Table 1 para 11D TC(DCI) Regs
 23 Reg 4(4) Table 1 para 8 TC(DCI) Regs
 24 Reg 4(1)(f) TC(DCI) Regs
 25 Reg 4(1)(g) TC(DCI) Regs
 26 Reg 4(1)(h) TC(DCI) Regs
 27 Reg 4(1)(h) TC(DCI) Regs
 28 Reg 4(1)(k) TC(DCI) Regs
 29 Reg 4(1)(i) TC(DCI) Regs
 30 Reg 4(4) Table 1 paras 14B, 14C and 14D TC(DCI) Regs
 31 Reg 4(4) Table 1 para 2B TC(DCI) Regs
 32 Reg 4(1)(j) TC(DCI) Regs
 33 Reg 4(1)(l) TC(DCI) Regs
 34 Reg 4(2A) and (2B) TC(DCI) Regs
 35 Reg 4(4) TC(DCI) Regs
 36 Reg 4(5) TC(DCI) Regs; s336 IT(EP)A 2003
 37 Reg 19 Table 7 para 1 TC(DCI) Regs
 38 Reg 4(1)(b) TC(DCI) Regs
 39 Reg 4(5) TC(DCI) Regs; s231 IT(EP)A 2003
 40 Reg 4(5) TC(DCI) Regs; s367 IT(EP)A 2003
 41 Reg 4(4) Table 1 para 17 TC(DCI) Regs
 42 Reg 4(5) TC(DCI) Regs; ss 337 and 338 IT(EP)A 2003
 43 Reg 4(4) Table 1 paras 2A and 2C TC(DCI) Regs
 44 Reg 4(4) Table 1 para 1 TC(DCI) Regs
 45 Reg 4(4) Table 1 para 4 TC(DCI) Regs
 46 Reg 4(4) Table 1 para 5 TC(DCI) Regs
 47 Reg 4(4) Table 1 para 6 TC(DCI) Regs
 48 Reg 4(4) Table 1 para 13 TC(DCI) Regs
 49 Reg 4(4) Table 1 para 14 TC(DCI) Regs
 50 Reg 4(4) Table 1 para 15 TC(DCI) Regs
 51 Reg 4(4) Table 1 para 8 TC(DCI) Regs
 52 Reg 4(4) Table 1 para 11E TC(DCI) Regs
 53 Reg 4(4) Table 1 para 10 TC(DCI) Regs
 54 Reg 4(5) TC(DCI) Regs; s377 IT(EP)A 2003
 55 Reg 4(4) Table 1 para 12 TC(DCI) Regs
 56 Reg 4(5) TC(DCI) Regs; s343 IT(EP)A 2003
 57 Reg 4(5) TC(DCI) Regs; s346 IT(EP)A 2003
 58 Regs 5(3) and 7(5A) TC(DCI) Regs
 59 Reg 4(5) TC(DCI) Regs; s713 IT(EP)A 2003

60 Reg 4(4) Table 1 para 11C TC(DCI) Regs
61 Reg 4(4) Table 1 para 14A TC(DCI) Regs
62 Reg 4(4) Table 1 para 18 TC(DCI) Regs
63 Reg 4(4) Table 1 para 19 TC(DCI) Regs
64 Reg 4(5) TC(DCI) Regs; ss370, 371 and 376 IT(EP)A 2003
65 Reg 4(5) TC(DCI) Regs; s373 IT(EP)A 2003
66 Reg 4(4) Table 1 para 3 TC(DCI) Regs
67 Reg 4(4) Table 1 para 7 TC(DCI) Regs
68 Regs 4(4) Table 1 para 9 and 5(2) Table 2 para 11 TC(DCI) Regs
69 Reg 4(5) TC(DCI) Regs; s352 IT(EP)A 2003
70 Reg 4(4) Table 1 para 11A TC(DCI) Regs
71 Reg 4(4) Table 1 para 11B TC(DCI) Regs
72 Reg 4(5) TC(DCI) Regs; s351 IT(EP)A 2003
73 Reg 4(4) Table 1 para 11 TC(DCI) Regs
74 Reg 3(7)(c) TC(DCI) Regs
75 Reg 6(a) TC(DCI) Regs
76 Reg 6(b) TC(DCI) Regs
77 Reg 6 TC(DCI) Regs
78 Reg 3(1) Step 4 TC(DCI) Regs
79 Reg 8 TC(DCI) Regs
80 Reg 19(c) Table 8 para 2 TC(DCI) Regs
81 Reg 19 Table 6 para 5(a) TC(DCI) Regs
82 Reg 9 TC(DCI) Regs
83 Reg 9 TC(DCI) Regs
84 Reg 18 TC(DCI) Regs
85 Reg 5(1)(a) TC(DCI) Regs
86 TC600 Notes
87 Reg 5(1)(b)-(m) TC(DCI) Regs
88 Reg 5(2) Table 2 para 9 TC(DCI) Regs
89 Reg 5(2) Table 2 para 10 TC(DCI) Regs
90 Reg 5(1)(a) TC(DCI) Regs
91 Reg 5(1)(a) TC(DCI) Regs
92 Reg 5(2) Table 2 paras 1-8 TC(DCI) Regs
93 Reg 10(1) TC(DCI) Regs
94 Reg 10(1)(a) TC(DCI) Regs
95 Reg 10(1)(d) TC(DCI) Regs
96 Reg 10(1)(c) TC(DCI) Regs
97 Reg 10(1)(e) TC(DCI) Regs
98 Reg 10(1)(b) TC(DCI) Regs
99 Reg 10(1)(a) TC(DCI) Regs
100 Reg 10(1)(a) TC(DCI) Regs
101 Reg 10(1)(a) TC(DCI) Regs
102 Reg 10(2)(a) Table 4 paras 1(b) and 2 TC(DCI) Regs
103 Reg 10(2)(a) Table 4 para 1(a) TC(DCI) Regs
104 Reg 10(2)(a) Table 4 para 3 TC(DCI) Regs
105 Reg 10(2)(c) TC(DCI) Regs
106 Reg 10(2)(d) TC(DCI) Regs
107 Reg 10(2)(e) TC(DCI) Regs
108 Reg 10(2)(a) Table 4 para 4 TC(DCI) Regs
109 Reg 10(2)(a) Table 4 paras 5 and 6 TC(DCI) Regs
110 Reg 10(2)(a) Table 4 para 7 TC(DCI) Regs
111 Reg 10(2)(a) Table 4 para 8 TC(DCI) Regs
112 TCTM para 4619
113 Reg 10(2)(a) Table 4 para 9 TC(DCI) Regs
114 Reg 10(2)(a) Table 4 para 10 TC(DCI) Regs
115 Reg 10(2)(a) Table 4 para 11 TC(DCI) Regs
116 Reg 10(2)(b) Table 5 TC(DCI) Regs
117 Reg 10(2)(a) Table 4 para 12 TC(DCI) Regs
118 Reg 11 TC(DCI) Regs
119 See Inland Revenue leaflet IR87 for information on the rent-a-room scheme
120 TCTM para 04700
121 TCTM para 04700
122 Reg 12(1) TC(DCI) Regs
123 Reg 12(3) TC(DCI) Regs
124 Reg 3(7)(a) TC(DCI) Regs
125 Reg 12(4) TC(DCI) Regs
126 Reg 3(3) TC(DCI) Regs
127 Reg 3(5A) TC(DCI) Regs
128 Reg 3(6A) TC(DCI) Regs
129 Reg 19 TC(DCI) Regs
130 Reg 19 Table 6 para 1 TC(DCI) Regs
131 Reg 19 Table 6 para 3 TC(DCI) Regs
132 Reg 19 Table 6 para 4 TC(DCI) Regs
133 Reg 19 Table 7 para 2(d) TC(DCI) Regs
134 Reg 19 Table 7 para 2(a)-(c) TC(DCI) Regs
135 Reg 19 Table 8 para 1 TC(DCI) Regs
136 Reg 19 Table 6 para 2 TC(DCI) Regs
137 Reg 19 Table 6 para 5 TC(DCI) Regs
138 Reg 19 Table 6 para 6 TC(DCI) Regs
139 Reg 19 Table 6 para 10 TC(DCI) Regs
140 Reg 19 Table 6 para 8 TC(DCI) Regs
141 Reg 19 Table 6 para 9 TC(DCI) Regs, as in force before the amendments in the Tax Credits (Miscellaneous Amendments No.2) Regulations 2003 SI No.2815
142 Reg 19 Table 6 para 9 TC(DCI) Regs
143 Reg 19 Table 6 para 11(a) TC(DCI) Regs
144 Reg 19 Table 6 para 11(b) TC(DCI) Regs
145 Reg 3(7)(c) TC(DCI) Regs
146 Reg 19 Table 6 para 12 TC(DCI) Regs
147 Reg 19 Table 6 para 13 TC(DCI) Regs
148 Reg 19 Table 6 para 14 TC(DCI) Regs
149 Reg 19 Table 6 para 14A TC(DCI) Regs
150 Reg 19 Table 6 para 15 TC(DCI) Regs
151 Reg 19 Table 6 para 16 TC(DCI) Regs
152 Reg 19 Table 7 para 1 TC(DCI) Regs
153 Reg 19 Table 8 para 6 TC(DCI) Regs

154 Reg 19 Table 8 para 4(b) TC(DCI) Regs
155 Reg 19 Table 8 paras 3 and 4 TC(DCI) Regs
156 Reg 19 Table 8 para 5(a) TC(DCI) Regs
157 Reg 19 Table 8 para 5(b) TC(DCI) Regs
158 Reg 3(7)(b) TC(DCI) Regs
159 Reg 19 Table 8 para 7 TC(DCI) Regs

4. **Notional income**
160 Reg 13 TC(DCI) Regs
161 Reg 15 TC(DCI) Regs
162 Reg 16 TC(DCI) Regs
163 Reg 17 TC(DCI) Regs
164 Reg 14 TC(DCI) Regs
165 Reg 14(2)(a)(i) TC(DCI) Regs
166 Reg 14(2)(a)(ii) TC(DCI) Regs
167 Reg 14(2)(a)(iii) TC(DCI) Regs
168 Reg 14(2)(a)(iv) TC(DCI) Regs
169 Reg 14(2)(a)(v) TC(DCI) Regs
170 Reg 14(2)(a)(vi) TC(DCI) Regs
171 Reg 14(2)(a)(vii) TC(DCI) Regs
172 Reg 14(2)(a)(viii) TC(DCI) Regs
173 Reg 14(2)(a)(ix)-(xi) TC(DCI) Regs
174 Reg 14(2)(a)(xii) and (xiii) TC(DCI) Regs
175 Reg 14(2)(a)(xiv) TC(DCI) Regs
176 Reg 14(2)(a)(xv) TC(DCI) Regs
177 Reg 14(2)(b) TC(DCI) Regs

Chapter 54

Claims, backdating and getting paid: tax credits

This chapter covers:

This chapter deals with who can claim child tax credit and working tax credit, how and when to make a claim, how your claim is dealt with and how you are paid. Tax credits are administered by the Revenue. Claims are dealt with by the Tax Credits Office.

1. Who should claim

You must be at least 16 years old to claim a tax credit.[1]

If you are a member of a married or unmarried couple, you must claim jointly with your partner. This is known as a 'joint claim'.[2] See p1331 for when you count as a member of a married or unmarried couple. Both partners must claim the tax credits jointly but there are special rules about who receives payment of the different tax credits. Note, however, that if you or your partner go abroad, either permanently or for more than a set period of time (see p1460), you will cease to be able to make a joint claim and instead must make a new claim as a single person. Failure to notify the Revenue of this may result in a penalty (see p1433).

If you are a single person, you make a 'single claim'.

If you have previously made a single or a joint claim for tax credits that leads to an award being made, and subsequently:

- if you made a joint claim, you are no longer part of a couple; *or*
- if you made a single claim, you are now part of a couple,

then your previous award ceases and you will need to make a new claim to reflect your new circumstances.[3] You should inform the Tax Credit Office about the changes within three months of the change taking place. Failure to do so could result in an overpayment being made. You could incur a financial penalty, or potentially lose out on tax credits to which you would otherwise be entitled.

Appointees

The following people can make a claim on your behalf if you are unable to make the claim yourself:[4]

- a receiver appointed by the Court of Protection with power to make a claim for tax credits on your behalf;
- in Scotland, a tutor, curator or other guardian acting or appointed in terms of law who is administering your estate;
- in Northern Ireland, a controller appointed by the High Court with power to make a tax credit claim on your behalf;
- a person who is your 'appointee' (see p1075) for social security purposes; *or*
- if there is no one who satisfies the above, a person aged 18 or over who applies to the Revenue in writing to act on your behalf and is appointed by the Revenue in that capacity.

2. How to make a claim

You have no entitlement to tax credits unless you make a claim.[5] You claim both child tax credit (CTC) and working tax credit (WTC) on one claim form. If you are entitled to receive pension credit (PC), in some circumstances you can be treated as having made a claim for CTC and do not have to fill in a claim form. This applies to you if, throughout the period from 22 August 2003 to 28 September 2003, you were:[6]

- in receipt of income support (IS);
- aged 60 or over;
- responsible for a child.

If this applies to you, you are deemed to have made a claim on 22 August 2003, for an 'initial decision' (see p1402) on your entitlement to CTC. For all other purposes, you will be treated as having made a claim for CTC on the first day of the benefit week beginning on or after 29 September 2003.

You must claim the tax credits in writing on form TC600, unless the above exception applies or you are renewing a claim (see p1399). In practice, the Revenue accepts written applications not on a claim form only in a few exceptional circumstances, although the Regulations provide discretion on this. You can obtain forms from Revenue enquiry centres, advice centres and directly from the Tax Credit Office (TCO – see Appendix 1), which can be contacted by telephone or in writing. The Revenue operates a Tax Credit Helpline service that can issue claim forms and answer questions about tax credits on 0845 300 3900 (0845 603 2000 in Northern Ireland), or if you have speech or hearing difficulties on 0845 300 3909 (0845 607 6078 in Northern Ireland). You can also make a claim online at the Revenue website (www.inlandrevenue.gov.uk/taxcredits).[7] An award of tax credits can be made on the basis of an online claim without you having to sign any document. This means that you should not, for example, make an online claim in order to find out whether you would be better off claiming CTC, as you cannot withdraw that claim once it has been decided.[8]

If you are just starting work after being unemployed, you can ask a Jobcentre Plus personal adviser to give you the form. Alternatively, you can obtain one from your local DWP office. Staff can help you complete the claim form.

If you have recently become sick or disabled there is a fast-track procedure that enables you to qualify for the disability element of WTC. For this to apply, you must have:

- recently become sick or disabled; *and*
- been receiving, for 20 weeks or more (this need not be a single continuous period as you can add together periods separated by eight weeks or less) statutory sick pay, occupational sick pay, short-term lower rate incapacity benefit, IS or national insurance credits because of incapacity for work. The last day of receipt must be no more than eight weeks before your WTC claim; *and*
- a disability which puts you at a disadvantage in getting a job that is likely to last for at least six months (see p1357 for more details); *and*
- gross earnings that are less than they were before the disability began by at least the greater of 20 per cent and £15 a week.

If you cannot complete all the details asked for on the claim form, you should phone the Helpline for further advice. You should send the completed claim form directly to the TCO in the pre-paid envelope provided with the claim form (or see Appendix 1 for the address). It is always best to return your form to the TCO. However, your claim may be sent instead, if necessary, to any Jobcentre Plus, DWP office or Revenue enquiry centre office.[9] Keep a copy of your claim form in case queries arise.

If you have sent your claim form to the Revenue and you later realise that the details on it need to be amended, you should contact the TCO as soon as possible. You can amend or withdraw your claim at any time before the claim has been decided.[10] Even if your claim has been decided, there are certain circumstances when your entitlement to tax credits can be amended. Once your claim has been decided and an award made, however, you cannot withdraw it.[11] For more details of when these changes in circumstances apply, see Chapter 55.

Information to support your claim

Your claim must contain all of the information requested on the claim form, unless the Revenue decides otherwise.[12] If you do not supply all the requested information, a decision may not be made on your claim until the required information is provided. If you need advice about the information required, contact the Helpline (see p1396).

National insurance number requirement

In particular, your claim must, in respect of each person for whom a claim is made, include:[13]

- her/his national insurance (NI) number plus information or evidence establishing that it is her/his NI number; *or*
- information or evidence to enable her/his NI number to be ascertained; *or*
- an application for an NI number to be allocated, with the necessary evidence or information to allow this.

Income

If you are receiving IS, income-based jobseeker's allowance or PC when you claim tax credits, you only need to inform the Revenue of this, and you do not need to provide any other income details.

Otherwise, when you make a claim for tax credits, you will need to provide details of your income during the previous tax year. If you are part of a couple and making a joint claim, your award is based on your joint income during the previous tax year, even in situations where you may not have been living as a couple during that previous tax year. For details of what counts as income, see Chapter 53.

If you think that your current tax year's income is going to be substantially different to the previous tax year's income, you should still complete the claim form with details of your previous tax year's income. When the Revenue makes a decision on your claim, you will be sent an award notice which tells you how to notify it of your estimated income for the current year. You can also request that your award be adjusted at any time during the year of the award. Where appropriate, the Revenue will then adjust your award of tax credits, using your estimated figure of your current year's income.

If you worked as an employee throughout the previous tax year, your P60 for that year will have details of your taxable income. If you received any payments in kind from your employer, you should have details of these on Form P9D or P11D, which your employer should give you. If you were self-employed throughout the previous tax year, you can use your tax return as the basis for your taxable income. If you were in receipt of taxable social security benefits, you should be able to obtain a statement of taxable benefit income from the DWP.

Bank account details

You are required to provide details of a bank, building society or post office card account into which the tax credits can be paid. This is because all payments of tax credits, with the exception of WTC for employees, are made into accounts. If you are a WTC claimant who is an employee, you will be paid by your employer, although the first few payments will usually be made directly into your bank account while your employer makes the necessary preparations. See p1404 for what happens if you do not have a bank or similar account.

Further information and evidence

The Revenue might need further information or evidence before making a decision (including one on a claim or on a revision). The information or evidence can be required from you or from your employer or childcare provider. If material is required, the Revenue gives notice to you (or another relevant person) that you are required to provide it within a specified time limit. In all cases except responses to final notices, you must be given at least 30 days. For responses to final notices there is an absolute time limit (see p1410).[14] The basic rule is that you can be required to provide any further information or evidence which the Revenue considers necessary. If you do not provide the material requested, you might be refused tax credit. If you provide incorrect information or fail to comply with requirements to provide information or evidence, you may be subject to a financial penalty or, in cases where you are considered to have acted fraudulently, a fine or imprisonment or both (see Chapter 42).

Renewing your claim

After 5 April the Revenue reviews all tax credit awards, including those where no award was put into payment because the amount awarded was too low, where there was a nil award because the claimant's income was too high or where the award ended before 5 April. This review process also invites you to renew your claim for tax credits. The Revenue will send you an annual review pack to allow it to review your claim and process your renewal claim. You can provide the Revenue with the information it asks for in the pack by returning the forms in the envelope provided, by registering to complete the forms online at the Revenue's website or by phoning the Tax Credits Helpline (see p1408).

Annual review

If you claimed tax credits for the tax year 2004/05, the Revenue should write to you between April and July 2005, enclosing an annual review form (TC603R). Unless you have an ongoing award of the family element only of CTC or a nil award, you should also receive an annual declaration form (TC603D – see p1400). Even if you did not actually receive any tax credits following your claim because your income was too high or the award too low, the Revenue should still write to you. While you are waiting for the forms to be sent to you and your renewal claim to be processed, you should continue to be paid tax credits at your existing rate.

If you made more than one claim for tax credits during the previous tax year (eg, because you separated from your partner during that year and had to make a new claim for tax credits as a single person), you will receive a separate annual review form and annual declaration form, if required, for each claim. If you are sent more than one set of forms covering different claims, you should reply to each separately, even if they both ask for the same information.

If the Revenue sends you an annual review form, but not an annual declaration form, you will be asked to check that all of the details on this form about your claim for the previous year are correct and to notify the Revenue of any changes of circumstances. You are also asked to confirm that your income for the tax year 2005/06 is likely to remain within the range indicated on the form. If your personal circumstances have not changed and you do not consider that your income in the coming tax year is likely to increase or drop below the amounts shown in your annual review form, you do not have to do anything further. You will then be deemed to have confirmed that all the details in the form are correct. The final decision on the award for 2004/05 and a new initial decision on an award for 2005/06 are as set out on the annual review form. However, you should always check the form and the notes accompanying it to see whether you need to return the forms.

If you do need to reply to the annual review form, you must do so by the date specified on the form. This will usually be 30 September 2005.

If you return your annual declaration after this but before 31 January 2006, and you have 'good cause' for returning it late, your renewal claim will be backdated to 6 April 2005.[15] 'Good cause' is not defined in the regulations. If you are returning your declaration late, you should explain why. However, this rule allowing late return of your declaration does not apply to you if:

- your previous claim was on the basis that you were single, and you are now a member of a couple; *or*
- your previous claim was made on the basis that you were a member of a couple, and you are now single.[16]

If the details set out on the forms sent to you about your claim and income are not correct and you fail to reply within the time allowed, you may not receive the correct amount of tax credit. If you are overpaid as a result, you may have to repay the overpayment. If you fail promptly to notify certain changes of circumstances, you may have to make a penalty payment(s) (see p1413).

Annual declaration

You may receive an annual declaration form (TC603D) which asks for details of your income in the previous tax year. Anyone whose 2004/05 award was more than just a family element of CTC or whose award ended before 5 April 2005 should get an annual declaration form.

If you are sent an annual declaration form you must always complete and return it by the date specified in the accompanying annual review form. This will usually be 30 September 2005. If you do not, your tax credit payments will stop, you may have to repay any overpaid tax credit and you may have to pay a penalty payment(s). You must also tell the Revenue of any changes in personal circumstances from those set out in the annual review form.

If, before this date, you do not know what your total income is for the period in question, you should not delay returning your forms. Instead, you should provide an estimate for the Revenue and then send details of your actual income as soon as you can. You must do this before 31 January 2006 or you may lose out on backdating (see below).

If you return your annual declaration form before the deadline (this will usually be 30 September 2005 for claims covering the tax year 2004/05), your renewal claim will be backdated to 6 April 2005. If you return your annual declaration after this but before 31 January 2006, and you have 'good cause' (see p1400) for returning it late, your renewal claim will be backdated to 6 April 2005.[17] However, this rule allowing late return of your declaration does not apply to you if:

- your previous claim was on the basis that you were single, and you are now a member of a couple; *or*
- your previous claim was made on the basis that you were a member of a couple, and you are now single.[18]

If you return your annual declaration form after 31 January 2006 you will only be able to backdate your claim for three months.

Final award notice

The Revenue aims to process your completed forms within 30 days of receiving them. You should receive a final notice confirming whether your award for 2004/05 was correct. If you did not have an annual declaration form to complete, the final notice is as set out in your annual review form (unless, having read your annual review form, you find that you have a change of circumstance to report, in which case the Revenue will send you details of your new award after it has dealt with the reported change).

The Revenue will also send you an initial award notice (TC602) setting out your award for the tax year 2005/06.

For information on what you can do if you are notified that you have been overpaid tax credits, see Chapter 56.

3. When to claim

You cannot make a claim for tax credits in advance of the tax year for which you are claiming.[19] The general rule is that claims for tax credits will run from the date they are received by the Revenue until the end of the tax year in which the claim is made.[20] Your claim can be backdated for a period of up to three months prior to the date it is received by the Revenue if you would have been entitled to tax credits throughout that period. Backdating is possible for a period of longer than three months where you become entitled to tax credit(s) following an award of disabilty living allowance or another qualifying benefit (see p1405).

Once a claim for tax credits has been made, it can automatically be renewed at the end of that tax year (see p1399).

4. How your claim is dealt with

Once you have made your claim for tax credits, the Revenue can make a decision on whether you are entitled to either of the tax credits, and if so, at what rate.[21] The Revenue may first require you, or your partner if you are making a joint claim, to provide any information or evidence that is needed to make a decision.[22]

You are notified of your award on form TC602. You are asked to check, sign and return this form. Failure to do so does not mean that you have not made a valid claim for tax credits, as returning this document is not necessary for a decision on entitlement to be made, or for an award to be paid. In particular, if you have submitted an online application for tax credits, you should not assume that failing to return this form has the effect of withdrawing or amending your application. No written signature is necessary for an online application to be complete.[23] You should, however, carefully check the information contained in the form before signing and returning it.

The first decision made after your claim is called the 'initial decision'. You can amend, orally or in writing, the details you have provided when making your claim at any time until the Revenue makes its initial decision and your date of claim will remain the same.

The initial decision is usually made on the basis of your circumstances at the date you make your claim and on your previous tax year's income. If your income or circumstances do not change, the award will run at the amount awarded on the initial decision until the end of the tax year. If the Revenue has not been able to make a decision on a new claim for tax credits by 6 April following a previous award of tax credits, your payment will continue at the previous rate until a decision on the new claim is made.[24] Certain changes in circumstances can mean that the initial decision will be changed. For more information on decisions and changes in circumstances, see Chapter 55.

5. Getting paid

As a general rule, the Revenue is responsible for making payments of tax credits, except if you are entitled to working tax credit (WTC) and working for an employer, in which case your employer will pay your WTC with your wages.[25]

In some cases, if you are entitled only to a small amount of tax credit(s), your award will be paid as a lump sum. This will apply to you if:[26]

- you are entitled to child tax credit (CTC) only, of less than £2 a week;
- you are entitled to be paid the childcare element of WTC (but no other element of WTC) and CTC together, and these come to less than £2 a week (this would occur, for example, where WTC, apart from the childcare element, is paid to your partner);
- you are entitled to WTC only, and the amount you are entitled to, not including any childcare element, is less than £2 a week;
- you have chosen to be paid CTC and WTC (not including the childcare element) at different intervals, *and*
  - the amount of any childcare element payable as part of your award plus your CTC is less than £2 a week; *or*
  - the amount of your WTC less any childcare element is less than £2 a week.

Who is paid

If you make a single claim, the general rule described above applies.

If you make a joint claim, CTC and the childcare element of WTC is paid to whoever is the 'main carer' of the children.[27] The **'main carer'** can be either you or your partner, depending on which one of you both of you agree should be paid CTC. If you and your partner are living at the same address and either you do not identify which one of you should be paid, or you cannot agree, the Revenue will decide. Where you and your partner are not currently living at the same address, or one of you is temporarily absent from that address, the Revenue will decide which of you will be paid.[28] If the main carer changes following an award of tax credits then the Revenue, if it considers it reasonable, can make the payments to that person instead.[29]

If you claim WTC as part of a joint claim and one of you is working, the payment of WTC (apart from any childcare amount payable) is made to the person who is engaged in full-time paid work (see Chapter 51). If you are both in full-time paid work you can decide who will receive the payment between you, or if you cannot agree, the Revenue will decide. If you both agree, you can write to the Revenue requesting that payment be made to the other person.[30]

If you make a joint claim and your partner subsequently dies, you will receive any outstanding amount of tax credits which would have been paid to your partner.[31]

If an appointee (see p1075) has claimed tax credits on your behalf, payment will be made to the appointee.

How and when payments are made

Payments of CTC, WTC if you are self-employed, and the childcare element of WTC are all usually made by direct credit transfer into a bank, building society (or similar) or post office card account.[32] The claim packs for tax credits should include a leaflet from the Financial Services Authority that explains the different types of account that you can open and how to do this. You can decide whether you want the payments to be made into your account every week or every four weeks, but CTC and the childcare element of WTC must be paid at the same time and at the same intervals.[33]

The post office card accounts have been phased in from April 2003 and if you would prefer to have your tax credit paid into this type of account the Revenue will pay you by girocheque until these accounts are available to everyone who wants one.

Where it is not considered appropriate for payments to be made into an account, the Revenue can decide on the manner and timing of payment by other means.[34] However, this will only take place in exceptional circumstances.[35] We understand that the Revenue may pay you by girocheque while your account is being set up or if there are problems with your account. There is a general rule that if details of an account are not supplied, your claim will cease until you supply the relevant details.[36] If you do not provide account details, the Revenue should write to you, giving you eight weeks to supply information on the account into which you want the tax credits to be paid. If you then require an authority from the Revenue to open an account, you will have three weeks from the date that the Revenue supplies you with the authority to provide details of your account. These periods can be extended if you have a 'reasonable excuse' for not being able to provide the details within the time limits.[37] 'Reasonable excuse' is not defined in the regulations. If you have not been able to provide details of an account within the time allowed, you should explain the reason.

If you are entitled to WTC and work for an employer, you will be paid WTC through your wage packet at the same time as your wages. Payments of WTC will be noted separately on your wage slip and the total WTC paid to you over the tax year will be entered on your P60.[38] If your employer fails to pay WTC, the Revenue can make payments directly to you.[39]*

Postponement of payment

Payment of tax credits may be postponed if you have lodged an appeal against a decision of the Revenue, or when there is an appeal for another tax credit claim lodged which may affect your own award.[40] The award may also be postponed if

* New claims from 7 November 2005 will be paid direct by the Revenue. By 1 April 2006, all WTC claimants will be paid direct by the Revenue rather than through the wage packet.

the details of the account into which you want the tax credits paid or your address appear to be incorrect.[41]

6. Backdating your claim

In general, your claim for tax credits can be backdated for up to three months (but see below), provided you would have satisfied the rules of entitlement throughout the three-month period.[42] The Revenue will look at your claim form for evidence of possible backdating. However, it is best to be clear and ask for your claim to be backdated to when you think your entitlement began (subject to the three-month limit).

If you were awarded tax credits but no payment was made because you failed to provide sufficient details of an account into which tax credits could be paid and you subsequently provide the necessary details, your award can be backdated for up to three months from the date that you supply the information.[43]

Backdating of your claim for tax credit(s) for more than three months is possible following an award of a disability benefit. This rule applies where your claim for tax credit is refused because you or a child included in your claim do not receive a qualifying disability benefit, and you notify the Revenue on your claim form that you have applied for a disability benefit. If that benefit is subsequently awarded, you should make a second tax credit claim within three months of the award of the disability benefit. Your tax credit claim will then be backdated to either the date that the disability benefit was awarded from or the date of your first tax credit claim, whichever is the later.[44]

Notes

NB You will not be able to backdate your claim to any day which is where the day to which you want to backdate your claim falls before 31 Dec 2006 *and* on that day, you were entitled to child amounts in your award of IS or income-based JSA.

1. **Who should claim**
 1 s3(3) TCA 2002
 2 s3(3)(a) and (8) TCA 2002
 3 s3(4) TCA 2002
 4 Regs 17 and 18 TC(CN) Regs

2. **How to make a claim**
 5 S3(1) TCA 2002
 6 Reg 2 Tax Credits Act 2002 (Child Tax Credit)(Transitional Provisions) Order 2003 SI No.2170
 7 Reg 3 TC(CN) Regs
 8 CIS/995/2004
 9 Reg 5(2) TC(CN) Regs
 10 Reg 5(7) TC(CN) Regs
 11 CIS/995/2004
 12 Reg 5(3) TC(CN) Regs
 13 Reg 5(4) TC(CN) Regs
 14 ss14, 15, 16, 17, 18, 19 and 22 TCA 2002; regs 30-33 TC(CN) Regs
 15 Reg 11 TC(CN) Regs
 16 Reg 11 TC(CN) Regs
 17 Reg 11 TC(CN) Regs
 18 Reg 11 TC(CN) Regs

3. **When to claim**
19 Reg 9 TC(CN) Regs
20 s5(2) TCA 2002

4. **How your claim is dealt with**
21 s14(1) TCA 2002
22 s14(2) TCA 2002
23 CIS/995/2004
24 s24(4) TCA; reg 7 TC(PB) Regs

5. **Getting paid**
25 ss24 and 25 TCA 2002
26 Reg 10 TC(PB) Regs
27 Reg 3 TC(PB) Regs
28 Reg 3(3) TC(PB) Regs
29 Reg 3(6) TC(PB) Regs
30 Reg 4 TC(PB) Regs
31 Reg 5 TC(PB) Regs
32 Reg 13(1) TC(PB) Regs
33 Reg 8(2) and (2A) TC(PB) Regs
34 Reg 9 TC(PB) Regs
35 Reg 14(3) TC(PB) Regs
36 Reg 14(1) TC(PB) Regs
37 Reg 14(4) TC(PB) Regs
38 Regs 4 and 6 Working Tax Credit (Payment by Employers) Regulations 2002 SI No.2172
39 Reg 6(14) WTC(PE) Regs
40 Reg 11(2) TC(PB) Regs
41 Reg 11(3) TC(PB) Regs

6. **Backdating your claim**
42 Reg 7 TC(CN) Regs
43 Reg 14(2) TC(PB) Regs
44 Regs 8, 26 and 26A TC(CN) Regs

Chapter 55

Decisions and changes in circumstances: tax credits

This chapter covers:

This chapter deals with the main tax credit decisions that are made on your claim – the initial and final decisions. Your award of tax credits may be affected by changes in your circumstances. This chapter also looks at those changes and when you should report them. This chapter does not deal with revisions or appeals (see Chapter 58), with how your tax credit award is calculated (see Chapter 52) or with decisions about penalties (see Chapter 57).

1. Making a decision

Decisions about tax credits are made by the Board of the Revenue[1] – not by the Secretary of State for Work and Pensions, who makes decisions about benefits (see p1180). In practice, decisions are made by civil servants in the Revenue.

The two main types of decision made on your claim are the initial decision and the final decision. The **initial decision** is made at the start of your claim, and is based on an estimate of what your tax credit entitlement is likely to be in the coming tax year (which runs from 6 April to 5 April). When the initial decision is made you are sent a tax credits award notice setting out your award. The **final decision** is made at the end of the tax year in which your claim is made. It is based on your actual circumstances during the year and thus is the decision that confirms what your entitlement actually was. Again, you are sent a tax credits award notice. In effect, therefore, you get two decisions on the same claim.

Unless the decision on your entitlement is changed either on **revision** or on **appeal**, the initial decision and the final decision are the only decisions on your claim that you will get. Revisions and appeals are described in Chapter 58.

Information and evidence

The Revenue requires certain information and evidence for making decisions. In individual cases, it might also need further information or evidence before making a decision. **Note:** if you do not supply such information, you might get an unfavourable decision. See p1398 for details of the information you may be required to provide. Also, if you provide incorrect information or fail to comply with requirements to provide information or evidence, you may be subject to a financial penalty or, in cases where you are considered to have acted fraudulently, a fine or imprisonment or both (see Chapter 57).

Delays, negligence and complaints

It is not possible to sue the Revenue for negligence in the way in which your claim is decided.[2] Instead, if a decision is wrong, you can seek a revision or appeal against it. The position is different if you are given wrong advice by an employee of the Revenue, in which case you may be able to seek compensation either through the courts or through the internal special payments scheme. See p1304 for information about seeking compensation.

If your claim has been received but not dealt with, ask why. If you are not satisfied with the explanation for the delay, make a **complaint** to the Revenue (see Chapter 47). You can also complain if, for example, you have been treated badly or your case has been mishandled. In some cases, it might be possible to seek a judicial review (see p1253). If there are unreasonable delays in processing your claim, you may be able to pursue a complaint with the Ombudsman.

If you disagree with a decision or your circumstances change

Most decisions about your entitlement to tax credits (including initial and final decisions) can be revised or appealed. If you think a decision is wrong you can seek a revision. You also have a right to appeal to a tribunal (see Chapter 58).

If you want to seek a revision or appeal against a decision, you should not delay. The time limit for appeals in particular is strict – normally 30 days. Some changes in your circumstances must be notified to the Revenue within three months or else you could be subject to a financial penalty. If you want your tax credit entitlement increased in full because of a change in your circumstances (other than a fall in your expected income), you normally have to report the change within three months (see p1413) if you want your increased entitlement backdated in full.

2. Contacting the Revenue

Writing to the Revenue is the best way to have your case dealt with. It ensures there is a permanent record of what you said and enables you to cover clearly all the points you want to make. Write to the Tax Credit Office that is handling your claim (the address should be on your tax credits award notice). Always put your name, address, the date and your national insurance (NI) number at the top of your letter as well as the type of tax credit your letter is about. Make it clear what it is you want to query, giving the date of the decision if this is relevant. Always try to make a copy of your letter. You should also keep all letters and forms sent to you. Such a record may help you or your adviser to work out later whether any decision can be challenged.

If there is a delay in getting a reply, you can telephone to find out why, but it may be better to write a short reminder and only telephone if you still receive no response.

On occasion, it may be necessary or preferable to telephone the Revenue. The Tax Credit Helpline number is 0845 300 3900 (0845 603 2000 in Northern Ireland). The textphone number is 0845 300 3909 (0845 607 6078 in Northern Ireland). If you telephone the Helpline:

- ask for the relevant section;
- be ready to give your surname, address and NI number;
- try to get the name and title of the person you speak to, as this may be useful in the future;
- make a brief note of what is said, together with the date.

If the information is important, follow up the telephone call with a letter confirming what was said so that any misunderstanding can be cleared up. Offices are usually reluctant to write merely to confirm a telephone conversation.

3. Initial decisions

On receiving an application for tax credits, the Revenue must make an initial decision as to whether an award should be made, and if so, the rate at which to award it.[3] The claim form for tax credits does not distinguish between child tax credit and working tax credit, so the Revenue must also decide on entitlement to both types of credit as well as the rate at which you are entitled.

The main evidence on which the initial decision is based is that on your claim form, unless you supply further evidence before the decision is made. You can be required to provide extra information or evidence (see p1398).

The evidence used is normally that which relates to your income in the tax year *previous* to the year in which you are claiming, but to your circumstances (eg, if you have a partner and/or children or if you are in full-time work) in the *current* tax year (ie, the one in which you are claiming). See Chapter 53 for more details about income.

You might want to have your initial decision based on your income in the current tax year – eg, because your income in the previous tax year was much higher. In such situations, we understand that the Revenue practice is still to make an initial decision based on your previous year's income, but then to revise it immediately when you give an estimate of what your income is likely to be in the current tax year. It can do this even where your entitlement on the previous year's income is nil, as the initial decision can be to make an award at a nil rate. Also, the Revenue can, if it wants to, make initial decisions using an estimate of income from *any* tax year.[4]

You must be notified of the initial decision. The notice must include the date on which it is given and your right of appeal against it.[5] If you had already claimed tax credits in the previous year, your initial decision for the coming year may be included in the final notice (see p1410).[6] See Chapter 58 for more information about appeals.

Once made, the initial decision sets the amount of tax credit you are due to receive for the remainder of the tax year until the final decision is made, unless it is changed on revision or appeal.

4. Final decisions

At the end of the tax year in which you claimed, the Revenue must make a final decision as to whether you were entitled to tax credit, and if you were, the amount of your award.[7] In effect, the final decision considers whether the initial decision on your claim was correct. Therefore the final decision can establish one of three things: that the initial decision was correct, that you were underpaid tax credit or you were overpaid tax credit.

Underpayments of tax credits are paid to you as a lump sum. **Overpayments** are usually recovered from you (for more information on overpayments, see Chapter 56). **Note:** you do not have the right of appeal against a decision that an overpayment is to be recovered from you. If you do not agree that you have been paid too much tax credit, it is important that you appeal against the lower award notified to you in the final decision.

The final decision is made in two main stages:

- A final notice is issued to gather information and evidence about what your income and circumstances were in the year.
- The information from the final notice is used to make a final decision on your entitlement for the year.

Final notice

At the end of the tax year in which you claimed, a final notice is sent to you. In the case of joint claims, the notice must be sent to all persons to whom the award was made (with separate copies of the notice if the Revenue considers that appropriate).[8] Your response to the final notice will form the basis of an automatic renewal of your claim for the following year (see p1402). The final notice may actually say what the final decision will be and when it will be made, unless you respond to the notice saying that the circumstances or income on which the decision is based are incorrect.

Regarding your circumstances during the year, the notice will either:

- require you to confirm that the circumstances taken into account by the Revenue which led to the award were correct. If they were not correct, you must specify in what way they were not correct; *or*
- inform you that unless you reply within the time allowed, you will be deemed to have confirmed that the circumstances were correct.[9]

For awards of tax credits covering the tax year 2004/05, you will usually be required to respond by 30 September 2005. However, if you reply after this, but before 31 January 2006, and you have 'good cause' for replying late, you may still be treated as having replied in time (see p1399).[10] 'Good cause' is not defined in the regulations. If you are replying late, you should explain why.

Current year's income

The final notice asks you about your current year's income – ie, your actual income for the year in which you have claimed. This is because your initial decision is usually based on your income in the previous year, and for the final decision the Revenue needs to check whether that proved an accurate forecast for the current year. It is therefore very important that you tell the Revenue if your actual current year's income is different from that used to make the initial decision, or any subsequent revision.

Sometimes (eg, if you are self-employed and cannot yet finalise your accounts) you may only be able to provide an estimate of your current year's income. The final notice allows for this.

You may be asked to make a declaration about your current year's income, or be informed that unless you respond you will be treated as having confirmed your income.

Specifically, you may be required:[11]

- to confirm that your current year's income was, or is estimated to be, the same as your previous year's income (as specified in the final notice); *or*
- to confirm that it was, or is estimated to be, lower than or no more than £2,500 higher than your previous year's income; *or*
- to state what your current year's income was or what your estimate of it is; *or*
- to declare that you were in receipt of income support, income-based jobseeker's allowance, minimum income guarantee or pension credit throughout the period of your award.

For awards of tax credits covering the tax year 2004/05, you will usually be required to respond by 30 September 2005. However, if you reply after this, but before 31 January 2006, and you have 'good cause' for replying late, you may still be treated as having replied in time (see p1399).[12] 'Good cause' is not defined in the regulations. If you are returning your declaration late, you should explain why.

Previous year's income

The final notice may ask you to confirm your previous year's income – ie, the income from the year previous to the year for which you have claimed. If it does so, you are either required to make a declaration, or are informed that the amount given in the final notice will be used unless you respond within the time allowed.[13]

Using estimated income

If you use an estimate of your current year's income, the final notice must inform you that your estimate will be treated as the actual amount of your current year's income, unless within the time allowed you state what it actually was.[14]

Responding to the final notice

Responses to the final notice must usually be on a form provided by the Revenue, although the Revenue can, if it wants, accept responses not on an official form. If you are unable to respond to the final notice (eg, because of illness) then responses can be accepted from receivers and people who are appointees for tax credit or benefit purposes.[15]

Final decision

The final decision is the decision on your actual entitlement to tax credits for the year. It is usually based on the information in your response to the final notice, but you can be required to provide extra information or evidence (see p1408).

Once a final notice has been issued, the Revenue must make a final decision. However, a final decision cannot be made before you have responded to the final notice, unless the time allowed for you to make such a response has passed. Once a final decision is made, it is usually the final decision on your entitlement for the tax year concerned unless it is changed either on revision or appeal (see Chapter 58). However, in addition to the usual revision and appeal rules, if you have responded to a final notice and a final decision has been made on or before the final date for your response, the final decision can be revised if you make a new response, as long as that new response is made on or before the final date your were given for your original response.[16]

You must be notified of a final decision.[17] However, your final notice may have said what the final decision will be and the date on which it will be made, unless you respond and say that the circumstances or income on which the decision is based are incorrect. Where you did not reply to such a final notice (eg, because there was no relevant change in your circumstances or income) the Revenue need not send you a separate notice of the final decision.[18] For more information about the way in which a final decision is made on your claim, see Chapter 54.

5. Change of circumstances after a claim

Your entitlement to tax credits depends on your family circumstances, childcare charges and your income. Changes to any of those during your award may lead to changes in your entitlement. If changes do affect your entitlement, this can be changed either soon after the change has occurred, or at the end of the year when the final decision is made and the Revenue makes a final check on your details. However, certain changes must be notified to the Revenue within three months or you may incur a penalty. Some other changes which increase your entitlement must be notified within three months if your increased award is to be backdated in full.

Once an initial decision has been made, there are three types of change which can affect your entitlement to tax credits:

- changes which must be notified to the Revenue;
- changes which affect your maximum entitlement to tax credits;
- changes in income.

Changes which must be notified to the Revenue

There are certain changes in circumstance about which you must notify the Revenue within three months of the date the change occurs. The requirement is that the notification is 'given' to the appropriate office (see p1417) within three months.[19] If you do not do this the Revenue may impose a financial penalty on you (see p1433). These changes are:

- you stop counting as a single claimant, or you stop being part of the couple in which you made a joint claim. In these circumstances, your tax credit entitlement comes to an end from the time the change occurred, and you must make a new claim; *or*
- you or your partner (if you have one) leave the UK permanently, or for more than eight weeks (12 weeks if the reason you had to leave was that you were ill, or a member of your family was ill or had died).[20] Again, in these circumstances your tax credit entitlement comes to an end and you must make a new claim (see p1460); *or*
- where you have made a claim for child tax credit (CTC) on or after 1 May 2004, you or your partner (if you have one) lose the right to reside in the UK. Note that this rule does not apply to cases where you are *treated* as making a claim by responding to a final notice.[21] If this rule applies to you, you are treated for tax credit purposes as though you were not in the UK. You are therefore no longer entitled to tax credits; *or*

- your weekly childcare costs either cease or reduce by £10 a week or more for four weeks in a row. For how your childcare costs are calculated, see p1360. If in doubt, notify the Revenue and give it the relevant details. You do not have to notify this change again if you have already notified it in advance (see p1417). The change in your entitlement takes effect from the first day of the week following the four weeks in a row in which the change occurred.[22] You may be overpaid tax credits and also liable to a penalty if you do not report the change within three months of the end of the four weeks in which your costs first reduced.

New relevant period

If any of these changes occur, the way your tax credits are calculated changes. All such changes mean that a new 'relevant period' is started from the time the change is treated as taking effect. This means that a new calculation of your entitlement for that period is made. See p1368 for details.

Changes which affect your maximum entitlement

There are certain other changes in circumstances which affect your maximum entitlement to tax credits – ie, they affect the tax credit elements to which you are entitled (see Chapter 52).

You do not have to notify the Revenue of these changes when they occur. If you choose to, you can notify instead at the end of the year when you are issued with your final notice. Some changes can be notified up to a week in advance (see p1417). However, most changes which *increase* your entitlement are only backdated for a maximum of three months from the time that you make the notification. The only exception concerns the disability and severe disability elements (see below). Changes that *decrease* your entitlement always take effect from the date of change, no matter when you notify the Revenue of them.[23] Delaying notifying these changes can, therefore, lead to you being underpaid or overpaid. Note that overpayments will usually be recovered from you (see Chapter 56).

The sorts of changes these rules apply to include:

- if you have a new baby, or another child joins your family;
- if one of your children leaves the family to live with someone else;
- if one of your children is given a custodial sentence of more than four months;
- if one of your children starts or stops full-time education after 1 September following her/his 16th birthday;
- if you change your employer or the number of hours you work;
- if your childcare costs increase by £10 or more a week for at least four weeks in a row. The change takes effect from the first week in which your costs increase, as long as you provide notification of the increase within three months of the first day of the first week in which the increase occurs. If you do not provide notification of the increase in your costs within that time, the change takes

effect from three months before the date that you do notify the Revenue.[24] You can report an increase of £10 or more a week as soon as one occurs, as long as you expect it to last for at least four weeks. For how your childcare costs are calculated, see p1360.

Entitlement to the disability or severe disability element of working tax credit

The rules on when your increased entitlement takes effect from are different in this circumstance. This applies where since your original claim for working tax credit, or since you asked for a revision to have the disability or severe disability element included in your claim, you have become entitled to a qualifying benefit which means you are now entitled to one or both of those elements. See p1405 regarding claims and p1441 regarding revisions.

Entitlement to the disability or severe disability element of child tax credit

A similar rule applies to CTC entitlement. If a child for whom you are responsible is awarded disability living allowance (DLA), you may be entitled to the severe disability element and/or the disability element with your award of CTC. This could increase the amount of CTC you get or mean that you now qualify for CTC when previously you had not qualified because your income was too high. See p1405 regarding claims and p1441 regarding revisions.

New relevant period

If any of these changes occur, the way your tax credits are calculated changes.[25] This is because they mean that a new 'relevant period' is started from the time the change is treated as taking effect. This means that a new calculation of your entitlement is made. For example, an increase in your childcare costs of the sort described above results in a new relevant period, so there will be a new calculation of your entitlement for the new period in which your childcare element is increased. See p1368 for details of the calculation.

Changes in income

The initial decision on your award of tax credit is usually based on your previous year's income. Your award can be changed to reflect:

- any expected fall in your annual income compared to that used to make the initial decision (eg, where your earnings fall during the year); *and*
- any expected rise in your income compared to that used to make the initial decision, where that rise is more than £2,500 a year.

Your award notice will advise you of what changes in income during the year will affect your award. Remember, though, the general rule is that any fall in your annual income can increase your award, but only an annual increase of more than £2,500 a year will decrease your award. See Chapter 53 for full details of how income affects your award.

You are not obliged to notify the Revenue during the year of your award that you expect your annual income either to fall, or to rise by more than £2,500 a year. It will require you to confirm your income for the year when it issues you with a final notice at the end of the year. The final decision that follows is about your entitlement for the whole year, so any underpayments or overpayments for the year are identified. However, you should consider carefully whether you should notify the Revenue during the year. Whether or not you are better off doing so will depend on your circumstances, and it is worth seeking advice. Consider the general points in the following two sections.

If you expect your annual income to fall

- If you notify the Revenue of this during the year, your tax credit award is increased. However, if you get housing benefit (HB) or council tax benefit (CTB), those benefits could be reduced as tax credits count as income (see Chapter 38).
- HB and CTB are based on the amount of tax credit you actually *receive*. At the end of the year it may turn out that your income did not fall as you predicted and, as a result, you have been overpaid tax credit, which you may have to repay. In these circumstances, HB and CTB are *not* increased for the period during which you were overpaid tax credit. Not only will you have been overpaid tax credit, you may have lost out on the additional HB and CTB which you would have been able to claim had you been receiving a lower award of tax credit.
- If you do *not* notify the Revenue of an expected fall in income during the year, your tax credit entitlement is not adjusted until the final decision at the end of the year. In this instance, you will have been underpaid tax credit for the year, and this will be paid to you as a lump sum. This lump sum counts as capital and is ignored for 52 weeks after you have received it. You will not, therefore, have been overpaid HB or CTB as a result of receiving these arrears. Lump sums of tax credit arrears can, in some circumstances, be disregarded for longer than 52 weeks, but only where the arrears arose as the result of an 'official error' (see p1035).

If you expect your annual income to rise by more than £2,500

- If you notify the Revenue of this during the year, your tax credit award is decreased. This may mean that you prevent an overpayment of tax credit building up further during the year (see Chapter 56). Your HB and CTB can then be increased to take account of the lower award of tax credit.
- If you do *not* notify the Revenue of such an expected rise in your income during the year, you will keep being paid the 'extra' tax credit during the year, and will incur an overpayment of tax credit. The overpaid tax credit is usually

recoverable from you by reduction in the tax credit you are paid in the following year, in which case your HB and CTB in that year are likely to increase.

- There is no penalty for incurring an overpayment of tax credit on the basis of an increase in income.
- All this, however, does not mean that you are always better off building up such an overpayment. You will not know for sure exactly how much you have been overpaid and at what rate it will be recovered from you until the final decision at the end of the year. Although the reduced tax credit entitlement in the following year may increase your HB and CTB, your increased earnings will also have the effect of reducing these benefits, and any further fluctuations in your income could complicate matters further.
- Ultimately, whether you are better off not notifying the Revenue of such an expected rise during the year will depend on matters such as how much the likely overpayment is, how recovery of that is likely to affect your HB and CTB in the next year, whether your income is likely to rise or fall again, and how comfortable you feel with building up a recoverable overpayment.

Notifying changes in circumstance

The notification may be given either orally or in writing. The rules also state that it must be given to an 'appropriate office', which is defined as an office of the Revenue or the DWP.[26] But in practice you should ensure that the Revenue has been informed, in order to be safe. The Revenue encourages claimants to telephone a Helpline if they have a query or want to report a change (see p1408). In practice, however, it is better to make the notification in writing to the Tax Credit Office of the Revenue and to keep a copy if you can. That way, you have a record of what you have said and when you said it.

Notification must be given by the person who claimed the tax credit. In joint claim cases, it can be given by either member of the couple.[27]

Some changes of circumstances can be notified up to a week in advance. These are:[28]

- if you have accepted an offer of work and expect to start work within seven days;
- if you have arranged childcare and will incur childcare costs during the current tax year;
- if there is going to be a change in your weekly childcare costs of £10 a week or more.

Your award can then be amended, provided that the change takes effect not more than seven days after the date you gave notification, and that it is within the current tax year.

You can amend the notification at any time before the initial award is revised, in which case the amended notification is taken as being notified at the time that your original notification was sent.[29]

Notes

1. **Making a decision**
1 s2 TCA 2002
2 *Jones v Department of Employment* [1989] QB 1 (CA)

3. **Initial decisions**
3 s14(1) TCA 2002
4 ss14(3) and 7(10) TCA 2002
5 s23 TCA 2002
6 S23(3) TCA 2002

4. **Final decisions**
7 s18 TCA 2002
8 s17(1) TCA 2002
9 s17(2) TCA 2002
10 Reg 11 TC(CN) Regs
11 s17(4) TCA 2002
12 Reg 11 TC(CN) Regs
13 s17(6) TCA 2002
14 s17(8) TCA 2002
15 Regs 34-36 TC(CN) Regs
16 s18 TCA 2002
17 s23 TCA 2002
18 s23(3) TCA 2002

5. **Change of circumstances after a claim**
19 ss6(3) and 32(3) TCA 2002; reg 21 TC(CN) Regs
20 Regs 3 and 4 TC(R) Regs
21 Reg 3 TC(R) Regs
22 Reg 16(5)(b) WTC(EMR) Regs
23 Regs 20 and 25 TC(CN) Regs
24 Reg 16(5)(a) WTC(EMR) Regs
25 Regs 7(2) and 8(2) TC(ITDR) Regs
26 Regs 22 and 2 TC(CN) Regs
27 Reg 23 TC(CN) Regs
28 Reg 27 TC(CN) Regs
29 Reg 24 TC(CN) Regs

Chapter 56

Overpayments of tax credits

This chapter covers all the rules about overpayments of tax credits. It contains:

For the rules on overpayments of benefits, see Chapter 41.

1. What is an overpayment of tax credits?

The main rules are the same for child tax credit (CTC) and working tax credit (WTC).[1] If you (and your partner, if you are making a joint claim) are paid more tax credit for a tax year than you are entitled to, that extra amount is regarded as an overpayment. The Revenue can decide to adjust your award during the year of your current tax credit award to prevent an overpayment building up (we call this an **'in-year overpayment'**), and/or recover all or some of the overpayment from you after the end of the tax year (we call this an **'end of year overpayment'**). There is no right of appeal, although you can appeal against a decision that your entitlement to tax credit has changed. This means that by challenging the new decision on your entitlement, you can in effect challenge the finding that there is an overpayment or challenge the amount of the overpayment.

When an overpayment occurs

There are a number of circumstances in which an overpayment can occur. The most likely are:

- Your income rises by more than £2,500 in the current tax year, compared to the previous tax year.
- You did not tell the Revenue in time about a change of circumstances reducing your entitlement (see p1413).
- The information you gave to the Revenue was incorrect.
- None of the above applies, but an overpayment occurred anyway because the Revenue made a mistake – ie, there was an 'official error'.

In-year overpayments

These are overpayments that arise during the year of your current tax credit award. They are sometimes also referred to as 'likely overpayments' (and sometimes are not referred to as overpayments at all). This is because, strictly speaking, they do not become actual overpayments until the end of the tax year (ie, become 'end of year overpayments'), when the Revenue finalises your award. Decisions on in-year overpayments can be made during the course of the tax year concerned, in the following circumstances:[2]

- If the Revenue thinks that there is likely to be an overpayment, it can adjust the award (or an award of another tax credit) in order to reduce or wipe out the overpayment. This may mean that your award is reduced for the rest of the year. If the Revenue thinks that you have already been paid all of the tax credits to which you are likely to be entitled for the whole year, it may stop paying you altogether.[3]
- If an award is terminated on the grounds that you did not satisfy the basic conditions for entitlement, the Revenue may decide that the amount already paid to you, or some of it, is to be regarded as an overpayment. The basic conditions of entitlement are, for CTC, that you are responsible for a child (see p1316) and, for WTC, that you are engaged in full-time work (see p1343).

End of year overpayments

These are overpayments that are identified at or after the end of the tax year concerned – ie, after your award for that year has been finalised.

The Revenue can decide that there has been an end of year overpayment when it makes any of the following decisions:[4]

- a final decision (see p1410);
- an enquiry decision (see p1444);
- a decision on discovery (see p1445);
- a revision for official error (see p1446).

Notification of overpayments

To decide that you have been overpaid, the Revenue must change the decision on your entitlement to tax credits. When it makes a new decision on your entitlement, it must notify you of the new decision.[5] Remember that you have the right of appeal against any decision regarding the amount of your entitlement to tax credit (see p1447). So if you think that the new decision on your entitlement is wrong, and that therefore you have not been overpaid as much as the Revenue says, or that you have not been overpaid at all, appeal against the new decision on your entitlement. If your appeal against the new decision on your entitlement is outside the 30-day time limit because you did not realise that you needed to appeal until you received a detailed calculation, the Revenue says that it will regard that as a reasonable excuse for the appeal being late.[6]

You may only find out about an **in-year overpayment** when the Revenue writes to you to say that your entitlement has changed and your payment has been adjusted. If the Revenue is going to recover an **end of year overpayment** from you, it must also give you notice of that, how much it is and how it is to be recovered from you. It usually does this at the same time as it writes to you about the final decision on your entitlement for the tax year. There is no right of appeal against the decision to recover an overpayment.[7] For what you can do, see p1425.

2. Recovery of overpayments

The basic rule is that the Revenue can recover all or part of any overpayment, even those caused by official error.

The Revenue can recover the overpayment by:

- adjusting your current award, in the case of an in-year overpayment; *and*
- requiring you to repay the overpayment, in the case of an end of year overpayment.

However, it does not have to recover an overpayment, and should exercise discretion, especially in cases of official error or hardship – see p1424. You must be given notice that you must repay an end of year overpayment. The notice must also say how much the overpayment is, and how it is to be recovered from you.[8] There is no right of appeal against the decision to recover an overpayment.[9] For what you can do, see p1425.

Also, the Revenue does not ask you if recovering an overpayment will cause you hardship, or if you think the overpayment should not be recovered from you. Instead, you have to tell it about such things. It is therefore important to contact the Revenue as soon as possible.

Overpayments and award notices

When an overpayment is recovered from you, the tax credit award notices that the Revenue sends out can be very complicated. This is especially so where you are also being paid 'additional payments' (see p1422). You can request a form (Form TC647) from the Revenue which gives more detail about how your payment has been worked out. Where it is still unclear, you can write to the Tax Credit Office (its address will be at the top of the award notice) requesting a 'tailored reply'. If your appeal against the new decision on your entitlement is outside the 30-day time limit because you did not realise that you needed to appeal until you received a detailed calculation, the Revenue says that it will regard that as a reasonable excuse for the appeal being late.[10]

If you still do not receive a satisfactory response, consider taking up the matter with your MP, or making a complaint (see Chapter 47).

From whom can an overpayment be recovered?

An end of year overpayment can be recovered from the person or persons to whom the tax credit award was made. This means:[11]

- if you made a single claim (ie, as a single person), the overpayment can be recovered from you;
- if you made a joint claim with your partner, the overpayment can be recovered from one or both of you. The Revenue can decide that each of you should pay a specified amount.

How much is recoverable

In-year overpayments

To recover an in-year overpayment, the Revenue adjusts the amount you are paid during the year, so that you receive less money. The adjustment it can make to your award may be to reduce the overpayment, or wipe it out altogether. There are no official limits to the amount by which your award can be reduced. Remember that you can appeal against any new decision on your entitlement (see p1447).

Official guidance says that the Revenue will 'normally' adjust your award.[12] This is even the case where **official error** or **hardship** is involved. In such cases, however, the Revenue will consider making 'additional payments' (see p1422).

End of year overpayments

The Revenue may recover all or part of an end of year overpayment, but does not have to.[13] Normally though, it wants to recover all of the overpayment. The main exception to this is where **official error** or **hardship** is involved (see p1424). However, if for any reason you think you will have difficulty repaying, tell the Revenue this and ask it to use its discretion not to recover all or some of the overpayment. It may be worth checking that the overpayment has been calculated correctly, especially if you are doubtful of the figures that have been used or do not understand how it has been worked out. Remember that you can appeal against any decision on your entitlement (see p1447). Seek advice (see Appendix 2) if you think you may need help with any of this.

Additional payments

If the Revenue adjusts your award to recover an in-year overpayment, it can pay you additional payments to bring your payments back nearer to the level they would have been had your award not been adjusted.

Official guidance sets out circumstances in which additional payments will and will not be made.[14] This guidance is not the law, and if you think that the Revenue has not exercised its discretion properly in adjusting your award, or in its decision about making additional payments, tell it so and ask it to exercise its discretion. If you remain unhappy, seek further advice (see Appendix 2), and consider making a complaint (see Chapter 47).

According to the official guidance,[15] the Revenue will not make additional tax credit payments if:

- your award is the family element of child tax credit (CTC) only; *or*
- your award has been adjusted because you have reported a rise in your income of £2,500 a year or more; *or*
- your award has been adjusted because the Revenue says there is something wrong with the information you provided about your claim (eg, where you deliberately supplied false information).

Again, according to the guidance,[16] the Revenue will make additional tax credit payments if your award has been reduced because of an in-year overpayment, and you ask for the Revenue to review your payments. The guidance says that additional payments will be made if:

- you are receiving income support or jobseeker's allowance and your CTC award has been adjusted. The additional payments will mean that your CTC is at least 90 per cent of what it would have been without the adjustment;
- your tax credit award includes a disability element, or you are entitled to maximum tax credits (working tax credit or CTC). The additional payments will mean that your award is at least 75 per cent of what it would have been without the adjustment;
- neither of the two bullets above apply. The additional payments will mean that your award is at least 50 per cent of what it would have been without the adjustment.

However, there is nothing in the law to say that the Revenue cannot make additional payments at a higher level. You could, for example, ask them to make additional payments to bring your award back to 100 per cent – ie, what it would have been without the adjustment.

If you get additional payments

If you get additional payments, when your award for the year is finalised, the Revenue will say that you have an end of year overpayment.[17] You can ask the Revenue not to recover the overpayment from you. You will have strong grounds for this if recovery of the overpayment would cause you hardship or if the overpayment actually resulted from an official error (see p1424), especially where the Revenue already accepted this during the year, when making the additional payments.

For the effect of additional payments on any means-tested benefit you receive, see p971. Additional payments do not affect non-means-tested benefits.

Official error and hardship

If an overpayment has been caused by official error, or where recovery would cause hardship, the Revenue may decide not to recover all or part of an overpayment.

These decisions are discretionary and do not carry the right of appeal. You need to explain your circumstances and ask the Revenue to exercise its discretion in your favour. If you remain unhappy with the decision, see p1425 for what you can do.

'Official error' is not defined for these purposes, but the official guidance is that the Revenue will not ask you to repay an overpayment if:

- the overpayment occured because of a mistake by the Revenue, *and*
- you could reasonably have thought that your award was right.[18]

For example, if you tell the Revenue about a change and it does not act upon it within 30 working days, and it was reasonable for you to think that your tax credit award was correct, then it will not ask you to repay any overpayment that results. On the other hand, if you are overpaid because the Revenue thinks you have got more children than you actually have, then it will expect you to notice that on your award notice and inform it. All will depend on the circumstances. Explain to the Revenue exactly what you did and why you assumed that your award was correct.

'Hardship' is not defined either, but the official guidance lists the following as the sort of things the Revenue will take into account in considering whether you may be in hardship:[19]

- your income and living expenses;
- savings, investments, etc.;
- other debts that you might have – eg, rent arrears, repayment of social security overpayments;
- other payments you are due to make to the Revenue;
- how long it would take you to repay the overpayment;
- your previous payment history;
- whether repaying would mean you could not afford essentials like gas, electricity or water;
- whether you have children aged under 5, or a chronically sick or disabled person in the family whose health could suffer;
- any other relevant factors.

Again, all will depend on the circumstances. It is in your interest to show the Revenue how repayment would cause you hardship.

How the overpayment is recovered

The Revenue recovers **in-year overpayments** by adjusting your payments during the year, so that you receive less money. You should be notified of the new decison on your entitlement.[20] There are no official limits to the amount by which your award can be reduced.

If the Revenue requires you (and/or your partner, if you have a joint claim) to repay an **end of year overpayment**, it must notify you (and your partner if it is also being recovered from her/him) of the amount to be repaid, and how the overpayment is to be repaid.[21]

There are two main ways in which it can require you to repay:[22]

- deductions from ongoing payments of any tax credit (see below) – this is the Revenue's preferred method of repayment;
- directly to the Revenue, due from 30 days of being given notice of the amount of the overpayment. You may pay in 12 monthly instalments if you wish.

Deductions from ongoing payments

If the Revenue asks you to repay an end of year overpayment by reducing the tax credit award you have for the current year, the *maximum* amounts by which it can reduce your award are:[23]

- 10 per cent of the award if you are receiving the maximum tax credits to which you could be entitled;
- 100 per cent of the award if you receive only the family element of CTC;
- 25 per cent of the award if neither of the above two bullet points apply.

Note that these are maximum amounts. If you accept that you should repay but cannot afford to repay at these rates, you should contact the Revenue and ask it to accept repayment at a lower rate. In order to persuade the Revenue, you may need to show why it would cause you hardship (see p1424 for how the Revenue defines that) to pay at the maximum rate. Even then, the Revenue is likely to pay you additional payments (see p1422) rather than use a lower rate.

Different parts of the overpayment can be recovered using different methods of recovery, as described above. Revised notices of overpayments, changing the method of recovery, can be issued at any time.[24]

Challenging recovery and negotiating repayment

Challenging recovery

There is no right of appeal against a decision to recover an overpayment. However, you do have the right of appeal against a decision on your entitlement to tax credits, including the amount of your entitlement. Do not assume that the Revenue always gets decisions on your entitlement right. If you have been overpaid and are unclear why, check the decisions about your entitlement (see p1421 for more on this). For more on appeals, see p1447.

You can ask the Revenue to use its discretion not to recover an overpayment. The official guidance suggests that the Revenue only considers this regarding end of year overpayments, but you can also ask it not to recover an in-year overpayment.

The Revenue is only likely not to recover an overpayment in cases involving official error or hardship (for more about those, see p1424). For in-year overpayments, the Revenue is likely to insist on reducing your award at least by some amount. The Revenue does not tell you about your ability to ask them not to take recovery action. However, you can contact the tax credit helpline to request an official form (Form TC846) on which you can ask them not to recover an overpayment. You do not have to use the form.

The only way to make a legal challenge to a decision to insist on recovering an overpayment is by judicial review in the courts. Usually, judicial review is only possible in extreme cases – eg, where the Revenue insists on making you repay an overpayment that was clearly caused by an official error, you could not reasonably have known that you were being overpaid, and there is some urgency in the need to make the Revenue change its decision. For more about judicial review, see p1253.

The only other way of making the Revenue change its mind is via complaints. You first need to use the Revenue's own complaints procedure. If you remain dissatisfied, you can complain to the Independent Adjudicator or to the Parliamentary Ombudsman (see Appendix 1 for the addresses and Chapter 47 for the details of making a complaint). They can recommend action and order financial compensation, but both are likely to take time to complete their investigaton. Both the Adjudicator and the Ombudsman can deal with complaints about tax credits, but it may be most appropriate to go to the Adjudicator with complaints about the Revenue's use of discretion (eg, on whether to recover an overpayment), and the Ombudsman about maladministration (eg, severe delays).

Negotiating repayment

If you do have to repay, then, except for cases involving official error or hardship (see p1424), the Revenue is unlikely to reduce the amount of the overpayment it is recovering from you. However, if you have difficulty repaying, the Revenue may agree to you repaying the overpayment over a longer period than normal, by making an repayment instalment plan. Contact the helpline at the number shown on your end of year notice, notice to pay, reminder or other letter about your overpayment. Usually, the Revenue would look to you paying something straight away, and the rest over a later period. It will take into account all the relevant circumstances, including your income, savings, other debts and outgoings.

Other methods of recovery

If the Revenue is not satisfied with recovery using the methods described above, including agreeing a repayment instalment plan with you, then it will consider taking legal action. If you miss a payment, the Revenue will contact you to remind you – official guidance says that it will do this twice before taking further action.[25] Further action will follow if the Revenue considers that you are refusing to repay, or neglecting to keep to an agreement to repay. All the circumstances will be taken into account before taking such action, but the Revenue may:[26]

- seize and sell your personal possessions. However, *unless you let the Revenue into your property*, authorised Revenue officers cannot enter your home and seize your personal possessions unless they have a warrant from the court; *or*
- take court action against you, including bankruptcy proceedings.

3. Interest on overpayments

In certain circumstances, the Revenue can add interest to the overpayment, with the effect of increasing the amount you have to repay.

When interest is added

Interest may be added to an overpayment being recovered from you (and/or your partner if you have a joint claim) if the Revenue considers that the overpayment is due to 'fraud or neglect' on the part of you (and/or your partner).[27]

If interest is added, it is added from 30 days after whichever of the following dates apply:[28]

- where you (or your partner) were treated during the tax year concerned as being overpaid due to termination of your award because of not satisfying the basic conditions of entitlement (see p1420), the date of the decision terminating the award; *or*
- if that did not apply, the date in the final notice that you were given until to confirm your actual income for the tax year.

When added to the overpayment, the interest is treated as if it were part of the overpayment. This means that it is subject to the same rules as the overpayment itself.[29]

How much interest is added

The amount of interest added to the penalty is 6.5 per cent a year or, if that is different from the average lending rate of the main banks, the bank lending rate plus 2.5 per cent.[30]

Challenging an interest decision

Decisions adding interest to an overpayment carry the right of appeal. For example, you might wish to argue on appeal that you did not act fradulently or negligently, or that the amount of the interest is wrong. You (and/or your partner if s/he is subject to the decision) must be given notice of a decision adding interest to an overpayment. The notice must be dated and include details of your right of appeal against the decision.[31] See Chapter 58 for appeals.

Notes

1. **What is an overpayment of tax credits?**
 1 s28 TCA 2002
 2 s28(5) and (6) TCA 2002; Inland Revenue Code of Practice COP 26, *What Happens if We Have Paid You Too Much Tax Credit*, p2
 3 Inland Revenue Code of Practice COP 26, *What Happens if We Have Paid You Too Much Tax Credit*, p2
 4 s28(1) TCA 2002
 5 s23 TCA 2002
 6 Inland Revenue Code of Practice COP 26, *What Happens if We Have Paid You Too Much Tax Credit*, p4
 7 ss29(1) and (2)and 38 TCA 2002

2. **Recovery of overpayments**
 8 ss28(1) and 29 TCA 2002
 9 s38 TCA 2002
 10 Inland Revenue Code of Practice COP 26, *What Happens if We Have Paid You Too Much Tax Credit*, p4
 11 s28(3) and (4) TCA 2002
 12 Inland Revenue Code of Practice COP 26, *What Happens if We Have Paid You Too Much Tax Credit*, p2
 13 s28(1) TCA 2002
 14 Inland Revenue Code of Practice COP 26, *What Happens if We Have Paid You Too Much Tax Credit*, pp3-4
 15 Inland Revenue Code of Practice COP 26, *What Happens if We Have Paid You Too Much Tax Credit*, p3
 16 Inland Revenue Code of Practice COP 26, *What Happens if We Have Paid You Too Much Tax Credit*, p4
 17 Inland Revenue Code of Practice COP 26, *What Happens if We Have Paid You Too Much Tax Credit*, p3
 18 Inland Revenue Code of Practice COP 26, *What Happens if We Have Paid You Too Much Tax Credit*, p8
 19 Inland Revenue Code of Practice COP 26, *What Happens if We Have Paid You Too Much Tax Credit*, p10
 20 ss28(5)and 23 TCA 2002
 21 s29(1) and (2) TCA 2002
 22 s29(3)-(5) TCA 2002; Inland Revenue Code of Practice COP 26, *What Happens if We Have Paid You Too Much Tax Credit*, p6
 23 Reg 12A TC(PB) Regs; Inland Revenue Code of Practice COP 26, *What Happens if We Have Paid You Too Much Tax Credit*, p6
 24 s29(2) TCA 2002
 25 Inland Revenue Code of Practice COP 26, *What Happens if We Have Paid You Too Much Tax Credit*, p11
 26 s29(3) TCA 2002 (overpayment of tax credit may be treated as if it were outstanding tax)

3. **Interest on overpayments**
 27 s37(1) TCA 2002
 28 s37(2)-(3) TCA 2002
 29 s37(6) TCA 2002
 30 Reg 4 TC(IR) Regs
 31 ss37(4) and 38(1)(d) TCA 2002

Chapter 57

Investigations, penalties and fraud: tax credits

This chapter covers the rules about tax credit investigations, penalties and fraud. It contains:

The Revenue has wide powers to investigate your claim. If you have made an incorrect statement or provided incorrect information, or have failed to comply with requirements, then in certain circumstances a financial penalty may be imposed on you. Also, if you are considered deliberately to have acted fraudulently, then you may be subject to a fine or imprisonment, or both.

1. Investigation of claims

The Revenue has powers to ask you to supply information and evidence and to gather evidence to help it check whether your claim is correct, and to investigate fraud. The Revenue refers to investigations into the accuracy of awards as **'examinations'** and **'enquiries'**. Examinations are carried out on some claims *during* the year in order to check that they are correct. Enquiries may be carried out *after* the year concerned to check that you were paid the correct amount. More serious investigations into **fraud** may also be carried out.

The Revenue might ask you to provide things like bank statements or your rent book but will usually explain why it needs them, and give you reasonable time to produce them. You can seek professional advice (eg, from a welfare rights adviser or a solicitor) and can be accompanied at meetings you have with the Revenue.

Not all investigations are fraud investigations. Fraud investigations tend only to happen in the more serious cases, and in such cases the Revenue has additional powers (see p1432).

Examinations

During the course of your award, or sometimes before your claim is decided, the Revenue may telephone or write to you requiring information or evidence. It may request a meeting with you in connection with your claim. Normally, the Revenue will write to you to say that they are examining your claim. You should be sent the booklet setting out the Revenue's Code of Practice on examinations.[1] If the examination is started before your claim is decided, then normally you will not be paid before the examination is complete. If it starts whilst you are already receiving tax credits, then normally you will continue to be paid whilst the examination is being carrried out.

If you prefer, the Revenue will deal with someone else on your behalf – eg, an adviser, accountant or a relative. The Revenue will need a short signed letter from you which confirms that that is what you want. However, you will still be regarded as personally responsible for the information provided.

There is nothing to say that you have to attend a **meeting**, but remember that the Revenue has powers to seek information or evidence (see below). At the meeting, the Revenue will take notes – it should let you have a copy later, when they have been typed up. If you do not co-operate with the examination (eg, by refusing to provide information) your claim might be refused or your award stopped, and you may be subject to a penalty (see p1433).

In some cases, it may ask you to sign the notes as an accurate record of the meeting. You do not have to sign this. Such signed notes may be used by the Revenue as evidence, so be very sure that you point out anything you disagree with in the notes before signing. If the Revenue finds your claim is incorrect or that you have not notified a change of circumstances that you must report, it might ask you to confirm the information by signing a Certificate of Full Disclosure. Be sure you are satisfied of the accuracy of information in such a certificate, as the Revenue will take a very serious view if you sign it when you know it is wrong.

You cannot stop an examination taking place, but if you are unhappy with the way you are being treated you can make a complaint - see Chapter 47.

Enquiries

After your tax credit award is finalised at the end of the tax year, the Revenue may carry out an enquiry into the award (a 'local office' enquiry). (Normally, this will not be until the May or June following, at the earliest. There is a deadline by which the Revenue must have initiated the enquiry – see p1444.) The Revenue must write to you about this. You should be sent a copy of the booklet setting out the Revenue Code of Practice on enquiries.[2]

If you prefer, the Revenue will deal with someone else on your behalf – eg, an adviser, accountant or a relative. The Revenue will need a short signed letter from you which confirms that that is what you want. However, you will still be regarded as personally responsible for the information provided.

As part of the enquiry the Revenue may request a **meeting** with you. The same points apply to such meetings as they do to meetings in connection with examinations (see above).

You can stop the enquiry by requesting the Revenue to complete it by making a decision on your tax credit entitlement for the year in question. If the Revenue wishes to continue making the enquiry, it will pass your request to an independent appeal tribunal. You can also appeal to the tribunal if you are unhappy with the decision following the enquiry. For more on when tribunals deal with requests and decisions regarding enquiries, see p1444.

Powers to seek information – examinations, enquiries and decisions

The Revenue can require you (and/or your partner if you have a joint claim) to provide information or evidence if during the course of your award it believes your award may be wrong – eg, for the purpose of an examination. It can also require information or evidence after your award has been finalised, for the purpose of an enquiry.

It can also do this if it is necessary for a decision relating to an initial claim (see Chapter 54), a revision during an award (see Chapter 58), a final notice and final decision (see Chapter 55), or (if you are an employee) regarding your employer's responsibility to pay you working tax credit.[3] You must be given at least 30 days to provide the information.[4] The Revenue does not have to suspect you of fraud in order to require information or evidence from you.

It is important that you co-operate with requests for information or evidence as far as you can. Even though you may not be the subject of a fraud investigation, the Revenue might refuse your claim or reduce your award (possibly to nil), and there are a number of circumstances in which you can be subject to a financial penalty or even a prosecution if you refuse to supply information, evidence, etc, or supply material which you know to be incorrect (see p1433). It is important that you are as truthful as possible when responding.

The Revenue can also require certain other people to provide information. They must be given at least 30 days to provide it. If they are subject to these requirements, they can also be subject to penalties (see p1433). The following people can be required to provide information and evidence relating to your claim or, for the purpose of a revision during an award or an enquiry (see pp1440 and 1447), your award:

- your employer (including your partner's employer if you have a joint claim); *or*
- someone whom the Revenue has reasonable grounds to believe is your (or your partner's) employer; *and*

- where your claim includes the childcare element, you (or your partner's) childcare provider; *or*
- someone whom the Revenue has reasonable grounds to believe is your (or your partner's) childcare provider.[5]

Where fraud is suspected

Fraud investigations are normally carried out by the Special Compliance Office of the Revenue. **Note:** if fraud is suspected, the Revenue will usually explain to you why your claim is being investigated, and that you can seek professional advice from someone who can attend any meetings you have with the Revenue. It is advisable to seek professional advice (eg, from a solicitor) if you are investigated on suspicion of fraud. If you are being investigated you should seek advice as quickly as possible. You are likely to be interviewed under caution.

In addition to the powers described above, the Revenue has specific powers when investigating fraud. Where the Revenue has 'reasonable grounds' for suspecting fraud, a court can make an order requiring that documents containing relevant evidence be delivered by you (or any other person who has them) to the Revenue within the time specified in the court order. An authorised Revenue officer must make the application to the court. You (or any other person if s/he has the documents) must be told of the application and are entitled to be heard when the court considers it, unless the court believes that would 'seriously prejudice' the investigation.

Failure to comply with a court order is treated in the same way as contempt of court. However, communications between a 'professional legal adviser' and her/his client are subject to legal privilege and cannot be subject to such an order. Deliberate falsification, concealment or disposal of documents that are the subject of such an order may be an offence with a penalty of a fine or imprisonment, or both.[6]

Where a court is satisfied that there is 'reasonable ground' for suspecting serious fraud, it can issue a warrant giving the Revenue authority to enter and search premises for evidence within 14 days. The Revenue can only apply for such a warrant where it is satisfied that asking the person in possession of the evidence to deliver it up might 'seriously prejudice' the investigation. Under the warrant, the Revenue can remove any things that there is 'reasonable cause' to believe may be required as evidence, and search any person on the premises of whom there is 'reasonable cause' to believe is in possession of such evidence. However, any such person must be searched by someone of the same sex. Also, communications between a 'professional legal adviser' and her/his client are subject to legal privilege and cannot be seized.[7]

2. Penalties

The Revenue can impose a financial penalty on you if:[8]

- you have fraudulently or negligently made an **incorrect statement or declaration** or supplied **incorrect information or evidence**; *or*
- you have **failed to comply** with requirements.

If you do not think a penalty should be imposed on you – eg, because you had a reasonable excuse for not declaring a change in circumstances, tell the Revenue. If a penalty is imposed, then you should be sent a leaflet setting out information about the penalty and what you can do.[9] You have the right of appeal against the imposition of a penalty (see p1454).

In making its decision, the Revenue will have regard to things like how much you have co-operated and how serious are the changes that need to be made. Here, we describe the rules on penalties and interest as they apply to you. However, in certain circumstances, these rules can also apply in the same way to your employer or your childcare provider (see p1431).

Incorrect statements and information

The Revenue can impose a financial penalty of up to £3,000 on you where you have acted fraudulently or negligently (note – the penalty is not applied where you have acted without alleged fault) in the following circumstances:[10]

- where you make an **incorrect statement or declaration** in connection with a claim, or a notification of a change of circumstances (see p1413) or in a response to a final notice (see p1410); *or*
- where you give **incorrect information or evidence** in connection with an initial decision (see p1409), a requirement to provide information or evidence during the course of your award, a revision during an award (see p1440), a final decision (see p1410), an enquiry (see p1444) or (if you are an employee) regarding your employer's responsibility to pay you working tax credit (WTC).

Penalties for incorrect statements and information

The maximum penalty is £3,000. You must be notified of the penalty, including the date on which it is given, and your right of appeal. The penalty is payable 30 days after the date you were notified of it.[11] The amount of the penalty may be increased by the addition of interest (see p1435).

If you are a member of a joint-claim couple (see p1395), the penalty may be imposed or partly imposed on your partner, unless s/he could not reasonably have been expected to have been aware that you had fraudulently or negligently made an incorrect statement or provided incorrect information or evidence. However, even if the penalty is imposed or partly imposed on your partner, the total penalty for the same incorrect statement cannot amount to more than £3,000.

If you are acting for someone else in connection with her/his claim and you fraudulently or negligently make an incorrect statement, the penalty applies to you.

Failure to comply

The Revenue can impose a financial penalty on you of up to £300 where you have failed to comply with requirements in the following circumstances:[12]

- where you **fail to provide information or evidence** for a decision on an initial claim (see p1409), a requirement to provide information or evidence during the course of your award, a revision during an award (see p1440), a final decision (see p1410), an enquiry (see p1444) or (if you are an employee) regarding your employer's responsibility to pay you WTC; *or*
- where you **fail to comply with a requirement regarding a final notice** (see p1410); *or*
- where you **fail to notify a specified change of circumstances.**[13] These are:
  - a decrease of £10 a week or more over four weeks in a row in your childcare costs or a stop in your childcare costs; *or*
  - you have stopped counting as a single claimant; *or*
  - you were claiming as a couple but are no longer part of that couple. This includes where you or your partner leave the UK permanently, or go abroad for more than a set period (see p1460); *or*
  - you (or, if you are claiming as a couple, your partner) lose your right to reside in the UK or stop being regarded as being in the UK.

Penalties for failure to comply[14]

The maximum penalty for this is £300. If the penalty is for failure to provide information or evidence there is a further daily penalty of up to £60 a day for each further day you continue to fail to comply. You must be notified of the penalty, including the date on which it is given, and your right of appeal. The penalty is payable 30 days after the date you were notified of it.[15] The amount of the penalty may be increased by the addition of interest (see p1435).

However, if the penalty is for failure to provide information or evidence, or for a failure regarding a final notice, then the Revenue cannot apply the penalty itself. Instead, it must write to the Appeals Service, which will then summons you to an appeal tribunal where it will decide whether the penalty should be applied.[16] You can appeal against the tribunal's decision to a commissioner (see p1453).

Once you have provided the information or evidence, a penalty cannot be imposed on you. You have not failed to provide information or evidence if you did so within any time that the Revenue has allowed you to, or if you had a 'reasonable excuse' for the failure, or if having had a reasonable excuse you later actually provided the information or evidence without unreasonable delay.

If you are a member of a joint-claim couple, and a £300 penalty has been imposed for failure to comply with a requirement regarding a final notice or for failure to report the specified change of circumstances, the total of that penalty applied to either or both of you is a maximum of £300.

If your employer fails to make correct payments of tax credits to you, s/he may be subject to a financial penalty up to a maximum of £3,000.[17]

Interest added to penalties

If a penalty is imposed on you, the Revenue has the power to apply interest to the penalty, with the effect of increasing the amount which you must pay. Although the Revenue does not have to apply a penalty, it can do so even where you are not considered to have acted fraudulently or negligently (ie, where the penalty is for failure to comply).[18]

If interest is added to the penalty, the amount becomes part of the penalty and is recoverable in the same way as the penalty itself (see p1435).

The amount of interest added to the penalty is 6.5 per cent per annum or, if that is different from the average of the lending rates of the main banks, the bank lending rate plus 2.5 per cent.[19]

You can appeal against the penalty itself and the amount of the penalty. However, the way the law is written suggests that there is no right of appeal regarding the addition of interest.[20]

Separately from the above rules, if the Revenue considers that an overpayment has arisen because of 'fraud or neglect' on your part (or, if you are a member of a joint-claim couple, on the part of one or both of you and your partner), it can decide to apply interest to all or some of the overpayment. See p1427 for details.

Recovery of penalties

The Revenue has discretion about whether to impose a penalty and – subject to the maximum amounts given above – the amount. Also, although the penalty itself can only be altered on appeal, the Revenue has discretion about whether actually to insist that you pay all or some of the penalty.[21] If you tried your best to fulfil all your obligations, or if the penalty would cause you hardship, tell the Revenue this and ask it to exercise its discretion not to recover all or some of the penalty.

If the Revenue does decide that a penalty may be imposed upon you, it will try to come to an agreement with you which involves you offering to pay the agreed amount. They call this agreement a 'contract'. It may be best to try to come to an agreement, as if the Revenue is not able to reach such an agreement with you, it may use its legal powers to recover the penalty. However, if you think you may want to challenge the penalty (see below) check to see if the contract means that the Revenue will not actually issue a decision imposing the penalty, as if you do not have a decision then you will not be able to challenge it on an appeal. If the Revenue uses its legal powers to recover a penalty, it can:

- seize and sell your personal possessions. However, *unless you let the Revenue into your property*, authorised Revenue officers cannot enter your home and seize your personal possessions unless they have a warrant from the court; *or*
- take court action against you, including bankruptcy proceedings.[22]

Challenging a penalty

Once imposed, a determination that a penalty has been made cannot be altered except on appeal. You have the right of appeal against all penalties. The appeal right includes the right of appeal against the determination that a penalty has been incurred and the amount of the penalty, although not against any addition of interest.

Note: subject to the maximum, the tribunal can increase as well as decrease the amount.

For more information on appeals, see p1447, and for more on penalty appeals, see p1454.

3. Fraud

You are regarded as having committed the offence of fraud if you deliberately take part in fraudulent activity in order to get a tax credit for you or anyone else. If you are convicted by a court, you are liable to a fine or to imprisonment, or both.[23]

Fines or imprisonment for fraud

If a court convicts you of fraud in connection with tax credits, you are liable to the following penalties:[24]

- if you are convicted in a magistrates' court, to a maximum of six months' imprisonment or a maximum fine of £5,000, or both; *or*
- if you are convicted in a Crown Court, to a maximum of seven years' imprisonment or a fine of an unlimited amount, or both.

Will you be prosecuted?

Whether or not you will be prosecuted is a discretionary decision for the Revenue. Not all cases of fraud end in prosecution. If you are being investigated by the Special Compliance Office *without* a view to prosecuting you, you are normally told about this. However, this does not mean that the Revenue cannot change its mind and decide that a prosecution should be made.

The factors that it may take into account are likely to include the strength of the evidence, the amount of tax credit involved, whether an offence was planned and your personal circumstances.

Official guidance[25] indicates that prosecutions are more likely where there is evidence of one or more of:

- extensive or substantial fraud;
- deliberate concealment or deception;
- false or forged documents prepared with the intention to deceive;
- conspiracy;
- corruption;
- in tax credit cases in particular, repeat offences, organised crime or multiple identity fraud.

Note: this is not a complete list and ultimately all depends on the circumstances of your case.

What to do if you are prosecuted

The most important thing to do is to get advice. You may be entitled to legal help and have a solicitor or barrister represent you in court. You should check carefully that the Revenue is able to prove all the parts of the offence you are charged with. Do not plead guilty until you have been able to get advice.

4. The effect of an investigation on tax credit claims

There is nothing to stop payment of your tax credits specifically because an investigation, whether for fraud or not, is underway. However, the Revenue is entitled to take the following action:

- revise a current award if it has 'reasonable grounds' for believing it is wrong (see p1440). Note that the Revenue might do this if you do not provide information or evidence that it has requested;
- change an award at the end of the tax year for which the award was made, when the final decision is made (see p1443);
- revise an award via an 'enquiry' or a 'decision on discovery' after the end of the tax year for which the award was made (see p1443);
- postpone payment where an appeal is pending on your claim or a similar claim, or it appears that your address or bank account details are incorrect (see p1404).

Also, the Revenue can ask you, and in certain cases other people, to provide information or evidence in connection with an award (see pp1433 and 1436), and impose a penalty (see p1433) if you do not respond within the given time.

The decision on whether you should be prosecuted is separate from a decision to recover an overpayment (see Chapter 56). Whether or not you are entitled to tax credits, the amount and recoverability of any overpayment is decided by the Revenue without regard to dishonesty of intention. Decisions on entitlement can in most cases be appealed (see p1447).

Whatever the result of an investigation or prosecution, the Revenue may take more time assessing future claims because it may check out your circumstances thoroughly. Again, if it takes too long for it to make a decision, you should complain. You could also apply for help from the social fund (see Chapter 21 or 22).

Notes

1. Investigation of claims

1 ss14(2), 15(2) and 16(2) and (3) TCA 2002; Inland Revenue Code of Practice COP 23, *Child Tax Credit and Working Tax Credit Local Office Examinations*
2 s19 TCA 2002; Inland Revenue Code of Practice COP 27, *Child Tax Credit and Working Tax Credit Local Office Enquiries*
3 ss14(2), 15(2), 16(3), 17, 19(2) and 22 TCA 2002
4 Reg 32 TC(CN) Regs
5 ss14(2)(b), 15(2)(b), 16(3)(b) and 19(2)(b) TCA 2002; regs 30 and 31 TC(CN) Regs
6 s36(1) TCA 2002
7 s36(2) TCA 2002

2. Penalties

8 ss31 and 32 TCA 2002
9 Inland Revenue leaflets WTC3 and WTC4
10 s31 TCA 2002
11 Sch 2 para 1 TCA 2002
12 s32 TCA 2002
13 ss32(3), 6(3) and 3(4) TCA 2002; reg 21(2) TC(CN) Regs
14 s32(2)(a)-(6) TCA 2002
15 Sch 2 para 1 TCA 2002
16 Sch 2 paras 1 and 3 TCA 2002
17 s33 TCA 2002
18 s37(5) and (6) TCA 2002
19 Reg 4 TC(IR) Regs
20 ss37(5)-(6) and 38 TCA 2002
21 Sch 2 paras 1 and 5 TCA 2002
22 Sch 2 para 7 TCA 2002

3. Fraud

23 s35(1) TCA 2002
24 s35(2) TCA 2002; reg 30 TC(CN) Regs
25 Prosecution Policy of the Board of the Inland Revenue

Chapter 58

Revisions and appeals: tax credits

This chapter covers revisions and appeals for child tax credit and working tax credit. It contains:

A decision made by the Revenue can be changed by:

- revision; *or*
- appeal.

A decision made by an appeal tribunal can be changed by:

- revision;
- appeal;
- being set aside; *or*
- correction of an accidental error.

This chapter explains how and when your award can be changed by these methods.

Rules for *revising* tax credit decisions are quite different from those for social security benefits. This chapter covers tax credit revisions in detail.

Tax credit *appeals* are heard by the same appeal tribunals that deal with social security benefits, and are administered by the Appeals Service, an agency of the Department for Work and Pensions. Many of the appeal rules are the same for tax credits as they are for social security benefits. Chapter 44 covers appeals for social security benefits. This chapter refers you to Chapter 44 where tax credit rules are the same as benefit rules. The footnotes in Chapter 44 also contain references to the child tax credit and working tax credit legislation where applicable.

1. Revisions

If you disagree with a decision, you may be able to have it revised by the Revenue. The circumstances in which a revision can be made depend on whether the decision with which you disagree is:

- an 'initial decision' on a claim (see p1440);
- a 'final decision' after the tax year has ended following an annual review (see p1443); *or*
- a decision of an appeal tribunal (see p1451).

Revision or appeal

Most decisions carry a right of appeal. An appeal must be made within 30 days after the date on which notice of the decision was given, although late appeals may be allowed in some circumstances. Unless you are simply reporting a change in circumstances, it is generally better to appeal than ask for a revision. You could be at a disadvantage if you ask for a revision before asking for an appeal because if the Revenue does not revise the award, you may have missed the deadline for appeal. On the other hand, if the Revenue does revise the award but you are still not happy with it, you have another 30 days to appeal. Asking for an appeal without first trying to have the decision revised does not mean your case will necessarily have to go to a tribunal. There is an opportunity to settle the dispute first with the Revenue (see p1449).

You will not have a choice between revision and appeal if you have missed the appeal deadline and cannot get a late appeal. In this situation, you may still be able to put your case to the Revenue and ask it to revise its decision. Which decisions can be revised is explained below.

Revising an initial decision during an award

When you claim a tax credit, the Revenue must decide whether to make an award and the rate at which to award it.[1] This is called an **'initial decision'**. If you disagree with it, you have the right to appeal (see p1447) or you may be able to ask the Revenue to revise the decision as described below. Your award can also be revised if your circumstances change.

Your claim is refused or award stopped

If your claim has been turned down altogether or your award has been terminated, you do not have the option to ask for the decision to be revised. You must appeal within 30 days if you want the decision to be changed. If you do not appeal or your appeal is unsuccessful, you will need to make a fresh claim to get any further tax credit in that tax year.[2]

No award because income too high

If your income in the previous year is too high to qualify for a tax credit, but you satisfy the other qualifying conditions, the decision will be to award a tax credit at a nil rate. This nil-rate award can be revised if your income is estimated to be lower in the current year.[3]

You disagree with an award

If you have been awarded a tax credit but you disagree with the amount, the initial decision can be revised if:

- your **circumstances have changed** so that you should get an additional or higher element (see p1441); *or*
- the Revenue has **reasonable grounds** for believing that you are entitled to a different rate of tax credit or that you are not entitled to a tax credit at all (see p1442); *or*
- there has been an **official error** (see p1443).

Changes in circumstances that increase entitlement to a tax credit element

If your circumstances change so that you should be getting an element you were not getting before, or a higher rate of an element, your award may be revised.[4] For example, if you have a new baby your child tax credit (CTC) award can be revised to include another child element and a baby element.

If you notify the Revenue of the change within three months, the increase in the award can be fully backdated.[5] There are specific rules dealing with the date from which an award is recalculated where there is a change in childcare charges or childcare provided (see p1414).

The increase in the award cannot be backdated for more than three months before the date you provide notification of the change, except in the following cases relating to the **disability or severe disability element of CTC and working tax credit** (WTC):

- If you claim disability living allowance (DLA) for a child, tell the Revenue straight away. Do not wait till it is awarded. Then tell the Revenue within three months of the decision that DLA has been awarded. That way, the disability or severe disability element of CTC is fully backdated to the date from which DLA is payable or, if later, the date you told the Revenue you had claimed DLA.
- If you are not already getting CTC when you claim DLA for your child, write on the tax credits claim form that you are waiting for a decision on the DLA claim (and keep a copy of the form). Tell the Revenue once DLA is awarded, within three months of the decision. The disability or severe disability element is backdated to the start of your CTC claim or, if later, to the start of the DLA award.
- If, when you claim WTC, you are waiting for a decision on a claim for one of the WTC disability or severe disability element qualifying benefits (eg, DLA, incapacity benefit or a disability premium), you should write this on the tax

credits claim form (and keep a copy). Notify the Revenue once the qualifying benefit is awarded. So long as you do so within three months of the date of the decision to award the qualifying benefit, the increase in your tax credit award can be backdated to the date of the original tax credit claim, or to the date the qualifying benefit is awarded if that is later.[6]

- If you are already getting WTC when you claim one of the WTC disability or severe disability element qualifying benefits, do not wait until it is awarded before notifying the Revenue. If you tell the Revenue that you are waiting for a decision on your qualifying benefit claim, then once it is awarded, the disability or severe disability element can be backdated to the date you first notified the Revenue that you had claimed the qualifying benefit or, if later, the start of the DLA award. You must notify the Revenue within three months of the date the qualifying benefit is decided.[7]

If you disagree with a revised decision, you have the right of appeal within 30 days to an appeal tribunal (see p1447) or to ask for another revision on 'reasonable grounds' (see below) or for official error (see p1446).

Reasonable grounds

The Revenue has the power to amend or terminate an award on its own initiative. It can do this if it has 'reasonable grounds for believing' that:[8]

- you are entitled to a different rate of tax credit; *or*
- you are not entitled to WTC or you are not entitled to CTC.

This could happen, for example, because you tell the Revenue about wrong information used in deciding your claim. Or it could happen because it has decided to examine your claim and has found errors (see p1430).

If the rate of tax credit is changed, the Revenue revises your award taking into account any changes in circumstance from the date they arose unless:

- it is a change that increases entitlement to tax credit elements, which can only be backdated for up to three months (see p1441);
- childcare charges go down by £10 a week or more. In this case there is a four-week run-on at the same rate before the award is reduced (see p1413).[9] **Note:** there may be a penalty if you do not provide notification of the change within three months (see p1433).

Decisions can only be revised in this way during the period of the award, not after an award has been terminated, nor after a final decision has been made.[10]

Example 1

Pauline provides an estimate of her income for the current year and this is less than the previous year's income on which the award was based. The initial decision can be revised and her award recalculated based on current year's income. The estimate she provides

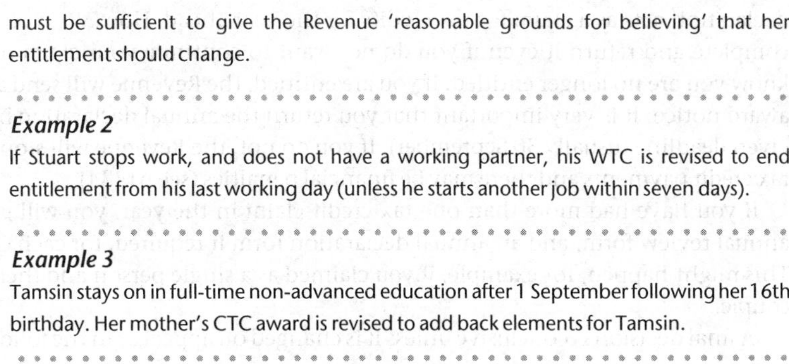
must be sufficient to give the Revenue 'reasonable grounds for believing' that her entitlement should change.

Example 2

If Stuart stops work, and does not have a working partner, his WTC is revised to end entitlement from his last working day (unless he starts another job within seven days).

Example 3

Tamsin stays on in full-time non-advanced education after 1 September following her 16th birthday. Her mother's CTC award is revised to add back elements for Tamsin.

If you disagree with the revised rate of tax credit, you can appeal within 30 days to an appeal tribunal (see p1447) or ask for another revision. However, if you disagree with a decision to end your tax credit entitlement, you have the right to appeal but not to a further revision.

Official error

An initial award can be revised where it is incorrect due to an official error.[11] See p1446 for details.

Annual review

After 5 April, the Revenue reviews your tax credit award for the year just ended and makes a **final decision** on your entitlement for that year. It sends you an annual review form (TC603R) which details the circumstances on which the award was based. You are asked to check that the details are correct and complete, and inform it about any changes or corrections. You might also be asked to complete an annual declaration form (TC603D) giving your income for the tax year just passed. You probably will not be sent an annual declaration form to complete if you only get the family element of CTC or a 'nil award'.

If the Revenue does not send you an annual declaration form and you have had no change in your personal circumstances and your income for the tax year just passed is within the range given on the annual review form, you do not need to do anything. Your annual review is complete. The Revenue will finalise your entitlement for the year just passed – ie, make a final decision. Your new award for the year ahead is set out in the annual review form. If your income or circumstances have changed, tell the Revenue as soon as you can, but no later than the deadline given on the form (usually 30 September) otherwise there may be financial penalties (see p1434).

If the Revenue sends you an annual declaration form, you must complete and return it by the deadline given on the form (usually 30 September). The Revenue will finalise your entitlement for the year just passed. Your completed annual declaration acts as a claim for tax credits for the year ahead. However, you must complete and return it even if you do not want to continue your claim or you know you are no longer entitled. If you are entitled, the Revenue will send a new award notice. It is very important that you return the annual declaration by the given deadline (usually 30 September). If you do not, the Revenue will stop your tax credit payments and there may be financial penalties (see p1434).

If you have had more than one tax credit claim in the year, you will get an annual review form, and an annual declaration form if required, for each claim. This might happen, for example, if you claimed as a single person and then as a couple.

A final decision is conclusive unless it is changed on appeal or in the following circumstances:

- If you **change your statement** about your income or circumstances before the deadline (see below), the final decision can be changed.
- Once a final decision is made, there is a period during which the Revenue can enquire into your entitlement. See below for details of **revision on enquiry**.
- Outside the period of enquiry, a final decision can be revised on 'discovery' of certain information to do with your tax liability or to do with fraud or neglect. There is a deadline for such revisions. See p1445 for details of **revision on discovery**.
- A final decision can be revised due to **official error**. See p1446 for details.

Changing your statement

If you reply to the annual review notice but then wish to change your statement, you may do so. If it is before the deadline given in the notice for replying (usually 30 September), but the Revenue has already made a final decision, the final decision may be revised.[12]

If the Revenue only had an estimate of your income for the current year (eg, because you are self-employed and have not yet finalised your accounts), you will have a later deadline (usually 31 January) in which to give details of your actual income for that year. If you do so, the Revenue must make a new final decision.[13] It can revise the new decision if you change your statement before the later deadline.[14] If you do not give further details of actual income, the Revenue must nevertheless make a new final decision once the later deadline is passed.

Revision on enquiry

The Revenue has the power to enquire into entitlement for any reason,[15] but it must begin its enquiry by giving you notice by a certain date. That is a year after the deadline by which you were to reply to the annual review notice, or a year after the later deadline for self-employed people or others to supply actual income details where only an estimate had been provided.[16] If you are required to submit an income tax return, the enquiry must begin by the day your tax return becomes final (for couples who are both required to submit a tax return, by whichever return is final last). Tax returns usually become final a year past 31 January after the end of the tax year – eg, for the tax year 2004/05, a return becomes final on 31 January 2007.

There is no deadline by which the enquiry must be completed. However, you have the right to apply for a 'direction' to get a decision made. You should apply in writing to the Revenue.[17] Your application is heard by an appeal tribunal. The appeal tribunal must grant the direction unless it is satisfied that the Revenue has reasonable grounds for not having made a decision.[18]

When the enquiry is completed, the Revenue will make a fresh decision on whether you are entitled and how much the award should be.[19]

Only one enquiry into entitlement can be conducted for any one tax year.[20]

For more details, see p1430.

If you disagree with an enquiry decision

If you disagree with the decision you have the right of appeal within 30 days to an appeal tribunal (see p1447). Alternatively, it may be revised if it is incorrect due to official error – see p1446.[21] The Revenue may also revise an enquiry decision by a 'revision on discovery' (see below).

Revision on discovery

If it is too late to 'enquire' into your entitlement, the Revenue can still revise a final decision, but only in specific circumstances, and there are further time limits by which such a revision must take place. A final decision or an enquiry decision may be revised outside the period allowed for an enquiry where the Revenue has 'reasonable grounds for believing' that tax credit entitlement is wrong:

- because of a revision of your income tax liability. The revision of your tax credit entitlement must take place within a year of your income tax liability being revised;[22] *or*
- for reasons attributable to fraud or neglect (see p1445).

There is nothing to stop the Revenue going through this process more than once.[23] Where a final decision, enquiry decision or discovery decision has been revised for official error, that too can be further revised in this way.[24]

Fraud or neglect

A decision can be revised if the Revenue has reasonable grounds for believing that an incorrect decision on tax credit entitlement is attributable to fraud or neglect.[25] The fraud or neglect may be on your part, or your partner's if it is a joint claim, or on the part of anyone acting for you (see p1396 for when a person may act for you).

Your tax credit entitlement in a tax year cannot be revised on this ground after five years from the end of the tax year.[26] For example, a tax credit award for 2004/05 cannot be revised after 5 April 2010.

If you disagree with a discovery decision

You have the right of appeal within 30 days to an appeal tribunal (see p1447). Alternatively, the decision may be revised if it is incorrect because of official error (see below).

Official error

An initial decision, final decision, enquiry decision or discovery decision can be revised if it is incorrect due to an official error.[27] The decision can be revised at any time up to five years after the end of the tax year to which the decision relates.

'Official error' means an error relating to a tax credit made by a Revenue or DWP officer or a person providing tax credit services for them. If you, or someone acting for you, materially contributed to the error, it does not count as an official error. An error of law can count as an official error. It would not count, however, if it was only shown to be an error of law because of a later decision of a commissioner or court.

Make sure you cover all the issues you want considered when you apply for a revision. The Revenue does not need to consider any issue that you do not raise.

How to seek a revision

If your circumstances change, rules lay down how the Revenue should be notified. These are described below. However, in other cases, there are no set rules to follow.

You, or your partner if you have a joint claim, must make the notification.[28] In some circumstances another person can act for you. If you have an appointee, either for tax credits or benefits, or someone legally appointed to act for you (see p1396), s/he can provide notification of the change on your behalf if you are unable to do it yourself.[29]

You should notify the Tax Credit Office. Your notification can also be accepted at any Revenue or DWP office. The notification need not be in writing; you can phone or tell the office in person.[30]

The date on which you notify the Revenue may be important – eg, for changes in circumstances that you are obliged to tell the Revenue about, or where the award can only be backdated for three months from the date of notification. The **'date of notification'** is defined as the date on which notification is given to the Revenue.[31] If you want to change any of the details, you can do so at any time before the Revenue has made a decision.[32] Your notification will still be taken as made on the original date.[33]

Keep a copy of any letter you send to the Revenue. If you call the Tax Credit Helpline it may be advisable to keep a log of your calls: when you made the call, information provided and what was agreed.

Normally you must provide notification of the change in circumstance after it has happened. But there are two cases where you can notify in advance:

- for WTC, if you are changing jobs and have a new job that you expect to start within seven days;
- where you are providing an estimate of childcare charges, or notifying an increase in charges.[34]

What happens after you seek a revision

Before making its decision, the Revenue may ask you to provide more information or evidence if it considers it needs this to help in the decision.[35] The Revenue may also contact your employer if it needs information from her/him too.[36]

It is very important that you respond to a request for information by the date given in the letter. If you do not provide the required information, you may have to pay a penalty of up to £300, and if you still do not comply, a further daily penalty of up to £60 a day could be imposed. See p1433 for more details of how these penalties are applied.

The Revenue must give notice of the decision to you, and to your partner if it is a joint claim. This must include details of your right to appeal.[37]

2. Appealing to a tribunal

At present, tax credit appeals are heard by the same appeal tribunals that deal with social security benefits, and are administered by the Appeals Service, an agency of the DWP.[38] The intention is that the tax appeals system will take over tax credit appeals from the Appeals Service once the system has been suitably reformed to accommodate them. It is not yet known when this changeover will happen, but it is not expected in the near future.

In the meantime, many of the tax credit appeals rules are the same as those for social security benefits. Chapter 44 deals with appeals for social security benefits. This chapter refers you to Chapter 44 where tax credit rules are the same as benefit rules.

Who can appeal

The following people have the right of appeal:[39]

- you, the tax credit claimant. For joint claimants, both of you together or either of you can make the appeal;
- for appeals about penalties, the person subject to the penalty;
- for an application for the Revenue to complete an enquiry into entitlement, the person making the application;
- an appointee, if you are unable to make the appeal yourself (see p1396). If you do not have an appointee, the person (who must be 18 or over) who is to act on your behalf in the appeal should write to the Revenue asking to be appointed;

- a receiver appointed by the Court of Protection with the power to make a tax credit claim for you;
- in Scotland, a judicial factor or guardian under the Adults With Incapacity (Scotland) Act 2000 who has the power to claim tax credits for you and is administering your estate.[40]

Decisions you can appeal

You can appeal against:[41]

- an initial decision;
- a final decision;
- a revised decision (for change in circumstances, on reasonable grounds or for official error);
- an enquiry decision;
- a discovery decision;
- a Revenue decision imposing a penalty;
- a decision charging interest on an overpayment.

If the Revenue decides you have been overpaid tax credit, it can recover all or part of it at its discretion, and you cannot appeal against the decision. You can, however, appeal against the amount of the award, but note that the time limit for appealing runs from the final decision on your award, rather than the date of the overpayment notice if the two dates are different. In some cases the Revenue may use its discretion not to recover an overpayment, or to reduce the amount – eg, where it was caused by official error or where recovery would cause hardship (see p1424 for details). You can complain to the Revenue if you are unhappy with the way your claim has been handled, and if your complaint is not resolved to your satisfaction you can ask the Independent Adjudicator to look into it (see p1300).

Time limit for appealing

Your appeal, including the details specified below, must be given to the Revenue within 30 days after the date given on the decision letter.[42]

You may not get a separate initial or final decision notice where the annual review notice states what the decision will be and the date on which it will be made, usually 30 September 2005 for awards in 2004/05 (eg, where there is no change to the information on which the award is based). This may apply where your award is made up of just the family element of child tax credit (CTC) and your circumstances have not changed. In this case your appeal must be made within 30 days after the date the annual review notice gives as the date on which the decision is made – eg, by 30 October.

Late appeals

You can appeal outside this 30-day time limit in limited circumstances. These circumstances are the same for tax credits as they are for benefits. You must appeal within an absolute time limit. This is one year after the date the 30-day time limit expired. See p1261 for details of late appeals, but note the following differences for tax credits:

- where the benefit rules refer to a one-month limit, that should be taken to be 30 days;
- where the benefit rules refer to a 13-month limit, that should be taken to be one year plus 30 days;
- your application for an extension to the time limit must be in writing, be signed by you (or on your behalf – eg, by an appointee) and include enough details to identify you (eg, your name and national insurance number), identify your appeal and your grounds for asking for an extension.[43]

There is no provision to ask for written reasons for a decision or to extend the time limit if you do. Nor is the time limit extended if you try unsuccessfully to get the decision revised by the Revenue before making an appeal.

How to appeal

You can appeal on the form inside the Revenue leaflet, WTC/AP, *How to Appeal Against a Tax Credit Decision or Award.* Alternatively, you can write a letter, but you must include the following details:[44]

- enough information to identify you (eg, your name and national insurance number);
- enough information to identify the decision being appealed – eg, the date of the decision and whether it is CTC or working tax credit (WTC);
- the grounds of your appeal – ie, you must say why the decision is wrong. If there is more than one reason why the decision is wrong, specify each one if you can. However, the tribunal may allow you to raise new grounds later if it considers that missing them out from this appeal notice was not 'wilful or unreasonable';[45]
- your signature (or someone can sign it on your behalf – eg, an appointee).

Send your appeal to the Revenue at the address given on the decision notice.

What happens after you appeal

Settling the appeal

Your appeal can be settled by the Revenue without going to an appeal tribunal.[46] You can point out to the Revenue where you think its decision is wrong and supply information or arguments you want it to consider. The Revenue may offer you terms on which to settle the appeal.

If you agree to settle the appeal, the Revenue should write to you setting out the terms of the agreement – eg, giving a new amount for your award. Your appeal then lapses unless you write to the Revenue within 30 days from the date of the written notice of agreement saying you have changed your mind and wish to proceed with your appeal.

If you are asked to settle the appeal, check first whether the proposed agreement gives you everything you think you are entitled to. Seek advice if you are not sure whether to agree. If in doubt, you should exercise your right to continue with the appeal.

Asking for a hearing

If your appeal is not settled, the Revenue prepares the appeal papers (this is referred to as its 'submission'). It sends a copy to you and a copy to your representative if you have one. At the same time, it sends you an enquiry form asking whether you want an oral hearing or not. You must return the form within 14 days of the date it was issued.[47] The clerk to the tribunal can extend this time limit but otherwise if you do not return the form in time, your appeal can be struck out.

For information and issues to consider when deciding whether to opt for an oral hearing, see p1227.

When your appeal can be struck out

Your appeal may be struck out:[48]

- 'for want of prosecution' – ie, you do not pursue the appeal; *or*
- if you do not comply with a direction and were warned that it could be struck out as a result – eg, you do not provide information requested to support your appeal; *or*
- if you do not return a pre-hearing enquiry form to tell the clerk whether or not you want an oral hearing, and were warned that the appeal could be struck out.

The decision to strike out may be made by the tribunal clerk, but the clerk could refer it to a legally qualified tribunal member to decide.

Reinstatement

If your appeal was struck out because you did not reply saying whether you wanted an oral hearing, you can write to the tribunal clerk to ask for your appeal to be reinstated. You must do so within a month of the decision to strike out the appeal, saying why you think it should not have been struck out. If the clerk is not satisfied that there are reasonable grounds to reinstate the appeal, s/he must pass your application to a legally qualified tribunal member. If the appeal was struck out for any other reason, you should still write to the clerk saying why it should not have been struck out. In either case, the tribunal member can reinstate the appeal if:

- your application was made within the month and there are reasonable grounds to reinstate; *or*

- there were not proper grounds for striking out the appeal; *or*
- although there were proper grounds for striking out the appeal, it is not in the interests of justice for it to be struck out.[49]

Withdrawing an appeal

You can ask to withdraw the appeal if you decide not to go ahead with it. You can tell the Revenue in writing or phone the Helpline. However, the Revenue can refuse to let you withdraw the appeal by writing to you within 30 days. If it has not written to you within 30 days, then the appeal is withdrawn.[50]

The hearing

The appeal tribunal holds an oral hearing if you have asked for one. Otherwise there is a paper hearing in your absence. For details of these and information on requesting a postponement or adjournment of the hearing, see p1231. The tax credit rules are the same as those for benefits except that there are no special 'test case' provisions for tax credits that can block your appeal or affect the outcome of your appeal (although payment can be postponed while there is an appeal pending in another case that could affect your own award).[51]

Tribunal procedures

Chapter 44 describes tribunal procedures for benefits, looking at:

- who is present at the hearing;
- what happens at an oral hearing;
- domiciliary hearings (hearings at home);
- what the tribunal can consider;
- changes in circumstances after you appeal;
- the tribunal decision;
- after the hearing;
- if you disagree with the tribunal's decision;
- when a decision can be set aside.

See pp1233–1243 for details. The tax credit rules are the same, with the following exceptions:

- **Medical examination.** The tribunal cannot refer you to a doctor for a medical examination.[52] However, where your appeal concerns a disability question it may be important to get your own medical evidence (see p1255).
- **What the tribunal can consider.** The rules on what tribunals need and need not consider are stricter for tax credits. They must consider grounds that you specified in your written application for appeal. After that, they may allow you to raise other issues if they are satisfied that it was not 'wilful or unreasonable' of you to have missed them out from the appeal notice.[53]

- **Changes in circumstance after you appeal.** These rules apply to tax credits in the same way as they do to benefits except:
  - wherever Chapter 44 refers to 'supersession' this should read 'revision' for tax credits;
  - if you reclaim or ask for a revision because of a change in circumstance after you appeal, there is no specific provision for a decision maker to revisit her/his decision on that claim/revision once the appeal has been heard on the grounds that s/he would have made a different decision had s/he known what the tribunal's decision would be.
- **After the hearing.** If the Revenue is considering an appeal to the commissioners or has decided to appeal, you are normally not paid until the commissioner decides the case. The Revenue has the power to 'postpone' payment in these circumstances, without any extra rules about notifying you of its intention (as there are for suspending benefits).[54]
- **If you disagree with the tribunal's decision.** A tribunal decision cannot be 'superseded' (because supersessions only apply to benefits, not to tax credits) but it can be revised in any of the ways described in this chapter except for official error (see p1440).

  If a tribunal made an error of law, you can appeal to the social security commissioners as you can in benefit appeals. For tax credits, the Revenue is not prevented from revising the tribunal's decision on 'reasonable grounds' which could also include an error of law (if it is still within the tax year of the award).
- **When a decision can be set aside.** If you appeal to the commissioners, there is no provision obliging a legally qualified tribunal member to set aside the decision where both you and the Revenue agree the tribunal made an error of law.[55]

Tribunal members

The tribunal is made up of one, two or three members depending on the type of issue under appeal.

- A lawyer, a doctor and someone with experience of disability hears your appeal if it is about:
  - the disability element or severe disability element of WTC or CTC;
  - for eligibility to WTC, whether you have a disability that puts you at a disadvantage in getting a job;
  - for the childcare element, the incapacity of a partner or disability of a child.[56]
- A lawyer and someone with financial expertise hears your appeal if it involves difficult financial issues about profit and loss accounts, revenue accounts, balance sheets, and accounts of trust funds.[57]
- A lawyer alone hears your appeal in any other case.

The lawyer acts as chair. The chair has the casting vote.[58] See p1244 for restrictions on the involvement of doctors known to you or to the tribunal members.

3. Appealing to a commissioner

You can appeal to the social security commissioners against a decision of an appeal tribunal, but only if the appeal tribunal made an error of law. In some penalty appeals, you can also appeal about the amount of the penalty (see p1454).

Chapter 44 explains what an error of law is and how to go about making your appeal (see p1245). The rules for tax credits are the same as those for benefits described in Chapter 44, with one exception that applies if you disagree with a commissioner's decision:

- it cannot be 'superseded' but it can be revised in any of the ways described above, except for revision for official error (see p1440).

4. Appealing to the courts

You can appeal to the Court of Appeal (in England and Wales) or to the Court of Session (in Scotland) against a decision of a social security commissioner, but only if there is an error of law. You have three months in which to apply.

Chapter 44 explains how to apply for permission to appeal (see p1251).

5. How to prepare an appeal

Suggestions for how to prepare your appeal and present your case are given in Chapter 44. Information in that chapter applies equally to tax credit appeals.

If you need to check the legislation for tax credits, the key Acts of Parliament are:

- Tax Credits Act 2002, which sets out the basic rules of entitlement to tax credits as well as how the scheme is administered;
- Social Security Act 1998 as amended by a set of Regulations, The Tax Credits (Appeals) Regulations 2002 No. 2926, which sets out the framework for appeals.

The detail of the law on tax credits is contained in Regulations, which are footnoted in the relevant chapters of this *Handbook*. Some Regulations refer to income tax legislation, in particular to:

- Income Tax (Earnings and Pensions) Act 2003;

- Income and Corporation Taxes Act 1988;
- Taxes Management Act 1970.

6. Penalty appeals

You have the right to appeal against a decision imposing a penalty. For information on penalties, see p1433.

For most types of penalty, the Revenue has the power to make its own decision imposing a penalty. You can appeal against this decision to an appeal tribunal in the normal way, with any further appeal going to the commissioners under the usual rules.[59] However, to impose a penalty of up to £300 for failing to provide required information or evidence, the Revenue cannot make the decision itself but must take 'proceedings' to an appeal tribunal. You have an opportunity to attend a hearing where the tribunal decides whether to apply a penalty. Your right of appeal then lies with the social security commissioners.[60]

In these penalty appeals to the commissioners (ie, where the decision was made by an appeal tribunal under penalty proceedings), you can appeal on a question of law *or* on the amount of the penalty.[61] You can appeal to the commissioners without needing leave to do so and you have a right to an oral hearing if you want one.[62] Send your notice of appeal directly to the commissioners' office. Because of a mistake in the way the law was drafted, there is no time limit for these appeals, although the usual time limits apply to other penalty appeals. However, it is advisable to appeal without delay.

On any penalty appeal, the appeal tribunal or the commissioner may decide to do the following:[63]

- set aside the decision imposing the penalty;
- confirm the decision if the amount of the penalty 'appears to be appropriate';
- reduce or increase the penalty if the amount appears to be excessive or insufficient.

The law sets the limit on maximum penalties but does not say when the maximum or a lesser penalty is appropriate. Therefore, if you think an issue is relevant then explain it at appeal – for example:

- if the penalty will cause you hardship; *or*
- if the Revenue contributed to the problem arising; *or*
- if your health or other personal circumstances was a factor.

Employers subject to a penalty also have the right of appeal. In this case the appeal is to the general or special commissioners who are appointed by the Lord Chancellor to hear tax appeals.[64]

Notes

1. **Revisions**

1 s14(1) TCA 2002
2 s3(2) TCA 2002
3 The Revenue intends to use the power in s14(3) TCA 2002 to award at a nil rate in these circumstances
4 s15(1) TCA 2002
5 Reg 25 TC(CN) Regs; reg 16(5)(a) WTC(EMR) Regs
6 Reg 26(2) TC(CN) Regs
7 Reg 26(3) TC(CN) Regs
8 s16(1) TCA 2002
9 Reg 16(5)(b) WTC(EMR) Regs
10 s16(1) TCA 2002
11 s21 TCA 2002
12 s18(5) TCA 2002
13 s18(6) TCA 2002
14 s18(9) TCA 2002
15 s19(1) TCA 2002
16 s19(4) TCA 2002
17 Reg 7 TC(A)(No 2) Regs
18 ss19(10) and 63(3) TCA 2002
19 s19(3) TCA 2002
20 s19(11) TCA 2002
21 s21 TCA 2002
22 s20(3) TCA 2002
23 s20(6)(a) TCA 2002
24 s20(6)(b) TCA 2002
25 s20(4) TCA 2002
26 s20(5) TCA 2002
27 s21 TCA 2002; reg 3 TC(OE) Regs
28 Reg 23 TC(CN) Regs
29 Regs 28 and 29 TC(CN) Regs
30 Reg 22(3) TC(CN) Regs
31 Reg 19 TC(CN) Regs
32 Reg 22(4) TC(CN) Regs
33 Reg 24 TC(CN) Regs
34 Reg 27 TC(CN) Regs
35 ss15(2)(b), 16(3)(b) and 19(2)(b) TCA 2002
36 Reg 30 TC(CN) Regs
37 s23 TCA 2002

2. **Appealing to a tribunal**

38 s63(2) TCA 2002
39 s12 SSA 1998, as amended by reg 4 TC(A) Regs
40 Reg 3 TC(A)(No 2) Regs
41 s38 TCA 2002
42 ss 39(1) and 23(2) TCA 2002
43 Reg 6 TC(A)(No 2) Regs
44 Reg 2 TC(NA) Regs
45 s39(2) and (5) TCA 2002
46 Reg 3 TC(A) Regs; s54 TMA 1970
47 Reg 12(3) TC(A)(No 2) Regs
48 Reg 16 TC(A)(No 2) Regs
49 Reg 17 TC(A)(No 2) Regs
50 s54 TMA 1970
51 Reg 11 TC(PB) Regs
52 The power to refer to a doctor in s20 SSA 1998 does not apply to tax credits
53 s39(5) TCA 2002
54 Reg 11 TC(PB) Regs
55 Reg 5(2) TC(A) Regs
56 Reg 9(2) TC(A)(No 2) Regs
57 Reg 9(3) TC(A)(No 2) Regs
58 s7 SSA 1998; s63(10) TCA 2002

6. **Penalty appeals**

59 s38 TCA 2002
60 s63 and para 4(1) Sch 2 TCA 2002
61 para 4(1) Sch 2 TCA 2002
62 Reg 18 SSCP(TCA) Regs
63 paras 2(1) and 4(2) Sch 2 TCA 2002
64 s63(2) TCA 2002

Chapter 59

Immigration and residence rules: tax credits

This chapter contains the immigration and residence conditions for tax credits. Many of the rules and terms used are similar to those for benefits. Therefore, for an overview of terms such as public funds, sponsorship and the rights of European Economic Area nationals, see Chapter 26. This chapter covers:

1. Introduction

It is important, before making a claim for tax credits, to know your immigration status. This is because your immigration status determines your right to tax credits. If you are unsure about your immigration status you should seek specialist advice.

Most people, apart from British citizens, are subject to some form of immigration control. This means that you cannot freely enter the UK, but will be subject to scrutiny by the immigration authority. The degree of control varies according to your nationality. European Economic Area nationals have enhanced rights by virtue of European Community law. They do not need leave to enter or remain and consequently cannot be subject to a public funds restriction. They can only be removed on very limited grounds and there are clear appeal rights against any attempts to remove them. They therefore have much greater security, particularly in respect of claims for benefit, than other migrants.

If you are subject to immigration control you require leave, or permission, to enter or remain. Such leave can be:

- limited leave to enter or remain;
- indefinite leave to enter or remain;
- exceptional leave to enter or remain;

- humanitarian protection or discretionary leave (see Chapter 26).

If you have limited leave you are only permitted to remain in the UK for a limited period of time. Certain conditions are frequently attached to a grant of limited leave. For example, a restriction may be made on you working or claiming certain benefits. If you breach these conditions you may put your right to remain in the UK at risk.

Public funds

Working tax credit (WTC) and child tax credit (CTC) have recently been listed as public funds.[1] However, the Immigration Rules state that a person who is eligible for tax credits will be treated as not having had recourse to public funds. Therefore, if you have a partner who is not subject to immigration control, your partner will be able to claim for you without affecting your right to remain in the UK. However, if you are single and you are subject to a public funds restriction, you will be defined as a 'person subject to immigration control' and would be subject to the public funds restriction.

Status of tax credits in EC law

CTC is a family benefit for EC Regulation 1408/71 (see p1461). Both CTC and WTC are covered by EC Regulation 1612/68 and would be considered a social advantage (see p1462).

2. The immigration status condition

You are not eligible for tax credits if you are a 'person subject to immigration control'.[2] This has the same meaning as for social security benefits[3] (see p654) and as with social security benefits there are certain groups who are exempt from the definition. There are also some important differences that arise for certain groups:

- Couples where one of the couple has settled status or is a British or European Economic Area (EEA) national but the other member of the couple is a 'person subject to immigration control' are eligible to claim (see p1459).
- Asylum seekers who are currently receiving income support (IS) because of transitional protection (see p666) are eligible for child tax credit (CTC) when all IS claimants are migrated onto CTC during 2005/06.
- Asylum seekers who receive pension credit (PC) because of transitional protection to means-tested benefits are entitled to CTC.

A **'person subject to immigration control'** is defined as someone who:

- requires leave to enter or remain but does not have it; *or*
- has leave to enter or remain in the UK which is subject to a public funds restriction (see p655); *or*

- has leave to enter or remain which has been given as a result of a maintenance undertaking (see p662); *or*
- is appealing a decision about her/his immigration status.

This definition therefore *does not* apply to:
- EEA nationals, whether or not they are 'workers';
- refugees;
- people with leave to enter or remain outside the immigration rules (exceptional, humanitarian or discretionary leave);
- British citizens;
- family members, whatever their nationality, of EEA workers.

Note: On 1 May 2004 the EEA expanded to include Cyprus, Czech Republic, Estonia, Hungary, Latvia, Lithuania, Malta, Poland, Slovakia and Slovenia.

Regulations exempt certain people from the definition of a 'person subject to immigration control'.

For both CTC and working tax credit (WTC) you are exempt if:
- you are a person with indefinite leave who is subject to a maintenance undertaking but the person who sponsored you has died, or you have been resident in the UK for a period of at least five years from the date of the undertaking or the date you arrived, whichever is later; *or*
- you are a person who has limited leave with a public funds restriction and you are temporarily without funds because money from abroad has been disrupted and there is a reasonable expectation that your supply of funds will resume. The maximum period during which tax credits can be paid under this rule is 42 days in any period of leave.

There is a further exemption for CTC if:
- you are a person who is lawfully working in Great Britain and are a citizen of a state with which the European Community has an agreement concerning equal treatment in social security. (This applies to citizens of Algeria, Morocco, Tunisia and Turkey.)

There is a further exemption for WTC if:
- you are a person who is lawfully present (see p697) in the UK and are a national of a state which has ratified the European Convention on Social and Medical Assistance or a state which has ratified the Council of Europe Social Charter of 1961 and who is lawfully present in the UK. (This includes all EEA countries, Croatia and Turkey.)

Refugees and asylum seekers

If you are recognised as a refugee you can claim backdated tax credits for the period before you were recognised, beginning with the date the claim for asylum was made. You must claim within three months of being notified that you have been granted refugee status.[4] Similar backdating rules apply for other benefits such as IS. The Government plans to remove the backdating provision of IS, housing benefit and council tax benefit but there are no plans to withdraw the backdating provision for tax credits.

Asylum seekers are generally excluded from entitlement to tax credits unless they fall within one of the exemptions listed above or they have a partner who has a different immigration status.

However, if you were entitled to IS urgent cases payments under transitional rules (see p667), you will be entitled to CTC instead of the child allowances in IS when IS claimants are 'migrated' to CTC. This will take place at some point between April 2005 and April 2006.[5] Asylum seekers not entitled to child benefit should also receive an additional payment in lieu of child benefit to top up their CTC.[6]

If you are an asylum seeker entitled to urgent cases payments of IS between 22 August 2003 and 8 September 2003 and are over 60 and now entitled to PC, you are also entitled to CTC for any children for whom you are responsible.[7]

Couples and families

If you are a 'person subject to immigration control', you are not entitled to any tax credits for yourself or for any members of your family, unless you qualify under one of the exemptions above (see p1457). However, where a couple have different immigration statuses, one of which allows the person to claim, the claim is determined as though both members of the couple are **not** subject to immigration control.[8] This means that you can make a couple claim (see p1395) and that you will be eligible for the second adult element of the tax credit. However, if you and your partner have different immigration statuses from one another and your partner is exempt from the 'person subject to immigration control' definition for CTC but not WTC, you will only be able to qualify for CTC. Equally, if your partner is only exempt from the 'person subject to immigration control' definition for WTC, you will only qualify for WTC.[9]

However, if you and your partner have a different immigration status from one another you may not be able to use the disability route to qualify for WTC. This is because the disability route to WTC usually depends on qualifying for incapacity or disability benefits and people who are subject to immigration control are usually excluded from entitlement to these benefits. Therefore, the disability element will not be met if the relevant person is a 'person subject to immigration control' (see p1457).

The immigration status of your children does not affect your entitlement. If you are eligible you can claim for any children regardless of their immigration status.

3. Residence conditions

Tax credits, like most social security benefits, have residence and presence conditions. This means that if you have recently arrived in Great Britain you may not qualify for tax credits immediately and if you go abroad the particular tax credit may no longer be payable. Special rules apply to both Crown servants (see p1461) and European Economic Area nationals; the latter may be protected by European Community (EC) law (see p1461).

In order to claim tax credits you must be 'present' (see p697) in the UK at the time of your claim and you must also be 'ordinarily resident' (see p698) in the UK.

For claims made from 1 May 2004, in order to qualify for child tax credit (CTC) you must have the right to reside. A person who does not have a right to reside will be treated as not present in the UK for the purposes of CTC. Many European Union nationals will have rights to CTC under EC Regulation 1408/71. See below and for full details of the requirement to reside, see Chapter 26.

General rules of presence, temporary absence and residence

It is possible to be treated as present and ordinarily resident during some temporary absences.

If you remain ordinarily resident in the UK and your absence is unlikely to exceed 52 weeks, tax credits continue to be paid during:

- the first eight weeks of any temporary absence;
- the first 12 weeks of any period when you are temporarily absent from the UK if that absence (or any extension to that period of absence) is in connection with:
  - the treatment of an illness or disability of you, your partner, a child for whom you are responsible, or another relative of either you or your partner; *or*
  - the death of your partner, a child for whom you are responsible, or another relative of you or your partner.

This means that you not only continue to satisfy the residence conditions for entitlement to tax credits during the period of an award, but you could also make a fresh or renewal claim while abroad (but see below if you are a member of a couple). If you spend longer abroad than certain permitted periods[10] you may no longer satisfy the residence condition for your tax credit.

If you are not entitled to tax credits while abroad or you have exceeded the permitted period for payment while you are abroad, your partner has to make a claim in her/his own right.

Crown servants[11]

You are exempt from the presence test if you are:

- a Crown servant posted overseas; *and*
  - immediately prior to your posting abroad you were ordinarily resident in the UK; *or*
  - immediately prior to your posting you were in the UK in connection with that posting; *or*
- you are the partner of a Crown servant posted overseas and you have accompanied her/him to the country where s/he is posted or you are temporarily absent from that country for one of the reasons set out above.

Couples

If you are temporarily absent for more than the period allowed or you are no longer ordinarily resident, and your partner remains in the UK, you or your partner must terminate the joint claim.[12] This is because to make a joint claim you must both be treated as being in the UK. The person who remains in the UK can make a fresh single claim if s/he meets the conditions for getting working tax credit (WTC) and/or CTC. If one of the couple fails to report that one of them has been temporarily absent for more than the allowed period and does not terminate the couple claim, the couple may be overpaid as a result and be subject to a penalty (see p1434). The single claim will be calculated on the basis of your past income, not that of your partner's. If your partner is abroad (even for a temporary absence and for no more than eight or 12 weeks) and s/he was the earning partner, you may lose entitlement to WTC if it is decided that s/he no longer satisfies the test of normally working full time (see p1343).

4. European Community law

European Economic Area (EEA) nationals have rights to tax credits under UK law but can also have enhanced rights under European Community (EC) law. What follows is a summary of EC rules as they apply to tax credits. For an overview of EC law and of the rights of EEA nationals, see Chapter 26.

EC Regulation 1408/71

Child tax credit (CTC) falls into the category of a family benefit for the purpose of EC Regulation 1408/71 (see p676).

The general principles of the Regulation in respect of family benefits are:

- You are covered by the Regulation if you or one of your family members has worked in any member state.
- All EEA nationals including those from A8 states (see p683) can potentially rely on the Regulation.

- You cannot export family benefits from another member state.
- You can receive family benefits for children who are not living with you but who are residing elsewhere in the EEA, including A8 States.
- If you are covered by the Regulation you are entitled not to be discriminated against in respect of benefits.
- There are no derogations from this area of EC law in respect of A8 nationals. Consequently A8 nationals are equally entitled to rely on the Regulation.
- If you are covered by the Regulation your family will also be covered, regardless of their nationality.

How this applies in practice

Claimants who have worked in the UK

If you are employed or self-employed in the UK (including A8 nationals), you cannot be denied CTC on the basis of your nationality or because you fail residence tests. A refusal under UK rules may be in breach of the Regulation and would therefore be unlawful. The Regulation expressly provides for a person who is no longer working but who is signing on and claiming jobseeker's allowance (JSA) to be entitled to family benefits[13] but the general non-discrimination provision[14] in the Regulation would mean that anyone who has worked, whether or not entitled to JSA, is entitled to non-discriminatory treatment in respect of family benefits.

Claimants who have worked in another EEA state

If you have not worked in the UK but you have worked elsewhere in the EEA, including A8 states, you may still have rights to CTC under EC Regulation 1408/71. However, the arguments are more complex because a decision has to be made about whether you are now habitually resident in the UK. This is determined in accordance with EC law rather than any UK test.

Claimants who have not worked in any member state

If you have not worked in any member state you will not be covered by the Regulation unless a family member has worked in the EEA.

Right of free movement and access to social advantage

Regulation 1612/68 covers freedom of movement and equality of treatment for 'workers' (see p673). It provides that those who have 'worker' status must not be discriminated against in respect of 'tax and social advantages'. Both tax credits fall into this category. There are equivalent Regulations and Directives that cover former workers (see p681) and self-employed people. EEA workers and family members cannot be discriminated against in terms of access to, and the rates of, tax credits. Family members of EEA workers may therefore qualify for tax credits in their own right. This applies whatever the nationality of the family member. You can also retain your rights as an EEA family member if you divorce. This applies if you are the primary carer of a dependent child who is attending an educational course in the UK.[15] The Government considers that working tax credit is covered by the EC social advantage rule. This is reflected in UK rules and EEA nationals who are workers will automatically be treated as ordinarily resident in the UK.

Association and co-operation agreements

The EEA has agreements with Algeria, Morocco, Tunisia and Turkey. These agreements are very similar to EC Regulation 1408/71 and specify that there should be equal treatment in social security. The benefits covered by the agreements are largely the same as those covered by EC Regulation 1408/71. Therefore, as the Revenue has decided that CTC is a family benefit for EC purposes it will also be covered by the association agreements. For details of who is covered by the agreements, see p684.

These agreements have the potential to assist asylum seekers qualify for tax credits. An asylum seeker who is a national from one of these countries and who has worked in the UK is eligible for CTC. The Government has ended the concession that allowed asylum seekers to take up work if their application for asylum was still outstanding after six months. This means that it has become increasingly difficult for asylum seekers to rely on the association agreements because they are not able to work lawfully. However, a new EC Directive has meant that the Government must allow asylum seekers who have been awaiting a decision on their asylum claim for more than a year the right to work.[16]

Notes

1. **Introduction**
   1 Statement of Changes in Immigration Rules HC 346, February 2005, coming into force 15 March 2005

2. **The immigration status condition**
   2 Reg 3(1) TC(Imm) Regs
   3 s115(9) IAA 1999
   4 Reg 4 TC(Imm) Regs
   5 Reg 5 TC(Imm) Regs
   6 At the time of writing there were no Regulations available, but we understand this to be the position
   7 Reg 5 TC(Imm) Regs
   8 Reg 3(2) TC(Imm) Regs
   9 Reg 3(3) TC(Imm) Regs

3. **Residence conditions**
   10 Reg 7(1) TC(R) Regs
   11 Reg 3 TC(R) Regs
   12 S3 TCA 2002

4. **European Community law**
   13 Articles 1(a), 13 and 75 EC Regulation 1408/71
   14 Article 3 Regulation 1408/71
   15 Immigration (European Economic Area) (Amendment) Regulations 2003
   16 Statement of Changes to Immigration Rules January 2005, para 360; Article 11 Council Directive 2003/9EC

Appendices

Appendix 1

Useful addresses

The President and regional chairs of The Appeals Service

The President
HH Judge Michael Harris
5th Floor
Fox Court
14 Grays Inn Road
London WC1X 8HN
Tel: 020 7712 2600
www.appeals-service.gov.uk

Chief Executive
Ms Christina Townsend
Contact as above

The President (Northern Ireland)
Mr C G MacLynn
6th Floor
Cleaver House
3 Donegal Square North
Belfast BT1 5GA
Tel: 02890 518 518

Regional chairs

Central
Ms Jessica Burns
3rd Floor
Auchinleck House
Broad St
Birmingham B15 1DL
Tel: 0121 634 7200
Minicom: 0121 634 7218

North East
Mr John Tinnion
3rd Floor
York House
York Place
Leeds LS1 2ED
Tel: 0113 251 9500
Minicom: 0113 251 9570

Eastern
Mr Robert Martin
The Pearson Building
57 Upper Parliament Street
Nottingham NG1 6AZ
Tel: 0115 909 3600
Minicom: 0115 909 3692

South East
Mr Jeremy Bennett
Copthall House
9 The Pavement
Grove Road
Sutton SM1 1DA
Tel: 020 8710 2900
Minicom: 020 8710 2966

North West
Mr Nick Warren
36 Dale Street
Liverpool L2 5UZ
Tel: 0151 243 1400
Minicom: 0151 243 1450

Wales and South West

Mr Jim Wood
Oxford House
Hills Street
The Hayes
Cardiff CF1 2DR
Tel: 029 2087 7200
Minicom: 029 2087 7296

Scotland

Mr Kenneth Kirkwood
Wellington House
134-136 Wellington Street
Glasgow G2 2XL
Tel: 0141 354 8400
Minicom: 0141 354 8413

Offices of the Social Security and Child Support Commissioners

England and Wales

3rd Floor
Procession House
55 Ludgate Hill
London EC4M 7JW
Tel: 020 7029 9850
Minicom: 020 7029 9820
www.osscsc.gov.uk

Scotland

Ms Susan M Niven
Secretary to the Commissioners
Office of the Social Security Commissioners
23 Melville Street
Edinburgh EH3 7PW
Tel: 0131 225 2201
www.ossc-scotland.org.uk

Northern Ireland

Office of the Social Security Commissioner and Child Support Commissioners
1st Floor
Headline Building
10-14 Victoria Street
Belfast BT1 3GG
Tel: 028 9033 2344
www.courtsni.gov.uk/en-GB

Inland Revenue* (tax credits)

England, Scotland and Wales

Inland Revenue
Tax Credit Office
Preston PR1 0SB
Tel: 0845 300 3900
Textphone: 0845 300 3909
www.inlandrevenue.gov.uk

Northern Ireland

Inland Revenue
Tax Credit Office
Dorchester House
52-58 Great Victoria Street
Belfast BT2 7WF
Tel: 0845 603 2000
Textphone: 0845 607 6078

**The Inland Revenue and Customs and Excise are merging in 2005 to create a new department called Her Majesty's Revenue and Customs*

Inland Revenue* (child benefit and guardian's allowance)

England, Scotland and Wales

Child Benefit Office
PO Box 1
Newcastle upon Tyne NE88 1AA
Tel: 0845 302 1444
Textphone: 0845 302 1474
www.inlandrevenue.gov.uk

Northern Ireland
Child Benefit Office
Windsor House
9–15 Bedford Street
Belfast BT2 7UW
Tel: 0845 603 2000
Textphone: 0845 607 6078

**The Inland Revenue and Customs and Excise are merging in 2005 to create a new department called Her Majesty's Revenue and Customs*

Inland Revenue* Solicitor's Office

Somerset House
Strand
London WC2R 1LB

**The Inland Revenue and Customs and Excise are merging in 2005 to create a new department called Her Majesty's Revenue and Customs*

National Insurance Contributions Office

Inland Revenue
National Insurance Contributions Office
Benton Park View
Newcastle upon Tyne NE98 1ZZ
Tel: 0191 213 5000

Department for Work and Pensions (benefits)

Chief Executive
David Andrews
Quarry House
Quarry Hill
Leeds LS2 7UA
Tel: 0113 232 4000
www.dwp.gov.uk

Department for Work and Pensions (policy)

The Adelphi
1–11 John Adam Street
London WC2N 6HT
Tel: 020 7962 8000

Department for Work and Pensions Solicitor's Office

New Court
48 Carey Street
London WC2A 2LS
Tel: 020 7962 8000

Benefit Enquiry Line

Victoria House
9th Floor
Ormskirk Road
Preston PR1 2QR
Tel: 0800 88 22 00
Textphone: 0800 24 33 55

The Decision Making and Appeals Unit

Quarry House
Quarry Hill
Leeds LS2 7UB
Tel: 0113 232 4855

The Guidance Team

Child Benefit Centre
PO Box 1
Newcastle upon Tyne NE88 1AA

Disability Benefits Unit

Government Buildings
Warbreck House
Warbreck Hill
Blackpool FY2 0YE
Tel: 0845 712 3456

Health Benefits Division

Sandyford House
Archbold Terrace
Jesmond
Newcastle upon Tyne NE2 1DB
Tel: 0191 203 5555

Department for Education and Skills

Sanctuary Buildings
Great Smith Street
London SW1P 3BT
Tel: 0870 000 2288
www.dfes.gov.uk

Under Eighteens Support Team

Level 4
Steel City House
West Street
Sheffield S1 2GQ
Tel: 01253 848 000

Compensation Recovery Unit

Durham House
Washington
Tyne and Wear NE38 7SF
Tel: 0191 213 5000
Textphone: 0191 225 2003

Independent Review Service for the Social Fund

4th Floor
Centre City Podium
5 Hill Street
Birmingham B5 4UB
Tel: 0121 606 2100
Freephone: 0800 096 1926
Minicom: 0800 096 1926
www.irs-review.org.uk

Health Service Ombudsman

Millbank Tower
Millbank
London SW1P 4QP
Tel: 0845 015 4033
www.ombudsman.org.uk

Local Government Ombudsman

England

10th Floor
Millbank Tower
Millbank
London SW1P 4QP
Tel: 020 7217 4620
www.lgo.org.uk

Scotland

4 Melville Street
Edinburgh EH3 7NS
Tel: 0870 011 5378
www.scottishombudsman.org.uk

Wales

Derwen House
Court Road
Bridgend CF31 1BN
Tel: 01656 661 325
www.ombudsman-wales.org

Northern Ireland

Progressive House
33 Wellington Place
Belfast BT1 6HN
Tel: 0800 343 424
www.ni-ombudsman.org.uk

Freepost address:
Freepost BEL 1478
Belfast BT1 6BR

The Parliamentary Ombudsman

Office of the Parliamentary
Commissioner
Millbank Tower
Millbank
London SW1P 4QP
Tel: 0845 0154 033
www.ombudsman.org.uk

The Independent Adjudicator

Dame Barbara Mills
Adjudicator's Office
Haymarket House
28 Haymarket
London SW1Y 4SP
Tel: 020 7930 2292
www.adjudicatorsoffice.gov.uk

Appendix 2

Information and advice

Independent advice and representation

It is sometimes difficult for unsupported individuals to get a positive response from the Department for Work and Pensions (DWP). You may be taken more seriously if it is clear you have taken advice about your entitlement or have an adviser assisting you.

If you want advice or help with a benefit problem, the following agencies may be able to assist.

- Citizens advice bureaux (CAB) and other local advice centres provide information and advice about benefits and may be able to represent you.
- Law centres can often help in a similar way to a CAB or advice centre.
- Local authority welfare rights workers provide a service in many areas and some arrange advice sessions and take-up campaigns locally.
- Local organisations for particular groups of claimants may offer help. For instance, there are unemployed centres, pensioners groups and centres for people with disabilities.
- Solicitors can give free legal advice to people on low incomes under the 'Legal help' scheme. This does not cover the cost of representation at an appeal hearing but can cover the cost of preparing written submissions and obtaining evidence such as medical reports. However, solicitors do not always have a good working knowledge of the benefit rules and you may need to shop around until you find one who does.

You can find details of advice centres and lawyers in the phone book either under 'advice' or in the 'community' section at the front of the book. Your library or community centre may have details of where to get advice in your area. The Community Legal Service has a list of many organisations who provide advice in different areas of law including welfare benefits. You can phone them on 0845 345 4345 or access this information over the internet at www.clsdirect.org.uk and search the 'directory' for advisers and lawyers within 5, 10 or 40 miles of your home.

Advice from CPAG

Unfortunately, CPAG is unable to deal with enquiries directly from members of the public, but if you are an adviser you can phone the advice line from 2pm to

4pm, Monday to Friday on 020 7833 4627. This is a special phone line; do not ring the main CPAG number. Alternatively, you can write to us at the Citizens' Rights Office, CPAG, 94 White Lion Street, London N1 9PF. Organisations based in Scotland can contact CPAG in Scotland at Unit 9, Ladywell, 94 Duke Street, Glasgow G4 0UW. A phone line is open for Scottish advisers on Tuesday, Wednesday and Thursday mornings between 10am and 12 noon on 0141 552 0552.

Advice from the DWP

You can find an address and phone numbers for your local DWP office in the phone book. They should be able to give you contact details for any office dealing with particular benefits. If you are disabled, you can obtain free telephone advice on benefits on 0800 882 200; minicom 0800 243 355 (in Northern Ireland 0800 220 674; minicom 0800 243 787). This is for general advice and not specific queries on individual claims.

If English is not your first language, ask your local DWP office to arrange for advice in your own language.

Finding help on the Internet

Some information about benefits and a selection of leaflets and forms is available on the DWP website at: www.dwp.gov.uk.

CPAG has a website which carries some articles about upcoming legislation and information about our publications, training and campaigning activities at www.cpag.org.uk.

The RightsNet website at www.rightsnet.org.uk carries details of new legislation and policies affecting social security benefits. It also has links to other useful sites.

Most Acts and Regulations can be found on the government information website at www.legislation.hmso.gov.uk and those for tax credits can be found at www.inlandrevenue.gov.uk.

You can find recent decisions of the social security commissioners at www.osscsc.gov.uk. You can also find many decisions from 1995 to the end of 2001 at www.hywels.clara.co.uk.

Appendix 3

Books, leaflets and periodicals

Many of the books listed here will be in your local public library. Stationery Office books are available from Stationery Office bookshops and also from many others. They may be ordered by post, telephone, fax or email from The Stationery Office, Post Cash Department, PO Box 29, Norwich, NR3 1GN (tel: 0870 600 5522, fax: 0870 600 5533, email: customer.services@tso.co.uk). It also has a website for further information at www.tso.co.uk. Many of the publications listed are available from CPAG; see below for order details, or order from www.cpag.org.uk. For social security information in electronic format see details of the *Welfare Benefits and Tax Credits CD-ROM* given below.

1. Textbooks

Compensation for Industrial Injury
R Lewis (Butterworths, 1987). An excellent study of industrial injury benefits.

The Law of Social Security
AI Ogus, EM Barendt and N Wikeley (Butterworths, 2002). Academic textbook on social security law.

Tolley's National Insurance Contributions 1994–95
(Tolley Publishing Company) A useful book on contributions.

2. Caselaw and legislation

Social Security Case Law – Digest of Commissioners' Decisions
D Neligan (Stationery Office, looseleaf in two vols). Summaries of commissioners' decisions grouped by subject. Also at www.dwp.gov.uk/advisers/docs/neligans/index.asp.

Welfare Benefits and Tax Credits CD-ROM
(CPAG) Includes: all social security legislation consolidated; tax credits legislation; over 2,000 commissioners' decisions, most with commentary; guidance; the *Welfare Benefits and Tax Credits Handbook* with links to the relevant legislation, decisions and guidance; CPAG's *Housing Benefit and Council Tax Benefit Legislation* (with commentary); housing benefit and council tax benefit circulars; transcripts of High Court judgments; the *Child Support Handbook* and child support regulations. Updated three times a year. Free trial disks are available from CPAG. The single user price for 2005, including updates, is £280 + VAT. Phone Liz Dawson on 020 7812 5212 for multi-user prices.

The Law Relating to Child Support
(Stationery Office, looseleaf) Also available at www.dwp.gov.uk/advisers/docs/lawvols/orangvol/index.asp.

The Law Relating to Social Security
(Stationery Office, looseleaf, 12 vols) All the legislation but without any comment. Known as the 'Blue Book'. Vols 6, 7, 8, 11 and 12 deal with means-tested benefits. Also available at www.dwp.gov.uk/advisers/docs/lawvols/bluevol/index.asp.

Social Security Legislation, Volume I: Non Means Tested Benefits
D Bonner, I Hooker and R White (Sweet & Maxwell). Legislation with

commentary. 2005/2006 edition available from October 2005: £74 for the main volume, reduced to £67 if you are a CPAG member and order from CPAG before 29 July 2005, or at full price from August.

Social Security Legislation, Volume II: Income Support, Jobseeker's Allowance, Pension Credit and the Social Fund
J Mesher, P Wood, R Poynter, N Wikeley and D Bonner (Sweet & Maxwell). Legislation with commentary. 2005/2006 edition available from October 2005: £74 for the main volume, reduced to £67 if you are a CPAG member and order from CPAG before 29 July 2005, or at full price from August.

Social Security Legislation, Volume III: Administration, Adjudication and the European Dimension
M Rowland and R White (Sweet & Maxwell). Legislation with commentary. 2005/2006 edition available from October 2005: £74 for the main volume, reduced to £67 if you are a CPAG member and order from CPAG before 29 July 2005, or at full price from August.

Social Security Legislation, Volume IV: Tax Credits and Employer-Paid Social Security Benefits
N Wikeley and D Williams (Sweet & Maxwell). Legislation with commentary. 2005/2006 edition available from October 2005: £74 for the main volume, reduced to £67 if you are a CPAG member and order from CPAG before 29 July 2005, or at full price from August.

Social Security Legislation – updating supplement to Volumes I, II, III & IV
(Sweet & Maxwell) The March 2006 update to the 2005/2006 main volumes, £47, reduced to £43 if you are a CPAG member and order from CPAG before 29 July 2005, or at full price from August.

CPAG's Housing Benefit and Council Tax Benefit Legislation
L Findlay, R Poynter, P Stagg, S Wright and C George (CPAG). Contains legislation with a detailed commentary. 2005/2006 edition (18th) available from December 2005, priced at £91 including Supplement. Reduced to £84 per set if ordered before 29 July 2005. The 17th edition (2004/2005) is still available at £89 per set. This publication is also on the *Welfare Benefits and Tax Credits CD-ROM* (see p1474).

Child Support: The Legislation
E Jacobs and G Douglas (Sweet & Maxwell). The 7th edition main volume is available from October 2005 at £75, reduced to £68 if you are a CPAG member and order from CPAG before 29 July 2005, or at full price from August.

Social Fund Directions
Available on the DWP website at www.dwp.gov.uk/advisers/socialfundguide/sfguide/part8.pdf.

3. Official guidance

Benefits Agency Guide, IS for 16/17-year-olds
(Stationery Office, amended February 1996)

Charging for Residential Accommodation Guide
(Department of Health, one vol)

Child Support Adjudication Guide
(Stationery Office, looseleaf)

Child Support: A Technical Guide
(Child Support Agency, looseleaf, 8 vols) Also available at www.csa.gov.uk/newcsaweb/techguide/index.asp.

Decision Makers Guide
(14 volumes, memos and letters) Also available at www.dwp.gov.uk/publications/dwp/dmg/cont.asp.

Field Officers' Guide
(Child Support Agency, looseleaf)

Handbook for Delegated Medical Practitioners
(Stationery Office, 1988)

Housing Benefit and Council Tax Benefit Guidance Manual
(Stationery Office, looseleaf) Also available at www.dwp.gov.uk/housingbenefit/manuals/hbgm/index.asp.

Industrial Injuries Handbook for Adjudicating Medical Authorities
(Stationery Office, looseleaf)

Income Support Guide
(Stationery Office, looseleaf, 8 vols) Procedural guide issued to DWP staff.

Notes on the Diagnosis of Prescribed Diseases (except pneumoconiosis and related occupational diseases and occupational deafness)
(Stationery Office, 1991)

Tax Credit Technical Manual
(available at www.inlandrevenue.gov.uk/manuals/index.htm)

The Social Fund Guide
(Stationery Office, looseleaf 2 vols) Also available at www.dwp.gov.uk/advisers/socialfundguide/sfguide/content.asp)

4. Leaflets

The DWP publishes many leaflets covering particular benefits or groups of claimants or contributors. They are free from your local DWP or Jobcentre Plus office. If you want to order large numbers of leaflets, or receive information about new leaflets, you can join the Publicity Register by writing to Publicity Register, Freepost, NWW 1853, Manchester, M2 9LU, tel: 0845 602 44 44 (9.00am to 6.00pm, Monday to Friday), fax: 0870 241 2634, email: publicity-register@dwp.gsi.gov.uk. Free leaflets on HB/CTB are available from the relevant department of your local council. A selection of leaflets can be found at www.dwp.gov.uk.

5. Periodicals

CPAG's *Welfare Rights Bulletin* is published every two months by CPAG. It covers developments in social security law, including commissioners' decisions, and updates this *Handbook* between editions. The annual subscription is £29 but it is sent automatically to CPAG Rights and Comprehensive Members. For subscription and membership details contact CPAG. Many features of the *Bulletin* are also reproduced on the *Welfare Benefits and Tax Credits CD-ROM*.

Articles on social security can also be found in *Legal Action* (Legal Action Group, monthly magazine) and the *Journal of Social Security Law* (Sweet & Maxwell, quarterly).

6. Other publications – general

Child Support Handbook
£21.50 (13th edition, summer 2005) (£6.00 for claimants). Also available on the *Welfare Benefits and Tax Credits CD-ROM*.

Personal Finance Handbook
£14.00 (1st edition, January 2005)

Paying for Care Handbook
£18.50 (5th edition, 2005)

Student Support and Benefits Handbook: England, Wales and Northern Ireland
£11.00 (3rd edition, autumn 2005)

Benefits for Students in Scotland Handbook
£11.00 (3rd edition, autumn 2005)

Council Tax Handbook
£15.00 (6th edition, autumn 2005)

Debt Advice Handbook
£16.50 (6th edition, November 2004)

Fuel Rights Handbook
£15.00 (13th edition, February 2005)

Migration and Social Security Handbook
£21.00 (4th edition, 2005)

Guide to Housing Benefit and Council Tax Benefit
£21.50 (Summer 2005)

Disability Rights Handbook
£16.50 (May 2005)

The Young Persons Handbook
£14.95 (2nd edition, September 2004)

Welfare to Work Handbook
£22.95 (2nd edition, July 2004)

For CPAG publications and most of those in Sections 2 and 6 contact:
CPAG, 94 White Lion Street, London N1 9PF, tel: 020 7837 7979, fax: 020 7837 6414. Order forms are also available at www.cpag.org.uk. Postage and packing: free for orders up to £10 in value; for order value £10.01–£100.00 add a flat rate charge of £3.99; for order value £100.01–£500.00 add £5.99; for order value £500.00+ add £9.99.

Appendix 4

Disabilities which may make a person incapable of work

Schedule to the Social Security (Incapacity for Work) (General) Regulations 1995

(1) *Activity*		*(2)* *Descriptor*	*(3)* *Points*
Part 1. Physical disabilities			
1. Walking on level ground with a walking stick or other aid if such aid is normally used.	1(a)	Cannot walk at all.	15
	(b)	Cannot walk more than a few steps without stopping or severe discomfort.	15
	(c)	Cannot walk more than 50 metres without stopping or severe discomfort.	15
	(d)	Cannot walk more than 200 metres without stopping or severe discomfort.	7
	(e)	Cannot walk more than 400 metres without stopping or severe discomfort.	3
	(f)	Cannot walk more than 800 metres without stopping or severe discomfort.	0
	(g)	No walking problem.	0
2. Walking up and down stairs.	2(a)	Cannot walk up and down one stair.	15
	(b)	Cannot walk up and down a flight of 12 stairs.	15
	(c)	Cannot walk up and down a flight of 12 stairs without holding on and taking a rest.	7
	(d)	Cannot walk up and down a flight of 12 stairs without holding on.	3
	(e)	Can only walk up and down a flight of 12 stairs if he goes sideways or one step at a time.	3
	(f)	No problem in walking up and down stairs.	0
3. Sitting in an upright chair with a back, but no arms.	3(a)	Cannot sit comfortably.	15
	(b)	Cannot sit comfortably for more than 10 minutes without having to move from the chair [*because the degree of discomfort makes it impossible to continue sitting].	15

(1) *Activity*	*(2)* *Descriptor*		*(3)* *Points*
	(c)	Cannot sit comfortably for more than 30 minutes without having to move from the chair [*because the degree of discomfort makes it impossible to continue sitting].	7
	(d)	Cannot sit comfortably for more than 1 hour without having to move from the chair [*because the degree of discomfort makes it impossible to continue sitting].	3
	(e)	Cannot sit comfortably for more than 2 hours without having to move from the chair [*because the degree of discomfort makes it impossible to continue sitting].	0
	(f)	No problem with sitting.	0
4. Standing without the support of another person or the use of an aid except a walking stick.	4(a)	Cannot stand unassisted.	15
	(b)	Cannot stand for more than a minute before needing to sit down.	15
	(c)	Cannot stand for more than 10 minutes before needing to sit down	15
	(d)	Cannot stand for more than 30 minutes before needing to sit down.	7
	(e)	Cannot stand for more than 10 minutes before needing to move around.	7
	(f)	Cannot stand for more than 30 minutes before needing to move around.	3
	(g)	No problem standing.	0
5. Rising from sitting in an upright chair with a back but no arms without the help of another person.	5(a)	Cannot rise from sitting to standing.	15
	(b)	Cannot rise from sitting to standing without holding on to something.	7
	(c)	Sometimes cannot rise from sitting to standing without holding on to something.	3
	(d)	No problem with rising from sitting to standing.	0
6. Bending and kneeling.	6(a)	Cannot bend to touch his knees and straighten up again.	15
	(b)	Cannot either bend or kneel, or bend and kneel as if to pick up a piece of paper from the floor and straighten up again.	15
	(c)	Sometimes cannot either bend or kneel, or bend and kneel as if to pick up a piece of paper from the floor and straighten up again.	3
	(d)	No problem with bending or kneeling.	0

(1) Activity	(2) Descriptor		(3) Points
7. Manual dexterity.	7(a)	Cannot turn the pages of a book with either hand.	15
	(b)	Cannot turn a sink tap or the control knobs on a cooker with either hand.	15
	(c)	Cannot pick up a coin which is 2.5cm or less in diameter with either hand.	15
	(d)	Cannot use a pen or pencil.	15
	(e)	Cannot tie a bow in laces or string.	10
	(f)	Cannot turn a sink tap or the control knobs on a cooker with one hand but can with the other.	6
	(g)	Cannot pick up a coin which is 2.5cm or less in diameter with one hand but can with the other.	6
	(h)	No problem with manual dexterity.	0
8. Lifting and carrying by the use of the upper body and arms (excluding all other activities specified in Part I of this Schedule).	8(a)	Cannot pick up a paperback book with either hand.	15
	(b)	Cannot pick up and carry a 0.5 litre carton of milk with either hand.	15
	(c)	Cannot pick up and pour from a full saucepan or kettle of 1.7 litre capacity with either hand.	15
	(d)	Cannot pick up and carry a 2.5 kilogramme bag of potatoes with either hand.	8
	(e)	Cannot pick up and carry a 0.5 litre carton of milk with one hand, but can with the other.	6
	(f)	Cannot pick up and carry a 2.5 kilogramme bag of potatoes with one hand, but can with the other.	0
	(g)	No problem with lifting and carrying.	0
9. Reaching.	9(a)	Cannot raise either arm as if to put something in the top pocket of a coat or jacket.	15
	(b)	Cannot raise either arm to his head as if to put on a hat.	15
	(c)	Cannot put either arm behind back as if to put on a coat or jacket.	15
	(d)	Cannot raise either arm above his head as if to reach for something.	15
	(e)	Cannot raise one arm to his head as if to put on a hat, but can with the other.	6
	(f)	Cannot raise one arm above his head as if to reach for something, but can with the other.	0
	(g)	No problem with reaching.	0

(1) Activity	(2) Descriptor	(3) Points
10. Speech.	10(a) Cannot speak.	15
	(b) Speech cannot be understood by family or friends.	15
	(c) Speech cannot be understood by strangers.	15
	(d) Strangers have great difficulty understanding speech.	10
	(e) Strangers have some difficulty understanding speech.	8
	(f) No problems with speech.	20
11. Hearing with a hearing aid or other aid if normally worn.	11(a) Cannot hear sounds at all.	15
	(b) Cannot hear well enough to follow a television programme with the volume turned up.	15
	(c) Cannot hear well enough to understand someone talking in a loud voice in a quiet room.	15
	(d) Cannot hear well enough to understand someone talking in a normal voice in a quiet room.	10
	(e) Cannot hear well enough to understand someone talking in a normal voice on a busy street.	8
	(f) No problem with hearing.	0
12. Vision in normal daylight or bright electric light with glasses or other aid to vision if such aid is normally worn.	12(a) Cannot tell light from dark.	15
	(b) Cannot see the shape of furniture in the room.	15
	(c) Cannot see well enough to read 16 point print at a distance greater than 20 centimetres.	15
	(d) Cannot see well enough to recognise a friend across the room at a distance of at least 5 metres.	12
	(e) Cannot see well enough to recognise a friend across the road at a distance of at least 15 metres.	8
	(f) No problems with vision.	0
13. Continence (other than enuresis (bed wetting)).	13(a) No voluntary control over bowels.	15
	(b) No voluntary control over bladder.	15
	(c) Loses control of bowels at least once a week.	15
	(d) Loses control of bowels at least once a month.	15
	(e) Loses control of bowels occasionally.	9

(1) Activity	(2) Descriptor		(3) Points
	(f)	Loses control of bladder at least once a month.	3
	(g)	Loses control of bladder occasionally.	0
	(h)	No problem with continence.	0
14. Remaining conscious without having epileptic or similar seizures during waking moments. **Note:** CIB/0884/2003 says that this wording is of no effect, and that the test should be: 'Remaining conscious other than for normal periods of sleep'.	14(a)	Has an involuntary episode of lost or altered consciousness at least once a day.	15
	(b)	Has an involuntary episode of lost or altered consciousness at least once a week.	15
	(c)	Has an involuntary episode of lost or altered consciousness at least once a month.	15
	(d)	Has had an involuntary episode of lost or altered consciousness at least twice in the 6 months before the day in respect to which it falls to be determined whether he is incapable of work for the purposes of entitlement to any benefit, allowance or advantage.	12
	(e)	Has an involuntary episode of lost or altered consciousness once in the 6 months before the day in respect to which it falls to be determined whether he is incapable of work for the purposes of entitlement to any benefit allowance or advantage.	8
	(f)	Has had an involuntary episode of lost or altered consciousness once in the 3 years before the day in respect to which it falls to be determined whether he is incapable of work for the purposes of entitlement to any benefit, allowance or advantage.	0
	(g)	Has no problems with consciousness.	0
Part II. Mental disabilities			
15. Completion of tasks.	15(a)	Cannot answer the telephone and reliably take a message.	2
	(b)	Often sits for hours doing nothing.	2
	(c)	Cannot concentrate to read a magazine article or follow a radio or television programme.	1
	(d)	Cannot use a telephone book or other directory to find a number.	1
	(e)	Mental condition prevents him from undertaking leisure activities previously enjoyed.	1
	(f)	Overlooks or forgets the risk posed by domestic appliances or other common hazards due to poor concentration.	1

(1) *Activity*	*(2)* *Descriptor*	*(3)* *Points*
	(g) Agitation, confusion or forgetfulness has resulted in potentially dangerous accidents in the 3 months before the day in respect to which it falls to be determined whether he is incapable of work for the purposes of entitlement to any benefit, allowance or advantage.	1
	(h) Concentration can only be sustained by prompting.	1
16. Daily living.	16(a) Needs encouragement to get up and dress.	2
	(b) Needs alcohol before midday.	2
	(c) Is frequently distressed at some time of the day due to fluctuation of mood.	1
	(d) Does not care about his appearance and living conditions.	1
	(e) Sleep problems interfere with his daytime activities.	1
17. Coping with pressure.	17(a) Mental stress was a factor in making him stop work.	2
	(b) Frequently feels scared or panicky for no obvious reason.	2
	(c) Avoids carrying out routine activities because he is convinced they will prove too tiring or stressful.	1
	(d) Is unable to cope with changes in daily routine.	1
	(e) Frequently finds there are so many things to do that he gives up because of fatigue, apathy or disinterest.	1
	(f) Is scared or anxious that work would bring back or worsen his illness.	1
18. Interaction with other people.	18(a) Cannot look after himself without help from others.	2
	(b) Gets upset by ordinary events and it results in disruptive behavioural problems.	2
	(c) Mental problems impair ability to communicate with other people.	2
	(d) Gets irritated by things that would not have bothered him before he became ill.	1
	(e) Prefers to be left alone for 6 hours or more each day.	1
	(f) Is too frightened to go out alone.	1

*In accordance with CIB/1239/2004, the wording 'because the degree of discomfort makes it impossible to continue sitting' in 3(b)–(e) does not apply from 15 July 2004.

Appendix 5

Statutory maternity pay, statutory paternity pay (birth) and maternity allowance

If your baby is expected during the week which begins on Sunday	*the 15th week before the EWC begins on Sunday+*	*and the earliest week for which you can get SMP or MA begins on Sunday++*	*Your 66-week test period for MA begins on Sunday*
3.4.05	19.12.04	16.1.05	28.12.03
10.4.05	26.12.04	23.1.05	4.1.04
17.4.05	2.1.05	30.1.05	11.1.04
24.4.05	9.1.05	6.2.05	18.1.04
1.5.05	16.1.05	13.2.05	25.1.04
8.5.05	23.1.05	20.2.05	1.2.04
15.5.05	30.1.05	27.2.05	8.2.04
22.5.05	6.2.05	6.3.05	15.2.04
29.5.05	13.2.05	13.3.05	22.2.04
5.6.05	20.2.05	20.3.05	29.2.04
12.6.05	27.2.05	27.3.05	7.3.04
19.6.05	6.3.05	3.4.05	14.3.04
26.6.05	13.3.05	10.4.05	21.3.04
3.7.05	20.3.05	17.4.05	28.3.04
10.7.05	27.3.05	24.4.05	4.4.04
17.7.05	3.4.05	1.5.05	11.4.04
24.7.05	10.4.05	8.5.05	18.4.04
31.7.05	17.4.05	15.5.05	25.4.04
7.8.05	24.4.05	22.5.05	2.5.04
14.8.05	1.5.05	29.5.05	9.5.04
21.8.05	8.5.05	5.6.05	16.5.04
28.8.05	15.5.05	12.6.05	23.5.04
4.9.05	22.5.05	19.6.05	30.5.04
11.9.05	29.5.05	26.6.05	6.6.04
18.9.05	5.6.05	3.7.05	13.6.04

If your baby is expected during the week which begins on Sunday	*the 15th week before the EWC begins on Sunday+*	*and the earliest week for which you can get SMP or MA begins on Sunday++*	*Your 66-week test period for MA begins on Sunday*
25.9.05	12.6.05	10.7.05	20.6.04
2.10.05	19.6.05	17.7.05	27.6.04
9.10.05	26.6.05	24.7.05	4.7.04
16.10.05	3.7.05	31.7.05	11.7.04
23.10.05	10.7.05	7.8.05	18.7.04
30.10.05	17.7.05	14.8.05	25.7.04
6.11.05	24.7.05	21.8.05	1.8.04
13.11.05	31.7.05	28.8.05	8.8.04
20.11.05	7.8.05	4.9.05	15.8.04
27.11.05	14.8.05	11.9.05	22.8.04
4.12.05	21.8.05	18.9.05	29.8.04
11.12.05	28.8.05	25.9.05	5.9.04
18.12.05	4.9.05	2.10.05	12.9.04
25.12.05	11.9.05	9.10.05	19.9.04
1.1.06	18.9.05	16.10.05	26.9.04
8.1.06	25.9.05	23.10.05	3.10.04
15.1.06	2.10.05	30.10.05	10.10.04
22.1.06	9.10.05	6.11.05	17.10.04
29.1.06	16.10.05	13.11.05	24.10.04
5.2.06	23.10.05	20.11.05	31.10.04
12.2.06	30.10.05	27.11.05	7.11.04
19.2.06	6.11.05	4.12.05	14.11.04
26.2.06	13.11.05	11.12.05	21.11.04
5.3.06	20.11.05	18.12.05	28.11.04
12.3.06	27.11.05	25.12.05	5.12.04
19.3.06	4.12.05	1.1.06	12.12.04
26.3.06	11.12.05	8.1.06	19.12.04
2.4.06	18.12.05	15.1.06	26.12.04
9.4.06	25.12.05	22.1.06	2.1.05
16.4.06	1.1.06	29.1.06	9.1.05
23.4.06	8.1.06	5.2.06	16.1.05
30.4.06	15.1.06	12.2.06	23.1.05
7.5.06	22.1.06	19.2.06	30.1.05
14.5.06	29.1.06	26.2.06	6.2.05
21.5.06	5.2.06	5.3.06	13.2.05
28.5.06	12.2.06	12.3.06	20.2.05
4.6.06	19.2.06	19.3.06	27.2.05
11.6.06	26.2.06	26.3.06	6.3.05
18.6.06	5.3.06	2.4.06	13.3.05

If your baby is expected during the week which begins on Sunday	*the 15th week before the EWC begins on Sunday+*	*and the earliest week for which you can get SMP or MA begins on Sunday++*	*Your 66-week test period for MA begins on Sunday*
25.6.06	12.3.06	9.4.06	20.3.05
2.7.06	19.3.06	16.4.06	27.3.05
9.7.06	26.3.06	23.4.06	3.4.05
16.7.06	2.4.06	30.4.06	10.4.05
23.7.06	9.4.06	7.5.06	17.4.05
30.7.06	16.4.06	14.5.06	24.4.05
6.8.06	23.4.06	21.5.06	1.5.05
13.8.06	30.4.06	28.5.06	8.5.05
20.8.06	7.5.06	4.6.06	15.5.05
27.8.06	14.5.06	11.6.06	22.5.05
3.9.06	21.5.06	18.6.06	29.5.05
10.9.06	28.5.06	25.6.06	5.6.05
17.9.06	4.6.06	2.7.06	12.6.05
24.9.06	11.6.06	9.7.06	19.6.05
1.10.06	18.6.06	16.7.06	26.6.05
8.10.06	25.6.06	23.7.06	3.7.05
15.10.06	2.7.06	30.7.06	10.7.05
22.10.06	9.7.06	6.8.06	17.7.05
29.10.06	16.7.06	13.8.06	24.7.05

+ EWC is the expected week of childbirth. The 15th week before the EWC is relevant to the continuous employment rule and the earnings condition for statutory maternity pay and statutory paternity pay (birth). See Chapter 23 for more information.

++ This is the 11th week before the baby is due (unless your baby is born earlier – see Chapters 17 and 23 for possible exceptions).

Appendix 6

Pensionable age for women aged between 40 and 45 on 6 April 1995

Date of birth	*Pensionable age (in years/months)*	*Date pensionable age reached*
06.04.50 – 05.05.50	60.1 – 60.0	06.05.2010
06.05.50 – 05.06.50	60.2 – 60.1	06.07.2010
06.06.50 – 05.07.50	60.3 – 60.2	06.09.2010
06.07.50 – 05.08.50	60.4 – 60.3	06.11.2010
06.08.50 – 05.09.50	60.5 – 60.4	06.01.2011
06.09.50 – 05.10.50	60.6 – 60.5	06.03.2011
06.10.50 – 05.11.50	60.7 – 60.6	06.05.2011
06.11.50 – 05.12.50	60.8 – 60.7	06.07.2011
06.12.50 – 05.01.51	60.9 – 60.8	06.09.2011
06.01.51 – 05.02.51	60.10 – 60.9	06.11.2011
06.02.51 – 05.03.51	60.11 – 60.10	06.01.2012
06.03.51 – 05.04.51	61.0 – 60.11	06.03.2012
06.04.51 – 05.05.51	61.1 – 61.0	06.05.2012
06.05.51 – 05.06.51	61.2 – 61.1	06.07.2012
06.06.51 – 05.07.51	61.3 – 61.2	06.09.2012
06.07.51 – 05.08.51	61.4 – 61.3	06.11.2012
06.08.51 – 05.09.51	61.5 – 61.4	06.01.2013
06.09.51 – 05.10.51	61.6 – 61.5	06.03.2013
06.10.51 – 05.11.51	61.7 – 61.6	06.05.2013
06.11.51 – 05.12.51	61.8 – 61.7	06.07.2013
06.12.51 – 05.01.52	61.9 – 61.8	06.09.2013
06.01.52 – 05.02.52	61.10 – 61.9	06.11.2013
06.02.52 – 05.03.52	61.11 – 61.10	06.01.2014
06.03.52 – 05.04.52	62.0 – 61.11	06.03.2014
06.04.52 – 05.05.52	62.1 – 62.0	06.05.2014
06.05.52 – 05.06.52	62.2 – 62.1	06.07.2014

Date of birth	*Pensionable age (in years/months)*	*Date pensionable age reached*
06.06.52 – 05.07.52	62.3 – 62.2	06.09.2014
06.07.52 – 05.08.52	62.4 – 62.3	06.11.2014
06.08.52 – 05.09.52	62.5 – 62.4	06.01.2015
06.09.52 – 05.10.52	62.6 – 62.5	06.03.2015
06.10.52 – 05.11.52	62.7 – 62.6	06.05.2015
06.11.52 – 05.12.52	62.8 – 62.7	06.07.2015
06.12.52 – 05.01.53	62.9 – 62.8	06.09.2015
06.01.53 – 05.02.53	62.10 – 62.9	06.11.2015
06.02.53 – 05.03.53	62.11 – 62.10	06.01.2016
06.03.53 – 05.04.53	63.0 – 62.11	06.03.2016
06.04.53 – 05.05.53	63.1 – 63.0	06.05.2016
06.05.53 – 05.06.53	63.2 – 63.1	06.07.2016
06.06.53 – 05.07.53	63.3 – 63.2	06.09.2016
06.07.53 – 05.08.53	63.4 – 63.3	06.11.2016
06.08.53 – 05.09.53	63.5 – 63.4	06.01.2017
06.09.53 – 05.10.53	63.6 – 63.5	06.03.2017
06.10.53 – 05.11.53	63.7 – 63.6	06.05.2017
06.11.53 – 05.12.53	63.8 – 63.7	06.07.2017
06.12.53 – 05.01.54	63.9 – 63.8	06.09.2017
06.01.54 – 05.02.54	63.10 – 63.9	06.11.2017
06.02.54 – 05.03.54	63.11 – 63.10	06.01.2018
06.03.54 – 05.04.54	64.0 – 63.11	06.03.2018
06.04.54 – 05.05.54	64.1 – 64.0	06.05.2018
06.05.54 – 05.06.54	64.2 – 64.1	06.07.2018
06.06.54 – 05.07.54	64.3 – 64.2	06.09.2018
06.07.54 – 05.08.54	64.4 – 64.3	06.11.2018
06.08.54 – 05.09.54	64.5 – 64.4	06.01.2019
06.09.54 – 05.10.54	64.6 – 64.5	06.03.2019
06.10.54 – 05.11.54	64.7 – 64.6	06.05.2019
06.11.54 – 05.12.54	64.8 – 64.7	06.07.2019
06.12.54 – 05.01.55	64.9 – 64.8	06.09.2019
06.01.55 – 05.02.55	64.10 – 64.9	06.11.2019
06.02.55 – 05.03.55	64.11 – 64.10	06.01.2020
06.03.55 – 05.04.55	65.0 – 64.11	06.03.2020
06.04.55	65.0	06.04.2020

Appendix 7

Prescribed degrees of disablement

Schedule 2 to the Social Security (General Benefit) Regulations 1982 SI No.1408

	Description of injury	*Degree of disablement %*
1	Loss of both hands or amputation at higher sites	100
2	Loss of a hand and a foot	100
3	Double amputation through leg or thigh, or amputation through leg or thigh on one side and loss of other foot	100
4	Loss of sight to such an extent as to render the claimant unable to perform any work for which eyesight is essential	100
5	Very severe facial disfiguration	100
6	Absolute deafness	100
7	Forequarter or hindquarter amputation	100

Amputation cases – upper limbs (either arm)

	Description of injury	*Degree of disablement %*
8	Amputation through shoulder joint	90
9	Amputation below shoulder with stump less than 20.5 cms from tip of acromion	80
10	Amputation from 20.5 cms from tip of acromion to less than 11.5 cms below tip of olecranon	70
11	Loss of a hand or of the thumb and 4 fingers of 1 hand or amputation from 11.5 cms below tip of olecranon	60
12	Loss of thumb	30
13	Loss of thumb and its metacarpal bone	40
14	Loss of 4 fingers of 1 hand	50
15	Loss of 3 fingers of 1 hand	30
16	Loss of 2 fingers of 1 hand	20
17	Loss of terminal phalanx of thumb	20

Amputation cases – lower limbs

	Description of injury	*Degree of disablement %*
18	Amputation of both feet resulting in end-bearing stumps	90
19	Amputation through both feet proximal to the metatarso-phalangeal joint	80
20	Loss of all toes to both feet through the metatarso-phalangeal joint	40
21	Loss of all toes of both feet proximal to the proximal inter-phalangeal joint	30
22	Loss of all toes of both feet distal to the proximal inter-phalangeal joint	20
23	Amputation at hip	90

	Description of injury	Degree of disablement %
24	Amputation below hip with stump not exceeding 13 cms in length measured from tip of great trochanter	80
25	Amputation below hip and above knee with stump exceeding 13 cms in length measured from tip of great trochanter, or at knee not resulting in end-bearing stump	70
26	Amputation at knee resulting in end-bearing stump or below knee with stump not exceeding 9 cms	60
27	Amputation below knee with stump exceeding 9 cms but not exceeding 13 cms	50
28	Amputation below knee with stump exceeding 13 cms	40
29	Amputation of 1 foot resulting in end-bearing stump	30
30	Amputation through 1 foot proximal to the metatarso-phalangeal joint	30
31	Loss of all toes of 1 foot through the metatarso- phalangeal joint	20
Other injuries		
32	Loss of 1 eye, without complications, the other being normal	40
33	Loss of vision of 1 eye, without complications or disfigurement of the eyeball, the other being normal	30
Loss of fingers of right or left hand		
Index finger:		
34	Whole	14
35	2 phalanges	11
36	1 phalanx	9
37	Guillotine amputation of tip without loss of bone	5
Middle finger:		
38	Whole	12
39	2 phalanges	9
40	1 phalanx	7
41	Guillotine amputation of tip without loss of bone	4
Ring or little finger:		
42	Whole	7
43	2 phalanges	6
44	1 phalanx	5
45	Guillotine amputation of tip without loss of bone	2
Loss of toes of right or left foot		
Great toe:		
46	Through metatarso-phalangeal joint	14
47	Part, with some loss of bone	3
Any other toe:		
48	Through metatarso-phalangeal joint	3
49	Part, with some loss of bone	1
2 toes of 1 foot, excluding great toe:		
50	Through metatarso-phalangeal joint	5
51	Part, with some loss of bone	2
3 toes of 1 foot, excluding great toe:		
52	**Through metatarso-phalangeal joint**	6
53	Part, with some loss of bone	3
4 toes of 1 foot, excluding great toe:		
54	Through metatarso-phalangeal joint	9
55	Part, with some loss of bone	3

The degree of disablement due to occupational deafness is assessed using tables and a formula to be found in regulation 34 of and Schedule 3 to the Social Security (Industrial Injuries) (Prescribed Diseases) Regulations 1985 as amended.

Appendix 8

Prescribed industrial diseases

Part I of Schedule 1 to the Social Security (Industrial Injuries) (Prescribed Diseases) Regulations 1985 SI No. 967 as amended

Prescribed disease or injury	*Occupation*
A – Conditions due to physical agents	**Any occupation involving:**
A1 Leukaemia (other than chronic lymphatic leukaemia) or cancer of the bone, female breast, testis or thyroid.	Exposure to electro-magnetic radiations (other than radiant heat), or to ionising particles, where the dose is sufficient to double the condition.
A2 Cataract.	Frequent or prolonged exposure to radiation from red-hot or white-hot material.
A3 Dysbarism, including decompression sickness, barotrauma and osteonecrosis.	Subjection to compressed or rarified air or from molten or red-hot material.
A4 Cramp of the hand or forearm due to repetitive movements.	Prolonged periods of handwriting, typing or other repetitive movements of the fingers, hand or arm.
A5 Subcutaneous cellulitis of the hand (beat hand).	Manual labour causing severe or prolonged friction or pressure on the hand.
A6 Bursitis or subcutaneous cellulites arising at or about the knee due to severe or prolonged external friction or pressure at or about the knee (beat knee).	Manual labour causing severe or prolonged external friction or pressure at or about the knee.
A7 Bursitis or subcutaneous cellulites arising at or about the elbow due to severe or prolonged external friction or pressure at or about the elbow (beat elbow).	Manual labour causing severe or prolonged external friction or pressure at or about the elbow.
A8 Traumatic inflammation of the tendons of the hand or forearm, or of the associated tendon sheaths.	Manual labour, or frequent or repeated movements of the hand or wrist.
A9 Miner's nystagmus.	Work in or about a mine.

Prescribed disease or injury	*Occupation*
A10 Sensorineural hearing loss amounting to at least 50dB in each ear, being the average of hearing losses at 1, 2 and 3 kHz frequencies, and being due in the case of at least one ear to occupational noise (occupational deafness).	Any occupation involving the use of, or work wholly or mainly in the immediate vicinity of the use of, a: *(a)* band saw, circular saw or cutting disc to cut metal in the metal founding or forging industries, circular saw to cut products in the manufacture of steel, powered (other than hand powered) grinding tool on metal (other than sheet metal or plate metal, pneumatic percussive tool on metal, pressurised air arc tool to gouge metal, burner or torch to cut or dress steel based products, skid transfer bank, knock out and shake out grid in a foundry, machine (other than a power press machine) to forge metal including a machine used to drop stamp metal by means of closed or open dies or drop hammers, machine to cut or shape or clean metal nails, or plasma spray gun to spray molten metal; *(b)* pneumatic percussive tool to drill rock in a quarry, on stone in a quarry works, used underground, for mining coal, for sinking a shaft, or for tunnelling in civil engineering works; *(c)* vibrating metal moulding box in the concrete products industry, or circular saw to cut concrete masonry blocks; *(d)* machine in the manufacture of textiles for weaving man-made or natural fibres (including mineral fibres), high speed false twisting of fibres, or the mechanical cleaning of bobbins; *(e)* multi-cutter moulding machine on wood, planing machine on wood, automatic or semi-automatic lathe on wood, multiple cross-cut machine on wood, automatic shaping machine on wood, double-end tenoning machine on wood, vertical spindle moulding machine (including a high speed routing machine) on wood, edge banding machine on wood, bandsawing machine (with a blade width of not less than 75 millimetres) on wood including one operated by moving the blade towards the material being cut, or chain saw on wood;

Prescribed disease or injury	*Occupation*
	(f) jet of water (or a mixture of water and abrasive material) at a pressure above 680 bar, or jet channelling process to burn stone in a quarry; *(g)* machine in a ship's engine room, or gas turbine for performance testing on a test bed, installation testing of a replacement engine in an aircraft, or acceptance testing of an Armed Service fixed wing combat aircraft; *(h)* machine in the manufacture of glass containers or hollow ware for automatic moulding, automatic blow moulding, or automatic glass pressing and forming; *(i)* spinning machine using compressed air to produce glass wool or mineral wool; *(j)* continuous glass toughening furnace; *(k)* firearm by a police firearms training officer; *(l)* shot-blaster to carry abrasives in air for cleaning.
A11 Episodic blanching, occurring throughout the year, affecting the middle or proximal phalanges or in the case of a thumb the proximal phalanx, of: *(a)* in the case of a person with 5 fingers (including thumb) on one hand, any 3 of those fingers; *or* *(b)* in the case of a person with only 4 such fingers, any 2 of those fingers; *or* *(c)* in the case of a person with less than 4 such fingers, any one of those fingers, *or* as the case may be, the one remaining finger (vibration white finger).	*(a)* The use of hand-held chain saws in forestry; *or* *(b)* the use of hand-held rotary tools in grinding or in the sanding or polishing of metal, or the holding of material being ground, or metal being sanded or polished by rotary tools; *or* *(c)* the use of hand-held percussive metal-working tools, or the holding of metal being worked upon by percussive tools, in riveting, caulking, chipping, hammering, fettling or swaging; *or* *(d)* the use of hand-held powered percussive drills or hand-held powered percussive hammers in mining, quarrying, demolition, or on roads or footpaths, including road construction; *or* *(e)* the holding of material being worked upon by pounding machines in shoe manufacture.
A12 Carpal tunnel syndrome.	The use of hand-held powered tools whose internal parts vibrate so as to transmit that vibration to the hand, but excluding those which are solely powered by hand.
A13 Osteoarthritis of the hip.	Work in agriculture as a farmer or farm worker for a period of, or periods which amount in aggregate to, 10 years or more.

Prescribed disease or injury	*Occupation*
B – Conditions due to biological agents	
B1 Anthrax.	*(a)* Contact with anthrax spores, including contact with animals infected by anthrax; *or* *(b)* handling, loading, unloading or transport of animals of a type susceptible to infection with anthrax or of the products or residues of such animals.
B2 Glanders.	Contact with equine animals or their carcases.
B3 Infection by leptospira.	*(a)* Work in places which are, or are liable to be, infested by rats, field mice or voles, or other small mammals; *or* *(b)* work at dog kennels or the care or handling of dogs; *or* *(c)* contact with bovine animals or pigs or their meat products.
B4 Ankylostomiasis.	Contact with a source of ankylostomiasis.
B5 Tuberculosis.	Contact with a source of tuberculous infection.
B6 Extrinsic allergic alveolitis (including farmer's lung).	Exposure to moulds or fungal spores or heterologous proteins by reason of employment in: *(a)* agriculture, horticulture, forestry, cultivation of edible fungi or malt-working; *or* *(b)* loading or unloading or handling in storage mouldy vegetable matter or edible fungi; *or* *(c)* caring for or handling birds; *or* *(d)* handling bagasse.
B7 Infection by organisms of the genus brucella.	Contact with: *(a)* animals infected by brucella, or their carcasses or parts thereof, or their untreated products; *or* *(b)* laboratory specimens or vaccines of, or containing, brucella.
B8*(a)* Infection by hepatitis A virus.	Contact with raw sewage.
(b) Infection by hepatitis B or C virus.	Contact with: *(a)* human blood or human blood products; *or* *(b)* any other source of hepatitis B or C virus.
B9 Infection by Streptococcus suis.	Contact with pigs infected by Streptococcus suis, or with the carcases, products or residues of pigs so infected.
B10*(a)* Avian chlamydiosis.	Contact with birds infected with chlamydia psittaci, or with the remains or untreated products of such birds.

Prescribed disease or injury	*Occupation*
(b) Ovine chlamydiosis.	Contact with sheep infected with chlamydia psittaci, or with the remains or untreated products of such sheep.
B11 Q fever.	Contact with animals, their remains or their untreated products.
B12 Orf.	Contact with sheep, goats or with the carcases of sheep or goats.
B13 Hydatidosis.	Contact with dogs.
B14 Lyme disease.	Exposure to deer or other mammals of a type liable to harbour ticks harbouring Borrelia bacteria.
B15 Anaphylaxis.	Employment as a healthcare worker having contact with products made with natural rubber latex.
C – Conditions due to chemical agents	
C1*(a)* Anaemia with a haemoglobin concentration of 9g/dl or less, and a blood film showing punctate basophilia. *(b)* Peripheral neuropathy. *(c)* Central nervous system toxicity.	The use or handling of, or exposure to the fumes, dust or vapour of, lead or a compound of lead, or a substance containing lead.
C2 Central nervous system toxicity characterised by parkinsonism.	The use or handling of, or exposure to the fumes, dust or vapour of, manganese or a compound of manganese, or a substance containing manganese.
C3 Poisoning by phosphorus or an inorganic compound of phosphorus or pseudo anti-cholinesterase action of organic phosphorus compounds.	The use or handling of, or exposure to the fumes, dust or vapour of, phosphorus or a poisoning due to the anti-cholinesterase or containing phosphorus.
C4 Primary carcinoma of the bronchus or lung.	Exposure to the fumes, dust or vapour of arsenic, a compound of arsenic or a substance containing arsenic.
C5*(a)* Central nervous system toxicity characterised by tremor and neuropsychiatric disease.	Exposure to mercury or inorganic compounds of mercury for a period of, or periods which amount in aggregate to, 10 years or more.
(b) Central nervous system toxicity characterised by combined cerebellar and cortical degeneration.	Exposure to methylmercury.
C6 Peripheral neuropathy.	The use or handling of, or exposure to carbon disulphide (also called carbon disulfide).
C7 Acute non-lymphatic leukaemia.	Exposure to benzene.
C12*(a)* Peripheral neuropathy. *(b)* Central nervous system toxicity.	Exposure to methyl bromide (also called bromomethane).
C13 Cirrhosis of the liver.	Exposure to chlorinated naphthalene.
C16*(a)* Neurotoxicity. *(b)* Cardiotoxicity.	Exposure to the dust of gonioma kamassi.

Prescribed disease or injury	*Occupation*
C17 Chronic beryllium disease.	Inhalation of beryllium or a compound of beryllium.
C18 Emphysema.	Inhalation of cadmium fumes for a period of, or periods which amount in aggregate to, 20 years or more.
C19(*a*) Peripheral neuropath. (*b*) Central nervous system toxicity.	Exposure to acrylamide.
C20 Dystrophy of the cornea (including ulceration of the corneal surface) of the eye.	Exposure to quinone or hydroquinone.
C21 Primary carcinoma of the skin.	Exposure to arsenic or arsenic compounds, tar, pitch, bitumen, mineral oil (including paraffin) or soot.
C22(*a*) Primary carcinoma of the mucous membrane of the nose or paranasal sinuses. (*b*) Primary carcinoma of a bronchus or lung.	Work before 1950 in the refining of nickel involving exposure to oxides, sulphides or water-soluble compounds of nickel.
C23 Primary neoplasm of the epithelial lining of the urinary tract (renal pelvis, ureter, bladder and urethra), including papilloma carcinoma-in-situ and invasive carcinoma.	(*a*) The manufacture of 1-naphtylamine, 2-naphthylamine, benzidine, auramine, magenta or 4 aminobiphenyl (also called biphenyl-4-ylamine); (*b*) work in the process of manufacturing methylenebis-orthochloroanile (also called MbOCA) for a period of, or periods which amount in aggregate to, 12 months or more; (*c*) exposure to 2-naphtylamine, benzidine, 4-aminobiphenyl (also called MbOCA) for a period of, or periods which amount in aggregate to, 12 months or more; (*d*) exposure to orthotoluidine, 4-chloro-2-methylaniline or salts of those compounds; *or* (*e*) exposure for a period of, or periods which amount in aggregate to, 5 years or more, to coal tar pitch volatiles produced in aluminium smelting involving the Sodeberg process (that is to say, the method of producing aluminium by electrolysis in which the anode consists of a paste of petroleum coke and mineral oil which is baked in situ).

Prescribed disease or injury	*Occupation*
C24(*a*) Angiosarcoma of the liver. (*b*) Acro-osteolysis characterised by: i) lytic destruction of the terminal phalanges; ii) in Raynaud's phenomenon, the exaggerated vasomotor response to cold causing intense blanching of the digits; *and* iii) sclerodermatous thickening of the skin. (*c*) Liver fibrosis.	Exposure to vinyl chloride monomer in the manufacture of polyvinyl chloride.
C25 Vitiligo.	The use or handling of, or exposure to, para-tertiary-butylphenol (also called 4-tert-butylphenol), para-tertiary-butylcatechol (also called 4-tert-butylcatechol), para-amyl-phenol (also called p-pentyl phenol isomers), hydroquinone monobenzyl ether of hydroquinone (also called 4-benzyloxyphenol), mono-benzyl ether of hydroquinone (also called 4-benzyloxyphenol) or mono-butyl ether of hydroquinone (also called 4-butoxyphenol).
C26(*a*) Liver toxicity. (*b*) Kidney toxicity.	The use of or handling of, or exposure to, carbon tetrachloride (also called tetrachloromethane).
C27 Liver toxicity.	The use of or handling of, or exposure to the fumes of, or vapour containing, trichloromethane (also called chloroform).
Deleted text	
C29 Peripheral neuropathy.	The use of or handling of, or exposure to, n-hexane or n-butyl methyl ketone.
C30(*a*) Dermatitiis. (*b*) Ulceration of the mucous membrane or the epidermis.	The use or handling of, or exposure to, chromic acid, chromates or dichromates.
D – Miscellaneous conditions	
D1 Pneumoconiosis.	[Occupations specified in reg 2(b) of, and Part II of Schedule 1 to, the Social Security (Industrial Injuries) (Prescribed Diseases) Regulations 1985 which are too numerous to set out here. They are all occupations involving exposure to dust, such as mining, quarrying, sand blasting, grinding, making china or earthenware, boiler-sealing and other work involving the use of stone, asbestos, etc.]

Prescribed disease or injury	*Occupation*
D2 Byssinosis.	Work in any room where any process up to and including the weaving process is performed in a factory in which the spinning or manipulation of raw or waste cotton or of flax, or the weaving of cotton or flax, is carried on.
D3 Diffuse mesothelioma (primary neoplasm of the mesothelium of the pleura or of the pericardium or of the peritoneum).	Exposure to asbestos, asbestos dust or any admixture of asbestos at a level above that commonly found in the environment at large.
D4 Allergic rhinitis which is due to exposure to any of the following agents: *(a)* isocyanates; *(b)* platinum salts; *(c)* fumes or dusts arising from the manufacture, transport or use of hardening agents (including epoxy resin curing agents) based on phthalic anhydride, tetrachlorophthalic anhydride, trimellitic anhydride or triethylenetetramine; *(d)* fumes arising from the use of rosin as a soldering flux; *(e)* proteolytic enzymes; *(f)* animals including insects and other anthropods used for the purposes of research or education or in laboratories; *(g)* dusts arising from the sowing, cultivation, harvesting, drying, handling, milling, transport or storage of barley, oats, rye, wheat or maize, or the handling, milling, transport or storage of meal or flour made therefrom; *(h)* antibiotics; *(i)* cimetidine; *(j)* wood dust; *(k)* ispaghula; *(l)* castor bean dust; *(m)* ipecacuanha; *(n)* azodice-bonamide; *(o)* animals including insects and other arthropods or their larval forms, used for the purposes of pest control or fruit cultivation, or the larval forms of animals used for the purposes of research, education or in laboratories; *(p)* glutaraldehyde; *(q)* persulphate salts or henna; *(r)* crustaceans or fish or products arising from these in the food processing industry; *(s)* reactive dyes;	Exposure to any of the agents set out in column 1 of this paragraph.

Prescribed disease or injury	*Occupation*
(t) soya bean; *(u)* tea dust; *(v)* green coffee bean dust; *(w)* fumes from stainless steel welding; *(x)* products made with natural rubber latex.	
D5 Non-infective dermatitis of external origin (excluding dermatitis due to ionising particles or electro-magnetic radiant heat).	Exposure to dust, liquid or vapour or any other external agent except chromic acid, chromates or bi-chromates capable of irritating the skin (including friction or heat but excluding ionising particles or electromagnetic radiations other than radiant heat).
D6 Carcinoma of the nasal cavity or associated air sinuses (nasal carcinoma).	*(a)* Attendance for work in or about a building where wooden goods are; *or* *(b)* attendance for work in a building used for the manufacture of footwear or components of footwear made wholly or partly of leather or fibre board; *or* *(c)* attendance for work at a place used wholly or mainly for the repair of footwear made wholly or partly of leather or fibre board.
D7 Asthma which is due to exposure to any of the following agents: *(a)* isocyanates; *(b)* platinum salts; *(c)* fumes or dusts arising from the manufacture, transport or use of hardening agents (including epoxy resin curing agents) based on phthalic anhydride, tetrachlorophthalic anhydride, trimellitic anhydride or triethylenetetramine; *(d)* fumes arising from the use of rosin as a soldering flux; *(e)* proteolytic enzymes; *(f)* animals including insects and other anthropods used for the purposes of research or education or in laboratories; *(g)* dusts arising from the sowing, cultivation, harvesting, drying, handling, milling, transport or storage of barley, oats, rye, wheat or maize, or the handling, milling, transport or storage of meal or flour made therefrom; *(h)* antibiotics; *(i)* cimetidine; *(j)* wood dust; *(k)* ispaghula; *(l)* castor bean dust; *(m)* ipecacuanha;	Exposure to any of the agents set out in column 1 of this paragraph.

Prescribed disease or injury	*Occupation*
(n) azodicarbonamide; *(o)* animals including insects and other arthropods or their larval forms, used for the purposes of pest control or fruit cultivation, or the larval forms of animals used for the purposes of research, education or in laboratories; *(p)* glutaraldehyde; *(q)* persulphate salts or henna; *(r)* crustaceans or fish or products arising from these in the food processing industry; *(s)* reactive dyes; *(t)* soya bean; *(u)* tea dust; *(v)* green coffee bean dust; *(w)* fumes from stainless steel welding; *(wa)* products made with natural rubber latex; *(x)* any other sensitising agent (occupational asthma).	
D8 Primary carcinoma of the lung where there is accompanying evidence of one or both of the following: *(a)* asbestosis; *(b)* unilateral or bilateral diffuse pleural thickening extending to a thickness of 5mm or more at any point within the area affected as measured by a plain chest radiograph (not being a computerised tomography scan or other form of imaging) which: i) in the case of unilateral diffuse pleural thickening, covers 50% or more of the area of the chest wall of the lung affected; *or* ii) in the case of bilateral diffuse pleural thickening, covers 25% or more of the combined area of the chest wall of both lungs.	*(a)* The working or handling of asbestos; or any admixture of asbestos; *or* *(b)* the manufacture or repair of asbestos textiles or other articles containing or composed of asbestos; *or* *(c)* the cleaning of any machinery or plant used in any of the foregoing operations and of any chambers, fixtures and appliances for the collection of asbestos dust; *or* *(d)* substantial exposure to the dust arising from any of the foregoing operations.
D9 Unilateral or bilateral diffuse pleural thickening extending to a thickness of 5mm or more at any point within the area affected as measured by a plain chest radiograph (not being a computerised tomography scan or other form of imaging) which: (i) in the case of unilateral diffuse plueral thickening, covers 50% or more of the area of the chest wall of the lung affected; *or* (ii) in the case of bilateral diffuse pleural thickening, covers 25% or more of the combined area of the chest wall of both lungs.	*(a)* The working or handling of asbestos; or any admixture of asbestos; *or* *(b)* the manufacture or repair of asbestos textiles or other articles containing or composed of asbestos; *or* *(c)* the cleaning of any machinery or plant used in any of the foregoing operations and appliances for the collection of asbestos dust; *or* *(d)* substantial exposure to the dust arising from any of the foregoing operations.

Prescribed disease or injury	*Occupation*
D10 Primary carcinoma of the lung.	*(a)* Work underground in a tin mine; *or* *(b)* exposure to bis(chloromethyl) ether produced during the manufacture of chloromethyl methyl ether; *or* *(c)* exposure to zinc chromate, calcium chromate or strontium chromate in their pure forms.
D11 Primary carcinoma of the lung where there is accompanying evidence of silicosis.	Exposure to silica dust in the course of: *(a)* the manufacture of glass or pottery; *(b)* tunnelling in or quarrying sandstone or granite; *(c)* mining metal ores; *(d)* slate quarrying or the manufacture of artefacts from slate; *(e)* mining clay; *(f)* using silicous materials as abrasives; *(g)* cutting stone; *(h)* stone masonry; *or* *(i)* work in a foundry.
D12 Except in the circumstances specified in regulation 2(d): *(a)* chronic bronchitis; *or* *(b)* emphysema; *or* *(c)* both, where there is accompanying evidence of a forced expiratory volume in one second (measured from the position of maximum inspiration with the claimant making maximum effort) of: i) at least one litre below the mean value predicted, obtained from the following prediction formulae which give the mean values predicted in litres: For a man, where the measurement is made without back-extrapolation, (3.62 x Height in metres) – (0.031 x Age in years) – 1.41; or, where the measurement is made with back-extrapolation, (3.71 x Height in meters) – (0.032 x Age in years) – 1.44. For a woman, where the measurement is made without back-extrapolation, (3.29 x Height in meters) – (0.029 x Age in years) – 1.42; or where the measurement is made with back-extrapolation, (3.37 x Height in meters) – (0.030 x Age in years) – 1.46; or ii) less than one litre.	Exposure to coal dust by reason of working underground in a coal mine for a period of, or periods amounting in the aggregate to, at least 20 years (whether before or after 5 July 1948) and any such period or periods of incapacity while engaged in such an occupation.

Appendix 9

Upper and lower earnings limits

Year	*Lower earnings limit*	*Upper earnings limit*
	£	£
1975–76	11.00	69.00
1976–77	13.00	95.00
1977–78	15.00	105.00
1978–79	17.50	120.00
1979–80	19.50	135.00
1980–81	23.00	165.00
1981–82	27.00	200.00
1982–83	29.50	220.00
1983–84	32.50	235.00
1984–85	34.00	250.00
1985–86	35.50	265.00
1986–87	38.00	285.00
1987–88	39.00	295.00
1988–89	41.00	305.00
1989–90	43.00	325.00
1990–91	46.00	350.00
1991–92	52.00	390.00
1992–93	54.00	405.00
1993–94	56.00	420.00
1994–95	57.00	430.00
1995–96	58.00	440.00
1996–97	61.00	455.00
1997–98	62.00	465.00
1998–99	64.00	485.00
1999–00	66.00	500.00
2000–01	67.00	535.00
2001–02	72.00 (zero rated to 87.00)	575.00
2002–03	75.00 (zero rated to 89.00)	585.00
2003–04	77.00 (zero rated to 89.00)	595.00
2004–05	79.00 (zero rated to 91.00)	610.00
2005–06	82.00 (zero rated to 94.00)	630.00

Appendix 10

Disability which puts a person at a disadvantage in getting a job

Schedule 1 Regulation 9(1) to the Working Tax Credit (Entitlement and Maximum Rate) Regulations 2002 SI No. 2005

PART 1

1. When standing he cannot keep his balance unless he continually holds onto something.

2. Using any crutches, walking frame, walking stick, prosthesis or similar walking aid which he habitually uses, he cannot walk a continuous distance of 100 metres along level ground without stopping or without suffering severe pain.

3. He can use neither of his hands behind his back as in the process of putting on a jacket or of tucking a shirt into trousers.

4. He can extend neither of his arms in front of him so as to shake hands with another person without difficulty.

5. He can put neither of his hands up to his head without difficulty so as to put on a hat.

6. Due to lack of manual dexterity he cannot, with one hand, pick up a coin which is not more than $2\frac{1}{2}$ centimetres in diameter.

7. He is not able to use his hands or arms to pick up a full jug of 1 litre capacity and pour from it into a cup, without difficulty.

8. He can turn neither of his hands sideways through 180 degrees.

9. He -

a) is registered as blind or registered as partially sighted in a register compiled by a local authority under section 24(9)(g) of the National Assistance Act 1948;

(b) has been certified as blind or as partially sighted and, in consequence, registered as blind or partially sighted in a register maintained by or on behalf of a council constituted under the Local Government (Scotland) Act 1994; or

(c) has been certified as blind and in consequence is registered as blind in a register maintained by or on behalf of a Health and Social Services Board in Northern Ireland.

10. He cannot see to read 16 point print at a distance greater than 20 centimetres, if appropriate, wearing the glasses he normally uses.

11. He cannot hear a telephone ring when he is in the same room as the telephone, if appropriate, using a hearing aid he normally uses.

12. In a quiet room he has difficulty in hearing what someone talking in a loud voice at a distance of 2 metres says, if appropriate, using a hearing aid he normally uses.

13. People who know him well have difficulty in understanding what he says.

14. When a person he knows well speaks to him, he has difficulty in understanding what that person says.

15. At least once a year during waking hours he is in a coma or has a fit in which he loses consciousness.

16. He has a mental illness for which he receives regular treatment under the supervision of a medically qualified person.

17. Due to mental disability he is often confused or forgetful.

18. He cannot do the simplest addition and subtraction.

19. Due to mental disability he strikes people or damages property or is unable to form normal social relationships.

20. He cannot normally sustain an 8 hour working day or a 5 day working week due to a medical condition or intermittent or continuous severe pain.

PART 2

21. As a result of an illness or accident he is undergoing a period of habilitation or rehabilitation.

Appendix 11

Abbreviations used in the notes

AC	Appeal Cases
All ER	All England Reports
Art(s)	Article(s)
CA	Court of Appeal
CAO	Chief Adjudication Officer
CCLR	Community Care Law Reports
CMLR	Common Market Law Reports
CS	Court of Session
CSBO	Chief Supplementary Benefit Officer
DC	Divisional Court
ECJ	European Court of Justice
ECR	European Court Reports
ECtHR	European Court of Human Rights
EHRR	European Human Rights Reports
ELR	Education Law Reports
EWCA	England and Wales Court of Appeal
EWHC	England and Wales High Court
FLR	Family Law Reports
HBRB	Housing Benefit Review Board
HC	High Court
HL	House of Lords
HLR	Housing Law Reports
ICR	Industrial Cases Reports
IRS	Independent Review Service for the Social Fund
JPR	Justice of the Peace Reports
KB	King's Bench Reports
para(s)	paragraph(s)
QB	Queen's Bench Reports
QBD	Queen's Bench Division
r	rule
RA	Rating Appeals Reports
reg(s)	regulation(s)
RSC	Rules of the Supreme Court
s(s)	section(s)
SBC	Supplementary Benefits Commission
Sch(s)	Schedule(s)
SLT	Scots Law Times
UKHL	United Kingdom House of Lords
WLR	Weekly Law Reports

Regulations and other statutory instruments

Each set of regulations has a statutory instrument (SI) number and a date. You ask for them by giving their date and number.

C(LC)AO No.2	The Children (Leaving Care) Act 2000 (Commencement No.2 and Consequential Provisions) Order 2001 No.3070
C(LC)(E) Regs	The Children (Leaving Care) (England) Regulations 2001 No.2874
C(LC)(W) Regs	The Children (Leaving Care) (Wales) Regulations 2001 No.2189 (W151)

C(LC)SSB Regs	The Children (Leaving Care) Social Security Benefits Regulations 2001 No.3074
C(LC)SSB(S) Regs	The Children (Leaving Care) Social Security Benefits (Scotland) Regulations 2004 No.747
CB Regs	The Child Benefit (General) Regulations 1976 No.965
CB(Amdt) Regs	The Child Benefit (General) Amendment Regulations 1987 No.35
CB(RPA) Regs	The Child Benefit (Residence and Persons Abroad) Regulations 1976 No.963
CB&GA(AA) Regs	The Child Benefit and Guardian's Allowance (Administrative Arrangements) Regulations 2003 No.494
CB&GA(Admin) Regs	The Child Benefit and Guardian's Allowance (Administration) Regulations 2003 No.492
CB&GA(DA) Regs	The Child Benefit and Guardian's Allowance (Decisions and Appeals) Regulations 2003 No.916
CB&SS(FAR) Regs	The Child Benefit and Social Security (Fixing and Adjustment of Rates) Regulations 1976 No.1267
CB&SS(FAR) Amdt Regs	The Child Benefit and Social Security (Fixing and Adjustment of Rates) (Amendment) Regulations 1998 No.1581
CC(DIS) Regs	The Community Charge (Deductions from Income Support) Regulations 1990 No.107
CS(AIAMA) Regs	The Child Support (Arrears, Interest and Adjustment of Maintenance Assessments) Regulations 1992 No.1816
CS(CEOFM) Regs	The Child Support (Collection and Enforcement of Other Forms of Maintenance) Regulations 1992 No.2643
CS(IED) Regs	The Child Support (Information, Evidence and Disclosure) Regulations 1992 No.1812
CS(MAP) Regs	The Child Support (Maintenance Assessment Procedure) Regulations 1992 No.1813
CS(MASC) Regs	The Child Support (Maintenance Assessments and Special Cases) Regulations 1992 No.1815
CS(MCP) Regs	The Child Support (Maintenance Calculation Procedure) Regulations 2000 No.2001/157
CS(MCSC) Regs	The Child Support (Maintenance Calculations and Special Cases) Regulations 2000 No.2001/155
CS(TP) Regs	The Child Support (Transitional Provisions) Regulations 2000 No.3186
CT(DD)O	The Council Tax (Discount Disregards) Order 1992 No.548
CT(DIS) Regs	The Council Tax (Deductions from Income Support) Regulations 1993 No.494
CTB Regs	The Council Tax Benefit (General) Regulations 1992 No.1814
CTB Amdt Regs	The Council Tax Benefit (General) (Amendment) Regulations 1997 No.1841
CTC Regs	The Child Tax Credit Regulations 2002 No.2007

DFA Regs	The Discretionary Financial Assistance Regulations 2001 No.1167
DWA&IS Regs	The Disability Working Allowance and Income Support (General) Amendment Regulations 1995 No.482
EA(C3TSP)O	The Employment Act 2002 (Commencement No.3 & Transitional and Savings Provisions) Order 2002 No.2866
EP(RUB&SB) Regs	The Employment Protection (Recoupment of Unemployment Benefit and Supplementary Benefit) Regulations 1977 No.674
F(DIS) Regs	The Fines (Deductions from Income Support) Regulations 1992 No.2182
FC Regs	The Family Credit (General) Regulations 1987 No. 1973. From 5 October 1999 the tax credit, WFTC, replaced family credit. However, the FC Regs remains the name of the regulations relating to this tax credit, but references within them are now all to WFTC.
GA(Gen) Regs	The Guardian's Allowance (General) Regulations 2003 No.495
HB Regs	The Housing Benefit (General) Regulations 1987 No.1971
HB(Amdt) Regs	The Housing Benefit (General) Amendment Regulations 1995 No.1644
HB(Amdt) Regs 1996	The Housing Benefit (General) Amendment Regulations 1996 No.965
HB(ILA) Regs	The Housing Benefit (Information from Landlords and Agents) Regulations 1997 No.2436
HB(RO) Regs	The Housing Benefit (Recovery of Overpayments) Regulations 1997 No.2435
HB&CTB(ABP)Amdt Regs	The Housing Benefit and Council Tax Benefit (Abolition of Benefit Periods) Amendment Regulations 2004 No.14
HB&CTB(Amdt) Regs	The Housing Benefit and Council Tax Benefit (General) Amendment Regulations 1997 No.852
HB&CTB(DA) Regs	The Housing Benefit and Council Tax Benefit (Decisions and Appeals) Regulations 2001 No.1002
HB&CTB(SPC) Regs	The Housing Benefit and Council Tax Benefit (State Pension Credit) Regulations 2003 No.325
I(EEA)O	The Immigration (European Economic Area) Order 1994 No.1895
IS Regs	The Income Support (General) Regulations 1987 No.1967
IS(AT) Regs	The Income Support (General) Amendment and Transitional Regulations 1995 No. 516
IS(JSACA) Regs	The Income Support (General)(Jobseeker's Allowance Consequential Amendments) Regulations 1996 No.206
JSA Regs	The Jobseeker's Allowance Regulations 1996 No.207
NA(AR) Regs	The National Assistance (Assessment and Resources) Regulations 1992 No.2977

NA(RA)(APAR)(A)(E) Regs	The National Assistance (Residential Accommodation) (Additional Payments and Assessment of Resources) (Amendment) (England) Regulations 2001 No.3441
NA(RA)(APRCAR)(W) Regs	The National Assistance (Residential Accommodation) (Additional Payments, Relevant Contributions and Assessment of Resources) (Wales) Regulations 2003 No.931
NA(RA)(RC)(E) Regs	The National Assistance (Residential Accommodation) (Relevant Contributions) (England) Regulations 2001 No.3069
NHS(CDA) Regs	The National Health Service (Charges for Drugs and Appliances) Regulations 2000 No.620
NHS(CDA)(S) Regs	The National Health Service (Charges for Drugs and Appliances) (Scotland) Regulations 2001 No.430
NHS(CDA)(W) Regs	The National Health Service (Charges for Drugs and Appliances) (Wales) Regulations 2001 No.1358 (W86)
NHS(DC) Regs	The National Health Service (Dental Charges) Regulations 1989 No.394
NHS(DC)(S) Regs	The National Health Service (Dental Charges) (Scotland) Regulations 1989 No.363
NHS(GOS) Regs	The National Health Service (General Ophthalmic Services) Regulations 1986 No.975
NHS(OCP) Regs	The National Health Service (Optical Charges and Payments) Regulations 1997 No.818
NHS(OCP)(S) Regs	The National Health Service (Optical Charges and Payments) (Scotland) Regulations 1998 No.642
NHS(TERC) Regs	The National Health Service (Travelling Expenses and Remission of Charges) Regulations 1998 No.551
NHS(TERC) Regs 2003	The National Health Service (Travelling Expenses and Remission of Charges) Regulations 2003 No.2382
NHS(TERC)(S) Regs	The National Health Service (Travelling Expenses and Remission of Charges) (Scotland) (No.2) Regulations 2003 No.460
PAL Regs	The Paternity and Adoption Leave Regulations 2002 No.2788
RO(HBF)O	The Rent Officers (Housing Benefit Functions) Order 1997 No.1984
RO(HBF)(S)O	The Rent Officers (Housing Benefit Functions) (Scotland) Order 1997 No.144
RR(CA)O	The Regulatory Reform (Carer's Allowance) Order 2002 No.1457
SF(App) Regs	The Social Fund (Applications) Regulations 1988 No.524
SF(AR) Regs	The Social Fund (Application for Review) Regulations 1988 No.34
SF(Misc) Regs	The Social Fund (Miscellaneous Provisions) Regulations 1990 No.1788
SF(RDB) Regs	The Social Fund (Recovery by Deductions from Benefits) Regulations 1988 No.35

SFCWP Regs	The Social Fund Cold Weather Payments (General) Regulations 1988 No.1724
SFM&FE Regs	The Social Fund Maternity and Funeral Expenses (General) Regulations 1987 No.481
SFWFP Regs	The Social Fund Winter Fuel Payment Regulations 2000 No.729
SMP Regs	The Statutory Maternity Pay(General) Regulations 1986 No.1960
SMP(MA) Regs	The Statutory Maternity Pay (General)(Modification and Amendment) Regulations 2000 No.2883
SMP(ME) Regs	The Statutory Maternity Pay (Medical Evidence) Regulations 1987 No.235
SMP(PAM) Regs	The Statutory Maternity Pay (Persons Abroad and Mariners) Regulations 1987 No.418
SPC Regs	The State Pension Credit Regulations 2002 No.1792
SPC(CTMP) Regs	The State Pension Credit (Consequential, Transitional and Miscellaneous Provisions) Regulations 2002 No.3019
SPC(CTMP) No2 Regs	The State Pension Credit (Consequential, Transitional and Miscellaneous Provisions) (No.2) Regulations 2002 No.3197
SPP(A)&SAP(AO)(No.2) Regs	The Statutory Paternity Pay (Adoption) and Statutory Adoption Pay (Adoptions from Overseas) (No.2) Regulations 2003 No.1194
SPP(A)&SAP(AO)(PAM) Regs	The Statutory Paternity Pay (Adoption) and Statutory Adoption Pay (Adoptions from Overseas) (Persons Abroad and Mariners) Regulations 2003 No.1193
SPPSAP(A) Regs	The Statutory Paternity Pay and Statutory Adoption Pay (Administration) Regulations 2002 No.2820
SPPSAP(G) Regs	The Statutory Paternity and Statutory Adoption Pay (General) Regulations 2002 No.2822
SPPSAP(PAM) Regs	The Statutory Paternity Pay and Statutory Adoption Pay (Persons Abroad and Mariners) Regulations 2002 No.2821
SPPSAP(WR) Regs	The Statutory Paternity Pay and Statutory Adoption Pay (Weekly Rates) Regulations 2002 No.2818
SS(AA) Regs	The Social Security (Attendance Allowance) Regulations 1991 No.2740
SS(BCO) Regs	The Social Security (Breach of Community Order) Regulations 2001 No.1395
SS(BTWB) Regs	The Social Security (Back to Work Bonus) Regulations 1996 No.193
SS(BTWB&LPRO) (Amdt) Regs	The Social Security (Back to Work Bonus and Lone Parent Run-on) (Amendment and Revocation) Regulations 2003 No.1589
SS(C1CCP)O	The Social Security (Class 1 Contributions – Contracted-out Percentages) Order 1992 No.795
SS(CatE) Regs	The Social Security (Categorisation of Earners) Regulations 1978 No.1689

SS(CMB) Regs	The Social Security (Child Maintenance Bonus) Regulations 1996 No.3195
SS(CMPMA) Regs	The Social Security (Child Maintenance Premium and Miscellaneous Amendments) Regulations 2000 No.3176
SS(Con) Regs	The Social Security (Contributions) Regulations 2001 No.1004
SS(C&P) Regs	The Social Security (Claims and Payments) Regulations 1987 No.1968
SS(C&P)A Regs	The Social Security (Claims and Payments) Amendment Regulations 2001 No.18
SS(Cr) Regs	The Social Security (Credits) Regulations 1975 No.556 (as amended)
SS(CTCNIN)Regs	The Social Security (Crediting and Treatment of Contributions, and National Insurance Numbers) Regulations 2001 No.769
SS(DLA) Regs	The Social Security (Disability Living Allowance) Regulations 1991 No.2890
SS(DLA) Amdt Regs	The Social Security (Disability Living Allowance) (Amendment) Regulations 2002 No.648
SS(EEEIIP) Regs	The Social Security (Employed Earners' Employment for Industrial Injuries Purposes) Regulations 1975 No.467
SS(EF) Regs	The Social Security (Earnings Factor) Regulations 1979 No.676
SS(EoFCoEF) Regs	The Social Security (Effect of Family Credit on Earnings Factors) Regulations 1995 No.2559
SS(GA) Regs	The Social Security (Guardian's Allowance) Regulations 1975 No.515
SS(GB) Regs	The Social Security (General Benefits) Regulations 1982 No.1408
SS(GRB) No.2 Regs	The Social Security (Graduated Retirement Benefit) (No.2) Regulations 1978 No.393
SS(HIP) Regs	The Social Security (Hospital In-Patients) Regulations 1975 No.555
SS(I)(MA) Regs	The Social Security (Incapacity) (Miscellaneous Amendments) Regulations 2002 No.491
SS(IA)CA Regs	The Social Security (Immigration and Asylum) Consequential Amendments Regulations 2000 No.636
SS(IB) Regs	The Social Security (Incapacity Benefit) Regulations 1994 No.2946
SS(IB)MA Regs	The Social Security (Incapacity Benefit) Miscellaneous Amendments Regulations 2000 No.3120
SS(IB)(T) Regs	The Social Security (Incapacity Benefit) (Transitional) Regulations 1995 No.310
SS(IB-ID) Regs	The Social Security (Incapacity Benefit – Increases for Dependants) Regulations 1994 No.2945
SS(IBWFI) Regs	The Social Security (Incapacity Benefit Work-focused Interviews) Regulations 2003 No.2439
SS(ICA) Regs	The Social Security (Invalid Care Allowance) Regulations 1976 No.409

SS(IFW) Regs	The Social Security (Incapacity for Work) (General) Regulations 1995 No.311
SS(II&D)MP Regs	The Social Security (Industrial Injuries and Diseases) Miscellaneous Provisions Regulations 1986 No.1561
SS(IIPD) Regs	The Social Security (Industrial Injuries) (Prescribed Diseases) Regulations 1985 No.967
SS(IIRE) Regs	The Social Security (Industrial Injuries) (Regular Employment) Regulations 1990 No.256
SS(IoM)O	The Social Security (Isle of Man) Order 1977 No.2150
SS(J&G)O	The Social Security (Jersey and Guernsey) Order 1992 No.1735
SS(JPI) Regs	The Social Security (Jobcentre Plus Interviews) Regulations 2002 No.1703
SS(JPIP) Regs	Social Security (Jobcentre Plus Interviews for Partners) Regulations 2003 No.1886
SS(LB) Regs	The Social Security (Loss of Benefit) Regulations 2001 No.4022
SS(LSTP) Regs	The Social Security (Literacy, etc. Skills Training Pilot) Regulations 2001 No.2710
SS(MA) Regs	The Social Security (Miscellaneous Amendments) Regulations 1998 No.563
SS(MAP) Regs	The Social Security (Maximum Additional Pension) Regulations 1978 No.949
SS(MatA) Regs	The Social Security (Maternity Allowance) Regulations 1987 No.416
SS(MatA)(E) Regs	The Social Security (Maternity Allowance) (Earnings) Regulations 2000 No.688
SS(MatA)(WA) Regs	The Social Security (Maternity Allowance) (Work Abroad) Regulations 1987 No.417
SS(ME) Regs	The Social Security (Medical Evidence) Regulations 1976 No.615
SS(NCC) Regs	The Social Security (Notification of Change of Circumstances) Regulations 2001 No.3252
SS(NDP) Regs	The Social Security (New Deal Pilot) Regulations 2000 No.3134
SS(NIRA) Regs	The Social Security (Northern Ireland Reciprocal Arrangements) Regulations 1976 No.1003
SS(OB) Regs	The Social Security (Overlapping Benefits) Regulations 1979 No.597
SS(PAOR) Regs	The Social Security (Payments on Account, Overpayments and Recovery) Regulations 1988 No.664
SS(PFA)MA Regs	The Social Security (Persons from Abroad) Miscellaneous Amendments Regulations 1996 No.30
SS(PN) Regs	The Social Security (Penalty Notices) Regulations 1997 No.2813
SS(RB) Regs	The Social Security (Recovery of Benefits) Regulations 1997 No.2205
SS(RB)App Regs	The Social Security (Recovery of Benefits) (Appeals) Regulations 1997 No.2237

SS(SDA) Regs	The Social Security (Severe Disablement Allowance) Regulations 1984 No.1303
SS(STB)(T) Regs	The Social Security (Short-Term Benefits) (Transitional) Regulations 1974 No.2192
SS(WB&RP) Regs	The Social Security (Widow's Benefit and Retirement Pensions) Regulations 1979 No.642
SS(WBRP&OB)(T) Regs	The Social Security (Widow's Benefit, Retirement Pensions and Other Benefits) (Transitional) Regulations 1979 No.643
SS(WFILP) Regs	The Social Security (Work-focused Interviews for Lone Parents) and Miscellaneous Amendments Regulations 2000 No.1926
SS(WTCCTC)(CA) Regs	The Social Security (Working Tax Credit and Child Tax Credit)(Consequential Amendments) Regulations 2003 No.455
SSAO No.8	The Social Security Act 1998 (Commencement No.8, and Savings and Consequential and Transitional Provisions) Order 1999 No.1958
SSA(F)AO No.5	The Social Security Administration (Fraud) Act 1997 (Commencement No.5) Order 1997 No.2766
SSA(SIB) Regs	The Social Security Amendment (Students and Income-related Benefits) Regulations 2002 No.1589
SS&CS(DA) Regs	The Social Security and Child Support (Decisions and Appeals) Regulations 1999 No.991 SSB(CE) Regs
SSB(CE) Regs	The Social Security Benefit (Computation of Earnings) Regulations 1996 No.2745
SSB(Dep) Regs	The Social Security Benefit (Dependency) Regulations 1977 No.343
SSB(MW&WSP) Regs	The Social Security (Benefit) (Married Women and Widows' Special Provisions) Regulations 1974 No.2010
SSB(PA) Regs	The Social Security Benefit (Persons Abroad) Regulations 1975 No.563
SSB(PRT) Regs	The Social Security Benefit (Persons Residing Together) Regulations 1977 No.956
SSBU(No.2)O 1991	The Social Security Benefits Up-rating (No.2) Order 1991 No.2910
SSC(DA) Regs	The Social Security Contributions (Decisions and Appeals) Regulations 1999 No.1027
SSC(NPPC1C)	The Social Security Contributions (Notional Payment of Primary Class 1 Contributions) Regulations 2000 No.747
SSCP Regs	The Social Security Commissioners (Procedure) Regulations 1999 No.1495
SSCP(TCA) Regs	The Social Security Commissioners Procedure (Tax Credit Appeals) Regulations No 2002 No.3237
SSFA(PM) Regs	The Social Security and Family Allowances (Polygamous Marriages) Regulations 1975 No.561

SSP Regs	The Statutory Sick Pay (General) Regulations 1982 No.894
SSP(HR) Regs	The Social Security Pensions (Home Responsibilities) Regulations 1994 No.704
SSP(MAPA) Regs	The Statutory Sick Pay (Mariners, Airmen and Persons Abroad) Regulations 1982 No.1349
SSP&SMP(D) Regs	The Statutory Sick Pay and Statutory Maternity Pay (Decisions) Regulations 1999 No.776
SSREFO	The Social Security Revaluation of Earnings Factor Order 2001 No.631
TC(A) Regs	The Tax Credits (Appeals) Regulations 2002 No.2926
TC(A)(No.2) Regs	The Tax Credits (Appeals) (No.2) Regulations 2002 No.3196
TC(ACCP)S	The Tax Credits (Approval of Child Care Providers) Scheme 2005 No.93
TC(C)O	The Tax Credits Act 2002 (Commencement No.4, Transitional Provisions and Savings) Order 2003 No.962 (C51)
TC(CN) Regs	The Tax Credits (Claims and Notifications) Regulations 2002 No.2014
TC(CTPA)O	The Tax Credits (Claims) (Transitional Provision) (Amendment) Order 2002 No.2158
TC(DCI) Regs	The Tax Credits (Definition and Calculation of Income) Regulations 2002 No.2006
TC(Imm) Regs	The Tax Credits (Immigration) Regulations 2003 No.653
TC(IR) Regs	The Tax Credits (Interest Rate) Regulations 2003 No.123
TC(ITDR) Regs	The Tax Credits (Income Thresholds and Determination of Rates) Regulations 2002 No.2008
TC(NA)Regs	The Tax Credits (Notice of Appeal) Regulations 2002 No.3119
TC(OE) Regs	The Tax Credits (Official Error) Regulations 2003 No.692
TC(PB) Regs	The Tax Credits (Payments by the Board) Regulations 2002 No.2173
TC(PM) Regs	The Tax Credits (Polygamous Marriages) Regulations 2003 No.742
TC(R) Regs	The Tax Credits (Residence) Regulations 2003 No.654
WF Regs	The Welfare Foods Regulations 1996 No.1434
WRP(PABWW) Regs	The Welfare Reform and Pensions (Persons Abroad: Benefits for Widows and Widowers) (Consequential Amendments) Regulations 2001 No.2618
WRPA(No.9)O	The Welfare Reform and Pensions Act 1999 (Commencement No.9, Transitional Provisions and Savings) Order 2000 No.2958
WTC(EMR) Regs	The Working Tax Credit (Entitlement and Maximum Rate) Regulations 2002 No.2005

Other information

See Appendix 3 for details of the following publications.

DMG	*Decision Makers Guide*, vols 1-14
GM	*TheHousing Benefit and Council Tax BenefitGuidance Manual*
IS GAP	*The Income Support Guidance and Procedure Manual*
SF Dir/SFI Dir	Direction(s) on the discretionary social fund. They are printed in the *Social Fund Guide* and Sweet and Maxwell's *Social Security Legislation* and are available on the DWP website.
SFG	*The Social Fund Guide*
TCTM	*Tax Credits Technical Manual*

References like CIS/142/1990 and R(SB) 3/89 are references to commissioners' decisions.

Acts of Parliament

CA 1989	Children Act 1989
C(LC)A 2000	Children (Leaving Care) Act 2000
C(S)A 1995	Children (Scotland) Act 1995
CCH(S)A 2002	Community Care and Health (Scotland) Act 2002
CJPOA 1994	Criminal Justice and Public Order Act 1994
CPA 2004	Civil Partnership Act 2004
CSA 1991	Child Support Act 1991
CSPSSA 2000	Child Support, Pensions and Social Security Act 2000
ECA 1972	European Communities Act 1972
ERA 1996	Employment Rights Act 1996
ETA 1973	Employment and Training Act 1973
GRA 2004	Gender Recognition Act 2004
HRA 1998	Human Rights Act 1998
HSS&SSA 1983	Health and Social Services and Social Security Adjudication Act 1983
IA 1978	Interpretation Act 1978
IAA 1999	Immigration and Asylum Act 1999
ICTA 1988	Income and Corporation Taxes Act 1988
IT(EP)A 2003	Income Tax (Earnings and Pensions) Act 2003
JSA 1995	Jobseekers Act 1995
LGFA 1992	Local Government Finance Act 1992
MCA 1973	Matrimonial Causes Act 1973
MHA 1983	Mental Health Act 1983
NAA 1948	National Assistance Act 1948
NHSA 1977	National Health Service Act 1977
NHS(S)A 1978	National Health Service (Scotland) Act 1978
NHSCCA 1990	National Health Service and Community Care Act 1990
NIA 1965	National Insurance Act 1965
PA 1995	Pensions Act 1995
PACEA 1984	Police and Criminal Evidence Act 1984
PSA 1993	Pension Schemes Act 1993
SPCA 2002	State Pension Credit Act 2002

SSA 1998	Social Security Act 1998
SS(IFW)A 1994	Social Security (Incapacity for Work) Act 1994
SS(RB)A 1997	Social Security (Recovery of Benefits) Act 1997
SSAA 1992	Social Security Administration Act 1992
SSA(F)A 1997	Social Security Administration (Fraud) Act 1997
SSC(TF)A 1999	Social Security Contributions (Transfer of Functions, etc) Act 1999
SSCBA 1992	Social Security Contributions and Benefits Act 1992
SSFA 2001	Social Security Fraud Act 2001
SW(S)A 1968	Social Work (Scotland) Act 1968
TCA 1999	Tax Credits Act 1999
TCA 2002	Tax Credits Act 2002
TMA 1970	Taxes Management Act 1970
WRPA 1999	Welfare Reform and Pensions Act 1999

European law

Secondary legislation is made under the Treaty of Rome 1957, the Single European Act and the Maastricht Treaty in the form of Regulations (EEC Reg) and Directives (EC Dir).

Index

How to use this Index

Because the Handbook is divided into separate sections covering the different benefits, many entries in the index have several references, each to a different section. Where this occurs, we use the following abbreviations to show which benefit each reference relates to:

AA	Attendance allowance	I-JSA	Income-based jobseeker's allowance
CA	Carer's allowance	JSA	Jobseeker's allowance
CTB	Council tax benefit	MA	Maternity allowance
CTC	Child tax credit	PC	Pension credit
DLA	Disability living allowance	SAP	Statutory adoption pay
HB	Housing benefit	SDA	Severe disablement allowance
IB	Incapacity benefit	SF	Social fund
IIDB	Industrial injuries disablement benefit	SMP	Statutory maternity pay
IS	Income support	SPP	Statutory paternity pay
C-JSA	Contribution-based jobseeker's allowance	SSP	Statutory sick pay
		WTC	Working tax credit

Entries against the bold headings direct you to the general information on the subject, or where the subject is covered most fully. Sub-entries are listed alphabetically and direct you to specific aspects of the subject.

Y

S